TEL:

GOOD HOUSEKEEPING
*Step-by-Step Encyclopaedia of*

# Needle
# Craft

GOOD HOUSEKEEPING
*Step-by-Step Encyclopaedia of*

# Needle Craft

*Judy Brittain*
assisted by Sally Harding

**BOOK CLUB ASSOCIATES LONDON**

The Good Housekeeping Step-by-Step Encyclopaedia of
Needlecraft was conceived, edited and designed by
Dorling Kindersley Limited, 9 Henrietta Street,
London WC2E 8PS.

**Managing Editor**   Amy Carroll
**Art Direction**   Stuart Jackman
**Project Editor**   Susan Berry
**Art Editors**   Douglas Wilson, Simon Jennings
**Editors**   Miren Lopategui, Alan Buckingham, Fiona MacIntyre,
Pamela Tubby
**Designers**   Helen Sampy, Sandra Schneider, Roger Twinn,
Dick Boddy, Linda Nash
**Design Assistant**   Gary Marsh
**Picture Research**   Caroline Lucas

This edition published 1980, Book Club Associates
By arrangement with Ebury Press, National Magazine House,
72 Broadwick Street London W1V 2BP

# CONTENTS

# INTRODUCTION

Since earliest times needles and yarns have been used to make beautiful works of art. As man developed, so did his skill with the needle: designs were introduced, stitch techniques were invented, yarns and threads were spun, and fabrics of all descriptions were woven. During the Middle Ages needlework reached such a high degree of skill that embroideries were regarded as the highest form of art and even surpassed the brushwork of the painter. By the time of the Renaissance, fabrics of all types, including lace, were made and worked with unbelievable diligence to reflect scenes from the imagination, literature and the Bible. This state of high art continued right down to the middle of the nineteenth century and then came the machines.

With the advent of machines life became easier for people generally. Fabrics could now be bought and not woven at home and there was no longer any need to hand decorate them as techniques were developed to print designs on fabrics. Slowly the needle was laid aside and skills which were commonplace in the past became rarities. The understanding of the workings of needle and yarn and their partnership with the texture of fabric were forgotten. Though mass-produced designs and patterns kept the needle busy, the freshness and spontaneity of original work was lost. The embroideries of the past fell into decay, beautiful works became worn and damaged and few people were capable of mending them. That is the state today.

This book, therefore, was undertaken to reinstate the craft of the needle — to set out the stages necessary to produce needlework as beautiful as that on display throughout the world. But needles and yarn on their own cannot work the magic. They have to be master-minded, and it is to the master mind that this book is directed. That is, to anyone who would like to study needlecraft techniques, to learn how many marvellous things can be made with the simple needle, and to discover that what looks complicated is, in fact, easy. And, I hope, that those who read the book, or sections of it, will later be able to make their own works of art so that new and beautiful needlework will once more come into being and become part of a future heritage.

*Judy Brittain*

# What you will find in this book

The Good Housekeeping Step-by-Step Encyclopaedia of Needle-craft deals with many different types of needlework and handcraft. Seven major chapters encompass the fifteen separate crafts of knitting, crochet, knotting, netting, macramé, tatting, rugmaking, weaving, embroidery, needlepoint lace, needlepoint, patchwork, appliqué, quilting and sewing. Each section starts with the first and simplest stage and gradually builds up into the most sophisticated form of that particular subject.

As a way of making each craft appealing and approachable to the reader, the material is organized into five categories. First, the *history* of each craft is discussed in order to trace the development of techniques included in this book, many of which had been abandoned in the last century. Second, the *materials and equipment* necessary to produce satisfactory results are shown. Before the advent of present-day technology with its mass produced products, it was understood by most needleworkers that subtle relationships existed between threads and fabrics. And although it is the rare worker today who will go so far as to use gold threads, jewels or hand-dyed yarns, one must pick and choose carefully among manu-factured products. Third, *how-to techniques,* mainly as step-by-step diagrams, cover all the working stages of a craft and simplify them so that successful results can be achieved by every worker. Fourth, separate *stitch glossaries* provide the handicrafter with an oppor-tunity for creating varied and individual work. Some patterns reproduce historical examples while others have been specially created for the book. Fifth, *projects and design ideas* should encourage and inspire readers to put new and old skills to work.

Needlemade lace (Punto in aria) of the seventeenth century; techniques for working lace are on pages 286-9.

One of the stages in working a simple oval pattern in cutwork; techniques begin on page 281.

A sampler of macramé patterns worked in fine threads in the eighteenth century; macramé begins on page 174.

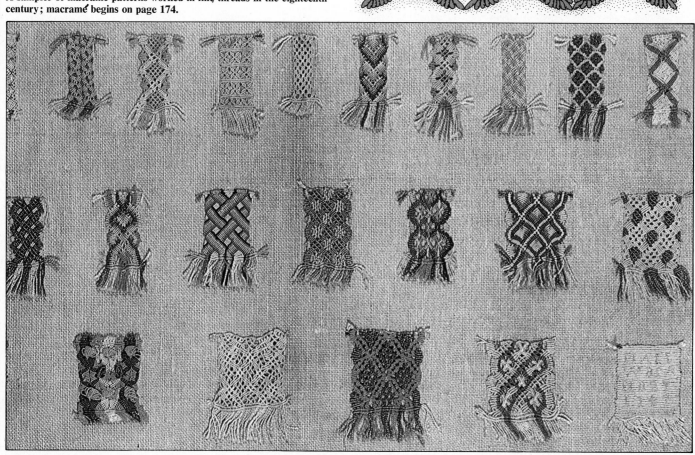

# Examples of pages

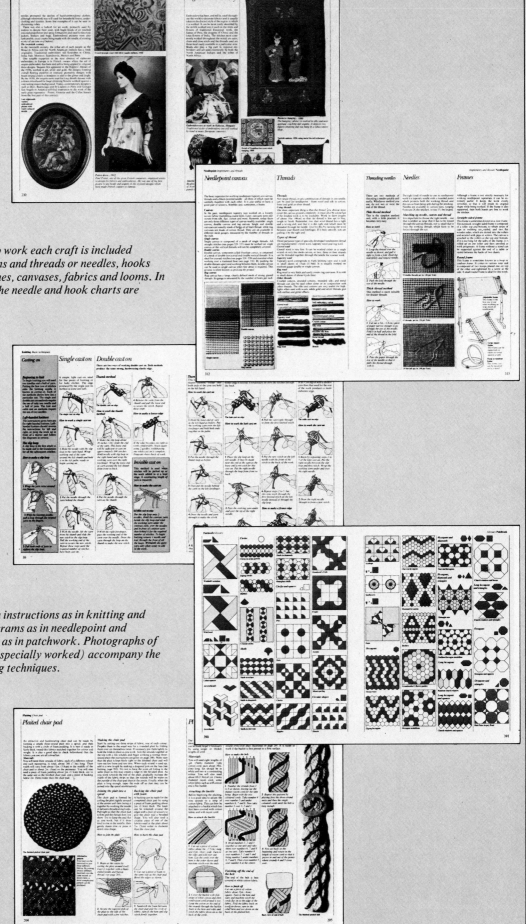

## Illustrated histories
The development of each craft is traced from its earliest known existing pieces through to the trends in its present-day applications. Where applicable, references to the best known examples are accompanied by photographs.

## Materials and equipment
The range of materials necessary to work each craft is included following the history. Not only yarns and threads or needles, hooks and pins but, where necessary, frames, canvases, fabrics and looms. In the knitting and crochet chapters, the needle and hook charts are drawn to size.

## How-to techniques
The necessary steps in beginning, working, diversifying and finishing each craft is the core matter of the book. Technique pages are lavishly illustrated, usually by step-by-step drawings of work in progress and by photographs of the desired effect. Where different techniques exist for certain effects, these are also illustrated. Technique pages appear throughout the chapter.

## Stitch glossaries
These may be in the form of written instructions as in knitting and crochet, or as stepped working diagrams as in needlepoint and embroidery, or as illustrations only as in patchwork. Photographs of each sample (whether historical or specially worked) accompany the text. Glossary pages follow working techniques.

## Projects and design ideas
These include garments, accessories and household items. The adult patterns are for sweaters, hats, gloves, socks, belts, purses and shawls while those for children refer to slipper socks, hats, sweaters, overalls and dresses. Projects for the home include cushions, quilts, curtains and linen. Projects are found following the necessary techniques.

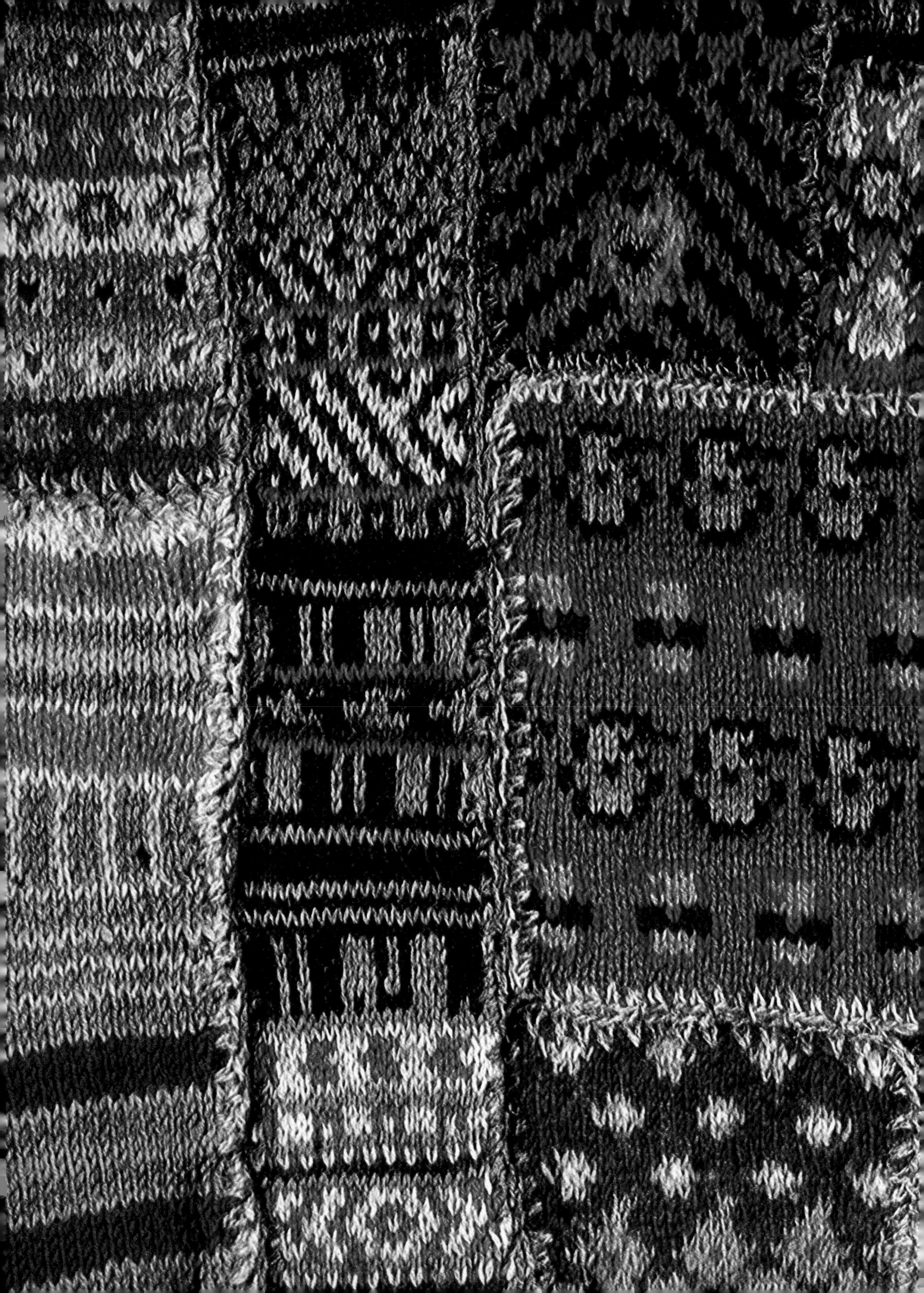

# 1
# KNITTING
*including Frame and Machine Knitting*

# History of knitting

Knitting has come back into popularity recently. Well-known fashion designers such as Kaffe Fassett, Bill Gibb, Chloë, Jap and Missoni, for example, have all turned to knitting to create new and exciting fabrics for their designs.

Knitting itself has an ancient and fascinating history, although its origins are difficult to trace because textiles perish with the passing of time and few early pieces have been found intact. It is not known how knitting first began – possibly it developed from looped sewing stitches. But "true" knitting is, in fact, the process of making a continuous looped fabric from a length of yarn and two or more eyeless needles.

Textiles from the early Peruvian cultures of about 900 BC to 600 AD are said to have been knitted, as are some fourth century AD Coptic sandal socks found in an Egyptian tomb. However, although these fabrics have the appearance of knitting, close inspection shows that they are not made from one continuous length of yarn, but are formed from separate lengths of thread looped together with a sewing needle.

Some scholars have suggested that knitting was a highly developed craft as far back as 900 BC. They refer to Homer's *Odyssey*, arguing that the web which Penelope worked by day and unpicked by night must have been knitted and not woven. If it were woven, they argue, far more time would have been required to unpick it than to weave it; whereas if it were knitted, then "the labour of the day, though long pursued, would be unwove in a few minutes without difficulty". (William Felkin, *History of Machine Wrought Hosiery and Lace Manufacturers, 1867*).

### The first true knitting
The earliest known pieces of knitting were discovered in Arabia and date back to the seventh century AD. The work is extremely sophisticated and the colourwork echoes the patterns of carpets and tiles of that time. The craft must have been in existence for much longer to have reached the skill and excellence found in these early fragments.

Although there is no evidence to show how knitting spread from the Middle East to Europe, it was presumably introduced as a craft by soldiers, sailors and traders from the East. One of the earliest European references is the fourteenth century painting by Master Bertram of the *Visit of the Angels* in the Buxtehude altarpiece where the Virgin Mary is depicted knitting on four needles.

### The formation of the guilds
It is only much later on that the history of knitting becomes easy to trace. In Europe, knitting had become sufficiently well-known by the mid-sixteenth century for the first knitting guild to be set up, in Paris in 1527. Not long after, there were knitting guilds in all the main cities of Europe. The guilds were dominated by men; in those days, the women were the spinners, and the men the weavers and knitters. The only women admitted to guild membership were widows who, on their husband's death, took on their work. The guilds exacted a high standard: each apprentice to guild membership had to study for six years and then had to submit for his final examination, a shirt, a felted cap, a pair of socks and a colourwork carpet.

By this time different types of garments had become popular in different countries. In southern Europe, the emphasis was on church work. France, Spain and Italy became famous for their fine, lacy stockings, gloves and knitted jackets. In Germany and Austria knitting was generally done in wool, and frequently embroidered, and these countries also became famous for their magnificent knitted carpets which were used as wall hangings.

The fashion for knitting spread from country to country, and the silk knitted stockings popular in the south of Europe became the fashion for courtiers in England after Elizabeth I was presented with a pair.

It was also at this time that knitting began to flourish both as a humble domestic craft and as a cottage industry, particularly in countries such as England where the wool trade was becoming increasingly important to the economy. Knitting must have been an accepted form of fabric-making in England by the mid-sixteenth century for a law of 1565 laid down that every person above the age of seven had to wear "upon the Sabbath or holyday (unless in the time of their travel out of town) upon their head a cap of wool knitted, thickened and dressed in England". Failure to do so would result in a fine for each day's transgression.

Many of these knit caps still exist in museums. They were knitted, then felted by immersion in water for four or five days. When the wool had thickened sufficiently the cap was blocked into shape, brushed with a teasel brush and even cut without fear that the knitting would unravel. The Turkish fez and French beret are still made in this way.

As knitting increased in popularity, and the demand for knitted garments grew, a Cambridge graduate, William Lee, watching his wife knit realized that the knitting process could be made much faster and in 1589 he invented the first knitting machine – a frame, for producing stockings. His invention revolutionized the knitting industry and the principles of his design remain the basis for the modern machine knitting industry.

As a result of the introduction of the knitting machine the hand knitting industry waned except in the more remote areas of Europe. By the mid-eighteenth century the schools and guilds of Europe were on the decline. However, hand knitting continued as a domestic craft.

**Knitting in the round**
*The Virgin Mary is shown picking up stitches on a shirt in a fourteenth century painting.*

**Stocking knitter**
*A drawing by Annibel Caracci (1560–1609) shows an itinerant stocking knitter. He was able to work two threads at a time by attaching a spool for each to a board located on his hip.*

### Knitting since the seventeenth century

Many beautiful examples of knitting still survive from the seventeenth century onwards although humbler, everyday articles have perished. From this time date the masterpiece carpets, probably knitted on frames, the richly worked ecclesiastical gloves knitted in red silks and golden threads and the silk vest which Charles I wore at his execution.

Later on, the nineteenth century wars also provided work for knitters throughout Europe. Knitted garments for the troops were made in some shapes which are still worn today. For example, the Battle of Balaclava in the Crimean War gave its name to the knitted helmets which covered the head, ears and necks of the soldiers who had to fight in extreme cold.

It was also during this time that the growth of a leisured class of women with time on their hands helped to reintroduce some very delicate needlecrafts including lace knitting. Many fine lace stitches were invented in the nineteenth century and used to make shawls, mittens, tablecloths, bonnets and layettes. Bead purses and pincushions, with the minutely beaded pastoral scenes and complex designs reached the realms of art and some experts feel that the intricate and delicate work of this period has never been surpassed.

The advent of the circulating library and ladies' journals and magazines helped to popularise the craft but in the more remote communities the traditional patterns and designs continued to be handed down by example and by word of mouth. It is claimed that the patterns of the Fair Isle knitters, for example, are virtually unchanged from the originals which are reported to have been taught to them by shipwrecked Spanish sailors after the attempted Armada invasion of Britain in the sixteenth century.

Some of these traditional patterns have since become commercialized. In the 1920s the multicoloured work of the Fair Isles became very fashionable in America and Europe. The popularity of authentic Fair Isle hand knitted sweaters is still widespread and even today the island knitters continue to work using patterns handed down by memory, rather than by using written instructions.

### History of implements

The earliest implements for knitting are unknown, but it is presumed that the very first types of knitting may have been worked by winding a thread in and out of the fingers and slipping loops off after repeated windings to form a simple knitted mesh. North American Indians are known to have worked knitting of this type on sticks either held in the hand or stuck vertically in the ground. This simple technique became highly sophisticated when a pegged frame was used instead of sticks or fingers,

and a hooked needle was used to slip the wool loops off the pegs.

The main types of frame were either rectangular or round, with the pegs set around a central slot or hole, through which the completed knitting dropped. Frames were built to many sizes and the yarn wound in different ways to create a variety of stitches. Knitting frames were used to create the large multi-coloured carpets produced by the knitting guilds in the Middle Ages. They were a particularly versatile method of working with colour as different colours were wound around each peg.

Since the mid-nineteenth century, frames have become a rarity. However, the technique survives in the spool or bobbin knitting still worked by children to make long knitted cords. Moreover, knitting frames are still sometimes used for making very wide fabric or tubular fabric.

The earliest knitting needles had a hook at one end, rather like a modern crochet hook. The first straight needles were made of a wide variety of materials: copper, wood, wire, ivory, and tortoiseshell. The needles were usually made by the knitters themselves and were carefully wrapped in leather folders to retain their polish or stowed away in cases of carved wood and ivory. Their ends were carefully ground from time to time to ensure their sharpness and protected with cork or wood stoppers when not in use.

To the professional hand knitters in the early days, speed was essential. Knitting sheaths or sticks were worn into which the right needle was inserted, leaving the right hand free to shuttle the stitches at high speed from needle to needle. Sometimes as many as 200 stitches a minute were knitted in this way.

These knitting sheaths or sticks were works of art, often elaborately carved and bearing the knitter's initials. They were worn on the right hip and tucked into the knitter's belt or apron strings. Knitting sticks and sheaths were often made by young men as gifts and love tokens for their sweethearts, and the carving included hearts, flowers and mottoes.

Some sheaths had chains attached with a hook at the end. The chain was wrapped around the back of the waist and the knitting attached to the hook. This served the double purpose of keeping the work under tension and it also meant that the knitter could drop the work at any time, leaving it to dangle safely from the hook at her waist.

These needles and methods of speed knitting continued right up to the twentieth century, until the advent of machine-made steel needles.

Today, knitting needles are manufactured in a comprehensive range of differing diameters and lengths. While most needles are straight, circular needles and double-pointed needles are also available. A range of needles is on page 14.

**Spanish ecclesiastical glove**
*Sixteenth century workers knitted many fine altar gloves in silk and gold thread on very fine needles.*

**Knit shirt of Charles I**
*Most probably knitted in Italy, this silk shirt was said to have been worn by the King on his death in 1649.*

**Silk thread pincushion**
*Very fine needles were used to produce this eighteenth century geometrically patterned pincushion.*

# Knitting implements

### Types of needles

The basic tools for knitting are called needles. All needles have a pointed tip to form the stitches and a long, cylindrical body to hold the stitches made. Modern needles are double pointed or knobbed at one end and are machine-made of steel, aluminium, plastic or wood. They are made in different sizes and types for different jobs but needle sizes have now been internationally standardized into 17 graded sizes, from 2 mm to 17 mm.

Knitting needles are used in pairs or sets of three or more. They can either be flexible or rigid. Rigid needles are best for speed. Flexible needles are more comfortable to use but bend easily. All needles must have a good sharp point. Blunt needles fray yarn, reduce speed and are difficult to use, especially with fine lace stitch patterns.

It helps to have a complete set of needles of every size so that a number of stitch gauge, or tension, samples can be worked in one session and the stitch gauge (page 69) adjusted immediately if necessary.

### Double pointed

Double pointed needles are sold in sets of four or six and sized in the usual way. They are used for knitting in the round, for tubular shapes such as socks, gloves or sweater sleeves, and for flat rounds or medallion shapes.

### Circular

Circular needles are a pair of pointed needles joined by a flexible length of wire or plastic. They are made in various sizes and lengths, and are used for knitting large tubular shapes like sweaters and skirts.

### Cable

Cable needles are much shorter than double pointed needles. Sized in the usual way, and pointed at both ends, they may also be curved. They are used for holding stitches at the back or front of the work when working twisted cable patterns.

### Other equipment

Five additional accessories are essential for successful knitting.

#### Needle gauge

A needle gauge is a piece of metal or plastic punched with holes which correspond to the standard sizes of needles. Each hole is marked with the international metric code as well as American and English sizings.

#### Row counter

A row counter is a small plastic cylinder which is pushed onto the end of a knitting needle and used to count rows or stitch groups. A small number register on the side is operated by twisting the top of the counter.

#### Stitch holder

A stitch holder resembles a large safety pin and is used to hold stitches not being worked.

#### Sewing needle

A blunt ended wool sewing needle is used to sew pieces of knitting together. The blunt end does not split the yarn. Fine pointed sewing needles should only be used for attaching a woven fabric to knitting.

#### Tape measure

A tape measure or a rigid ruler is essential for measuring stitch gauge and for checking the length of a piece of knitting.

## Popular knitting needle sizes

| English | Metric |
|---|---|
| 14 | 2mm |
| 13 | 2¼mm |
| 12 | 2¾mm |
| 11 | 3mm |
| 10 | 3¼mm |
| 9 | 3¾mm |
| 8 | 4mm |
| 7 | 4½mm |
| 6 | 5mm |
| 5 | 5½mm |
| 4 | 6mm |
| 3 | 6½mm |
| 2 | 7mm |
| 1 | 7½mm |
| 0 | 8mm |
| 00 | 9mm |

1/2 Stitch holders
3 Double pointed needles
4 Wool needles 5 Cable needle
6 Circular needles
7 Standard knitting needles
8 Row and stitch counters
9 Needle gauge 10 Cable needle
11 Wool pins
12 Measuring device
13 Scissors 14 Tape measure

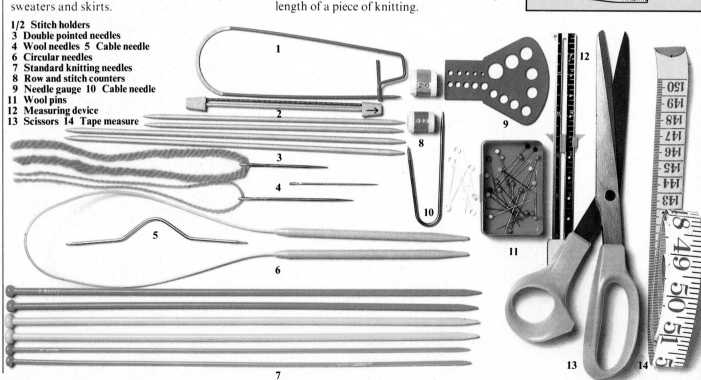

## How to wind knitting yarns

# Knitting yarn

Most yarn is sold already wound into balls but occasionally it is necessary to wind from the coiled hank or skein into a ball before knitting can begin. Carefully unfold the hank then stretch it around 2 chairs placed back to back, or loop it over the fingers of a helper, leaving the thumbs free to manoeuvre the yarn. Begin winding with the end of the hank: winding from the inside causes tangles.

Wind all yarns, especially natural ones, loosely. Wool is an elastic fibre and, if it is tightly wound into balls it will knit up stretched and then relax, or shrink back, disastrously when it is washed.

Yarn is the name for the spun strands of fibre which can either be animal, vegetable or mineral. The most common types of yarn fibre are shown below.

Each strand of knitting yarn is known as a ply.

Two or more strands can be combined to form yarns of different thicknesses.

There are several methods of spinning the strands of fibre so that yarns of varying textures are produced, from corded to curled.

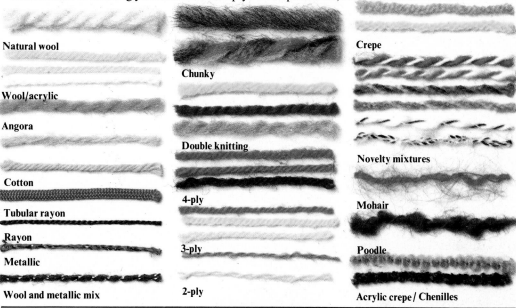

**Natural wool**

**Wool/acrylic**

**Angora**

**Cotton**

**Tubular rayon**

**Rayon**

**Metallic**

**Wool and metallic mix**

**Chunky**

**Double knitting**

**4-ply**

**3-ply**

**2-ply**

**Crepe**

**Novelty mixtures**

**Mohair**

**Poodle**

**Acrylic crepe / Chenilles**

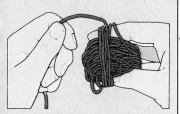

***How to wind so that the working end is on top***
*Wrap wool tightly around 3 fingers. Slip the coils off. Change position of wool and continue, adding more layers and forming a well-shaped ball.*

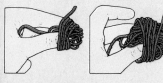

***How to wind so that the working end comes from the centre***
*Hold the end of yarn across the palm. Wind the yarn in a figure of eight over thumb and forefinger. Slip yarn off, fold over and wind loosely into a ball.*

**Wound yarns**
Hand knitting yarn is commonly sold in "balls", **1**, **2**, and **3**, or "hanks", **4** and **5**. Cone and cylinder shapes, **6**, **7**, and **8**, are best for machine knitting

15

## Casting on

### Beginning to knit

To begin knitting you will need two needles and a ball of yarn. Putting the first row of stitches onto the knitting needle is known as *casting on*. Each of the methods shown here has a particular use. The single and double cast on methods require the use of only one needle and a ball of yarn. The knit and cable cast on methods require the use of two needles.

### Left-handed knitters

The instructions given here are for right-handed knitters. Left-handed knitters should reverse the instructions for left and right, or prop the book up in front of a mirror and follow the diagrams in reverse.

### The slip loop

A slip loop is the first stitch to be made and is the foundation for all the subsequent stitches.

### How to make a slip loop

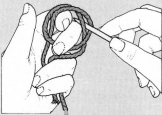

**1** *Wrap the yarn twice around two fingers.*

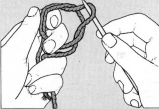

**2** *With the knitting needle, pull a loop through the twisted yarn on the fingers.*

**3** *Pull both ends of yarn to tighten the slip loop.*

## Single cast on

A simple, light cast on, ideal for fine pieces of knitting or for baby clothes. The edge produced by the single cast on method is loose and soft.

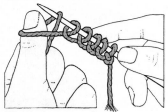

**The single cast on edge**

### How to work a single cast on

**1** *Hold the needle with the slip loop in the right hand. Wrap working end of the yarn around the left thumb and hold it in the left palm, ready to begin casting on.*

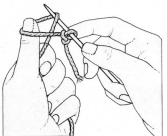

**2** *Put the needle through the yarn behind the thumb.*

**3** *With the needle, lift the yarn from the thumb and slide the new stitch to the slip loop. Pull the working end of the yarn to secure the new stitch. Repeat these steps until the required number of stitches have been cast on.*

## Double cast on

### Thumb method

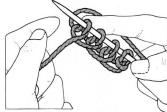

**The double cast on edge**

### How to work the thumb method

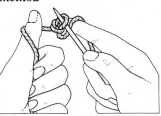

**1** *Make the slip loop about 36 inches (1m) from the end of the yarn. This loose end will be sufficient to cast on approximately 100 stitches. Hold needle with slip loop in the right hand and wrap the working yarn over the right forefinger. Wrap the loose end of yarn around the left thumb from front to back.*

**2** *Put the needle through the yarn on the thumb.*

**3** *With the right forefinger, pass the working end of the yarn over the needle. Draw the yarn through the loop on the thumb to make the new stitch.*

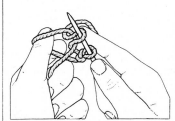

**4** *Release the yarn from the thumb and pull the loose end to secure the stitch. Repeat these steps.*

### How to make a looser edge

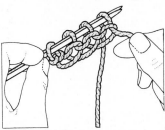

*If the edge becomes too tight to work comfortably, begin again using 2 needles, withdrawing one when cast on is complete. Diagram shows back of work.*

## Invisible cast on

This method is used when stitches will be picked up or the work added to at a later stage. A contrasting length of yarn is required.

### How to make the cast on

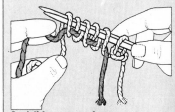

**Invisible cast on edge**

*Put the slip loop onto 2 needles. Hold the contrast yarn beside the slip loop and wind the working yarn under the contrast yarn, over the needles and in front of contrast yarn then behind it for the required number of stitches. To begin knitting remove 1 needle and knit through the front of all the loops. Withdraw the spare yarn only when ready to add to the work.*

# Knit stitch cast on

# Cable cast on

## Thumb and finger method

This is exactly the same as the thumb method, except that both ends of the yarn are held in the left hand.

### How to work the cast on

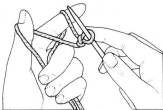

**1** Hold the loose end of yarn in the left hand as before. Put the working yarn over the left forefinger and hold both ends together in the palm.

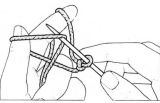

**2** Put the needle through the thumb loop as before.

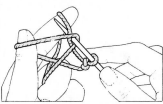

**3** Then put the needle behind the yarn on the left forefinger.

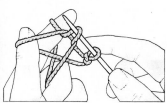

**4** Draw the needle and yarn through to make the stitch.

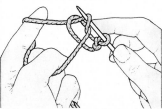

**5** Release the yarn from the thumb and pull both ends to secure the new stitch.

---

The knit stitch cast on produces a soft, loose edge suitable for fine lace stitches. Two needles are needed for this cast on. If a firmer edge is desired, it is necessary to cross the stitches through the back.

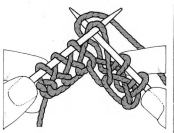

**The knit cast on edge**

### How to work the knit cast on

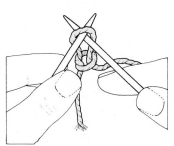

**1** Place the slip loop on the left needle. It may be made near the end of the yarn as the loose end is not used for this cast on. Put the right needle through the loop from front to back.

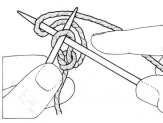

**2** Pass the working yarn under and over the tip of the right needle.

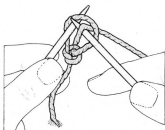

**3** Draw the right needle with the yarn at its tip back through the slip loop.

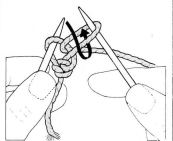

**4** Pull the yarn right through to form the first knitted stitch.

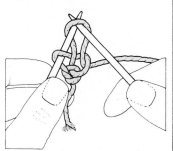

**5** Put the new stitch on the left needle with the front of the stitch to the back of the work.

**6** Repeat steps 2 to 5, but this time work through the first knitted stitch on the left needle instead of through the slip loop.

### How to make a firmer edge

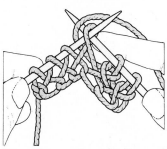

For a firmer edge, knit the first row through the back of the stitches, as shown, crossing them.

---

The cable cast on produces the strongest and most elastic edge of all. Casting on with a thicker yarn than that used for the rest of the work produces a more elaborate edge.

**The cable cast on edge**

### How to work the cast on

**1** Begin by repeating steps 1 to 5 of the knit cast on. Put the right needle between the slip loop and first stitch. Wrap the working yarn under and over the right needle.

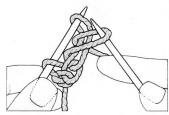

**2** Draw the right needle through to form a new stitch.

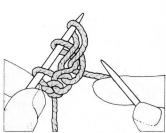

**3** Place the new stitch on the left needle. Continue, until the required number of stitches have been cast on.

## *Holding needles and yarn*

There are many ways of holding needles and yarn. Some methods make knitting faster, but all that matters is that each knitter finds a comfortable personal style. Threading the working end of yarn through the fingers controls tension and helps produce a firm, even fabric.

### *Yarn in right hand*

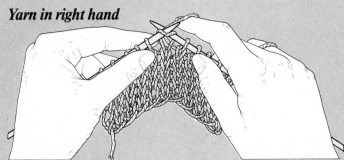

*Hold the needles as shown with the working yarn in the right hand. Use the right forefinger to wrap the working yarn over the needles.*

#### *How to work purl stitch*

*The right forefinger wraps the yarn around the needle. Hold the right needle like a pen for light work with short needles.*

#### *How to thread yarn*

*Thread the working yarn through the fingers of the right hand in either of the ways shown here.*

### *Yarn in left hand*

*The stitches are identical to those of right hand method. The left forefinger positions the yarn, the right needle moves to encircle the yarn when forming a new loop.*

#### *How to work purl stitch*

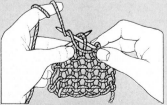

*The right needle encircles yarn before drawing loop through.*

#### *How to thread yarn*

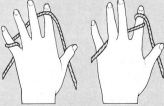

*Thread the working yarn in either of the ways shown.*

## *The basic knit stitch*

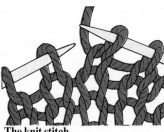

**The knit stitch**

### *How to knit*

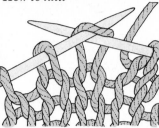

**1** *With the yarn to the back, insert the right needle from right to left through the front of the first stitch on the left-hand needle.*

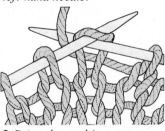

**2** *Bring the working yarn up and over the right needle.*

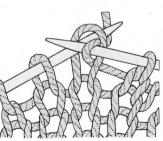

**3** *Draw the right needle and the yarn through the stitch, discarding the stitch on the left needle and at the same time forming a new stitch on the right needle. Continue in this way, knitting into the next and every subsequent stitch on the left needle until the end.*

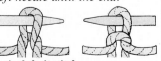

**A single knit stitch**
*The front of a knit stitch (left) and the reverse (right).*

### *Knitting the second row*

When the first row of knitting is complete, turn the work around and take the needle carrying the stitches, the right needle, in the left hand. The empty needle is held in the right hand ready to begin a new row of knitting. The back of the work now faces the knitter.

### *Garter stitch*

When every row is knitted back and forth on two needles, this fabric (below) called garter stitch is formed.

**Garter stitch**

### *Stocking stitch*

Stocking stitch (below) is made by knitting the first and every alternate row and purling the second and every alternate row.

**Stocking stitch**

### *Working stocking stitch in the round*

Knitting in the round on 3 or more needles does not require the work to be turned around, so the knit stitch is always on the front, or outside, of the work and the ridged purl will always be on the inside.

# The basic purl stitch

**The purl stitch**

*2 Bring the working yarn up over the right needle.*

### How to purl

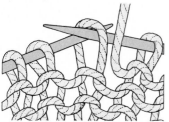

*1 With the yarn to the front of the work, insert the right needle from right to left through the front of the first stitch on the left needle.*

*3 Draw the right needle and the yarn through the stitch, discarding the stitch on the left needle and at the same time forming a new stitch on the right needle. Continue in this way, exchanging needles at the end of each row.*

### Knit and purl stitches combined

*When the first row of purl stitch is complete, turn the work around and begin a new row. If the purl row is succeeded by a knit row, and the two are worked alternately, Stocking stitch is formed. When every row is purled, Garter stitch is formed in the same way as knitting every row. The fabric above is formed from rows of knit stitches and rows of purl stitches.*

## Learning to knit if you are left handed

Follow the diagrams for holding needles and yarn (left) in a mirror. To knit as shown in right hand method, the working yarn is threaded through the fingers of the left hand. To knit, hold the needle bearing the stitches in the right hand and insert the left needle through the stitches. The left forefinger then moves the working yarn over the needles.

# Knit and purl variations

### Close knit and purl
This variation produces a very tight and even fabric. When worked with the yarn held in the left hand it is one of the fastest ways of knitting.

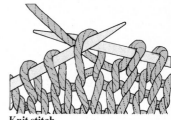

#### Knit stitch
*With the yarn in left hand and to back of work, insert right needle through back of stitch and knit in the usual way.*

**Knit stitch**

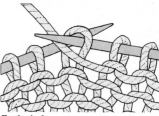

#### Purl stitch
*With yarn to front of work, insert right needle through front of stitch and purl in the usual way.*

**Purl stitch**

### Crossed knit and purl
Crossing or twisting the stitches produces a stronger, more elastic fabric. Both the knit and purl stitches are worked by knitting and purling into the *back* of the stitch.

#### Knit stitch
*With the yarn to the back of the work, insert the right needle through the back of the stitch and knit in the usual way.*

**Knit stitch**

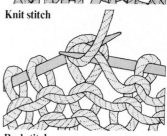

#### Purl stitch
*With the yarn to the front of the work, insert the right needle through the back of the stitch and purl in the usual way.*

**Purl stitch**

### Plaited stocking stitch
This is a very old and decorative stitch. It is sometimes used for bead knitting (page 63). The plaiting action is worked on every row which is purled.

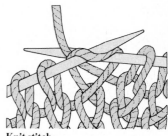

#### Knit stitch
*This is knitted through the front, in the same way as the basic knit stitch.*

**Knit stitch**

#### Purl stitch
*With the yarn to the front of the work, insert the right needle through the back of the stitch. Bring the yarn beneath the needle and draw through to form the crossed purl stitch.*

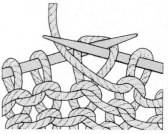

**Purl stitch**

# Picking up dropped stitches

Now that you have learnt how to knit and purl, you are ready to begin work on your first piece of knitting. These two pages contain a mixture of important information. Below are a number of general tips which will help you with your first pattern.

On the right is a detailed step by step guide showing how to pick up and replace dropped stitches and how to unpick the knitting to correct mistakes.

Five different ways of making a selvedge, or side edge, are shown on the facing page.

Finally, you must learn how to take the finished piece of knitting off the needles, this is known as *casting off*. There are four different cast off methods to choose from.

## Points to remember

**1** If possible use the brand and type of yarn specified in your knitting pattern.

**2** If you are buying several balls of yarn in one colour make sure that each ball comes from the same dye lot. Tones of colour vary slightly from dye bath to dye bath. The dye lot number is always marked on the yarn ball band.

**3** Always read the complete pattern instructions before beginning to work.

**4** Use long needles if you are knitting a pattern with a large number of stitches. If short needles are overloaded the stitches will slip off.

**5** Knit long fibred yarns, such as angora and mohair, loosely to allow the fibres to lie freely so that the fibres stand up.

**6** If you have any doubts about the length of a piece of knitting use the invisible cast on method (page 16). With this method you can always lengthen the work by picking up the stitches and knitting as many more rows as required in the opposite direction.

**7** Never leave off work in the middle of a row as this will stretch the knitting and make it easier for stitches to drop off.

## Picking up a knit stitch

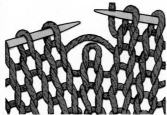

**A dropped knit stitch**

### How to pick up the stitch

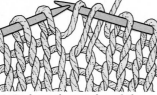

**1** *Pick up the stitch and the strand on the right needle, inserting the needle from the front to the back.*

**2** *Insert left needle from back to front through the stitch only.*

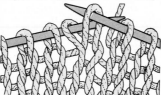

**3** *With the right needle, pull the strand through to re-form the stitch on the row above.*

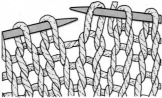

**4** *The stitch is on the right needle, but it is twisted.*

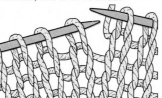

**5** *Place the stitch in the correct position on the left needle ready to begin knitting.*

## Picking up a purl stitch

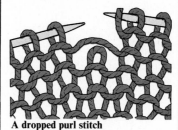

**A dropped purl stitch**

### How to pick up the stitch

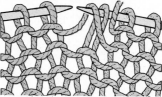

**1** *Pick up the stitch and the strand on the right needle, inserting the needle from the back to the front.*

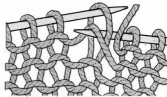

**2** *Insert the left needle from front to back through the stitch.*

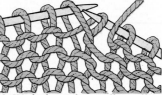

**3** *With the right needle, pull the strand through the stitch. Drop stitch from left needle.*

**4** *The re-formed stitch is now on the right needle.*

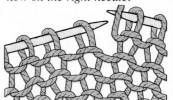

**5** *Place the re-formed stitch on the left needle, ready to begin purling.*

## Correcting a ladder

When a dropped stitch is not picked up it forms a ladder. This can easily happen, especially if work is left off in the middle of a row. Any patterned stitches using knit and purl combinations will need both the pick-up methods.

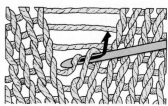

**Picking up a knit stitch**
*Insert a crochet hook through the front of the fallen stitch. Hook up one strand, pulling it through the stitch to form a new stitch one row further up. Continue to the top of the ladder. Secure any other dropped stitches with safety pins while picking up the first.*

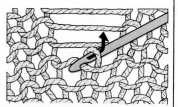

**Picking up a purl stitch**
*This is rather more difficult than on a knit row. After each strand has been picked up the hook must be taken out and re-inserted for the next stitch.*

## Unpicking mistakes

Mistakes can easily occur when following a pattern and remain unnoticed for several rows.

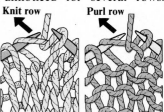

**Knit row**          **Purl row**

### How to unpick stitches

*Carefully, unpick the stitches, putting the needle into the row below and undoing the stitch above until the mistake is reached. The needle position is shown for a knit row (left), a purl row (right).*

# Selvedges

## Stocking stitch selvedge

The most common edge of all. The first and last stitches must be knitted firmly to keep the edge straight.

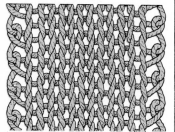

**How to knit the selvedge**
*All knit row stitches are knitted and all purl row stitches are purled.*

## Open selvedge

This makes a neat but decorative edge.

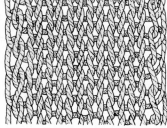

**How to knit the selvedge**
*Slip the first and last stitches of every knit row knitwise. Purl all the edge stitches in the purl row.*

## Slip stitch selvedge

Use when a neat edge is required on cardigans.

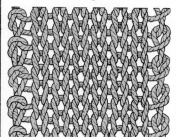

**How to knit the selvedge**
*Slip the first stitch of each row knitwise then knit the last stitch of each row. This forms even "pips" along the edge which look neat and make row counting easier as each "pip" counts for 2 rows. Sewing up is also made easy.*

## Flat selvedge

Prevents edges curling on ties, scarves, mats and shawls.

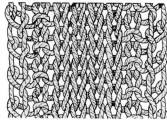

**How to knit the selvedge**
*Purl the second and next to last stitches on all knit rows. The purl rows do not alter.*

## Fancy selvedge

Use on openwork and lace knitting patterns.

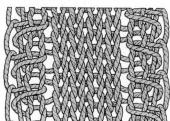

**How to knit the selvedge**
*First row Take yarn to front of work and once over needle to make a stitch (yarn over increases, page 34). Slip next stitch, knit one, pass slipped stitch over. Continue in pattern.*
*Second row Take yarn to back of work and once around needle, purl 2 stitches together. Continue in pattern.*

## Sewing up selvedges

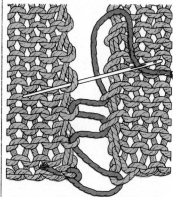

*Sew into the "pips" of the slip stitch selvedge when sewing up. A neatly worked selvedge makes sewing up much easier. See Finishing (page 84).*

# Casting off

## Quick and easy cast off

### Knit row

**1** *Knit the first 2 stitches and insert the tip of the left needle through the first stitch.*
**2** *Lift the first stitch over the second stitch and discard it. Continue discarding in this way to the end of the row and the last stitch. Cut yarn, slip end through stitch and pull tight to fasten off.*

### Purl row

*The method is exactly the same as for a knit row. Purl the first 2 stitches and insert the left needle through the first stitch. Lift it over the second stitch and discard. When casting off in rib, knit stitches are knitted and the purl stitches are purled.*

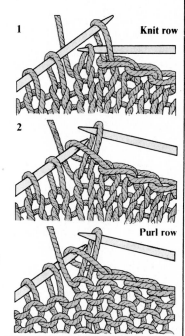

Knit row

Purl row

## Suspended cast off

Slower and looser than the method above.
*Knit first 2 stitches and insert tip of left needle through first stitch and lift over as though to cast off, but hold stitch instead. Knit third stitch and discard held stitch at the same time as completing the new stitch.*

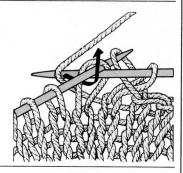

## Crochet cast off

This cast off is suitable for cotton and silk yarns which are less elastic than wool. A crochet hook is needed.
**1** *Knit the first stitch using the crochet hook. With the yarn at the back, insert the hook through the front of the second stitch. Take the yarn under and over the hook.*
**2** *With the hook, draw the yarn through the second and first stitches. Discard both, retaining the stitch just formed.*
**3** *Continue, drawing yarn through next stitch on needle and stitch on crochet hook.*

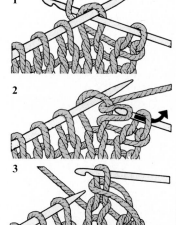

## Invisible cast off

Use when more work will be done on a piece of knitting.
*Break working yarn, thread on a wool sewing needle. Draw yarn through all the stitches on the knitting needle.*

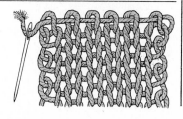

# Knit and purl patterns

Many different and richly textured patterns can be made simply by a combination of the basic knit and purl stitches.

## Reading knitting instructions

Knitting patterns may appear incomprehensible at first, but they are in fact a very logical shorthand. Instructions usually guide the knitter through a pattern row by row, if the instructions were written out in full even the simplest pattern would run for pages. So a standard set of abbreviations has evolved. An instruction reading k5, p3 means knit five stitches then purl three. An asterisk, *, means the following instruction must be repeated: for example; p1, *k5, p3; repeat from *, end p2. This means purl the first stitch in the row then repeat the k5, p3 sequence up to the last two stitches which are purled. Brackets are also used to indicate repeats: for example; k1, p1 (k5, p3) twice, k1, p1. This means that k5, p3 must be repeated twice before you move on to k1, p1. Each stitch pattern is preceded by the words "multiple of *x* sts". This indicates the number of stitches required to complete one repeat of the pattern in each row. Thus, "multiple of 8 sts plus 5", means cast on 16+5, 24+5, or 32+5 stitches, and so on. See page 97 for a complete list of abbreviations.

## Making a pattern sampler

The best way to learn a new stitch or stitch pattern is to try it out with needles and yarn. Make each sample large enough to show off the complete pattern and allow you to become thoroughly familiar with the pattern. Aim to work at least three complete repeats of the pattern in your sample. Use any yarn you like. As a general guide, using 4-ply yarn, 60 stitches cast on to No. 10 (metric size 3·25 mm) needles would give a sample approximately 8 in. (20·5 cm) wide. The samples can be knitted all together, one after the other to make a scarf or sewn together into a blanket.

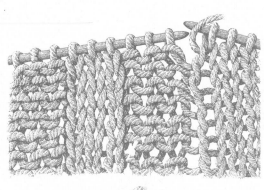

**Changing from a knit stitch to a purl stitch**
Having knit 3 stitches, take yarn to the front of the work then purl next 3 stitches in the usual way.

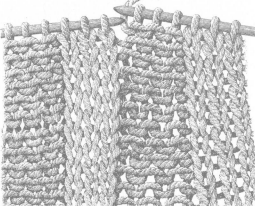

**Changing from a purl stitch to a knit stitch**
Having purled 3 stitches, take yarn to the back of the work then knit next 3 stitches in the usual way.

### One by one rib

Multiple of 2 sts plus 1.
**Row 1** *K1, p1; rep from *, end k1.
**Row 2** P1, *k1, p1; rep from *.
Repeat rows 1 and 2

### Three by three rib

Multiple of 6 sts plus 3.
**Row 1** *K3, p3; rep from *, end k3.
**Row 2** P3, *k3, p3; rep from *.
Repeat rows 1 and 2

### Knife pleat rib

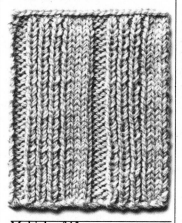

Multiple of 13 sts.
**Row 1** *K4, (p1, k1) 3 times, p3; rep from *.
**Row 2** *K3, (p1, k1) 3 times, p4; rep from *.
Repeat rows 1 and 2

### Reversible shadow rib

Multiple of 3 sts plus 2.
**Row 1** (WS) Knit.
**Row 2** P2, *k1-b, p2; rep from *.
Repeat rows 1 and 2.

### Sailor's rib

Multiple of 5 sts plus 1.
**Row 1** (RS) k1-b, *p1, k2, p1, k1-b; rep from *.
**Row 2** P1, *k1, p2, k1, p1; rep from *.
**Row 3** K1-b, *p4, k1-b; rep from *.
**Row 4** P1, *k4, p1; rep from *.
Repeat rows 1 to 4.

### Seeded rib check

Multiple of 4 sts plus 3.
**Row 1** K3, *p1, k3; rep from *.
**Row 2** K1, *p1, k3; rep from *, end p1, k1.
**Rows 3 and 5** Repeat row 1.
**Rows 4 and 6** Repeat row 2.
**Rows 7, 9 and 11** Repeat row 2.
**Rows 8, 10 and 12** Repeat row 1.
Repeat rows 1 to 12.

## Moss stitch

Cast on an uneven number of stitches.
**Row 1** *K1, p1; rep from *,
end k1
Repeat row 1.

## Double moss stitch

Multiple of 4 sts.
**Rows 1 and 2** *K2, p2; rep
from *.
**Rows 3 and 4** *P2, k2; rep
from *.
Repeat rows 1 to 4.

## Window pane check

Multiple of 8 sts plus 1.
**Row 1** (WS) and all other WS
rows purl.
**Row 2** P1, *k1, p1; rep from *.
**Rows 4, 8 and 12** Knit.
**Rows 6 and 10** P1, *k7, p1;
rep from *.
Repeat rows 1 to 12.

## Basket rib

Multiple of 4 sts plus 1.
**Row 1** (RS) K1, *p1, k1; rep
from*
**Row 2** K2, *p1, k3; rep from *,
end p1, k2.
**Row 3** P2, *k1, p1; rep from *,
end k1, p2.
**Row 4** P1, *k1, p1; rep from *.
**Row 5** K1, *p3, k1; rep from *.
**Row 6** P1, *k3, p1; rep from *.
Repeat rows 1 to 6.

## Basketweave

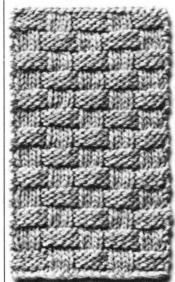

Multiple of 8 sts plus 5.
**Row 1** (RS) Knit.
**Row 2** K5, *p3, k5; rep from *.
**Row 3** P5, *k3, p5; rep from *.
**Row 4** Repeat row 2.
**Row 5** Knit.
**Row 6** K1, *p3, k5; rep from *,
end last rep k1 instead of k5.
**Row 7** *k3, p5; rep from *,
end last rep p1 instead of p5.
**Row 8** Repeat row 6.
Repeat rows 1 to 8.

## Ridge variations

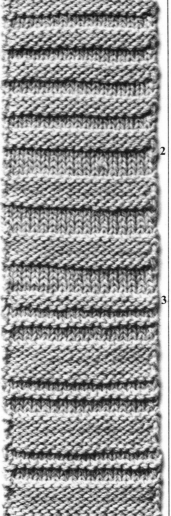

1
2
3

### Ridge variation 1

Any number of sts.
**Rows 1 and 2** (RS) Knit.
**Row 3** Purl.
**Rows 4 and 5** Knit.
**Row 6** Purl.
Repeat rows 1 to 6.

### Ridge variation 2

Any number of sts.
**Rows 1 and 2** Knit.
**Rows 3 and 5** Purl.
**Rows 4, 6, and 7** Knit.
**Rows 8 and 10** Purl.
**Row 9** Knit.
Repeat rows 1 to 10.

### Ridge variation 3

Any number of sts.
**Row 1** (RS) Knit.
**Rows 2 and 3** Purl.
**Row 4** Knit.
**Row 5** Purl.
**Row 6** Knit.
**Row 7** Purl.
**Rows 8 and 9** Knit.
**Row 10** Purl.
**Rows 11 and 12** Knit.
Repeat rows 1 to 12.

## Quaker ridge

Any numbers of sts.
**Rows 1, 3 and 5** (RS) Knit.
**Rows 2 and 4** Purl.
**Row 6** Knit.
**Rows 7, 9 and 11** Knit.
**Rows 8 and 10** Purl.
**Row 12** Knit.
**Row 13** Purl.
**Row 14** Knit.
Repeat rows 1 to 14.

## Staircase

Multiple of 32 sts.
**Rows 1 and 3** (RS) *K5, p11;
rep from *.
**Row 2** *K11, p5; rep from *.
**Rows 4 and 6** Purl.
**Row 5** Knit.
**Rows 7 and 9** P4, *k5, p11; rep
from *, end k5, p7.
**Row 8** K7, *p5, k11; rep from *,
end p5, k4.
**Rows 10 and 12** Purl.
**Row 11** Knit.
**Rows 13 and 15** P8, *k5, p11;
rep from *, end k5, p3.
**Row 14** K3, *p5, k11; rep
from *, end p5, k8.
**Rows 16 and 18** Purl.
**Row 17** Knit.
**Rows 19 and 21** K1, p11,
*k5, p11; rep from *, end k4.
**Row 20** P4, *k11, p5; rep
from *, end k11, p1.
**Row 22** Purl.
**Row 23** Knit.
**Row 24** Purl.
Repeat rows 1 to 24.

## Vandyke check

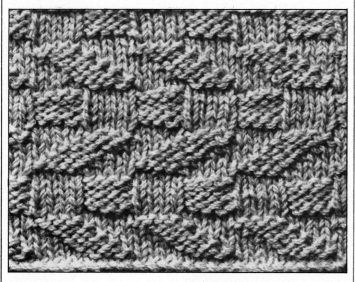

Multiple of 8 sts.
**Row 1** (RS) Knit.
**Row 2** *K4, p4; rep from *.
**Row 3** P1, *k4, p4; rep from *, end last rep p3 instead of p4.
**Row 4** K2, *p4, k4; rep from *, end last rep k2 instead of k4.
**Row 5** P3, *k4, p4; rep from *, end last rep p1 instead of p4.
**Row 6** *P4, k4; rep from *.
**Row 7** Knit.
**Rows 8, 9, 10 and 11** *K4, p4, rep from *.

**Row 12** Purl.
**Row 13** *P4, k4; rep from *.
**Row 14** K1, *p4, k4; rep from *, end last rep k3 instead of k4.
**Row 15** P2, *k4, p4; rep from *, end last rep p2 instead of p4.
**Row 16** K3, *p4, k4; rep from *, end last rep k1 instead of k4.
**Row 17** *K4, p4; rep from *.
**Row 18** Purl.
**Rows 19, 20, 21 and 22** *P4, k4; rep from *.
Repeat rows 1 to 22.

## Reversible diagonal

Multiple of 8 sts.
**Row 1** *K1, p1, k1, p5; rep from *.
**Row 2** *and all other even-numbered rows* Knit all knit sts and purl all purl sts.
**Row 3** K1, p1, *k5, p1, k1, p1; rep from *, end k5, p1.
**Row 5** K1, *p5, k1, p1, k1; rep from *, end p5, k1, p1.
**Row 7** *K5, p1, k1, p1; rep from *.

**Row 9** P4, *k1, p1, k1, p5; rep from *, end (k1, p1) twice.
**Row 11** K3, *p1, k1, p1, k5; rep from *, end p1, k1, p1, k2.
**Row 13** P2, *k1, p1, k1, p5; rep from *, end k1, p1, k1, p3.
**Row 15** *P1, k1, p1, k5; rep from *, end p1, k1, p1, k4.
**Row 16** See row 2.
Repeat rows 1 to 16.

## Diagonal rib

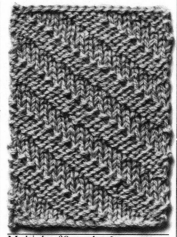

Multiple of 8 sts plus 6.
**Row 1** K1, *p4, k4; rep from *, end p4, k1.
**Row 2** K4, *p4, k4; rep from *, end p2.
**Row 3** K3, *p4, k4; rep from *, end p3.
**Row 4** K2, *p4, k4; rep from *, end p4.
**Row 5** P1, *k4, p4; rep from *, end k4, p1.
**Row 6** P4, *k4, p4; rep from *, end k2.
**Row 7** P3, *k4, p4; rep from *, end k3.
**Row 8** P2, *k4, p4; rep from *, end k4.
Repeat rows 1 to 8.

## Steep diagonal rib

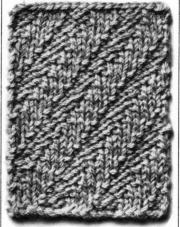

Multiple of 6 sts.
**Row 1** *P3, k3; rep from *.
**Row 2** *and all other even-numbered rows* Knit all knit sts and purl all purl sts.
**Row 3** P2, *k3, p3; rep from *, end k3, pl.
**Row 5** Pl, *k3, p3; rep from *, end k3, p2.
**Row 7** *K3, p3; rep from *.
**Row 9** K2, *p3, k3; rep from *, end p3, k1.
**Row 11** K1, *p3, k3; rep from *, end p3, k2.
**Row 12** See row 2.
Repeat rows 1 to 12.

## Double pennant

Multiple of 10 sts plus 1.
**Row 1** (RS) K1, *p7, k3; rep from *.
**Row 2** *P4, k6; rep from *, end p1.
**Row 3** K1, *p5, k5; rep from *.
**Row 4** *P6, k4; rep from *, end p1.
**Row 5** K1, *p3, k7; rep from *.
**Row 6** *P8, k2; rep from *, end p1.
**Row 7** K1, *p1, k9; rep from *.
**Rows 8, 9, 10, 11, 12 and 13** Repeat Rows 6, 5, 4, 3, 2, 1.
**Row 14** P2, *k7, p3; rep from *, end k7, p2.
**Row 15** *K3, p7; rep from *, end k1.
**Row 16** P1, *k6, p4; rep from *, end k6, p4; rep from *,
**Row 17** *K5, p5; rep from *, end k1.
**Row 18** P1, *k4, p6; rep from *, end k1.
**Row 19** *K7, p3; rep from *, end k1.
**Row 20** P1, *k2, p8; rep from *.
**Row 21** *K9, p1; rep from *, end k1.
**Rows 22, 23, 24, 25, 26, 27 and 28** Repeat rows 20, 19, 18, 17, 16, 15 and 14.
Repeat rows 1 to 28.

## *Zigzag*

| | |
|---|---|
| Multiple of 6 sts. | end last rep p1 instead of p3. |
| **Row 1** (WS) *and all other WS rows* Purl. | **Row 8** *P3, k3; rep from *. |
| **Row 2** *K3, p3; rep from *. | **Row 10** P2, *k3, p3; rep from *, end last rep p1 instead of p3. |
| **Row 4** P1, *k3, p3; rep from *, end last rep p2 instead of p3. | **Row 12** P1, *k3, p3; rep from *, end last rep p2 instead of p3. |
| **Row 6** P2, *k3, p3; rep from *, | Repeat rows 1 to 12. |

## *Ripple stitch*

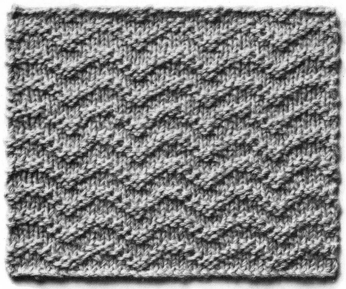

| | |
|---|---|
| Multiple of 8 sts plus 6. | **Row 6** P6, *k2, p6; rep from *. |
| **Row 1** (RS) K6, *p2, k6; rep from *. | **Row 7** P1, *k4, p4; rep from *, end k4, p1. |
| **Row 2** K1, *p4, k4; rep from *, end p4, k1. | **Row 8** K2, *p2, k2; rep from *. |
| **Row 3** P2, *k2, p2; rep from *. | **Row 9** K1, *p4, k4; rep from *, end p4, k1. |
| **Row 4** P1, *k4, p4; rep from *, end k4, p1. | **Row 10** P2, *k2, p6; rep from *, end k2, p2. |
| **Row 5** K2, *p2, k6; rep from *, end p2, k2. | Repeat rows 1 to 10. |

## *Chevron*

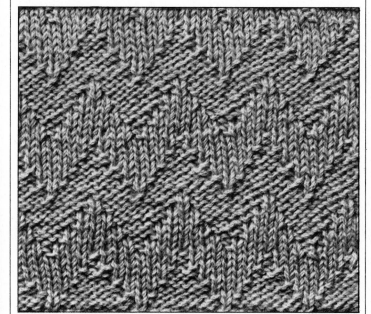

| | |
|---|---|
| Multiple of 8 sts. | **Row 9** *P1, k7; rep from *. |
| **Row 1** *K1, p7; rep from *. | **Row 11** P2, *k5, p3; rep from *, end k5, p1. |
| **Row 2** *and all even-numbered rows.* Knit all knit sts and purl all purl sts. | **Row 13** P3, *k3, p5; rep from *, end k3, p2. |
| **Row 3** K2, *p5, k3; rep from *, end p5, k1. | **Row 15** P4, *k1, p7; rep from *, end k1, p3. |
| **Row 5** K3, *p3, k5; rep from * end p3, k2. | **Row 16** See row 2. |
| **Row 7** K4, *p1, k7; rep from *, end p1, k3. | Repeat rows 1 to 16. |

## *Dotted chevron*

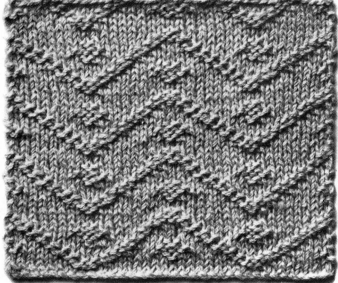

| | |
|---|---|
| Multiple of 18 sts. | **Row 6** *P3, (k2, p3) 3 times; rep from *. |
| **Row 1** (RS) *K8, p2, k8; rep from *. | **Row 7** *K2, p2, k3, p4, k3, p2, k2; rep from *. |
| **Row 2** *P7, k4, p7; rep from *. | **Row 8** *P1, k2, (p5, k2) twice, p1; rep from *. |
| **Row 3** *P1, k5, p2, k2, p2, k5, p1; rep from *. | **Row 9** P2, k14 p2; rep from *. |
| **Row 4** *K2, p3, k2, p4, k2, p3, k2; rep from *. | **Row 10** *K1, p16, k1; rep from *. |
| **Row 5** *P1, k3, p2, k6, p2, k3, p1; rep from *. | Repeat rows 1 to 10. |

## Lozenge brocade

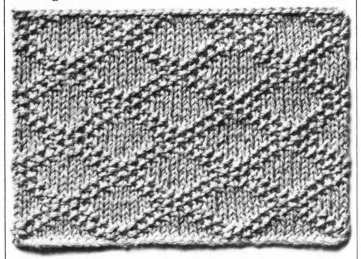

## Diamond block

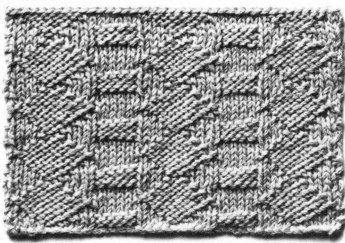

Multiple of 12 sts plus 1.
**Row 1** (RS) K1, *p1, k9, p1, k1; rep from *.
**Row 2** K1, *p1, k1, p7, k1, p1, k1; rep from *.
**Row 3** K1, *p1, k1, p1, k5, (p1, k1) twice; rep from *.
**Row 4** P1, *(p1, k1) twice, p3, k1, p1, k1, p2; rep from *.
**Row 5** K1, *k2, (p1, k1) 3 times p1, k3; rep from *.

**Row 6** P1, *p3, (k1, p1) twice, k1, p4; rep from *.
**Row 7** K1, *k4, p1, k1, p1, k5; rep from *.
**Row 8** Repeat row 6.
**Row 9** Repeat row 5.
**Row 10** Repeat row 4.
**Row 11** Repeat row 3.
**Row 12** Repeat row 2.
Repeat rows 1 to 12.

Multiple of 14 sts plus 5.
**Row 1** (RS) P5, *k4, p1, k4, p5; rep from *.
**Row 2** K5, *p3, k3, p3, k5; rep from *.
**Row 3** K7, *p5, k9; rep from *, end last rep k7.

**Row 4** P6, *k7, p7; rep from *, end last rep p6.
**Row 5** K5, *p9, k5; rep from *.
**Row 6** Repeat row 4.
**Row 7** Repeat row 3.
**Row 8** Repeat row 2.
Repeat rows 1 to 8.

## Parquet

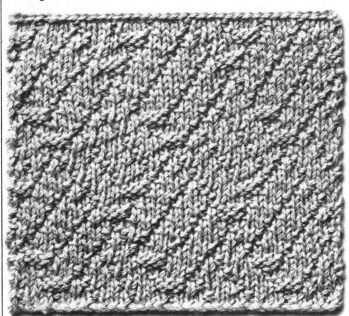

## Diamond check

Multiple of 12 sts.
**Row 1** *K2, (p1, k3) twice, p1, k1; rep from *.
**Row 2** *and all other even-numbered rows* Knit all knit sts and purl all purl sts.
**Row 3** *K3, p1, k1, p3, k3, p1; rep from *.
**Row 5** *P1, K3; rep from *.
**Row 7** *(K1, p1) twice, k3, p3, k2; rep from *.
**Row 9** *K2, (p1, k3) twice, p1, k1; rep from *.
**Row 11** *K1, (p1, k3) twice, p1, k1, p1; rep from *.

**Row 13** *P1, k3; rep from *.
**Row 15** *P2, k1, (p1, k3) twice, p1; rep from *.
**Row 17** *K2, (p1, k3) twice, p1, k1; rep from *.
**Row 19** *K3, p1, k1, p1, k3, p3; rep from *.
**Row 21** *P1, k3; rep from *.
**Row 23** *K1, p1, k3, (p1, k1) twice, p1, k2; rep from *.
**Row 24** See row 2.

Repeat rows 1 to 24.

Multiple of 18 sts plus 2.
**Row 1** (RS) P2, *k4, p4, k2, p2, k4, p2; rep from *.
**Row 2** K3, *p4, k2, p2, k2, p4, k4; rep from *, end last repeat k3.
**Row 3** K2, *p2, k4, p4, k4, p2, k2; rep from *.
**Row 4** P1, *k4, (p4, k2) twice, p2; rep from *, end k1.
**Row 5** P2, *k2, p2, k8, p2, k2, p2; rep from *.
**Row 6** K1, *p2, k4, p5, k2, p2, k2; rep from *, end p1.
**Row 7** K2, *p2, k2, p2, k4, (p2, k2) twice; rep from *.
**Row 8** P1, *k2, p2, k2, p6, k4, p2; rep from *, end k1.
**Rows 9, 11 and 12** Repeat rows 5, 3 and 2.

**Row 10** K1, *p2, (k2, p4) twice, k4; rep from *, end p1.
**Row 13** P2, *k4, p2, k2, p4, k4, p2; rep from *.
**Row 14** P5, *(k2, p2) twice, k2, p8; rep from *, end last repeat p5.
**Row 15** K4, *(p2, k2) twice, p4, k6; rep from *, end last repeat k4.
**Row 16** P3, *(k2, p2) 3 times, k2, p4; rep from *, end last repeat p3.
**Row 17** K4, *p4, (k2, p2) twice, k6; rep from *, end last repeat k4.
**Row 18** Repeat row 14.

Repeat rows 1 to 18.

## Double window pane

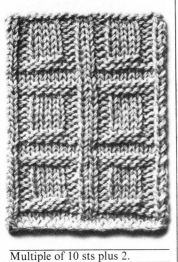

Multiple of 10 sts plus 2.
**Row 1** (RS) Knit.
**Row 2** Purl.
**Row 3** K2, *p8, k2; rep from *.
**Row 4** P2, *k8, p2; rep from *.
**Rows 5, 7 and 9** K2, *p2, k4, p2, k2; rep from *.
**Rows 6, 8 and 10** P2, *k2, p4, k2, p2; rep from *.
**Row 11** Repeat row 3.
**Row 12** Repeat row 4.
Repeat rows 1 to 12.

## Moss rib

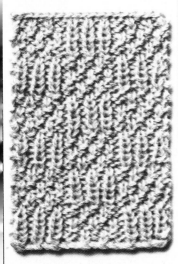

Multiple of 12 sts plus 7.
**Row 1** (P1, k1) 3 times, *p2, k1, p1, k1, p2, (k1, p1) twice, k1; rep from * end p1.
**Row 2** *and all other even-numbered rows.* Knit all knit sts and purl all purl sts.
**Row 3** P1, *k1, p1; rep from *.
**Row 5** Repeat row 1.
**Row 7** (K1, p1) twice, k1, *p2 (k1, p1) twice, k1, p2, k1, p1, k1; rep from * end p1, k1.
**Row 9** Repeat row 3.
**Row 11** Repeat row 7.
**Row 12** See row 2.
Repeat rows 1 to 12.

## Double basket pattern

Multiple of 18 sts plus 10.
**Row 1** (RS) *K11, p2, k2, p2, k1; rep from * end k10.
**Row 2** P1, k8, p1, *p1 (k2, p2) twice, k8, p1; rep from *.
**Row 3** *K1, p8, (k2, p2) twice, k1; rep from * end k1, p8, k1.
**Row 4** P10, *p1, k2, p2, k2, p11; rep from *.
**Rows 5, 6, 7 and 8** Repeat rows 1, 2, 3 and 4.
**Row 9** Knit.
**Row 10** (P2, k2) twice, p 2, *p10, (k2, p2) twice; rep from *.
**Row 11** *(K2, p2) twice, k2, p8; rep from *, end (k2, p2) twice, k2.
**Row 12** (P2, k2) twice, p2, *k8 (p2, k2) twice, p2; rep from *.
**Row 13** *(K2, p2) twice, k10; rep from *, end (k2, p2) twice, k2.
**Rows 14, 15, 16 and 17** Repeat rows 10, 11, 12 and 13.
**Row 18** Purl.
Repeat rows 1 to 18.

## Ripple rib

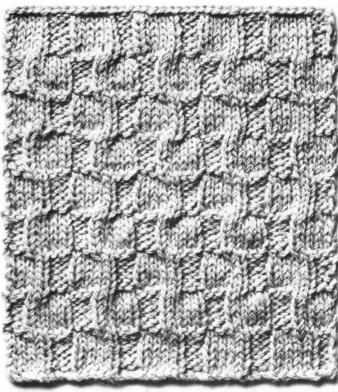

Multiple of 8 sts.
**Rows 1, 3 and 5** (RS) *P3, k5; rep from *.
**Rows 2, 4 and 6** *P5, k3; rep from *.

**Rows 7, 9 and 11** *K5, p3; rep from *.
**Rows 8, 10 and 12** *K3, p5; rep from *.
Repeat rows 1 to 12.

## Long rib check

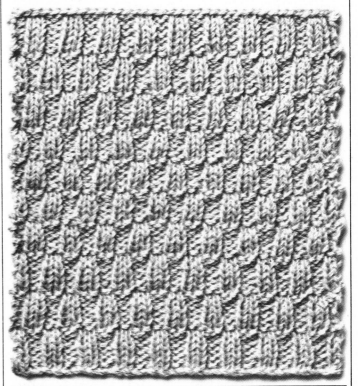

Multiple of 4 sts plus 2.
**Rows 1, 3 and 5** K2, *p2, k2; rep from *.
**Rows 2, 4 and 6** P2, *k2, p2; rep from *.

**Rows 7, 9 and 11** P2, *k2, p2; rep from *.
**Rows 8, 10 and 12** K2, *p2, k2; rep from *.
Repeat rows 1 to 12.

# Cable patterns

The basis of all cable patterns is a simple technique by which stitches are moved from one position to another in the same row. The knit and purl patterns are made by knitting the stitches in the order in which they come off the needle. Cabling alters this order because a number of stitches are slipped on to a cable needle and are held either at the back or the front of the work while the next few stitches are worked. The held stitches are then knitted off the cable needle which is shorter than a regular needle and pointed at both ends. This creates a plaited rope-like pattern called a cable. Cables can be as simple as the One over one rib (right), or very intricate and distinctive, like the fishermen's sweaters from Guernsey and Aran. Originally these complicated cables served as a means of identification for fishermen, and each area had its own cable or stitch pattern. Once the principle of working cables is understood, even the most complicated ones present no difficulty.

## Left over right cable

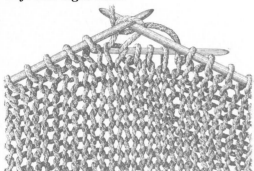

When 2 or more stitches must be crossed, the cable needle is used and the stitches that are to be crossed are transferred to it and held until it is their turn to be knitted. A 3 over 3 stitch cable is worked as follows: *Slip the first 3 stitches on to the cable needle, abbreviated as* cn, *and hold at back of work. Knit the next 3 stitches. Then knit the first 3 stitches off the* cn.

**Left over right cable**
This forms a left over right cable. Repeat cable row on every alternate row for a close cable.

## Right over left cable

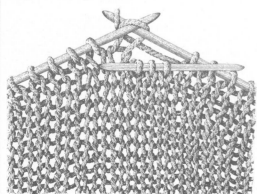

*Slip the first 3 stitches on to the* cn *and hold at the front of the work. Knit the next 3 stitches and then knit the 3 stitches from the cable needle. This right over left cable is the best one to use when knitting in the round as it is more convenient to hold stitches to the front.*

**Right over left cable**
The right over left cable is formed as shown.

### Four stitch cable

Centre panel of 8 sts.

**Rows 1 and 3** (WS) K2, p4, k2.

**Row 2** P2, k4, p2.

**Row 4** P2, sl next 2 sts to cn and hold at back (or for reverse at front); k2, then k2 from cn, p2.

Repeat rows 1 to 4.

### Five rib cable

Centre panel of 14 sts.

**Note** *Front Cross (FC): sl 2 sts to cn and hold at front, k2, then k2 from cn.*
*Back Cross (BC): sl 2 sts to cn and hold at back, k2, then k2 from cn.*

**Rows 1 and 3** (WS) K2, p10, k2.

**Row 2** P2, k2, (FC) twice, p2.

**Row 4** P2 (BC) twice, k2, p2.

Repeat rows 1 to 4.

### Six stitch cable

Centre panel of 10 sts.

**Rows 1 and 3** (WS) K2, p6, k2.

**Row 2** P2, k6, p2.

**Row 4** P2, sl next 3 sts to cn and hold at back (or at front); k3, then k3 from cn, p2.

**Row 5** As 1 and 3.

**Row 6** As 2.

Repeat rows 1 to 6.

### Six stitch cable 2

Centre panel of 10 sts.

**Rows 1 and 3** (WS) K2, p6, k2.

**Row 2** P2, k6, p2.

**Row 4** P2, sl next 3 sts to cn and hold at back (or at front); k3, then k3 from cn, p2.

**Rows 5 and 7** As 1 and 3.

**Rows 6 and 8** As 2.

Repeat rows 1 to 8.

## Eight stitch cable

Centre panel of 12 sts.
**Rows 1 and 3** (WS) K2, p8, k2.
**Row 2** P2, k8, p2.
**Row 4** P2, sl next 4 sts to cn and hold at back (or at front); k4, then k4 from cn, p2.
**Rows 5, 7 and 9** As 1 and 3.
**Rows 6, 8 and 10** As 2.
Repeat rows 1 to 10.

## Eccentric cable

Centre panel of 10 sts.
**Rows 1 and 3** (WS) K2, p6, k2.
**Row 2** P2, k6, p2.
**Row 4** P2, sl next 3 sts to cn and hold at back (or at front); k3, then k3 from cn, p2.
**Rows 5, 7, 9, 11, 13, 15 and 17** as 1 and 3.
**Rows 6 and 8** As 2.
**Row 10** As 4.
**Rows 12, 14, 16 and 18** As 2.
Repeat rows 1 to 18.

## Making a simple cable

Two very simple cable techniques which do not use the cable needle are shown below. You could introduce either into a plain stocking stitch pattern for a change of texture.

### One over one cable

The simplest cable of all is the one over one stitch cable which does not require a special cable needle. Try this method first as it illustrates the principle of cable work. The larger cables require a cable needle.

**Knit row cross over**

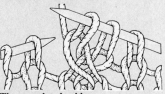

**The completed cable**
*The K1 over 1 movement has crossed the first stitch over the second from right to left.*

**How to make the cross-over**

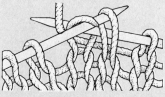

**1** *Miss the first stitch, take the needle behind it and insert the needle knitwise into the second stitch. Knit second stitch but do not discard it, instead hold it on the left needle.*

**2** *Knit the first stitch and at the same time slip the second stitch off the left needle. This is abbreviated as K1 over 1.*

**Purl row cross over**

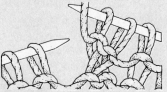

**The completed cable**
*The first stitch has crossed over the second. This will show on the front of the knitting as a cross-over from left to right.*

**How to make the cross-over**

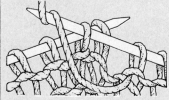

**1** *Miss the first stitch, take the needle in front and insert it purlwise into the second stitch. Purl this stitch, and hold it on the left needle.*

**2** *Purl the first stitch and at the same time slip the second off the left needle. This is abbreviated as P1 over 1.*

### Making a knotted rib

The knit cross-over produces a right over left cross. The purl cross-over only produces a left over right cross.

#### Right over left cross

Cast on a multiple of 5sts plus 3.
**Row 1** *P3, (k1 over 1)*. Rep from *, end p3.
**Row 2** K3, *p2, k3*. Rep from *.
Continue with these two rows.

#### Left over right cross

**Row 1** *P3, k2*. Rep from *, end p3.
**Row 2** K3, *(p1 over 1), k3*. Rep from *.

**Right over left cross**

**Left over right cross**

## Twisted cable

Centre panel of 16 sts.

**Rows 1, 3 and 5** (RS) K2, (p1, k1) 3 times, p6, k2.
**Rows 2, 4 and 6** K8, (p1, k1) 3 times, k2.
**Row 7** K2, sl next 7 sts to cn and hold at back, p5, then (p1, k1) 3 times, p1 (the 7 sts from cn); k2.
**Rows 8, 10, 12 and 14** K3, (p1, k1) 3 times, k7.
**Rows 9, 11 and 13** K2, p6, (k1, p1) 3 times, k2.
**Row 15** K2, sl next 5 sts to cn and hold at back (p1, k1) 3 times, p1 – the next 7 sts – then p5 from cn; k2.
**Row 16** Repeat row 2.
Repeat rows 1 to 16.

## Four rib cable

Panel of 17 sts.
**Note** *Back Cross (BC) : sl 1 st to cn and hold at back, k2, then p1 from cn. Front Cross (FC) : sl 2 sts to cn and hold at front, p1, then k2 from cn.*
**Row 1** (WS) (K2, p2) twice, k1, (p2, k2) twice.
**Row 2** P2, k2, p2, sl next 3 sts to cn and hold at *back*, k2, sl the purl st from cn back to left-hand needle and purl it, then k2 from cn; p2, k2, p2.
**Row 3** Repeat row 1.
**Row 4** P2, FC, BC, p1, FC BC, p2.
**Row 5** (K3, p4) twice, k3.
**Row 6** P3, sl next 2 sts to cn and hold at back, k2, then k2 from cn; p3, sl next 2 sts to hold at front, k2, then k2 from cn; p3.
**Row 7** Repeat row 5.
**Row 8** P2, BC, FC, p1, BC, FC, p2.
**Row 9** Repeat row 1.
**Row 10** P2, k2, p2, sl the next 3 sts to cn and hold at *front*, k2, then sl the purl st from cn back to left-hand needle and purl it, then k2 from cn; p2, k2, p2.
**Rows 11 to 16** Repeat rows 3 to 8.
Repeat rows 1 to 16.

## Framed cable

Panel of 18 sts.
**Note** *Front Cross (FC) : sl 3 sts to cn and hold in front, k3 then k3 from cn.*
*Single Front Cross (SFC) : sl 1 st to cn and hold at front, p1, then k1-b from cn.*
*Single Back Cross (SBC) : sl 1 st to cn and hold at back, k1-b, then p1 from cn.*
**Row 1** (WS) K5, p8, k5.
**Row 2** P4, SBC, k6, SFC, p4.
**Row 3** *and all subsequent WS rows* Knit all knit sts and purl all purl sts.
**Row 4** P3, SBC, p1, k6, p1, SFC, p3.
**Row 6** P2, SBC, p2, FC, p2, SFC, p2.
**Row 8** P1, SBC, p3, k6, p3, SFC, p1.
**Row 10** P1, SFC, p3, k6, p3, SBC, p1.
**Row 12** P2, SFC, p2, FC, p2, SBC, p2.
**Row 14** P3, SFC, p1, k6, p1, SBC, p3.
**Row 16** P4, SFC, k6, SBC, p4.
Repeat rows 1 to 16.

## Crossing cables

Panel of 24 sts.
**Note** *Front Cross (FC) : sl 3 sts to cn and hold at front, k3, then k3 from cn.*
*Back Cross (BC) : sl 3 sts to cn and hold in back, k3, then k3 from cn.*
*Single Front Cross (SFC) : sl 3 sts to cn and hold at front, p1, then k3 from cn.*
*Single Back Cross (SBC) : sl 1 st to cn and hold at back, k3, then p1 from cn.*
**Row 1** (WS) K2, p3, k4, p6, k4, p3, k2.
**Row 2** P2, k3, p4, BC, p4, k3, p2.
**Row 3** *and all subsequent WS rows* Knit all knit sts and purl all purl sts.
**Row 4** P2, (SFC, p2, SBC) twice, p2.
**Row 6** P3, SFC, SBC, p2, SFC, SBC, p3.
**Row 8** P4, FC, p4, BC, p4.
**Row 10** P3, SBC, SFC, p2, SBC, SFC, p3.
**Row 12** P2 (SBC, p2, SFC) twice, p2.
**Row 14** P2, k3, p4, FC, p4, k3, p2.
**Rows 16 and 18** Repeat rows 4 and 6.
**Row 20** P4, BC, p4, FC, p4.
**Rows 22 and 24** Repeat rows 10 and 12.
Repeat rows 1 to 24.

## *Aran cable*

Centre panel of 12 sts.
**Row 1** (WS) *and all other WS rows* K2, p8, k2.
**Row 2** P2, k4, sl 2 sts to cn and hold at front, k2, then k2 from cn; p2.
**Row 4** P2, k8, p2.
**Row 6** Repeat row 2.
**Row 8** P2, sl 2 sts to cn and hold at back, k2, then k2 from cn; k4, p2.
**Row 10** Repeat row 4.
**Row 12** Repeat row 8.
Repeat rows 1 to 12.

## *Banjo cable*

Centre panel of 12 sts.
**Row 1** (WS) K4, p4, k4.
**Row 2** P4, k5, p4.
**Row 3** K4, p1, sl 2 wyif, p1, k4.
**Row 4** P2, sl next 3 sts to cn and hold at back, k1, then p1, k1, p1 from cn; sl next st to cn and hold at front, k1, p1, k1, then k1 from cn; p2.
**Rows 5, 7 and 9** K2, (p1, k1) 3 times, p2, k2.
**Rows 6, 8 and 10** P2, (k1, p1) 3 times, k2, p2.
**Row 11** K2, sl 1 wyif, (k1, p1) 3 times, sl 1 wyif, k2.
**Row 12** P2, sl next st to cn and hold at front, p2, k1, then k1 from cn; sl next 3 sts to cn and hold at back, k1, then k1, p2 from cn, p2.
**Rows 13, 14, 15 and 16** Repeat rows 1 and 2 twice.
Repeat rows 1 to 16.

## *Bobble cable*

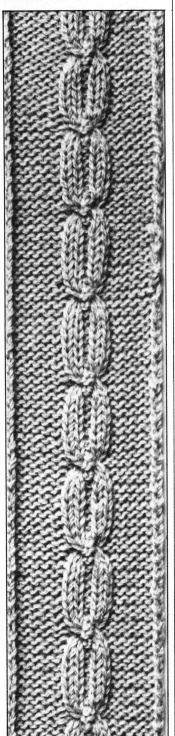

Centre panel of 10 sts.
**Row 1** (RS) (P2, k2) twice, p2.
**Row 2** (K2, p2) twice, k2.
**Row 3** P2, sl next 4 sts to cn and hold at front, k2, then sl the 2 purl sts from cn back to left-hand needle, then pass the cn with 2 remaining knit sts to back of work; p2 from left-hand needle, then k2 from cn; p2.
**Rows 4, 6 and 8** Repeat row 2.
**Rows 5, 7 and 9** Repeat row 1.
**Row 10** Repeat row 2.
Repeat rows 1 to 10.

## *Double cable*

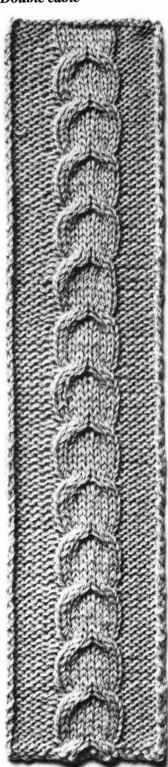

Centre panel of 12 sts.
**Rows 1, 3, 5 and 7** (WS) K2, p8, k2.
**Row 2** P2, sl next 2 sts to cn and hold at front, k2, then k2 from cn; sl next 2 sts to cn and hold at back, k2, then k2 from cn; p2.
**Rows 4, 6 and 8** P2, k8, p2.
Repeat rows 1 to 8.

## *Leaf rib*

## *Patchwork cable*

**Note** *Right Twist (RT): K2 tog, leaving sts on left needle. Insert right needle from the front between the two sts knitted together. Knit the first st again, then slip both sts from needle together.*
*Left Twist (LT): With right needle behind left needle, miss one st and knit second st through the back. Insert right needle into backs of both the missed st and the second st, and k2 tog-b.*

Multiple of 16 sts plus 1.

**Row 1** *(WS) and all other WS rows* Purl.

**Row 2** K1, *LT, (RT) twice, k3, (LT) twice, RT. k1; rep from *.

**Row 4** K2, *LT, (RT) twice, k1, (LT) twice, RT, k3; rep from *, end last repeat k2.

**Row 6** K1, *(LT) twice, RT, k3, LT, (RT) twice, k1; rep from *.

**Row 8** K2, *(LT) twice, RT, k1, LT, (RT) twice, k3; rep from *, end last repeat k2.

**Row 10** K1, *(LT) 3 times, k3, (RT) 3 times, k1; rep from *.

**Row 12** K2, *(LT) 3 times, k1, (RT) 3 times, k3; rep from *, end last repeat k2.

**Rows 14, 16, 18, 20 and 22**
Repeat rows 10, 8, 6, 4 and 2.

**Row 24** K2, *(RT) 3 times, k1, (LT) 3 times, k3; rep from *, end last repeat k2.

**Row 26** K1, *(RT) 3 times, k3, (LT) 3 times, k1; rep from *.

**Row 28** Repeat row 24.

Repeat rows 1 to 28.

Multiple of 18 sts plus 1.
**Note** *Back Cross (BC): sl 3 sts to cn and hold at back, k3, then k3 from cn.*

**Row 1** (RS) K1, *p8, k1, p1, k6, p1, k1; rep from *.

**Row 2** P1, *k1, p6, k1, p1, k8, p1; rep from *.

**Row 3** K2, *p6, k2, p1, BC, p1, k2; rep from *, end last repeat k1.

**Row 4** P1, *k1, p6, k1, p2, k6, p2; rep from *.

**Row 5** K3, *p4, k3, p1, k6, p1, k3; rep from *, end last repeat k1.

**Row 6** P1, *k1, p6, k1, p3, k4, p3; rep from *.

**Row 7** K4, *p2, k4, p1, k6, p1, k4; rep from *, end last repeat k1.

**Row 8** P1, *k1, p6, k1, p4, k2, p4; rep from *.

**Row 9** *K10, p1, BC, p1; rep from *, end k1.

**Rows 10 to 17** Repeat rows 8, 7, 6, 5, 4, 3, 2 and 1.

**Row 18** P1, *k1, p6, k1, p1; rep from *.

**Row 19** K1, *p1, k6, p1, k1, p8, k1; rep from *.

**Row 20** P1, *k8, p1, k1, p6, k1, p1; rep from *.

**Row 21** K1, *p1, BC, p1, k2, p6, k2; rep from *.

**Row 22** P2, k6, p2, k1, p6, k1, p2; rep from *, end last repeat p1.

**Row 23** K1, *p1, k6, p1, k3, p4, k3; rep from *.

**Row 24** P3, *k4, p3, k1, p6, k1, p3; rep from *, end last repeat p1.

**Row 25** K1, *p1, k6, p1, k4, p2, k4; rep from *.

**Row 26** P4, *k2, p4, k1, p6, k1, p4; rep from *, end last repeat p1.

**Row 27** K1, *p1, BC, p1, k10; rep from *.

**Rows 28 to 36** Repeat rows 26, 25, 24, 23, 22, 21, 20, 19 and 18.

Repeat rows 1 to 36.

# Big cross cable

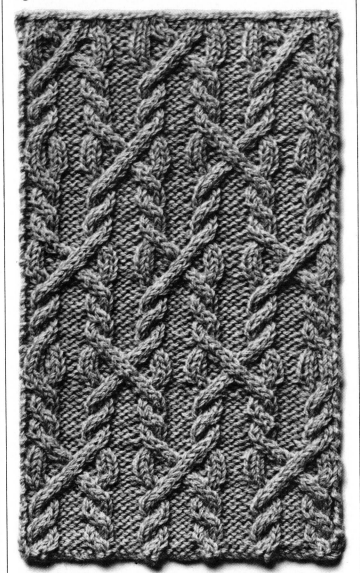

# Aran lattice

Multiple of 6 sts plus 2.

**Rows 1 and 3** (WS) K1, *k2, p4; rep from *, end k1.

**Row 2** K1, *sl next 2 sts to cn and hold at front, k2, then k2 from cn; p2; rep from *, end k1.

**Row 4** K1, p2, *k2, sl next 2 sts to cn and hold at back, k2, then p2 from cn; rep from *, end k5.

**Rows 5 and 7** K1, *p4, k2; rep from *, end k1.

**Row 6** K1, *p2, sl next 2 sts to cn and hold at back, k2, then k2 from cn; rep from *, end k1.

**Row 8** K5, *sl next 2 sts to cn and hold at front, p2, then k2 from cn; k2; rep from *, end p2, k1.

Repeat rows 1 to 8.

# Lattice cable

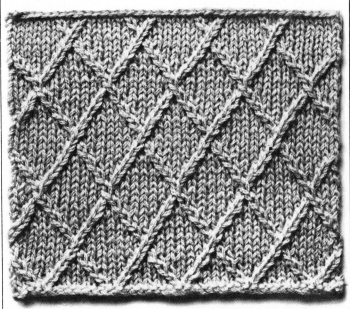

Multiple of 16 sts.

**Note** *Front Cross (FC): sl 2 sts to cn and hold at front, k2, then k2 from cn.*

*Front Purl Cross (FPC): sl 2 sts cn and hold at front, p2, then k2 from cn.*

*Single Front Cross (SFC): sl 2 sts to cn and hold at front, p1, then k2 from cn.*

*Back Cross (BC): sl 2 sts to cn and hold at back, k2, then k2 from cn.*

*Back Purl Cross (BPC): sl 2 sts to cn and hold at back, k2, then p2 from cn.*

*Single Back Cross (SBC): sl 1 st to cn and hold at back, k2, then p1 from cn.*

**Rows 1, 3, 5, 7, 9 and 11** (WS) K2, *p4, k4; rep from *, end p4, k2.

**Rows 2, 6 and 10** P2, *FC, p4, BC, p4; rep from *, end last repeat p2.

**Rows 4 and 8** P2, *k4, p4; rep from *, end k4, p2.

**Row 12** P1, *SBC, FPC, BPC, SFC, p2; rep from *, end last repeat p1.

**Rows 13 and 15** K1, *p2, k3, p4, k3, p2, k2; rep from *, end last repeat k1.

**Row 14** P1, *k2, p3, BC, p3, k2, p2; rep from *, end last repeat p1.

**Row 16** P1, *SFC, BPC, FPC, SBC, p2; rep from *, end last repeat p1.

**Rows 17, 19, 21, 23, 25 and 27** Repeat odd-numbered rows 1 to 11.

**Rows 18, 22 and 26** P2, *BC, p4, FC, p4; rep from *, end last repeat 2.

**Rows 20 and 24** Repeat rows 4 and 8.

**Row 28** P1, SBC, SFC, *p2, SBC, FPC, BPC, SFC; rep from *, end p2, SBC, SFC, p1.

**Rows 29 and 31** K1, (p2, k2) twice, *p2, k3, p4, k3, p2, k2; rep from *, end p2, k2, p2, k1.

**Row 30** P1, (k2, p2) twice, *k2, p3, FC, p3, k2, p2; rep from *, end k2, p2, k2, p1.

**Row 32** P1, SFC, SBC, *p2, SFC, BPC, FPC, SBC; rep from *, end p2, SFC, SBC, p1.

Repeat rows 1 to 32.

Multiple of 8 sts plus 2.

**Row 1** *(WS) and all other WS rows* Purl.

**Row 2** K1, *LT, k4, RT; rep from *, end k1.

**Row 4** K2, *LT, k2, RT, k2; rep from *.

**Row 6** K3, *LT, RT, k4; rep from *, end last repeat k3.

**Row 8** K4, *RT, k6; rep from *, end last repeat k4.

**Row 10** K3, *RT, LT, k4; rep from *, end last repeat k3.

**Row 12** K2, *RT, k2, LT, k2; rep from *.

**Row 14** K1, *RT, k4, LT; rep from *, end k1.

**Row 16** K8, *LT, k6; rep from *, end k2.

Repeat rows 1 to 16.

For LT and RT see p. 33

## *Increasing and decreasing*

To increase is to add, or to make stitches. To decrease means to lose stitches. Increasing and decreasing serve two purposes, either to shape the knitted fabric into a piece of clothing – a sweater front, sleeve or sock, or to make the decorative texture in lace, embossed and fancy stitches. For shaping clothes, increases or decreases are worked in pairs, so that the garment widens or narrows equally on both sides. Methods of using increases and decreases for shaping are explained fully on page 72.

There are many different ways of increasing and decreasing. It is worthwhile examining the various methods and trying each one out. An understanding of increasing and decreasing is the first step towards designing a piece of knitting. None of the methods are difficult, but, as with all knitting techniques, they must be followed exactly to achieve the correct result.

An increase can be made visible or invisible. Visible increases are usually used in lace and fancy patterns where the increase itself makes the openwork pattern by the hole or gap it creates in the knitting. Invisible increases are worked by making one stitch from another so that no hole or gap is left in the fabric. They are most often used for shaping garment pieces.

Decreases are always visible. The decreased stitch slants at an angle, either to the left or to the right. These angled stitches are important in the construction both of fancy textured fabric and clothes. It is important to pair your decreases so that the direction of slant of the various decreases is balanced. For example, if your first decrease is a slip stitch decrease which slants from right to left, your second decrease should be knitting two stitches together which will slant from left to right.

# *Visible increases*

### *Yarn over in a knit row*

This increase is created by a forward movement of the working yarn. It is abbreviated in knitting patterns as *yo*, yarn over; or, specifically in knit rows as *yfwd*, yarn forward.

#### *How to make the yarn over*

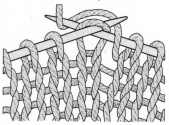

**1** *Bring the yarn forward to the front, loop it over the right needle, knit the next stitch.*

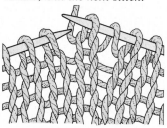

**2** *With the loop and the new stitch on the right needle, knit to the end of the row.*

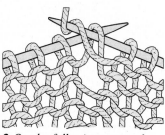

**3** *On the following row purl the yarn over loop in the usual way together with all the original stitches.*

### *Yarn over in a purl row*

The purl row increase is created by an over and under movement of the yarn. It is abbreviated as *yo* or, specifically in purl rows as *yrn*, yarn round needle.

#### *How to make the yarn over*

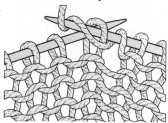

**1** *Take the yarn over the right needle to the back of the work and under the needle to the front of the work. Purl next stitch.*

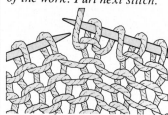

**2** *With the loop and the new stitch on the right needle, purl to the end of the row.*

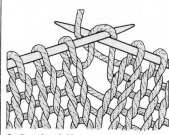

**3** *On the following row knit the yarn over loop in the usual way together with all the original stitches.*

### *Yarn over between knit and purl stitches*

The abbreviation for this yarn over needle movement is *yo* or *yon*.

#### *How to make the yarn over*

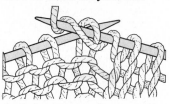

**1** *After a purl stitch and before a knit stitch, the yarn is already in the correct position at the front of the work. Knit the next stitch in the usual way.*

**2** *After a knit stitch and before a purl stitch, bring the yarn forward and under the needle then back over and around the needle again to the front. Purl the next stitch.*

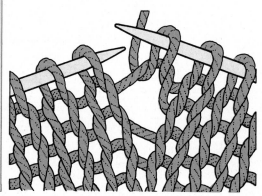

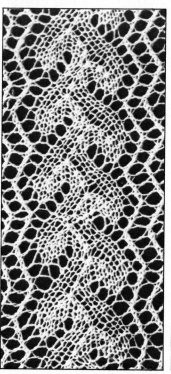

**The completed yarn over increase** The hole made by the yarn over increase is clearly visible once the loop has been knitted into on the following row.

### Yarn over on crossed fabrics

This increase is used with crossed knit and purl stitches (page 19). The result is the same as the basic yarn over. The increase is abbreviated as *yfwd* or *yrn*.

#### Yarn over in a crossed knit row

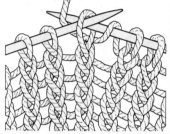

*Take the yarn over the right needle to the front and then around to the back again. Knit next stitch through the back. On the following row the loop is purled through the back in the same way as the other crossed purl stitches.*

#### Yarn over in a crossed purl row

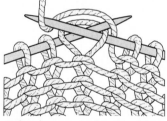

*Take the yarn under the right needle and to the back of the work. Purl the stitch through the back, taking the yarn over the right needle.*

### Lacy motifs

*The patterns on the centre panel (left) and border panel (right) of the Shetland shawl shown complete on page 101 are both made using the increasing and decreasing techniques set out in this section. The repeating tree motif on the border is formed by simple slanting faggot stitches which are further explained on page 43.*

### Yarn over on a selvedge

This increase can be used to form looped or picot edges, as well as selvedge increases.

#### Yarn over in a knit row

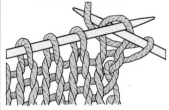

*With yarn forward, knit the first stitch in the usual way.*

#### Yarn over in a purl row

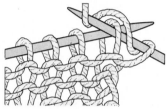

*Loop the yarn around the right needle from front to back. Purl the first stitch in the usual way.*

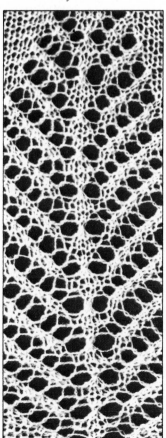

### Yarn over made invisible by crossing

This increase does not cause a hole and is not visible. The yarn movement is the same as that for a crossed stitch but the needle is inserted through the front as for an ordinary knit or purl stitch. Because it is crossed, the new stitch tightens up and closes the hole that would have appeared if the yarn over had not been knitted crossed.

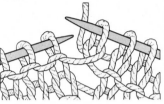

**The crossed yarn over**

#### How to make the yarn over

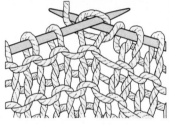

**1** *Take yarn over the right needle to front and then under to back of the work. Knit the next stitch through the front.*

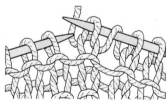

**2** *Continue to the end of the row in pattern.*

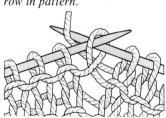

**3** *On the following row, insert the right needle through the front of the stitch, crossing it, and then knit the stitch in the usual way.*

Any number of stitches may be increased by the yarn over method. Take care that the newly-made stitches are knitted off in the correct order on the subsequent row.

### Double increase in a knit row

This increase is abbreviated as *yo2* or *yfwd2*. Take the yarn forward then take it around the needle, knit the next stitch and complete the row. *On the subsequent purl row the first new stitch is purled and the second stitch is knitted.*

### Double increases in a purl row

This is abbreviated as *yo2* or *yrn2*. Take the yarn around the needle as for a single yarn over, then take it completely around a second time and complete the purl row. *On the subsequent knit row, the first new stitch is knitted and the second purled.*

### Multiple increases in a knit row

This is abbreviated as *yo3*, or *yfwd3,4,5* depending on the number of increases required in the pattern. Take the yarn forward and then 3, 4 or more times around the needle according to the pattern. Knit to the end of the row. On the subsequent purl row the new stitches are knitted and purled alternately, but the last new stitch is *always knitted so the order of knitting and purling will depend on how many new stitches there are.*

### Multiple increases in a purl row

This is abbreviated as *yo3*, or *yrn3,4,5* depending on the pattern. Take the yarn around the needle then around again for the number of increases directed by the pattern, then purl to the end of the row. On the subsequent knit row, knit and purl the new stitches alternately remembering that *the last new stitch is always purled.*

# Invisible increases

### Make a new stitch by knitting two stitches from one

This increase is abbreviated as *Inc 1*, increase 1. Two stitches are made from one and a small horizontal bar is just visible below the first stitch on the right needle. This method is sometimes known as a "bar" increase.

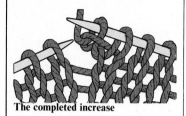

**The completed increase**

### How to increase in a knit row

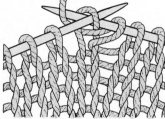

Knit into the front of the stitch in the usual way, then, without discarding the stitch on the left needle, knit into the back of it and discard it.

### How to increase in a purl row

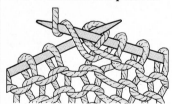

**1** Purl into the front of the stitch in the usual way, then without discarding the stitch on the left needle, purl into the back of it and discard it.

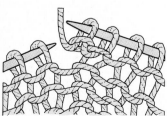

**2** Two stitches have been made from one.

### Make a new stitch by knitting into the stitch below

This increase, which is often called a "lifted increase", is abbreviated as *K up 1* or *P up 1*. In the completed increase the new stitch is on the right needle. Its origins are barely visible.

**The completed increase**

### How to increase in a knit row

**1** Insert right needle from front to back into top of stitch below the next one to be knitted. Knit the stitch in the usual way.

**2** Then knit the next stitch on the left needle and continue to the end of the row.

### How to increase in a purl row

**1** Insert right needle from back to front into top of stitch below the next one to be purled. Purl it in the usual way.

**2** Then purl the next stitch on the left needle and continue to the end of the row.

### Make a new stitch by knitting into the running thread below

This increase, which is often called a "raised increase", is abbreviated as *M1*, make one.

#### How to increase in a knit row

**1** Insert the left needle from front to back under the running thread between the left and right needles.

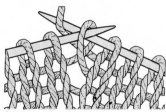

**2** Knit into the back of the raised running thread.

#### Visible variation

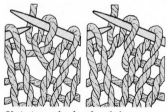

Knit into the back of the running thread, crossing it to make an invisible increase (left). Knit into the front for a visible increase (right).

#### How to increase in a purl row

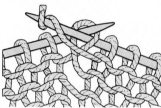

**1** Insert the left needle from front to back under the running thread between the left and right needles.

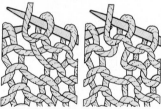

**2** Purl into the back of the raised running thread.

#### Visible variation

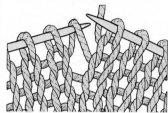

Purl into the back of the running thread, crossing it to make an invisible increase (left). Purl into the front for a visible increase (right).

## Double and multiple increases

### Invisible double increases

Two stitches are increased at the same time instead of one. The abbreviation for this method is *M2*, make two.

**Making two stitches from one**
Knit, purl and knit into the front of the same stitch before discarding it.

**Combining increases**
Make any 2 single increases in immediate succession.

### Invisible multiple increases

To make more than two extra stitches from one the method is the same as the double increase. Continue to knit, purl, knit, purl into the same stitch for the number of stitches that must be made. This technique of multiple increasing is used to make bobble and embossed patterns (page 38).

# Decreases

## Knitting two stitches together

This decrease is abbreviated as *K2 tog* or *P2 tog*. If the two stitches are knitted together through the front they form a decrease slanting from left to right. If knitted together through the back, the decrease will slant from right to left.

**The completed decrease**

### How to decrease in a knit row

Insert right needle through the front of the first 2 stitches on the left needle. Knit them together as a single stitch.

### How to decrease in a purl row

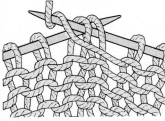

**1** Insert right needle through the front of the first 2 stitches on the left needle. Purl them together as a single stitch.

**2** The 2 stitches purled together through the front slant from left to right. If purled together through the back, the decrease slants from right to left.

## Knitting two stitches together on crossed fabrics

Knit two together in this way when you are using crossed knit and purl stitches.

### How to make the decrease

Insert the right needle through the back of the 2 stitches on the left needle and knit. This forms a decrease which slants from right to left.

## Knitting two together in knit and purl combinations

This method is used when a right to left slant is needed for shaping knitting, or when a knit and purl stitch must be decreased together

### How to make the decrease

Insert the right needle purlwise into the front of the first stitch and knitwise into the front of the second stitch. Knit both stitches together. One stitch will be crossed and the other one will be uncrossed.

## Double decreases

For rapid decreasing, use the slip and K2tog methods together. The double decrease is abbreviated as follows: on a knit row as *sl 1, k2 tog, psso* on a purl row as *s 1, p2 tog, psso* Alternatively, the decreases can be worked in a different order, as follows: *sl 2, k1, p2sso: sl 2, p1, p2sso;*

## The slip stitch decrease

This decrease is abbreviated as *Sl 1, k1, psso*, slip one, knit one, pass slipped stitch over. On a purl row the abbreviation is *Sl 1, p1, psso*. The decrease slants from right to left on the front of the knitting.

**The completed decrease**

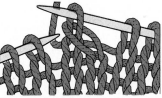

**The completed decrease**

### How to decrease in a knit row

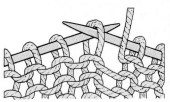

**1** Insert the right needle knitwise into the stitch on the left needle and then slip the stitch onto the right needle.

**2** Hold the slipped stitch and knit the next stitch in the usual way.

**3** Insert the left needle through the front of the slipped stitch and lift it over the stitch just knitted.

### How to decrease in a purl row

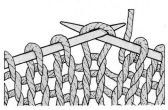

**1** Insert the right needle purlwise into the first stitch on the left needle and slip it onto the right needle.

**2** Hold the slipped stitch and purl the next stitch in the usual way.

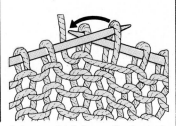

**3** Insert the left needle through the front of the slipped stitch, lift it over the stitch just purled.

## Pairing decreases

A purl row decrease slants from left to right on the front or knit side of the fabric. If you want a purl decrease to slant from right to left on the front, purl the first stitch on the left needle and replace it purlwise on the left needle. Lift the second stitch on the left needle over the first stitch, making a slant from right to left. Put the first stitch back on the right needle. This is abbreviated as: *P1, ret to LN, pnso*. In this way, decreases can be paired to form a pattern or to be used in shaping (page 72).

# Bobble and embossed patterns

In bobble and embossed patterns a single stitch is used repeatedly, and increased into to form a cluster of stitches. This cluster is knitted in a variety of ways according to the pattern. The stitches are then decreased and all but one stitch discarded. In this way the surface of the knitting is raised to a greater or lesser extent depending on whether the pattern calls for a round fat bobble or an embossed leaf design.

Like cables, many of these patterns were invented by fishing communities as a form of identification for any fishermen lost at sea. On the next few pages there are a variety of bobble and embossed patterns to work. The simple cluster principle used to raise the knitting remains the same as that shown below. It is important never to begin making an embossed stitch on the first stitch in a row as this makes an uneven selvedge which will be difficult to sew up later.

## How to make a simple bobble

**Row 1** *Knit two, take the yarn forward to the front of the work and over the needle, knit one but do not discard the stitch, instead continue working into the stitch twice more. In a knitting pattern this instruction would read:*
K2, *yo, k1*; rep from * twice more.

**Row 2** *Turn the work. Slip the first stitch purlwise onto the right needle and purl 5 stitches. Turn. Sl 1 pwise, p5.*

**Row 3** *Turn. Slip the first stitch knitwise onto the right needle and knit 5. Turn. Sl 1, kwise, k5.*

**Row 4** *Turn. Purl 2 stitches together 3 times. Turn. P2 tog 3 times.*

**Row 5** *Turn. Slip 1 stitch knitwise, knit 2 stitches together pass the slipped stitch over. One stitch remains on the needle. Turn. Sl 1 kwise, k2 tog, psso. I st rem.*

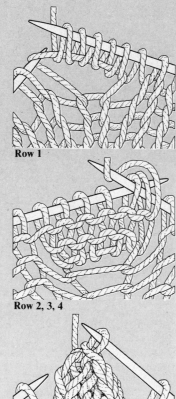

**Row 1**

**Row 2, 3, 4**

**Row 5**

### The finished bobble

These five rows form a simple bobble. In the patterns which follow, different types of bobble and embossed stitches are produced, but the basic principle remains the same.

## Berry stitch

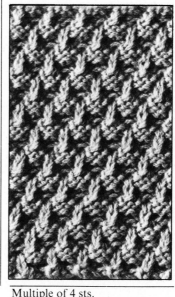

Multiple of 4 sts.
**Row 1** (WS) *(K1, yo, k1) in same st, p3 tog; rep from *.
**Row 2** *K1, p3; rep from *.
**Row 3** *K3, p1; rep from *.
**Row 4** *P1, k3; rep from *.
**Row 5** *P3 tog, (k1, yo, k1) in same st; rep from *.
**Row 6** *P3, k1; rep from *.
**Row 7** *P1, k3; rep from *.
**Row 8** *K3, p1; rep from *.
Repeat rows 1 to 8.

## Gooseberry pattern

Odd number of sts.
**Row 1** (RS) Knit.
**Row 2** K1, *(p1, yo, p1, yo, p1) in next st, making 5 sts from one; k1, rep from *.
**Row 3** Purl.
**Row 4** K1, *sl 2 wyif, p3 tog, p2sso, k1; rep from *.
**Row 5** Knit.
**Row 6** K2, *(p1, yo, p1, yo, p1) in next st, k1; rep from *, end k1.
**Row 7** Purl.
**Row 8** K2, *sl 2 wyif, p3 tog, p2sso, k1; rep from *, end k1.
Repeat rows 1 to 8.

## Puffball pattern

| Multiple of 10 sts plus 2. | **Rows 5, 6 and 7** Repeat rows 1, 2 and 3. |
|---|---|
| **Rows 1 and 3** (WS) Purl. | |
| **Row 2** Knit. | **Row 8** K6, rep from * of row 4; end last repeat k6 instead of k10. |
| **Row 4** K1, *(k5, turn, p5, turn) 3 times, k10; rep from *, end k1. | Repeat rows 1 to 8. |

## Bluebell pattern

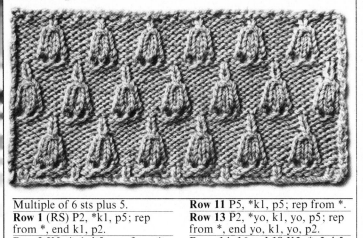

Multiple of 6 sts plus 5.
**Row 1** (RS) P2, *k1, p5; rep from *, end k1, p2.
**Row 2** K2, *p1, k5; rep from *, end p1, k2.
**Row 3** P5, *yo, k1, yo, p5; rep from *.
**Rows 4, 6 and 8** K5, *p3, k5; rep from *.
**Rows 5 and 7** P5, *k3, p5; rep from *.
**Row 9** P5, *sl 1, k2 tog, psso, p5; rep from *.
**Rows 10 and 12** K5, *p1, k5; rep from *.
**Row 11** P5, *k1, p5; rep from *.
**Row 13** P2, *yo, k1, yo, p5; rep from *, end yo, k1, yo, p2.
**Rows 14, 16 and 18** K2, *p3, k5; rep from *, end p3, k2.
**Rows 15 and 17** P2, *k3, p5; rep from *, end k3, p2.
**Row 19** P2, *sl 1, k2 tog, psso, p5; rep from *, end sl 1, k2 tog, psso, p2.
**Row 20** Repeat row 2.
Repeat rows 1 to 20.

## Grape pattern

Multiple of 20 sts plus 1.
**Note** *Throughout pattern MB (Make Bobble) as follows: (k1, yo, k1, yo, k1) into the same st forming 5 bobble sts; turn work around and p5 across the bobble sts; turn again and k5, then pass the 4th, 3rd, 2nd, and first sts separately over the last st knitted, completing bobble.*
**Row 1** (RS) K1, *(p4, k1) twice, p4, MB, p4, k1; rep from *.
**Row 2** P1, *k4, p1-b (into bobble st); (k4, p1) 3 times; rep from *.
**Row 3** K1, *(p4, k1) twice, p3, MB, p1, MB, p3, k1; rep from *.
**Row 4** P1, *k3, p1-b, k1, p1-b, k3, p1, (k4, p1) twice; rep from *.
**Row 5** K1, *(p4, k1) twice, p2, MB, (p1, MB) twice, p2, k1; rep from *.
**Row 6** P1, *k2, p1-b, (k1, p1-b) twice, k2, p1, (k4, p1) twice; rep from *.
**Row 7** K1, *p4, MB, (p4, k1) 3 times; rep from *.
**Row 8** P1, *(k4, p1) twice, k4, p1-b, k4, p1; rep from *.
**Row 9** K1, *p3, MB, p1, MB, p3, k1, (p4, k1) twice; rep from *.
**Row 10** P1, *(k4, p1) twice, k3, p1-b, k1, p1-b, k3, p1; rep from *.
**Row 11** K1, *p2, MB, (p1, MB) twice, p2, k1, (p4, k1) twice; rep from *.
**Row 12** P1, *(k4, p1) twice, k2, (p1-b, k1) twice, p1-b, k2, p1; rep from *.
Repeat rows 1 to 12.

## Tassel pattern

Panel of 15 sts.
**Row 1** (RS) Purl.
**Row 2** Knit.
**Row 3** P7, Make Bobble (MB) as follows: (k1, yo, k1, yo, k1) in next st, turn and p5, turn and k5, turn and p2 tog, p1, p2 tog; turn and sl 1, k2 tog, psso, completing bobble; p7.
**Row 4** K7, p1-b, k7.
**Row 5** P4, MB, p2, k1-b, p2, MB, p4.
**Row 6** K4, p1-b, k2, p1, k2, p1-b, k4.
**Row 7** P2, MB, p1, sl next st to cn and hold in front, p1, then k1 from cn (Front Cross, FC); p1, k1-b, p1, sl next st to cn and hold at back, k1, then p1 from cn (Back Cross, BC); p1, MB, p2.
**Row 8** K2, p1-b, k2, (p1, k1) 3 times, k1, p1-b, k2.
**Row 9** P2, FC, p1, FC, k1-b, BC, p1, BC, p2.
**Row 10** K3, BC, k1, p3, k1, FC, k3.
**Row 11** P4, FC, Make One (M1) pwise by purling into the back of running thread; sl 1, k2 tog, psso, M1 pwise, BC, p4.
**Row 12** K5, BC, p1, FC, k5.
**Row 13** P5, purl into front and back of next st, sl 1, k2 tog, psso, purl into front and back of next st, p5.
**Row 14** K7, p1, k7.
**Rows 15 and 16** Repeat rows 1 and 2.
Repeat rows 1 to 16.

## Looped knitting

To knit a sample;
Cast on an odd number of stitches and knit one row.
Row 2 (WS) K1, *insert needle knitwise into next st, take yarn away from you twice around the point of the right hand needle and the finger (or two fingers if you want longer loops) then around the needle again, draw the 3 loops through the st on the left hand needle but do not drop this stitch off the needle, sl the 3 loops on to the left hand needle, then knit tog this stitch and the 3 loops, k1, rep from * to the end.
Work either one or 3 rows of stocking stitch between the loop rows.
    The size of the loops can be varied depending on how many fingers the yarn is looped over. A different coloured or textured yarn can be used for the loops. This should be held in the left hand, looped around the fingers and then knitted off in the original yarn.

**Making the loop**

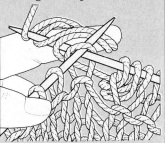

*The yarn is twisted around the right needle 3 times. When combined with stitch on left hand needle, the loops are secured.*

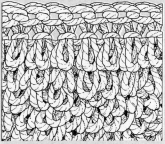

**The completed knitting**
*Shaggy textured knitting is easy to work and makes a thick, warm fabric.*

**Bobble and diamond cable**

**Bouquet pattern**

## Bobble and diamond cable

Panel of 17 sts.

**Note** *Front Cross (FC): sl 2 sts to cn and hold in front, p1 then k2 from cn.*

*Back Cross (BC): sl 1 st to cn and hold at back, k2, then p1 from cn.*

**Rows 1 and 3** (WS) K6, p2, k1, p2, k6.

**Row 2** P6, sl next 3 sts to cn and hold at back, k2, then sl the purl st from cn back to left needle and purl it, then k2 from cn; p6.

**Row 4** P5, BC, k1, FC, p5.

**Row 5** *and all subsequent WS rows* Knit all knit sts and purl all purl sts.

**Row 6** P4, BC, k1, p1, k1, FC, p4.

**Row 8** P3, BC, (k1, p1) twice, k1, FC, p3.

**Row 10** P2, BC, (k1, p1) 3 times, k1, FC, p2.

**Row 12** P2, FC, (p1, k1) 3 times, p1, BC, p2.

**Row 14** P3, FC, (p1, k1) twice, p1, BC, p3.

**Row 16** P4, FC, p1, k1, p1, BC, p4.

**Row 18** P5, FC, p1, BC, p5.

**Row 20** Repeat row 2.

**Row 22** P5, BC, p1, FC, p5.

**Row 24** P4, BC, p3, FC, p4.

**Row 26** P4, k2, p2. Make Bobble as follows: (k1, yo, k1, yo, k1) in next st, turn and p5, turn and k5, turn and p2 tog, p1, p2 tog, turn and sl 1, k2 tog, psso, completing bobble; p2, k2, p4.

**Row 28** P4, FC, p3, BC, p4.

**Row 30** Repeat Row 18.

Repeat rows 1 to 30.

## Bouquet pattern

Panel of 16 sts.

**Note** *Front Cross (FC): sl 1 st to cn and hold in front; p1, then k1 from cn.*

*Front Knit Cross (FKC): same as FC but knit both sts.*

*Back Cross (BC): sl 1 st to cn and hold at back, k1, then p1 from cn.*

*Back Knit Cross (BKC): same as BC, but knit both sts.*

**Row 1** (WS) K7, p2, k7.

**Row 2** P6, BKC, FKC, p6.

**Row 3** K5, FC, p2, BC, k5.

**Row 4** P4, BC, BKC, FKC, FC, p4.

**Row 5** K3, FC, k1, p4, k1, BC, k3.

**Row 6** P2, BC, p1, BC, k2, FC, p1, FC, p2.

**Row 7** (K2, p1) twice, k1, p2, k1, (p1, k2) twice.

**Row 8** P2, Make Bobble (MB) as follows: (k1, p1) twice into next st, turn and p4, turn and k4, turn and (p2 tog) twice, turn and k2 tog, completing bobble; p1, BC, p1, k2, p1, FC, p1, MB, p2.

**Row 9** K4, p1, k2, p2, k2, p1, k4.

**Row 10** P4, MB, p2, k2, p2, MB, p4.

Repeat rows 1 to 10.

## Bead pattern

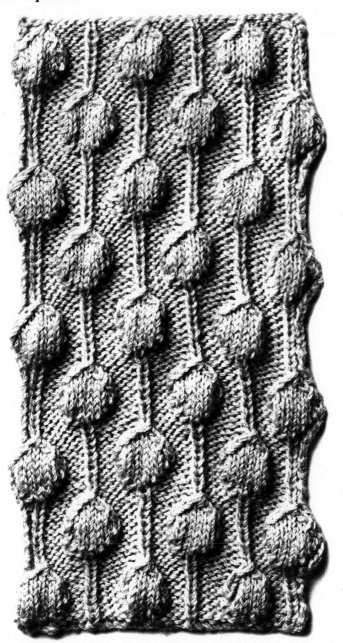

Multiple of 10 sts plus 4.

**Row 1** (RS) P4, *k1, p4, yo, k1, yo, p4; rep from *.

**Row 2** K4, *yo, p3, yo, k4, p1, k4; rep from *.

**Row 3** P4, *k1, p4, yo, k5, yo, p4; rep from *.

**Row 4** K4, *yo, p7, yo, k4, p1, k4; rep from *.

**Row 5** P4, *k1, p4, yo, k9, yo, p4; rep from *.

**Row 6** K4, *p2 tog, p7, p2 tog-b, k4, p1, k4, rep from *.

**Row 7** P4, *k1, p4, sl 1, k1, psso, k5, k2 tog, p4; rep from *.

**Row 8** K4, *p2 tog, p3, p2 tog-b, k4, p1, k4; rep from *.

**Row 9** P4, *k1, p4, sl 1, k1, psso, k1, k2 tog, p4; rep from *.

**Row 10** K4, *p3, tog, k4, p1, k4; rep from *.

**Row 11** P4, *yo, k1, yo, p4, k1, p4; rep from *.

**Row 12** K4, *p1, k4, yo, p3, yo, k4; rep from *.

**Row 13** P4, *yo, k5, yo, p4, k1, p4; rep from *.

**Row 14** K4, *p1, k4, yo, p7, yo, k4; rep from *.

**Row 15** P4, *yo, k9, yo, p4, k1, p4, rep from *.

**Row 16** K4, *p1, k4, p2 tog, p7, p2 tog-b, k4; rep from *.

**Row 17** P4, *sl 1, k1, psso, k5, k2 tog, p4, k1, p4; rep from *.

**Row 18** K4, *p1, k4, p2 tog, p3, p2, tog-b, k4; rep from *.

**Row 19** P4, *sl 1, k1, psso, k1, k2 tog, p4, k1, p4; rep from *.

**Row 20** K4, *p1, k4, p3 tog, k4; rep from *.

Repeat rows 1 to 20.

## *Twining vine pattern*

## Kiss stitch

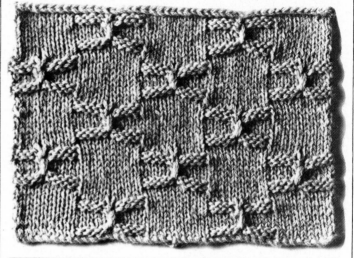

Multiple of 18 sts plus 9.
**Row 1** (RS) K9, *p9, k9; rep from *.
**Row 2** P9, *k9, p9; rep from *.
**Rows 3 and 5** Knit.
**Rows 4 and 6** Purl.
**Rows 7 and 8** Repeat rows 1 and 2.
**Row 9** K13, *insert needle into front of next st 9 rows below, and draw up a loop; slip this loop onto left needle and knit it tog with next st; k17; rep from *, end last repeat k13.

**Row 10** Purl.
**Row 11** P9, *k9, p9; rep from *.
**Row 12** K9, *p9, k9; rep from *.
**Rows 13 and 15** Knit.
**Rows 14 and 16** Purl.
**Rows 17 and 18** Repeat rows 11 and 12.
**Row 19** K4, *draw up a loop from 9th row below and knit it tog with next st as before; k17; rep from *, end last repeat k4.
**Row 20** Purl.
Repeat rows 1 to 20.

## *Sheaf stitch*

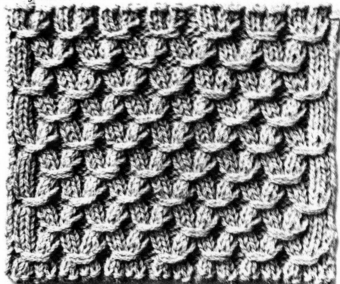

Multiple of 8 sts plus 2.
**Rows 1 and 3** (WS) K2, *p2, k2; rep from *.
**Row 2** P2, *k2, p2; rep from *
**Row 4** P2, *insert right needle from front between 6th and 7th sts on left needle and draw through a loop; sl this loop onto left needle and knit it together with first st on left needle; k1, p2, k2, p2; rep from *

**Rows 5 and 7** Repeat rows 1 and 3.
**Row 6** Repeat row 2.
**Row 8** P2, k2, p2, *draw loop from between 6th and 7th sts as before and knit it together with first st, then k1, p2, k2, p2; rep from *, end k2, p2.
Repeat rows 1 to 8.

---

Centre panel of 26 sts
**Row 1** (WS) K12, p5, k4, p3, k16.
**Row 2** P14, p2 tog, knit into front and back of next st, k2, p4, k2, yo, k1, yo, k2, p12.
**Row 3** K12, p7, k4, p2, k1, p1, k15.
**Row 4** P13, p2 tog, k1, purl into front and back of next st (purl inc), k2, p4, k3, yo, k1, yo, k3, p12.
**Row 5** K12, p9, k4, p2, k2, p1, k16.
**Row 6** P12, p2 tog, k1, purl inc, p1, k2, p4, sl 1, k1, psso, k5, k2 tog, p12.
**Row 7** K12, p7, k4, p2, k3, p1, k13.
**Row 8** P11, p2 tog, k1, purl inc, p2, k2, p4, sl 1, k1, psso, k3, k2 tog, p12.
**Row 9** K12, p5, k4, p2, k4, p1, k12.
**Row 10** P12, yo, k1, yo, p4, k2, p4, sl 1, k1, psso, k1, k2 tog, p12.
**Row 11** K12, p3, k4, p2, k4, p3, k12.
**Row 12** P12, (k1, yo) twice, k1, p4, k1, knit into the *back* of running thread (M1), k1, p2, sl 2 kwise, k1, p2sso, p12.
**Row 13** K16, p3, k4, p5, k12.
**Row 14** P12, k2, yo, k1, yo, k2,

p4, k1, knit into front and back of next st, k1, p2 tog, p14.
**Row 15** K15, p1, k1, p2, k4, p7, k12.
**Row 16** P12, k3, yo, k1, yo, k3, p4, k2, purl inc, k1, p2 tog, p13.
**Row 17** K14, p1, k2, p2, k4, p9, k12.
**Row 18** P12, sl 1, k1, psso, k5, k2 tog, p4, k2, p1, purl inc, k1, p2 tog, p12.
**Row 19** K13, p1, k3, p2, k4, p7, k12.
**Row 20** P12, sl 1, k1, psso, k3, k2 tog, p4, k2, p2, purl inc, k1, p2 tog, p11.
**Row 21** K12, p1, k4, p2, k4, p5, k12.
**Row 22** P12, sl 1, k1, psso, k1, k2 tog, p4, k2, p4, yo, k1, yo, p12.
**Row 23** K12, p3, k4, p2, k4, p3, k12.
**Row 24** P12, sl 2 kwise, k1, p2sso, p2, p2 tog, k1, M1, k1, p4, (k1, yo) twice, k1, p12.
Repeat rows 1 to 24.

# Eyelet and lace patterns

# Eyelet variations

Small holes or "eyelets" are the basis of all lace patterns. Like bobble and embossed patterns, lace patterns are made by increasing and decreasing. However, to make eyelets the increases and decreases are worked beside each other in the same row causing a hole without reducing the number of stitches. Eyelets form discreet individual holes and are arranged into patterns like broderie anglaise. They must have three rows of knitting in between them otherwise they loose their individuality and become faggot motifs (see facing page). Eyelets can also be used as tiny buttonholes, as slotting for ribbons and to make decorative picot hemlines (page 83).

Eyelet and lace stitches are used to make traditional Shetland lace shawls. There is a complete pattern for a shawl on page 100.

There are two kinds of simple eyelet, the chain eyelet and the open eyelet. In both cases, start working the eyelet at least two stitches in from the beginning of a row, and finish the eyelet two stitches before the end of a row, otherwise an uneven selvedge will be formed, making the knitting difficult to sew up.

Eyelets can be made larger by repeating the decrease to make a double eyelet. Heart-shaped picot eyelets are particularly decorative, while very large eyelets, called bold eyelets, can be made as buttonholes or part of large-scale designs. Eyelets can be made even larger by knitting more stitches together and then increasing more on the following row to compensate. Up to four or five stitches can be knitted together, more than that and the knitting becomes uncomfortable to work. The yarn over increases in the row following the multiple decreases are knitted and purled into until the stitches have been made up to the original number. The grand eyelet is a very good example of the large multiple increase and decrease eyelet.

## Making two simple eyelets

### The chain eyelet
This is the simplest and most common eyelet used in knitting patterns. When combined with the open eyelet it forms the basis for many more intricate lace stitches.

### The open eyelet
This method is useful for making a single row of eyelets to form slots through which a ribbon can be threaded.

#### How to make the eyelet

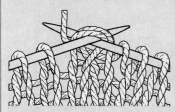

**1** *K2, yo, k2tog.*

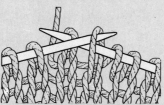

**1** *K2, yo, sl 1 kwise (slip the next stitch knitwise onto the right needle), k1, psso.*

**2** *The yo increase has replaced the stitch which was decreased by knitting 2 together.*

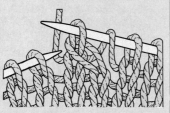

**2** *The yo increase has replaced the stitch which was decreased by slipping.*

**Chain eyelet**
A detail of the finished chain eyelet shows how it is constructed.

**Open eyelet**
A detail of the finished open eyelet shows how it is constructed.

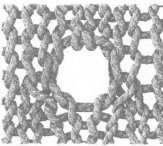

**Double eyelet**

**Picot eyelet**

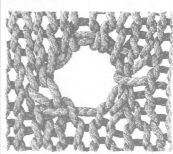

**Bold eyelet**

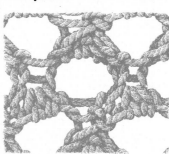

**Grand eyelet**

### Double eyelet
Cast on a minimum of 8 sts.
**Row 1** K2, k2 tog, yo, sl 1, k1, psso, k2
**Row 2** Purl. Purl and then knit into the yo stitch.

### Picot eyelet
Cast on a minimum of 8 sts.
**Row 1** K2, k2 tog, yo2, sl 1, k1, psso, k2.
**Row 2** Purl. Purl the first yo but knit the second, so forming the little picot dot to make the heart shape.

### Bold eyelet
Because this is so large, it takes four rows to make. Cast on a minimum of 10 sts.
**Row 1** K3, k2 tog, yo2, sl 1, k1, psso, k3.
**Row 2** P3, p2 tog, (one st is first yo), k2 tog (one st is 2nd yo), p3.
**Row 3** K4, yo2, k to end.
**Row 4** P3, p2 tog (one st is first yo) and at the same time, purl through the strand below, k1, p1 into 2nd yo and at the same time, knit and purl through strand below. Purl to end of row.

### Grand eyelet
Cast on a multiple of 4 sts, plus 2 sts each for beg. and end of row. Minimum of 8 sts.
**Row 1** (WS) P2, *yo, p4 tog, rep from * end p2.
**Row 2** K2, *k1, (k1, p1, k1) into yo, rep from *, end k2.
**Row 3** P2, *p4 tog, yo, rep from *, end p2.
**Row 4** K2 *(k1, p1, k1) into yo, k1, rep from *, end k2.
Rep rows 1 to 4.

# Faggot stitches

### How faggoting is used in knitting

Knitted faggoting is composed of eyelets arranged so that the eyelet holes run together to form an openwork pattern. The technique originated in the sixteenth century when it was designed to resemble the fashionable decorative seams of faggot embroidery stitches.

Faggoting is used in two ways. **1** To form decorative faggot motifs, in which case the increases and decreases are worked on alternate rows. **2** To form a lacy openwork fabric, in this case the increases and decreases are worked on every row. Faggoting is the basis of many of the eyelet and lace, and lace edging patterns which appear on pages 44-47 and pages 96–99.

This type of knitting is not only very decorative but is also a useful way of making lightweight summer garments and baby clothes which not only look good but are also cool to wear, even on the hottest days as the little eyelet holes act as ventilation.

### Faggot motifs

Either the chain or the open eyelet can be used to make faggot motifs. Motifs can be arranged into vertical or diagonal patterns, but not into horizontal lines as the characteristic strands between the holes would be lost and a row of simple eyelets would appear instead of the intended faggots .

### Vertical faggot motifs

In vertical motifs, the succession of eyelets worked one above the other creates a bias in the knitted fabric. A bias to the *right* will form if the increase is continually worked *before* the decrease. A bias to the *left* will form if the increase is continually worked *after* the decrease. The bias can be avoided by working motifs composed of short vertical lines where the bias will not be noticed. If long vertical lines are required, the bias can be neutralized by working the increases alternately before and after the decrease. The Beginners' lace pattern (page 46) is a good example of a pattern composed of vertical faggot motifs.

### Diagonal faggot motifs

Diagonal lines of faggoting can be arranged into chevron, diamond and lattice patterns. The direction of the diagonal is determined by the order in which the increases and decreases are worked. The diagonal will slant to the *right* if the increase is placed *after* the *decrease*. The diagonal will slant to the *left* if the increase is placed *before* the decrease. The Vienna lace pattern (page 46) is an example of a pattern which contains both diagonal and vertical faggot motifs.

When faggots are arranged into chevron, diamond and lattice patterns, the edges of the eyelet holes form a pattern of their own. There are three types of edge pattern: chain edge, soft edge and crossed edge. **Note** In all three patterns, the position of the increase changes in Row 9. This causes the diagonal to change direction.

### Lace faggoting

To produce a very lacy openwork fabric, the increases and decreases are worked on every row. In lace stitch patterns, lace faggoting forms the ground mesh while solid motifs create the design. Examples of lace faggoting are Ricrac pattern (page 44) and the Mesh pattern shown (right). Purse stitch was often used as the background in bead knitting (page 63) and gets its name from the purses which were very popular in Victorian times.

# Faggot variations

1 Chain edge
2 Soft edge
3 Crossed edge
4 Mesh pattern
5 Purse stitch

### Chain edge

Cast on a minimum of 7 sts.
Purl all even-numbered rows.

**Row 1** K1, yo, sl 1, k1, psso, k4.

**Row 3** K2, yo, sl 1, k1, psso, k3.

**Row 5** K3, yo, sl 1, k1, psso, k2.

**Row 7** K4, yo, sl 1, k1, psso, k1.

*****Row 9** K3, k2 tog, yo, k2.

**Row 11** K2, k2 tog, yo, k3.

**Row 13** K1, k2 tog, yo, k4.

### Soft edge

Cast on a minimum of 7 sts.
Purl all even-numbered rows.

**Row 1** K1, yo, k2 tog, k4.

**Row 3** K2, yo, k2 tog, k3.

**Row 5** K3, yo, k2 tog, k2.

**Row 7** K4, yo, k2 tog, k1.

*****Row 9** K3, sl 1, k1, psso, yo, k2.

**Row 11** K2, sl 1, k1, psso, yo, k3.

**Row 13** K1, sl 1, k1, psso, yo, k4.

### Crossed edge

Cast on a minimum of 7 sts.
Purl all even-numbered rows.

**Row 1** K1, yo, k2 tog-b, k4.

**Row 3** K2, yo, k2 tog-b, k3.

**Row 5** K3, yo, k2 tog-b, k2.

**Row 7** K4, yo, k2 tog-b, k1.

*****Row 9** K3, k2 tog-b, yo, k2.

**Row 11** K2, k2 tog-b, yo, k3.

**Row 13** K1, k2 tog-b, yo, k4.

### Mesh pattern

Cast on an odd number of sts.
Purl all even-numbered rows.

**Row 1** K1, *yo, k2 tog, rep from * to end.

The increase comes before the decrease and creates a bias to the right.

**Row 3** *Sl 1, k1, psso, yo, rep from * to end. End k1.

The increase coming after the decrease creates a bias to the left which forms the pattern.

### Purse stitch

Cast on an even number of sts. Minimum 8 sts.

**Row 1** *Yo, p2 tog, yo, p2 tog, rep from *.

Repeat on every row.

## Drop loop mesh

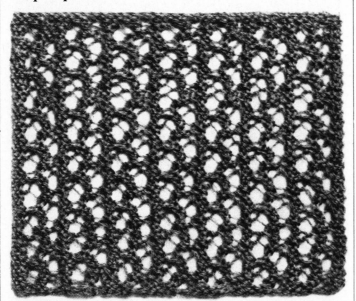

Multiple of 5 sts plus 3.
**Note** *Drop Loop (DL): drop the second loop of the double yo of previous row off the needle. The first loop is already knitted.*
**Preparation Row** K3, *(yo) twice, k2 tog, k3; rep from *.
**Row 1** K5, *DL, (yo) twice, k2 tog, k3; rep from *, end last repeat k1.
**Row 2** K3, *DL, k2, (yo) twice, k2 tog, k1; rep from *.
**Row 3** K3, *DL, (yo) twice, k2 tog, k3; rep from *.
Repeat rows 1 to 3.

## Lace cable

Multiple of 11 sts plus 7.
**Row 1** *(WS) and all other WS rows* Purl.
**Row 2** K1, *yo, sl 1, k1, psso, k1, k2 tog, yo, k6; rep from * to last 6 sts, end yo, sl 1, k1, psso, k1, k2 tog, yo, k1.
**Row 4** K2, *yo, sl 1 – k2 tog – psso, yo, k1, sl next 3 sts to cn and hold at back, k3, then k3 from cn, k1; rep from * to last 5 sts, end yo, sl 1 – k2 tog – psso, yo, k2.
**Row 6** Repeat row 2.
**Row 8** K2, *yo, sl 1 – k2 tog – psso, yo, k8; rep from * to last 5 sts, end yo, sl 1 – k2 tog – psso, yo, k2.
Repeat rows 1 to 8.

## Cobweb

Multiple of 6 sts plus 5.
**Row 1** *(WS) and all other WS rows* Purl.
**Row 2** K2, *yo, sl 1, k1, psso, k1, yo, sl 1, k1, psso, k1-b; rep from *, end yo, sl 1, k1, psso, k1.
**Row 4** K3, *k2 tog, yo, k1-b, yo, sl 1, k1, psso, k1-b; rep from *, end k2.
**Row 6** K2, k2 tog, *yo, sl 2 – k1 – p2sso, yo, sl 1 – k2 tog – psso; rep from *, end yo, sl 2 – k1 – p2sso, sl 1, k1, psso, k2.
**Row 8** K3, *k1-b, yo, k1, yo, k1-b, k1; rep from *, end k2.
**Row 10** K2, *yo, sl 1, k1, psso, k1-b, yo, sl 1, k1, psso, k1; rep from *, end yo, sl 1, k1, psso, k1.
**Row 12** *K2 tog, yo, k1-b, yo, sl 1, k1, psso, k1-b; rep from *, end k2 tog, yo, k1-b, yo, sl 1, k1, psso.
**Row 14** K1, *yo, sl 2 – k1 – p2sso, yo, sl 1 – k2 tog – psso; rep from *, end yo, sl 2 – k1 – p2sso, yo, k1.
**Row 16** K1-b, *k1, yo, k1-b, k1, k1-b, yo; rep from *, end k1, k1-b, k1.
Repeat rows 1 to 16.

## Ricrac

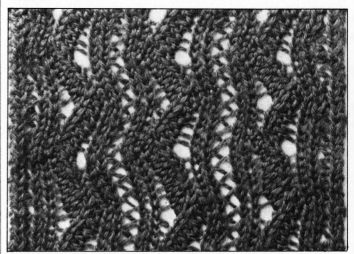

Multiple of 10 sts plus 5.
**Row 1** *(RS)* K1, *sl 1, k1, psso, yo, k5, k2 tog, yo, k1; rep from *, end sl 1, k1, psso, yo, k2.
**Row 2** P1, *p2 tog, yo, p2, yo, p1, p2 tog, p3; rep from *, end p2 tog, yo, p2.
**Row 3** K1, *sl 1, k1, psso, yo, k3, k2 tog, k2, yo, k1; rep from *, end sl 1, k1, psso, yo, k2.
**Row 4** P1, *p2 tog, yo, p2, yo, p3, p2 tog, p1; rep from *, end p2 tog, yo, p2.
**Row 5** K1, *sl 1, k1, psso, yo, k2, sl 1, k1, psso, k3, yo, k1; rep from *, end sl 1, k1, psso, yo, k2.
**Row 6** P1, *p2 tog, yo, p2, yo, p3, p2 tog-b, p1; rep from *, end p2 tog, yo, p2.
**Row 7** K1, *sl 1, k1, psso, yo, k2, yo, sl 1, k1, psso, k4; rep from *, end sl 1, k1, psso, yo, k2.
**Row 8** P1, *p2 tog, yo, p4, p2 tog-b, p1, yo, p1; rep from *, end p2 tog, yo, p2.
**Row 9** K1, *sl 1, k1 psso, (yo, k2) twice, sl 1, k1, psso, k2; rep from *, end sl 1, k1, psso, yo, k2.
**Row 10** P1, *p2 tog, yo, p2, p2 tog-b, p3, yo, p1; rep from *, end p2 tog, yo, p2.
**Row 11** K1, *sl 1, k1, psso, yo, k2, yo, k3, k2 tog, k1; rep from *, end sl 1, k1, psso, yo, k2.
**Row 12** P1, *p2 tog, yo, p2, p2 tog, p3, yo, p1; rep from *, end p2 tog, yo, p2.
Repeat rows 1 to 12.

## *Shooting star*

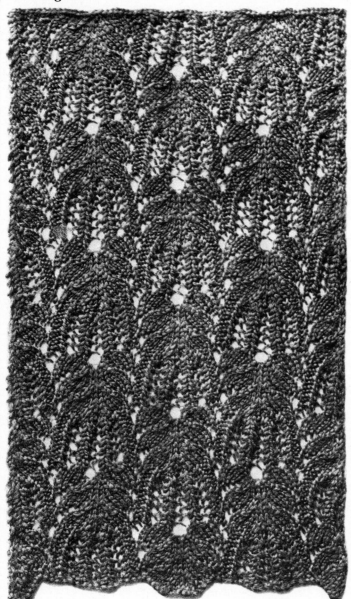

## *Crazy check*

| Multiple of 16 sts plus 2. |
| --- |

**Rows 1, 3, 5 and 7** (RS) k1, *(sl 1, k1, psso, yo) 4 times, k8; rep from *, end k1.

**Rows 2, 4, 6 and 8** k1, *K 8 , p 8 rep from *, end k1.

**Rows 9, 11, 13 and 15** K1, *k8, (yo, k2 tog) 4 times; rep from *, end k1.

**Rows 10, 12, 14 and 16** K1, *p8, k8; rep from *, end k1.
Repeat rows 1 to 16.

## *Chinese lantern*

Multiple of 34 sts plus 2.

**Row 1** (RS) K1, *k3, k2 tog, k4, yo, p2, (k2, yo, sl 1, k1, psso) 3 times, p2, yo, k4, sl 1, k1, psso, k3; rep from *, end k1.

**Row 2** K1, *p2, p2 tog-b, p4, yo, p1, k2, (p2, yo, p2 tog) 3 times, k2, p1, yo, p4, p2 tog, p2; rep from *, end k1.

**Row 3** K1, *k1, k2 tog, k4, yo, k2, p2, (k2, yo, sl 1, k1, psso) 3 times, p2, k2, yo, k4, sl 1, k1, psso, k1; rep from *, end k1.

**Row 4** K1, *p2 tog-b, p4, yo, p3, k2, (p2, yo, p2 tog) 3 times, k2, p3, yo, p4, p2 tog; rep from *, end k1.

**Rows 5 to 12** Repeat rows 1 to 4 twice more.

**Row 13** K1, *yo, sl 1, k1, psso, k2, yo, sl 1, k1, psso, p2, yo, k4,

sl 1, k1, psso, k6, k2 tog, k4, yo, p2, k2, yo, sl 1, k1, psso, k2; rep from *, end k1.

**Row 14** K1, *yo, p2 tog, p2, yo, p2 tog, k2, p1, yo, p4, p2 tog, p4, p2 tog-b, p4, yo, p1, k2, p2, yo, p2 tog, p2; rep from *, end k1.

**Row 15** K1, *yo, sl 1, k1, psso, k2, yo, sl 1, k1, psso, p2, k2, yo, k4, sl 1, k1, psso, k2, k2 tog, k4, yo, k2, p2, k2, yo, sl 1, k1, psso, k2; rep from *, end k1.

**Row 16** K1, *yo, p2 tog, p2, p2 tog, k2, p3, yo, p4, p2 tog, p2 tog-b, p4, yo, p3, k2, p2, yo, p2 tog, p2; rep from *, end k1.

**Rows 17 to 24** Repeat rows 13 to 16 twice more.
Repeat rows 1 to 24.

Multiple of 13 sts plus 2.

**Row 1** (WS) K2, *p5, k1, p5, k2; rep from *.

**Row 2** P2, *k1, (yo, k2 tog) twice, p1, k5, p2; rep from *.

**Rows 3 and 5** K2, *p4, k2, p5, k2; rep from *.

**Row 4** P2, *k1, (yo, k2 tog) twice, p2, k4, p2; rep from *.

**Row 6** P2, *k1, (yo, k2 tog) twice, p2, sl next 2 sts to cn and hold at back, k2, then k2 from cn, p2; rep from *.

**Rows 7, 8, 9, 10, 11 and 12** Repeat rows 3, 4, 5 and 6, then repeat rows 3 and 4 again.

**Row 13** Repeat row 1.

**Row 14** P2, *k5, p1, (sl 1, k1, psso, yo) twice, k1, p2; rep from *.

**Rows 15 and 17** K2, *p5, k2, p4, k2; rep from *.

**Row 16** P2, *k4, p2, (sl 1, k1, psso, yo) twice, k1, p2; rep from *.

**Row 18** P2, *sl next 2 sts to cn and hold at back, k2, then k2 from cn; p2, (sl 1, k1, psso, yo) twice, k1, p2; rep from *.

**Rows 19, 20, 21, 22, 23 and 24** Repeat rows 15, 16, 17 and 18, then rows 15 and 16 again.
Repeat rows 1 to 24.

## *Beginners' lace*

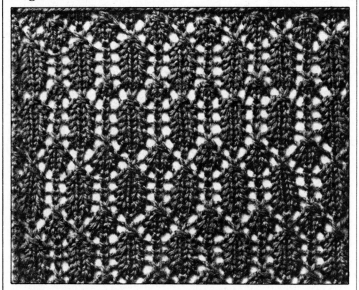

Multiple of 6 sts plus 1.
**Row 1** *(WS) and all other WS rows* Purl.
**Rows 2, 4 and 6** K1, *yo, sl 1, k1, psso, k1, k2 tog, yo, k1; rep from *.
**Row 8** K2, *yo, sl 1 – k2 tog – psso, yo, k3; rep from *, end last repeat k2.

**Row 10** K1, *k2 tog, yo, k1, yo, sl 1, k1, psso, k1; rep from *.
**Row 12** K2 tog, *yo, k3, yo, sl 1 – k2 tog – psso; rep from *, end yo, k3, yo, sl 1, k1, psso.
Repeat rows 1 to 12.

## *Cascade*

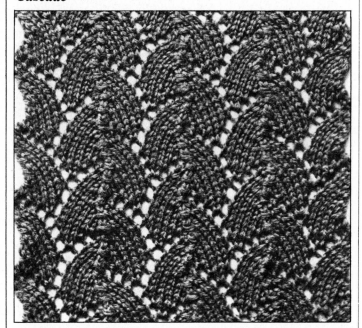

Multiple of 11 sts plus 1.
**Row 1** *(WS) and all other WS rows* Purl.
**Row 2** K2 tog, *k5, yo, k1, yo, k2, sl 1 – k2 tog – psso; rep from * to last 2 sts, end last repeat sl 1, k1, psso.
**Row 4** K2 tog, *k4, yo, k3, yo, k1, sl 1 – k2 tog – psso; rep from * to last 2 sts, end last repeat sl ., k1, psso.
**Row 6** K2 tog, *k3, yo, k5, yo, sl 1 – k2 tog – psso; rep from * to last 2 sts, end last repeat sl 1, k1, psso.

**Row 8** K2, tog, *k2, yo, k1, yo, k5, sl 1 – k2 tog – psso; rep from * to last 2 sts, end last repeat sl 1, k1, psso.
**Row 10** K2 tog, *k1, yo, k3, yo, k4, sl 1 – k2 tog – psso; rep from * to last 2 sts, end last repeat sl 1, k1, psso.
**Row 12** K2 tog, *yo, k5, yo, k3, sl 1 – k2 tog – psso; rep from * to last 2 sts, end last repeat sl 1, k1, psso.
Repeat rows 1 to 12.

## *Vienna lace*

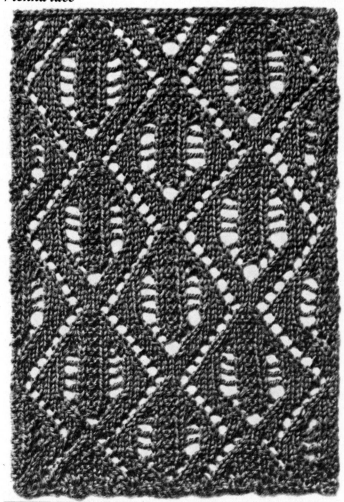

Multiple of 20 sts plus 2.
**Row 1** *(WS) and all other WS rows* Purl, always working (k1, p1) into each double yo of a previous row.
**Row 2** K1, yo, *sl 1, k1, psso, k2, yo, sl 1, k1, psso, k1, yo, k2 tog, p2, sl 1, k1, psso, yo, k1, k2 tog, yo, k2, k2 tog, (yo) twice; from *, end last repeat yo, k1 instead of (yo) twice.
**Row 4** P2, *(yo, sl 1, k1, psso, k2) twice, p2, (k2, k2 tog, yo) twice, p2; rep from *.
**Row 6** P2, *k1, yo, sl 1, k1, psso, k2, yo, sl 1, k1, psso, k1, p2, k1, k2 tog, yo, k2, k2 tog, k1, p2; rep from *.
**Row 8** P2, *sl 1, k1, psso, (yo) twice, sl 1, k1, psso, k2, yo, sl 1, k1, psso, p2, k2 tog, yo, k2, k2 tog, (yo) twice, k2 tog, p2; rep from *.
**Row 10** P2, *sl 1, k1, psso, (yo) twice, k2 tog, k3, yo, sl 1, k1, psso, k2, yo, k3, sl 1, k1, psso, (yo) twice, k2 tog, p2; rep from *.
**Row 12** P2, *sl 1, k1, psso, (yo) twice, k2 tog, k1, k2 tog, yo, k4, yo, sl 1, k1, psso, k1, sl 1, k1, psso, (yo) twice, k2 tog, p2; rep from *.
**Row 14** P2, *sl 1, k1, psso, (yo) twice, (k2 tog) twice, yo, k6, yo, (sl 1, k1, psso) twice, (yo) twice, k2 tog, p2; rep from *.

**Row 16** P2, *sl 1, k1, psso, yo, k1, k2 tog, yo, k2, k2 tog, (yo) twice, sl 1, k1, psso, k2, yo, sl 1, k1, psso, k1, yo, k2 tog, p2; rep from *.
**Row 18** P2, *(k2, k2 tog, yo) twice, p2, (yo, sl 1, k1, psso, k2) twice, p2; rep from *.
**Row 20** P2, *k1, k2 tog, yo, k2, k2 tog, yo, k1, p2, k1, yo, sl 1, k1, psso, k2, yo, sl 1, k1, psso, k1, p2; rep from *.
**Row 22** P2, *k2 tog, yo, k2, k2 tog, (yo) twice, k2 tog, p2, sl 1, k1, psso, (yo) twice, sl 1, k1, psso, k2, yo, sl 1, k1, psso, p2; rep from *.
**Row 24** K1, *k2 tog, yo, k3, sl 1, k1, psso, (yo) twice, k2 tog, p2, sl 1, k1, psso, (yo) twice, k2 tog, k3, yo, sl 1, k1, psso; rep from *, end k1.
**Row 26** K3, *yo, sl 1, k1, psso, k1, sl 1, k1, psso, (yo) twice, k2 tog, p2, sl 1, k1, psso, (yo) twice, k2 tog, k1, k2 tog, yo, k4; rep from *, end last repeat k3.
**Row 28** K4, *yo, (sl 1, k1, psso) twice, (yo) twice, k2 tog, p2, sl 1, k1, psso, (yo) twice, (k2 tog) twice, yo, k6; rep from *, end last repeat k4.
Repeat rows 1 to 28.

## Willow pattern

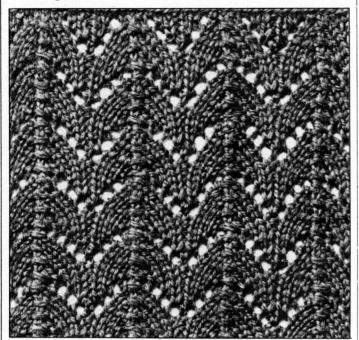

Multiple of 10 sts plus 1.
**Rows 1 and 3 (WS)** Purl.
Row 2 K1, *yo, k3, sl 1 – k2 tog – psso, k3, yo, k1; rep from *.
**Row 4** P1, *k1, yo, k2, sl 1 – k2 tog – psso, k2, yo, k1, p1; rep from *.
**Rows 5 and 7** K1, *p9, k1; rep from *.

**Row 6** P1, *k2, yo, k1, sl 1 – k2 tog – psso, k1, yo, k2, p1; rep from *.
**Row 8** P1, *k3, yo, sl 1 – k2 tog – psso, yo, k3, p1; rep from *.
Repeat rows 1 to 8.

## Victory

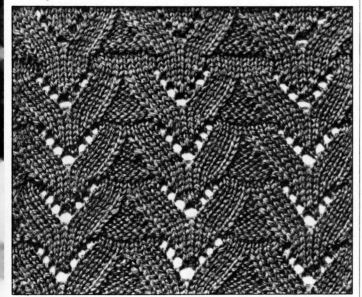

Multiple of 16 sts.
**Row 1 (RS)** Knit.
**Row 2** *K4, p8, k4; rep from *.
**Row 3** *P3, k2 tog, k3, (yo) twice, k3, sl 1, k1, psso, p3; rep from *.
**Row 4** *K3, p4, purl into front and back of double yo, p4, k3; rep from *.
**Row 5** *P2, k2 tog, k3, yo; k2, yo, k3, sl 1, k1, psso, p2; rep from *.

**Row 6** *K2, p12, k2; rep from *.
**Row 7** *P1, k2 tog, k3, yo, k4, yo, k3, sl 1, k1, psso, p1; rep from *.
**Row 8** *K1, p14, k1; rep from *.
**Row 9** *K2 tog, k3, yo, k6, yo, k3, sl 1, k1, psso; rep from *.
**Row 10** Purl.
Repeat rows 1 to 10.

## Butterfly lace

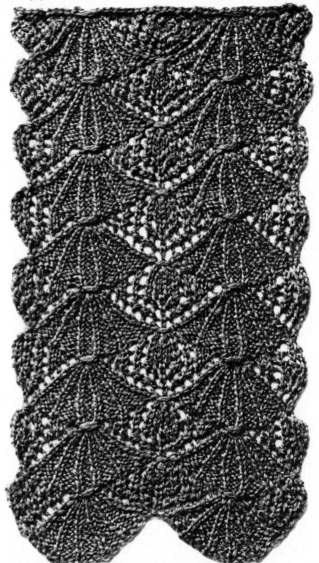

Multiple of 22 sts plus 1.
**Note** *Cluster – sl the given number of sts wyib, pass yarn to front, sl the same number of sts back to left needle, pass yarn to back, sl the same sts again wyib.*
**Row 1 (RS)** K1, *yo, (k1-b, p3) 5 times, k1-b, yo, k1; rep from *.
**Row 2** P3, *(k3, p1) 4 times, k3, p5; rep from *, end last repeat p3.
**Row 3** K1, *yo, k1-b, yo, (k1-b, p3) 5 times, (k1-b, yo) twice, k1; rep from *.
**Row 4** P5, *(k3, p1) 4 times, k3, p9; rep from *, end last repeat p5.
**Row 5** K1, *yo, k1-b, yo, sl 1, k1, psso, yo (k1-b, p2 tog, p1) 5 times, k1-b, yo, k2 tog, yo, k1-b, yo, k1; rep from *.
**Row 6** P7, *(k2, p1) 4 times, k2, p13; rep from *, end last repeat p7.
**Row 7** K1, *k1-b, (yo, sl 1, k1, psso) twice, yo, (k1-b, p2) 5 times, k1-b, yo, (k2 tog, yo) twice, k1-b, k1; repeat from *.
**Row 8** P8, *(k2, p1) 4 times, k2, p15; rep from *, end last repeat p8.

**Row 9** K2, *(yo, k2 tog) twice, yo, k1-b, yo, (k1-b, p2 tog) 5 times, (k1-b, yo) twice, (sl 1, k1, psso, yo) twice, k3; rep from *, end last repeat k2.
**Rows 10 and 12** P10, *(k1, p1) 4 times, k1, p19; rep from *, end last repeat p10.
**Row 11** Sl 1, k1, psso, *(yo, k2 tog) 3 times, k1-b, yo, (k1-b, p1) 5 times, k1-b, yo, k1-b, (sl 1, k1, psso, yo) 3 times, sl 2 – k1 – p2sso; rep from *, end last repeat k2 tog instead of sl 2 – k1 – p2sso.
**Row 13** K1, *(k2 tog, yo) twice, k2 tog, k1, k1-b, yo, (sl 1, k1, psso) twice, sl 1 – k2 tog – psso, (k2 tog) twice, yo, k1-b, k1, sl 1, k1, psso, (yo, sl 1, k1, psso) twice, k1; rep from *.
**Row 14** Cluster 2, *p7, Cluster 5, p7, Cluster 3; rep from *, end last repeat Cluster 2 instead of Cluster 3.
Repeat rows 1 to 14.

# Working in colour

The use of more than one colour dates back to the earliest known pieces of knitting. A fragment found at Fostat in Egypt was probably made in the seventh century. This piece was worked on a ground of gold silk with a sophisticated pattern in maroon silk resembling the tile and carpet designs of the period.

Colourwork reached its height in the late sixteenth century. The knitting guilds at that time required their apprentices, who were all men, to study for six years. To gain admission to the guild each apprentice had to submit, among other items, a colourwork carpet measuring 6 feet by 5 feet (2m by 1.5m) and showing pictorial scenes, rather like a tapestry. These carpets had to be made in 13 weeks together with a beret, a shirt and a pair of stockings. It was an immense undertaking and many of the results are rightly regarded as masterpieces.

## Brocade knitting

Later on brocade knitting became fashionable. This involved working with both different colours and different stitches. Usually the background would be knitted in one colour while the pattern would be knitted in another colour and a different stitch; the pattern would then be outlined in a third colour. Brocade knitting was made to resemble the brocade fabric of the day as much as possible and was usually worked in silk.

## International colourwork patterns

It is interesting to note that the main pattern motifs of international knitting are always taken from the important aspects of everyday life. For instance in Peru, the llama which is not only the national animal but also the bearer of the wool, always plays a big part in their patterns; whereas in Norway the snowflake is often used for all-over designs, whilst in the Alpine countries reindeer, fir trees and tiny flowers are the themes.

## Working with colour

Colour in knitting can be as flexible as colour in painting. There is no limit to the number of effects you can achieve once you have mastered the techniques that make it possible to combine colours in any way you choose. The simplest way to start working with colour is to make horizontal stripe patterns for which the new colour is added at the beginning of a row and the unused colours are either broken off or carried up the side of the work until they are needed again. For more complicated colourwork designs, the new colour or colours can be added either at the beginning of a row or during a row, depending on where they are needed. The best methods to use for adding in colour are shown opposite.

## Modern yarns for colour

There are an enormous quantity of different yarns on the market today, far more than were available in the sixteenth century when the finest colourwork was produced. Yarns not only come in a wide variety of colours and colour blends, they are also produced in a range of different spins, starting with the basic 2-plys, 3-plys, 4-plys, double and triple knittings. These different plys can be spun in various ways, for instance into a crepe yarn which is tightly spun and gives a slightly clearer look to the individual knitted stitches. Modern yarn manufacturers, called spinners, produce yarns ranging from chenilles which knit up into a velvety fabric, to heavily textured slubs and bouclés, to tweedy and flecked yarns for a fabric look, and twinkling metallic and metal mixture yarns.

## Joining in new colours

Add the new colours in one of the ways shown below. These methods apply to all colourwork and ensure that the added colours are both neatly and safely secured. Darn all loose ends of yarn into the selvedge or back of work.

### How to add a new colour at the beginning of a row
Use this method to knit horizontal stripe patterns.

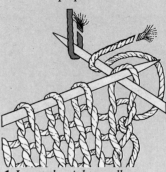

1 *Insert the right needle through the first stitch on the left needle and wrap first the old and then the new over it. Knit the stitch using both yarns.*

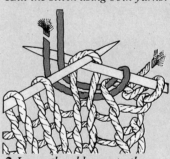

2 *Leave the old yarn to the back and knit the next 2 stitches using the doubled length of new yarn.*

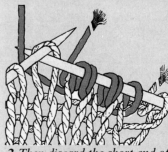

3 *Then discard the short end of new yarn and continue knitting. On the following row, the 3 double stitches are each treated as single stitches. If the old yarn is to be used again, leave it at the side of the work, ready to pick up and use when next required.*

### How to add new colour in the middle of a row
Use this method for patterns where the old colour will be used again in the same row.

1 *Insert the right needle through the next stitch on the left needle. Wrap the new yarn over the right needle and knit the stitch with the new yarn. Leave the old yarn to the back of the work.*

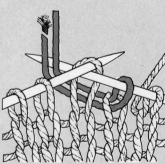

2 *Knit the next 2 stitches using the new yarn double.*

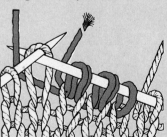

3 *Discard the short end and continue knitting with the new colour. Use the new and old yarns as required by the pattern. On the following row the 2 double stitches are each treated as single stitches and knitted in the usual way.*

# Stripe variations

The simplest and most basic patterns can be changed into unique and colourful designs just by knitting the pattern up in horizontal stripes instead of a single colour. The stripes can be wide or narrow, regular or irregular; in toning colours or bold contrast. Experiment with stripes before you start knitting more complicated colour patterns, simple patchwork patterns can be made at the same time as you try out colour combinations. Some different stripe variations are shown below.

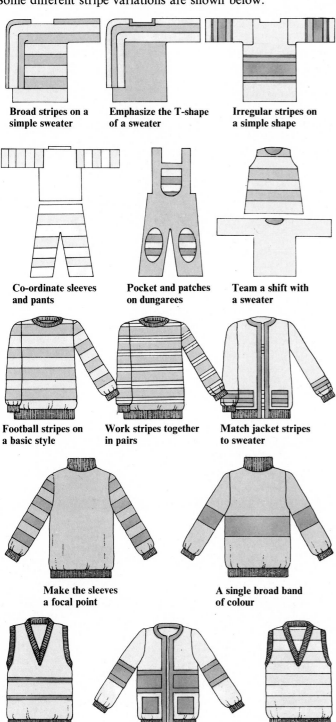

**Broad stripes on a simple sweater**

**Emphasize the T-shape of a sweater**

**Irregular stripes on a simple shape**

**Co-ordinate sleeves and pants**

**Pocket and patches on dungarees**

**Team a shift with a sweater**

**Football stripes on a basic style**

**Work stripes together in pairs**

**Match jacket stripes to sweater**

**Make the sleeves a focal point**

**A single broad band of colour**

**Stripe details on a pullover**

**Match stripes to buttonbands**

**Regular bands of colour on a pullover**

# Slip patterns

Using the slip method you can create the greatest number of different effects with the least amount of difficulty. The slip method can be used in three distinct ways: **1** To form textured patterns in a single colour. **2** To form multi-colour patterns. **3** To form multi-colour textured patterns.

### How the slip method works

Patterns are formed by knitting some stitches and slipping others. You slip a stitch by transferring it from one needle to another without working it. Stitches are slipped purlwise, i.e. as if the stitch was about to be purled, from the left to the right needle and the yarn is brought either in front or behind the slipped stitches. Stitches are always slipped purlwise unless the pattern specifically states knitwise. When the yarn is brought to the front of the slipped stitches the pattern reads: With yarn in front, abbreviated as *Wyif*. When the yarn is brought behind, the pattern reads: With yarn in back, *Wyib*.

### Using the slip method for textured patterns

For texture, stitches can be slipped for several rows, bringing the knitted stitches closer together making a thicker fabric. It is not advisable to slip stitches for more than three rows without knitting them as they become stretched.

Further textured effects can be made depending on whether the yarn is brought in front of or behind the slipped stitches. When the yarn is brought in front of the slipped stitches, it forms a bar across them which partially conceals them. This bar can be worked over a number of rows and stitches to make a variety of patterns. When the yarn is brought behind the slipped stitches it can be pulled tight, making the knitting fold into pleats. The size of the pleats can be varied according to the spacing of the slipped stitches.

### Using the slip method for colour patterns

When using the slip method only for changing colours, the stitches of one colour are knitted for two rows while the stitches of the second colour are slipped for two rows. On the following two rows the stitches which were previously knitted are slipped and the stitches which were previously slipped are knitted. In this way, only one colour is knitted at a time, and a neat and even back is formed on the work automatically. For changing colours, the method can only be used over small blocks of colour.

### Using the slip method for colour and texture

When the slip method is used for both coloured and textured effects, many elaborate patterns can be made. A selection of slip patterns are shown over the page, with pattern instructions on page 52. Some patterns, such as the Rainbow zigzag, shown on the next page, call for a further technique, called bias knitting.

### Bias knitting

In bias knitting each row slants diagonally to left or right. This is done by working decreases and increases with an interval of stitches between them. On the subsequent rows increases are worked directly above the first increase, and decreases are worked directly above the first decrease.

A bias to the right is formed by working the decrease at the beginning of a right side row, or group of stitches, then working the increase after the intervening stitches. A bias to the left is formed by working the increase at the beginning and the decrease at the end of a right side row.

# Colour slip patterns

All the multi-colour patterns on this page are worked using the slip technique. For an explanation of the technique, turn to page 49; for pattern instructions, see page 52.

**The front of the knitting**
*If the strands are handled correctly, the patterns will be easy to see on the face of the work.*

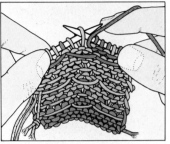

**The back of the knitting**
*The different coloured strands must be caught up in the back of the work to keep them getting tangled.*

1 **Dot and dash**  2 **Chevron stripes**  3 **Window pane**

4 **Sporting check**  5 **Hamburger check**  6 **Persian check**

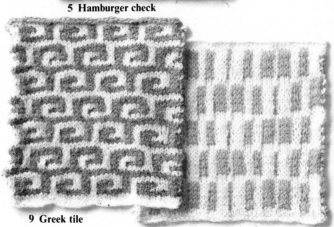

7 **Interlacing stripe**  8 **Florentine**  9 **Greek tile**  10 **Variegated check**

### Double-ended pattern

*Certain patterns like Peppermint and Plaid are double ended. This means that they are not turned at the end of each row; instead, two consecutive rows are worked on the same side. Patterns of this kind must either be knitted on double pointed needles or knitted in the round.*

11 **Peppermint**

12 **Plaid**

13 **Rainbow zig zag**

# Using slip patterns

## Multi-colour cap

Any pattern can be knitted up in a slip pattern. The stocking cap (right), which is an adaptation of the basic beret pattern (page 94) has been knitted in plain stripes, and in two different chevron patterns, a three-colour Chevron stripes slip pattern and a reversible knit and purl Chevron pattern. Details of the three patterns are shown (far right).

By adding patterns and by varying their combinations you can turn an essentially simple garment into something much more interesting.

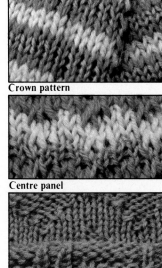

Crown pattern

Centre panel

Cap brim

## Patterned baby sweater

An unusual baby jacket knitted in bright colours (bottom right) instead of the usual pastels. The full pattern for the jacket is on page 70. To convert a plain pattern into a colour pattern always make a stitch gauge sample first (page 68) using the yarn and colour pattern of your choice. From the sample you can calculate how many stitches to cast on and how many rows to knit to make the garment in the size you want. This is particularly easy with a simple pattern like this one which is composed of rectangles with no shaping.

The jacket has been finished off with an edging and ties in red yarn. To knit the edging, pick up stitches along the two front edges and around the neck. To pick up stitches, follow the instructions on page 96 for attaching a knitted edging, then use the cast on stitches formed in this way to knit one row in red yarn.

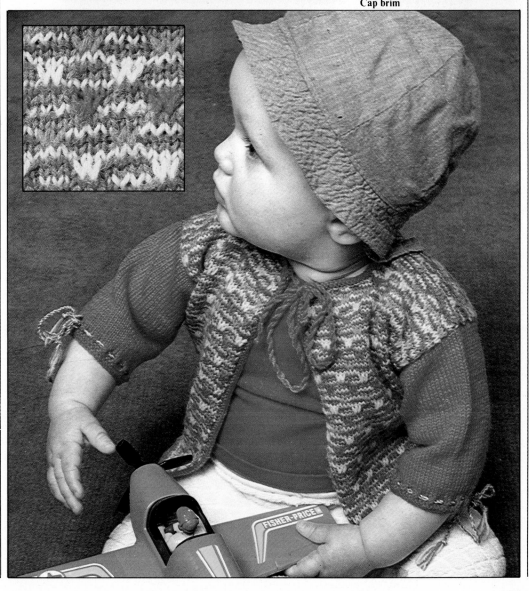

# Colour slip pattern instructions

The slip method is the easiest way of creating multi-coloured and textured patterns. The key (below) shows the position of each pattern on the colour page (50).

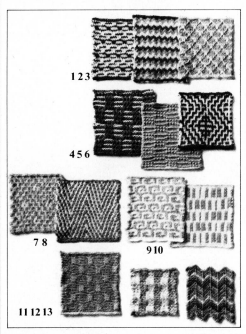

1 Dot and dash
2 Chevron stripes
3 Windowpane stripes
4 Sporting check
5 Hamburger check
6 Persian check
7 Interlacing stripe
8 Florentine
9 Greek tile
10 Variegated check
11 Peppermint
12 Plaid
13 Rainbow zigzag

## 1 Dot and dash

Multiple of 6 sts plus 4.
Colours A, B and C.
Cast on with C.
**Row 1** (RS) With A, knit.
**Row 2** With B, purl.
**Row 3** With C, k1, *sl 2 wyib, k4; rep from *, end sl 2, k1.
**Row 4** With A, p1, *sl 2 wyif, p4; rep from *, end sl 2, p1.
**Row 5** With B, knit.
**Row 6** With C, purl.
**Row 7** With A, k4, *sl 2 wyib, k4; rep from *.
**Row 8** With B, p4, *sl 2 wyif, p4; rep from *.
**Rows 9 to 24** Repeat rows 1 to 8 twice more, changing colours every row. Colour sequence remains A, B, C, A, B, C, etc.
Repeat rows 1 to 24.

## 2 Chevron stripes

Multiple of 4 sts.
Colours A, B and C.
Cast on with A and purl one row.
**Row 1** (RS) with B, *k1, sl 3 wyib; rep from *.
**Row 2** With B, *p1, sl 1 wyif, p3; rep from *, end sl 1, p2.
**Row 3** With B, knit.
**Row 4** With B, purl.
**Rows 5 to 8** With C, repeat rows 1 to 4.
**Rows 9 to 12** With A, repeat rows 1 to 4.
Repeat rows 1 to 12.

## 3 Window pane stripes

Multiple of 6 sts plus 5.
Colours A, B and C.
**Row 1** (WS) With A, p4, *sl 3 wyib, p3; rep from *, end p1.
**Row 2** With B, knit.
**Row 3** With B, repeat row 1.
**Rows 4 and 5** With C, repeat rows 2 and 3.
**Row 6** With A, k5, *insert needle from front under the 3 loose strands and upward to knit next st, catching all 3 strands behind st as it is knitted; k5; rep from *.
**Row 7** With A, p1, *sl 3 wyib, p3; rep from *, end last repeat p1.
**Row 8** With B, knit.
**Row 9** With B, repeat row 7.
**Rows 10 and 11** With C, repeat rows 8 and 9.
**Row 12** With A, k2, rep from * of row 6; end last repeat k2 instead of k5.
Repeat rows 1 to 12.

## 4 Sporting check

Multiple of 10 sts plus 2.
Colours A and B.
**Row 1** (RS) With A, knit.
**Row 2** With A, (k1, p1) twice, k1, *p2, k1, p1, k1; rep from *, end p2.
**Row 3** With B, k1, *k5, (sl 1 wyib, k1) twice, sl 1 wyib; rep from *, end k1.
**Row 4** With B, k1, *(sl 1 wyif, k1) twice, sl 1 wyif, k5; rep from *, end k1.
**Row 5** With A, knit.
**Row 6** With A, k1, *(p1, k1) twice, p1, k5; rep from *, end k1.
**Rows 7, 8, 9, 10, 11 and 12** Repeat rows 3, 4, 5 and 6, then rows 3 and 4 again.
**Rows 13 and 14** With A, repeat rows 1 and 2.
**Row 15** With B, k1, *(sl 1 wyib, k1) twice, sl 1 wyib, k5; rep from *, end k1.
**Row 16** With B, k1, *k5, (sl 1 wyif, k1) twice, sl 1 wyif; rep from *, end k1.
**Row 17** With A, knit.
**Row 18** With A, k1, *k5, (p1, k1) twice, p1; rep from *, end k1.
**Rows 19, 20, 21, 22, 23 and 24** Repeat rows 15, 16, 17 and 18, then rows 15 and 16 again.
Repeat rows 1 to 24.

## 5 Hamburger check

Multiple of 16 sts plus 9.
Colours A and B.
**Note** *Odd-numbered rows are RS rows.*
**Rows 1, 2, 5, 6, 9, 10, 13 and 14** With A, knit.
**Rows 3 and 7** With B, (k1, sl 1 wyib) 4 times, *k9, (sl 1 wyib, k1) 3 times, sl 1 wyib; rep from *, end k1.
**Rows 4 and 8** With B, (k1, sl 1 wyif) 4 times, *p9, (sl 1 wyif, k1) 3 times, sl 1 wyif; rep from *, end k1.
**Rows 11 and 15** With B, k9, *(sl 1 wyib, k1) 3 times, sl 1 wyib, k9; rep from *.
**Rows 12 and 16** With B, p9, *(sl 1 wyif, k1) 3 times, sl 1 wyif, p9; rep from *.
Repeat rows 1 to 16.

## 6 Persian check

Multiple of 30 sts plus 3.
Colours A and B.
**Note** *On all RS rows, sl all sl sts wyib.*
Cast on with A and knit one row.
**Row 1** (RS) With B, k8, *(sl 1, k3) 4 times, sl 1, k13; rep from *, end last repeat k8.
**Row 2** *and all other WS rows* (purl) the same sts worked on the previous row, k wize with the same colour; sl all the same sl sts wyif.
**Row 3** With A, k1, *(sl 1, k3) 3 times, sl 1, k1, (sl 1, k3) 4 times; rep from *, end sl 1, k1.
**Row 5** With B, k6, *(sl 1, k3) 5 times, sl 1, k9; rep from *, end last repeat k6.
**Row 7** With A, k1, sl 1, k1, *(sl 1, k3) 3 times, sl 1, k1, (sl 1, k3) 3 times, (sl 1, k1) twice; rep from *.
**Row 9** With B, k4, *(sl 1, k3) 6 times, sl 1, k5; rep from *, end last repeat k4.
**Row 11** With A, k1, *(sl 1, k3) 3 times, sl 1, k5, (sl 1, k3) 3 times; rep from *, end sl 1, k1.
**Row 13** With B, k2, *(sl 1, k3) 3 times, (sl 1, k1) twice, (sl 1, k3) 3 times, sl 1, k1; rep from*, end k1.
**Row 15** With A, k3, *(sl 1, k3) twice, sl 1, k9, (sl 1, k3) 3 times; rep from *.
**Row 17** With B, k2, *sl 1, k1, (sl 1, k3) 7 times; rep from *, end k1.
**Row 19** With A, k1, *(sl 1, k3) twice, sl 1, k13, (sl 1, k3) twice; rep from *, end sl 1, k1.
**Row 21** With B, k4, *(sl 1, k3) 6 times, sl 1, k1, sl 1, k3; rep from *, end last repeat k2.
**Rows 23 and 24** With A, repeat rows 15 and 16.
**Rows 25 and 26** With B, repeat rows 13 and 14.
**Rows 27 and 28** With A, repeat rows 11 and 12.
**Rows 29 and 30** With B, repeat rows 9 and 10.
**Rows 31 and 32** With A, repeat rows 7 and 8.
**Rows 33 and 34** With B, repeat rows 5 and 6.
**Row 35** With A, k1, *(sl 1, k3) 4 times, sl 1, k1, (sl 1, k3) 3 times; rep from *, end sl 1, k1.
**Row 36** See row 2.
Repeat rows 1 to 36.

## 7 Interlacing stripe

Multiple of 16 sts plus 3.
Colours A and B.
**Note** *On all RS rows, sl all sl sts wyib.*
Cast on with A and knit one row.
**Row 1** (RS) With B, k1, *(k1, sl 1, k3, sl 1) twice, k3, sl 1; rep from *, end k2.
**Row 2** *and all other WS rows* Knit all the same sts you worked on previous row, with the same colour; sl all the same sl sts wyif.
**Row 3** With A, k1, *sl 1, k3; rep from *, end sl 1, k1.

**Interlacing stripe continued**

**Row 5** With B, k4, *sl 1, k1, (sl 1, k3) twice, sl 1, k5; rep from *, end last repeat k4.

**Row 7** With A, k2, *sl 2, k3, (sl 1, k3) twice, sl 2, k1; rep from *, end k1.

**Row 9** With B, k4, *(sl 1, k3) twice, sl 1, k1, sl 1, k5; rep from *, end last repeat k4.

**Row 11** With A, repeat row 3.

**Row 13** With B, k2, *(sl 1, k3) twice, sl 1, k1, sl 1, k3, sl 1, k1; rep from *, end k1.

**Row 15** With A, k3, *sl 1, k3; rep from *.

**Row 17** With B, k2, *(sl 1, k1, sl 1, k3) twice, sl 1, k3; rep from *, end k1.

**Row 19** With A, repeat row 3.

**Row 21** With B, k4, *sl 1, k1, sl 1, k5, (sl 1, k3) twice; rep from *, end last repeat k2.

**Row 23** With A, k3, *sl 1, k3, sl 2, k1, sl 2, k3, sl 1, k3; rep from *.

**Row 25** With B, k2, *sl 1, k3, sl 1, k5, sl 1, k1, sl 1, k3; rep from *, end k1.

**Row 27** With A, repeat row 3.

**Row 29** With B, k4, *(sl 1, k3, sl 1, k1) twice, sl 1, k3; rep from *, end last repeat k2.

**Row 31** With A, repeat row 15.

**Row 32** See row 2.

Repeat rows 1 to 32.

## 8 Florentine

Multiple of 24 sts plus 2.
Colours A and B.

**Note** *On all RS (odd-numbered) rows all sl sts are slipped wyib. On WS (even-numbered) rows all sl sts are slipped wyif.*

Cast on with A and purl one row.

**Row 1** (RS) With B, k1, *sl 1, k2; rep from *, end k1.

**Row 2** With B, k1, *p2, sl 1; rep from *, end k1.

**Row 3** With A, k1, *k1, sl 1, (k2, sl 1) 3 times, k3, (sl 1, k2) 3 times, sl 1; rep from *, end k1.

**Row 4** With A, k1, *sl 1, (p2, sl 1) 3 times, p3, (sl 1, p2) 3 times, sl 1, p1; rep from *, end k1

**Row 5** With B, k1, *k2, (sl 1, k2) 3 times, sl 1, k1, sl 1, (k2, sl 1) 3 times, k1; rep from *, end k1.

**Row 6** With B, k1, *p1, (sl 1, p2) 3 times, sl 1, p1, sl 1, (p2, sl 1) 3 times, p2; rep from *, end k1.

**Rows 7 and 8** With A, repeat rows 1 and 2.

**Rows 9 and 10** With B, repeat rows 3 and 4.

**Rows 11 and 12** With A, repeat rows 4 and 6.

Repeat rows 1 to 12.

## 9 Greek tile

Multiple of 10 sts plus 2.
Colours A and B.

**Note** *On all RS (odd-numbered) rows slip all sl sts wyib; on all WS (even-numbered) rows slip all sl sts wyif.*

**Row 1** (RS) With A, knit.

**Row 2** With A, purl.

**Row 3** With B, k1, *k8, sl 2; rep from *, end k1.

**Row 4** *and all subsequent WS rows* Using the same colour as in previous row, purl across, slipping wyif all the same sts that were slipped on previous row.

**Row 5** With A, k1, *sl 2, k4, sl 2, k2; rep from *, end k1.

**Row 7** With B, k1, *k2, sl 2, k4, sl 2; rep from *, end k1.

**Row 9** With A, k1, *sl 2, k8; rep from *, end k1.

**Row 11** With B, knit.

**Row 13** With A, *k4, sl 2, k4; rep from *, end k2.

**Row 15** With B, k2, *sl 2, k2, sl 2, k4; rep from *.

**Row 17** With A, *k4, sl 2, k2, sl 2; rep from *, end k2.

**Row 19** With B, *k6, sl 2, k2; rep from *, end k2.

**Row 20** See row 4.

Repeat rows 1 to 20.

## 10 Variegated check pattern

Multiple of 22 sts plus 1.
Colours A and B.

**Note** *on the RS (odd-numbered) rows sl all sl sts wyib; on WS (even-numbered) rows sl all sl sts wyif.*

**Row 1** (RS) With A, knit.

**Row 2** With A, purl.

**Row 3** With B, k1, *sl 3, k2, sl 2, k3, sl 1, sl 2, k2, sl 3, k1; rep from *.

**Row 4** With B, p1, *sl 3, p2, sl 2, p3, sl 1, p3, sl 2, p2, sl 3, p1; rep from *.

**Row 5** With A, k1, *k3, sl 2, k2, sl 3, k1, sl 3, k2, sl 2, k3, sl 1; rep from *, end last repeat k1 instead of sl 1.

**Row 6** With A, p1, *p3, sl 2, p2, sl 3, p1, sl 3, p2, sl 2, p3, sl 1; rep from *, end last repeat p1 instead of sl 1.

**Rows 7 to 14** Repeat rows 3 to 6 twice more.

**Row 15** With A, knit.

**Row 16** With A, purl.

**Rows 17 and 18** With B, repeat rows 5 and 6.

**Rows 19 and 20** With A, repeat rows 3 and 4.

**Rows 21 to 28** Repeat rows 17 to 20 twice more.

Repeat rows 1 to 28.

## Double-end patterns

Peppermint and Plaid are "double-ended" patterns. They are not always turned at the end of a row, sometimes there are two consecutive rows on the wrong side. Therefore, these patterns must be worked on a circular needle or on a pair of double-pointed needles (*dpn*). If the patterns are knitted in the round, there is no need to worry about which strand is dropped at the end of the row, because at the end of a round, either strand can be used to continue.

## 11 Peppermint

Multiple of 10 sts plus 5.
Colours A and B.

**Row 1** (WS) With A, purl.

**Row 2** With B, knit. Sl sts to other end of needle.

**Row 3** With A, knit.

**Row 4** With B, p1, *sl 3 wyif, p7; rep from *, end sl 3, p1. Sl sts to other end of needle.

**Row 5** With A, purl.

**Row 6** With B, k1, *sl 3 wyib, k7; rep from *, end sl 3, k1. Sl sts to other end of needle.

**Row 7** With A, knit.

**Row 8** With B, repeat row 4. Sl sts to other end of needle.

**Rows 9, 10 and 11** Repeat rows 1, 2 and 3.

**Row 12** With B, p6, *sl 3 wyif, p7; rep from *, end sl 3, p6. Sl sts to other end of needle.

**Row 13** With A, purl.

**Row 14** With B, k6, *sl 3 wyib, k7; rep from *, end sl 3, k6. Sl sts to other end of needle.

**Row 15** With A, knit.

**Row 16** With B, repeat row 12. Sl sts to other end of needle.

Repeat rows 1 to 16.

## 12 Plaid

Multiple of 10 sts plus 2.
Colours A and B.

Cast on with A and purl one row.

**Row 1** (RS) With B, k1, *(sl 1 wyif, sl 1 wyib) twice, sl 1 wyif, k5; rep from *, end k1. Sl sts to other end of needle.

**Row 2** With A, k1, *k5, sl 5 wyib; rep from *, end k1. Turn.

**Row 3** With B, k1, *p5, (sl 1 wyif, sl 1 wyib) twice, sl 1 wyif; rep from *, end k1. Sl sts to other end of needle.

**Row 4** With A, k1, *sl 5 wyif, p5; rep from *, end k1. Turn.

**Rows 5, 6, 7, 8 and 9** Repeat rows 1, 2, 3, 4 and row 1 again.

**Row 10** With A, k1, *k5, (sl 1 wyif, sl 1 wyib) twice, sl 1 wyif; rep from *, end k1. Turn.

**Row 11** With B, k1, *p5, sl 5 wyif; rep from *, end k1. Sl sts to other end of needle.

**Row 12** With A, k1, *(sl 1 wyif, sl 1 wyib) twice, sl 1 wyif, p5; rep from *, end k1. Turn.

**Row 13** With B, k1, *sl 5 wyib, k5; rep from *, end k1. Sl sts to other end of needle.

**Rows 14, 15, 16, 17 and 18** Repeat rows 10, 11, 12, 13 and row 10 again.

**Row 19** With B, k1, *p5, (sl 1 wyib, sl 1 wyif) twice, sl 1 wyib; rep from *, end k1. Sl sts to other end of needle.

**Row 20** With A, k1, *sl 5 wyif, p5; rep from *, end k1. Turn (same as row 4).

**Row 21** With B, k1, *(sl 1 wyib, sl 1 wyif) twice, sl 1 wyib, k5; rep from *, end k1. Sl sts to other end of needle.

**Row 22** With A, k1, *k5, sl 5 wyib; rep from *, end k1. Turn (same as row 2).

**Rows 23, 24, 25, 26 and 27** Repeat rows 19, 20, 21, 22 and row 19 again.

**Row 28** With A, k1, *(sl 1 wyib, sl 1 wyif) twice, sl 1 wyif, p5; rep from *, end k1. Turn.

**Row 29** With B, k1, *sl 5 wyib, k5; rep from *, end k1. Sl sts to other end of needle (same as row 13).

**Row 30** With A, k1, *k5, (sl 1 wyib, sl 1 wyif) twice, sl 1 wyib; rep from *, end k1. Turn.

**Row 31** With B, k1, *p5, sl 5 wyif; rep from *, end k1. Sl sts to other end of needle (same as row 11).

**Rows 32, 33, 34, 35 and 36** Repeat rows 28, 29, 30, 31 and row 28 again.

Repeat rows 1 to 36.

## 13 Rainbow zigzag

Rainbow zigzag is a bias knitting pattern. For an explanation of bias knitting, see page 49.

Multiple of 12 sts plus 3.
Colours A and B.

Cast on with A and knit one row.

**Row 1** (RS) With B, k1, sl 1, k1, psso, *k9, sl 2, k1, p2sso; rep from *, end k9, k2 tog, k1.

**Row 2** With B, k1, *p1, k4 (k1, yo, k1) in next st, k4; rep from *, end p1, k1.

**Rows 3 and 4** With A, repeat rows 1 and 2.

Repeat rows 1 to 4.

# International patterns

Here are a variety of colourful patterns from many parts of the world. Use the colour schemes and designs to decorate your own knitted garments and household items.

Information on how to knit from charts is to be found on page 60.

Mexican motif

Italian motif

Scandinavian motif

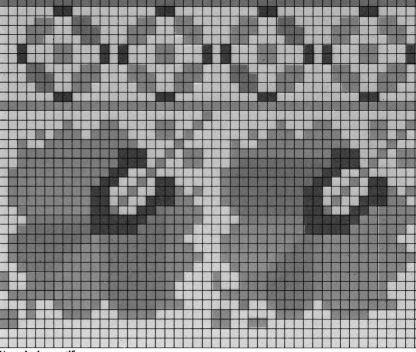
Yugoslavian motif

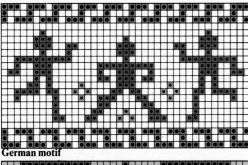
German motif

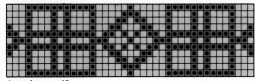
Austrian motif

Scandinavian motif

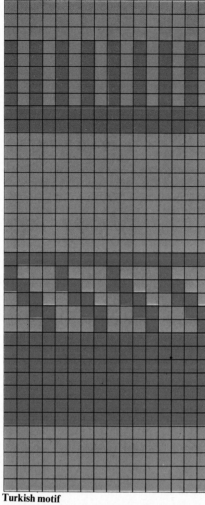

**Turkish motif**

Turkish motif

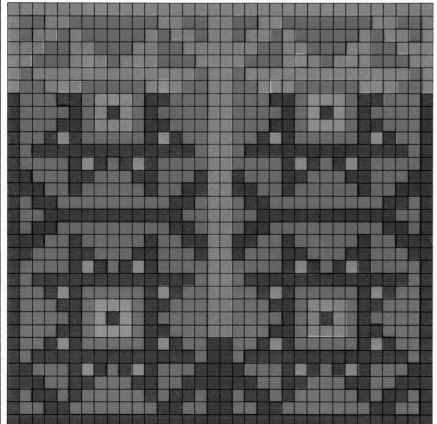

**Yugoslavian motif**

# Translating motifs

Motifs can be charted from existing garments and used on similar or different items.

### Turkish gloves
The patterns found on these boldly coloured gloves have been charted on the left. Use the same patterns to enliven a sweater.

**Turkish gloves worked in boldly contrasting colours**

### Argyll socks

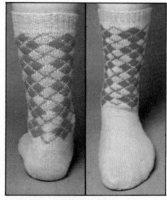

**Argyll socks**
Traditionally patterned socks are made by combining a charted design with the sock instructions on page 89.

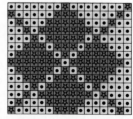

**Pattern chart**
Once the pattern has been charted out, the repeating design can be put to other uses. For instance, a thick afgan of Argyll squares.

# Materials and colour schemes

### Using different colours and yarns

Building up a colour scheme of your own is far more satisfying than copying one planned by someone else. Colour is a matter of individual taste, and rules about colour often do little except deflate an original enthusiasm. Use any colours together, but bear in mind that two or three tones of one colour will give a more subtle effect than a single tone. A change of texture, for example, using a tawny brown 4-ply yarn together with a tawny brown mohair yarn will soften the harsh lines of colour into a light, diffuse haze.

### Choosing a colour scheme

If in doubt about which colours to use, the natural wool colours, browns, blacks, greys and off-whites are the safest. These colours are frequently used in the traditional knitting of Peru, Iceland and the Shetland Islands. If these shades are not bright enough, use tones of one colour, for example, knit a pink sweater with the palest to the deepest shades of rose, or a sweater using all the shades of orange and lemon. Nature is the best guide to colour, so if you find it difficult to plan a colour scheme, try looking at a fruit bowl or around the garden for inspiration. If you want to try an unusual colour combination, knit up a small test piece using the yarn and stitch pattern for your design in exactly the same way as you would make a stitch gauge sample before beginning to knit any pattern.

The choice of colour and colour schemes depends also on the fashion of the times. For instance, what was considered right in Victorian times might look quite wrong today. However, bear in mind that when strong contrasting colours such as black, white, turquoise and orange are used together, each will jump out and form a strong vivid pattern on its own.

### Using up leftover yarns

Working with many colours is an excellent way of using up odd balls of yarn. However, do not mix different types of yarn in one piece of knitting as the yarns will not wash and wear in the same way. It is best to use all the synthetic fibres together and all the wool or hair fibres together.

An easy and effective way of using leftover balls of yarn is to make a patchwork, planning it in exactly the same way as a fabric one. The knitted patches do not have to be all one colour but can be striped horizontally, vertically or diagonally or can be patterned with dots, flowers and fleur de lys, or any kind of motif you choose. You could work out all the patterns in sketch form beforehand. Plan your own multi-colour designs on graph paper, taking each small square to represent one stitch, like the colour pattern charts on page 61. You could also take some of the slip patterns from the previous page and include them in your patchwork, using your own colour scheme.

### Knitting with unusual materials

You do not have to knit only with the materials packaged and sold as "knitting yarn". You can knit with anything, from ribbons to rags, so long as it is flexible and long enough to form a loop. There are all kinds of unusual materials to experiment with. Try knitting with string, combining rough and smooth string in natural colours to make mats, hammocks or bags.

As an economy measure, old clothes can be cut into strips and knitted up into rugs, blankets and even clothes. If it is carefully knitted in well-chosen colours this rag knitting need not be used just for economy, some very beautiful knitting can be made using the most unlikely materials.

# Advanced colour techniques

### Knitting intricate colour patterns

Colours can be used in a much more flexible way than is possible with the slip method. The three techniques for combining colours, stranding, weaving and crossing yarns (right) have evolved for two reasons. 1 To keep the back of the knitting free from long loops of unworked yarn. 2 To keep the knitting together and prevent a hole appearing when one colour joins with another.

### Stranding colour across the back of the work

For small regular patterns such as dots, small checks and flower shapes, the stranding method is used to carry the unworked colour across the back of the work until it is needed again. It is the ideal method to use when you are working with only two colours, alternating them every few stitches. The pattern can then be worked by feeding one colour in from the right hand and the other from the left hand (threading hands, page 18). Although the yarns are automatically stranded for colour change in the slip method, the slipped stitches cause a pulled texture and so this simple stranding is a much better method to use when you need an even texture.

### Weaving colour across the back of the work

When the range of colour and pattern extends to more than two colours, or when each colour is worked for more than four stitches, then the yarn must be woven into the back of the work. The weaving prevents long strands of unused yarn being carried across the back of the work, getting caught up and distorting the knitting. A woven back can also be used to form a thicker fabric regardless of colour. This was a favourite way of making men's warm waistcoats in the nineteenth century.

### Crossing yarns for separate blocks of colour

When the colour is only being used in one area, for example, in diagonal or vertical stripes, or blocks of colour, then the yarn is not required to travel across the back of the work and neither the stranding nor the weaving methods are necessary. To prevent a hole forming where two colours meet, the yarns are crossed over each other, joining the two colour areas together.

To knit blocks of colour you will need a separate ball or length of yarn for each pattern block. A vertical black stripe on a white ground, for example, calls for two balls of white and one of black yarn. To knit squares and tartan patterns, knit as the pattern dictates, crossing the yarns for diagonal and vertical areas of pattern and weaving or stranding if required.

### Using embroidery with colourwork

Sometimes only a thin, one stitch line of colour is needed – for example in Argyll patterns, window pane checks or in patterns with tiny patches of different colour. It is often easier to leave this colour out during knitting and then embroider it in later when the knitting is completed. Use the Swiss darning technique, explained on page 65.

Embroidery can also be used in other ways. The outline of an eyelet can be emphasized by stitching in a contrasting colour (see page 65); large motifs or alphabets to decorate knitting can be added using the cross stitch method (see page 66); honeycombing can be used to shape smocking while bullion knots can imitate needlemade lace (see page 67).

# Stranding colours

Use the stranding method for patterns with small repeats of only two or three colours.

### How to work in a knit row

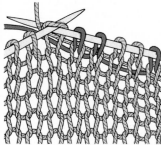

*With both yarns at the back of the work, knit 2 with the first colour and then drop it to the back. Pick up the second colour and knit 2, then drop it to the back. Continue working the colours alternately and keeping the yarns stranding loosely along the back.*

### How to work in a purl row

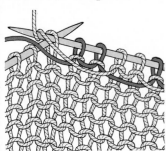

*Work in the same way but with the yarns held to the front of the work.*

### Stranding at correct tension

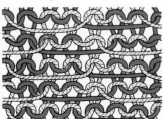

*If stranding is worked correctly the yarns run evenly across the back of the work at the same tension as the knitting. If the stranding yarns are strained the knitting will be puckered. When knitting in the round, the work is not turned, so all stranding is as for a knit row.*

# Weaving colours

Use the weaving method for large pattern repeats and when three or more colours are being used in a row. When working with more than three colours, try threading each colour through an empty cotton reel. The weight will help prevent the yarns from becoming tangled.

### How to work in a knit row

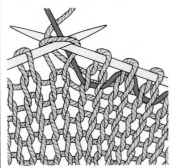

**1** *Thread both hands with yarn (holding yarn, page 18). Knit 1 with the first colour and at the same time, with the left hand, bring the second colour over the top of the first.*

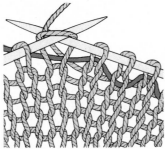

**2** *Knit 1 again with the first colour, and this time bring the second colour below the first. Continue to weave the second colour while working the first When the second colour is being worked, weave the first.*

### How to work in a purl row

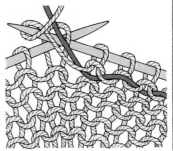

**1** *Work the purl row in exactly the same way as the knit row, holding the yarns to the front of the work. Thread both hands with yarn. With the left hand bring the second colour over the top of the first and purl 1 with the first colour.*

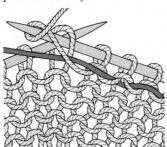

**2** *Purl 1 again with the first colour, but this time keep the second colour below the first.*

## Weaving yarns at the correct tension

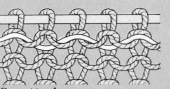

**Correct tension**

*The yarn here is woven at the same tension as the knitting, with the strands crossing evenly and undulating to the same depth.*

**Incorrect tension**

*The woven yarn is stretched too tightly across the back of the work. The knitting will be pulled and look "smocked" on the front. It is better to weave too loosely rather than too tightly.*

# Crossing colours

### Diagonal colour change

Use the crossing method when a colour is used only in one particular part of the knitting. The colours are not taken across the work, but cross when they join their neighbours. Each block of colour therefore needs a separate ball of yarn.

### When a pattern slants diagonally to the right

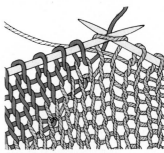

*The right-hand yarn is crossed in front of the left-hand yarn on the knit row and then dropped to the back. The left-hand yarn is then picked up. On the return purl row the diagonal encroaches and the yarns automatically loop together.*

### When a pattern slants diagonally to the left

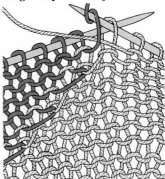

*The yarns are crossed on the purl row only. On the knit row the diagonal encroaches and the yarns automatically loop together.*

### Vertical colour patterns

The colours are crossed with their neighbours on every row, because in vertical work the pattern does not encroach. The method of crossing yarn is the same as for diagonals.

# *Modern colourwork*

Knitting today is more colourful than ever before. The choice of colours and patterns is infinite, and once you have mastered the technique of working with more than one colour, you can devise your own patterns. For inspiration, look at the work of Kaffe Fasset on page 62. Charts for the patterns shown here are on page 61. You can adapt any garment pattern and knit it up in many colours. Variations of the basic glove pattern (page 90) are shown opposite; while two sweaters knitted in a variety of the colourwork patterns are on page 75.

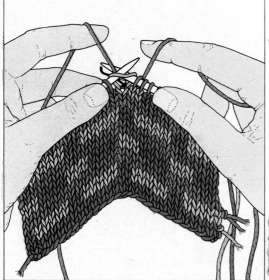

**Knitting with more than one colour**
*Successful colourwork depends upon keeping the different strands tangle-free as well as using them at the right tension. Techniques for knitting with colours are explained on page 56.*

**1 Dots**

**2 Check and stripe**

**5 Bars and stripes**

**6 Checkers**

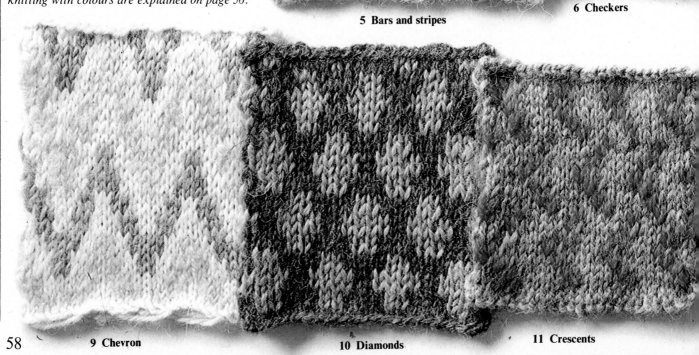

**9 Chevron**

**10 Diamonds**

**11 Crescents**

# Patterned gloves & mittens

**3 Balloon**

**4 Cross and stripe**

**7 Bird**

**8 Brocade**

**12 Diagonals**

**13 Lattice**

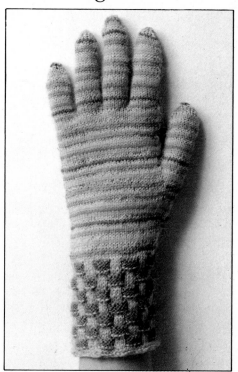

*Striped gloves*
*A pair of gloves is a challenge to any knitter and a basic glove pattern provides endless decorative possibilities and a great chance to play with colours and patterns. Full instructions for making this glove and the mitten below are shown on pages 90–91.*

*Fingerless mittens*
*Fingerless mittens are fun to wear and easier to knit than full gloves. Mittens take very little yarn and are an ideal way of using up colourful scraps of yarn.*

# Pattern charts

Chart instructions for knitting form the picture of a pattern whereas the written instructions are the story. Although intricate colour patterns are always shown in chart form, knitting patterns are usually written out. But some designers and publications prefer to use charts so an understanding of the principles of stitch pattern charts is important. *All* charts for both stitch and colour patterns are read from the bottom of the chart upwards, so the bottom row of the chart represents the first row of the knitting.

## Stitch pattern charts

Stitch pattern charts are not particularly difficult to understand. Each square represents a stitch and each line represents a row or round of knitting. In chart patterns for example, a knit stitch can be represented by a blank square and a purl stitch by a solid square. Each pattern instruction has a different symbol, and the chart will always have a visual key to explain the symbols used. The instructions will read differently for flat knitting, the chart is read from right to left for the rows when the right side of the work is facing you; and from left to right when the back of the work is facing you. With knitting in the round, the front of the fabric always faces the knitter, so the work is always read from the front, from right to left. Each line of the chart represents each new row or round of knitting.

## Colourwork charts

A chart is essential in colourwork if you are to understand when to introduce the different coloured yarns. The squares each represent one stitch and each row of squares represents one row of knitting. Each colour has its own symbol on the chart, and a key to the symbols is printed beside the chart.

The charts are usually based on stocking stitch where the first and all odd numbered rows are knitted from right to left and the second and all even numbered rows are purled from left to right. If the fabric is to be knitted in the round, then each round is knitted from right to left with the right side facing out.

In order for the pattern to work, the correct multiple of stitches must be adhered to. Edge stitches, which do not necessarily have to be repeated, are given at the beginning and ends of rows and it is often possible to adjust these. Bear in mind that extra rows which are not always included in a chart may also be required to finish off a pattern.

## Using charts for designing

You can very easily design colourwork patterns of your own. The best way is to use blank squares for the main colour background and blacked out squares for the second colour. Crosses, dots, diagonal lines and other symbols can be used for third and subsidiary colours. Or you can work directly with colour, using crayons or paints. Once you have worked out your colourwork chart, knit a sample piece before beginning the main work. Knit at least two pattern repeats in order to test the pattern for colour and style.

Stitch pattern designs follow the same principle. Each stitch should be represented by one square. Each different stitch must have a different symbol.

A decrease (or an increase) instruction will always occupy only one square on the chart whether the instruction is to decrease only one or several stitches. The complementary increase then occupies the vacant square whether it is adjacent to the decrease or not. Also consider the pairing of increases and decreases (page 72) when plotting garment shapes on a chart.

# Stitch pattern chart

As an example of the way in which pattern symbols are used, the Crazy check pattern (page 45) from the eyelet and lace stitch glossary has been translated into chart form.

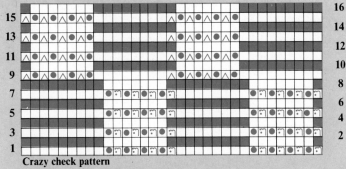

Crazy check pattern

## Symbols for knitting charts

A selection of stitch pattern symbols are shown below. Use these for designing your own patterns. Different sets of symbols are used by different designers, but a key to the symbols will always be printed with a charted pattern

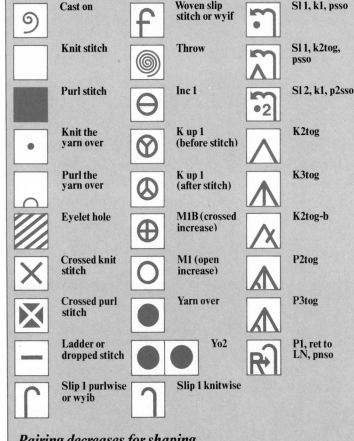

| | | |
|---|---|---|
| Cast on | Woven slip stitch or wyif | Sl 1, k1, psso |
| Knit stitch | Throw | Sl 1, k2tog, psso |
| Purl stitch | Inc 1 | Sl 2, k1, p2sso |
| Knit the yarn over | K up 1 (before stitch) | K2tog |
| Purl the yarn over | K up 1 (after stitch) | K3tog |
| Eyelet hole | M1B (crossed increase) | K2tog-b |
| Crossed knit stitch | M1 (open increase) | P2tog |
| Crossed purl stitch | Yarn over | P3tog |
| Ladder or dropped stitch | Yo2 | P1, ret to LN, pnso |
| Slip 1 purlwise or wyib | Slip 1 knitwise | |

## Pairing decreases for shaping

| | |
|---|---|
| K2tog | Sl 1, k1, psso |
| P2tog | P1, ret to LN, pnso |

# Colourwork charts

Following colourwork charts is as easy as painting by numbers. Each of the charts on this page relates to the colourwork patterns shown on page 58 and in the key below. To see how these patterns look when knitted up into clothes, turn to the modular sweater variations on page 74. Each colour is represented on the charts by a different symbol. Use the colours shown on page 58, or make up your own colour schemes.

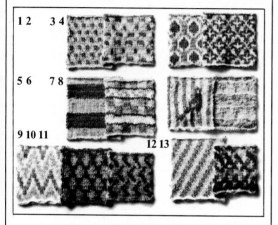

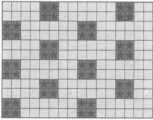

**1 Dots**

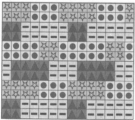

**2 Check and stripe**

**3 Balloons**

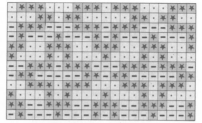

**4 Cross and stripe**

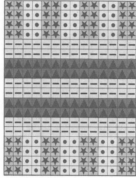

**5 Bars and stripes**

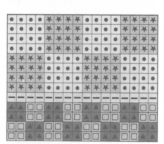

**6 Checkers**

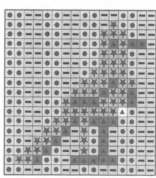

**7 Bird**

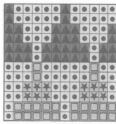

**8 Brocade**

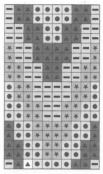

**9 Chevron**

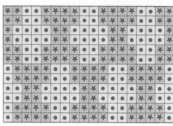

**10 Diamonds**

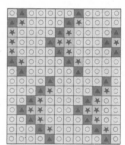

**11 Crescents**

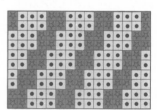

**12 Diagonals**

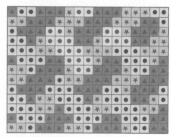

**13 Lattice**

# Traditional Fair Isle

# Colourwork variations

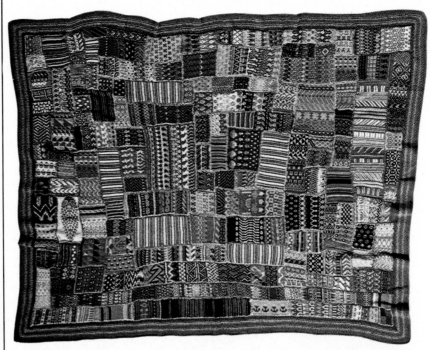

The origins of the Fair Isle patterns are obscure. They have been handed down without written instructions amongst knitters in the islands for centuries. Some say the patterns were taught to the Islanders in the sixteenth century by the Spanish sailors from the shipwrecked Armada. Others suggest the patterns are older still, brought over by the Vikings. The patterns have been spread through trade and fishing contacts. In the 1920s Fair Isle sweaters became fashionable, particularly as V-necked golfing sweaters. Fair Isle knitted garments have now become classic fashion, but they are still made in the traditional way in the Islands today.

**Nineteenth century Tam O'Shanter in authentic Fair Isle pattern**

Much of the charm of traditional colourwork patterns stems from the use of natural-dyed wool and the juxtapositioning of contrasting small patterns. This patchwork blanket, designed and worked by Kaffe Fassett, uses motifs inspired from nature and worked into a multiplicity of patterns.

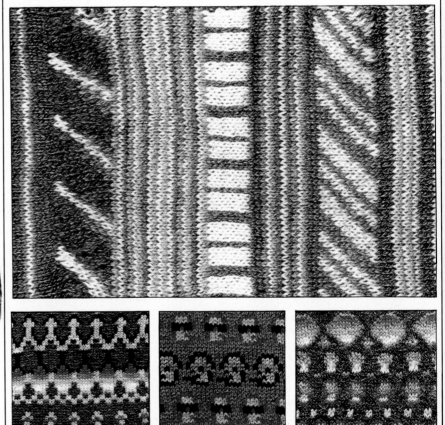

**Details showing the wide variety of small patterns used in the patchwork blanket**

# Knitting with beads and sequins

Beads and sequins can be used in knitting in two ways: as a decorative finish or as a more solid fabric. There are two techniques for applying the beads, beaded knitting and purse knitting (page 64).

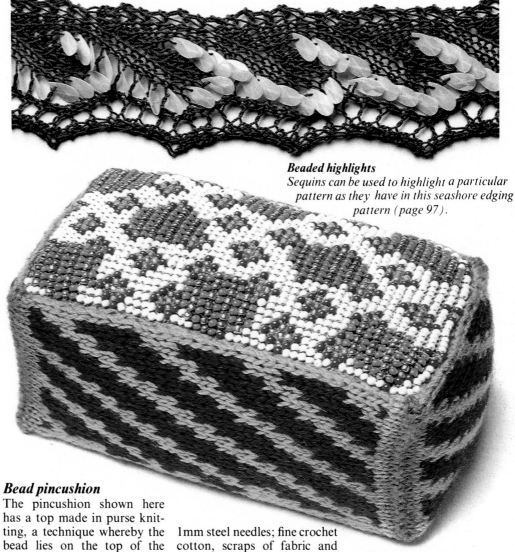

**Beaded highlights**
Sequins can be used to highlight a particular pattern as they have in this seashore edging pattern (page 97).

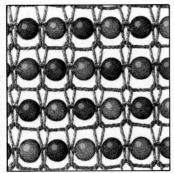

**Beaded fabric**
Beaded knitting can be used to decorate the whole fabric.

**Beaded motif**
Beads can also be used to form a more complex design such as a beaded motif. The motif must be charted in the same way as colourwork patterns (page 61) and the beads added to the yarn when the motif is reached in the pattern.

**Bead pincushion**
The pincushion shown here has a top made in purse knitting, a technique whereby the bead lies on the top of the stitches. (see page 64).

**How to make the pin cushion**
You will need approx 700 2mm glass beads for the background colour and 250 each for each of the other colours; a pair of 1mm steel needles; fine crochet cotton, scraps of fabric and wool, and sawdust for filling. Make a purse knitted top using the chart instructions below. Then make a cotton box to fit the measurements of the top and fill it with sawdust. Knit a strip in diagonal pattern (page 61) to go round the sides of the box with contrasting stripes at each corner. Apply top, base and knitted sides to the box.

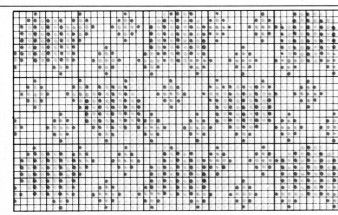

The pincushion top measures 5 in. (12.7 cm) by 2¾ in (7 cm)

## How to make the pin cushion top

The pincushion top is worked in crossed stocking stitch. Be sure to thread first the last bead to be knitted, as indicated in the diagram below. The chart on the left shows the pattern for the pincushion top, each square representing one stitch and one bead.

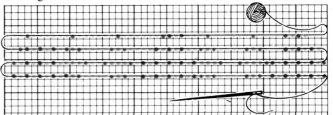

# Knitting with beads

With purse knitting you can knit entire bead fabrics, or with beaded knitting simply give a slight shimmer or highlight to a design. The secret of success lies in the exact placing of each bead so that it lies securely and in full view in the position for which it was intended. Both techniques were developed in the eighteenth and nineteenth centuries. Beaded knitting was used on exquisitely fine lace stitch patterns to highlight the knitting with crystals or pearls, or worked into flower motifs. Purse knitting was used to depict tiny beaded scenes, landscapes and stories on pin cushions, bags and purses.

### Choosing beads and yarn

You can knit with any type of bead, but remember that the knitted fabric will carry the weight of all the beads together, so the lighter the beads the less they will weigh down the knitting. Sequins, used in beaded knitting must be the type which have a hole at the side not a hole in the centre. The knitting yarn must be strong enough to carry the weight of the beads but fine enough to be threaded through them. Use crochet cotton with small beads, and knitting yarn with wooden beads and large sequins. Make sure that the knitting needles make stitch loops smaller than the beads or they will slip through to the back.

The beads, yarn and needles must all work together and be in proportion to each other. Crochet cotton was used to knit the pin cushion on page 63. This was threaded with 2mm glass beads. The stitches were knitted on home-made steel needles. You can make these by buying a length of 1mm steel wire and cutting it into needles, then filing the tips to points. This is not the ordeal that it sounds; before the machine age all needles were made by hand.

### Threading beads onto the knitting yarn

In beaded knitting the beads and sequins are usually all one colour and, unlike the beads in purse knitting, do not have to be threaded in order. They can be threaded direct from the string.

Threading beads for purse knitting needs perfect accuracy to ensure that the beads will be knitted off the yarn in the correct order to form the design. First, the whole design must be drawn onto graph paper with each square representing one bead. Thread the beads reading the chart from the *top left corner for odd rows* and *top right for even rows* to the *bottom right corner*. When following a knitting chart, work always begins at the bottom right corner.

## How to thread beads onto knitting yarn

**Threading the beads**

*Thread some sewing cotton through a loop of knitting yarn and then thread both ends of sewing cotton through a sewing needle. Now proceed to thread the beads along the sewing needle to reach the knitting yarn. When beads and sequins are not on a thread, but loose, each one has to be picked up individually and threaded onto the needle.*

### Beaded knitting

Add beads or sequins on the second and every alternate row, from the back of the fabric. If they are added on every row the knitting is likely to curl. The knitting will also curl if beads are put on with the first stitch in a row.

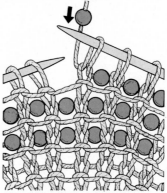

**Slip the bead close to the stitch**

### Knitting in the beads

Start knitting in the beads 2 or 3 stitches from the beginning of each beaded row. Use garter stitch (page 18) when working an all-over pattern. Work as follows:

**Row 1** Knit.
**Row 2** Knit the first 2 stitches, to make a plain selvedge, then slip a bead up to the front of the work, close to the stitch just knitted, as shown (above). Knit the next stitch and then add a bead once again. Continue in this way up to the selvedge.
**Row 3** Knit.
**Row 4** Bead. Take care that the beads sit firmly to the front of the work.

### Working beaded motifs

When working beaded motifs the beads are added at the back of the work on every alternate row as before and the stitches before and after the bead are knitted in order to push the bead to the front of the work. All other stitches are worked in pattern.

### Purse knitting

In purse knitting the beads are added on every row so that they completely cover the knitted ground. Each bead lies vertically on top of a crossed knit stitch which prevents the bead from slipping to the back of the work.

Designs must be charted if more than one colour bead is used and the beads threaded carefully as explained (left). Instructions for making a pin cushion in purse knitting are given on page 63.

### Working purse knitting

Purse knitting is always worked using crossed stocking stitch (page 19) so as to prevent the beads from slipping to the back of the work. Beads are added on both the knit and the purl rows, between the first and last two stitches on each row, and with every stitch. Knit two rows of stocking stitch before adding the beads.

### How to bead in a knit row

*Push the bead through to the front of the work with the left forefinger as the new loop is drawn through. The needle keeps the stitch open while the bead is manoeuvred into place.*

### How to bead in a purl row

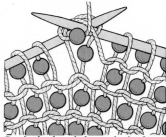

*Push the bead through the loop with the left thumb as the new loop is drawn through.*

# Embroidery on knitting

There are many ways of using embroidery on knitting. All are simple to work and all turn plain knitting into something far richer. Seven different techniques are shown here and in colour on pages 66 and 67. The most common ways of decorating knitting are with Swiss darning and cross stitch embroidery, both of which add more colour and pattern to knitting. Embroidered bullion knots add texture and look particularly effective worked on lacy patterns. The eyelet holes in lace patterns can be decorated by surrounding them with stitching in a contrast colour. Ladder weaving is useful for decorating dropped stitches and dropped stitch patterns. Honeycombing, which resembles smocking, can be used as a decoration on ribbed knitting and as a means of shaping. Finally, with appliqué you can make intricate patterns by applying one piece of knitting on top of another.

When embroidering on knitting, always use a blunt-ended wool or tapestry needle to avoid splitting the yarn, and make sure that the embroidery stitches are worked to the same tension as the knitting.

## Three ways to decorate knitting

Here are three unusual but very simple-to-work methods of decorating knitting. Use them all to emphasize features of the knitted fabric and make your knitting more colourful.

### Ladder weaving

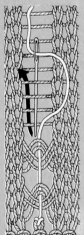

**Method of working**
Secure yarn to the dropped stitch at the bottom. Insert the needle downwards under the second two strands then over the lower two strands. Invert the needle, twisting the two pairs of strands around the embroidery yarn. Continue working up the ladder.

### Embroidery around eyelets

Knitted eyelets (page 42) can be emphasized and finished off in a different colour simply by stitching around each one.

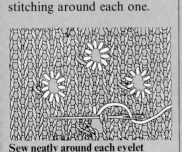

**Sew neatly around each eyelet**

### Bullion knots on lace knitting

Fine needle laces were the height of fashion in the eighteenth century. But they were extremely expensive, so skillful knitters developed a clever imitation. Fine lace patterns were knitted in gossamer thin yarn and then embroidered with bullion knots.

For a modern adaptation of this old idea, use a thick yarn. Knit it up into a lace stitch pattern and then embellish the solid parts of the pattern with fat bullion knots. The Beginner's lace pattern on page 67 has been decorated in this way.

### How to work bullion knots

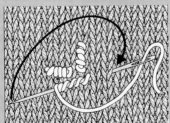

Push the needle through as far as possible twisting the yarn around it and then invert needle as shown.

## How to work Swiss darning

If the stitches are to be covered completely, embroider with yarn of exactly the same type as the base fabric. For a contrast or highlight, embroider with any type of yarn.

### Embroidery on knit stitches in horizontal rows

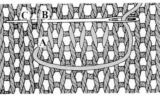

**1** Secure the embroidery yarn at the back of the work. Bring needle out to the front of the work at A. Insert the needle at B, under the base of the stitch above, to emerge at C.

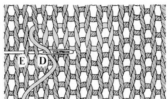

**2** Insert the needle at D and emerge at E ready to embroider the next stitch.

### Embroidery on knit stitches in vertical rows

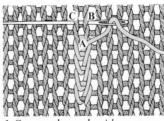

**1** Secure the embroidery yarn and bring the needle out to the front of the work at A. Insert the needle at B, bringing it out at C.

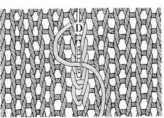

**2** Then take the needle under the head of the stitch below and emerge above it at D ready to form the next stitch.

### Embroidery on purl stitches in horizontal rows

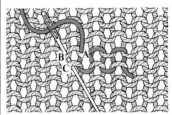

**1** Secure the embroidery yarn and bring the needle out at A. Take it across the head of the stitch and insert at B. Bring it out at C, under the head of the stitch, in the row below.

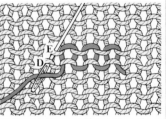

**2** Insert the needle at D, take it up to the row above, to emerge at E ready to cover the head of the next stitch.

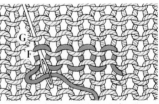

**3** To complete the embroidery insert the needle at F under the head of the last stitch to be embroidered and bring it out 1 row above at G.

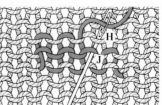

**4** Working from left to right take the needle across and insert at H, covering the head of the stitch and coming out at J under the head of the stitch in the row below.

# Embroidery on knitting

## Swiss darning

Swiss darning embroidery imitates knitting. With Swiss darning colour can be added to a piece of knitting easily and in far less time than it takes to knit it in. Swiss darning can be used to add spots of colour, highlights, special motifs, messages, flowers and symbols. It can be used for any design that is given in chart form and it is the easiest way to add single lines of colour in tartans and Argyll patterns, and to outline and emphasize a motif in brocade knitting. Swiss darning can only be distinguished from knitting on close inspection when the embroidery stitch can be seen to be in slight relief from the knitted stitch which it covers.

Swiss darning forms a double fabric and is therefore an effective way of reinforcing certain areas of a garment, such as the elbows on a man's sweater or the knees on a child's trousers.

Step by step diagrams showing how to work Swiss darning on knit and purl stitches, in vertical and horizontal rows are on page 65.

## Cross stitch

Cross stitch is worked on knitting in the same way as it is on woven fabrics, and any cross stitch embroidery motif can be worked onto knitting. Each stitch should be sewn firmly but not so tightly that the elasticity of the knitting pulls the embroidery out of shape.

### How to work cross stitch

*1 Make a diagonal from A to B. Emerge at C and insert needle at D.*

*2 For the second cross, emerge at E, insert again at D and re-insert at A.*

### Working cross stitch in rows

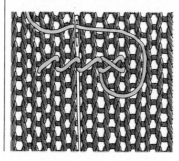

*Work one row of diagonals and on the return journey, cross them with a second row.*

## Honeycombing on ribbed knitting

Honeycombing is a form of smocking worked on ribbed knitting. It can be used as a means of shaping, drawing in extra fullness with the embroidery stitches. Allow 1½ times the required width of the finished knitting to work the embroidery. Honeycombing can be worked in the same or a contrast yarn.

### How to work honeycombing

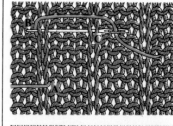

*1 Insert needle at A and emerge at B. Insert at C, re-emerge at B. Draw tight and repeat B–C once more.*

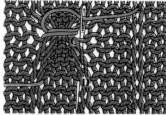

*2 Insert at C and emerge at D.*

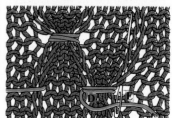

*3 Insert at E and emerge at D. Draw tight and repeat once more.*

## Bullion knots on lace knitting

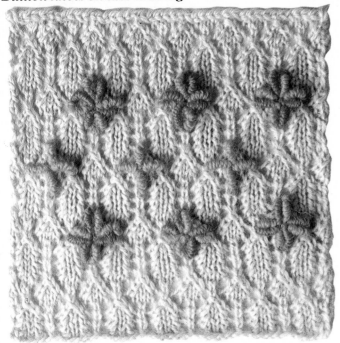

## Applique with knitted shapes

Lace knitting decorated with embroidered bullion knots is an old idea dating from the eighteenth century when it was worked in imitation of expensive needlemade lace. For a modern adaptation, sew several squares together to make a bedspread. The knitted lace pattern (above) is called Beginner's lace and is on page 46. Diagrams showing how to make bullion knots are on page 65.

Plain stocking stitch squares can be built up into extravagant designs by applying simple knitted shapes like squares, diamonds and triangles. Strips of striped knitting on the sample (above) have been arranged into a Celtic motif. Apply the shapes using the running stitch of Swiss darning. The decorated squares can be joined together to make cushion covers, blankets, afgans or bedspreads.

### Swiss darning on a plain beret

An embroidered motif makes a plain stocking stitch design much richer and more colourful. Use the method to add bright patterns to simple garments such as children's clothes, gloves, scarves or hats. The hexagonal beret project given on page 94 has been made much more decorative by the addition of a simple repeating motif.

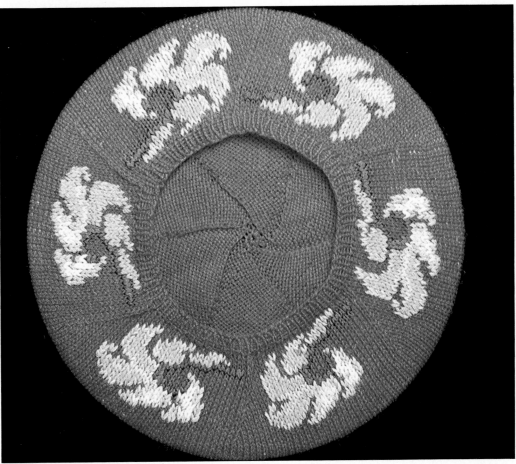

### The embroidery motif

Swiss darning is such excellent knitting forgery, even a simple motif can be most impressive. This stylized flower pattern is embroidered on each of the six sides of the beret. A graph chart for the pattern can be found on page 94.

# Shaping knitting

## The essentials of shaping

Shapes can be made with or without increases and decreases. Square or rectangular shapes are determined by the number of stitches cast on and the number of rows worked. Scarves, cushion covers, bedspreads, and even simple garments can be made in this way. Instructions for making an adult's sweater and a baby's jacket without increases or decreases are given on page *70*. More tailored shapes require increases and decreases to be worked into the knitting. To make any shape you must first decide on the dimensions of the design in inches or centimetres, and then calculate how many stitches and rows are needed to the inch or centimetre. The knitting is made to fit these measurements.

Calculating the number of stitches and rows is known as *stitch gauging*. Three factors influence stitch gauge. **1** The size of needles and type of yarn. **2** The type of stitch pattern. **3** The knitter.

## The size of needles and type of yarn

The selection of yarn and needles is one of the first decisions to be made when knitting a design. This combination is vitally important in determining the size of the stitch. The nine samples (right) demonstrate the importance of that combination and their role in calculating measurements for a design. All the samples have been worked with eight stitches over eight rows, but with different yarns and needles.

## The stitch pattern

Some stitch patterns form a loose fabric while others form a tight one. The three pattern samples (right) have all been knitted using the same needles, yarn, number of stitches and number of rows, yet each works out to a different final size.

## The knitter

The flow of yarn is controlled by the knitter. This control is known as *tension*, and is as personal as handwriting. Some knitters put more stress on the yarn, making a smaller stitch and tighter knitted fabric; others put less stress on the yarn and make a looser fabric. Both the samples (right) have been made with the same needles, yarn, number of stitches and number of rows by two knitters. The sample on the left is slightly bigger than that on the right. Though the difference in size on these small pieces is only $\frac{1}{8}$ inch (3mm) it could be drastic if you are working from a knitting pattern where the stitch gauge has been worked out to the designer's tension.

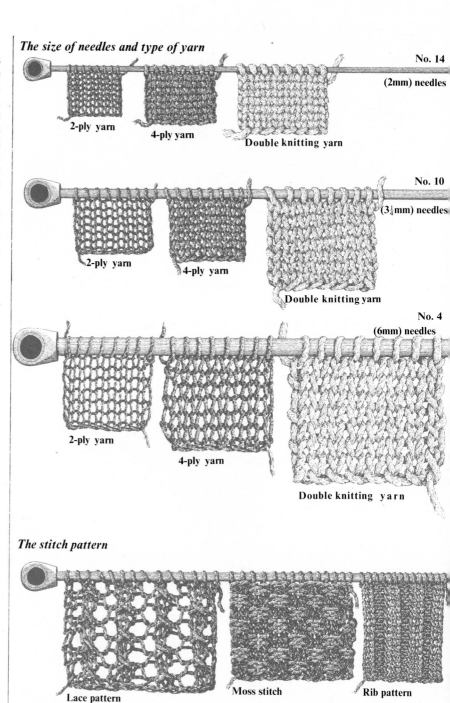

**The size of needles and type of yarn**

No. 14
(2mm) needles

2-ply yarn

4-ply yarn

Double knitting yarn

No. 10
(3¼mm) needles

2-ply yarn

4-ply yarn

Double knitting yarn

No. 4
(6mm) needles

2-ply yarn

4-ply yarn

Double knitting yarn

**The stitch pattern**

Lace pattern

Moss stitch

Rib pattern

**The knitter**

Knitter A

Knitter B

# Measuring stitch gauge

### Why stitch gauge is important

You must always measure stitch gauge before you start to make anything. This is necessary for two reasons: to check your tension against stitch gauge given in a pattern, and to calculate the number of stitches to cast on and rows to work when you are planning a design of your own. The stitch gauge or tension is always given at the beginning of a pattern and states the number of stitches and rows to the inch or centimetre using the yarn, needles and stitch pattern for a given design.

### Making a stitch gauge sample

Use the same yarn, needles and stitch pattern as those to be used for the main work. Knit a sample at least 3 inches (7.5cm) square. Smooth out the finished sample on a flat surface but do not stretch it.

### Measuring the number of stitches

This determines the width of the knitting. Place a steel ruler or tape measure across the sample and mark 2 inches (5cm) in the centre of the fabric with pins. Count the number of stitches between the pins. For complete accuracy pin out the sample several times. An extra half stitch will prove to be vital when you are working from a knitting pattern or when you are gauging the number of stitches to cast on for your own design. If the knitting is 20 inches (50cm) wide and the stitch gauge is $5\frac{1}{2}$ stitches to the inch, then the correct number of stitches to be cast on would be 20 inches $\times$ $5\frac{1}{2}$ stitches, a total of 110 stitches. If the half stitch is ignored and 20 $\times$ 5, a total of 100, stitches are cast on then the knitting will be 10 stitches short, a difference of more than $1\frac{1}{2}$ inches (3.8cm).

### Adjusting stitch gauge

The stitch gauge can be adjusted by changing the size of needles and working another sample. Changing to needles one size larger or smaller makes a difference of one stitch usually every 2 inches (5cm). If there are too many stitches to the inch your tension is too tight and you should change to needles a size larger. If there are too few stitches, your tension is too loose and you should change to needles a size smaller.

### Measuring the number of rows

This determines the depth of the knitting. The stitch gauge also determines the number of rows to the inch or to the centimetre. Place a ruler vertically along the fabric and mark out 2 inches (5cm) with pins. Count the number of rows between the pins. From this count you can gauge the number of rows needed to reach the planned length of a design. You can also calculate where shaping is required and the position of increases and decreases.

### Altering a pattern

Always make a stitch gauge sample if you intend to alter a pattern – for example, changing from stocking stitch to a lace stitch, or adding a cable panel. Also check the stitch gauge when changing from a single colour to a multi-colour pattern.

### Planning your own design

To plan your own design, first take the body measurements (right), remembering that you will be knitting for a finished garment so the measurements must be easy and not skin tight. Then calculate the stitch gauge against the body measurements.

## Taking measurements

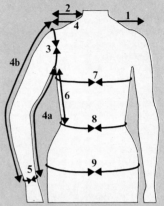

**1 Shoulders** Measure across back from shoulder tip to tip.
**2 Top of shoulder** Measure from shoulder point to neck edge. From this you calculate neck shaping.
**3 Armhole** Measure loosely from the highest point of the shoulders.
**4 a & b Sleeve** Measure with elbow bent from armpit to wrist, and outside arm from shoulder to wrist.
**5 Wrist** Measure around the wristbone.
**6 Waist to underarm** Measure with arm raised.
**7 Chest** Measure around the fullest part.
**8 Waist** For easy movement, measure with a finger between waist and tape measure.
**9 Hip** Measure around the broadest part.

### Measuring for skirts

**10 Waist-hip** Most of the shaping takes place in this area.
**11 Hem, straight skirts** Hip measurement plus 10 inches (25cm) gives average hem width.

### Measuring for hats, gloves, and socks

Details of measurements are on pattern pages. For socks page 88, gloves page 90 and hats page 94.

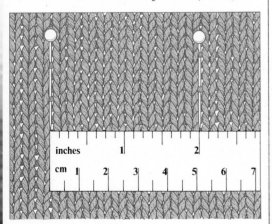

**How to count stitches**
*Place the ruler along a row of stitches, mark the stitches with pins and measure accurately, not forgetting to include any half stitches.*

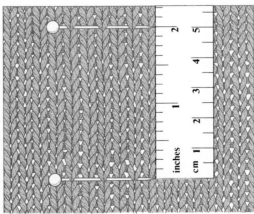

**How to count rows**
*Place the ruler vertically over the stitch gauge sample and insert the pins. Note how the pins are placed, between each row.*

# Baby jacket and sweater

## Simple garments

Many traditional garments throughout the world are based on straight lines without any curves. Here are patterns for a baby's jacket and an adult sweater made entirely of rectangles and squares. Both patterns can easily be adapted to fit different sizes. Working with the needles, yarn and tension, or stitch gauge, given in the pattern, add or subtract as many stitches and rows as required to fit the body measurements. Stitch gauge and measurements are explained on page 69. Both patterns can be varied with different colours, stitch patterns and trims. The baby's jacket is shown knitted in a multi-colour pattern on page 51.

**Baby's jacket**
This simply shaped jacket is made entirely of rectangles and squares. Once the stitch gauge is established simply add or subtract rows to match the baby's size.

### Baby's jacket

**Materials** 3-ply baby wool, 4 × 1 oz (113gr) or 5 × 25 gram balls. Yarn for ties. 12 buttons. **Needles** One pair No. 14 (2mm). **Stitch gauge** 20 sts and 44 rows to 2 inches (5cm). **Size** To fit 18 inch (46cm) chest. **Note** Work in garter st throughout.
**Back** Cast on 100 sts. K 220 rows (10in/25cm). Cast off. **Fronts** Cast on 55 sts. K 198 rows (9in/22·5cm). Cast off 23 sts at beg of next row, k to end. K 21 rows (1in/2·5cm) on rem 32 sts. Cast off. Rep for other side. **Sleeves** Cast on 80 sts, k 3 rows. To make eyelets: k2, *yo, k2tog; rep from * to last 2 sts, k2. K 106 rows (5in/12·5cm). Cast off. **Making up** Press each piece (page 84), join shoulder seam using edge to edge seam (page 84). Match centre of sleeve top with shoulder seam and sew in place. Join sleeve and side seams. Make 2 × 14 inch (35·5cm) cords and thread through eyelets at wrists. Make 12 button loops (page 82) at ½ inch (12mm) intervals along left front edge. Sew buttons in place.

### Rectangular sweater

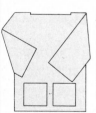

**Yarn** Double knitting wool, 7 × 2 oz (397gr) or 8 × 50 gram balls colour A; 6 balls each colours B and C. **Needles** One pair No. 3 (6¼mm). **Stitch gauge** 8 sts and 14 rows to 2 inches (5cm). **Size** To fit 36 inch (92cm) chest. **Note** Yarn is used double throughout.
**Pattern** Work in garter st throughout. Stripe sequence consists of 4 rows each colour. Join in colours for stripes using the method on page 49.
**Back and Front** Using 2 ends of colour A together, cast on 80 sts. K 1 row. Work in pattern for 196 rows (27½in/70cm) ending with 3 rows A. Cast off in A. **Sleeves** With A cast on 72 sts. Work in pattern for 122 rows (17½in/43·5cm) ending with 2 rows A. Cast off in A. **Pockets** With A cast on 24 sts. Work in pattern for 40 rows. Cast off in A. **Making up** Press each piece (page 84). Leaving an 11 inch (30cm) neck opening, join shoulder seams using back stitch seam (page 84). Match centre sleeve with shoulder seams, sew in place. Join side and sleeve seams. Attach pockets to front, 3 inches (7·5cm) from side seams and bottom edge, matching stripes on both pieces.

**Pale blue variation**
*Make this simple sweater more interesting by stitching on the buttons in a contrasting colour and adding multi-coloured beads to the sleeve cords to decorate them.*

**Olive green variation**
*Further interesting effects can be obtained by knitting the sweater in a darker colour, adding boldly striped patch pockets and more decorative buttons.*

# Rectangular sweater

### Optional pockets

*Simple square patch pockets can be added to the sweater after the garment is finished. They can be a solid colour or striped to match the overall design as shown (left). Sewing up technique is shown on page 83.*

# Knitted poncho

The poncho is the first project to use increases and decreases to create a garment shape. Methods of increasing and decreasing are given on page 36. The pattern for the poncho is given on page 72, while on the facing page there is an explanation of how increases and decreases can be used to create different shapes.

### Multi-colour stripe patterns

*Knit the sweater in any combination of colours and stripes. In this variation (left), each colour is knitted for only 2 rows instead of 4. Instructions and ideas for many stripe patterns begin on page 49.*

### Adding fringe to the poncho

*Use odd balls of yarn to decorate the poncho with a bright multi-coloured fringe. Loop the yarn through the edge of the poncho with a crochet hook. The fringe can be knotted into patterns for a more decorative effect.*

## Poncho project

The poncho consists of a simple triangular shape. The pattern begins with only one cast on stitch. The triangle is made by increasing one stitch at each end of every right side row. When one side of the poncho is complete, a neck opening is made in the centre by casting off a number of stitches. On the next row, these stitches are cast on again and the second side of the poncho is knitted in exactly the same way as the first, except that stitches are decreased instead of increasing until finally only one stitch remains.

The poncho is worked in Trinity stitch with a narrow border of Moss stitch. Trinity stitch, composed of regular, closely worked bobbles, is a very old popular pattern often worked on fishermen's sweaters. It gets its name from the way in which the bobbles are formed, by making "three in one and one in three", (k1,p1,k1, into next st, p3tog).

You can adapt this basic pattern in a number of ways. For example, by knitting only one side of the poncho to make a thick warm shawl (remembering to cast off very loosely), or, by omitting the neck opening to make a rug.

### Pattern instructions

**Yarn** 30 × 25gm balls double knitting wool. **Needles** One pair extra long No. 6 (5mm) needles. **Stitch gauge** 10 sts and 12 rows to 2 inches (5cm) over st-st. **Measurements** The completed poncho measures 74 inches (187cm) from point to point; and is therefore 37 inches (94cm) long at front and back. **Note** The crossed raised increase is used throughout. To work it, raise the running thread between 2 sts, and knit into the back of it (see page 37). Abbreviated as m1(RC). **Front point** Cast on 1 st. **Row 1** Knit. **Row 2** (K1, p1, k1) into the one st. **Row 3** Knit. **Row 4** K1, (k1, p1, k1) into middle st. K1. **Row 5** K1, p3, k1. **Row 6** K2, m1(RC), p1, m1(RC), k2. **Row 7** K1, p5, k1. **Row 8** K2, m1(RC), k1, p1, k1, m1(RC), k2. **Row 9** K1, p2, k1, p1, k1, p2, k1. **Row 10** K2, m1(RC), p1, k1, p1, k1, p1, m1(RC), k2. **Row 11** K1, p3, k1, p1, k1, p3, k1. **Row 12** K2, m1(RC), (k1, p1) 3 times, k1, m1(RC), k2. **Row 13** K1, p2, (k1, p1) 3 times, k1, p2, k1. **Row 14** K2, m1(RC), (p1, k1) to last 3 sts, p1, m1(RC), k2. **Row 15** K1, p3, (k1, p1) to last 5 sts, k1, p3, k1. **Row 16** K2, m1(RC), (k1, p1) to last 3 sts, k1, m1(RC), k2. **Row 17** K1, p2, (k1, p1) to last 4 sts, k1, p2, k1. **Row 18** K2, m1(RC), (p1, k1) to last 3 sts, p1, m1(RC), k2. **Row 19** K1, p3, (k1, p1) to last 5 sts, k1, p3, k1. **Row 20** K2, m1(RC), (k1, p1) to last 3 sts, k1, m1(RC), k2. **Row 21** K1, p2, (k1, p1) 3 times, k1, (k1, p1, k1) into next st, (k1, p1) 3 times, k1, p2, k1. **Row 22** K2, m1(RC), (p1, k1) 4 times, p3, (k1, p1) 3 times, m1(RC), k2. **Row 23** K1, p3, (k1, p1) 3 times, (k1, p1, k1) into next st, p3tog, (k1, p1, k1) into next st, (p1, k1) 3 times, p3, k1. **Row 24** K2, m1(RC), (k1, p1) 4 times, p7, (p1, k1) 4 times, m1(RC), k2. **Row 25** K1, p2, (k1, p1) 3 times, k1, [(k1, p1, k1) into next st, p3tog] twice, (k1, p1, k1) into next st, (k1, p1) 4 times, p1, k1. **Row 26** K2, m1(RC), (p1, k1) 4 times, p11, (k1, p1) 4 times, m1(RC), k2. **Row 27** K2, p3, (k1, p1) 3 times, (k1, p1, k1) into next st, p3tog] 3 times, (k1, p1, k1) into next st, (p1, k1) 3 times, p3, k1. **Row 28** K2, m1(RC), (k1, p1) 4 times, p15, (p1, k1) 4 times, m1(RC), k2. Cont in patt, inc 1 st at each end of every RS row. Keep the 10 st Moss st border on either side of main Trinity st patt until poncho measures 37 inches (94cm) from point to needles, with 56 "bobbles" vertically and 111 across needles (plus borders) ending with a RS row. **Neck opening Next row** Work in patt across 46 bobbles. For next 19 bobbles [k1, p3tog] instead of [(k1, p1, k1) into next st, p3tog]. K1, cont in patt to end of row. **Next row** Inc and work Moss st border. P to 11 inch (28cm) neck opening in centre. Cast off 39 sts very loosely. P to last 10 sts. Work Moss st border, inc at end of row. **Next row** Work in patt to centre opening, turn, so RS faces up. Cast on 39 sts very loosely, turn, knit back so WS faces. Work to end of row. **Next row** K1, k2tog, k1tb1, work 8 sts Moss st. P to last 11 sts, Moss st 8 sts, k2tog, k1. **Next row** Work border [p3tog, (k1, p1, k1) into next st] up to cast on sts, then [p1, (k1, p1, k1) into next st] 19 times, p1, [(k1, p1, k1) into next st, p3tog] to last 10 sts. Work in Moss st. **To complete poncho** Work back half to match front. Decrease at each end of RS rows instead of increasing. Continue 10 st Moss st border.

# Increasing and decreasing for shape

Increasing invisibly by making two stitches from one is shown on page 36 and to shape garments equally on both sides, increases and decreases must be paired, with one placed on either side of the knitting. This technique is explained here; once you understand it, you will be able to follow shaping instructions more easily and even design your own patterns in any style, to fit any figure. First, the construction of simple triangles is explained below.

## Making triangular shapes

Triangles can be made by building up a shape with increases and diminishing it with decreases. The poncho is made like this, with increases on one side and decreases on the other.

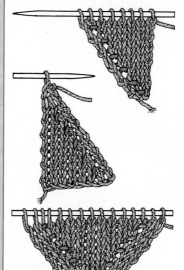

### Right angle triangle made by increasing

Cast on 2 stitches. Increase 1 at the end of every knit row.

### Left angle triangle made by decreasing

Cast on stitches for the base of the triangle. Sl 1, k 1, psso at the beginning of every knit row.

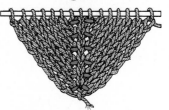

### Double triangle with horizontal stitches made by increasing

Cast on 3 stitches. Increase 1 on the second stitch at the beginning of every row.

### Double triangle in bias knitting made by increasing

Cast on 3 stitches. Increase 1 on the first and centre stitch. On the following row purl all stitches. Repeat, increasing the stitch next to the central stitch and the central stitch itself.

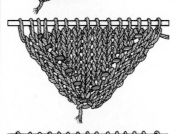

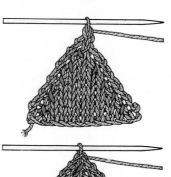

### Double triangle with horizontal stitches made by decreasing

Cast on the required number of stitches. Decrease on the second stitch at the beginning of every row.

### Double triangle in bias knitting made by decreasing

Cast on the required number of stitches. *Work to the central stitch, k2tog, k to end. On alternate rows *work to central stitch, p2 tog, p to end.

## *Pairing increases and decreases*

Paired increases and decreases are sometimes termed "fully fashioned" and form a discreet pattern at the same time as shaping the knitting. It is essential that both increases and decreases are correctly paired, otherwise the pattern will not be symetrical, and the shaping will pull against the knitted fabric and may distort it. Three methods of working paired increases are shown.

### *Knitting into the front and back of a stitch*

This bar increase is most often used for garment shaping. It is abbreviated as *Inc 1*.

### *Knitting into the stitch below*

Use this increase for invisible increasing. It is abbreviated. *K up 1*. Ease the tension slightly when working as it is inclined to contract the knitting.

### *Knitting into the running thread below*

This raised increase is most widely used for knitting gloves. It is abbreviated as *M1*.

### *Paired decreases*

Pairing decreases is even more important than pairing increases. When a decrease is made, the top of the decreased stitch forms an angle. This angle must always slope in the same direction as the decreasing. On the left side a decrease slopes towards the right, and on the right a decrease slopes towards the left. If the decreased stitch slopes against the line of decreasing, it may strain against the knitting and perhaps break. The various decrease combinations are paired to prevent this happening.

### *Single decreases*

The decreases shown right are worked three stitches in from each end of the rows.

### *Double decreases*

Because two stitches are decreased at once, a double decrease makes a more acute angle.

### *Chained decreases*

These are made by working two decreases in every row.

## *Working paired increases*

### *Knitting into the front and back of a stitch*

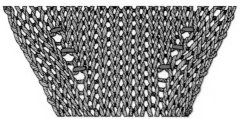

#### *Working the increase*

Make the first increase on the third stitch from the right, with its partner formed on the left on the fourth stitch from the end. The bars appear in the same position on each side. The method of working is the same on a purl row with the bars showing on the front of the fabric. The little bars formed beneath the new stitch make a decorative increase and are useful for counting the number of increase rows.

### *Knitting into the stitch below*

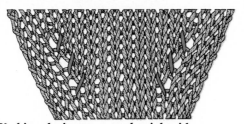

#### *Working the increase on the right side*

Knit the edge stitches and then knit into the head of the stitch below.

#### *Working the increase on the left side*

Knit into the head of the stitch below before knitting into the edge stitches. The same applies on the purl row.

### *Knitting into the running thread below*

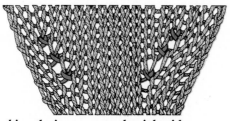

#### *Working the increase on the right side*

Pick up the running thread *after* knitting the third stitch.

#### *Working the increase on the left side*

Pick up the running thread *before* knitting the third last stitch.

## *Working paired decreases*

### *Single decreases*

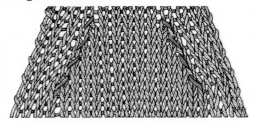

#### *Working the decrease on the right side*

On knit row, either sl 1 k1, psso; or k2tog through back of stitch. On purl row, p1, return it to the left needle and pass the next stitch over. This is abbreviated as *p1, ret to* LN, *pnso*. Alternatively, p2tog through back of stitch.

#### *Working the decrease on the left side*

On knit row, either k2tog; or k1, ret to LN, pnso. On purl row, p2tog; or sl 1, p1, psso.

### *Double decreases*

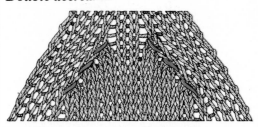

#### *Working the decrease on the right side*

On knit row, sl 1, k2tog, psso. On purl row, p2tog, ret to LN, pnso.

#### *Working the decrease on the left side*

On knit row, sl 1, k1, psso. On purl row, sl 1, p1, then slip the next stitch on the left needle purlwise and return it to the left needle again. This turns it to reverse way. Transfer the purled stitch to the left needle and slip the turned stitch over it. Return the stitch to the right needle and pass the first slipped stitch over it.

### *Chained decreases*

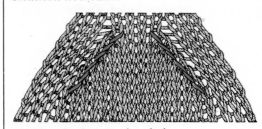

#### *Working the decrease in a knit row*

Sl 1, k1, psso, continue to the last 2 stitches, k2tog.

#### *Working the decrease in a purl row*

P1, ret to LN, pnso, continue to the last 2 stitches, p2tog. When knitting in the round, only the knit row decrease is used.

# *Modular sweater*

Crew neck with
set in sleeves

Polo neck with
set in sleeves

Cardigan style
with set in sleeves

Placket and collar
with set in sleeves

V-neck with
set in sleeves

Crew neck with
raglan sleeves

Polo neck with
raglan sleeves

V-neck with
raglan sleeves

Crew neck with
saddle shoulder sleeves

The ten sweaters on these pages are all made from the same basic pattern. Five different necklines (shown far right) and three different sleeve styles (below) as well as a sleeveless version are all included in the pattern. All of these styles are classic and all have been designed to interchange with each other. Using the basic pattern you can make a very large number of different sweaters.

The front and back of the sweater remain the same in all variations except for the cardigan front which is worked in two panels. To use the modular pattern, all you have to do is select the neckline and sleeve style you want and then work the basic back and front until you reach the shaping instructions for your chosen style. The full pattern instructions on page 76 are coded with clear diagrams showing each variation so you can easily select the pattern for each style.

The basic pattern has been designed to be worked in stocking stitch. This can be varied with textured, bobbled, cable or lace stitch patterns. When using a different stitch take care that the number of stitches in the stitch pattern divides equally with the number of stitches to be cast on. You must make a stitch sample using the needles and yarn specified in the pattern to ensure that your chosen stitch pattern works out to the same gauge as that given for the stocking stitch pattern. If it works out too large then change to smaller size needles; if it is too small, use larger size needles. Instructions for working out stitch gauge are on page 68.

You can also use colour and slip stitch patterns to change the basic sweater. The nine sweaters (left) illustrate the patterns from the modern colourwork glossary (page 58). The sleeveless version is shown opposite.

### Modular sweater variations
*These nine sweaters illustrate some of the styles that can be made using the modular sweater patterns.*

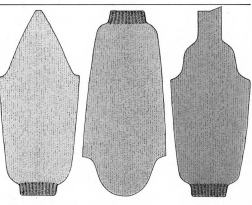

### Sleeve variations
*The three sleeve styles given in the pattern are (from left to right) raglan sleeve, set in sleeve and saddle shoulder sleeve.*

# Neckline styles

The five classic neckline styles included in the modular sweater pattern are the crew, V-neck, polo neck, cardigan front, and placket with collar as shown below.

**Crew neck**

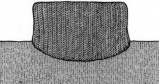

**Polo neck**

**Cardigan style**

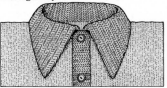

**Placket and collar**

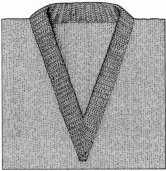

**V-neck**

## Neckline variations

*You can combine any one of these necklines with any of the sleeve variations. The polo neck can be made longer or shorter by knitting more or less rows. These neckline shapes can be varied by being knit in a different colour from the main body of the sweater.*

## Two knitted variations

*Two variations from the modular pattern have been knitted using patterns from the modern colourwork glossary. The V-neck sleeveless pullover (above left) is in the four-colour chevron pattern. The crew neck sweater with set in sleeves (above right) is knitted in four colours in bands of different patterns. A detail of the chevron pattern is shown (left) as well as a detail of the separate patterns used for the crew neck sweater (right).*

## General information for all patterns

**Yarn** For basic sweater or cardigan approx 18 (19) 19 (20) 1oz (25g) balls of 4-ply wool. For polo sweater allow one extra ball. For sleeveless sweater approx 12 (13) 13 (4) balls. One pair each of No. 9 (3¾mm) and No. 10 (3¼mm) knitting needles. 10 buttons for cardigan, 3 buttons for sweater with placket and collar.

**Stitch gauge** 13 sts and 17 rows to 2 inches (5cm) over st-st on No. 9 needles.

**Measurements** To fit 34 (36) 38 (40) 42 inch bust/chest [86 (91) 97 (102) 107cm]. Length of basic sweater 24 (24½) 25 (25½) 26 inches [60 (61) 62 (63.5) 64.5cm]. Sleeve seam 17½ (18) 18½ (19) 19½ inches [44 (45) 46 (47) 48cm].

**Note.** The cm equivalent of imperial measurements are approximate.

### Basic sweater with crew neck or polo neck

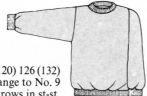

**Back** With No. 10 needles cast on 114 (120) 126 (132) 138 sts. Work 14 rows in k1, p1 rib. Change to No. 9 needles and beg with a k row work 122 rows in st-st.
**Shape armholes** Cast off 5 sts at beg of next 2 rows, then 2 (2) 3 (3) 4 sts at beg of next 2 rows. Dec 1 st at each end of next and foll 4 (5) 5 (6) 6 alt rows. [90 (94) 98 (102) 106 sts.** Cont without shaping until 68 (72) 76 (80) 84 rows have been worked from beg of armhole shaping. **Shape shoulders** Cast off 5 (6) 7 (6) 7 sts at beg of next 6 rows, then 7 (6) 5 (7) 6 sts at beg of next 4 rows. Cast off rem 32 (34) 36 (38) 40 sts. **Front** Work as given for back to **. Cont without shaping until 50 (52) 54 (56) 58 rows have been worked from beg of armhole shaping. **Shape neck** Next row K37 (39) 41 (43) 45, turn and leave rem sts on spare needle.*** Cast off 2 sts at beg of next row, then dec 1 st at neck edge on next and foll 5 (6) 7 (8) 9 alt rows. [29 (30) 31 (32) 33 sts.] Cont without shaping until armhole measures the same as back, ending with a purl row. **Shape shoulder** Cast off 5 (6) 7 (6) 7 sts at beg of next and foll 2 alt rows, then 7 (6) 5 (7) 6 sts at beg of foll alt row. Work 1 row, then cast off rem 7 (6) 5 (7) 6 sts. Return to the sts on spare needle, with right side facing rejoin yarn and cast off 16 sts, knit to end. Cont to match left side, reversing shaping. **Sleeves** With No. 10 needles cast on 58 (60) 62 (64) 66 sts. Work 14 rows in k1, p1 rib. Change to No. 9 needles and beg with a knit row cont in st-st, inc 1 st at both ends of 11th (9th) 7th (5th) 3rd and every foll 12th row until there are 76 (80) 84 (88) 92 sts, then cont without shaping until 134 (138) 142 (146) 150 rows have been worked in st-st.**** **Shape top** Cast off 5 sts at beg of next 2 rows, then 2 (2) 3 (3) 4 sts at beg of next 2 rows. Dec 1 st at each end of next and every alt row until 40 sts rem, ending with a purl row. Cast off 2 sts at beg of next 8 rows, 3 sts at beg of next 2 rows, then 4 sts at beg of next 2 rows. Cast off rem 10 sts. **Neckband** Join right shoulder seam. With No. 10 needles and right side facing pick up and k112 (116) 120 (124) 128 sts around neck. For single crew neck work 10 rows in k1, p1 rib. Cast off in rib. For double crew neck work 20 rows in k1, p1 rib. Cast off in rib. For polo neck work 20 rows in k1, p1 rib, then change to No. 9 needles and work a further 20 rows. Cast off loosely in rib. **To make up** Press work according to instructions on ball band. Join left shoulder seam and neckband. Sew in sleeves. Join side and sleeve seams. Fold double crew neckband in half to inside and sl-st. Press seams.

### Basic cardigan

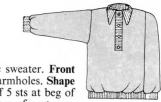

Work back and sleeves as for sweater. **Left front** With No. 10 needles cast on 62 (65) 68 (71) 74 sts. Work 14 rows in k1, p1 rib. Change to No. 9 needles. Next row K53 (56) 59 (62) 65, turn and leave rem 9 sts on safety pin. Cont in st st until 122 rows have been worked. **Shape Armhole** Cast off 5 sts at beg of next row, then 2 (2) 3 (3) 4 sts at beg of foll alt row. Dec 1 st at armhole edge on foll 5 (6) 6 (7) 7 alt rows. 41 (43) 45 (47) 49 sts. Cont without shaping until 49 (51) 53 (55) 57 rows have been worked from beg of armhole shaping. **Shape neck** Cast off 4 sts at beg of next row, then k1 row. Cont as given for front of sweater from ***. **Right front** With No. 10 needles cast on 62 (75) 68 (71) 74 sts. Work 14 rows in k1, p1 rib, making a buttonhole (page 82) on 5th st of 5th row. Next row rib 9 and sl these sts on to a safety pin, change to No. 9 needles and knit to end. Cont to match left front, reversing shaping. **Left front band** Sl the 9 sts from safety pin on to No. 10 needle and cont in rib until band, when slightly stretched, reaches to neck edge, ending with a wrong side row. Break off yarn and leave sts on safety pin. Tack band in place and mark position of buttons – 1st button on 5th row from beg, 2nd button will be in neckband, on 5th row above sts on safety pin, then 8 more at equal distance between these 2. **Right front band** Work to match Left front band, making buttonholes as before to correspond with position of buttons. **Neckband** Join shoulder seams. With No. 10 needles and right side facing rib the 9 sts of right front band, pick up and K102 (106) 110 (114) 118 sts around neck, then rib the 9 sts of left front band. 120 (124) 128 (132) 136 sts. Work 9 rows in rib, making a buttonhole on 5th st of 4th row. Cast off in rib. **To make up** Press work according to instructions on ball band. Sew in sleeves. Join side and sleeve seams. Sew on front bands. Press seams. Sew on buttons.

### Sweater with placket and collar

Work back and sleeves as for basic sweater. **Front** Work as for basic sweater as far as armholes. **Shape armholes and divide for neck** Cast off 5 sts at beg of next 2 rows, then 2 (2) 3 (3) 4 sts at beg of next row. Next row cast off 2 (2) 3 (3) 4, p until 47 (50) 52 (55) 57 sts on needle, sl these sts on to a spare needle, sl next 6 sts on to a safety pin, then p to end. Cont on last 47 (50) 52 (55) 57 sts, dec 1 st at beg of next and foll 4 (5) 5 (6) 6 alt rows. 42 (44) 46 (48) 50 sts. Cont without shaping until 49 (51) 53 (55) 57 rows have been worked from beg of armhole. **Shape neck** Cast off 5 sts at beg of next row, then k1 row. Cont as given for basic sweater from ***. Return to the other 47 (50) 52 (55) 57 sts and work to match, reversing shaping. **Button band** With No. 10 needles cast on 7 sts and work in k1, p1 rib until band measures the same as front edge. Cast off. **Buttonhole band** Mark position of buttons on button band – the first ¾ inch (2cm) from beg, the second ¾ inch (2cm) from top, then one more halfway between. Sl the 6 sts from safety pin on to No. 10 needles; with right side facing (k1,p1) twice, k1, inc in last st. 7 sts. Cont in rib to match button band, making buttonholes (page 82) on centre st to correspond with position of buttons. **Collar** Join shoulder seams. With No. 10 needles and right side facing pick up and K104 (108) 112 (116) 120 sts around neck. Work in k1, p1 rib, inc one st at each end of 2nd and every alt row until collar measures 4 inches (10cm). Cast off in rib. **To make up** Press work according to instructions on ball band. Sew in sleeves. Join side and sleeve seams. Sew on front bands. Press seams. Sew on buttons.

## *Sleeveless V-neck sweater*

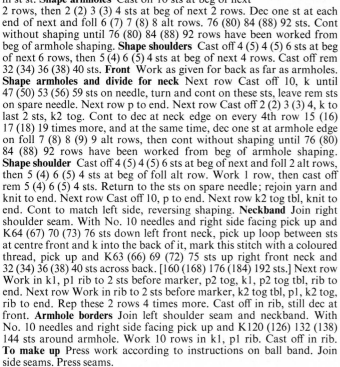

**Back** With No. 10 needles cast on 114 (120) 126 (132) 138 sts. Work 14 rows in k1, p1 rib. Change to No. 9 needles and beg with a k row work 114 rows in st st. **Shape armholes** Cast off 10 sts at beg of next 2 rows, then 2 (2) 3 (3) 4 sts at beg of next 2 rows. Dec one st at each end of next and foll 6 (7) 7 (8) 8 alt rows. 76 (80) 84 (88) 92 sts. Cont without shaping until 76 (80) 84 (88) 92 rows have been worked from beg of armhole shaping. **Shape shoulders** Cast off 4 (5) 4 (5) 6 sts at beg of next 6 rows, then 5 (4) 6 (5) 4 sts at beg of next 4 rows. Cast off rem 32 (34) 36 (38) 40 sts. **Front** Work as given for back as far as armholes. **Shape armholes and divide for neck** Next row Cast off 10, k until 47 (50) 53 (56) 59 sts on needle, turn and cont on these sts, leave rem sts on spare needle. Next row p to end. Next row Cast off 2 (2) 3 (3) 4, k to last 2 sts, k2 tog. Cont to dec at neck edge on every 4th row 15 (16) 17 (18) 19 times more, and at the same time, dec one st at armhole edge on foll 7 (8) 8 (9) 9 alt rows, then cont without shaping until 76 (80) 84 (88) 92 rows have been worked from beg of armhole shaping. **Shape shoulder** Cast off 4 (5) 4 (5) 6 sts at beg of next and foll 2 alt rows, then 5 (4) 6 (5) 4 sts at beg of foll alt row. Work 1 row, then cast off rem 5 (4) 6 (5) 4 sts. Return to the sts on spare needle; rejoin yarn and knit to end. Next row Cast off 10, p to end. Next row k2 tog tbl, knit to end. Cont to match left side, reversing shaping. **Neckband** Join right shoulder seam. With No. 10 needles and right side facing pick up and K64 (67) 70 (73) 76 sts down left front neck, pick up loop between sts at centre front and k into the back of it, mark this stitch with a coloured thread, pick up and K63 (66) 69 (72) 75 sts up right front neck and 32 (34) 36 (38) 40 sts across back. [160 (168) 176 (184) 192 sts.] Next row Work in k1, p1 rib to 2 sts before marker, p2 tog, k1, p2 tog tbl, rib to end. Next row Work in rib to 2 sts before marker, k2 tog tbl, p1, k2 tog, rib to end. Rep these 2 rows 4 times more. Cast off in rib, still dec at front. **Armhole borders** Join left shoulder seam and neckband. With No. 10 needles and right side facing pick up and K120 (126) 132 (138) 144 sts around armhole. Work 10 rows in k1, p1 rib. Cast off in rib. **To make up** Press work according to instructions on ball band. Join side seams. Press seams.

## *Raglan sweater with crew or polo neck*

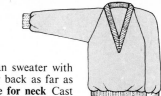

**Back** With No. 10 needles cast on 114 (120) 126 (132) 138 sts. Work 14 rows in k1, p1 rib. Change to No. 9 needles and beg with a knit row work 118 rows in st-st. **Shape armholes** Cast off 5 sts at beg of next 2 rows. Dec 1 st at each end of next and every alt row until 32 (34) 36 (38) 40 sts rem, ending with a purl row. Cast off. **Front** Work as given for back until 54 (56) 60 (62) 66 sts rem, ending with a purl row. **Shape neck** Next row k2 tog, k19 (19) 21 (21) 23, turn and leave rem sts on spare needle. **Next row** Purl to end. Dec 1 st at each end of next and foll 7 (7) 8 (8) 9 alt rows, then cont to dec at armhole edge only on every alt row until 2 sts rem, ending with a purl row. Cast off. Return to the sts on spare needle; cast off 12 (14) 14 (16) 16 sts, knit to last 2 sts, k2 tog. Cont to match left side. **Sleeves** Work as for sleeves of basic sweater to ****. **Shape top** Cast off 5 sts at beg of next 2 rows. Dec 1 st at each end of next row and every foll 4th row 6 times more, then at each end of every alt row until 6 sts rem, ending with a purl row. Cast off. **Neckband** Join raglan seams, leaving left back seam open. Work as for neckband on basic sweater. **To make up** Press according to instructions on ball band. Join left back raglan seam and neckband. Join side and sleeve seams. Press seams.

## *Raglan sweater with V-neck*

Work back and sleeves as for raglan sweater with crew neck. **Front** Work as given for back as far as armholes. **Shape armholes and divide for neck** Cast off 5 sts at beg of next 2 rows. Next row k2 tog, k50 (53) 56 (59) 62, turn and leave rem sts on spare needle. Next row Purl to end. Dec 1 st at neck edge on next and every foll 4th row 13 (14) 15 (16) 17 times more, and at the same time dec at armhole edge on every alt row until 2 sts rem, ending with a purl row. Cast off. Return to the sts on spare needle; rejoin yarn and knit to last 2 sts, k2 tog. Cont to match left side. **Neckband** Join raglan seams, leaving left back seam open. With No. 10 needles and right side facing pick up and k6 sts across sleeve, 60 (63) 66 (69) 72 sts down left front neck, pick up loop between sts at centre front and knit into the back of it, pick up and k60 (63) 66 (69) 72 sts up right front neck, 6 sts across sleeve and 33 (35) 37 (39) 41 sts across back neck. [166 (174) 182 (190) 198 sts.] Work 10 rows as given for sleeveless V-neck sweater. Cast off in rib, still dec at front. **To make up** Press according to instructions on ball band. Joint left back raglan seam and neckband. Join side and sleeve seams. Press seams.

## *Sweater with saddle shoulders and crew neck*

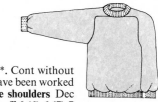

**Back** Work as for basic sweater to **. Cont without shaping until 58 (62) 66 (70) 74 rows have been worked from beg of armhole shaping. **Shape shoulders** Dec 1 st at each end of next 6 rows. Cast off 6 (6) 6 (7) 7 sts at beg of next 6 rows, then 5 (6) 7 (5) 6 sts at beg of next 2 rows. Cast off rem 32 (34) 36 (38) 40 sts. **Front** Work as for back until 52 (54) 56 (58) 60 rows have been worked from beg of armhole shaping. **Shape neck** Next row K37 (39) 41 (43) 45, turn and leave rem sts on spare needle. Cast off 2 sts at beg of next and foll alt row, then dec 1 st at beg of foll 1 (2) 3 (4) 5 alt rows, ending with a purl row. **Shape shoulder** Dec 1 st at each end of next row, then dec 1 st at armhole edge only on next row. Rep the last 2 rows twice more. Cast off 6 (6) 6 (7) 7 sts at beg of next and foll 2 alt rows. Work 1 row, then cast off rem 5 (6) 7 (5) 6 sts. Return to the sts on spare needle; cast off 16 sts, knit to end. Cont to match left side, reversing shaping. **Sleeves** Work as for sleeve of basic sweater to ****. **Shape top** Cast off 5 sts at beg of next 2 rows, then 2 (2) 3 (3) 4 sts at beg of next 2 rows. Dec 1 st at each end of next and every alt row until 40 sts rem, ending with a purl row. Cast off 2 sts at beg of next 8 rows. Cont on rem 40 sts, work 36 (38) 40 (42) 44 rows. **Right sleeve** Cast off 17 sts at beg of next row, 3 sts at beg of foll alt row, then dec 1 st at beg of every alt row until 2 sts rem. K2 tog and fasten off. **Left sleeve** K1 row, then work as given for right sleeve. **Neckband** Sew saddles to shoulders, leaving left back seam open. Work as given for neckband of basic sweater. **To make up** Press work according to instructions on ball band. Join left back saddle seam. Sew in sleeve heads. Join side and sleeve seams. Press seams.

# Fishermen's sweaters

The patterns for the fishermen's sweaters which follow have been carefully researched and use authentic patterns and wools. The instructions for making an adult's Guernsey are on the facing page and instructions for an Aran sweater in adult and child sizes begin on page 80.

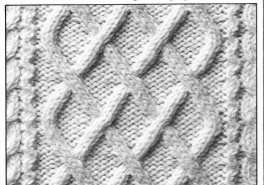

**Detail of Aran cables**

**Sheringham sweaters**
*These early twentieth century boatmen from Norfolk, England were photographed in their traditional cabled sweaters.*

**Aran sweaters**
*Aran sweaters are knitted back and forth on two needles, although the body may be knitted in the round as far as the armhole shaping.*

*Traditionally, the wool used is either natural cream or grey, or it is dyed a soft green from the island mosses or brown from the seaweed.*

# Man's Guernsey sweater

**Yarn** 19 × 50gm hanks 0½ combed 5-ply wool.
**Needles** 2 No. 14 (2mm) circular needles lengths
36 inches (91cm) and 20 inches (51cm); 1 pair long
No. 14 (2mm) needles; 2 sets of 4 No. 14 (2mm) dpn
(one set long, one short); 2 stitch holders (optional).
**Stitch gauge** 16 sts and 20 rows to 2 inches over st-st
on No. 14 (2mm) needles. **Measurements** To fit chest
38–40 inches (96.5–101cm). Length: 25 inches
(63.5cm). Sleeve: 20 inches (51cm) from the shoulder
to cuff edge.
**Body** With 36 inch (91cm) No. 14 (2mm) circular
needle cast on 320 sts. Work 2 rounds plain, 2
rounds purl. Work these 4 rounds 6 times. Cont
with plain knitting, making imitation seams up each
side by working 157 sts, p1, k1, p1 (front and right
"seam"); 157 sts, p1, k1, p1 (back and left "seam"),
until guernsey measures 12½ inches (32cm) from
lower edge. **Yoke** Start the underarm gussets in the
first round of the yoke pattern by increasing one st
in the centre of the seam sts (on both sides of guernsey) making 2 plain sts in the centre with 1 purl st
on each side. These 2 plain sts are the beginning of
the gusset. It is worked in plain knitting throughout.
Increase one st either side of both gussets every 4th
round until there are 20 sts. The yoke is worked in
pattern from commencement of gussets – see detail
of yoke pattern. Divide the knitting at the armholes: 180 sts for the front and the same for the back.
Slip the gussets and purl sts on either side (22 sts for
each) onto wool or st-holders. For the front, continue in pattern on 2 needles but at each armhole
edge work the first 3 and last 3 sts in garter st.
When you reach the neck (25 inches (63.5cm) from
cast on edge) put 57 sts in centre on a holder for the
neck. For the shoulders, work 50 sts each side in
garter st for 12 rows finishing on a plain row. Work
the back in the same way. Cast off the back and
front shoulders together on the right side, making
a ridge. **Neck band** (use set of 4 long needles) 57 sts
are left in the centre for the neck – back and front –
with 15 sts from each shoulder, total 144 sts. Work
17 rounds of k2, p2, then 1 round plain; 2 rounds
purl; 1 round plain then cast off plain with a double
thread for extra strength.
**Sleeves** Use 20 inch (50cm) No. 14 (2mm) circular
needle. Pick up 142 sts for the sleeve not counting
the gusset. The sleeve starts with 2 rounds plain;
2 rounds purl, repeated once (but working gussets
and seam sts in their own pattern) and decreasing
one st on each side every 4th row. Work 1¾ inches
(4.5cm) plain then one band of yoke pattern. Start
sleeve decreasings after pattern is finished – decrease
one st each side of seam st every 7 rounds (5 times);
every 5 rounds (13 times) every 3 rounds (11 times)
until 80 sts remain. Work 3 inches (7 6mm) in k2,
p2 rib for cuff on set of 4 short No. 14 (2mm)
needles. Cast off plain with a double thread. **Yoke
pattern Ridge** 2 rounds purl, 2 rounds plain, rep
once. **\*\*Row 1** \*P2, k2, rep from \*. **Row 2** Knit.
**Row 3** \*K2, p2, rep from \*. **Row 4** Knit. Work these
4 rows 5 times for each panel. For the next 10 rows:
knit 2 rows, purl 2 rows, knit 2 rows, purl 2 rows,
knit 2 rows. Rep from \*\* until 5 panels are completed. The pattern band on the sleeves is worked
in the same way, from the beginning, once only
(with ridge at beginning and end). **Note** When on
2 needles, work the last pattern row (RS facing);
then purl 1 row, knit 2 rows, purl 2 rows, knit 1 row,
purl 2 rows, knit 2 rows, purl 1 row. Begin pattern
over again.

### Guernsey sweaters

*Guernseys are knitted in the
round, although false seams
are always worked up the
sides and down the sleeves to
the cuff. Increases are worked
into the "seam" stitches to
make the underarm gusset, a
detail which adds years to the
life of these sweaters. The
sleeves are picked up at the
shoulder and knitted downwards to the cuff.*

# Child's Aran sweater

The traditional Guernsey, from the Channel Island of the same name, is square in shape with loose sleeves for easy working. It is knitted in 5-ply worsted wool on fine needles. The finished fabric is thick, close, wind and waterproof, and strong enough to last a lifetime. The patterns on the yoke vary from village to village and even from family to family.

Aran sweaters, from the three islands off the western coast of Ireland – Inishmore, Inishmaan and Inisheer – are knitted in thick wool which retains its natural oils, making the finished garment waterproof. The patterns symbolize aspects of the fisherman's life, as do the patterns on Guernseys: cables represent ropes, diamonds the meshes of fishing nets, zigzags are cliff paths or forked lightning. The rich patterns on Aran sweaters are reminiscent of the swirling and interlacing bands typical of Celtic art. Some people say that the art of knitting and the patterns came to the islands originally from the Coptic sect in Egypt via the old trade routes across the Mediterranean to France. From there, monks brought the knowledge to the islands.

## Pattern instructions

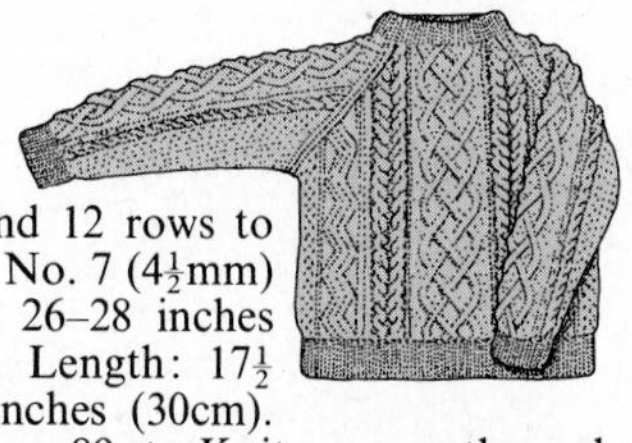

**Yarn** 8 × 50gm balls Aran wool. **Needles** One pair each No. 9 (3¾mm) and No. 7 (4½mm); 1 cable needle; stitch holder and 2 safety pins. **Stitch gauge** 10 sts and 12 rows to 2 inches (5cm) over reversed st-st on No. 7 (4½mm) needles. **Measurements** To fit chest 26–28 inches (66–71cm). Approx age 6–8 years. Length: 17½ inches (44.5cm). Sleeve seam: 12 inches (30cm).

**Back** with No. 9 (3¾mm) needles cast on 89 sts. Knit one row through the back of the sts. **Row 1** *K1, p1, rep from * to last st, k1. **Row 2** K2, *p1, k1, rep from * to last st, k1. Work these 2 rows 5 times. Then work Row 1 again. Change to No. 7 (4½mm) needles. **Pattern** (right side facing) **Row 1** K1, (k1, p1) twice, k1-b, p2, (sl 1b, k1-b, pss) 3 times, k1, p1, k1, k1-b, p1, tw2b, (p1, k4) twice, p1, tw2f, p4, k4, p4, inc into next st pwise, k4, p4, tw2b, (p1, k4) twice, p1, tw2f, p1, k1-b, k1, p1, k1, (sl 1f, p1, kssb) 3 times, p2, k1-b, (p1, k1) twice, k1. **Row 2** (K1, p1) twice, k1, p1-b, k2, (p1-b, k1) 3 times, p1, k1, p1, p1-b, k1, p2, k1, (p4, k1) twice, p2, k4, p4, k6, p4, k4, p2, (k1, p4) twice, k1, p2, k1, p1-b, (p1, k1) twice, (p1-b, k1) 3 times, k1, p1-b, (k1, p1) twice, k1. *Row 3 K1, (p1, k1) twice, k1-b, p3, (sl 1b, k1-b, pss) 3 times, (k1, p1) twice, k1-b, p1, tw2f, p1, c4b, p1, c4f, p1, tw2b, p4, c4f, p6, c4f, p4, tw2f, p1, c4b, p1, c4f, p1, tw2b, p1, k1-b, (p1, k1) twice (sl 1f, p1, kssb) 3 times, p1, k1-b, (k1, p1) twice, k1. **Row 4** K1, (k1, p1) twice, p1-b, k1, (p1-b, k1) 3 times, (p1, k1) twice, p1-b, k1, p2, (k1, p4) twice, k1, p2, k4, p4, k6, p4, k4, p2, (k1, p4) twice, k1, p2, k1, p1-b, k1, (p1, k1) twice, (p1-b, k1) 3 times, p1-b, (p1, k1) twice, k1. **Row 5** K1, (k1, p1) twice, k1-b, p1, (sl 1f, p1, kssb) 3 times, (p1, k1) twice, k1-b, p1, tw2b, p1, (k4, p1) twice, tw2f, p3, t3b, t3f, p4, t3f, p3, tw2b, (p1, k4) twice, p1, tw2f, p1, k1-b, (k1, p1) twice, (sl 1b, k1-b) pss) 3 times, p1, k1-b, (p1, k1) twice, k1. **Row 6** (K1, p1) twice, k1, p1-b, k2, (p1-b, k1) 3 times, p1, k1, p1, p1-b, k1, p2, k1, (p4, k1) twice, p2, k3, p2, k2, p2, k4, p2, p2, k3, p2, (k1, p4) twice, k1, p2, k1, p1-b, (p1, k1) twice, (p1-b, k1) 3 times, k1, p1-b, (k1, p1) twice, k1. **Row 7** K1, (p1, k1) twice, k1-b, p2, (sl 1f, p1, kssb) 3 times, p1, k1, p1, k1-b, p1, tw2f, p1, (k4, p1) twice, tw2b, p2, t3b, p2, t3f, p2, t3b, p2, t3f, p2, tw2f, (p1, k4) twice, p1, tw2b, p1, k1-b, p1, k1, p1, (sl 1b, k1-b, pss) 3 times, p2, k1-b, (k1, p1) twice, k1. **Row 8** K1, (k1, p1) twice, p1-b, k3, (p1-b, k1) 3 times, p1, k1, p1-b, k1, p2, k1, (p4, k1) twice, p2, k2, p2, k4, p2, k2, p2, k2, p2, (k1, p4) twice, k1, p2, k1, p1-b, k1, p1, k1, (p1-b, k1) 3 times, k2, p1-b, (p1, k1) twice, k1. **Row 9** K1, (k1, p1) twice, k1-b, p3, (sl 1f, p1, kssb) 3 times, p1, k1, k1-b, p1, tw2b, p1, c4b, p1, c4f, p1, tw2f, p1, t3b, p4, t3f, t3b, p4, t3f, p1, tw2b, p1, c4b, p1, c4f, p1, tw2f, p1, k1-b, k1, p1, (sl 1b, k1-b, pss) 3 times, p3, k1-b, (p1, k1) twice, k1. **Row 10** (K1, p1) twice, k1, p1-b, k4, (p1-b, k1) 3 times, p1, k1, p1, (p1-b, k1) twice, k1, (p4, k1) twice, p2, k6, p4, k6, p2, k1, p2, (p4, k1) twice, p2, k1, p1-b, p1, k1, (p1-b, k1) 3 times, k3, p1-b, (k1, p1) twice, k1. **Row 11** K1, (p1, k1) twice, k1-b, p4, (sl 1f, p1, kssb) 3 times, p1, k1-b, p1, tw2f, p1, (k4, p1) twice, tw2b,

p1, k2, p6, c4b, p6, k2, p1, tw2f, (p1, k4) twice, p1, tw2b, p1, k1-b, p1, (sl 1b, k1-b, pss) 3 times, p4, k1-b, (k1, p1) twice, k1. **Row 12** K1, (k1, p1) twice, p1-b, k5, (p1-b, k1) 3 times, p1-b, k1, p2, k1, (p4, k1) twice, p2, k1, p2, k6, p4, k6, p2, k1, p2, k1, (p4, k1) twice, p2, k1, p1-b, k1, (p1-b, k1) 3 times, k4, p1-b, (p1, k1) twice, k1. **Row 13** K1, (k1, p1) twice, k1-b, p4, (sl 1b, k1-b, pss) 3 times, k1, k1-b, p1, tw2b, p1, (k4, p1) twice, tw2f, p1, t3f, p4, t3b, t3f, p4, t3b, p1, tw2b, (p1, k4) twice, p1, tw2f, p1, (sl 1f, p1, kssb) 3 times, p4, k1-b, (p1, k1) twice, k1. **Row 14** (K1, p1) twice, k1, p1-b, k4, (p1-b, k1) 3 times, p1, p1-b, k1, p2, k1, (p4, k1) twice, p2, k2, p2, k4, p2, k2, p2, k4, p2, k2, p2, (k1, p4) twice, k1, p2, k1, p1-b, p1, k1, (p1-b, k1) 3 times, k3, p1-b, (k1, p1) twice, k1. **Row 15** K1, (p1, k1) twice, k1-b, p3, (sl 1b, k1-b, pss) 3 times, k1, p1, k1-b, p1, tw2f, p1, c4b, p1, c4f, p1, tw2b, p2, t3f, p2, t3b, p2, t3f, p2, tw2f, p1, c4b, p1, c4f, p1, tw2b, p1, k1-b, p1, k1, (sl 1f, p1, kssb) 3 times, p3, k1-b, (k1, p1) twice, k1. **Row 16** K1, (k1, p1) twice, p1-b, k3, (p1-b, k1) 3 times, p1, k1, p1-b, k1, p2, k1, (p4, k1) twice, p2, k3, p2, k2, p2, k4, p2, k2, p2, k3, p2, k1, (p4, k1) twice, p2, k1, p1-b, k1, p1, k1, (p1-b, k1) 3 times, k2, p1-b, (p1, k1) twice, k1. **Row 17** K1, (k1, p1) twice, k1-b, p2, (sl 1b, k1-b, pss) 3 times, k1, p1, k1, k1-b, p1, tw2b, (p1, k4) twice, p1, tw2f, p3, t3f, t3b, p4, t3f, t3b, p3, tw2b, (p1, k4) twice, p1, tw2f, p1, k1-b, p1, k1, (sl 1f, p1, kssb) 3 times, p2, k1-b, (p1, k1) twice, k1. **Row 18** As row 2. Repeat from row 3 (a 16 row repeat) until you have completed 60 rows from end of rib, turning cables either side of the middle panel on row 21 and every following 6th row. **Shape raglan** Cast off 5 sts at beg of next 2 rows. Next row, sl 1, sl 1, k1, psso, pattern to last 3 sts, k2tog, k1. Next row, sl 1, p1, pattern to last 2 sts, p1, k1. Repeat last 2 rows until 34 sts remain. Put onto st holder and leave.

**Front** Work as for back, including raglan shaping, until you have completed 96 rows from end of rib (46 sts). **Shape neck** (continuing pattern and raglan shaping). Work 18 sts and leave on st holder. Cast off 10 sts, work to end. Work one row. *Cast off 5 sts at beg of next row, work to end. Dec one st at neck edge of next 3 rows and foll 2 alt rows (3 sts). Work 2 more rows dec once on raglan edge. Cast off last 2 sts. With WS facing pick up 17 sts from st holder and complete for right side from *.

**Sleeves** With No. 9 (3¾mm) needles cast on 36 sts. Knit one row tbl. K1, p1, rib for 12 rows. Then work one more row rib, increasing: *rib 3, inc into next st, rib 6, inc into next st; rep from * to last 3 sts, rib 3 (42 sts). Change to No. 7 (4½mm) needles. **Row 1** P1, k1, p1, k4, p1, tw2f, p4, k4, p6, k4, p4, tw2b, p1, k4, p1, k1, p1. **Row 2** K1, p1, k1, p4, k1, p2, k4, p4, k6, p4, k4, p2, k1, p4, k1, p1, k1. **Row 3** K1, p2, c4f, p1, tw2b, p4, c4f, p6, c4f, p4, tw2f, p1, c4b, p2, k1. **Row 4** P1, k2, p4, k1, p2, k4, p4, k6, p4, k4, p2, k1, p4, k2, p1. **Row 5** P1, k1, p1, k4, p1, tw2f, p3, c3b, c3f, p4, c3b, c3f, p3, tw2b, p1, k4, p1, k1, p1. **Row 6** K1, p1, k1, p4, k1, p2, k3, p2, k2, p2, k4, p2, k2, p2, k3, p2, k1, p4, k1, p1, k1. **Row 7** K1, p2, k4, p1, tw2b, p2, c3b, p2, c3f, p2, c3b, p2, c3f, p2, tw2f, p1, k4, p2, k1. **Row 8** P1, k2, p4, k1, p2, k2, p2, k4, p2, k2, p2, k4, p2, k2, p2, k1, p4, k2, p1. **Row 9** Inc in first st, k1, p1, c4f, p1, tw2f, p1, c3b, p4, c3f, c3b, p4, c3f, p1, tw2b, p1, c4b, p1, k1, inc into last st. **Row 10** Knit all k sts, purl all p sts. **Row 11** Moss st 3, p1, k4, p1, tw2b, p1, k2, p6, c4b, p6, k2, p1, tw2f, p1, k4, p1, moss st 3. **Row 12** Knit all k sts, purl all p sts. **Row 13** Moss st 3, p1, k4, p1, tw2f, p1, c3f, p4, c3b, c3f, p4, c3b, p1, tw2b, p1, k4, p1, moss st 3. **Row 14** Knit all k sts, purl all p sts. **Row 15** Inc in first st, moss st 2, c4f, p1, tw2b, p2, c3f, p2, c3b, p2, c3f, p2, c3b, p2, tw2f, p1, c4b, p1, moss st 2, inc into last st. **Row 16** Knit all k sts, purl all p sts. **Row 17** Moss st 4, p1, k4, p1, tw2f, p3, c3f, c3b, p4, c3f, c3b, p3, tw2b, p1, k4, p1, moss st 4. **Row 18** Knit all k sts, purl all p sts. Cont with patt, inc at either end of every 6th row until there are 62 sts [12 inches (30cm)] working increased sts in double moss. **Shape raglan** Cast off 5 sts at beg of next 2 rows. **Row 1** Sl 1, k2tog tbl, pattern to last 3 sts, k2tog, k1. **Row 2** Knit all k sts, purl all p sts. **Row 3** Sl 1, k2, pattern to end. **Row 4** Knit all k sts, purl all p sts. Repeat last 4 rows once more then dec on every alt row until there are 14 sts left. Sl 1, k3tog, patt to last 4 sts, k3tog, k1. Knit all k sts, purl all p sts. Sl 1, k2tog, pattern to last 3 sts, k2tog, k1. Put rem 8 sts on st holder.

**Neck and making up** Press pieces. Join all raglan seams except for right back. With RS facing pick up 34 sts from st holder (back), 8 sts from top of left sleeve, 40 sts across top of front, 8 sts from top of right sleeve (90 sts). Work 16 rows in rib. Cast off in rib loosely. Stitch right back raglan seam (including neck). Turn cast off edge of neck to inside and stitch down. Stitch sleeve and side seams.

# *Woman's Aran sweater*

**Yarn** 16 × 50gm· balls Aran wool.
**Needles** One pair each No. 9 (3¾mm) and No. 7 (4½mm); 1 cable needle; stitch holder and 2 safety pins. **Stitch gauge** 10 sts and 12 rows to 2 inches (5cm) over reversed st-st on No. 7 (4½mm) needles. **Measurements** To fit bust 36–38 inches (91–96.5cm). Length: 26 inches (66cm). Sleeve seam: 18 inches (46cm).

**Back** With No. 9 (3¾mm) needles cast on 111 sts. Knit one row tbl. **Row 1** *K1, p1, rep from * to last st, k1. **Row 2** K2, *p1, k1, rep from * to last st, k1. Work these 2 rows 5 times. Then row 1 again. Change to No. 7 (4½mm) needles. **Pattern** (RS facing) **Row 1** K1, (p1, k1) 4 times, k1-b, p1, k1-b, p2, (sl 1b, k1-b, pss) 3 times, k1, p1, k1, k1-b, p1, tw2b, (p1, k4) twice, p1, tw2f, p4, (k4, p6) twice, k4, p2, inc into next st pwise, tw2b, (p1, k4) twice, p1, tw2f, p1, k1-b, k1, p1, k1, (sl 1f, p1, kssb) 3 times, p2, k1-b, p1, k1-b, (k1, p1) 4 times, k1. **Row 2** K1, (k1, p1) 4 times, p1-b, k1, p1-b, k2, (p1-b, k1) 3 times, p1, k1, p1, p1-b, k1, p2, k1, (p4, k1) twice, p2, k4, (p4, k6) twice, p4, k4, p2, (k1, p4) twice, k1, p2, k1, p1-b, (p1, k1) twice, (p1-b, k1) 3 times, k1, p1-b, k1, p1-b, (p1, k1) 4 times, k1. **Row 3** K1, (k1, p1) 4 times, k1-b, p1, k1-b, p1, (sl 1b, k1-b, pss) 3 times, (k1, p1) twice, k1-b, p1, tw2f, p1, c4b, p1, c4f, p1, tw2b, p4, (c4f, p6) twice, c4f, p4, tw2f, p1, c4b, p1, c4f, p1, tw2b, p1, k1-b, (p1, k1) twice, (sl 1f, p1, kssb) 3 times, p1, k1-b, p1, k1-b, (k1, p1) 4 times, k1. **Row 4** K1, (p1, k1) 4 times, p1-b, k1, p1-b, k1, (p1-b, k1) 3 times, (p1, k1) twice, p1-b, k1, p2, (k1, p4) twice, p2, k4, p4, (k6, p4) twice, k4, p2, (k1, p4) twice, k1, p2, k1, p1-b, (k1, p1) twice, (p1-b, k1) 3 times, k1, p1-b, k1, p1-b, (p1, k1) 4 times, k1. **Row 5** K1, (p1, k1) 4 times, k1-b, p1, k1-b, p1, (sl 1f, p1, kssb) 3 times, (p1, k1) twice, k1-b, p1, tw2b, p1, (k4, p1) twice, tw2f, p3, (t3b, t3f, p4) twice, t3b, t3f, p3, tw2b, (p1, k4) twice, p1, tw2f, p1, k1-b, (k1, p1) twice, (sl 1b, k1-b, pss) 3 times, p1, k1-b, p1, k1-b, (k1, p1) 4 times, k1 **Row 6** K1, (k1, p1) 4 times, p1-b, k1, p1-b, k2, (k1, p4) twice, k1, p2, k3, (p2, k2, p2, k4) twice, p2, k2, p2, k3, p2, (k1, p4) twice, k1, p2, k1, p1-b, (p1, k1) twice, (p1-b, k1) 3 times, k1, p1-b, k1, p1-b, (p1, k1) 4 times, k1. **Row 7** K1, (k1, p1) 4 times, k1-b, p1, k1-b, p2, (sl 1f, p1, kssb) 3 times, p1, k1, p1, k1-b, p1, tw2f, p1, (k4, p1) twice, tw2b, p2, (t3b, p2, t3f, p2) 3 times, tw2f, (p1, k4) twice, p1, tw2b, p2, k1-b, p1, k1-b, (p1, k1) 4 times, k1. **Row 8** K1, (p1, k1) 4 times, p1-b, k1, p1-b, k3, (p1-b, k1) 3 times, p1, k1, p1-b, k1, p2, k1, (p4, k1) twice, p2, (k2, p2, k4, p2) 3 times, k2, p2, (k1, p4) twice, k1, p2, k1, p1-b, k1, p1, k1, (p1-b, k1) 3 times, k2, p1-b, k1, p1-b, (k1, p1) 4 times, k1. **Row 9** K1, (p1, k1) 4 times, k1-b, p1, k1-b, p3, (sl 1f, p1, kssb) 3 times, p1, k1, k1-b, p1, tw2b, p1, c4b, p1, c4f, p1, tw2f, p1, (t3b, t3f) 3 times, p1, tw2b, p1, c4b, p1, c4f, p1, tw2f, p1, k1-b, k1, p1, (sl 1b, k1-b, pss) 3 times, p3, k1-b, p1, k1-b, (k1, p1) 4 times, k1. **Row 10** K1, (k1, p1) 4 times, p1-b, k1, p1-b, k4, (p1-b, k1) 3 times, p1, p1-b, k1, p2, k1, (p4, k1) twice, p2, k1, p2, (k6, p4) twice, k6, p2, k1, p2, k1, (p4, k1) twice, p2, k1, p1-b, k1, p1, (p1-b, k1) 3 times, k3, p1-b, k1, p1-b, (p1, k1) 4 times, k1. **Row 11** K1, (k1, p1) 4 times, k1-b, p1, k1-b, p4, (sl 1f, p1, kssb) 3 times, p1, k1-b, p1, tw2f, p1, (k4, p1) twice, tw2b, p1, k2, (p6, c4b) twice, p6, k2, p1, tw2f, (p1, k4) twice, p1, rw2b, p1, k1-b, p1, (sl 1b, k1-b, pss) 3 times, p4, k1-b, p1, k1-b, (p1, k1) 4 times, k1. **Row 12** K1, (p1, k1) 4 times, p1-b, k1, p1-b, k5, (p1-b, k1) 3 times, p1-b, k1, p2, k1, (p4, k1) twice, p2, k1, p2, (k6, p4) twice, k6, p2, k1, p2, k1, (p4, k1) twice, p2, k1, p1-b, k1, p1-b, k1, (p1-b, k1) 3 times, k4, p1-b, k1, p1-b, (k1, p1) 4 times, k1. **Row 13** K1, (p1, k1) 4 times, k1-b, p1, k1-b, p4, (sl 1b, k1-b, pss) 3 times, k1, k1-b, p1, tw2b, p1, (k4, p1) twice, tw2f, p1, (t3f, p4, t3b) 3 times, p1, tw2b, (p1, k4) twice, p1, tw2f, p1, k1-b, k1, (sl 1f, p1, kssb) 3 times, p4, k1-b, p1, k1-b, (k1, p1) 4 times, k1. **Row 14** K1, (k1, p1) 4 times, p1-b, k1, p1-b, k4, (p1-b, k1) 3 times, p1, p1-b, k1, p2, k1, (p4, k1) twice, p2, (k2, p2, k4, p2) 3 times, k2, p2, (k1, p4) twice, k1, p2, k1, p1-b, k1, p1-b, (p1, k1) 4 times, k1. **Row 15** K1, (k1, p1) 4 times, k1-b, p1, k1-b, p3, (sl 1b, k1-b, pss) 3 times, k1, p1, k1-b, p1, tw2f, p1, c4b, p1, c4f, p1, tw2b, p2, (t3f, p2, t3b, p2) 3 times, tw2f, p1, c4b, p1, c4f, p1, tw2b, p1, k1-b, p1, k1, (sl 1f, p1, kssb) 3 times, p3, k1-b, p1, k1-b, (k1, p1) 4 times, k1. **Row 16** K1, (p1, k1) 4 times, p1-b, k1, p1-b, k3, (p1-b, k1) 3 times, p1, p1-b, k1, p2, k1, (p4, k1) twice, p2, k1, p1-b, k1, p1, k1, (p1-b, k1) 3 times, k2, p1-b, k1, p1-b, (k1, p1) 4 times, k1. **Row 17** K1, (p1, k1) 4 times, k1-b, p1, k1-b, p2, (sl 1b, k1-b, pss)

3 times, k1, p1, k1, k1-b, p1, tw2b, (p1, k4) twice, p1, tw2f, p3, (t3f, t3b, p4) twice, t3f, t3b, p3, tw2b, (p1, k4) twice, p1, tw2f, p1, k1-b, k1, p1, k1, (sl 1f, p1, kssb) 3 times, p2, k1-b, p1, k1-b, (k1, p1) 4 times, k1. **Row 18** As row 2. Repeat from row 3 (a 16 row repeat) until you have completed 108 rows from end of rib, turning cables either side of middle panel on row 21 and every following 6th row. **Shape raglan** Cast off 3 sts at beg of next 2 rows. **Next Row** Sl 1, sl 1, k1, psso pattern to last 3 sts, k2tog, k1. **Next Row** Sl 1, p1, pattern to last 2 sts, p1, k1 **. Repeat last 2 rows until 36 sts remain, put on st holder and leave.
**Front** Work as for back as far as **. Repeat last 2 rows until 50 sts rem on left needle. Pattern 16 sts. Cont working on these 16 sts, dec 1 st at raglan edge every alt row as before and dec 1 st at neck edge on every row for 5 rows then every alt row till 1 st remains. Cast off. Leave central 18 sts on st holder and work right side to match left side.
**Sleeves** With No. 9 (3¾mm) needles, cast on 50 sts. Knit one row through back of the sts. Sl 1, *k1, p1, rep from * to last st, k1. Work this row 16 times. Change to No. 7 (4½mm) needles. **Pattern** (right side) Cont with pattern, inc 1 st at both ends of every 6th row until there are 80 sts, working increased side edges in double moss st as on back and front. **Row 1** P1, k1, p1, k4, p1, tw2f, p4, k4, (p6, k4) twice, p2, inc into next st pwise, p1, k2, inc into next st kwise, p1, k1, p1. **Row 2** K1, p1, k1, p4, k1, p2, k4, (p4, k6) twice, p4, k4, p2, k1, p4, k1, p1, k1. **Row 3** K1, p2, c4b, p1, tw2b, p4, (c4f, p6) twice, c4f, p4, tw2f, p1, c4f, p2, k1. **Row 4** For this and every foll alt row knit all k sts and purl all p sts. **Row 5** P1, k1, p1, k4, p1, tw2f, p3, (t3b, t3f, p4) twice, t3b, t3f, p3, tw2b, p1, k4, p1, k1, p1. **Row 7** K1, p2, k4, p1, tw2b, p2, (t3b, p2, t3f, p2) 3 times, tw2f, p1, k4, p2, k1. **Row 9** P1, k1, p1, c4b, p1, tw2f, p1, (t3b, p4, t3f) 3 times, p1, tw2b, p1, c4f, p1, k1, p1. **Row 11** K1, p2, k4, p1, tw2b, p1, k2, (p6, c4b) twice, p6, k2, p1, tw2f, p1, k4, p2, k1. **Row 13** P1, k1, p1, k4, p1, tw2f, p1, (t3f, p4, t3b) 3 times, p1, tw2b, p1, k4, p1, k1, p1. **Row 15** K1, p2, c4f, p1, tw2b, p2, (t3f, p2, t3b, p2) 3 times, tw2f, p1, c4b, p2, k1. **Row 17** P1, k1, p1, k4, p1, tw2f, p3, (t3f, t3b, p3, tw2b, p1, k4, p1, k1, p1. Rep from row 3 (16 row repeat) turning cables on either side of middle panel on row 21 and every foll 6th row. **Shape raglan** Work exactly as for back only continue until there are only 10 sts left, leave on safety pin.
**Neck and making up** Press pieces. Join all raglan seams except for right back. With RS facing pick up 36 sts from st holder (back), 10 sts from top of left sleeve, 11 sts down left side of neck, 18 sts from st holder (front), 11 sts up right side of neck and 10 sts from top of right sleeve (96 sts). Work 16 rows in rib. Cast off loosely. Stitch right back raglan seam (including neck). Turn cast off edge of neck to inside and stitch down. Stitch side and sleeve seams.

## *Aran abbreviations*

**Sl 1f:** Slip a st onto cn at the front of the work.

**Sl 1b:** Slip a st onto cn at the back of the work.

**Kssb:** Knit slipped st into the back of the loop.

**Cable 4 back (c4b):** Slip next 2 sts onto cn and leave at back of work, k2, then knit sts from cn.

**Cable 4 front (c4f):** Slip next 2 sts onto cn and leave at front of work, k2, then knit sts from cn.

**Twist 2 front (tw2f):** Knit into the front of 2nd st then into the front of the first st on the left-hand needle then slip 2 sts off needle together.

**Twist 2 back (tw2b):** Knit into the back of the 2nd st then the back of the first st on the left-hand needle then slip 2 sts off the needle together.

**Twist 3 front (t3f):** Slip next 2 sts onto cn at front, p1 then knit sts from cn.

**Twist 3 back (t3b):** Slip next st onto cn at back of work; k2 then purl sts from cn.

**Pss:** Purl slipped stitch.

# Buttonholes and buttonbands

# Pockets

### Buttonbands

Buttonbands can be worked in a variety of knit and purl stitches. The best stitches to use, however, are garter or moss stitches as they do not curl. They can be worked in the same colour as the main fabric or in toning and contrasting colours.

If buttonbands are knitted separately and sewn to the garment later, both sides can be knitted at the same time, using separate balls of yarn. Both buttonbands will then be exactly the same length. When the buttonholes are reached on one band, the other band can be marked off with a pin to give accurate button positions.

### Horizontal buttonholes

Horizontal buttonholes are usually used on sweaters, cardigans and jackets.

### Knitting the buttonhole

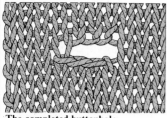
**The completed buttonhole**

Knit up to the position of the buttonhole, which should be about 3 or 4 stitches in from the edge of the main fabric or the buttonband. Cast off 2 or more stitches according to the size of the button and knit to the end of the row.

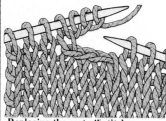
**Replacing the cast off stitches**

On the following row work up to the cast off stitches. Then replace them by casting on the same number of new stitches, and complete the row. This forms a horizontal buttonhole.

### Reinforced horizontal buttonholes

This is a firm hardwearing buttonhole. Use it on chunky outdoor garments.

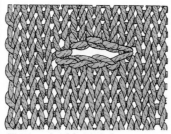
**The completed buttonhole**

### Knitting the buttonhole

Work up to the buttonhole position. Bring yarn to front, slip 1 stitch, take yarn back and drop it. Then: *Slip a second stitch, pass first slip stitch over casting it off; repeat from * until the required number of stitches have been cast off. Slip the remaining stitch back on the left needle.

Turn, pick up the yarn, and pass it between the needles to the back. Using the cable cast on method (page 17) replace the cast off stitches, plus 1. Before placing the last new stitch on the left needle bring the yarn through to the front, to form a dividing strand between the last stitch and the first stitch next to last. Turn again, slip from left to right needle, pass the last cast on stitch over. The buttonhole is now complete. Work to the end of the row.

### Eyelet buttonholes

These are the simplest buttonholes to make and are used primarily for baby clothes and lace stitch designs where small buttons are used. Knit a sample eyelet and check it for size against the buttons. For tiny buttons, work either of the simple eyelets, the open or chain eyelet. For larger buttons use one of the larger eyelets, the double, bold or grand eyelet. Instructions for making all these eyelets are given on page 42.

### Vertical buttonholes

Vertical buttonholes are made on pocket and tab flaps.

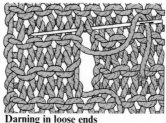
**Darning in loose ends**

### Knitting the buttonhole

Knit up to the buttonhole position, divide fabric and knit each side separately. On the right side, turn and knit back, turn and knit back, to the depth of the button. Knit an odd number of rows to finish with the needle pointing in the correct direction to knit the left side. Add a new ball of yarn and knit left side up. Knit 1 row less than right side. Discard new ball and knit across. Darn in loose ends.

### Buttonstand

Sometimes when the knitting divides to form the opening of a garment, you will need to knit in an extra area of fabric to form the base for a button. This is known as a buttonstand.

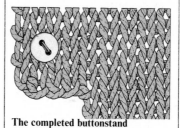
**The completed buttonstand**

### How to knit a buttonstand

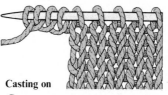
**Casting on**

*Cast on an extra number of stitches at the end of a row, and work these along with the rest of the stitches until you reach the depth required. Cast off the extra stitches.*

### Inset pockets

Inset pockets are worked with the main fabric.

### Knitting the pocket

Work up to position for the top of the pocket, ending with a knit row. Then knit a strip the same width as the pocket, transferring the stitches on the left and right sides of the pocket to stitch holders. Work to the required length, ending with a knit row. (See diagram top right.)

Fold over to form a pocket at the back. Restore the stitches on the left stitch holder to the needle and continue to knit across these stitches. On the following row, restore the stitches on the right holder to the needle and work them. (See Sewing up, right.)

If a border is needed for this pocket, it should be added later by picking up the stitches along the top fold line of the pocket. To avoid forming holes, add 1 extra stitch at each end. Knit across these stitches for the required depth. (See Making a border, right.)

### Patch pockets

Patch pockets knitted in cable, lace or bobble stitch pattern can enhance a plain stocking stitch design. The pocket is knitted first and then attached invisibly using Swiss darning (page 65). The flap is knitted with the main fabric.

### Knitting the pocket

Knit a square or rectangular patch to size. Knit the garment as far as the top of the patch pocket and finish with a purl row. Attach the patch pocket then knit the flap separately. Cast on the same number of stitches as for the patch, plus 2, and knit to the required depth of the flap. Place the needle carrying the flap against the needle carrying the main garment stitches and knit the 2 pieces together, knitting 2 stitches together as one. (See Patch pocket, right.)

# *Hemlines*

The most usual form of hemline for sweaters is ribbing which gives a close fit around cuffs, waist and hipline. However, there are other types of hem which can be used.

## *Making a stocking stitch hem*

Working from the bottom of the garment upwards, cast on using the loose knit stitch or invisible cast on methods (page 17). Knit to the depth of the hemline then knit a row of purl stitches on the front or knit side to mark the fold line.

Knit the same number of rows again, plus one row extra so that the work ends on a purl row. With the second needle, pick up loose cast on stitches. Place both needles together and with a third needle, knit them together, counting two stitches as one. This joins the fabric, creating a folded hemline, and places the stitches on the needle, ready for the knitting to continue.

## *Making a picot hem*

Work in the same way as the stocking stitch hem to the required depth. On the fold line, knit a row of eyelets as follows: K1, *sl 1, kwise, k1, psso.* Repeat from *, end k1.

On the following row, purl the yo increases as ordinary stitches. Knit the same number of rows again, plus one extra row so as to end on a purl row. Complete as for stocking stitch hem.

## *Fancy stitch hems*

Patterned borders and edges can be used for hems. Borders must have the same number of stitches as the main fabric and edges must be the length required. See pages 28 to 33 for examples.

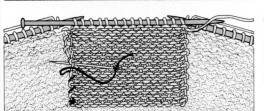

**Making an inset pocket**
Knit a strip the length and width of the pocket, keeping the main garment stitches on stitch holders.

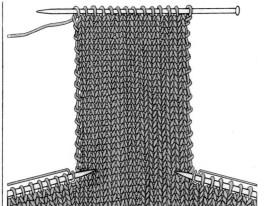

**Sewing up·**
Fold the strip over to form the pocket. Sew up the sides of the pocket separately.

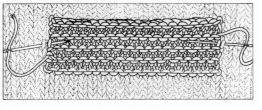

**Making a border**
For a border, pick up stitches along the top fold line of the pocket, adding two extra stitches.

**Completing the pocket**
Sew the border down to the base fabric to form the inset pocket with a garter stitch border.

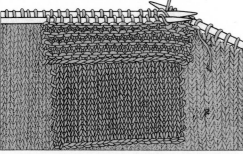

**Attaching a patch pocket flap**
Place the needle carrying the flap stitches against the main garment stitches and knit them off together.

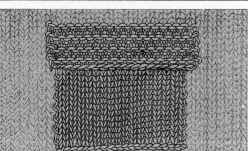

**Patch pocket with flap**
The finished patch pocket with contrasting garter stitch flap.

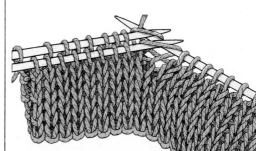

**Stocking stitch hemline**
Pick up the cast on stitches, place both needles together and knit both sets of stitches off together.

**Picot hemline**
The eyelet holes worked on the fold line form a line of picots when the hem is folded over.

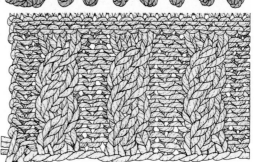

**Fancy hemline**
A cable stitch pattern is used here to make a more decorative hemline. See pages 28 to 33 for other fancy stitches.

# Blocking and pressing

Before the knitting can be sewn up into a garment, it should be blocked and pressed. When you have finished any piece of knitting, first darn in all loose ends to the back of the work.

### How to block a piece of knitting
To block a piece of knitting, pin it out to the correct size and shape on a padded surface. A table covered with a folded blanket under a sheet is ideal. Using rustless pins, pin each piece of knitting wrong side up to the padding. Do not stretch or distort the fabric. Check the length and width of each piece against the pattern measurements. Make sure that all the rows run in straight lines, then pin closely all around the knitting.

### How to press knitting
Wool should be pressed lightly under a damp cloth with a warm iron. Do not move the iron over the surface, but lay it on the cloth and lift it up again. Leave the knitting pinned in position until it has cooled and dried completely. Some yarns other than wool may need to be treated differently, if so, the ball band will give pressing instructions. Highly textured knitting like embossed, cable and rib patterns should be treated differently from flat fabrics like stocking stitch and garter stitch. They need gentle pressing and careful treatment.

### Pressing embossed patterns
Press raised and embossed patterns under a damp cloth. Remove the cloth and the pins, and immediately adjust the knitting, easing and patting it into shape while it is still hot. Swift action will prevent the raised patterns being flattened.

### Pressing ribbing
Ribbing should be lightly stretched and pinned before ironing. Iron it under a heavy cloth and remove the cloth and pins immediately afterwards then gently ease the ribbing into its correct position while it is still warm.

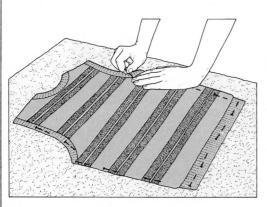

**Blocking the knitting**
Pin the knitting at the corners, check the length and width against the measurements given in the pattern, then pin all around.

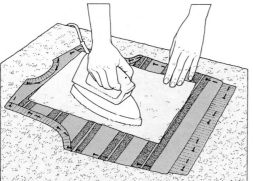

**Pressing the knitting**
Press each section of the blocked piece of knitting evenly under a damp cloth.

# Seams and zips

### Edge to edge seam

This seam gives a soft edge on light garments and baby clothes.

This method gives an almost invisible seam, forms no ridge, and is the best seam to use for baby clothes or where a hard edge must be avoided.

Place the pieces to be joined edge to edge with the heads of the knit stitches locking together. Match the pattern pieces carefully row for row and stitch for stitch.

Using the same yarn and sewing at the same tension as the knitting, sew into the head of each stitch alternately.

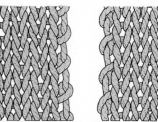

**Place the edges together**

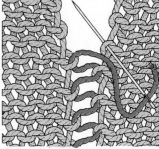

**Sew into the edge stitches**

### Back stitch seam

This seam gives a strong, firm edge on all garments.

Place the pieces to be seamed together with right sides facing and carefully match pattern to pattern, row to row and stitch to stitch. Work back stitch as for sewing along the seam, sewing into the centre of each stitch to correspond with the same stitch on the opposite piece. Sew $\frac{1}{4}$ inch (6mm) from the edge of the knitting.

### Zip fasteners

Zip fasteners need to be sewn onto a firm selvedge.

Use a firm selvedge (page 21) if you intend to fit a zip fastener to a garment. The stocking stitch and flat selvedges are both suitable.

Pin the zip fastener to the opening, making sure that the knitting fits easily on top of it and is not wrinkled or stretched. The knitted edges should come right up to the sides of the zip mechanism. Work back stitch with sewing thread along the edge. Be sure to use a fastener that is the correct weight for the garment.

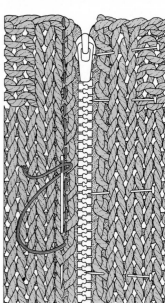

# Waistbands and facings

## Elastic waistbands

Use a wide and fairly soft elastic for waistbands.

Cut the elastic to fit the waist measurement and sew it into a circle. Then place it around the waistline on the inside of the skirt and pin at each quarter around the waist. Ease the knitting evenly between the quarters and secure the elastic with more pins. Sew the elastic to the skirt using herringbone sewing stitch . Hold the knitting over the fingers of the left hand, slightly stretching the elastic and catching the knitting above and below it.

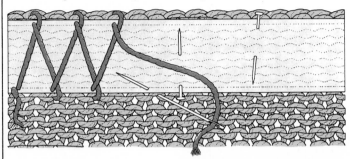

## Ribbon facings

Use ribbon facings to give neatness and strength, and to prevent the knitting being stretched out of shape. Facings are most often used to line the inside edges or buttonbands of cardigans and jackets.

A soft grosgrain ribbon is the best type to use. Turn in a small hem at top and bottom of the ribbon then pin it to the buttonbands. Ease the knitting along the ribbon. Make sure that it is neither stretched nor too loose and that the button-holes are evenly spaced. With sewing thread attach the facing. When the sewing is complete mark out the buttonholes with pins and cut the ribbon through to them. Then lightly oversew around the buttonholes to prevent fraying and then work buttonhole stitch around them using sewing thread.

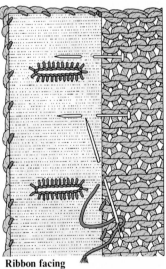

**Ribbon facing**

## Mitred corners

When facing ribbon must be sewn around right angles, stitch the outside edges first and then fold the ribbon into a mitred corner, sew over this and then stitch the inside edges.

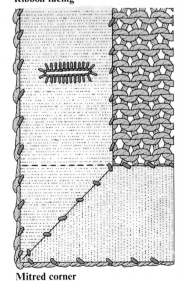

**Mitred corner**

# Invisible joining

Use grafting method to join knitting horizontally but invisibly. Keep the pieces on the needles. Hold them back to back with both working ends of yarn at the same end and with the stitches evenly spaced to correspond one with the other on opposite sides. Break the yarn on the front needle to $1\frac{1}{2}$ times the length of the seam to be joined. Thread it on a blunt-ended sewing needle.

## Stocking stitch

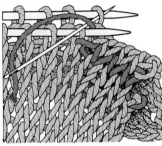

**Stocking stitch**

### Front knitting needle

*First stitch* Insert sewing needle knitwise through stitch, slip it off knitting needle.
*Second stitch* Insert needle purlwise through the stitch and keep it on the knitting needle.

### Back knitting needle

*First stitch* Insert needle purlwise through stitch, slip it off.
*Second stitch* Insert needle knitwise through the stitch and keep it on the knitting needle. Repeat from * to last stitch.
Gently ease the grafted stitches and the yarn to the same tension as the knitting. Pull the yarn through the last stitch and fasten off. Break off ends and darn into back of work.

## Garter stitch

The order of knitwise and purlwise is changed.

### Front knitting needle

*First stitch* Insert needle knitwise, slip the stitch.
*Second stitch* Insert needle purlwise, keep the stitch.

### Back knitting needle

*First stitch* Insert needle knitwise, slip the stitch.
*Second stitch* Insert needle purlwise, keep the stitch.

# Order of seaming

**1 Shoulder seams**
**2 Set in sleeves** Mark the centre top of the sleeve, match it up to the shoulder seam and pin in position. Pin the pieces together, easing in the fullness.
**3 Side and sleeve seams** Sew together in one long seam.
**4 Collars** Sew the right side of the collar to the wrong side of the neckline, matching centre back of both pieces.
**5 Buttonbands**
**6 Pockets** These can be sewn on invisibly by pinning the pocket along a line of stitches and rows, matching the base fabric exactly. Work Swiss darning (page 65) around the pocket to attach it.
**7 Hems** Hems should be sewn neatly so as not to make a bulky line (see below). When edges have been made with ribbing, cables or any fancy stitch then hemming is not necessary.

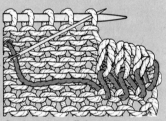

**Sewing a hem off the needle**

## Making a folded hem

For a skirt or any piece of knitting requiring a sewn hem, end with a knit row, keeping the stitches on the knitting needle. Sew the stitches off the needle onto the base fabric. Sew the first stitch to the very edge of the base so that each stitch is sewn to its fellow on the base.

To ensure the hemline is straight a contrast yarn can be knitted or woven into the row on to which the hem will be turned. When the cast on edge needs to be hemmed, use the invisible cast on method (page 16). Insert a knitting needle through the stitches, and withdraw the contrast yarn. Sew hem down directly from knitting needle onto the base.

# Knitting in the round

Circular knitting and tubular knitting are worked in a continuous round to make a seamless fabric. Round knitting is much older than the flat knitting which is more common today. All the traditional peasant styles of knitting are worked in the round. It can be worked on sticks, spools, sets of double pointed needles, a single circular needle, on two needles, or on a frame.

## Knitting with a circular needle

Knitting with a circular needle is the best way to make very large tubular shapes like skirts. Two circular needles can also be used as straight needles for large, flat shapes such as afgans. Modern circular needles consist of a flexible nylon tube joining a pair of metal needles.

Cast on the stitches in the usual way. Follow the diagram opposite for closing the circle.

**Closing the circle**
*Knit into the slip loop or first cast on stitch marking the beginning of each round with the loose end of the slip loop.*

## Knitting with two needles

It is possible to knit a tubular fabric with a pair of double pointed needles by slipping and knitting stitches alternately. The knitting can be worked with either a closed or open end depending upon the cast on used. A closed end should be used for borders and double-faced fabrics while an open end is for sleeves, gloves and socks.

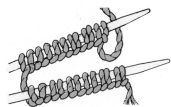

**Correct needle position**
*Hold the needle so that the working yarn is to the beginning of the back needle.*

### Working a closed end
Cast on an even number of stitches on one needle and work either the slip stitch stocking or rib stitches as set out below. Knit to the desired length then cast off the stitches in the usual way to close the top edge.

### Working an open end
Cast on an even number of stitches then slip half the stitches onto a second needle. Fold the work, holding the needles parallel; the working yarn should be at the beginning of the back needle (see above). Using a third needle slip first one stitch from the front needle and then one from the back needle. Slip stitches alternately from front and back needles until they are all on one needle. Knit to desired length using either the slip stocking or rib stitch as set out below. To cast off divide the stitches onto two needles. Slip the first stitch to one needle and the second onto the other, alternately dividing them equally between both needles. Cast off each side separately with a third needle so that the work remains open at the top.

### Basic stitches for two needle method
In both slip stocking stitch and slip rib stitch the stitches are always slipped purlwise. As with all knitting in the round directions are given for one row only which is repeated until the desired length is reached.
*Slip stocking stitch:* *P1, sl 1, rep from *
*Slip rib stitch:* Worked on a multiple of 4 sts P1, sl 1, * ybk, k1, yfwd, sl 1, p1, sl 1; rep from * to last 2 sts, end ybk, k1, yfwd, sl 1.

## Knitting with three or more needles

Knitting with three or more needles is the most common method of producing a tubular fabric for sweaters, socks and gloves. As many as six needles can be used. When knitting with, for example, four needles, the stitches are held on three of the needles and are knitted off with the fourth.

Knitting instructions usually state the number of stitches to be cast on for each needle, but it is much easier to cast the total number of stitches onto one needle and then redistribute them to the other needles according to the pattern.

**Beginning a round**
*When using 4 needles divide the cast on stitches between 3 and knit off with the 4th.*

### Working method
The first round of knitting closes the circle. Draw the last and the first needle as close together as possible and then insert the spare needle through the first cast on stitch. Knit with the working yarn from the last cast on stitch. Keep this first knitted stitch close to the last needle so that no gap forms in the joining of the circle, and continue to knit the stitches off the first needle.

When the first needle is empty, use it to knit the stitches off the second needle. Continue to work the round in this way, keeping the correct number of stitches on each needle and knitting with the spare needle. Hold the two working needles as you would normally, in the left and right hands, and drop the needles not in use to the back of the work.

## Spool knitting

Spool knitting is worked on a hollowed cork, a spool or a cotton reel and it is a good way to make cords and braids. Spool knitting is worked in the same way as frame knitting (see facing page) although it is simpler and less versatile.

### Knitting on a spool
Loop the yarn around the nails at the top of the spool. After the second winding, lift the lower loops over the nails using a darning needle or crochet hook.

Both stocking stitch and crossed stitch can be worked on spools. Discard the stitches down the central hole and pull the finished cord through from below. Cast off in the same way as frame knitting.

**Spool knitting**
Today spools are often used by children learning to knit. They are also a simple way of making cords and trims for garments.

## Stick knitting

Stick knitting is the earliest form of circular knitting. Sticks are held vertically in the hand or stuck in the ground and the yarn is wound around them. Any number of sticks can be used – arranged in a circle to make tubular fabric or in a line to make a flat fabric.

### Knitting on sticks
Wrap the yarn around the sticks as illustrated. After the third winding, lift the bottom loop over the sticks and drop it. Repeat winding and drop loops after each round.

**Stick knitting**
Stick knitting may have developed like the game of cat's cradle, from grass or wool twisted around the fingers.

# Frame knitting

In frame knitting the stitches are looped around pegs mounted on a rectangular or circular frame. The principle is the same as stick or spool knitting, but the method is much more sophisticated and is capable of producing large and elaborately coloured fabrics.

Frames were used by the knitting guilds in the Middle Ages to make their master-works – multi-coloured carpets. Even with the advent of machines, frame knitting remains a versatile way of working with colour, as different colours can be wound individually around each peg.

## Types of frames

Rectangular frames are used to make flat and tubular fabrics. They can be from 12 to 60 inches (30 to 52·5 cm) long with a $\frac{1}{4}$ to $\frac{3}{4}$ inch wide (6 to 18 mm) slot cut along the centre. Circular frames produce a tubular fabric only and vary in diameter from 6 to 14 inches 15 to 35.5 cm) with a circle of the required diameter cut from the centre. Pegs or nails, placed $\frac{1}{4}$ inch (6 mm) apart are arranged around the slot or circle of the frame. The old frames held from 70 to 200 pegs and each peg represented a stitch. Frames are mounted on a trestle so that the knitted fabric falls easily through the slot or circle. The size of the frame dictates the maximum size of the knitting, although fewer pegs can be employed to make small pieces.

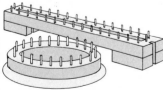
**Round and rectangular frames**

## Materials and tools

Any yarn or fibre, from thick string for hammocks to finest silks for stockings, can be used. A bent nail or a crochet hook is required to lift the stitches from the pegs.

## Using crossed stitch

A fabric which is similar to the crossed stocking stitch is formed by using the method shown below.

### Making the crossed stitch

Knot the yarn to one of the pegs or secure it to a slit on the outside edge of the frame. Wind the yarn once around each peg. Make a second winding.

To make a tubular piece of knitting on a straight frame continue the second and all subsequent windings in the same direction.

To make a flat fabric, make the second winding in the opposite direction and the subsequent windings alternately clockwise and anti-clockwise.

After the second winding, lift the bottom loop up and over the top loop, discarding it into the centre. Continue to wind and discard until the knitting is the required length.

## Using stocking stitch

A closer fabric is formed using this stitch rather than the crossed stitch so it is often known as the close stitch.

### Making the stocking stitch

Cast on the first round, then make the second and subsequent windings by winding the yarn along the outside of the pegs. When this winding is complete, lift the bottom loop over the strand and discard it into centre slot.

## Using stocking stitch rib

This introduces the purl stitch, but the ribbing can only be used to make flat fabrics on a straight frame.

### Making the stocking stitch rib

Cast on from right to left, and cast on diagonally back and forth across the slot. Work the next and subsequent windings alternately from left to right and right to left. You can make wider ribs by winding the pegs in groups, taking 2 from the back and 2 from the front for a 2 by 2 rib, and so on.

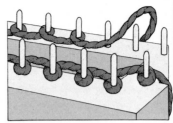
**Winding the yarn**
*Secure the yarn to the frame before winding it once around each peg.*

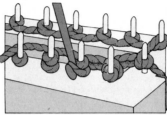
**Discarding a stitch**
*Use a crochet hook or darning needle to lift the bottom loops over the top ones, making sure to discard them down the centre.*

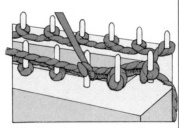
**Winding the yarn**
*Yarn in the second and subsequent rows should be wound along the outside of the pegs.*

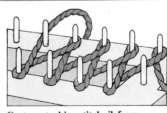
**Cast on stocking stitch rib from right to left**

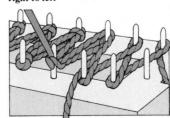
**Work next winding from left to right, then alternate**

## Increasing stitches

1 Wind on an extra peg at the beginning or end of each row. When working on a circular frame, change to a bigger frame.
2 Pick up the running thread between the stitches and place it on the next peg, redistributing the other stitches onto the following pegs.
3 Change to a thicker yarn.
4 Change from stocking stitch to crossed stitch.

## Decreasing stitches

1 Change from crossed stitch to stocking stitch.
2 Change to a finer yarn.
3 Change to a frame where the pegs are closer together.
4 Knit two stitches together.

## Casting off

When the knitting is complete wind each peg separately and cast off.

### Working method

Knit the stitch on peg B and lift it over to peg A. Then lift the bottom loop on peg A over and off, return the stitch to peg B. Repeat the process with the next loop on peg C. Continue up to the last stitch. Cut the yarn, draw it through the stitch, fasten off. Alternatively, draw a thread through all the stitches and gather the work together.

The cast on edges in frame knitting are always loose but can be made firmer by picking up the edge loops and returning them to the frame and casting them off. The cast on and cast off edges can be joined together to make a double fabric if both edges are returned to the frame and cast off together.

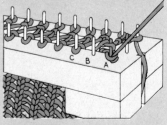
**Casting off**

87

## Sock construction

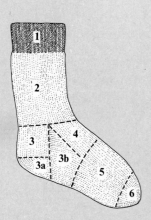

**1 Sock top** Socks are worked from the top to the toe. The top can be knitted in any stitch pattern divisible by the number of stitches cast on. Rib stitches are generally preferred as they are elastic and provide a good grip on the leg.
**2 The leg** Stocking stitch, as its name suggests, is the most common stitch used, although like the top, any pattern may be used. The leg finishes at the ankle bone where the stitches are divided; some are used to form the heel while the rest are held, to be used to knit the gusset later.
**3 The heel** This is knitted back and forth on two needles. The heel receives more wear than any other part of the sock so it should be reinforced. Two methods are shown in the pattern. The heel itself is composed of two separate parts.
**3a The heel flap** This forms the back of the heel.
**3b The heel turning** This forms the base of the heel.
**4 The gusset** This fits over the instep and is made by uniting the heel and leg stitches.
**5 The foot** The circumference of the foot is always the same as that of the ankle. The top of the foot can be knitted in any pattern, but the base should always be knitted in smooth stocking stitch.
**6 The toe** Two alternative methods of shaping the toe are included in the basic pattern.

# Sock patterns

### Plain sock pattern

The instructions for the plain socks offer a choice of two types of heel and two types of toe. Following the plain sock pattern, instructions are given for an Argyll sock and a sock with a lace insert.

### Materials and measurement

**Yarn** 5 × 25 gm balls of 4-ply yarn. **Needles** Set of four No. 11 (3 mm) and No. 10 (3¼ mm) dpns. **Stitch gauge** 14 sts and 18 rows to 2 inches (5 cm) over st-st on No. 10 (3¼ mm) needles. **Measurements** Knitted at this stitch gauge the socks will fit a 9 inch (23 cm) ankle. To vary the size, alter the stitch gauge: at 16 sts to 2 inches (5 cm) the socks will fit an 8 inch (20.5 cm) ankle; at 18 sts to 2 inches (5 cm) the socks will fit a 7 inch (18 cm) ankle. Lengths are adjustable as required.

### Top of sock

Using a set of 4 No. 11 (3 mm) needles and the cable cast on method (page 17), cast on 64 sts and work in rounds of k1, p1, rib for 2 inches (5 cm), or length reqd.

### Leg

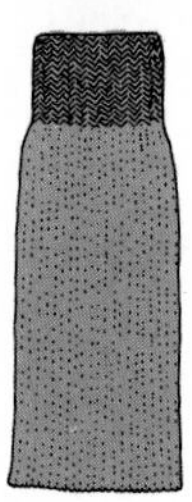

Change to No. 10 (3¼ mm) needles and cont in rounds of st-st until work measures the reqd length to ankle bone, ending at the end of a round.

### Heel

The heel is composed of the heel flap and the heel turning, and is worked back and forth and not in the round. The heel is made on half the number of stitches in the round plus one, and the beginning of the round is placed in the middle of the heel flap. **Next row** K17, turn and sl the last 16 sts of round onto the other end of this needle; divide the rem 31 sts onto 2 needles and leave for gusset.

### Heel flap

The heel flap is usually a square. It can be worked in st-st or reinforced by working in hard-wearing heel stitch. Another way of reinforcing the heel is by weaving in an extra length of the same yarn during knitting (see colour weaving, page 56). **Plain heel flap** Cont in rows of st-st for 3 inches (7.5 cm) ending with a p row. **Heel flap in heel stitch Row 1** (WS) P to end **Row 2** K1, *sl 1, k1; rep from * to end. **Row 3** P to end. **Row 4** K2, *sl 1, k1; rep from * to last st, k1. Rep these 4 rows for 3 inches (7.5 cm) ending with a purl row.

### Turning the heel

After the heel flap is completed, the heel is turned. Two alternative heel turnings are given below, Round and Coptic. **Round heel turning Row 1** K18, sl 1, k1, psso, k1, turn. **Row 2** P5, p2tog, p1, turn. **Row 3** K6, sl 1, k1, psso, k1, turn. **Row 4** P7, p2tog, p1, turn. Cont to work one more st on every row until all sts are worked, and 19sts rem, ending with a p

Turning heel continued

row. **Next row** K10. This completes the heel. **Coptic heel turning Row 1** K22, sl 1, k1, psso, turn. **Row 2** P12, p2tog, turn. **Row 3** K12, sl 1, k1, psso, turn. Rep rows 2 and 3 until all sts are worked, and 13 sts rem, ending with a p row. **Next row** K7.

### Gusset and foot

Sl the instep sts back onto one needle; with the spare needle k9 sts (round·heel) or 6 sts (coptic heel), pick up and k18 sts along side of heel; with the second needle k the instep sts; with the third needle pick up and k18 sts along side of heel, then k the rem 10 sts (round heel) or 7 sts (coptic heel). **Next round** K to end. **Next round** On first needle k to last 3 sts, k2tog, k1; on second needle k to end; on 3rd needle k1, sl 1, psso, k to end. Rep the last 2 rounds until 64 sts rem, then cont without shaping until foot measures 2 inches (5 cm) less than final length reqd, ending at the end of a round.

### Shape toe

Two alternative methods of shaping the toe are given – the round toe and flat toe. **Round toe Rd 1** *Sl 1, k1, psso, k14; rep from * to end. **Rd 2** K to end. **Rd 3** *Sl 1, k1, psso, k13; rep from * to end. Cont to dec in this way on alt rounds, working one st less between the decs each time, until 16 sts rem. Break off yarn, thread through sts, draw up and fasten off. **Flat toe** Sl the first st from the 3rd needle onto the end of the 2nd needle; there will now be 32 sts on 2nd needle and 16 sts each on first and 3rd needles. **Rd 1** On first needle k to last 3 sts, k2tog, k1; on 2nd needle k1, sl 1, k1, psso, k to last 3 sts, k2tog, k1; on 3rd needle k1, sl 1, k1, psso, k to end. **Rd 2** K to end. Rep these 2 rds until 16 sts rem, then k the sts from first needle onto 3rd needle and graft sts tog (page 85).

### Socks with lace inset

**Yarn** 2 × 25 gm balls of 2-ply yarn. **Needles** Set of four No. 14 (2 mm) and No. 13 (2¼ mm) dpns. **Stitch gauge** 20 sts and 24 rows to 2 inches (5 cm) over st-st on No. 13 (2¼ mm) needles. **Measurements** Knitted at this stitch gauge the sock will fit a 6½ inch (16.5 cm) ankle. The length is adjustable as on plain socks. Using No. 14 (2 mm) needles cast on 64 sts and work in k1, p1 rib for ¾ inch (2 cm). Change to No. 13 (2¼ mm) needles and work as for plain sock, but work a panel of 16 sts at outside leg in Victory pattern (page 47). Note that as you are working in rounds, when working the 2nd and alt rows, read k for p and p for k throughout. Cont with panel in patt as far as ankle, then cont as given for plain socks, using the round heel and the spiral toe.

## Argyll sock

The chart for this pattern is shown in colour on page 54. **Yarn** 4 × 25 gm balls of 4-ply yarn in main colour A. 2 balls in contrast colour B. **Needles** Set of four No. 11 (3 mm) and No. 10 (3¼ mm) dpns. **Stitch gauge and measurements** As for plain socks. With No. 11 (3 mm) needles and colour A, cast on 64 sts and work in k1, p1 rib for 1½ inches (4 cm) or length reqd. Change to No. 10 (3¼ mm) needles and cont in rounds of st-st, working in patt from chart, until work measures reqd length to ankle, ending if possible at the end of a patt repeat. Cont in colour A as given for plain socks, using the round heel and spiral toe.

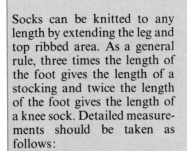

## Measuring for socks

Socks can be knitted to any length by extending the leg and top ribbed area. As a general rule, three times the length of the foot gives the length of a stocking and twice the length of the foot gives the length of a knee sock. Detailed measurements should be taken as follows:

**1 Calf** Measure around the fullest part.

**2 Ankle** Measure around the widest part. This is often the same width as the foot.
**3 Width of foot** Measure around the widest part.
**4 Length of foot** Measure from centre back of heel to the longest point at the toes. When in doubt, make this measurement generous rather than mean.
**5 Length** Take this measurement up the outside leg from the bottom of the heel to the top of the stocking or sock.

### 1 Sock with lace pattern insert
*This sock is a modern interpretation of the lacy full length stockings much admired by the Elizabethans.*

### 2 Plain pattern sock in Egyptian style.
*The pattern for this sock is based on a sixth century Coptic sock found in an Egyptian tomb.*

### 3 Argyll sock.
*Contrasting diamonds intersected by diagonal lines make up the classic Argyll pattern. Because the unworked yarn is stranded across the back, the socks are warmer than the plain pattern.*

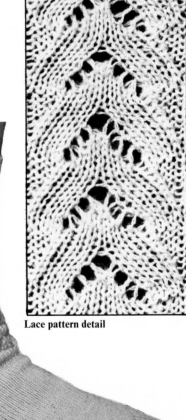

**Lace pattern detail**

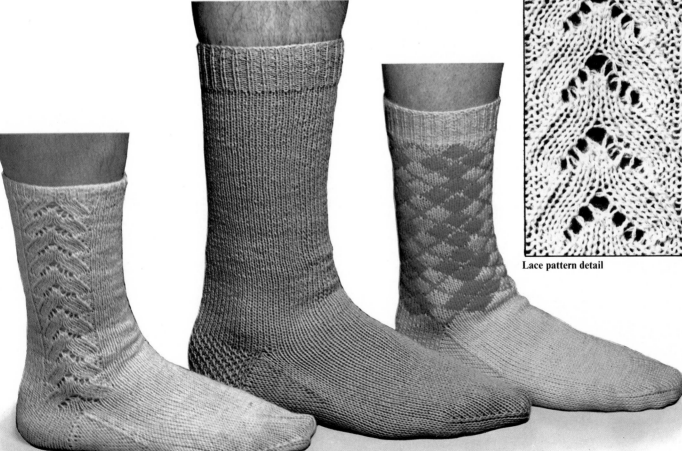

## Mitten and glove construction

### Mittens

Measure around the widest part of the knuckles. Measure length from the tip of the longest finger to the centre wrist or desired length. The length of thumb is taken from the tip of the outside thumb to the lower thumb joint.

### Gloves

All measurements are taken as for mittens except that the length of palm and fingers are measured separately and the circumference of each finger is measured.

### Method of construction

Gloves and mittens are made in the same way up to the thumb separation.

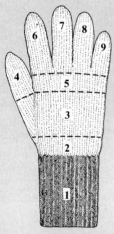

**1 Cuff** Gloves and mittens are worked from the cuff to the fingers. The circumference should be the same as around the widest part of the knuckles. **2 Wrist** This is knitted without shaping for a short distance. **3 Palm and thumb gusset** The shaping for the base of the thumb is knitted at the same time as the palm until the thumb separation is reached. **4 Thumb** The stitches are divided and the thumb is worked separately and shaped off at the tip. **5 Mid-palm to base of fingers** This area is knitted without shaping until the base of the fingers is reached. **6, 7, 8, & 9 Fingers** Each finger is worked separately in order.

# Glove patterns

The patterns given here are for three pairs of mittens and a pair of gloves. The pattern is given for stocking stitch but it can be knitted in any stitch pattern which is divisible by the number of stitches cast on. The size can be adjusted by altering the stitch gauge.

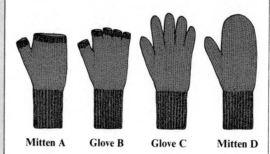

Mitten A    Glove B    Glove C    Mitten D

## Materials and measurements

**Yarn** 2 × 25 gm balls of 3-ply yarn for each style. **Needles** Set of 4 No. 14 (2 mm) and No. 13 (2¼ mm) dpns. **Stitch gauge** 18 sts and 24 rows to 2 inches (5 cm) over st-st on No. 13 (2¼ mm) needles. **Measurements** Width around palm 6 (7) inches 15 (18) cm.

## Cuff ribbing and wrist

With four No. 14 (2 mm) needles cast on 52 (60) sts and work in rounds of k1, p1 rib for 3 (3½) inches [7.5 (9) cm]. Change to four No. 13 (2¼ mm) needles and cont in rounds of st-st for ½ inch (1 cm).

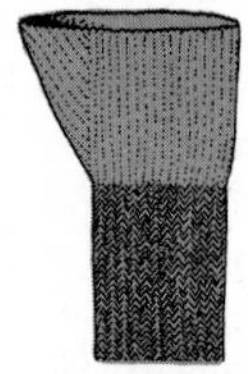

## Thumb gusset

The increasing for the thumb now begins.
**Rd 1** M1B (by picking up the loop between sts and knitting into the back of it), K to end.
**Rds 2 & 3** Knit.
**Rd 4** M1B, k1, M1B, k to end.
**Rds 5 & 6** Knit.
**Rd 7** M1B, k3, M1B, k to end.
Cont to inc in this way on every 3rd round until there are 71 (81) sts, then knit 3 rounds.

## Thumb

A number of sts are separated from the rest and the thumb is worked. **Next round** K 19 (21), sl rem 52 (60) sts onto a thread. Cast on 3 sts and join these 22 (24) sts into a round. **For styles A and B** Cont in rounds of st-st for ⅝ inches (1.5 cm) then work four rounds in k1, p1 rib and cast off loosely in rib.

**Thumb continued**
**Styles C and D** Cont in rounds of st-st for approx 1½ (½) inches [4 (1) cm] less than final length reqd, ending with the first of the 3 cast on sts. **Shape top Rd 1** *Sl 1, k1, psso, k7 (8), k2tog, rep from * once more. **Rd 2** K to end. **Rd 3** * Sl 1, k1, psso, k5 (6), k2tog, rep from * once more. Cont to dec in this way on alt rounds twice more. Break off yarn, thread through sts, draw up and fasten off securely. Sl rem 52 (60) sts back onto three needles, pick up and k4 sts from the cast on sts at base of thumb, then k to end, 56 (64) sts.

## Mittens

**Style A** Cont in rounds of st-st, work 10 rounds (or the length reqd) then work 6 rounds in k1, p1 rib. Cast of loosely in rib. **Style D** Cont in rounds of st-st for 3 (1½) inches [7.5 (4) cm] **less** than final length reqd. **Left hand** End after the 4 cast on sts; **Right hand** End before the 4 cast on sts. **Shape top Rd 1** *K1, sl 1, k1, psso, k22 (26), k2tog, k1; rep from * once more. **Rd 2** Knit to end. **Rd 3** * K1, sl 1, k1, psso, k20 (24), k2tog, k1; rep from * once more. Cont to dec in this way on every round until 16 (20) sts rem, then divide the work onto 2 dpns with the shaping at each end of the needles and graft sts together (page 85).

## Gloves

Cont in rounds of st-st for 3 (1½) inches [7.5 (4) cm] less than final length reqd. **Left hand** End after the 4 cast on sts; **Right hand** End before the 4 cast on sts.

### First finger

K8 (9), sl the next 40 (46) sts onto a thread, cast on 2 sts, then k the rem 8 (9) sts, 18 (20) sts. **Style B** Cont in rounds of st-st for ½ inch (1 cm) then work 4 rounds in k1, p1 rib and cast off loosely in rib. For style B finish all fingers in this way. **Style C** Cont in rounds of st-st for 2½ (½) inches [6.5 (1) cm] less than final length reqd, ending in the centre of the 2 cast on sts. **Shape top Rd 1** *Sl 1, k1, psso, k5 (6), k2tog, rep from * once more. **Rd 2** K to end. **Rd 3** *Sl 1, k1, psso, k3 (4), k2tog, rep from * once more. Cont to dec in this way on foll alt round. Break off yarn, thread through sts, draw up and fasten securely.

### Second and third fingers

Sl the first and last 7 (8) sts from thread onto needles, k7 (8), pick up and k2 from base of previous finger, k the other 7 (8) sts, then cast on 2, 18 (20) sts. Cont as for first finger, but making the length 2¾ inches (7 cm) instead of 2½ inches (6.5 cm). **Third finger** Work as for second finger, but making the length the same as the first finger.

### Fourth finger

K the rem 12 (14) sts, pick up and k2 sts from base of previous finger, 14 (16) sts. Cont in rounds of st-st for 2 inches (5 cm), ending in centre of outside of hand. **Shape top** Work as for first finger, but starting with 3rd round of shaping.

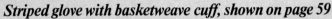

## Patterned mitten and glove projects

### Fingerless mitten in five colours, shown on page 59

The mitten is knitted in 5 colours of 4-ply yarn. **Yarn** Approximately 50 gm of 4-ply yarn. **Needles** 4 No. 13 (2¼ mm) dpns; 4 No. 12 (2¾ mm) dpns. **Stitch gauge** 17 sts to 2 inches (5 cm) over st-st in horizontal stripes using No. 12 (2¾ mm) dpns. **Measurements** This pattern with the above stitch gauge will fit a 6¾/7¾ inch (17/19.5 cm) palm circumference. Follow the instructions for the plain fingerless mitten A. Knit the cuff in colour A. Work the thumb and palm in horizontal stripes of colours B and C. Then change to No. 12 (2¾ mm) needles and work the top of the palm and the finger area in vertical stripes of colours D and E. Use colour B and No. 13 (2¼ mm) needles for ribbing around the fingers. Use colour C and No. 12 (2¾ mm) needles for the ribbing around the thumb.

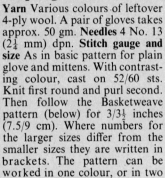

### Striped glove with basketweave cuff, shown on page 59

**Yarn** Various colours of leftover 4-ply wool. A pair of gloves takes approx. 50 gm. **Needles** 4 No. 13 (2¼ mm) dpn. **Stitch gauge and size** As in basic pattern for plain glove and mittens. With contrasting colour, cast on 52/60 sts. Knit first round and purl second. Then follow the Basketweave pattern (below) for 3/3½ inches (7.5/9 cm). Where numbers for the larger sizes differ from the smaller sizes they are written in brackets. The pattern can be worked in one colour, or in two colours (A and B). If you prefer 2 colours, use colour A for all knit sts and colour B for all purl sts, while loosely stranding the colour not in use to the back of the work (see page 57). **Basketweave cuff Rd 1** Knit. **Rd 2, 3 and 4** *P5, k3; rep from *, end p4. **Rd 5** Knit. **Rd 6, 7 and 8** P1, *k3, p5; rep from *, end k3 Repeat rounds 1 to 8.

After completing the above, follow the instructions for the plain glove, beginning with the wrist and working in random stripes throughout.

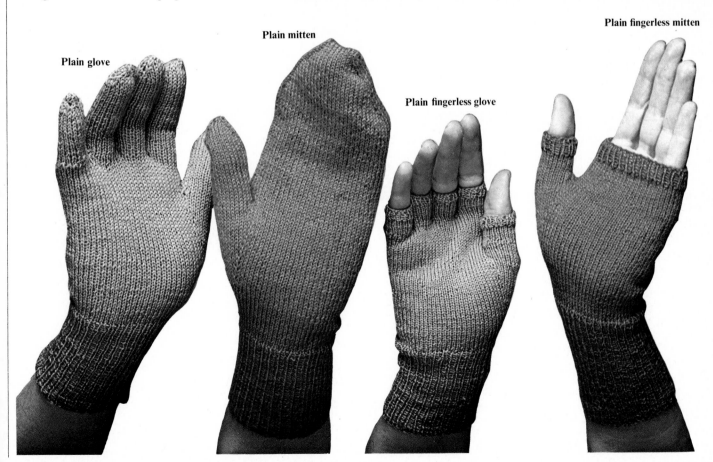

**Plain glove**

**Plain mitten**

**Plain fingerless glove**

**Plain fingerless mitten**

# Medallion knitting

### Introduction to medallion knitting

Knitted medallions can be worked in squares, circles, hexagons, pentagons or octagons. They are knitted on four, five or six needles. Circles can also be worked on just two needles. Large medallions are used as shawls and tablecloths, small ones are used singly for mats and doilys or sewn together to make bedspreads, rugs, tablecloths or cushion covers. Medallions can be knitted up in any type of yarn, from fine cottons and silks to fleecy Shetland wools for blankets and shawls. Medallions are made either by increasing from the centre outwards or by decreasing from the circumference inwards. The increasing method is easier to handle, but both can be used in one piece of knitting to make berets or seamless double-sided designs like cushion covers and pouch bags or purses.

### How a medallion shape is formed

The shape of a medallion is determined by the position of the increases or decreases. These can be made to form straight or swirling lines, or they can be scattered so that they become completely invisible. To form straight lines two increases or decreases are used at every point. To form swirling lines only one increase or decrease is used at each point Any method of increasing can be used, although the "inc 1" method, making one stitch from another (page 36) is commonly used for solid fabrics; and the yarn over method (page 34) is used for lacy openwork patterns.

### Where to place invisible increases

When the pattern instructions for a medallion read "inc 1 at the beginning and end of every needle", this means work into the *first* and *next to last* stitch on each needle so that the "bars" fall in the correct positions.

### Where to place visible increases

The yarn over increase (page 34) is usually placed before the *first* and the *last* stitch on each needle. When the increase comes before a knit stitch use the knit or "yfwd" increase. When the yarn over needle increase comes before a purl stitch use the purl or "yrn" increase.

### Hints on knitting medallions

Use the knit cast on method (page 17). When casting on with four or five needles it is easier to cast all the stitches on to one needle and then distribute them, according to the pattern instructions, on the other needles. A firm, tightly spun cotton is the best yarn to experiment with, the easiest needle size to use is size No 9 (3¾mm). The first few rounds may be awkward to handle but with a little practice you will soon become used to holding four or five needles. Push the stitches well to the middle of each needle and knit as tightly as possible to prevent them falling off. After casting on always knit the first round into the back of all stitches to flatten them. If the medallion becomes frilly, work an extra round of plain stitches without increases or decreases. If it becomes too tight then omit a round of plain stitches. The extra rounds must be continued throughout the work to retain the balance of the design. Cast off in the usual way then break the yarn and draw the end through the last stitch and through the first stitch to close the round. Finish off the hole in the centre of the medallion by threading a sewing needle with either the same or a contrast yarn and drawing the hole in the centre together.

# Medallion shapes

### The basic medallions

These nine patterns show how to work the different medallion shapes. The instructions are given for stocking stitch in order to emphasize the positions of the increases and decreases for the various shapes. Once you understand these positions you can use any fancy stitch pattern to make medallions.

### Square with straight increase lines

Cast on 2 sts on each of 4 needles and knit with a 5th.

| | |
|---|---|
| **Round 1** Knit into the back of all sts. | |
| **Round 2** Inc 1 into every st. | |
| **Round 3** Knit. | |
| **Round 4** Inc 1 at the beginning and the end of each needle. | |

Repeat rounds 3 and 4 until square is required size.

### Square with swirling increase lines

Cast on 2 sts on each of 4 needles and knit with a 5th.

| | |
|---|---|
| **Round 1** Knit into the back of all sts. | |
| **Round 2** Yo at the beginning of all 4 needles. | |

Repeat round 2 until square is required size. Knit the yo's as ordinary sts.

### Pentagon with straight increase lines

Cast on 2 sts on each of 5 needles and knit with a 6th.

| | |
|---|---|
| **Round 1** Knit into the back of all sts. | |
| **Round 2** Inc 1 into every 2nd st. | |
| **Round 3** Knit. | |
| **Round 4** Inc 1 at beginning and end of all 5 needles. | |
| **Rounds 5 and 6** Knit. | |
| **Round 7** Inc 1 at beginning and end of all 5 needles. | |
| **Round 8** Knit. | |

Repeat rounds 4 to 8 until pentagon is required size.

### Square with straight decrease lines

Cast on 20 sts on each of 4 needles and knit with a 5th.

**Round 1** K2 tog at beginning of each needle, sl 1, k1, psso at the end of each needle.

**Round 2** Knit.

Repeat these 2 rounds until 2 sts rem on each needle. Cast off, then break the yarn and thread it through a sewing needle. Sew through first stitch to complete circle. This method of decreasing applies to all medallions. The decreases will always be positioned in the same places as those given for the increases.

## Hexagon with swirling increase lines

Cast on 4 sts on each of 3 needles and knit with a 4th.

**Round 1** Knit into back of all sts.

**Round 2** Yo before first and 3rd sts on each needle.

**Round 3 and all odd-numbered rounds** Knit.

**Round 4** Yo before first and 4th sts on each needle.

**Round 6** Yo before first and 5th sts on each needle.

Continue to knit all odd-numbered rounds. In all even-numbered rounds increase on the first and the 6th, 7th and 8th sts and so on.

## Octagon with straight increase lines

Cast on 2 sts on each of 4 needles and knit with a 5th.

**Round 1** Knit into the back of all sts.

**Round 2** Inc 1 into each stitch.

**Round 3 and all odd-numbered rounds** Knit.

**Round 4** Inc 1 into first and 3rd st on each needle.

**Round 6** Inc 1 into 3rd and last st on each needle.

**Round 8** Inc 1 into 4th and last st on each needle.

**Round 10** Inc 1 into 5th and last st on each needle.

Continue in this way.

## Circle with radiating increases

Cast on 2 sts on each of 4 needles and knit with a 5th.

**Round 1** Knit into the back of all sts.

**Round 2** Inc 1 into each st.

**Rounds 3, 4 and 5** Knit.

**Round 6** Inc 1 into each st.

**Rounds 7 to 11** Knit.

**Round 12** Inc 1 into each st.

**Rounds 13 to 19** Knit.

**Round 20** Inc 1 into every 2nd st.

**Rounds 21 to 25** Knit.

**Round 26** Inc 1 into every 3rd st.

**Rounds 27 to 31** Knit.

**Round 32** Inc 1 into every 4th st.

Continue in this way to knit 5 rounds plain, and then increase for a round making next increases on every 5th st and so on.

## Circle with invisible increasing

Cast on 2 sts on each of 4 needles and knit with a 5th.

**Round 1** Knit into the back of all sts.

**Round 2** Inc 1 into each st (16 sts).

**Round 3 and all odd-numbered rounds** Knit.

**Round 4** Inc 1 into every 2nd st in round (24 sts).

**Round 6** K1, inc 1 into next st then *inc 1 into every 3rd st. Repeat from * to end of round (32 sts).

**Round 8** Inc 1 into every 4th st (40 sts).

**Round 10** K1, inc 1 into next st then *inc 1 into every 5th st. Repeat from * to end of round (48 sts).

**Round 12** Inc 1 into first st then *inc 1 into every 6th st. Repeat from * to end of round (56 sts).

**Round 14** K4, inc 1 into next st then *inc 1 into every 7th st. Repeat from * to end of round (64 sts).

**Round 16** K1, inc 1 into next st then *inc 1 into every 8th st. Repeat from * to end of round (72 sts).

**Round 18** Inc 1 into first st then *inc 1 into every 9th st. Repeat from * to end of round (80 sts).

**Round 20** K5, inc 1 into next st then *inc 1 into every 10th st. Repeat from * to end of round (88 sts). Continue, increasing alternately with previous round.

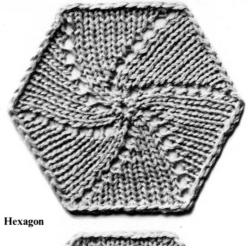

**Hexagon**

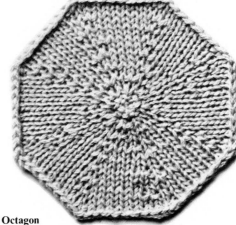

**Octagon**

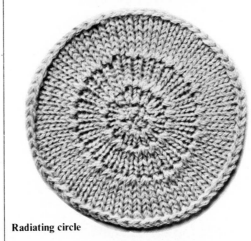

**Radiating circle**

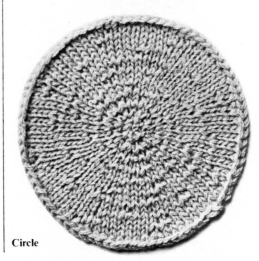

**Circle**

## Making a medallion in sections

### Circle made in sections on two needles

This medallion is made section by section with work being "turned" at regular intervals before the end of the row. When the directions say "turn, leaving 2 sts" this means that these two stitches are not worked. In order to prevent a gap forming where stitches have been left the following method has evolved:

Slip one of the two last stitches from the left to the right needle without knitting it. Take the yarn around this stitch and to the back, then return the slipped stitch to left needle. Turn and knit back. The yarn wrapped around the stitch fills in the gap.

**Section on needle**

**Complete medallion**

### How to make the medallion

Using the Invisible cast on (page 16) cast on 12 sts on 1 needle.

**Row 1 and all odd-numbered rows** Knit.

**Row 2** Purl. Turn leaving 2 sts.

**Row 4** Purl. Turn leaving 4 sts.

**Row 6** Purl. Turn leaving 6 sts.

**Row 8** Purl. Turn leaving 8 sts.

**Rows 10 to 12** Purl.

This forms one section of the circle. Repeat from row 1 eleven times more to complete the circle. Cast off and join together by grafting (page 85) the last section to the first. A lace edging (page 96) can be worked along the edge at the same time as the circle is being knitted.

# Knitted hat projects

### Plain knitted beret

The beret is worked from the centre of the top outwards in a hexagonal swirl then in again to the headband. It is an extended version of the hexagonal medallion on page 93. The techniques for working medallions, together with a variety of other medallion shapes are shown on pages 92 and 93. Once you understand this beret pattern, any of the medallion shapes could be easily adapted to it.

### Stocking cap

The basic pattern can also be used to make a stocking cap of any length. To do this, stop increasing at the point indicated in the pattern and work round and round without increasing or decreasing until the required length is reached. Instructions are given for working a border of Double moss stitch on the cap.

### Patterned cap

The third version of the pattern is a multi-coloured cap worked in three different stitch patterns. Beginning with the main colour, the hexagonal swirl is then worked in three-colour stripes. The straight part of the cap is worked first in a colour slip pattern and then, in the main colour, in the Chevron and Reversible diagonal knit and purl patterns. Both of these patterns are reversible so that the cap can be worn with the brim folded back if you wish.

## Famous knitted hats

Throughout history, home knitters have produced a wide range of hat styles. Most styles were developed to provide protection against the weather, but others were produced to meet social or religious conventions.

In Tudor England felted knitted caps were an essential part of the wardrobe for the majority of the people, anyone found not wearing one was fined.

The French beret is another type of felted knitting and though not a must by law is worn by men throughout France in preference to any other form of headgear.

**French beret**

Italian caps of the seventeenth century were mostly worn in private by men who had shaved their heads to accommodate the heavy, fashionable wigs of the time.

The Balaclava helmet, invented at the time of the Crimean War was designed to keep the troops warm in Arctic conditions and remains the warmest type of headwear.

**Balaclava helmet**

The Fisherman's roll brim cap, worn throughout the world was also developed as protection against the weather and can be worn pulled down over the ears or rolled back according to the temperature. The Fair Isle beret is a far more decorative version of the roll brim cap having as it does the decorative colourwork crowns, but it too is worn pulled down over the ears in cold weather.

**Fair Isle beret**

**Patterned cap**

**Plain knitted beret with swiss darned motif**

**Stocking cap**

# *Pattern instructions*

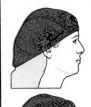

### *Plain beret and stocking cap*

**Yarn** Approximately 75 gm 3-ply wool for beret. Approximately 75 gm 4-ply wool for cap. **Needles** 4 No. 10 (3¼mm) dpns. 4 No. 12 (2¾mm) dpns. **Stitch gauge** 14 sts to 2 inches (5cm). **Measurements** The beret knit with the above stitch gauge will fit a head circumference of 20 inches (51cm). The cap pattern will fit a head circumference of 20 inches. To make the beret or cap larger or smaller you could vary the stitch gauge. Cast 12 sts onto three No. 10 (3¼mm) needles, 4 on each needle, and knit with a fourth. The knit cast on page 17 is preferable. Leave a long end of yarn to draw up central hole afterwards.
**Rd 1** Knit. **Rd 2** MIB into first and 3rd sts on each needle (knit all other sts). **Rd 3** MIB into first and 4th sts on each needle. **Rd 4** MIB into first and 5th sts on each needle. **Rd 5** MIB into first and 6th sts on each needle. **Rds 6 to 14** Continue increasing in this way in every round (**Rd 6** Increase into first and 7th sts. **Rd 7** Increase into first and 8th sts, etc.) until there are 30 sts on each needle, 90 sts in the ground. **Rd 15** Knit all odd rounds until Rd 50. **Rd 16** MIB into first and 16th sts on each needle. **Rd 18** MIB into first and 17th sts on each needle. **Rd 20** MIB into first and 18th sts on each needle, 90 sts in the ground. **Rds 22 to 49** Knit odd rounds plain and increase this way on even rounds (**Rd 22** Increase into first and 19th sts, **Rd 24** Increase into first and 20th sts etc). **For stocking cap** stop increasing when there are **144 sts** in the round. Work round in Double moss stitch pattern (page 23) to required length. Finish with 5 rounds of ribbing, k1, p1 using No. 12 (2¾ mm) dpns and then cast off. **For beret** continue increasing until there are 64 sts on each needle, 192 sts in the round, then proceed as follows. **Rds 50 to 58** Knit. **Rd 59** Knit 30, k2tog, knit to last 2 sts on needle, k2tog, on each needle. **Rd 60** Knit all even-numbered rounds until Rd 76. **Rd 61** K29, k2tog, knit to last 2 sts on needle, k2tog, on each needle. **Rd 63** K28, k2tog, knit to last 2 sts on needle, k2tog, on each needle. **Rd 65** K27, k2tog, knit to last 2 sts on needle, k2tog, on each needle. **Rds 67 to 75** Continue knitting all even rounds and decreasing in this way on odd rounds (**Rd 67** K26, k2tog, knit to last 2 sts, k2tog. **Rd 69** K25, k2tog, knit to last 2 sts, k2tog, etc.) until there are 46 sts on each needle, 138 in the round. **Rds 76 to 79** Using No. 12 (2¾ mm) dpns *k1, p1, rep from * to end of round. **Rd 80** Cast off all sts. **To finish off**, block the beret into a flat round shape. A good idea for pressing is to cut a piece of card the size of the beret and stretch the beret over this and block it.

### *Patterned cap*

**Yarn** 3 × 25 gm balls 3-ply wool in main colour A. Oddments of 3-ply wool (slightly less than colours B, C and D. **Needles** 4 No. 8 (4 mm) dpns. **Stitch gauge** 14 sts to 2 inches (5 cm) over st-st stripes. **Measurements** The cap will fit a head circumference of 20 inches (51 cm). By working the hexagonal swirl longer until there are the required number of stitches in the round the cap can be made larger. But the number of stitches must be a multiple of 8 stitches in order to suit the Chevron stripes, the Chevron and the Reversible diagonal patterns.

The pattern for this cap is the same as for plain cap above with the following additions to the instructions. Cast on in colour A and work the first few rounds of the pattern. Then continue working the hexagonal swirl but in stripes in 3 colours (B, C and D). Work in stripes until there are 144 stitches in the round. At the beginning of the next round begin working the Chevron stripes pattern. (See page 52 in colour slip glossary.) Remember that this cap is knit in rounds and not rows, therefore when applying a pattern which is written for rows the pattern must be read differently. All right side rows read the same but wrong side rows should be read from the end of the row to the beginning and all knit stitches should be read as purl stitches and all purl stitches as knit stitches.

Work the Chevron stripes pattern with colours B, C and D for 2 inches (5 cm). Then begin working Chevron pattern (see page 25 in knit and purl glossary) with colour A. This is a reversible knit and purl pattern and this edge can therefore be worn folded up or unfolded. Work to the desired length and finish off with 12 rounds of Reversible diagonal pattern (see page 24 in the knit and purl glossary). Cast off.

## *Measuring for hats*

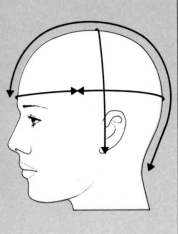

The beret and caps have been worked so that they fit a head circumference of 20 inches (51 cm). The size can be adjusted by altering the stitch gauge; or in the caps, by working the hexagonal swirl to a greater or lesser extent.

To calculate the size for a hat or cap: measure around the head at the widest part to obtain the circumference. Measure across the top of the head from ear tip to ear tip and from mid-forehead to the base of the skull to obtain the diameter.

### *Making the Swiss darned motif*

The beret is decorated with a simple motif worked in Swiss darning on each of the six segments. The chart for the motif is shown (below). For an explanation on how to work Swiss darning, see page 65.

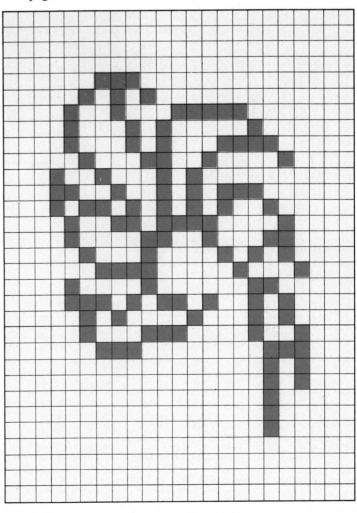

# Lace edgings and borders

Lacy edgings and borders are a beautiful way of finishing off a piece of knitting or of trimming household linen and clothes. Edgings are knitted vertically and can be sewn to the edges of woven fabrics as well as attached to knitting. Borders are knitted horizontally and are often worked as an integral part of the main body of the knitting. These patterns look best knitted in fine crochet cotton or 2-ply wool on No.14 (2mm) needles.

## Making a picot edge

The picot cast on edge is the simplest of all the knitted edgings. It is quick to work and makes a neat and delicate looped edging. The loops formed along the side can be picked up and used to knit the main fabric.

### How to make the edge

**1** *Make a slip loop and knit 1 stitch. Then take the yarn over (yo) the right needle to make an edge stitch.*

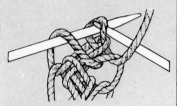

**2** *Slip the first stitch purlwise off the left needle and on the right needle.*

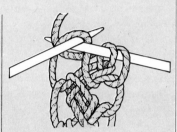

**3** *Knit 1 stitch in the usual way. Then pass the slipped stitch over.*

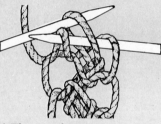

**4** *The complete pattern reads: K1, \*yo, sl 1 pwise, k1, psso\*. Repeat from \* for the required length of the picot edging strip.*

### Attaching a lace edging to knitting

The main body of the knitting can be worked directly from an edging by picking up stitches as shown below.

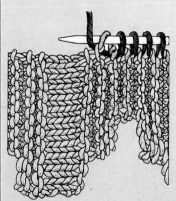

### How to attach the edge

Knit the lace edging to the required length and cast off. With the yarn to be used for the main body of the knitting held at the back of the edging, insert the knitting needle between each row, from front to back.

Draw a loop of yarn through to form a stitch. Continue until the required number have been cast on ready to begin the main body of work.

## Leaf edging

Cast on 8 sts.

**Row 1** (RS) K5, yo, k1, yo, k2.
**Row 2** P6, knit into front and back of next st (inc), k3.
**Row 3** K4, p1, k2, yo, k1, yo, k3.
**Row 4** P8, inc in next st, k4.
**Row 5** K4, p2, k3, yo, k1, yo, k4.
**Row 6** P10, inc in next st, k5.
**Row 7** K4, p3, k4, yo, k1, yo, k5.
**Row 8** P12, inc in next st, k6.
**Row 9** K4, p4, sl 1, k1, psso, k7, k2 tog, k1.
**Row 10** P10, inc in next st, k7.
**Row 11** K4, p5, sl 1, k1, psso, k5, k2 tog, k1.
**Row 12** P8, inc in next st, k2, p1, k5.
**Row 13** K4, p1, k1, p4, sl 1, k1, psso, k3, k2 tog, k1.
**Row 14** P6, inc in next st, k3, p1, k5.
**Row 15** K4, p1, k1, p5, sl 1, k1, psso, k1, k2 tog, k1.
**Row 16** P4, inc in next st, k4, p1, k5.
**Row 17** K4, p1, k1, p6, sl 1, k2 tog, psso, k1.
**Row 18** P2 tog, cast off next 5 sts using p2 tog st to cast off first st; p3, k4.
Repeat rows 1 to 18.

## Garter stitch point

Cast on 2 sts.

| Row 1 K2. |
| Row 2 Yo, k2. |
| Row 3 Yo, k3. |
| Row 4 Yo, k4. |
| Row 5 Yo, k5. |
| Row 6 Yo, k6. |
| Row 7 Yo, k7. |
| Row 8 Yo, k8. |
| Row 9 Yo, k9. |
| Row 10 Yo, k10. |
| Row 11 Yo, k11. |
| Row 12 Yo, k12. |
| Row 13 Yo, k13. |
| Row 14 Yo, k14. |

Break yarn and leave the finished point at the non-working end of the needle. On the same needle, cast on 2 sts and work another point the same as the first 14 rows. Continue until there are as many points as desired on the needle or on stitch holders; do not break yarn upon completing the last one. Turn and knit across all sts on needle, joining all points together; then work a few more rows of garter stitch to complete border. To finish, weave all loose ends of yarn through border.

## Faggot and scallop

Cast on 13 sts.

**Row 1** *(WS) and all other WS rows* K2, purl to last 2 sts, k2.
**Row 2** K7, yo, sl 1, k1, psso, yo, k4.
**Row 4** K6, (yo, sl 1, k1, psso) twice, yo, k4.
**Row 6** K5, (yo, sl 1, k1, psso) 3 times, yo, k4.
**Row 8** K4, (yo, sl 1, k1, psso) 4 times, yo, k4.
**Row 10** K3, (yo, sl 1, k1, psso), 5 times, yo, k4.
**Row 12** K4, (yo, sl 1, k1, psso) 5 times, k2 tog, k2.
**Row 14** K5, (yo, sl 1, k1, psso) 4 times, k2 tog, k2.
**Row 16** K6, (yo, sl 1, k1, psso) 3 times, k2 tog, k2.
**Row 18** K7, (yo, sl 1, k1, psso) twice, k2 tog, k2.
**Row 20** K8, yo, sl 1, k1, psso, k2 tog, k2.
Repeat rows 1 to 20.

## *Pinnacle edging*

Cast on 8 sts and knit one row.
**Row 1** Sl 1, k1, (yo, k2 tog) twice, yo, k2.
**Row 2** K2, yo, k2, (yo, k2 tog) twice, k1.
**Row 3** Sl 1, k1, (yo, k2 tog) twice, yo, k2.
**Row 4** K2, yo, k4, (yo, k2 tog) twice, k1.
**Row 5** Sl 1, k1, (yo, k2 tog) twice, k4, yo, k2.
**Row 6** K2, yo, k6, (yo, k2 tog) twice, k1.

**Row 7** Sl 1, k1, (yo, k2 tog) twice, k6, yo, k2.
**Row 8** K2, yo, k8, (yo, k2 tog) twice, k1.
**Row 9** Sl 1, k1, (yo, k2 tog) twice, k8, yo, k2.
**Row 10** K2, yo, k10, (yo, k2 tog) twice, k1.
**Row 11** Sl 1, k1, (yo, k2 tog) twice, k10, yo, k2.
**Row 12** Cast off 11 sts, k2, (yo, k2 tog) twice, k1.
Repeat rows 1 to 12.

## *Castle edging*

Cast on 6 sts.
**Rows 1, 2 and 3** Knit.
**Row 4** Cast on 3 sts, knit.
**Rows 5, 6 and 7** Knit.
**Row 8** Cast on 3 sts, knit.
**Rows 9, 11, 13, 14 and 15** Knit.

**Rows 10 and 12** Purl.
**Row 16** Cast off 3 sts, knit.
**Rows 17, 18 and 19** Knit.
**Row 20** Cast off 3 sts, knit.
Repeat rows 1 to 20.

## *Ripple and cube*

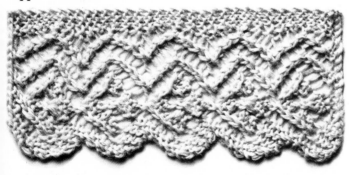

Cast on 17 sts and knit one row.
**Row 1** (RS) K4, (yo, k1, k2 tog) twice, yo, k3, yo, k4.
**Row 2** K4, yo, k5, (yo, p2 tog, k1) twice, yo, k4.
**Row 3** K4, (yo, k1, k2 tog) twice, k1, yo, sl 1, k1, psso, k1, k2 tog, yo, k4.
**Row 4** K4, yo, k3, yo, p3 tog, yo, k3, (yo, p2 tog, k1) twice, yo, k4.
**Row 5** K5, k2 tog, yo, k1, k2 tog, yo, k11, yo, k4.
**Row 6** K2 tog, k3, yo, p2 tog, k1, p2 tog-b, yo, k1, yo, p2 tog, k1, p2 tog-b, (yo, k1, p2 tog) twice, k4.
**Row 7** K4, (yo, sl 1, k1, psso,

k1) twice, yo, sl 1, k2 tog, psso, yo, k3, yo, k3 tog, yo, k3, k2 tog.
**Row 8** K2 tog, k3, yo, p2 tog, k3, p2 tog-b, (yo, k1, p2 tog-b) twice, yo, k2 tog, k3.
**Row 9** K3, k2 tog, yo, sl 1, k1, psso, (k1, yo, sl 1, k1, psso) twice, k1, k2 tog, yo, k3, k2 tog.
**Row 10** K2 tog, k3, yo, p3 tog, (yo, k1, p2 tog-b) twice, yo, k2 tog, k3.
**Row 11** K3, k2 tog, yo, sl 1, k1, psso, yo, sl 1, k1, psso, k2, yo, k3, k2 tog.
**Row 12** K2 tog, k3, yo, k1, (yo, p2 tog, k1) twice, yo, k4.
Repeat rows 1 to 12.

## *Peak edging*

Cast on 17 sts and knit one row.
**Section A** of pattern: K2, k1-b, yo, k1, p2 tog, (yo) twice, (p2 tog) twice, yo. (10 stitches increased to 11.)
**Section B** of pattern: K2, p2 tog, yo, (p2 tog) twice, (yo) twice, p2 tog, yo, p2 tog. (12 stitches decreased to 11.)
**Row 1** (RS) K4, yo, p2 tog, k2, yo, k2, p1, k3, yo, k1-b, k2.
**Row 2** A, k5, yo, p2 tog, k2.
**Row 3** (K4, yo, p2 tog) twice, k1, p1, k3, yo, k1-b, k2.
**Row 4** A, k7, yo, p2 tog, k2.
**Row 5** K4, yo, p2 tog, k6, yo, p2 tog, k1, p1, k3, yo, k1-b, k2.
**Row 6** A, k9, yo, p2 tog, k2.
**Row 7** K4, yo, p2 tog, k5, k2 tog, yo, k1, yo, p2 tog, k1, p1, k3, yo, k1-b, k2.
**Row 8** A, k3, yo, p2 tog, k6, yo, p2 tog, k2.
**Row 9** K4, yo, p2 tog, k3, k2 tog, yo, k5, yo, p2 tog, k1, p1, k3, yo, k1-b, k2.
**Row 10** A, k7, yo, p2 tog, k4, yo, p2 tog, k2.
**Row 11** K4, yo, p2 tog, k1, k2 tog, yo, k9, yo, k3, p1, k3, yo, k1-b, k2.
**Row 12** K2, k1-b, yo, k1, p2

tog, (yo) twice, p2 tog, p3 tog, yo, k1, (yo, p2 tog, k2) twice.
**Row 13** K4, yo, p2 tog, k2, yo, sl 1, k1, psso, k7, k2 tog, yo, k4, p1, p2 tog, yo, p2 tog, k2.
**Row 14** K2, p2 tog, yo, (p2 tog) twice, (yo) twice, p2 tog, k1, yo, p2 tog, k5, p2 tog-b, yo, k5, yo, p2 tog, k2.
**Row 15** K4, yo, p2 tog, k4, yo, sl 1, k1, psso, k3, k2 tog, yo, k1, p2 tog, k1, p1, p2 tog, yo, p2 tog, k2.
**Row 16** B, k1, p2 tog-b, yo, k7, yo, p2 tog, k2.
**Row 17** K4, yo, p2 tog, k6, yo, k3 tog, yo, k3, p1, p2 tog, yo, p2 tog, k2.
**Row 18** B, k8, yo, p2 tog, k2.
**Row 19** K4, yo, p2 tog, k5, k2 tog, yo, k3, p1, p2 tog, yo, p2 tog, k2.
**Row 20** B, k6, yo, p2 tog, k2.
**Row 21** K4, yo, p2 tog, k3, k2 tog, yo, k3, p1, p2 tog, yo, p2 tog, k2.
**Row 22** B, k4, yo, p2 tog, k2.
**Row 23** K4, yo, p2 tog, k1, k2 tog, yo, k3, p1, p2 tog, yo, p2 tog, k2.
**Row 24** B, k2, yo, p2 tog, k2.
Repeat rows 1 to 24.

## *Seashore edging*

Cast on 13 sts.
**Row 1** *and all other odd-numbered rows* K2, purl to last 2 sts, k2. (Number of purl sts will vary on different rows.)
**Row 2** Sl 1, k3, yo, k5, yo, k2 tog, yo, k2.
**Row 4** Sl 1, k4, sl 1, k2 tog, psso, k2, (yo, k2 tog) twice, k1.
**Row 6** Sl 1, k3, sl 1, k1, psso, k2, (yo, k2 tog) twice, k1.
**Row 8** Sl 1, k2, sl 1, k1, psso, k2, (yo, k2 tog) twice, k1.
**Row 10** Sl 1, k1, sl 1, k1, psso,

k2, (yo, k2 tog) twice, k1.
**Row 12** K1, sl 1, k1, psso, k2, yo, k1, yo, k2 tog, yo, k2.
**Row 14** Sl 1, (k3, yo) twice, k2 tog, yo, k2.
Repeat rows 1 to 14.

97

## Partridge edging

**Notes** Cable needle required. DL Drop Loop: drop the yo of previous row off needle. Inc. increase: knit into front and back of the same st (in this pattern it will be a yo of previous row).

Cast on 2 and cast off 2 – Knit first st, leaving it on needle, and place new st on left needle; then knit this st and place next new st on left needle. Then k2 (the 2 new sts) and pass the first st over the second; then knit the third st (the original first st) and pass the second st over it. This completes one picot point.

Cast on 18 sts and knit one row.

**Preparation Row** K5, k2 tog, k2, yo, k1, k2 tog, yo, k2 tog, k1, yo, k3.

**Row 1** Sl 1, k2, yo, slip the yo of previous row, k2, inc, k3, sl next 2 sts to cn and hold in front, k3, then k2 from cn, yo, k2 tog, k1.

**Row 2** Cast on 2 and cast off 2, k6, k2 tog, yo, k2 tog, k4, (k1, p1) into both yo loops together, as if they were a single loop, k3.

**Row 3** Sl 1, k1, k2 tog, yo, k2 tog, k10, yo, k2 tog, k1.

**Row 4** K5, (yo, k1) twice, k2 tog, yo, k2 tog, k3, yo, DL, k3.

**Row 5** Sl 1, k2, (k1, p1) into the yo of previous row, k7, inc, k1, inc, k2, yo, k2 tog, k1.

**Row 6** Cast on 2 and cast off 2, k4, yo, k2 tog, k1, k2 tog, k1, yo, (k1, k2 tog, yo, k2 tog) twice, k2.

**Row 7** Sl 1, k2, yo, DL, k6, (yo, k2 tog, k1) 4 times.

**Row 8** K5, (yo, k2 tog, k1) 3 times, yo, k2 tog, k2, (k1, p1) into the yo of previous row, k3.

**Row 9** Sl 1, k1, k2 tog, yo, k2 tog, k5, (yo, k2 tog, k1) 4 times.

**Row 10** Cast on 2 and cast off 2, k4, (yo, k2 tog, k1) 3 times, yo, k2 tog, k2, yo, DL, k3.

**Row 11** Sl 1, k2, (k1, p1) into the yo of previous row, k6, (yo, k2 tog, k1) 4 times.

**Row 12** K5, (yo, k2 tog, k1) 4 times, k2 tog, yo, k2 tog, k2.

**Rows 13 and 15** Repeat rows 7 and 9.

**Row 14** Cast on 2 and cast off 2, k4, (yo, k2 tog, k1) 3 times, yo, k2 tog, (k1, p1) into the yo of previous row, k3.

**Row 16** K5, (yo, k2 tog, k1) 3 times, yo, k2 tog, k2, yo, DL, k3.

**Row 17** Sl 1, k2, (k1, p1) into the yo of previous row, k6, yo, (k2 tog, k1) twice, (yo, k2 tog, k1) twice.

**Row 18** Cast on 2 and cast off 2, k4, yo, k2 tog, k1, k2 tog, yo, k2 tog, k1, yo, k3, k2 tog, yo, k2 tog, k2.

**Row 19** Sl 1, k2, yo, DL, k7, yo, k2 tog, k2, (yo, k2 tog, k1) twice.

**Row 20** K5, yo, (k2 tog) twice, yo, k2 tog, k5, (k1, p1) into the yo of previous row, k3.

**Row 21** Sl 1, k1, k2 tog, yo, k2 tog, k7, (k2 tog, k1) twice, yo, k2 tog, k1.

**Row 22** K5, k2 tog, k2, yo, k1, k2 tog, yo, k2 tog, k1, yo, DL, k3.

Repeat rows 1 to 22.

## Diagonal picot

Cast on 17 sts and knit one row.

**Row 1** Sl 1, k1, yo, k2 tog, yo, k1, yo, (k2 tog) twice, (yo) twice, (k2 tog) twice, yo, k1, yo, k3.

**Row 2** Sl 1, k8, p1, k9.

**Row 3** Sl 1, k1, yo, k2 tog, yo, k2, yo, k2 tog, k4, k2 tog, yo, k2, yo, k3.

**Row 4** Sl 1, k20.

**Row 5** Sl 1, k1, yo, k2 tog, yo, k3, yo, k2 tog, k4, k2 tog, (yo, k3) twice.

**Row 6** Sl 1, k22.

**Row 7** Sl 1, k7, yo, (k2 tog) twice, (yo) twice, (k2 tog) twice, yo, k1, yo, k2 tog, k1, yo, k3.

**Row 8** Sl 1, k11, p1, k11.

**Row 9** Cast off 3, k4, yo, k2 tog, k4, k2 tog, yo, k2, yo, k2 tog, k1, yo, k3

**Row 10** Sl 1, k21.

**Row 11** Sl 1, k1, yo, k2 tog, yo, k1, yo, k2 tog, k4, k2 tog, yo, k3, yo, k2 tog, k1, yo, k3.

**Row 12** Sl 1, k23.

**Row 13** Sl 1, k1, yo, k2 tog, yo, k2, yo, (k2 tog) twice, (yo) twice, (k2 tog) twice, yo, k1, (yo, k2 tog, k1) twice, yo, k3.

**Row 14** Sl 1, k14, p1, k10.

**Row 15** Sl 1, k1, yo, k2 tog, yo, k3, yo, k2 tog, k4, k2 tog, yo, k2, (yo, k2 tog, k1) twice, yo, k3.

**Row 16** Sl 1, k27.

**Row 17** Sl 1, k7, yo, k2 tog, k4, k2 tog, yo, k3, (yo, k2 tog, k1) twice, yo, k3.

**Row 18** Sl 1, k28.

**Row 19** Cast off 3, k4, yo, (k2 tog) twice, (yo) twice, (k2 tog) twice, yo, k1 (yo, k2 tog, k1) 3 times, yo, k3.

**Row 20** Sl 1, k17, p1, k8.

**Row 21** Sl 1, k1, yo, k2 tog, yo, k1, yo, k2 tog, k4, k2 tog, yo, k2, (yo, k2 tog, k1) 3 times, yo, k3.

**Row 22** Sl 1, k28.

**Row 23** Sl 1, k1, yo, k2 tog, yo, k2, yo, k2 tog, k4, k2 tog, yo, k3, (yo, k2 tog, k1) 3 times, yo, k3.

**Row 24** Sl 1, k30.

**Row 25** Sl 1, k1, yo, k2 tog, yo, k3, yo, (k2 tog) twice, (yo) twice, (k2 tog) twice, yo, k1, (yo, k2 tog, k1) 4 times, yo, k3.

**Row 26** Sl 1, k20, p1, k11.

**Row 27** Sl 1, k7, yo, k2 tog, k4, k2 tog, yo, k2, (yo, k2 tog, k1) 4 times, yo, k3.

**Row 28** Sl 1, k33.

**Row 29** Cast off 3, k4, yo, k2 tog, k4, k2 tog, yo, k18.

**Row 30** Cast off 14 (loosely), k16.

Repeat rows 1 to 30.

## Christmas tree

Cast on 16 sts and knit one row.

**Row 1** Yo, k2 tog, k1, yo, k10, yo, k2 tog, k1.

**Row 2** K2, yo, k2 tog, k12, p1.

**Row 3** Yo, k2 tog, k1, yo, k2 tog, yo, k9, yo, k2 tog, k1.

**Row 4** K2, yo, k2 tog, k13, p1.

**Row 5** Yo, k2 tog, k1, (yo, k2 tog) twice, yo, k8, yo, k2 tog, k1.

**Row 6** K2, yo, k2 tog, k14, p1.

**Row 7** Yo, k2 tog, k1, (yo, k2 tog) 3 times, yo, k7, yo, k2 tog, k1.

**Row 8** K2, yo, k2 tog, k15, p1.

**Row 9** Yo, k2 tog, k1, (yo, k2 tog) 4 times, yo, k6, yo, k2 tog, k1.

**Row 10** K2, yo, k2 tog, k16, p1.

**Row 11** Yo, k2 tog, k1, (yo, k2 tog) 5 times, yo, k5, yo, k2 tog, k1.

**Row 12** K2, yo, k2 tog, k17, p1.

**Row 13** Yo, k2 tog, k1, (yo, k2 tog) 6 times, yo, k4, yo, k2 tog, k1.

**Row 14** K2, yo, k2 tog, k18, p1.

**Row 15** Yo, k2 tog, k1, (yo, k2 tog) 7 times, yo, k3, yo, k2 tog, k1.

**Row 16** K2, yo, k2 tog, k19, p1.

**Row 17** Yo, (k2 tog) twice, (yo, k2 tog) 7 times, k3, yo, k2 tog, k1.

**Rows 18, 20, 22, 24, 26, 28, 30** Repeat rows 14, 12, 10, 8, 6, 4 and 2.

**Row 19** Yo, (k2 tog) twice, (yo, k2 tog) 6 times, k4, yo, k2 tog, k1.

**Row 21** Yo, (k2 tog) twice, (yo, k2 tog) 5 times, k5, yo, k2 tog, k1.

**Row 23** Yo, (k2 tog) twice, (yo, k2 tog) 4 times, k6, yo, k2 tog, k1.

**Row 25** Yo, (k2 tog) twice, (yo, k2 tog) 3 times, k7, yo, k2 tog, k1.

**Row 27** Yo, (k2 tog) twice, (yo, k2 tog) twice, k8, yo, k2 tog, k1.

**Row 29** Yo, (k2 tog) twice, yo, k2 tog, k9, yo, k2 tog, k1.

**Row 31** Yo, (k2 tog) twice, k10, yo, k2 tog, k1.

**Row 32** K2, yo, k2 tog, k11, p1.

Repeat rows 1 to 32.

## Diamond eyelet

Cast on 17 sts.

**Note:** Yo2, a double yo. All single purl sts on even-numbered rows go into the *second* loop of a double yo made on a preceding row.

**Row 1** K3, (yo, p2 tog) twice, k10.

**Row 2** K12, (yo, p2 tog) twice, k1.

**Row 3** K3, (yo, p2 tog) twice, k6, k2 tog, yo2, k1, inc in last st.

**Row 4** K4, p1, k9, (yo, p2 tog) twice, k1.

**Row 5** K3, (yo, p2 tog) twice, k4, k2 tog, yo2, (k2 tog) twice, yo2, k1, inc in last st.

**Row 6** K4, p1, k3, p1, k7, (yo, p2 tog) twice, k1.

**Row 7** K3, (yo, p2 tog) twice, k2, k2 tog, yo2, (k2 tog) twice, [yo2, (k2 tog) twice] twice, yo2, k1, inc in last st.

**Row 8** K4, (p1, k3) twice, p1, k5, (yo, p2 tog) twice, k1.

**Row 9** K3, (yo, p2 tog) twice, k2 tog, [yo2, (k2 tog) twice] 3 times, yo2, k2 tog.

**Row 10** K2, (p1, k3) 4 times, (yo, p2 tog) twice, k1.

**Row 11** K3, (yo, p2 tog) twice, k2, k2 tog, [yo2, (k2 tog) twice] 3 times.

**Row 12** K2 tog, k1, (p1, k3) twice, p1, k5, (yo, p2 tog) twice, k1.

**Row 13** K3, (yo, p2 tog) twice, k4, k2 tog, [yo2, (k2 tog) twice] twice.

**Row 14** K2 tog, k1, p1, k3, p1, k7, (yo, p2 tog) twice, k1.

**Row 15** K3, (yo, p2 tog) twice, k6, k2 tog, yo2, (k2 tog) twice.

**Row 16** K2 tog, k1, p1, k9, (yo, p2 tog) twice, k1.

Repeat rows 1 to 16.

## Faggot and diamond

Cast on 34 sts and knit one row.

**Row 1** Sl 1, k3, yo, sl 1, k1, psso, k3, k2 tog, yo, p3, yo, sl 1, k1, psso, k3, k2 tog, yo, sl 1, k1, psso, (yo, k2 tog) 6 times, k1.

**Row 2** Sl 1, k23, p5, k3, (k1, p1) in next st, k1.

**Row 3** Sl 1, k5, yo, sl 1, k1, psso, k1, k2 tog, yo, p5, yo, sl 1, k1, psso, k3, (yo, k2 tog) 6 times, k2.

**Row 4** Sl 1, k24, p3, k5, (k1, p1) in next st, k1.

**Row 5** Sl 1, k7, yo, sl 1, k2 tog, psso, yo, p7, yo, sl 1, k1, psso, k3, (yo, k2 tog) 6 times, k1.

**Row 6** Sl 1, k25, p1, k7, (k1, p1) in next st, k1.

**Row 7** Sl 1, k6, k2 tog, yo, k3, yo, p2 tog, p3, p2 tog-b, yo, k3, k2 tog, yo, k1-b, (yo, k2 tog) 5 times, k2.

**Row 8** Sl 1, k24, p3, k6, k2 tog, k1.

**Row 9** Sl 1, k4, k2 tog, yo, k5, yo, p2 tog, p1, p2 tog-b, yo, k3, k2 tog, yo, k1-b, (yo, k2 tog) 6 times, k1.

**Row 10** Sl 1, k23, p5, k4, k2 tog, k1.

**Row 11** Sl 1, k2, k2 tog, yo, k7, yo, p3 tog, yo, k3, k2 tog, yo, k1-b, (yo, k2 tog) 6 times, k2.

**Row 12** Sl 1, k21, p7, k2, k2 tog, k2.

Repeat rows 1 to 12.

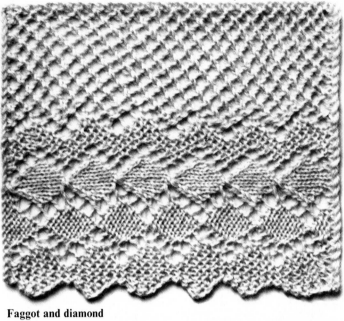

**Faggot and diamond**

**Partridge edging**

**Diagonal Picot**

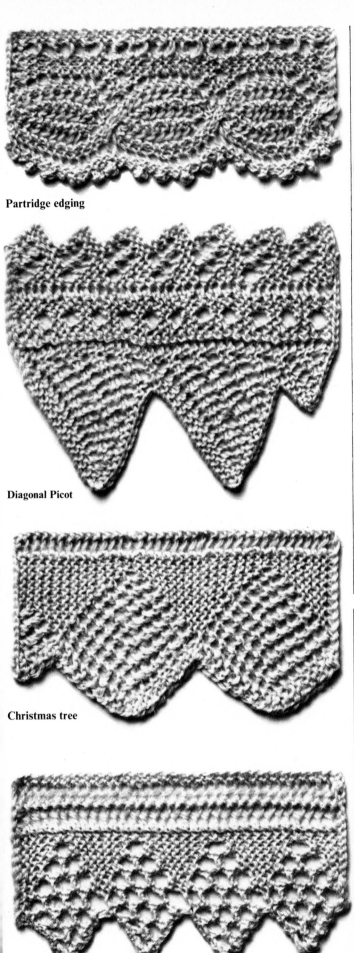

**Christmas tree**

**Diamond eyelet**

### *Purl scallop edging*

**Step 1** Foundation—Knit 8 rows stocking stitch

**Step 2** Work in reverse stocking stitch (knit on the wrong side, purl on the right side) for *twice* the desired width of border. Do not cast off.

**Step 3** Fold border in half with the purl side out. Break yarn, leaving a long end.

**Step 4** On the wrong side of work, sew stitches off needle one by one, attaching each stitch to the corresponding stitch in foundation row. At even intervals (i.e. every 8th stitch or every 10th stitch) pass sewing strand over the top of border and pull tight to form scallop.

## *Victorian pattern sampler*

Instead of writing down stitch patterns, as is common today, Victorian needlewomen knitted their patterns for reference. Pattern squares were made and joined together to form decorative stitch samplers.

# *Making a traditional shawl*

Traditional Shetland shawls are worked using an edging pattern, a border pattern and a central square pattern. They have neither cast on nor cast off edges, are worked from the outside inwards and were originally as light as gossamer when knitted with handspun yarn as fine as human hair. Today they are made either in fine Shetland 2-ply for babies or soft fleecy Shetland 4-ply for warmer shawls.

The construction is always the same. It is made on very fine long wire needles and is worked in the following way: a small number of stitches are cast on and a scalloped edging worked for the shawl. When the edging is completed, the stitches along the straight edge are picked up to form the base of the inner border. The border pattern is knitted and then decreased at the sides to form mitred edges. It is completed with a line of eyelet holes and the central square panel is started. The central panel is often knitted in garter stitch, although it can be in any stitch pattern as long as it forms a perfect square. The Shetlander's golden rule is to knit as many double rows as there are stitches on the needle.

When the square is completed a second set of needles is used to knit up a second edging and border in exactly the same way. When completed, this edging, instead of being finished with a row of eyelet holes is grafted to the central square. This makes an openwork pattern very similar to the eyelet holes.

The third and fourth edging and border are worked in exactly the same way. The edging for this shawl is knitted in one long strip, then folded in four. Two borders are knitted, followed by the central panel and then the remaining two borders. When the shawl is completed, the mitred corners remain to be joined together. The shawl is then washed gently.

## *Making up*

Lay all the pieces flat. Graft together with a herringbone stitch the 2 mitred corners of the border (where B joins C, and where D joins A). Then join together the stitches from the remaining 3 edges of the border to the 3 sides of the centre panel. Pin out and block.

## *Materials and measurements*

**Yarn** 7 × 25 gm balls 2-ply Shetland wool. **Needles** 2 pairs extra long No. 8 (4 mm). **Measurements** Finished shawl approx. 44 inches (111 cm) square.

## *The edging pattern*

Edging pattern is worked 65 times. Cast on 9 sts. **Row 1** K3 (yo, k2tog) twice, yo, k2. **Row 2** and all even numbered rows knit. **Row 3** K3, (yo, k2tog) twice, yo, k3. **Row 5** K3, (yo, k2tog) twice, yo, k4. **Row 7** K3, (yo, k2tog) twice, yo, k5. **Row 9** K3, (yo, k2tog) twice, yo, k6. **Row 11** K3, (yo, k2tog) twice, yo, k7. **Row 13** K3, (yo, k2tog) twice, yo, k8. **Row 15** Cast off 7 sts loosely, k to end. **Row 16** Knit. Repeat rows 1 to 16 64 times – 65 in all – ending on row 15. Cast off all sts. Sew two ends together. Fold edging into 4. Pick up sts for border sections (see page 96) on these 4 lengths of edging in 2 parts i.e. sides A and B then C and D so knitting 2 sections of the border at the same time.

## *The border pattern*

Around two sides of edging pick up 261 sts; i.e. 129 sts along side A; 3 sts for herringbone mitre; 129 sts. along side B. **Row 1** K16, (yo, k4tog, yo, k27) 3 times, yo, k4tog, yo, k16, k1, yo, k2tog, k16, (yo, k4tog, yo, k27) 3 times, yo, k4tog, yo, k16. **Row 2** And all even-numbered rows k to centre 3 sts, (mitred corner) k1, yo, k2tog, k to end. **Row 3** *K14, (k2tog, yo, k3, yo, k2tog, k23) 3 times, k2tog, yo, k3, yo, k2tog, k14**; k1, yo, k2tog, rep from * to **. **Row 5** *K13, (k2tog, yo, k5, yo, k2tog, k21) 3 times, k2tog, yo, k5, yo, k2tog, k13**; k1, yo, k2tog; rep from * to **. **Row 7** *K12, (k2tog, yo, k2, yo, k3tog, yo, k2, yo, k2tog, k19) 3 times, k2tog, yo, k2, yo, k3tog, yo, k2, yo, k2tog, k12**, k1, yo, k2tog; rep from * to **. **Row 9** *K11, (k2tog, yo, k1, k2tog, yo, k3, yo, k2tog, k1, yo, k2tog, k17) 3 times, k2tog, yo, k1, k2tog, yo, k3, yo, k2tog, k1, yo, k2tog, k11**, k1, yo, k2tog; rep from * to **. **Row 11** *K10, (k2tog, yo, k1, k2tog, yo, k5, yo, k2tog, k1, yo, k2tog, k15) 3 times, k2tog, yo, k1, k2tog, yo, k5, yo, k2tog, k1, yo, k2tog, k10**, k1, yo, k2tog; rep from * to **. **Row 13** *K9, (k2tog, yo, k1, k2tog, yo, k2, yo, k3tog, yo, k2*, yo, k2tog, k1, yo, k2tog, k13) 3 times, k2tog, yo, k1, k2tog, yo, k2, yo, k3tog, yo, k2, yo, k2tog, k9**, k1, yo, k2tog; rep from * to **. **Row 15** *K8, ([k2tog, yo, k1] twice, k2tog, yo, k3, yo, k2tog, [k1, yo, k2tog] twice, k11) 3 times (k2tog, yo, k1) twice, k2tog, yo, k3, yo, k2tog, (k1, yo, k2tog) twice, k8**, k1, yo, k2tog; rep from * to **. **Row 17** *K7, ([k2tog, yo, k1] twice, k2tog, yo, k5, yo, k2tog, [k1, yo, k2tog] twice, k9) 3 times (k2tog, yo, k1) twice, k2tog, yo, k5, yo, k2tog, (k1, yo, k2tog) twice, k7**, k1, yo, k2tog; rep from * to **. **Row 19** *K6 ([k2tog, yo, k1] twice, k2tog, yo, k2, yo, k3tog, yo, k2, yo, k2tog, [k1, yo, k2tog] twice, k7) 3 times (k2tog, yo, k1) twice, k2tog, yo, k2, yo, k3tog, yo, k2, yo, k2tog, (k1, yo, k2tog) twice, k6**, k1, yo, k2tog; rep from * to **. **Row 21** *K5, ([k2tog, yo, k1] 3 times, k2tog, yo, k3, yo, k2tog, [k1, yo, k2tog] 3 times, k5) 3 times (k2tog, yo, k1) 3 times, k2tog, yo, k3, yo, k2tog, (k1, yo, k2tog) 3 times, k5**, k1, yo, k2tog; rep from * to **. **Row 23** *K4 ([k2tog, yo, k1] 3 times, k2tog, yo, k5, yo, k2tog, [k1, yo, k2tog] 3 times, k3) 3 times (k2tog, yo, k1) 3 times, k2tog, yo, k5, yo, k2tog (k1, yo, k2tog) 3 times, k4**, k1, yo, k2tog; rep from * to **. **Row 25** *K3 ([k2tog, yo, k1] 3 times, k2tog, yo, k2, yo, k3tog, yo, k2, yo, k2tog, [k1, yo, k2tog] 3 times k1) 3 times (k2tog, yo, k1) 3 times, k2tog, yo, k2, yo, k3tog, yo, k2, yo, k2tog, (k1, yo, k2tog) 3 times, k3**, k1, yo, k2tog; rep from * to **. **Row 27** *K2, k2tog, yo, k1, ([k2tog, yo, k1] 3 times, k2tog, yo, k3, yo, k2tog, [k1, yo, k2tog] 3 times, k1, yo, k3tog, yo, k1) 3 times, (k2tog, yo, k1) 3 times, k2tog, yo, k3, yo, k2tog, (k1, yo, k2tog) 4 times, k2** k1, yo, k2tog; rep from * to **. **Row 29** *K2, k2tog, ([k2tog, yo, k1] 3 times, k2tog, yo, k5, yo, k2tog, [k1, yo, k2tog] 3 times, k3) 3 times, (k2tog, yo, k1) 3 times, k2tog, yo, k5, yo, k2tog, (k1, yo, k2tog) 3 times, k2tog, k2**, k1, yo, k2tog; rep from * to **. **Row 31** *K2, ([k2tog, yo, k1] 3 times, k2tog, yo, k2, yo, k3tog, yo, k2, yo, k2tog, [k1, yo, k2tog] 3 times, k1) 3 times, (k2tog, yo, k1) 3 times, k2tog, yo, k2, yo, k3tog, yo, k2, yo, k2tog, (k1, yo, k2tog) 3 times, k2**, k1, yo, k2tog; rep from * to ** **Row 33** *K2, k2tog, ([k2tog, yo, k1] 3 times, k2tog, yo, k3, yo, k2tog, [k1, yo, k2tog] 3 times, k5) 3 times (k2tog, yo, k1) 3 times, k2tog, yo, k3, yo, k2tog, (k1, yo, k2tog) 3 times, k2tog, k2**, k1, yo, k2tog; rep from * to **. **Row 35** *K2, ([k2tog, yo, k1] 3 times, k2tog, yo, k5, yo, k2tog, [k1, yo, k2tog] 3 times, k3) 3 times, (k2tog, yo, k1) 3 times, k2tog, yo, k5, yo, k2tog, (k1, yo, k2tog) 3 times, k2**, k1, yo, k2tog; rep from * to **. **Row 37** *K2, k2tog, ([k2tog, yo, k1) twice, k2tog, yo, k2, yo, k3tog, yo, k2, yo, k2tog, [k1, yo, k2tog] twice, k7) 3 times,

### The Shetland shawl

*A Shetlander knitted the finished shawl from memory. Centre panel and border motif details.*

**The border pattern continued**

(k2tog, yo, k1) twice, k2tog, yo, k2, yo, k3tog, yo, k2, yo, k2tog, (k1, yo, k2tog) twice, k2tog, k2**, k1, yo, k2tog; rep from * to ** **Row 39** *K2, ([k2tog, yo, k1] 3 times, k2tog, yo, k3, yo, k2tog, [k1, yo, k2tog] 3 times, k5) 3 times, (k2tog, yo, k1) 3 times, k2tog, yo, k3, yo, k2tog, (k1, yo, k2tog) 3 times, k2**, k1, yo, k2tog; rep from * to **. **Row 41** *K2, k2tog, ([k2tog, yo, k1] twice, k2tog, yo, k5, yo, k2tog, [k1, yo, k2tog] twice, k9) 3 times, (k2tog, yo, k1) twice, k2tog, yo, k5, yo, k2tog, (k1, yo, k2tog) twice, k2**, k1, yo, k2tog; rep from * to **. **Row 43** *K2, ([k2tog, yo, k1] twice, k2tog, yo, k2, yo, k3tog, yo, k2, yo, k2tog, [k1, yo, k2tog] twice, k7) 3 times, (k2tog, yo, k1) twice, k2tog, yo, k2, yo, k3tog, yo, k2, yo, k2tog, (k1, yo, k2tog) twice, k2**, k1, yo, k2tog; rep from * to **. **Row 45** *K2, k2tog, ([k2tog, yo, k1] twice, k2tog, yo, k3, yo, k2tog, [k1, yo, k2tog] twice, k11) 3 times, (k2tog, yo, k1) twice, k2tog, yo, k3, yo, k2tog, (k1, yo, k2tog) twice k2tog, k2**, k1, yo, k2tog; rep from * to **. **Row 47** *K2, ([k2tog, yo k1] twice, k2tog, yo, k5, yo, k2tog, [k1, yo, k2tog] twice, k9) 3 times, (k2tog, yo, k1) twice, k2tog, yo, k5, yo, k2tog, (k1, yo, k2tog) twice, k2**, k1, yo, k2tog; rep from * to **. **Row 49** *K2, k2tog, (k2tog, yo, k1, k2tog, yo, k2, k3tog, yo, k2, yo, k2tog, k1, yo, k2tog, k13) 3 times, k2tog, yo, k1, k2tog, yo, k2, yo, k3tog, yo, k2, yo, k2tog, k2tog, k2**, k1, yo, k2tog; rep from * to **. **Row 51** *K2, ([k2tog, yo, k1] twice, k2tog, yo, k3, yo, k2tog, [k1, yo, k2tog] twice, k11) 3 times, (k2tog, yo, k1) twice, k2tog, yo, k3, yo, k2tog, (k1, yo, k2tog) twice, k2**, k1, yo, k2tog; rep from * to **. **Row 53** *K2, k2tog, (k2tog, yo, k1, k2tog, yo, k5, yo, k2tog, k1, yo, k2tog, k15) 3 times, K2tog, yo, k1, k2tog, yo, k5, yo, k2tog, k1, yo, k2tog, k2tog, k2**, k1, yo, k2tog; rep from * to **. **Row 55** *K2, (k2tog, yo, k1, k2tog, yo, k2, yo, k3tog, yo, k2, yo, k2tog, k1, yo, k2tog, k13) 3 times, k2tog, yo, k1, k2tog, yo, k2, yo, k3tog, yo, k2, yo, k2tog, k1, yo, k2tog, k2**, k1, yo, k2tog; rep from * to **. **Row 57** *K2, k2tog, (k2tog, yo, k1, k2tog, yo, k3, yo, k2tog, k1, yo, k2tog, k17) 3 times, k2tog, yo, k1, k2tog, yo, k3, yo, k2tog, k1, yo, k2tog, k2tog, k2**, k1, yo, k2tog; rep from * to **. **Row 59** *K2, (k2tog, yo, k1, k2tog, yo, k5, yo, k2tog, k1, yo, k2tog, k15) 3 times, k2tog, yo, k1, k2tog, yo, k5, yo, k2tog, k1, yo, k2tog, k2**, k1, yo, k2tog; rep from * to ** **Row 61** *K2, k2tog, (k2tog, yo, k2, yo, k3tog, yo, k2, yo, k2tog, k19) 3 times, k2tog, yo, k2, yo, k3tog, yo, k2, yo, k2tog, k2tog, k2**, k1, yo, k2tog; rep from * to ** **Row 63** *K2, (k2tog, yo, k1, k2tog, yo, k3, yo, k2tog, k1, yo, k2tog, k17) 3 times, k2tog, yo, k1, k2tog, yo, k3, yo, k2tog, k1, yo, k2tog, k2**, k1, yo, k2tog; rep from * to **. **Row 65** *K2, (k2tog, yo, k5, yo, k2tog, k21) 3 times, k2tog, yo, k5, yo, k2tog, k2tog, k2**, k1, yo, k2tog; rep from * to **. **Row 67** *K2, (k2tog, yo, k2, yo, k3tog, yo, k2, yo, k2tog, k19) 3 times, k2tog, yo, k2, yo, k3tog, yo, k2, yo, k2tog, k2**, k1, yo, k2tog; rep from * to **. **Row 69** *K4, (k2tog, yo, k3, yo, k2tog, k23) 3 times, k2tog, yo, k3, yo, k2tog, k4**, k1, yo, k2tog; rep from * to **. **Row 71** *K2, k3tog, (yo, k5, yo, k2tog, k21, k2tog) 3 times, yo, k5, yo, k3tog, k2**, k1, yo, k2tog; rep from * to **. **Row 73** *K2, k2tog, (yo, k2tog, k1, k2tog, yo, k25) 3 times, yo, k2tog, k1, k2tog, yo, k2tog, k2**, k1, yo, k2tog; rep from * to **. **Row 75** K2, k2tog, (yo, k3tog, yo, k27) 3 times, yo, k3tog, yo, k2tog, k2 *, k1, yo, k2tog; rep from * to **. **Row 76** K99, k1, yo, k2tog, k99. **Row 77** *K2tog, k2tog, (yo, k2tog) 46 times, k2tog, k1**, k1, yo, k2tog; rep from * to **. 195 sts. **Row 78** (k2tog, yo) 48 times, k1, yo, k2tog, (yo, k2tog) 48 times. End of border – now slip the first 99 sts onto a thread; remaining 96 sts form beginning of central panel. Repeat border pattern along sides C and D of edging leaving all stitches on a thread.

### The centre panel pattern

Starting with 96 sts remaining from side A or border. **Row 1** K7, k2tog, (k2, [yo, k2tog] twice, yo, k1, yo, k2, k3tog, k3, k3tog) 4 times, k2, (k2tog) twice, yo, kl, yo, k2, k2tog, k4. **Row 2** and all even-numbered rows, knit. **Row 3** K6, (k2tog, k2 [yo, k2tog] twice, yo, k3, yo, k2, k2tog, k1) 4 times, k2tog, k2, (yo, k2tog) twice, yo, k3, yo, k2, k2tog, k3. **Row 5** K5, k2tog, (k2, [yo, k2tog] twice, yo, k5, yo, k2, k3tog) 4 times, k2, (yo, k2tog) twice, yo, k5, yo, k2, k2tog, K2. **Row 7** K4, k2tog, k1, (k1, yo, k1, [yo, k2tog] twice, yo, k2, k2tog, k3, k2tog, k1) 4 times, k1, yo, k1, (yo, k2tog) twice, yo, k2, k2tog, k7. **Row 9** K3, k2tog, k2, (yo, k3, [yo, k2tog] twice, yo, k2, k2tog, k1, k2tog, k2) 4 times, yo, k3, (yo, k2tog) twice, yo, k2, k2tog, k6. **Row 11** K2, k2tog, k2, yo, (k5, [yo, k2tog] twice, yo, k2, k3tog, k2, yo) 4 times, k5 (yo, k2tog) twice, yo, k2, k2tog, k5. **Row 13** K6, (k1, k2tog, k2, [yo, k2tog] twice, yo, k1, yo, k2, k2tog, k2) 4 times, k1, k2tog, k2 (yo, k2tog) twice, yo, k1, yo, k2, k2tog, k4. **Row 14** Knit. Now repeat from row 3 (12 row pattern) 15 times (16 repeats in all). Leave sts on a thread.

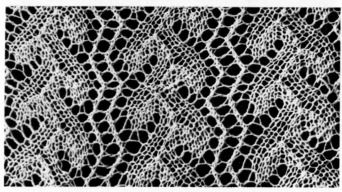

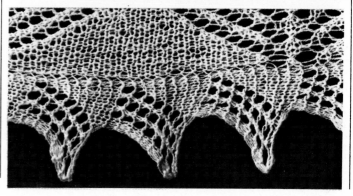

# Machine knitting

*Advantages of machine knitting*

Machine knitting is a craft in its own right and success does not depend on a knowledge of hand knitting. The main advantages of machine knitting over hand knitting are speed and ease of patterning.

### Speedier knitting

Because machine knitting is many times faster than hand knitting, you can experiment without too much loss of time. When uncertain about size, shape or stitch, you can knit up one section so quickly that it is no hardship to unravel and re-knit if necessary. You can knit straight or partly shaped lengths of fabric, and complete the garment with cut-and-sew (page 103). This involves some waste fabric, and is undesirable where every stitch has to be knitted by hand.

Speed means that large projects can be completed in a few days spare time. This greatly widens the scope of what can be knitted—not only outsize garments, long, full skirts and kaftans, but also soft furnishings such as bed spreads, divan covers and curtains. Speed also means that it is practical to use very fine yarns such as industrial synthetics which most hand knitters hesitate to use. With these yarns very fine underwear, cobweb shawls and stoles can be made quickly.

### Ease of patterning

Patterning in hand knitting involves either frequent reference to instructions, memorizing the pattern, or visual checking. With an automatic knitting machine, the knitter can concentrate on the shaping of the garment; the machine, once set, takes care of the stitch pattern. In hand knitting, care must be taken when increasing to work in extra stitches so that the pattern remains correct. In automatic machine knitting, the stitch pattern remains correct even when stitches are increased or decreased. A good knitting machine, in good working order, produces perfect fabric. There will be no variation in tension as may happen even with an experienced hand knitter.

### Method of knitting

The hand knitter has one needle with a number of stitches on it which are gradually knitted off on to a second needle. The machine knitter has a number of needles, each of which holds one stitch. It follows that shaping within the row, which is so common in hand knitting will involve removing the knitting from the machine and replacing it so that some needles hold two stitches. This way of shaping can be avoided, if the shaping is done at each end, or if sections of needles are put into a holding position and shaping is done one section at a time, or by changing the tension or stitch pattern.

A typical knitting machine consists, basically, of a *needle bed*, into which are cut a number (usually between 166 and 200) of *channels or grooves*. Each of these channels holds a *latched needle*. A *cam box* (or carriage) is moved across the needle bed causing selected needles to slide forward. The yarn, the flow of which is controlled by a *mast*, *tension spring* and *tension disc*, is caught in the hook of the needle, held in position by the latch which closes on to the yarn as the needle slides back and pulls the yarn, held in the hook, through the previous stitch to form a new stitch.

This is a simplified explanation of how a knitting machine works, but it should enable even a beginner to work out the solution to some problems which may arise in the early days. For example, it should be obvious that it is essential for the yarn to flow freely, neither too slackly nor too tightly. Therefore, a fault may often be rectified by adjusting the flow of the yarn in accordance with the instructions for the machine. Also, if the machine does not produce perfect stitches it is probably that a needle is broken or bent in such a way that it cannot slide backwards and forwards in its groove, or that a latch is damaged.

### The wool winder

Because the yarn flow is so vital to good machine knitting it is unwise to try to knit from a ball of yarn that has been wound for hand knitters. Most machine knitters nowadays use coned yarn but many types of hand knitting yarn can be used satisfactorily on a knitting machine, as long as the yarn is re-wound into balls which allow it to flow without interuption from the centre of the ball. To re-wind yarns use a *wool winder*.

1  Needle bed
2  Cam box or carriage
3  Channels or grooves
4  Mast
5  Tension spring
6  Tension disc

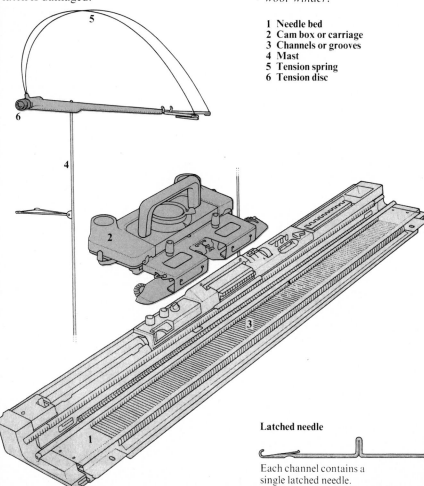

### Latched needle

Each channel contains a single latched needle.

## *Choosing a machine*

There are a number of knitting machines on the market, from the simple to the sophisticated.

Even the simplest machine should knit perfect stocking stitch and mock rib. Semi-automatic and automatic machines offer a much wider stitch variety, including colour work (all-over designs or single motifs), knit-weaving, slip stitch, tuck stitch, plating and lace knitting (either by transferring stitches to adjacent needles or by using a fine thread). Some of the most modern machines use punched cards which make stitch patterns as easy as stocking stitch.

Accessories, such as a ribbing attachment or colour changer, widen the scope of the machine still further and make it possible to produce beautiful fabrics in various textures.

Before making a final choice, ask for a demonstration and check the following points:

**1** Does the cam box move smoothly and easily across the needle bed?

**2** Are stitch patterns produced quickly and easily? Generally speaking, the cheaper the machine the more manual selection will be needed to produce stitch patterns.

**3** How much tuition is available? Will this be private tuition, a postal instruction course, or an instruction book only? The last is enough for the simplest machines, as long as it is a good one. Even if other tuition is provided, look carefully at the instruction book before buying the machine. It should be so clearly illustrated that you should be able to solve small problems with its help.

**4** Does the machine produce even fabric with neat edges?

**5** Does the machine have a holding position which makes it easy to shape necklines, shoulders and sleeve caps?

These points apply whether you buy a new or second-hand machine. Every machine should be thoroughly checked and covered by a guarantee.

## *Types of machine*

### *The single bed machine*

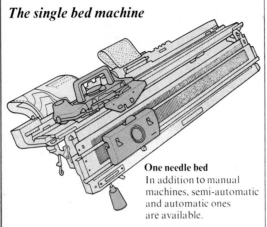

**One needle bed**
In addition to manual machines, semi-automatic and automatic ones are available.

Single bed machines have one needle bed. They cannot do "true" ribbing, but they do mock rib, which is satisfactory for welts, cuffs, and neckbands. Some of their stitch patterns such as tuck stitch and slip stitch "thicken" the yarn and produce warm garments from fine yarns.

### *Ribbing attachments*

Ribbing attachments can be fitted to many single bed machines, enabling them to work ribbing, tubular and various rib-based stitches. Models vary in their performance, so study sales literature. Many experts advise beginners to master the single bed machine before adding a ribbing attachment.

### *The double bed machine*

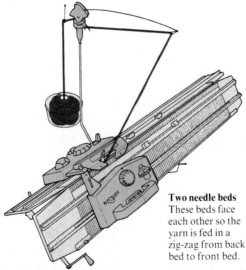

**Two needle beds**
These beds face each other so the yarn is fed in a zig-zag from back bed to front bed.

Double bed machines have two needle beds, and work "true" rib, tubular knitting, and many rib-based stitches, which make a thick fabric from fine yarn. Both beds can be used separately. Some beginners find a double bed machine more difficult to master than a single bed.

Most knitting machines are manually operated (the knitter has to push the cam box to and fro) but some can be fitted with an electric motor for automatic operation.

## *Special machine techniques*

### *Shaping*

Shaping on a machine can be done by changing tension (comparable to a hand knitter changing to larger or smaller needles) or by changing stitch pattern. For example: a band of simple colourwork at the waistline of a stocking stitch sweater will pull the knitting in and give the garment a waisted look because the number of stitches to the inch is usually more for colourwork than for stocking stitch in the same yarn at the same tension. Baby dresses can have the skirts knitted in tuck stitch with the bodice in plain stocking stitch. Even though the stitch size and the number of needles in the work remain the same, the bodice will be narrower than the skirt and give a gathered effect because the number of stitches to the inch is usually fewer for tuck stitches than it is for stocking stitch.

### *Knit-weaving*

This technique is often called weaving. One yarn, usually a 4-ply or finer, is knitted while a second yarn, another 4-ply in a toning or contrasting colour, or a double knit, chunky or fancy yarn, is woven under and over selected needles. Needle selection may be by punch card and therefore fully automatic. This knit-weaving produces a firm, good looking fabric which stretches less than most knitting, hand or machine, and can be used for skirts, trousers or upholstery fabric. It frays very little and is therefore very suitable for the cut-and-sew technique as set out below.

### *Cut-and-sew*

In its true form, cut-and-sew means knitting, or knit-weaving, straight lengths of material, pressing them (where the yarn is suitable for pressing) and then cutting out and stitching up on a sewing machine exactly as a dressmaker uses bought fabric.

In practice, cut-and-sew is often adapted to suit various yarns and knitters. With very soft, fine yarns, or with synthetics which cannot be pressed, many knitters machine stitch around the pattern outline before cutting. Either straight stitch or zigzag stitch can be used.

With soft yarns which can be pressed, an iron-on interfacing gives body to the fabric and makes cutting and sewing much easier. It also produces a better looking garment.

To avoid waste, especially with expensive yarns, as well as to save time on neatening seams, many knitters use a modified form of cut-and-sew. They knit to shape as long as this is easy and trouble free and use cut-and-sew for the difficult parts. In practice this often means knitting the garment in the conventional way as far as the shoulder shaping, and using cut-and-sew for the neckline.

## First steps to machine knitting

As soon as you have chosen your machine, carefully study the instruction book provided for that particular machine. Make yourself familiar with the names of the parts and try the processes such as casting on, increasing and decreasing.

### Tension squares

Pay particular attention to the instructions for making and measuring tension squares, or stitch gauge. Correct tension is the basis of good machine knitting; you cannot produce a piece of fabric to the required size unless you know how many stitches to cast on and how many rows to knit. Study the function of the tension discs too, because these, as well as the stitch dial, affect tension.

### Holding position

You should also make sure that you understand what is meant by holding position. This is not the same as the non-working position (when the needles are pushed right back and do not knit at all). Holding position needles have stitches on them, but are temporarily out of action. This makes it easy to knit first one, then the other side of a neck opening, and also to knit partial rows, to shape a heel or a hem.

### Beginning to knit

When beginning, first make a few items in plain stocking stitch. This will give you the "feel" of the machine; you will learn, by experience, that it is best to work at a steady rhythmical pace. You will see that if your stitch size is too small the fabric will be hard and stiff and that if it is too large, the fabric will stretch and lose its shape.

A smooth 4-ply yarn on cone is best for beginners. If this is not available, use a smooth, good quality 4-ply hand knitting yarn, but this should be rewound on a wool winder. Most hand knitting yarns benefit from being waxed. To do this, hold a piece of wax in your hand and allow the yarn to slide over it as you wind.

## Simple projects

Choose something simple for your first project. Rectangular cushions, scarves, bags, T-shirts with slit necklines are all very easy to knit to the required size.

Assume your tension square gives you 28 stitches and 40 rows to 4 inches (10 cm) square. This means that to produce one inch (2.5 cm) in width, you will need 7 stitches; and to produce one inch (2.5 cm) in length you will need 10 rows. You can now calculate any size.

### Cushion

To make a cushion cover measuring 15 by 16 inches (38 by 40.5 cm): 7 stitches equal one inch (2.5 cm) so for 15 inches (38 cm) you will need 105 stitches. It is usually easier to work with an even number, so call it 106 stitches. Ten rows equal one inch (2.5 cm) so for 16 inches (40.5 cm) you will need 160 rows.

If you are going to make the cover in two pieces and machine them together (see Making up) it is advisable to add two extra stitches each side and two extra rows top and bottom, to allow for the seams.

The pattern for the cushion cover would be as follows:
Cast on 110 stitches (106 + 2 + 2).
Knit 164 rows (160 + 2 + 2).
Cast off.
This is your first machine knitting pattern, and shows you how easy it is to produce a rectangle of knitting to required measurements. Scarves, bags and casual garments without shaping are just as easy, and simple shapes can be trimmed with embroidery or braid, or knitted in shapes or stitch patterns.

### Making a T-shirt

Your tension square will tell you how many stitches and rows you need for the required measurements. Back and front each consist of a rectangle. Knit these and then decide how wide you want the neckline to be. Leaving this amount free, join the shoulder seams. Now decide how deep you wish the armholes to be and mark this depth, back and front on each side, with a coloured thread.

You can finish the armhole with a simple crochet edging. Or you can pick up the stitches between the marked points and knit either an armhole band or a sleeve (no shaping is required for this type of garment). Or you may knit sleeves separately and sew them in.

Join side seams, turn up hem at the bottom and on the sleeves, if you have knitted them. Or you can bind all the edges with purchased or knitted braid, or trim with crochet. You now have a serviceable garment, which can be trimmed with embroidery as suggested for the cushion cover. You are now ready to follow simple machine knitting patterns.

## Patterns for machine knitting

Machine knitting patterns may be: **1** written out in words, similar to hand knitting patterns, **2** in diagram form or **3** a combination of words and diagrams.

### Written Patterns

The modern tendency is to move away from words, toward diagrams. But written patterns are still available, and you should learn to understand these.

#### Understanding a written pattern

If you have studied your instruction book, most of the technical terms will be clear to you. "Cast on by hand" means to wind the yarn around each needle, as described in the instruction book. Sometimes this is written as "Cast on with closed edge" to distinguish it from "cast on with waste yarn". Here the knitting is started with a piece of contrast (waste) yarn which is afterwards discarded. This is quick and easy; it produces an untidy edge but as the waste yarn does not form part of the finished knitting this does not matter.

These instructions for casting on refer to single bed machines. Double bed machines or ribbing attachments usually cast on automatically by means of a zigzag followed by two or four rows of circular knitting. This will be described in your instruction book.

The instructions for increasing, decreasing, and shaping by partial knitting (putting some needles into holding position and so knitting only part of a row), will all be clear if you have studied you manual.

### Stripping off

"Stripping off" is not always included in instruction books. It simply means that instead of casting off, remove the work from the machine by knitting a number of rows (usually seven or eight) in waste yarn, then remove the yarn from the yarn feeder, moving the cam box across the needle bed and so "stripping off" the knitting. This means that the open stitches from the last row knitted in the main yarn will have to be finished in some way—by grafting, by putting them back on to the machine and knitting them off together with another set of stitches, or by back stitching through the open loops. All these processes should be explained in your instruction book.

Beginners are often dismayed by the apparent complexity of written patterns. This may be because the pattern covers a very wide range of sizes. Go through such patterns, either underlining the figures you need, or writing out the pattern in your size. Some patterns give row counter readings at the end of each section, enabling the knitter to check as she works; try to choose such patterns for early attempts.

## Diagram Patterns

Diagram patterns have a language of their own using various signs and symbols. A key to the symbols is always given although the symbols may vary with the different makes of machine.

### Reading a diagram pattern

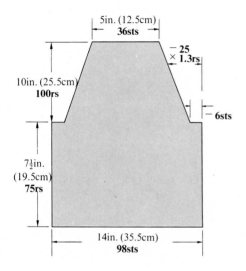

This typical diagram pattern for the back of a child's raglan sweater or cardigan is easy to understand without any specialized knowledge of machine knitting. Measurements are given and the number of stitches or rows which will produce these measurements are shown in brackets. Only the instructions marked (1) and (2) may need some explanation, but even these are simple:

— (minus sign) means "decrease".

× (multiplication sign) means multiply or "times".

¨ means "every"; so that

$-25 × \ddot{1}3$ rows means "decrease 1 stitch every 3 rows, 25 times". You may also see this instruction written as follows:

$-25 × 1 \boxed{3}$

It is important to remember that when you buy a pattern book which uses sign language like this, a key is always provided. Do not feel you have to memorize the symbols. After you have knitted a few garments, working from diagram patterns, you will find you can read them as easily as the written word.

For most knitters, the diagram pattern, once understood, is easier to work from; it makes it easier to alter or adapt patterns and means that if you cannot achieve the given tension, it will be simple to re-write based on your actual tension.

Another advantage of learning to use diagram patterns is that as soon as you begin to design your own garments (which is very easy with machine knitting), you will find it convenient to work with diagrams.

## Charting Devices

An off-shoot of the diagram pattern, and one which has made machine knitting faster, easier and more creative than it has ever been, is the charting device. Some machines work with a diagram which is the actual size of the garment, others work with half-scale diagrams. But the principle is the same.

### How charting devices work

With all makes the charting device, which is fitted onto the machine (or sometimes built into it), holds a sheet on which is drawn the outline of the item to be knitted. The appropriate stitch scale, depending on the number of stitches to the inch or centimetre, is clipped in; the row indicator is set in accordance with the number of rows to the inch or centimetre. The diagram moves down one space each time a row is knitted, and the knitter simply reads off the number of stitches to be increased or decreased. There is no need to count rows, or even to consult a row counter on the machine—because as the sheet moves down the knitter can see at a glance how far to knit and where to increase or decrease. Charting devices are usually supplied with a set of basic shapes, in a good range of sizes, but it is easy to alter or adapt these, or to draw your own shapes.

### Advantages of a charting device

The advantages of the charting device are speed, simplicity, and the fact that once you have found a shape that you like, you can knit it again and again, varying yarn, stitch size, and stitch pattern, subject only to the laws of common sense and suitability (a garment designed to be knitted in a firm 4-ply crepe will be unsuitable in gossamer-fine baby yarn).

Simple dressmaking patterns, including diagram patterns, can provide suitable shapes for use with your charting device. So can worn-out items such as favourite toys, garments, or clothing accessories.

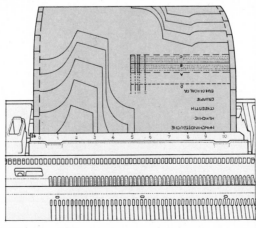

**Charting device**
*This fitted accessory enables the knitter to work from a charted design*

Many machine knitters start by trying to adapt hand knitting patterns. It is often possible to copy a stocking stitch garment, designed for hand knitting, although machine knitted stitches are usually shorter than hand knitted ones, so that while it is not difficult to match stitch tension, it may not be possible to match row tension. When this happens, the number of rows has to be increased to reach the same length.

For example, if the hand knitting tension is 7 stitches and 9 rows to 1 inch (2.5cm), machine knitting tension may be 7 stitches and 10 rows to 1 inch (2.5cm). If the hand knitting pattern tells you to knit 63 rows, you know this will produce a piece of knitting 7 inches (18 cm) long ($63 \div 9 = 7$). So to produce the same length on the machine you would have to knit 70 rows ($7 \times 10$).

### Using a charting device

Some hand knitting patterns can be adapted for use with the charting device. To do this, feed a blank sheet into the device, setting to correct stitch and row tension. Then turn the roller by hand and read off the pattern while marking the paper with dots until the proper shape is achieved. Hand knitting patterns which shape within the row should be avoided.

Usually a machine knitter quickly loses the desire to adapt hand-knitting patterns. There is now no shortage of good machine knitting patterns, many of them in diagram form, and many of them suitable for use with most machines. Adapting hand knitting patterns to machine knitting, which is a different craft, may confuse and discourage the beginner.

# Yarns for machine knitting

A wide variety of yarns can be used successfully on a knitting machine. Even knop yarns, or chunky knits, which may not knit successfully on every needle, can often be used, on every other needle, or for the knit-weaving that most modern machines do.

### Coned yarns
Coned yarns have several advantages: You can knit straight from the cone (hand knitting yarn usually has to be rewound for machine knitting); they are usually already waxed (hand knitting yarns may need waxing, which means holding a piece of wax in the hand and allowing the yarn to slide over the wax as you wind); there will be very few short ends to darn in, and no time is wasted joining in new balls.

Most knitting machine centres keep a stock of coned yarns, or there are mail order firms which supply. The yarns range from cheap, serviceable yarns for school, play and work garments, to luxury yarns for top fashion knitwear. Never use harsh, coarse or "whiskery" yarns. They will not produce good knitwear, and may damage the needles. Two types of coned yarn need special mention: they are both excellent for making inexpensive, attractive knitwear, but neither is suitable for the very new knitter.

### Shetland wool
Coned wool sometimes appears to be oily and dirty. It should be knitted at a fairly loose tension, so that the knitting, as it comes off the machine, appears to be too open. Wash it in hot water and washing up liquid, and the stitches will "swell", giving a soft, warm, and good-looking fabric. As the washing alters the size of the knitting, the tension square should not be measured until after it has been washed. The hot water and detergent is for the initial degreasing wash only. After that, treat Shetland as any other wool, wash it by hand in a mild liquid. Shetland normally comes in two thicknesses. Experienced knitters use the finer yarn to make beautiful lacy garments, or they mix two or three strands together to produce beautiful tweed or random effects.

### Fine coned synthetics
These are not the regular 3- or 4-ply, repeatable coned synthetics which are stocked by many knitting machine centres and mail order firms. They may be oddments left over from industrial use, which can be bought, often very cheaply, in markets, from mail order firms, and from some knitting machine centres. Some mail order firms also supply these fine yarns on large cones in repeatable colours.

They are too fine to knit singly (except for special effects), but when two, three, four—or even more, strands are used together, they make attractive, hard-wearing easy-care garments at an inexpensive price.

Most of them cannot be steam pressed, which means that hems, for example, must be knitted on a firm tension so that they will retain their shape. If you wish to iron, experiment with a warm iron and a dry cloth, on a small piece of waste knitting. By using a number of strands of different colours marl, random, tweed and ombre effects can be obtained.

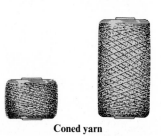
**Coned yarn**

**Wound yarn**

# Making up machine knitted garments

When it comes to the making up of knitted garments, machine knitting is closer to dressmaking than to hand knitting. The over-sewing and back stitching which many hand knitters rely on to finish their garments are seldom suitable for machine knitting.

This aspect of machine knitting is still to some extent in the experimental stage. Many ways have been tried—crocheting the pieces together, picking up the stitches on the machine and knitting two pieces together; "weaving" the pieces together; sewing with a firm back stitch. The majority of successful knitters now rely mainly on two methods:

### Mattress stitch
The method of working mattress stitch should be clearly explained and illustrated in your instruction book. When done correctly it gives a beautiful finish—but it may take considerably longer to make up the garment this way than it did to knit it, which nullifies one of the advantages of machine knitting—speedier knitting.

Essentially mattress stitching involves working backwards and forwards between two pieces, making running stitches between the last and next-to-last stitch on each side.

### Stitching by sewing machine
Using a sewing machine to make up machine knitting is becoming more and more popular, and the results can be excellent. Care and practice is necessary—use up all waste knitting this way. Keen knitters will evolve their own favourite methods, but here are a few hints.

Always use a good quality synthetic thread which will "give" with the knitting.

Pin the pieces together, with pins at right angles to the seam; work fairly slowly and remove the pins as you go.

Use the zipper foot on your sewing machine; this enables you to make a neat seam not wide enough to be clumsy, not so narrow that it tends to run off the edge of the knitting. Some knitters prefer to use a roller foot, especially with colour work as they claim it makes the strands of yarn at the back of the work less likely to catch in the foot.

Use a very light pressure.

Use a medium length stitch width—if you have a swing-needle machine—the very narrowest possible zigzag. You can still achieve good results with a straight stitch machine.

### Hand finishing
There will still be some hand finishing to be done. Fully fashioned raglan sleeves should be mattress stitched. Collars and armhole bands may be turned to the inside and slip stitched into position, or turned to the outside and secured by backstitching into the open loops of the last row knitted in main yarn (this is if you have stripped, rather than cast off). Pocket tops and side vents may need to be carefully hand-sewn. Front bands knitted in stocking stitch can be machine stitched and then caught down by hand on the inside; ribbed bands are more difficult to sew by machine but the really careful worker can achieve excellent results. Practice is the only way to learn.

More and more machine knitters are using their sewing machines in conjunction with their knitting machines, for instance in the cut and sew technique, and so enormously extending the range of garments and soft furnishings which the keen amateur, in her own home, can now produce to really professional standards.

# Caring for woollen articles

Careful maintenance of knitted articles can greatly extend their years of use. Never hang garments as their weight can pull them out of shape, but store them flat in a drawer.

## Washing knitwear

Use mild soap especially designed for knitwear and luke-warm water. Before washing strong colours, check that they are colour-fast by dipping a small piece of the article into the soapy water and pressing it out in a white cloth. If it leaves a stain, wash in cold water only.

Remove the knitting from the water when thoroughly cleaned and squeeze out excess soapy water. It is very important to rinse woollens thoroughly. Keep on rinsing with cold water until it remains clear. A fabric softener can be added to the last rinse.

Do not wring the article out but squeeze gently removing as much water as possible. Place the garment on a white turkish towel. Smaller towels can be placed inside the garment and under sleeves and pockets to prevent coloured areas touching. Roll the article up in the towel and press the roll to extract more water. It is sometimes necessary to use a second towel. Finish drying by placing the article out flat on another clean towel, making sure it is correctly shaped. Dry the knitting away from direct heat.

## Re-using yarn

The major problem in re-using yarn is being able to unpick knitting stitches without making cuts along the seam line. You can prevent this by marking the seam line with a small amount of contrasting yarn, which is only visible on the inside. Once the seams are unpicked, locate the last cast off stitch, and begin to unravel the knitting. To keep the yarn from getting tangled or stretched, re-wind it around the back of a chair. Fasten the hank at two ends, catching the end of the yarn and hand wash it. When it is dry, rewind the yarn into loose balls.

**Correct washing technique**
*Always squeeze the suds into the garment and never rub the wool or felting will result. Do not let the garment soak but remove it quickly.*

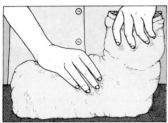

**Removing excess water**

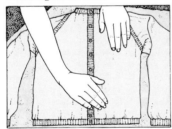

**Re-shaping the garment**

**Seam marked with a contrasting colour**

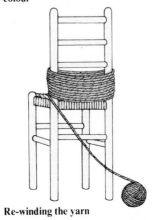

**Re-winding the yarn**

# Knitting abbreviations

| | | | |
|---|---|---|---|
| **BC** | Back cross: In cabling, the cn is held to the back of the work while other stitches are worked in front | **p2sso** | Pass two slipped stitches over |
| **beg** | Beginning | **patt** | Pattern |
| **col** | Colour | **p** | Purl |
| **cont** | Continue or continuing | **pl-b** | Purl into back of stitch |
| **cn** | Cable needle | **p2tog** | Purl two stitches together |
| **dec** | Decrease | **p-wise** | Purlwise |
| **dpn** | Double pointed needle | **rem** | Remain or remaining |
| **FC** | Front cross: In cabling, the cn is held to the front of the work while other stitches are worked behind. | **rep** | Repeat |
| | | **Rep from\*** | Repeat all the instructions that follows\* |
| **foll** | Following | **RN** | Right needle |
| **gm** | Gram | **RS** | Right side |
| **g-st** | Garter stitch | **sl** | Slip |
| **inc** | Increase | **sl st** | Slip stitch |
| **Inc 1** | Increase one stitch by knitting into the front then the back of a stitch | **sl 1f** | Slip a stitch onto a cable needle at the front of the work |
| **k** | Knit | **sl 1b** | Slip a stitch onto cn at back of work |
| **k1-b** | Knit one into the back of the stitch | **st** | Stitch |
| **k2tog** | Knit two stitches together | **sts** | Stitches |
| **Kssb** | Knit slip stitch through the back | **st-st** | Stocking stitch |
| **k up 1** | Pick up and knit the stitch in the row below | **tbl** | Through back of loop |
| **k-wise** | Knitwise | **throw** | To make an elongated stitch, yarn is thrown, or wrapped, twice or more around point of needle. Throws are dropped in the subsequent row |
| **LN** | Left needle | | |
| **M1, M1-b** | Make one. Pick up loop or running thread below and knit into back of it. | **tog** | Together |
| | | **turn** | Turn the work around as the point indicated, *before* the end of the row. |
| **MB** | Make bobble | | |
| **m-st** | Moss stitch | **WS** | Wrong side |
| **no** | Number | **Wyib** | With yarn in back |
| **nos** | Numbers | **Wyif** | With yarn in front |
| **oz** | Ounces | **ybk** | Yarn back |
| **()** | Parentheses: Repeat all the material between parentheses as many times as indicated | **yfwd** | Yarn forward |
| | | **yrn** | Yarn around needle |
| | | **y2rn** | Yarn twice around needle |
| **pnso** | Pass next stitch over | **yo** | Yarn over |
| **psso** | Pass slipped stitch | **yo2** | A double yarn over |
| | | **yon** | Yarn on needle |

# 2
# CROCHET

*including Tunisian, Filet and
Broomstick Techniques*

# History of crochet

The word "crochet" comes from the French *croc* meaning a hook. Like all textiles, its origins are difficult to trace and few examples of early crochet remain.

It is formed, like knitting, into a looped fabric from one continuous length of yarn. But whereas knitting uses two or more needles onto which a number of stitches are cast, crochet uses only one hook on which one stitch at a time is worked. There is a different form of crochet, known as *Tunisian crochet*, which is worked in much the same way as knitting – on a long hook onto which a number of loops are cast, then worked off and cast on again for the next row. As it seems more than likely that the origins of knitting and crochet are the same, possibly Tunisian crochet was the point of departure between the two.

The technique of crochet appears to have travelled extensively as early samples of it have been found across the world in China, Turkey, Africa and Europe as well as in both the United States and South America. It has two very distinctly different appearances: it can be worked using very fine yarns and the finest hooks to form a fine, open fabric that is very similar to lace or it can be worked with thicker yarn on larger hooks to make a dense fabric.

The denser type of crochet was the more well known of the two. The Chinese used it to make three-dimensional sculptural dolls; the Africans used it for making caps for their chieftains; the Turks also used it for making hats and in Scotland it was used to make both caps and heavy cloaks, worn amongst others by shepherds, hence the name for it in Scotland of *shepherd's knitting*. This dense type of crochet is also very popular today for all sorts of clothing: sweaters, coats, jackets, socks and caps, for example. It is also very useful for making warm rugs, blankets and shawls.

The crochet fabric can either be worked in flat pieces or in rings from which tubular shapes and medallions can be made. In the United States, in the days of the pioneering families when new wool was in short supply, old scraps of wool were re-used to make multi-coloured medallions which were then pieced together, like a patchwork to make blankets, rugs and shawls. The popularity of this type of crochet is still very great today. Known as *granny squares* or *afghan squares*, these brightly coloured medallions can be used to make clothes and bags as well.

## Crochet lace

The more delicate, lace-like form of crochet originated in Italy in the sixteenth century where it was worked by the nuns to make church trimmings and vestments, hence the name for it at that time of *nun's lace*. It was made in very fine cotton yarn on the finest crochet hooks. The technique spread to Spain and to Ireland where it was also worked by the nuns for the church.

It was not until the early nineteenth century that crochet lace became used for garments and for household use. Its popularity may largely have stemmed from the work of a French emigrée, Eleanore Riego de la Branchardière, who, when she settled in Ireland, became interested in the lace crochet work of the nuns in a Dublin convent. She developed their craft and invented many new stitches, publicizing the work in her own magazine called *The Needle*.

Another factor which influenced the development of this type of crochet was the setting up in Carrickmacross of a home industry to help impoverished people by a Mrs Gray Porter, in the first half of the nineteenth century. A similar industry was set up in Clones by a Mrs Hand. The work in these two areas

**Child's dress**
Late nineteenth-century English child's dress, with raised motifs on yoke and as a border on the sleeve.

**Handbag**
Late nineteenth-century Irish crochet handbag worked in fine white cotton.

**Crochet collar**
Nineteenth-century lace collar, probably Irish lace crochet, with raised motifs.

flourished and is still carried on today, the crochet having become world famous under the name of its places of origin, as *Carrickmacross lace* and *Clones lace*. It has a very distinctive appearance worked in fine cotton yarn with relief motifs of roses and shamrocks, for example, on a fine lattice background. This kind of lace is used to make both complete fabrics, such as tablecloths and bedspreads, or as a trimming or insertion on clothes and household items.

There are several other lace-like forms of crochet. *Filet* crochet, for example, is very simple to work and has become popular recently for clothes and for edgings. It is formed in a lattice-like mesh made of treble stitches. The mesh is filled in with a denser stitch at certain points to make motifs on the lattice background. *Hairpin* crochet also has a lace-like appearance and is worked with the help of a special shaped device on which the stitches are formed. *Broomstick* crochet is similarly worked, but in this case the looped stitches are formed on a thick needle before they are worked off with a crochet hook.

The simplest forms of crochet are very easy to work once the basic technique has been mastered. Because only one loop is on the hook at a time, it will not unravel and can therefore be carried around more easily than knitting. Crochet is very useful as an edging fabric because it is easy to pick up stitches on an existing piece of fabric. Knitting and crochet could easily be combined to provide a crochet border on a knitted blanket for example. Crochet can, of course, be worked using a variety of fabrics from cotton and silk ribbon to thick wool yarn.

**Crochet jacket**
*Modern crochet in a patchwork type jacket.*

# Hooks and yarns

Below are illustrated the range of crochet hook sizes available and a small selection of the many yarns suitable for crochet.

## Hook sizes

0.60mm
0.75mm
1.00mm
1.25mm
1.50mm
1.75mm
2.00mm
2.50mm
3.00mm
3.50mm
4.00mm
4.50mm
5.00mm
5.50mm
6.00mm
7.00mm
8.00mm
9.00mm
10.00mm

## Types of yarn

Crochet cottons

Knitting wools

Knitting cottons

Novelty yarns

# Holding the hook and yarn

### Threading yarn

Threading the yarn through the fingers is important as this helps to give extra tension, controlling the yarn while allowing it to flow easily from hand to hook. If you are left-handed the method is exactly the same. Thread the yarn in either of the two methods shown, whichever is the more comfortable.

**How to thread yarn around the little finger**

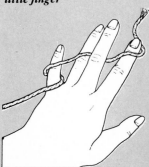

*Pass the working end of yarn around the little finger, over the next finger, under the middle finger and finish with it resting over the forefinger.*

**How to thread yarn over the little finger**

*Pass the working end of yarn over the little finger, under the next 2 fingers and finish with it resting over the forefinger.*

### Holding the hook

The crochet hook can be held in either the knife or the pencil position. Both ways are equally good and the choice depends on which position feels most comfortable in the hand.

**How to hold the hook in the pencil position**

**1** *Hold the hook in the right hand like a pencil. If you are left-handed hold the hook in the same way, but in the left hand.*

**2** *Prepare to make the first chain by drawing the yarn from the left forefinger with the hook through the slip loop.*

**How to hold the hook in the knife position**

**1** *Hold the hook in the right hand like a knife. If you are left-handed hold the hook in the same way, but in the left hand.*

**2** *Prepare to make the first chain by drawing the yarn from the left forefinger with the hook through the slip loop.*

# Casting on

To begin to crochet a slip loop is placed on the hook and the yarn is then threaded through the left hand. Both hands are then brought together so that the hook in the right hand and the yarn threaded over the left forefinger are in easy contact.

### The slip loop

The slip loop is the first crochet stitch and is made in the same way as the slip loop in knitting. In crochet, however, a hook instead of a knitting needle is used to draw the loop through the twists of yarn.

**How to make a slip loop**

**1** *Twist the yarn twice around 2 fingers and insert the hook between the 2 twists of yarn.*

**2** *Using the hook, draw one twist through the other.*

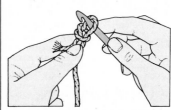

**3** *Pull both ends of yarn to tighten the slip loop and secure it on the hook.*

# Chain stitch

Chain stitch is used for the foundation row, upon which the next row or round will be worked. It is also used to make spaces between stitches, and for bars in open and lace work (page 122). At the beginning of the instructions, all crochet patterns give the hook size, type of yarn to use and number of chains to cast on. When learning the basic stitches, 20 chain stitches are sufficient.

The abbreviation for a chain stitch is *ch*.

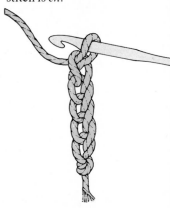

**How to make a chain stitch**

**1** *Thread the yarn in the left hand and hold the hook with the slip loop in the right hand. Twist the hook first under and then over the yarn to make a loop.*

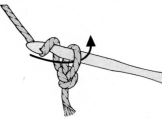

**2** *Draw the hook with the yarn on it through the slip loop to form a chain stitch. The chain stitch is now complete. Repeat this process until the movement becomes easy and feels quite natural to work.*

# Double chain stitch

For garments which will have to endure strain on the edges, such as socks, hats and gloves, a firmer foundation row can be made by working a double chain stitch.

The abbreviation for a double chain stitch is *dch*.

**How to make a double chain stitch**

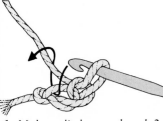

**1** *Make a slip loop and work 2 chain stitches. With the yarn at the back insert the hook between the 2 halves of the first chain stitch, twist the hook around the yarn and draw it through. There are now 2 loops on the hook.*

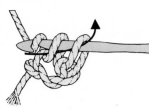

**2** *Twist the hook around the yarn and draw through both loops to form a double chain. Continue in this way to form more double chain stitches, each time inserting the hook into the left side of the stitch just made.*

# Finishing off

When the work has been completed the yarn must be finished off properly, otherwise it will come undone. This is also known as casting off.

**How to finish off**

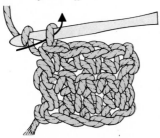

**1** *When the final stitch has been completed, cut the working yarn and pull it through the last loop on the hook. Pull it tight to close the loop.*

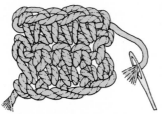

**2** *Thread the working end of the yarn into a sewing needle and darn it neatly into the back of the work.*

**Counting stitches**

Counting stitches in crochet is more difficult than in knitting, for the stitches are not left on the hook. The sample above is worked in double crochet. Each stitch is numbered to show how to count the stitches. Counting treble stitches is easier, because each treble forms 1 upright or post which is counted as a single stitch.

A chain stitch counts as 1, and if between 2 trebles, 3 stitches should be counted.

# Working from patterns

To save space all crochet instructions are written with symbols and abbreviations. These are easy to follow and each pattern gives a key to them in the instructions. The codes normally used are given below:

## Pattern abbreviations

| | | | |
|---|---|---|---|
| **alt** | alternate | **lp(s)** | loop(s) |
| **beg** | begin or beginning | **patt** | pattern |
| **bet** | between | **pc** | picot |
| **ch(s)** | chain(s) or chain stitch(es) | **rem** | remaining |
| | | **rep** | repeat |
| **cl** | cluster | **rnd** | round |
| **col** | colour | **sp(s)** | space(s) |
| **cont** | continue | **ss** | slip stitch or single crochet |
| **dc** | double crochet | | |
| **dch(s)** | double chain(s) or double chain stitch(es) | **st(s)** | stitch(es) |
| | | **tbl** | through back of loop |
| **dec** | decrease | **t-ch(s)** | turning chain(s) |
| **dtr** | double treble | **tog** | together |
| **foll** | following | **tr** | treble |
| **gr** | group | **tr tr** | triple treble |
| **htr** | half treble | **yrh** | yarn around hook |
| **inc** | increase | | |

## Pattern symbols

The most common symbols in crochet patterns are given below. Take care to read the printed pattern thoroughly in case there is a variation from the standard methods of giving instructions.

### Commas

These separate two kinds of stitches, e.g. if the instructions read 2dc, 1ss, you work 2 double crochet into 2 stitches of the previous row and then 1 slip stitch into the next stitch of the previous row.

### Hyphens

These refer to stitches which have already been made but which will be used as the base for the next stitch, e.g. if the instructions read 2tr into 2-ch sp, you work 2 trebles into the space made by the 2 chain stitches worked in the previous row. The use of hyphens is optional rather than general.

### Brackets

These are used for several reasons. Brackets at the end of a row, e.g. (5dc) indicate the number of stitches which have been made at the end of a row or round, and in this case 5 double crochet stitches have been made.

If brackets enclose a certain stitch combination and then have a number with or without an x immediately beyond them, the stitch combination must be repeated by the number of times stated just outside the brackets, e.g. (1ch, 2dc, 1tr) 3 x means that 1ch, 2dc, 1tr are to be made in that order three times.

Brackets also denote size ranges and the number of stitches to use, e.g. 5 (7,9) ss means that 5 slip stitches are worked for the smallest size, and 7 or 9 slip stitches for the larger sizes.

### Inc (dec) evenly

This indicates that increases (decreases) can be placed where convenient to you, so long as they are evenly spaced.

### Stars or asterisks

A star or asterisk in instructions means that the instructions should be repeated from the * to the end of a row or round, or as specified in the pattern instructions.

# Basic stitches

Crochet stitches are always made in the same way, whether the work is flat and turned at the end of each row, or circular and never turned at the end of the round. The texture of some stitches does, however, differ, according to whether they are worked flat or in a circle. In flat work because the work is turned the direction of the stitches is also turned, whereas for work in the round the direction of the stitches always remains the same, for the work is never turned. This texture change is more apparent in stitches which are based on single and double crochet stitches.

Before beginning to work the basic stitches you should remember that all first row stitches are worked through the back half of the chain stitch foundation row. On the following rows, unless specifically instructed otherwise, all the stitches are worked through both halves of the top of the stitches below, and the hook is always inserted from front to back.

## Turning chains

At the end of the foundation row of chain stitches, or at the end of the following rows of crochet stitches, the work is turned so that the working yarn is behind the hook and the next row of stitches can be worked back into the top of the previous row's stitches. Each basic crochet stitch is formed from a different number of loops giving each one a different height. Extra chains must therefore be added at the beginning of each row in order to bring the hook level with the height of the next stitch to be worked. Each basic stitch has its own particular number of extra chains which are called *turning chains*, abbreviated to *t-ch*.

Having made the turning chains at the end of a foundation row of chain stitch, the hook is inserted into the second, third, fifth, sixth or seventh chain from the hook, depending on the stitch being worked for the next row. After completion of this row, the next and all following rows should be worked with the correct number of turning chains for the appropriate stitch. The hook is inserted into either the first or second stitch depending on the stitch being used.

The chart below gives the correct number of turning chains and the hook positions needed for all stitches and subsequent rows.

### Turning chain instructions for basic stitches

| Type of stitch | Turning chains at the end of each row | After foundation row of chain make first stitch into: | At beginning of a row make first stitch into: |
|---|---|---|---|
| Slip stitch | 1 t-ch | 2nd chain from hook | First stitch |
| Double crochet | 1 t-ch | 2nd chain from hook | First stitch |
| Half treble | 2 t-ch | 3rd chain from hook | First stitch |
| Treble | 3 t-ch | 5th chain from hook | Second stitch |
| Double treble | 4 t-ch | 6th chain from hook | Second stitch |
| Triple treble | 5 t-ch | 7th chain from hook | Second stitch |

A foundation row of approximately 20 ch is sufficient to try out any of the stitches.

# Single and double crochet

### Slip stitch
Also known as single crochet (abbr. as *ss*).

**Finished slip stitch**

### Double crochet
Also known as plain stitch (abbr. as *dc*).

**Finished double crochet**

*How to work slip stitch*

**1** *Make a foundation row of chs. Insert hook through back of 2nd chain from hook.*

**2** *Twist the yarn around the hook (yrh) and draw through the 2 loops now on hook, making an ss. Continue working into the next and following chains.*

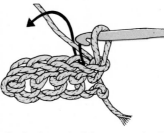

**3** *At the end of the row make 1 t-ch, turn work and insert hook through back half of first stitch in row below to make first ss. Continue in this way for all the following rows.*

*How to work double crochet*

**1** *Make a foundation row of chs. Insert hook through back of 2nd chain from hook, yrh and draw through.*

**2** *With 2 loops now on hook, yrh and draw through both loops, making a dc.*

**3** *Continue working dc into the next and following chains to end of row.*

**4** *At the end of the row make 1 t-ch, turn the work and insert the hook through both halves of the first stitch in the row below to make the first dc.*

# *Treble crochet*

## *Half treble*
This is abbreviated as *htr*.

**Finished half treble**

*How to work half treble*

**1** *Make a foundation row of chs. Yrh and then insert hook through back of 3rd chain from the hook.*

**2** *Yrh and draw through. There are now 3 loops on hook. Yrh and pull through all 3 loops, making a htr.*

**3** *Continue working htr into every chain.*

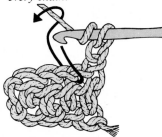

**4** *At the end of the row make 2 t-ch, turn work and make first htr into first stitch in row below. Continue in this way for all the following rows.*

## *Treble*
This is abbreviated as *tr*.

**Finished treble**

*How to work treble*

**1** *Make a foundation row of chs. Yrh and insert hook through back of 5th chain from the hook.*

**2** *Yrh and draw through (3 loops on hook), yrh and draw through first 2 loops.*

**3** *There are now 2 loops on hook. Yrh and draw through these 2 loops to complete the tr.*

**4** *Continue to make tr to end of row. Then make 3 t-ch, turn work and make first tr into 2nd stitch in row below.*

## *Double treble*
This is abbreviated as *dtr*.

**Finished double treble**

*How to work double treble*

**1** *Make a foundation row of chs. Yrh twice and insert hook into back of 6th chain from hook.*

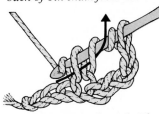

**2** *Yrh and draw through. There are now 4 loops on hook. Yrh and draw through first 2 loops.*

**3** *There are now 3 loops on hook. Yrh and draw through first 2 loops, yrh and draw through rem 2 loops to complete the dtr.*

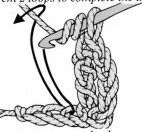

**4** *Continue to make dtr to end of row. Then make 4 t-ch, turn work and make first dtr into 2nd stitch in row below.*

## *Triple treble*
This is abbreviated as *tr tr*.

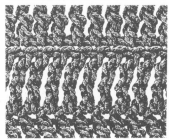

**Finished triple treble**

*How to work triple treble*

**1** *Make a foundation row of chs. Yrh three times and insert hook through back of 7th chain from hook.*

**2** *Yrh and draw through. There are now 5 loops on hook. Yrh and draw through first 2 loops. Repeat this process three more times.*

**3** *Continue to make tr tr to end of row. Then make 5 t-ch, turn work and make first tr tr into 2nd stitch in row below.*

# Stitch techniques

Variations to basic stitches are made by inserting the hook into different parts of the stitches below and manipulating the yarn in different ways. The following diagrams illustrate some of the variations.

## Making crossed double crochet
By reversing the normal hook under yarn process, crossed double crochet is made.

### How to work crossed double crochet

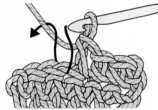

*Take the hook over the yarn each time a loop is drawn through.*

## Working into half the stitch below
Ridged effects are made by continually working into the back half or the front half of the stitch below. Patterns are made by varying the intervals between the ridges.

### How to work into the back half

*Insert the hook into the back half of the stitch in the row just below.*

### How to work into the front half

*Insert the hook into the front half of the stitch in the row just below.*

## Reversing the stitches
By inserting the hook from the back to the front the stitches will be reversed.

### How to work the reversed stitch

*Insert the hook from the back to the front of the stitch in the row below.*

## Working between stitches
Many different effects can be achieved by working into the spaces between the stitches rather than by working into the stitches themselves.

### How to work between two stitches

*Insert the hook through the space between the 2 stitches in the row below.*

### How to work into the chain space

*Insert the hook into the space made by the chain stitch in the row below.*

## Working into several rows below
Variations can be made by working into more than one row below and by working into different parts of the stitch.

### How to work through the stitch two rows below

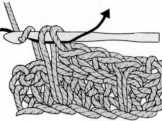

*Insert the hook from front to back into the space between the 2 stitches 2 rows below.*

### How to work into the side of the stitch three rows below

*Insert the hook into the side of the stitch 3 rows below.*

## Working around the stitch
Crochet stitches can be given a raised appearance by working around the stitches below from the front or an indented effect by working around stitches from back.

### How to make a raised effect

*Insert the hook from the front around the stitches below. To obtain an indented effect, work around stitches from back.*

## Russian stitch

This is the same as plain dc, except that it is worked in the round, so that every row is a right side row. Make any number of ch, then join into a ring with a ss into first ch.

**Round 1** 1ch as first dc, 1dc into each ch to end, join with a ss to first ch.

**Round 2** 1ch as first dc, * 1dc into next st, inserting hook through both halves of st, rep from * to end, join with a ss to first ch.

Rep rnd 2 throughout.

## Double stitch

Make any number of ch, 1ch, turn.

**Row 1** Insert hook into 2nd ch from hook, yrh, draw lp through, insert hook into next ch, yrh, draw lp through, yrh, draw through all 3 lps on hook, * insert hook into same ch as 2nd lp of previous st, yrh, draw lp through, insert hook into next ch, yrh, draw lp through, yrh, draw through all 3 lps on hook, rep from * to end, 1ch, turn.

**Row 2** Insert hook into first st, yrh, draw lp through, insert hook into next st, yrh, draw lp through, yrh, draw through all 3 lps on hook, * insert hook into same st as 2nd lp of previous st, yrh, draw lp through, insert hook into next st, yrh, draw lp through, yrh, draw through all 3 lps on hook, rep from * to end, 1ch, turn.

Rep row 2 throughout.

## Ridge stitch

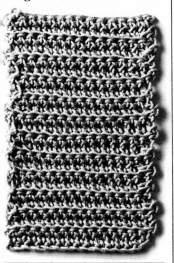

Make any number of ch, 1ch, turn. Work a row of dc on foundation ch, 1ch, turn.

**Row 1** *1dc into next dc, inserting hook through back half only of st, rep from * to end, 1ch, turn.

Rep row 1 throughout.

## Crossed half trebles

Make an odd number of ch, 2ch, turn.

**Row 1** Yrh, insert hook into 3rd ch from hook, yrh, draw lp through, yrh, insert hook into next ch, yrh, draw lp through, yrh, draw through all 5 lps on hook, 1ch, * (yrh, insert hook into next ch, yrh, draw lp through) twice, yrh, draw through all 5 lps on hook, 1ch, rep from * to last ch, 1htr into last ch, 2ch, turn.

**Row 2** Yrh, insert hook into first ch sp, yrh, draw lp through, yrh, insert hook into next ch sp, yrh, draw lp through, yrh, draw through all 5 lps on hook, 1ch, * yrh, insert hook into same ch sp as last lp of previous st, yrh, draw lp through, yrh, insert hook into next ch sp, yrh, draw lp through, yrh, draw through all 5 lps on hook, 1ch, rep from * to end, 1htr into t-ch, 2ch, turn.

Rep row 2 throughout.

## Double half trebles

Make any number of ch, 1ch, turn. Work 1 row of dc on foundation ch, 2ch, turn.

**Row 1** Yrh, insert hook into first st, yrh, draw lp through, yrh, insert hook into next st, yrh, draw lp through, yrh, draw through all 5 lps on hook, 1ch, * yrh, insert hook into same st as 2nd lp of previous st, yrh, draw lp through, yrh, insert hook into next st, yrh, draw lp through, yrh, draw through all 5 lps on hook, 1ch, rep from * to end, 1htr into t-ch, 1ch, turn.

**Row 2** * 1dc into ch sp, rep from * to end, 1dc into t-ch, 2ch, turn.

Rep rows 1 and 2 throughout.

## Trebles in relief

This is more commonly called *raised treble*.

Make an odd number of ch, 3ch, turn. Work a row of tr on foundation ch, 1ch, turn.

**Row 1** 1dc into each tr to end, 1dc into t-ch, 2ch, turn.

**Row 2** * Yrh, keeping hook at front of work, insert hook from right to left round stem of next tr on foundation row and work a tr – called RTF – miss dc above this tr, 1dc into next dc, rep from * to end, ending with 1RTF round stem of last tr, 1dc into t-ch, 1ch, turn.

**Row 3** 1dc into each st to end, 1dc into t-ch, 2ch, turn.

**Row 4** * 1RTF round stem of RTF on row 2, 1dc into next dc, rep from * to end, working last dc into t-ch, 1ch, turn.

Rep rows 3 and 4 throughout.

## Spider stitch

Make an even number of ch, 2ch, turn.

**Row 1** (1dc, 1ch, 1dc) into 3rd ch from hook, * miss 1ch, (1dc, 1ch, 1dc) into next ch, rep from * to last ch, 1dc into last ch, 2ch, turn.

**Row 2** * (1dc, 1ch, 1dc) into ch sp, rep from * to end, 1dc into t-ch, 2ch, turn.

Rep row 2 throughout.

## Cable stitch

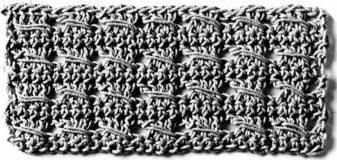

Make a number of ch divisible by 4 plus 2, 1ch, turn. Work a row of dc on foundation ch, 3ch, turn.

**Row 1** * Miss next st, 1tr into each of next 3 sts, yrh, insert hook from front to back into the st which was missed and work a tr, rep from * to end, 1tr into t-ch, 1ch, turn.

**Row 2** 1dc into each st to end, 3ch, turn.

Rep rows 1 and 2 throughout.

## Basket stitch

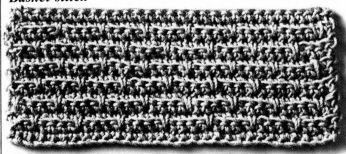

Make a number of ch divisible by 4 plus 3, 1ch, turn.
Work first 2 rows as given for ridge stitch, 1ch, turn.

**Row 3** 1dc into back half of each of first 3dc, * insert hook into st below next dc (i.e. 1 row down) and work a dc, miss this dc, 1dc into back half of next 3dc, rep from * to end, 1ch, turn.

## Ridged trebles

These are also called *stand trebles*. Make any number of ch, 3ch, turn.
Work a row of tr on foundation ch, 3ch, turn.

**Row 1** *1tr into next st, inserting hook through back half only of st, rep from * to end, 3ch, turn.

Rep row 1 throughout.

**Row 4** 1dc into back half of each st to end, 1ch, turn.

**Row 5** 1dc into back half of first dc, * 1dc into dc below next dc, miss this dc, 1dc into back half of next 3dc, rep from * to last 2 sts, 1dc into dc below next dc, 1dc into back half of last dc, 1ch, turn.

**Row 6** As row 4.

Rep rows 3 to 6 throughout.

# Textured stitches

Textured effects are created in crochet either by working into the same stitch several times or by wrapping the yarn around the hook several times and then drawing a loop through the wrappings. Various standard techniques for making textured stitches are shown below.

### Making a pineapple stitch
Each pineapple stitch is made into every other stitch on a row of chains.

#### How to make a pineapple stitch

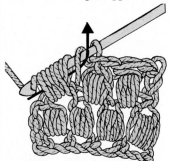

*(Yrh, insert hook into ch, yrh, draw through) 4 times into same st, 9 loops on hook, yrh, draw through 8 loops, yrh, draw through rem 2 loops, 1 ch.*

### Making a popcorn stitch
Each popcorn stitch is separated by trebles and made on a row of chains.

#### How to make a popcorn stitch

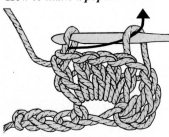

**1** *5tr into next st, withdraw hook from loop, insert hook into first of 5 tr, pick up dropped loop and draw it through.*

**2** *Finish with 1 ch.*

### Cabling around the stitch
Each cable is made by wrapping the hook around the treble below.

#### How to make a cable around the stitch

*Yrh, insert hook from back to front and through to back again around the tr of previous row, yrh, draw through, 3 loops on hook, yrh, draw through 2 loops on hook, yrh, draw through rem 2 loops.*

### Making a bullion stitch
A bullion stitch is made by wrapping the yarn several times around the hook before drawing a loop through. Use a hook thicker at the handle and finer at the working end and hold the loops in position with thumb and forefinger of left hand. The size of the bullion depends on the number of loops. Begin with a row of loose chain stitches and make one bullion into each stitch.

#### How to make a bullion stitch

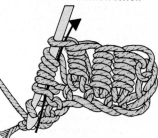

*Yrh evenly several times, insert hook into ch, yrh, draw through, yrh and draw through all loops on hook.*

### Making a shell stitch
Each shell is made of a cluster of trebles worked into spaces on the previous row.

#### How to make a shell stitch

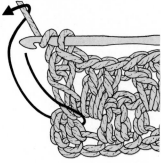

*(2 tr, 1 ch, 2 tr) into the space between 2 tr below.*

### Weaving around the stitch
Weave around each treble as shown below.

#### How to weave around the stitch

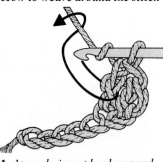

**1** *1tr, yrh, insert hook around tr just made, yrh, draw through.*

**2** *(Yrh, insert hook again around tr, yrh, draw through) twice more. Yrh, draw hook through all loops on hook.*

**3** *The hook and yarn are now in position ready to make the treble into next chain below.*

### Making a loop stitch
Loop stitches are formed on the back of the work on every second row with a row of double crochet in between. Loops can be of any size but, to keep them even, use a cardboard template, a pencil, or your finger. Finished loops can be left as they are, or they can be cut open to make a fringe. Begin by making a row of double crochet.

#### How to make a loop stitch

**1** *Wrap yarn from back to front around left forefinger, insert hook through first st and pass it behind yarn on forefinger. Catch both strands on forefinger.*

**2** *Draw both loops through and drop loop from forefinger, 3 loops on hook, yrh.*

**3** *Draw through all 3 loops on hook to complete loop stitch. Continue in this way to the end of the row. Then work one row of dc before next loop row.*

## Pineapple stitch

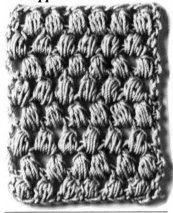

Make an odd number of ch, 3ch, turn.

**Row 1** Yrh, insert hook into 4th ch from hook, yrh, draw lp through (yrh, insert hook into same ch, yrh, draw lp through) 3 times, yrh, draw through 8 lps on hook, yrh, draw through rem 2 lps, 1ch, * miss 1ch, (yrh, insert hook into next ch, yrh, draw lp through) 4 times, yrh, draw through 8 lps, yrh, draw through rem 2 lps, 1ch, rep from * to last 2ch, miss 1ch, 1tr into last ch, 3ch, turn.

**Row 2** *(yrh, insert hook into ch sp, yrh, draw lp through) 4 times, yrh, draw through 8 lps, yrh, draw through rem 2 lps, 1ch, rep from * to end, 1tr into t-ch, 3ch, turn.

Rep row 2 throughout.

## Raised dots in pineapple stitch

Make a number of ch divisible by 4 plus 3, 1ch, turn.
Work 3 rows in dc, 1ch, turn.

**Row 4** 1dc into each of first 3 sts, * insert hook into next st, yrh, draw lp through, (yrh, insert hook into the same st 2 rows below – i.e. first row – yrh, draw lp through, yrh, draw through 2 lps) 6 times, yrh, draw through all 8 lps on hook – called 1 pineapple – 1dc into each of next 3dc, rep from * to end, 1ch, turn.
Work 3 rows in dc, 1ch, turn.

**Row 8** 1dc into first dc, * 1 pineapple into next dc, 1dc into each of next 3dc, rep from * to last 2 sts, 1 pineapple into next dc, 1dc into next dc, 1ch, turn.

Rep rows 1 to 8 throughout.

## Raised diagonal pineapple

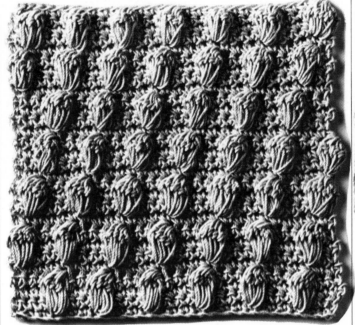

Make a number of ch divisible by 4 plus 3, 1ch, turn.
Work 3 rows in dc, 1ch, turn.

**Row 4** As row 4 of raised dots in pineapple stitch.
Work 3 rows in dc, 1ch, turn.

**Row 8** 1 pineapple into next st, * 1dc into each of next 3dc, 1 pineapple into next dc, rep from * to last 2 sts, 1dc into each of next 2dc, 1ch, turn.
Work 3 rows in dc, 1ch, turn.

**Row 12** As row 8 of raised dots in pineapple stitch.
Work 3 rows in dc, 1ch, turn.

**Row 16** 2dc, * 1 pineapple, 3dc, rep from * to last st, 1 pineapple into last dc, 1ch, turn.

Rep rows 1 to 16 throughout.

## Raised puff balls

Make a number of ch divisible by 6 plus 5, 1ch, turn.
Work 3 rows in dc, 1ch, turn.

**Row 4** 1dc into each of next 5dc, * 1ch, (1tr into next st 2 rows below) 6 times (all into the same st), take hook out of last tr, insert it into the first ch of this gr, pull the lp of the tr through the ch – called puff ball – miss this dc, 1dc into each of next 5dc, rep from * to end, 1ch, turn. Work 3 rows in dc, 1ch, turn.

**Row 8** 1dc into each of first 2dc, * 1ch, 1 puff ball below next dc, miss this dc, 1dc into each of next 5dc, rep from * to last 3 sts, 1 puff ball below next dc, 1dc into each of last 2dc, 1ch, turn.

Rep rows 1 to 8 throughout.

## Honeycomb stitch

Make a number of ch divisible by 3, 1ch, turn.
Work a row of dc on foundation ch, 1ch, turn.

**Row 1** *Yrh, insert hook into next st, (yrh, draw lp through, yrh, draw through 2 lps) 5 times, yrh, draw through 6 lps, 1dc into each of next 2dc, rep from * to end, 1ch, turn.

**Row 2** 1dc into each st to end, 1ch, turn.

**Row 3** *1dc into each of next 2dc, yrh, insert hook into next st, (yrh, draw lp through, yrh, draw through 2 lps) 5 times, yrh, draw through 6 lps, rep from * to end, 1ch, turn.

**Row 4** As row 2.

Rep rows 1 to 4 throughout.

## Cluster stitch

Make an odd number of ch, 3ch, turn.

**Row 1** Yrh, insert hook into 4th ch from hook, yrh, draw lp through, yrh, draw through 2 lps, (yrh, insert hook into same ch, yrh, draw lp through, yrh, draw through 2 lps) twice, yrh, draw through 4 lps on hook, 1ch, * miss 1ch, (yrh, insert hook into next ch, yrh, draw lp through, yrh, draw through 2 lps) 3 times into the same ch, yrh, draw through 4 lps on hook – called 1cl or cluster – 1ch, rep from * to last 2ch, miss 1ch, 1tr into last ch, 3ch, turn.

**Row 2** * 1cl into ch sp, 1ch, rep from * to end, 1tr into t-ch, 3ch, turn.

Rep row 2 throughout.

### Canary stitch

Make an even number of ch, 3ch, turn.

**Row 1** Yrh, insert hook into 4th ch from hook, yrh, draw lp through, yrh, draw through 2 lps, yrh, miss 1ch, insert hook into next ch, yrh, draw lp through, yrh, draw through 2 lps, yrh, draw through all 3 lps on hook, 1ch * yrh, insert hook into same ch as last lp of previous st, yrh, draw lp through, yrh, draw through 2 lps, yrh, miss 1ch, insert hook into next ch, yrh, draw lp through, yrh, draw through 2 lps, yrh, draw through all 3 lps, 1ch, rep from * to last ch, 1tr into last cn, 3ch, turn.

**Row 2** Yrh, insert hook into first ch sp, yrh, draw lp through, yrh, draw through 2 lps, yrh, insert hook into next ch sp, yrh, draw lp through, yrh, draw through 2 lps, yrh, draw through all 3 lps, 1ch, * yrh, insert hook into same ch sp as last lp of previous st, yrh, draw lp through, yrh, insert hook into next ch sp, yrh, draw lp through, yrh, draw through 2 lps, yrh, draw through all 3 lps, 1ch, rep from * to end, 1tr into t-ch, 3ch, turn.

Rep row 2 throughout.

### Close shell stitch

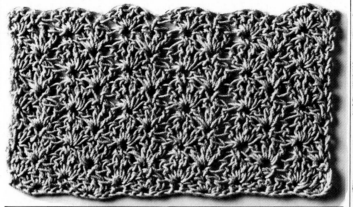

Make a number of ch divisible by 6, plus 4, 3ch, turn.

**Row 1** 3tr into 4th ch from hook, miss 2ch, 1dc into next ch, * miss 2ch, 4tr into next ch, miss 2ch, 1dc into next ch, rep from * to end, 3ch, turn.

**Row 2** 2tr into dc, * 1dc bet 2nd and 3rd tr, 4tr into dc, rep from * to end, 1dc bet last tr and t-ch, 3ch, turn.

Rep row 2 throughout.

### Blossom stitch

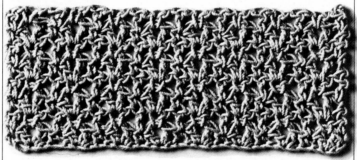

Make a number of ch divisible by 4 plus 3, 2ch, turn.

**Row 1** (1tr, 1ch, 1tr) into 3rd ch from hook, miss 1ch, 1dc into next ch, * miss 1ch, (1tr, 1ch, 1tr) into next ch, miss 1ch, 1dc into next ch, rep from * to end, 2ch, turn.

**Row 2** * 1tr into dc, 1ch, 1dc into ch sp, 1ch, rep from * to end, 1tr into t-ch, 2ch, turn.

**Row 3** * (1tr, 1ch, 1tr) into dc, 1dc into tr, rep from * to end, working last dc into t-ch, 2ch, turn.

Rep rows 2 and 3 throughout.

### Paris stitch

Make a number of ch divisible by 3 plus 1, 3ch, turn.

**Row 1** (1tr, 2ch, 1dc) into 4th ch from hook, * miss 2ch, (2tr, 2ch, 1dc) into next ch, rep from * to end, 3ch, turn.

**Row 2** (1tr, 2ch, 1dc) into 2ch sp, * (2tr, 2ch, 1dc) into next 2ch sp, rep from * to end, 3ch, turn.

Rep row 2 throughout.

### Spray stitch

Make a number of ch divisible by 3 plus 1, 2ch, turn.

**Row 1** 2tr into 3rd ch from hook, * miss 2ch, (1dc, 2tr) into next ch, rep from * to last 3ch, miss 2ch, 1dc into last ch, 2ch, turn.

**Row 2** 2tr into first dc, *(1dc, 2tr) into next dc, rep from * to end, 1dc into t-ch, 2ch, turn.

Rep row 2 throughout.

### Sprig stitch

Make an odd number of ch, 2ch, turn.

**Row 1** (1dc, 2ch, 1dc) into 3rd ch from hook, * miss 1ch, (1dc, 2ch, 1dc) into next ch, rep from * to last 2ch, miss 1ch, 1dc into last ch, 2ch, turn.

**Row 2** * (1dc, 2ch, 1dc) into 2ch sp, rep from * to end, 1dc into t-ch, 2ch, turn.

Rep row 2 throughout.

### Tulip stitch

Make a number of ch divisible by 4, plus 1, 3ch, turn.

**Row 1** 3tr into 4th ch from hook, * miss 3ch, (1dc, 3ch, 3tr) into next ch, rep from * to last 4ch, miss 3ch, 1dc into last ch, 3ch, turn.

**Row 2** 3tr into first dc, * (1dc, 3ch, 3tr) into 3ch lp, rep from * to last lp, 1dc into last lp, 3ch, turn.

Rep row 2 throughout.

### Rope stitch

Make a number of ch divisible by 3, 3ch, turn.

**Row 1** 1tr into 4th ch from hook, 1ch, 1tr into next ch, * miss 1ch, 1tr into next ch, 1ch, 1tr into next ch, rep from * to last ch, 1tr into last ch, 3ch, turn.

**Row 2** (1tr, 1ch, 1tr) into each ch sp to end, 1tr into t-ch, 3ch, turn.

Rep row 2 throughout.

# Peacock stitch

Make a number of ch divisible by 14, plus 1, 1ch, turn.

**Row 1** 1dc into 2nd ch from hook, * miss 6ch, 13 long tr into next ch (drawing lp up to ½in. to form a long tr), miss 6ch, 1dc into next ch, rep from * to end, 4ch, turn.

**Row 2** 1 long tr into dc, * 5ch, 1dc into 7th of 13 long tr, 5ch, 2 long tr into dc, rep from * to end, 1ch, turn.

**Row 3** * 1dc bet 2 long tr, 13 long tr into dc, rep from * to end, 1dc bet long tr and t-ch, 4ch, turn.

Rep rows 2 and 3 throughout.

# Loop stitch

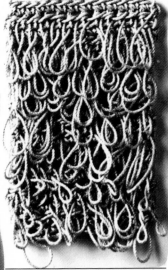

Make any number of ch, 1ch, turn. Work a row of dc on the foundation ch, 1ch, turn.

**Row 1** (wrong side of work) * Yrh, insert hook into next st, take yarn round finger, yrh, draw lp through, yrh, draw through 3 lps on hook, rep from * to end, 1ch, turn.

**Row 2** 1dc into each st to end, 1ch, turn.

Rep rows 1 and 2 throughout.

# Parquet stitch

Make a number of ch divisible by 3 plus 1, 1ch, turn.

**Row 1** 1dc into 2nd ch from hook, * 2ch, miss 2ch, 1dc into next ch, rep from * to end, 3ch, turn.

**Row 2** 1tr into first dc, * 3tr into next dc, rep from * to end, 2tr into last dc, 1ch, turn.

**Row 3** 1dc into first tr, * 2ch, 1dc into 2nd of 3tr, rep from * to end, 2ch, 1dc into t-ch, 3ch, turn.

Rep rows 2 and 3 throughout.

# Scallop stitch

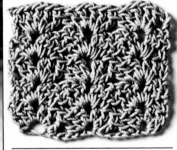

Make a number of ch divisible by 6 plus 2, 3ch, turn.

**Row 1** (2tr, 1ch, 2tr) into 4th ch from hook, * yrh, insert hook into next ch, yrh, draw lp through, yrh, draw through 2 lps, yrh, miss 3ch, insert hook into next ch, yrh, draw lp through, (yrh, draw through 2 lps) 3 times, (2tr, 1ch, 2tr) into next ch, rep from * to last ch, 1tr into last ch, 3ch, turn.

**Row 2** * (2tr, 1ch, 2tr) into ch sp, yrh, insert hook into next tr, yrh, draw lp through, yrh, draw through 2 lps, yrh, miss 3 sts, insert hook into next tr, yrh, draw lp through, (yrh, draw through 2 lps) 3 times, rep from * to end, ending with (2tr, 1ch, 2tr) into ch sp, 1tr into t-ch, 3ch, turn.

Rep row 2 throughout.

# Sweet pea stitch

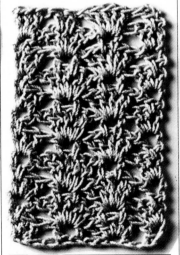

Make a number of ch divisible by 7 plus 4, 3ch, turn.

**Row 1** 1tr into 4th ch from hook, * miss 2ch, 5tr into next ch, miss 2ch, 1tr into each of next 2ch, rep from * to last 3ch, miss 2ch, 3tr into last ch, 3ch, turn.

**Row 2** 1tr bet first 2tr, * 5tr bet the 2 single tr, 1tr bet 2nd and 3rd of 5tr, 1tr bet 3rd and 4th of 5tr, rep from * to end, 3tr bet last tr and t-ch, 3ch, turn.

Rep row 2 throughout.

# Turtle stitch

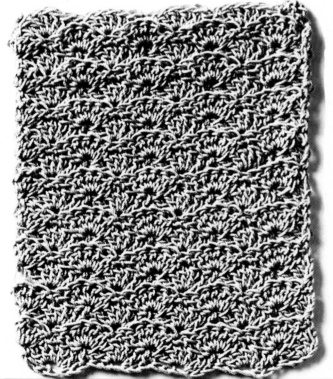

Make a number of ch divisible by 6 plus 4, 3ch, turn.

**Row 1** 3tr into 4th ch from hook, miss 2ch, 1dc into next ch, * miss 2ch, 5tr into next ch, miss 2ch, 1dc into next ch, rep from * to end, 3ch, turn.

**Row 2** Working into the back half only of each st, 3tr into dc, * 1dc into 3rd of 5tr, 5tr into dc, rep from * to end, 1dc into t-ch, 3ch, turn.

Rep row 2 throughout.

# Openwork techniques

Openwork crochet is formed by missing stitches and making chains over the spaces left. Various patterns can be made with openwork by altering the combinations of stitches and spaces. For example, chains can be used to make simple net ground. They can also be used to form bars onto which subsequent stitches are worked to form more intricate patterns, the simplest of which are worked with double crochet and trebles to form lattices. Other openwork patterns can be made by connecting trebles and crossing them to give a fretwork effect.

## Making a simple openwork pattern
The spaces in the pattern below are formed by missing stitches and making chains over them.

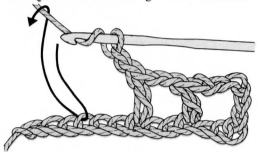

*Work 1 tr, 2 ch, miss 2 ch in previous row, 1 tr into next ch in previous row.*

## Making a simple net ground
The net ground below is made with chain and double crochet stitches.

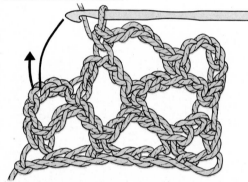

*Work 1 dc into middle of 5 ch of previous row, 5 ch, 1 dc into middle of 5 ch of previous row.*

## Making a bar and lattice
The lattice is formed on a bar of chains.

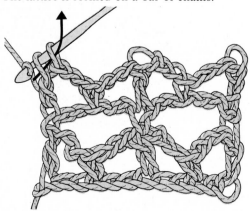

*Work 1 tr, 3 ch, miss 2 ch in previous row, 1 dc into next ch, 3 ch, miss 2 ch, 1 tr into next st.*

## Making crossing trebles
A fretwork effect is formed by making a row of crossing trebles on a foundation chain.

### How to make crossing trebles

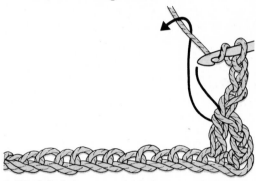

**1** *Work 3 ch (to act as 1tr), 1tr into 5th ch from hook, 4 ch, yrh, insert hook into junction of tr and 3 ch as shown in diagram above.*

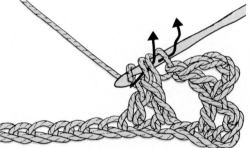

**2** *Complete tr in usual way, 1ch, * yrh twice, miss 1ch, insert hook into next ch, yrh, draw through, yrh, draw through 2 lps, 3 lps now on hook, yrh, miss 1ch, insert hook into next ch, yrh, draw through, 5 lps now on hook, (yrh, draw through 2 lps) 4 times as shown in diagram above.*

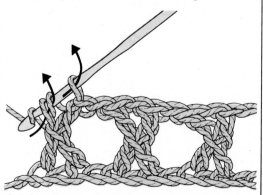

**3** *1ch, yrh, insert hook through upper part of connected trebles, complete tr in usual way, 1ch, rep from * to complete row.*

## Simple net ground

Make a number of ch divisible by 4 plus 1, 5ch, turn.

**Row 1** 1dc into 10th ch from hook, * 5ch, miss 3ch, 1dc into next ch, rep from * to end, 5ch, turn.

**Row 2** 1dc into 5ch lp, * 5ch, 1dc into next lp, rep from * to end, 5ch, turn.
Rep row 2 throughout.

## Solomon's knot

There is no foundation ch for this stitch. Make a slip lp and put onto hook.

**Row 1** *Draw lp up to ½in., yrh, draw lp through, insert hook bet double and single threads of lp just made, yrh, draw lp through, yrh, draw through both lps on hook, rep from * for length reqd, making an even no. of knots, turn. knots, turn.

**Row 2** Miss knot on hook and next 3 knots, work 1dc into next knot, * make 2 knots as on row 1, miss 1 knot on row 1, work 1dc into next knot, rep from * to end, working last dc into first ch on row 1.

**Row 3** Make 3 knots, 1dc into next free knot along last row, * make 2 knots, 1dc into next free knot along last row, rep from * to end.

Rep row 3 throughout.

## Ladder stitch

Make a number of ch divisible by 6 plus 1, 1ch, turn.

**Row 1** 1dc into 2nd ch from hook, * 5ch, miss 5ch, (1dc, 3ch, 1dc) into next ch, rep from * to last 6ch, 5ch, miss 5ch, 1dc into last ch, 1ch, turn.

**Row 2** 1dc into first dc, * 5ch, (1dc, 3ch, 1dc) into 3ch lp, rep from * to end, ending with 5ch, 1dc into last dc, 1ch, turn.

Rep row 2 throughout.

## Bar and lattice stitch

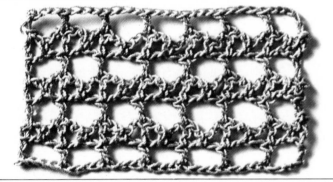

Make a number of ch divisible by 4 plus 1, 5ch, turn.

**Row 1** 1tr into 10th ch from hook, * 3ch, miss 3ch, 1tr into next ch, rep from * to end, 4ch, turn.

**Row 2** * 1dc into 2nd of 3ch, 2ch, 1tr into tr, 2ch, rep from * to end, ending with 2dc into 2nd ch, 2ch, 1tr into t-ch, 5ch, turn.

**Row 3** 1tr into next tr, * 3ch, 1tr into next tr, rep from * to end, working last tr into t-ch, 4ch, turn.

Rep rows 2 and 3 throughout.

## Reseau stitch

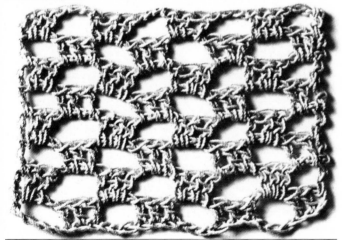

Make a number of ch divisible by 6 plus 1, 3ch, turn.

**Row 1** 1tr into 4th ch from hook, 1tr into next ch, * 3ch, miss 3ch, 1tr into each of next 3ch, rep from * to last 4ch, 3ch, miss 3ch, 1tr into last ch, 3ch, turn.

**Row 2** 2tr into first 3ch sp, * 3ch, 3tr into next 3ch sp, rep from * to end, ending with 3ch, 1tr into t-ch, 3ch, turn.

Rep row 2 throughout.

## Paddle stitch

Make a number of ch divisible by 6 plus 1, 3ch, turn.

**Row 1** (1tr, 2ch, 1tr) into 7th ch from hook, * miss 2ch, (2tr, 1ch, 2tr) into next ch, miss 2ch, (1tr, 2ch, 1tr) into next ch, rep from * to last 3ch, miss 2ch, 1tr into last ch, 3ch, turn.

**Row 2** * (2tr, 1ch, 2tr) into 2ch sp, (1tr, 2ch, 1tr) into 1ch sp, rep from * to end, ending with (2tr, 1ch, 2tr) into 2ch sp, 1tr into t-ch, 3ch, turn.

**Row 3** * (1tr, 2ch, 1tr) into 1ch sp, (2tr, 1ch, 2tr) into 2ch sp, rep from * to end, ending with (1tr, 2ch, 1tr) into 1ch sp, 1tr into t-ch, 3ch, turn.

Rep rows 2 and 3 throughout.

## Irish net stitch

Make a number of ch divisible by 4 plus 1, 5ch, turn.

**Row 1** (1dc, 3ch, 1dc) into 10th ch from hook, * 5ch, miss 3ch, (1dc, 3ch, 1dc) into next ch, rep from * to last 4ch, 5ch, miss 3ch, 1dc into last ch, 5ch, turn.

**Row 2** * (1dc, 3ch, 1dc) into 3rd of 5ch, 5ch, rep from * to end, 1dc into t-ch, 5ch, turn.

Rep row 2 throughout.

## Venetian stitch

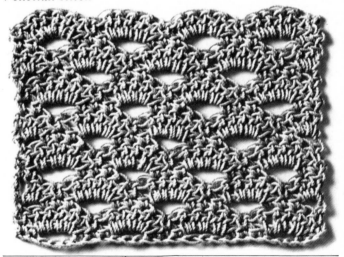

Make a number of ch divisible by 6 plus 1, 1ch, turn.

**Row 1** 1dc into 2nd ch from hook, 1dc into next ch, * 3ch, miss 3ch, 1dc into each of next 3ch, rep from * to last 5ch, 3ch, miss 3ch, 1dc into each of last 2ch, 1ch, turn.

**Row 2** 1dc into first dc, * 5tr into 3ch sp, miss 1dc, 1dc into next dc, rep from * to end, 3ch, turn.

**Row 3** * 1dc into 2nd, 3rd and 4th of 5tr, 3ch, rep from * to end, ending with 1dc into 2nd, 3rd and 4th of 5tr, 2ch, 1dc into last dc, 3ch, turn.

**Row 4** 2tr into 2ch sp, miss 1dc, 1dc into next dc, * 5tr into 3ch sp, miss 1dc, 1dc into next dc, rep from * to end, 3tr into last ch sp, 1ch, turn.

**Row 5** 1dc into each of first 2tr, * 3ch, 1dc into 2nd, 3rd and 4th of 5tr, rep from * to end, ending with 3ch, 1dc into each of last 2tr, 1ch, turn.

Rep rows 2 to 5 throughout.

123

## Crown stitch

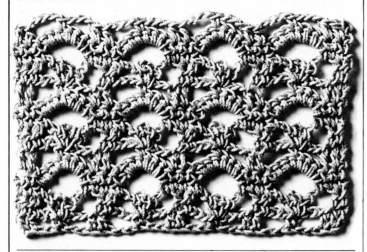

Make a number of ch divisible by 7 plus 2, 2ch, turn.

**Row 1** 1htr into 3rd ch from hook, 1htr into next ch, * 3ch, miss 2ch, 1dc into next ch, 3ch, miss 2ch, 1htr into each of next 2ch, rep from * to end, 2ch, turn.

**Row 2** 1htr into each of first 2htr, * 3ch, (1dc, 3ch, 1dc) into dc, 3ch, 1htr into each of next 2htr, rep from * to end, 1ch, turn.

**Row 3** 1dc into each of 2htr, * 1dc into 3ch sp, 5ch, 1dc into next 3ch sp, 1dc into each of 2htr, rep from * to end, 1ch, turn.

**Row 4** 1dc into each of first 2dc, * miss 1dc, 7dc into 5ch sp, miss 1dc, 1dc into each of next 2dc, rep from * to end, 2ch, turn.

**Row 5** 1htr into each of first 2dc, * 3ch, miss 3dc, 1dc into next dc, 3ch, miss 3dc, 1htr into each of next 2dc, rep from * to end, 2ch, turn.

Rep rows 2 to 5 throughout.

## Star stitch

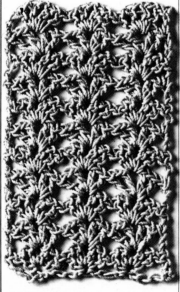

Make a number of ch divisible by 4 plus 1, 3ch, turn.

**Row 1** 1tr into 8th ch from hook, (1ch, 1tr) 3 times into same ch, * miss 3ch, 1tr into next ch, (1ch, 1tr) 3 times into same ch, rep from * to last 4ch, miss 3ch, 1tr into last ch, 3ch, turn.

**Row 2** * 1tr into 2nd ch sp of shell, (1ch, 1tr) 3 times into same ch sp, rep from * to end, 1tr into t-ch, 3ch, turn.

Rep row 2 throughout.

## Diamond stitch

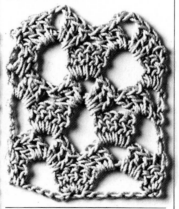

Make a number of ch divisible by 6 plus 1, 3ch, turn.

**Row 1** 2tr into 4th ch from hook, * 4ch, miss 5ch, 5tr into next ch, rep from * to last 6ch, 4ch, miss 5ch, 3tr into last ch, 1ch, turn.

**Row 2** * (3tr, 3ch, 3tr) into 4ch sp, rep from * to end, 1dc into t-ch, 6ch, turn.

**Row 3** * 5tr into 3ch sp, 4ch, rep from * to end, ending with 5tr into 3ch sp, 3ch, 1tr into t-ch, 5ch, turn.

**Row 4** 3tr into 3ch sp, * (3tr, 3ch, 3tr) into 4ch sp, rep from * to end, ending with (3tr, 2ch, 1tr) into t-ch, 3ch, turn.

**Row 5** 2tr into 2ch sp, * 4ch, 5tr into 3ch sp, rep from * to end, 4ch, 3tr into t-ch, 1ch, turn.

Rep rows 2 to 5 throughout.

## Picot lace ground

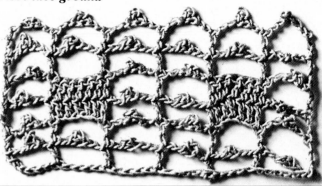

Make a number of ch divisible by 15 plus 1, 7ch, turn.

**Row 1** 1dc into 3rd ch from hook – called picot – 2ch, miss 9ch, 1tr into next ch, * 5ch, pc, 2ch, miss 4ch, 1tr into next ch, rep from * to end, 8ch, pc, 2ch, turn.

**Row 2** Miss first tr, 1tr into next tr, * 5ch, 1tr into next tr, (5ch, pc, 2ch, 1tr into next tr) twice, rep from * to last 2pc, 5ch, 1tr into next tr, 5ch, pc, 2ch, 1tr into 3rd ch beyond pc, 8ch, pc, 2ch, turn.

**Row 3** Miss first tr, 1tr into next tr, * 1tr into each of next 5ch, 1tr into next tr, (5ch, pc, 2ch, 1tr into next tr) twice, rep from * ending with 1tr into each of next 5ch, 1tr into next tr, 5ch, pc, 2ch, 1tr into 3rd ch beyond pc, 8ch, pc, 2ch, turn.

**Row 4** Miss first tr, 1tr into next tr, * 1tr into each of next 6tr, (5ch, pc, 2ch, 1tr into next tr) twice, rep from * ending with 1tr into each of next 6tr, 5ch, pc, 2ch, 1tr into 3rd ch beyond pc, 8ch, pc, 2ch, turn.

**Row 5** Miss first tr, 1tr into next tr, * 5ch, pc, 2ch, miss 5tr, 1tr into next tr, (5ch, pc, 2ch, 1tr into next tr) twice, rep from * ending with 5ch, pc, 2ch, miss 5tr, 1tr into next tr, 5ch, pc, 2ch, 1tr into 3rd ch beyond pc, 8ch, pc, 2ch, turn.

**Row 6** Miss first tr, 1tr into next tr, * 5ch, pc, 2ch, 1tr into next tr, rep from * to end, working last tr into 3rd ch beyond pc, 8ch, pc, 2ch, turn.

Rep rows 2 to 6 throughout.

## Palm lace ground

Make a number of ch divisible by 13 plus 6, 3ch, turn.

**Row 1** 3tr into 4th ch from hook, * miss 4ch, 4tr into next ch, 5ch, miss 3ch, 1dc into next ch, 5ch, miss 3ch, 4tr into next ch, rep from * to last 5ch, miss 4ch, 4tr into last ch, 3ch, turn.

**Row 2** 3tr into first tr, * miss 6tr, 4tr into next tr, 3ch, 1dc into 5ch lp, 1dc into next 5ch lp, 3ch, 4tr into next tr, rep from * to end, miss 6tr, 4tr into t-ch, 3ch, turn.

**Row 3** 3tr into first tr, * miss 6tr, 4tr into next tr, 5ch, 1dc bet 2dc, 5ch, 4tr into next tr, rep from * to end, miss 6tr, 4tr into t-ch, 6ch, turn.

**Row 4** 1dc bet gr of tr, * 5ch, 4tr into each of next 2 5ch lps, 5ch, 1dc bet gr of tr, rep from * to end, 3ch, 1tr into t-ch, 6ch, turn.

**Row 5** 1dc into first lp, * 1dc into next lp, 3ch, 4tr into next tr, miss 6tr, 4tr into next tr, 3ch, 1dc into next lp, rep from * to end, 1dc into next lp, 3ch, 1tr into 3rd of 6ch, 6ch, turn.

**Row 6** 1dc bet 2dc, * 5ch, 4tr into next tr, miss 6tr, 4tr into next tr, 5ch, 1dc bet 2dc, rep from * to end, 5ch, 1dc into 3rd of 6ch, 3ch, turn.

**Row 7** 3tr into first lp, * 4tr into next lp, 5ch, 1dc bet gr of tr, 5ch, 4tr into next lp, rep from * to end, 4tr into t-ch lp, 3ch, turn.

Rep rows 2 to 7 throughout.

## *Ruby lace ground*

Make a number of ch divisible by 8, 1ch, turn.

**Row 1** Starting into 2nd ch from hook * 1dc into next 4ch, 3ch, ss into first of these 3ch – called picot – 1dc into each of next 4ch, turn, 9ch, ss to first dc, turn, into the 9ch lp work 7dc, 3pc, 7dc, rep from * to end, 9ch, turn.

**Row 2** * 1dc into 2nd of 3pc, 8ch, rep from * to end, 1dc into 2nd of

3pc, 4ch, 1tr tr into t-ch, 1ch, turn.

**Row 3** 1dc into each of next 4ch, turn, 5ch, ss to first dc, turn, 2pc, 7dc into 5ch lp, rep from * on first row to last 9ch, 1dc into each of next 4ch, turn, 5ch, ss into first dc, turn, 7dc into 5ch lp, 2pc, turn.

**Row 4** * 8ch, 1dc into 2nd of 3pc, rep from * to end, 3ch, turn.

Rep rows 1 to 4 throughout.

## *Daisy stitch*

Make a number of ch divisible by 8 plus 1, 3ch, turn.

**Row 1** Starting into 8th ch from hook, ** yrh twice, insert hook into st, yrh, draw lp through, (yrh, draw through 2 lps) twice ** 3 times into the same ch, yrh, draw through 4 lps, * 7ch, rep from ** to ** 3 times into same ch as before, yrh, draw through 4 lps, 3ch, miss 3ch, 1dc into next ch, 3ch, miss 3ch, rep from ** to ** 3 times into next ch, yrh, draw through 4 lps, rep from * to end, ending after a dc into last ch, 3ch, turn.

**Row 2** Rep from ** to ** 3 times into ch before first petal, yrh, draw through 4 lps, 3ch, rep from ** to ** twice into top of petal just worked, yrh, draw through 3 lps, * 1dc into 4th of 7ch, 3ch, rep from ** to ** twice into dc just worked, rep from ** to ** 3 times into ch after next petal, rep from ** to ** 3 times into ch before foll petal, yrh, draw through 9 lps, 3ch, rep from ** to ** twice into top of gr just worked, yrh, draw through 3 lps, rep from * to end, ending with 1dc into 4th of 7ch, 3ch, rep from ** to ** twice into dc just worked, rep from ** to ** 3 times into ch after next petal,

yrh, draw through 6 lps, 3ch, turn.

**Row 3** Rep from ** to ** twice into top of petal just worked, yrh, draw through 3 lps, * 3ch, 1dc into dc, 3ch, rep from ** to ** 3 times into centre of next gr, yrh, draw through 4 lps, 7ch, rep from ** to ** 3 times into same place, yrh, draw through 4 lps, rep from * to end, ending with 3ch, 1dc into dc, 3ch, rep from ** to ** 3 times into top of gr at end, yrh, draw through 4 lps, 7ch, turn.

**Row 4** Rep from ** to ** twice into 4th of 7ch just worked, * rep from ** to ** 3 times into ch after next petal, rep from ** to ** 3 times into ch before foll petal, yrh, draw through 9 lps, 3ch, rep from ** to ** twice into top of gr just worked, yrh, draw through 3 lps, 1dc into 4th of 7ch, 3ch, rep from ** to ** twice into dc just made, rep from * to end, ending after 1dc into t-ch, 3ch, turn.

**Row 5** * Rep from ** to ** 3 times into top of next gr, yrh, draw through 4 lps, 7ch, rep from ** to ** 3 times into top of same gr, yrh, draw through 4 lps, 3ch, 1dc into dc, rep from * to end, ending after 1dc into t-ch, 3ch, turn.

Rep rows 2 to 5 throughout.

## *Border stitch*

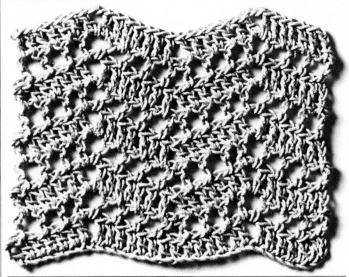

Make a number of ch divisible by 14, 2ch, turn.

**Row 1** 1tr into 4th ch from hook, 1tr into each of next 5ch, * 2ch, 1tr into each of next 14ch, rep from * to last 7ch, 2ch, 1tr into each of next 7ch, turn.

**Row 2** Ss into 2nd tr, 4ch, (miss next tr, 1tr into next tr, 1ch) twice, miss next tr, * (1tr, 3ch, 1tr) into 2ch sp, (1ch, miss 1tr, 1tr into next tr) 3 times, miss 2tr, (1tr into next tr, 1ch, miss 1tr) 3 times, rep from

* to end, ending with (1tr, 3ch, 1tr) into 2ch sp, (1ch, miss 1tr, 1tr into next tr) 3 times, turn.

**Row 3** Ss into ch sp, 3ch, (1tr into tr, 1tr into ch sp) twice, 1tr into tr, *(1tr, 2ch, 1tr) into 3ch sp, (1tr into tr, 1tr into ch sp) 3 times, miss 2tr, (1tr into ch sp, 1tr into tr) 3 times, rep from * to end, ending with (1tr, 2ch, 1tr) into 3ch sp, (1tr into tr, 1tr into ch sp) 3 times, turn.

Rep rows 2 and 3 throughout.

## *Sea stitch*

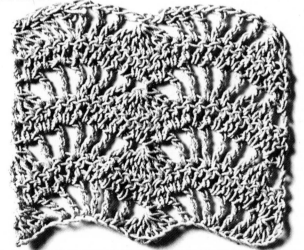

Make a number of ch divisible by 12, 3ch, turn.

**Row 1** Yrh, insert hook into 4th ch from hook, yrh, draw lp through, yrh, draw through 2 lps, ** yrh, insert hook into next ch, yrh, draw lp through, yrh, draw through 2 lps ** rep from ** to ** once more, yrh, draw through 4 lps, *(1ch, 1dtr into next ch) twice, (1ch, 1dtr) twice into next ch, (1ch, 1dtr into next ch) twice, 1ch, rep from ** to ** into each of next 7ch, yrh, draw through 7 lps, yrh, draw through rem 2 lps – called 7tr tog – rep from * to end, but ending with 4tr tog instead of 7, 3ch, turn.

**Row 2** (1tr into ch sp, 1tr into dtr) 6 times, * rep from ** to ** into each of next 2 ch sps, yrh, draw through 3 lps, 1tr into dtr, (1tr into ch sp, 1tr into dtr) 5 times, rep from * to end, rep from ** to ** into next ch sp and into t-ch, yrh, draw through 3 lps, 3ch, turn.

**Row 3** Miss first tr, work next 3tr tog, * (1ch, 1dtr into next tr) twice, (1ch, 1dtr) twice into next tr, (1ch, 1dtr into next tr) twice, 1ch, work 7tr tog, rep from * to end, but ending with 4tr tog instead of 7, 3ch, turn.

Rep rows 2 and 3 throughout.

125

# Shaping crochet

Crochet is easy to shape as only one stitch is worked at a time. This makes the fabric both easy to handle and easy to measure, either held against a person or flat on a paper pattern. Crochet shapes and designs can be worked in three ways: firstly, by making simple squares and rectangles which can be put together in different ways; secondly, by increasing and decreasing the number of stitches according to the pattern, and thirdly by varying the heights of the basic stitches. But whatever method is used, the size of the stitch must be first determined.

### Gauging stitch size

Whatever the design, you will have to measure the size of the work. Three factors will always govern the size of the stitch. **1** The size of hook and type of yarn. **2** The type of stitch pattern. **3** The individual worker. Before you begin to crochet, whether you are following pattern instructions or whether you are creating an original design, these three points must be taken into account so that you can calculate accurately the number of stitches and rows you will need. This process is known as *stitch gauging* (see opposite page for how to measure stitch gauge). No one factor is more important than any other in stitch gauging, so all three must be taken into consideration.

### The size of hook and type of yarn

The selection of hook and yarn is among the first decisions to be made. The combination of yarn and hook is vital in determining the size of the stitch. The six samples of double crochet (right) show how hook and yarn combinations alter the size of the design. All the samples were worked with eight stitches over eight rows.

### The stitch pattern

The stitch pattern in crochet can make a very large difference to the size of the work. Some patterns form a loose fabric, while others form a tight one. The three pattern samples (right) have all been worked with eight stitches over eight rows with the same hook and yarn combination, yet each works out to a different size.

### The crochet worker

The flow of yarn is controlled by the worker. This control, known as *tension*, varies according to the individual: a beginner's crochet, for example, is often a little tense and this can result in the stitches becoming small and tight. This fault can be corrected by changing to a larger hook. Both the samples (right) have been worked with the same hook, yarn and stitch pattern by two different workers. Although the difference in size is small, over a large area of work it could be crucial: a difference of half a stitch over 1 in. can make all the difference between success or disaster when making crochet garments, for example.

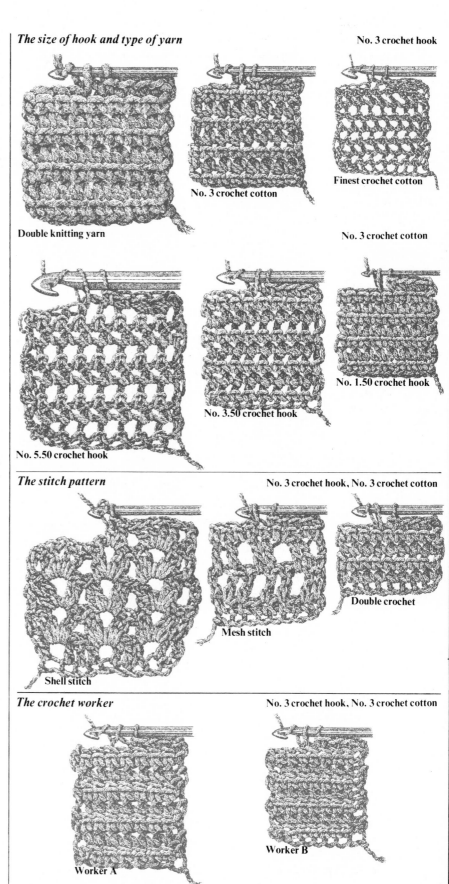

**The size of hook and type of yarn**

No. 3 crochet hook

No. 3 crochet cotton

Finest crochet cotton

Double knitting yarn

No. 3 crochet cotton

No. 5.50 crochet hook

No. 3.50 crochet hook

No. 1.50 crochet hook

**The stitch pattern**　　No. 3 crochet hook, No. 3 crochet cotton

Double crochet

Mesh stitch

Shell stitch

**The crochet worker**　　No. 3 crochet hook, No. 3 crochet cotton

Worker A

Worker B

## Stitch gauging

You must always measure the stitch gauge before you start to crochet. This is necessary in order to check the tension against the instructions in a pattern or to calculate the number of stitches to use and rows to work if you are creating a new design. The number of stitches and the number of rows determine the size of the crochet. If you have more stitches per inch (cm) on your test piece than required, try a larger hook. If less you should try a smaller hook.

### Width gauging

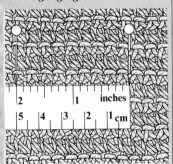

Lay a test piece of crochet on a flat surface and place the pins vertically 2 in. (5 cm) apart. Now count the number of stitches between the pins. For total accuracy, pin out the distance several times. You should now be able to calculate correctly the number of stitches per inch (cm).

### Length gauging

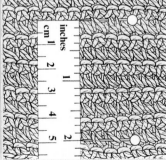

Lay the test piece of crochet out as above but place the pins horizontally 2 in. (5 cm) apart. Then count the number of rows between the pins. Continue testing until the number of stitches is accurate.

# Using increasing to shape

By increasing the number of stitches in a row or round you can widen the crochet. Increases are usually worked on basic stitches but when they are used in conjunction with a special stitch, the instructions will be included in the stitch pattern you are working from.

### Increasing by working twice into one stitch

The simplest form of increasing is to work twice into the same stitch, making 2 stitches from one. This can be done in the beginning, middle and end of rows, either as a single increase or a double increase. To shape a sleeve, for example, you would make the increase gradually at the sides into the first and last stitches of a row.

### Single increases at the beginning and end of the row

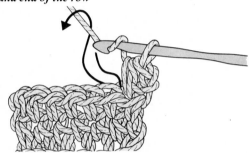

Where the increase is required, insert the hook into the stitch in the row below. Make a stitch; insert the hook again into the same stitch and make a second stitch.

When increasing at the beginning of the row, work twice into the first stitch and at the end of the row twice into the last stitch.

### Single increases in the middle of the row

When working an increase in the middle of a row or round, follow the same method but mark the position of the increase with a piece of coloured thread so that further increases can take place at the same point on subsequent rows. When increasing more than once in a row or round, make sure the increases are spread evenly across the work. The abbreviation for this is *inc evenly*.

### Double increases

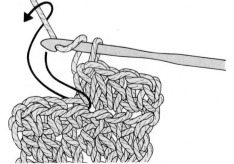

To make 2 increases instead of one, work three times into the same stitch where the double increase is needed.

### Adding stitches at the edge

If several stitches need to be added at edge of work, a different method is used: additional chain stitches are made.

### Multiple increases at the beginning of the row

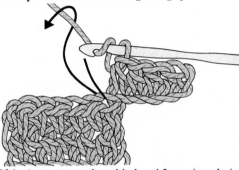

If 4 stitches are to be added and 2 turning chains are required for the stitch being worked, make a chain of 6 stitches. Then insert hook into 3rd chain from the hook, and work the 4 new crochet stitches.

### Multiple increases at the end of the row

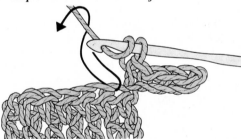

The same method is used, but the chain of extra stitches must be made at beginning of previous row to ensure that, if both ends are being increased, the increases will be at the same level. In order to do this a base of ss has to be worked over the new stitches added. To form a base of 4 stitches, for example, make a chain of 4 stitches plus a turning chain at beginning of previous row, insert hook into 2nd chain from hook and work ss over new chains. Then continue to work in required stitch.

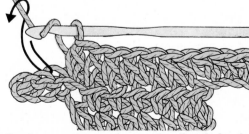

On the next row work over the slip stitches in required stitch.

# Using decreasing to shape

Decreasing the number of stitches in a row or round narrows the crochet. Like increases decreases are usually worked in basic stitches.

## Decreasing by missing a stitch

This is the simplest method of decreasing. The decrease is worked by missing a stitch. One stitch is missed for a single decrease and two for a double.

### Single decreases at the beginning of the row

Miss one stitch, leaving it unworked, and then work into the next stitch.

### Single decreases at the end of the row

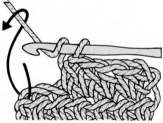

Miss the next to last stitch and work into the final stitch.

### Decreasing in the middle of the row

The method is the same, but the decreases must be evenly spaced. The abbreviation is *dec evenly.*

### Double decreases

The method is exactly the same as for single increases but two stitches are missed instead of one. When working double decreases in the middle of the row be sure to space the decreases evenly. If holes left by the decrease are too visible it may be better to use several single decreases.

## Decreasing by working two stitches as one

Another method of decreasing is to work two stitches as one. This method can be used on all the basic crochet stitches either at the beginning, the middle or the end of the row.

### Decreasing in double crochet

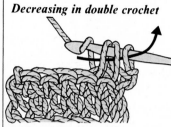

Make a turning chain and insert the hook into the first stitch, yrh and draw through. Insert the hook into the next stitch, yrh and draw through (3 loops on the hook), yrh and draw through all the loops on the hook. This makes one decrease. Use the same method at the middle or end of row.

### Decreasing in half trebles

Make 2 turning chains. Yrh, insert hook into the first stitch, yrh and draw through, yrh and insert hook into next stitch, yrh and draw through (5 loops on hook). Yrh and draw through all 5 loops. This makes one decrease. Use the same method at the middle or end of row.

### Decreasing in trebles

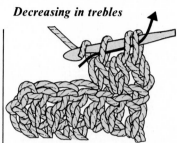

Make 3 turning chains, yrh and insert hook into first stitch and draw through, yrh and draw through 2 loops on hook, yrh and insert hook into next stitch, yrh and draw through, yrh and draw through 2 loops (3 loops on hook), yrh and draw through all 3 loops on the hook. This makes one decrease.

### Decreasing in the middle of the row

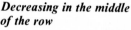
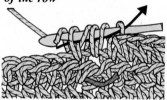

Whatever the stitch being used, decreases in the middle of rows or rounds should be marked with a coloured thread, so that the same position can be found easily on subsequent rows if further decreases are to be made.

## Decreasing at the edge

A third method of decreasing is worked by leaving stitches unworked at the beginning and end of rows.

### Multiple decreases at the beginning of the row

Work slip stitch over the stitches to be decreased and then make the required number of turning chains (depending on stitch pattern) to form next stitch and finish row in pattern.

### Multiple decreases at the end of the row

Work in pattern until the stitches to be decreased at the end of the row are reached. Leave these stitches unworked and make turning chains for the first stitch of the next row.

## Shaping by using different stitch lengths

Each of the basic stitches are of different heights. Used in the same or subsequent rows, they automatically shape the crochet.

This technique is often used in shaping medallions.

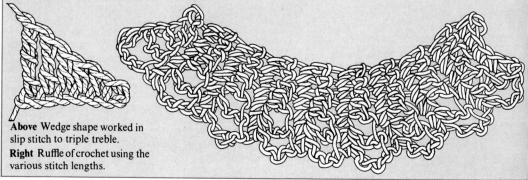

**Above** Wedge shape worked in slip stitch to triple treble.

**Right** Ruffle of crochet using the various stitch lengths.

# *Shaping pattern instructions*

The following are the pattern instructions for the child's dungarees, pram suit and crochet dress shown on page 131.

## *Child's dungarees*

**Materials** 10 (13) × 25g balls of double knitting in main colour, A; 1 (1) ball in each of 3 contrasting colours, B, C and D; No. 3.50 and No. 4 crochet hooks; 2 buttons. **Stitch gauge** 14 sts and 14 rows to 4 inches (10cm), adjustable. **Measurements** To fit chest 22 (24) inches (56[61]cm). Length from shoulder to crotch: 16 (17½) inches (40[45]cm), adjustable. Inside leg: 12½ (14½) inches (32[37]cm), adjustable. **Front** With No. 4 hook and A make 22(25)ch. **Right leg** For first row work 1htr into 3rd ch to end, 1htr into each ch to end (21 [24] sts). **Row 2** 2ch, 1htr between each htr to end. Rep the 2nd row 3 times more, do not break off A. **Row 6** Using B, 3ch, 1tr bet each htr to end. **Row 7** Using C, 1ch, 1dc bet each tr to end. **Row 8** Using A, 2ch, 1htr bet each dc to end. **Row 9** Using A, 2ch, 1htr bet each htr to end. **Row 10** Using D, as row 6. **Row 11** Working in dc, and always working between sts of previous row, work (3A, 3B) 3 (4) times, then on first size only work 3A. **Row 12** As row 11 but working colours as set. **Row 13** As row 11. **Row 14** As row 11 but working (3C, 3A) 3 (4) times, then on first size only work 3C. **Rows 15 and 16** As row 11 working colours as set. **Rows 17 to 19** As rows 11 to 13. **Row 20** Using D, 3ch, 1tr bet each dc to end. Break off B, C and D and cont in A only, work in htr, always working bet the sts of previous row, until work measures 12½ (14½) inches (32[37]cm) from beg, or length reqd, ending with a wrong side row. Break off yarn and leave this piece for the present. **Left leg** Work as given for right leg, but do not break off yarn at the end. **Join legs** For the next row work across left leg, 2ch, then work across right leg (44[50] sts). Cont in htr as before, dec 1 st at each end of next row and every foll 6th row until 36 (42) sts rem, then cont without shaping until work measures 7½ (8½) inches (19[22]cm) from crotch, or length reqd, dec 1 st in centre of last row on 2nd size only (36 [41] sts). **Shape armholes** For the next row work ss over first 2 (3) sts, patt to last 2 (3) sts, turn. Dec 1 st at each end of next row, then on 2nd size only work 1 row (30 [33] sts). Work rows 6 to 20 as on legs, but allowing for the different no. of sts on rows 11 to 19, then work 1 (3) rows htr in A. ** **Shape neck** For next row work patt over first 9 (10) sts, turn and cont for shoulder strap. Dec 1 st at neck edge on next 3 (2) rows (6[8] sts rem) then work 6 (8) rows without shaping. Fasten off. Miss the centre 12 (13) sts, rejoin yarn and patt to end. Cont to match first shoulder strap. **Back** Work as given for front, but reading right for left and vice versa until 36 (42) sts rem, ending with the dec row. **Shape back** For next row work in patt over first 30 (34) sts, turn. **Next row** Ss over next 6 (5) sts, patt over next 12 (16) sts, turn. **Next row** Patt to end. Cont to match front, taking measurement from crotch to armholes at side edge of work, as far as **. Work 3 more rows in htr in A, then shape neck as for front until 6 (8) sts rem on first shoulder strap. Work 4 (5) rows without shaping. **Buttonhole row** Work 2(3)htr, 2ch, miss 2 sts, work 2(3)htr. On next row work 1htr into each of the 2ch. Work 2 rows, rep the buttonhole row and next row. Fasten off. Miss centre 12 (13) sts; rejoin yarn and patt to end. Cont to match first strap. **Making up** Press work, if necessary, with a warm iron over a damp cloth (or according to instructions on ball band). Join side seams and inside leg seams. With No. 3.50 hook and C(D) work 1 row of dc round neck and armhole edges and round bottom of legs. Press seams. Sew on buttons.

## *Child's pram suit*

**Materials** 13 × 50g balls of chunky knit in main colour, A; 2 balls in first contrasting colour, B; 1 ball in each of 3 contrasting colours, C, D and E; No. 5.50 and No. 6 crochet hooks; zip fastener for bottom edge (optional). **Stitch gauge** 10 sts and 10 rows to 4 inches (10cm) over main patt on No. 5.50 hook. **Measurements** To fit 18 inches (46cm) chest (actual measurement 26 inches [66cm]). Length to shoulder: 24 inches (61cm); sleeve seam 10 inches (25cm). **Front** With No. 6 hook and A make 41ch. **Row 1** 1htr into 3rd ch from hook, 1htr into each ch to end (40htr). **Row 2** 2ch, 1htr, bet each htr to end. Rep row 2, 4 times. Dec 1 st at each end of next row, then work 1 row. Change to No. 5.50 hook. **Row 9** Using B, 1ch, 1dc into back half of each st to end. **Row 10** Using B, as row 9. Rep the last 2 rows, working 2 rows in E, 2 rows in A, 2 rows in D, 2 rows in C, 2 rows in B. Change to No. 6 hook and cont in A. **Row 21** 2ch, 1htr bet each dc to end. Cont in patt as row 2, work 3 rows. Dec 1 st at each end of next and every foll 6th row until 30 sts rem, then work 2 rows (25 rows in A). ** **Divide for front opening** Work next row

## *Child's pram suit continued*

in patt over first 15 sts, turn and work 13 more rows on these sts, ending at side edge. **Shape neck** Work in patt to last 5 sts, turn. **Next row** Ss over first 3 sts, patt to end (7 sts rem). **Next row** Patt to end. Fasten off. Return to where work was left, with right side facing rejoin yarn and patt to end. Cont to match first side. **Back** Work as given for front to **, then work a further 16 rows without shaping. **Shape neck** Work in patt over first 7 sts, break off yarn, miss 16 sts, rejoin yarn and patt over rem 7 sts. Fasten off. **Sleeves** With No. 5.50 hook and A make 33ch and work first 4 rows as on front (32htr). Change to No. 6 hook and work rows 9 to 20 as on front. Change to No. 5.50 hook and work row 21 as on front, then cont in patt, work 9 more rows. Fasten off. **Hood** With No. 5.50 hook and A make 51ch and work first 2 rows as on front (50htr). Change to No. 6 hook and work rows 9 to 20 as on front. Change to No. 5.50 hook and work row 21, then work 2 more rows. **Next row** Patt over first 18 sts, turn and work 9 more rows on these sts. Fasten off. Miss centre 14 sts, rejoin yarn and patt over rem 18 sts. Work 9 more rows. Fasten off. **Making up** Do not press. Join all pieces using A and ss as follows: Join shoulder seams. Join in sleeves, placing the centre of sleeve to the shoulder seam. Join side and sleeve seams. Join the two cast-off edges of hood, then sew the side edges of this piece to the centre 14 sts. Join hood to neck edge. With No. 5.50 hook and B work a row of dc along each edge of front opening. Using B make 4ch approx 6 inches (15cm) long and sew to front edges to tie in pairs. Sew zip fastener into lower edge if required.

## *Child's crochet dress*

**Materials** 4(6) × 25g balls of medium crochet cotton in each of 3 colours, A, B and C; No. 2 and No. 2.50 crochet hooks. **Stitch gauge** 1 patt rep of 20 sts at beg measures 3 inches (8cm) on No. 2.50 hook; 1 patt rep of 12 sts at top measures 2 inches (5cm) on No. 2.50 hook. **Measurements** To fit chest 26 (30) inches (65[75]cm). Length: 24 (27) inches (61[69]cm), adjustable. **Back** With No. 2.50 hook and A make 145(165)ch. **Row 1** Yrh, insert hook into 4th ch from hook, yrh, draw 1p through, yrh, draw through 2 lps, yrh, insert hook into next ch, yrh, draw 1p through, yrh, draw through 2 lps, yrh, draw through all 3 lps on hook – called 2tr tog – *1tr into each of next 8ch, 3tr into next ch, 1tr into each of next 8ch, yrh, insert hook into next ch, yrh, draw lp through, yrh, draw through 2 lps, miss next ch, yrh, insert hook into next ch, yrh, draw lp through, yrh, draw through 2 lps, yrh, draw through all 3 lps on hook – called 3tr tog – rep from * to last 20ch, 1tr into each of next 8ch, 3tr into next ch, 1tr into each of next 8ch, 2tr tog over next 2ch, 1tr into last ch (143[163] sts). **Row 2** 3ch, 2tr tog, inserting hook into the sps between the sts, *1tr into each of next 8 sps between tr, 3tr into next sp, 1tr into each of next 8 sps, 3tr tog over next 3 sps, rep from * to end, but ending with 2tr tog over last 2 sps, 1tr into t-ch, drawing B through on last tr. Rep row 2 12 (14) times more, working throughout in stripes of 2 rows in B, 2 rows in C, 2 rows in A. **Shape skirt** (still working in stripe patt throughout). **Next row** 3ch, 2tr tog, *1tr into each of next 17 sps, 3tr tog over next 3 sps, rep from * ending with 2tr tog, 1tr into t-ch (129 [147] sts). **Next row** 3ch, 2tr tog, *1tr into each of next 7 sps, 3tr into next sp, 1tr into each of next 7 sps, 3tr tog over next 3 sps, rep from * ending as before. Rep the last row 12 (14) times more. **Next row** 3ch, 2tr tog, *1tr into each of next 15 sps, 3tr tog over next 3 sps, rep from * ending as before (115 [131] sts). **Next row** 3ch, 2tr tog, *1tr into each of next 6 sps, 3tr into next sp, 1tr into each of next 6 sps, 3tr tog over next 3 sps, rep from * ending as before. Rep the last row 10 (12) times more. **Next row** 3ch, 2tr tog, *1tr into each of next 13 sps, 3tr tog over next 3 sps, rep from * ending as before (101 [115] sts). **Next row** 3ch, 2tr tog, *1tr into each of next 5 sps, 3tr into next sp, 1tr into each of next 5 sps, 3tr tog over next 3 sps, rep from * ending as before. Rep the last row 8 (10) times more. **Next row** 3ch, 2tr tog, *1tr into each of 11 sps, 3tr tog over next 3 sps. rep from * ending as before (87[99]sts). **Next row** 3ch, 2tr tog, *1tr into each of next 4 sps, 3tr into next sp, 1tr into each of next 4 sps, 3tr tog over next 3 sps, rep from * ending as before. Rep the last row 14 times more. Adjust length here if reqd. **Shape armholes** For next row work ss over first 6 sts, patt to last 6 sts, turn. Keeping patt correct, dec 1 st at each end of next 1 (4) rows (73[79] sts). Cont without shaping (taking care to keep ends of rows correct) until armholes measure 3 (3½) inches (8[9]cm). **Shape neck** Work next row in patt over first 10 sts, turn. Keeping the ends of rows correct, cont on these sts until armhole measures 5½ (6½) inches (14[16]cm), ending at armhole edge. **Next row** 1ch, 1dc into each of next 5 sps, 1tr into each sp to end. Fasten off. Miss centre (53[59]sts), rejoin yarn and patt to end. Work to match first strap. **Front** Work as given for back, but shape neck when armholes measure 2 (2½) inches (5[6]cm) instead of 3 (3½) inches (8[9]cm). **Making up** Press work lightly with a warm iron over a damp cloth. Join shoulder seams and side seams. Using No. 2 hook work a row of ss along back and front neck, using the same colour as the last row worked. Using C work 2 rows of dc round each armhole and 1 row of dc along side edges of neck. Press all seams.

# Child's dungarees

The dungarees illustrated on this page need only a little simple shaping at the armholes. They are worked in double knitting wool, using one main colour for the body of the dungarees and three contrasting colours for the pattern on the yoke and on the trouser legs. The patterns on the preceding page are given in two sizes – a 22in. (56cm) and 24in. (61cm) chest. The length of the body and legs can be adjusted to fit those of the child.

**Left**
Front view

**Right**
Back view

**Fastening the straps**
The dungarees are fastened on the shoulders with two buttons. To prevent the fabric stretching, attach a small circle of felt to the back of the fabric behind the button and stitch securely.

*Contrasting patterns*
The patterns on the yoke and legs, shown in detail left and below, could be altered by using any of the colourwork patterns shown on pages 136–137 or by using different colour contrasts.

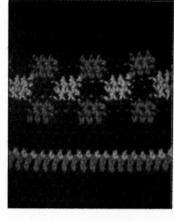

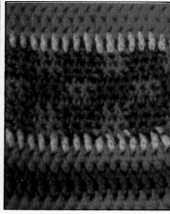

**Left, leg detail**
Yellow, green and blue on a red background.

**Right, leg detail**
Green, beige and maroon on a brown background.

# Pram suit

The pram suit (to fit an 18in. (46cm) chest) can be used as a sleeping bag or dressing gown. It is zipped at the foot and converted to a dressing gown by removing the zip. Pattern instructions are on the preceding page.

**Front fastening detail**

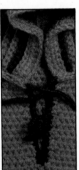

**Sleeve shape detail**

# Child's dress

The child's dress shown below is given in two sizes, to fit a 26in. (65cm) and a 30in. (75cm) chest. Made in finer yarn on finer hooks than the dungarees or pram suit, it is also a more difficult pattern to work (see page 129).

The pattern of the dress is worked in two rows of trebles in each of three colours and is reversible. The length can be adjusted by working more or fewer rows as required keeping the pattern in the same order throughout.

**Detail of neck and shoulders**

**Hem detail showing scalloped edge**

# Finishing details

# Buttonholes and button loops

The finishing details of a crochet design are as important as the actual working of the crochet. You can, if you choose, make a design entirely of crochet from the buttons to the loops, cords and final seaming together. But you can, of course, also use bought buttons and the seams can be stitched together with needle and yarn.

## Making crochet buttons

Crochet buttons can be made onto either a plastic ring or a button mould, or alternatively they could be stuffed with cotton wool. When making ring buttons any suitably sized plastic ring can be used as a base for the crochet.

### How to make ring buttons

Work dc around the ring and join with ss to the first dc (left). Turn the stitches to the inside of the ring, and sew the stitches together. For further decoration work another round of dc over first round (right).

### How to make covered buttons

Having decided the size of the button, make a medallion to width required (see page 138) and insert the button mould. Then decrease as necessary to cover the back of the button and finish off. If the button is to be stuffed with cotton wool, decrease until the round is just big enough to insert the stuffing. Pack tight and finish off. These coverings can be worked in decorative colour designs, or finished with cross or satin stitch embroidery.

## Making vertical buttonholes

There are two methods of making vertical buttonholes: one for small stitches (up to half trebles); the other for larger stitches.

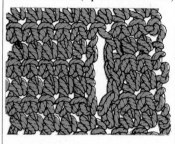

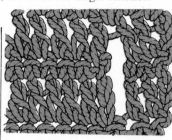

### How to make buttonholes for small stitches

**1** Work to the buttonhole position and turn. Work back and repeat on this and all the subsequent rows until buttonhole is of required length, ending at inner edge.

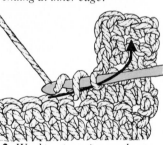

**2** Work ss down inner edge to last complete row.

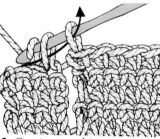

**3** Continue working these stitches to and fro until they are level with the first side. Then continue across all stitches in the pattern, closing the slit to form the buttonhole.

### How to make buttonholes for large stitches

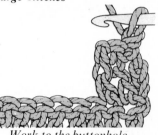

**1** Work to the buttonhole position and complete the first side of the buttonhole in the same way as for smaller stitches ending at outer edge.

**2** Using a separate ball of yarn, begin working from inner edge of buttonhole and form second side to match first. Break off new yarn and continue with original yarn across all stitches to complete buttonhole.

## Making horizontal buttonholes

This is the simplest method for making crochet buttonholes.

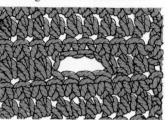

### How to make horizontal buttonholes

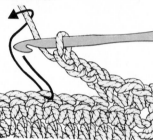

**1** Work from the side edge to the buttonhole position – 3 to 4 stitches is usually enough. Make 2 or more chains, depending on the size of the button. Miss the same number of stitches in the row below.

**2** Work in pattern to the end of the row. On the following row work in pattern over the chains to the end of the row.

## Making button loops

Button loops are worked as an edging after the main fabric has been completed. Mark the position for the buttons. Work slip stitch and then chain stitches for the required length, missing the same number of stitches beneath.

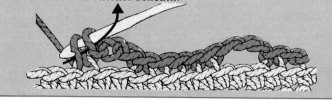

# Crochet cords

Crochet cords or chains are made in several ways and are used for gathering, tying, or as frogging, and for belts. They can be made in various colours to add decorative interest.

### Coloured chains

A simple two-coloured chain is worked like a single chain but using each colour alternately.

Place both colours in the left hand and over the left forefinger. Pick each one up and drop it alternately, making one chain with each colour. Thicker chains can be made in the same way, using several coloured strands at a time to give a more hardwearing cord.

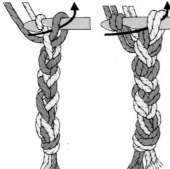

**Single 2 colour chain   Thick 2 colour cord**

### Round cords or chains

Round cords or chains are useful for belts and for tying back curtains. They can be widened as required by increasing the number of chains cast on for the basic ring. Work 5 chains and join them into a ring with a ss. Slip stitch into each stitch until the cord reaches the length required. Use several colours for a decorative effect.

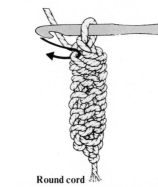

**Round cord**

### Using single chains

Make a single chain as shown on page 112. Then, with a safety pin fixed at one end, thread the chain as shown, through a row of double trebles, to gather up a cuff, neckline or waistline, for example.

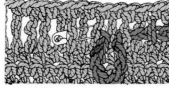

**Single chain**

## Pressing and blocking

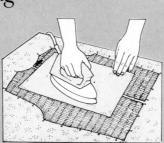

*When the pieces of crochet are completed they should be pressed before being seamed together. Take care not to stretch fabric while pressing. Place each piece right side down on a padded surface. Pin evenly around edges, so that rows and stitches are straight.*

*Using a damp cloth, and a warm iron, press each piece of crochet evenly, or as instructed on the ball band. Lift the iron up and down (not to and fro) until each piece is well pressed. Leave the pieces to cool, and then remove pins. The pieces are now ready to be seamed.*

# Seams and edges

Seaming can be done in any of the ways shown below. For sewing cardigans, sweaters and dresses, first the shoulder seams are sewn, then the sides and sleeves are made up in one continuous seam. The top of the sleeve is then marked and that point is attached to the shoulder seam. The sleeves are then eased into place and secured, first with pins and then tacked into position before stitching.

### Slip stitch seams

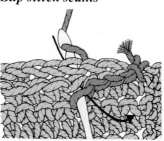

If the ridge of slip stitch is to be shown on the right side of the work, place the pieces with the wrong sides facing. Or, if the ridge is to be on the inside, place the pieces with right sides facing. Insert the hook from front to back through the edge stitches of both pieces, yrh and draw through. Work 1 ss in the usual way, then insert the hook into the next stitch along, ready to make the next ss. Continue in this way to the end and fasten off.

### Double crochet seams

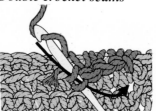

Place the pieces of crochet to be joined with right sides together. Insert the hook from front to back through the edges of both pieces. Yrh and draw through, work 1 dc in the usual way and then insert the hook into the next stitch along ready to make the next dc. Continue in this way to the end of the edge and fasten off.

### Back stitch seams

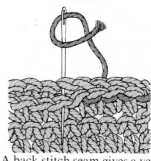

A back stitch seam gives a very firm seam and can be particularly useful for making seams for hardwearing garments. Place the pieces to be joined with right sides facing. Thread a wool needle with matching yarn and work back stitch as shown, inserting the needle between two crochet stitches.

### Woven seams

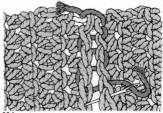

Woven seams are best for fine work and baby clothes. Lay the pieces wrong side up with edges touching. Thread a wool needle with matching yarn and weave it loosely around centres of the edge stitches of both pieces as shown in the diagram.

### Double crochet edging

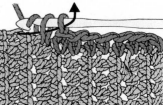

Double crochet edging is used mainly for necklines or borders. Insert the hook from front to back through the edge. Yrh and draw through. Work a double crochet and then continue along the edge, inserting the hook row by row. This edging can be worked in a contrasting colour.

# Coloured stitch patterns

Colours can be used in crochet either in conjunction with textured stitches, in which case only one colour is used in each row, or in conjunction with simple stitches such as double crochet or trebles, in which case two or more colours can be used in a row (see opposite page).

When textured stitches are used with colour the instructions are written out. We have called these *coloured stitch patterns*. Examples of some are given on this page and their written instructions are on page 136. The stitches are formed to make irregular shapes and overlapping lines so the impression is given of more than one colour being used in each row. This can be further enhanced by changing the colours in every row.

There are various methods of joining in new colours in crochet and these are given in detail on page 137.

| | |
|---|---|
| **1** Dot stitch | **4** Brick stitch |
| **2** Pinnacle stitch | **5** Speckle stitch |
| **3** Almond stitch | **6** Petal stitch |

**3**

**4**

**5**

**1**

**6**

**2**

## Charts for colourwork patterns

Below are the charts for the colourwork patterns (see right) which are all worked in double crochet. Instructions for working from charts are given on page 136.

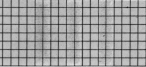

**1 Horizontal stripes**

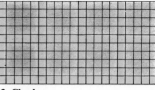

**2 Vertical stripes**

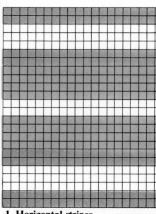

**3 Checks**

**4 Zigzags**

*Alternative patterns*

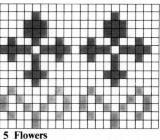

**5 Flowers**

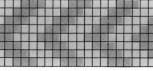

**6 Scales**

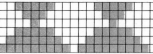

# Colourwork patterns

When simple stitches are being used with two or more colours the instructions are usually given in chart form, which makes them easier to read. Each square represents one stitch. We have called these *colourwork patterns* and show examples of them on this page. (The charts are shown left on the opposite page.) The patchworked, colourwork scarf (right) shows how effective these simple colourwork patterns can be when used together. The instructions for making the scarf are given on page 136. Colourwork patterns can also be used in this patchworked form to make cushion covers and bedspreads for example. By a careful choice of colours, these can be worked either in many tones of one colour to give shaded effects, in a number of brilliant colours for really bright designs or in several colours to blend with a particular colour scheme for a room.

The various ways of joining crochet pieces together are given in detail on pages 132–133. The joining can be made more decorative by using a contrasting thread or, alternatively, before joining, each patch can be finished with a single row of double crochet in a contrasting colour or with a deep border of several rows of double crochet.

**1 Horizontal stripes**

**2 Vertical stripes**

**3 Checks**

**4 Zigzags**

**5 Flowers**

**6 Scales**

**The scarf above could also be made in school or club colours**

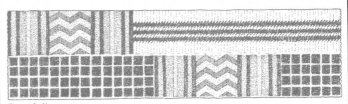

*Scarf diagram*
*The diagram above shows one pattern repeat of the scarf. A bedspread could be made by adding more strips side by side.*

**Detail of scarf pattern**

# Crochet stitch patterns

The patterns given below are all shown in colour on page 134. The instructions for joining in new colour and working with more than one colour are shown on the opposite page. The pattern abbreviations are all listed on page 113.

## 1 Dot stitch

This pattern uses 2 colours, A and B.

Using A, make a number of ch divisible by 3 plus 1, 1ch, turn.

**Row 1** 1dc into 2nd ch from hook, *2ch, miss 2ch, 1dc into next ch, rep from * to end, joining in B on last dc.

**Row 2** Using B, 4ch, *3tr into 2ch sp, 1ch, rep from * to end, 1tr into last dc.

**Row 3** Return to beg of row 2, draw A through under 4th of 4ch, 1ch as first dc, *2ch, 1dc into 1ch sp, rep from * to end, drawing B through on last dc.

**Row 4** Using B, as row 2.

Always starting each row at the end where the correct colour was left, rep rows 3 and 4 throughout.

## 2 Pinnacle stitch

This pattern uses 2 colours, A and B.

Using A, make a number of ch divisible by 14 plus 1, 2ch, turn.

**Row 1** 1dc into 3rd ch from hook, *1dc into each of next 5ch, miss 3ch, 1dc into each of next 5ch, 3dc into next ch, rep from * to end, but ending with 2dc into last ch instead of 3.

**Row 2** 1ch, 1dc into same place, *1dc into each of next 5dc, miss 2dc,1dc into each of next 5dc, 3dc into next dc, rep from * to end, but ending with 2dc into t-ch.

Rep row 2 throughout, working 2 more rows in A, then 4 rows in B, 4 rows in A throughout.

## 3 Almond stitch

This pattern uses 2 colours, A and B.

Using A make a number of ch divisible by 10 plus 1, 1ch, turn.

**Row 1** 1dc into 2nd ch from hook 1dc into each ch to end, joining in B on last dc.

**Row 2** Using B, 1ch, *1dc into next st, 1htr into next st, 1tr into each of next 5 sts, 1htr into next st, 1dc into next st, 1ch, miss 1 st, rep from * to end, ss into t-ch, turn.

**Row 3** Using B, 1ch, *1dc into dc, 1htr into htr, 1tr into each of 5tr, 1htr into htr, 1dc into dc, 1ch, rep from * to end, ss into t-ch, drawing A through.

**Row 4** 3ch, *1dc into each of next 9 sts, 1tr into missed st of row 1, rep from * to end, ending with 1tr into t-ch.

**Row 5** Using A, 1ch,1dc into each st to end, drawing through B on last dc.

## 4 Brick stitch

This pattern uses 3 colours, A, B and C.

Using A, make a number of ch divisible by 4 plus 2, 2ch, turn.

**Row 1** 1tr into 4th ch from hook,*2ch, miss 2ch, 1tr into each of next 2ch, rep from * to end, joining in B on last tr.

**Row 2** Using B, 2ch, *1tr into each of the 2 missed ch on row 1, 2ch, rep from * to end, ending

with 1ch instead of 2, then ss into 3rd of 3ch at beg of row 1, joining in C.

**Row 3** Using C, 3ch, 1tr into missed tr on last row, *2ch, 1tr into each of 2 missed tr on last row, rep from * to end, drawing A through on last tr.

**Row 4** Using A, as row 2.

Working 1 row in each colour throughout rep rows 3 and 4.

## 5 Speckle stitch

This pattern uses 3 colours, A, B and C.

Using A, make a number of ch divisible by 3 plus 2, 1ch, turn.

**Row 1** 1dc into 3rd ch from hook, 1dc into each ch to end.

**Row 2** 1ch, 1dc into each dc to end. Do not break off A.

**Row 3** Join in B, 1ch,1dc into each dc to end.

**Row 4** As row 2. Do not break off B.

**Row 5** Return to beg of row 4, join in C, 1ch, 1dc into each dc to end. Do not break off C.

**Row 6** Draw A through first st, 1ch, 1dc into next dc, *1dtr insert-

ing hook from right to left in front of corresponding st on row 2, 1dc into each of next 2dc, rep from * to end.

**Row 7** As row 2.

**Row 8** Draw C through first st, 1ch, 1dc into each dc to end.

**Row 9** Return to beg of row 8, draw B through first st, 1ch, 1dc into next dc, *1dtr, inserting hook from right to left in front of dtr on row 6, 1dc into each of next 2dc, rep from * to end.

**Row 10** As row 2.

Always starting each row at the correct end where yarn was left, rep rows 5 to 10 throughout.

## 6 Petal stitch

This pattern uses 2 colours, A and B.

Using A make a number of ch divisible by 6 plus 1, 3ch, turn.

**Row 1** 2tr into 4th ch from hook,* miss 2ch, 1dc into next ch, miss 2ch, 5tr into next ch, rep from * to end, ending with 3tr into last ch instead of 5.

**Row 2** Join B to top of 3ch at beg of row 1, 1dc into this st, *2ch, ** yrh, insert hook into next tr, yrh, draw lp through, yrh, draw through 2 lps **rep from ** to **

into next tr, into dc, then into each of next 2tr, yrh, draw through 6 lps on hook, 2ch, 1dc into next tr, rep from * to end, drawing through A on last dc.

**Row 3** Using A, 3ch, 2tr into first dc, *1dc into top of gr, 5tr into next dc, rep from * to end, but ending with 3tr into last dc.

**Row 4** Return to beg of row 3, draw B through top of 3ch and work as row 2.

Rep rows 3 and 4 throughout.

## 6 Using B, 3ch, 1tr into each of next 2 sts, *1htr into next st, 1dc into next st, 1ch, miss 1st, 1dc into next st, 1htr into next st, 1tr into each of next 5 sts, rep from * to end, but ending with 3tr instead of 5.

**Row 7** 3ch, 1tr into each of next 2tr, *1htr into htr, 1dc into dc, 1ch,1dc into dc, 1htr into htr, 1tr into each of 5tr, rep from* to end, but ending with 3tr instead of 5 and draw through A on last tr.

**Row 8** Using A, 1ch as first dc, 1dc into each of next 4 sts, *1tr into miss st of row 5, 1dc into each of next 9 sts, rep from * to end, but ending with 1dc into each of next 5 sts.

**Row 9** As row 5.

Rep rows 2 to 9 throughout.

# Working with colourwork charts

Colourwork patterns are always worked in basic stitches such as double crochet or treble using more than one colour in a row or round.

Colourwork patterns are often shown on charts which are easier to follow than written patterns as the whole design is visible in symbol form. Each colour has its own symbol or colour on the chart. Each square represents a stitch and each line represents a row or round. Charts should be read in the direction the crochet is worked – from bottom to top, right to left and left to right when working in rows, and from right to left only when working in rounds.

## Colourwork scarf

**Yarn** 4-ply wool throughout: 2 25g balls each of brown and cream for vertical stripes and checks patterns; 1 25g ball each of yellow and rose for zigzag pattern; 1 25g ball each of pale blue, dark blue, pale orange, orange and lime or for horizontal stripes pattern use scraps of 4-ply wool.

**Hooks** No. 3.50 and no. 4 crochet hooks

**Stitch gauge** 11 stitches to 2in. (5cm).

### Making the scarf

The scarf is worked in two strips entirely in double crochet (charted instructions for patterns on page 134). Each strip has a width of 20 sts. Use No. 4 hook for all patterns except horizontal stripe pattern which requires a No. 3.50 hook. Begin the first strip with *24 rows of horizontal stripe pattern. This is followed by 20 rows of zigzag pattern, 24 rows of horizontal stripe pattern, then 100 rows of vertical stripe pattern. Repeat from * until strip is the required length. Begin the second strip with 70 rows of check pattern. Follow with **24 rows of horizontal stripe pattern, 20 rows of zigzag pattern, 24 rows of horizontal stripe pattern, then 100 rows of check pattern. Repeat from ** until second strip is same length as first strip. Join the strips with slip stitch. For a wider scarf or a shawl, add first strip and second strip alternately.

# Working with colours

Colours can be introduced at any point and either carried along the top of the previous row and passed over until they are needed, or introduced in the middle of a row. Horizontal stripes are made by joining in a new colour at the beginning of rows or rounds, and vertical stripes are worked with the colours being carried along the top when not in work. They are then exchanged with the original colour which itself is now carried along the top while the second colour is in work. Diagonals and chevrons are worked in the same way as striped patterns.

Random patterns can be created by introducing the colours as required and either carrying them along the top of the work and using them when needed, or by introducing them and leaving them hanging at the back of the work, picking them up on the subsequent row at the same point and working them from that position.

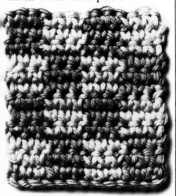

**Colourwork in double crochet**

**Colourwork in treble crochet**

## Adding new yarn when working double crochet

This is done to replace an old yarn which has run out or to introduce a new colour.

***How to add new yarn before a stitch***

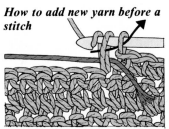

**1** *Carry new yarn loosely along top of previous row and work over it as though it were part of row. When needed new yarn is introduced with final yrh of dc.*

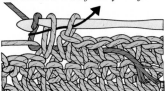

**2** *If old yarn is to be used again in this row carry it along top of previous row. If not, carry it along top of row for a few stitches and snip off end. If old yarn will only be required in same place in next row, leave it hanging to back of work and then pick it up again on the subsequent rows.*

***How to add new yarn after a stitch***

**1** *Work stitch with old yarn to final yrh and introduce the new yarn.*

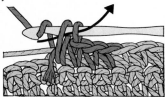

**2** *Lay loose end of new yarn along top of row and work over it. If old yarn is required again in this row lay it along the top and work over it until needed.*

## Working with more than one colour in the same row

When working with two colours in a row the yarns are changed by working in the new colour and carrying the old one along top of previous row and working over it.

***How to change colours in double crochet***

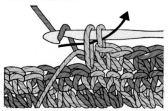

**1** *Introduce the second colour with final yrh of previous stitch. The first colour is then carried along top of previous row.*

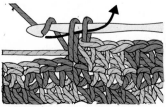

**2** *The 2 yarns exchange roles when the old colour is required again. When several colours are worked in this way a dense stitch such as dc must be used if the carried yarns are to remain hidden.*

***How to change colours in trebles***

**1** *Introduce second colour with 2nd yrh of treble. Carry the old colour at the base of the stitches, working over it with the new colour.*

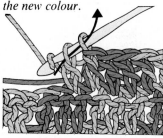

**2** *When the old yarn is required again, reintroduce it and carry the new yarn at the base of the stitches.*

## Adding new yarn when working trebles

This method of adding a new yarn is used for all types of treble colourwork, including filet crochet.

***How to work***
**1** *Carry the new yarn along the top of the previous row until it is required.*
**2** *Yrh with the old yarn and insert the hook in the usual way. Yrh with both yarns and draw both through. Yrh with the new yarn only and draw through the double and the single loop, yrh with the new yarn and draw it through the remaining 2 loops.*
**3** *If the old colour is to be discontinued, carry it along at the base of the stitches and then snip it off. If it is required again later, continue to carry it along at the base of the stitches.*

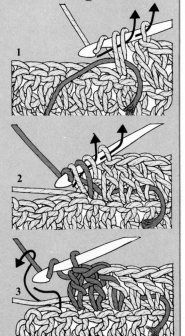

## Working in the round

Working in the round instead of in rows means that the foundation row of chains is made into a circle or ring and the crochet stitches are then worked from this circle in a continuous round without turning and working back and forth. Many different shapes can be made from this simple foundation ring. The crochet can be worked outwards for flat medallions, and increased and then decreased for rounded shapes such as balls or berets. It can also be worked upwards to form tubular shapes for sleeves, socks and gloves.

### Working foundation rings

To begin working either medallion or tubular crochet make a foundation ring of chains.

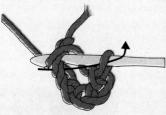

**How to work a single chain ring**
Make a foundation chain to required length and then close ring with a slip stitch into the first chain.

### Double crochet rings

If a large number of chains are needed for a medallion, work the ring in double crochet.

**How to work a double crochet ring**
**1** After making circle as shown, insert hook through from underneath. Yrh and draw hook through circle, yrh again and draw through loop on hook.

**2** Work double crochet around circle and over both strands.

**3** When required number of dc have been worked, pull loose end tight to draw circle together. Close ring with slip stitch.

## Simple medallions

These are worked from the centre and increased outwards. The positioning of the increase forms the shapes. They can be plain, relief or lacy, in one colour or multicoloured. (For coloured medallions, see pages 144–145; for relief medallions, pages 148–149.)

Square medallions are made by increasing at four regular intervals. Round medallions are made by increasing evenly around the circle. Hexagons are made by increasing at six regular intervals. Octagons are made by increasing at eight regular intervals.

The working instructions for the medallions on these two pages are on pages 140–141.

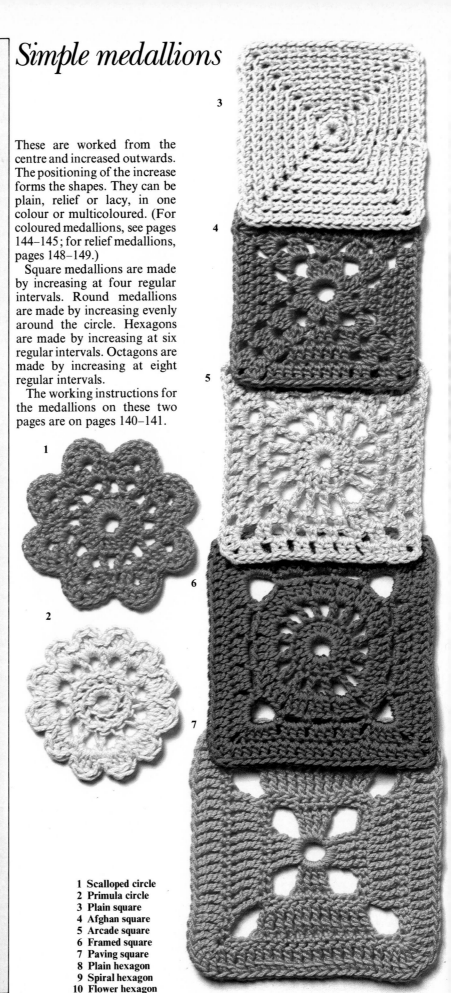

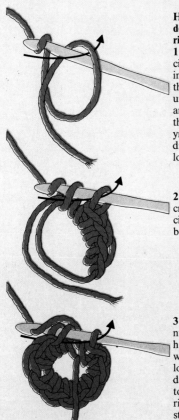

1 **Scalloped circle**
2 **Primula circle**
3 **Plain square**
4 **Afghan square**
5 **Arcade square**
6 **Framed square**
7 **Paving square**
8 **Plain hexagon**
9 **Spiral hexagon**
10 **Flower hexagon**

# *Lace medallions*

These are constructed in the same way as simple medallions but are quicker to work. For the most lace-like, a fine crochet cotton is best.

**Large medallions**
One large medallion can be worked as a lace cover for a cushion and stitched to a fabric backing of the same or a contrasting colour.

1

**Small medallions**
Many small medallions can be made and joined together to form a bed cover. The foundation ring can be shaped to make a central motif such as a shamrock, as in the medallion below. The patterns for the medallions left and below are given on page 141.

**1 Willow lace square**
**2 Irish lace square**

**Joining medallions**
Place the patches face to face and join with slip stitch or with one of the methods shown on page 133.

2

8

9

10

# Plain medallions

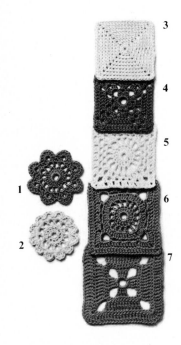

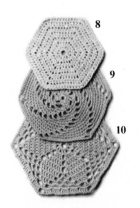

1 Scalloped circle
2 Primula circle
3 Plain square
4 Afghan square
5 Arcade square
6 Framed square
7 Paving square
8 Plain hexagon
9 Spiral hexagon
10 Flower hexagon

## 1 Scalloped circle

Make 6ch and join into a ring with a ss into first ch.

**Round 1** 3ch, 23tr into ring, join with a ss to 3rd of first 3ch.

**Round 2** 5ch, 1tr into ss, 1ch, * miss 2tr, (1tr, 2ch, 1tr) into next tr, 1ch, rep from * 6 times more, join with a ss to 3rd of first 5ch.

**Round 3** Ss into 2ch sp, 3ch, (1tr, 2ch, 2tr) into same sp, * 1dc into 1ch sp, (2tr, 2ch, 2tr) into 2ch sp, rep from * 6 times more, 1dc into 1ch sp, join with a ss into 3rd of first 3ch.

**Round 4** Ss into 2ch sp, 3ch, (2tr, 1ch, 3tr) into same sp, * 1dc before next dc, 1dc after the same dc, (3tr, 1ch, 3tr) into 2ch sp, rep from * 6 times more, 1dc before next dc, 1dc after the same dc, join with a ss to 3rd of first 3ch.

Fasten off.

## 2 Primula circle

Make 4ch and join into a ring with a ss into first ch.

**Round 1** 1ch, 11dc into ring, join with a ss to first ch.

**Round 2** 1ch, 1dc into same place, inserting hook into back half of each st work 2dc into each st to end, join with a ss to first ch.

**Round 3** 3ch, * miss 1dc, 1dc into back half of next dc, 2ch, rep from * to end, join with a ss to first of first 3ch.

**Round 4** Into each 2ch sp work 1dc, 1tr, 2dtr, 1tr and 1dc, join with a ss to first dc.

Fasten off.

## 3 Plain square

Make 4ch and join into a ring with a ss into first ch.

**Round 1** 1ch, 11dc into ring, join with a ss to first ch.

**Round 2** 1ch, working into the back half of each st throughout, 1dc into next dc, * 3dc into next dc, 1dc into each of next 2dc, rep from * to last dc, 3dc into next dc, join with a ss to first ch.

**Round 3** 1ch, working into the back half of each st throughout, 1dc into each of next 2dc, * 3dc into next dc, 1dc into each of next 4dc, rep from * twice more, 3dc into next dc, 1dc into next dc, join with a ss to first ch.

**Round 4** 1ch, working into the back half of each st throughout, 1dc into each of next 3dc, * 3dc into next dc, 1dc into each of next 6dc, rep from * twice more, 3dc into next dc, 1dc into each of next 2dc, join with a ss to first ch.

Cont in this way, working 2 more dc along each side in each rnd, until square is the required size. Fasten off.

## 4 Afghan square

Make 8ch and join into a ring with a ss into first ch.

**Round 1** 3ch, ** yrh, insert hook into ring, yrh, draw lp through, yrh, draw through 2 lps ** rep from ** to **, yrh, draw through 3 lps, 5ch, * rep from ** to ** 3 times, yrh, draw through 4 lps – called 1 cluster – 2ch, 1cl, 5ch, rep from * twice more, 1cl, 2ch, join with a ss to 3rd of first 3ch.

**Round 2** Ss into 5ch sp, 3ch, rep from ** to ** twice, yrh, draw through 3 lps, 2ch, 1cl into same sp, * 2ch, 3tr into 2ch sp, 2ch, (1cl, 2ch, 1cl) into 5ch sp, rep from * twice more, 2ch, 3tr into 2ch sp, 2ch, join with a ss into 3rd of first 3ch.

**Round 3** Ss into corner 2ch sp, 3ch, rep from ** to ** twice, yrh, draw through 3 lps, 2ch, 1cl into same sp, * 2ch, 2tr into 2ch sp, 1tr into each of next 3tr, 2tr into 2ch sp, 2ch, (1cl, 2ch, 1cl) into corner 2ch sp, rep from * twice more, 2ch, 2tr into 2ch sp, 1tr into each of next 3tr, 2tr into 2ch sp, 2ch, join with a ss to 3rd of first 3ch.

**Round 4** Work in the same way as rnd 3, but working 1tr into each of 7tr instead of 3tr along each side.

Cont in this way, working 4 more tr along each side in each rnd, until square is the required size.

Fasten off.

## 5 Arcade square

Make 6ch and join into a ring with a ss into first ch.

**Round 1** 3ch, 15tr into ring, join with a ss to 3rd of first 3ch.

**Round 2** 5ch, * 1tr into next tr, 2ch, rep from * 14 times more, join with a ss to 3rd of first 5ch.

**Round 3** Ss into first sp, 3ch, (1tr, 3ch, 2tr) into same sp, * (2ch, 1dc into next sp) 3 times, 2ch, (2tr, 3ch, 2tr) into next sp, rep from * twice more, (2ch, 1dc into next sp) 3 times, 2ch, join with a ss to 3rd of first 3ch.

**Round 4** Ss into next 3ch sp, 3ch, (1tr, 3ch, 2tr) into same sp, * (2ch, 1dc into next sp) 4 times, 2ch, (2tr, 3ch, 2tr) into 3ch sp, rep from * twice more, (2ch, 1dc into 2ch sp) 4 times, 2ch, join with a ss to 3rd of first 3ch.

**Round 5** Ss into 3ch sp, 3ch, (2tr, 2ch, 3tr) into same sp, * (1ch, 2tr into 2ch sp) 5 times, 1ch, (3tr, 2ch, 3tr) into 3ch sp, rep from * twice more, (1ch, 2tr into 2ch sp) 5 times, 1ch, join with a ss to 3rd of first 3ch.

Fasten off.

## 6 Framed square

Make 8ch and join into a ring with a ss into first ch.

**Round 1** 3ch, 15tr into ring, join with a ss to 3rd of first 3ch.

**Round 2** 5ch, (1tr into next tr, 2ch) 15 times, join with a ss to 3rd of first 5ch.

**Round 3** Ss into first 2ch sp, 3ch, 2tr into same sp, 1ch, * 3tr into next sp, 1ch, rep from * to end, join with a ss to 3rd of first 3ch.

**Round 4** Ss into first ch sp, * (3ch, 1dc into next sp) 3 times, 6ch, 1dc into next sp, rep from * 3 times more, omitting last dc and join with a ss to ss at beg of rnd.

**Round 5** Ss into first 3ch sp, 3ch, 2tr into same sp, 3tr into each of next 2 3ch sps, * (5tr, 2ch, 5tr) into 6ch sp, 3tr into each of next 3 3ch sps, rep from * twice more, (5tr, 2ch, 5tr) into 6ch sp, join with a ss to 3rd of first 3ch.

**Round 6** 3ch, 1tr into each tr to corner, * (1tr, 1dtr, 1tr) into 2ch sp, 1tr into each tr to next corner, rep from * twice more, (1tr, 1dtr, 1tr) into 2ch sp, 1tr into each tr to end, join with a ss to 3rd of first 3ch.

Fasten off.

## 7 Paving square

Make 10ch and join into a ring with a ss into first ch.

**Round 1** 11ch, * 4dtr into ring, 7ch, rep from * twice more, 3dtr into ring, join with a ss to 4th of first 11ch, ss into each of next 3ch, turn.

**Round 2** 1ch, 1dc into each of next 2ch, * 1dc into each of 4dtr, 1dc into each of next 3ch, 1ch, 1dc into each of next 3ch, rep from * twice more, 1dc into each of 4dtr, 1dc into each of 3ch, 1ch, join with a ss to first ch, turn.

**Round 3** 11ch, * 2dtr into next dc, 1dtr into each of next 8dc, 2dtr into next dc, 7ch, rep from * twice more, 2dtr into next dc, 1dtr into

# Lace medallions

**Paving square continued**

each of next 8dc, 1dtr into same place as the 11ch, join with a ss to 4th of 11ch, ss into each of next 3ch, turn.

**Round 4** As rnd 2, but working 1dc into each of 12dtr instead of 4.

## 8 *Plain hexagon*

Make 4ch and join into a ring with a ss into first ch.

**Round 1** 1ch, 11dc into ring, join with a ss to first ch, turn.

**Round 2** 2ch, * 3htr into next dc, 1htr into next dc, rep from * 4 times more, 3htr into next dc, join with a ss to 2nd of first 2ch, turn.

**Round 3** 2ch, 1htr into next htr, * 3htr into next htr, 1htr into each of next 3htr, rep from * 4 times more, 3htr into next htr, 1htr into

## 9 *Spiral hexagon*

Make 5ch and join into a ring with a ss into first ch.

**Round 1** * 6ch, 1dc into ring, rep from * 5 times more, ss over first 3ch of first lp.

**Round 2** * 4ch, 1dc into 6ch lp, rep from * 5 times more, working last dc into ss before first 4ch.

**Round 3** * 4ch, 2dc into 4ch lp, 1dc into dc, rep from * 5 times more, working last dc into last dc at end of last rnd.

## 10 *Flower hexagon*

Make 6ch and join into a ring with a ss into first ch.

**Round 1** 4ch, (1tr into ring, 1ch) 11 times, join with a ss to 3rd of first 4ch.

**Round 2** 3ch, 2tr into sp, 1tr into tr, 2ch, * 1tr into tr, 2tr into sp, 1tr into tr, 2ch, rep from * 4 times more, join with a ss to 3rd of first 3ch.

**Round 3** 3ch, 1tr into same place, 1tr into each of next 2tr, 2tr into next tr, 2ch, * 2tr into next tr, 1tr into each of next 2tr, 2tr into next tr, 2ch, rep from * 4 times more, join with a ss to 3rd of first 3ch.

**Round 4** 3ch, 1tr into same place, 1tr into each of next 4tr, 2tr into next tr, 2ch, * 2tr into next tr, 1tr into each of next 4tr, 2tr into next tr, 2ch, rep from * 4 times more, join with a ss to 3rd of first 3ch.

**Round 5** 3ch, 1tr into each of next 7tr, * 3ch, 1dc into 2ch sp, 3ch, 1tr into each of next 8tr, rep from * 4 times more, 3ch, 1dc into 2ch sp, 3ch, join with a ss to 3rd of first 3ch.

**Round 5** Ss into 1ch sp, 4ch, 5dtr into same ch sp, * 1dtr into each dc to next corner, 6dtr into ch sp at corner, rep from * twice more, 1dtr into each dc to end, join with a ss to 4th of first 4ch.

Fasten off.

next htr, join with a ss to 2nd of first 2ch, turn.

**Round 4** 2ch, 1htr into each of next 2htr, * 3htr into next htr, 1htr into each of next 5htr, rep from * 4 times more, 3htr into next htr, 1htr into each of next 2htr, join with a ss to 2nd of first 2ch, turn.

Cont in this way, working 2 more htr along each side in each rnd until hexagon is the required size.

Fasten off.

**Round 4** * 4ch, 2dc into 4ch lp, 1dc into each of next 2dc, rep from * to end.

**Round 5** * 4ch, 2dc into 4ch lp, 1dc into each of next 3dc, rep from * to end.

Cont in this way, working 1 more dc in each group on each rnd until motif is the required size, ending with a ss into next dc.

Fasten off.

**Round 6** Ss into next tr, 3ch, 1tr into each of next 5tr, * 3ch, (1dc into 3ch sp, 3ch) twice, miss next tr, 1tr into each of next 6tr, rep from * 4 times more, 3ch, (1dc into 3ch sp, 3ch) twice, join with a ss to 3rd of first 3ch.

**Round 7** Ss into next tr, 3ch, 1tr into each of next 3tr, * 3ch, (1dc into 3ch sp, 3ch) 3 times, miss next tr, 1tr into each of next 4tr, rep from * 4 times more, 3ch, (1dc into 3ch sp, 3ch) 3 times, join with a ss to 3rd of first 3ch.

**Round 8** Ss between 2nd and 3rd tr of group, 3ch, 1tr into same place, * 3ch, (1dc into 3ch sp, 3ch) 4 times, 2tr between 2nd and 3rd tr of gr, rep from * 4 times more, 3ch, (1dc into 3ch sp, 3ch) 4 times, join with a ss to 3rd of first 3ch.

**Round 9** Ss into 3ch sp, 3ch, 3tr into same sp, (4tr into 3ch sp) 4 times, * 3ch, miss 2tr, (4tr into 3ch sp) 5 times, rep from * 4 times more, 3ch, join with a ss to 3rd of first 3ch.

Fasten off.

## 1 Willow lace square
## 2 Irish lace square

**1 Willow lace square**
**2 Irish lace square**

### 1 Willow lace square

Make 5ch and join into a ring with a ss into first ch.

**Round 1** 1ch, 11dc into ring, ss to first ch.

**Round 2** * 15ch, ss into next dc, rep from * 11 times more, working last ss into ss at end of rnd 1.

**Round 3** Ss along to centre of first lp, * 4ch, 1dc into next lp, 4ch, (yrh, insert hook into next lp, yrh, draw 1p through, yrh, draw through 2 lps) 3 times, yrh, draw

through all 4 lps on hook – called cluster – 4ch, cl into same lp, 4ch, 1dc into next lp, rep from * 3 times more, working last dc into ss at beg of rnd.

**Round 4** Ss along to centre of first 4ch 1p, 3ch, cl into this same 1p, * 4ch, 1dc into next 1p, 4ch, (cl, 4ch, cl) into next 1p, 4ch, 1dc into next lp, 4ch, cl into next lp, rep from * 3 times more, but omit last cl and ss to 3rd of first 3ch.

Fasten off.

### 2 Irish lace square

Make 16ch.

**Round 1** 1dc into first of the 16ch, to make a 1p, (15ch, 1dc into same ch as before) twice. 3 lps now made.

**Round 2** 24dc into each 1p, join with a ss to first dc.

**Round 3** 1dc into each dc all round, join with a ss to first dc.

**Round 4** Ss into each of next 3dc, * 1dc into next dc, ** 4ch, 1dc into 3rd ch from hook, 5ch, 1dc into 3rd ch from hook, 1 ch ** – called 1 picot loop – miss 4dc, 1dc into next dc, (1 picot loop, miss 4dc, 1dc into next dc) twice, 1 picot lp, 1dc into 5th dc of next leaf, rep from * twice more, omitting the last dc and working a ss into first dc of rnd. 12 picot lps now made.

**Round 5** Ss along to centre of first picot 1p, * 8ch, 1dc into centre of next lp, turn, ss into lp just made, 3ch, 9tr into same 1p, 1tr into next dc, turn, 4ch, miss first 2tr, 1tr

into next tr, (1ch, miss 1tr, 1tr into next tr) 3 times, 1ch, miss 1tr, 1tr into 3rd of 3ch, 4ch, 1dc into 3rd ch from hook, 2ch, 1dc into same 1p, (1 picot 1p, 1dc into centre of next 1p) twice, rep from * 3 times more, but omitting last dc and working a ss into ss at base of first 8ch.

**Round 6** Ss up side of tr and into each of next 3ch, * 1 picot lp, 1dc into centre 1ch sp, 1 picot lp, 1dc into last tr of "crown" (1 picot lp, 1dc into centre of next lp) twice, 1 picot lp, 1dc into 3rd of 3ch at beg of "crown" rep from * 3 times more, omitting last dc and working a ss into ss before first picot lp.

**Round 7** Ss along to centre of first picot lp, work as rnd 5, but working 4 picot lps between each "crown" instead of 2.

**Round 8** As rnd 6 but working 2 more picot lps along each side of square.

Fasten off.

# Colour medallions

Colourwork medallions are composed of two or more colours. As well as being decorative, they are an economic way of using up odd scraps of yarn. They can be made in many different shapes such as squares, circles and hexagons and joined together to make blankets, shawls and bags or made larger and used individually as cushion covers. In colourwork medallions, new colours are added at the beginning of rounds. When breaking off the old yarn at the end of a round and joining in the new colour, secure the ends carefully.

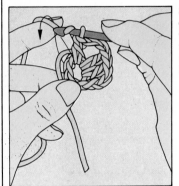

**Securing loose end on first round**
On first round of medallion work stitches over loose end.

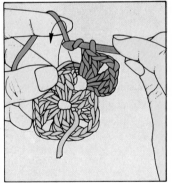

**Securing loose ends on subsequent rounds**
When joining in new colours on subsequent rounds work several stitches over loose ends of new and old yarn. When medallion is completed trim ends.

**1**

Pattern instructions for the above colourwork medallion and for medallions opposite are given on pages 144–145.

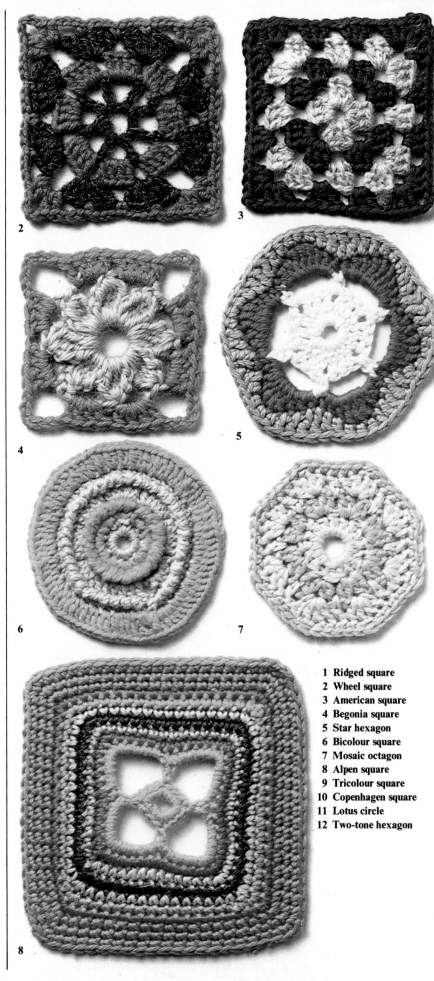

**2**

**3**

**4**

**5**

**6**

**7**

**8**

1 **Ridged square**
2 **Wheel square**
3 **American square**
4 **Begonia square**
5 **Star hexagon**
6 **Bicolour square**
7 **Mosaic octagon**
8 **Alpen square**
9 **Tricolour square**
10 **Copenhagen square**
11 **Lotus circle**
12 **Two-tone hexagon**

# Granny square afghans

These were originally made by the first American settlers who, because of shortage of supplies, had to use up any odd scraps of yarn. At first the designs of these came second to their serviceability and warmth but later more thought went into the overall patterns of the medallions resulting in very beautiful finished pieces of work.

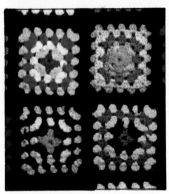

### Joining medallions

The small square medallions are very striking when worked with carefully graded bright colours at the centre and edged and joined in one dark colour like those in the afghan above to give the effect of stained glass windows. Using the square medallion patterns make your own afghan, joining the squares together using the method on page 133.

143

# Colourwork medallions

1 Ridged square
2 Wheel square
3 American square
4 Begonia square
5 Star hexagon
6 Bicolour circle
7 Mosaic octagon
8 Alpen square
9 Tricolour square
10 Copenhagen square
11 Lotus circle
12 Two-tone hexagon

## 1 Ridged square

This square uses 5 colours, A, B, C, D and E.

Using A, make 8ch and join into a ring with a ss.

**Round 1** 4ch, 3dtr into ring, * 5ch, 4dtr into ring, rep from * twice more, 5ch, join with a ss to 4th of first 4ch. Fasten off.

Make 3 more squares in the same way, one each in B, C and D.

Using E, join squares as follows: place 2 squares tog with wrong sides tog, join E to 1 corner, work 3dc into sp, 1dc bet each dtr, 3dc into sp. Fasten off.

## 2 Wheel square

This square uses 2 colours, A and B.

Using A, make 8ch and join into a ring with a ss into first ch.

**Round 1** Using A, 6ch, * 1tr into ring, 3ch, rep from * 6 times more, join with a ss to 3rd of first 6ch. Break off A.

**Round 2** Join in B to any sp, 3ch, 3tr into same sp, * 2ch, 4tr into next sp, rep from * 6 times more, 2ch, join with a ss to 3rd of first 3ch. Break off B.

**Round 3** Join in A to any sp, 3ch, 5tr into same sp, * 1ch, 6tr into next sp, 3ch, 6tr into next sp, rep from * twice more, 1ch, 6tr into next sp, 3ch, join with a ss to 3rd of first 3ch. Break off A.

**Round 4** Join in B to a 1ch sp, * 3ch, 1dc between 3rd and 4th tr of gr, 3ch, (2tr, 3ch, 2tr) into 3ch sp, 3ch, 1dc bet 3rd and 4th tr of gr, 3ch, 1dc into 1ch sp, rep from * 3 times more, omitting last dc and join with a ss to first ch. Fasten off.

## 3 American square

This square uses 2 colours, A and B.

Using A, make 6ch and join into a ring with a ss into first ch.

**Round 1** Using A, 3ch, 2tr into ring, * 3ch, 3tr into ring, rep from * twice more, 3ch, join with a ss to 3rd of first 3ch. Break off A.

**Round 2** Join in B to any sp, 3ch, (2tr, 3ch, 3tr) into same sp, * 1ch, (3tr, 3ch, 3tr) into next sp, rep from * twice more, 1ch, join with a ss to 3rd of first 3ch. Break off B.

**Round 3** Join in A to a 3ch sp, 3ch, (2tr, 3ch, 3tr) into same sp, * 1ch, 3tr into 1ch sp, 1ch, (3tr, 3ch, 3tr) into 3ch sp, rep from * twice more, 1ch, 3tr into 1ch sp, 1ch, join with a ss to 3rd of first 3ch. Break off A.

**Round 4** Join in B to a 3ch sp, 3ch, (2tr, 3ch, 3tr) into same sp, * (1ch, 3tr into 1ch sp) twice, 1ch, (3tr, 3ch, 3tr) into 3ch sp, rep from * twice more, (1ch, 3tr into 1ch sp) twice, 1ch, join with a ss to 3rd of first 3ch. Fasten off.

## 4 Begonia square

This square uses 2 colours, A and B.

Using A, make 4ch and join into a ring with a ss into first ch.

**Round 1** Using A, 4ch, ** yrh twice, insert hook into ring, yrh, draw lp through, (yrh, draw through 2 lps) twice ** rep from ** to ** 3 times more, yrh, draw through 5 lps, * 4ch, rep from ** to ** 5 times, yrh, draw through 6 lps, rep from * 6 times more, 4ch, join with a ss to 4th of first 4ch. Break off A.

**Round 2** Join in B to a 4ch lp, 3ch,

3tr into same sp, * 4tr into next sp, 6ch, 4tr into next sp, rep from * twice more, 4tr into next sp, 6ch, join with a ss to 3rd of first 3ch.

Fasten off.

## 5 Star hexagon

This motif uses 3 colours, A, B and C.

Using A, make 6ch and join into a ring with a ss into first ch.

**Round 1** 4ch, 2dtr into ring, * 1ch, 3dtr into ring, rep from * 4 times more, 1ch, join with a ss to 4th of first 4ch, turn.

**Round 2** Using A, * 1dc into 1ch sp, 7ch, rep from * 5 times more, join with a ss to first dc. Break off A.

**Round 3** Join B to a 7ch lp, into each lp work 1htr, 2tr, 3dtr, 2tr, 1htr, join with a ss to first htr. Break off B.

**Round 4** Join C to first htr of a petal, 4ch, 1tr into each of 2tr, 1htr into each of 3dtr, 1tr into each of 2tr, 1dtr into htr, * 1dtr into htr, 1tr into each of 2tr, 1htr into each of 3dtr, 1tr into each of 2tr, 1dtr into htr, rep from * 4 times more, join with a ss to 4th of first 4ch.

Fasten off.

## 6 Bicolour circle

This motif uses 2 colours, A and B.

Using A, make 4ch and join into a ring with a ss into first ch.

**Round 1** Using A, 1ch, 15dc into ring, join with a ss to first ch. Break off A.

**Round 2** Join B to any dc, 1ch, 2dc into same dc, * miss 1dc, 3dc into next dc, rep from * to last dc, miss 1dc, join with a ss to first ch.

**Round 3** Working from *left* to *right* work 1dc into each dc, join with a ss to first dc. Break off B.

**Round 4** Join A to a missed st of rnd 2, 5ch,* working behind previous rnds, 1htr into next missed st of rnd 2, 3ch, rep from * to end, join with a ss to 2nd of first 5ch.

**Round 5** Using A, work 5tr into each 3ch lp.

**Round 6** Using A, as rnd 3.

**Round 7** Using A, 1ch, working behind previous row, work 1dc into each tr to end, join with a ss to first ch. Break off A.

**Round 8** Join B to any dc, 3ch, 1tr into same place, 2tr into each dc to end, join with a ss to 3rd of first 3ch.

Fasten off.

## 7 Mosaic octagon

This motif uses 2 colours, A and B.

Using A, make 6ch and join into a ring with a ss into first ch.

**Round 1** Using A, 3ch, 15tr into ring, join with a ss to 3rd of first 3ch. Break off A.

**Round 2** Join B to any tr, 3ch, (1tr, 1ch, 2tr) into same place, * miss 1tr, (2tr, 1ch, 2tr) into next tr, rep from * 6 times more, join with a ss to 3rd of first 3ch. Break off B.

**Round 3** Join A to a 1ch sp, 3ch, (1tr, 1ch, 2tr) into same sp, * 1tr bet gr, (2tr, 1ch, 2tr) into 1ch sp, rep from * 6 times more, 1tr bet gr, join with a ss to 3rd of first 3ch. Break off A.

**Round 4** Join B to any st, 1ch, 1dc into each st all round, join with a ss to first ch.

Fasten off.

## 8 Alpen square

This square uses 4 colours, A, B, C and D.

Using A, make 6ch and join into a ring with a ss into first ch.

**Round 1** Using A, 1ch, 15dc into ring, join with a ss to first ch.

**Round 2** Using A, 11ch, * miss 3dc, 1dc into next dc, 10ch, rep from * twice more, join with a ss to first of first 11ch.

**Round 3** Using A, 1ch, * 11dc into 10ch lp, 1dc into dc, rep from * 3 times more, but omit last dc and join with a ss to first ch. Break off A.

**Round 4** Join in B to 6th of 11dc, 1ch, 1dc into same place, 1dc into each dc all round and 2dc into each corner, join with a ss to first ch. Break off B.

**Round 5** Join in C to corner and work as rnd 4. Break off C.

**Round 6** Join in D to corner and work as rnd 4. Break off D.

Cont in the same way, working 1 rnd each in C, A and B, then 3 rnds in A.

Fasten off.

## 9 Tricolour square

This square uses 3 colours, coded A, B and C.

Using A, make 8ch and join into a ring with a ss into first ch.

**Round 1** Using A, 4ch, 5dtr into ring, * 3ch, 6dtr into ring, rep from * twice more, 3ch, join with a ss to 4th of first 4ch.

**Tricolour square continued**

**Round 2** Using A, 5ch, ** yrh twice, insert hook into next dtr, yrh, draw lp through, (yrh, draw through 2 lps) twice, ** rep from ** to ** into each of next 4dtr, yrh, draw through 6 lps, * 5ch, 1ss into 2nd of 3ch, 5ch, rep from ** to ** into each of next 6dtr, yrh, draw through 7 lps, rep from * twice more, 5ch, 1ss into 2nd of 3ch. Break off A.

**Round 3** Join in B to top of a cl, work (3dtr, 1ch, 3dtr, 2ch, 3dtr, 1ch, 3dtr) into 3ch sp of rnd 1, 1ss into top of next cl, rep from * 3 times more, working last ss into same place as yarn was joined, and joining in A at the same time. Break off B.

**Round 4** Using A, 4ch, 5dtr into same ss, * (6dtr, 2ch, 6dtr) into 2ch sp, 6dtr into ss at top of next cl, rep from * twice more, (6dtr, 2ch, 6dtr) into 2ch sp, join with a ss to 4th of first 4ch. Break off A.

**Round 5** Join in C to last ss of rnd 4, 1ch, 1dc into each of next 5dtr, 1tr into 1ch sp between gr of dtr on rnd 3, * 1dc into each of next 6dtr, 3dc into 2ch sp at corner, (1dc into each of next 6dtr, 1tr into 1ch sp bet gr of dtr on rnd 3) twice, rep from * twice more, 1dc into each of next 6dtr, 3dc into 2ch sp at corner, 1dc into each of next 6dtr, 1tr into 1ch sp bet gr of dtr on rnd 3, join with a ss to first ch.

**Round 6** Using C, 3ch, 1tr into each st all round, working 3tr into centre st of each corner, end by joining with a ss to 3rd of first 3ch.

Fasten off.

## 10 Copenhagen square

This square uses 4 colours, A, B, C and D.

Using A, make 10ch and join into a ring with a ss into first ch.

**Round 1** Using A, 1ch, 19dc into ring, join with a ss to first ch.

**Round 2** Using A, 9ch, * miss 4dc, 1dc into next dc, 8ch, rep from * twice more, miss 4dc, join with a ss to first of first 9ch.

**Round 3** Using A, 1ch, * 9dc into 8ch sp, 1dc into dc, rep from * to end, omitting last dc and join with a ss to first ch. Break off A.

**Round 4** Join in B to 5th of 9dc (corner), 1ch, 1dc into same dc, * 1dc into each of next 9dc, 2dc into next dc, rep from * twice more, 1dc into each of next 9dc, join with a ss to first ch. Break off B.

**Copenhagen square continued**

**Round 5** Join in C to last ss, 1ch, 1dc into same place, * 1dc into each of next 10dc, 2dc into next dc, rep from * twice more, 1dc into each of next 10dc, join with a ss to first ch. Break off C.

**Round 6** Join in D to last ss, 4ch, 1tr into same place, * 1ch, (1tr into next dc, 1ch, miss 1dc) 5 times, 1tr into next dc, 1ch, (1tr, 1ch, 1tr) into next dc, rep from * twice more, 1ch, (1tr into next dc, 1ch, miss 1dc) 5 times, 1tr into next dc, 1ch, join with a ss to 3rd of first 4ch.

**Round 7** Using D, 1ch, 2dc into 1ch sp, 1dc into tr, * (1dc into 1ch sp, 1dc into tr) 7 times, 2dc into 1ch sp, 1dc into tr, rep from * twice more, (1dc into 1ch sp, 1dc into tr) 6 times, 1dc into 1ch sp, join with a ss to first ch. Break off D.

**Round 8** Join in A to one corner, 1ch, 1dc into same place, 1dc into each dc all round and 2dc into each corner, join with a ss to first ch. Break off A.

**Round 9** Join in C to corner, 4ch, 1tr into same place, * (1ch, miss 1dc, 1tr into next dc) 8 times, 1ch, miss 1dc, (1tr, 1ch, 1tr) into next dc, rep from * twice more, (1ch, miss 1dc, 1tr into next dc) 8 times, 1ch, join with a ss to 3rd of first 4ch.

**Round 10** Using C, 1ch, 2dc into 1ch sp, 1dc into tr, * (1dc into 1ch sp, 1dc into tr) 9 times, 2dc into next sp, 1dc into tr, rep from * twice more, (1dc into 1ch sp, 1dc into tr) 8 times, 1ch, join with a ss to first ch. Break off C.

**Round 11** Join in B to one corner and work as rnd 8.

Fasten off.

## 11 Lotus circle

This uses 2 colours, coded as A and B.

Make 3ch in A and join into a ring with a ss into first ch.

**Round 1** 1ch 5dc into ring, join with a ss to first ch.

**Round 2** 1ch, join in B and work 1dc into same place, * 1dc in A and 1dc in B into next st, rep from * to end, join with a ss in A into first ch.

**Round 3** 1ch, working into the back half only of each st on *every* rnd, *2dc in B into next dc, 1dc in A into next dc, rep from * to last st, 2dc in B into last st, join with a ss in A into first ch.

**Lotus circle continued**

**Round 4** 1ch, * 2dc in B into next dc, 1dc in B into next dc, 1dc in A into next dc, rep from * to last 2 sts, 2dc in B into next dc, 1dc in B into next dc, join with a ss in A to first ch.

**Round 5** 1ch, * 2dc in B into next dc, 1dc in B into each of next 2dc, 1dc in A into next dc, rep from * to last 3 sts, 2dc in B into next dc, 1dc in B into each of next 2dc, join with a ss in A into first ch.

Cont in this way, working 1 more st in B in each gr on every rnd until there are 8 sts in B in each gr (54 sts in the rnd).

**Round 10** 1ch, * 2dc in A into next dc, 1dc in B into each of next 7dc, 1dc in A into next dc, rep from * to end, but omit the last dc in A and join with a ss in A into first ch.

**Round 11** 1ch, * 2dc in A into next dc, 1dc in A into each of next 2dc, 1dc in B into each of next 6dc, 1dc in A into next dc, rep from * to end, but omit the last dc in A and join with a ss in A into first ch.

Cont in this way, still inc 6 sts in every rnd, but working 1 st less in B in each gr on every rnd until only 1 st in B remains (96 sts in the rnd).

Fasten off.

## 12 Two-tone hexagon

This motif uses 2 colours, A and B.

Using A, make 6ch and join into a ring with a ss into first ch.

**Round 1** Using A, 3ch, 2tr into ring, * 3ch, 3tr into ring, rep from * 4 times more, 3ch, join with a ss to 3rd of first 3ch. Break off A.

**Round 2** Join B to 3ch sp, 5ch, (2tr tr, 2ch, 3tr tr) into same sp, * (3tr tr, 2ch, 3tr tr) into next sp, rep from * 4 times more, join with a ss to 5th of first 5ch. Break off B.

**Round 3** Join A to same place as ss, 1tr into next 2tr tr, * (2tr, 2ch, 2tr) into 2ch sp, 1tr into each of next 6tr tr, rep from * 4 times more, (2tr, 2ch, 2tr) into 2ch sp, 1tr into each of next 3tr tr, join with a ss to 3rd of first 3ch. Break off A.

**Round 4** Join B into any st, 3ch, 1tr into previous st, * miss 1 st, 1tr into next st, 1tr into the missed st, rep from * all round, join with a ss to 3rd of first 3ch.

Fasten off.

**Materials** 100g of No. 3 cotton; No. 3.50 crochet hook. **Stitch gauge** 14 sts and 15 rows to 4in. (10cm) over htr. **Size** 12½in. (32cm) square. Make 4ch and join into a ring with a ss into first ch. **Round 1** Work 8htr into ring, but do *not* join at end of this or any rounds. **Round 2** 2htr into each htr to end (16 sts). **Round 3** *1ch, (yrh, insert hook between next 2htr, yrh, draw lp through) 4 times into the same place, yrh, draw through all 9 lps on hook – called 1cl (cluster) – 1ch, 1htr bet 3 times, rep from * 3 times more. **Round 4** *1ch, 1cl in top of cl, 1ch, 1htr bet cl and next htr, 1htr bet htr twice, 1htr bet htr and cl, rep from * 3 times more. **Round 5** As rnd 4, but having 5htr along each side instead of 4. **Round 6** As rnd 4, but working 2ch instead of 1ch before and after cl and having 6htr along each side. **Round 7** *2ch, (1cl, 1ch, 1cl) into top of cl, 2ch, 7htr, rep from * 3 times more. **Round 8** *2ch, (1cl, 1ch, 1cl) into 1ch sp, 2ch, 8htr, rep from * 3 times more. **Round 9** As rnd 8 but with 9htr along each side. **Round 10** *2ch, (2cl, 1ch, 2cl) into 1ch sp, 2ch, 10htr, rep from * 3 times more. **Round 11** *2ch, (2cl, 1ch, 2cl) into 1ch sp, 2ch, 5htr, 1cl between next 2htr, 5htr, rep from * 3 times more. **Round 12** *2ch, (2cl, 1ch, 2cl) into 1ch sp, 2ch, 5htr, 1cl on each side of cl in previous rnd, 5htr, rep from * 3 times more. **Round 13** *2ch, (3cl, 1ch, 3cl) into 1ch sp, 2ch, 5htr, 3cl, 5htr, rep from * 3 times more. **Round 14** *2ch, 1cl bet 1st and 2nd cl, 1cl bet 2nd and 3rd cl, (3cl, 1ch, 3cl) into 1ch sp, (1cl bet cl) twice, 2ch, 5htr, 4cl, 5htr, rep from * 3 times more. **Round 15** *2ch, (1cl bet cl) 4 times, (3cl, 1ch, 3cl) into 1ch sp, (1cl bet cl) 4 times, 2ch, 5htr, 5cl, 5htr, rep from * 3 times more. **Round 16** *2ch, (1cl bet cl) 6 times, (3cl, 1ch, 3cl) into 1ch sp, (1cl bet cl) 6 times, 2ch, 5htr, 6cl, 5htr, rep from * 3 times more. **Round 17** *1htr into each cl to corner, 1htr between each cl to corner, (2htr, 1ch, 2htr) into 1ch sp, 1htr bet each cl, 1htr into 2ch sp, 5htr, 5cl, 5htr, rep from * 3 times more. **Round 18** As rnd 17, but working 4cl above each 5 cl in previous rnd. **Round 19** As rnd 17 but working 3cl in each grp. **Round 20** As rnd 17 but working 2cl in each grp. **Round 21** As rnd 17 but working 1cl in each grp. Work 3 rnds in htr, working (2htr, 1ch, 2htr) into each corner. After 24th rnd, join with ss to next htr. Fasten off.

# Relief medallions

Medallions can be made in relief patterns by working the stitches in fluted groups, by working twice into the same round, by using looped stitches and by making bobbles. They can be used as shown below and opposite.

Large medallion as a cushion cover (pattern instructions on page 145)

A single small medallion can be made in fine yarn and used as a brooch.

### Medallion patterns
*The following numbered medallions are made using different techniques and the instructions for each are given on page 148.*

**1 Bobble square**

**2 Cineraria**

**3 Magnolia**

**4 Dandelion**

**5 Flower square**

**6 Looped nosegay**

### Joined medallions
*Many medallions can be joined together to form a bed or cushion cover or a small number can be joined and applied to the surface of an existing quilt as shown below. The corners can be decorated with individual medallions. The different ways of joining are shown on page 132. When making many medallions which are later to be used together make sure that the same type of yarn, size of hook and tension are used throughout, otherwise the size of the medallions will vary, and it will be difficult to join them.*

# Relief medallions with lace edges

Frequently in the past lace crochet edgings were used to finish off medallion crochet as shown on the doll's bedspread below. The detail at the bottom of the page is worked in bobble squares (see page 148) and with a fan edging (page 165).

**Doll's bedspread**

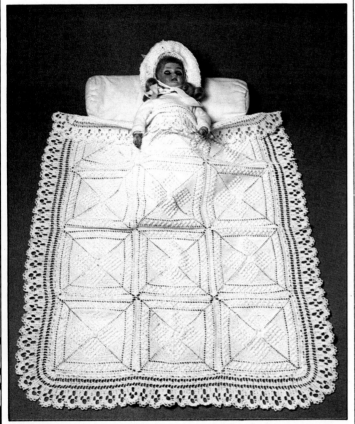

**Bobble square bedspread with fan edging**

# Crochet motifs

1  **Spray of leaves**

2  **Hibiscus**

3  **Four leaf clover**

4  **Rose**

5  **Shamrock**

**Child's sweater with four leaf clover motifs attached**

## Crochet motifs
*Crochet motifs such as those seen in Irish crochet are usually used on bed and table linen, worked in fine crochet cotton. They can be sewn onto ground fabric or worked in lace patterns and joined with decorative chains. The instructions for the above motifs are on page 148.*

# *Relief medallions and motifs instructions*

## Relief medallions

1 Bobble square
2 Cineraria
3 Magnolia
4 Dandelion
5 Flower square
6 Looped nosegay

### 1 Bobble square

Make 12ch and join into a ring with a ss into first ch.

**Round 1** 3ch, 1tr into ring * (yrh, insert hook into ring, yrh, draw 1p through, yrh, draw through 2 lps) 6 times, yrh, draw through 6 lps, yrh, draw through rem 2 lps – called bobble – 4tr into ring, rep from * twice more, bobble, 2tr into ring, ss to 3rd of first 3ch.

**Round 2** 3ch, 1tr into same place, * 1tr into each of next 3 sts, 2tr into next tr, 1ch, 2tr into next tr, rep from * 3 times more, but omit the last 2tr and ss to 3rd of first 3ch.

**Round 3** 3ch, 1tr into same place, * (1tr into next tr, bobble into next tr) twice, 1tr into next tr, 2tr into next tr, 2ch, 2tr into next tr, rep from * 3 times more, but omit the last 2tr and ss to 3rd of first 3ch.

**Round 4** 3ch, 1tr into same place, * 1tr into each of next 7 sts, 2tr into next tr, 3ch, 2tr into next tr, rep from * 3 times more, but omit last 2tr and ss into 3rd of first 3ch.

**Round 5** 3ch, 1tr into same place, * 1tr into each of next 2tr, (bobble into next tr, 1tr into next tr) 3 times, 1tr into next tr, 2tr into next tr, 4ch, 2tr into next tr, rep from * 3 times more, but omit last 2tr and ss to 3rd of first 3ch.

**Round 6** 3ch, 1tr into same place * 1tr into each of next 11 sts, 2tr into next tr, 4ch, 2tr into next tr, rep from * 3 times more, but omit last 2tr and ss to 3rd of first 3ch.
Fasten off.

## 2 Cineraria

Make 8ch and join into a ring with a ss into first ch.

**Round 1** 3ch, 17tr into ring, ss into 3rd of 3ch.

**Round 2** 8ch, (1tr into next tr, 5ch) 17 times, ss into 3rd of first 8ch.

**Round 3** * 1dc into each of next 2ch, (1dc, 1ch, 1dc) into next ch, 1dc into each of next 2ch, miss 1tr, rep from * 17 times more.

**Round 4** * 1dc into each of next 3dc, (1dc, 1ch, 1dc) into 1ch sp, 1dc into each of next 3dc, rep from * 17 times more.

**Rounds 5, 6, 7, 8 and 9** As rnd 4, working one more dc in each gr on each round.

**Round 10** * 5ch, 1dc bet 8th and 9th of next 16dc (i.e., above the tr which was missed in rnd 3) rep from * 16 times more, 5ch, ss into base of first 5ch.

**Round 11** * 5ch, 1dc into 3rd ch of lp, 5ch, 1dc into next dc, rep from * 17 times more, omitting last dc and working a ss into base of first 5ch.

**Round 12** Ss along to 3rd ch of lp, * 5ch, 1dc into next lp, rep from * 35 times more, omitting last dc and working a ss into ss before first 5ch.

**Round 13** As rnd 12.
Fasten off.

## 3 Magnolia

This medallion uses 3 colours, A, B and C.
Using A, make 5ch and join into a ring with a ss into first ch.

**Round 1** 1ch, 4dc into ring, ss to first ch.

**Round 2** 1ch, 1dc into same place, 2dc into each dc to end, ss to first ch.

**Round 3** 2ch, 1htr into same place, 2htr into each dc to end, ss to 2nd of first 2ch.

**Round 4** Inserting hook into front strand only of each st, * 3ch, 1dtr into same place, 2dtr into each of next 2htr, (1dtr, 3ch, 1ss) into next htr, 1ss into next htr, rep from * 4 times more. Break off A.

**Round 5** Join B behind the centre of one petal, then inserting hook into back strand only of each st of rnd 4, work as rnd 4 but working tr tr instead of dtr. Break off B.

**Round 6** Join C *in front of* work into a dc of rnd 1, (3ch, 1dc into next dc) 4 times, 3ch, ss into same place as join.
Fasten off.

## 4 Dandelion

Make 4ch and join into a ring with a ss into first ch.

**Round 1** 1ch, 11dc into ring, ss to first ch.

**Round 2** Working into front half only of each dc, work (1dc, 4ch, 1dc) into each dc.

**Round 3** Working into back half only of each dc of rnd 1, * 6ch, (1dc, 6ch, 1dc) into next dc, rep from * to end.
Fasten off.

## 5 Flower square

This square uses 3 colours, A, B and C.

Using A, make 4ch and join into a ring with a ss into first ch.

**Round 1** * 2ch, 4tr into ring, ss into ring, rep from * 3 times more.

**Round 2** Using A, ss into back of 3rd tr, * keeping yarn at back of work, 4ch, ss into back of 3rd tr of next gr, rep from * twice more, 4ch, join with a ss to first ss. Break off A.

**Round 3** Join B to a 4ch lp, into each lp work 1ss, 5tr, 1ss.

**Round 4** Using B, * 6ch, 1ss into back of ss between petals, rep from * 3 times more. Break off B.

**Round 5** Join A to a 6ch lp, 3ch, (2tr, 3ch, 3tr) into same lp, * 1ch, (3tr, 3ch, 3tr) into next lp, rep from * twice more, 1ch, join with a ss to 3rd of first 3ch. Break off A.

**Round 6** Using B, as rnd 3 of American square.

**Round 7** Using C, as rnd 4 of American square (see page 144).
Fasten off.

## 6 Looped nosegay

This medallion uses 3 colours, A, B and C.
Using A, make 3ch and join into a ring with a ss into first ch.

**Round 1** 1ch, 3dc into ring, ss into first ch.

**Round 2** 1ch, 1dc into same place, 2dc into each dc to end, ss into first ch.

**Round 3** As rnd 2. Break off A.

**Round 4** Join in B, 1ch, * 2dc into next dc, 1dc into next dc, rep from * 7 times more, but omit last dc and work a ss into first ch. Break off B.

**Round 5** Join in C, 1ch, * 2dc into next dc, 1dc into each of next 2dc, rep from * 7 times more, but omit last dc and work a ss into first ch.

**Round 6** Using C, 1ch, * 2dc into next dc, 1dc into each of next 3dc, rep from * 7 times more, ending as before. Break off C.

**Round 7** Turn work and join in A with wrong side facing, 1ch, * yrh, insert hook into next st, hold a pencil behind work and take the yarn round it to form a loop, yrh, draw lp through, yrh, draw through 3 lps on hook, rep from * to end, ss to first ch. Break off A.

**Round 8** Join in B and work as rnd 7, but inc 8 sts evenly in the round. Break off B.

**Round 9** Join in C and work as rnd 8. Fasten off.

## Motifs

1 Spray of leaves
2 Hibiscus
3 Four leaf clover
4 Rose
5 Shamrock

### 1 Spray of leaves

For first leaf make 16ch.

**Row 1** 1dc into 2nd ch from hook, 1dc into each of next 13ch, 3dc into next ch, cont along other side of foundation ch, 1dc into each of next 14ch, 1ch, turn.

**Row 2** Working throughout into the back half only of each st, 1dc into each of next 11dc, 1ch, turn.

**Row 3** 1dc into each of next 11dc, 3dc into next st, 1dc into each of next 12dc, 1ch, turn.

**Row 4** 1dc into each of next 12dc, 3dc into next dc, 1dc into each of next 10dc, 1ch, turn.

**Row 5** 1dc into each of next 10dc, 3dc into next dc, 1dc into each of next 10dc, 1ch, turn.

**Row 6** 1dc into each of next 10dc, 3dc into next dc, 1dc into each of next 8dc, 1ch, turn.

**Spray of leaves continued**

**Row 7** 1dc into each of next 8dc, 3dc into next dc, 1dc into each of next 8dc, 1ch, turn.

**Row 8** 1dc into each of next 8dc, 3dc into next dc, 1dc into each of next 6dc.

Fasten off.

Make 2 more leaves in the same way.

For stalk make 30ch, ss into base of one leaf, 8ch, ss into base of second leaf, turn; working over 3 strands of yarn work 1dc into each ch to end, turn, ss into each of first 30 sts, then ss to base of third leaf (this will now be opposite to the first leaf).

Fasten off.

## 2 Hibiscus

This medallion uses 2 colours, A and B.

Using A, make 6ch and join into a ring with a ss into first ch.

**Round 1** 3ch, 19tr into ring, ss to 3rd of 3ch. Break off A.

**Round 2** Join in B, * 1ch, 1tr into next tr, 2tr into next tr, 1tr into next tr, 1ch, 1dc into next tr, rep from * 4 times more, but omit last dc and work a ss into same place as join.

Fasten off.

Cut a few strands of each colour and join to back of work to form stalk.

## 3 Four leaf clover

Make 5ch and join into a ring with a ss into first ch.

**Round 1** 1ch, 13dc into ring, ss to first ch.

**Round 2** 1ch, 1dc into next dc, * 4ch, ** yrh twice, insert hook into next st, yrh, draw lp through, (yrh, draw through 2 lps) twice ** rep from ** to ** twice more into same st, yrh, draw through 4 lps on hook, 3ch, 1dc into each of next 2dc, rep from * 3 times more, make 6ch for stalk, turn and work 1ss into each ch, then 1ss into next dc on flower.

Fasten off.

## 4 Rose

Wind the yarn 3 or 4 times round a finger, remove the loop from finger and fasten with a ss.

**Round 1** 1ch, 17dc into ring, ss to first ch.

**Round 2** 6ch, miss 2dc, 1htr into next dc, * 4ch, miss 2dc, 1htr into next dc, rep from * 3 times more, 4ch, ss into 2nd of first 4ch.

**Round 3** Into each 4ch lp work (1dc, 1htr, 3tr, 1htr, 1dc), end with a ss into first dc.

**Round 4** Ss into back of htr on rnd 2, * 5ch, keeping yarn at back of work 1ss into back of next htr on rnd 2, rep from * 4 times more, 5ch, ss into same htr as first ss.

**Round 5** Into each 5ch lp work (1dc, 1htr, 5tr, 1htr, 1dc), end with a ss to first dc.

**Round 6** Ss into back of ss on rnd 4, * 6ch, keeping yarn at back of work 1ss into back of next ss on rnd 4, rep from * to end.

**Round 7** Into each 6ch lp work (1dc, 1htr, 7tr, 1htr, 1dc), end with a ss into first dc.

Fasten off.

## 5 Shamrock

Make 16ch.

**Round 1** 1dc into first of the 16ch, to make 1 lp, (15ch, 1dc into same ch as before) twice (3 lps now made).

**Round 2** Lay a separate length of yarn along the work, then working over this thread, work 22dc into each 15ch lp, ss into first dc.

**Round 3** Working again over a separate length of yarn, miss 1dc, * 1dc into each of next 20dc, miss 2dc (1dc of this lp and 1dc of next lp) rep from * twice more, ss into first dc, 25ch, turn.

**Stalk** 1dc into 2nd ch from hook, then working over separate length of yarn work 1dc into each ch, then work 1ss into first dc of shamrock.

Fasten off.

# Filet crochet

Filet crochet is extremely easy to work and is made with chains and trebles only. The principle is to make an openwork mesh of chains and trebles and to fill in the chain spaces with trebles to make solid blocks. These solid blocks are then built up into designs against the mesh background. It can also be worked with different colours so that the motif or solid block is in one whilst the mesh background is in another.

## Making the filet mesh

The following gives the principle of the mesh but some patterns call for two chain spaces instead of one for each mesh hole.

**Row 1:** 1tr into 7th ch from hook, *1ch, miss 1ch, 1tr into next st, rep from * to end, 4ch, turn.

**Row 2** and all foll rows: Miss first tr, *1tr into next tr, 1ch, miss 1ch, rep from * ending with 1tr into 3rd ch of 4 t-chs. On 2nd row work final tr into 2nd of 6ch at beg of previous row.

## Filet crochet charts

Filet crochet is nearly always worked from charts instead of written instructions. These charts are either worked on graph paper with the solid blocks of trebles shown in black, or in symbol form with the crochet symbols shown in a key.

## Crochet symbols

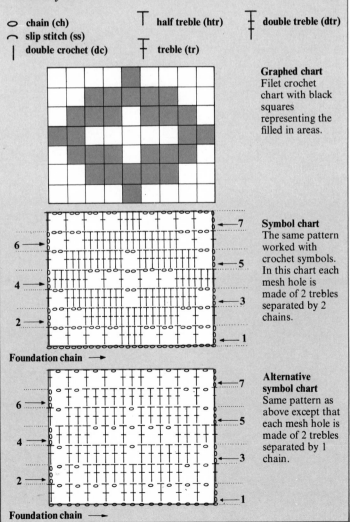

**Graphed chart**
Filet crochet chart with black squares representing the filled in areas.

**Symbol chart**
The same pattern worked with crochet symbols. In this chart each mesh hole is made of 2 trebles separated by 2 chains.

**Alternative symbol chart**
Same pattern as above except that each mesh hole is made of 2 trebles separated by 1 chain.

# Filet crochet

Filet crochet is useful for both clothes and household items such as curtains, tablemats and as an edging for tablecloths for example. The motifs in filet crochet are easy to work and the instructions for making filet crochet are given on the preceding page. Three of the motifs have been charted (see right) and these could be used as a panel in a dress or on a pocket, for example.

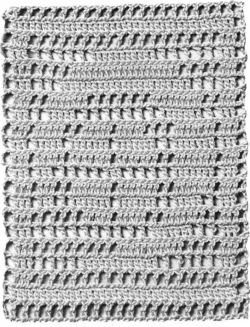

**Geometric pattern motif**

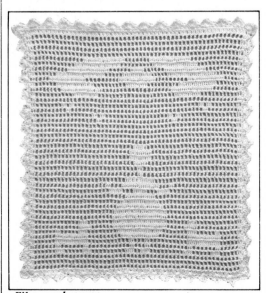

**Filet crochet mat**
*Stylized figures can be worked in filet crochet, and Scandinavian-type cross stitch designs, for example, can easily be translated into this type of crochet, using a chart.*

**Baby rabbit motif**

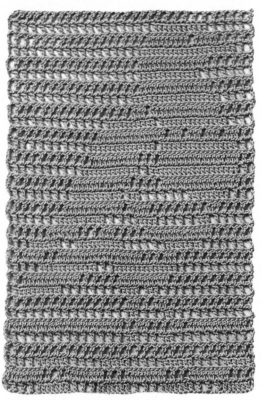

**Bird motif**

# Charted motifs

The instructions for reading filet crochet charts are given on the preceding page. There are two methods for charting filet crochet but the type of chart below is the easiest to make for your own designs.
The following charts are for the crochet motifs (see left).

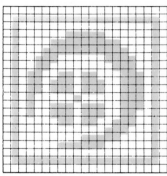

**Geometric pattern motif**

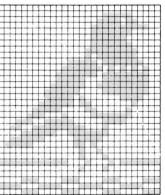

**Baby rabbit motif**

**Bird motif**

# Café curtains

Half curtains, or café curtains as they are also known, can look very attractive on a suitable window. They can be hung from a bamboo pole or curtain rod, which can either be inserted through the curtain itself or attached with rings sewn to the top edge of the curtain. Measure your window to get the correct size and work out your tension first.

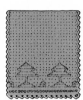

**Materials** 8 × 25g balls of crochet cotton No. 3; No. 2·50 crochet hook.
**Measurements** Width 15½in. (39cm). Length 16½in. (42cm), adjustable. **Stitch gauge** 27 sts and 11 rows to 4in. (10cm).
**Curtain** With No. 2.50 hook make 110ch.
**Row 1** 1tr into 8th ch from hook, *2ch, miss 2ch, 1tr into next ch, rep from * to end (35 sps).
**Row 2** 3ch, 2tr into first sp, 1tr into next tr, *2tr into next sp, 1tr into next tr, rep from * to end, ending with 2tr into last sp, 1tr into 5th of 7ch.
**Row 3** 5ch, miss next 2tr, 1tr into next tr, *2ch, miss next 2tr, 1tr into next tr, rep from * to end, working last tr into 3rd of 3ch.
**Row 4** As row 2, working last tr into 3rd of 5ch.
Cont in patt from chart until the 21 rows have been completed, then rep row 21 until work measures 16½ in. (42cm) from beg, or length reqd. Fasten off.
**Edging** With right side facing join yarn to top left hand corner of curtain, work 1dc into this st, 3ch, 3tr into first sp, *miss 1 sp, (1dc, 3ch, 3tr) into next sp, rep from * down left side, across bottom edge and up right side, working (1dc, 3ch, 3tr) twice into the space at each bottom corner and ending with 1dc into last st at top of right hand side. Work 1dc into each st along top edge. Fasten off.
Press work with a warm iron over a damp cloth.

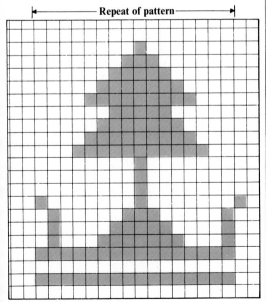

**── Repeat of pattern ──**

### Working from chart
*When working from this chart work 5 chs at the start of each row beginning with a space and work 3 chs at the start of each row beginning with a block of trebles. Read from right to left on odd rows and from left to right on even ones.*

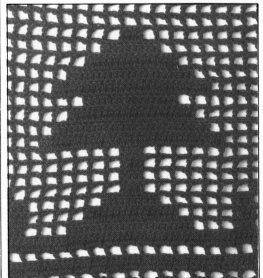

### Filet crochet curtains
*These can also be made with fine cotton on a small gauge hook. Originally all filet crochet was made fine in this way so that it resembled lace as closely as possible.*

### Curtain detail
*The solid blocks in filet crochet can also be worked in a contrasting colour, for example this tree could be green and the mesh white (see joining in colours, page 137).*

151

# Tunisian crochet

This type of crochet – also known as *afghan* and *tricot stitch* – could be said to be the fundamental link between knitting and ordinary crochet and might even be the forerunner of both. Like knitting it is worked with many stitches but these are carried on a single hook, much like a crochet hook except that it is longer and the same thickness throughout. The stitches are always worked from a foundation row of chains and are picked up on the first row, made into stitches and these are discarded on the next row and so on alternately. It forms a dense, thick fabric and is largely used for shawls, bedspreads and blankets. Any of the usual knitting or crochet yarns can be used for Tunisian crochet but it was originally worked in wools to give greater warmth.

**Finished Tunisian crochet**

### Working Tunisian crochet

The following is the basic stitch technique of Tunisian crochet. For a sample piece, cast on a foundation row of chains: 20 is sufficient.

### How to work the plain stitch

**1** *For the first row (also called the loop row), with yarn at back of work insert hook into 2nd ch from hook, yrh and draw 1 loop through. Continue making loops into each ch to end of row.*

**2** *With yarn at back of work, yrh and draw hook through first loop, \*yrh and draw hook through next 2 loops. Repeat from \* to end of row.*

**3** *With yarn at back of work insert hook through vertical loop of 2nd stitch in previous row, yrh and draw through 1 loop.*

**4** *Continue making loops in the same way to end of row. Repeat from Step 2 making loop rows and return rows.*

# Shaping Tunisian crochet

Tunisian crochet can be shaped in the same way as ordinary crochet, by either increasing or decreasing the number of stitches.

### Single increases on the right side edge

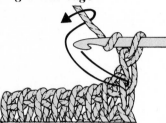

To increase at the beginning of a row make 1ch and insert hook behind vertical thread of edge stitch. Yrh and draw through a new loop. Continue making loops in the usual way to the end of the row.

### Multiple increases on a right side edge

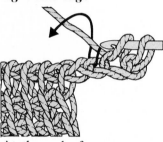

At the end of a return row work the required number of ch for the number of stitches to be increased. Work the basic stitch into each ch and into the vertical edge stitch of the previous row. Then continue making loops in the usual way to the end of the row.

### Decreasing on a right side edge

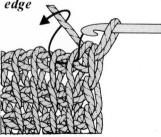

At the beginning of a loop row insert the hook through 2 vertical threads instead of 1 and work them together as if they were 1. Continue making loops in the usual way to the end of the row.

### Single increases on the left side edge

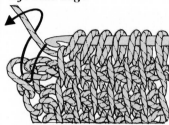

At the beginning of the previous return row yrh and draw through 1 loop, 1ch, \*yrh and draw through 2 loops. Repeat from \* to end of row. In next loop row work to last stitch, insert hook into extra ch, draw loop through. Work last loop in the usual way.

### Multiple increases on a left side edge

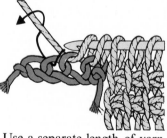

Use a separate length of yarn and work required number of ch for number of stitches to be increased. At the end of a loop row make loops into each of the new ch. Then work the return row in the usual way.

### Decreasing on a left side edge

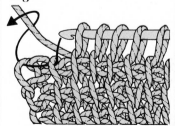

At the end of a loop row work 2 loops off together as if they were 1. Then work the return row in the usual way.

# Tunisian stitch patterns

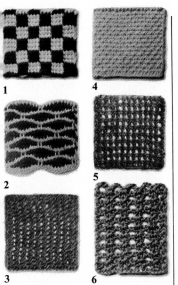

1
4
2
5
3
6

## 1 Colour squares

This pattern uses 2 colours, A and B.

Make a no. of ch divisible by 8.

**Row 1** Using A, insert hook into 2nd ch, yrh, draw lp through, (insert hook into next ch, yrh, draw lp through) twice; using B, (insert hook into next ch, yrh, draw lp through) 4 times, cont in this way working 4 lps in A and 4 lps in B.

**Row 2** Using B, yrh, draw through one lp, (yrh, draw through 2 lps) 3 times, using A, (yrh, draw through 2 lps) 4 times, cont in this way to end.

Cont in this way, work 4 more rows, then alternate the colours and work 6 rows.

Rep these 12 rows throughout.

## 2 Brocade stitch

This pattern uses 2 colours, A and B.

Using A, make a no. of ch divisible by 10, plus 2.

Work first 2 rows of plain Tunisian stitch.

**Row 3** Using B, insert hook into first lp without drawing yarn through – called 1 sl st – *work 2 plain sts, (yrh, insert hook into next st, draw lp through, draw through 2 lps – called tr st –) 4 times, 2 plain sts, 2 sl sts, rep from * to end.

**Row 4** Using B, as row 2.

**Rows 5 and 6** Using A, as plain Tunisian stitch.

**Row 7** Using B, 2 tr sts, * 2 plain sts, 2 sl sts, 2 plain sts, 4 tr sts, rep from * to end.

**Row 8** Using B, as row 2.

Rep these 8 rows throughout.

## 3 Sage lace stitch

Make an odd no. of ch.

**Row 1** Yrh, insert hook into 3rd ch from hook, draw lp through, *yrh, miss 1ch, insert hook into next ch, yrh draw lp through, rep from * to end.

**Row 2** As plain Tunisian stitch.

**Row 3** *Yrh, insert hook into next st, yrh draw lp through, rep from * to end.

**Row 4** As row 2.

Rep rows 3 and 4 throughout.

## 4 Tweed stitch

Make an odd no. of ch and work first 2 rows of plain Tunisian stitch.

**Row 3** *Insert hook from right to left in front of next st, yrh, draw lp through, insert hook from left to right in front of next st, yrh, draw lp through, rep from * to end.

**Row 4** As row 2.

**Row 5** *Insert hook from left to right in front of next st, yrh, draw lp through, insert hook from right to left in front of next st, yrh, draw lp through, rep from * to end.

**Row 6** As row 2.

Rep rows 3 to 6 throughout.

## 5 Queen lace stitch

Make an even no. of ch and work first 2 rows of plain Tunisian stitch.

**Row 3** *Lay yarn across front of work, insert hook from right to left in front of first 2 sts tog, yrh and draw lp through purlwise, insert hook between sts, yrh and draw lp through, rep from * to last st, insert hook into last st, yrh, draw lp through.

**Row 4** As row 2.

Rep rows 3 and 4 throughout.

## 6 Narcissus lace stitch

Make a no. of ch divisible by 4, and work first row of plain Tunisian stitch.

**Row 2** Yrh, draw through 2 lps, *4ch, yrh, draw through 5 lps, rep from * until 3 lps rem on hook, 3ch, yrh, draw through 3 lps, 1ch.

**Row 3** Insert hook into first ch, yrh, draw lp through, rep into each of next 2ch, *(insert hook into next ch, yrh and draw lp through) 4 times, rep from * to end.

Rep rows 2 and 3 throughout, ending with row 2.

## Project instructions

The project instructions below are for the socks and hats shown on page 155.

### Slipper socks in Tunisian crochet

**Materials** Approx. 50 (50:75)g of double knitting in colours as reqd; No. 5.50 Tunisian crochet hook; 1 pair of No. 9 (3¾mm) knitting needles. Suede or soft leather for soles. **Stitch gauge** 11 sts and 9 pairs of rows to 2in. (5cm) over Tunisian crochet on No. 5.50 hook. **Measurements** Length of foot 4¾(5½:6½)in. (12[14:16]cm). **Note** Instructions are given for one colour throughout. Colours can be varied as required, changing colour at either end of rows to achieve a different effect.

### Version with knitted ankle

With No. 5.50 hook make 16(18:20)ch and work 2 rows (one pair) in plain Tunisian crochet. **Row 3** Work 5 sts, yrh to make a st, work to last 5 sts, yrh, work to end. **Row 4** Work sts off as row 2, making an extra st where the yrh is. (18[20:22] sts). Cont to inc in the same way, keeping the inc in line on next and every odd numbered row until there are 32(36:40) sts then cont without shaping until 12(15:18) pairs of rows have been worked from beg. **Divide for ankle** For next row, work patt over first 12(13:14) sts, then cont on these sts until 9(10:11) pairs of rows have been worked. **Next row** Patt 2(3:3) sts, work 2 tog, patt to end. **Next row** Work back as row 2. **Next row** Patt 1(2:2) sts, work 2 tog, patt to end. **Next row** Work back as row 2. On 2nd and 3rd sizes only **Next row** Patt one st, work 2 tog, patt to end, then work back. On all sizes fasten off. Miss centre 8(10:12) sts, rejoin yarn and patt to end. Cont to match first side, reversing shaping. **Ankle** With No. 9 (3¾mm) knitting needles and right side facing pick up and k35(39:43) sts round ankle and top of front. Beg first row with p1, work in k1, p1 rib for 5(6:7)cm or length reqd. Cast off loosely in rib. **Making up** Fold work in half and join sides to form centre of sole. Join toe. Join seam at back of heel and join rib at back of ankle. Cut sole to size reqd, make holes all round with a leather punch, then sew to foot with cross stitch.

### Crochet hats

**Materials** For both versions approx. 50g of double knitting in colours A, B, C and D; No. 4.50 crochet hook; button for helmet. **Stitch gauge** 12 sts and 16 rows to 4in. (10cm) over htr on No. 4.50 hook. **Note** The htr are worked *between* the sts, not into them, throughout. **Measurements** To fit approx. two-year-old child.

### Hat with turned-up brim

With No. 4.50 hook and colour A make 4ch and form ring with a ss. **Round 1** 2ch, 7htr into ring, ss to 2nd of 2ch (8 sts). **Round 2** Ss into sp bet first 2 sts, 2ch, 1htr into same sp, 2htr into each sp to end, ss to 2nd of 2ch (16 sts). **Round 3** Join in B to a sp bet 2 sts, 2ch, 2htr into next sp, *1htr into next sp, 2htr into next sp, rep from * to end, ss to 2nd of 2ch (24 sts). **Round 4** Join in C to a sp, 2ch, 1htr into next sp, 2htr into next sp, *1htr into each of next 2 sps, 2htr into next sp, rep from * to end, ss to 2nd of 2ch (32 sts). **Round 5** Using C, ss into first sp, 2ch, 1htr into each sp to end, ss to 2nd of 2ch. **Round 6** Join in D to a sp, 2ch, 1htr into each of next 2 sps, 2htr into next sp, *1htr into each of next 3 sps, 2htr into next sp, rep from * to end, ss to 2nd of 2ch (40 sts). **Round 7** Join in A and work as rnd 6 (50 sts). Cont without shaping, work 1 rnd in C, 2 rnds in B, 1 rnd in D, then 20 rnds in A, inc 2 sts in last rnd (52 sts). **Scalloped edge** With wrong side facing, join in B to a sp, 1dc into same place, *1ch, miss 1 sp, 3tr into next sp, 1ch, miss 1 sp, 1dc into next sp, rep from * to end, omitting last dc and ss to first dc. Fasten off.

### Helmet

Work 7rnds as given for first hat, but working 2 rnds B, 1 rnd A, 1 rnd C, 2 rnds D, 1 rnd B (50 sts). Cont without shaping, work 1 rnd C, 1 rnd D, then 14 rnds A. **Ear flaps** With right side facing miss first 4 sts from join, join in B to sp bet 2 sts, 2ch, 1htr into each of next 12 sps, turn and cont in rows of htr on these 13 sts. Work 2 rows without shaping, then dec one st at end of every row until 3 sts rem, then work 1 row. **Next row** 3ch, miss 2 sts, 1htr into end st, turn and work 2 more rows on these 3 sts. Fasten off. With right side facing miss next 17 sts, join in B bet sts, 2ch, 1htr into each of next 12 sps. Cont on these 13 sts as for first flap until 3 sts rem, then work 4 rows and fasten off. Sew on button to correspond with buttonhole.

# Tunisian crochet stitch patterns

Horizontal buttonholes as shown below are the easiest type to work in Tunisian crochet. For vertical buttonholes use the method for ordinary crochet (see page 132).

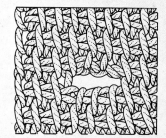

**The completed buttonhole**

*How to work*

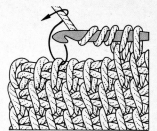

**1** *On the loop row work the pattern to the position of the buttonhole, then yrh once for every stitch required to fit the button.*

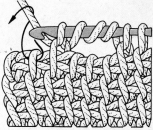

**2** *Miss the same number of stitches on the row below and then complete the loop row.*

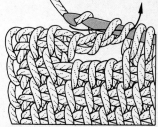

**3** *On the return row treat the yrhs as stitches and work in the usual way.*

The instructions for the following stitch samples are given on page 153. New colours are always added at the beginning of rows using the same technique as that given for ordinary crochet on page 137.

**4 Tweed stitch**

**1 Colour squares**

**5 Queen lace stitch**

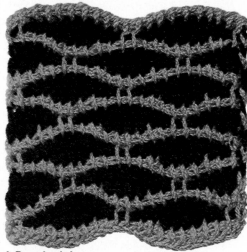

**2 Brocade stitch**

**3 Sage lace stitch**

**6 Narcissus lace stitch**

# Slippers in Tunisian crochet

# Hats in tubular crochet

The pattern instructions for the slippers shown here are given on page 153. These can be made bigger by making a longer foundation row and working more rows. The legs of the slippers can be made longer by working more rows.

The pattern instructions for these two children's hats are given on page 153. They are both worked in the round from the same basic pattern but are finished with different brim shapes. The ear flaps for the helmet are added after the cap shape has been completed.

**Slipper with green and blue stripes**

**Slipper with grey, blue and yellow stripes**

**The slipper legs are worked in a knitted rib**

**Hat with turned-up brim**

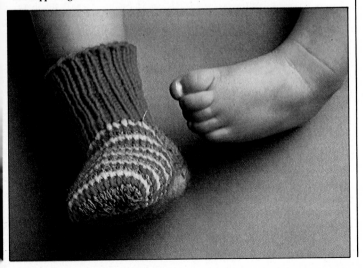

**Helmet with ear flaps**

# Beads and sequins

# Hairpin crochet

Beads and sequins can be used to make glittering motifs or entirely beaded fabrics. They are always threaded onto the yarn before beginning bead-work so that the yarn does not have to be broken every time the beads need to be threaded.

### Working with beads or sequins in double crochet
When working flat crochet row by row the beads are added on alternate rows at the back of the work. In double crochet the beads will lie at a slant owing to the structure of the stitch.

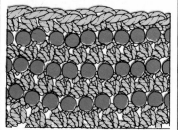

**Beads in double crochet**

### How to add beads in double crochet

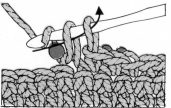

*When a bead is required insert the hook through the stitch of the previous row in the usual way, yrh and draw a loop through. Then slide the bead close to the work, yrh and draw through both loops at the same time pushing the bead firmly on top of stitch in previous row.*

### Working with beads or sequins in treble crochet
When working half treble and treble the beads lie straight with the holes upwards.

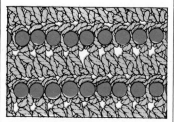

**Beads in half treble**

### How to add beads in half treble

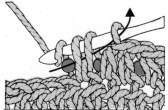

*Yrh and insert hook through stitch in row below, yrh and draw through. Slide bead up to work, yrh and draw through all 3 loops.*

### Adding beads or sequins when working in the round
When working sequins in this way they can be used in each round and will overlap each other.

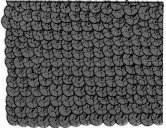

**Sequins in the round**

Hairpin crochet takes its name from the two-pronged steel fork on which it is worked. It forms braids or bands for trimmings as edgings or insertions, or, when the bands are joined together, it forms a light, airy fabric for shawls and scarves. The size of the forks will vary according to the width of the braid to be worked. Any light-weight yarn is suitable for hairpin crochet, from silk, cotton and fine wool to ribbon, cord and raffia.

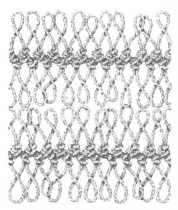

**Finished hairpin crochet**

### Making hairpin crochet
The stitches are worked with a crochet hook between the prongs of the fork, which is turned from right to left after each stitch has been formed, making loops on each prong alternately.

#### How to work hairpin crochet

**1** *Make a slip loop in the usual way (page 112) and place it on the right prong of fork with knot inside, passing thread behind left prong.*
*Thread left hand as for ordinary crochet (page 112) and hold the fork between the forefinger and thumb of the left hand.*

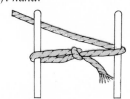

**2** *Turn the fork from right to left so that the thread passes behind both prongs.*

**3** *Insert crochet hook under front strand of loop on left prong, yrh and draw a loop through, yrh again and draw a 2nd loop through first one. This forms a dc and completes the first round.*

**4** *With loop still on hook turn fork from right to left. Insert hook under front thread on left prong and work a dc in the usual way.*

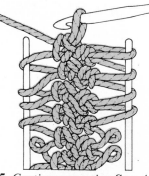

**5** *Continue repeating Step 4 and turning fork from right to left after completing each stitch. When fork is filled, carefully take off all loops. Replace last 4 or 5 to be completed, leaving rest hanging behind fork, and continue working as before. When braid is required length, fasten off by breaking yarn and drawing it through final stitch.*

## Threading beads or sequins

*Fold a length of sewing thread in half and thread 2 cut ends through a fine sewing needle. Pass end of crochet yarn through loop of thread and fold it down. Now pick up beads or sequins with needle and slide them down onto yarn. The last bead threaded will be the first to be used.*

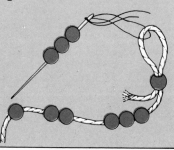

## Finishing hairpin braids

When the hairpin braids are completed the outer loops can be finished off with a row of double crochet.

### How to finish braids

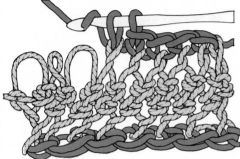

**Finishing braids**
Insert hook into first loop, turn loop to twist it, yrh and draw through. Then insert hook through 2nd loop, turn this loop to twist it, yrh and draw through, yrh and draw through both loops. Continue, and repeat method for second side.

## Joining braids to form fabrics

Below are two methods for joining hairpin braids in order to form a fabric, one using slip stitch, the other using chain stitch.

**Using slip stitch**
Lay braids together side by side. With a slip loop on hook, insert hook into loop below and then into loop above. Slip stitch them together, taking thread through all 3 loops. Continue until the braids are joined.

**Using chain stitch**
Lay braids together side by side. With a slip loop on hook, insert hook into loop above, yrh and draw through both loops, work 1ch and then insert hook into loop below, yrh and draw through both loops. Then work 1ch. Continue until the braids are joined.

## Hairpin pattern instructions

### Rose braid

Make 2 strips of hairpin crochet, having a multiple of 3 lps in each.
Work along one side of each strip as follows:
Make a slip loop, insert crochet hook through the first 3 lps, twisting them, draw the lp through and work a dc, *3ch, 1dc into next 3 lps tog, rep from * to end of strip.
To join the 2 strips, place them side by side, join yarn to first dc on one strip, *3ch, 1dc into 2nd of 3ch on 2nd strip, 3ch, 1dc into 2nd of next 3ch on first strip, rep from * to end, ending with 3ch, 1dc into last dc. Fasten off.

### Sienna braid

Make a strip of hairpin crochet the required width and length, closing each lp with 2htr worked into the front strand of the left lp.
Work along each side of braid as follows:
**Row 1** Join yarn to first lp, work 1dc into each lp, twisting the lp each time, 1ch, turn.
**Row 2** 1dc into first dc, *2ch, 1dc into same st, 1dc into next dc, rep from * to end.
Fasten off.

### Hairpin insertion

Work exactly as for rose braid, but working the edging along both sides of each strip.
Join the 2 strips in the same way as rose braid, then work a row of dc along the outer edges of the insertion.

### Zigzag braid

Make 2 strips of hairpin crochet, having a multiple of 12 lps in each.
Work a border along one side of first strip as follows:
Join yarn to first lp, work a dc into this lp, (1ch, 1dc into next lp) 5 times, twisting the lp each time, *1ch, insert hook into next 12 lps tog, twisting each lp as you insert the hook, and work a dc into these 12 lps tog, (1ch, 1dc into next lp, still twisting the lps)12 times, rep from * to end, but ending with 6 lps instead of 12.
Work along the other side of this strip, but starting with 6 lps tog, *(1ch, 1dc into next lp) 12 times, 1ch, 1dc into 12 lps tog, rep from * to end, but ending with 6 lps tog.
Work along each side of the 2nd strip in the same way then join the 2 strips: place the 2 strips side by side, join yarn to first dc of one strip, *2ch, 1dc into next dc of 2nd strip, 2ch, 1dc into next dc of first strip, rep from * to end.
Fasten off.

### Scalloped hairpin lace

Make 2 strips of hairpin crochet with 2tr in each lp, and having an even no. of lps in each strip. To join the strips, place them side by side, insert hook into 2 lps on right-hand strip and work a dc, *2ch, insert hook into 2 lps on the left and work a dc, 2ch, insert hook into 2 lps on the right and work a dc, rep from * until strips are joined.
To work the heading, insert hook into first 2 lps and work a dc, *2ch, insert hook into next 2 lps and work a dc, rep from * to end.
To work the scalloped edge, insert hook into first 2 lps along other side of strip and work a dc, *5ch, insert hook into next 2 lps and work a dc, rep from * to end, turn.
Into each 5ch lp work 1dc, 1htr, 3tr, 5ch, ss into first of these 5ch, 3tr, 1htr, 1dc.

### Topaz braid

Make a strip of the required length, closing each loop with a dc worked into the front strand of the left lp, and having a multiple of 4 lps in the strip.

Work edging along each side of strip as follows:
**Row 1** Insert hook into 4 lps tog, twisting them tog and work a dc, *3ch, insert hook into next 4 lps tog, twisting them and work a dc, rep from * to end, turn.
**Row 2** 3ch, 1dc into first dc, *3ch, 1dc into 2nd of 3ch, 3ch, 1dc into dc, rep from * to end.
Fasten off.

### Hairpin fringe

This uses 2 colours, A and B, or 2 different yarns.
Using A, make 2 strips, closing each lp with a dc worked into the front strand of the left lp, and having a multiple of 3 lps in each strip.
Place the strips side by side, insert hook into the first 3 lps of left strip, *insert hook into 3 lps on right strip and draw them through the lps on hook, insert hook into next 3 lps on left strip and draw them through the lps on hook, rep from * to end.
Fold work in half along the join. This will now produce a thick chain along the top edge of work.
Using B, join to first ch along top edge, 1dc into same place, 1dc into each ch to end, turn.
**Row 2** 3ch, 1dc into first dc, *miss 1dc, (1dc, 3ch, 1dc) into next dc, rep from * to end.
Fasten off.
Cut loops along free edge to make fringe.

# Hairpin crochet patterns

The instructions for the following stitch samples are given on page 157. Samples 1 to 6 can be made into large pieces for bedcovers or shawls by working them longer and adding further strips to the sides. Sample 7 is suitable only as a fringe. All the samples can be used in the width shown but worked longer for edgings to crochet, knitting and fabric. The edgings can be joined to knitting and crochet using slip stitch (see page 114) and to fabric by hand-stitching.

1 **Rose braid**
2 **Siena braid**
3 **Hairpin insertion**
4 **Zigzag braid**
5 **Scalloped hairpin lace**
6 **Topaz braid**
7 **Hairpin fringe**

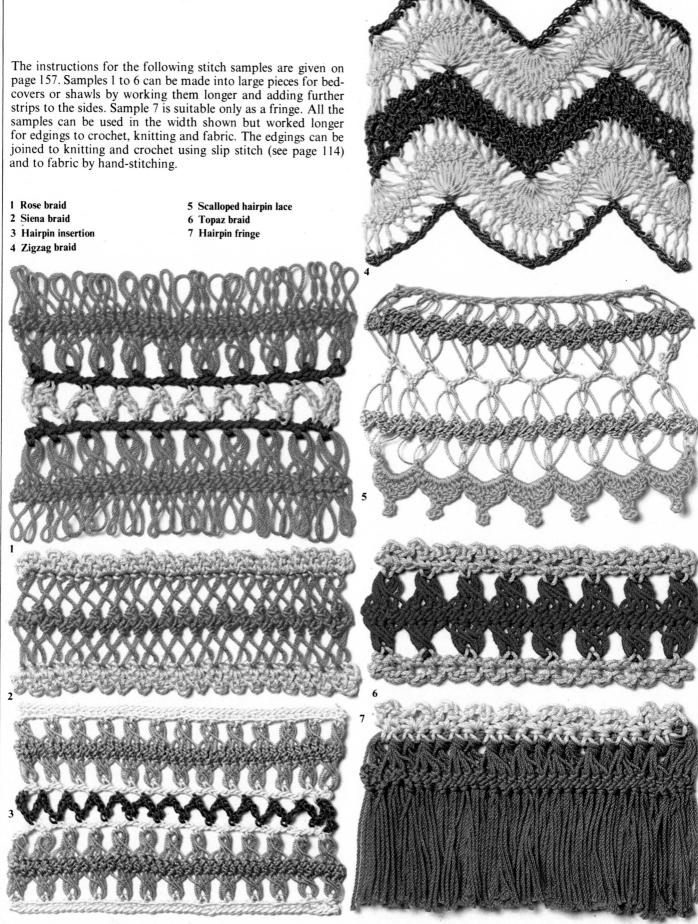

# Embroidery on crochet

Embroidery stitches can be used to great effect in crochet either to give further texture or to add spots of colour as highlights or as motifs. Embroidery stitches can be worked in matching or contrasting yarn using a blunt sewing needle.

### Working faggot insertion stitches to join crochet

Faggot seams can be used to join up granny squares in matching or contrasting yarn. White wool or cotton textured squares joined with faggot stitch in matching yarn look particularly attractive (Fig. 1).

### Using darning stitch around trebles

Any pattern formation can be made by darning in and out of a mesh of trebles (Fig. 2). Filet mesh could also serve as a ground for darning stitch (see filet crochet, page 151).

### Using buttonhole stitch around trebles

Trebles can be corded with buttonhole stitch in different colours (Fig. 3).

### Working chain stitch motifs

Chain stitch motifs are worked around the edges or in the centre of an area of double crochet (Fig. 4).

### Using cross stitch to emphasize a colour change

Using a third colour, a row of cross stitch can be worked between two bands of colour (Fig. 5).

### Using satin stitch patterns

Blocks of satin stitch can be worked in various colours and in geometric patterns (Fig. 6).

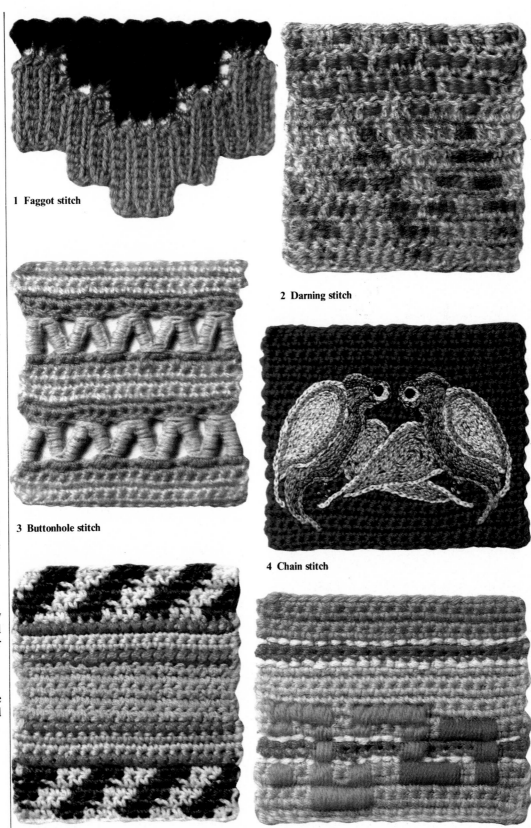

1 Faggot stitch

2 Darning stitch

3 Buttonhole stitch

4 Chain stitch

5 Cross stitch

6 Satin stitch

159

# Broomstick crochet

There is only one stitch in broomstick crochet and this forms an openwork fabric. It is worked with a hook and the aid of a giant knitting needle. The size of the implements, together with the number of loops being used, will determine the size of the stitch pattern. Recommended sizes of hook and needle will be given in the relative pattern instructions.

### Making broomstick crochet

Make a foundation row of chains divisible by 5. The multiple can be varied to make smaller or larger stitch patterns.

*How to work broomstick crochet*

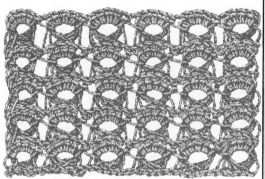

**Finished broomstick crochet**

**1** *Pull last loop out and extend it over the knitting needle held in the left hand.*

**2** *Miss 1 chain, then insert hook into next chain, yrh, draw through a loop and place this on the needle. Continue making loops in this way to end of chain. Do not turn work.*

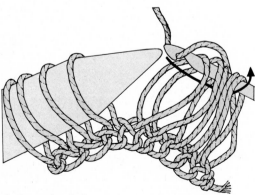

**3** *Insert hook from right to left through first 5 loops on needle and remove them from needle, yrh and draw a loop through the 5 loops.*

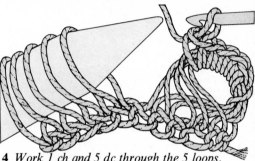

**4** *Work 1 ch and 5 dc through the 5 loops.*

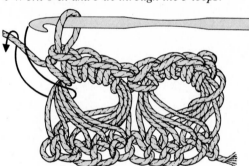

**5** *\*Then insert hook through next 5 loops on needle, yrh and draw a loop through 5 loops, yrh and draw through 2 rem loops. Then work 4dc through the 5 loops. Repeat from \* to end of row.*

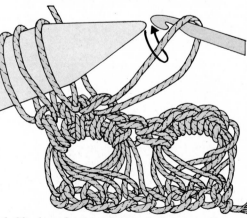

**6** *Slip loop from hook onto knitting needle, \*then insert hook through the next dc, yrh and draw a loop through and place it on needle. Continue from \* to end of row. Do not turn work. Continue making loop and return rows.*

## Sleeveless pullover pattern

**Back and front** (both alike) With No. 4 hook make 95(100: 105:110:115)ch. **Foundation row** Pull up last loop and put on to knitting needle, \*insert hook into next ch, yrh, draw lp through and put onto knitting needle, rep from \* to end, 95(100:105:110: 115) loops on needle. **Row 1** Holding the needle in left hand, insert the crochet hook from right to left into the first 5 lps, yrh, draw lp through, yrh, draw through lp (to complete a dc) slipping the 5 lps off the knitting needle, work 4 more dc into the same 5 lps, \*insert crochet hook into the next 5 lps and work a dc, slipping the lps off the needle, work 4 more dc into the same 5 lps, rep from \* to end, do not turn (19[20:21:22:23] groups of lps). **Row 2** Draw up the lp on hook and put onto knitting needle, \*keeping the knitting needle in the left hand, insert hook into next dc to the right, yrh, draw lp through and put onto needle, rep from \* to end, working always into the back half only of each dc. Rep rows 1 and 2 15 times more, then row 1 again. **Next row** Inc 2 lps at each end by working twice into each of first 2 and last 2 dc. **Next row** Work 2dc into first 2 lps, 5dc into each 5 lps to last 2 lps, 2dc into last 2 lps. **Next row** Inc 2 lps at each end as before. **Next row** Work 4dc into first 4 lps, 5dc into each 5 lps to last 4 lps, 4dc into last 4 lps. **Next row** Inc 1 lp at each end by working twice into first and last dc. **Next row** Patt to end as row 1 (21[22:23:24:25] groups of lps). Cont in patt until work measures 21(21:22½:22½: 23½)in. (54[54:57:57:60]cm) from beg, ending with row 1, turn. **Next row** 1ch, miss first dc, 1dc into each of next 3dc, \*miss 2dc, 1dc into each of next 3dc, rep from \* to last dc, 1dc into last dc, turn. **Next row** 1ch, 1dc into each dc to end, turn. Rep the last row once more. Fasten off. **Making up** Pin out work to size and press. Join shoulders for 4½ (4½:4¾:4¾:5½)in. (11[11:12:12:13] cm) from each end, leaving centre open. Join side seams to beg of shaping. **Lower edge** Work in dc round lower edge, working 7dc into each 2 groups of lps, then join with a ss to first dc. **Next round** 1ch, 1dc into each dc to end, ss to first ch. Rep the last rnd once more. Fasten off. **Armholes** With right side facing join in yarn at side seam, work in dc round armhole, working 3dc into every lp row and 1dc into each dc row, join with a ss to first dc. Work 2 more rnds as on lower edge. Fasten off.

# Broomstick pullover

# Crochet edgings

For the project below, (see instructions, left) which can be made in sizes 32(34:36:38:40)in. bust (81[86:91:97:102]cm), you will need 3(4:4:4:5) × 50g balls of 4-ply wool; a No. 4 crochet hook and a knitting needle ¾in. (2cm) in diameter. The stitch gauge is 3 groups of loops and 3 rows to 2¾in. (7cm). The length measures 22½(22½:23½:23½:25)in. (57[57:60:60:63]cm).

Crochet edgings at their most decorative were designed to resemble as closely as possible the needle- and bobbin-made laces and were originally worked in the finest cottons on the smallest gauge hooks. However, they can look just as good though not so lace-like when worked in wools on larger gauge hooks. They are used to finish off or decorate a piece of crochet, knitting or any other fabric and can be worked directly onto either a crocheted or knitted fabric or separately in a strip and when completed joined to the fabric.

### Working the edging directly onto a piece of crochet

When working an edging directly onto a piece of crochet or knitting the first row is worked into the existing stitches.

*How to work*

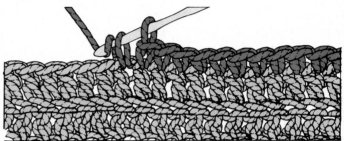

**1** *First work a row of double crochet in same or contrasting yarn along edge to serve as a base to edging.*

**2** *Then work the edging back and forth in rows until complete.*

### Joining the edging to a piece of crochet with slip stitch

When an edging is worked vertically along the strip it can only be joined to a fabric after completion. It should be applied to ordinary fabric with overcast or running stitch and to a piece of crochet or knitting with double crochet or with slip stitch (see page 114).

*How to work*

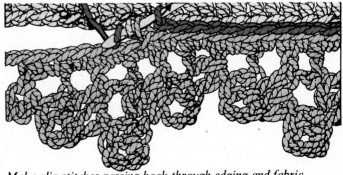

*Make slip stitches passing hook through edging and fabric.*

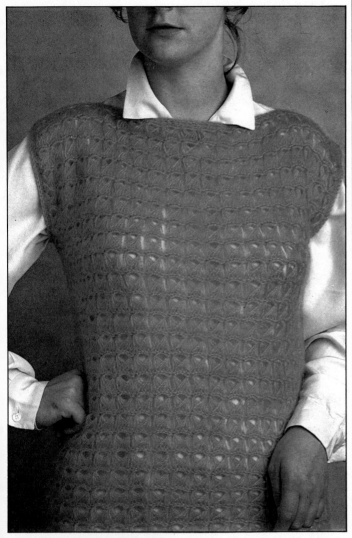

***Detail of broomstick lace***
*Broomstick lace (see detail, left) can be made using a larger or smaller knitting needle to form the loops. The example left has been worked on a ¾in. (2cm) knitting needle. For a tighter, more dense effect use a smaller needle to form the loops.*

# Edging patterns

## Scallop edging

Worked into a row of dc on edge of work, having a multiple of 6dc plus 1.

1ss into first dc, *miss 2dc, 5tr into next dc, miss 2dc, 1ss into next dc, rep from * to end.

## Plain picot edging

Worked into a row of dc on edge of work.

*1dc into each of next 3dc, 4ch, ss into last dc made, rep from * to end.

## Cluster edging

Worked into a row of dc on edge of work, having an even no. of dc.

Join yarn to first dc, 2ch, *1htr into next dc, (yrh, insert hook round stem of htr, yrh, draw lp through) 3 times, yrh, draw through all 7 lps on hook, 1ch, miss 1dc, rep from * to end, 1htr into last dc.

## Arch edging

Worked into a row of dc on edge of work.

1dc into next dc, *3ch, miss 1dc, 1dc into next dc, rep from * to end.

## Twisted edging

Worked into a row of dc on edge of work, having a no. of dc divisible by 3 plus 1.
**Row 1** Using A, 1dc into first dc, *3ch, miss 2dc, 1dc into next dc, rep from * to end. Break off A and return to beg of row.

**Row 2** Using B, 1dc into first dc, *3ch, take hook out of last ch, insert it under the 3ch lp of row 1, pick up lp of last ch and draw it through, yrh and draw through lp, rep from * to end, ending with a dc into last dc.

## Wave edging

Worked into a row of dc on edge of work, having a number of dc divisible by 18, plus 1.

Ss into first st, *1dc, 1htr, 1tr, 1dtr, 1tr, 1htr, 1dc, 1ss, 1dc, 1htr, 1tr, 1dtr, 1tr tr, 1dtr, 1tr, 1htr, 1dc, 1ss, rep from * to end.

## Picot arch edging

Make a ch the length reqd, having a no. of ch divisible by 3 plus 1, 2ch, turn.
**Row 1** 1tr into 4th ch from hook, 1tr into each ch to end.
**Row 2** *3ch, miss next 2tr, 1tr into next tr, rep from * to end.
**Row 3** Ss into first lp, *6ch, ss into 4th ch from hook, 2ch, 1dc into next lp, rep from * to end.
Fasten off.

## Bicolour loop edging

Worked into a row of dc on edge of work, having a number of dc divisible by 4 plus 1.

This border uses 2 colours, A and B.
**Row 1** Using A, work in dc to end of row. Break off yarn and return to beg of row.
**Row 2** Using B, work in dc to end of row. Break off yarn and return to beg of row.

**Row 3** Using A, 1dc into first dc, *6ch, miss 3dc, 1dc into next dc, rep from * to end. Break off yarn and return to beg of row.
**Row 4** Using B, 1dc into first dc, *1ss into back half only of each of next 6ch, 1dc into next dc, rep from * to end.
Fasten off.

## Triangle edging

Make a ch the length reqd, having a no. of ch divisible by 4 plus 1, 2ch, turn.
**Row 1** 1tr into 4th ch from hook, 1tr into each ch to end.
**Row 2** 3ch, 3tr into first tr (edge st), *miss 3tr, 1dc into next tr, 3ch, 3tr into same tr, rep from * to end, ending with miss 3tr, 1dc into t-ch.
Fasten off.

## Stripe edging

Worked into a row of dc on edge of work.
Using 2 or more colours as reqd,

work a row of ss in each colour, always working each row with right side of work facing.

## Bouquet edging

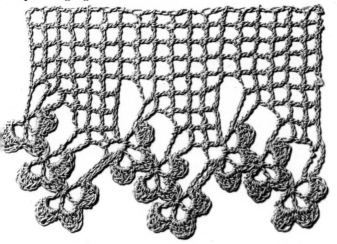

Make 21ch.

**Row 1** 1tr into 8th ch from hook, 2ch, miss 2ch, 1tr into next ch) 3 times, 5ch, miss 3ch, (1tr, 3ch) 3 times into next ch, 1tr into same ch, 1ch, turn.

**Row 2** (1dc, 1htr, 1tr, 1dtr, 1tr, 1htr, 1dc) into each of 3 3ch sps – shamrock made – 5ch, 1tr into 5ch lp, (2ch, 1tr into next tr) 4 times, 2ch, miss 2ch, 1tr into next ch, 5ch, turn.

**Row 3** Miss first tr, 1tr into next tr, (2ch, 1tr into next tr) 4 times, 2ch, 1tr into 5ch lp, 7ch, (1tr, 3ch) 3 times into centre of 2nd petal, 1tr into same place, 1ch, turn.

**Row 4** Make a shamrock as before, 5ch, 1tr into 7ch lp, *2ch, 1tr into next tr, rep from * to end, working last tr into 3rd of 5ch, 5ch, turn.

**Row 5** As row 3 but working 2ch, 1tr into next tr) 6 times instead of 4 times.

**Row 6** As row 4.

**Row 7** Miss first tr, 1tr into next tr, (2ch, 1tr into next tr) 3 times, 7ch, miss 4 sps, (1tr, 3ch) 3 times into next sp, 1tr into same sp, 1ch, turn.

Rep rows 2 to 7 for length reqd, ending with a 6th row.

Fasten off.

## Diamond filet edging

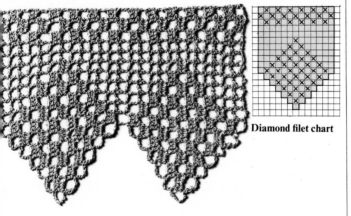

**Diamond filet chart**

Make 38ch.

**Row 1** 1tr into 8th ch from hook, *2ch, miss 2ch, 1tr into next ch, rep from * to last 6ch, 1tr into each of next 3ch, 2ch, miss 2ch, 1tr into next ch, 3ch, turn.

**Row 2** 2tr into 2ch sp, 1tr into next tr, 2ch, miss 2tr, 1tr into next tr, 2tr into 2ch sp, 1tr into next tr, (2ch, 1tr into next tr) 7 times, 2tr into 2ch sp, 1tr into 5th of 7ch, 6ch, 1dtr into base of last tr, ss into each of last 3ch (1 sp

increased), 7ch, turn.

**Row 3** 1tr into last ss (1 sp increased), 2tr into 2ch sp, 1tr into next tr, 2ch, miss 2tr, 1tr into next tr, 2tr into 2ch sp, 1tr into next tr, (2ch, 1tr into next tr) 6 times, 2ch, miss 2tr, 1tr into next tr, 2tr into 2ch sp, 1tr into next tr, 2ch, miss 2tr, 1tr into 3rd of first 3ch, 3ch, turn.

Cont working in patt from chart for length reqd.

Fasten off.

## Irish shamrock edging

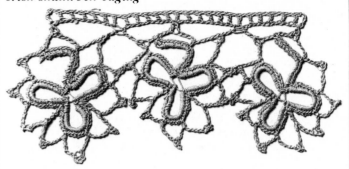

### First shamrock

Make 29ch.

**Round 1** Ss into 14th ch from hook, (13ch, ss into same ch) twice.

**Round 2** Working over a cord, or 4 strands of the same thread, work 25dc into each lp, then still working over the thread work 15dc over rem part of ch for stem, working last dc into last ch. Cut off cord.

**Round 3** 1dc into same place as last dc, (6ch, 1dc into 4th ch from hook – called picot – 3ch, miss 9dc on next petal, 1dc into next dc, 8ch, pc, 3ch, 1dc into next dc, 8ch, pc, 3ch, 1dtr bet petals) twice, 8ch, pc, 3ch, miss 9dc on next petal, 1dc into next dc, **8ch, pc, 3ch, miss 5dc, 1dc into next dc, 8ch, pc, 3ch, 1dc into centre dc on stem, 8ch, pc, 3ch, 1ss into first dc.

Fasten off.

### Second shamrock

Work as given for first shamrock as far as **, 4ch, ss into pc on lp at end of first petal on first shamrock, 2ch, 1dc into 3rd of 4ch, 3ch, miss 5dc on 2nd shamrock, 1dc into next dc, complete as for first shamrock.

Make as many shamrocks as reqd, joining each as shown.

### Heading

With wrong side facing join yarn to picot on last lp of end shamrock (the lp below end of stem). *11ch, leaving the last lp of each on hook, work 1dtr into each of next 2pc, yrh and draw through 3 lps on hook – called a joint dtr – 11ch, 1dc into next pc, rep from * to end, 4ch, turn.

**Row 2** *(miss 1ch, 1tr into next ch, 1ch) 5 times, miss 1ch, 1tr into top of joint dtr, 1ch, rep from * to end, omitting last ch.

Fasten off.

## Richelieu edging

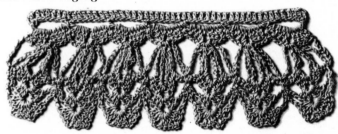

Make a ch the length reqd, having a number of ch divisible by 7 plus 1, 2ch, turn.

**Row 1** 1tr into 4th ch from hook, 1tr into each ch to end.

**Row 2** *6ch, miss 6tr, 1dc into next tr, rep from * to end.

**Row 3** Ss into first lp, 3ch, (3tr, 2ch, 4tr) into same lp, * (4tr, 2ch, 4tr) into next lp, rep from * to end.

**Row 4** * 3ch, 1dc into 2ch sp, (15ch, 1dc into same sp) 3 times, 3ch, 1dc between groups of tr,

rep from * to end, working last dc into 3rd of 3ch at beg of row 3.

**Row 5** 8ch, * 3dc into first 15ch lp, (3tr, 2ch, 3tr) into next lp, 3dc into next lp, rep from * to end.

**Row 6** *3ch, (3tr, 2ch, 3tr) into 2ch sp, 3ch, 1dc bet groups of dc, rep from * to end, working last dc into 8th of 8ch.

**Row 7** *3ch, (3tr, 2ch, 3tr, 2ch, 3tr) into 2ch sp, 3ch, 1dc into dc, rep from * to end, omit last dc and end with a ss into first of 3ch.

Fasten off.

## *Pansy edging*

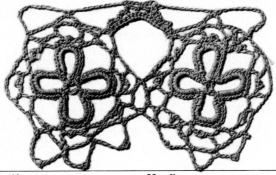

### First motif

Make 6ch and join into a ring with a ss into first ch.

**Round 1** (1dc into ring, 12ch) 4 times, ss into first dc.

**Round 2** Working over a cord, or 4 strands of the same thread, work 20dc into each lp, ss into first dc. Fasten off.

**Round 3** Join yarn to 8th dc of a petal, 1dc into same place, *5ch, 1dc into 3rd ch from hook – called picot – 3ch, miss 4dc, 1dc into next dc, 5ch, pc, 3ch, miss 7dc on next petal, 1dc into next dc, rep from * all round, omitting last dc at end and ss into first dc.

**Round 4** Ss over first ch and into lp, 8ch, 1tr into same lp on other side of pc,*3ch, (1dc, 5ch, 1dc) into next lp, 3ch, (1tr, 5ch, 1tr) into next lp, rep from * all round, omitting (1tr, 5ch, 1tr) on last rep, ss into 3rd of 8ch.

Fasten off.

### Second motif

Work as for first motif until 3 rnds have been completed.

**Round 4** Ss over first ch and into lp, 8ch, 1tr into same lp, 3ch, (1dc, 5ch, 1dc) into next lp, 3ch, 1tr into next lp, 2ch, ss into corresponding 5ch lp on first motif, 2ch, 1tr into same lp on 2nd motif, complete rnd as on first motif.

Make as many motifs as reqd, joining each as shown.

### Heading

**Row 1** Join yarn to 2nd 5ch lp counting from the outer edge of end motif, 1dc into same place, *5ch, (1dc, 5ch, 1dc) into next 5ch lp, 5ch, 1dc into next 5ch lp, 12ch, 1dc into corresponding lp on next motif, turn, 15dc into 12ch lp just made, ss into lp, turn, 1dc into first dc, (3ch, miss 1dc, 1dc into next dc) 7 times, ss into same 5ch lp, rep from * to last motif, 5ch, (1dc, 5ch, 1dc) into next lp, 5ch, 1dc into next lp, 13ch, turn.

**Row 2** Miss first lp, 1dc into next lp, *10ch, miss 2 3ch lps, (1dc into next lp, 3ch) twice, 1dc into next lp, 10ch, miss next 5ch lp, 1dc into next lp, rep from * to end, ending with 10ch, 1tr into last dc.

Fasten off.

### Scalloped edge

**Row 1** Miss 3 lps after end of heading on end motif, join yarn to next lp, 1dc into same place, *5ch, pc, 3ch, miss next lp, (1dc, 5ch, 1dc) into next lp, 5ch, pc, 3ch, miss next lp, 1dc into next lp, 3ch, leaving the last lp of each on hook, work 1tr into next lp and 1tr into corresponding lp on next motif, yrh and draw through all 3 lps on hook, 3ch, 1dc into next lp, rep from * to end, but omitting 3ch, 2tr and 3ch at end of last rep.

Fasten off.

## *Nugget edging*

Make a ch the length reqd, having a no. of ch divisible by 8 plus 3, 2ch, turn.

**Row 1** 1tr into 4th ch from hook, 1tr into each ch to end.

**Row 2** 3ch, 1tr into each of next 2tr, *(2ch, miss 2tr, 1tr into next tr) twice, 1tr into each of next 2tr, rep from * to end, working last tr into t-ch.

**Row 3** 4ch, leaving last lp of each on hook work 3dtr into next sp, yrh, draw through all 4 lps on hook, *9ch, leaving last lp of each on hook work 3dtr into next sp, then 3dtr into next sp after the 3tr, yrh, draw through all 7 lps on hook, rep from * to end, ending with 9ch, work a 3dtr cluster into last sp, 1dtr into t-ch.

**Row 4** Ss into top of first cluster, work (1dc, 1htr, 7tr, 1htr, 1dc) into each 9ch lp, ss into top of last cluster.

Fasten off.

## *Piranesi edging*

Make 8ch and join into a ring with a ss into first ch.

**Row 1** 3ch, 8tr into ring, turn.

**Row 2** 4ch, 1tr into 2nd tr, *1ch, 1tr into next tr, rep from * 5 times more, 1ch, 1tr into 3rd of 3ch.

**Row 3** 5ch, 1tr into 2nd tr, *2ch, 1tr into next tr, rep from * 5 times more, 2ch, 1tr into 3rd of 4ch.

**Row 4** 6ch, 1tr into 2nd tr, * 3ch, 1tr into next tr, rep from * 5 times more, 3ch, 1tr into 3rd of 5ch.

**Row 5** *(1dc, 3tr, 1dc) into 3ch sp, rep from * 7 times more, 8ch, turn and ss into 2nd of first 3tr, turn.

**Row 6** 3ch, 8tr into 8ch lp, turn.

**Row 7** 4ch, 1tr into 2nd tr, * 1ch, 1tr into next tr, rep from * 5 times more, 1ch, 1tr into 3rd of 3ch, ss

into 2nd tr of next group of 3 turn.

**Row 8** 5ch, miss first tr, 1tr into next tr, work as row 3 from * to end.

**Row 9** Work as row 4, then s into 2nd tr of next group of 3 turn.

Rep rows 5 to 9 for the lengt reqd, then work row 5, omitting the 8ch at end of row.

### Heading

Working along straight edge o work, 5ch, 1tr into next row-end *2ch, 1tr into next row-end, re from * to end, turn.

**Next row** 3ch, *2tr into 2ch sp 1tr into next tr, rep from * to end working last tr into 3rd of 5ch.

Fasten off.

## *Elm edging*

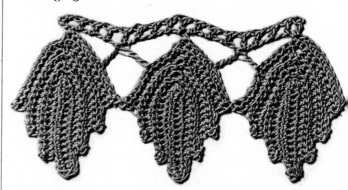

### First leaf

Make 16ch.

**Row 1** 1dc into 2nd ch from hook and into each of next 13ch, 3dc into last ch, cont along the other side of ch, 1dc into each ch to end, 2dc into same ch as first dc, turn.

From here, work always into the back half only of each st.

**Row 2** 1dc into each of next 13dc, 1ch, turn.

**Row 3** 1dc into each dc, 3dc into centre dc of gr of 3dc, 1dc into each dc along other side to 1dc before next 3dc gr, 1ch, turn.

**Row 4** 1dc into each dc to 3rd dc from end, working 3dc into centre dc of 3dc gr, 1ch, turn.

**Rows 5, 6, and 7** As row 4.

**Row 8** 1dc into each dc to centre of 3dc gr, ss into centre dc. Fasten off.

### Second leaf

Work as for first leaf until 7 rows have been completed, 1ch, turn.

**Row 8** 1ss into corresponding d on first leaf, 1dc into each dc t centre of 3dc gr, ss into centre dc. Fasten off.

Make as many leaves as reqd joining each as shown.

### Heading

**Row 1** Join yarn to centre dc o first leaf, 1dc into same place *7ch, keeping the last lp of each on hook, work 1dtr into centr dc along side of this leaf, the 1dtr into centre dc along side o next leaf, yrh and draw throug all 3 lps on hook – called a join dtr – 7ch, 1dc into centre dc at top of this leaf, rep from * to end 4ch, turn.

**Row 2** *(miss 1ch, 1tr into nex ch, 1ch) 3 times, miss 1ch, 1t into top of joint tr, 1ch, (mis 1ch, 1tr into next ch, 1ch) 3 times, miss 1ch, 1tr into dc, re from * to end.

Fasten off.

## *Rose edging*

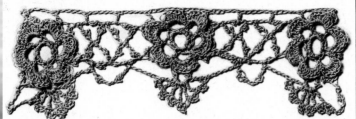

### First motif
Make 8ch and join into a ring with a ss into first ch.

**Round 1** 1ch, 11dc into ring, ss to first ch.

**Round 2** *5ch, miss 1dc, 1dc into next dc, rep from * 4 times more, 5ch, 1dc into ss at end of rnd 1.

**Round 3** Into each 5ch lp work 1dc, 1htr, 5tr, 1htr and 1dc.

**Round 4** Keeping hook behind petals just worked, work 1dc into first dc on rnd 2, *4ch, 1dc into 3rd ch from hook – called picot – 5ch, pc, 2ch, 1dc into dc on rnd 2 bet next 2 petals, rep from * all round, ending with 1ss into first dc.

Fasten off.

### Second motif
Work as given for first motif until the 4 rnds have been completed, but do not break off yarn.

To join motifs, work in rows as follows:

**Row 1** Ss along to centre of next pc lp, 1dc into same lp, 4ch, pc, 5ch, pc, 2ch – called picot loop – 1dc into centre of next pc lp, turn.

**Row 2** 1 pc lp, 1dc into centre of next pc lp, 1 pc lp, 1dc into dc at base of pc lp on previous row, turn.

**Row 3** Ss to centre of next pc lp, 1dc into same lp, 1 pc lp, 1dc into centre of next pc lp, turn.

**Row 4** 4ch, pc, 1ch, ss into centre any lp on first motif, 3ch, pc, 2ch, 1dc into next pc lp on 2nd motif, 3ch, pc, 2ch, 1dc into dc at base of previous row.

Fasten off.

Make as many motifs as reqd, joining each as shown, leaving one pc lp free at each side of join.

### Heading
With right side facing join yarn to pc lp at top of first motif, 1dc into same place as join, *(5ch, 1tr into next pc lp) 4 times, 5ch, 1dc into next pc lp, rep from * to end.

Fasten off.

### Scalloped edge
With right side of other edge facing join yarn to loop before the top lp of first motif, 5ch, pc, 3ch, *into next lp (at top of motif) work (1dtr, 3ch, 1dc into top of dtr) 6 times, then 1dtr, 5ch, 1dc into pc lp at join of motifs, 1 pc lp, 1dc into next lp, 5ch, rep from * along edge, ending with dtr gr as before, 5ch, pc, 2ch, 1dc into next pc lp.

Fasten off.

## *Fan edging*

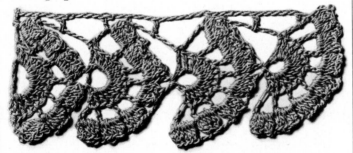

Make 10ch and join into a ring with a ss into first ch.

**Row 1** 3ch, 14tr into ring, 5ch, turn.

**Row 2** Miss first 2tr, (1tr into next tr, 2ch, miss 1tr) 6 times, 1tr into 3rd of 3ch, 3ch, turn.

**Row 3** *7tr into next sp, take hook out of lp, insert it into 3rd of 3ch, then into the lp and draw lp through – called popcorn st – 3ch, rep from * 5 times more, 1 popcorn st into last sp, 10ch, turn.

**Row 4** Miss first 2 sps, (1dc, 5ch, 1dc) into next sp, 3ch, turn.

**Row 5** 13tr into 5ch lp, 1dc into 10ch lp, 5ch, turn.

**Row 6** Miss dc and first tr, (1tr into next tr, 2ch, miss 1tr) 6 times, 1tr into 3rd of 3ch, 3ch, turn.

Rep rows 3 to 6 for the length reqd, ending with a 3rd row. Do not turn or break off yarn.

### Heading
1tr into sp below last popcorn st, *5ch, 1tr into 10ch lp, 5ch, 1tr into sp below next popcorn st, rep from * to end.

Fasten off.

## *Sunflower edging*

### First motif
Wind yarn about 10 times round one finger, then sl loop off finger.

**Round 1** Work 40dc into ring, ss to first dc.

**Round 2** 1ch, 1dc into each dc to end, ss to first ch.

**Round 3** As rnd 2.

**Round 4** *5ch, miss 1dc, 1dc into next dc, rep from * to end, working last dc into ss at end of rnd 3 (20 lps).

**Round 5** Ss into first lp, 4ch, leaving last lp of each on hook, work 2dtr into same lp, yrh, draw through all 3 lps on hook, * 5ch, leaving the last lp of each on hook, work 3dtr into next lp, yrh, draw through all 4 lps on hook, rep from * to end, 5ch, ss to top of first cluster.

Fasten off.

### Second motif
Work as for first motif until 4 rnds have been completed.

**Round 5** Ss into first lp, 4ch, work a 2dtr cluster as on first motif, *2ch, ss into a 5ch lp on first motif, 2ch, work a 3dtr cluster into next lp on 2nd motif, rep from * twice more, then complete as for first motif.

Make as many motifs as reqd, joining each in the same way. Take care to leave 7 lps free at top and bottom of motifs between the 3 lps joining the motifs.

### Heading
With right side facing join yarn to 7th lp before join on first motif, 9ch, 1dtr into next lp, *(4ch, 1dc into next lp) 3 times, 4ch, 1dtr into next lp, 4ch, leaving the last lp of each on hook work 1tr tr into next lp and 1tr tr into first free lp on next motif, yrh, draw through all 3 lps on hook, 4ch, 1dtr into next lp, rep from * to last motif, (4ch, 1dc into next lp) 3 times, 4ch, 1dtr into next lp, 4ch, 1tr tr into next lp, 7ch, turn.

**Next row** *1tr into dtr, (4ch, 1tr into dc) 3 times, 4ch, 1tr into dtr, 4ch, 1tr into joined tr tr, 4ch, rep from * to end, working last tr into 5th of 9ch.

Fasten off.

## *Picot loop edging*

Make a length of ch as reqd, 1ch, turn.

**Row 1** 1dc into 2nd ch from hook, *1ch, draw this ch up to the reqd length, and to keep the lps even put onto a pencil or a thick knitting needle, take hook out of lp, insert hook into the st below the lp, then into next ch along foundation ch, yrh, draw lp through ch, yrh, draw through 2 lps on hook, rep from * to end.

Fasten off.

## *Crescent border*

Make a ch the length reqd, having a no. of ch divisible by 8 plus 5, 2ch, turn.

**Row 1** 1tr into 4th ch from hook, 1tr into each ch to end.

**Row 2** *5ch, miss next 3tr, 1tr into next tr, rep from * to end.

**Row 3** Ss into first lp, *3ch, 1tr into next lp, (5ch, 1tr into same lp) 3 times, 3ch, 1dc into next lp, rep from * to end.

Fasten off.

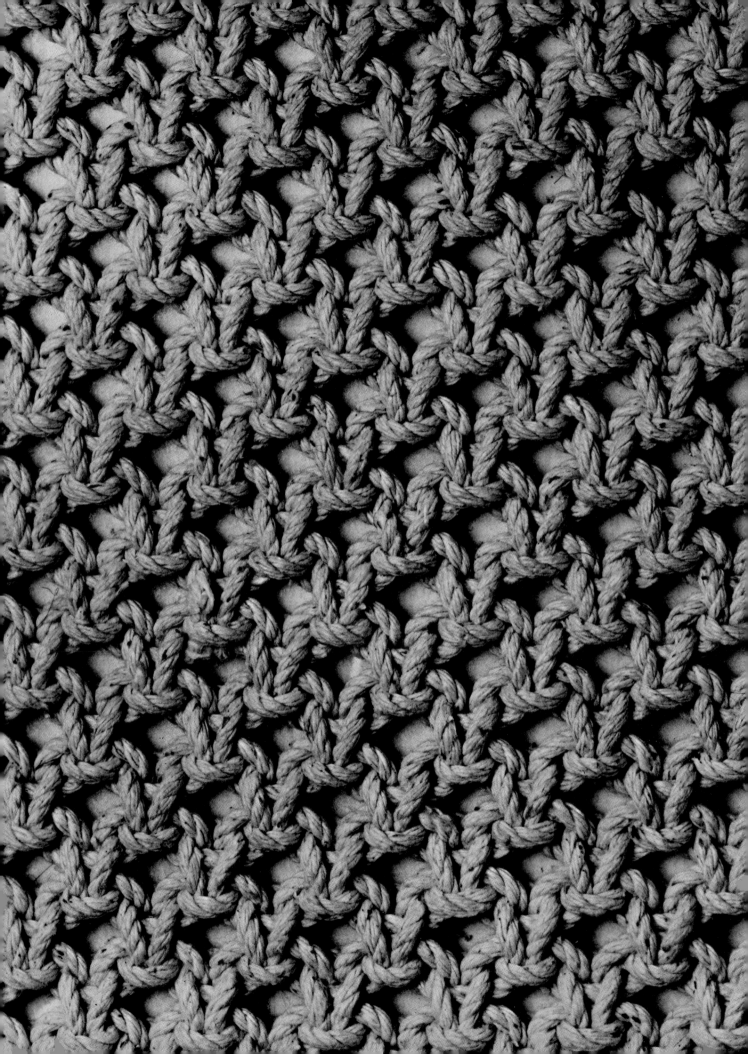

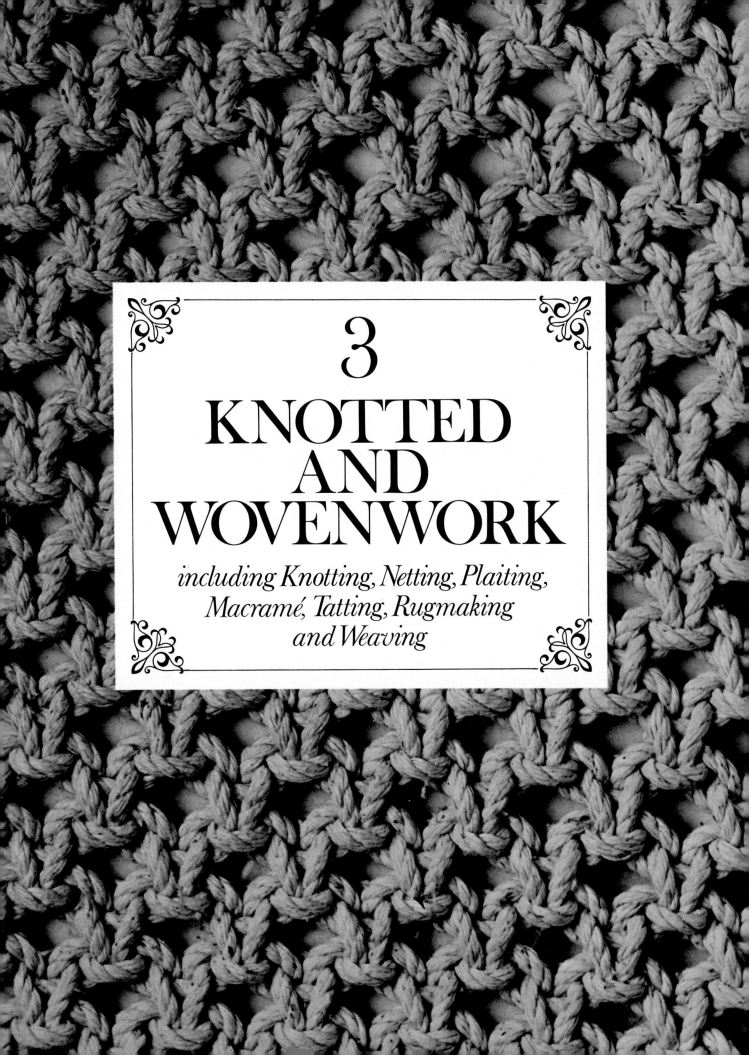

# 3
# KNOTTED
# AND
# WOVENWORK

*including Knotting, Netting, Plaiting,
Macramé, Tatting, Rugmaking
and Weaving*

# History of knotting

The tying of knots is probably the oldest of all handicrafts. From the earliest days, readily available materials such as vines and grasses or the hair and skin of animals were used as simple ropes. Thereafter, it was just a matter of time before these single strands were twisted and plaited into longer and thicker lengths, and the art of rope-making became well-known to all the world's great civilizations.

As soon as man discovered that he could make some sort of rope, he must have devised methods of tying the knots that he needed. Indeed, we know that fishing nets were made by Stone Age lake-dwellers using the netting knot. In Egypt and Persia, bridges were built and ships were rigged out using a wide variety of knots. And in Peru, the Incas developed a decimal system of numbers on the basis of tying different kinds of knots in strings suspended from a horizontal cord. These were called *quipus* or knot-records and were "read" according to the type of the knot, its position on the cord and the colour of the strings. They enabled the Incas to keep records of dates, astronomical events and other sums and figures.

It is impossible to say when knots first began to be designed for decorative purposes. At some stage in the past, as knots became more complicated and the techniques more sophisticated, they must have been made for their own sake. Knotting has long been established in the sailor's trade and, in the days when single voyages lasted several months, sailors took advantage of the spare time and of the miles of rope which every ship had on board to develop knotting into an intricate and decorative art.

## Materials

All ropes are made out of fibres. These fibres may be vegetable in origin (for example, manila hemp, sisal or cotton), animal (wool or silk) or man-made (nylon). In the process of making rope, the fibres are first spun into yarn, the yarns are wound into strands, and, finally, the strands are twisted into rope.

The choice of materials for knotting is almost unlimited. The sort of rope, string, cord or yarn that you decide to use will depend entirely on what you are making and on the particular effect that you are aiming to achieve.

**1 Flax hemp**

**2 Manila**

**3 Cotton**

**4 Nylon**

**5 Plaited nylon**

**6 Polythene**

**7 Polypropylene**

# Basic knots

Out of the thousands of different knots which exist, the ones given in this section are the simplest and the most common. They are all easy to tie and have a wide variety of uses. It is a good idea to become familiar with them since, to a large extent, they form the basis of many of the more complicated knots.

## Overhand knot

This is the simplest and most basic of all knots. Sometimes called the *thumb knot*, it is tied in a single piece of rope and is used for a wide range of purposes, from tying up parcels to preventing the end of a rope from fraying. It is often employed as a "stopper" knot, to stop a piece of rope from slipping through a hole, but it is not the best knot to use for this purpose.

**Overhand knot**

### How to work

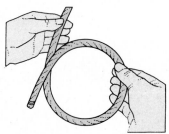

**1** *Hold the rope in one hand. Take the end across the face of the standing part so that it forms a loop as shown.*

**2** *Pass the end around the rope and back through the loop. Tighten into position.*

## Figure of eight knot

This knot is also tied in a single piece of rope and has been called the "perfect" knot – on account of its symmetrical construction. It is bulkier and makes a better "stopper" than the overhand knot since it does not jam so hard when it is tightened and is therefore much easier to undo.

**Figure of eight knot**

### How to work

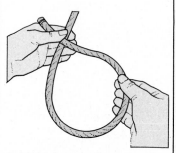

**1** *Hold the rope in one hand. Take the end across the face of the standing part so that it forms a loop as shown.*

**2** *Pass the end up behind the rope in another loop and then down through the first. Tighten the knot into position.*

## Reef knot

Also known as *square knot*, this is commonly used for tying two ends of rope together. The knot lies flat, does not jam, and is easy to untie. However, it should not be used if the strain on the knot comes at an angle or if the ropes are of different thicknesses. Two left-handed or two right-handed knots together will produce a "granny knot", which tends to slip and can be dangerous.

**Reef knot**

*How to work*

**1** *Take an end in each hand. Pass left over right and under.*

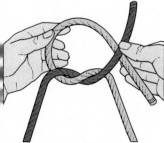

**2** *Now bring the ends up again. Pass right over left and under.*

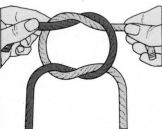

**3** *Tighten the 2 half knots to make the finished reef knot.*

## Sheet bend

This is also known as the *netting knot*. It is widely used for tying together two pieces of rope of the same thickness and also in making nets. The instructions for tying it are given in the section on netting (see page 187).

**Sheet bend**

## Lark's head knot

Also known as the *cow hitch*, this is a useful knot for mounting a doubled length of rope on to a pole or another piece of rope. It is widely used in macramé and tatting (see page 175). However, it will remain secure only if equal tension is put on both hanging ends.

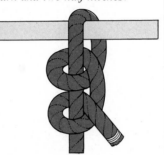

**Lark's head knot**

*How to work*

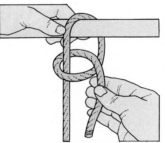

*Double the rope over and lay it across the top of the rope or pole to which it is being tied. Bring the loop under and tuck the ends through it so that they hang vertically.*

## Double half hitch

This knot provides a quick way of securing a rope to a pole or to a ring, and it is often used as a temporary fixing. It is composed of two identical half hitches beside one another. The knot can be made more secure by taking the end twice around the pole or ring before tying the hitches, in which case it is called a *round turn and two half hitches.*

**Double half hitch**

*How to work*

**1** *Pass the end of the rope over the top of the pole, around the back and then out to the front again. Pass it around the standing part of the rope and through the loop from the back to the front so that it forms one half hitch.*

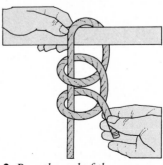

**2** *Pass the end of the rope around the standing part again to form another identical half hitch. Pull the knot tight.*

## Bowline

This knot represents the best way of forming a loop or "eye" in the end of a rope. The knot will not slip and yet is easy to untie. There are several variations on the bowline, of which this is the simplest.

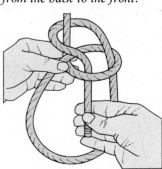

**Bowline**

*How to work*

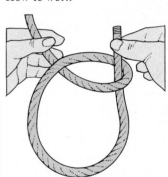

**1** *Hold the rope in one hand. Form a small loop some distance from the end and hold in place with the thumb. Pass the end up through the loop, from the back to the front.*

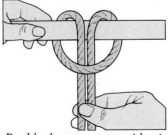

**2** *Take the end up behind the standing part, from the right to the left. Then pass it back through the original loop, this time from the front to the back. Tighten into position.*

# Whipping

Whipping is a method of preventing the strands of a rope from fraying by winding thin twine around the end. There are other methods, such as tying an overhand or figure of eight knot or, with nylon ropes, burning the end, but whipping is the most effective and most permanent. It should be done with special whipping twine, which is available from any chandler.

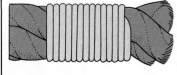

**The whipped end of rope**

*How to work*

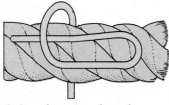

*1 Lay the twine along the rope in a loop. Take the working end over the top and around the back of the rope.*

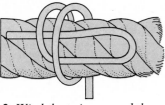

*2 Wind the twine around the rope again as shown.*

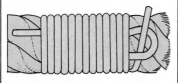

*3 Continue winding for 12 or 13 turns, keeping the coils tight and close together. Insert the working end through what is left of the original loop. Then pull the other end so that the loop and working end disappear beneath the coils. Trim off the protruding end.*

# Short splice

Splicing is the technique of joining two ropes together by meshing the separate strands into each other. It makes for a much stronger join than any knot.

**The finished splice**

*How to work*

*1 Tie a short length of whipping twine around each of the rope ends. Unravel the strands back to this point. Place the ropes together so that each strand lies between 2 others.*

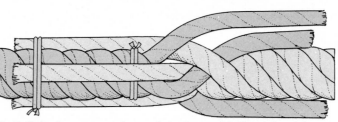

*2 Pull the 2 ropes together and tie the strands from the right-hand side on to the left-hand rope as shown. Remove the twine from the right-hand rope. Take the nearest loose strand and thread it under the first strand in the right-hand rope, either using a marlin spike or twisting the rope to open the strands.*

*3 Work around the rope, moving towards the right and threading the next loose strand from the left-hand rope under successive strands on the right-hand rope. Continue until each strand has been threaded through at least 3 times. Then remove the twine from the left-hand rope and splice the strands on that side in the same way. Trim off the ends.*

# Eye splice

This splice enables a permanent loop to be worked on the end of a piece of rope.

**The finished eye splice**

*How to work*

*1 Tie whipping twine around the rope about 6in. (15cm) from the end. Unravel the strands back to this point. Make the loop in the rope. Take one strand and thread it through the standing part, using a marlin spike or twisting the rope to open the strands. Take the strand on the left of the previous one and thread it under the next strand up in the standing part.*

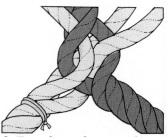

*2 Turn the work over and thread the remaining strand into the rope as shown. Continue in the same way until all the strands are spliced back into the rope. Finally, trim off the protruding ends.*

# Turk's head knots

There are many different knots of the Turk's head type, and together they make up a large family of knots all sharing the same basic characteristics. In most cases, they are made with a single length of thread that is laced around and around in the distinctive "over and under" sequence. Indeed, Turk's head knots probably take their name from their resemblance to turbans. The basic pattern can vary, but, once established by the first round, it can be repeated several times to produce finished knots of three, four or five strands. Turk's head knots can be worked either in the hand, in which case they will be cylindrical or spherical in shape, or they can be pinned out on a soft board, in which case they will be flat.

## Flat Turk's head knot

This knot is usually worked on a flat surface, so that the loops can be pinned in place if necessary. Its form varies according to the number of crossings you make in the centre and the number of strands you use. As with all Turk's head knots, the first round marks out the shape of the knot and is then simply repeated as many times as is required. These knots make ideal decorative table mats.

**Three-strand flat Turk's head knot**

### How to work

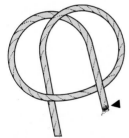

**1** *Start at arrow and lay the working thread out on a flat surface so that it forms 2 overlapping loops as shown. Pin in place if necessary.*

**2** *Form a third loop to the right of the other 2 by taking the working thread around through the previous loops – passing it over, over, under, under and then over again.*

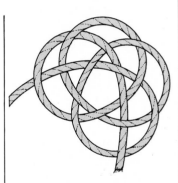

**3** *Form a fourth loop down to the bottom right by threading the working end under and over the previous coils as shown.*

**4** *Insert the thread back into the knot at the starting point to make the final loop. Repeat the same route twice for a 3-strand knot. Stitch or glue the ends down at the back.*

## Cylindrical Turk's head knot

This knot is worked in the hand. The first complete round dictates the knot's structure; after that, any subsequent rounds simply follow exactly the same route as the first. These Turk's head knots can be used for napkin rings and bracelets or for making decorative handgrips on ropes, fishing rods and archery bows.

**Three-strand cylindrical Turk's head knot**

### How to work

**1** *Loosely wind the thread twice around the fingers of the left hand. Then slip the first coil over the second coil to form a loop as shown.*

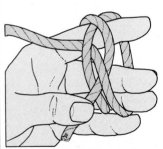

**2** *Insert the working end through the loop from right to left, taking it over and under.*

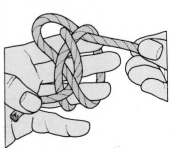

**3** *Take the working end up over the top of the knot and then pass it from left to right between the two coils so that it crosses over the first and then under the second.*

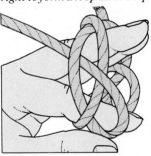

**4** *Turn the knot over in your hand. Take the coil on the left over the top of the coil on the right to form a loop as in Step 1.*

**5** *Bring the working end up and pass it through this loop from right to left as shown.*

**6** *Turn the knot over again. Insert the working end back into the coils at the starting point. Follow the same course exactly to make a multi-strand knot. Either stitch or glue the ends down on the inside.*

# Buttons

There is a wide range of ball-shaped knots, usually called *knob knots*, which can be used to make decorative buttons. They are best worked in silk or cotton cords or leather thonging.

## Monkey's fist

This is one of the easiest of the knob knots to work and, when pulled tight, makes an ideal button. It is best worked in the hand, winding the coils around the fingers, and can be made in either a three- or a four-strand version.

**Four-strand monkey's fist**

**How to make a four-strand monkey's fist knot**

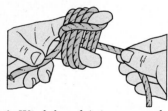

**1** *Wind thread 4 times around first 2 fingers of left hand, and then 4 times over previous coils, between fingers.*

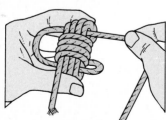

**2** *Remove fingers and wind 4 more coils into previous ones.*

**3** *Tighten into small ball by pulling each loop through knot.*

## Chinese button

This knot is worn as a button throughout China. It is best worked by laying the loops out on a flat surface, and can be either one- or two-strand.

**Two-strand Chinese button**

### How to make a two-strand Chinese button

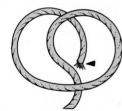

**1** *Start at arrow and form thread into shape as above.*

**2** *Take working end from left to right, under, over, under and then over again.*

**3** *Take working end down and then up into centre of knot, crossing under, over and under, to arrive back at starting point. Follow same route once more. Tighten into small ball.*

# Turkish mat

Flattened *prolonged knots* can be used to make Turkish mats in a wide variety of sizes and thicknesses. They can be used either as doormats or as table mats. To make the two-strand doormat illustrated here, you will need 12ft (3.7m) of 1in. (2.5cm) diameter rope. The finished mat will measure approximately 29in. (74cm) by 15in. (38cm).

**Two-strand Turkish mat**

### How to make a Turkish mat

**1** *Form the rope into 3 loops as shown, so that the top of the middle loop is in the centre of the length of rope.*

**2** *Extend the 2 outside loops by pulling them downwards.*

**3** *Cross the loop on the left over itself by twisting it to the right. Do the same to the other loop, also by twisting it over to the right.*

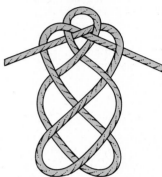

**4** *Pass the loop on the right over the loop on the left.*

**5** *Thread the ends of the rope into the bottom loops as shown.*

**6** *Follow same route once more for a 2-strand mat. Take the ends to the back, whip them and stitch them down.*

# *Hanging curtain*

This hanging curtain is made from lengths of string worked into simple knotted chains, interspersed at regular intervals with wooden beads. A chevron pattern can be formed by varying the number of knots between the first and the second beads. The strings are worked from the bottom upwards, starting with an overhand knot, a round bead and then the slip knot which begins the knotted chain. When completed the strings are all looped over a horizontal pole which can then be hung above a doorway.

*Materials*

The hanging curtain illustrated here is worked in simple parcel string. For each string of the curtain you will need nine round wooden beads, twelve oval-shaped wooden beads, about 10yds (9.2m) of parcel string and some whipping twine. The finished curtain should then measure about 6ft (1.9m) from top to bottom, although this will vary since, when hung, the strings will tend to stretch. The number of strings you make will depend on the width of the doorway and the thickness which you intend the curtain to have.

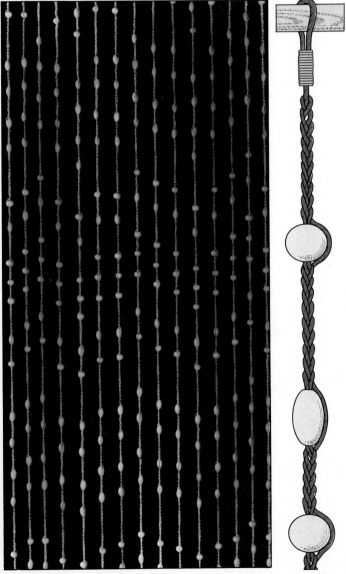

**The finished hanging curtain**

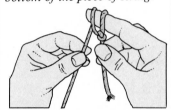

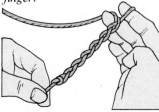

**Knotted chain**

## *The knotted strings*

Working from the bottom, a simple knot is repeated along the length of string to produce a decorative knotted chain.

### *How to make the knots*

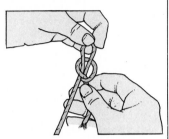

**1** *Make a slip knot at the bottom of the piece of string.*

**2** *Insert finger through loop and take string over finger.*

**3** *Pull the slip loop over the second loop and off finger.*

**4** *Take the working end up over finger again. Slip the previous loop over it and off finger.*

**5** *Continue in the same way, to produce a knotted chain.*

## *The beads*

Beads can be threaded on to the string and, by varying the number of knots between the first two, a pattern can be built up in the curtain.

### *How to thread the beads*

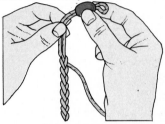

**1** *Extend the loop. Pinch the end and thread it through bead.*

**2** *Insert finger through loop above bead. Take string around bead and up over finger.*

**3** *Pull loop over working end and off finger. Tighten.*

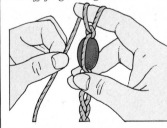

**4** *Continue working the knotted chain above the bead in the normal way.*

### *Finishing off*

The finished strings are looped over a pole. The loops are made by whipping the end of the string back on itself with a length of fine twine.

173

# History of macramé

Macramé almost certainly originated in very early days in the Middle East. It would have been a natural development from basic knots to more sophisticated decorative work. In ancient Turkey, weavers often finished off the threads on towels with decorative knotted fringes, and their word for towel was *maqrama*. It is possible that the name also derives from the Arab word, *migramah*, meaning decorative fringe or braid. From the Middle East macramé spread to Spain with the Moors, to Italy with the returning Crusaders, and so into Europe. Thereafter, sailors must have helped to spread the knowledge of macramé to countries all around the world.

When William of Orange came to the throne of England his wife Mary taught macramé to the women of the court and it enjoyed a popularity which stretched right through to the late Victorian period. The Victorians usually worked in very fine thread to produce an almost lace-like quality, and macramé was one of the acceptable accomplishments for a gentlewoman of the time. Hardly a home in Britain was complete without macramé decorating its mantelpiece, piano, lampshades and the women's clothing.

In the nineteenth century finished macramé work began to be exported to South America and California, particularly from the Italian Riviera around Genoa. The technique was not unknown there, however, since the Spaniards had already taken it over to Mexico, and the Indians on the east coast of Canada had undoubtedly picked it up from French sailors.

After something of a decline in its popularity, macramé has experienced a revival in the last decade or so. Nowadays, with the increased interest in all things ethnic and a growing awareness of yarns and textures, the craft is taking on a slightly different look, with bright colours and often very thick yarns. However, the basic techniques are still the traditional ones – simple for the beginner to learn and with plenty of scope for the more experienced worker to develop ideas of his or her own.

**Specimens of mid-eighteenth century macramé work**

# Tools and materials

One could almost say that the only tools required are a pair of hands: certainly no other implement is needed to form the working threads into knots.

However, the work does need to be mounted securely – to take the tension of tightening the knots and to help keep the work even. The Victorians had macramé desks which comprised a wooden board with raised side pieces in which holes had been drilled. The work was suspended on pegs which were inserted into these holes at the required level. These days the simplest foundation on which to work is a piece of soft board. This should be flat and solid enough to support the work but soft enough to take pins pushed in by hand. Composition soft-board is ideal and several thicknesses of cork board glued together also work very well. If you are a beginner it is a good idea to have a piece of paper attached to the face of the working board and lined off into equal squares. This provides a guide which helps to keep the work straight, both horizontally and vertically. Special macramé boards, marked out like this, are available from craft shops.

There are also special pins for securing macramé to the working surface. They are called *T-pins*, since they are shaped like a letter "T" to prevent the threads from slipping off, and are larger and stronger than normal pins.

Other tools you may need are a tape measure, a pair of scissors and sometimes a needle and thread.

## Threads

Your choice of working thread is almost unlimited, since macramé can be worked in more or less anything which can be formed into knots. Obviously, the thread you decide to use will be determined by the effect you want to achieve, but it is worth bearing in mind that some threads are much easier to work with than others.

The ideal thread will be strong and have a firm twist so that it will not break or stretch to an uneven tension when you are tightening the knots. It will not have too rough a texture since this would obscure the knots and might hurt the hands after working with it for a while. The thickness of the yarn will vary according to the type of work, but it should be fairly even as a lumpy texture is difficult to knot.

It is possible to buy many special macramé threads, but ordinary, everyday string can also look very attractive, as can some of the yarns available for knitting and crochet. The best thread to use if you are a beginner is probably a medium thickness, smooth string.

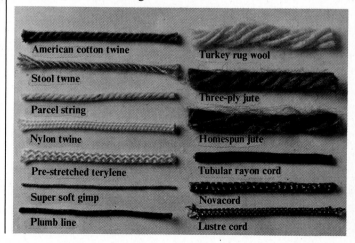

# Setting up the work

Before any macramé can be worked it has to be set up. The working threads must be hung vertically and supported securely. What you are making will determine the length and the number of working threads that you need, and these must be carefully measured and cut. As a rough guide, allow four times the length of the finished project for each working thread, i.e. eight times for each thread before it is doubled and mounted. However, some knots take up more thread than others, and the thicker the thread the more will be needed.

The threads can be set up either on to a foundation cord on the working surface or, if you are making something like a curtain hanging for example, they can be suspended directly from the curtain rod.

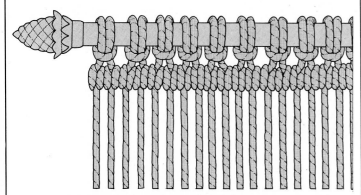

**A row of working threads mounted on a curtain rod**

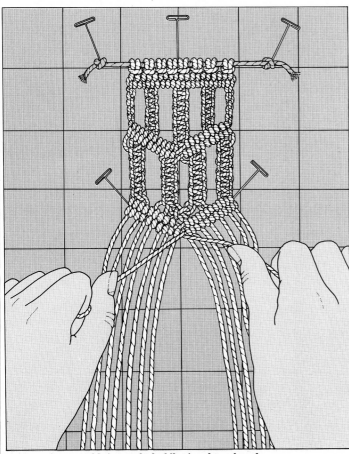

**A piece of macramé being worked while pinned to a board**

## Foundation cord

When the work is not mounted directly on to a piece of fabric or a solid object such as a buckle or a handle, a foundation cord is required on to which the first knots can be mounted. Once the work has been completed, it can either be retained and the ends fastened off, or it can be removed.

A double foundation cord (two threads used together as one) will make for larger mounting knots and added strength if it is retained in the work.

### How to work

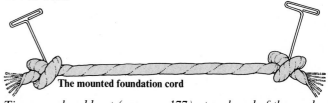

**The mounted foundation cord**

*Tie an overhand knot (see page 177) at each end of the cord and pin it to the working surface, ensuring that it is taut.*

### Mounting knot

The macramé mounting knot (also known as the *lark's head* knot) is used to position the working threads on to the foundation cord.

**Finished mounting knot secured over foundation cord**

### How to work the mounting knot

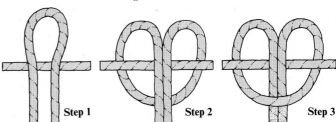

Step 1  Step 2  Step 3

*Fold each thread in half (unless otherwise stated in the instructions). Place the loop of the folded thread in front of the foundation cord. Then fold it over and behind the cord and tuck the 2 ends through the loop. Pull tight to secure the knot in position on the foundation cord.*

### Double mounting knot

A row of double mounting knots will produce a wider piece of work with more space between the working threads.

**Finished double mounting knot secured over foundation cord**

### How to work the double mounting knot

Step 1  Step 2

*First, work a reversed single mounting knot as shown. Then, work a half hitch over the foundation cord on either side of the first knot, using the ends of the working threads. Pull the knot tight to secure it in position on the foundation cord.*

# Half hitch

The half hitch forms one of the basic techniques of macramé and most of the knots are built around it, either vertically or horizontally. It is a simple movement, which is easy to master, and it can be worked either clockwise or anti-clockwise with one or more threads around a central core. It is also sometimes known as the *simple knot*, the *cording knot*, the *tatting knot*, a *clove hitch* or *buttonhole knot*.

**Half hitch**

### How to work anti-clockwise half hitch

Using the right-hand thread as a core and keeping it taut, knot the left-hand thread over it, behind and through to the front between the core and itself. This forms 1 anti-clockwise half hitch. Continue in this way to form a spiral which twists to the right.

### How to work clockwise half hitch

Using the left-hand thread as a core and keeping it taut, knot the right-hand thread over it, behind and through to the front between the core and itself. This forms 1 clockwise half hitch. Continue in this way to form a spiral which twists to the left.

### How to work single knotted chain

Work an anti-clockwise half hitch by knotting the left-hand thread around the right-hand core, and then a clockwise half hitch by knotting the right-hand thread round the left-hand core. Continue working half hitches alternately to form a flat braid.

### How to work double knotted chain

Use 4 threads, divided into 2 groups of 2 threads each. Work each pair of threads together as if they were 1 thread, and form alternate anti-clockwise and clockwise half hitches in the same way as for single knotted chain.

# Horizontal cording

A row of horizontal cording is usually used to secure the mounting knots in position. This is done by working each thread in a double half hitch over a horizontal core. The core can either be the first working thread or a separately introduced thread; in either case it is called the *leader*.

### How to work horizontal cording

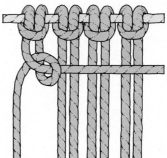

**1** Use the first working thread as the leader. Start at the left, and knot the second hanging thread around the leader in a half hitch as shown.

**3** Move on to the next hanging thread. Work it over the same leader in another double half hitch as shown. Draw it tight and make sure that it is positioned as closely as possible to the previous knot.

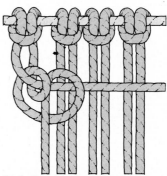

**2** Still using the same hanging thread, work another half hitch over the leader. This forms a double half hitch and will secure the knot in place.

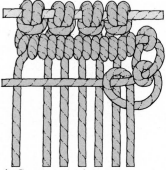

**4** Continue in the same way to the end of the row, working each hanging thread over the leader in a double half hitch. Work second row from right to left, using the same leader.

## Alternative method of cording

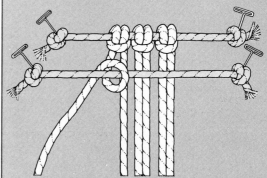

Instead of using the first working thread as the leader, pin a new thread taut immediately under the mounting knots. Work each double half hitch over this new thread as shown.

# Diagonal cording

Diagonal cording is worked in exactly the same way as horizontal cording, except that the leader is held diagonally downwards, either to the left or to the right.

### *How to work diagonal cording*

**1** Use the first working thread, held diagonally, as the leader. Work second thread over it in a double half hitch.

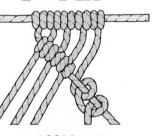

**2** Continue down the row, working each hanging thread in double half hitches over the leader.

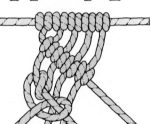

**3** Work second diagonal row in the same way, but use second working thread as the new leader.

### *How to work opposing diagonal rows*

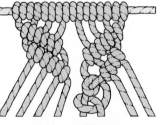

**Unjoined**
Work first half of threads over leaders slanting diagonally down to right. Work second half so that they slant down to left.

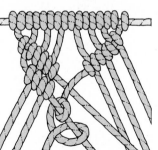

**Joined**
**1** Work as above, but cross leaders in centre, then work second diagonals so that original leaders become working threads in opposite group.

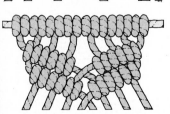

**2** When finished, the opposing diagonal rows will be joined together in the centre as shown.

# Vertical cording

In vertical cording, the working thread becomes the core and the leader works the half hitches. When vertical cording is combined with horizontal cording only, it is known as *Cavandoli* work (see page 182).

### *How to work vertical cording*

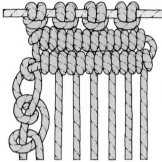

**1** *Work 2 rows of horizontal cording. At the start of the third row, hold the first working thread taut and knot the leader around it in a vertical double half hitch.*

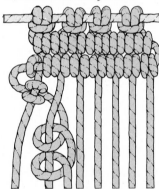

**2** *Take the leader behind the next working thread and work another double half hitch over it as shown.*

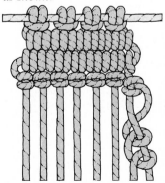

**3** *Continue to the end of row. Work next row in the same way but from right to left, with anti-clockwise knots.*

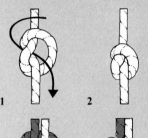
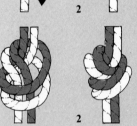
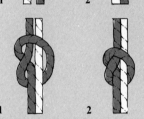

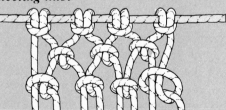

# Flat knot

This knot, also known as *Solomon's knot*, is worked with three or more threads (four is usual) and is used to make braids or *sinnets*, open meshes and solid fabrics. The knot is formed by working the two outer threads around a central core. Any additional threads go into the core.

**Flat knot**

### How to work a flat knot braid

**1** *Holding the core threads taut, take the left-hand thread over to the right, threading it behind the core threads and in front of the right-hand thread.*
**2** *Take the right-hand thread over to the left, threading it in front of the core threads and into the loop formed by the left-hand thread.*
**3** *Take the right-hand thread over to the left, threading it behind the core and in front of the left-hand thread. Take the left-hand thread over to the right, threading it in front of the core and into the loop of the right-hand thread.*
**4** *Tighten the threads to lock the knot in place, and continue down the row.*

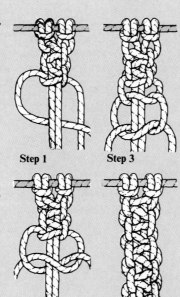

**Step 1**   **Step 3**

**Step 2**   **Step 4**

### Alternating flat knots

This is a method of working along a group of several hanging threads and forming horizontal rows of flat knots. The alternating pattern is made by forming the flat knots over different groups of four threads. The knots can either be worked close together to give a solid fabric or spaced apart for an open mesh and both techniques look good if decreased to a point.

### How to work closed

*First, work a horizontal row of 4 flat knots, each knot formed over 4 working threads in the way described above.*

*On the second row, re-group the threads so that there are 2 spare at each end. Work a flat knot on each new group of 4 threads, pulling it tight so that it lies close under the knots in the previous row.*

*On the third row, re-group the threads as for the first row.*

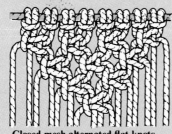

**Closed-mesh alternated flat knots**

### How to work open

*Work in exactly the same way as for the closed method, but leave more space between each row of flat knots so that an open-mesh effect is produced.*

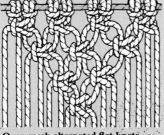

**Open-mesh alternated flat knots**

# Braids and spirals

Braids of simple flat knots can be varied to produce much more complex and decorative braids and spirals. Below are shown five different ways in which these can be worked.

### Flat knot spiral

*You can form the braid into a spiral by repeating only one half of the flat knot. The direction in which the spiral twists will vary according to whether you use only the first half or only the second half of the flat knot.*

### Knotted edge braid

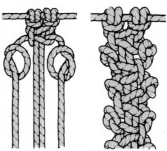

*To form this variation on the simple flat knot braid, work an overhand knot on each of the outer threads in between the flat knots.*

### Picot edged braid

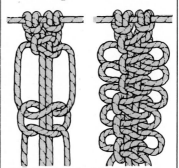

*Work a braid of flat knots so that a space is left between each separate knot. When you push the knots up together, the outer threads form into decorative loops or picots.*

### Intertwined flat knot braid

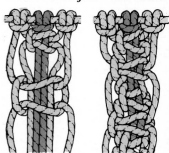

*Work a braid of flat knots over 6 threads. Alternate so that the first knot uses only the centre 4 threads and the next uses the outer 2 threads over a 4-thread core.*

### Blackberry ball braid

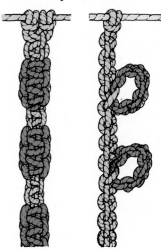

**Front view**   **Side view**

*After making, say, about ten flat knots, push the two core threads through to the back of the work with a blunt needle or a crochet hook, just above the fifth flat knot. Then pull the ends so that the knots roll up into the blackberry ball.*

**Forming the knots into a ball**

# Simple headings

When starting a piece of macramé, you need not necessarily begin just with simple mounting knots secured by horizontal cording. Simple picots or loops can be used to make decorative headings.

### *Plain picot*

*Double the working thread over and pin it above the foundation cord in a loop. Then secure it to the foundation cord with two cording knots as shown.*

### *Multiple picot*

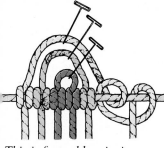

*This is formed by pinning successively larger loops above the foundation cord. The smallest picot is knotted first, and the largest, outer one last.*

### *Knotted picot*

*This method gives a simple decoration to the plain picot. After securing the thread with one cording knot, make an overhand knot in the centre of the loop, pin it in place, and make the second cording knot.*

# Decorative headings

The techniques for making three decorative headings are shown below and to the right. The headings are all worked by building up a pattern of knots above the foundation cord.

### *Scalloped picot*
This heading is worked on two doubled threads in a series of double half hitches.

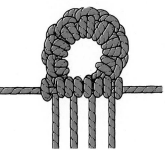

### *How to work*

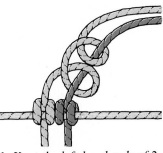

**1** *Knot the left-hand ends of 2 working threads on to the foundation cord. Allow about double the length for the outer thread. Work a double half hitch with the outer thread on to the inner thread.*

**2** *Work double half hitches all around the picot.*

**3** *Pull tight and knot the ends on to the foundation cord.*

### *Flat knot picot*
This heading is worked on three doubled threads to give a shape like a *fleur-de-lys*.

### *How to work*

**1** *Pin 3 doubled threads in position above the foundation cord, the centre one higher than the other two.*

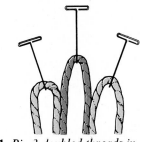

**2** *With a 4-thread core, work the outer threads into one or more flat knots.*

**3** *Mount each thread on to the foundation cord with a cording knot to secure the heading.*

### *Double knotted picot*
This heading is worked on two doubled threads and is quick and easy to make.

### *How to work*

**1** *Knot the left-hand ends of 2 working threads on to the foundation cord. Holding the 2 threads together knot them in an overhand knot at the top of the picot.*

**2** *Work a half hitch below the overhand knot as shown.*

**3** *Knot the right-hand ends on to the foundation cord.*

179

# Decorative knots

## Josephine knot

This decorative knot can be made with two single threads, but it is much more effective when worked in two groups of several threads, each laid side by side and kept flat.

**Four-thread Josephine knot**

### How to work

**1** *Pin one group of threads in a flat loop as shown.*

*2 Weave the other group over and under it. Tighten carefully.*

## Japanese knot

This is a more complicated decorative knot. It too can be worked in four single threads or in four groups of threads. The knot is easier to form if the working threads are all mounted on a foundation cord and pinned to a soft board. Additional pins can then be added at various points so that the knot is kept in shape while it is being worked.

**Two-thread Japanese knot**

### How to work

**1** *Work the outer threads into a flat knot around the centre threads. Then pin the centre threads into loops around the outer threads as shown.*

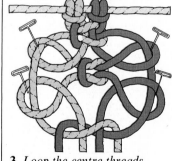

*3 Loop the centre threads around the outer ones. Work a flat knot over centre threads.*

**2** *Work the centre threads into a central, coreless flat knot.*

*4 Finish off by tightening the whole knot into shape as shown.*

# Working in the round

Macramé lends itself particularly well to being worked in the round. The work can be either flat (as for a place mat) or cylindrical (as for a lampshade, hanging basket or gazebo). In either case, the method of mounting the threads at the start will be slightly different from ordinary macramé.

## Mounting on to a solid ring

Rings are one of the best methods of mounting when working in the round. They are available in plastic, metal and wood, and can be used horizontally or vertically, either completely covered by the threads or partially revealed. The rings can be used to shape the work or, when finished, to suspend it (for example, see hanging basket, page 184).

**Working threads mounted on to a ring with simple mounting knots**

## Mounting on to a flat thread ring

The foundation ring need not be specially purchased; it can be made from a length of thread. This is done by forming the thread into a circle of one or more loops and then either tying it with a reef knot or incorporating the ends with the other working threads. This method is very useful for a flat piece of macramé, where extra bulk at the centre would be undesirable.

**Working threads mounted on to a triple-thickness thread ring**

## Mounting with an overhand knot

Sometimes it is enough simply to tie all the threads together in a giant overhand knot. The ends can be left hanging to produce a decorative tassel. Alternatively, the threads can be doubled over and the overhand knot tied so that it leaves a loop as shown below.

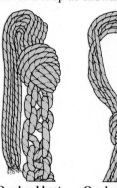

**Overhand knot with tassel**   **Overhand knot with loop**

## Increasing

When working macramé in flat rounds, extra threads must be added as the work spreads out. In the example shown here, threads are added at the bottom right-hand corner with simple mounting knots.

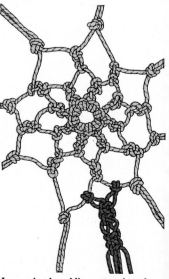

**Increasing by adding extra threads**

# Fringes, tassels and beads

The decorative effects of all macramé can be enhanced by making fringes or tassels or by including beads in the work.

## Fringes

Forming a fringe is one neat way of finishing off your work. However, macramé fringes can also be made separately and used as decorative finishes for lampshades, roller blinds and articles of clothing. It is important to choose a yarn which will hang softly but heavily: silky threads such as tubular rayon are ideal.

By removing the weft threads from the edge of a piece of fabric, a fringe can be worked on the warp threads.

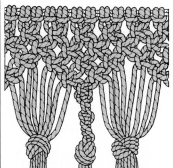

**A fringe made up of flat knots and multiple overhand knots and spirals**

**A fringe mounted on crochet chain**

**A fringe worked on the warp threads of a piece of fabric**

## Tassels

Tassels are simple to make and can be part of the work or can be made separately and tied in place. A number of threads are held together with an overhand knot, a collecting knot, a flat knot or they are bound together with a separate length of thread. The ends are then trimmed level and can also be frayed if necessary. When choosing the yarn for your tassel, bear in mind the same considerations as for fringing.

**Overhand knot**       **Collecting knot**

**Flat knots**       **Bound tassel**

## Beads

The addition of beads can give extra colour and texture to macramé. Once threaded, they can be secured in place with a knot underneath or by being incorporated into the core of a flat knot. Sometimes the yarn may be so thick that once it has been threaded the bead will stay in place without an additional knot being needed.

# Joining and finishing

## Joining

If a working thread turns out to be too short – either because you have underestimated the length or because it has broken during the knotting – a new piece can be joined in.

### How to join vertically

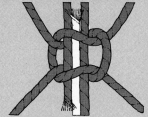

*Introduce the new length of thread into the core of a flat knot or vertical cording knot. Work the knot over the join and take the ends to the back.*

### How to join horizontally

*Lay the new length of thread along beside the leader in a row of horizontal cording. Work the knots over the join and take the ends to the back.*

## Finishing

If your piece of macramé ends in a fringe, all that is needed is to trim the loose ends of thread. However, if a fringe is not part of the design, there are several methods for securing the loose ends, and finishing the work off neatly.

### How to finish off by darning
*Cut the loose ends to a length of about 2in. (5cm). Turn them over to the back of the work and darn each one into the back of the knots. Use either a crochet hook or thread the ends through with a needle as shown. Be careful not to darn them into the first knot or the bottom row will unravel.*

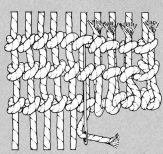

**Darning into the back of the work**

### How to finish off by stitching
*Turn the loose ends of thread over to the back of the work in the same way as in the method above. However, instead of darning them in, secure them firmly to the back of the work with a few small stitches as shown, using a needle and fine but strong thread.*

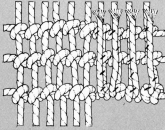

**Stitching to the back of the work**

### How to finish off by hemming
*Cut the loose ends to a length of about ¼in. (6mm) and sew them on to the side of a strip of seam or bias binding as shown. When you have finished stitching right across the width of the work, fold the binding over and sew the remaining edges to the back of the macramé as shown.*

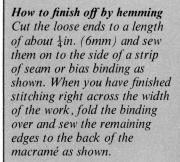
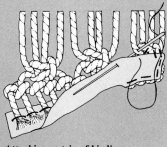

**Attaching a strip of binding**

# Cavandoli

This type of macramé originated in Italy in the late nineteenth century. It is reputed to have been discovered by a Madame Valentina Cavandoli, who taught it to children there. The technique is very simple indeed and consists of a combination of just two different knots – horizontal and vertical cording. It produces a close, firm texture which makes a very hardwearing fabric, ideal for belts or for bags.

In its best-known form, Cavandoli work is made up in two colours. The method, explained in detail below, is very simple. A number of working threads in one colour are suspended vertically from a mounting cord. A single length of thread in a contrasting colour is then introduced from the left-hand side of the work. Thereafter, horizontal and vertical cording knots are alternated. The vertical threads are worked into horizontal cording knots using the contrasting colour as the leader; and the contrasting colour is worked into vertical cording knots using the vertical threads as leaders.

When designing a piece of Cavandoli work it is a good idea to draw it out on squared graph paper, each square representing a separate knot. Usually, the horizontal cording is used for the background and the vertical cording for the actual design. It is worth bearing in mind that because of the shape of the knots the finished article will be longer and thinner than the squared-off design and that this should be allowed for.

### How to work Cavandoli

**1** *Suspend the working threads from a horizontal mounting cord in the usual way. Each working thread should be 4 times the estimated length of the finished work. Introduce the contrast colour separately by pinning it to the left of the work. It should be all in one ball of thread totalling the same length as all the working threads added together. Using the first working thread as the leader, work the contrast colour over it in a double half hitch as shown.*
**2** *Work another double half hitch over the next working thread so that you have formed 2 vertical cording knots. Now make the contrast colour the leader, and take the next 2 working threads over it in double half hitches so that you have formed 2 horizontal cording knots.*
**3** *Continue alternating in this way to the end of the row, working over the hanging threads in vertical cording and over the contrast colour in horizontal cording. At the end of the row, leave a small picot as shown and work back again alternating the 2 types of cording in the same way.*

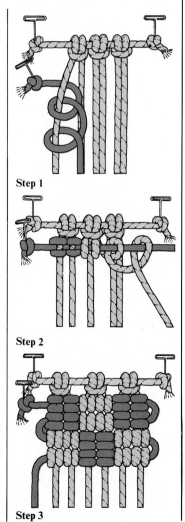

Step 1

Step 2

Step 3

# Angling

Angling is a method which is often used in conjunction with Cavandoli work. The actual shape of the piece of macramé can be altered by increasing or decreasing the number of knots in the row to the left or right. The colour patterns can be changed and angled strips can be made and then interlocked.

*How to work*

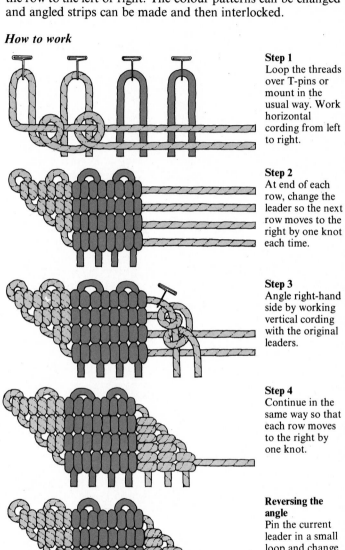

**Step 1**
Loop the threads over T-pins or mount in the usual way. Work horizontal cording from left to right.

**Step 2**
At end of each row, change the leader so the next row moves to the right by one knot each time.

**Step 3**
Angle right-hand side by working vertical cording with the original leaders.

**Step 4**
Continue in the same way so that each row moves to the right by one knot.

**Reversing the angle**
Pin the current leader in a small loop and change direction. Work horizontal cording from right to left.

**Changing the colour pattern**
Change to vertical cording and use the contrasting coloured threads as leaders.

When making up certain projects, it is often best not to mount the work on to a foundation cord but to mount it straight on to the object itself.

## Bags

For bags, the macramé threads can be mounted directly on to the handles using simple mounting knots.

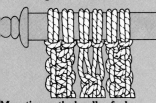

Mounting on the handle of a bag

## Belts

Belts will be much stronger if the threads are mounted on to the buckle, again using simple mounting knots.

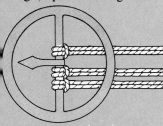

Mounting on the buckle of a belt

## Hangings

A brass or wooden curtain rod is an ideal foundation on which to work a window covering or a wall hanging (see page 175). If you are working in the round and making a gazebo or a hanging basket, then mount the threads on to a ring (see page 180).

## Fabrics

The threads for a macramé edging can be mounted directly on to the fabric using a needle or fine crochet hook.

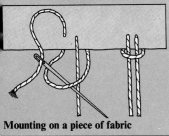

Mounting on a piece of fabric

# *Macramé belt*

This macramé belt is both inexpensive and easy to make. It is worked entirely in a repeated sequence of vertical and horizontal cording which forms a very simple two-colour Cavandoli pattern. You can, of course, vary this to your own design if you wish. The belt is worked away from the pointed end, towards the end which is tied to the buckle.

## *Materials*

The belt is best worked in something like parcel string or American cotton twine. For a belt measuring about 33in. by 2in. (84cm by 5cm), you will need the following materials: four lengths of black thread, each measuring 25ft (7.6m) in length; two lengths of white thread, each measuring 25ft (7.6m); one length of white thread, measuring 40ft (12.2m), to use as a leader; and a suitable flat buckle.

## *Starting the belt at the pointed end*

Take the two 25ft (7.6m) lengths of white string, fold them in half and pin them on to a board. Work a flat knot over the two central core threads (Step 1). Fold one of the lengths of black string in half and position it over the four threads just below the tightened flat knot. Work the four white strings over the black in a row of horizontal cording as shown (Step 2). Taking one for each new row, centre the other three lengths of black over the hanging strings as before. Work three rows of horizontal cording, the ends of each new leader becoming hanging strings on the next row. Finally, introduce the white leader from the left and work the twelve hanging threads over it in two rows of horizontal cording (Step 3). Secure the short loose end of the leader by threading it into the knots at the back of the work.

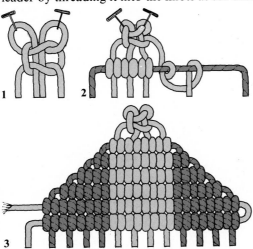

**Step 1**
A flat knot using the four white threads.

**Step 2**
The first black thread secured with horizontal cording knots.

**Step 3**
The other black threads and the white leader joined in with horizontal cording.

## *Working the main section of the belt*

Work the main part of the belt by repeating a sequence of two rows of vertical cording followed by four rows of horizontal cording. For the vertical cording, the original white leader is worked over each of the twelve hanging threads in turn; for the horizontal cording, the twelve hanging threads are all worked over the original white leader.

## *Finishing off and attaching the buckle*

To finish off, mount the twelve working strings on to the central strut of the buckle by winding each string twice around the strut and then tying pairs of them together at the back with a reef knot (see page 169). Trim off the ends.

The finished macramé belt

# Hanging basket

A very effective hanging basket can be made using fairly simple macramé techniques. The one given here is worked in the round, from top to bottom, and is suspended from a vertical wooden ring. It has two baskets, one larger than the other, although by using longer lengths of thread you can vary the pattern for as many as you like.

**Hanging basket**

## Materials

You will need at least 128yds (118m) of macramé thread and three wooden rings, one measuring 2¼in. (6cm) in diameter and the other two measuring 3½in. (9cm) in diameter. A wide variety of macramé threads would be suitable, but the hanging basket is perhaps best worked in a soft, fairly thick yarn such as jute or Turkey rug wool. The dimensions of the hanging basket will vary according to the macramé thread you use and the length of the tassels at the bottom; worked in rug wool, it is about 5ft (1.5m) in height.

## Making the hanging basket

Start at the top and work downwards. Begin by securing the working threads on to the wooden ring from which the basket will hang. To do this, cut out 8 lengths of thread, each 12yds (11m) long. Lay them together and, using the 2 outer threads on each side, work a **flat knot** in the middle of the length over a core of the 4 central threads. Make 5 flat knots to one side of the centre knot, and 6 to the other side. Double the threads through the 2¼in. (6cm) diameter wooden ring and secure them in place by winding a separate length around the double thickness of knots about half way down their length. Separate the 16 hanging threads into 4 groups of 4 threads each. Work a **flat knot spiral** of 23 knots on each group. Then thread a **bead** on to each spiral, taking all 4 threads through the bead. Secure the beads in place by continuing the **flat knot spirals,** working 23 more knots on each group of threads.

*Re-group the threads: take 2 threads from each spiral together with 2 threads from the one next to it. Leave a space of about 3½in. (9cm) below the previous flat knot spirals and work 4 **flat knots** on each group. Using **horizontal cording,** work all the threads on to a 3½in. (9cm) diameter wooden ring. Cut 8 more lengths of thread, each 2yds (1.9m) long, double them over and mount them on to the wooden ring with **cording knots,** placing 2 lengths between each group. This will leave you with 32 hanging threads. Keeping to the same groups as before, and forming the additional threads into new groups, make one **flat knot** on each group of 4 threads. Follow with 6 rows of **alternated flat knots.** After the third row, begin decreasing to a point from centre front to centre back on each side. Cross the 2 centre front and 2 centre back threads to use as leaders and work 2 rows of **diagonal cording** outlining the points.*

Divide the 8 threads from each point into 2 groups of 4 threads each. Make a **flat knot spiral** of 32 knots on each group. Place a **bead** on each group as before, and then continue the **flat knot spiral** with another 32 knots. Pass the 16 threads remaining in the centre of the work through a **large bead.** The thickness of the threads themselves should hold it in place. Fray out the ends and trim them so that they are all the same length.

Repeat from * to *, but leave a space of 5in. (12.5cm) below the spirals and then follow with 9 flat knots on each group. Trim and fray all the threads in the same way as above.

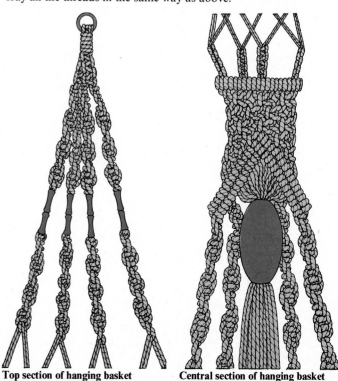

**Top section of hanging basket**          **Central section of hanging basket**

# Director's chair

To make up the patterns for a chair back and chair seat, you will need at least 340yds (312m) of strong macramé thread or string. When complete, the back measures about 18in. (46cm) by 12½in. (32cm) and the seat 18in. (46cm) by 15in. (38cm).

**Director's chair with macramé seat and back**

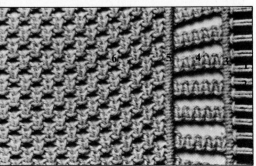

**Chair back**

1 Flat knot braids
2 Wooden strut
3 Horizontal cording
4 Flat knot braids
5 Horizontal cording
6 Alternated flat knots
7, 8 Diagonal cording
9 Alternated flat knots
10 Diagonal cording
11 Josephine knot

**Chair seat**

1 Mounting knots
2 Wooden strut
3 Horizontal cording
4 Flat knot braids
5 Horizontal cording
6 Alternated flat knots

## Making the chair back

Cut 24 lengths of thread, each 7yds (6.4m) long. Divide them into 6 groups of 4 threads each. Make a flat knot in the middle of each group and then 6 more on either side of the first, so that you have **flat knot braids** of 13 knots (1). These form the **loops** which go over the wooden struts (2). Cut 6 more lengths of thread, also 7yds (6.4m) long. Use one as a leader. Double it over and place the centre at the right-hand side, thus leaving 2 extra working threads at the left-hand edge. Double the flat knot loops over the wooden strut so that there are 8 threads hanging from each. Taking 1 thread at a time, alternately from the front and from the back of the loop, knot them over the leader in a row of **horizontal cording** from left to right. At the same time, add the other 5 lengths of thread. Double them over and secure them onto the leader with a reversed mounting knot, one in between each of the flat knot loops. At the end of the row, work back again from right to left over the same leader, so that you have 2 rows of horizontal cording (3) from which are suspended 60 working threads. Divide the threads into 15 groups of 4. Work 4 flat knots on each group of 4 threads (4). Using the left-hand thread as the leader, work 1 row of **horizontal cording** (5).

The **central section** is based on 29 rows of alternated flat knots (6). Begin by working 2 complete rows of **alternated flat knots.** On the third row, introduce 3 rows of **diagonal cording** (7) slanting down to the left and to the right of the centre. Leave about 1½in. (3.8cm) of the vertical threads unworked and then, with the 2 central threads as leaders, work the next 12 adjacent threads on either side over them in a row of **diagonal cording** (8). Form the central diamond with the threads that were used for the last row of diagonal cording. Work in the following sequence, completing one half first and then repeating the same rows in reverse: **alternated flat knots** (9); 1 row of **diagonal cording** centred to the left and right (10); and in the centre a **Josephine knot** over 4 threads (11). Work the other half of the chair back to correspond exactly with the first half.

To form the **final loops,** sort out 6 groups of 4 from the 60 working threads. This is done by numbering them off as follows: 2, 4, 6 and 8; 12, 14, 16 and 18; 22, 24, 26 and 28; 32, 34, 36 and 38; 42, 44, 46 and 48; 52, 54, 56 and 58. Work 13 **flat knots** over each of these groups. Take the completed loops around the wooden strut and secure them by knotting their loose ends to the ends still hanging from the last row of horizontal cording. Secure the final loose ends by trimming them off and, if necessary, gluing them down.

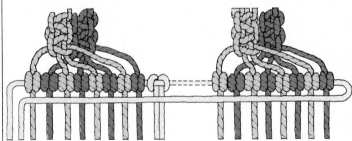

**Working the first row of horizontal cording**

## Making the chair seat

Cut 32 lengths of thread, each 4yds (3.7m) long. Double them over and mount them (1) onto the wooden strut (2) in the usual way. Cut 2 lengths of thread each 1yd (1m) long to use as separate leaders. Introduce one from the left and work 1 row of **horizontal cording** (3) over it. Divide the working threads into 16 groups of 4 and work 5 **flat knots** on each group (4). Introduce the other leader from the left and work another row of **horizontal cording** (5) over it. Omitting the outer 2 threads at each end, divide the working threads into 15 groups of 4 and work 31 rows of **alternated flat knots** (6). Work the other side of the chair seat in exactly the same way. Mount the final threads onto the wooden strut with a knot as shown.

**Tying to strut**

**Finish with reef knot**

# History of netting

Netting was one of the earliest crafts, originally being used by primitive man to trap animals and fish. The Romans used nets in the arena when the gladiators fought either one another or wild animals. Fishing nets just as we know them today were in use at least a thousand years before Christ, and, although the materials may have become more sophisticated over the centuries, the method of making them has not. Today's fishermen still make their nets by hand and carefully mend them when they become torn.

At some stage, various kinds of netting also came to be used for clothing. The ancient Egyptians decorated their tunics with it, often embroidering the loops with coloured silks or gold and silver thread to create an early form of lace. Examples of decorative netting were brought to Europe from the Orient by the returning Crusaders in the eleventh and twelfth centuries. Thereafter, a very fine form of embroidered netting developed between the thirteenth and the sixteenth centuries, particularly in England, France, Germany, Scandinavia and Italy. In England it was known by various names, such as *opus areneum* or *spiderwork*; in France it was called *filet* or *lacis*, where the meshes were embroidered in geometric patterns; in Germany and Scandinavia the embroidery of net became much more elaborate, with a vast variety of embroidery stitches, thread thicknesses and colours combining to make a dense, rich fabric; in Italy, too, many different embroidery stitches were used with netting that was often made in different-sized meshes to give added variety to the patterns. The *filet* crochet and Scandinavian *Hardanger* work done today must surely have their origins in basic netting techniques.

Since the age of the Victorians, however, netting has tended to return to its more practical form. Strong, basic meshes are now used unadorned for shopping bags, garden and sports nets or hammocks. And, of course, simple nets are still used by fishermen around the world.

## Tools and materials

The principal tool in all netting is the *netting needle*. This is used to hold the working yarn and to form the knots. Netting needles are usually long and pointed at one end where there is a large eye with a central prong. At the other end there is an indented heel over which the thread is wound. The needles vary in width, depending on the scale of the meshes, but the one you use should always be slightly smaller than the width of a half mesh so that it will pass through the loop easily and will not distort the work. Although the shape of individual netting needles may vary, they all work on exactly the same principle and are used in the same way.

The only other really essential tool in netting is the *mesh stick*. This is used to guarantee that all the meshes are worked over the same length of thread and that they are therefore made to a uniform size. Mesh sticks are rectangular in shape, and their width will equal half the finished mesh size. They must always be slightly wider than the needle being used. Various sizes are available, usually made in firm, smooth wood or plastic, but if you do not want to or cannot buy one then they can be easily improvised from a suitable piece of wood or stiff cardboard.

The *thread* with which you decide to work must be strong and firm, with a good twist to it so that it will withstand the tension during the knotting and will form clean knots. Plain string is ideal although many of the modern macramé twines are suitable and often make for a more interesting or attractive effect, especially if the netting is to be used for a decorative purpose.

# Setting up the work

## Securing the work

As with most crafts which involve the making of knots, netting requires a certain amount of tension while it is being worked. It is a good idea, therefore, to attach the work to a secure base. There are several methods of doing this.

A macramé board makes an ideal base for netting, since it is both firm enough for a good support and soft enough to take pins. Macramé T-pins are large and strong enough to hold the netting securely in place while it is being worked.

Alternatively, the netting can be anchored to a kitchen worktop or to a heavy table using a clamp. But this obviously means that you can only work in the one place.

For coarse, heavy work or large projects, a loop of cord slipped under the worker's foot gives a good base on which to anchor the foundation loop. Once the work has reached a certain size, the original loop will have to be shortened and perhaps eventually attached further up the netting.

## Loading the needle

The netting needle carries the string while the knots are being worked. It is important that the needle is not overloaded otherwise it will be too bulky to handle and may distort the netting. The string should be wound on to it very tightly.

### How to load the needle

**1** *Hold the netting needle in your left hand, so that the point is facing upwards. Position the end of the string against the solid part of the needle with your left thumb. Pass the string up the needle, around the prong and down the same side of the needle over the starting end of the string. This holds the end in place against the needle.*

*Then take the string under the bottom of the needle in the centre of the curve.*

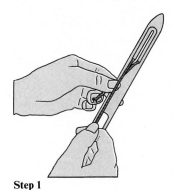
**Step 1**

**2** *Turn the needle over in your hand so that the other side of it is now facing you. Take the string up the face of the needle, pass it around the prong again, and bring it down the same side of the needle.*

*Then once again take the string under the bottom of the needle in the centre of the curve, ready for the needle to be turned over again.*

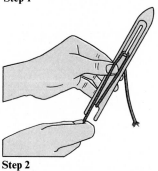
**Step 2**

**3** *Keep repeating the same movement, taking the string in loops around the prong, first on one side of the netting needle and then on the other. Continue building up layers of string on the needle in this way until it is full.*

**Step 3**

# Netting knot

This knot, also known as the *mesh knot* or the *sheet bend*, is the basic knot in all netting.

**The tightened netting knot**

*How to work*

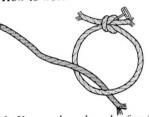

**1** Knot a short length of string into a loop and pin it to the working surface. This forms the foundation loop. Pass the working string up through this loop from back to front.

**2** Take the working string to the left, hold it there with your thumb, and then take it to the right over the top of the foundation loop.

**3** Take the working string behind the foundation loop and bring it out to the front through the loop on the left.

**4** Tighten the knot by pulling the working string down to the right, taking care that it seats itself correctly.

# Diamond mesh

Diamond mesh is the most frequently used mesh shape in netting. It is quick and easy to work and uses simple netting knots. The actual size of the mesh will vary according to the width of the mesh stick, and your choice of this may depend on the thickness of the string.

**Diamond mesh**

*How to work*

**1** Make a foundation loop and pin it to the working surface. The circumference of the loop should be at least double the width of the number of knots that you plan to make. Load the netting needle and attach the working string to the bottom of the foundation loop with a netting knot.

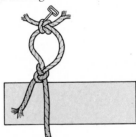

**2** Hold the mesh stick as shown and bring the working string down over the front.

**3** Take the string under and behind the mesh stick and pass it through the foundation loop from back to front. Pull the needle downwards so that the mesh stick is positioned close up against the lower edge of the netting knot again. With your thumb and first finger, hold the working string in place where it crosses the foundation loop.

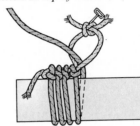

**4** Work a second netting knot as shown, and tighten it into position at top of mesh stick.

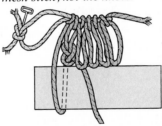

**5** Continue for as many meshes as are required – counting the loops around the mesh stick, not the knots.

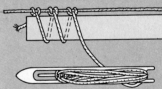

**6** For the 2nd row, remove the mesh stick and turn the work over so that the loop which was made last is now on the left-hand side. Place the mesh stick directly below the loops of the 1st row. Pass the working string around the mesh stick and, taking care to omit the descending thread, knot into the first loop as before.

Continue along the row, working a netting knot into each loop of the previous row. The 2nd and 1st row loops combine to form full meshes.

Work the 3rd and subsequent rows in the same way, turning the work over at the end of each row, and always moving from left to right.

# Alternative mounting method

This alternative method of mounting the netting is ideal for wide pieces of diamond mesh. It involves attaching the first row of loops on to a horizontal foundation cord instead of a foundation loop. Because the foundation cord is single thickness, once it is removed and the mounting knots opened out, the difference in the size of the meshes is kept to a minimum. Again, it can be left in place if desired.

**The working string attached to a horizontal foundation cord**

*How to work*

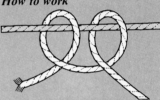

**1** Support a single foundation cord of the required length horizontally, by pinning it to the working surface at either end. Attach the working string at the left-hand end with a double half hitch as shown.

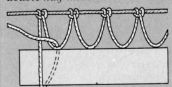

**2** Tighten the knot and place the mesh stick directly below it. Pass the string around the stick in the usual way and secure the mesh with another double half hitch.

**3** When the 1st row has been completed, turn the work over and work the 2nd and subsequent rows as before, using netting knots.

# Mesh variations

By altering the size of the meshes row by row, patterns can be built up in the netting. The simplest way of doing this is to use different sizes of mesh stick, but the two methods below show how to vary the mesh when just using one.

## Double loop
This is worked in the same way as diamond mesh, but the string is taken around the mesh stick twice (or more) to produce a double-sized mesh.

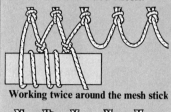

**Working twice around the mesh stick**

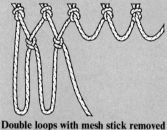

**Double loops with mesh stick removed**

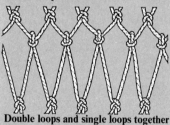

**Double loops and single loops together**

## Oblong loop
The netting knots are worked slightly above the mesh stick.

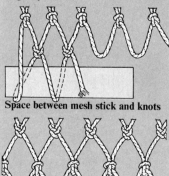

**Space between mesh stick and knots**

**Finished oblong loops in diamond mesh**

# Increasing or decreasing

Increasing or decreasing the number of loops in a row enables the work to be shaped. This is useful for more imaginative netting projects; and it is also essential for working square mesh netting.

## How to increase

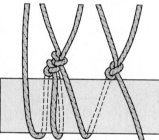

**1** Work 1 netting knot into the loop of the previous row as usual. Then take the string around the mesh stick again, pass it through the same loop, and make a 2nd netting knot close to the 1st one.

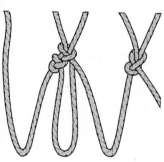

**2** This will produce 1 extra mesh in the row.

## How to decrease

Pass the working string through 2 loops of the previous row, draw them together, and secure them both with a single netting knot.

# Square mesh

This is made in the same way as diamond mesh, except that it is worked diagonally from one corner in a series of increases and decreases. The end result is a piece of netting with straight, reinforced edges, ideal for the garden, games or fishing.

*How to work*

**1** Make a foundation loop in the same way that you would for diamond mesh and pin it to the working surface. Leaving an end of about 6in. (15cm) free, attach the working string to the foundation loop with a netting knot. Work 2 loops in the usual way.

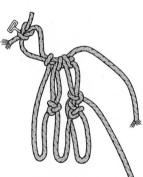

**2** For the 2nd row, turn the work over and mesh once into the 1st loop of the previous row and twice into the 2nd loop. This will produce 3 loops when the mesh stick is removed.

For the 3rd and subsequent rows, mesh once into each loop except the last. Mesh twice into the last loop so that each row increases by 1 loop.

Continue in this way, working 1 more row than the number of squares that you wish to have across the top of the net. For example, when you have completed 6 rows, the finished net will measure 5 squares across the top. At this point you will be ready to work the first corner.

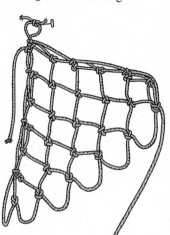

**3** To turn the corner, mesh once into each loop of the row except the last 2. Mesh the last 2 loops together as one.

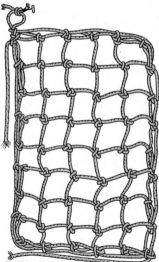

**4** Work subsequent rows so that you alternately increase and decrease by 1 loop at the end of each row. Continue until the net is 1 mesh longer than the number of squares required down the side.

To turn the last corner, decrease at the end of every row until only 2 loops remain. Work these 2 loops together with a netting knot without using the mesh stick.

Finally, remove the foundation loop and, using the 6in. (15cm) loose end, tie the first 2 loops together with a single netting knot.

# Working in the round

# String bag

This method is used for making either circular or closed-end tubular netting. It is worked from the centre outwards, and the first row forms a circular foundation round called a *grommet*. Subsequent rounds on flat netting will require an increase in the number of meshes.

*How to work*

1 *Unwind a length of string from the netting needle and make a slip knot in it as shown. The loose end must measure either twice the radius of the finished piece of circular netting or twice the depth of a tubular piece. The loop above the knot must be more than large enough to take the number of netting knots planned for the 1st round.*

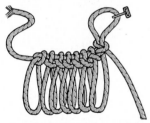

2 *Pin the loop to the working surface so that the loose end is at the left. Work netting knots on to the loop in the usual way. Make 1 mesh less than required for the 1st round.*

3 *After completing the last mesh, take the loose end over the top of the work and pass it through what is left of the original loop. Hold the loose end just before the slip knot, at arrow, and pull it to the left so that the foundation loop tightens over it at the other end of the work.*

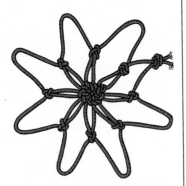

**Circular netting**

4 *Now hold the loose end where it comes out of the tightened loop and pull it further, so that it tightens over the top of the knots and makes the loops fan out into a circle. This forms the grommet. Secure it by tying the loose end and the working string in a reef knot (see page 169) close to the netting knots in the centre of the grommet.*

5 *For a circular piece, pin the loops evenly in position on the working surface.*

*For a tubular piece, suspend the grommet over a toggle made from a button.*

*In both cases, make the final loop by tying the loose end and the working string in an overhand knot level with the outer edges of the other meshes.*

*Continue working in rounds, increasing where necessary. At the end of each round, make the final loop by knotting together the loose end and the working thread as before.*

Several different objects can be made from netting worked in the round, but one of the easiest is the simple string bag. As with all circular and tubular netting, it is worked from the centre outwards. The bottom of the bag, which is formed from the foundation round, is worked first and measures eight meshes in circumference. The handles are worked last.

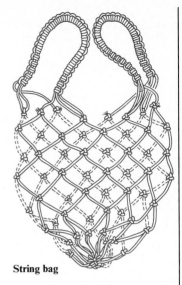

**String bag**

*Making the handles*

Each handle is worked across four meshes. Numbering 1 to 4 from the left, secure the end of the working string with a netting knot to the base of mesh 2. Form it into a loop the size of the required handle and knot to mesh 3. Take the string back around the loop, keeping it even with the first, and knot to mesh 1. Use double half hitches as shown and begin knotting over the double loop, leaving a space of about half a mesh before working the first knot.

Continue in double half hitches all around the handle, ending level with the first knot. Secure with a netting knot into mesh 4.

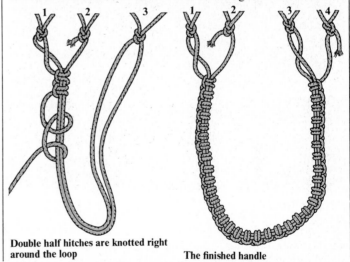

**Double half hitches are knotted right around the loop**

**The finished handle**

## Joining in new working string

As there is a limit to how much working string the netting needle can hold, it is inevitable that a new length of string will have to be joined in at some stage during the work.

*How to join*
*Finish off the old length of working string with a netting knot in the usual way. Cut off a new length and load it on to the netting needle. With the new string, work another netting knot into the same mesh, on top of the netting knot made with the old end.*

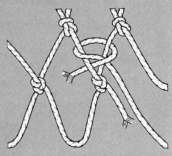

# Making a hammock

This hammock is easy and inexpensive to make. Apart from a knowledge of the basic techniques of netting and knotting, it requires only some simple carpentry.

**Measurements**

The central section of netting measures about 6ft 5in. (2m) by 2ft 9in. (84cm). The distance from the spreader to the outer edge of the ring is about 18in. (46cm).

**Materials**

You will need the following: 160yds (146.4m) of 3mm string; 24ft (7.3m) of 6mm cord; 12ft (3.7m) of 10mm rope; a 2½in. (6.5cm) mesh stick; a large netting needle; 2 pieces of wood, each measuring 3ft by 1½in. by ¾in. (91.5cm by 4cm by 2cm); 2 metal or wooden rings, each 3½in. (9cm) in diameter.

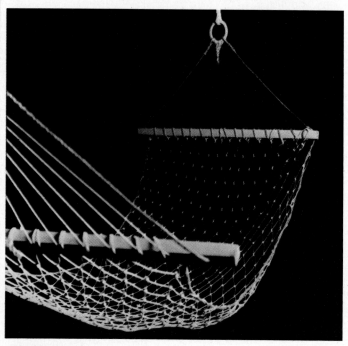

**The finished hammock**

## The central netting

Cut a length of about 20in. (51cm) of 3mm string, make a foundation loop and attach it to a secure base. Load the netting needle with 3mm string. Attach the string to the foundation loop with a netting knot and continue meshing until there are 16 loops. Continue for 32 rows (16 full meshes).

**Finishing off**

Fold double a 60ft (18.3m) length of string and load it onto the netting needle as shown. Join in the string with a netting knot and mesh one row in double string. Then remove the foundation loop and work one row in double string at the other end of the piece of netting in the same way.

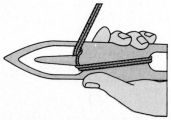

**Loading needle with double string**

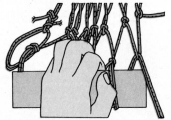

**Working final row in double string**

## Rings

These are the rings to which the clews, the side cords and the ropes are attached. They are made by completely covering two 3½in. (9cm) diameter wooden or metal rings with string.

### How to cover the rings

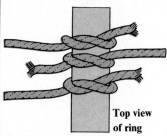

**Top view of ring**

**1** Cut 3 lengths of string, each 8ft (2.4m) long. Working away from yourself, tie the 3 threads on to the ring as shown – the first working thread to the left, the second to the right, and the third to the left.

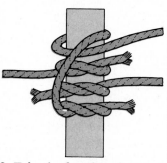

**2** Take the first thread up to the right across the top of the other two. Pass the end through the ring from right to left, so that a small loop is formed to the right of the ring. Take the end back over the top of the ring and through the loop. Pull tight.

**5** When the ring is completely covered, end with 2 threads to the right and 1 thread to the left. Undo the original knots which tied the string to the ring. Take the end nearest to you on the right-hand side and tie it, using a reef knot, to the first thread so that it lies as close to the ring as possible.

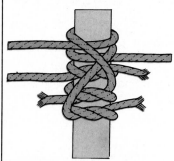

**3** Take the second thread up to the left across the top of the other two. Make another half hitch around the ring in the opposite direction from the previous one and tighten.

**4** Work the third thread in the same way as the first. Continue around the ring in this coxcombing pattern, always keeping 2 threads to one side and 1 to the other alternately. The thread nearest to you of a pair is worked next.

**6** Tie the left-hand end to the beginning of the second thread. Then tie the last 2 ends together. Trim the ends and glue for extra strength.

## Clews

The triangular-patterned set of strings joining the rings to the spreaders are called *clews*.

### How to make the clews

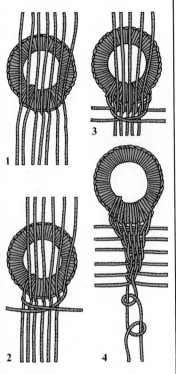

**1** Cut 7 pieces of string, each 7ft (2.2m) long. Double them over and set them on to the ring with reversed mounting knots so they cover the join on the coxcombing. On each pair of threads, position one upwards and one downwards.

**2** Lay the downward thread of the right-hand pair across all the other downward threads and the upward thread of the left-hand pair over it.

**3** On each pair, exchange the upward thread with the downward thread so that they all change places. Now lay the right-hand down thread across all the other down threads and the left-hand up thread over it.

**4** Exchange the up threads with the down threads again. Continue in this way until there are 6 horizontal threads on each side and 2 hanging down vertically. Secure the 2 vertical threads in a single knotted chain, using the left-hand thread as the first core.

## Spreaders

Two pieces of wood are used to spread out the meshes of the netting and to keep them in place. The strings of the clews are then threaded through holes in the wooden strip.

### How to work

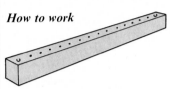

**1** Drill 14 equally-spaced, counter-sunk holes in each piece of wood, the first and last of which are 4in. (10cm) from the ends. Each hole must be just large enough to take one piece of 3mm string. About 1½in. (4cm) from each end drill another hole, this time ½in. (1.5cm) in diameter.

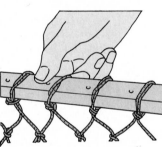

**2** Slide the pieces of wood through the 16 double-string meshes at each end of the central netting. Position the meshes so that they fall between the holes as shown.

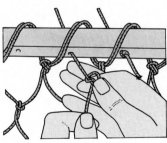

**3** To attach the clews to the spreaders, position the ring centrally to the spreader so that the bottom of the triangular pattern is about 12in. (30.5cm) from the wood. Pass each of the clew threads through a hole in the spreader and secure them by tying overhand knots as shown.

## Side cords

The sides of the hammock are supported by two pieces of 6mm cord, each measuring 12ft (3.7m) in length. They stretch between the two rings, passing through the large holes in the spreaders and along the sides of the netting. At one end of the hammock the cords are secured to the ring with an eye splice. At the other end the strands of the cord are prevented from fraying with a back splice, and the cords are tied to the ring with a double half hitch. This can then be altered if you need to adjust the sag in the hammock.

### How to make an eye splice

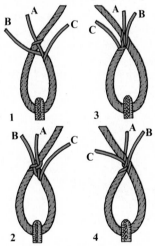

**1** Unravel about 2½in. (6.5cm) of the strands, make a loop and splice them back along the cord. Tuck A from right to left under nearest strand of the cord.

**2** Tuck B from right to left under the next strand of the cord in the same way.

**3** Turn the loop over.

**4** Then tuck strand C from right to left under the unoccupied strand of the cord. Turn the loop over again and continue until the strands are spliced into the cord.

**The completed eye splice**

## How to thread the side cords

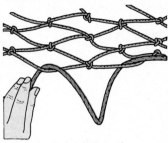

*When both cords have been secured to one ring with an eye splice, pass them through the large holes in the spreader and thread through each mesh at the side of the netting as shown. Secure the cords to the other ring with double half hitches and back splice the ends as described below.*

### How to make a back splice

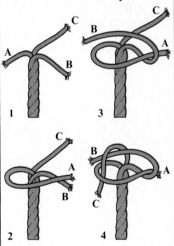

**1** Unravel about 3½in. (9cm) of the strands and work a crown knot as follows. Separate the 3 strands.

**2** Loop strand A from left to right over strand B as shown.

**3** Loop strand B around strand A then over strand C.

**4** Loop strand C around strand B and down through the loop formed by A. Then splice the ends back along the cord as before. For more details on splicing, see page 170.

## Ropes

Cut two lengths of rope, each 6ft (1.8m) long. Work a back splice on one end of each piece of rope and join the other ends to the rings with an eye splice.

# History of tatting

As with many traditional needlecrafts, the origins of tatting are obscure. It certainly evolved from knotting, which originated in the East, and was extremely popular for several hundreds of years but particularly in the seventeenth century.

Knotting was a technique whereby a length of thread was tied in a series of decorative knots and then couched to a fabric background to outline embroidery. Threads of varying thicknesses were used and it was done with the aid of either a needle or a shuttle. These shuttles were much larger than their modern counterparts so that quite thick threads could be used.

Towards the end of the eighteenth century this pastime was dying out but, by the mid-nineteenth century, tatting as we know it today was beginning to evolve. This involved using the knots to create patterns and trimmings for use without embroidery.

Even more obscure than the history of the technique is the origin of the name "tatting". There are many theories. It could come from the English "tatters" as this intricate form of lace is made up of bits and pieces of rings, ovals, chains, picots and scallops. It could be from the French *tater*, to feel or handle. Or the English "tattle" as the movement of the shuttle is similar to a gossiping tongue. And, indeed, the modern French word for either tatting or knotting is *frivolité*.

What is in no doubt is that the result is an attractive form of lace which can be used for edgings or worked into a full fabric. Modern designers are developing the craft further, taking it away from its traditional look of fine lace and, by returning to the use of larger shuttles, are making it into more of an art form.

**An eighteenth-century French knotting shuttle**

## Basic equipment

Tatting equipment is minimal and so can easily be carried around and used in your spare time. You will need the following basic equipment:

**Shuttle**
This comprises two flat, boat-shaped pieces separated by a central spool around which the thread is wound. Never fill the shuttle so full that the thread projects beyond the sides.

**Thread**
A suitable thread which has a good twist is essential so that it is firm and will not stretch. Mercerized cotton is ideal.

**Crochet hook**
A fine crochet hook is used to make joins.

**Scissors and tape measure**
You will also need scissors and sometimes a tape measure.

**A modern tatting shuttle**

# Tatting technique

Although a completed piece of tatting can look extremely complex, it is really only made up of one knot; it is the different ways in which a number of these knots can be combined which alter the design. Despite being a knot, it is generally called a stitch, known as *double stitch*, and is worked in two stages.

### Single stitch

Single stitch is the first stage of the double stitch. Step 5, when the knot is transferred, is the key movement in making the stitch.

*How to make the single stitch*

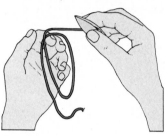
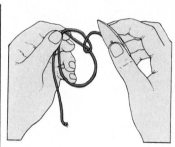

**1** *With the shuttle in the right hand, hold the thread towards its end between the thumb and forefinger of the left hand. Wind it over the top of the left hand, underneath and back between the thumb and forefinger to form a loop.*

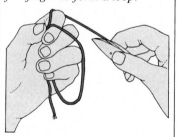

**2** *Place the left thumb over the crossing point of the threads. This loop is called the* ring thread.

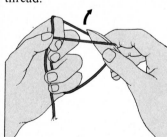

**3** *Form the shuttle thread into a loop like the letter "C" over the top of the left hand and pass the shuttle from right to left under the ring thread and out between it and the loop. Unwind the shuttle as more thread is required.*

**4** *The shuttle thread is now looped around the ring thread.*

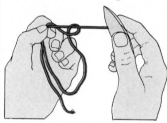

**5** *Still holding the threads firmly with the left hand and keeping the ring thread slack, pull the shuttle thread taut to the right. The knot will transfer so that the ring thread is now looped around the shuttle thread.*

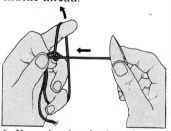

**6** *Keep the shuttle thread taut and still. Raise the middle finger of the left hand to slide the knot close to the left thumb and forefinger. This completes the single stitch. The shuttle thread can run freely through the stitch so that the ring thread can be made larger or smaller as required. Always hold the last stitch that has been made with the left hand.*

## Double stitch

The second stage of the knot, which is worked in the opposite direction to the first, completes the double stitch.

### How to make the double stitch

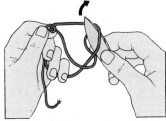

**1** First make a single stitch. Pass the shuttle thread under the ring as shown and through from back to front.

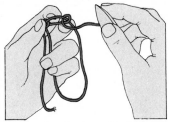

**2** The shuttle thread is looped around the ring thread.

**3** Still holding the single stitch with the left hand and with the ring loose, pull the shuttle thread taut to the right. This transfers the knot.

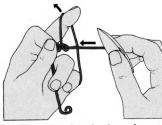

**4** Keep the shuttle thread taut and still. Raise the left-hand middle finger to slide the knot close to the previous one. This completes the double stitch.

# The picot

The picot is a small loop between double stitches which is used both as decoration and as a means of joining motifs. Pattern instructions will specify the number of double stitches to work before a picot but for the purposes of learning, start with two double stitches.

### How to make the picot

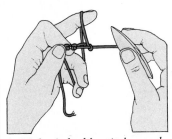

**1** Make 2 double stitches and then make the first stage of a third double stitch but leave a space of at least $\frac{1}{4}$in. (6mm) between it and the previous stitch. The size of the space determines the size of the picot loop that will be formed.

**2** Complete the second stage of the double stitch, sliding it up close to the first stage.

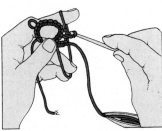

**3** Slide the completed double stitch close up to the previous one so that the length of thread between them loops up into a picot. Remember that the picot is formed with the following double stitch so that if a pattern reads "1 picot, 4ds", once the picot is drawn up there will only be 3 more double stitches to do.

# Joining

Individual motifs are always joined at a picot. Some tatting shuttles are made with a long point which can be used to pick up and draw the thread through the picot loops. A fine crochet hook can be used instead if the shuttle has no point, and a crochet hook is sometimes provided with the shuttle.

### How to make the joins

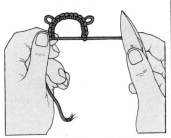

**1** Make a scallop of 4 double stitches, 1 picot, 8 double stitches, 1 picot and 4 double stitches by pulling the shuttle thread up until the stitches have formed a semi-circle.

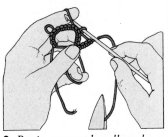

**2** Begin a second scallop close up to the base of the first one, making 4 double stitches.
Insert the crochet hook or point of the shuttle from front to back through the last picot of the previous scallop and catch the ring thread of the new scallop ready to draw it through the picot.

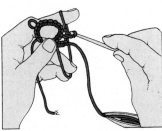

**3** Pull the thread through and draw it out into a loop large enough for the tatting shuttle to pass through. This will pull the ring thread tighter.

**4** Pass the shuttle through this loop from back to front.

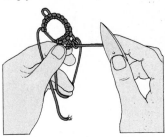

**5** Draw the shuttle thread through and tighten the loop around it by pulling the ring thread back. This takes the place of the first stage of the following double stitch.

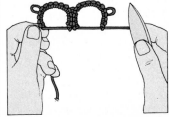

**6** Work the second stage of the double stitch in the usual way. This secures the join. Complete the scallop by making 7 more double stitches, 1 picot, 4 double stitches and drawing them into a semi-circle. Once again, remember that by making the join you are also completing the first double stitch to follow it. A pattern for the above scallop would read "... join to previous scallop, 8ds", but once the join is completed, so also is the first of the 8 double stitches and only 7 more remain to be done.

# Working with a ball and shuttle

A straight length of tatting (known as a *chain*) needs two threads. The second thread can be taken directly from the ball or introduced on a second shuttle but there are occasions when two shuttles must be used (see right). As most tatting patterns require a combination of chains and rings, the instructions below illustrate how to carry this out. When the technique uses two threads, a second colour can be used if desired.

### How to make a chain with two threads

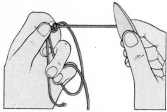 

**1** *Tie the 2 ends together and hold the knot under the left thumb. Wind the ball thread over the top of the left hand and around the little finger, leaving the ball hanging loose.*

**2** *With the loop over the hand taking the place of the ring thread in the one thread technique, make several doubl stitches to form a chain.*

### Joining the chain to rings or scallops

When the chains are used with rings or scallops the work has to be turned where the two join. This is known as *reversing*.

### How to combine motifs by reversing

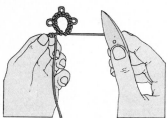 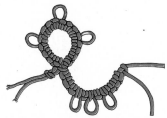

**1** *Knot the 2 threads together as before and ignore the ball thread. Wind shuttle thread around the left hand in the usual way to make a ring, and make (4 double stitches, 1 picot) 3 times, 4 double stitches, draw into a ring.*

**3** *Make a chain of 4 double stitches, (1 picot, 2 double stitches) twice, 1 picot, 4 double stitches. Release shuttle thread and reverse work again so that the ring is uppermost and newly made chain beneath.*

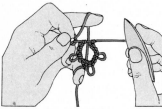 

**2** *Turn the ring downwards, and hold the reversed ring between the thumb and forefinger of the left hand. Wind the ball thread over the left hand as in step 1.*

**4** *To make a second ring as before but joining at the side picot of first ring, work 4 double stitches, join to first ring, 4 double stitches, 1 picot, 4 double stitches, 1 picot, 4 double stitches.*

# Working with two shuttles

When the second thread is used to form the knots, two shuttles must be used because the ball thread would be too big to pass through the ring thread. When chains of different colours are being worked, two shuttles are essential. When working with two shuttles for the first time, particularly if the threads are both of the same colour, it helps to use shuttles of contrasting colours or to make an identifying mark on one of them.

### How to use two shuttles

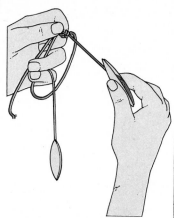 

**3** *Change the shuttles over and work 12 double stitches, 1 picot, 2 double stitches. Reverse work.*

**1** *Tie the 2 threads together as before and wind the thread from the second shuttle over the left hand as for the ball thread.*

**4** *Change shuttles and work 2 double stitches, join to first picot worked, 12 double stitches, 1 picot, 2 double stitches. Reverse the work.*

**2** *Knotting with the main shuttle around the second shuttle thread, make 2 double stitches, 1 picot, 2 double stitches. Then reverse the work.*

**5** *Change shuttles and work 2 double stitches, join to picot of adjacent scallop, 12 double stitches, 1 picot, 2 double stitches.*

## Attaching tatting to fabric

Use a very fine needle and thread to stitch the tatting onto the fabric. If it is to be used as an edging, stitch a fine, rolled hem on to the fabric first.

**How to work**
Slip stitch the tatted edging on to the right side of the hemmed fabric.

# Using single and double stitches

It is possible to make Josephine knots and scallops using the single stitch, with the knots either widely spaced or close together. The detached scallops and detached rings are made with double stitches and form a more solid edging.

### How to make Josephine knots

*Make 4 single stitches. Slip the ring thread off the left hand and pull the shuttle thread, easing the stitches into a ring. For a larger version work in the same way with 10 single stitches.*

### How to make Josephine scallops

*Work as for the Josephine knot but leave a short length of ring thread, so that the knots form a semi-circle.*

### How to make detached scallops

*Work 12 double stitches. Pull the shuttle thread until the knots form a semi-circle. Work the next 12 double stitches so that the two scallops touch.*

### How to make detached rings

*Work 16 double stitches and pull the shuttle thread tight to form a circle. Work the next 16 stitches close to the previous group.*

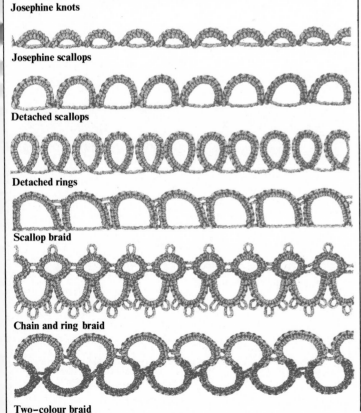

**Josephine knots**

**Josephine scallops**

**Detached scallops**

**Detached rings**

**Scallop braid**

**Chain and ring braid**

**Two–colour braid**

# Joining with picots

More interesting effects can be achieved by adding picots to scallops and rings, and using them for joins. The scallop braid is made with one thread, and the chain and ring braid and the two-colour braid with two threads. When working the chain and ring braid, you can use a ball and shuttle but two shuttles must be used for the two-colour braid.

### How to make a scallop braid

*To make the first scallop work 4ds, lp, 8ds, lp, 4ds, draw into a semi-circle. To make the second and subsequent scallops, work 4ds, join to second p of previous scallop, 8ds, lp, 4ds, draw into a semi-circle.*

### How to make a chain and ring braid

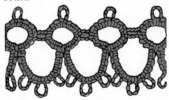

*Make a r of (4ds, lp) 3 times, 4ds. Rw. \*Make a ch of 4ds, lp, 2ds, lp, 2ds, lp, 4ds. Rw, make another r of 4ds, join to last p of previous r, 4ds, lp, 4ds, lp, 4ds. Repeat from \*.*

### How to make a two-colour braid

*Using the right hand of two shuttles, 2ds, lp, 2ds. Rw, change shuttles. 12ds, lp, 2ds. Rw, change shuttles. 2ds, join to first p worked, 12ds, lp, 2ds. Rw, change shuttles. \*2ds, join to p of adjacent scallop, 12ds, lp, 2ds. Rw, change shuttles. Repeat from \**

# Joining in new threads

### Joining with a weaver's knot
To make a weaver's knot, follow steps 1 to 4 below, pulling the knot taut to finish.

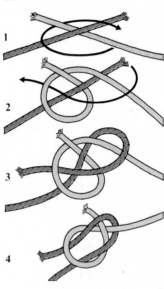

### Joining with a reef knot
To make a reef knot, follow steps 1 and 2 below.

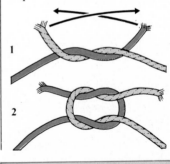

### Abbreviations
Tatting instructions have their own abbreviations. Those normally used are given below.

| | |
|---|---|
| **ch** | chain |
| **cl** | close |
| **ds** | double stitch |
| **lp** | long picot |
| **lr** | large ring |
| **p** | picot |
| **r** | ring |
| **rw** | reverse work |
| **sep** | separated |
| **sh** | shuttle |
| **sp** | space |
| **sr** | small ring |
| **ss** | single stitch |

# *Tatted edgings*

Tatting is particularly suitable for making border strips which can be used to edge collars and cuffs, for example, or as a decorative finish to tablecloths, pillowcases and handkerchiefs. When planning a tatted edge, make sure it is not too wide nor the yarn too coarse or the result will look clumsy and unbalanced.

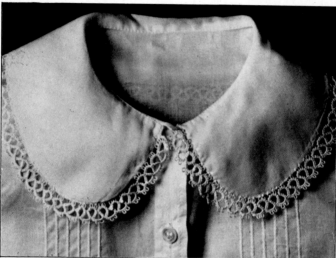

Collar with braided edging

## Brocade edging

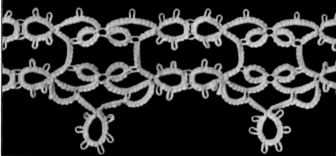

### First motif

Tie ball and shuttle threads together.
Make a r of 2ds, 6p sep by 3ds, 2ds, cl, rw.
Ch of 4ds, 2p sep by 6ds, 4ds, rw.
R of 2ds, 6p sep by 3ds, 2ds, cl.
Ch of 6ds, 1p, 6ds, rw. Sr of 6ds, join to first p of adjacent ch, 6ds, cl.
Sr of 6ds, 1p, 6ds, cl, rw.
Ch of 6ds, 1p, 6ds.
R as first r, rw.
Ch of 4ds, join to p of previous sr, 6ds, 1p, 4ds, rw.
R as 2nd r.
Ch of 6ds, 1p, 6ds, rw.
Sr of 6ds, join to free p of adjacent ch, 6ds, cl.
Sr of 6ds, join to free p of first ch worked, 6ds, cl. rw.
Ch of 6ds, 1p, 6ds, join by shuttle thread to base of first r of motif, rw.
Ch of 10ds, join by shuttle thread to p of previous ch.

Ch of 6ds.
R of 2ds, 6p sep by 3ds, 2ds, cl.
Ch of 6ds, join by shuttle thread to p of next ch.
Ch of 10ds, join by shuttle thread to base of next r. Finish off.

### Second motif

Tie ball and shuttle threads together.
R of 2ds, 2p sep by 3ds, 3ds, join to corresponding p on 4th r worked on previous motif, 3ds, join to next p, 3ds, 2p sep by 3ds, 2ds, cl, rw.
Ch of 4ds, 2p sep by 6ds, 4ds, rw.
R of 2ds, 2p sep by 3ds, 3ds, join to corresponding p on 3rd r worked on previous motif, 3ds, join to next p, 3ds, 2p sep by 3ds, 2ds, cl.
Complete as for first motif.

Repeat motifs for length required, joining each as second motif was joined to first.

## Eyelet edging

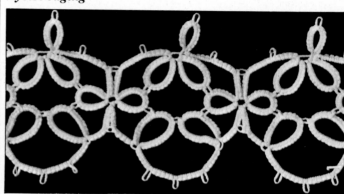

Tie ball and shuttle threads together.
**Row 1** R of 8ds, 2p sep by 4ds, 8ds, cl, rw.
Ch of 6ds, 2p sep by 6ds, 6ds.
*R of 8ds, 1p, 8ds, cl, rw.
R of 12ds, join to first p of adjacent r, 12ds, cl.
R of 12ds, 1p, 12ds, cl, rw.
Ch of 6ds, 2p sep by 6ds, 6ds, rw.
R of 8ds, join to p of previous r, 4ds, 1p, 8ds, cl.
R of 8ds, 2p sep by 4ds, 8ds, cl, rw.
Ch of 6ds, join to first p of adjacent ch, 6ds, 1p, 6ds.
Repeat from * for length required, omitting r and ch at end of last repeat, rw.

**Row 2** Ch of 5ds, 1p, 5ds, rw.
*R of 10ds, join to free p of previous r, 6ds, 1p, 14ds, cl, rw.
Ch of 6ds, 3p sep by 6ds, 6ds.
R of 14ds, join to free p of previous r, 6ds, join to next free p on first row, 10ds, cl, rw.
Ch of 5ds, 1p, 5ds, join by shuttle thread to base of next 2rs on first row.
Ch of 5ds, join to adjacent p, 5ds, rw.
Repeat from * to end, omitting ch at end of last repeat and joining last ch to base of first r worked. Finish off.

## Pointed edging

**Row 1** Tie ball and shuttle threads together. R of 8ds, 1p, 8ds, cl, rw. Ch of 6ds, p, 6ds, 3ps sep by 1ds, p, 6ds, rw. *R of 8ds, join to p on previous r, 8ds, cl. R of 8ds, 1p, 8ds, cl, rw. Ch of 6ds, join by ball thread to last p on previous ch, 6ds, 3ps sep by 1ds, p, 6ds, rw, repeat from * 17 times more or length required, ending with r of 8ds, join to p on previous r, 8ds, cl. Tie ends, cut and oversew neatly on wrong side.

**Row 2** Tie ball and shuttle threads together, attach to base of first r on previous row. *Ch of 10ds, 1p, 10ds, join by shuttle thread to base of next 2 rs, repeat from * joining last ch to base of last r on previous row. Tie ends, cut and oversew neatly on wrong side.

**Row 3** Tie ball and shuttle threads together. Attach ball thread to p on first ch on previous row. Ch of 6ds. R of 4ds, 3ps sep by 4ds, 4ds, cl. *R of 4ds, join to last p of previous r, 2ds, 6ps sep by 2ds, 4ds, cl. R of 4ds, join to last p on previous r, 4ds, 2ps sep by 4ds, 4ds, cl. Ch of 6ds, 1p, 6ds, join by shuttle thread to next p, **ch of 6ds, 1p, 6ds. R of 4ds, 1p, 4ds, join to centre p on previous r, 4ds, 1p, 4ds, cl, repeat from * ending last repeat at **. Tie ends, cut and oversew neatly on wrong side.

## Stepped edging

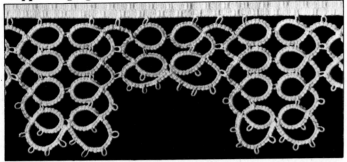

Tie ball and shuttle threads together. R of 4ds. 3ps sep by 8ds,
4ds, cl, rw. (ch of 4ds, 1p, 4ds, rw.
R of 4ds, join to last p of previous
r, 8ds, 2ps sep by 8ds, 4ds, cl, rw)
three times.
*Ch of 4ds, 4ps sep by 4ds, 4ds,
join by shuttle thread to centre p
of previous r, ch of 4ds, 4ps sep
by 4ds, 4ds, rw. R of 4ds, 1p, 8ds,
join to centre p of previous r,
8ds, 1p, 4ds, cl, rw, (ch of 4ds, 1p,
4ds, rw. R of ds, join to last p of
previous r, 8ds, join to free p of
adjacent r, 8ds, 1p, 4ds, cl, rw)
twice. Ch of 4ds, 1p, 4ds, rw. R of
4ds, join to last p of previous r,
8ds, join to free p of adjacent r,
8ds, 1p, 4ds, cl.** Ch of 4ds, 1p,
4ds. R of 4ds, 3ps sep by 8ds, 4ds,
cl, rw. Ch of 4ds, join to p of adjacent ch, 4ds, rw. R of 4ds, join
to last p of previous r, 8ds, 2ps

sep by 8ds, 4ds, cl, rw. Ch of 4ds,
join to p of adjacent ch, 4ds, 3ps
sep by 4ds, 4ds, join by shuttle
thread to centre p of previous r,
ch of 4ds, 4ps sep by 4ds, 4ds,
rw. R of 4ds, 1p, 8ds, join to
centre p of previous r, 8ds, 1p, 4ds,
cl, rw. Ch of 4ds, 1p, 4ds, rw. R of
4ds, join to last p of previous r,
8ds, join to free p of adjacent r,
8ds, 1p, 4ds, cl. Ch of 4ds, 1p, 4ds.
R of 4ds, 3ps sep by 8ds, 4ds, 4ds,
cl, rw, (ch of 4ds, join to next p of
adjacent ch, 4ds, rw. R of 4ds,
join to last p of previous r, 8ds,
2ps sep by 8ds, 4ds, cl, rw) twice.
Ch of 4ds, 1p, 4ds, rw. R of 4ds,
join to last p of previous r, 8ds,
2ps sep by 8ds, 4ds, cl, rw, repeat
from * 4 times more, or length
required, ending last repeat at **.
Tie ends, cut and oversew neatly
on wrong side.

## Looped edging

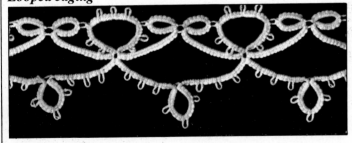

Tie ball and shuttle threads to-
gether.
**Row 1** Lr of 4ds, 9p sep by 4ds,
4ds, cl, rw.
*Ch of 18ds, rw.
R of 8ds, join to 3rd p of previous
r, 8ds, cl.
R of 8ds, 1p, 8ds, cl, rw.
Ch of 18ds, rw.
Lr of 4ds, 2p sep by 4ds, 4ds, join
to p of previous r, 4ds, 6p sep by

4ds, 4ds, cl, rw.
Repeat from * for length required, omitting rw at end of last
repeat.
**Row 2** *Ch of 4ds, 3p sep by 4ds,
4ds.
R of 5ds, 3p sep by 5ds, 5ds, cl.
Ch as before, join by shuttle
thread to base of next lr on first
row.
Repeat from * to end. Finish off.

## Braided edging

*The tatted edging pattern below makes a very suitable narrow
border for cuffs or collars, as shown on the collar of the child's
blouse opposite.*

Tie ball and shuttle threads together.
R of 4ds, 4p sep by 2ds, 4ds, cl,
rw.
Ch of 2ds, 3p sep by 2ds, 4ds,
join by shuttle thread to last p of
r, rw.
*Ch of 2ds, 3p sep by 2ds, 4ds,

join by shuttle thread to last p of
previous ch, rw.
Repeat from * for length required.
Finish off.

# Tatted insertions

If tatting is to be used as an insertion, a mirror image design,
like the one shown below, should be used. Tatted insertions are
often used on fine clothes such as lingerie or baby wear.

## Fleur-de-lys insertion

Join ball and shuttle threads.
**Row 1** *R of 6ds, 1p, 6ds, close,
repeat from * twice more, rw.
Ch of (6ds, 1p) twice, 3ds, rw.
**R of 3ds, 1p, 3ds, join to p of
previous r, (3ds, 1p) 3 times, 3ds,
close, rw.
Ch of 3ds, (1p, 6ds) twice, rw.
R of 6ds, join to 4th p of previous
r, 6ds, close, *r of 6ds, 1p, 6ds,
close, repeat from * once more,
rw.***

Ch of 6ds, join to p on previous
ch, 6ds, 1p, 3ds, rw.
Rep from ** for length required
but ending at ***.
**Row 2** Ch of 6ds, join to p of
previous ch, 1p, 6ds, rw.
Repeat pattern from beginning
but joining ch to corresponding p
each time and ending with ch of
6ds, join to p of previous ch,
join to first p of first ch, 6ds.

## Attaching a tatted insertion

If the tatting is to be inserted
between two pieces of fabric,
the raw edges of the fabric
must be hemmed first.
   Turn under the raw edges of
the seam ¼in. (6mm) to the
wrong side, and then turn
under ¼in. (6mm) again. Press,
pin and stitch close to the
seam line. Then attach the
tatted strip on the right side
of the fabric using small
overcast stitches.

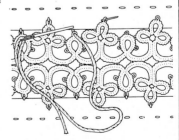

**Stitching the tatted insertion**

# Tatted tablecloth project

Tatting can be used to form motifs which can be joined together to make a lace-like fabric. Tablemats, tablecloths and dressing table sets, for example, can be made in this way. The tablecloth illustrated below is made from the hexagonal motif pattern shown right and the motifs are joined as they are worked. The motif patterns on the opposite page can be used instead of the hexagonal motifs to make a similar cloth, or they can be used separately as coasters. Alternatively, small groups of any of the motifs can be joined together to make tablemats or doilies.

## Hexagonal tablecloth

**Materials** 6 × 2oz (50g) medium heavy crochet cotton; tatting shuttle.
**Measurements** Motif, approx. 3in. (7.4cm) across; cloth, at widest point, approx. 24in. (61cm).

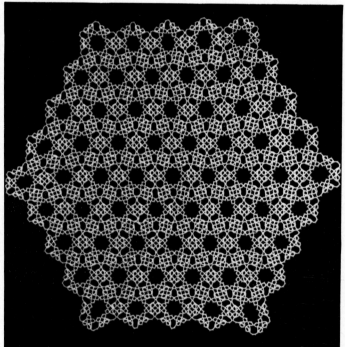

**The finished cloth**

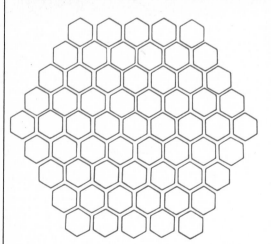

**Hexagonal cloth chart**
The chart shows the number of motifs required to make the cloth illustrated above and the position for joining them.

## Hexagonal motif

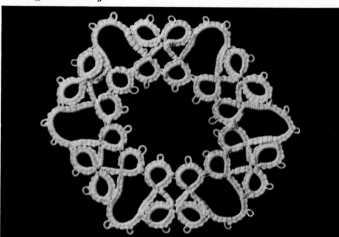

### First motif

Join ball and shuttle threads.
R of (4ds, 1p) 3 times, 4ds, close, rw.
Long ch of 6ds, 1p, (4ds, 1p) 3 times, 6ds, rw.
*Ring A of 4ds, join to last p of previous r, (4ds, 1p) twice, 4ds, close, rw.
Ch of 4ds.
Ring B of 8ds, join to last p of long ch, 4ds, 1p, 4ds, close.
Ring C of (4ds, 1p) twice, 8ds, close.
Ch of 4ds, rw.
R of 4ds, join to last p of ring A, (4ds, 1p) twice, 4ds, close, rw.

Long ch of 6ds, join to last p of ring C, (4ds, 1p) 3 times, 6ds, rw.**
Repeat from * to ** 4 times more.
R of 4ds, join to last p of previous r, 4ds, 1p, 4ds, join to first p of first r made at beginning of motif, 4ds, close, rw.
Ch of 4ds.
Work ring B as before.
Join ring C to the first ch at beginning of motif: rw, r of 8ds, join to first p of long ch, 4ds, 1p, 4ds, close.
Ch of 4ds.
Cut and tie ends to beginning of motif.

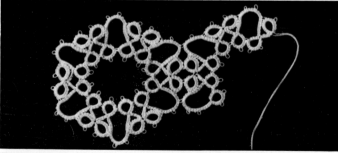

### Second motif

Join ball and shuttle threads.
R of (4ds, 1p) 3 times, 4ds, close, rw.
Long ch of 6ds, (1p, 4ds) twice, join to corresponding p on any long ch of first motif, 4ds, 1p, 6ds, rw.
Ring A of 4ds, join to last p of previous r, (4ds, 1p) twice, 4ds, close, rw.
Ch of 4ds.
Ring B of 8ds, join to last p of previous long ch, 4ds, join to corresponding p of ring C on first motif, 4ds, close.
Ring C of 4ds, join to corresponding p of ring B on first motif, 4ds, 1p, 8ds, close.

Ch of 4ds, rw.
R of 4ds, join to last p of ring A, (4ds, 1p) twice, 4ds, close, rw.
Long ch of 6ds, join to last p of ring C, 4ds, join to corresponding p on long ch of first motif, (4ds, 1p) twice, 6ds, rw.
Complete second motif as for first.

### To make the cloth

Work 61 motifs in all, joined in a formation of a central row of 9, with rows of 8, 7, 6 and 5 motifs on either side as shown, and joining each motif to the previous one(s) as required.

# Tatted medallion patterns

## Rose motif

**Materials** No. 10 crochet cotton; tatting shuttle.
**Measurements**
Each motif measures approx. 3in. (7.4cm) across.

R of 8ds, 1p, (4ds, 1p) 3 times, 8ds, close.
*R of 8ds, join to last p of previous r, (4ds, 1p) 3 times, 8ds, close.**
Repeat from * to ** 6 times more, omitting last p of final r and instead joining to first p of first r. Tie threads to connect the centre of the rosette.
Keep the shuttle thread at the back of the rosette and join it to the p connecting first and last rs as follows:
Insert hook in p, catch thread and pull out a loop, pass the shuttle through the loop and adjust knot. In the same way join shuttle thread to second p of first r.
Leave a space of ⅛in. (3mm).
Josephine knot of 4ss, join to same p as last shuttle thread join, 4ss, close, rw.
Leave a space of ⅜in. (1cm).
R of (4ds, 1p) 3 times, 4ds, close.
Leave a space of ⅜in. (1cm).

*R of 4ds, join to last p of previous r, (4ds, 1p) twice, 4ds, close, rw. Space of ⅜in. (1cm).
Josephine knot of 4ss, join to next p on centre rosette, 4ss, close, rw. Space of ⅜in. (1cm).
R of 4ds, join to last p of previous r, (4ds, 1p) twice, 4ds, close, rw. Space of ⅜in. (1cm).
Josephine knot of 4ss, join to next p on centre rosette, 4ss, close, rw. Space of ⅜in. (1cm).
R of 4ds, join to last p of previous r, (4ds, 1p) twice, 4ds, close. Space of ⅜in. (1cm).**
Repeat from * to ** all round, joining first and last rs of outer edge. Cut and tie thread to first Josephine knot.

### To make a cloth
Make 61 motifs in all, joining them in formation as given for hexagonal motif by linking 3 rings at outer edges as shown.

## Circular motif

**Materials** No. 10 crochet cotton; tatting shuttle.
**Measurements**
Each motif measures approx. 3¾in. (9.5cm) across.

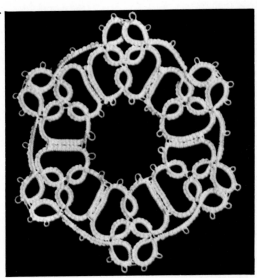

Join ball and shuttle threads.
R of 7ds, 1p, 7ds, close, rw.
Long ch of 3ds, 1p, 2ds, 1p, 9ds, 1p, 7ds, rw.
R of 7ds, join to p of previous r, 7ds, close.
Large r of 10ds, 1p, 2ds, 1p, 4ds, 1p, 4ds, close.
*Ch of 7ds, 1p, 7ds.
Large r of (4ds, 1p) twice, 2ds, 1p, 10ds, close.
R of 7ds, 1p, 7ds, close, rw.
Long ch of 7ds, join to last p of previous long ch, 9ds, join to next p of same ch, 2ds, 1p, 3ds, rw.
R of 7ds, join to p of previous r, 7ds, close, rw.
Long ch of 3ds, 1p, 2ds, 1p, 9ds, 1p, 7ds, rw.
R of 7ds, join to junction of previous 2 rs, 7ds, close.

Large r of 10ds, join to last p of previous large r, 2ds, 1p, 4ds, 1p, 4ds, close.**
Repeat from * to ** 4 times more.
Ch of 7ds, 1p, 7ds.
Large r of (4ds, 1p) twice, 2ds, join to first large r, 10ds, close.
R of 7ds, join to junction of first and second rs, 7ds, close, rw.
Long ch of 7ds, join to first long ch, 9ds, join to same ch, 2ds, 1p, 3ds.
Cut and tie thread to beginning of motif.

### To make a cloth
Make 61 motifs in all, joining them in formation as given for hexagonal motif by linking the 2 outermost ps of pairs of rs as shown.

**Joined rose motifs**

**Joined circular motifs**

# History of plaiting

Plaiting is the technique of weaving single strands into *plaits* or *braids*. The method by which this is done varies according to the number of strands with which you are working and the pattern you want to create. A wide variety of materials can be used for the strands. Plaiting gives a very hard-wearing surface as well as an interesting texture.

Traditionally, the history of plaiting lies with industrial England, particularly the north, and with the early settlers who emigrated to North America. It began as a way of using odd scraps of material, such as old clothes, which were then cut into strips to make an economical new fabric.

In most cases, the single plaits were joined together, either in strips or in the round, to make an excellent fabric for rugs, mats, bedcovers and cushion-covers. Nowadays, with the increase in popularity of plaiting, fabrics are often specially bought with particular colour schemes in mind and then cut into the required number of strips.

## Tools

Plaiting is easiest when the strands are firmly anchored. The simplest way of doing this is to mount them on to a board with T-pins. A macramé board is ideal since it is firm enough to support the work but soft enough to take the pins. To join plaits into a fabric you will need heavy-duty thread and a large needle. Otherwise, basic sewing equipment, such as pins, scissors and a tape measure, is also useful.

## Materials

For single braids, any string-like cord with a firm twist to it can be used. These days a wide variety of macramé threads are available and most of them are ideal for plaiting. Leather thongs can be used too. For soft furnishings, almost any pliable fabric is suitable, although natural fibres are better than man-made and wool makes for the hardest wear. Always check that the colours will not run – by dabbing a piece of damp cotton wool on to the material – and make certain that combined fabrics each have the same washing requirements.

*Plaits worked in macramé stool twine from instructions on the opposite page. They are, from left to right: three-strand plait, four-strand round cord, four-strand plait, five-strand plait, double plait, eight-strand alternating plait, eight-strand cross-over plait, and eight-strand twisted plait.*

# Making the plaits

Plaiting techniques can be used to make many different braids, from the everyday three-strand plait to the six-strand circular plait. The simpler braids can be worked with either cords or fabrics, but the more complicated ones are better suited to working in string-like cords that have a firm twist and no stretch to them. They make interesting belts, bracelets and replacement handles, as well as braids for stitching to clothes.

### How to make a three-strand plait

**1** *Tie 3 strands together with an overhand knot and pin to a soft board with a T-pin.*

**2** *Take the strand on the left over the top of the strand in the middle.*

**3** *Take the strand on the right over the top of the strand in the middle.*

**4** *Continue in this way, alternately taking the strand from the left and then the strand from the right over the one in the middle. Pull the plait tight as you go.*

### How to make a six-strand circular plait

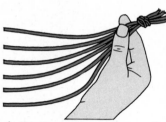

**1** *Tie 6 strands together with an overhand knot. Number them off from 1 to 6.*

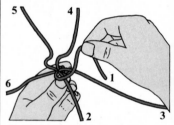

**2** *Hold the work in the left hand and arrange the strands as shown. Work anti-clockwise and take strand 1 up over strands 2 and 3.*

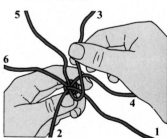

**3** *Now take strand 3 up over strands 1 and 4.*

**4** *Continue in this way, taking the strand immediately behind the newly-positioned one and moving it anti-clockwise over the 2 strands in front of it.*

# *Various types of plaits*

Tie the strands together, pin to a board and number them off from the left. Work them over one another, following the numbers through so that their order changes as shown. In each case, the broken line shows the end of the basic sequence. After this, repeat the same movements from the beginning. Eventually, as can be seen in the exploded diagrams of the two simplest plaits, each strand will return to its original position.

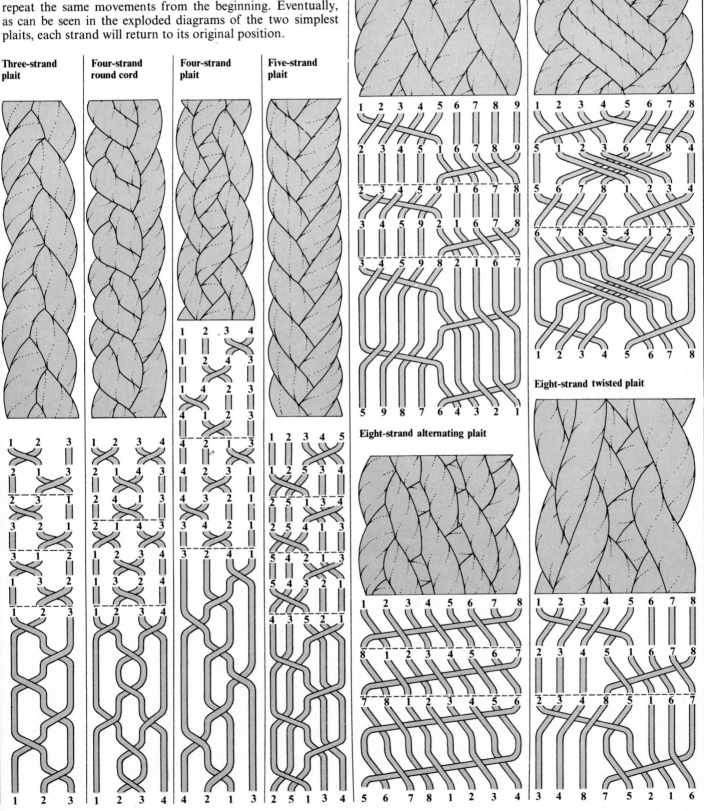

**Three-strand plait**

**Four-strand round cord**

**Four-strand plait**

**Five-strand plait**

**Double plait**

**Eight-strand cross-over plait**

**Eight-strand alternating plait**

**Eight-strand twisted plait**

# Plaiting with fabrics

Plaiting with fabric is not quite as straightforward as working with string or cord since there are several stages of preparation before the actual plaiting can begin. Instructions are given below explaining how to cut the fabric and fold it into strips.

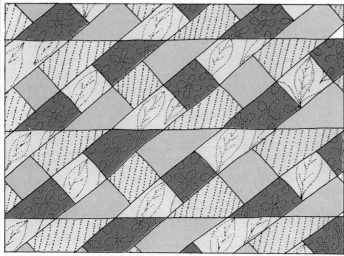

**Four-strand plaits joined to make a patterned fabric**

## Preparing the fabric

Any used materials should be washed and new ones should be pre-shrunk before plaiting. The working strands are made by cutting the fabric into bias strips. These are usually 1 to 1½in. (2.5 to 4cm) wide, although this will of course depend on the width of the plait you plan to make.

### How to join the strips

**1** To join the strips together, cut diagonally across the bias on the straight grain.
**2** Place the 2 strips together, matching them up on the diagonal as shown. Sew along the join with back stitch.
**3** Press seams open, trim off corners and unfold the pieces into a continuous length and trim off any surplus material.

### How to fold the strips

**1** Lay the strips out flat, right side downwards.
**2** Fold the strips sides to middle as shown.
**3** Fold them in half again down the centre line. Tack them into place if you want to produce a rounded effect, or press them lightly with an iron if you want the finished plait to look more flattened.

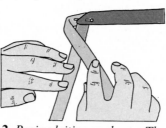

**1  Strips cut on the diagonal**

**2  Stitching along the diagonal**

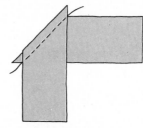

**3  The opened-out join**

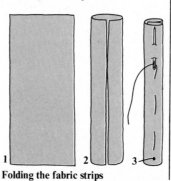

**1**      **2**      **3**
**Folding the fabric strips**

# Beginning the plait

The first thing to do is to secure the strands together at the top before beginning the plait. There are three methods for doing this.

### How to secure a 3-strand plait

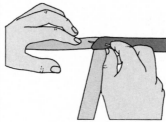

**1** *For a 3-strand plait, join two strips together. Slot a third strip into the fold of the other two at the centre. Secure with a pin or a few stitches.*

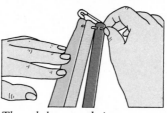

**2** *Begin plaiting as shown. The left half of the top strip becomes the first strand of the plait, the vertical strip the second, and the right half of the top strip the third.*

### How to secure with safety pin

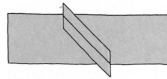

*Thread the strands in sequence on to a safety pin as shown.*

### How to secure with tacking stitches

*Lay the strands next to each other and secure them along the top with tacking stitches.*

# Working the plait

Plaited fabrics are worked in exactly the same way as plaited string or cord. However, by varying the technique slightly, it is possible to produce either a rounded or a flattened effect on the finished plait. In both cases, it is essential to mount the tops of the strands firmly to the working surface before beginning the plaiting.

### How to make a rounded plait

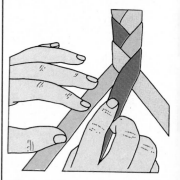

*Work in the normal way, treating each strand as if it were a simple cord. Keep the open edges to the right throughout. To produce even fatter, rounder plaits, make each strand bulkier by lining it with another strip of fabric before folding it over and beginning to plait.*

### How to make a flattened plait

*Work in the normal way, but this time fold the strands over in a sharp crease at the outer edges of the plait. This will guarantee that they lie flat. Start off by setting the open edges of the fabric strands to the right. If this is done you will find that as the work progresses, the open edges always face up towards the top of the plait.*

# *Making up projects*

Any number of fabric plaits can be joined together to make articles such as rugs, bedspreads or cushion covers. The various techniques for joining the plaits together – either by lacing or by interbraiding – and for finishing and backing the completed work are given below.

## *Gauging the quantities*

In general, each plait requires strands of about one-and-a-half times its finished length, but it is difficult to be accurate about the figure since the quantity will vary according to the width and thickness of the plait.

If you are making a continuous spiral, you will find that each round will take up about 7 or 8in. (18 to 20.5cm) more than the previous one. On top of this, you will need a further 7in. (18cm) or more for joining the ends.

## *Lacing*

Whether you are joining plaits in a straight line, in rounds or in ovals, lacing is the best method of sewing them together. It is easier and stronger than stitching through the fabric itself. Always use strong carpet thread on rugs and heavy-weight bedspreads, and a strong linen thread for other items. Begin by securing the thread to the fabric with a heavy darning needle. Then remove the darning needle and replace it with either a blunt-ended tapestry needle or a lacing needle that is specially designed for plaited work.

## *Making a straight join*

Lay the plaits side by side. Insert the needle through the first loop of the right-hand plait, without penetrating the fabric, and take it down and across to the base of the corresponding loop on the left-hand plait. Pass it up inside this loop and then cross to the base of the next loop on the right-hand plait. Always pull the thread tight to make the lacing as secure and as invisible as possible.

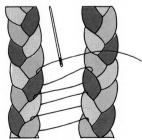
**Lacing on a straight join**

## *Making a join on a curve*

Work in the same way, but miss out the occasional loop on the outer plait as shown. Check that the article will lie flat and if not adjust the positioning of the missed loops.

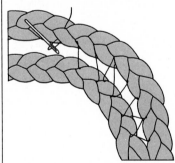
**Lacing on a curved join**

## *Joining an oval shape*

For an oval shape, work in the same way. Begin about half way down the straight centre plait and work downwards as shown. When you reach the first curve, change direction and lace upwards towards the second curve. Continue round in the usual way.

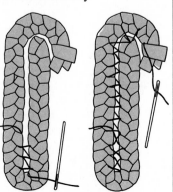
**Lacing on an oval shape**

## *Interbraiding*

An alternative method of joining plaits in a straight line is to work them into one another as they are being plaited.

### *How to work*

*Work the plaits side by side. In between loops on each plait, pull the strands through a loop of the adjoining plait with a crochet hook as shown.*

## *Butting*

This is a method of joining together the ends of two finished plaits. It is worked by splicing together the strands of each plait so that the join is not visible when finished.

### *How to work*

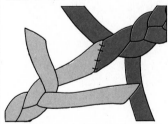

*1 Open out the ends of the strands on both plaits. Attach one strand from the top plait to the matching strand from the bottom plait by stitching them together along a diagonal join. Fold the joined strands back over again in the usual way. Repeat for 2 of the other strands, keeping to the pattern.*

*2 Finally, join the last 2 strands, plaiting them into the others so that the pattern follows through correctly.*

## *Finishing off*

When the plait has been worked to the required length, it must be finished off by darning back and securing the ends of the strands.

### *How to finish off a straight plait*

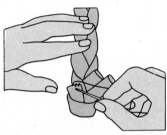

*Thread the ends of the strands back into the loops of the plait on the wrong side of the work. Secure them by stitching over the ends, keeping the stitches out of sight.*

### *How to finish off a spiral*

*The neatest way to finish off a spiral is to taper the end of each strand before completing the plait. The plait will then become thinner and thinner until it can be unobtrusively joined into the spiral.*

## *Backing*

Attaching a backing on to a plaited article will make it more hard-wearing. For a plaited rug, use a conventional hessian rug backing. Either cut out a piece slightly smaller than the rug and stick it in place with carpet tape, or cut out a piece slightly larger than the rug, turn the edges under and stitch it in place. Bedspreads, too, are both warmer and stronger if backed. The best material to use is a thin lining fabric, turned under at the edges and stitched to the back of the bedspread.

# Plaited chair pad

An attractive and hardwearing chair pad can be made by forming a simple three-strand plait into a spiral, and then backing it with a circle of foam padding. It is best if made in fairly thick, tweed-like fabrics matched together for colour and weight. It is also a good idea to check beforehand that the fabrics you use are all colourfast.

### Materials

You will need three strands of fabric, each of a different colour and each measuring, in total, about 24ft (7.3m) long. Their width will vary from about 1½in. (3.8cm) in the middle of the chair pad to about 2in. (5cm) on the perimeter. You will also need a piece of foam padding about ½in. (1.3cm) thick, cut to the same size as the finished chair pad, and a piece of backing fabric 2in. (5cm) wider than the chair pad.

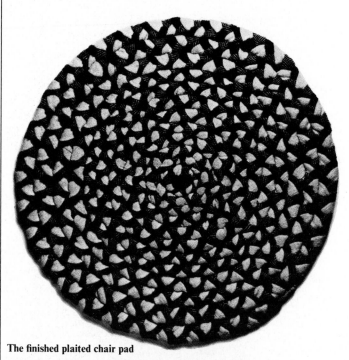

**The finished plaited chair pad**

**Alternative pattern**
You need not be restricted to just three different fabrics. By joining several different materials into the same strand, as shown here, a more complicated pattern can be produced.

### Making the chair pad

Start by cutting out three strips of fabric, one of each colour. Prepare them in the usual way for a rounded plait by folding them over on themselves twice. If necessary pin them lightly to hold the folds in place as you work. Join the strands together at the top with a few stitches and begin working a normal three-strand plait (the instructions are given on page 200). Make sure that the plait is kept fairly tight or the finished chair pad will turn out too loose and too thin. When each strand is used up, add in a new length by making a diagonal join on the bias (see butting, page 203). Try not to have the joins all falling in the same place as this may create a ridge in the finished plait. As you work towards the end of the plait, gradually increase the width of the fabric strips so that the rounds will be wider on the outside of the chair pad than in the centre. Finally, when the plait is long enough, taper the ends off so that they can be joined into the spiral unobtrusively.

### Joining the plait into a spiral

The chair pad is formed by coiling the plait tightly around at the centre and then lacing it together by working the needle in between the adjoining loops. Pull tight so that the chair pad is firm and the thread does not show. Try to keep the pad flat as you work, but if it does tend to rise in the middle, then gently steam iron or press it down into shape.

*How to join the plait*

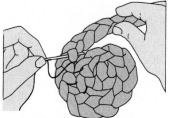

**1** *Begin at the centre by coiling the plait around itself. Lace it together with a blunt-ended needle and button thread (see page 203).*

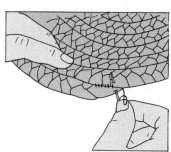

**2** *Secure the tapered ends of the plait to the side of the chair pad with a few stitches.*

### Backing the chair pad with foam

A backing can be made for the completed chair pad by using a piece of foam padding about ½in. (1.3cm) thick. The foam can be trimmed around the edges with a pair of scissors to give the chair pad a bevelled shape. You will also need a circular piece of one of the fabrics used in the plait about 2in. (5cm) wider in diameter than the chair pad.

*How to back the chair pad*

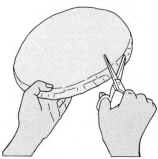

**1** *Cut out a piece of foam to the same size as the chair pad. Bevel the edges as shown.*

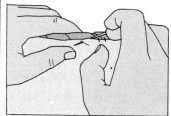

**2** *Sandwich the foam between the chair pad and the circle of fabric, turn in the hem and slip stitch firmly together.*

# Plaited belt

The plaited belt given here is about 28½in. (72cm) long. It can be made larger if necessary by using longer or thicker lengths of cord.

## Materials

You will need eight lengths of $\frac{3}{16}$in. (5mm) diameter 3-ply cotton cord, each about 39in. (1m) long. Six should be in white and two in a contrasting colour. You will also need about 6ft (1.9m) of $\frac{1}{8}$in. (3mm) diameter rayon cord, some white fabric such as stiff cotton and a flat buckle.

## Attaching the buckle

Before beginning the plaiting, it is a good idea to secure the nine strands to a strip of cotton fabric. This can then be attached to a buckle which has first been covered with cotton fabric and with rayon cord.

### How to attach the buckle

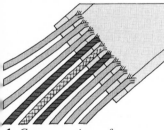

**1** *Cut out a piece of cotton fabric about 3in. (7.5cm) long and 1½in. (4cm) wide. Turn in the sides and fold over one hem. Lay the cords over the hem in the order shown and machine stitch over the ends.*

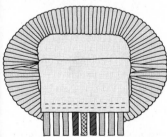

**2** *Cover the buckle with thin strips of white cotton and then wind rayon cord around it too. Loop the cotton on the end of the strands through the buckle. Turn in the hem and sides and stitch the fabric down on to the back of the cords.*

## Making the belt

The basic pattern for the plaited belt is the same as the eight-strand cross-over plait illustrated on page 200. It is easier to work if the buckle is first pinned to a firm surface.

### How to make the belt

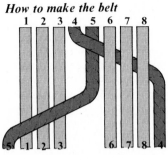

**1** *Number the strands from 1 to 8 as shown, leaving out the thinner rayon cord for the time being. Begin with the two coloured cords. Take number 4 over number 5 and under numbers 6, 7 and 8. Now take number 5 over 3, 2 and 1.*

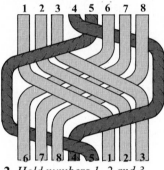

**2** *Hold numbers 1, 2 and 3 together as one unit and take them over numbers 6, 7 and 8 as one unit. Take number 4 over numbers 3, 2 and 1 and bring number 5 under numbers 6, 7 and 8. Then cross number 5 over number 4 at the centre.*

## Finishing off the end of the belt

The end of the belt is best covered in white cotton fabric.

### How to finish off

*Cut out a piece of cotton fabric about 1½in. (4cm) square. Turn in the hem and sides and machine stitch the cords flat on to the edge of the fabric. Fold the fabric back on itself as shown, turn in the other hem and sew down on the back of the plaited belt.*

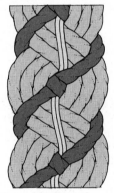

**3** *Repeat this pattern by plaiting first the three-strand units and then the single coloured cords until the belt is long enough.*

**4** *Now go back to the beginning and weave in the length of rayon cord so that it passes in and out of the points where strands 4 and 5 cross over.*

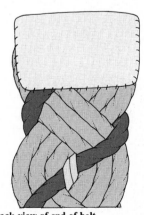

**Back view of end of belt**

**The finished plaited belt**

# History of rugmaking

Many rugs have been discovered which date back to at least 2000 BC. They were nearly all made by tying short lengths of yarn on to the warp threads of a loom to create a piled fabric, and the invention of this technique for making woven rugs has been variously attributed to the Chinese, the Egyptians and the Mayas. The knot that was used for these rugs, the "Oriental" or "Ghiordes" knot, was developed in Scandinavia into the "rya" knot – thus enabling shaggy piled rugs to be worked with a needle on special ready-made backings. Rya fabrics were made in unwashed woollen yarns and, because they stood up to water so much better than animal skins, they were used by fishermen as raincoats. Their thickness and warmth meant that they were also used as wall hangings to keep out the draughts and as floor coverings and bedspreads.

Hooked rugs, too, which most people think of as being a specifically American art, have their origins in Scandinavia. The method has been traced back to the Vikings who used fur-like piled fabrics as clothing to withstand the cold. They took the technique of rug hooking to the British Isles, from where it spread to the American colonies with the early settlers. Some of the most beautiful hooked rugs date from eighteenth- and early nineteenth-century New England. They were made with thin strips of used fabric, in bold, colourful designs that portray flowers, animals and landscapes.

## Rugmaking techniques

The rugmaking techniques included in this section are confined to those which are made by working yarns or strips of fabric on to a ready-woven backing such as canvas or hessian. The six different types are illustrated below.

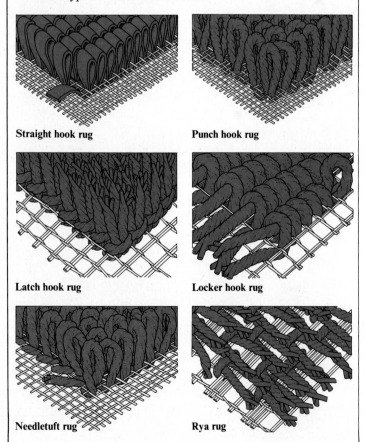

Straight hook rug

Punch hook rug

Latch hook rug

Locker hook rug

Needletuft rug

Rya rug

# Tools and materials

The six types of rug are differentiated according to the way in which they are worked and the tools which are used to form the pile. They fall into two broad categories: *hooked* and *needle-made*. The first four are hooked and the last two are needlemade.

## Tools

The *straight hook* has an end shaped like a crochet hook to pull the yarn into loops through the backing fabric; the *punch hook* is threaded with yarn and pushed through the backing fabric; the *latch hook* enables special knots to be made with pre-cut lengths of yarn; the *locker hook* has a crochet hook on one end and an eye on the other; and *rug needles* are thick and blunt.

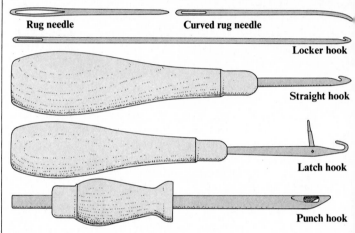

Rug needle

Curved rug needle

Locker hook

Straight hook

Latch hook

Punch hook

## Yarns

Heavy, 6-ply rug yarns are most commonly used for rugmaking. They are thick and have a firm twist to them which makes them very hardwearing. Wool is undoubtedly the best fibre, although synthetic yarns and mixtures are also available. As illustrated below, rug yarns come in heavy, medium and light weights and in a wide variety of colours and textures.

Strips of fabric can also be used, in particular for straight hook rugs, but the fabrics you choose must be strong and quite firmly woven in order to withstand wear. Any medium-weight fabrics can be salvaged from discarded garments or household linens, as was the custom when making traditional rag rugs.

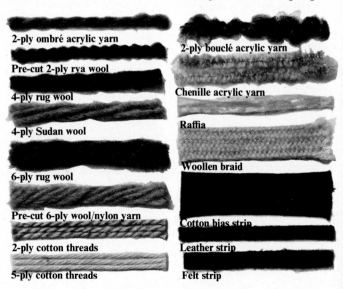

2-ply ombré acrylic yarn

2-ply bouclé acrylic yarn

Pre-cut 2-ply rya wool

4-ply rug wool

Chenille acrylic yarn

4-ply Sudan wool

Raffia

6-ply rug wool

Woollen braid

Pre-cut 6-ply wool/nylon yarn

Cotton bias strip

2-ply cotton threads

Leather strip

5-ply cotton threads

Felt strip

# Backings

# Designing

The *backing* is the foundation fabric on which the rug is worked. The stronger your backing fabric, the better. All hand-made rugs involve a lot of work and this would be wasted if the backing canvas wore out before the surface. A wide variety of backings are available and the most common are shown below. When buying, you should choose the one most suitable for your technique. Before starting any rug, it is advisable to work a small sample so that any practical problems can be sorted out at an early stage. Try out various gauges and types of canvas and also different yarns and plys. When deciding on the width of your backing, always allow a hem of about 1½in. to 2½in. (3.8cm to 6.5cm) on each side. Even if you are working from selvedge to selvedge, leave at least ½in. (1.3cm) for a narrow hem. Either bind the hem with tape or fold it back and work over it with rug stitches as shown below.

The scope for rug design is completely unlimited. It can take the form of anything from abstract shapes or formal borders to pictorial scenes such as the one below. Unless you are making up your pattern as you go, there are two methods of working out a planned design. You can either draw the shapes straight on to the backing fabric on the side that you are working with an indelible crayon or you can lay out the design on graph paper before you start working. The first method is better for straight hook, punch hook and needletuft techniques on fabric backings; the second is more suited to open-mesh canvas.

### Drawing out the design on the backing
Begin by drawing the pattern on to the backing fabric in pencil. You can use cut-out cardboard shapes to trace around if you like. When you have the design looking as you want it, go over the outlines with an indelible crayon or felt-tipped pen. Remember that any small details in your design will be obscured if you are working a shaggy, long-piled rug.

### Drawing out the design on graph paper
Draw out the design you want on the graph paper. Then go over it and square it off as shown. Let each square on the paper represent one stitch, loop or knot and establish a colour or symbol code to identify the types and colours of yarn.

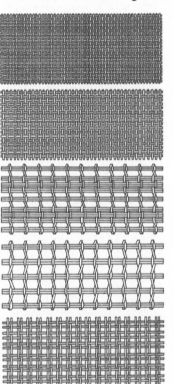

**1 Hessian**
*Widely used for hooked rugs, it is evenly woven but not so firm that it is difficult to pass the hook through it.*

**2 Evenweave cotton/linen**
*Ideal for hooking, it is more expensive than hessian, but is stronger and more durable.*

**3 Scandinavian backing**
*Made for rya rugs, it has rows of unwoven warp spaces in which the individual rya knots are worked.*

**4 Open-mesh canvas**
*Three holes per in. (2.5cm). This canvas, stiffened with size and composed of doubled threads, is ideal for rugs made with the latch hook method.*

**5 Open-mesh canvas**
*Five holes per in. (2.5cm). This is used for finer latch hook rugs and for the locker hook method as well.*

### Binding the canvas edges

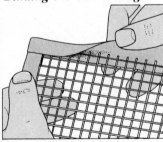

To prevent the edges of the backing from fraying, either bind them with adhesive tape or machine stitch on strips of bias binding. These bindings can then be hemmed to the backing for a neat finish.

### Working over the hems

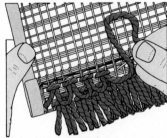

To make an invisible hem, fold the allowance to the right side of the backing and tack it in place so that the warp and weft threads lie directly above one another. Work the rug stitches through the two thicknesses.

**Detail of early nineteenth-century American rug**
*Note how the direction in which the yarn is worked has been varied so that the outlines of the shapes are emphasized. See directional hooking, page 209.*

# Straight hook rugs

The *straight hook* method is the simplest of the rugmaking techniques and was the one used in the making of traditional rag rugs. Apart from its handle, the straight hook (also known as the *hand hook*) is very similar to a crochet hook, and it works by pulling the yarn up through the backing fabric to form loops on the surface.

## Backings

Any even, firmly woven fabric with apparent warp and weft threads is suitable. An evenweave mixture of cotton and linen is the best. Hessian can be a little too weak and uneven to give good results, although it was nevertheless the traditional backing fabric for American hooked rugs.

## Yarns

Thin strips of cloth make the best yarns, as this hook tends to separate the strands of rug wools when pulling them through the backing. Almost any closely woven fabric will do – indeed the traditional rag rugs were often made from old clothes. Wool, flannel and tweed make the most hardwearing rugs; cotton, linen and some synthetics are also suitable; satins and silks, however, tend to be too slippery to work well.

Straight hook rug worked in felt on evenweave cotton/linen

## Frames for hooked rugs

When working with a straight or punch hook, the backing fabric should be stretched tautly over a frame to ensure even hooking. Frames are available in various sizes or you can make your own. Secure the work to them with strong thumb tacks.

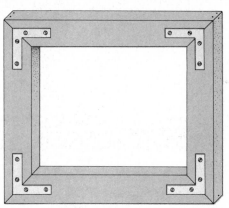

**Small lap frame**
A simple frame can be made from 2in. by 1in. (5cm by 2.5cm) wooden strips. Mitre the corners, nail the pieces into a rectangle and reinforce with metal brackets.

## Preparing the fabric

The first thing to do is to wash the fabric – whether you have bought it new or whether you plan to make use of old scraps of material. If you are using old clothes, remove any buttons or zips, open up all the seams and hems, and cut away any badly worn patches. Do not worry if the fabric shrinks: it will be less likely to fray or unravel.

Your fabric must now be cut into strips. The width of the strips will depend on the type of fabric, the kind of backing you are using and the effect you want to achieve. Experiment with different widths: flannels and fairly fine fabrics can be cut to about ½in. (1.3cm) wide; medium-weight woven materials to about ¼in. (6mm); and heavier tweeds and wools can be as thin as ⅛in. (3mm). Remember, however, that if the strips are too narrow the fabric may fray when hooked through.

### How to cut the strips

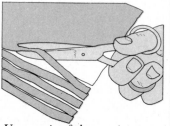

Use a pair of sharp scissors. Measure out the width of the strip and cut woven fabrics along the grain and knitted fabrics along their length.

### How to join the strips

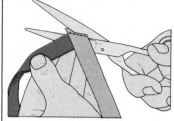

If you must join strips together, lay 2 at right angles, stitch across the top on the diagonal, open up the seam and trim off the edges.

## Hooking

In this method, the yarn or strip of fabric is held beneath the work. The hook is then inserted through the backing and the yarn pulled through from the underside to the top in small loops. Each loop is controlled by hand and regulated by eye. With practice, you can hook in any direction and thus create linear patterns or rhythms in the pile.

### How to use the hook

**1** *Hold the yarn or the strip of fabric beneath the backing so that it is taut. Push the hook down through the backing from the right side, passing between warp and weft threads.*

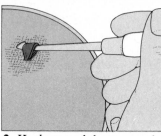

**2** *Hook around the yarn and pull it up through the backing to form a loop of the desired height on the right side.*

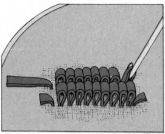

**3** *Advance the hook by 1 or 2 backing threads and push it through again ready to pull up another loop. Continue in this way, always starting and finishing a length of yarn by pulling the ends up to the top.*

# Punch hook rugs

The *punch hook* technique is similar to that of the straight hook, but it is faster and easier to manipulate. You work with the backing fabric stretched on a frame and with what will be the underside of the rug towards you. The loops are then pushed through from the back to the front and their height is regulated automatically by the punch hook.

## Backings
Any strong, evenly woven fabric is suitable for punch hooking as long as the threads will allow the hook to pass through. Hessian and evenweave cotton/linen are probably the most commonly used backings. If you choose hessian, use the heavy variety – its unevenness will not affect the hooking.

## Yarns
Yarns are easier to use with a punch hook than strips of fabric since they will slide more freely up and down the centre of the hook. However, very thin strips of fabric can be used successfully. Various thicknesses and combinations of yarns used together produce interesting textures, and there is scope for using novelty yarns, braids and ribbons as well.

**Punch hook rug worked in various rug wools on hessian**

## Hooking
The punch hook is really a large hollow needle with an eye on one side of the tube. The size of the loop that it makes can be adjusted from about $\frac{1}{4}$in. (6mm) to $\frac{3}{4}$in. (2cm) by a turning and locking movement of the wooden handle. The most important thing to remember is not to lift the hook above the surface when you pull it out of the backing fabric.

### How to thread the hook

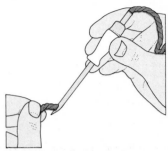

**1** *Holding the slotted side of the hook towards you, insert the end of the yarn down into the hollow needle from the top to the bottom.*

**2** *As the end of the yarn appears, thread it through the eye. Make sure that the yarn is free to move through the needle with ease.*

### How to use the hook

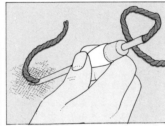

**1** *Hold the hook in an upright position, like a pencil. Keep the slotted side facing in the direction you are going.*

**3** *Hold the backing steady and withdraw the hook. Do not raise it above the surface of the backing. Slide it along and plunge it in again.*

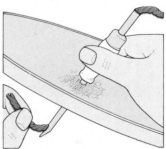
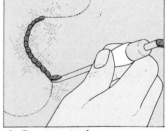

**2** *Push the hook down through the backing, between the warp and weft threads, until it will not go any further.*

**4** *Continue in the same way, changing direction when necessary and pushing the ends of each length of thread through to the front.*

## Directional hooking
Changing the direction in which you are hooking enables patterns to be built up in the pile of the rug. Thus, you will obtain a different effect according to whether you are hooking in straight lines, in diagonals or in curves. When working to a design, begin by following the outline of the shape for a few rows. Then gradually work in towards the centre, filling in with curves, circles or swirls.

# *Latch hook rugs*

*Latch hook* rugs are made by knotting lengths of yarn onto an open-mesh canvas. The yarn is pre-cut and the result is a dense piled rug. The height of the pile can be varied either by using different lengths of yarn or by trimming certain areas when complete. If you want to work a pattern, chart out your design on graph paper first, but remember that it is difficult to obtain curves and circles and that small details tend to get lost in the thick pile. Simple coloured and textured designs are the best. Because of the stiffness of the canvas no frame is needed.

**Latch hook rug**
This rug has been worked in assorted yarns on open-mesh canvas. A hem has been added at the top and a fringe at the bottom.

## *Backings*

The open-mesh canvas used for latch hooking is made up of doubled threads. The warp threads are twisted and the weft threads, over which the knots are worked, are not. The canvas is available in gauges of 3 to 5 holes per in. (2.5cm).

## *Yarns*

Any yarn that fits through the canvas mesh when doubled can be used. You can try mixtures of different types and different thicknesses as well as fabric strips or ribbon. The minimum length convenient for hooking is 2½in. (6.5cm) which works into a pile of about 1in. (2.5cm). Pre-cut yarn can be bought in packets sold by weight, but it is cheaper to buy hanked yarn and then cut it yourself using the method described below.

### *How to cut the yarn*

*Yarn gauges and mechanical cutters are available but it is easy to make your own. Fold a piece of cardboard in half – the size depends on the desired length of yarn. Wrap the yarn carefully around it without overlapping. Then cut along the open edge of the cardboard with a pair of scissors or sharp blade as shown.*

## *Hooking*

Begin by trying a few sample knots to test out the length and thickness of your yarns. Work horizontally, starting at the bottom and hooking right along each row as you go. Make sure that all the knots face the same way and check that every space in the backing canvas has been filled.

### *How to use the hook*

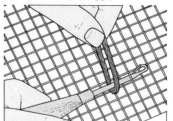

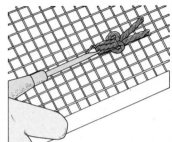

**1** *Take a piece of pre-cut yarn and fold it in half around the shaft of the hook. Now insert the hook and pass it up underneath one horizontal canvas thread as shown.*

**3** *Pull the hook towards you so the latch closes around the yarn. Continue pulling until both ends of the yarn have been drawn through the loop to form the completed knot.*

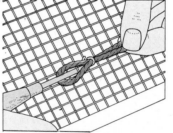

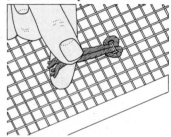

**2** *Take the two ends of yarn through the open latch and tuck them down under the hook itself as shown.*

**4** *Check that the knot is tight by giving the two ends of the yarn a sharp tug with your free hand.*

## *Finishing*

A lining is not strictly necessary for this type of rug. However, the edges of the canvas must be protected by turning over a hem of about 1in. to 2in. (2.5cm to 5cm) to the right side. This is done at the beginning of the work. If you like, leave one row unworked at the edge so that a fringe can be added. The rug will be more hardwearing if you also sew a strip of rug binding over the back of the hem on all sides.

### *How to make a hem*

*Fold the hem allowance up over the right side of the canvas. Align the warp and weft threads and work through the double thickness.*

### *How to add a fringe*

*Leave the first weft of the hem unworked. When the rug is completed knot longer lengths of yarn on to the edge as shown to form a fringe.*

# Locker hook rugs

The *locker hook* is a long thick needle with a crochet hook at one end and a large eye at the other. It is used to work rows of stitches which are caught in place by a continuous thread running through a series of loops. The rug that it produces has a flat-stitched, very dense surface and the added advantage that the tightly looped pile cannot be pulled out. As this method produces definite straight lines of loops, it is best to work to a strong geometric pattern.

## Backings
Either an open-mesh canvas of about 4 or 5 holes per in. (2.5cm) or an evenly woven canvas of heavy linen or jute is suitable. The choice will depend on the weight of the yarns.

## Yarns
Any heavy rug wool can be used. On open-mesh canvas, use 6-ply so that the backing threads are completely covered between rows. On linen, 4-ply will usually be thick enough.

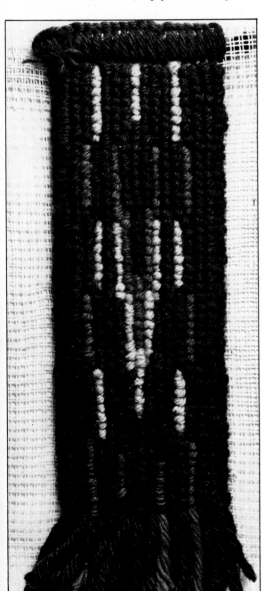

**Locker hook rug**
This rug has been worked in 6-ply rug wool on open-mesh canvas. It is bound at the top with buttonhole stitch and decorated at the bottom with a fringe.

## Hooking
It is best to work in straight rows across the canvas, rather than in curves or circles. When turning corners or starting a new row, take the locker hook to the back of the canvas and up again through a hole in the next row. Take care that you do not enlarge the first loop of each group as this will tighten the last loop of the previous group.

### How to use the hook

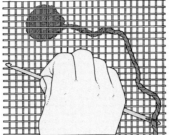

**1** *Thread one end of the yarn through the eye of the hook. Push the hook through the canvas from back to front, drawing through several feet of yarn and holding end at back.*

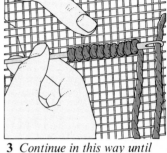

**3** *Continue in this way until you have about 10 loops on the locker hook. Then draw the hook from right to left through the loops that you have just made, as shown.*

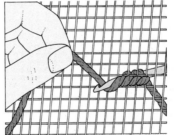

**2** *Insert the hook down through successive holes in the canvas, each time picking up a loop of yarn from beneath and slipping it on to the shaft.*

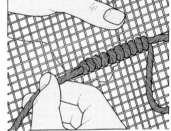

**4** *Keep pulling so that the yarn threaded through the hook comes through the row of loops and "locks" them on to the right side of the canvas.*

## Finishing
Either finish the edges of the rug with a buttonhole stitch hem or add a decorative fringe. On open-mesh canvas it is not essential to have a lining, but it is a good idea for linen.

### How to make a hem

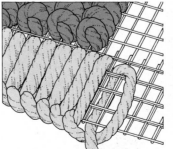

*Turn 1in. (2.5cm) of the backing to the wrong side. Work around the hem with braid or buttonhole stitch.*

### How to make a fringe

*Pull both ends of yarn through to the front of the backing fabric at the end of each row. Trim off the ends evenly.*

# Needletuft rugs

This is a piled rug which is worked on even-weave canvas with a long, blunt-ended rug needle and continuous lengths of strong yarn. It is advisable to use a frame – preferably a small one which will leave both your hands fairly free. When choosing your design bear in mind that the rug is worked along straight lines or in diagonal rows and that simple patterns are generally the best. If you do want to work a complicated design, draw it out first on graph paper, marking out each separate stitch. Remember that when you work horizontally the rows encroach on each other and blur any design motif. Therefore, for any pattern with precise, well-defined lines, it would be best to work the stitches in diagonal rows.

## Backings
Strong linen canvas or evenweave mixtures of cotton and linen are all suitable for this method. The linens stiffened with size are the easier to handle if the rug is not too large.

## Yarns
Whatever yarn you decide to use must be strong enough to withstand the constant friction of being passed through the small holes in the backing fabric and the tension of the strong pull needed to secure the knot. Sturdy 3-, 4- or 6-ply rug wools are ideal. Textured yarns can also be used but they need to have some elasticity to help them spring out into tufts when the loops are all cut.

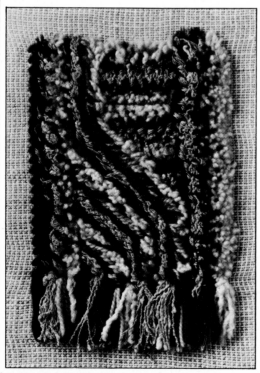

**Needletuft rug worked in various yarns on evenweave cotton/linen**

## Making the rug
Always work upwards, above the previous row. If you are going to cut the loops, do so after every two or three rows.

### How to make the stitch

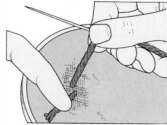

**1** *Start at left. Insert the needle diagonally up under 2 mesh intersections. Pull the yarn through, holding down the last ¾in. (2cm) with finger.*

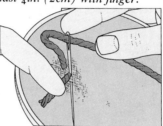

**2** *Insert the needle at the starting point again. Take it down under 2 horizontal backing threads and pull tight.*

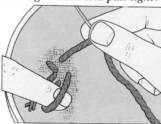

**3** *Move a few threads to the right and make another diagonal stitch on the same level. Leave a loop about ¾in. (2cm) deep as shown, using finger as a gauge.*

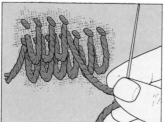

**4** *Continue making loops to end of row. Take yarn to back and work next row above previous one as shown.*

# Rya rugs

*Rya* rugs are long-piled, shaggy rugs worked on a special canvas with a blunt-ended rug needle and a continuous length of yarn. The knot used is a form of the "Ghiordes" knot. It is best to choose simple textural designs as the length of the pile tends to blur any but the most basic patterns. If you want the pile to be of an even length then use a pile gauge and cut the loops after each row. However, interesting effects can be obtained by cutting the pile into different lengths. Because the canvas is fairly thick a frame is not essential and rya rugs rarely need to be lined.

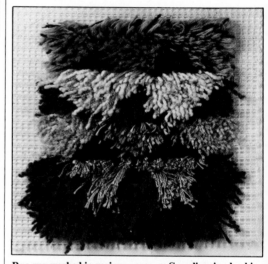

**Rya rug worked in various yarns on Scandinavian backing**

## Backings
There is a special canvas for all rya rugs called "Scandinavian" backing. The weft threads are doubled and woven closely in place but with spaces every so often for the knots to be worked over the open warps. The canvas comes in various widths and sometimes even in pre-finished standard rug sizes.

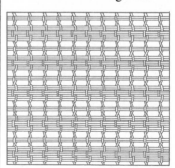

**Scandinavian rya backing**
Note how the warp threads are spaced out and twisted around the weft threads.

## Yarns
Special 2-ply woollen yarns from Scandinavia are available and when used they are generally threaded through the needle several at a time. However, any yarns can be used. The rug will look more luxurious if you use multiple strands of yarns that have different textures.

# *Finishing*

### *Making the rug*

It is best to work from the bottom upwards since the long pile needs to be held down if you are going to work each row easily. A pile gauge is essential if you want to regulate the height of the pile accurately; if not, it is sufficient simply to wrap the yarn around your fingers each time. Begin by turning over about 1in. (2.5cm) of the canvas to the right side so as to form a hem along each edge. Work the rya knots over the double thickness of canvas.

### *How to make the knot*

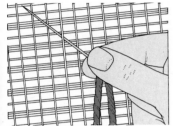

**1** *Start at left. Insert the needle from right to left under 1 warp thread as shown.*

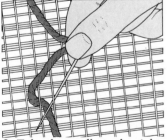

**2** *Take the needle to the right over 2 warp threads and insert it up under the second warp in the same way. Secure the knot by pulling it tight.*

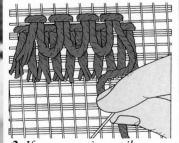

**3** *If you are using a pile gauge, wrap the yarn around it before starting each knot. Continue to the end of the row and then cut through the loops.*

### *Blocking*

Blocking is a technique that enables a rug which has become distorted while being worked to be stretched firmly back into shape. It is only rarely necessary, since working on a frame usually prevents the canvas from becoming badly misshapen. To block a rug, lay it face down on a soft board. Dampen it evenly with cold water from a wet sponge. Gradually stretch it into shape and pin around each side with strong, rustproof tacks. Allow two or three days for it to dry completely before removing.

### *Joining*

To join two pieces of rug, begin by making a row of machine stitching around each single edge of unworked backing about 1in. (2.5cm) from the rug stitches. Trim off the excess. Overlap the two strips of backing, matching up the meshes above and below, and then sew them together with overcasting stitch. Now work across the join, through the double thickness, in the appropriate rug stitches. Match up the yarns and the pattern so that the seam is invisible.

### *Binding*

If the backing finishes with a raw edge, it must be bound and hemmed to prevent it from fraying or unravelling. Sewing on a strip of rug binding or tape is the best way of doing this. Begin by sewing the rug binding on to the right side of the backing fabric as close to the edge of the rug stitches as possible. Use strong thread and running or back stitch. Cut off the excess backing to within about ¾in. (2cm) on each side. Fold the edges to the back and sew the binding to the back of the rug, making sure that the stitches do not show on the surface. Make a triangular mitre at the corners. When binding round or oval rugs, use bias strips. Turn the hems to the back and ease them around the curves by making small, V-shaped slits in the backing fabric.

### *Lining*

Rugs worked on stiff canvas and those that have been properly bound should not need lining. However, if you do want to line your rug, use heavy hessian or any strong, closely woven fabric. Cut out a piece of fabric 1½in. (3.8cm) larger all around than the rug. Turn back the edges of unworked canvas to make a hem in the usual way. Pin the lining at intervals to the back of the rug, starting at the centre and working outwards. Check that the grain of the lining and the canvas is the same. Sew the lining to the hem of the rug about ½in. (1.3cm) from the edge on each side using strong thread and herringbone stitch.

For unlined hooked rugs, you can apply a latex backing. This will make the rug slip-proof and firmer and it will stabilize the stitches. Spread the latex very thinly on to the back of the rug using a palette knife or a paintbrush. Trim the unworked edges of canvas down to about 2in. (5cm) on each side. The corners can be either mitred or folded. Stitch down with cotton or linen carpet thread or use a special adhesive to paste the hem securely to the back of the rug.

### *Fringes*

Many rugs look much better with the addition of a fringe; indeed some look unfinished without one. The size and weight of the fringe should be matched carefully to the rug and you should therefore choose the length, colour and texture accordingly. Since the fringe is added after the rug has been completed, you can experiment by trying out various ideas first. When you have decided how long the fringe is to be and what kind of yarn to use, cut the strands to double the length plus an extra 1in. (2.5cm) for the knot. Fold the strands in half and pull them through the backing fabric with a crochet hook to form a loop. Slip the ends through the loop and tighten the knot.

### *Tassels*

Rather than adding a fringe, it is sometimes better to decorate the finished rug with tassels. These should be somewhere between 5in. (12.5cm) and 10in. (25.5cm) long and be made from an appropriate matching yarn. They are formed by winding the yarn around a piece of cardboard cut to the same length as the required tassel. A separate piece of yarn is then used to tie the strands together at the top and they are all cut at the bottom. The tassel is attached to the rug by stitching it to the hem on the underside.

### *Cleaning*

To remove everyday dust and dirt, use a vacuum cleaner which does not have a beating action. Vacuum first on the surface and then on the underside as well. If something is spilt on the rug, remove as much of it as you can immediately with an absorbent cloth. For food stains such as tea, milk, chocolate or egg, and for ink and blood stains, make up a solution of one teaspoonful of white vinegar and one teaspoonful of soap flakes to 1 quart (1.1 litre) of cool water. Test that the rug is colourfast (by dabbing the back with dampened cotton wool) and then apply the mixture gently with a sponge. Warm water alone should remove most stains caused by alcohol and non-greasy food, although you may find that you have to apply it more than once. Afterwards, allow the rug to dry thoroughly and then gently brush up the pile. For chewing gum, tar and other greasy stains, use dry-cleaning fluid.

### *Storing*

Never fold rugs to store them as this weakens the backing and may cause it to split. Ideally, they should be kept flat. Large rugs, however, should be rolled up, right side inwards, around a polythene-covered roll of cardboard. Wrap this up securely to keep it free from dust.

# Weaving

Weaving is one of the oldest methods of constructing a fabric. In its simplest form it is the interlacing of two distinct and separate sets of threads at right angles to each other. The weaving loom is basically a frame used to hold a vertical set of threads (known as the *warp*) taut and parallel, while a horizontal set of threads (known as the *weft*) is woven backwards and forwards between them.

Despite its primitive origins, the principle of hand weaving remains essentially unchanged, even with the mechanization of the craft through the introduction of power machinery.

## History

Weaving has existed in a very primitive form from earliest days, with different types of textiles being produced, for practical reasons, in different parts of the world. In general, hot countries, like India and Egypt, wove lighter fabrics, using cotton and flax, whereas colder regions like Scandinavia, Germany and Britain produced coarser fabrics – usually from sheep's wool, which was spun into yarn from a distaff, and then woven into cloth. The subsequent introduction of dyeing, and weaving looms, led to a greater quantity and variety of cloths.

Although the actual origins of weaving are unknown, ancient Greek and Egyptian records show evidence that primitive looms were being used in these societies. Early weaving was done on a warp suspended from an upper bar and weighted at the bottom. Next came the *two-bar loom* with the warp stretched from bar to bar – or, for extended length, wound onto the bars. The warp, which could be vertical or horizontal, was held taut by a framework or stakes in the ground. (Early Egyptian records indicate a preference for this type of loom.)

A method of achieving a more adjustable tension then developed simultaneously in various parts of the world. This was the *backstrap loom* (still used in parts of Asia and Central and South America) in which the lower bar was attached to a belt around the waist of the weaver who, leaning forwards or backwards, could slacken or tighten the warp. In this loom the horizontal thread, or weft, was first inserted across the warp in small bundles. Later it was wound onto sticks and released as it crossed through the warp. Finally, in order to give the process more speed and continuity, the weft was wound onto bobbins which were inserted into boat-shaped shuttles.

The first device for speeding up the positioning of warp threads was the *shed rod*. The next step, obviously, was to raise the alternate warp threads, and so the *heddle* was introduced. The warp threads that passed under the shed rod were tied with string loops to a second rod – the *heddle rod* – and they consequently could be raised past those on the shed rod with one upward movement. Later, a series of heddle rods replaced the shed rods altogether and so allowed the faster production of different and more interesting fabric structures.

The loom which is most commonly used for hand weaving today is probably the *four-shaft pedal loom*, which has basically remained unchanged from its earliest ancestors. On this, the heddle rods are suspended on a frame and the warp, stretched horizontally between two rollers, passes through them. The weft is held in position and beaten up to the fabric by a reed, which is also suspended from the frame. Although more complex looms can be made, even the simplest hand weaving looms can produce satisfactory results.

# Weaving yarns

## Warp yarn

Two important things to bear in mind when setting up warp threads are, firstly, that they must be strong, as they are held permanently under tension, and, secondly, that they must be smooth, since they must be capable of being individually lifted or left down. If a warp yarn is at all hairy it will stick to the other warp yarns and will be difficult to separate.

## Weft yarn

Weft yarn can be made of anything that is reasonably pliable. It does not even have to be a yarn in the strictest sense of the word, but can be cord, raffia, cane, plastic or paper, depending on what you want your finished fabric to be.

## Samples of weaving yarns

Below are some examples of weaving yarns. These, in fact, are suitable as weft rather than warp threads.

**Woollen gimp**

**Novelty spiky yarn**

**Rayon slub**

**Acrylic marl**

**Chenille**

# *Weaving implements*

Certain pieces of equipment will be necessary, whatever type of weaving is used, although warp and weft yarn is common to all three types we describe. Other articles which may be required are listed below.

### *For card weaving*
A strong piece of card; a darning needle.

### *For frame weaving*
A weaving frame; a shed stick; a shuttle stick.

### *For tabby loom weaving*
A tabby loom; warping posts; lease threads; 2 shed sticks.

## *Weaving terms*
Below are definitions of some of the more commonly used weaving terms.

### *Cross*
This is the shape formed by the warp yarns when they are wound around the warping posts. It keeps the threads in their correct sequence.

### *Heddle*
This is used for positioning the warp threads and making the sheds.

### *Lease thread*
This is tied through the warp to mark the "cross" or an end of the warp. It can also be used to mark specific sections of the warp for ease during raddling. It should be more than double the width of the warp.

### *Pick*
The name given to a single weft thread.

### *Plying*
The name given for twisting several yarns together.

### *Raddle*
This is used for spreading the warp evenly.

### *Shaft*
This is a frame to which heddles are attached. (The warp threads pass through the heddles.)

### *Shed*
This is the space between the alternating warp threads through which the weft yarn is passed.

### *Shuttle stick*
This is a flat stick, preferably of the same length as the width of the warp, with a notch cut at each end. It is used to pass the weft yarn through the shed.

### *Warp*
The name given to the lengthwise or vertical threads in woven cloth.

### *Warping post*
This is a vertical or horizontal peg (which can be attached to the edge of a table) used for making warps.

### *Weft*
The name given to the horizontal threads interlaced through the warp in a piece of fabric.

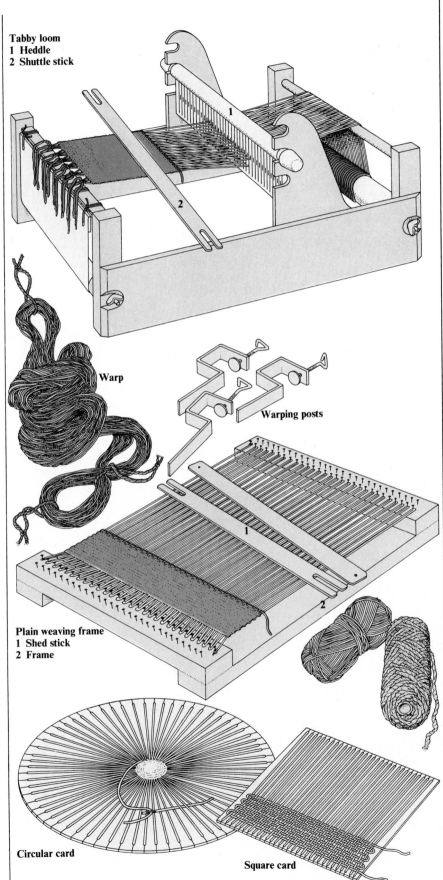

**Tabby loom**
1 **Heddle**
2 **Shuttle stick**

Warp

Warping posts

**Plain weaving frame**
1 **Shed stick**
2 **Frame**

Circular card

Square card

# Card weaving

Card weaving can be done on either square or circular cards. Any size or type of card can be used, as long as it is thick and strong enough to take the threads without bending: hardboard or plywood may be used if necessary. You will have to prepare the cards before beginning to weave, and there are several methods of doing this. The two we illustrate below can be used on either square or circular cards. After weaving, the warp threads are cut away from the card and stitched into the fabric.

## Using both sides of the card
One method of preparing the card for weaving is to wind the warp threads across both sides of the card.

### How to work

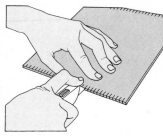

**1** *Cut a piece of cardboard to the size required and mark and cut small, evenly spaced slits at top and bottom.*

**2** *Fasten warp yarn at back of card with adhesive tape and pass through first slit.*

**3** *Carry yarn up across card, bring through opposite slit, wrap around back of card and bring up through 2nd slit.*

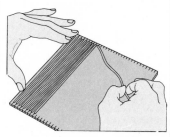

**4** *Repeat, fastening warp yarn (last slit top right) at back with adhesive tape.*

## Using one side of the card
The warp threads can also be wrapped around the tongues formed by the slits, instead of around the back of the card.

### How to work

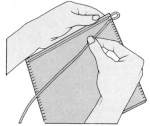

**1** *Repeat Steps 1 and 2 as above. Take yarn up through first slit (top left), wrap around tongue of card and back through 2nd slit.*

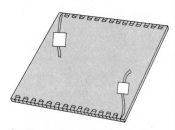

**2** *Continue until one side of card is covered with threads. The back of the card will show short horizontal threads behind alternate tongues.*

# Weaving on square cards

When weaving on square cards, the warp threads are attached to the card and the weft threads then woven into them from right to left.

**Finished woven fabric**

### How to weave

**1** *Using a weaving needle and starting from the right, darn the weft threads under and over the warp threads.*

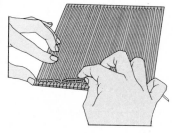

**2** *Using the blunt end of the needle, push the threads together, to ensure that they are straight.*

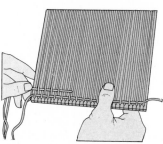

**3** *Repeat Step 1 from the left, this time taking the needle over and under the warp threads. Continue in this way until weaving is completed.*

## Finishing off
When finishing off card weaving the fabric is removed from the card and the loose strands then woven back into the fabric. If the warp threads cover both sides of the card the fabric is removed by cutting away the warp threads at the back of the card. If the warp threads cover only one side of the card, the fabric is unhooked from it.

### How to finish off

*When the fabric has been removed from the card thread the loose strands (or loops) onto the needle, using this to push them back into fabric.*

## Introducing a new weft
If the weft thread is thick, this is best done from the opposite side to the one where the previous weft has ended. If thin, it is done from the same side.

### How to introduce new weft

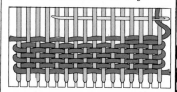

*Leaving about $\frac{3}{4}$in. (2cm) of both new and old weft threads at edge of card, tuck loose strands of old weft over next pick to secure them.*

## Incorrect tension

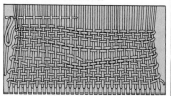

Weaving the weft threads too tightly causes the warp threads to pull towards the centre and the edges to pull inwards.

# Circular card weaving

As in square card weaving, warp threads are attached to the card and weft threads then woven in. Make sure to cut an odd number of slits when preparing circular cards, otherwise a plain weave cannot be produced. Punch the central hole (which will eventually be used to fasten the yarn) before attaching warp threads to card.

### How to prepare the cards

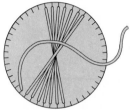 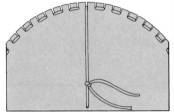

**1** *Fasten yarn at back with adhesive tape, pass it to front of card (crossing centre) and behind opposite tongue, working clockwise.*

**2** *Pass warp thread through central hole and attach it to the back of the card either with adhesive tape or by tying it to starting thread.*

### How to weave

**1** *Starting at any point in the centre, and using a fine thread weave in and out of warp threads going under/over.*

**3** *Push weft threads towards centre with blunt end of needle.*

 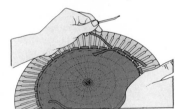

**2** *Tighten the thread initially at the centre to make sure correct shape is formed.*

**4** *Continue circular weaving, not pulling weft too tightly as this will buckle the weaving. You will need thicker threads at edge of circle.*

### How to introduce new weft    ### How to finish off

 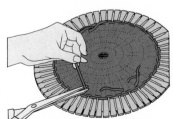

*Start new weft at least 3 warp threads before previous finished warp threads. Cut off weft threads or stitch them into weaving.*

*Cut loose weft ends as shown then snip the warp threads at back of card and stitch into edge of weaving, crossing each thread with the next.*

## Card weaving patterns

Circular plain weaving sample worked in 2 colours in varying numbers of picks.

Circular plain weaving sample worked in 5 different-coloured yarns of differing thicknesses.

Square plain weaving sample worked in rug wool with knots at regular intervals.

Plain weaving sample worked in space-dyed bouclé yarn.

Plain weaving sample worked in 4 grey picks and 1 white pick alternately.

# Simple frame weaving

After weaving on cards, the next simplest form of weaving is frame weaving. Frame weaving is easy to work: the warp threads are wound onto nails at each end of the frame and the weft is woven in with a shuttle stick. A wide range of fabrics can be woven with a frame, including *plain* or *tabby weaving* and *tapestry weaving* (samples of which are described and shown below). Although the size of the fabric woven is limited by the size of the frame, many variations in texture, colour and pattern can be achieved by adding new weft threads when required (see opposite page). There are several different types of frame. The one shown below is the simplest in construction and the easiest to use.

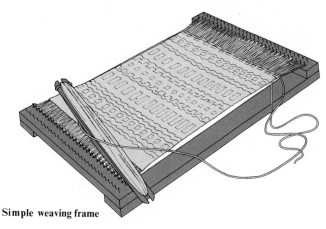

**Simple weaving frame**

**Plain weaving**
This type of frame weaving is based on the principle of weaving "over one, under one". The sample shown left is made up of varying numbers of picks worked in thick and thin undyed cotton.

**Tapestry weaving**
This variation of plain weaving is worked "over two, under two" In the sample shown left, made in 2 colours, 2 threads have been worked per 10 mm (cm).

# Preparing the warp

Before beginning to weave, the warp must be prepared. This is done by wrapping the yarn around the inner rows of nails. The outer row is used only if a finer warp is required (see below).

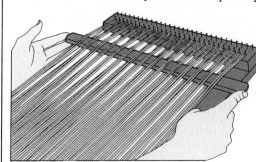

**The prepared warp**
The shed stick is shown ready in position for weaving.

***How to prepare the warp***

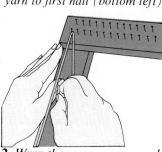

**1** *Fasten the first thread by securely tying one end of warp yarn to first nail (bottom left).*

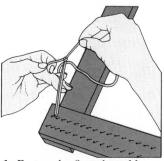

**2** *Wrap the warp yarn around the opposite nail (top left) from left to right.*

**3** *Pass yarn around 2nd nail (bottom left) from left to right. Continue across width of frame, checking that the tension is even.*

**4** *Finish by fastening yarn to last nail, fairly near bottom.*

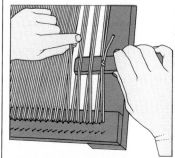

**5** *Weave in shed stick from right to left, passing it over one pair of warp threads, and under next, alternately.*

***Using a finer warp***

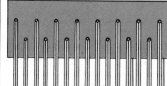

To achieve a finer warp with more threads to the inch (cm) you must use both rows of nails. Wind the yarn first around the two inner rows, then the two outer rows so that all four rows are covered.

# *Filling the shuttle stick*

This method of attaching the yarn to the shuttle stick will ensure that the weft does not get tangled. Do not overfill the stick, otherwise it will not weave through the warp threads easily.

### *How to fill the stick*

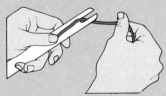

**1** *Holding yarn down with left thumb, insert it through fork.*

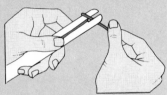

**2** *Wrap yarn anti-clockwise around left prong and re-insert through fork.*

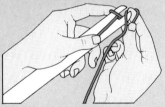

**3** *Wrap yarn clockwise around right prong, forming a figure of eight around fork.*

**4** *Pass yarn back through fork of shuttle stick and wind it lengthwise on stick.*

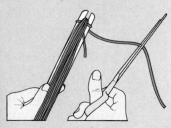

**5** *Cut off end of yarn.*

# *Starting to weave*

As in card weaving, the weft threads are woven in from right and left. Different textures of fabric can be woven by using varying thicknesses of warp and weft threads as required, and changing the positioning of the shed stick.

### *How to weave on a frame*

**1** *Turn shed stick on its side and pass shuttle stick from left and right through shed (see page 215), leaving about 2in. to 3in. (5cm to 7cm) of weft yarn loose on the left side of the warp.*

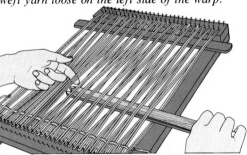

**2** *Turn shed stick back to its original position and use it to push your first weft thread into place at front of frame. Insert next weft thread by darning shuttle stick in and out of the alternate warp threads from right and left.*

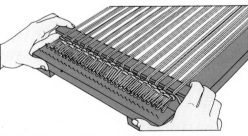

**3** *Push 2nd weft thread into place with the shed stick.*

**4** *Continue in the same way, repeating the process from Step 1.*

# *Finishing off*

When finishing off frame weaving, the work is first removed from the frame (either by unhooking it from the nails, or cutting the warp yarn at each end), and the loose strands then woven into fabric.

### *How to finish off*

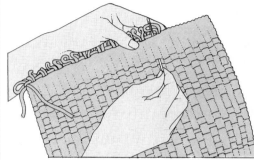

*Having removed work from frame, thread each loose strand of yarn through needle. Push needle down into fabric, drawing yarn through with it. Pull needle out, leaving loose strand hidden in fabric.*

## *Introducing a new colour*

A new colour can be added at any point when required, by adding a new weft thread with a second shuttle stick, ensuring that the colour wefts are interlocked at the edges. This will make the edges tidier and the weaving easier.

### *How to weave in a second colour*

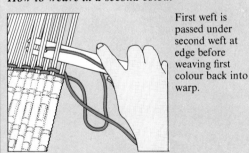

First weft is passed under second weft at edge before weaving first colour back into warp.

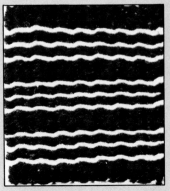

**Finished sample worked in two colours**

# Tabby loom weaving

# Setting up the warp

Tabby loom weaving is the simplest of all forms of mechanized weaving. A tabby loom is basically a frame loom but with the nails replaced by two rollers – one at each end of the loom. This means that the warp can be longer than the frame, although the width of the fabric is still limited by the actual width of the loom. As you weave, the fabric is wound onto the front roller and the warp is released from the back roller.

### How the heddle is used

The warp threads on a tabby loom pass through a rigid heddle (also known as a *split reed* or *metlyx heddle*) which replaces the shed stick used in frame weaving. This heddle not only makes both sheds automatically but also holds each warp thread in place, and is used to beat each new weft thread up to the already woven fabric (known as the *fell*). Because these two sheds are fixed this loom will only make plain weaves.

It takes a little longer to set up a tabby loom than a simple frame loom because the warp has to be made first and then attached to the rollers (see right for instructions).

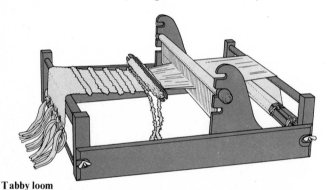

**Tabby loom**

*Front view*

*Side view*

The heddle is pierced with slits and holes through which the warp threads are passed alternately.

The position of the heddle can be altered to provide the sheds on the loom. Use the central position to attach the warp.

### Fastening the heddle

Before you attach the warp to the loom, you must first make sure that the heddle, which is adjustable, is fixed in the central position. Tie each end of the heddle bar with a piece of string to secure it. Once the warp threads have been secured onto both rollers, the string can be removed.

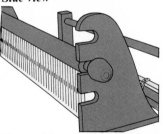

**Heddle fastened in central position**

Winding the warp threads for a roller frame is more complex than winding them for a simple frame, but taken in stages it can be mastered quite easily.

First of all, you will have to decide how much warp you will need. This will depend on the design of the fabric you are making and the texture of the yarn. However, your design will be limited to some extent by the number of holes and slits to the inch (cm) on your particular heddle as this will govern the number of warp threads the loom can take. Bear in mind that if you want to make a coarser fabric you can use a thicker yarn and half the number of slits and holes on the heddle.

Once you have determined the overall length of the warp and the number of threads per inch (cm), you are ready to make it. You must first attach three posts about 4in. to 6in. (10cm to 15cm) high to the edge of a table (which should be long enough to take the warp although you can go around the corners provided you put in an extra post there). Two of the posts should always be about 10in. (25cm) apart, but the third post is placed at whatever distance is required to make the length of the warp, so for a warp of 50in. (125cm) the first two posts should be 10in. (25cm) apart and the third 40in. (100cm) from the second.

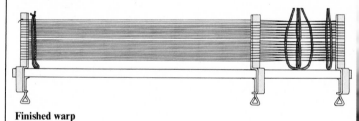

**Finished warp**

*How to make the warp*

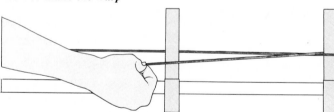

**1** *Attach warp yarn to extreme left hand post.\* Pass yarn around back of 2nd post and then around 3rd post from front to back. Bring yarn forward again in front of 2nd post and back around 1st post from front to back. Repeat the process from \* until you have enough warp threads. End by fastening the yarn to 1st post (left hand post). An even number of warp threads should be wound.*

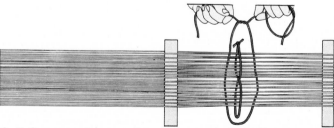

**2** *Before removing warp from posts, mark the half-way point with a lease thread and insert a cross thread through the warp on either side of the cross. Make sure that the lease threads are long enough to allow the warp to be stretched out to its full width and make sure they are tied securely.*

# Attaching the warp to the loom

The next step is to attach the warp to the back roller of the loom. You must take care when handling the warp not to tangle the threads.

## *How to attach the warp*

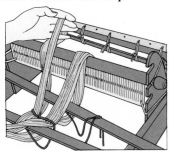 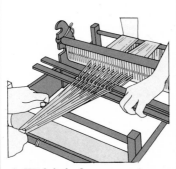

**1** *Tie the heddle into the central position and suspend cross end of warp over the length of the loom and hold "cross" lease thread taut. Slip roller stick into each side of cross and rest across width of loom. Mark the slit to the right of the centre on the heddle. Divide the warp in two halves.*

**4** *With help from an assistant, holding the front end of the warp taut, wind it through the heddle onto the back roller. Move cross sticks carefully towards the front roller as you do so. Continue winding until there is just 6in. (15cm) left lying over the front roller.*

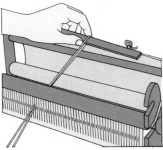 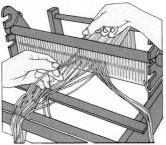

**2** *Then working from centre take first loop on right and thread it through marked slit from front to back, passing the back roller stick (which has been released from the roller) through the end of the loop.*

**5** *Then cut front end of warp threads and rethread heddle by taking alternate threads out of slits and passing them through holes in heddle. Use the cross to help you.*

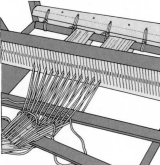 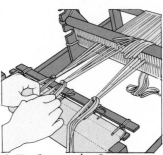

**3** *Continue in this way, completing right side of warp, and then work from the centre to the left. Then undo the "cross" lease thread, leaving sticks in place.*

**6** *Tie front ends of warp to front roller. As an even tension is very important, support front roller stick by temporarily tying central section of warp. Then starting with small even sections of about ¾in. (2cm) at a time, work from both edges to centre.*

# Weaving

Weaving on the tabby loom is almost the same as on the frame, but much quicker. As there is no "darning process" it does not matter in which direction the shuttle stick is passed.

## *How to weave*

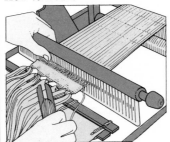 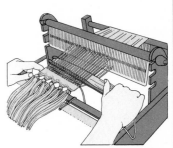

**1** *Push the heddle down for one shed and then pass shuttle through warp. Beat up to front roller stick.*

**2** *Lift the heddle up for the alternate shed and then pass shuttle through warp. Beat up to last thread.*

## *Winding on the warp*

The warp must be wound on when there is not enough space between the fabric and heddle to continue weaving.

## *How to wind on*

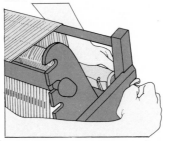 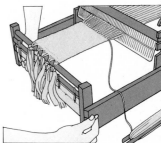

**1** *Release roller clamps at front and back and wind front roller towards you until the fell is about 4in. (10cm) from the front roller. Then fix front roller.*

**2** *Turn back roller away from you to ease tension on warp and then reclamp. Continue to weave and wind on until completed.*

## *Introducing a second colour*

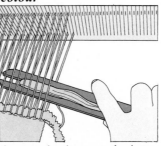

A second colour can be introduced from either side. The previous colour can either be cut off and the end tucked into the next shed or the thread can be left and reintroduced later, leaving a float along the side of the work.

## *Securing the warp*

To make sure the newly threaded warp does not slip out of the heddle, tie threads into bundles with a slip knot.

## *Finishing off*

Untie or cut off the surplus warp threads and darn them in or overlock stitch the end of the woven fabric to secure.

# Tabby weave patterns

The samples of tabby weaving, right, are made with different types of yarn. Some are made using a plain warp, and others with a striped warp. When winding a striped warp, follow the usual instructions for winding the warp, but work in the sequence required for forming the stripes.

All the samples are worked in plain weave, i.e. under one, and then over one.

### Sample patterns

Samples 1 to 4 are in plain weave and have 13 warp threads per in. (5 per cm).

**1** Grey in every pick (background) with small pieces of white yarn woven backwards and forwards where desired, placed in warp before grey pick.

**2** Striped warp. Picks: *8 grey, 4 white, 4 grey, 4 black. Rep from *.

**3** Picks: *25 beige, 1 white, 4 black, 1 white, 42 beige, 1 white, 4 black, 1 white, 25 beige. Rep from *. Brush after weaving.

**4** Picks: *6 grey, 6 white, 6 black. Rep from *.

Samples 5, 6 and 7 have been worked with a thicker yarn in the alternate spaces and holes in the heddle. They have 13 warp threads per 2in. (5 per 2cm).

**5** White with small pieces of dark grey woven in at random.

**6** Striped warp. Picks: *7 white, 1 grey. Rep from *. Plain weave. Picks: *9 white, 1 grey. Rep from *.

**7** Picks: *13 white, 1 grey, 3 white, 1 grey. Rep from *.

**8** Striped warp. Picks: *4 grey, 4 white, 4 grey. Rep from *. Threaded through heddle in groups of 12 with 8 spaces/holes left empty between each set of stripes. Plain weave.

# Knotting and tufting

Knotting and tufting can be used to give a more decorative finish to plain weaving. The most satisfactory knot to use is the one illustrated below because it can be used for loops, tufts or fringes, and will not pull out if worked correctly. The spacing between the loops or tufts can be varied to give a dense or open effect.

## Making tufts with short lengths of yarn

The yarn should be cut into specific lengths – generally, about 3in. (7.5cm) is the minimum. The tufts can always be trimmed later if required.

### How to work

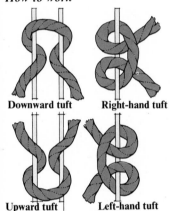

**Downward tuft**   **Right-hand tuft**

**Upward tuft**   **Left-hand tuft**

*Lay 1 length of thread over 1 or 2 warp threads. With your fingers, take the 2 ends behind and then up in between the 1 or 2 warp threads, pulling the ends towards you. Work in any of the four directions shown above.*

## Cutting equal lengths of yarn

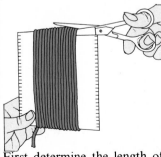

First determine the length of the tufts, and then cut a piece of card to half this size. Wind the yarn around the card and cut along one edge as shown.

## Varying the colour sequence

If a pattern using different colours is required, plan the sequence out first in a diagram, as shown above.

## Making looped fabric

A continuous length of yarn is used for making a looped fabric. The yarn is worked over a gauge which determines the size of the loops. A large knitting needle, for example, makes a suitable gauge for medium-sized loops. When working loops, remember that yarn length should be about 5 times the width of the warp, depending on the size of the gauge used.

### How to work

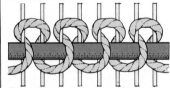

*Tie the yarn at one side and then thread over the gauge, around 2 warp threads and back over the gauge again. At the end of the row, cut and darn yarn into work or carry yarn up one side until next looped row is worked.*

## Cutting tufts to make loops

Slit through each row of loops with a pair of sharp scissors.

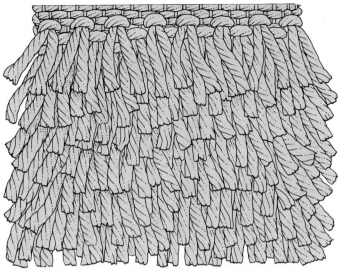

**Tufted fabric**

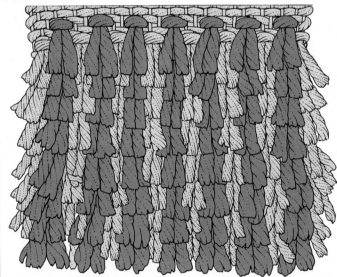

**Two-colour tufted fabric**

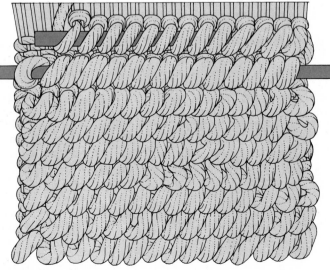

**Looped fabric with gauge**

# Woven shoulder bag

Many articles can be woven in plain or tapestry weave (see page 218). Below is a shoulder bag 12in. (30cm) long by 14in. (36cm) wide, woven in tapestry weave in varying picks of white, grey and black (see below for weaving pattern instructions, and right for instructions on how to make the bag). Rug wool has been used for the weft threads and string for the warp threads (set at two threads per ⅗in. [cm]). Any colours can be used, as long as the correct number of picks is kept to.

## Weaving instructions

Using three colours, black (B), grey (G) and white (W), first weave 3in. (7cm) of black yarn, then the border pattern, which is as follows: 6 picks W; 4 picks G; 6 picks W; 4 picks G; 6 picks W; 10 picks B; 6 picks W; (1 pick G, 1 pick W) × 10; 6 picks W; 10 picks B; 4 picks G; 6 picks B; 4 picks G. Then work 4in. (10cm) in B, then work the border pattern again, this time reversing order.

**Woven shoulder bag**

**Detail of bag**

## Making the bag

Weave the two pieces as described left. Fold all but ¾in. (2cm) of black at beginning and end to the inside and stitch down. Then cut a piece of lining to match the size of the bag, fold and stitch down sides. Stitch sides and bottom of bag firmly. Then position lining inside and stitch into place. Make a strong decorative cord (see below) and stitch it into place along the sides of the bag. Alternatively, the bag can easily be woven in one piece and folded.

## Making the cord

The cord can be made either thick or thin, depending on how many threads are used, and how much twist is put into them. (The more twisted the threads are, the harder and tighter the cord will be: if the cord has very few twists it will be soft and look more bulky, but it will not be as strong as a tight cord, nor will it wear as well.) Prepare a number of threads approximately four times the required length of the finished cord. Knot them together at one end and secure to a fixed point such as a door handle. Then, holding the other end, twist the threads together in a clockwise direction. Do this until you have the required number of twists. Keeping hold of the loose end of cord in one hand, firmly grip the twisted thread at about the halfway point with the other. Then join the two ends together, at the same time releasing the secured end. The two halves of the cord will automatically twist around one another. Tidy the ends by knotting and trimming.

## Alternative patterns

**Tapestry weave sample**
Worked in varying picks of brown and white.

**Tapestry weave sample**
Worked in varying picks of brown and grey.

# Child's tufted waistcoat

The child's waistcoat shown right has been woven using tufts (see page 223 for technique). It is made to fit a four-year-old child with a 22in. (55cm) chest measurement. It is made on a tabby loom with a woollen warp set at five threads per $\frac{3}{8}$in. (cm).

### Weaving instructions

Cut wefts of Aran wool 3in. (7cm) long and put them into warp two at a time (as in sample shown on page 223), i.e. around two warp threads in a downward direction, leaving six warp threads between each tuft, and four picks of Aran wool between each row of tufts, the alternate rows of tufts being half spaces.

## Making the waistcoat

The waistcoat is woven directly into shape as shown in the plan below. (The left front is worked in the same way as the right front, except that the shapings are reversed.) The warp ends are then darned in and the pieces stitched together at the shoulders and sides. The waistcoat can be lined if required: the lining is simply stitched directly to the finished edge of the weaving. (The back can also be woven in two pieces – with a central seam – if required.)

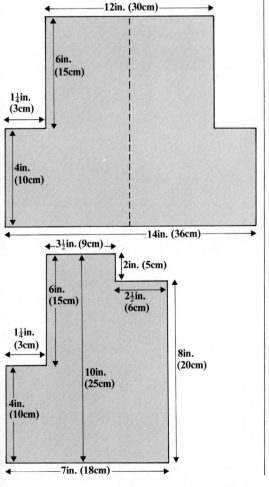

*Child's waistcoat*
*This attractive and hardwearing child's waistcoat can be made in any plain weave pattern, using the measurements shown left. Many additions can be made if required. For example, the edges can be bound with leather or tape binding, and fastenings, such as toggles, can also be added.*

**Detail of waistcoat**

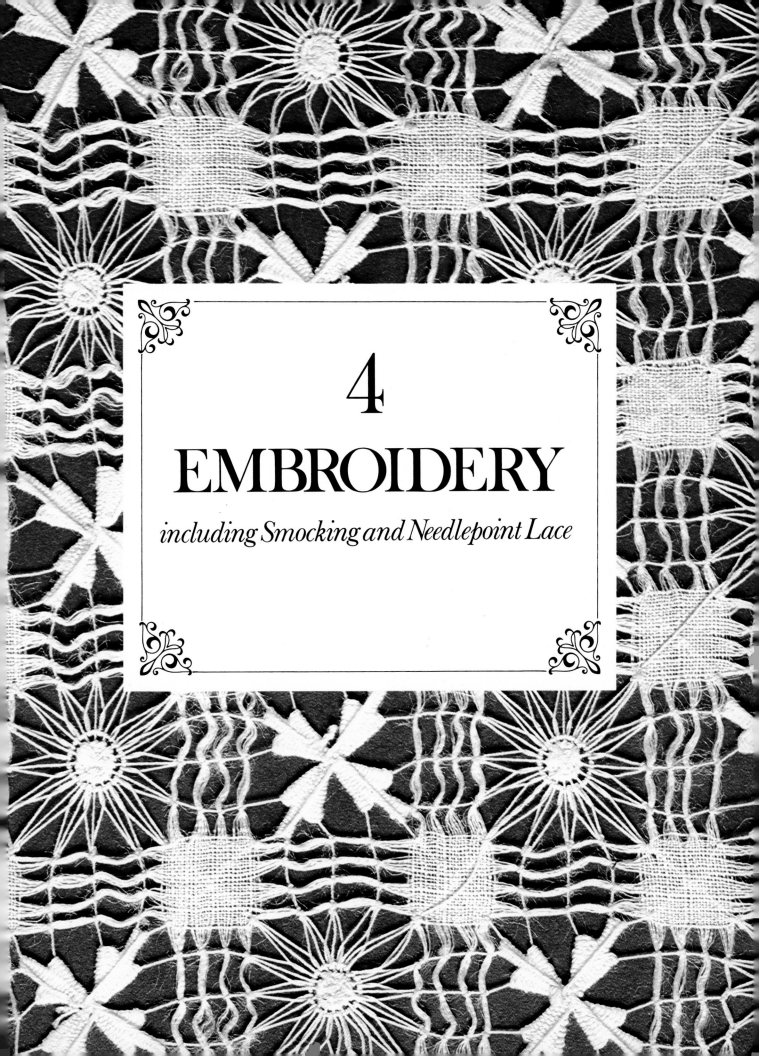

# 4

# EMBROIDERY

*including Smocking and Needlepoint Lace*

# History of embroidery

Embroidery is the art of decorating a ground fabric with stitches to enrich it and add to its beauty. It can be worked on any pliable material from leather to gauze, in threads ranging from wool to the finest gold, and it can be embellished with jewels, pearls and enamels. The very richness of embroidery has led to its undoing in the past, as greedy fingers unstitched precious works to remove the golden threads and jewels.

The origins of embroidery, as of all needlework, are obscure owing to the perishable nature of fabric. It is difficult to give an exact history of it: the Greeks attributed it to Minerva, the Peruvians to Mama Ella, the consort of their first sovereign Mango Capac, and the Chinese say it was founded by the wife of the Emperor Yao. Contemporary accounts, sculpture and paintings, however, remain to tell the story of the past art of the needle.

### Ancient embroidery

In many countries, most notably China, embroidery was used as a symbolic language, not just for decoration. It could denote rank and circumstance, or offer praise and good wishes to the wearer. This symbolic language has had the effect of crystallizing the designs so that the styles of 2,000 years ago remain more or less the same today. In Chinese embroidery the symbols include, for example, the butterfly for conjugal bliss or flirtation, pink bats for happiness, the crane for longevity, mandarin ducks for conjugal affection, the goose for domestic happiness and the parrot as a warning to unfaithful wives. The phoenix was reserved for the empress as a symbol of beauty and good fortune, while the five-clawed or Lung Dragon and the colour yellow were for Imperial use alone. Flowers and fruit also played their parts with the peach and convolvulus being used on marriage garments, the pomegranate for hopes of fertility and the lotus for fruitfulness and purity.

In India, embroidery was defined by the Code of Manu, issued over 2,500 years ago, in which strict rules were laid down as to its uses and types of design, and the areas in which certain types of embroidery could be worked. In this way embroidery became the livelihood and inherited profession for men and women in large areas of India, with skills and techniques passed down from generation to generation.

In ancient Peru, isolated from Europe and the Orient, embroidery stitches resembling knitting were used to create elaborate ritualistic embroideries, worked in brightly coloured llama wools. The Peruvians not only worked extremely sophisticated fabrics from embroidery stitches, they also used the stitches to make three-dimensional fringes and borders depicting little birds and doll-like figures.

The Greeks and Romans sometimes used embroidery to border their tunics and togas and worked it in straight, geometric patterns. They also liked to wear richly embroidered vests of gold, worked for them in Phrygia, an Aegean seaport which is now part of Turkey. The Phrygians were, in fact, famous for their gold embroideries. The circular medallion patterns used in these vests were echoed centuries later in early English work. Gradually geometric and circular patterns gave way to figurative designs: botanical motifs, animals and people were introduced. There are no remaining pieces of this work and it is only known from contemporary accounts and, in particular, a sermon by St Asterius, the fourth-century Bishop of Amasia, who upbraided his parishioners with the following words: "Strive to follow in your lives the teachings of the Gospel rather than the miracles of our Redeemer embroidered upon your outward dress."

### Medieval embroidery

In Europe, in the eleventh century, France produced the Bayeux tapestry, an epic work measuring 227ft by 20in. stitched in wools on a linen ground. It depicts the victories of William the Conqueror and was probably made by the ladies of his court. The simplicity of the materials used for this great work may account for its existence to this day, as it did not prove a temptation to despoilers. An account written by Baldric, Abbot of Bourgueil, describes a far richer contemporary embroidery. The Abbot tells of bed hangings made for William the Conqueror's daughter, Adela, and describes them as being stitched in gold, silver and silk threads, so finely worked that they were scarcely visible. "Skilful care had made the threads of gold and silver so fine that I believe that nothing could have been thinner. The web was so subtle that nothing could be more so . . . Jewels with red marking were shining amidst the work, and pearls of no small price . . . so great was the glitter and beauty of the tapestry that you might say it surpassed the rays of Phoebus. Moreover by reading the inscriptions you might recognize upon the tapestry histories true and novel . . ." Presumably, as it has not survived, this was one of the embroideries whose richness could not stand the test of avarice.

From the eleventh to the thirteenth centuries, England grew rich under the Normans and its embroidery flourished, becoming famous throughout Europe as *opus Anglicanum* and being primarily used for ecclesiastical purposes. It was sought by popes and given as the gift of kings. Fortunately, it was regarded as precious more for the delicacy of its execution and the detailing of its figures than for the richness of its threads, which were mainly silks. The high regard in which it was held has meant that many specimens of it have been carefully preserved to this day and can be seen in museums and cathedrals throughout Europe. The earliest designs were worked with the motifs encircled by rondeaux which were worked with leaves, fruit and birds, the style echoing the far earlier Phrygian work. Later these rondeaux gave way to Gothic arches which sheltered the realistically worked biblical figures, depicted in stem stitch. In the fourteenth century English embroidery declined and did not revive again until the sixteenth century.

Meanwhile in the embroideries of medieval Germany, beads and glass were being used instead of jewels and pearls and linen grounds and threads replaced the rich silks and golds. These humbler materials gave birth to two new types of embroidery. One was beadwork which, by the eighteenth and nineteenth centuries, was used for bead pictures, purses and even cushions. The other was whitework or openwork, known then as *opus Teutonicum*, which used linen grounds and threads. This type of embroidery was mainly worked by nuns, using white threads on white linen with the designs drawn by wandering painters. The stitches were used not only to decorate the ground but also to pull it apart, opening it into lace designs. Gradually the fame of the work spread and the techniques were adopted first by Switzerland and later by the Scandinavian countries where it still flourishes in such places as Hardanger in Norway and Hedebo in Denmark.

The Italians, too, were interested in the openwork techniques and used them in a much more open style, developing from them their famous reticella cutwork embroideries and later, in the fifteenth century, inventing needlepoint lace by coupling the techniques of reticella and needlepoint edgings.

At about the same time they also developed a completely new style of embroidery, known as *voiding*, in which the outlines

**Detail from the Bayeux tapestry, "Odo cheers on his troops"**

and ground of the design were filled with coloured silks, worked in long-armed or Italian cross stitch, leaving the ground fabric within the outlines exposed. This was developed at Assisi in Italy but is also seen in Greek Island embroideries and in modern Scandinavian work.

### Renaissance influence

In the fifteenth century the Renaissance had an immediate effect upon embroidery. Up to this time, it had been allowed to follow its own course – the various stitches determined the textural design and the silks, golds, wools and linens made up the richly surfaced patterns. With the advent of the Renaissance the needle was used like a brush and the threads as paints so that the embroideries became realistic pictures with architecture being shown, and perspective introduced, for the first time. This new, realistic style was greatly aided by the rich patrons of the time, such as the Dukes of Burgundy and the Medicis, who bore the cost of the work and employed the painters of the day, such as Veronese and Botticelli, to make the designs.

### The sixteenth century

In sixteenth-century Spain paintings were used as a guide for the embroiderer with the stitches being worked in gold and jewels to give the sumptuous effects and sharp definitions. At this time a new style of work was invented in Spain known as *blackwork*, in which black silk was used on white linen to make swirling stem designs decorated with intricately filled leaves and occasionally lightened with gold and spangles. This style quickly caught on in other parts of Europe and many fashionable portraits of the day show blackwork used on garments.

In Germany, the desire for realism reached its height with raised and padded techniques being used to give relief effects to motifs, and wiring incorporated to raise the stitches away from the ground. This technique, known as *stump work*, was taken up in other parts of Europe where it was used for altar fronts, and for covering boxes and books or for framing mirrors.

### The seventeenth century

By the seventeenth century extravagance had given way to comfort: embroidered hangings were worked in wool and were necessary as draught excluders. At this time, too, chairs were upholstered for the first time and this opened up a new area for needle craft. In England a style was developed, probably taken from Oriental printed cottons, and known as *Jacobean work*, in which coloured wools were used to make sprawling designs of trees, leaves, fruit, flowers and birds, all stylized and oversized. The fashion for lace, too, was gathering momentum: bobbin lace had been invented in Saxony in the middle of the sixteenth century, and needlepoint lace had spread from Italy to Spain, France and Belgium.

### The eighteenth century

By the eighteenth century, embroidery was being used extensively for clothing. In women's clothes, it was used to cover skirts and bodices, cuffs and necklines. In men's clothing it was used with even greater effect and with more originality: brocade waistcoats were entirely embroidered with the designs repeated on coats at the cuffs, edgings and pockets. The designs ranged from minutely detailed flowers to scenes such as cockfights, complete with flying feathers. Even the buttons were covered with the embroidery motifs of the main design. Whitework was also extensively used for bed linens, night gowns and layettes.

### The nineteenth century

By the nineteenth century manufactured embroidery designs and needlework magazines had come into being along with the introduction of machines. The influx of new machine-made

**Needlework picture of "Cain and Abel", early seventeenth century**

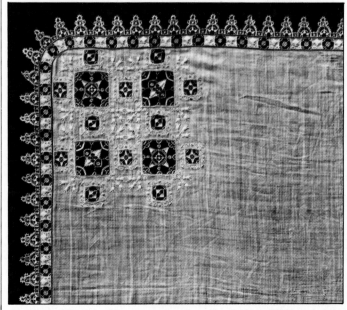

**Detail of whitework with cut squares and needlepoint lace fillings and edges**

textiles prompted the decline of hand-embroidered clothes, although whitework was still used for household linens, under-clothing and layettes. Some fine examples of it can be seen in christening robes.

There was also a fashion for jet work, primarily used by widows to denote their state, with bugle beads of jet stitched into elaborate flower and spray formations and used to decorate jackets, bodices and bags. Embroidered pictures were also fashionable, exact copies being made with the needle of existing works of art (see oval below).

### The twentieth century

In the twentieth century, the tribal art of such people as the Masai in Africa and the North American Indians has a fresh originality. Traditional embroidery still flourishes in China, India, Iran, Morocco, Scandinavia, Mexico and Peru.

One notable exception to the near absence of elaborate embroidery in Europe is in French *couture* where the art of sequin embroidery has been and still is being applied to original dress designs. Sequins first appeared in the flappers' dresses of the 1920s, worked in jet, silver and gold, the designs forming overall flowing patterns or intricate geometric designs with beads strung loosely at hemlines to add to the glitter and jingle. By the 1930s, the sequins were used for long sheath dresses with colours introduced for huge glittering flowers worked against a contrasting sequin background. Today, contemporary designers such as Dior, Balenciaga and St Laurent in Paris and Giorgio San Angelo in America still find inspiration in the work of the early great exponents – Poiret, Vionette and the Callot Soeurs from the first part of this century.

**French brocade scarf with silver sequin outlines, 1920**

**Late eighteenth-century embroidered picture with water-coloured details**

*Poiret dress , 1912*
*Paul Poiret, one of the great French couturiers, employed artists to design his fabrics and embroideries. He was one of the first people to use beads and sequins in the stylized designs which have made French couture so famous.*

# *Regional embroidery*

Embroidery has been, and still is, used throughout the world to decorate fabrics and it usually takes on the distinct style of the region in which it is worked. It can be most easily identified by the motifs worked into it such as the trees and flowers of traditional European work, the llamas of Peru, the dragons of China and the lotus flowers of India. The stitches most commonly worked throughout the world are satin, chain and cross stitch and the threads used are those most easily available in a particular area. Beads also play a big part in regional embroidery and are used extensively by both the North American Indians and the tribes of North Africa.

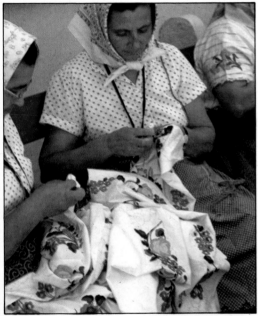

***Embroideresses at work in Kalocsa, Hungary***
*Traditional styles of embroidery are still worked by hand in many European countries.*

***American Indian beadwork saddle***
*Beadwork saddle stitched by the Plains Indians of North America. Note the geometric design panels similar to Indian blanket patterns.*

**Burmese hanging , 1880**
*The hanging (above) is worked in silks and uses appliqué, couching and sequins. It depicts two figures smoking and was hung in a tobacconists' shop.*

**Detail of Scandinavian cross stitch hanging, 1800**

**Turkish cushion, 1850, using metal thread techniques**

**Detail of Cretan satin stitch skirt border, 1820**

# Embroidery frames

Embroidery frames are used to support the ground fabric while it is being embroidered. Although frames are not necessary for all types of work, they do help to make the work easier in various ways. For example, if you use a frame the ground fabric is kept permanently taut and evenly stretched, which helps ensure the stitches worked will be even as well. Also, because work in a frame is handled less, it will stay cleaner. A frame on a stand allows both hands to be free to manipulate the stitches.

There are a number of different types of frame, and the choice depends on the size and the type of the work and, to some extent, on personal preference. For example, a frame on a stand will usually be necessary for large pieces of work to keep the work steady. Hand-held frames, on the other hand, will be better for smaller pieces of work because they can be carried around and worked at will.

### Round frames

These are sometimes known as *tambour frames* because of the drum or tambourine shapes from which they were derived. They come in various sizes and are composed of two hoops placed one on top of the other and tightened by a screw at the side.

### Straight-sided frames

These are sometimes known as *slate frames*, and are constructed in different ways. They are suitable for all types of embroidery. They stretch the ground fabric very evenly and allow a large part of the work to be visible, which is important when working freehand designs. The standard frames are composed of a roller top and bottom to which strips of tape or webbing are nailed and two flat wood sides, which are slotted into the rollers and secured with pegs or screws.

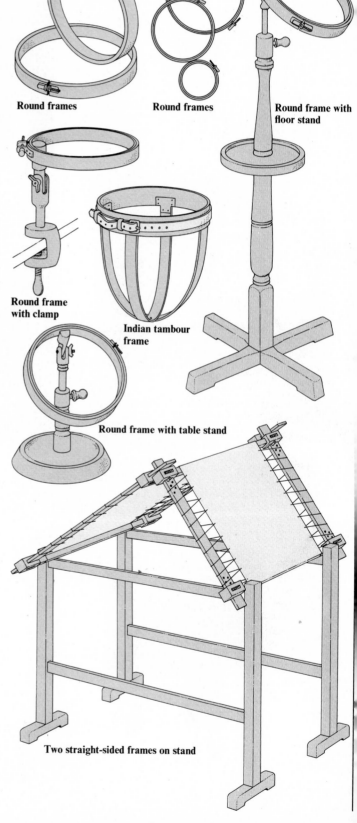

Round frames      Round frames      Round frame with floor stand

Round frame with clamp

Indian tambour frame

Round frame with table stand

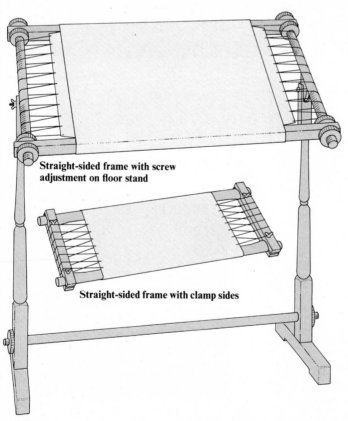

**Straight-sided frame with screw adjustment on floor stand**

**Straight-sided frame with clamp sides**

**Two straight-sided frames on stand**

# Mounting round frames

Round frames are generally used for smaller pieces of embroidery, and can be mounted very easily.

## *How to mount a round frame*

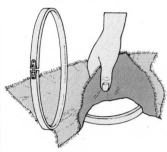

**1** *Place the fabric to be embroidered on top of the lower hoop and place the upper hoop over it.*

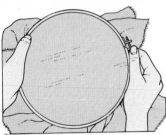

**2** *Tighten the upper hoop by turning the screw until the fabric is both secure and evenly stretched. Do not pull the fabric once the top hoop is secure as this may snag or form stretch marks on it.*

## Binding the frame

When working with a fine fabric there is a tendency for the material to sag in the progress of work. Binding the lower hoop will give the fabric a better grip.

## *How to bind*

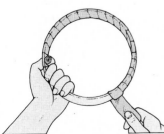

*Before mounting the work, bind the lower hoop with woven tape, as shown, and fasten the end with a few stitches.*

## *Remounting embroidery*

When working larger pieces of embroidery, such as long border strips, the fabric is moved along as each area is completed. This necessitates remounting the piece and care must be taken not to damage the completed stitching.

### *How to remount*

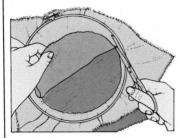

*Place the fabric on the lower hoop and then cover it with a spare piece of fabric such as muslin. Secure the upper hoop and then cut away the muslin to expose the area being worked.*

### *Mounting odd shapes*

In order to frame small cut shapes, the pieces have to be attached to a supporting fabric.

### *How to mount odd shapes*

**1** *Sew the piece onto a larger supporting fabric and then mount in the usual way.*

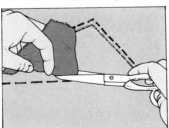

**2** *When firmly in place cut away the supporting fabric inside the shape from underneath, leaving the shape ready for embroidering.*

# Mounting straight-sided frames

These are more complicated to mount and dismount than round frames and before fabric can be mounted on them it must be prepared: the edges of the fabric can be folded back and hemmed or a $\frac{3}{4}$in. (2cm) tape can be stitched all around the edges and dispensed with later.

### *Attaching the fabric to the frame*

After preparing the fabric mark the centre of both the rollers and the top and bottom of the fabric. Then stitch the fabric to the roller webbing starting from the centre and working outwards, using a herringone or diagonal stitch and taking the stitching through the folded hem or tape (see Fig. 1). If the fabric is too long for the frame when both top and bottom are stitched to the roller webbing, wind it around on one roller.

Then slot the sides into the rollers and pull the fabric taut by adjusting the pegs or screws. Lace the sides of the fabric to the sides of the frame, using a needle and a strong thread such as a crochet cotton or button thread (see Fig. 2 below). Lace the sides loosely at first and then tighten them alternately, getting an equal pull on either side. Then tighten the top by altering the peg or screw holes if necessary and give the lacing a final pull before securing it by firm knotting. It is essential to get an even stretch across the whole surface of the fabric, and several adjustments may be necessary to lacing and pegs before it is satisfactory.

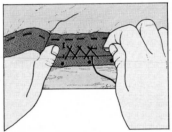
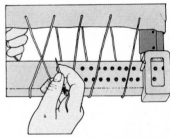

**1 Stitching fabric to roller webbing**   **2 Lacing fabric to sides of frame**

# Lighting for embroidery

**Setting up**
When setting up an embroidery stand it is important to position it in a well-lit area. It should be within range of a direct light source, or directed spotlight. Good lighting conditions are essential for working embroidery, both to protect the eyes from strain and as an aid to working subtle blends and tones of colours.

# Threads, fabrics and needles

Much of the beauty of embroidery depends on a harmonious working partnership between ground fabric and threads, with the stitches being worked from a needle of the correct gauge and type for the job in hand. In the old days, both the fabrics and threads were made in the home, which led to an intimate understanding of their construction, and consequently it was almost second nature to the embroiderers to choose the right needle, thread and ground fabric for the stitch techniques being worked. With the arrival of spinning and weaving machines this intimate understanding was lost and, as a result, a great deal of modern embroidery has suffered from stitches being worked in an unsuitable thread and needle combination for the ground fabric. Ideally, the thread should be worked easily in and out of the ground fabric on a needle which neither splits the woven threads nor forces them apart. The exception to this rule is openwork embroidery (see pages 274–285). The thread, fabric and needle samples on the right show those most commonly used for embroidery together with their partnership combinations.

## Threads
Threads come in silks, cottons, linens, wools, metals and synthetics, which usually imitate their natural counterparts. They are spun in different ways to give different effects to the stitching. The important point to remember when buying thread is its weight and thickness. It should never be so heavy as to distort the ground nor so light as to be invisible.

## Fabrics
Any surface can be embroidered as long as it is firm enough to retain the stitches, supple enough to allow the thread to pass in and out and strong enough to sustain the constant working of the stitching. The most suitable embroidery fabrics are given here and range from finest silks to thickest wools. Printed fabrics and woven designs, too, can be used for embroidery, with the designs acting as useful patterns to embroider over or around.

## Needles
Needles have progressed a long way since the first days of sewing when thorns or fish bones were used to do the job of joining two pieces of fabric together. Today they are made in a wide range of types, sizes and gauges designed for different uses. The different types of embroidery needles are shown on the opposite page: each category has its own size range so that fine gauge needles can be used on fine grounds and large gauges for coarser grounds. In most cases the eye of the needle is long to make threading easier. The exception to this is the needle used for metal work. This has a round eye so that the precious threads are held still and protected during work.

## Thread
The threads shown below are the different types used for embroidery. Metal threads are shown on pages 266–267.

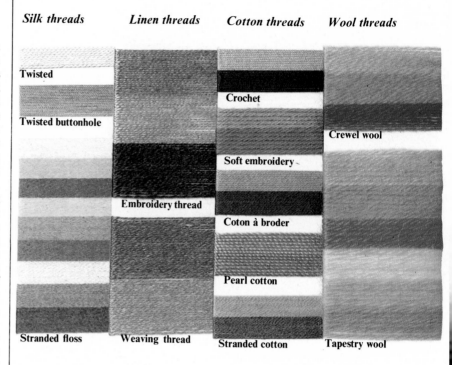

**Silk threads**   **Linen threads**   **Cotton threads**   **Wool threads**

Twisted

Twisted buttonhole

Crochet

Soft embroidery

Crewel wool

Embroidery thread

Coton à broder

Pearl cotton

Stranded floss   Weaving thread   Stranded cotton   Tapestry wool

## Fabric
The examples of fabric (see below) show the four types of natural fabrics used for embroidery.

**Cottons**
1 Cotton lawn 2 Cotton velvet
3 Cotton mull 4 Cotton satin

**Silks**
1 Jap silk 2 Silk chiffon 3 Silk shantung 4 Silk net 5 Raw silk

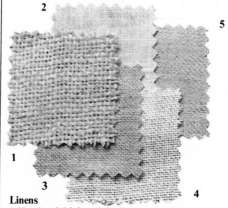

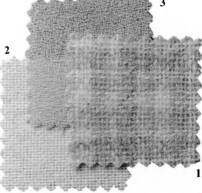

**Linens**
1 Hessian 2 Lightweight linen
3 Linen canvas 4 Evenweave linen 5 Linen twill

**Wools**
1 Wool tweed 2 Wool hopsack
3 Wool georgette

# Implements

## Samples

The following working illustrations show suitable combinations of threads, fabrics and needles using different stitches.

To get the best results in embroidery it is important to use good quality implements. Embroidery scissors should be small and sharp. Thimbles should always fit the finger comfortably; they are used to hold the needle steady as it is being pushed through the fabric. Pins and needles should be stored in sand- or sawdust-filled pin cushions.

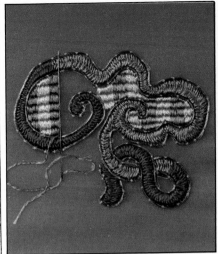

*Silk floss and metal thread worked with a darning needle in double running stitch and couching on silk chiffon.*

*Cotton floss and linen thread worked with a crewel needle in satin and chain stitch and French knots on printed cotton.*

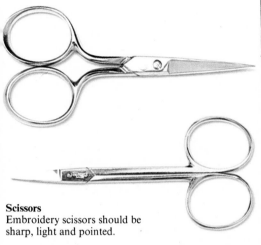

**Scissors**
Embroidery scissors should be sharp, light and pointed.

*Silk twist worked with a crewel needle and crewel wool worked with a chenille needle in cross stitch on wool tweed.*

*Soft embroidery cotton and pearl cotton worked with a chenille needle in chain and back stitch on hessian.*

**Thimbles**
Thimbles need well defined indentations.

**Pincushions**
Pincushions protect pins and needles from rust.

## Needles

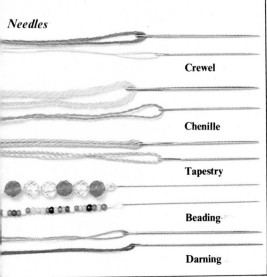

**Crewel**

**Chenille**

**Tapestry**

**Beading**

**Darning**

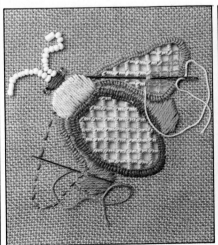

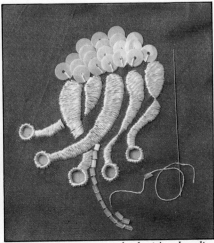

*Crochet cotton and coton à broder worked with tapestry and crewel needles in openwork and satin stitch on evenweave linen.*

*Beads and sequins worked with a beading needle and cutwork in silk floss on silk.*

## Transferring

# Reproducing original designs

Before starting work on your embroidery you will have to determine the kind of design, type of ground fabric and the type of yarn or threads you will use (see pages 234–235). Having chosen these, you will then have to decide how to reproduce, or *transfer*, the design onto the fabric, unless, of course, you are working with a bought pattern (see below). Various methods of transferring designs are given here and on the next page.

### Bought patterns

Embroidery designs can, of course, be created by the embroiderer, but beginners would do best to use a bought pattern and then, as confidence grows, gradually begin to make original embroideries.

Manufactured designs can come in several different forms:

#### Ready printed designs

These are already marked onto a ground fabric and are styled for a specific purpose such as a table cloth, bag or cushion.

#### Transfers

These are designs drawn onto a type of tissue paper with a special waxy ink. They are worked onto the fabric by placing the inked side of the transfer on the surface of the fabric and then ironing over it.

#### Counted thread designs

These designs include cross stitch and openwork (see pages 242, 274). They are worked with the warp (lengthwise) and weft (crosswise) threads of the ground fabric as a guide. The pattern instructions will give the type of stitches to use and the number of threads to cover per stitch.

#### Graphed designs

These designs are shown on squared paper and are worked by tacking squares of the same size onto the ground fabric and then embroidering each square, section by section, copying the design lines contained therein. The process is similar to that in enlarging (see opposite page).

If you are using an original design or wish to copy a design you will have to decide how best to transfer the design onto the fabric. Here are six methods of doing this: **1** Freehand embroidery. **2** Tracing with carbon paper. **3** Tracing direct onto fine fabric. **4** Tacking the design through tissue paper. **5** Pricking and pouncing. **6** Using light.

### Freehand embroidery

For someone already at ease with drawing and the various stitches, the original design can simply be stitched and designed at the same time.

#### How to work

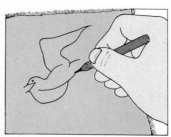

*As a guide to stitching, make a finished coloured drawing of the design, or draw directly onto the fabric using a pencil and then follow these lines.*

### Tracing with carbon paper

This method is suitable for smooth fabrics. Use dressmaker's carbon paper – dark for light fabrics and light for dark fabrics.

#### How to transfer by tracing

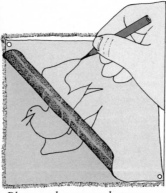

*Place carbon paper between drawing and fabric. Draw over the outlines.*

### Tracing direct onto fine fabrics

This method of transferring is particularly suitable for fine fabrics like gauze, lawn, muslin and organdie.

#### How to trace direct

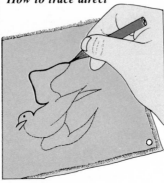

*Lay fabric over design and draw design directly onto it.*

### Tacking through tissue paper

This is the best method to use on coarse or uneven ground fabrics or pile fabric like velvet and towelling.

#### How to tack through tissue paper

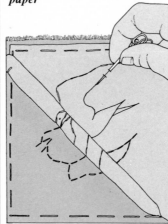

*After tracing the design onto tissue paper, pin the paper to the fabric and tack over the traced lines, using small stitches so as to retain the details. Pull the tissue paper away, leaving the design outlines in tacking stitches. If the finished embroidery completely covers the stitches, leave them in; otherwise pull them out, using tweezers.*

### Pricking and pouncing

This is a traditional and very accurate method of copying designs onto fabric, and is suitable for use on any flat surface fabric. You will need: powdered tailor's chalk, a thick pin or needle for pricking, tracing paper, drawing pins, a piece of felt (or a drawing board) and a pad of cloth or felt rolled into a bundle for pouncing.

#### How to prick and pounce

**1** *Lay the drawing or tracing on a table top covered with a piece of felt or on a drawing board. Prick closely around the outline of the drawing with the pin so that even the most intricate parts of the drawing will show through.*

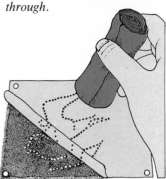

**2** *Lay the pricked design on the ground fabric and secure with drawing pins. Dip the pad into powdered chalk and dab it over the design, forcing chalk through holes and onto fabric. Then remove the paper carefully. Fix the dotted lines by lightly drawing over them with a pencil.*

# *Enlarging, reducing and repeating designs*

Existing designs can be enlarged, reduced or repeated in bands and strips. None of these is difficult to do but accurate measuring and correct positioning is vital. To reduce a design, follow the enlarging procedure below, but in reverse order.

### *Enlarging*

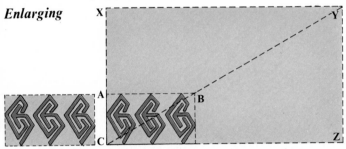

First enclose the design in a square or rectangle (above left). Then take a large piece of paper and lay the original picture at the corner of it (above right). Next draw a diagonal line from C, through B to Y. This line can be extended to any length, but to get the required height for a particular enlargement extend the line CA and measure off on this the desired height at the point called X. From here a line is drawn from X to Y and must be parallel to the base of the original design and meet the diagonal line CBY. This gives the correct position for the final line YZ and will give the required new proportion.

The next step is to divide the original design into equal squares (above left). Then make the same number of squares on the enlargement paper making them proportionately larger (above right). The design is then drawn freehand over the enlargement, square by square.

### *Repeating designs*

A repeating design can be used for borders and edges. In order to judge where to repeat the motif on edges place a mirror on the design and move it around until the best pattern repeat is reached. Mark this point with a line on the design and transfer the marked design onto the ground fabric. When the line is reached in the embroidery repeat the motif by working it again in mirror image.

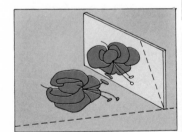

**How to work**
*For corners place mirror at an angle to design until a corner shape is reflected. Mark angle on design and repeat motif in mirror image on other side.*

# *Using light to reproduce designs*

Designs can be reproduced most effectively by using light, both artificial and natural, for tracing.

| **How to trace designs using artificial light** | **How to trace designs using natural light** |
|---|---|
| 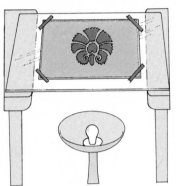 | 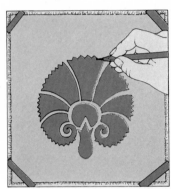 |

*Place a strong light under a sheet of glass. Lay the design on top of the glass and cover it with tracing paper or the ground fabric if it is fine enough. The light will reflect the design through the tracing paper or fabric and the lines can then be traced accurately.*

*Attach the picture to be copied to the inside of a window with adhesive tape. Make sure the sun is shining brightly through the window. Attach the tracing paper or fine fabric over the picture. Then, with a pencil, make the tracing over the lines of the design.*

### *Projecting designs onto fabric*

Many different objects and shapes can be transferred accurately onto fabric with the use of a photographic projector. Portraits, houses, animals, landscapes and intricate tile and carpet patterns can all be copied.

### *How to trace projected designs onto fabric*
*Pin the fabric to a wall, place a transparency in the projector and project it onto the fabric. Focus the projector until the image is the required size. Draw over the image with a pencil directly onto the fabric.*

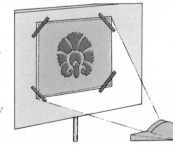

## *Tracing from embossed designs*

An old embroidery or embossed design can be reproduced by tracing it onto a piece of firm but fine paper.

### *How to trace*
*Pin the piece of paper onto the embroidery, which has been fastened to a drawing board. With a soft pencil, work back and forth over the surface of the paper until an impression has been taken. Remove the paper and draw around the outline. Then take a tracing and transfer it to the fabric.*

# Embroidery stitches

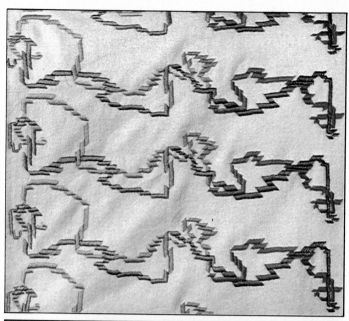

There are hundreds of embroidery stitches, some of which are universally used, such as satin, cross, darning, chain, stem and split, and others which were originally more localized and used in the regions of their invention such as Cretan, Ceylon, French knot, Pekinese stitch and Maltese cross interlacing stitch. However, no matter how localized or intricate a stitch may be, it is interesting and revealing to know that all stitches break down into four basic stitch structures: flat, crossed, looped or knotted.

## Flat stitches

Flat stitches are composed of straight surface stitches worked in different lengths and directions and spaced at varying intervals. The main stitches in this group are *running, back, stem, split, satin* and *long and short.*

## Crossed stitches

Crossed stitches are formed of two or more stitches which cross each other in many different ways. The main crossed stitches are *cross, long-armed cross* and *herringbone.*

## Looped stitches

Looped stitches are made by the thread being looped on the surface of the fabric and held down with a stitch. The main looped stitches are *chain, feather* and *buttonhole.*

## Knotted stitches

Knotted stitches are worked by twisting or knotting the thread on the surface of the fabric to form many different textured effects. The main knotted stitches are *French* and *bullion* knots; *coral* and *tailor's buttonhole* stitches.

## Stitch developments

The basic stitches, in these four groups have been developed for specific effects or uses.

### Composite stitches

These consist of two or three different stitches used in partnership to get raised, threaded, whipped or interlacing effects.

### Couching·

This is a technique used to secure one layer of threads, known as *laid threads*, with overcast stitches, known as *couching stitches.*

### Needlepoint lace

Basic stitches are used in needlepoint lace to make a fabric without using any supporting ground fabric.

### Openwork

In openwork stitches have been developed to hold back the fabric and open it up.

### Smocking

Basic stitches are used in smocking to decorate and hold back the gathered fabric.

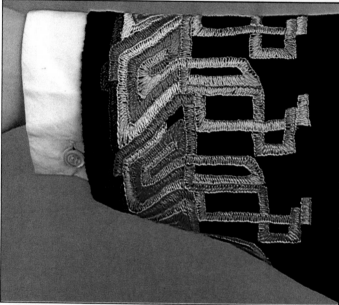

# Embroidered samplers

The word "sampler" comes from the French *exemplaire*, meaning a pattern. Samplers were originally made as a means of stitch reference. The early fifteenth-century samplers were unsigned and the stiches, which were mostly devoted to openwork patterns to be used on the embroidery of household linens, were worked in parallel bands on narrow strips of linen. In the sixteenth century the first stitch pattern book was published and this heralded the end of the original practical purpose of the sampler for by the seventeenth century they had become square and picturesque and were signed by their workers. Flowers, birds and repeating patterns began to be introduced. A little later borders started to appear and by the eighteenth century they had become a schoolroom discipline for carefully worked stitches combined with the first lessons on design and presentation. Gradually a sampler style was developed so that eventually by the twentieth century standard sampler patterns were produced to be worked with specified embroidery stitches.

A late sixteenth-century English sampler signed Jane Bostocke and dated 1598 – one of the earliest signed pieces.

**Detail of sampler**

**Knotted stitch: French knot stitch cat in miniature landscape**
The flowers are also made in French knots amidst a satin stitch background.

**Couching: couched strings of beads in pattern formation**
Detail of cuff from traditional Carpathian skirt.

**Openwork: cutwork border in broderie anglaise style**
Nineteenth-century English cutwork linen edging.

239

# *Flat stitches*

Flat stitches are the earliest of all sewing and embroidery stitches and the easiest to work. They are formed by making straight, flat stitches, worked in a number of different sizes and directions and at various intervals. When used as filling stitches, they can be arranged in different ways to catch the light and make subtle shaded and patterned effects.

The Chinese are probably the greatest exponents of the art of flat stitching and use satin stitch for many of their pictorial embroideries. Darning stitch, double running stitch, back stitch, stem stitch, split stitch and satin stitch all date back to the world's earliest known embroideries. Stem stitch, for example, was being worked in Egypt and Peru as far back as 900 BC.

## Running stitch

Detail from early 17th-century English coif

The simplest of all the stitches, running stitch is the basic stitch for hand sewing. It is used in embroidery for making lines, outlining, and as a foundation for other stitches. It is also used for hand quilting.

It is worked in and out of the ground fabric at regular intervals.

Several small, neat, even stitches are worked at a time.

## Back stitch

Detail from early 17th-century Italian sampler

This is also known as *point de sable stitch*. Used for lines and outlines, it should be worked in small, even stitches. It is more raised than double running stitch.

It is worked by first making a stitch forwards and then a stitch backwards.

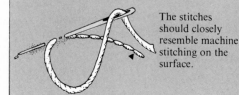

The stitches should closely resemble machine stitching on the surface.

## Stem stitch

Detail from early 18th-century English bag

This is also known as *crewel stitch*. One of the principal embroidery stitches, it can be used in many different ways: for backgrounds, fillings, outlines, and lines. It is also used for shading.

It is worked with the thread kept on the same side of the needle. Place the rows close together for fillings and backgrounds. For wider effects the needle enters the ground fabric at a slight angle.

Narrow stitch            Wide stitch

## Split stitch

This is an important stitch for all forms of figurative work and is also used for outlines and for filling. As its name suggests, the thread is split in the working of the stitch, making its formation invisible and giving a brush stroke quality and smooth, flat surface to the embroidery.

It is worked in the same way as stem stitch, but the thread is split by the needle as it emerges from the short back stitch.

## Satin stitch

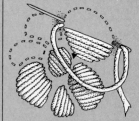

Detail from 18th-century Chinese roundel

This is a major embroidery stitch and, although it appears simple, it is difficult to get the stitches to lie evenly and close together to give a neat edge. It is used for outlining, filling, geometric patterns and shaded effects.

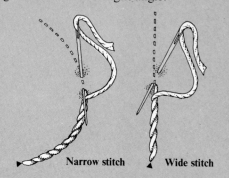

The stitch can be worked in varying lengths, but very long stitches can become loose and untidy.

## Long and short stitch

Detail from early 18th-century shoe panel

This is also known as *embroidery stitch, plumage stitch, shading stitch* and *brick stitch* when used in geometric filling patterns. It is used for edges and outlines and as a filling stitch.

The first row is worked in long and short satin stitches. When used as a filling stitch, the subsequent rows are worked in satin stitches of equal length.

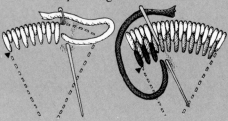

240

# Darning stitch

**Detail from 18th-century Dodecanese hanging**

This is also known as *tacking stitch*. It is a long running stitch, forming big surface stitches. It can be used as a filling stitch by working lines of the stitches close together, or as a decorative stitch (known as *damask stitch*) to form geometric patterns by altering the length of the stitches.

# Double running stitch

**Detail from 19th-century Turkish wedding veil**

This is also known as *Holbein stitch* and *Romanian stitch*. When used as a filling stitch, it is known as *double darning stitch* or *pessante stitch*. It can be used for making outlines and fillings.

It is worked with stitches and spaces of equal length on both sides of the fabric.

# Dot stitch

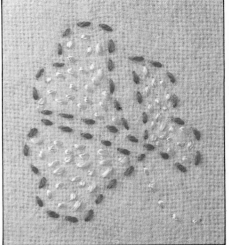

**Dot stitch worked in silk on wool**

This is used for outlines and fillings and gives a more raised surface than running stitch. It can be used to give dotting, beading, seeding and powdering effects.

It is worked by making two back stitches into the same holes, leaving a space before the next pair of stitches is worked.

# Encroaching satin stitch

**Detail from 19th-century Japanese box cover**

This is used for blending colours and soft tonal effects.

The first row is worked as for satin stitch, but subsequent rows are worked so that the head of the new stitch is placed between the bases of the stitches above.

For really subtle effects, the tones can be changed in every row.

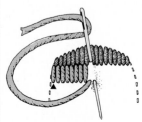

# Fishbone stitch

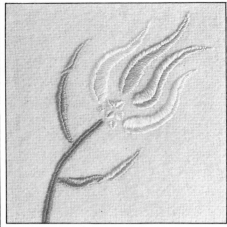

**Fishbone stitch worked in silk on wool**

Although often used as a filling stitch for leaves and petals, it is a useful stitch for borders when it is worked with equal length stitches.

It is worked with a small central stitch at the tip of the motif and then sloping stitches worked alternately on the right and left sides under the base of the previous stitches. By using two needles alternately it can be worked in more than one colour.

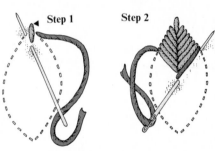

Step 1       Step 2

# Arrowhead stitch

**Arrowhead stitch worked in silk on silk**

This is used as a light filling stitch and for lines of stitching. It is also worked in pairs for powdering effects. It can be worked either vertically or horizontally and is composed of two straight stitches at right angles to each other. Work subsequent rows touching the previous ones.

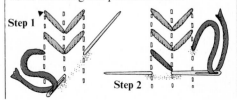

Step 1       Step 2

### Open fishbone stitch

This is used in the same way as fishbone stitch except that more space is left between the stitches.

It is worked in two steps.

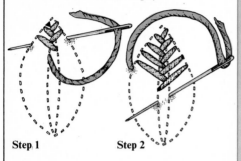

Step 1          Step 2

### Fern stitch

Fern stitch worked in silk on silk

This is used for feathery fillings and fern-like sprays and outlines.

Three equal length stitches are worked at angles to each other, followed by a similar group. If the outside stitches are worked closer together, the central stitch is shortened.

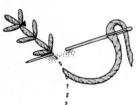

All 3 stitches in each group are worked into same base hole.

### Chevron stitch

This is used for borders and for light lattice fillings.

Even length diagonal stitches are worked at angles to each other, starting and finishing with a short back stitch. It is helpful to work between traced or stitched design lines.

# Crossed stitches

Crossed stitches are formed by two or more stitches crossing each other. The angle of crossing can vary from the simple right angles of cross stitch to the oblique angles of the herringbone and fishbone groups.

Cross stitch, one of the oldest of all embroidery stitches, was widely used by the Phrygians and ancient Egyptians. Also, the traditional embroideries of many countries, including the Greek Islands, Turkey, Romania, Austria, Sweden, Norway and Denmark, all use cross stitch as their principal stitch. The herringbone group of stitches is widely favoured in Algeria and the Yemen.

### Cross stitch

Detail from 18th-century Greek pillowcase

This is also known as *sample stitch*, and is the best known of all embroidery stitches. It is used for outlines, fillings, voiding, borders and motifs. The top stitches should always pass in the same direction, unless deliberate light and shade effects are required, in which case their direction can be varied to catch the light.

It can be worked individually or in a series, when it is worked in two journeys.

#### Worked individually
In this method a complete cross is made before going on to the next. This creates neat, raised crosses.

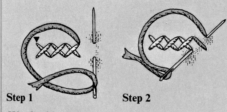

Step 1          Step 2

#### Worked in a series
In this method a line of diagonal stitches is worked in one direction and then covered by a line worked in the other direction.

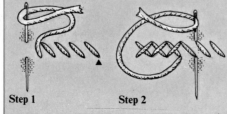

Step 1          Step 2

### Long-armed cross stitch

Detail from Greek Island hanging

This is also known as *Slav stitch* and is used for borders and fillings.

It is worked in long and short diagonal stitches whose subsequent crosses overlap.

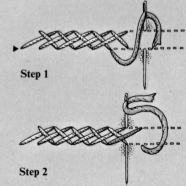

Step 1

Step 2

### Herringbone stitch

This is also known as *Russian cross stitch*. It is used for edgings and fillings and is also the foundation for many other stitches.

It is worked from left to right. The back of the work looks like parallel rows of running stitches.

## *Double-sided cross stitch*

This produces an identical stitch on both sides of the fabric and is used for fine work and reversible work.

It is worked in four steps, with the important half diagonals being made at the end of the first journey and before the last. The dotted line shows the reverse side crosses. Occasionally it is necessary to re-cross a cross in order to get to a point of continuation, and this should be done as invisibly as possible.

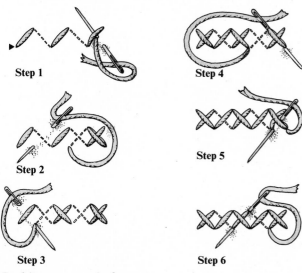

**Step 1**

**Step 2**

**Step 3**

**Step 4**

**Step 5**

**Step 6**

## *Marking cross stitch*

**Back**

This reversible stitch forms a cross on one side of the fabric and a square on the other.

It is worked by covering one cross twice to get a double-sided effect. Occasionally it is necessary to make further re-crosses, especially when working lettering. At the right of each step the back of the stitch is shown.

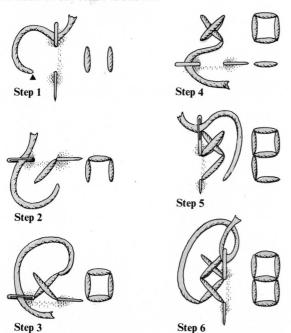

**Step 1**

**Step 2**

**Step 3**

**Step 4**

**Step 5**

**Step 6**

## *St George cross stitch*

This stitch has the same uses as cross stitch, which is shown on the opposite page.

It is worked by making horizontal stitches which are then covered by vertical stitches of the same length.

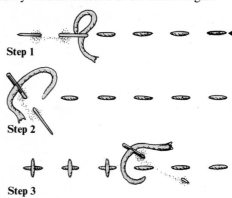

**Step 1**

**Step 2**

**Step 3**

## *Star filling stitch*

This stitch is used as a light filling stitch and for motifs and borders. It can also be used alone as a star.

It is worked by making a St George cross which is then covered by an equal sized cross stitch and topped with a tiny central cross. Each cross can be worked in a different colour.

The tiny central cross is worked to a third the size of the base cross.

## *Ermine stitch*

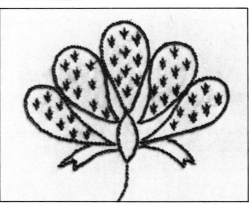

**Ermine stitch worked in silk floss on silk fabric**

This stitch gets its name from the ermine tail effect which is produced when it is worked in black on white. Often used in Spanish blackwork, it is used for fillings and borders.

It is worked by making a straight stitch which is then covered by an elongated cross stitch that is about one-third shorter.

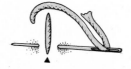

The elongated cross stitch is worked a fraction up from the base of the straight stitch.

## Zigzag stitch

This stitch is used for edgings and fillings and for geometric lattice backgrounds.

It is worked in two journeys of alternate upright and diagonal stitches. On the return journey the upright stitches are made into the same holes as the previous journey and the diagonals cross each other.

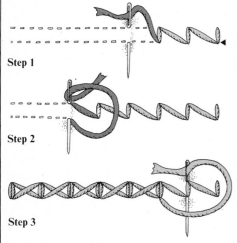

**Step 1**

**Step 2**

**Step 3**

**Zigzag stitch worked in silk on linen**

## Basket stitch

**Basket stitch worked in silk on silk**

This stitch produces a braided effect and is useful for both fillings and edgings.

It can be worked to give an open or closed effect. The back of the work will show a series of parallel stitches.

It is worked with a forwards and a backwards stitch, like the long-armed cross stitch but closer together.

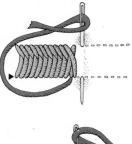

**Step 1**
The forwards stitch is worked diagonally up to the right with the needle inserted vertically downwards through the design lines.

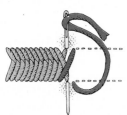

**Step 2**
The backwards stitch is made into the same holes as the 2 previous stitches.

## Raised fishbone stitch

**Raised fishbone stitch worked in silk on silk**

This is also known as *overlapping herringbone stitch*. It is used for padded and raised effects and for filling such shapes as petals, leaves and lozenges.

It is worked by making a straight central stitch and then building up interlacing diagonal stitches worked from side to side. These should be placed as close together as possible to give a smooth surface.

**Step 1**
A central stitch is made first, and then crossed with the diagonal stitches.

**Step 2**
Subsequent diagonal stitches are worked close together and cross over each other at the centre.

## Leaf stitch

**Leaf stitch worked in silk on silk**

This is a light, open stitch ideal for filling leaves and when so used looks good finished off with an outline stitch. It is also used for borders and can be varied in size if required.

It is worked upwards from side to side.

**Step 1**
The needle is brought out left of centre, is inserted at right margin and brought out a little to right of centre.

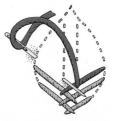

**Step 2**
The needle is inserted at left margin and brought out to left of centre below stitch just formed.

244

## Close herringbone stitch

This is also known as *shadow stitch*. It is used for fine work, with either the back or the front of the stitch being used on the front of the fabric. It can also be used for shadow work on fine fabric with the back of the stitches on the front of the work and the herringbone showing through in shadow form.

It is worked in the same way as herringbone stitch except that the diagonals touch at the top and bottom.

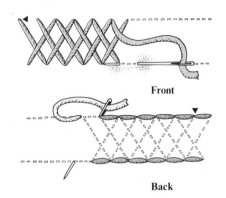

**Front**

**Back**

**Detail from 18th-century Greek bolster cover**

## Flat stitch

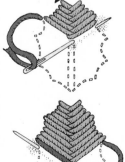

**Flat stitch worked in silk on cotton**

This stitch is used in the same way as leaf stitch, but it is worked closer giving a denser effect. When worked in rows as a filling the outer edges interlock slightly, giving more substance.

It is made in a similar way to leaf stitch except that it is worked from the inner margin to the outer margin.

**Step 1**
The needle is brought out at left margin, inserted to right of centre and brought out at right margin.

**Step 2**
The needle is inserted to left of centre and brought out at left margin.

## One-sided insertion stitch

This is an intricate form of cross stitch suitable for fancy bordering and not an insertion stitch as its name implies.

It is worked in regular and irregular cross stitches and is best used on counted threads to make even stitches.

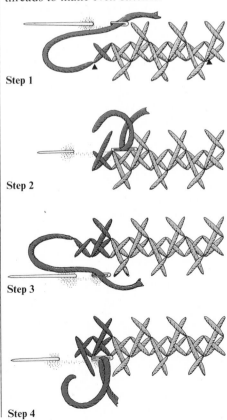

**Step 1**

**Step 2**

**Step 3**

**Step 4**

## Two-sided insertion stitch

**Front**

**Back**

This, like the one-sided insertion stitch, is used for bordering and not insertion work. The back of the stitch forms a lattice pattern, making it reversible.

It is worked in five steps from left to right with the top part being worked first.

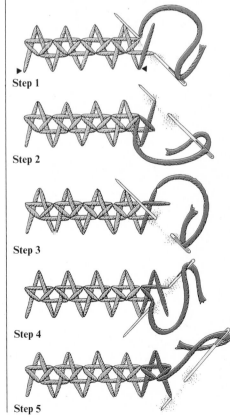

**Step 1**

**Step 2**

**Step 3**

**Step 4**

**Step 5**

245

# Looped stitches

In looped stitches the thread is looped on the surface of the fabric and held in place with a stitch. Chain stitch and buttonhole stitch are the most universally known members of this group. They are frequently used in Spanish blackwork and in Jacobean or crewel work. Both are equally effective as line, outline and filling stitches. Buttonhole stitch is used for all types of edgings and particularly in broderie anglaise. It is also the principal stitch for needlepoint lace (see page 286). Chain stitch can be used to work entire designs and is sometimes used over large areas with a tambour hook (see page 292 for tambouring). It is frequently seen in Chinese and Indian embroideries and is one of the most effective of all the embroidery stitches. It has several variations which are used for both colour and texture changes.

## Chain stitch

This is the fundamental stitch of this group and is used for fillings, edgings, outlines and lines. It is also particularly good for spiral and curved shapes.

It is made with the working thread looped under the tip of the needle and held down with the left thumb, the needle picking up the same-sized piece of ground fabric for each stitch and giving a neat line of back stitches on the reverse side.

The needle is inserted into the same hole from which it has emerged to make the next stitch.

## Detached chain stitch

This is also known as *lazy daisy stitch*. It is commonly used to make leaf and flower shapes, and is also a good filling stitch. It is particularly useful for powdering effects when the individual stitches are scattered.

It is worked in the same way as chain stitch, except that each loop is fastened with a small tying stitch.

**Step 1**
The needle is brought out at arrow, inserted back into same hole and brought out with loop under needle.

**Step 2**
The needle is taken over loop and inserted under it, making a small tying stitch.

Chain stitch detail from 17th-century Mughal coat

Chain stitch detail from 18th-century French waistcoat

Buttonhole stitch detail from 18th-century English coverlet

## Feather stitch

This is also known as *single coral stitch*. It is a light, delicate filling stitch which is useful for feather effects. It can also be used for backgrounds and outlines. Feather stitch is often seen on smocks both for surface embroidery and as the smocking stitch.

A loop stitch is made alternately to the left and the right.

## Buttonhole stitch

This is known as *blanket stitch* when the stitches are further apart. It is widely used for the practical purposes of edging hems and buttonholes. It is also an important stitch for decorative embroidery, used for scallop edgings, all forms of couching, laid work and cut work (see pages 260, 262, 279), and is a very useful filling stitch.

It is worked from left to right.

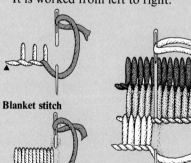

**Blanket stitch**

**Buttonhole stitch**

**Encroaching in rows**

## Chequered chain stitch

This is a more ornate version of chain stitch which is worked alternately in two contrasting coloured threads.

The needle is threaded with two threads; the one not in use is kept above the point of the needle.

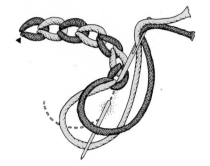

## Broad chain stitch

This is also known as *reverse chain stitch*. It has the same uses as the chain stitches above, but gives a bolder effect. It looks best in a thick thread.

It is worked by first making a running stitch and then bringing the needle out further along the line.

The first chain is made by passing the needle under the running stitch. Subsequent chains are made by passing the needle under the previous chain.

## Heavy chain stitch

This is a broad, decorative stitch which is suitable for bold lines and outlines.

It is worked by first making a straight stitch and subsequently always passing the needle back under two chains to form the next chain.

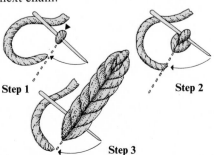

Step 1   Step 2   Step 3

## Double chain stitch

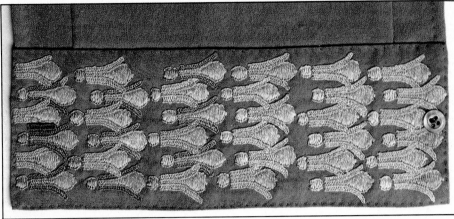

**Double chain stitch worked in silk on silk**

This is a variation of the common chain stitch and can be used for wide borders and for fillings.

It is worked by forming a chain to the right and a chain to the left, starting by making a small vertical stitch to the left with the loop under the needle. A similar stitch is then made at the left margin. Subsequent stitches are made into the loops of the previous ones.

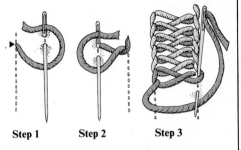

Step 1   Step 2   Step 3

## Open chain stitch

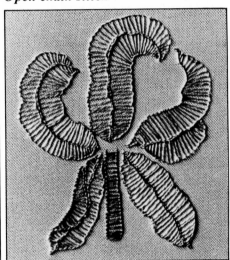

**Open chain stitch worked in silk on silk**

This is also known as *square chain stitch* and *ladder stitch*. Used for bandings, this stitch is often worked in Indian embroideries and can also be formed in varying widths to fill graduating motifs.

It is worked from top to bottom.

The needle is brought out at left margin, inserted at right margin and then brought out at left margin again with thread under needle.

## Zigzag chain stitch

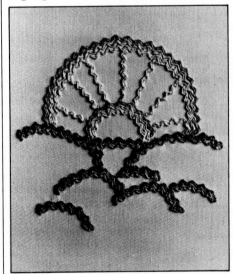

**Zigzag chain worked in silk on fine cotton**

This is also known as *Vandyke chain*. It is used for borders, lines and decorative outlines. It was the original chain stitch of the ancient Chinese embroideries.

It is worked in the same way as chain stitch, except that each stitch is made at an angle to the previous one. In order to keep the chain flat the needle pierces the previous loop whilst forming the next.

247

## Twisted chain stitch

Twisted chain stitch worked in cotton on viyella

This stitch is very useful for curving lines and outlines.

It is worked with the stitches close together, giving a very decorative chain stitch, less linked-looking than the basic chain stitch.

The needle is brought out at arrow and, with thread held down to left, is inserted under thread and then brought out over it.

## Feathered chain stitch

Feathered chain stitch worked in cotton on cotton

This is a neat border stitch which is made up of central zigzags that have a chain at each of their points.

It is worked by making slanting chain stitches to the left and right alternately, and joining them with diagonal stitches.

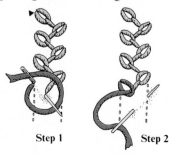

Step 1          Step 2

## Wheat-ear stitch

This stitch is used for decorative lines or, when detached, as a powdering background stitch. It is often used on smocks.

It is worked by making two diagonal stitches joined with a chain stitch. When made as a detached chain stitch for powdering effects, it is worked by making one looped stitch divided by a detached chain.

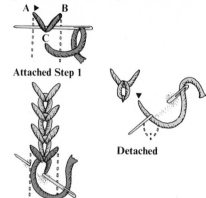

Attached Step 1

Detached

Attached Step 2

## Petal stitch

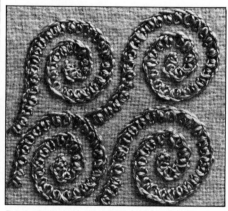

Petal stitch worked in silk on wool

This pendant chain stitch is used for circular and spiral effects as well as for scrolling linework.

It is worked by making a stem stitch and a detached chain stitch.

The detached chain stitch is made halfway along the stem stitch.

Step 1

Step 2          Step 3

## Rosette chain stitch

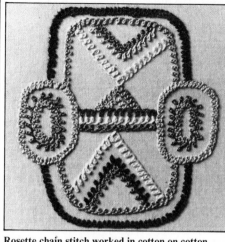

Rosette chain stitch worked in cotton on cotton

This is also known as *bead edging*. It is a decorative stitch which is used for making individual flower shapes. It is also good for borders, edgings and as a delicate finishing touch to babies' clothes.

It is worked by passing the thread to the left and holding it down loosely while making the loop.

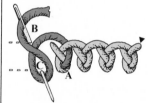

**Step 1**
A crossed loop is made to the left from A. Needle is inserted at B and brought out at C inside loop.

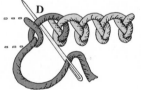

**Step 2**
To complete stitch pass needle under top thread at D, but not through fabric. Continue in the same way.

## Braid stitch

This is an ornamental border stitch which looks best when worked with coarse thread.

**Step 1**
The needle is brought out at A, and twisted around the thread up towards B to make a loop.

**Step 2**
The needle is then inserted at B and brought out at C ready to make the next braid stitch.

## *Plaited braid stitch*

This stitch produces a very ornate surface and is ideally suited to goldwork as most of the stitch is shown on the surface, so there is little waste. It is attractive when worked with a silk corded thread.

**Step 1**
The needle is brought out at arrow and, after making a loop as shown, is inserted at A, brought out at B and pulled through, leaving a loop.

**Step 2**
The needle is then passed under crossed threads without piercing fabric, leaving a loose loop.

**Step 3**
Finally, the needle is inserted at C and brought out at D and pulled through, leaving a loop.

## *Sword edging*

This is a simple stitch which is used for both softening edges and for powdering effects when sprinkled over an area.

It is worked by making a loose stitch which is then looped through with a second stitch, pulling the first into a V-shape.

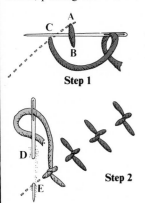

**Step 1**

**Step 2**

The needle is brought out at A, inserted at B and brought out again at C. The second stitch is then looped through first stitch. The needle is then inserted at D and brought out at E.

## *Single feather stitch*

This stitch is similar to blanket or buttonhole stitch, except that the arms are angled. It is often used for smocking as well as for edgings and borders.

It is worked by making loops to the right.

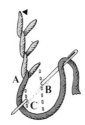

The needle is brought out at A and, with the thread held to the left, is inserted at B and brought out at C, with the loop under the needle.

## *Double feather stitch*

This is also known as *double coral stitch*. It is another variation of feather stitch, and is worked in zigzags to give a light, lacy effect for borders and grounds.

It is worked in the same way as feather stitch, except that, instead of making single stitches, two or more are made to the right and left alternately. It can also be worked irregularly with unequal numbers of stitches to the left and right.

Three feather stitches are made down to right, then 2 to left and 2 to right alternately.

## *Closed feather stitch*

This is a good border stitch which can be made more decorative by laying contrasting threads underneath (see couching and laid work, pages 260–265).

It is worked in the same way as feather stitch, except that the needle is inserted vertically instead of at an angle and close up to the previous stitch.

**Step 1**          **Step 2**

## *Cretan stitch*

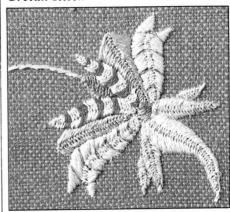

**Cretan stitch worked in silk on linen**

This is also known as *long-armed feather stitch*. It is a very decorative filling stitch which can be easily adapted to fit broad or narrow shapes by simply varying the size of the stitches.

It can be worked with the stitches close together, or further apart to show the ground fabric, or as a line stitch.

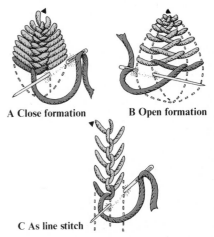

**A Close formation**          **B Open formation**

**C As line stitch**

## *Open Cretan stitch*

**Open Cretan stitch worked in silk on wool**

This is a variation of Cretan stitch which is used for simple borders or as a lattice ground stitch when worked in rows.

It is worked by making short vertical stitches downwards and upwards alternately, with the working thread always held down to the right under the needle. The stitches can be worked close together or far apart.

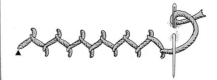

### Fly stitch

**Fly stitch worked in silk on cotton**

This is also known as *open loop* or *Y stitch*. It is a diminutive border stitch which makes an excellent, delicate finishing touch to babies' clothes.

It is worked, either vertically or horizontally, by making detached loop stitches.

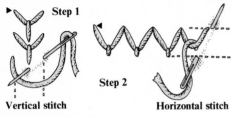

**Vertical stitch**      **Horizontal stitch**

### Loop stitch

This is a good stitch for making broad lines and may also be used for fillings.

The first vertical stitch is made by bringing the needle out at the centre, then inserting it at the top margin and bringing it out at the bottom. The needle is then passed under the stitch just made and over the working thread.

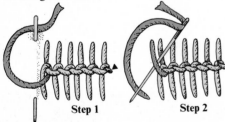

**Step 1**      **Step 2**

### Vandyke stitch

**Vandyke stitch worked in silk on cotton**

This is similar to loop stitch but is plaited along the central vein.

It is worked from top to bottom, with the needle piercing the fabric only at the left and right margins, and not at the centre.

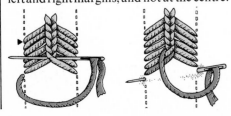

### Ladder stitch

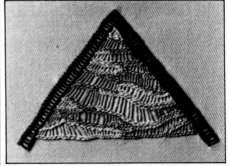

**Ladder stitch worked in silk on cotton**

This broad border and filling stitch is also used for making geometric patterns.

It is worked from the top downwards, stranding and plaiting alternately from right to left.

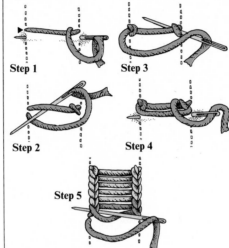

**Step 1**      **Step 3**

**Step 2**      **Step 4**

**Step 5**

### Ceylon stitch

This stitch, also a needlepoint lace stitch, gives a dense filling and has the appearance of knitting. It is, in fact, identical to the crossed knit stitch of knitted fabrics and may have been the forerunner of two-needle knitting. It can be used for broad lines and was used in early Peruvian work.

**Step 1**
The thread is stranded across area to be covered and stitches are looped onto this.

**Step 2**
At the end of each row the needle is brought back to left margin. Stitches in subsequent rows are looped into bases of stitches in previous row.

### Wave stitch

**Wave stitch worked in silk on viyella**

This is also known as *looped shading stitch*. It is an effective filling stitch and is also excellent for shading and colour effects.

After beginning with a row of satin stitches the second and subsequent rows are looped into the base of the previous rows. The diagram below shows the stitches worked far apart for clarity, but they can be placed close together.

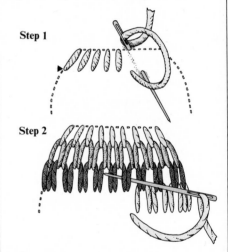

**Step 1**

**Step 2**

### Closed buttonhole stitch

This is a variation of the buttonhole stitch used for borders and hems.

It is worked with pairs of stitches made into the same hole.

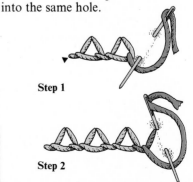

**Step 1**

**Step 2**

## Up and down buttonhole stitch

This is a simple buttonhole variation and it is worked by first pulling the needle through downwards and then inserting it upwards to make a second buttonhole stitch into the same hole.

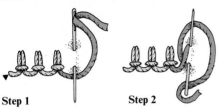

**Step 1**    **Step 2**

## Detached buttonhole stitch

This detached needlepoint lace stitch is used for relief work where motifs are intended to stand away from the ground fabric. It is also used in other types of embroidery as a filling stitch.

It is worked by making rows of buttonhole stitch into the stitches of previous rows without picking up any ground fabric.

When used to fill a graduating motif shaping is achieved by increasing or decreasing stitches at the end of a row.

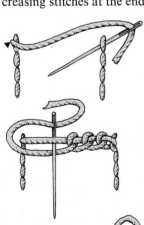

**Step 1**
One row of back stitch is worked at each side of outline and thread is stranded from left to right passing needle under top right back stitch.

**Step 2**
Buttonhole stitches are worked over strand with purled edge below.

**Step 3**
At end of row needle is passed under back stitch, then taken across and looped around other side.

**Step 4**
In subsequent rows the stitches are worked through loops of previous stitches and under strand.

# Knotted stitches

These are formed by knotting or twisting the working thread on the surface of the fabric and securing the twist or knot with a stitch. They can be used as relief stitches for single motifs or massed over larger areas. They can also often be used for entire embroideries. The principal stitches in this group are the French knot and the coral stitch and they are found in Chinese embroideries, Spanish blackwork, crewel work and Mountmellick embroidery.

## French knot

**Detail from 17th-century Italian hanging**

This is also known as *French, dot* and *knotted stitch*. It is commonly used for powdering and sprinkling effects, to denote dots, as a solid filling for motifs, and as a decorative outline finishing stitch. It is also very effective when used massed together for landscape and abstract designs.

This stitch is best worked on a frame so both hands are free. To make the knot, twist the needle two or three times around the thread.

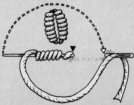

The needle is twisted several times around thread, turned and inserted into hole from which it emerged.

## Coral stitch

This is also known as *beaded stitch, German knot, snail trail* and *knotted stitch*. It is used for irregular lines, outlines and borders. It can also be used for open fillings and is often seen in the Jacobean wool work of seventeenth-century England.

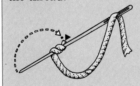

The needle is inserted under the working thread and is brought out over it.

## Bullion knot stitch

This is also known as *knot stitch, caterpillar stitch, worm stitch, coil stitch, Puerto Rico rose, roll stitch* and *post stitch*.

This large, long knot is used in much the same way as the French knot but gives greater emphasis.

It is used singly to form rosettes and is particularly decorative when worked with a needle threaded with different colours as is done in certain Chinese embroideries.

It is worked using a thick needle and pushing it through as far as possible when twisting so as to accommodate the twists.

The needle is pulled through the twists, inverted and inserted at arrow.

## Tailor's buttonhole stitch

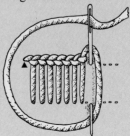

**Tailor's buttonhole stitch worked in silk on wool**

This is a simple variation of the buttonhole stitch which gives a stronger and more hardwearing edge.

It is worked in the same way as buttonhole stitch, except that an additional knot is formed at the head of each stitch. The length of stitches can be varied.

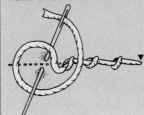

The needle is inserted over and brought out over the working thread.

## Double knot stitch

**Double knot stitch worked in silk on wool**

This is also known as *Palestrina, tied coral, old English* and *Smyrna stitch*. It is used as a continuous stitch for knotted lines and borders or isolated to form diminutive flower shapes.

It is worked from left to right by making a straight stitch, under and over which the thread is looped to form a knot. For best results the knots should be kept evenly spaced along the design lines.

**Step 1**    **Step 2**    **Step 3**

## Zigzag coral stitch

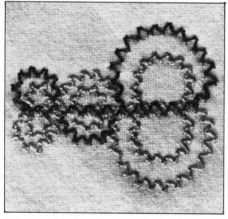

**Zigzag coral stitch worked in silk on wool**

This stitch is used for decorative bands and wide borders.

It is worked in the same way as coral stitch, but from top to bottom, and making a zigzag trail.

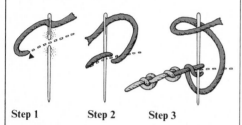

The needle is inserted at right margin and brought out in the centre of the loop. A similar stitch is then made at left margin, and so on alternately.

## Scroll stitch

**Scroll stitch worked in silk on wool**

This stitch is used where flowing lines are required, such as in the depiction of water, and also for borders or banding.

It is worked from left to right, or right to left for a flatter effect. After making the loop around to the right, the needle is inserted inside the loop and brought out (still inside the loop) over the working thread, making sure that the thread is not pulled too tightly.

## Four-legged knot stitch

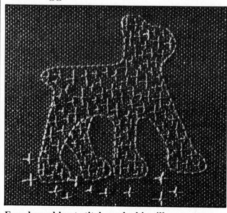

**Four-legged knot stitch worked in silk on cotton**

This stitch can be used for powdering fillings or, when in rows, for borders.

The knot is made after the vertical stitch by passing the needle, without piercing the fabric, first under the initial vertical stitch, then over the working thread. The last leg of the cross is then made.

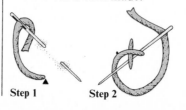

**Step 1**    **Step 2**    **Finished stitch**

## Cable chain stitch

**Cable chain stitch worked in silk on viyella**

This is a fancy chain stitch with intervening links and is often used in conjunction with a contrasting stitch on either side.

The first loop is made by a twist of the needle around the thread. The needle is then inserted downwards under this loop and is brought out ready to make the next stitch in the same way.

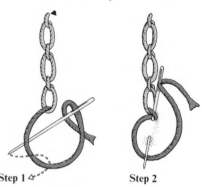

**Step 1**    **Step 2**

## Knotted chain stitch

This is also known as *link stitch*. It gives a bold decorative line and is shown off best when worked with a thick thread.

The needle is brought out at A, inserted at B and brought out at C. It is then passed downwards under the stitch just made and drawn through, leaving the thread slightly slack. The needle is now passed downwards under the loop and over the working thread. It is then pulled through, forming a knot ready to make next stitch.

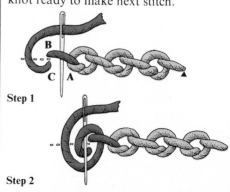

**Step 1**

**Step 2**

## Knotted cable chain stitch

This is more decorative than cable chain stitch and is used for wide curving lines and borders. Familiarity with coral stitch would help before beginning this stitch.

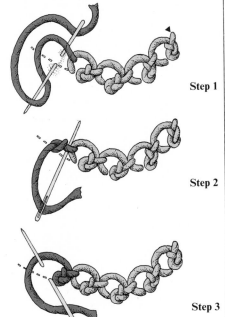

Step 1

Step 2

Step 3

## Diamond stitch

This stitch is used for borders and as an insertion stitch. It can also be used as a filling stitch.

It is worked by making a stranding stitch from left to right (A–B) and bringing out the needle just below (C). A knot is then formed to right and left and then centre.

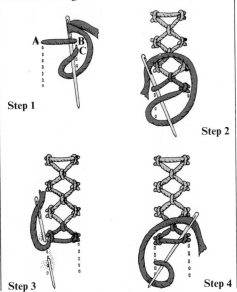

Step 1

Step 2

Step 3

Step 4

## Crested chain stitch

This is also known as *Spanish coral stitch*. It is a combination of chain and coral stitch and is a fancy stitch which is used for decorative bands and wide borders.

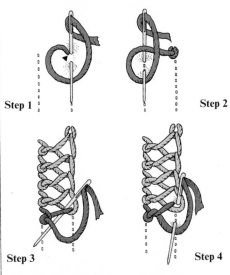

Step 1

Step 2

Step 3

Step 4

## Knotted buttonhole stitch

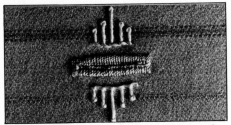

**Knotted buttonhole stitch worked in silk on wool**

This is a variation of the buttonhole stitch and is made with knotted tips. It is used for fancy edges in lines or circles or for fringe effects, and looks best when worked with a coarse thread.

It is worked from left to right by making a loop around the finger through which the needle is passed, and then making a simple buttonhole stitch with the loop still on the needle to make the knot.

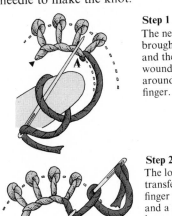

**Step 1**
The needle is brought out at A and the thread is wound once around the finger.

**Step 2**
The loop is transferred from finger to needle and a simple buttonhole stitch is made.

## Spanish knotted feather stitch

This is also known as *twisted zigzag chain stitch*. It is used for bands and wide decorative borders.

It is worked downwards and consists of a series of twisted loops. With practice the stitch will become even.

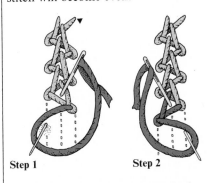

Step 1

Step 2

## Portuguese knotted stem stitch

**Portuguese knotted stem stitch worked in silk on cotton**

This stitch, used for raised lines and medium heavy outlines, gives a knobbly effect when worked with a coarse thread.

It is worked by making stem stitches and tying them together with whipping stitches.

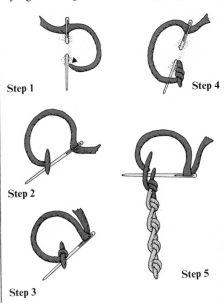

Step 1

Step 2

Step 3

Step 4

Step 5

253

### Rope stitch

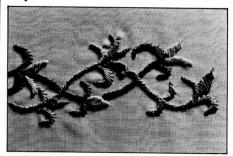

**Rope stitch worked in silk on silk**

This is a raised stitch which otherwise is very similar in appearance to satin stitch. It is used for spirals, curving lines and rope-like effects.

It is worked from top to bottom by making slanting stitches placed very close together with the needle coming through over the working thread to form small knots on the base line.

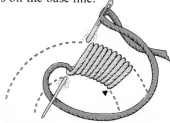

### Pearl stitch

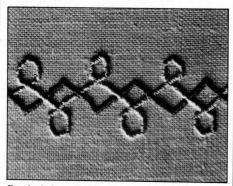

**Pearl stitch worked in silk on linen**

This is used for bead and pearl effects or, when worked far apart, to form ragged lines. It is also used for making geometric patterns and looks best when worked with a coarse thread.

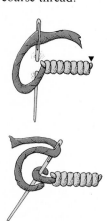

**Step 1**
The needle is inserted vertically downwards and is brought out under thread. The needle is pulled through, leaving a small loop.

**Step 2**
The needle is inserted downwards through small loop and under thread, pulled through and tightened.

# Composite stitches

Composite stitches are combinations of stitches used together to create a raised, bolder and more decorative effect. They are made either by *whipping* one stitch over another or by *threading* one stitch through another. Certain stitches are worked with the second one merely going around the first without picking up the ground fabric. With these stitches it is easier to use a blunt-pointed needle as a safeguard against piercing the ground fabric or splitting the threads of the stitch being covered.

Whipped stitches are used for both raised and decorative effects, with one stitch being imposed upon another. Threaded stitches are used for purely decorative effects, with one stitch being threaded through another, without picking up any ground fabric. One example of each is shown below.

### Overcast stitch

This whipped stitch is best worked on a frame and is extensively used for all forms of open work, such as withdrawn thread, pulled thread and cut work (see pages 274–285). It is also used for raised lines and outlines and is particularly useful for making letters, initials and monograms and for figurative designs or where the lines cross over one another.

It is worked by making a foundation row of running stitches which are then whipped over with the overcast stitches.

**Overcast stitch worked in silk on cotton**

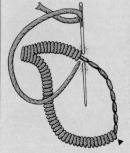

Lines are covered with double running stitches. Overcast stitches are then worked over these, picking up a minimum of ground fabric with each stitch.

### Pekinese stitch

This threaded stitch is also known as *Chinese stitch*. A braid-like stitch, it is one of the principal Chinese embroidery stitches and is used by them for entire works which are closely stitched in subtle shades. Pekinese stitch is most effective when worked in gold and metal threads.

It is worked by making a foundation row of back stitches through which a second thread is laced.

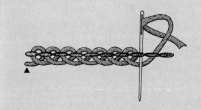

**Detail from 19th-century Chinese bag**

## Whipped running stitch

This is also known as *cordonnet stitch*. It is similar in appearance to overcast stitch but the whipping is worked farther apart and does not pick up any ground fabric. It gives a very simple raised line or outline and can also be used for fillings. Sometimes it is used exclusively, as in the fine muslin embroideries of India.

It is worked by making a foundation row of double running stitches which are then whipped over with overcast stitches.

Work widely spaced overcast stitches around running stitches.

## Whipped satin stitch

In this stitch the whipping gives a corded finish to the satin stitch foundation, making it a useful stitch for textured lines and bars over a motif.

After making a foundation row of satin stitches, work these over with whipping stitches placed diagonally to them.

## Whipped stem stitch

This stitch is used for bold lines and can be made more decorative using a contrasting thread for the whipping.

It is worked by making a foundation row of stem stitches which are covered with regularly placed whipping stitches.

Whipping stitches are worked over and under the stem stitches without picking up any ground fabric.

## Whipped chain stitch

This stitch is used for borders and bold outlines. Like the whipped stem stitch, it can be made more decorative by using a contrasting whipping thread.

It is worked by making a foundation row of chain stitches which are covered with regularly placed whipping stitches, taking care not to pierce the ground fabric.

## Threaded back stitch

This stitch is used for decorative lines and edges in the same or a contrasting thread.

It is worked by making a foundation row of back stitches which are then threaded through in two separate journeys.

## Guilloche stitch

This is an ornamental border stitch which consists of three different stitches.

It is worked by making the outer lines in stem stitch and the inner ones in groups of three satin stitches which are threaded in two journeys. The circles are finished with a French knot.

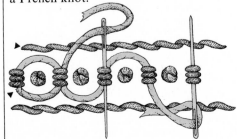

## Interlacing band stitch

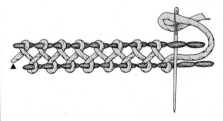

This is also known as *herringbone ladder filling stitch*. It is used for bands and trellis fillings and can also be worked as a reversible stitch by making the lacing stitches on both sides of the fabric.

It is worked by making two lines of double running stitches (see page 241), placing the second line so that the stitches do not lie opposite those in the first line.

These stitches are then threaded through alternately up and down. When used as a filling, further lines of double running stitch are worked one below the other and threaded in the same way.

## Cloud filling stitch

**Cloud filling stitch worked in silk on linen**

This is also known as *Mexican stitch*. It is an easy and effective stitch to work and is used for crewel embroideries, having been much used in Jacobean designs. It is also widely used in Denmark on huckaback towelling, with much bolder effects being achieved by working the subsequent rows of threading in different colours.

It is worked by making a foundation row of equal sized and regularly placed vertical darning stitches (see page 241) and then threading through these to form a trellis. Cloud filling can be worked in pattern formation by threading up and down, several lines at a time, as in Danish work.

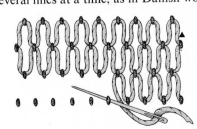

255

### Raised chevron stitch

When needed for bold borders and bands chevron stitch (see page 242) can be given more prominence by using it as a threading stitch on a foundation of diagonal stitches worked in V formations.

The V shapes are worked with the needle always in a horizontal position. It is brought out at A, inserted at B, brought out at C, inserted at A or the first V; then brought out at D, inserted at E, brought out at F and inserted at D for the second V. The chevron threading is then worked in either the same or contrasting thread.

Step 1

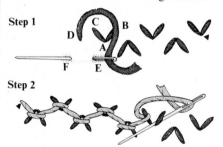

Step 2

### Threaded detached chain stitch

This stitch, used for light borders or decorative lines, can be threaded in a single or double line to form interlinking chains.

It is worked by making a line of detached chains (see page 246) and then threading through them with the same or contrasting coloured thread.

### Raised lattice band

This forms a really firm, raised band and is ideal for rich, padded borders.

It is worked using herringbone stitch over padded satin stitches, and then lacing through it.

### Twisted lattice band

Twisted lattice band worked in cotton on coarse linen

This light border stitch can also be used as a rich background stitch when interlaced with gold.

It is worked by making a foundation of two rows of herringbone stitch which are then threaded in two journeys.

### Tied herringbone stitch

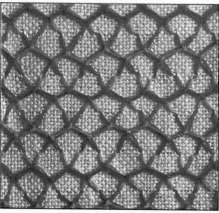

Tied herringbone stitch in cotton on coarse linen

This is used for neat, formal borders or as a light filling stitch.

It is worked by making a foundation row of the herringbone stitches and threading them with zigzag coral stitch (see page 252). The knots of these are made on the intersections of the herringbone stitches (as shown in the diagram below).

### Interlacing crossed stitches

The following three stitches are worked with intricate crossed stitches as the framework for the decorative interlacings which are worked subsequently.

### Laced herringbone stitch

This is also known as *German interlacing stitch*. It is a good border stitch, worked with an unusual circular threading.

It is worked by making a foundation of herringbone stitches and then turning the work upside down ready to begin the threading. In order to work the threading correctly it is important to follow the given formation of the herringbone foundation. When threading, make two complete circles around each upper cross and one and a half around each lower cross.

### Interlacing stitch

This old and very beautiful stitch can be used for borders to form geometric patterns and as an insertion stitch for a decorative seam to join two pieces of fabric together. The interlacing thread can be in a contrasting colour and looks particularly good when blue is used on a white ground.

The herringbone formation of this stitch is slightly different to that of the common herringbone stitch, and the trick in working it correctly is to study its formation carefully. When working the stitch make sure that the herringbone stitches are worked under and over each other in the order given. Thread by working one side and the middle and then the second side and the middle again.

## Maltese cross interlacing stitch

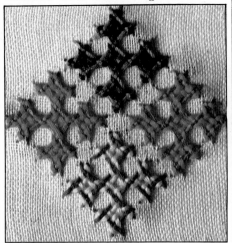

**Maltese cross interlacing stitch worked in cotton on coarse linen**

Fine or coarse threads can be used for this stitch, which can be used either for individual motifs or as a more elaborate border stitch.

It is worked by making a foundation framework of crossed stitches and then threading through in the order given, using either the same or contrasting thread.

**Step 1**
The grid is worked starting from large arrow.

**Step 2**
Then grid is laced, starting from arrow at centre.

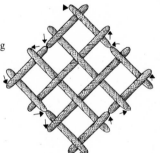

**Step 3**
The lacing forms a cross shape filling on grid. Finished stitch with contrasting lacing.

## Bands and ladders

Bands and ladder effects are made by working a foundation of horizontal stitches and then threading through these in various ways as shown in the following three stitches.

### Chequered chain band

This is used for checked borders and fillings. It can also be worked as a raised stitch by making a padding of laid threads beneath the horizontal stitches. The threading is worked with two blunt-pointed needles, each threaded double with contrasting threads, but an embroidery needle and single thread are used for working the foundation stitching.

A foundation of horizontal stitches is made and then the first double-threaded needle is brought to the surface at the top of the ladder and passed over the first bar and under the second bar. It is then laid to one side and the second double-threaded needle is brought through between first and second bars and is pulled through the threads on the first needle. This is then laid to one side and the first needle is worked into the next bar. The process is then repeated, using alternate threads to work down the ladder.

When used as a filling, lines of chequered chain band are worked side by side with stripes being formed by starting each new line in the same colour and checks being made by starting each alternate line in the alternate colour.

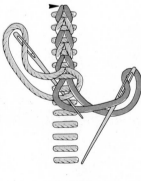

**Step 1**
The first needle is held to the side and the second one is passed under the bar and through the threads of the first needle.

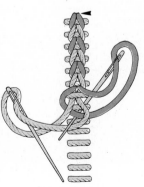

**Step 2**
The second needle is then held to the side and the first one is taken up and used in the same way.

## Raised chain band

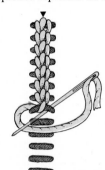

This solid little banding stitch is worked by making a looped stitch onto each bar.

After working the foundation stitches the needle is brought through above the first bar and passed under the centre of the bar. A loop stitch is then made as shown and the sequence repeated down the ladder.

Starting at arrow take needle over and under first bar and work loop stitch as shown. Continue in this way.

## Singalese chain stitch

**Singalese chain stitch worked in silk on wool**

This stitch, found in the traditional embroideries of Sri Lanka, is an adaptation of open chain stitch (see page 247) worked with contrasting threads at either side. It is used for borders and as a decorative casing for ribbon fillings.

Before working, trace two lines and then place the contrasting threads loosely along these and work the open chain stitches over them.

Starting at arrow work open chain stitch over the loosely laid threads.

# Designing motifs

In the past, ideas for embroidery were often taken from nature. This still remains one of the best sources for inspiration for both colour and line. In the example below, a Peruvian lily was studied and the outline drawn, transferred to fabric and worked first in cross stitch (Fig. 1) and then in satin stitch (Fig. 2).

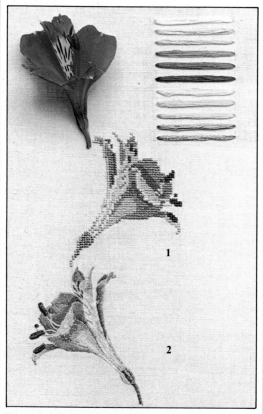

1

2

**The embroidery threads matched to the original lily**

**Charted design for the cross stitch lily**

## Positioning motifs

Embroidered motifs can be placed anywhere on a garment to make something plain into something special. Take care to use appropriate threads for the ground fabric, working on it whenever possible before the garment is made up.

**Motif designed and worked by a contemporary artist**

*Embroidery can be used on jeans as a decoration or to cover worn areas.*

*The above motif can be repeated around the collars and cuffs and is worked in Vandyke stitch (see page 250).*

*The birds above and below are details from a South American embroidery, worked on coarse fabric.*

## Shirt motifs

Printed and woven fabrics are also a useful source for embroidery designs. These can be copied exactly or stylized, as in Jacobean embroidery. The motifs right and below were adapted from modern Indian printed fabric and can be used alone or together to decorate clothes. When working motifs make sure that the threads chosen are suitable for the ground fabric. When the motifs are repeated each one could be coloured slightly differently or worked in different stitches. Beads and sequins could also be incorporated into the design (see pages 296–297 for techniques).

**Silk thread in Cretan stitch on linen**

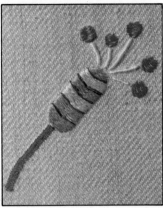

**Silk thread in flat stitch on cotton**

**Silk motif in chain, ermine and satin stitch**

## Embroidered waistcoat

Styles of embroidery too can be used as inspiration for new designs. The waistcoat above, embroidered in stranded silk floss, is reminiscent of old Chinese work. A tambour hook (see page 292) has been used to work the tiny chain stitches. The detail left shows the motif of a stylized bird amidst the twining vine leaves border. The position of main motifs is important as they should always be placed at a focal point. This design could also be repeated in panels to cover a whole ground or the birds could be isolated and used alone.

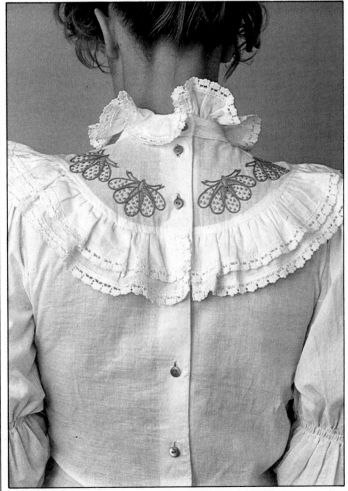

**Motif (above left) worked around a blouse yoke**

259

# Couching

Couching and laid work (page 265) are two similar techniques which have been developed to show off threads that are either too valuable, too brittle or too delicate to be worked in and out of the fabric in the usual way. Both are used almost exclusively when working with gold and metal threads, which also require special treatment (see pages 268–269).

In couching one or more threads are laid down on the surface of the fabric and stitched into position with another less precious, more supple thread. This technique can be used to make bold lines and outlines for filled motifs. It can also be used to finish appliqué work and to make decorative patterns with the colour and design formation of the couching stitches.

### Threads

Although any threads can be couched, the glossy texture of silk and the glitter of metal threads will be shown off best by this technique. Various thread combinations can be used. For example, metal threads can be laid down and couched with contrasting silk; alternatively, several different coloured strands of silk can be threaded through the same needle and laid down and couched with silk of yet another colour. When worked in a contrasting colour the couching stitches become visible and form additional patterns above the laid threads. Invisible couching stitches can be worked in matching colours to the laid threads when the texture of the laid threads is already sufficiently ornate, or when laying down cords which will form their own pattern and need no extra decoration.

Chinese sleeve detail showing couching techniques on the birds

# Plain couching

Couching should always be worked on a supported frame, as both hands need to be free to manipulate the laid and couching threads. Couched lines and outlines are easy to work, but make sure that the laid threads lie neatly under the couching stitches, which must secure them firmly and at regular intervals. In simple couching the laid threads are brought to the surface and worked along the design line. As work progresses the laid threads are guided along loosely with the left hand while the right hand makes small overcast stitches with the couching thread. When the line of stitches is complete the laid threads are brought to the back of the work and secured. When making a curve the couching stitches are placed closer together, so that the threads lie flat; when making an angle, a couching stitch is placed at the point of the angle.

A bunching effect can be achieved by couching several thick threads with a tight overcast stitch (see below). This effect is used for pronounced decorative outlines.

### How to work simple couching

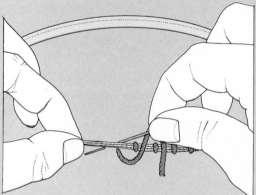

**Simple couching**
Bring both the laid threads and the couching thread to the surface. Then secure the laid threads at regular intervals with couching stitches. Finish by taking threads to back of work and securing.

### How to work bunched couching

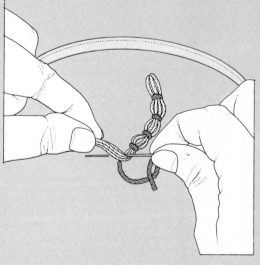

**Bunched couching**
Bring the laid threads to the surface as for simple couching and secure them at intervals with short overcast stitches which are pulled tightly to bunch the threads.

# Couching with embroidery stitches

One way of making simple couching more decorative is by using embroidery stitches instead of overcasting to couch the laid threads. Many embroidery stitches which form broad bands can be used, including cross stitch, buttonhole stitch, feather stitch and satin stitch (see pages 240–257 for stitch techniques). These stitches are used to secure the laid threads and must therefore be worked in and out of the ground fabric.

## Feather stitch
This is worked by making a loop stitch alternately from side to side.

*How to work*
1 *Lay 2 groups of threads, with a gap between them. Then work feather stitch over both lines of threads, beginning over the top group.*
2 *Make a second stitch over the bottom group and continue in this way alternately.*

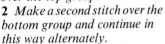

## Satin stitch
This stitch can be used to make different patterns according to the length and grouping of the embroidery stitches over the laid threads.

*How to work*
*Secure the laid threads by working regular groups of satin stitch over them and through the fabric.*

**Couching with satin stitch**

## Buttonhole stitch
This stitch can be used to give a firm, yet decorative edge to outlines and borders.

*How to work*
*Keeping the purled side to the outer edge work regularly spaced buttonhole stitches over a group of laid threads.*

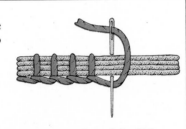

**Couching with buttonhole stitch**

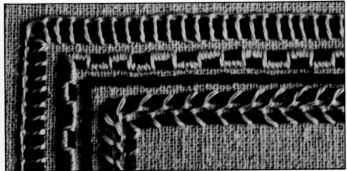

**Embroidery stitches used to couch down laid threads on a border**

# Couching for fillings

Couching can be used to make light and solid fillings. Decorative effects can be achieved by contrasting the laid and couching threads.

## Light fillings
Light fillings can be made by stitching the laid threads in an open grid pattern and then securing them by working cross stitches over them.

*How to work*

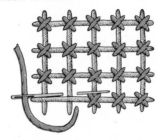

*Make the grid pattern with long laid stitches across the fabric. Then work cross stitches in the same or contrasting colours over the intersections.*

## Solid fillings
When making solid couched fillings for motifs the lines of the laid thread can be made to go in any direction: vertical, horizontal, slanting, or simply following the contours of the shape to be filled.

*How to work*

*Bring the thread to be couched to the front of the work. Take it back and forth across the motif, securing it at intervals with a second thread in the same or a contrasting colour.*

# Single thread couching

In couching a continuous thread is often used for both the laid and the couching stitches. There are two main types, Bokharan couching and Romanian. In Bokharan couching the slackly stitched laid threads are couched with short tying stitches but in Romanian couching the tying stitches are long and loose.

*How to work Bokharan couching*

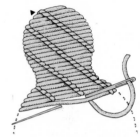

*Put down the laid thread one line at a time and couch on the return journey with short overcast stitches placed at regular intervals to build up a pattern with subsequent lines.*

*How to work Romanian couching*

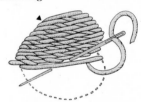

*Put down the laid thread slackly one line at a time and couch on the return journey with long loose overcast stitches.*

*How to work Romanian stitch*

*Work as for Romanian couching but with only one overcast stitch in each line.*

261

# Couching and laid work

Both couching and laid work have been used since early times to secure precious threads on the top fabrics. They are quick and effective ways of covering entire grounds with surface threads. Couching too is one of the best methods for making outlines either to define them or to cover the raw edges as in appliqué. It is also the ideal technique for securing any threads, ribbons, cords or braids which cannot be stitched through the fabric.

**Nineteenth-century Dodecanese panel in Bokharan couching**

***Sixteenth-century English screen made by Mary Queen of Scots***
*The large vases are filled with laid threads couched in trellis designs. Couching is also used to outline the shapes and secure the gold cords on the background.*

***Late sixteenth-century Swiss satchel***
*The satchel above is worked with silk and gold threads in a number of stitches including split, stem and satin. Laid work is used on the houses and well. The scrolled metal threads are couched.*

# Couched borders

The border below is made using Bokharan couching, Romanian stitch and simple couching (see pages 260–261). It would be suitable as a decorative edging to the bottom of a skirt, to a cuff or cushion cover. Be sure when choosing the threads to be used that they are matched to the ground fabric and are neither too thin nor too thick for it.

### Working the couched border
Trace the pattern from the diagram below and transfer it to the ground fabric. If a coarse thread and ground fabric are being used then the design should be enlarged (see page 237). Stretch the fabric tautly in a frame and begin by working the orange shapes with Bokharan couching. Next work the beige shapes with Romanian stitch. Lastly outline the orange shapes in simple couching using two contrasting colours.

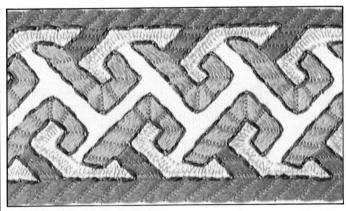

**Finished sample of the border design**

**The design can be traced from the drawing above**

**Detail of late sixteenth-century English stool cover**
*The detail above is worked in silk and metal threads on a linen ground and applied to a damask background with couching used to conceal the edges.*

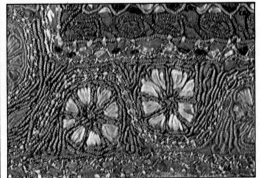

**Border of Palestinian dress**
*The detail left shows couched cords arranged in pattern to enclose the little satin stitch petals.*

**Detail of eighteenth-century Chinese robe**
*The Lung dragon above is worked in concentric circles of couched gold threads.*

# Invisible couching

This old form of couching shows no surface couching stitch and is very hardwearing and flexible. It is an excellent technique for gold and metal threads, but a beginner would be wise to try it out first on less expensive threads. As the turned threads are hidden at the back of the work, giving a neat edge, it is also useful for turning threads at the end of a row (see page 268).

Work on a finely woven linen or cotton firmly stretched on a supported frame, and use a strong, fine couching thread.

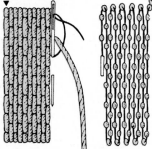

**Finished motif in invisible couching**

*How to work*

**Front of work          Back of work**

*Secure the laid thread at the back of the work, then bring to surface at top left. Next bring out couching thread a little below it. Encircle laid thread with the couching thread and return it through same hole, pulling through a fraction of the laid thread with it. During this process hold laid thread firmly in left hand above work and couching thread in right hand underneath work, keeping an equal tension between the two so that just enough laid thread goes through to back. Continue to work like this, making a solid covered surface.*

# Motifs and backgrounds

Motifs can be introduced into solid couching by padding the motif to raise it from the background (see below).

### Raised couching

This method of couching is particularly effective when using metal threads. The motif is worked in satin stitch. Then the background and the motif are couched over using a separate contrasting tying thread and working at right angles to the satin stitches.

*How to work*

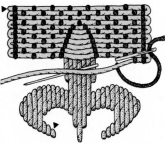

*Make the tying stitches at regular intervals for the background and, when the motif is reached, make extra stitches along the outline only.*

### Changing the direction of stitches

Further patterns can be made by changing the direction of the stitches and using horizontal stitches for the motif and vertical ones for the background. The threads over the background are couched at regular intervals and those over the padded motif along the outline only.

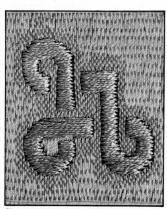

**Changing stitch direction**

# Laidwork

Laid work is an extension of couching and is used for covering large areas. It is a very quick and effective way of filling both motifs and backgrounds, and is made with long, loose satin stitches secured on subsequent journeys with couching stitches. The sheen of silk and golden threads is often a sufficient point of decoration so that the couching stitches can be quite simple, worked in matching thread.

### Simple laidwork

The long threads covering the motif or background are first laid on the fabric in satin stitch and then fastened to the fabric with couched lines as in plain or trellis couching.

To ensure that the satin stitches lie evenly along the surface of the fabric they are best worked in two journeys.

*How to lay the threads*

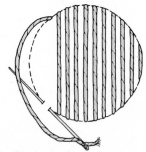

**1** *Work the first journey of satin stitches to and fro across the area to be filled, picking up only a small piece of fabric at each edge.*

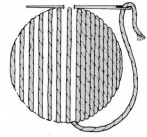

**2** *When the first journey is completed work the needle back, filling in the spaces left.*

### Securing the laid threads

Either of the methods described below can be used to secure the laid threads.

*How to secure with plain couching*

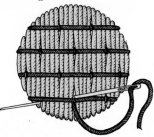

*Work the couched threads at right angles to the satin stitches one at a time. Lay the thread across and then couch it at regular intervals on the return journey as in Bokharan couching.*

*How to secure with trellis couching*

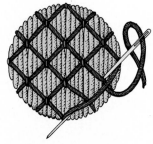

*Lay the threads at intervals diagonally across the satin stitches. Cover these with a second layer of diagonal stitches a line at a time, couching them on the return journey at the intersections of the trellis pattern.*

# Decorative laidwork

Rich patterns in laid work can be made by working a second layer of stitches in various formations with a contrasting thread. Make sure to work the couched threads in the opposite direction to the laid threads underneath so that they act as anchorage as well as decoration.

## Couching in swirls

A second layer of laid stitches can be worked to form swirling patterns in harmony with the shape being covered. Where the satin stitches are short (as on the clover leaf stem below) they do not need to be secured further.

*How to work*

*Work the motif in satin stitch in 2 journeys. Once the motif is filled secure these stitches with swirling lines, each laid and tied with a continuous thread. When laying the swirl before couching it, be sure to leave it slack as the thread will be taken up as it is couched.*

## Couching in chevrons

Regular patterns such as chevrons can be used to cover abstract motifs or to make backgrounds more interesting.

*How to work*

*Cover the motif with long satin stitches in 2 journeys, then work couched zigzag lines across the first layer of threads, making the overcast stitches at the points of the angles.*

## Couching in features

The second layer of threads can also be used to create the special features of a motif.

*How to work scales*

*Cover the motif with satin stitches. Then make the features with a contrasting thread, working the laid thread slackly and then couching on the return journey.*

## Weaving laid threads

Further patterns can be made by weaving under and over the laid threads. In this pattern the laid threads are worked vertically and the second layer horizontally. Many variations of this theme can be worked simply by altering the number of threads woven into. With this technique the second layer does not pierce the ground fabric.

*How to work*

*Lay the first layer of stitches using satin stitch in 2 journeys. Then, using a blunt-pointed needle, weave under and over each satin stitch alternately. At the end of each row make a short vertical stitch downwards under the fabric at the margin of the motif coming out at the right level for the next row.*

**Detail of a Chinese sleeve ribbon**
*The illustration above is a detail of the silk sleeve ribbon which is purported to have belonged to the Empress Dowager Tz'u-hsi in China in the nineteenth century. The petals, flower centres, the veins on the leaves and the feathers of the birds have been worked using laid and couched threads, showing how effective the technique is for creating textures and patterns. Old embroideries provide a very useful source of ideas for motifs, stitches and thread combinations.*

265

## Metalwork threads

Various types of gold and metal wires and threads are available today, but beginners would do well to work with imitations rather than real gold threads as these are very expensive and can be easily damaged by over-handling.

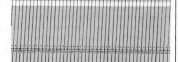

1  **Smooth gold coil**

2  **Bright check or crinkle gold coil**

3  **Rough or dull gold coil**

4  **Medium-gauge bright bullion**

5  **Large-gauge bright bullion**

6  **Medium-gauge dull gold purl**

7  **Fine-gauge dull gold purl**

8  **Medium twisted gold cord**

9  **Fine twisted gilt cord**

10  **Gold passing**

11  **Fine tambour passing**

12  **Imitation jap passing**

13  **Imitation gold passing**

14  **Imitation silver passing**

15  **Smooth gold lurex passing**

16  **Fine aluminium passing**

17  **Copper lurex passing**

18  **Gold lurex passing**

## Goldwork embroidery

Goldwork embroidery can be used for borders, motifs or complete designs. Whenever it is used it transforms the design into something rich and rare. The fascination with it dates back to early times throughout the world and it has always been used to denote rank in church, state, military and civilian life. It can be worked in conjunction with beads, sequins, mirrors, appliqué and silk embroidery. When working with real gold threads, time and care should be taken as this type of work is an investment of time and money.

**Modern Tunisian work**
*Gold worker in the medina at Tunis. Note the way he uses his leg as a support instead of the usual frame.*

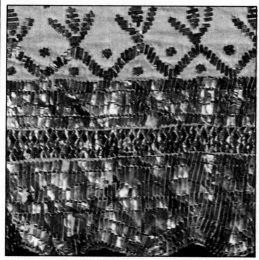

**Goldwork from the Ottoman empire, 1850**
*The beaten gold strips in the embroidery above were cut from plate – an ancient practice.*

**Nineteenth-century Afghanistan purse**
*Contrasting coloured couching threads have been used to make the pattern on the gold threads. Mirrorwork has also been incorporated into the design.*

**Chair cover**
*Detail of a nineteenth-century Chinese chair cover embroidered with gold threads and depicting a chhi-lin, an animal of good omen.*

# Gold embroidered yoke

This design contains several goldwork techniques and incorporates most of the threads and techniques used in goldwork to make the different textural patterns. The design could be adapted for use on dress yokes, cuffs and borders. For a richer effect, the trellis ground between the circles could be extended to cover all the exposed ground. The design could also be made brighter by working the border in many different colours. General working instructions for it are given on page 268. For working with gold threads, see page 268.

**Yoke panel design**
*The design is repeated on both sides of the yoke.*

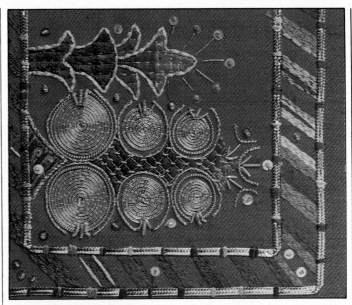

**Detail of finished yoke panel**

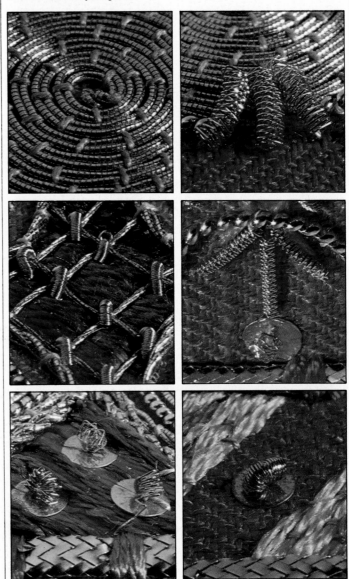

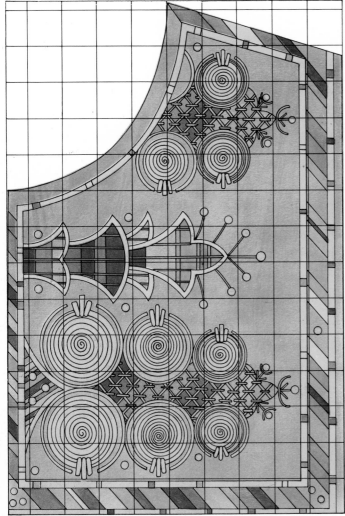

**Yoke chart**
*To enlarge the chart above to the size required for your garment follow the instructions given on transferring on pages 236–237.*

**Details of goldwork on yoke**
*Above are details of the gold threads, spangles and purls couched into positon. The coloured silk used for couching often wears thin from contact with the metal threads and is best strengthened with beeswax to ensure a longer life for the work.*

# Goldwork

# *Working with metal threads*

The use of gold in fabric dates back to the times of the ancient Egyptians, Hebrews and Romans. In those days, it was worked in solid strips cut from thinly beaten gold plates. Later, in early Christian times, the gold strips were spun around filaments of silk or flax to make the first gold threads. It was not, however, until the invention of the wire-drawing machine in Nuremberg in 1360 that the thin strips were replaced by wires.

Real gold and silver threads need to be treated with care: they should be handled as little as possible so as not to tarnish them, and worked carefully to avoid piercing them. When laying down gold and silver threads, it is usual to work them two at a time.

The yoke is best suited for application to a simple loose fitting collarless shirt or robe. After choosing your pattern enlarge yoke design to fit it using chart given on page 267 (see enlarging, page 236–237). Transfer design to fabric allowing a wide border for mounting. Stitch fabric to backing and stretch tautly in a frame. Begin embroidery with plant shapes. Lay silk embroidery threads in stripes, fill shapes and secure in place with couched lines (see laid work, pages 264–265). Finish plant shapes with outline of couched silk. For sprays at ends of shapes, couch fine passing (for detailed instructions on how to work with metal threads, see right). Next work circular shapes using medium passing, doubled. Couch in place with silk sewing thread beginning on outer edge of circle working toward centre. Make couching stitches fit between stitches of previous row. When circles are complete, fill spaces between them with laid silk threads in stripes. Lay fine passing diagonally over silk in parallel lines, first in one direction and then at right angles to it. Secure lines at intersections with bullion. Couch fine cord outline around circles adding an extra outline of purl where desired. Sew all spangles in place with bullion. Then work details of bullion and purl. Work border last by making couched silk stripes and outlining with braid. When complete stitch yoke to garment.

## Metal threads

Gold or metal can be made into threads of varying gauges – from fine to coarse – by coiling, twisting or spinning. There are also several imitation metal threads which are far less valuable, and as such would be better for beginners.

*Coiled threads* can be coiled in three different ways to create different effects: **1** bright, or smooth, where the flat wires are coiled edge to edge to make a flexible, shining tube; **2** check, where the wire is crinkle-coiled to give an irregular glitter and an uneven surface; **3** rough, or dull, where the wire is coiled like a spring to give a ridged, less bright surface. All three types come in two qualities: bullion and purl. Bullion is the oldest type of coil and is used principally for church embroideries, decorating uniforms, and heraldic devices. The coiled wire is made so that it can be pulled out to any size, and then cut into varying lengths. It should be handled as little as possible and the separate pieces should be picked up on the needle and attached in their drawn-out coils to the surface of the fabric in the same way as spangles or sequins. Purl is more expensive than bullion and is used as a coiled edging to it. It is too delicate to be drawn through the fabric, is cut to varying lengths, and is laid down in its coiled form and attached to the surface with couching stitches.

*Twisted wires* give a cord effect and are used for lines and outlines. Several wires can be twisted together to form a thread. The number of strands will depend on the thickness of the finished thread.

*Spun wires*, known as *passings*, are used for all types of metal embroidery. The gold or metal threads are spun around a filament of silk, flax or cotton to make the thread.

Gold and metal threads are usually sold in *skeins*, which are twisted in such a way as to allow the ends to be withdrawn at the same time making it easier to cut the strands required to the same length, which is important as two strands are always worked at the same time.

## Fabrics

You should always use closely woven fabrics as these are the easiest to work on. Any fabric you use should have a backing fabric, preferably of strong linen or cotton, which should be tacked to the back of the ground fabric. Make sure you use good-quality ground fabric to make best use of the expensive threads.

## Implements

You will need a needle with an eye wide enough to take the metal threads and some fine embroidery needles for the couching threads. A stiletto to punch fine holes in the ground fabric may be needed if working on very closely woven fabrics or leather, in which case the marked design lines should be pierced before the work is begun.

## *Preparation*

Two points to bear in mind when working with gold and metal threads are, firstly, that they are always worked on a frame, and, secondly, that the ground fabric must be attached to a backing fabric. Stretch a strong fabric such as linen onto the frame. (This will act as a lining for the embroidered ground.) Then stitch the ground fabric to this backing and transfer the design onto it (see transferring, page 236). If you are using a very stiff fabric, first pierce the design lines to ease the subsequent stitching and prevent the threads from being damaged. When working filled motifs on a velvet ground embroider directly onto the linen backing and then apply the finished motifs to the velvet, using a couching outline stitch to cover the edges (see couching, page 260). In this way the pile of the velvet is disturbed as little as possible.

## *Types of work*

There are four different types of work using metal threads: **1** outline work; **2** flat work; **3** raised work; **4** mixed work with beads, sequins and gems (see beadwork, page 296).

## *Outline work*

Outlining with gold and metal threads is done in exactly the same way as outline couching and gives a rich effect without wasting the thread. The silk couching threads can be in either a matching or a contrasting colour to the laid metal threads.

# Flat work

Flat work can be used either to cover the surface of the fabric, or for motifs. It can be worked with a looped edge, known as *turning*, or a clean edge.

## Making a looped edge

This is quick to work, but the looped edges may need to be covered later with an outline of couching. Insert a wide-eyed needle at arrow and push through so that only eye shows. Then pass ½in. (1.3cm) of doubled metal threads through eye, pull needle through to back and unthread it. The threads are then couched down with silk. The first stitch made on design line should secure threads underneath. When the edge of the design is reached the metal threads are turned and worked back.

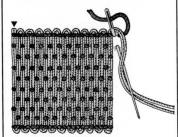

**Looped edge flat work**

## Making a clean edge

To make a neater edge work in the same way as for the looped edge but make each line separately. When the end of a line is reached, the threads are cut leaving ½in. (1.3cm) extra, and are threaded to the back, and secured with a couching thread.

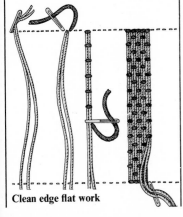

**Clean edge flat work**

# Decorative flat work

Flat work can be made more decorative by arranging couching stitches in different pattern formations and also by using a contrasting couching thread. The patterns used for the couching can be used not only to secure the threads but also as a design feature in their own right.

## Making filling patterns

Mosaic and geometric designs are formed by the regular patterns of the couching stitches. When working these patterns the design for the couching stitches is marked on the ground fabric and followed as the couching progresses. More pronounced patterns can be made by using a sharply contrasting couching thread.

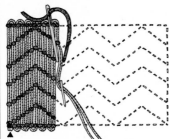

**Chevrons made by couching stitches**

## Making motif patterns

Motif patterns can be made with the couching stitches by using a contrasting silk for the motif couching and working the stitches densely over the area of the motif. The background couching stitches are worked at regular intervals in the usual way to contrast with the motif.

**Letter made by couching stitches**

# Raised goldwork

A further dimension can be added to goldwork by padding the surface of the ground fabric before working it. This padding can be made with satin stitches, cardboard, or string. Raised work can be used to cover the entire surface or the motif only.

## Using satin stitch padding

The motifs to be raised are worked in satin stitch with a thick cotton. When an entire surface is to be covered the metal threads are then couched to the edge of the padding. They are then carried over the motif and silk couching thread is passed underneath it, coming up on the opposite edge. The couching is then continued as before.

## Using cardboard padding

Individual raised motifs can be worked directly onto the ground, using it as the background to the motifs. Pad with a cardboard cut-out which is secured with a small tying stitch at either end. The metal threads are couched alternately on either side of it.

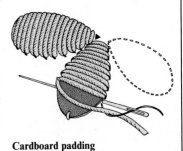

**Cardboard padding**

## Using string padding

Both woven and interlacing patterns can be worked by using string as the padded foundation. A good firm string such as that used for macramé is ideal.

## Making woven patterns

The string is cut into required lengths and placed at evenly spaced intervals across area to be covered. It is then couched in position with cotton thread. The metal threads are then taken over strings and couched down between them in pattern formation. This pattern is worked by taking the metal threads over 2 strings at a time and couching and alternating this on next row.

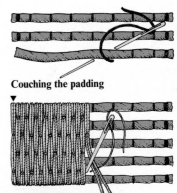

**Couching the padding**

**Couching the metal threads and the string padding**

## Making interlacing patterns

The design is traced in channel lines onto the ground fabric. The string is then couched down between the channels and cut at intersections so that one string does not cross another. The metal threads are taken over string. Couching stitches are placed on either side, and as near to it as possible so as to keep the covering metal threads as taut as possible to bring the pattern into high relief.

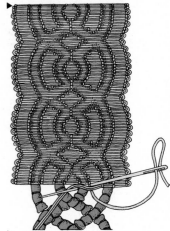

**Interlacing string padding pattern**

# Alphabets and monograms

The use of embroidered initials and monograms on clothes and gifts turns the most mundane article into a personal and prized possesion. The designs shown on these two pages, are all made by a contemporary artist, and can be traced and used as illustrated in the sizes shown or they can be reduced or enlarged (see page 237), and put to further uses. Very large initials can be worked across the back of kimonos, robes and jackets whilst tiny ones look good on shirts. Lettering can also be used on fabric coverings for household articles such as boxes, wastepaper baskets and writing paper folders. Elaborate initials and monograms, together with the relative date, can be used to sign a piece of embroidery, adding an extra ornament in the process. Valentine, Christmas, birthday and anniversary cards too can have their messages worked in embroidered letters thus making them into presents as well as greeting cards.

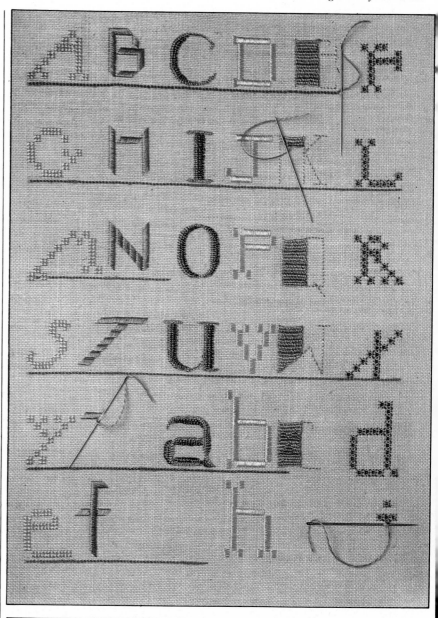

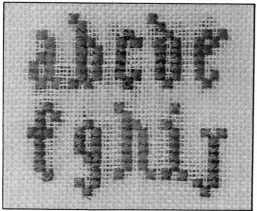

**Cross stitch alphabet**
*Worked detail of the alphabet shown in chart on page 273.*

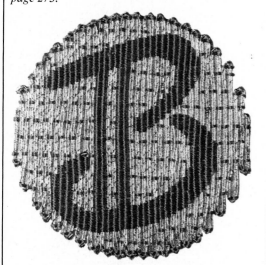

**Medallion monogram**
*Couching is used here for both the background and the monogram with the couching stitches, worked close together to form the letters.*

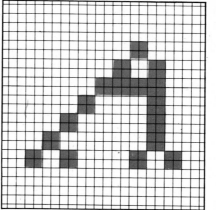

**Chart for A**
*Cross stitch A from sampler shown above.*

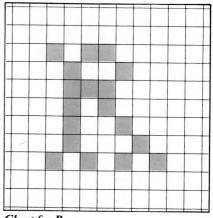

**Chart for R**
*Algerian eye stitch R from sampler shown above.*

### Satin stitch shirt monogram
*The monogram shown below is worked in satin stitch with voiding to make the pattern. Chain stitch is used for the circular frame.*

### Pillowcase initialling
*The letter S shown left is worked in padded satin stitch outlined in back stitch. The scroll pattern is worked in chain stitch in the shape of a Y.*

### Handkerchief initialling
*The padded satin stitch P is worked on a pulled thread work ground within a frame of long cross stitch.*

### Initial and flowers on scarf
*Satin stitch is used for the K and encroaching satin stitch is worked for the flowers which are finished with bead details at the centres.*

The initial is placed in the corner to fill it.

### Pocket lettering
*Both the stylized lettering and the rabbit design are worked in cross stitch in different-coloured threads on an evenweave linen ground. The chart for working this design is shown left.*

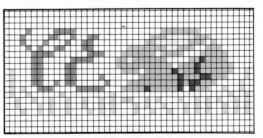

### Original Designs
When making original designs for letters and monograms it is best to sketch them out first on tissue paper and then place this in position to make sure the design both fits and is suitable. Select an embroidery stitch which will make clearly defined letters, and avoid using fluffy threads.

# Alphabets and monograms

From the earliest times lettering has been used in embroidery as a practical form of identification. Up till quite recently all household linens were marked with initials and dated with the time of purchase. The marks were made in the same or a contrasting thread and were usually placed on the top right-hand corner of sheets, pillowcases and towels. Today there is a growing fashion for working more elaborate initials and monograms in the central border of top sheets and best towels and on pillowcases. (However, when working impressive monograms on pillowcases which are going to be slept on it is best not to work them centrally, for embroidery is uncomfortable to sleep against.) Lettering is also used in badges, banners and heraldic work to convey the ideals of church, state and family and in these circumstances it is usually stitched in gold threads on raised grounds.

### History

Embroidered letters have also been used in the past to convey messages, usually of a rather high tone. This was popular in the sixteenth century and a unique example of it was found on a fragment of fine white linen embroidered in silks and silver purl and interlaced with bands worked in an almost invisible thread and bearing axioms on the nature of riches such as "Covet not to wax riche through deceit", "He that hath lest witte is most poore" and many more along these lines. This high tone was also used in eighteenth- and nineteenth-century samplers with the purpose of instilling morals into young minds at the same time that the fingers learnt the stitching techniques.

Less moral use was made of lettering in the nineteenth century when Valentine cards and souvenir postcards were often embroidered with sentimental rhymes and sprigged with red roses and forget-me-nots. This same style was also used for hearthside pictures with inscriptions such as "Home is where the Heart is".

Today, with messages being spread across T-shirts there is ample opportunity for the needle to make more lasting and certainly more decorative statements with embroidery.

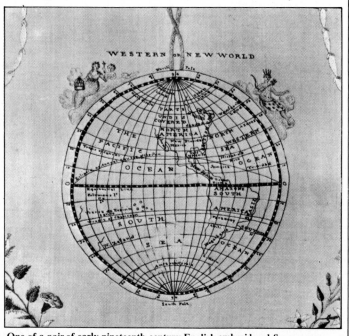

One of a pair of early nineteenth-century English embroidered firescreens

# Stitch techniques for lettering

To be effective lettering must be legible, with all the letters stitched evenly in clearly defined lines. It should ideally be worked on a frame, to prevent the fabric from puckering. Trace the letters first and then mark them onto the ground. Many stitches can be used: below are four examples, each worked in different ways.

### Simple initials and monograms

The quickest way to work over the marked letters is to use cross, chain or satin stitch. The initials or monograms can be set in isolation upon the ground or framed with further stitching.

*Chain stitch*

*This is the easiest stitch for free-style lettering. The edges of the lettering can be neatened and finished off with an outline of stem stitch.*

### Padded lettering

Padding is used to emphasize lettering by raising it. It is often seen in goldwork where the lettering is the same colour as the ground.

*Padded satin stitch*

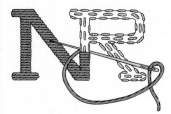

*The letters can be raised by working a padding of running or chain stitches first and covering these with satin stitch.*

### Braid or soutache lettering

Fine ribbon or braids make effective lettering. The braid is attached with small, invisible running stitches starting at a place where the join will be least noticeable. It should be carried over design lines from start to finish without a break.

*Couched braid*

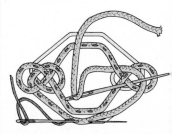

*When intersections are reached leave a gap in running stitches on first journey and on returning to this point thread braid through gap.*

### Openwork lettering

Openwork can be used on fine, even-weave fabrics either for lettering or the background.

*Openwork background with satin stitch lettering*

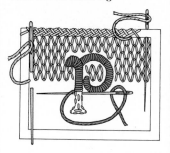

*When openwork is used for the background embroider the lettering first and then work background. When it is used for lettering work the openwork stitches within the lettering outlines. The background can be framed with further embroidery.*

# Designing | Alphabets

The lettering or initials can be set amidst flowers, animals, leaves or any subject which is either decorative or significant to the lettering. For instance, if the name of a flower is being worked then flowers of that name can be used for the ground. Similarly, if the bearer of the initials has a particular fondness for a certain fruit, flower or animal or is interested in a particular sport then that subject can be worked into the ground to make a more personal design. These ideas do not need to be restricted to the ground but can become an integral part of the lettering with flowers being introduced into the letters or twined around them. In the same way birds and butterflies can "flit" in and out of the words. Club stripes, too, can be used to colour the letters. When embroidering chess or backgammon boards lettering and names can be introduced on the ground and then the chess or backgammon patterning worked around them.

Below and right we give a cross stitch alphabet and an alphabet for satin stitch and a set of numerals for chain stitch. The cross stitch alphabet can be worked directly from the chart but the other two will need to be traced and then transferred to the ground fabric. Any lettering can be traced and used as long as it is defined enough to be legible with embroidery stitches. The instructions for transferring are given on page 236 and those for satin stitch and for crossed stitches are on pages 240–242. If the satin stitch alphabet is to be worked with gold threads, follow the instructions on page 268.

**Letter D with encroaching foliage**

**Figurative letter R**

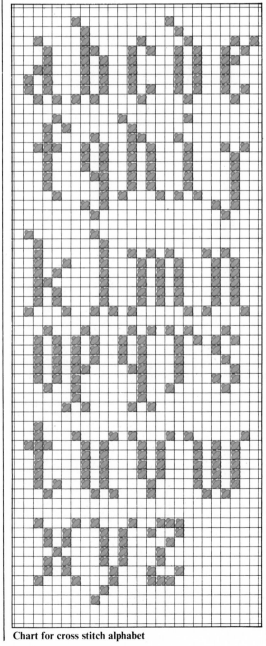

**Chart for cross stitch alphabet**

**Letters for satin stitch alphabet**

**Numerals for working in chain stitch**

# *Openwork*

Openwork embroidery, sometimes known as *whitework* as it is principally worked in white stitches on a white ground fabric, is the collective name for all forms of embroidery which have the appearance of lace and yet are worked on fabric.

It is mainly used for table and bed linen and for decoration on fine clothing, lingerie and layettes. It is also used for openwork seaming, known as *faggotting* (see pages 284–285).

There are three distinct techniques for making openwork embroidery, each of which is described below.

### *Pulled thread work*

This technique is the finest and most lace-like of openwork embroideries and is sometimes known as *drawn fabric work*. It also goes under such regional names as *point de Dresde, point de Saxe* and *Flemish work*.

In this technique the threads of the ground fabric are pulled back with special embroidery stitches to make decorative holes or perforations.

### *Withdrawn thread work*

This form of openwork embroidery, dating as far back as the twelfth century, was originally widely used throughout Europe but gained its greatest popularity in Scandinavia. It is still famous under such regional names as Danish *Hedebo work* and Norwegian *Hardanger work*.

In this technique a few threads are withdrawn from the fabric and embroidery stitches are used to group the loose strands into patterns.

### *Cutwork*

This is the most open of all openwork and is well known as *broderie anglaise* or *eyelet lace*. It is also the basic technique used for Madeira, Swiss, Renaissance and Richelieu work.

In cutwork the embroidery designs are worked first and the fabric is then cut away from around the stitches. In Renaissance and Richelieu work so much of the background is cut away that needlepoint bars are needed to join the solid motifs. The most decorative form of cutwork is Italian and is composed of small cut squares which are then elaborately filled with needlepoint lace motifs (see page 286).

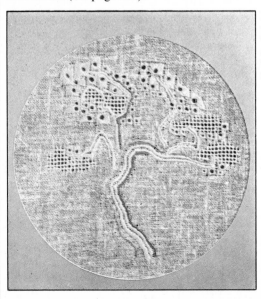

Pulled thread work techniques are used in the olive tree motif (see left)

# *Pulled thread work*

The fine, lace-like appearance of pulled thread embroidery is achieved by the ground fabric being pulled apart with specially developed stitches. The instructions for some of these special stitches are shown right, and on the opposite page. Although the diagrams for the working of the stitches show the fabric threads being pulled only slightly you should bear in mind that this is done merely to make the diagrams easier to read. When worked correctly the stitches will distort the appearance of the fabric more.

## *Materials*

The essence of pulled thread work is correctly counted threads, therefore soft even-weave fabrics which have easily counted threads, such as organza, muslin, voile and finely woven cotton and linen are ideal.

The working thread should be of the same texture and thickness as the ground fabric, but strong enough to hold back the pulled threads of the fabric securely. Remember that it is the pulled back fabric which will nearly always form the patterns and not the thread of the embroidered stitches, so a closely matched thread is necessary.

A thick and blunt-pointed needle should be used: the thickness of the needle makes the holes and the blunt point prevents the ground threads from being split when working the stitches.

## *Preparation*

The work should be mounted on a frame (see page 233), taking care not to stretch the fabric too tightly over the frame. The warp and weft threads should lie at right angles to each other and be clearly visible for counting. When working, it may be necessary to loosen the fabric on the frame to get the threads to pull correctly.

# *Pulled thread stitches*

All the following stitches should be worked tautly so that the working thread pulls the fabric apart to make holes.

### *Antique hemstitch*

This shows the principle of pulled work and is used to secure a folded hem.

#### *How to work*

*On wrong side of fabric, insert needle 2 threads down into folded hem. Then insert needle up to right and pass it to left under 3 threads of single layer. Next take it back to fold line, pulling 3 threads together to form a hole.*

### *Single faggot stitch*

This is used for patterning or background filling. The rows can be worked in the same direction, in which case the frame should be turned after each row is completed.

#### *How to work single faggot*

**1** *Work diagonally, making horizontal and vertical pulling stitches alternately.*

**2** *On the next row make squares by working into the holes of the previous row.*

## Chained border stitch

This stitch, also known as *cable stitch*, can be worked both horizontally and diagonally.

*How to work horizontally*

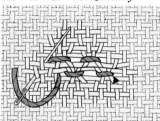

**1** Work small horizontal stitches tautly from right to left and from bottom to top alternately, working in 4 vertical thread clusters and moving along 2 vertical threads with each stitch.

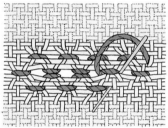

**2** The top line of the next and subsequent rows is always worked into the base of the previous row.

*How to work diagonally*

**1** Take needle down to left over 2 vertical and 2 horizontal threads. Then insert it up under 2 horizontal threads and make a second diagonal stitch. Continue in this way to the end of the row.

**2** On return row work upwards with top line of stitches being made into the holes of the previous row.

## Three-sided stitch

This is composed of equal length back stitches worked tightly to draw the ground threads together and making perforations where the stitches meet each other.

*How to work*

**1** Make 2 horizontal back stitches over the same threads and, bringing needle out at starting point, make another pair of back stitches diagonally upwards to the right over the same number of threads. Then take needle to upper line.

**2** Work 2 horizontal back stitches. Then work 2 diagonal back stitches down to the right.

**3** Continue working in this way alternately on lower and upper lines to end of row.

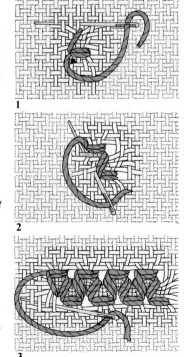

## Four-sided stitch

This neat line stitch draws the fabric together in squares.

*How to work*

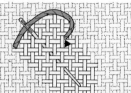

**1** Make a horizontal stitch and bring the needle out diagonally down to right.

**2** Bring needle up, insert it again at starting point and pass it diagonally down to left.

**3** Form third side of square passing needle down to right. Continue working Steps 1 and 2 downwards.

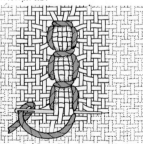

**4** To start the next row bring needle out at right.

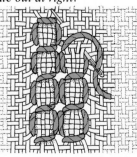

**5** Then work upwards into sides of previous row.

## Close herringbone stitch

Squares, triangles and chevron patterns can be made using close herringbone stitch (see page 245). Work the patterns as shown in the diagrams below, pulling the stitches taut.

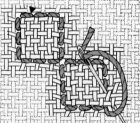

**Working squares**

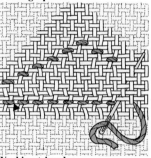

**Working triangles**

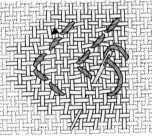

**Working chevrons**

## Diagonal raised band

This stitch is used when slightly raised bands are needed.

*How to work raised band*

*Work as shown in diagonal stitches in 2 journeys up and then down the fabric pulling the working thread taut between each stitch.*

275

### Algerian eye stitch

This star-shaped stitch can be used as a single motif or as a filling stitch. It is perforated at the centre and looks best when it is worked in silks on loosely woven ground fabric.

#### How to work as a single motif

*Work 8 equal length pulling stitches into the central hole.*

#### How to work as a filling stitch

*Work the pulling stitches in 2 journeys, making the first side of the star on the downward journey and the second on the upward one.*

### Indian drawn ground stitch

This gives a very open effect and looks best on a lightweight open-weave fabric. It can be worked over an entire surface or in rows, stripes, blocks or diagonal patterns.

#### How to work

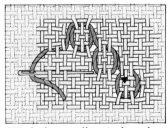

*Work diagonally, circling the threads for one stitch before moving on to the next. When worked in rows, it is easiest to start at the top and then work downwards.*

### Honeycomb darning stitch

This stitch is very easy to work and forms a lattice pattern with regular perforations.

#### How to work

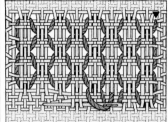

*Bring the needle out at arrow, insert it down over 3 horizontal threads and bring out to left under 3 vertical threads. Take up and insert over 3 horizontal threads and bring out 3 vertical threads to left. Finish row and work next row into the base of the previous one.*

### Greek cross filling stitch

This stitch completely changes the weave of the fabric. It is made up of four buttonhole stitches radiating from the same central hole.

#### How to work

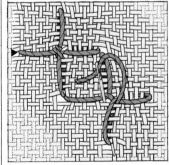

*Bring the needle out, insert it to right over 6 horizontal and 6 vertical threads and bring out 6 threads down to left of stitch. Pull tight. Insert needle 6 vertical threads to right, bring out at central point above stitch just made and pull tight. Insert 6 horizontal threads down, coming out again at centre to right of stitch just made. Complete stitch with a tying stitch over central threads and bring out at base ready to make next cross.*

# Withdrawn thread work

Withdrawn thread work is sturdier and less lace-like than pulled thread work. It is worked by withdrawing threads from the ground fabric and then securing the remaining ones into clusters and grouping them with embroidery stitches to make regular patterns. It is sometimes known as *needleweaving* as some of its main patterns are made by weaving the needle in and out of the fabric threads, filling in the gap left by the withdrawn threads and making a further fabric in their place.

It is used to decorate sheets, pillowcases, bedspreads, towels, table cloths, mats, napkins and curtains. It can also be used for decorative hems and borders on clothes.

Although withdrawn work is most often worked in white thread on white ground fabric, it can also be worked using coloured thread or fabric as a contrast.

*Preparation*

Before the stitches can be worked in withdrawn thread work some of the fabric threads must be removed. On the opposite page the instructions for withdrawing threads for borders are given. On the following pages are the instructions for working withdrawn thread work stitches for backgrounds and motifs.

**Withdrawn thread work**

# *Withdrawing threads for borders*

# *Mitering corners*

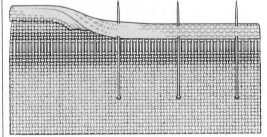

**1 Withdrawing threads across fabric**

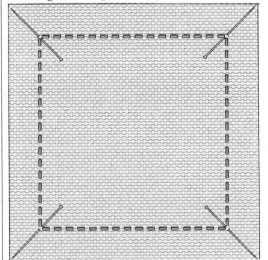

**2 Pinning and tacking the hem in position**

**3 Marking the corners**

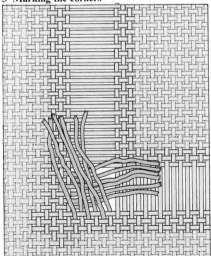

**4 Withdrawing threads**

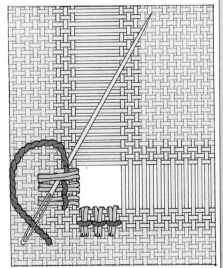

**5 Tacking down corner threads**

### *Making single borders*

Single borders are usually found on towels, sheets and skirts. On this type of border, the threads can be withdrawn to the limit of the fabric.

### *How to work*

*Measure the hem allowance and slip a pin under thread marking hemstitching line. Withdraw this thread across the fabric and then withdraw any further threads as required (Fig. 1). Turn the hem up to drawn thread line, fold over and pin and tack ready for hemstitching (Fig. 2).*

### *Making borders with corners*

Borders with corners are used for square designs, such as tablecloths and napkins.

### *How to work*

*Measure the depth of the hemline and mark the outer corner of the border with a pin (Fig. 3). The thread should only be withdrawn to these limits. Then cut each thread 2in. to 3in. (5cm to 7.5cm) away from the corner points (Fig. 4) and withdraw the centre portions leaving the loose ends. To finish: either cut off the loose ends and secure raw edges with closely worked buttonhole stitch or trim, fold back, tack down loose ends (Fig. 5), and secure them under the hem.*

Before a hem is turned down, the corners can be mitred as shown in the steps below.

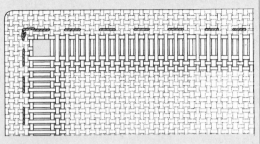

### *How to work*

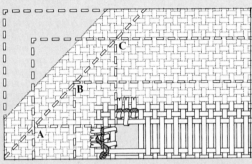

**1** *Crease fabric along required hemline and mark the corner point. Then fold fabric diagonally over this point on line ABC. Unfold fabric and cut off corner just above crease line.*

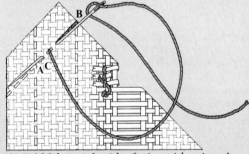

**2** *Fold fabric right sides facing with points A and C touching and point B on the fold line. Backstitch from B to AC through both layers.*

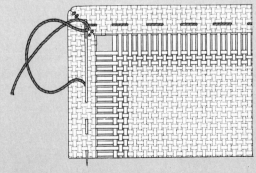

**3** *Open fabric and turn stitched corner inside out. Repeat procedure on all corners, then turn down hem and tack in place ready for subsequent hemstitching.*

# Withdrawn thread work for borders

Once the threads have been withdrawn to the required depth for the border, the remaining threads are ready to be grouped into clusters. Hemstitching can be used as a decorative border on its own, to prevent fringed edges from fraying, or as a means of grouping threads into clusters before decorating them further. For each of the following hemstitches the number of threads withdrawn for the border will depend on the desired effect. A deeper border will be necessary if the hemstitching is being used as a preparation for crossing or embroidered clusters (see right).

### Single hemstitch

For single hemstitch withdraw about 4 or 5 threads. Fold hem down and begin stitching from left to right on wrong side of fabric. Insert needle under 2, 3, or more of the loose strands, depending on the pattern being worked. Then pick up 2 threads of the ground fabric on the folded edge and pull the working thread through fairly tightly so as to cluster the loose strands. Continue in this way, drawing the strands into clusters along folded hem.

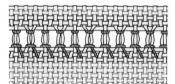

**Front:** Finished single hemstitch

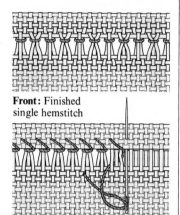

**Back:** Working single hemstitch

### Ladder hemstitch

For simple ladder hemstitch withdraw 4 or 5 threads. On wrong side of fabric, work top as above for single hemstitch grouping the loose strands into equal clusters. For bottom edge insert needle under each cluster formed by the top hem, then pick up 2 threads of the ground fabric below and pull the working thread between each stitch. On the bottom line the small diagonal stitches will show through to the front of the fabric as it is not being worked through a folded hem.

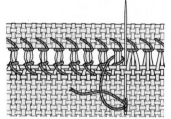

**Front:** Finished ladder hemstitch

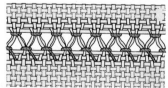

**Back:** Working ladder hemstitch

### Trellis hemstitch

Withdraw 4 or 5 threads then hemstitch along top line in 4-strand clusters, then work single hemstitch along the bottom line but form the separate 4-strand clusters by taking 2 strands from each cluster above, so that the clusters form a chevron pattern along the border.

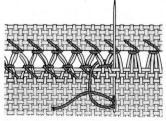

**Front:** Finished trellis hemstitch

**Back:** Working trellis hemstitch

# Crossing and embroidered clusters for borders

### Crossing clusters

The loose strands of a withdrawn thread border can be patterned by crossing the clusters. For the following stitches withdraw enough threads to enable the loose strands to be pulled across each other. Before working them, ladder hemstitch the loose strands into two-strand clusters. For the crossing, use a slightly coarser thread than that of the ground.

### Single crossing clusters

Secure working thread into fold line, insert needle from left to right behind 2nd cluster, twist it back, inserting behind first cluster. Bring out after 2nd cluster ready to cross following two clusters.

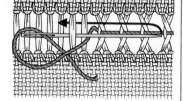

### Double crossing clusters

Work as for simple crossing clusters but cross the first cluster with the 3rd and the 2nd cluster with the 4th.

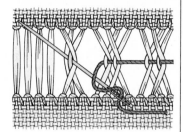

### Embroidered clusters

Embroidery stitches can also be used to group clusters decoratively. Before beginning the following stitches ladder hemstitch the loose strands into two- or three-strand clusters.

### Knotted clusters

Draw every 3 clusters together with coral stitch (see page 251) by inserting needle above the working thread behind 3 clusters and bringing it out through loop. Pull tight and repeat to end of border.

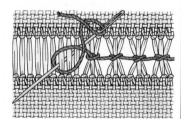

### Knotted lattice pattern

Work this stitch at back of fabric so that only knots are visible at front. Using coral stitch as above draw the first and 2nd clusters together at top and then 2nd and 3rd clusters together at bottom. Repeat to end.

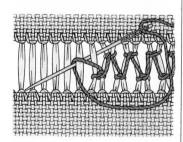

### Buttonhole stitch border

Work buttonhole stitch over 6 clusters, taking in one more cluster with each stitch until 6 are covered, then decreasing back to single cluster.

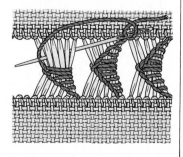

# Corded and needlewoven clusters for borders

# Withdrawing threads for grounds

## Corded clusters

Cording, or wrapping, is used to make solid clusters and can be worked without previously hemstitching the border.

### Corded cluster pattern

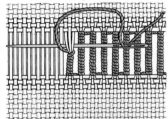

Work up and down as shown with thread being closely and tightly wrapped around 3 strands at a time.

### Decorative corded pattern

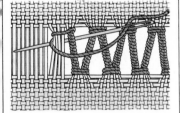

Begin at the top and cord twice around 8 strands. Then divide and work down 4 strands. At the bottom join in 4 more strands and wrap twice around these 8. Divide again and cord upwards around 4 strands. Continue in this way to form V shapes along the border.

### 4-cluster cording pattern

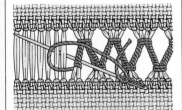

Ladder hemstitch into 2-strand clusters. Then cord twice around 4 clusters, divide in half and cord up the 2 clusters. Join in 2 more clusters and cord twice around all four, then divide and cord down 2. Continue in this way to make the pattern along the border.

## Needleweaving clusters

Needleweaving is used to make solid decorative patterns, and is worked by weaving the needle in and out of the loose strands of the withdrawn thread border. The following stitches are examples of this technique but more complicated patterns can be made by using more colours and a deeper border. A blunt-ended tapestry needle should be used to ensure that the threads do not split. Hemstitching is not necessary as the weaving forms the cluster.

### Simple weaving

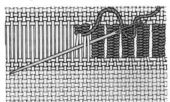

Work from top to bottom and bottom to top, weaving under and over 2 strands at a time in a figure of eight.

### Pattern weaving in one colour

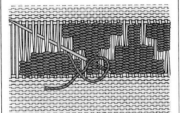

Weave in and out of 2-strand clusters in pattern formation.

### Pattern weaving in several colours

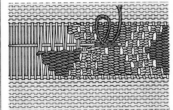

Work in the formation shown using 3 different coloured weaving threads.

So far we have only dealt with borders of various depths but complete grounds (see below), backgrounds and individual motifs (see page 280) can also be worked over withdrawn threads. All the techniques are the same but are used differently in order to cover the open fabric. The preparation of the ground fabric is more involved as the threads are withdrawn in both directions over the surface of the fabric.

Withdrawn thread work over a complete piece of fabric is interesting to work, with rewarding results. Typical of this type of work is the Danish Hedebo embroidery and the Norwegian Hardanger embroidery. The latter is further decorated with surface satin stitches worked in geometric patterns.

### Preparing fabric for withdrawn grounds

The threads can be withdrawn in regular grid formations as shown or in certain areas only to form patches, panels or frames with intervening solid fabric.

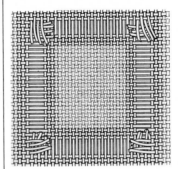

***How to withdraw threads in both directions***
*1 Mark the limits to which the threads may be withdrawn and then withdraw all border threads as shown on page 277. The ground threads are then ready to be withdrawn.*

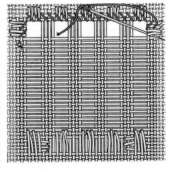

*2 Start with vertical (warp) threads, withdrawing 4 threads and leaving 4 threads. Cut threads 3in. (7.5cm) away from limits and withdraw these central threads the whole way up fabric. Cut back, trim and secure loose 3in. (7.5cm) ends.*

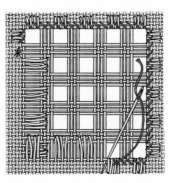

*3 Then withdraw 4 and leave 4 horizontal (weft) threads in the same way. Use overcast stitch around the perimeter of the fabric if it is to be covered with a subsequent hem, otherwise use buttonhole stitch. The withdrawn threads are now ready to be grouped using any of the withdrawn thread techniques given for borders or in the ground stitches given on the next page.*

# Withdrawn thread work for motifs and backgrounds

Withdrawn thread work is equally effective for openwork motifs on solid backgrounds and for openwork backgrounds to solid motifs. It is a major part of the design in Russian, Sicilian and Rodi embroideries. When working withdrawn backgrounds or motifs the design is always outlined in buttonhole stitch before the threads are withdrawn. The buttonhole stitch is worked inwards for withdrawn motifs and outwards for withdrawn backgrounds. In both cases the threads are withdrawn as for grounds, shown on the previous page. There is endless scope for making original withdrawn thread work designs as the technique lends itself equally well to geometric and figurative patterns.

Although the patterns illustrated show two threads being withdrawn in each direction, the number can vary according to the gauge of the fabric and the openness of the effect desired.

### Preparing fabric for withdrawn background and solid motifs

Mark the shape of the motif and work running stitch around it. Then buttonhole stitch over the running stitches making the stitch with the purled edge to the outside. When the buttonhole stitching is complete cut and withdraw the threads, withdrawing two and leaving two in each direction. Be sure to cut the threads as close as possible to the buttonhole stitch. The background is now ready to receive any of the ground stitches (see right for various types of ground stitches).

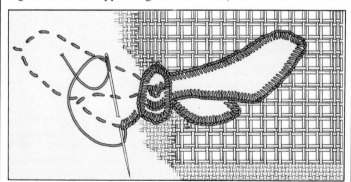

Working a withdrawn background

### Preparing fabric for withdrawn motifs and solid background

Mark the shape of the motif and work running stitch around it. Then buttonhole stitch over the running stitches forming the stitch with the purled edge to the inside. When the buttonhole stitching is complete cut and withdraw the threads, withdrawing two and leaving two in each direction. The motif is now ready to be worked with ground stitches (see right).

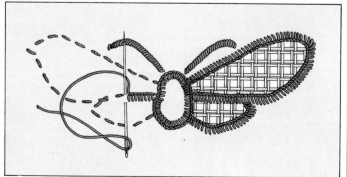

Working a withdrawn motif

# Stitches for grounds, backgrounds and motifs

Withdrawn grounds, backgrounds and motifs are worked with the same techniques as used for borders with knotting, cording and needleweaving clustering the strands. The advanced stitches below can all be worked by withdrawing threads in each direction as desired. The numbers stated in the instructions are the numbers used for each of the samples illustrated.

### How to work lace pattern with knotting

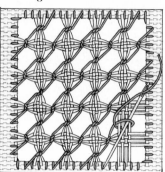

*Withdraw 4 and leave 4 threads in each direction. Then work single knot stitch diagonally connecting clusters.*

### How to work lace pattern with cording

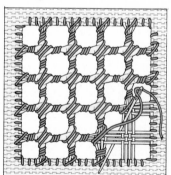

*Withdraw 4 and leave 4 threads in each direction. Then work cording diagonally making a slanting stitch at intersections.*

### How to work loop stitch pattern

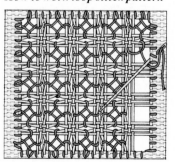

*Withdraw 4 and leave 4 threads in each direction. Then work loop stitches up and down over open spaces.*

### How to work openwork pattern with needleweaving

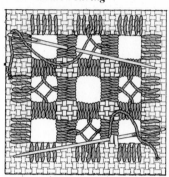

*Withdraw 4 and leave 4 threads in each direction. Then needleweave over 2 and under 2 threads in figure of 8 to cluster strands. The intervening spaces can be filled wth looped stitches or wheel (see opposite).*

### How to work cobweb pattern

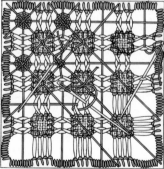

*Withdraw 8 and leave 8 threads in each direction. Then hemstitch the loose strands into 2-strand clusters around the perimeter and also around the solid squares. Next cross all the 2-strand clusters (see page 278) with the thread being carried over the open spaces and making vertical and horizontal lines. Now make diagonal lines in both directions covering the open spaces and attaching them to the corners and centres of the solid squares with coral stitch. Finally needleweave wheels around the threads in the open spaces (see opposite for detail of needleweave wheel).*

# Corners

When working borders around all four sides of the ground fabric the fabric threads are withdrawn in both directions and a hole is formed at each corner. If this hole is small it can be left as it is but if it is big it can be made secure and decorated with an embroidery or needleweaving stitch.

### How to work loop stitch filling

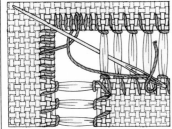

**1** *Work loop stitches into all 4 sides, working around clusters on withdrawn sides.*

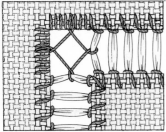

**2** *Complete the corners and then work the borders in any of the ways shown on pages 278–279.*

### How to work needleweave wheel

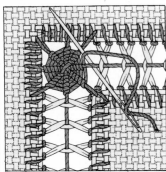

*First cross the border clusters making horizontal and vertical lines in corners then make diagonal lines across corners. Finally, needleweave around crossed threads starting at centre and working outwards.*

# Cutwork

Cutwork, along with needlepoint edges, forms the origins of needlepoint lace. It is made by cutting holes in the ground fabric in pattern formation. The holes can be cut inside the motifs, as in broderie anglaise, or outside the motifs to form the backgrounds, as in Renaissance and Richelieu work. When all the background is cut away it is replaced with needlepoint lace bars attached to the motifs which make a very open and lacy fabric.

Cutwork is used for all types of decorative table and bed linens as well as for the borders, hems, collars and cuffs of clothing.

## Materials and implements

Firm, tightly woven fabrics which do not fray easily are essential for cutwork. For whitework use cambric, lawn and fine linen. For coloured work flannels and crêpes de chine are also suitable. All cutwork should be mounted on a frame to ease the stitching.

A pair of sharp embroidery scissors or a stiletto should be used to form neatly cut shapes and clean edges.

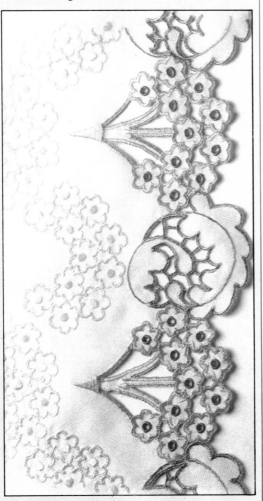

**Detail of cutwork border**

# Cutwork motifs with solid backgrounds

In this type of cutwork the motif is cut away and the raw edges are covered with overcasting or buttonhole stitches. Broderie anglaise is the best known example of this type of work.

### Eyelet holes

The holes in cutwork motifs are known as eyelets and can be made in various different shapes such as circles, ovals and triangles.

### How to make circles

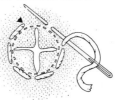 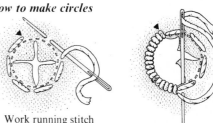

**1** Work running stitch around the outline, then snip centre twice (as shown).

**2** Turn corners to back and overcast around edge.

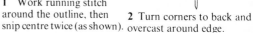

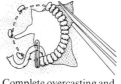 

**3** Complete overcasting and cut away corners at back.

**4** The finished circle.

### How to make ovals

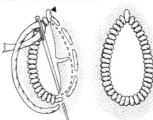

Work in the same way as circles but be sure to make them pointed at one end and rounded at the other.

### How to make triangles

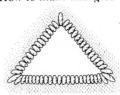 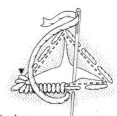

Work in the same way as circles but make overcast stitches longer at the points.

### Shadow eyelets

These eyelets are worked with the overcasting made over several rows of running stitches.

### How to work

*Outline eyelet in rows of running stitches. Then cover the running stitches with overcast stitches, grading them for a shadow effect.*

281

# Eyelet patterns

The eyelet **shapes** shown on the previous page can be grouped together to make patterns. The simple patterns below illustrate how the eyelet designs are prepared, but more complicated motifs can be made by using different shapes together.

When making eyelet patterns you should first plan the over-all design on paper. Geometry instruments such as set squares and compasses may often be helpful for drawing the motifs. When the design is complete transfer it onto the fabric (see transferring, pages 236–237). Then stretch the fabric tautly on an embroidery frame.

*How to work a simple circle pattern*

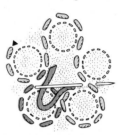
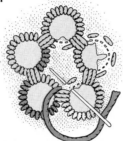

**1** *Work a continuous line of running stitch around the eyelet outlines in 2 anti-clockwise journeys. Starting at arrow, work outside first eyelet, inside 2nd, outside 3rd, inside 4th and outside 5th. On 2nd journey (see dark thread) fill in spaces left on previous journey, ending at arrow.*

**2** *When running stitches are complete snip centres of eyelets and turn edges to back. Then work overcast stitch in the same 2 journeys as the running stitches. Where eyelets touch work 3 long overcast stitches to join them. When overcasting is complete cut away the edges at the back.*

*How to work a simple oval pattern*

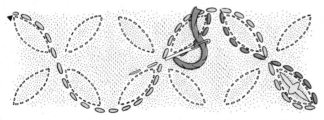

**1** *Starting at arrow work running stitch around outlines of ovals in 4 journeys. When complete snip centres of eyelets and turn edges to back.*

**2** *Cover running stitches with overcast stitch, making longer stitches at each end of the eyelets. Then cut away edges at back.*

# Cutwork edges

Scalloped edges are very often used in broderie anglaise and make beautiful finishes for all types of linen and clothing. They should be designed in clean, well-defined shapes with the outer fabric cut away to the very edge of the embroidery stitches leaving no frayed ends.

*Working scalloped edgings*

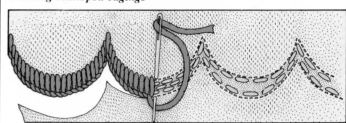

Mark pattern onto fabric, then outline inner and outer edges and fill with running stitches. Work buttonhole stitch over outlines. Finally, cut away outer fabric.

*Working oval edgings*

Mark pattern onto fabric, then outline and fill with running stitches. Work graduated buttonhole stitch over outlines. Cut away outer fabric.

*Working eyelet scallops*

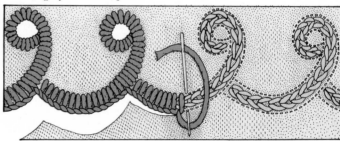

Mark pattern onto fabric and fill between outlines with chain stitches. Then work overcast stitch over the inner pattern and buttonhole stitch along the edge. Cut away outer fabric and eyelet centres.

*Working oval eyelet scallops*

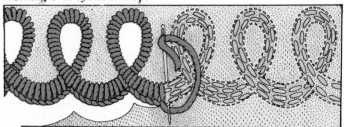

Mark pattern onto fabric, then outline and fill with running stitches. Work overcast stitch over the inner pattern and buttonhole stitch along the edge. Cut away outer fabric and then cut out the eyelet centres.

# Cutwork backgrounds with solid motifs

When making cutwork backgrounds with solid motifs make sure that the motifs touch if needlepoint lace bars are not being used to join them.

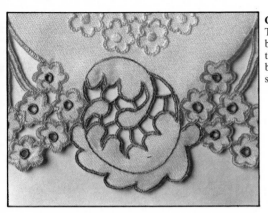

**Cutwork border**
This cutwork border illustrates the use of cutwork background with solid motifs.

### How to prepare a solid motif

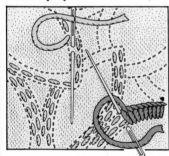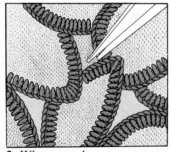

**1** Work 2 lines of running stitch along motif outlines and cover with buttonhole stitch.

**2** When complete, cut away background fabric as near to buttonhole edging as possible.

## Making cutwork backgrounds with needlepoint lace bars

If a very open background is required, the motifs can be joined with needlepoint lace bars. The origins of needlepoint lace and instructions on how to make it are shown on page 286.

### Making plain bars

The motifs should be outlined in running stitch at the same time that the bars are made. The outlines are then covered with buttonhole stitch and the background cut away afterwards.

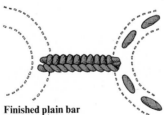

**Finished plain bar**

### How to work

*Work running stitch around the motif until a bar is reached on the design. Then strand the thread 3 times back and forth between the motifs. Cover the strands with buttonhole stitch and then continue the running stitch around the motif until the next bar is reached.*

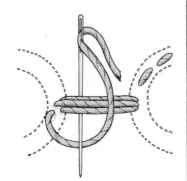

### Simple picot bar

This is a rather more decorative form of bar.

### How to work

*Strand the thread between motifs as for a plain bar. Cover with buttonhole stitches to centre. Insert pin and make loop around it as shown. Secure loop by passing needle under it, bringing it out over working thread and pulling tight. Then complete the bar.*

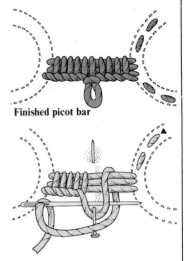

**Finished picot bar**

### Buttonhole scallop bar

This bar is worked like a plain bar but with an additional scallop on one side.

### How to work

*Strand the threads as for a plain bar. Cover with buttonhole stitch almost to end of strands. Then strand thread back and forth 3 times to form small scallop under bar. Buttonhole stitch over strands to bar. Then complete the bar.*

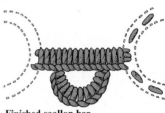

**Finished scallop bar**

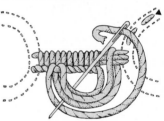

### Branched bar

This is used if three motifs are to be joined together. The method of working is basically the same as for a plain bar.

### How to work

*Start as for a plain bar and then work buttonhole stitch over the strands to the centre of the bar. Then strand 3 times back and forth to the third motif. Work in buttonhole stitch over the branched strands back up to the first bar and complete the bar. Continue the running stitch around the motif.*

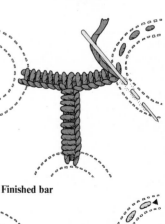

**Finished bar**

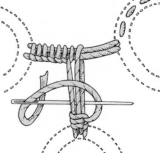

# Faggoting

Faggoting is the technique used to make openwork seams. It was originally developed as a decorative way of joining two widths of narrow hand-woven fabric to make large articles such as sheets. It is easy to work and makes even plain pieces of fabric look decorative.

### Preparation

Before beginning the faggot stitches the fabric pieces must be hemmed if they are not to be joined at the selvedges. The pieces are then tacked to a firm brown paper backing leaving a space of about ¼in. (6mm) to 1¼in. (3.1cm) according to the width of the stitch being used. This will guarantee that regular stitches are made and that the space between the pieces remains even.

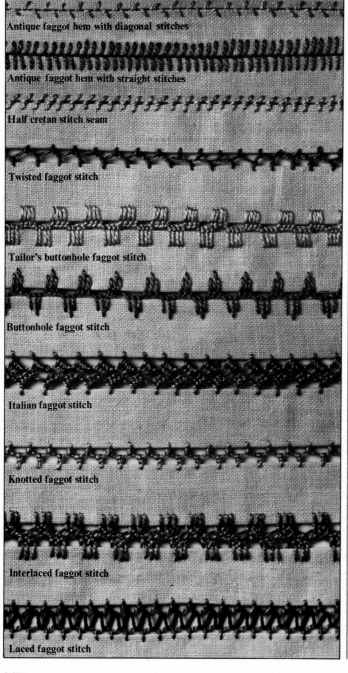

Antique faggot hem with diagonal stitches

Antique faggot hem with straight stitches

Half cretan stitch seam

Twisted faggot stitch

Tailor's buttonhole faggot stitch

Buttonhole faggot stitch

Italian faggot stitch

Knotted faggot stitch

Interlaced faggot stitch

Laced faggot stitch

# Faggot stitches

The stitches given below and on the next page are examples of various types of faggot stitches. Both antique hem with diagonal stitches and antique hem with straight stitches are especially suitable for joining two selvedges together when a flat seam is required. The other stitches all give an openwork effect.

A slightly thicker thread than that of the ground fabric is necessary in order to emphasize the stitching but it should not be so thick that it does not pass easily through the fabric.

### Antique faggot hem with diagonal stitches

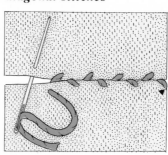

Work diagonal stitches from edge to edge picking up a small piece of fabric edge with each of the stitches.

### Antique faggot hem with straight stitches

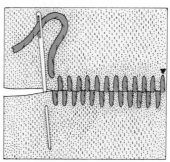

Work straight stitches from edge to edge picking up a small piece of fabric edge with each of the stitches.

### Half cretan stitch seam

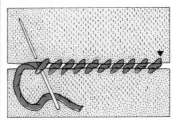

Make diagonal stitches between two edges, crossing them with a second diagonal stitch on each return journey. Pick up only a small piece of fabric edge with each stitch.

### Twisted faggot stitch

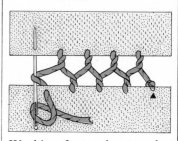

Working from edge to edge pick up a small piece of fabric edge with each stitch. Pass needle under and over the stranded thread to twist it on each journey as shown.

### Tailor's buttonhole faggot stitch

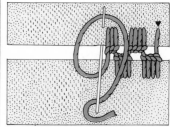

**1** *Work 4 tailor's buttonhole stitches (see page 251) from edge to edge alternately. On top edge insert needle upwards under fabric edge and bring it out on surface over loop made by working thread.*

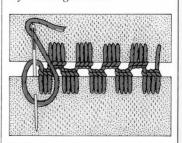

**2** *On bottom edge insert needle downwards under fabric edge and bring out on surface over loop made by working thread.*

## Buttonhole faggot stitch

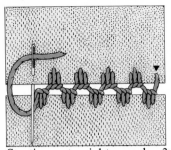

Starting at right work 3 buttonhole stitches alternately from edge to edge, making central stitch slightly longer.

## Italian faggot stitch

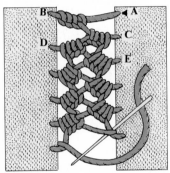

Bring needle out at A and insert at B. Work 4 close buttonhole stitches from left to right, on strand just made. Make buttonhole loop (as shown at bottom of diagram) at C. Make another buttonhole loop at D and work 4 close buttonhole stitches over buttonhole loop at C from centre to right. Then make buttonhole loop at E and work 4 close buttonhole stitches over buttonhole loop at D from centre to left. Continue in this way from side to side.

## Knotted faggot stitch

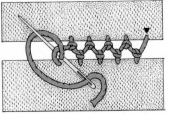

Starting at right work alternately from edge to edge making loops knotted in place with buttonhole stitch.

## Interlaced faggot stitch

This is one of the most ornate of the faggot stitches. It was often used on fine church vestments and Victorian bed linen.

It can be used to join a contrasting fabric or ribbon to the edge or hem of a piece of work. The only point to remember when doing this is that the fabric being joined should be of the same weight as the main ground, otherwise it will not hang or lie correctly.

When working the stitch use a coarser thread than the ground. Tack the pieces to strong brown paper, leaving a space of ¾in. (2cm) for fine fabrics to 1¼in. (3.1cm) for coarse fabrics between the pieces.

### How to work

**1** *Secure thread to bottom edge at arrow. Then leaving a space insert needle downwards at top edge bringing it out over strand just made. Leave a space and insert needle upwards at bottom edge bringing it out over the strand which has just been made.*

**2** *Take needle up under first strand and insert downwards at top edge to left of previous stitch bringing it out under strand which has just been made and over first strand.*

**3** *Insert needle upwards at bottom edge to left of previous stitch bringing it out over the strands.*

**4** *Pass needle upwards under middle strand. Leave a space and insert downwards at top edge bringing it out over strand just made.*

**5** *Pass needle down to left under first and third strands and insert upwards to left of previous stitches, bringing it out over strands.*

**6** *Pass needle upwards under middle strand and insert downwards at top edge to left of previous stitch bringing it out over strands. Pass needle downwards under middle strand. Leave a space and continue in this way.*

## Laced faggot stitch

First work loop stitch on both edges. Leave a small space and insert needle downwards through loop of working thread and edge of fabric, bringing it out over thread. Continue in this way for both edges. Then tack pieces to strong brown paper and work lacing with contrasting thread as shown.

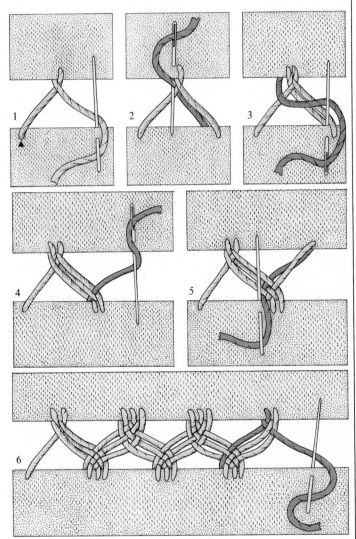

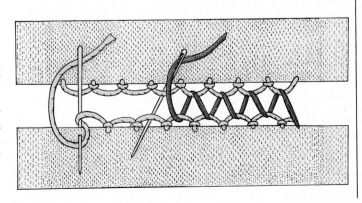

# Needlepoint lace

Detail of seventeenth-century Venetian needlepoint lace

Detail of Italian seventeenth-century "punto in aria"

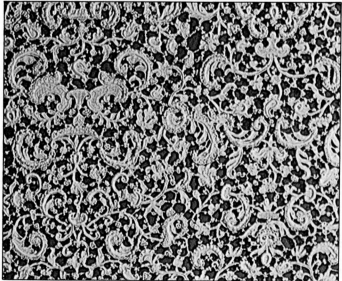

Detail of Italian seventeenth-century gros point

The word "lace" comes from the Latin, *lacinia*, meaning hem or fringe. In a primitive form, lace has been known since early history: the Egyptians used it to fringe their garments and passed the technique on to the Hebrews, the Greeks and the Romans, who in turn handed it on to the early Christians. The Christians reserved their lace entirely for church use, treating it as precious and often working it in silver and gold threads.

It was not until the Renaissance that the particular type of lace known as *needlepoint lace* came into general use. It is constructed without any supporting ground fabric, the lace being formed with a needle and thread alone – hence the Italian name for it, *punto in aria* (point in the air). In fact, both the Italians and the Spanish lay claim to having invented the technique. The Italians maintain they learnt it from the Greeks while the Spanish assert it was taught to them by the Moors. However, the early Italian needlepoint laces are generally recognized as the forerunners of all needlepoint lace and look very similar to the Italian reticella cutwork designs which pre-dated them.

With its development, the popularity of needlepoint lace grew and it became more widely used as part of the wardrobe of the rich. The texture changed according to the fashion: in seventeenth-century Spain and Italy it was rich and heavy – with raised outlines and decorated bars joining the motifs. In eighteenth-century France it became gossamer-fine, a net or *reseau* ground having been introduced to replace the bars which had previously been used to join the motifs.

Another change in needlepoint lace took place after the introduction of the net-making machine in Hamburg in the last century. Machine-made grounds were then used instead of the more time-consuming hand-made grounds.

Although hand-made lace declined in popularity from the mid-nineteenth century onwards, interest in it has revived recently. It is similar in appearance to bobbin lace, which is worked using an entirely different technique. In bobbin lace, a number of threads are used. These are attached to bobbins, and plaited around pins which are arranged in a pattern formation on a supporting pillow or cushion.

## The construction of needlepoint lace

Needlepoint lace is always made in stages. First the individual motifs are filled with lace stitches and then these are joined to make an overall design either with bars, or hand-made net ground. Alternatively, they can be applied to a machine-made net ground.

Any design can be worked provided it is organized into sections and, although the very fine thread used formerly is no longer available, fine crochet cotton can be used instead. The lace can be worked in different coloured threads, although traditionally, of course, it was always worked in white, cream or black threads.

## Implements and threads

Long, fine needles with a ball or blunt point, such as tapestry needles, are used. You will also need a strong flax thread or fine crochet cotton; tracing paper for marking the design; strong paper such as brown wrapping paper for a foundation on which to work the lace and, lastly, an embroidery frame mounted with coarse linen.

# *Making needlepoint segments*

The complete design must be marked out onto a firm glazed paper. In small designs which are to be joined with bars or hand-made net, all the motifs can be worked in their correct position on the overall design. For clarity in the following instructions we have shown how to make the motifs individually, in the stages illustrated below.

### *Pricking the motifs*

Lay the tracing of the motif over the firm paper and secure it in place. Then, using a needle or a pin, prick holes at regular intervals around the outline of the motif through the tracing paper and the paper below. When completed, remove the tracing paper.

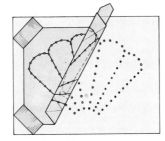

**Removing the tracing**

### *Mounting the pricked design*

To work the lace stitches, the pricked design must be supported so that it is kept smooth and flat. Mount an embroidery frame with backing fabric, such as coarse linen, and stretch it taut. Pin the pricked design on top and tack around the edges to secure it as shown in the diagram (right).

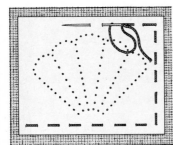

**Tacking down the design**

### *Making the fil de trace*

Once the pricked design is tacked to the backing fabric a thread is couched down around the motif outline. This is known as the *fil de trace* and is used as a support for the lace stitches, so use a thick thread or two or three strands of the thread used for the filling stitches.

Lay the fil de trace along the pricked outline and with a finer thread couch it down at each pricked hole with an overcast stitch which enters and leaves through the same hole. Secure the fil de trace all around the outline of the design.

The couching thread secures the fil de trace to the backing. At a later stage, the motif can be removed without pulling it or damaging the stitches, by simply snipping the couching thread at the back of the stretched linen.

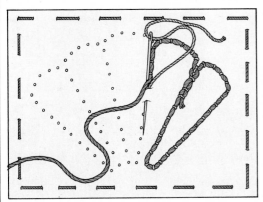

**Couching the fil de trace**
Using a fine thread couch down a thicker thread to form the outline of the motif.

### *Filling the motifs*

After the fil de trace is secured, the filling stitches are worked (see page 289 for filling stitch instructions). The filling stitches are almost always made with variations of buttonhole stitch which are built up row by row. The designs formed depend on the number of stitches worked at stated intervals. The stitching always begins and ends at the fil de trace and care must be taken not to pierce either the small couching stitches or the backing paper as this will make it difficult to remove the motif from the backing at a later stage.

The first row is worked along the fil de trace. The subsequent rows are worked into the stitches of the previous row and stitched to the fil de trace only at the sides. When the outline narrows or widens the number of stitches are decreased or increased in order to fill the space correctly. It is important always to make the stitches of the same uniform size.

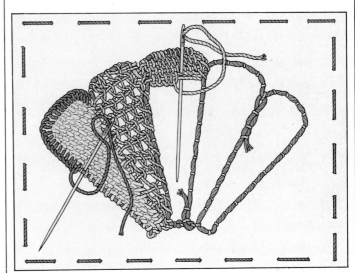

**Working the filling stitches (right) and the cordonnet (left)**

### *Finishing the edges of the motif*

The edges of all motifs are always outlined with close buttonhole stitch which can be padded to give a corded effect and which is also known as the *cordonnet*. The stage at which the buttonhole edging is worked depends on the method of joining used. It is used to secure the lace fillings and to emphasize the shape of the outlines.

If the lace motif is to be applied to fabric or to machine-made net, work the cordonnet after the fillings have been completed and before the motif is removed from its backing. If the motifs are to be joined by bars or hand-made net then the cordonnet is worked after the joining has been completed.

### *Removing the motifs from the backing*

Once the motifs have been completely filled, the couching stitches are cut away from behind the backing fabric and the lace motif released. Remove the couching threads carefully so as not to pull the finished motif out of shape.

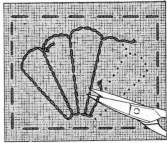

**Back: snipping the couching thread**

# *Joining needlepoint lace motifs*

Needlepoint lace motifs can be joined in several ways to form the overall pattern. They can be applied direct to a ground fabric as decoration, or added as a decorative edging on a collar or cuff, for example. Alternatively, they can be worked into an overall design, either by applying the motifs to a machine-made net ground or by joining with bars or with a hand-made net ground. When the motifs have been completed, if they are to be joined with bars or a hand-made lace (see opposite page for stitch instructions), they should be set in position on the overall paper design. However, if they are to be applied to a net ground or fabric, they should be arranged in position on the fabric and then stitched down. Although the joining methods below show a pattern being made of a single repeating motif, more ornate patterns can be made using a variety of shapes.

## *Applying motifs to fabric*

The lace motifs can be stitched to a ground fabric directly as an applied motif or as a decorative edging. The lace motifs are joined together where they touch with overcast stitches.

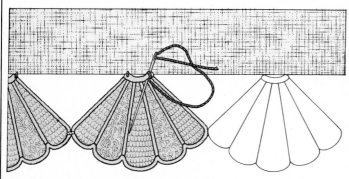

**Attaching motif to fabric**

## *Applying motifs to a machine-made net ground*

The simplest method of joining the filled motifs into a pattern formation is by applying them to a machine-made net ground.

The net ground should be tacked down over a tracing of the overall design which in turn is tacked onto a mounted backing fabric. The completed motifs, outlined with cordonnets, are then arranged on top of the net ground in the correct position. Then pin and tack the motifs in position and oversew them with invisible stitching through the lace motif and net ground only. If a more decorated design is required, additional embroidery stitches can be worked over the net.

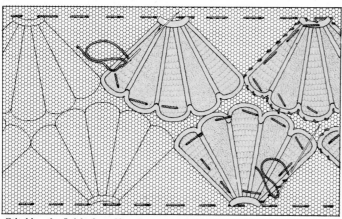

**Stitching the finished motif to the net ground**

## *Joining motifs with bars*

The bars which join the motifs are made with buttonhole stitch. They can be worked plain without picots and as such are known as *brides claires* or they can be decorated with picots, in the style of the Venetian and Spanish needlepoints, in which case they are known as *brides ornées*. Early needlepoint laces were worked in heavy, embossed patterns, surrounded with thick, raised buttonhole edgings and richly decorated picot bars.

The motifs should be removed from their backing after the filling stitches have been worked but before the cordonnet has been made. The motifs are then pinned and tacked in position on top of a tracing of the overall design on a mounted backing fabric. Work the bars at the places indicated on the design. Make sure no pieces of lace are left unattached. When they have all been worked the cordonnet is worked around the outlines of all the motifs.

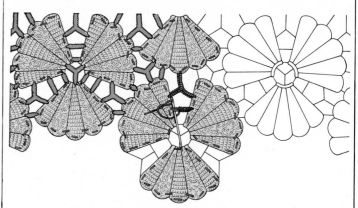

**Working the bars to join the motifs**

## *Joining motifs with a hand-made net ground*

For a hand-made net or *reseau* ground, the tracing of the overall design must be tacked onto a stretched backing fabric. The motifs are removed from their backing after the filling stitches have been worked but before the cordonnet has been made. The filled motifs are tacked to the traced design and a second fil de trace worked around the perimeter of the whole design, where the lace motifs do not serve as an edge.

The lace ground should be worked from one corner of the design, in rows. Work the first row until the fil de trace of the first motif is reached and then work into the fil de trace at this point and make the next row back. Continue to make the net ground, filling all the spaces. When completed, work the cordonnet round the edges of all the motifs.

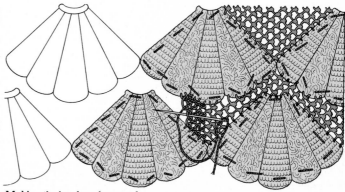

**Making the hand-made ground**

# Lace fillings

These are worked in buttonhole stitch variations (see detached buttonhole stitch on page 251). They can be worked far apart or close together depending on whether a dense or open effect is required. The same number of stitches is always worked in each row except where the motif narrows or widens in which case fewer or more stitches will be needed. All the following stitches can be used either for fillings or for net grounds. If they are being used as net grounds they should be worked further apart to give a light, lacy texture.

### Detached buttonhole filling stitch

This is the commonest of all the needlepoint lace stitches. Work first row of buttonhole loops over fil de trace from left to right. At end of row pass needle under fil de trace, carry it back to left side and pass it under fil de trace there. On next row of loops pass needle under both the stretched thread and loops of previous row. Continue to fill the motif in this way.

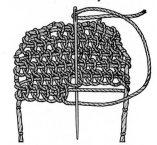

**Working detached buttonhole stitch**

### Hollie stitch

This twisted buttonhole stitch is simple to work.

Work first row of loops over fil de trace from left to right making an extra twist on loop before passing needle through. At end of row pass needle under fil de trace, take it back to left and pass it under fil de trace there. On next row of loops pass needle under thread just stretched and loops of previous row. Continue to end.

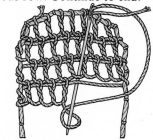

**Working hollie stitch**

### Venetian filling stitch

This is worked in clusters of 4 buttonhole stitches. Work first row from left to right over fil de trace making a loose buttonhole loop then working a group of 4 buttonhole stitches over it. Continue like this to end of row. Work 2nd row from right to left making loose loops between each group of 4 buttonhole stitches. Work 3rd row like first but over loops of previous row. Continue working 2nd and 3rd rows back and forth.

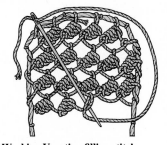

**Working Venetian filling stitch**

### Net filling stitch

This easy stitch is ideal for net grounds. Work first row of loose buttonhole loops from left to right over fil de trace. At end of row pass needle under fil de trace. Then work another row of loose buttonhole loops from right to left over the loops of the previous row. Work next and subsequent rows back and forth in this way.

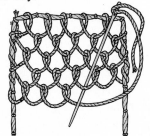

**Working net filling stitch**

# Bars

Bars are made in closely worked buttonhole stitches and are used to join the motifs. They can be made in any direction and are branched when necessary (for plain and branched bars see page 283).

### Double buttonhole bar

This gives a double purled edge to a bar. Strand thread 2 times between motifs. Then work pairs of buttonhole stitch over strands from left to right leaving spaces in between. Before making second stitch of pair pass thread behind strands (Fig. 1).

Fill spaces on return row, working from right to left (Fig. 2).

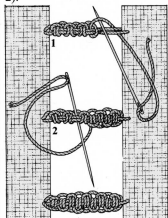

**Working double buttonhole bars**

### Venetian picot bar

This was used in Venetian and Spanish laces. Strand thread 2 or 3 times between motifs. Work buttonhole stitches over strands from top to bottom to middle of bar. Put pin in position. Make a loop around pin. Then pass needle behind strands and out through loop. Make another loop around pin. Work buttonhole stitches up to bar and complete bar.

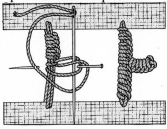

**Working Venetian picot bar**

# Lace edges

These edges worked on fabric illustrate the beginnings of needlepoint lace.

### Picot edging

Work from left to right. Make a buttonhole stitch then make a first loop to form picot. Make a second loop and pass needle downwards through buttonhole stitch and 2nd loop. Leave space and make next stitches in same way.

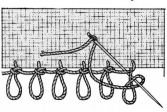

**Working picot edging**

### Scallop edging

For A make 2-strand loop. Work buttonhole stitch over strands from right to left. Make 2-strand loop for B. Work buttonhole stitch to middle. Make 3 strand loop for C. Cover with buttonhole stitches and complete B. Continue in this way.

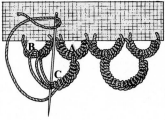

**Working scallop edging**

### Bullion picot scallop

Make a 4-strand loop. Work buttonhole stitch over strands with bullion picots at intervals. Make bullions by twisting needle several times around thread and drawing it through.

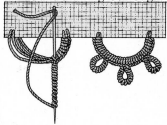

**Working bullion picot scallop**

# Designing embroidery

In the past, when embroidery and tapestry were both rated highly as art forms, most of the designs for them were made either by special embroidery designers or by the painters of the time. The resulting designs were then worked by skilled professionals or by the ladies of the house so that only the choice of thread, stitch and ground fabric was left for them to decide. But for those not rich enough to have their own designers, inspiration for their designs came from a range of different sources, such as biblical stories, drawings copied from books, wild flowers and so on. The embroideries also commemorated events of national or domestic importance, and a stream of original designs was produced for use on clothes and on household articles, as well as for pictures in their own right.

These old embroideries are worth studying, as much for their brilliant use of stitch, thread and ground subject as for their subject matter, because it is the successful partnership between all these factors that can turn a simple embroidery into a work of art. There are very few rules which have to be observed, and the scope is enormous, thanks to the range of fabrics, threads and stitches which can be used.

For less-experienced embroiderers, a smaller design is probably better as a starting point. The embroideries by Jonathan Langley (a painter and embroiderer) on the opposite page are all, in fact, quite small – they measure approximately 5in. (12.5cm) by 3in. (7.5cm).

If you are making an embroidered picture to display, the choice of both border and frame is very important so as to set off the embroidery to its best advantage. The instructions for framing embroidery are on page 233.

**Chinese badge of office**
*In the seventeenth-century Chinese embroidered mandarin square (above), used as a badge of office, the pictorial design is deliberately stylized.*

**Children's pictures**
*Children's drawings can be an excellent source for original designs. The embroidery (above left) was copied from the drawing above which was done by a child of six. The simplicity of the drawing has been retained in the embroidery by the fresh colours and the clever use of outlines and exposed ground. Stitches worked in chain, satin and French knots.*

**Kutch Indian wall hanging**
*The detail (left) of the wall hanging has been worked in chain stitches. Note the way the direction of the stitches helps to form the simple shapes of horse and rider.*

# Designing an embroidered picture

The step-by-step construction of one of Jonathan Langley's pictures is shown on the right. First of all, a fine linen sheet is stretched on a hoop frame and then the design is marked out in pencil. Next, the colours are filled in using coloured pencils. When the design is fully coloured, the embroidery is begun by filling in the top background and then all the other large areas. Once these have been completed, the details such as the hair, face and stars are worked and the picture is finished finally with a border. The process used is very simple and the order of work very logical. Although it is more satisfying to work from one of your own designs, if you are not able to draw freehand then a tracing of a drawing or painting could easily be used instead (see transferring instructions on pages 236–237).

**Stitches and threads**

1 Satin stitch
2 Satin with long and short stitch.
3 Brick stitch
4 Brick stitch
5 Speckling
6 French knots
7 Chain stitch
Stitches 1, 2, 3 and 7 in 2-strand; 4, 5 and 6 in 1-strand.

## How to work

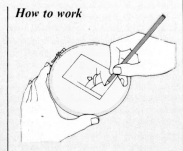

**1** *Using a pencil, mark out the chosen design.*

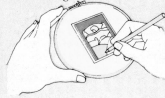

**2** *Then, with coloured pencils, block in the areas of colour.*

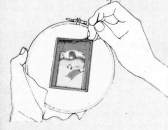

**3** *Start to work the main areas of the background.*

**4** *Then work the more detailed parts of the design, using the appropriate stitches for each part.*

**5** *Finally, stitch around the design to make a border for the completed picture.*

**The Farmer.**
*This picture within a picture, measuring 6¾in. by 5in. (17cm by 12.5cm), was made by surrounding a painted plaster miniature with an embroidery in satin stitch. The perspective is achieved by shortening the stitches at the top.*

**The Clown.**
*This embroidery measures 6in. by 4in. (15cm by 10cm) and is worked in rich, bright colours using coloured inks for the details on the arch and the border.*

# Designing in embroidery

### Uses and forms of embroidery

Embroidery can be used to decorate the ground fabric in many different ways. At its most simple just a single flower can be embroidered. Progressing from the single flower, small motifs can then be worked as edgings on clothing and household linen. Single motifs can also be enlarged and used as separate designs in themselves, for the central medallion on cushions and bed-covers, for example. If the motifs are repeated at regular intervals or arranged in patterns an entire embroidered ground is made. Stitches can also be worked in different-coloured bands of stripes, checks and chevrons and used in borders. Alternatively, wide panels of embroidery can be worked with intervening spaces of plain ground fabric. The scope is enormous, but when embarking on an original design there is no need to use all the stitch techniques for a massive piece of work. It is far better to start with a simple motif worked in one or two stitches and then gradually progress to more ambitious designs. Quite a good idea is to select one stitch for working the main part of the motif and a second for lines and outlines, whilst a third can be held in reserve for special textural effects.

### Inspiration for designs

Inspiration for embroidery designs can come direct from the imagination or from nature, paintings, drawings, photographs, printed textiles, porcelain, pottery and tiles. They can also come from already existing embroideries. These are the most helpful of all sources as they alone tell the textural story of the workings of the stitches and threads, and it is well worthwhile studying old pieces of embroidery in order to see just how effective a well-chosen combination of stitches, threads, ground fabric and colours can be.

---

## Working embroidery over large areas

The quickest way to cover large areas of fabric with embroidery is by *tambouring*. In this method of embroidery, a tambour hook – which is small, metal and slightly pointed at the tip – is used instead of a needle to work chain stitches through the ground fabric. It should be worked on a frame, as the surface of the fabric needs to be tautly stretched in order to work the hook easily in and out of the fabric.

#### How to work

**1** *Knot the end of the working thread and hold it in the left hand underneath the ground fabric. Insert the hook downwards, from front to back of fabric, and draw through a loop of working thread and pull it up through fabric.*

**2** *Then, with loop still on hook, insert hook a little further along design line and draw through another loop of the thread. Draw this 2nd loop through first, forming a chain stitch and continue in this way.*

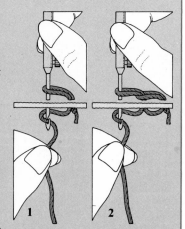

---

# Preparing the designs

### Preparing the designs

When the design has been planned it is transferred to the ground fabric by any of the methods described on page 236, depending on the type of fabric being covered. The ground fabric is then mounted onto an embroidery frame, where it is stretched firmly and evenly into position for the subsequent stitching. When embroidery is being worked on clothing or small articles the ground fabric should be worked uncut, and cut into shape later. Pieces which are too small to be mounted onto a frame on their own should be mounted onto a supporting fabric, which is then placed and stretched on the frame. The following design points may be helpful if you are planning a new design.

### Type of ground fabric

The choice of ground fabric will depend on the type of design being worked and the kind of stitches and threads being used. The various fabric and thread combinations are given on page 234.

Prints and brocades can be used to form the design if their motifs are worked over with embroidery stitches. The motifs can be raised by using the same coloured thread as the ground fabric, or filled with contrasting coloured threads to give brilliant multicoloured effects. Alternatively, the motifs can be outlined with embroidery stitches for emphasis or increased in size by extending the stitches beyond their limits.

### Voiding

The ground fabric itself can be used as part of the design by working stitches over the background and around the outlines of the motif but leaving the ground within the motif exposed. This is known as *voiding*, and is found in Greek Island and Assisi embroideries. This theme can be developed further by couching the outlines with the same or contrasting coloured threads. Voiding can also be used to make geometric patterns by working blocks of stitches with intervals of exposed ground.

### Outlines

Outlines are used to define the pattern shapes. They can be made almost invisible by using a thread which is only slightly different in colour to the ground, or emphasized by using a sharply contrasting thread or even couched metal threads. Modern Danish embroideries sometimes use a thin black outline to define fine cross stitch embroideries. When several rows of outlining are used they greatly emphasize the motif. Outlines can also be made more decorative by using raised, whipped or threaded stitches. They can be made to undulate by using stitches such as scroll, zigzag and coral stitch. Finally, they can be used for covering over badly worked edges.

### Backgrounds

Backgrounds can be either left exposed to emphasize the embroidered design or worked over in various ways. They can be entirely covered with quick filling stitches, such as chain or darning stitch, or tambouring. The backgrounds can be shaded from dark to pale by introducing paler threads or made richer by darning with gold and metal threads. They can be given an "antiqued" look by working with different shades of one colour, or decorated with motifs to harmonize with the main design. Beads and sequins can also be scattered over them to give light and glitter effects.

# Stitch combinations

# Pictorial embroidery

## Same stitch, same thread

Very often the rich patterning of embroideries is worked with one stitch in the same colour throughout, with the pattern being formed by the arrangement of the stitches. This is found in many traditional cross stitch embroideries. The use of one stitch and one thread is also found in pictorial embroideries, where the image is formed by the directional change of the stitch. For example, if satin stitch is worked in silks with some areas worked horizontally and others vertically, the tones of the colour will change from area to area, according to how the light hits them. This can be taken a stage further by working a third area in diagonal formation. This treatment is less effective when worked in wools but is shown off best when metal threads are used.

## Same stitch, different threads

The types of threads can be changed but the same colour and stitch retained. Highlights can be introduced on wool embroideries with glossy threads while matt effects can be created by using wool threads with silks. Metal threads can be used when glitter is needed.

## Same colour, different stitches

Many different stitches can be used together to give rich, patterned effects, as seen in Spanish blackwork and any of the whitework embroideries.

## Different colour effects

Toning and shading is worked by using many tones of one colour. The new tones are introduced in easy stages, slowing down to one stitch at a time for very subtle effects. Several needles can be kept threaded for this purpose.

For diffused effects several colours can be threaded into one needle. The strength of one colour can be increased by adding more strands whilst discarding others.

## Pictorial embroidery

In pictorial work certain subjects, such as animals and birds, lend themselves well to embroidery, as fur and feathers can easily be translated into stitches, whereas other subjects are more difficult to capture, such as features and skin tones in human faces.

### Feathers

These can be copied exactly by working satin stitches in different lengths and directions to follow the line of the feather.

### Fur

Straight-haired fur is best worked in satin stitch, with the length of the stitches being varied according to the type of fur: wavy fur can be worked in chain stitch; ridged fur can be formed in fillings of buttonhole stitch; wool can be shown in bullion or French knots.

### Sky and water

Use flat stitches or laid threads for calm effects, and coiling, swirling stitch arrangements for storms. Water is often shown in stylized form: in Chinese embroidery, where coiled couched gold threads were used, and in eighteenth-century embroideries, where strips of dark to pale blues and white were used. Stripes can also be used for stylized skies. Clouds can be introduced, emphatically shaped and filled with white chain stitches. Sometimes, too, clouds can be created by applying net to the ground to give a misty effect.

### Wind and rain

Gusts of wind can be interpreted by a sudden change of stitch direction on the subject matter. Rain can be shown by top stitching in light-coloured glossy threads, using irregular-sized stroke stitches.

### Landscapes

When portraying landscapes the stitches can be changed and graded so that those in the foreground are longer than those in the background, giving a sense of distance.

### Faces

People are the most difficult subjects to reproduce in embroidery, for flesh and skin tones do not easily lend themselves to translation into stitches. In fact, old embroideries often make no attempt to disguise these difficulties and show the features merely painted in – with the ground being used for the skin tones. Not all embroidery workers, however, have been so faint-hearted and the following methods have all been worked successfully. For example, in the fifteenth century flesh was portrayed by the unworked ground fabric but the features were worked in outlines, using black or brown threads. In Chinese embroideries faces are often worked in solid, closely worked satin stitches covering both the front and the back of the fabric to give a plump, raised texture. The features are then worked through this padding and are tightly pulled so that they sink down to give moulding to the face as well as colour definition to the eyes, nose and mouth.

In early English embroidery stem stitch was used to portray faces and worked in concentric circles, starting at the cheekbone and working outwards in ever-widening circles to give roundness to the face. Sometimes shading was used with tones being added here and there to emphasize the bone structure. Features were finally added on top and worked in different-coloured threads to give fine detailing to eyes, nose and mouth. Split stitch can also be used and worked in carefully graded skin tones, for the main ground, with the features added later in short satin stitches. Alternatively, short straight satin stitches can be used to fill the face area and then the features can be worked over these in brown threads. The facial bone structure can be modelled by using darker threads where shadows fall.

Detail of a Kutch Indian wall hanging in which the direction of the chain stitching has been used to form the features on the faces, as well as the main outlines and fillings of the embroidery.

# Beads and sequins

Beads and sequins are probably the most effective way of transforming quite simple patterns into rich, exotic designs. When working with them, the main point to bear in mind is that they should lie neatly together in prearranged order. Not only beads and sequins but buttons, shells and pebbles can be used in embroidery provided they have holes of a convenient size to secure them to the fabric. Make sure the fabric is strong enough to support the weight of heavy beads, for example.

A small cross-section of the different types of beads and sequins is shown below. Sequins are almost always made to glitter and catch the light and are therefore usually of gold or metal. Beads, on the other hand, are either made to glitter in clear, coloured glass or plastic, or used simply to add colour in bright wood or opaque plastic.

Because the beads and sequins are fragile, it is best to keep them in separate containers. They should be stored away from direct light. As the gold and silver sequins are inclined to tarnish, try to handle them as little as possible so that they do not lose their glitter or sheen.

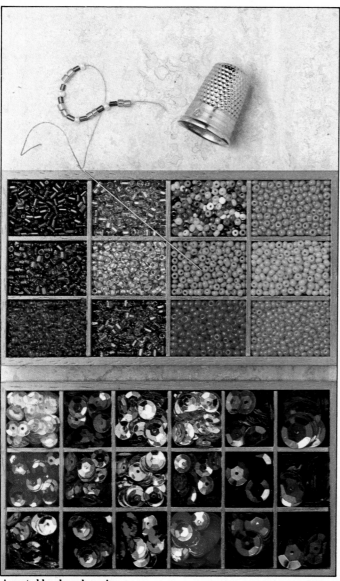

**Assorted beads and sequins**

**Seventeenth-century English beadwork picture**

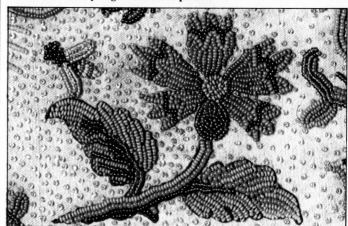

**Detail of the brightly beaded motif**

**Modern beadwork belt**
The pattern has been taken from a Sioux chief's headband

**Masai warrior's apron**
Shells and beads have been used for a traditional Masai apron

294

# Bead and sequin purse

In the purse design below, sequins are used to imitate the fish scales while beads are used for all the other parts of the design. This fish motif can also be used to make a border by repeating the design and using it either with or without the sea background. The instructions for making the purse are given below.

**Spanish cope**
*The cope, showing the grid emblem of St Lorenzo, has been worked using a mixture of gold and silver threads and gold and silver sequins. Sequins can be used with metal threads to give a particularly lustrous texture.*

**Traditional Hungarian head-dress**
*The sequins in the ceremonial head-dress above are stitched with gold thread, on top of applied silk and velvet.*

## Making the sequin purse

The purse measures $4\frac{3}{4}$in. (12cm) by $10\frac{1}{8}$in. (26cm) in the strip and when folded it measures $4\frac{3}{4}$in. (12cm) by $3\frac{7}{8}$in. (10cm). The materials required are: $\frac{1}{4}$yd (30cm) each of silk ground fabric and lining; 1 packet each of the following beads and sequins: 2 shades small beads for waves, using lighter shade for wave peaks; 2 shades medium-sized beads for fins; 1 shade sequins for fish and 2 small contrasting beads for eyes.

Leave a 2in. (5cm) seam allowance all around and trace fish design above and transfer to the ground fabric as shown right. Then stretch fabric on frame and apply the beads for waves, fins and eyes first. Then fill in fish with sequins (see page 297 for applying beads and sequins). When completed, remove from frame and trim seam allowance to $\frac{5}{8}$in. (1.5cm) and cut lining to same size. Then place beaded fabric and lining face to face and work running stitch around 3 sides. Turn right sides out and fold in unstitched edges and stitch to close. Now fold to form purse at line AB and stitch sides. Finish off with cord or button at middle of flap.

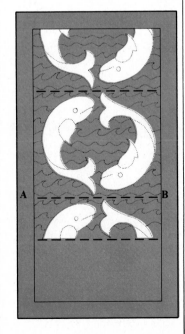

# Bead work

Bead work is the only type of embroidery which has remained undiminished in style, design and imagination with the advent of machines. In fact, modern bead and sequin work is as beautiful as any of the older embroideries. The sparkling dresses, embellished with beads and sequins, produced by the French couture houses in the 1920s must have been greeted with just as much astonishment as the heavily-bejewelled robes and tents of the kings and courtiers at the Field of the Cloth of Gold in France in 1520. The only major difference between bead work now and formerly is that in the old days the glitter and sparkle came from real jewels, and gold and silver spangles; now it is provided by tin, glass and plastic.

The earliest sequins were those found in a Greek tomb. Made of gold and silver, they had been worked into a variety of shapes: stars, crescent moons (complete with a man in the moon) and circles, squares and wedge-shapes. Later these shapes were further adorned with enamels of different colours to provide added lustre.

In the sixteenth century, the spangles used by Queen Isabella of Castile were made of gold and silver and, unlike modern flat sequins, were convex. These sequins were stitched down over-lapping one another, in the same way that roof tiles are laid.

Anything that glitters can be stitched to fabric, from beetle wings in Bangkok to abalone shells in Borneo. Various countries have made particular use of beads and sequins. The Masai tribes of Kenya and the North American Indians are probably the most liberal in their use of brightly-coloured beads, while the street traders of London, for their costumes as pearly kings and queens, make use of thousands of pearl buttons as decoration. The most dramatic use of beads and sequins is probably by the clowns of the Commedia dell'Arte in Naples.

Ceremonial decoration, using sequins, for an elephant at the Festival of Kandy

# Applying sequins

Sequins can be attached to the ground fabric so that the stitching is either visible or invisible. The choice of method depends on whether a contrasting yarn is used for special effect, such as gold or metal threads, or whether the patterns are built up with the sequins overlapping each other and thus hiding the stitches.

You can scatter the sequins all over the fabric or use them to highlight a part of an embroidery (for example, to make a drop of dew on an embroidered flower). Alternatively, they can be used in broad bands to give a richly textured effect to the fabric.

Sequins are generally bought threaded on cotton. As they are fragile, keep them carefully until they are used.

### Applying sequins with stitches on one side only

This method is best when the thread is to be a decorative feature. It gives a slightly raised effect.

*How to work*

*Bring the needle with the thread to the surface from the back of the fabric and insert it through the eye of the sequin. Work a back stitch over the right side of the sequin and bring needle out to left, ready to thread through eye of next sequin which is placed edge to edge with the previous one. Continue until all the sequins are secured.*

### Applying sequins with stitches on both sides

This method gives a more flattened effect.

*How to work*

*Work back stitch over right side of sequin and then bring needle out at left edge of sequin and work another back stitch through the eye of the sequin, bringing needle out to left to be threaded through eye of next sequin, which is placed edge to edge with the previous one. Continue in this way.*

### Applying sequins with invisible stitches

To apply sequins so that the stitches are invisible, the sequins must be overlapped.

*How to work*

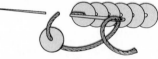

*Work a back stitch into the left side of the first sequin and place next sequin so that the right edge covers the eye of the previous one. Bring the needle out exactly at the left edge of it and work back stitch through the eye, inserting needle into hole of previous back stitch.*

### Securing sequins with a small bead

As a decorative feature the sequins can be stitched down with a bead. This also means that the thread is invisible because it is the bead which secures the sequin.

*How to work*

*Bring the needle out through the eye of the sequin and thread a small bead onto it, then insert the needle through the eye of the sequin again and pull tight so that the bead rests firmly over the eye, securing the sequin.*

# Applying beads

Beads can be used to decorate the fabric in a wide variety of ways, either as braids or to form blocks of coloured patterns, or as tassels and fringes. The beads can be applied singly or in rows by couching the laid row or beads to the fabric. Beads are always secured invisibly.

### *How to apply individually*

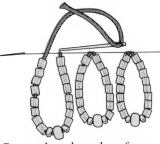

*Bring needle to surface and thread bead onto it. Then insert needle back through the same hole, make a stitch slightly longer than the length of the bead. Alternatively make a stitch the length of the bead so that next bead can be secured edge to edge with the previous one.*

### *How to couch beads*

*Cut 2 lengths of thread and bring one thread to surface and thread beads onto it. Slide first bead into position. With a separate needle and thread make an overcast stitch as close as possible to edge of bead. Slide 2nd bead up to first. Continue in this way until all beads have been couched into position.*

### *How to apply loop fringe*

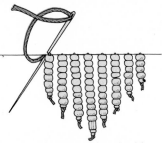

*Secure thread to edge of fabric and thread on required number of beads. Insert needle back into hole from which it emerged and bring it out a little to left ready to make next loop.*

### *How to apply dangling fringe*

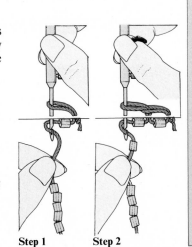

*Knot end of thread and add a small bead to it. Then thread on required number of beads for dangle and secure to edge of fabric with a small back stitch. Continue adding dangles in this way.*

### Applying beads with a tambour hook

In this technique the beads are applied onto a tightly stretched fabric from the underneath.

### *How to work*

*1 Thread beads and secure thread to fabric. Insert hook downwards through fabric and wrap thread around it. With hook draw loop through to surface. Push first bead up to fabric below work. Insert hook back through fabric and again draw loop through.*

*2 Continue in this way along the design line.*

**Step 1**     **Step 2**

# Mirrorwork

This type of work is seen in the traditional embroideries of Afghanistan and in Baluchistan and Sind in India. It is worked with little discs of mirror or tin being secured around their circumference on the surface of the fabric with a special embroidery stitch known as *shisha stitch*.

### *How to work*

*1 Lay disc on surface of fabric and hold it secure with left thumb. Bring needle out at A. Carry thread across from left to right over disc and insert needle at B, bringing it out at point C.*

*2 Carry thread back across disc and insert needle at D, bringing it out at E.*

*3 Pass needle over and under the first horizontal thread. Draw it through and take it up and pass it over and under 2nd horizontal thread in same way. Then insert needle at F and bring it out at G.*

*4 Again pass needle over and under both horizontal threads.*

*5 Insert needle at H and bring it out at I.*

*6 Pass needle under intersection on first horizontal thread and bring it out to right of working thread.*

*7 Insert needle at I and bring it out at J over working thread.*

*8 Pass needle under vertical thread and bring out over working thread.*

*9 Insert needle at J and bring it out at K over working thread.*

*10 Repeat steps 8 and 9 around the disc until it is completely encircled with stitches.*

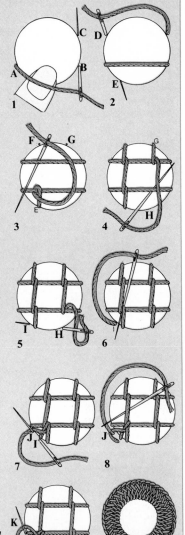

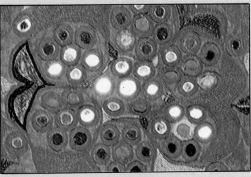

**Baluchi head-dress**
Detail of head-dress showing mirrorwork with shisha stitch

# Smocking

Smocking is the only form of embroidery which has a practical as well as a decorative function, with the smocking stitches being used to gather in the fullness at the same time as decorating the surface of the folds. For traditional smocks (which were really work overalls), special motifs and stitches were used as symbols of the wearer's trade. These were worked along the borders of the smocked panels and on the shoulders, collars and cuffs. Later, smocking was used on nightdresses and children's clothes and today it is used in many parts of the world on all types of clothing. Smocking is usually worked on the yoke of a blouse, at the front of a skirt or to gather up fullness at the wrist of a sleeve. It can be worked on most light or medium weight fabrics.

**Apron from Dorset, England**
*Traditional motifs used with smocking and worked in Dorset feather, wheat-ear and buttonhole stitches.*

**Traditional smock**
*Many different smocking patterns are used for the panel. Hearts have been used to decorate the collar.*

**Modern smocking**
*Different colours are used for each of the smocking stitches and the panels are outlined with embroidered motifs in subdued colours. A thin line of contrasting coloured stem stitch frames the honeycombing. The instructions for working honeycomb stitch are on page 301.*

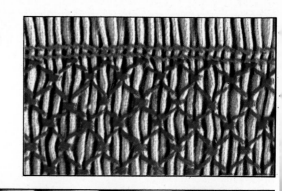

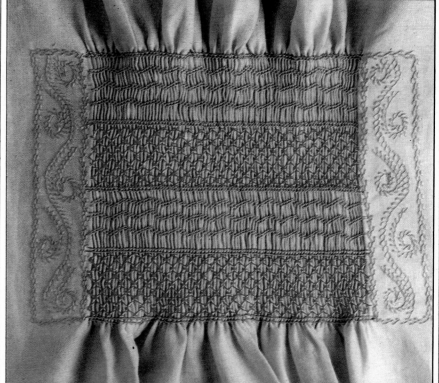

**Close up of the smocked fabric**

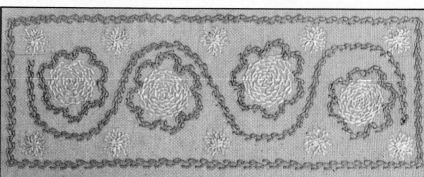

**Feather stitch flower panel**

**Feather stitch scroll panel**

Traditional smock with modern stitches added

### *Enhancing a traditional pattern*

Both the back and the front panels of traditional smocks were usually gathered with the smocking stitches worked in one colour throughout. In this modern version, further colours are added to enhance the basic stitching and flower motifs are used in feather stitch for the panels, cuffs, shoulders and collar. The extra fullness at the wrist is also taken in with a small area of smocking. It is interesting to note that although large gathered work shirts were used in many parts of the world, it was only in England that they were made decorative with smocking stitches.

Detail of back of smock

# *Smocking stitches*

Smocking can be worked on many different types of patterned fabrics with the patterns, such as dotted and checked designs, acting as the guides for the gathering. Areas of fabric can be left unsmocked and later embroidered with motifs in the same or contrasting colours. When making a garment with smocking, the smocked areas should always be worked first, before the whole garment is made up.

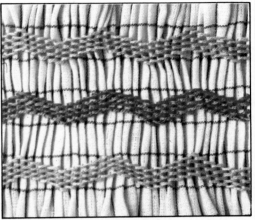

Vandyke stitch on windowpane checks

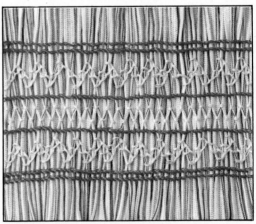

Stem, honeycomb and feather stitches on stripes

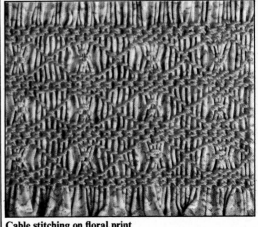

Cable stitching on floral print

# Smocking

The word "smocking" comes from the old English word, smock, meaning a shift or chemise. The technique of smocking was invented in England and used on the big, square-cut shirts worn by rural workers in Britain from Anglo-Saxon times onwards. It was, and still is, the most practical way of gathering fullness around the chest and wrists giving extra warmth to these places, while permitting the easy movement so necessary for working men such as shepherds, woodmen, wheelwrights and gardeners.

The smocks were usually made in strong linen, in either green, blue, white or black. Special Sunday smocks and wedding smocks were made in much finer fabric; generally fine white linen was used.

At first, the smocked gathering was worked without any form of embroidered decoration, but gradually the women who made the smocks added embroidery stitches to the smocked surfaces, surrounding the collars, cuffs and shoulders with embroidered motifs. These motifs often symbolized the trade of the wearer: for example, wheels for the wheelwright, ears of wheat for the ploughman, crossed crooks and hurdles for the shepherd and paths and flowers for the gardener. These motifs were sometimes interspersed with marks of wifely affection: lover's knots or hearts perhaps. The borders were worked in chain, feather and wheat ear stitch.

With the advent of the Industrial Revolution, traditional smocks were replaced by machine-made overalls, but the art of smocking has not been lost and it is still used today, particularly for children's dresses.

## Materials

Any fabric, from plain linen to cottons and printed silks, can be smocked provided it is supple enough to be gathered. Gingham and patterned fabric such as stripes and polka-dot prints, are particularly easy to smock as the pattern forms a ready-made guide for making gathers at regular intervals.

The smocking stitches, although traditionally worked in matching cotton thread to the ground fabric, can be of any colour or of several different contrasting colours. Stranded cotton thread is the best to use. You will also need a suitable sewing needle and the usual sewing implements.

There are two basic types of smocking: the traditional method, shown below left, and the lattice smocking method, shown below right. The techniques are given on the opposite page.

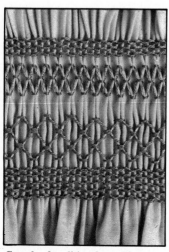

**Sample of traditional smocking using a variety of smocking stitches**

**Sample of lattice smocking, often used for making cushion covers**

# Method of working

### Preparing to smock

Smocking is worked by gathering the fabric into even-size folds. It is always worked before the garment is assembled. The amount of fabric needed is usually about three times the actual finished width of the smocking, but less fabric may be necessary if a thicker fabric such as a soft, woollen weave is used.

Traditionally the position of the folds was calculated by counting the horizontal and vertical threads in the ground fabric and marking them with ruled chalk lines. The gathering was done with a waxed thread worked over the chalk marks, with small pieces of ground fabric being picked up at regularly spaced intervals. This still remains the best method as it ensures that the gathers are on the same straight-weave lines.

Nowadays, printed transfers are readily available in the shops. They consist of a piece of transfer paper marked with equally spaced dots which are transferred onto the back of the fabric. Make sure that each dot falls on the weave line of the fabric, because if not the fabric will be strained and wrinkled when gathered.

If printed transfers are not available, you could make your own on a piece of card by marking evenly-spaced dots in rows along the card, and piercing each dot. This template is then placed on the ground fabric to be smocked, and each dot is marked through the holes with a dressmaker's pencil. The template can be kept and used again.

Once the fabric has been marked, it is ready for gathering.

### Gathering the fabric

You need enough thread to amply complete each full row of gathers. Using a knotted thread, bring the needle through the fabric from back to front and pick up a small piece of ground fabric at each dot, as shown. Then at the end of each row, leave the surplus thread hanging loose. Rethread the needle with new thread and complete all the rows. Then pull the loose ends up a row at a time, gathering the fabric until the required width has been achieved. Tie the thread ends in pairs and stroke the gathers gently with a pin to even them out.

The fabric is now ready for smocking. The gathering threads are removed when the smocking has been completed.

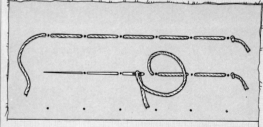

**How to work**
**1** Gather the back of fabric in rows, picking up a small piece of fabric at each dot.

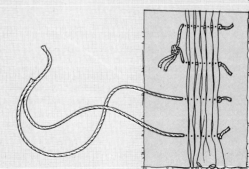

**2** When all the rows are worked, tie the thread ends together in pairs.

# Smocking stitches

A wide variety of patterns can be formed from any of the basic stitches below.

### *Rope stitch*

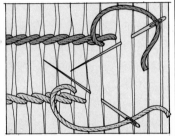

Bring the needle to the surface through first fold on left. Work stem stitch (see page 240) with thread above needle, across row picking up small piece of fabric on each fold.

To slant stitch in opposite direction, keep thread below needle as shown.

### *Cable stitch*

Bring needle to surface through first fold on left. Insert needle horizontally and work in stem stitch into each fold with thread alternately above and below needle.

### *Vandyke stitch*

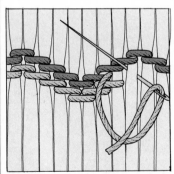

Work in 2 rows of stem stitch in chevron pattern. Keep thread below needle when working upwards and above needle when working downwards.

### *Honeycomb stitch with working thread hidden*

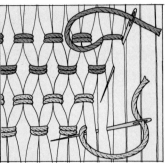

Work from left to right. Bring needle out on 1st line and make a back stitch to draw 2nd and 1st folds together on top line. Then inserting needle beneath fabric emerge at 2nd fold on line below. Make a back stitch to draw 3rd and 2nd folds together. Return needle to 1st line at 3rd fold and draw 4th and 3rd folds together. Continue working alternately up and down to end of row. Work next and following rows in same way.

### *Feather stitch*

Work from right to left. Bring needle out at 1st fold and insert lower down on same fold. Take needle through 1st and 2nd folds bringing it out over working thread. Make two more stitches in the same way working down to left, make the first over 2nd and 3rd folds and next over 3rd and 4th folds. Then work two feather stitches upwards to left over next two folds. Continue in this way working two feather stitches upwards and two downwards drawing in one more fold with each stitch (see feather stitch, page 246).

### *Honeycomb stitch with working thread on surface*

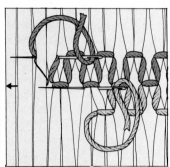

Work from right to left. Bring needle out on 2nd fold on 2nd line and make a back stitch over 1st and 2nd folds. Then take needle up on surface to 1st line making a back stitch over 2nd and 3rd folds. Return over surface to 2nd line and make a back stitch over 3rd and 4th folds. Continue to end of row. On subsequent rows make back stitches on lower lines but on upper lines, which are connected to previous rows, just pass needle under back stitches already made.

### *Chevron honeycomb stitch*

Work from left to right. Bring needle out on 2nd line then take it up to 1st line over two folds and insert it under 2nd fold. Make a back stitch over 2nd and 3rd folds emerging between the two. Take needle down over two folds and insert in 2nd line between 4th and 5th folds and bring out between 3rd and 4th. Make a back stitch over 4th and 5th folds. Continue to end of row. On next row make first stitch beneath 1st stitch of previous row and work next stitch downwards to 3rd line and so on. Repeat these two rows.

This is worked on the back of the fabric and requires no prior gathering. Mark position of gathers with dots.

### *How to work*

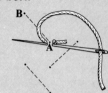

**1** *Make stitch at A.*

**2** *Make stitch at B. Return to A and make another stitch.*

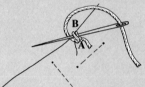

**3** *Pull A and B together and knot securely.*

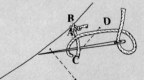

**4** *Make stitch at C. Then knot securely keeping intervening fabric flat.*

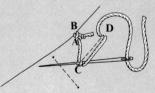

**5** *Make stitch at D. Return to C and make another stitch.*

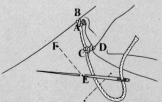

**6** *Pull C and D together and knot securely. Continue in this way stitching and knotting.*

# Braidwork

The word "braid" comes from the same Anglo Saxon word meaning to weave or entwine. Braids, cords and ribbons have been used since earliest times to decorate clothes and denote rank on uniforms. The important points to bear in mind when working braid patterns are to make sure that neither the braids nor the ground fabric pucker, that the corners are neatly turned and that the curves are accurately formed.

## *Preparation and stitching*

Mark the pattern onto the ground fabric and when it is in place lay the braids on top and tack down. Where possible conceal the ends at start and finish by inserting narrow cords and braids through the fabric, and broad braids and ribbons through the seam lines or under crossings. The braids are then secured with running or back stitches. Narrow braids and cords only require to be stitched along the centre except where curves are reached, when the stitching is worked along both edges. Broad braids and ribbons are stitched on both edges so that they lie down evenly.

### *How to work interlacing patterns*
*When an intersection is reached leave a small area untacked and on returning to this point thread the braid through a bodkin and insert it under the unworked area and carry on tacking.*

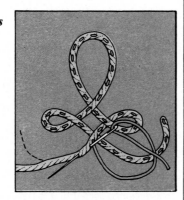

### *How to work angles*

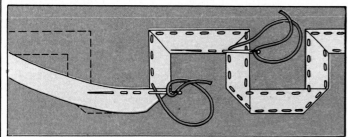

*Corners and angles are formed by twisting the braid over.*

### *How to work curves*

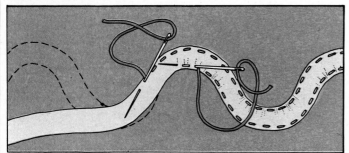

*Tack the outer edge first, then gather the inner edge until it fits and tack into position.*

**Turret pattern in tartan ribbon on striped cotton ground**

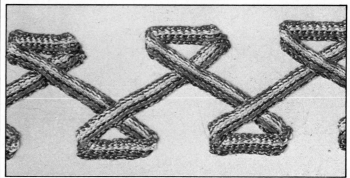

**Wave pattern in striped ribbon on plain linen ground**

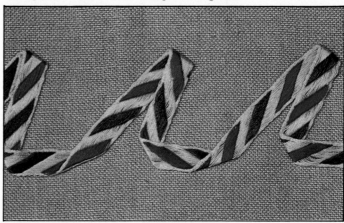

**Herringbone pattern in rainbow silk cord on wool felt ground**

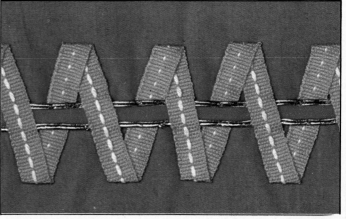

**Zigzag pattern in velvet and cotton ribbons and metal cord on plain cotton ground**

# Shadow work

Shadow work originated in India as a means of decorating fine cotton gauzes and muslins and is still in use today on lightweight shirts and tunics. The stitching is worked on the back of fine, transparent fabrics to produce a shadow tracery which is outlined on the front with back stitches. It is mostly worked in white threads on a white or coloured ground but very beautiful pastel shadow effects can be achieved by working with brightly coloured threads. Shadow work can be used to embroider shirts, blouses, lingerie and table linen.

## *Preparation and stitching*

Trace the design on the wrong side of the fabric and then work over it in close herringbone stitch (see page 245). The design lines should be followed closely from start to finish in order to show the back-stitched shape on the front of the fabric. Occasionally it may be necessary to add a few back stitches to the front of the fabric when the close herringbone has been completed in order to finish off the outlined shape. Stitched lines for stalks, stems and scrolls can be added later on the right side of the fabric by using either back stitch or stem stitch. Marking cross stitch (see page 243) can also be used to form geometric shadow designs with the cross making the shadow.

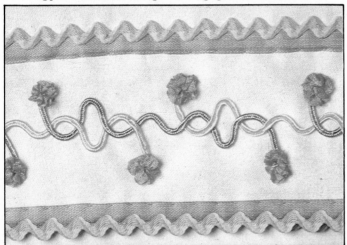

**Entwining pattern in silk cord with gold cord edging for neckline on wool**

**Voile ground with motifs worked in yellow, pink and green silks**

**Rosette pattern using silk ribbons and cords with ric rac braid on silk ground**

**Celtic knot pattern in silk cords on silk ground**

**Silk chiffon ground with motifs worked in blue and gold silks**

# Washing embroidery

Embroideries should always be properly looked after if they are to be preserved. All embroideries should be washed or cleaned regularly as a protection against dust, dirt and moths, which are the three great enemies of all textiles. Old and valuable pieces should not be washed at home unless you have first sought the advice of a dry-cleaning specialist concerning the embroidery you intend to clean.

Before beginning to wash any piece of embroidery you should first test whether it is colour-fast. This can be done in two ways: you can either press a swab of wet cotton wool against the various colours and see if any colour comes off, or cut small pieces of colour threads and immerse these separately in hot water, and note whether any one of these colours the water. If, in either case, you find that the colours run, then washing should be avoided.

Fabrics with painted designs incorporated on the embroideries, such as flags and banners, should never be washed, nor should silk which has been treated with a dressing.

### How to wash embroideries

Dissolve some pure soap flakes in hot water to make a good lather and dilute with cold water until lukewarm. Then soak the embroidery and move it around but do not squeeze it. Rinse in warm water followed by cold until the water is completely clear. Always drain away water before removing embroidery (this applies especially to delicate pieces). Rinsing can be made a great deal easier by using a shower attachment and sprinkling water over the surface of the fabric. Hang out or dry flat. Dry as quickly as possible and never leave in a wet and crumpled heap.

### How to wash delicate embroideries

Delicate, colour-fast embroideries should be soaked overnight in warm, salted water, and then removed and washed as above. When rinsed roll them up in a towel and leave them for a few hours, then iron in the usual way.

### How to wash lined embroideries

If the embroidery is lined, then both the lining and interlining should be removed and all should be washed separately.

### How to wash upholstery covers

When these require washing they should be removed carefully and a paper pattern or template made of each piece so that they can be stretched back into the correct shape after washing. Submerge covers in softened, luke-warm soapy water, sponge gently over the surface and then rinse in the usual way. When rinsed, dry flat with right side up, smooth into shape, using the templates as guides to size. When dry, iron in the usual way with the embroidery face downwards on a padded surface and covered with a damp cloth.

### How to wash lace

Make a paper template of the lace before washing. Then wind lace carefully around a corked or stopped bottle which has been half-filled with sand. Cover with muslin, lightly tacked to secure it. Immerse bottle in saucepan of cold water and add soap flakes. If the lace is really dirty, add a pinch of salt. Boil for one hour, replacing water as it becomes dirty. When the hour is up or the water is clear, allow to cool, then remove bottle, take off the muslin covering, unwind the lace and roll it up in a dry cloth. Pin it out on template, leave to dry and then press under a damp cloth with a medium-hot iron. Hold the iron on the cloth-covered lace until each area is dry. In order to stretch the lace, several ironings may be needed, the lace being pulled out crossways and lengthways between each pressing.

### How to wash fine lace

If stained or greasy, first soak the lace for a few days in a bath or bowl of best olive oil, to revive the threads. Then wash and iron the lace, following the method described above.

### How to restore colour brilliance

If old embroideries lose their initial, fresh brilliance the colours can be easily restored by soaking the embroidery in a solution of half a glass of white vinegar mixed with $1\frac{1}{4}$ pints (1 litre) of water. Stir the embroidery in the solution for a few minutes, then rinse in clean water and wash and iron in the usual way.

### Ironing embroidery

Press on wrong side of embroidery with work face downwards on a padded surface. (The padded surface prevents the stitches from being flattened.) Place a damp cloth over the embroidery and press with a warm or hot iron according to the type of fibres in the embroidery and ground fabric.

## Blocking embroidery

**How to work**
Before washing, make a paper template of the embroidery. After washing, lay the embroidery face up on a soft board covered with polythene. Smooth it into shape using the paper template and then pin it in place with brass lace pins. Leave to dry.

# Cleaning embroidery

In some cases it may not be advisable to wash the embroideries in water. We list alternative methods of cleaning below, and the circumstances in which each may be useful. Remember never to brush embroideries, as this may damage the stitches.

### Dry-cleaning

Large pieces of embroidery such as hangings, raised work, or those which do not stand the colour-fast test, should be dry-cleaned and not washed.

### Vacuum cleaning

Dusty as opposed to badly soiled embroideries can be vacuum cleaned, using the nozzle attachment on your vacuum cleaner. Cover the embroidery with a piece of nylon mono-filament screening, hold both these down and move the vacuum cleaner back and forth a little above the surface of the embroidery.

### Cleaning raised work

Raised or gold work embroideries can be cleaned where the dust has collected by using a sable-haired brush and stroking it in and out of the crevices between the stitches.

### Badly soiled hangings

As long as these are strong and in good condition they can be cleaned in a coin-operated dry-cleaning machine. First remove anything that may catch or snag the stitches, such as curtain hooks, curtain rings or nails. Then place the prepared hanging in a nylon net bag, which can be made from old net curtains, and sew around it to keep the embroidery secure. Place the bag in the machine and clean in the usual way. Then hang it out in fresh air on a padded hanger until the fumes have completely evaporated.

### Valuable embroideries

You should not attempt to clean old or valuable embroideries yourself. The risk of damaging the fragile stitches is too high. Instead, they should be sent to a specialist cleaner.

# Storing and mounting

## Storing

Embroideries not in use should be carefully stored in a dark place and packed between ample layers of white acid-free tissue paper. They should be kept clean, examined regularly for moths and, if folded, rearranged from time to time. If a piece is too large to be stored flat it should be loosely folded or, even if the piece is lined, rolled with the right side out over layers of tissue.

## Mounting

Embroideries made for pictures, screens and fire screens should be mounted on a hardboard backing before framing. A margin of unworked ground all around the embroidery will be needed so that it can be folded to the back of the hardboard. The hardboard should be $\frac{1}{4}$in. (6mm) larger than the work on all sides so that an overlapping frame will not obscure the embroidery.

### How to mount on hardboard

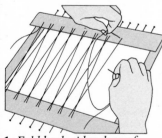

**1** *Fold back side edges of fabric and, using a strong thread, lace back and forth. Then pull stitches to tighten.*

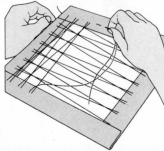

**2** *Fold back top and bottom edges and lace in same way. The embroidery is now ready to be framed.*

# Removing stains

The following list offers advice on removing common stains. If the embroidery is valuable or you are in doubt about the origins of a particular stain do not treat it at home but send it off to a specialist cleaner. Always test for colour-fastness before attempting to remove any stains from embroideries.

### Blood
Rinse in cold water until the stain is partly removed, then wash in warm soapy water in the usual way. If badly stained rinse in cold salted water and then wash in the usual way. If the stain is on heavy material, make a thick paste of starch and warm water and apply this to it. Leave it to dry and then very gently shake the mixture off. Repeat the process several times if necessary.

### Candle wax
First harden the wax with an ice-cube and gently scrape away the excess, being careful not to damage any of the embroidery stitches. Then lay the embroidery face down on a padded surface, between two sheets of blotting paper. Then press with a warm iron, moving the blotting paper as the wax soaks into it. For coloured candle wax remove the colouring with a sponge dipped in alcohol after the wax itself has been removed.

### Candy or sweets
Spot clean thoroughly with cold water. Delicate fabrics should be spot cleaned with a wad of cotton wool soaked in distilled water or rain water.

### Chewing gum
For non-washable fabrics soften the gum with petrol or methylated spirits and then gently remove it from the fabric. For washable fabrics rub lard onto stain, then wash in warm soapy water.

### Chocolate
Cover the stain with a small quantity of dry borax and wash in cold water. For delicate fabrics sponge with warm water, being careful to rinse the sponge between each separate application.

### Coffee and tea
If stain can be treated immediately, wash in warm soapy water. Treat silk and wool in the same way as given for chocolate. Treat any stubborn stains on strong fabrics by placing the stained area over a bowl and then pouring boiling water on it.

### Fruit, berries and wine
Cover the stain with table salt and rub over it with a piece of damp soap. Leave for a few hours and then rinse. For strong fabrics pour boiling water from a height as for coffee. For silk and wool cover the stain with borax and wash in warm water. For white cotton and linen apply lemon juice to the stain and pour hot water on it.

### Glue
Soak in warm water until the glue dissolves or sponge with white vinegar.

### Grease
Wash thoroughly in warm soapy water or spot clean with soft cloth soaked in alcohol. Or treat as for candle wax. If stain can be treated immediately cover it with talcum powder and leave it on for several hours, then shake it off. For black grease or tar spot clean with a soft cloth soaked in eucalyptus oil.

### Indelible pencil
Soak stains for three to five minutes in alcohol, then wash in warm soapy water.

### Ink
For coloured fabrics soak for several hours in milk, changing milk as it colours, then wash in warm soapy water. For whites, moisten stain with salt and lemon juice and place in sun. Then wash in warm soapy water, or hold stained area over the spout of a steaming kettle. For ballpoint and felt pen stains spot clean with a soft cloth soaked in methylated spirits.

### Lipstick
Spot clean with vaseline or a soft cloth soaked in glycerine or eucalyptus oil. Then, if possible, wash in soapy water.

### Mildew
Fresh stains can be easily removed by washing in cold or warm soapy water. Mildew on whites is best removed with lemon juice and then dried in the sun. Finally, it is washed in warm soapy water.

### Mud
Washing in warm soapy water will remove most mud stains.

### Pet stains
Spray wet stain immediately with soda water. Leave for a few minutes and then sponge off. If possible, wash in warm soapy water as well.

### Rust
For rust stains on whites spread the stained area over a bowl of steaming water and squeeze lemon juice on it. Leave for a few minutes, then rinse in hot water. Repeat several times if necessary. Alternatively you can moisten stain with salt and lemon juice, adding more lemon juice as it dries. Wash in warm soapy water.

### Scorch marks
Wash as quickly as possible in warm soapy water or moisten with a mixture of salt and fresh lemon juice applied to the stain. For wool wet the stain, apply powdered chalk and then dry in the sun. For white flannel rub fresh lemon juice and pulp into the scorch mark at once, then dry in the sun.

### Transfer marks
Wash finished embroidery in warm soapy water. If fabric is non-washable remove the marks by rubbing gently with a soft, clean rag dipped in benzine and then place the embroidery by a closed window in the sun and allow it to dry thoroughly.

### Water marks
Sponge entire surface evenly, moistening fabric but not soaking it. Then press. For silk, satin and velvet shake the fabric over steam. Fill the kettle with only a small quantity of water and cover the spout with a piece of cloth. Keep water boiling until the fabric is thoroughly steamed.

# 5

# NEEDLEPOINT

*including Florentine Work*

# History of needlepoint

Needlepoint tapestry, which is also known as *canvas work* and, in the nineteenth century, as *Berlinwork*, is the strongest and most hardwearing of all types of needlework. Throughout the ages it has been used primarily in the house for chair covers, wall hangings and cushion coverings.

It is worked with a needle and thread on a strong canvas or even-weave linen. In the past it was often worked on softer grounds of silk and cotton weaves and stitched in a hard-spun thread which made it stiff and strong enough to withstand the wear on seating, hassocks and cushions.

### The stitches

The stitches used in needlepoint tapestry have been specially devised over the years, not only to decorate and cover the ground, but also to strengthen it. The earliest stitches, which are still used today, were tent stitch (also known as *petit point*) and cross stitch (also known as *gros point*).

The threads can range from wools (the most common), to cottons, silks and metal threads. Metal threads were often used in the sixteenth and seventeenth centuries for the ground work to set off the silk stitched motifs and give a really rich look. Beads, too, were used on the canvas, either to cover it completely or as motifs and highlights.

Needlepoint tapestry is one of the oldest forms of embroidery. It was known to the Egyptians and the Phrygians. The Romans knew it as *opus pulvinarium*, meaning cushion work, and, as the name suggests, used it to cover the cushions on which they lounged as they feasted at their banquets.

Needlepoint has long been associated with church work where it was used for hangings, kneelers and altar frontals as well as for the vestments of priests. A beautiful chasuble from Germany made in the twelfth century still exists. It is designed pictorially with figures from the scriptures outlined in bands of geometric patterns. Needlepoint was also frequently used in England in the twelfth and thirteenth centuries as the borders for their famous *opus Anglicanum* embroideries.

In fifteenth-century Florence needlepoint was developed along quite different lines. Long stitches were used in bright zigzag patterns, flame-like in character and highly decorative. This type of work has since become known as *Florentine* or *Bargello* embroidery and was used then, as now, for the covering of chairs, for wall hangings, altar frontals and as borders to pictorial works. It is reported as having come to Italy through the marriage of one of the Medicis to a Hungarian bride, who brought the work with her and taught it to her Court.

Needlepoint tapestry really came into its own in sixteenth-century Europe. Trade routes had been well established with India, China, Turkey and Persia and embroideries and carpets were being imported to decorate the houses of the rich. Carpets were used to replace the rushes on the floor and to cover tables as the fashion of that time dictated. For the not so rich, the price of these imported goods was too high. So they were copied skilfully in embroidery by the ladies of the time. Fine wool threads were used for the table carpets and thicker threads developed for the floor coverings. Velvet stitch was invented to resemble the rich pile of Turkey carpets. It subsequently became known as *Turkey work*.

The designs for the needleworked table carpets then began to be developed along original lines with the top covering being made in geometric and trellis patterns, often intertwined with vine leaves, bunches of grapes and flowers. The drop along the sides of the table, forming the border of the carpet, was designed

English seventeenth-century christening cushion showing the finding of Moses

Detail from the seventeenth-century picture "The Judgement of Solomon" with Charles I as Solomon

with pastoral scenes from everyday life being minutely worked in tent stitch and showing landscapes, hunting scenes and houses and castles, probably portraits of the owners' homes.

## Practical uses of needlepoint

Not only carpets but also woven tapestries and bedhangings were also copied by these ingenious needlewomen using new stitches to imitate the woven textures. Hangings, both woven and embroidered, were essential as draught excluders in cold northern climates and as a protection against the heat in the hot, southern countries. They were also used as a means of dividing up large areas to give privacy.

In the seventeenth century, with the introduction of upholstered chairs, needlepoint expanded into a new area. At first the designs were made in the same style as for crewel work or Jacobean embroidery, with dark grounds and sprawling stem and tree designs lavishly blooming and bearing flowers and fruit in brightly coloured wools. Later, the designs became more refined with paler grounds and less strident patterns.

In the eighteenth century, with the advent of more rounded chairs, the designs, too, became circular: rondos of flowers in pinks, blues and creams replaced the stylized Jacobean designs. In Germany, a more figurative style was adopted with pictures depicting classical scenes used for chair backs, the seats scattered with flowers, fruit and leaves.

French workers, too, favoured a more classical approach and succeeded in making the figures as realistic as possible, even giving relief effects to the faces. Pastoral scenes with nymphs and shepherds surrounded by circlets of pale full-blown roses became popular towards the end of the century and echoed in colouring the Aubusson carpets of that time.

Also at this time in Holland, some of the most interesting needlepoint designs were being produced for hangings, portraying scenes from everyday life, such as busy market scenes, minutely observed.

By the nineteenth century more sophisticated designs were being sought. The Berlin print seller, Wittich, must have sensed this for in 1810 he produced a series of coloured patterns of copies of famous paintings which met with immediate success. The patterns were bought by the score and were worked in German wool, known as *Berlin wool*, which was far superior in both texture and colour to anything else available on the market. This fashion led to these manufactured designs being called *Berlinwork*. Turkey work, too, became popular again and was used for reliefwork flower pictures, cushions and chairbacks with huge, cabbage roses being worked in tufted velvet stitch on a tent or cross stitch background.

## Art nouveau

At the end of the nineteenth century, William Morris in England fostered a new style in needlepoint and woven tapestry design. Madonna lilies took the place of overworked roses, soft blues and greens were used for backgrounds, and classical, Pre-Raphaelite figures began to appear. This style became part of the art nouveau school.

During the years of war and depression in Europe in the twentieth century there was a lull in needlepoint activity. Then, at the beginning of the 1960s, needlepoint tapestry began to flourish once more in Europe and America. This new interest has led to a proliferation of designs and pattern ideas which in turn ensure the continued popularity of needlepoint.

**Eighteenth-century panel worked with silks in minute tent stitch**

**Nineteenth-century wool rug in Berlinwork style**

# History of needlepoint

In the past needlepoint has played a major part in the interior decoration of houses with the designs for them being made either by the professional painters of the time or by the needleworkers themselves.

These old pictorial needlepoints are fascinating to study, not only as a source of inspiration for future works, but also because of their contribution to the history of a particular society. Much of their charm stems from the simplicity of some of the figurative images coupled with the intricacy of the stitch patterns and textures used.

Seventeenth-century English needlepoint design, "Abraham and the Angels", worked in silk and wools on canvas.

Detail of late sixteenth-century Spanish design, "Galceran de Pinos disembarks at Salona near Tarragona", worked in silk, wool and metal thread on canvas.

**Detail of back of American eighteenth-century Queen Anne wing chair**
The needlepoint measures 46¾in. by 31½in. (119cm by 80cm). There are many modern examples of needlepoint-upholstered chairs: they look particularly effective when the design flows down the chair back and on to the chair seat in a continuous picture.

# Needlepoint canvas

The basic requisites for working needlepoint tapestry are canvas, threads and a blunt-pointed needle – all three of which must be carefully matched with each other. It is also useful to have a good pair of scissors, thimbles and, sometimes, a frame.

### Canvas
In the past, needlepoint tapestry was worked on a loosely woven fabric resembling coarse linen. Later, canvases were also woven from silk, flax, cotton and wool. However, today there are only three different types of canvas readily available: single canvas, double canvas and rug canvas. Single and double canvases are usually made of hemp or of linen thread, while rug canvases are made of cotton thread. They are all available in different mesh gauges, measured by the number of threads to the inch.

### Single canvas
Single canvas is composed of a mesh of single threads. All straight stitches (see pages 329–331) must be worked on single canvas or the vertical threads will not be completely covered.

### Double canvas
Double canvas, sometimes called *Penelope canvas*, is composed of a mesh of double horizontal and double vertical threads. It is ideal for crossed stitches (see pages 324–329) and essential when working over a trammed base (see page 316). By pushing the double threads apart and working between them, double canvas can be used as single canvas when fine detail is required. This process is often known as *pricking the ground*.

### Rug canvas
Rug canvas has a large, clearly defined mesh of strong, glazed threads. Its gauge is measured by the number of holes per inch.

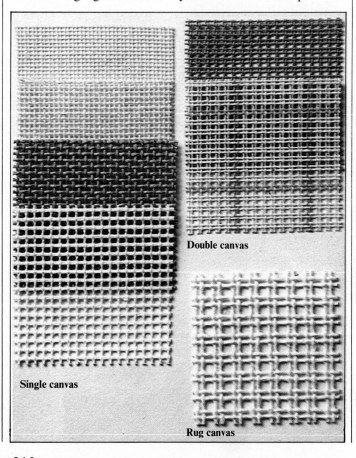

**Double canvas**

**Single canvas**

**Rug canvas**

# Threads

### Threads
Any single thread, or any combination of threads in one needle, can be used for needlepoint – from wool and silk to cotton, linen and gold or silver thread.

### Using threads
The most important thing is that the thread you choose must cover the canvas ground completely. It must also be colourfast if the finished work is to be washable. Work in short lengths of about 18in. (46cm) so that the thread is less apt to fray, tangle or break. Remember, too, that wool thread has a right and a wrong end, and that it is the right end which must be threaded through the needle. Test for this by running the wool between your thumb and forefinger. If it feels smooth, you are pulling it by the right end.

### Types of thread
Three particular types of specially developed needlepoint thread are manufactured: crewel wool, tapestry wool and rug wool.

### Crewel wool
Crewel wool is very fine. It can be worked either in a single strand on very fine mesh canvas, or two, three or four strands can be threaded together through the needle for coarser work.

### Tapestry wool
Tapestry wool corresponds to 4-ply knitting yarn and is sold in small skeins of 15yds (13.8m). It is usually worked on medium-gauge double or single canvas.

### Rug wool
Rug wool is very thick and easily covers rug canvases. It is sold in small skeins of about 6½yds (6m).

### Other threads
Crochet cottons, stranded cottons, stranded silks and metal threads can also be used either alone or in conjunction with other threads. The silks and cottons are very useful for highlights when used with wools, while gold and silver threads give rich outline and glitter effects.

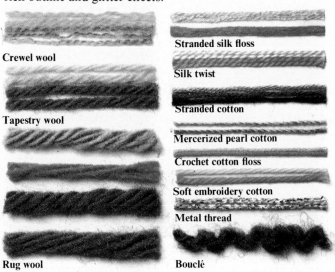

**Crewel wool**

**Tapestry wool**

**Rug wool**

**Stranded silk floss**

**Silk twist**

**Stranded cotton**

**Mercerized pearl cotton**

**Crochet cotton floss**

**Soft embroidery cotton**

**Metal thread**

**Bouclé**

## Threading needles

There are two methods of threading a needle quickly and easily. Whichever method you use, do not wet or twist the end of the thread.

### Thin thread method

This is the simplest method and, with a little practice, it becomes very easy.

### How to work

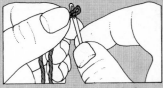

**1** *Loop the thread over the needle as shown, and pull it tight to form a fold. Hold the fold firmly and remove needle.*

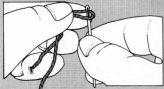

**2** *Push the fold through the eye of the needle.*

### Thick thread method

This method is more suitable for thicker threads.

### How to work

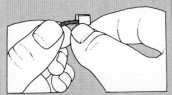

**1** *Cut out a 1in. (2.5cm) piece of paper narrow enough to go through the eye of the needle. Fold it in half and place the end of the thread in the fold.*

**2** *Pass the paper through the eye of the needle so that it pulls the thread through with it.*

## Needles

The right kind of needle to use in needlepoint work is a tapestry needle with a rounded point which protects both the working thread and the canvas from being split during the stitching. Needles are available in various sizes, ranging from size 24, the smallest, to size 13, the largest.

### Matching up needle, canvas and thread

It is important to choose the right needle – one that is neither so large that it has to be forced through the canvas threads, nor so small that it frays the working threads which have to be forced through the eye.

**10 double threads per in. (20 per 5cm)**

**12 threads per in. (24 per 5cm)**

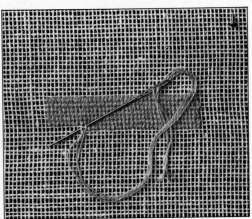

**24 threads per in. (48 per 5cm)**

## Frames

Although a frame is not strictly necessary for working needlepoint tapestries, it can be extremely useful. It keeps the work evenly stretched, so that it will retain its original shape while being worked. If the frame is also supported, then both hands are free to work the stitches.

### Straight-sided frame

This frame is sometimes known as a *slate frame*. The standard, straight-sided frame is composed of a roller top and bottom, to which strips of tape or webbing are nailed, and two flat wooden sides, which are slotted into the rollers and secured with pegs or screws. The canvas is attached to the rollers at the top and bottom. If it is too long for the sides of the frame, it is rolled up on one roller and then unrolled as work progresses. A frame without a stand can be supported against the end of a table or rested between the backs of two chairs.

### Round frame

This frame is sometimes known as a *hoop* or *tambour frame*. It comes in various sizes and is composed of two hoops placed one on top of the other and tightened by a screw at the side. A small round frame is ideal for fine work.

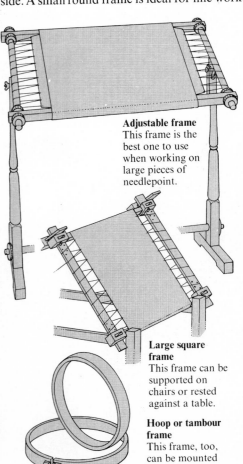

**Adjustable frame**
This frame is the best one to use when working on large pieces of needlepoint.

**Large square frame**
This frame can be supported on chairs or rested against a table.

**Hoop or tambour frame**
This frame, too, can be mounted on to a stand.

# Needlepoint ideas

The items illustrated on these two pages have been chosen to represent some of the many articles that can be made using needlepoint techniques. If, like the sofa (right) or many of the articles shown below, your work will be subject to heavy wear, take care to use canvas and threads of a suitable quality and strength. For information on finishing the work, see pages 356–361.

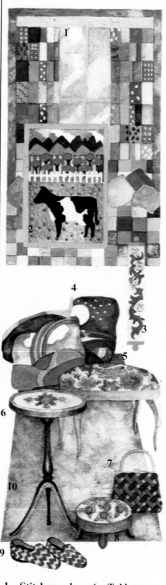

| | | | |
|---|---|---|---|
| 1 | Stitch sampler | 6 | Table top |
| 2 | Picture | 7 | Bag |
| 3 | Bell pull | 8 | Foot stool |
| 4 | Cushions | 9 | Slippers |
| 5 | Stool cover | 10 | Carpet |

## Simple figurative designs

It is possible to transfer fairly complex figurative designs into needlepoint by simplifying them into broad areas of similar colour and tone. The examples shown here have all been worked in tent stitch. The designs can either be made into pictures or used for such things as cushion covers.

**Twelve needlepoint panels**
This series of panels shows landscapes at various times of the day and in different weathers.

**Sofa cushions worked in simple needlepoint designs**

**Rainbow**

**Twilight**

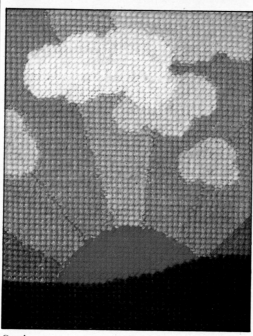

**Sunrise**

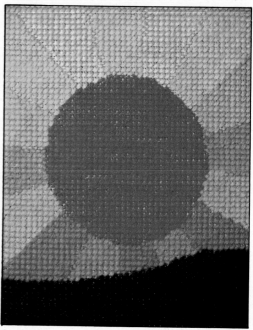

**Sunset**

*Modern cushion cover*
*This contemporary design for a cushion cover has been worked in brightly coloured tapestry wools on single canvas in a variety of stitches.*

A needlepoint evening bag, made in England in the early twentieth century

**Traditional cushion cover**
Although this cushion cover, which comes from Spain, is a contemporary piece of work, it is derived from a traditional design.

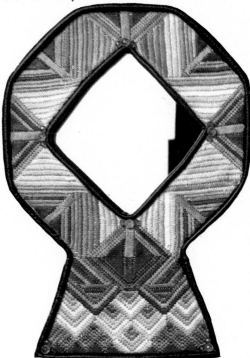

A needlepoint border, trimmed with leather and used to frame a small hand mirror

A figurative needlepoint border, used as a photograph frame

315

## *Bought patterns*

When starting to work needlepoint tapestry it is often best to buy a ready-made design in order to become familiar with the needlepoint techniques. Patterns can be bought with the designs painted on them, worked out in trammed stitches on the canvas, or marked out on charts.

### *Painted canvas*
The design is already painted on the canvas and the needlepoint is worked over the design. All that is required is to work the stitches in matching colours. The threads are usually sold with the canvas.

### *Charts*
With charted designs each square on the chart represents one square or mesh of the canvas. The stitches are marked in coloured inks or symbols with a key at the side of the chart. Charts are often used for Florentine work.

### *Trammed canvas*
With trammed (or *trammé*) canvas, the design is worked in coloured horizontal threads (see right), over which the needlepoint is worked in corresponding colours. Trammed canvases are therefore particularly hardwearing and so are especially suitable for chair coverings.

**Painted design on canvas**

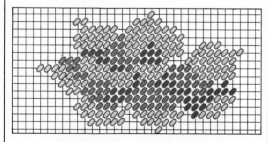

**Charted design**

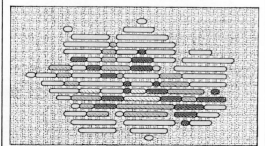

**Trammed design on canvas**

## *Working your own designs*

Creating your own designs for needlepoint can be much more rewarding than following a ready-made design. By creating an original design you have far greater control over the colours you use and can therefore fit them in with a colour scheme in a room. Personal patterns, favourite pictures and lettering can also be depicted. Use the methods shown opposite to transfer a chosen design to the working canvas. Make sure the threads are suitable for the canvas mesh (see canvas and threads, page 312).

### *Setting up*
When preparing to work an original design always allow for a 3in. (7.5cm) wide area to be left unworked all around the edges, as this is used to stretch the canvas into shape when finished. If an embroidery frame is not being used, bind the edges with adhesive tape or fold and tack them down to prevent the canvas from fraying.

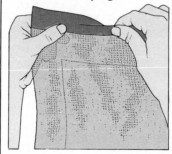

**Binding the edges with tape**

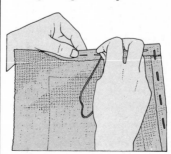

**Tacking down the folded edges**

## *Making charts and tramming*

### *Making charts*
Abstract designs such as geometric patterns, Bargello and Florentine patterns can be charted out on graph paper with each square on the graph paper representing a square of the canvas mesh. The length, direction and colour of the stitches should be marked out until the area to be covered is filled. When designing for specific areas such as chair seats, measure the area to be worked first. Then select the correct canvas size, remembering that wide meshed canvas has less threads per inch (cm) than finer meshed canvas and that the holes or lines on the charted design must correspond to the holes or threads on the canvas. Finally, work out the design on graph paper. Colourwork designs and textured stitch designs can be made in the same way by using symbols and plotting them on graph paper. The proportions of the stitches must always be observed so that they cover the correct space on the graph and flow in the right directions, filling the design.

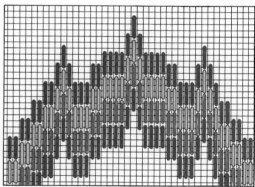

**Charting a Florentine design**

### *Making trammed designs*
An original design for chair or stool covers (which need a hardwearing surface) should be worked onto a double canvas. Before starting to work, the design is covered with tramming stitches in the relevant colours. Tramming stitches are horizontal stitches of various lengths worked between the horizontal double threads to indicate the design.

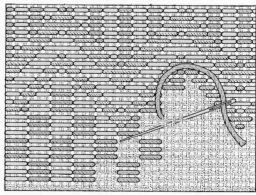

**Tramming a geometric design**

# Freehand designs

Designs can evolve from the stitching or be drawn directly onto the canvas, in the manner of a painting.

## Stitching directly onto canvas

If you wish to work your own design directly onto canvas you can select the colours you would like to use, start stitching and let the pattern gradually emerge. Alternatively you can sketch out the outline of the design first with a line of stitches and then work the filling, using textured stitches as well as coloured threads.

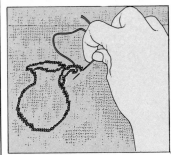

**Stitching outline directly onto canvas**

## Drawing directly onto canvas

For anyone who can draw or paint easily, it is very simple to either pencil the outlines of the proposed design directly onto the canvas or to paint the whole canvas as though it were a picture. Use oil paints mixed quite thinly with turpentine and be sure they are thoroughly dry before you begin the needlepoint. The design can then be stitched accordingly. There is no reason why, if the canvas is fine and well painted, areas of it should not be left unworked to combine the techniques of needlepoint and painting.

**Painting directly onto canvas**

# Transferring

## Using a lightbox

If you want to use an existing picture as a pattern, the easiest method of transferring it is to use a lightbox. A home-made version of a lightbox can be made by placing a sheet of glass between two chairs and putting a lamp with a strong bulb beneath it.

### How to work

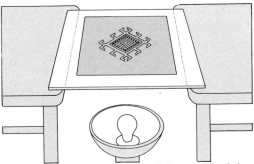

**1** *Place the drawing on top of the glass and the canvas on top of the drawing.*

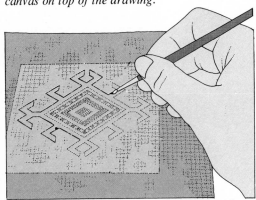

**2** *Using Indian ink, mark the design onto the canvas. The original can be used as the guide for colouring the needlepoint stitches.*

## Using carbon paper

Tracing with carbon paper only works successfully on a smooth, fine-gauge canvas.

*Make a tracing of an original drawing and then place a sheet of dressmaker's carbon between it and the canvas and retrace the outline.*

# Large designs

Large scale designs, such as those for carpets, may need to be worked in sections, since one width of canvas may not be wide enough to take the complete design. This is not a difficult process but it does require a little more precision and some careful planning.

## Working in sections

First draw the whole design on plain or graph paper, then divide it into equal sized sections and label them. Cut the canvas into equivalent sized sections and label them, remembering to allow the essential 3in. (7.5cm) unworked border all around each piece. When the canvas sections are cut and prepared, mark the design from each paper section onto the corresponding sections of canvas and start to work in the usual way. If the design has been marked out on graph paper it is unnecessary to mark it onto the canvas, so merely read the graph for each section of the design.

When the work is completed, each section must be stretched, mounted and sewn together edge to edge in the correct order (see blocking and finishing, pages 356–361).

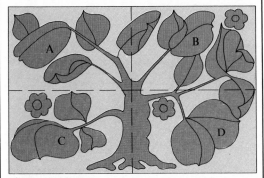

**Dividing the design**

**Prepared canvas sections**

# Needlepoint samplers

The five samplers illustrated here have been worked to show the different categories into which needlepoint stitches fall: crossed, diagonal, straight, looped and star. They have all been worked in stranded silk yarns on single canvas, and, apart from the straight stitch sampler, the canvasses all measure 18 threads to the inch (36 per 5cm); the straight stitch canvas has 24 threads per inch (48 per 5cm). The stitches are all identified on the right. Instructions for them can be found in the needlepoint stitch glossary on pages 320–335.

**Star stitches**

**Crossed stitches**

**Diagonal stitches**

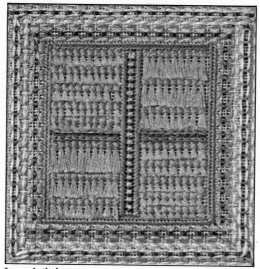

**Looped stitches**

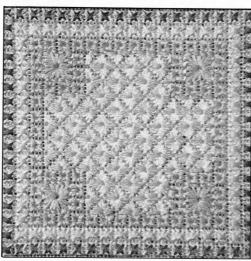

**Straight stitches**

## Stitch details

The illustrations below show details of individual stitches used in the five needlepoint samplers pictured left.

### Crossed stitches

**Cross stitch**

**Oblong cross with back stitch**

**Rice stitch**

### Diagonal stitches

**Scottish stitch**

**Milanese stitch**

**Graduated diagonal stitches**

**Jacquard stitch**

### Straight stitches

**Hungarian stitch variation**

**Graduated upright Gobelin stitch**

**Gobelin filling stitch**

**Florentine stitch**

### Looped stitches

**Velvet stitch**

**Chain stitch and straight stitches**

**Shell stitch**

**Knitting stitch**

### Star stitches

**Star stitch**

**Eye stitch**

# Working stitch samplers

Stitch samplers were traditionally worked to show off the different types of needlepoint stitches. They were either abstract (see left) or pictorial (as shown here). They give endless scope for variation since you can use existing stitches alone, combine them with other ones or make up your own. The stitch chart below identifies the ones given in the stitch glossary on pages 320–335; the others were devised by the artist who worked the picture.

## Stitch chart

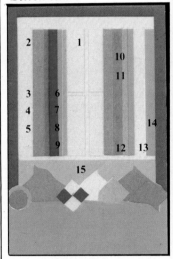

1. **Diagonal Gobelin filling stitch**
2. **Mosaic stitches with diagonal stitch background**
3. **Jacquard stitch**
4. **Tent stitch with French knots and Smyrna cross stitch**
5. **Reversed cross stitch**
6. **Hungarian stitch variation**
7. **Gobelin stitch**
8. **Cross stitch**
9. **Milanese stitch**
10. **Knitting stitch**
11. **Tent stitch variation**
12. **Knotted stitch**
13. **Oblong cross with back stitch**
14. **Diagonal stitch**
15. **Blocks of graduated diagonal stitches**

**Patchwork stitch sampler**
*This contemporary needlepoint picture of a sofa in front of a window has been worked in a patchwork pattern using stranded cottons on single canvas.*

319

# Needlepoint stitch glossary

The stitches in needlepoint tapestry are worked over the canvas threads either vertically, diagonally or horizontally. They vary in size and shape according to the number of canvas threads over which they are worked. The following stitch instructions state the number of threads in each direction over which the stitches should be formed, but these can, of course, be extended or reduced as long as the proportions of the stitch are retained and the canvas is covered. It is inadvisable, however, to extend a flat stitch beyond about ten threads as it is likely to either get snagged up or work loose and droop.

The most important point to bear in mind when working needlepoint tapestry is that the stitches should cover the canvas threads. When in doubt about this it is best to make a test sample before starting on the main work. If the stitch does not cover the canvas properly then use a thicker thread, or if the thread is fine then add a second or even a third strand to the needle. Alternatively, the canvas can be worked over with trammed stitches (see page 316); this will not only ensure that the canvas is covered but will also add strength to the work.

## Categories of stitches

The stitch glossary is divided into the following categories: *diagonal stitches,* of which tent stitch is the prime example; *crossed stitches,* led by cross stitch itself; *straight stitches*; *looped stitches*; *star stitches*; *grounds* and *colour patterns.*

Where the instructions for the stitches do not state the type of canvas to be used, either a double or a single canvas is suitable. The small arrows on the diagrams point to the place where the work was started.

## Hints on working needlepoint canvas

Never work with too long a thread as it will not only be difficult to handle but will get frayed in the process of being worked. A length of about 18in. (45cm) is sufficient.

When starting or ending a length of working thread, do not tie a knot at the end. Knots create bumps at the back of the work and they may come undone or be pulled through the canvas. Instead, secure the end of the yarn as shown below.

Do not start and end new threads in the same place row after row – the extra thickness of the covered ends will produce a ridge at this point throughout the work. To ensure that this does not happen vary the lengths of the thread a little each time.

**How to start a thread**

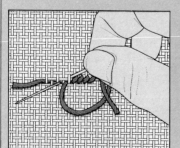

Hold end of thread at back of canvas. Work a few stitches over it to secure it. Cut off any surplus thread.

**How to end a thread**

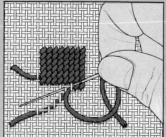

When thread has been used up, hold end at back of canvas and work a few stitches over it to secure it. Cut off surplus.

# Diagonal stitches

## Tent stitch

This is also known as *petit point.* It is the best known of all needlepoint stitches and is used for backgrounds, fillings, outlines and for colour-work patterns. Tent stitch is usually worked on a single canvas and forms a small diagonal stitch which is always made in the same direction over one canvas intersection. Ideally, it should be worked diagonally rather than horizontally across the canvas, as this gives the work extra strength and prevents the canvas from being pulled.

### How to work diagonal method

1 *Work diagonally, starting at top right. Bring needle out and take it up to right over 1 canvas intersection. Insert downwards under 2 horizontal threads and bring needle out ready to form the next stitch. Continue in this way to the end of the row.*

2 *On the return row work back up the line of stitches filling in the spaces left on the previous journey. Take needle up to right over 1 canvas intersection and insert it horizontally under 2 vertical threads. Bring needle out again ready to form the next stitch in the same way.*

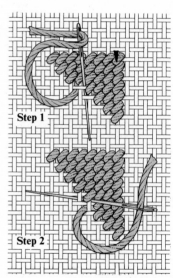

Step 1

Step 2

### How to work horizontal method

This method is used when small areas cannot be filled by working diagonally. It can be worked either from left to right or from right to left.

1 *Bring needle out and then take it up to right over 1 canvas intersection. Insert downwards under 2 vertical threads and 1 horizontal one. Bring needle out ready to form the next stitch.*

*Continue in this way to the end of the row.*

2 *On all subsequent rows work into the heads of the stitches in the previous rows.*

### Back of work

*The back of the work is made up of long diagonal stitches all slanting in the same direction.*

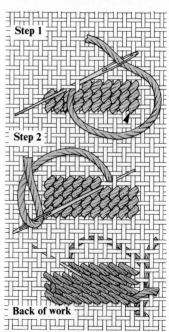

Step 1

Step 2

Back of work

## Trammed tent stitch

This is used when tent stitch is worked on double canvas in order to ensure that the tent stitch covers the canvas threads completely. It forms a slightly ridged effect, and gives a very hardwearing surface which is particularly useful for covering the seats of chairs and stools.

### How to work

*Bring needle out and make a long horizontal stitch, known as a trammed stitch, across the canvas, from left to right. Then, starting from the right, go back along the trammed stitch and work horizontal tent stitch over it as shown.*

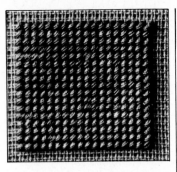

## Half cross stitch

This has the appearance of tent stitch but is worked differently. The two stitches should not be used together as the different textures on the back of the work will make the surface uneven. It is worked on double canvas.

### How to work

*Work horizontally, starting at top left. Bring needle out and take it up to right over 1 canvas intersection. Insert downwards under 1 horizontal double thread and bring needle out ready to form next stitch.*

*Continue in the same way for all subsequent rows.*

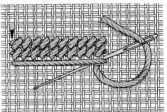

### Back of work

*The back of the work is made up of short vertical stitches.*

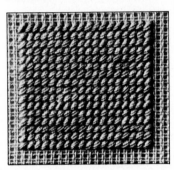

## Rep stitch

This stitch is also known as *Aubusson stitch*. It is a very small tent stitch, worked on double canvas and used for fine detail work. It consists of stitches that are worked diagonally over the canvas intersections and which use even the spaces between the horizontal double threads as well as the wider meshes. As the rep stitches are less slanted than half cross and tent stitches, the final texture will produce a ridged effect.

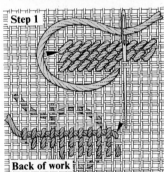

### How to work

*Work as shown, taking the needle in between the horizontal double threads but always over the complete vertical double threads each time a stitch is made.*

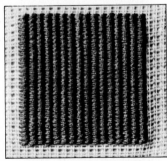
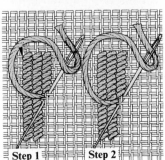

## Gobelin stitch

This stitch is also known as *oblique Gobelin stitch*, and sometimes as *gros point* since it forms a larger version of tent stitch or *petit point*. It is worked on single canvas and each stitch covers two horizontal threads and one vertical one.

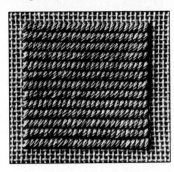

### How to work

**1** *Work horizontally, starting at bottom left of canvas. Bring needle out and take it down to left over 2 horizontal threads and 1 vertical one. Insert needle up to right under 2 canvas intersections and bring it out again ready to form the next stitch in the same way.*
**2** *Continue making Gobelin stitches to end of row. Finish row by inserting needle upwards under 2 horizontal threads and bringing it out at top of previous stitch as shown.*
**3** *Work next row from right to left in the same way but insert needle down to left under 2 vertical and 2 horizontal threads working into the heads of the stitches in the previous row.*

*Continue up the canvas, working rows from left to right and from right to left alternately until the required area of canvas has been covered.*

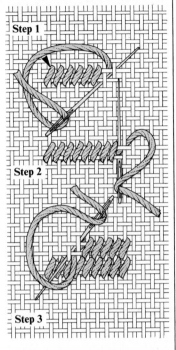

## Encroaching Gobelin stitch

This is a good stitch for filling large areas and for shading and blending colours. The stitches are much bigger than those used in Gobelin stitch since they are usually worked over five horizontal threads and one vertical thread. It is worked on a single canvas with the subsequent rows overlapping the stitches in the previous rows by one horizontal thread.

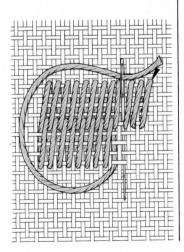

### How to work

*Work horizontally, as for a large half cross stitch, starting at left or right. Bring needle out and then take it up to right over 5 horizontal threads and 1 vertical one. Insert needle downwards under 5 horizontal threads and bring it out again ready to form the next stitch.*

*On all subsequent rows overlap by working the stitches over the same horizontal canvas thread used at the bottom of the previous row of stitches.*

### Diagonal stitch

This stitch can be used to give a patterned surface when it is worked in one colour or a striped and patterned surface when worked in two or more different colours.

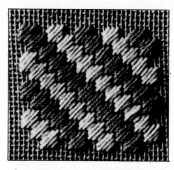

#### How to work

*Work diagonally, starting at top right of canvas. Begin at arrow by bringing needle out and forming diagonal stitches in groups of 4. These vary in length and should be worked in a repeated sequence over 2, 3, 4 and 3 canvas intersections.*

*On the next and subsequent rows work back so that the shortest stitches meet the longest stitches of the previous row as shown.*

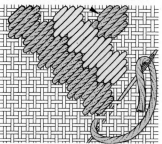

### Chequer stitch

This is a combination of alternate squares of tent stitch and graduated diagonal stitch. Each square covers four horizontal and four vertical canvas threads. The stitch is particularly useful for both colour-work and textural effects.

#### How to work

*Work diagonally, starting at top left of canvas. Begin at arrow with a square of diagonal stitches, worked in groups of 7 in a repeated sequence over 1, 2, 3, 4, 3, 2 and 1 canvas intersections.*

*Work the next row in squares of 16 tent stitches. On all subsequent rows work the 2 types of square alternately.*

### Scottish stitch

This is a combination of tent stitch and graduated diagonal stitch. It is formed by working small squares of diagonal stitch and framing them with tent stitch. It can be worked either all in one colour to give a woven texture, or in several colours to produce coloured squares that are framed in a contrasting colour.

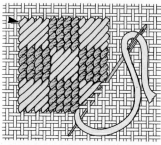

#### How to work

*Form the inner squares first by working groups of 5 diagonal stitches in a sequence over 1, 2, 3, 2 and 1 canvas intersections as shown.*

*Then outline these squares by working single lines of tent stitch around them.*

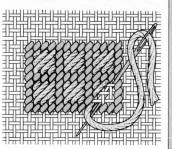

### Mosaic stitch

This is a quick and effective stitch composed of short and long diagonal stitches over two rows. When worked upright it is known as *Hungarian stitch* (see page 331). The stitch gets its name because intricate patterns can be built up by using different colours for the little squares – much like mosaic work. (See page 335 for an example of a coloured mosaic stitch pattern.)

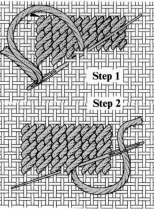

#### How to work

**1** *Work horizontally, starting with a short diagonal stitch down over 1 canvas intersection followed by a long diagonal stitch down over 2 intersections.*
**2** *Work second row as a line of short stitches filling in the spaces left on the previous row.*

*Continue in the same way for all subsequent rows.*

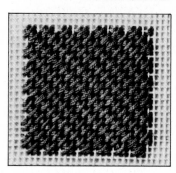

### Diagonal mosaic stitch

This is sometimes known as *Florentine stitch* but is not the one used for bargello work.

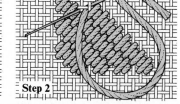

#### How to work

**1** *Work down diagonally in alternate long and short diagonal stitches. Cover 1 canvas intersection with the short stitch and 2 intersections with the long stitch.*
**2** *Work second row upwards so that the short stitches run beside the long stitches of the previous row.*

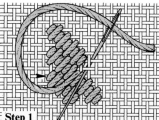

### Working graduated diagonal stitches

By using diagonal stitches of different lengths together, various patterns can be formed.

The square here is worked over the number of canvas intersections indicated in the diagram. Our instructions in the text for this would read "work in groups of 7 in a repeated sequence over 1, 2, 3, 4, 3, 2 and 1 canvas intersections"

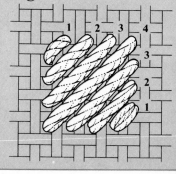

## Cashmere stitch

This will give a steep stripe if worked in two colours.

### How to work

**1** Work diagonally, starting with 1 short diagonal stitch up over 1 canvas intersection followed by 2 long diagonal stitches up over 2 intersections. **2** Work second row in the opposite direction using the same sequence and matching up to previous row as shown.

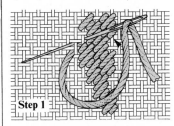

Step 1

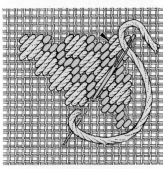

Step 2

## Moorish stitch

This is a combination of short diagonal stitches and squares of graduated diagonal stitches. It gives a zigzag and check pattern if the different stitches are worked in contrasting colours. For best results, work it on double canvas.

### How to work

Work diagonally, starting at arrow. Begin by working groups of 4 diagonal stitches in a repeated sequence over 1, 2, 3 and 2 canvas intersections. Work the zigzag line of short diagonal stitches in between the squares, each stitch covering just 1 canvas intersection.

Continue in this way, working subsequent rows beside the previous ones.

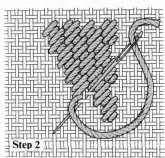

## Milanese stitch

This is a brocade stitch which is worked in graduated back stitches to form alternating triangles and reverse triangles.

### How to work

Work back stitches diagonally over 4 rows in the following order: in the first row work stitches over 1 and 4 canvas intersections alternately; in second row over 2 and 3 canvas intersections alternately; in third row over 3 and 2 canvas intersections alternately; and in fourth row over 4 and 1 canvas intersections alternately. This completes the sequence and forms the triangles.

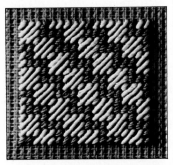

## Byzantine stitch

This is a quick filling stitch which is particularly useful for large areas of background. It gives a regular zigzag pattern of equal-sized steps and consists of diagonal stitches over four vertical and four horizontal threads.

### How to work

Work diagonally, starting at arrow and moving up to top left. Form the zigzags or steps by working 5 diagonal stitches to the left followed by 5 diagonal stitches upwards.

Continue in this way, working subsequent rows beside the previous ones. Fill in the corners and the edges with graduated diagonal stitches.

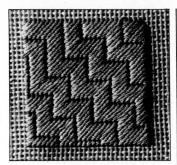

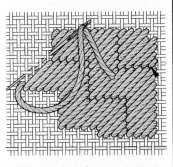

## Jacquard stitch

This is another quick filling stitch which is useful for covering large areas. It is worked in two zigzag rows of diagonal stitches, the first over one canvas intersection and the second over two intersections.

### How to work

Work diagonally, starting at arrow. Form zigzags by working 5 diagonal stitches, each over 1 intersection, across the canvas and then 5 diagonal stitches, each over 1 intersection, up or down the canvas.

Work second row in the same way but cover 2 canvas intersections with each stitch.

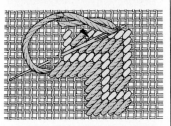

## Canvas stem stitch

This stitch gets its name from its stem-like appearance. It is formed by two vertical lines of diagonal stitches set at right angles to each other and divided by a row of back stitches. It should be worked on double canvas.

### How to work

Work vertically, starting at bottom right. Work the first row in diagonal stitches slanted to the left over 2 canvas intersections. At the top work downwards, forming the same stitches but slanted the other way and placed at right angles to the previous row.

When completed work a row of back stitches over the horizontal canvas threads between the rows.

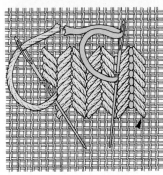

# Crossed stitches

## Cross stitch

This, along with tent stitch, is one of the two principal stitches in needlepoint tapestry. It is worked on double canvas for both fine or coarse work, the size of the crosses varying with the gauge of the canvas and the thickness of the thread. Each cross is worked separately before going on to the next, and it is essential that it completely covers the canvas. The crosses should be cleanly formed, with the top stitch pointing in the same direction throughout the work. Cross stitch can be worked either horizontally or diagonally but the formation of the actual stitch always remains the same.

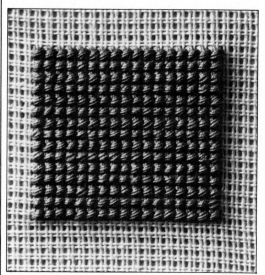

**Cross stitch**

A sample square of needlepoint tapestry worked in cross stitch. Note how the thread has been matched to the canvas so that the mesh is not visible through the stitches.

## How to work horizontal method

**1** Bring needle out at arrow and take it up to left over 1 canvas intersection. Insert downwards under 1 horizontal double thread.
**2** Take needle up to right, over the stitch that has just been formed, and insert down to left under the canvas intersection. Bring needle out again in the same spot ready to make the next cross stitch.

## How to work diagonal method

Start at bottom left and work diagonally. Bring needle out and take it up to left over 1 canvas intersection. Insert downwards under 1 horizontal double thread. Bring needle out and take it up to right, over 1 intersection and across the stitch just made, and insert under 1 vertical double thread. Bring needle out again in position ready to make the next cross stitch.

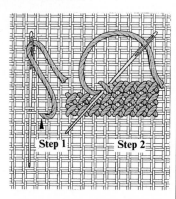

Step 1    Step 2

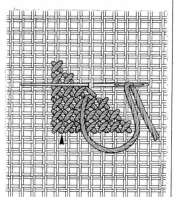

## Upright cross stitch

This stitch is worked in two diagonal journeys, the first in vertical stitches and the second in horizontal stitches which cover the previous ones. It should be worked on double rather than single canvas.

### How to work

**1** Start at bottom right and work diagonally. Bring needle out and work a row of vertical stitches by taking needle over 2 horizontal double threads, inserting down to left under 1 canvas intersection and bringing it out again ready to make the next vertical stitch.
**2** At top of row work the return journey in horizontal stitches. Bring needle out as if making another vertical stitch, but take it to right over 2 vertical double threads and across the stitch of the previous journey. Insert down to left under 1 canvas intersection and bring needle out again ready to make a further crossing.

Continue to end of row and then work subsequent rows next to each other in the same way.

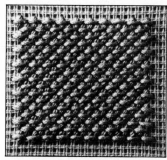

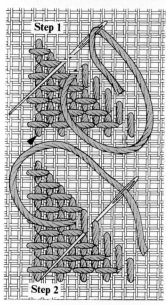

Step 1

Step 2

## Oblong cross stitch

This is a very quick covering stitch. It is worked in two journeys of diagonal stitches, each covering four horizontal and two vertical threads, and forming a row of elongated cross stitches. It can be worked on either single or double canvas as long as it covers the canvas threads.

### How to work

**1** Work the first journey of diagonal stitches horizontally, starting at top right. Bring needle out and take it up to left over 4 horizontal and 2 vertical threads. Insert downwards under 4 horizontal threads and bring needle out ready to form the next stitch in the same way.
**2** At end of row bring needle out as if to make next diagonal, but take it back up to right over 4 horizontal and 2 vertical threads. Insert downwards under 4 horizontal threads and bring needle out ready to form the next stitch.

Continue to end of row and then work all subsequent rows into the bases of the stitches in the previous rows.

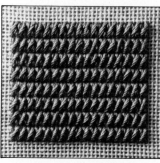

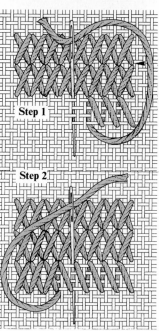

Step 1

Step 2

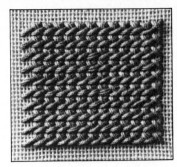

## Two-sided Italian cross stitch

This is also known as *Italian cross stitch* and *arrowhead cross stitch*. It is worked by framing an ordinary cross stitch with four straight stitches.

### How to work

**1** Work horizontally, starting at bottom left. Bring needle out at arrow and make a back stitch from left to right over 3 vertical threads. Bring needle out again at starting point.
**2** Make a diagonal stitch up to right over 3 canvas intersections and bring needle out again at starting point.
**3** Make a vertical stitch over 3 horizontal threads. Insert needle down to right under 3 canvas intersections and bring it out ready to make the second diagonal of the cross stitch.
**4** Finally, make a diagonal stitch up to left over 3 canvas intersections and bring needle out ready to form the last vertical side.

Take needle up over 3 horizontal threads, insert downwards under the same 3 threads and bring it out ready to form the next stitch.

This stitch can alternatively be worked in 2 journeys. First work along the row repeating Steps 1 to 3 as above. Then add the top diagonal of the cross on the return journey.

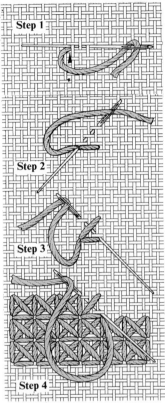

## Diagonal cross stitch

This consists of a series of upright cross stitches separated by diagonal stitches.

### How to work

**1** Work diagonally, starting at bottom left of canvas. Bring needle out at arrow and make a vertical stitch up over 4 horizontal threads. Insert needle downwards and bring it out again at arrow.
**2** Make a diagonal stitch up to right over 2 canvas intersections. Bring needle out 4 vertical threads to left ready to form the next step.
**3** Make a back stitch over 4 vertical threads, crossing the vertical stitch that has just been formed and bringing the needle out again in the same spot ready to form the next stitch.

Work subsequent rows diagonally side by side in the same way.

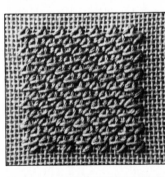

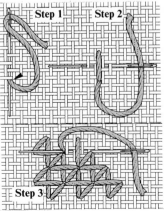

## Long-armed cross stitch

This is also known as *long-legged stitch* and *plaited Slav stitch*. It can also be used as an embroidery stitch for working on a fabric ground. It is made up of a long diagonal stitch which is then crossed by a slightly shorter one.

### How to work

**1** Work horizontally, starting at top left. Bring needle out at arrow and make a long diagonal stitch up to right over 6 vertical and 3 horizontal threads. Insert downwards under 3 horizontal threads and bring needle out ready to form the next stitch.
**2** Make a second, short diagonal stitch up to left over 3 canvas intersections. Insert downwards under 3 horizontal threads and bring needle out ready to form the next stitch.

On all subsequent rows work into the bases of the stitches in the previous row as shown.

The back of the work is composed of rows of vertical stitches at regular intervals.

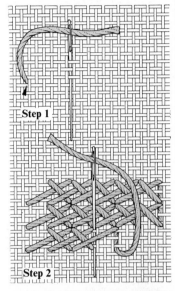

## Plait stitch

This stitch is also known as *Spanish stitch*. It is very quick and easy to work and gives a dense and slightly raised surface which is useful both for filling in backgrounds and for lines and outlines. It looks best worked on double canvas in a fairly thick thread.

### How to work

**1** Work horizontally, starting at top left. Bring needle out at arrow and make a diagonal stitch up to right over 2 canvas intersections. Insert downwards under 2 horizontal double threads and bring needle out again ready to form the next, shorter diagonal stitch.
**2** Make a second diagonal stitch up to left over 1 vertical and 2 horizontal double threads. Insert downwards under 2 horizontal double threads and bring needle out again ready to form the next stitch.

On all subsequent rows work into the bases of the stitches in the previous row as shown.

The back of the work, like long-armed cross stitch, is composed of rows of vertical stitches which are spaced out at regular intervals.

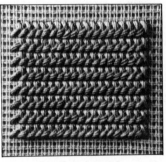

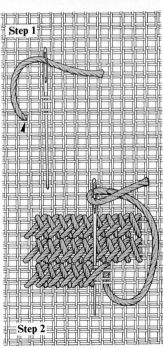

### Algerian plaited stitch

This looks the same as plait stitch on the surface, but it is worked like herringbone stitch and forms channels of back stitches on the back of the work. For best results, work it on double canvas.

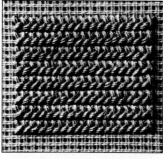

#### How to work

**1** *Work horizontally, starting at bottom left. Bring needle out at arrow and make a diagonal stitch down to right over 1 vertical and 2 horizontal double threads. Insert to left under 1 vertical double thread and bring needle out ready to form the next stitch.*
**2** *Make a diagonal stitch up to right over 2 canvas intersections. Insert to left under 1 vertical double thread and bring needle out ready to form the next stitch.*

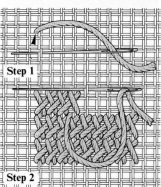

### Montenegrin cross stitch

This looks similar to long-armed cross stitch but is made by working additional vertical stitches along the row. It is quick to work, and it is reversible since either side can be used as the surface stitch. It is best worked with a coarse thread on double or single canvas, but it can also be used as an embroidery stitch on evenweave linen.

#### How to work

**1** *Work horizontally, starting at bottom left. Bring needle out at arrow and make a long diagonal stitch up to right over 8 vertical and 4 horizontal threads. Insert down to left under 4 canvas intersections and bring needle out ready to form the next stitch.*
**2** *Make a second, short diagonal stitch up to left over 4 canvas intersections. Insert down to right and bring needle out again in the same spot.*
**3** *Finally, make a vertical stitch up over 4 horizontal threads. Insert downwards and bring needle out in the same spot ready to form next stitch.*

*Continue in this way to end of row, and then work subsequent rows into the heads of the stitches in the previous rows.*

#### Back of work

*The back of the work forms a slightly different pattern but is equally decorative.*

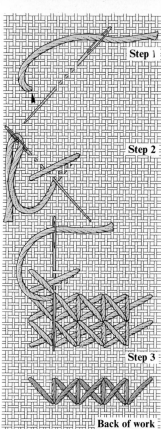

### Greek stitch

This stitch should be worked in a coarse thread on double canvas. It is worked like herringbone stitch and forms channels of back stitches on the back of the work.

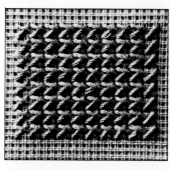

#### How to work

**1** *Work horizontally, starting at top left. Bring needle out at arrow and make a diagonal stitch up to right over 2 canvas intersections. Insert to left under 2 vertical double threads and bring needle out ready to form the next stitch.*
**2** *Make a diagonal stitch down to right over 4 vertical and 2 horizontal double threads. Insert to left under 2 vertical double threads and bring needle out ready to form next stitch.*

*Continue in this way to end of row, and then work next row from right to left so that the stitches are worked into the bases of those in the previous row.*

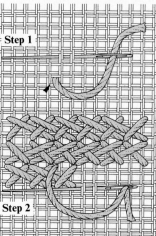

### Oblong cross stitch with back stitch

This stitch consists of a combination of both oblong cross stitches and back stitches. It is a quick filling stitch which needs to be worked on a single canvas. The back stitches can be made in a contrasting colour if wished. In this case the oblong cross stitches are all worked first and are then covered subsequently with back stitches.

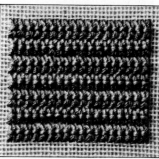

#### How to work

**1** *Work horizontally, starting at top left. Bring needle out at arrow and make a diagonal stitch up to right over 2 vertical and 4 horizontal canvas threads. Insert to left under 2 vertical threads and bring needle out again. Make another diagonal stitch down to right over 2 vertical and 4 horizontal threads. Insert needle and bring it out again 2 canvas intersections up to left ready to form the next stitch.*
**2** *Make a horizontal stitch over the top of the oblong cross stitch by taking needle to right over 2 vertical threads. Insert downwards under 2 horizontal threads and bring needle out on the base line again ready to form the next oblong cross stitch in the same way.*

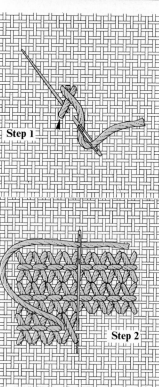

## Smyrna cross stitch

This is also known as *Leviathan stitch*. It is an effective stitch which is simple to work and which gives a dense texture formed by a combination of cross stitch and upright cross stitch on top of one another.

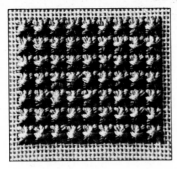

### How to work

1 *Work horizontally, starting at top left. Bring needle out at arrow and work a large cross stitch by making 2 diagonal stitches over 4 canvas intersections. After taking needle up to form the second diagonal stitch, insert it down to right under 2 vertical and 4 horizontal threads and bring it out again ready to form the upright cross stitch.*
2 *Make a vertical stitch over 4 horizontal threads.*
3 *Make a horizontal stitch over 4 vertical threads to complete an upright cross stitch on top of the cross stitch formed in Step 1. Bring the needle out on the base line ready to form the next complete stitch.*

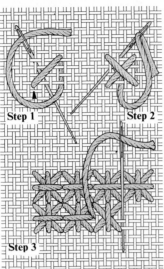

## Alternating cross stitch

This is a combination of cross stitch and oblong cross stitch which is worked either in the same or in contrasting colours.

### How to work

1 *Work horizontally, starting at top right. Bring needle out and make a diagonal stitch up to left over 2 vertical and 6 horizontal threads. Bring needle out again on the base line, and make another diagonal stitch up to right over 2 vertical and 6 horizontal threads. Insert needle down to left under 2 vertical and 4 horizontal threads and bring it out ready to form the small cross.*
2 *Work a small cross stitch by making 2 diagonal stitches over 2 canvas intersections as shown. After taking needle up to form the second diagonal of the small cross, bring it out again on base line, 2 vertical and 4 horizontal threads down to left ready to form the next oblong cross stitch.*

*Continue in this way, working oblong cross stitch and cross stitch alternately.*

*On all subsequent rows overlap the 2 different stitches by working them as shown.*

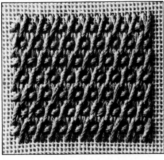

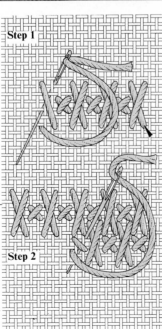

## Reversed cross stitch

This is formed by cross stitches and upright cross stitches in alternate sequence on top of one another. The top layer is worked in a contrasting colour. It is excellent for texture or colourwork, and for grounds.

### How to work

1 *Start at bottom left and work diagonal rows of cross stitch over 4 canvas intersections, with unworked spaces between the stitches as shown.*
2 *Start at bottom left again and work diagonal rows of upright cross stitch over 4 canvas threads into the spaces left by the previous rows.*
3 *Repeat both stitches in reverse sequence in a contrasting colour, so that the cross stitches are covered with upright cross stitches and the upright cross stitches are covered with cross stitches.*

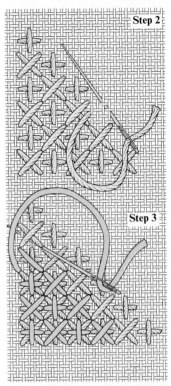

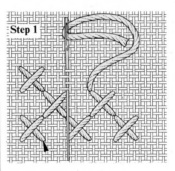

## Rice stitch

This is also known as *crossed corners cross stitch*. It is an excellent stitch for colourwork or for dense background textures and is made up of cross stitch and back stitch. The back stitch can be worked in a contrasting colour and is particularly good for metal threads as well.

### How to work

*Work horizontally in 2 journeys. Start the first journey at top left and work a row of large cross stitches over 4 canvas intersections as shown, completing each cross stitch before going on to the next.*

*When the crosses are complete, work a return journey of back stitches at right angles over the corners of the cross stitches. Each back stitch covers 2 canvas intersections.*

*Work all subsequent rows into the bases of the stitches in the previous rows.*

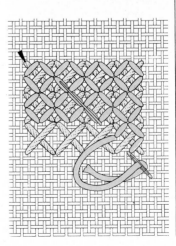

327

### Plaited Gobelin stitch

This stitch, as its name suggests, gives a plaited texture and is worked in a coarse thread so that it covers the canvas. It is quick to work and is useful for filling large areas. It looks best when it is worked on double canvas.

#### How to work

**1** *Work horizontally, starting at top right. Bring needle out and take it up to left over 1 vertical and 2 horizontal double threads. Insert downwards under 2 horizontal double threads and bring needle out ready to form the next stitch.*

*Continue in the same way to end of row, working diagonal stitches all slanting up to left.*
**2** *On the return journey work a row of similar diagonal stitches, from left to right, but slant them in the opposite direction and overlap the bases of the stitches in the previous row by 1 horizontal double thread.*

*Work all subsequent rows in this pattern of overlapping diagonal stitches slanted alternately to the left and then to the right.*

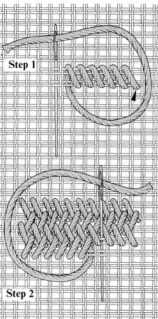

### Fishbone stitch

This forms a chevron pattern that consists of long diagonal stitches crossed alternately at the top and base by a short diagonal stitch. For the best result, work on double canvas.

#### How to work

**1** *Work the first row vertically downwards. Bring needle out at arrow and make a diagonal stitch up to right over 3 canvas intersections. Bring needle out again 1 vertical double thread to left.*
**2** *Make a short diagonal stitch down to right over 1 canvas intersection so that it crosses the top of the long diagonal stitch. Then bring needle out again 3 canvas intersections down to left, just underneath the previous long diagonal, ready to form the next stitch.*

*Continue in the same way to bottom of row.*

*On all subsequent rows work long diagonal stitches into the heads of those in the previous row and slant them in the opposite direction to form the zigzag patterning.*

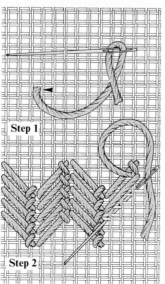

### Fern stitch

This stitch gives a decorative ridged effect and is worked down the canvas in overlapping diagonal stitches set at right angles to each other. Work it on double canvas.

#### How to work

**1** *Work vertically downwards. Bring needle out at arrow and make a diagonal stitch down to right over 2 canvas intersections. Bring needle out again 1 vertical double thread over to the left as shown.*
**2** *Make a diagonal stitch up to right over 2 canvas intersections. Bring needle out again 1 horizontal and 3 vertical double threads down to left ready to form the next stitch in the same way as the one above it.*

*Work all subsequent rows into the sides of the stitches in the previous row.*

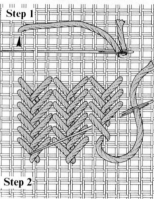

### Web stitch

This is a very closely woven background filling stitch which needs to be worked on double canvas. It is composed of diagonal stitches secured at regular intervals by tying stitches which cross at right angles and are worked through the middle of the canvas intersections. As the rows progress so the diagonal stitches get longer and require more tying stitches to secure them.

#### How to work

**1** *Work diagonally, starting at top left. Bring needle out at arrow and make a diagonal stitch up to right across 1 canvas intersection. Make another, parallel diagonal stitch, 1 horizontal double thread below, across 2 canvas intersections. Insert needle down to left and bring it out in between the double threads of the first canvas intersection.*
**2** *Tie down the diagonal stitch just made by taking needle over it and inserting in between the double threads 1 canvas intersection down to right. Bring needle out again 1 canvas intersection down to left ready to form the next diagonal stitch. Work this over 3 canvas intersections and tie with stitches at regular intervals, arranged so that they alternate with the tying stitches of the previous row as shown.*

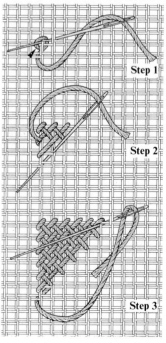

**3** *Continue in this way down across the work, making longer diagonal stitches for each row and securing them with regularly placed tying stitches.*

## Knotted stitch

This stitch gives a "railroad" texture and is best worked on double canvas. It is composed of diagonal stitches slanted in the same direction and each tied down by short diagonal stitches which are set at right angles to them.

### How to work

**1** Work horizontally, starting at top right. Bring needle out at arrow and make a diagonal stitch up to right over 1 vertical and 3 horizontal double threads. Insert downwards under 2 horizontal double threads and bring needle out again ready to form the tying stitch.
**2** Take needle up to left over 1 canvas intersection. Insert down to left under 1 vertical and 2 horizontal double threads and bring needle out again ready to form the next knotted stitch in the same way.
**3** Continue to end of row and then work next and all subsequent rows into the spaces left between the long diagonal stitches, so that they overlap the previous rows by 1 horizontal double thread.

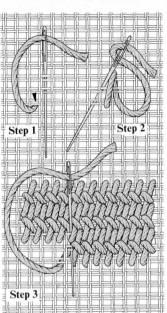

## Stitch patterns

*In the simple needlepoint picture, above, the stitch direction has been changed to bring out the different features of the design.*

# Straight stitches

These stitches, which are in general quick and easy to work, look best when worked on single canvas.

## Upright Gobelin stitch

This is sometimes known as *straight Gobelin stitch*. It is the simplest and quickest of all canvas stitches to work, and it gives a close, ridged surface. It can be given a more hard-wearing surface by working the stitches over a trammed stitch.

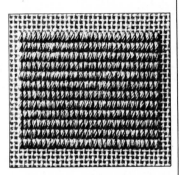

### How to work

*Work horizontally, starting at top left. Bring needle out and take it up over 2 horizontal threads. Insert down to right under 1 vertical and 2 horizontal threads and bring needle out ready to form the next stitch.*
*Work all subsequent rows into the bottom of those above.*

### How to work over trammed stitch

*Work a horizontal stitch along the length of the row, and then on the return journey work the straight gobelin stitches over it as shown.*

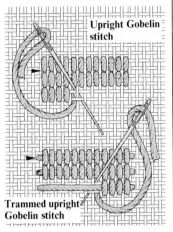

## Gobelin filling stitch

This is a very quick stitch to work and, when using more than one colour, is very good for shading and blending effects since the rows overlap each other by three canvas threads. Gobelin filling stitch can also be used for pulled thread work. It is important to match up the thickness of the thread with the gauge of the canvas so that, when finished, the canvas mesh does not show.

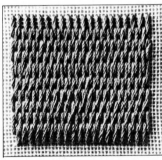

### How to work

**1** Work horizontally, starting at top left. Bring needle out and make a straight stitch up over 6 horizontal threads. Insert down to right under 2 vertical and 6 horizontal threads and bring needle out again ready to form the next upright stitch to the same size and in the same way.
**2** Work next and all subsequent rows so that they overlap the previous rows by 3 horizontal threads and so that the heads of the upright stitches are worked into the spaces left in the row above.

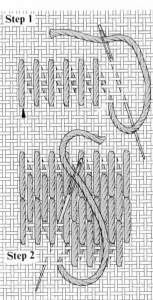

329

### Renaissance stitch

This is similar in appearance to upright Gobelin stitch, but it is always worked over a laid thread and is formed completely differently. It is worked in groups of three stitches, with each group placed vertically beneath the last.

*How to work*
**1** *Start at top left and work downwards. Bring needle out at arrow and make a horizontal stitch to left over 2 vertical threads. Insert downwards under 1 horizontal thread and bring needle out again ready to form the next stitch.*
**2** *Work a straight stitch up over 2 horizontal threads. Insert needle down to right under 1 vertical and 2 horizontal threads and bring it out again ready to form the next stitch.*
**3** *Work a second straight stitch up over 2 horizontal threads. Insert needle down to right under 1 vertical and 3 horizontal threads and bring it out again ready to form the next group of stitches.*
**4** *Work all subsequent rows into the same holes as the edge stitches of the previous rows.*

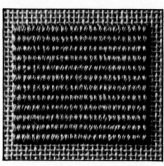

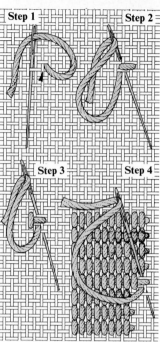

### Parisian stitch

This stitch is quick and easy to work and is particularly useful for filling large areas of background. It is composed of both long and short straight stitches which are worked alternately and it looks best when it is worked on single canvas.

*How to work*
*Work horizontally, starting at top left. Bring needle out and make a long straight stitch up over 6 horizontal threads. Insert down to right under 1 vertical and 4 horizontal threads and bring needle out again ready to form the next stitch as shown.*

*Work another, shorter straight stitch, this time up over 2 horizontal threads only. Insert needle down to right under 1 vertical and 4 horizontal threads and bring it out again on the base line ready to form the next long straight stitch.*

*Continue alternating the 2 stitches in this way, working a long one first and then a short one until you reach the end of the row.*

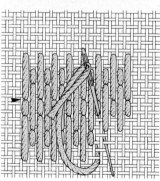

*Work all subsequent rows so that they overlap. The stitches alternate so that the long ones fall beneath the short ones in the previous row and the short ones fall beneath the long ones in the previous row.*

### Long stitch

This stitch gives a brocade pattern and is formed by working graduated straight stitches in a series of triangles and reverse triangles over two rows.

*How to work*
*Work horizontally, starting at top left. Continue along row, working groups of 6 straight stitches in a repeated sequence over 4, 3, 2, 1, 2 and 3 horizontal threads.*

*Work the return row from right to left in the same sequence but so that the longest stitches fall beneath the shortest ones in the previous row. In this way the stitches will fill the spaces left by the first row and will thus complete the pattern of interlocking triangles.*

*On subsequent rows work into the bases of the stitches in the previous row.*

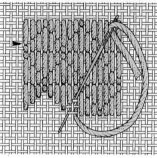

### Long stitch variation

This stitch gives a tweed-like texture which is quite quick and easy to work. It is formed by first working a row of long straight stitches in a chevron formation and then working two rows of shorter straight stitches directly underneath them. It is best when it is worked on a single canvas.

*How to work*
**1** *Work horizontally, starting at top left. Bring needle out and begin with the row of long straight stitches. Take needle up over 4 horizontal threads, insert down to right under 1 vertical and 3 horizontal threads, and bring it out again ready to form the next stitches. Work all these over 4 horizontal threads, moving up 1 horizontal thread with each stitch until 4 stitches have been made. Then work 3 more stitches in the same way but moving down 1 horizontal thread with each stitch. Continue to end of row,*

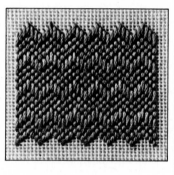

*working in groups of 3 stitches alternately ascending and descending.*
**2** *Work the next 2 rows in exactly the same sequence but in shorter straight stitches, each covering only 2 horizontal threads. Work the short straight stitches into the bases of the long straight stitches of the previous row.*

*Follow this pattern of 1 row of long straight stitches and then 2 rows of shorter ones until the required area of canvas has been completely covered.*

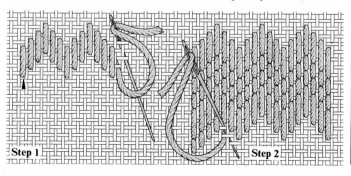

## Florentine stitch

This is also known as *bargello stitch*, *cushion stitch*, *flame stitch* and *Irish stitch*. It is worked in zigzag rows of stitches to form multicoloured bands, often worked in graduating tones. The characteristic flame patterns produced are known as *bargello* or *Florentine* work.

When working these multicoloured designs, it is useful to keep several needles threaded with the different colours so that they can be picked up and used when required.

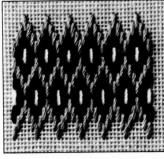

### How to work

**1** Work horizontally, starting at the left. Bring needle out at arrow and work a straight stitch up over 4 horizontal canvas threads. Follow this with 3 more stitches, each worked 2 threads higher up than the base of the previous one. Work the next 3 stitches downwards, the next 3 upwards, and so on. Continue in this way to end of row.
**2** Work second row in the same way and in the same colour but start working downwards first and then upwards to form a diamond pattern with the first row.
**3** Work third and fourth rows in a new colour in the same way as the first and second, filling in the diamond pattern. Finish off the final central stitch of each diamond with a third colour.

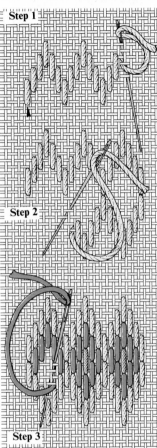

Step 1

Step 2

Step 3

## Hungarian stitch

This is also known as *mosaic stitch* when worked diagonally (see page 322). It produces a diamond-patterned brocade surface and is composed of graduated straight stitches. It can be worked all in one colour or in bands of different colours.

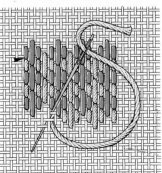

### How to work

Work horizontally, starting at top left. Work groups of 3 graduated straight stitches in a repeated sequence over 2, 4 and 2 horizontal threads, leaving a space of 2 vertical threads between each group.

On all subsequent rows overlap by working the groups of 3 stitches into the spaces left in the previous rows as shown.

Use a different colour for each row for a striped effect.

## Hungarian stitch variation

This is worked in the same way as Hungarian stitch but forms a larger diamond pattern. It too can be worked all in one colour or in bands of different colours.

### How to work

Work horizontally, starting at top left. Work groups of 4 graduated straight stitches in a repeated sequence over 2, 4, 6 and 4 horizontal threads.

Continue in the same way to end of row, without leaving a space between the separate groups of 4 stitches.

On all subsequent rows work the long stitches into the bases of the short stitches in the previous rows so that they overlap and fill the spaces.

Use a different colour for each row for a striped effect.

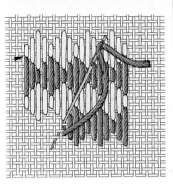

## Tent stitch needlepoint

In the needlepoint, above, worked in England around 1600, the only stitch used is tent stitch. Relief has been added to the design, however, by careful toning of colours to give a three-dimensional effect to the fruit.

# Looped stitches

## Chain stitch

This stitch is worked on canvas in exactly the same way as when it is used as an embroidery stitch on fabric. It is worked vertically so that each successive looped stitch ties down the one preceding it. It forms a texture rather like knitting and is used as a filling stitch.

### How to work

Start at top left and work downwards. Bring needle out and hold working thread down to left under thumb. Insert needle back into the same hole and bring it out again 2 horizontal threads lower down, taking it over the loop of the working thread as shown. Draw needle through the loop to make the first chain stitch.

Continue in this way to end of row, finishing off with a small straight stitch to tie down the final chain.

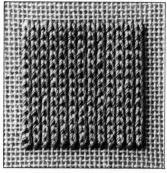

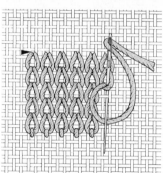

## Knitting stitch

This is also known as *tapestry stitch*. When worked in a coarse thread it has a texture like knitting, but when worked in a fine thread it looks more like woven tapestry. It is best when worked on single canvas.

### How to work

**1** Work vertically in 2 journeys, starting at bottom right. Bring needle out and take it up to right over 1 vertical and 4 horizontal threads. Insert down to left under 1 vertical and 2 horizontal threads and bring needle out again ready to form the next stitch.
**2** Finish off row by taking needle up to right over 1 vertical and 4 horizontal threads. Insert to left under 2 vertical threads and bring needle out again ready to start working the return journey.
**3** Then work stitches downwards, taking needle down to right over 1 vertical and 4 horizontal threads, inserting up to left under 1 vertical and 2 horizontal threads and bringing it out again ready to form the next knitting stitch.

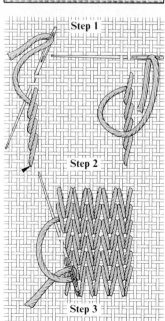

## Velvet stitch

This stitch resembles the pile of carpets, and can be used in colourwork patterns as a filling stitch or to work motifs in relief. It must be worked on a double canvas and looks best when worked in either a thick wool or in several strands of wool threaded through one needle. The loops are all cut and trimmed to length when the work is completed.

### How to work

**1** Work horizontally, starting at bottom left. Bring needle out at arrow and take it up to right over 1 canvas intersection. Insert needle down to left and bring it out at arrow again.
**2** Take needle up to right again and insert in the same place as before, but this time either leave a loop of thread at the bottom, or work the loop over a mesh stick or knitting needle. Bring needle out again 1 horizontal thread down.
**3** Take needle up to left over 1 canvas intersection. Insert down to right and bring needle out again in the same place ready to form the next stitch.

When the work is completed cut the loops and trim them if necessary so that they are all the same length.

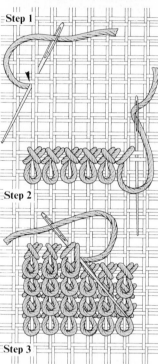

## Single knotted stitch

This stitch also has the texture of carpet pile. It is best worked on single canvas, the threads of which should be completely covered by the stitches.

### How to work

**1** Work horizontally, starting at bottom left. Insert needle through the front of the canvas at arrow, leaving a short end on the surface held down with the thumb. Take needle up to left under 1 horizontal and 2 vertical threads and bring it out again. Take needle to right over 3 vertical threads and insert down to left under 1 horizontal and 2 vertical threads. Bring needle out and pull working thread tight to close the knot.
**2** Work next stitches in the same way, forming loops over a mesh stick or knitting needle.
**3** Work subsequent rows 1 horizontal thread up. Cut and trim the loops when the work is completed.

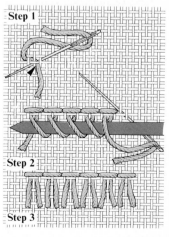

## Eastern stitch

This is a lacy filling stitch which looks good when worked with a stranded silk thread. For best results, work it on a single canvas.

### How to work

1 *Work horizontally, starting at top left. Bring needle out at arrow and take it to right over 4 vertical threads. Insert down to left under 4 canvas intersections and bring the needle out again ready to form the next stitch.*
2 *Take needle up over 4 horizontal threads and insert at original starting point. Take needle down to right under 4 canvas intersections and bring it out again ready to form the next stitch.*
3 *Take needle up to left. Pass it from left to right underneath the vertical stitch, without piercing the canvas and keeping working thread under needle in order to form a loop.*
4 *Pass needle downwards underneath the horizontal stitch, without piercing the canvas and keeping both working thread and first loop under needle in order to form a second loop.*
5 *Insert needle on base line again as shown. Take it up under 4 horizontal threads and bring needle out again ready to form the next Eastern stitch.*

*Continue in the same way to end of row, working next and subsequent stitches into the side of the previous ones.*

*Work all subsequent rows into the bases of the stitches in the previous rows.*

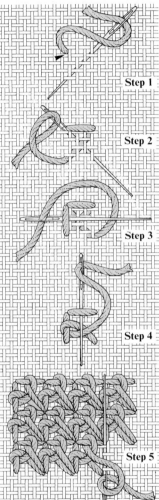

## Rococo stitch

This stitch needs to be worked on a wide-mesh double canvas since it consists of bundles of four stitches grouped together and formed over the same canvas threads. The bundles are each worked into alternating squares that overlap to give a dense texture perforated by small holes. It makes a very decorative ground stitch.

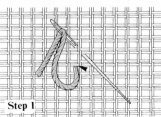

### How to work

1 *Work diagonally, starting at bottom right. Bring needle out at arrow, take it up over 2 horizontal double threads, and bring it out down to right under 1 canvas intersection.*

**Rococo stitch continued**
2 *Insert needle to left over vertical stitch just made. Bring it out 1 horizontal double thread below.*
3 *Insert needle up over 2 horizontal double threads and, keeping working thread to left of needle, bring it out 1 horizontal double thread below.*
4 *Again insert needle down under 1 horizontal double thread and make 2 more stitches in the same way over the same threads.*
5 *Take needle to left over 1 vertical double thread. Insert needle downwards under 2 horizontal double threads and bring it out again ready to form the next rococo stitch.*
6 *Continue diagonally in the same way. Work subsequent rows into the tops of the stitches in the previous rows.*

## Shell stitch

This is a very decorative border and filling stitch. It is worked in two journeys, using a contrasting colour or type of thread for the second journey.

### How to work

1 *Work horizontally, starting at top right. Bring needle out at arrow, take it up over 6 horizontal threads, and insert to left under 1 vertical thread.*
2 *Take needle down over 6 horizontal threads and insert to left under 1 vertical thread.*
3 *Take needle up over 6 horizontal threads and insert to left under 1 vertical thread again. Take needle down over 6 horizontal threads. Insert up to right under 1 vertical and 3 horizontal threads and, keeping thread to right of needle, bring it out again.*
4 *Pass working thread over 4 stitches just made and insert needle under them 1 vertical thread to right. Bring needle out again 3 canvas intersections down to left ready to form the next complete shell stitch.*
5 *Link the row of completed shells with a contrasting thread. Starting at right, pass needle down through 1st back stitch, up through 2nd, down through 1st again, up through 2nd, and then on to the next shell stitch. This forms 2 loops at the bottom and 1 at the top. The next stitch will have 2 loops at the top and 1 at the bottom.*

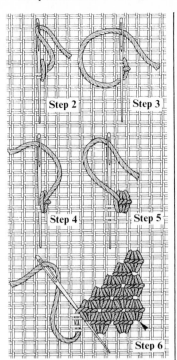

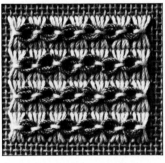

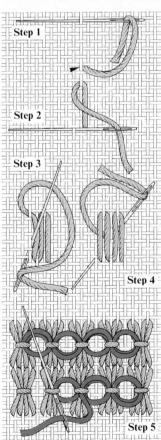

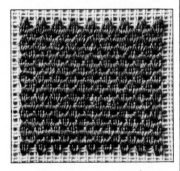

333

# Star stitches

## Star stitch

This stitch is used for both canvaswork and openwork embroidery on linen. It forms a star within a square and consists of eight stitches all worked into the same central point. It is best worked on single canvas in a coarse thread.

### How to work

*Work either vertically or horizontally. Starting from the outer edge of the square, bring needle out and work each stitch into the centre over 2 canvas threads or over 2 canvas intersections when coming from the corners. Leave 2 canvas threads unworked between each converging stitch so that each star occupies a square 4 horizontal threads by 4 vertical threads.*

*Work next and subsequent stitches into the side edge of the previous ones.*

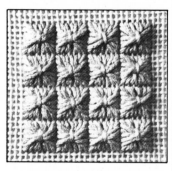

## Rhodes stitch

This stitch also forms a star shape within a square and gives a raised surface. It consists of diagonal stitches worked around a square in an anti-clockwise direction so that they all cross each other over the same central point. It is best worked on a single canvas.

### How to work

*1 Work either vertically or horizontally. Starting from the outer edge of the square, bring needle out at arrow. Take it up to right over 6 canvas inter-sections, insert down to left, and bring needle out again 1 vertical thread to right of original starting point.*

*Work the next stitch over the previous one, inserting needle 1 vertical thread to left at top and bringing it out 1 vertical thread to right again at bottom. Continue in this way as shown, working anti-clockwise until the square is filled.*

*2 Finish off each square with a small vertical stitch over 2 horizontal threads at the centre.*

*Work next stitches beside the previous ones as shown.*

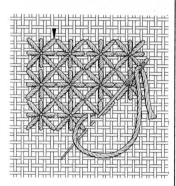

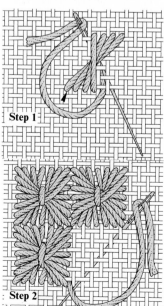

**Step 1**

**Step 2**

## Eye stitch

This stitch can be used both for canvaswork and as a pulled work stitch for embroidering on linen. It consists of sixteen diagonal stitches all converging into the same central point, with their outer ends arranged around a square. The square is marked out in a frame of small back stitches.

### How to work

*1 Work either vertically or horizontally. Starting from the outer edge of the square, bring needle out at arrow. Take it down to left over 4 canvas intersections, insert at centre of square, and bring it out again up to right, 2 vertical threads to left of original starting point.*

*Continue in this way, working each stitch into the centre over 4 canvas threads or over 4 canvas intersections when coming from the corners. Leave 2 canvas threads unworked between each converging stitch so that the square finally measures 8 horizontal threads by 8 vertical threads.*

*2 When the squares are completed surround them with a frame of back stitches, each worked over 2 canvas threads.*

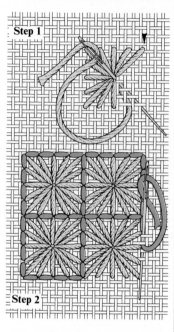

**Step 1**

**Step 2**

## Fan stitch

This stitch can be formed with either five or nine stitches depending on the thickness of the thread and the gauge of the canvas being used. The stitches which form the fan-shape are worked so that they all radiate in the opposite direction in alternate rows.

### How to work

*1 Work either vertically or horizontally. Bring needle out at arrow, take it up over 4 horizontal threads, insert downwards and bring it out again at original starting point. Work the next 4 stitches all radiating from the same corner as shown. Leave 2 canvas threads unworked between each stitch so that the 5 stitches cover a square 4 horizontal threads by 4 vertical threads.*

*Continue in the same way to end of row, working each group of 5 stitches into the side of the previous group.*

*2 On subsequent rows alternate the fans so that they radiate in the opposite direction.*

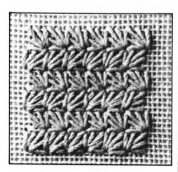

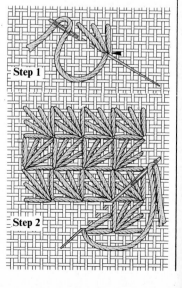

**Step 1**

**Step 2**

# Grounds

This section gives an idea of how different stitches can be worked together to give interesting background textures.

### Straight stitch and fern stitch

This ground is best worked on double canvas. It is composed of two rows of straight stitch, worked up and down the canvas in an overlapping triangle pattern, alternated with one row of fern stitch which can be worked in a contrasting colour.

### How to work
*Work 2 rows of straight stitches up and down the canvas. On the first row, work the stitches in a repeated sequence over 1, 2, 3, 4, 5, 6, 7, 6, 5, 4, 3 and 2 vertical double threads as shown. This forms the first row of triangles. On the second row, work the stitches in the same sequence, but overlap the triangles by working the longest stitches next to the shortest in the previous row.*

*Work the row of fern stitches vertically as well (see page 328). Each stitch covers 2 horizontal and 3 vertical double threads and is worked into the side of the straight stitch pattern as shown.*

*Continue in this way, working the 2 stitches alternately.*

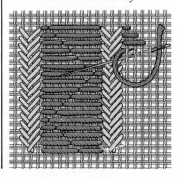

### Fishbone and tent stitch

This ground is best worked on double canvas in two colours.

### How to work
*Work a vertical row of fishbone stitch (see page 328). Then work a row of tent stitch (see page 320) next to it.*

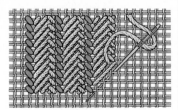

### Stem and fern stitch

This ground is best worked on double canvas in two colours.

### How to work
*Alternate rows of canvas stem stitch (see page 323) with fern stitch (see page 328).*

# Colour patterns

All these patterns are worked in a combination of simple straight and diagonal stitches. They are effective when worked both in yarns of different colours and in yarns of different textures too.

### Chequer pattern

This pattern is worked on single canvas in squares of seven diagonal stitches over 1, 2, 3, 4, 3, 2 and 1 canvas intersections. A chequer pattern is formed by alternating both the direction in which the diagonal stitches slant and their colour or texture.

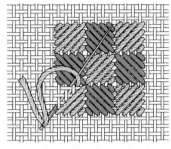

### Jacquard stitch pattern

This pattern consists of alternating rows of short diagonal stitches, each covering two canvas intersections, and of long diagonal stitches, each covering four canvas intersections. Each row is worked for nine stitches up and nine stitches across on double canvas.

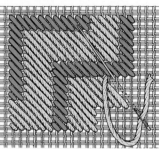

### Diagonal stripe pattern

This pattern is worked on double canvas. The first row forms a stepped pattern of tent stitches and is worked diagonally, from bottom left to top right. The second row is worked in graduated diagonal stitches in a repeated sequence over 1, 2, 3, 4, 3 and 2 canvas intersections.

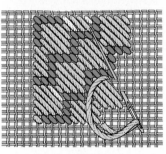

### Mosaic stitch pattern

This pattern is worked on single canvas and is composed wholly of mosaic stitches (see page 322), each over two canvas intersections. The actual pattern is formed by using contrasting colours as shown. Any other crossed stitch can be adapted to this pattern.

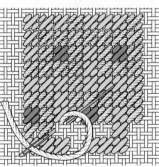

### Hungarian stitch pattern

This pattern can be worked either on single or double canvas. It is composed wholly of Hungarian stitches (see page 331), each worked over 2, 4 and 2 horizontal threads. The actual pattern is formed by using contrasting colours as shown. It is best to work all the stitches in one colour first, and then the others afterwards.

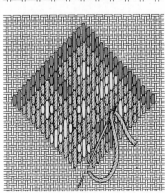

# Florentine work

This is also known as *Bargello* work and *fiamma* or *flame* stitch. A very popular type of needlepoint, it forms irregular patterns and is always worked in many different colours. The straight stitches are placed in graduating zigzags and once the first line is worked the following lines of stitches are used to fill in the canvas above and below it, following its contours. It is purported to have come to Florence from Hungary, brought there in the fifteenth century by a Hungarian girl who married a Medici prince.

### Working Florentine stitches

A single-thread canvas should be used for best results and worked in wools or silks thick enough to cover the canvas. The grouping of the stitches up and down in zigzag lines forms the pattern. The zigzag is first worked upwards and when the required height is reached the stitches are then worked downwards in the same way. The stitch used for Florentine work is Florentine stitch (see page 331). The most usual stitch size for Florentine work extends upwards over four horizontal threads and back down under two horizontal threads. Though the method of working the stitches is always the same, the stitch itself can be made longer or shorter, with the longest workable stitch being taken up over six horizontal threads and back under one. And the smallest workable stitch being taken up over three threads and back down under two threads. Although the stitch size can be varied as shown below it is always best to use the same size throughout a pattern, so that each row can be worked in the same way. Variations of stitch sizes can be used for certain patterns (see page 338) although this is not authentic Florentine work.

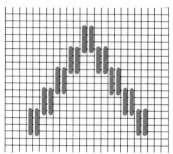

**Average stitch size** Up over 4 horizontal canvas threads and back down under 2.

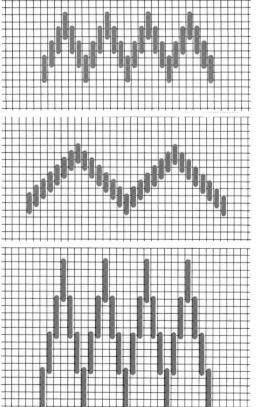

**Shortest stitch size** Up over 3 horizontal canvas threads and back down under 2.

**Longest stitch size** Up over 6 horizontal canvas threads and back down under 1.

# Types of zigzags

The zigzag lines forming the pattern can be made in steps, pinnacles or curves used separately or together to form any number of different designs. It is important to remember when planning patterns with the three simple formations shown below that the actual stitch size used should be the same throughout otherwise the rows will vary.

### Step formation

Stepped zigzags are made by working several stitches along the same horizontal threads.

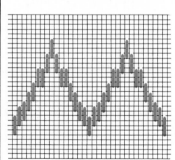

**Two stitch steps**

**Three stitch steps**

### Pinnacle formation

Sharper effects are made by using a longer stitch throughout and finishing the pinnacle with a single stitch at the peak. The height of the pinnacle can be graduated by using a shorter stitch worked in steps.

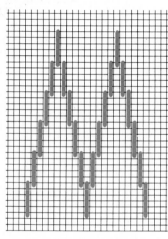

*The steepest pinnacles are made by working over six horizontal canvas threads and back under one horizontal canvas thread.*

**Graduated pinnacle**

### Curved formation

Pinnacles can be converted into curves by doubling and tripling the number of stitches at the peak. Curves can also be made more gradual by working in step formation.

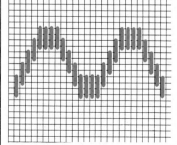

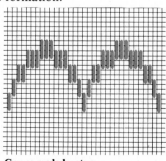

**Curves made by flat tops**

**Curves made by steps**

# Combination of patterns

# Making Florentine patterns

Steps, pinnacles and curves can be worked large or small, in regular or irregular sizes, along a zigzag. Curves can be worked downwards to form deep wells and can be followed by steps or steep pinnacles. Random patterns can be made by using pinnacles and curves together in varying heights. Undulating effects can be made by introducing curves in the middle of pinnacles. The combinations are endless and making original patterns is part of the pleasure of Florentine work. Below are three examples of combinations.

Once the first zigzag line has been worked, the subsequent lines are made in graduating colour sequence above and below it. In this way the first line can be thought of as the skeleton of the pattern and the subsequent lines as the flesh. The skeleton line can be worked in different directions: horizontally, as shown in the previous illustrations; diagonally; or in mirror image, when a second skeleton is reversed and worked immediately below the first. Finally, the Florentine patterns can be worked in four different directions, either from the four sides inwards or from the centre outwards (see pages 340–341).

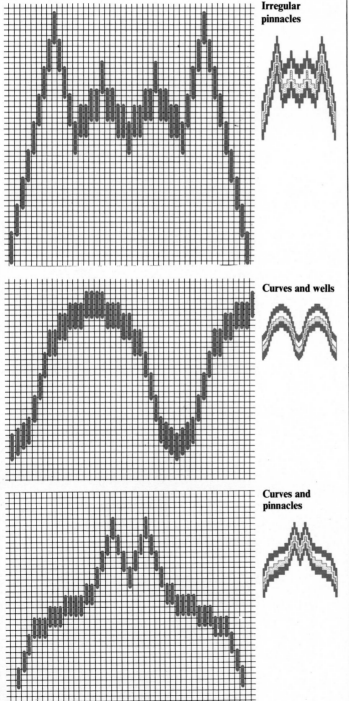

**Irregular pinnacles**

**Curves and wells**

**Curves and pinnacles**

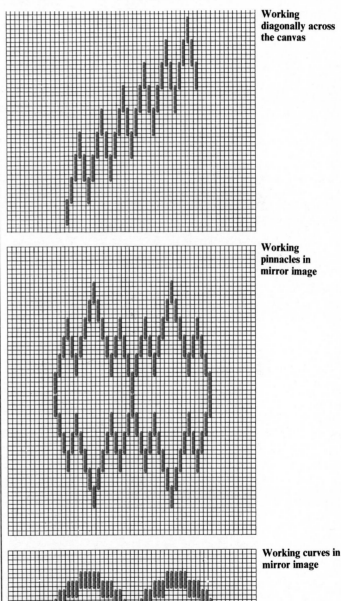

**Working diagonally across the canvas**

**Working pinnacles in mirror image**

**Working curves in mirror image**

# Florentine patterns

The patterns here (charts on pages 340–341) can be worked in the colours shown or in new colourways as long as the same number of colours are used. The choice of colour is yours but remember that bright areas graduating to dark ones look the most dramatic. In fact, the line of the zigzag looks more marked if it is started with the darkest colour and then graduated to lighter shades.

**Gothic pinnacles**

**Undulating pinnacles**

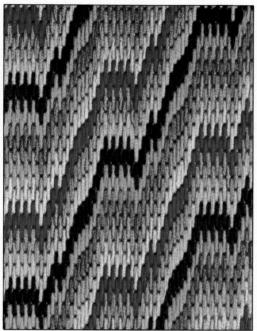

**Diagonal pinnacles**

**Pinnacles with stripes**

**Mirror image pinnacles**

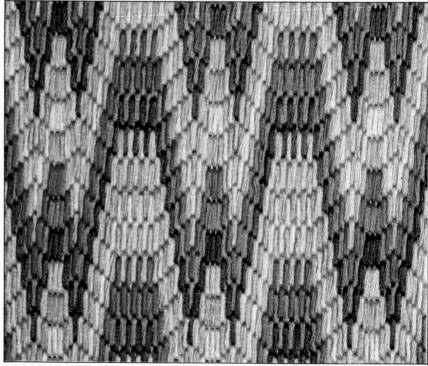

**Pinnacles with wells**

**Pinnacles and curves**

**Four-way Florentine**

**Florentine sampler**
This is made up
of a random
choice of different
Florentine
patterns outlined
with darker
thread.

# *Florentine pattern charts*

The charts on these pages are for the patterns on pages 338–339. On needlepoint tapestry charts the graph paper represents the canvas threads and the stitches are marked accordingly.

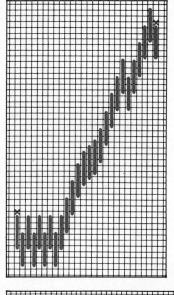

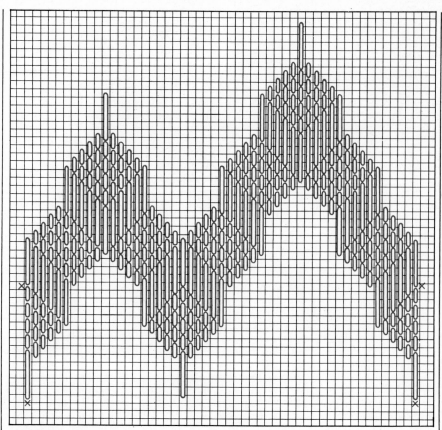

**Diagonal pinnacles**
Worked in stitches over 6 threads in varying steps using 8 colours.

**Mirror image pinnacles**
Worked in stitches over 3, 4, 6 and 8 threads using 7 colours.

**Gothic pinnacles**
Worked in stitches over 6 and 2 threads using 8 colours.

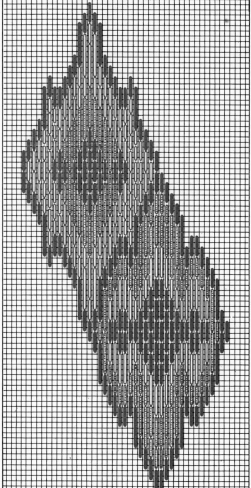

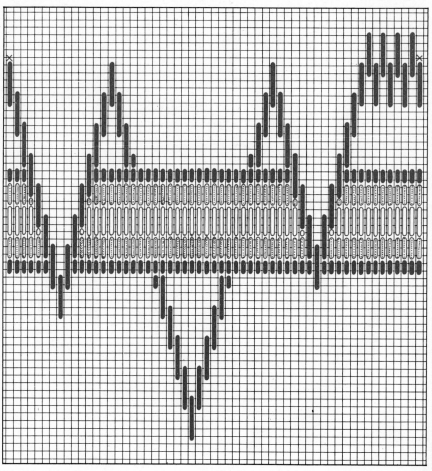

**Pinnacles and stripes**
Worked in stitches over 6 threads in steps of 4 threads using 7 colours and stripes worked over 2, 3 and 4 threads using 3 colours.

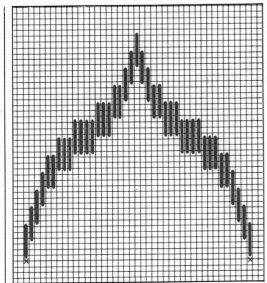

**Pinnacles and curves**
Worked in stitches over 6 threads in steps of 3 threads using 7 colours.

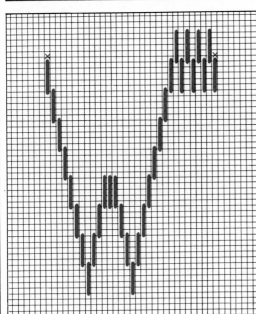

**Pinnacles and wells**
Worked in stitches over 6 threads in steps of 5 threads using 7 colours.

**Undulating pinnacles**
Worked in stitches over 6 threads in steps of 3 threads using 8 colours.

# Working in four directions

In four-way Florentine the pattern is worked in four directions either from or towards the centre of the canvas. In both cases the canvas is divided into four equal triangles. The sections are filled either separately up to the diagonal line or worked in rounds with the direction of the stitches being changed when the diagonal line is reached.

### Preparing the canvas
Mark the centre of the canvas and draw two diagonal lines from corner to corner crossing the canvas intersections.

### Working towards the centre
When working towards the centre the pattern is set at the beginning. Select the skeleton pattern and work this along all four sides. Then repeat in colour sequence inwards.

**Working towards the centre**
When working the skeleton pattern make sure that its centre is lined up with the centre of the canvas.

### Working from the centre
When working from the centre the pattern gradually emerges as work progresses and more stitches are added at the sides.

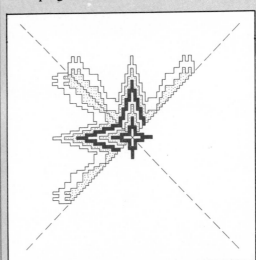

**Working from the centre**
Start with 4 stitches made into the centre hole placed at right angles to each other and develop the pattern as you work outwards filling each quarter identically.

# Backgrounds

Needlepoint designs often need a plain background to show up the main figurative part of the work. This large area can be dull to work unless it is treated imaginatively.

## Plain backgrounds

Either tent or cross stitch are very often used on backgrounds but many other quick and interesting stitches can be used instead, such as upright GobelinHungarian, Byzantine, Milanese and long stitch. Any of these or similar stitches will break the monotony of a plain background without interfering with the focal point of the work.

## Toned backgrounds

Subtly blended tones can be introduced into plain backgrounds without distracting from the design. This can be done either by buying special threads which are already shaded or by dividing the strands of different coloured threads and twisting them into different combinations.

### How to twist the strands

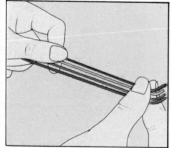

**1** *Select 3 or 4 closely toning threads of stranded cotton or tapestry wool.*

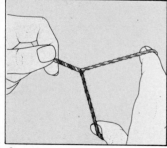

**2** *Untwist the threads and then twist the different strands together to make a new thread.*

## Shading techniques

The techniques of shading are very simple. The choice of method depends on the overall design of the work. If an "antiqued" appearance is required, as in the needlepoint above, very subtle, uneven patterns of shaded colours can be used with the rethreading method described.

This method can also be used when trying to match an old, faded piece of needlepoint. A simpler method of shading is worked with a pre-shaded bought thread. Two different ways of using pre-shaded thread are shown below.

*Pre-shaded silks in tones of dark green to white are used above to create a random shaded effect and make a play of shadows on the grass. Encroaching Gobelin stitch is used to give the grass a more "realistic" texture.*

*Similarly the same stitch and type of thread has been used in the sky of the needlepoint above. Different delicately shaded tones have been used to produce the effect of clouds and sky and give a retreating skyline to the picture.*

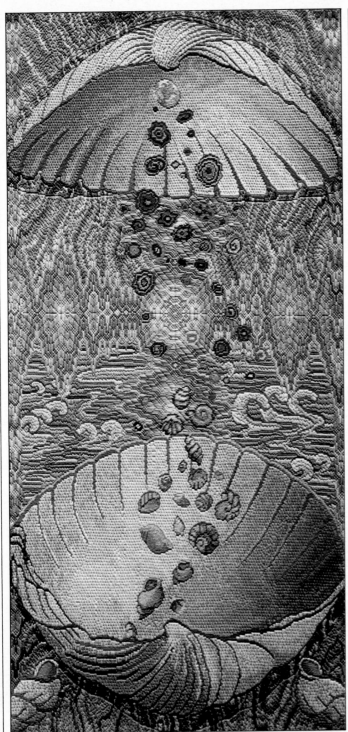

**Shell carpet**

## *Marbled effects*

Marbled and mother of pearl effects are difficult to work but are very beautiful. Use pale shades and subtle tonal blends to achieve the delicate, irregular patterning. When working with wools highlights can be introduced with similar tones of silk threads. These effects are shown very clearly in the centre of the bedspread (right) and on the shells in the carpet (above).

## *Patterned backgrounds*

Elaborate backgrounds can be designed to become an integral part of the whole design. Geometric patterns such as Greek key designs, trellises, checks and chevrons can all be incorporated. Traditional flame or bargello patterns are also very useful. Take care that the colours in the background do not overpower the subject. Bargello techniques are on page 336.

**Detail of flower panel**
Soft diagonal stripes are used to set off the flowers in the foreground.

**Detail of butterfly carpet**
Bargello patterns have been used as a surround to the central butterfly.

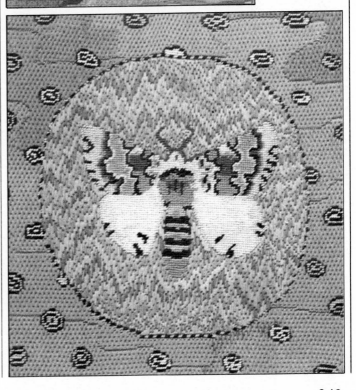

# Unworked backgrounds

Worked backgrounds can be dispensed with altogether by using fabric instead. This can be done either by working the needlepoint directly onto an evenweave linen or by working it through both the canvas and the fabric and then removing the canvas threads. This latter method is particularly suitable for cushion covers.

**Needlepoint on fabric**

*How to work*

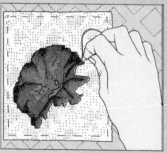

**1** *Mark the design onto canvas and tack this securely to the fabric. Then work the needlepoint stitches through both the canvas and the fabric.*

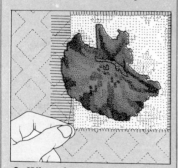

**2** *When the stitching is finished pull the canvas threads away, until only the stitching and fabric remain.*

# Textures

The combination of canvas, stitch and thread makes up the many different textural effects which can be achieved with needlepoint tapestry. The different stitches worked separately or in combination with each other form patterns on the surface of the canvas with more pronounced effects being made by a careful choice of colours. When designing needlepoint pictures particular attention should be paid to the various stitches so that they are used to give exactly the right textures in the different parts of the work.

Diagonal, brick and satin stitches have been used in opposite directions on the garden and house walls to create tonal changes on large monochrome areas

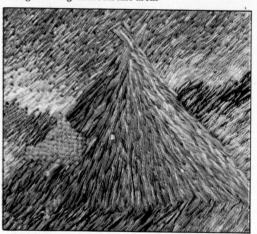

**Stitch direction**
*The stitch direction can be used to emphasize the form and nature of a motif in needlepoint. In the above detail of a haystack, free stitching has been used to show its rough texture.*

**Tonal changes**
*Textures can be depicted with a clever use of colour. The background is lighter behind the lace curtains and darker on the window panes.*

## Raised effects

The surface of the needlepoint can also be changed by using raised or relief effects. This can be done either by using tramming stitches beneath the needlepoint stitching or by using special stitches which form relief effects themselves.

The best stitches to use for making relief effects are velvet and single knotted stitch (see page 332). In the needlepoint panel opposite, both techniques have been used in different areas. The leaves of the plant have been trammed first before being worked over in satin stitch to give them a raised appearance.

The tablecloth has been worked in velvet stitch and the loops of the stitch cut to give a similar effect to carpet pile. Velvet stitch can also be left uncut to form a looped pile as in the detail on the relief tile pattern (below).

Single knotted stitch can be used to give tassel or fringe effects as shown on the tablecloth edging.

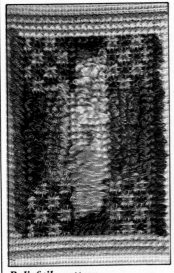

**Relief tile pattern**
*The pattern is worked in cross, eye and uncut velvet stitch.*

### Textured flower pattern

*This flower motif can be used for borders and is worked with a background of cross stitch, flower petals of cut velvet stitch, flower centre of beads attached with uncut velvet stitch, and leaves of graduated upright gobelin stitch.*

**Needlepoint picture with relief work**

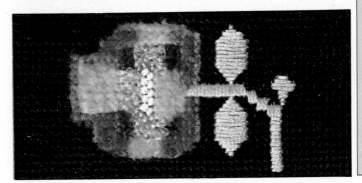

## Beads

Beads can be used in needlepoint either to cover an entire surface or to work backgrounds, as in the bead curtain below. They can also be used for motifs, details and highlights. Always use small, easily threaded beads and a strong buttonhole twist thread to secure them, using either couching or tent stitch.

**Detail of bead curtain**

### Securing with couching

This method is used for covering large areas with beads. String the beads onto the thread first.

*How to work*

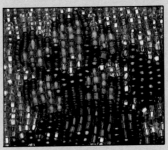

*Lay the string of threaded beads on the surface and secure with couching stitches at regular intervals.*

### Securing with tent stitch

This method is mainly used for details and highlights.

*How to work*

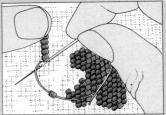

*Take the needle through to the front of the canvas. Then thread the bead and work the tent stitch in the usual way.*

# *Borders*

Borders are used to edge the main design and can be made in many different sizes, shapes and styles so that they become either discreet frames, decorative surrounds or an important part of the main design. Therefore, when working out a design, the choice of border should be taken into account and carefully planned so that it works in harmony with the whole design.

### *Border effects*

By altering the depth of a border from the average 3in. (7.5cm) to a narrow 1in. (2.5cm), or to a deep band which almost engulfs the main design, quite dramatic changes can be made to the appearance of the whole needlepoint. Borders which are lighter or darker in tone than the main design can also be used to reduce or enhance the importance of the central design.

### *Border width*
*The deep border on the needlepoint above gives a sense of distance to the main design. The same design, this time with a very narrow border, appears stronger. A similar effect could be achieved on the trellis and flower needlepoint on the opposite page, if the wider border were removed.*

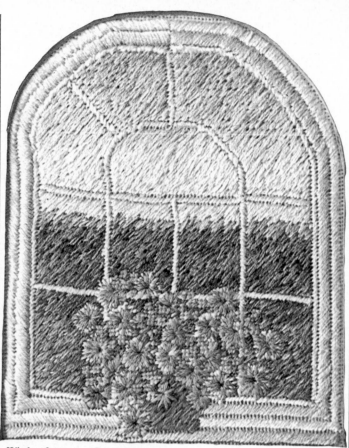

**Window frame on a flower picture**

### *Shaped borders*

Borders, when used as frames, can be made in many different shapes, from classic squares, rectangles, circles and ovals to the figurative shapes of stars, flowers, windows and doors. Windows and doors, in fact, make excellent borders for designing needlepoint pictures. The borders can also be made in shapes which relate to the pictures within, for instance by using a ship for a seascape or a star, as in the illustration below, for a skyscape. For these specially shaped borders, both the main picture and border should be planned together, as part of the whole design.

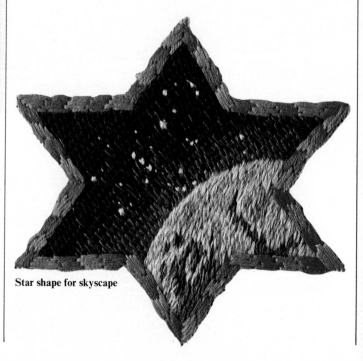

**Star shape for skyscape**

## Formal borders

Formal borders can be worked in one colour throughout or in many different colours to complement the main design. The stitching can be simple or textured, using any of the stitches in the glossary (pages 320–335). Formal borders can be designed using geometric patterns, such as stripes, checks, chevrons and diamonds or motifs, such as flowers, can be worked at regular intervals.

## Overflowing borders

Borders can be designed to become an integral part of the main design either by allowing them to overflow into the central area or by making the main design flow into the border. In the needlepoint below, the leaves from the border encroach upon the central design while the flowers from the central part spill into the border. In the illustration at the bottom of the page, the window frame is used as a border for the whole design and the pots of flowers overlap it.

**Trellis and flower needlepoint**

**Vase of flowers with overflowing border**

## Corners

When continuous patterns are being used in borders, the corners need careful planning. They can be left unpatterned and filled with a simple coloured square or they can be worked with a single flower, as seen right in the detail from a contemporary carpet. The pattern could also be repeated in mirror image at the corners.

**Cabbage rose corner detail**

**Geraniums on a window ledge**

347

# *Needlepoint carpets*

**Modern carpet**
The carpet on the left was specially designed to the owner's requirements in a pattern made up of bold geometric forms.

From the sixteenth century, needlepoint carpets were made as copies of the more expensive woven or knotted Oriental ones. This can still be done today by studying the motifs and colours in existing carpets. The motifs all have their individual special meanings. Colours, too, have their significance: for example, white is the colour of sorrow; red the colour of joy, happiness and wealth; and yellow is the colour of piety, although in China it was used to indicate land, gold and wealth. Blue is the colour of strength in Mongolia but signifies sky in Persian carpets. Green is the sacred colour of Islam and in prayer rugs signifies Paradise.

## *Doll's house carpet*

The miniature carpet shown below in actual size can be made and used for a doll's house by working from the chart on the left. It is worked entirely in tent stitch on double canvas with 12 threads per in. (24 per 5cm). The five colours, for which a key is given below, can be altered to fit any colour scheme.

### *Key to colours*

| | |
|---|---|
| ⊡ | **Coral** |
| ⊡ | **Scarlet** |
| ◪ | **Bright yellow** |
| ☐ | **Autumn yellow** |
| ▼ | **Bright peacock blue** |
| ■ | **Peacock blue** |

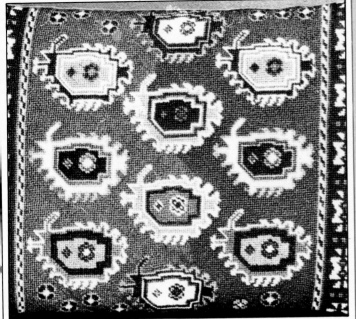

**Needlepoint cushion**
*It is possible to design and make cushions to reflect traditional carpet patterns. The cushion shown above is a modern interpretation made in Spain and worked in tent stitch using authentic motifs and vegetable dyes.*

**Needlepoint carpet**
*This needlepoint carpet comes from Portugal and was made in the eighteenth century. It is worked in crossed stitches on a form of double canvas in traditional motifs.*

# Carpet motifs

Numerous different motifs are used in Oriental carpets: some are symbolic, others are derived from natural forms. They have been developed over hundreds of years and provide a source for inspiration when making new designs. They can be used as backgrounds or borders or in the actual style of existing carpets.

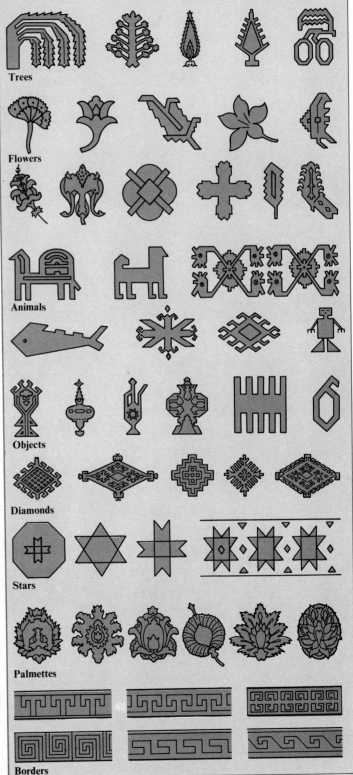

Trees

Flowers

Animals

Objects

Diamonds

Stars

Palmettes

Borders

# Needlepoint projects

These two designs are worked in bold colours using simple needlepoint stitches. Charts and instructions for them both are given on page 352.

All the items shown here (below and right) have been worked by contemporary artists and can be made using the needlepoint techniques described in the preceding pages. Charts showing the stitches and instructions explaining how each of the articles can be made appear as follows: the beaded book cover on page 352; the pin cushion on page 353; the purse on page 355; and the belt on page 354.

**Book cover**

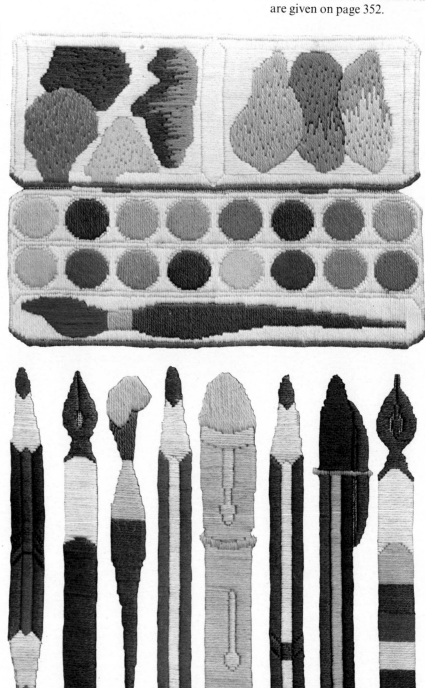

**Purse**

**Pin cushion**

**Belt**

# *Making a bookmark*

The bookmark below measures about 6in. by 1⅞in. (15cm by 4.7cm) and is backed with a piece of leather.

### *Making the bookmark*

Use single-mesh canvas with 24 threads per in. (2.5cm). Mark out the dimensions of the bookmark, leaving ½in. (1.3cm) extra all around, and work to the pattern illustrated below, using seven different colours of stranded cotton. When complete, turn back the hems, mitre the corners (see page 360) and stitch down. Cut out a piece of thin leather to the same size and stick to the back of the work.

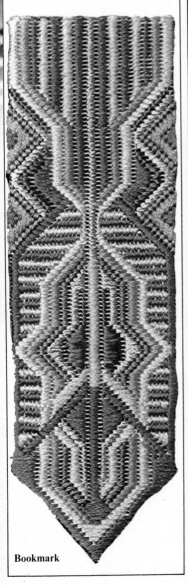

**Bookmark**

***Picture of cow***
Embroidered grass and flowers set off the needlepointed cow and background in this small picture project. Brightly coloured stranded cotton is used for both types of stitches. The instructions are on page 353.

# *Project instructions*

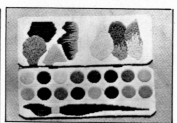

## Book cover

An attractive book cover can be made with a piece of needlepoint decorated with beads and sequins. The book cover shown here measures about 6in. by 4½in. (15cm by 11.5cm).

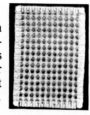

### Materials

You will need a piece of single canvas measuring at least 8in. by 7in. (20.5cm by 18cm); five different coloured skeins of stranded silk; some thick card; and some satin-like fabric.

### Making the book cover

Mark out the design on the canvas and work over it in graduated upright Gobelin stitches following the pattern from the chart given below. Finish off with beads between the large rust-coloured circles and sequins around the border. When complete, cut out three pieces of thick card: two 6in. by 4½in. (15cm by 11.5cm) and one 6in. by ⅝in. (15cm by 1.5cm). Choose some suitable satin fabric for the inside of the cover and cut out four pieces each measuring 7in. by 7½in. (17.3cm by 19cm). Place two of the pieces together and machine stitch along three edges. Turn right side out, fold back 2in. (5cm) and stitch up the sides to form a flap. Slip a piece of card inside and stitch down the raw edge. Repeat with the other two pieces of fabric. Cover the small strip of card with fabric and hand sew it to the other larger pieces so that it forms the spine. Then hem the needlepoint and slip stitch it onto the front. Finally, insert the book.

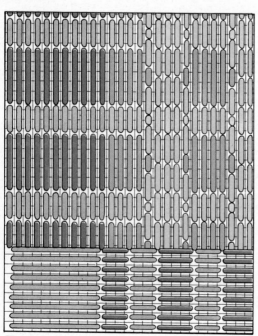

The stitch chart shows bottom left-hand corner of the book cover; the rest of the design is a simple repeat p. 376

### Picture of paintbox

This design is worked in four needlepoint stitches: graduated upright Gobelin stitch worked vertically (1) and horizontally (2); graduated Gobelin filling stitch worked vertically (3) and horizontally (4). It measures 14in. by 12in. (35cm by 30cm) and is worked in tapestry wools in the colours shown on page 350.

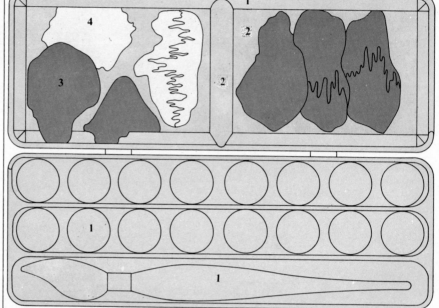

### Picture of pens and pencils

This design is worked in two different needlepoint stitches: graduated upright Gobelin stitch worked vertically (1) and horizontally (2). It measures 14in. by 12in. (35cm by 30cm) and is worked in tapestry wools. Trace the design onto single canvas using the method given on pages 316–317. For the colours, see page 350.

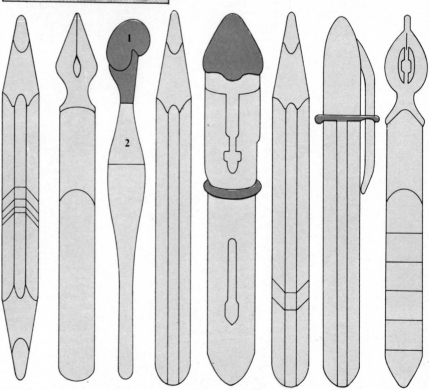

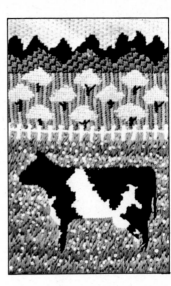

## Pin cushion

This simple pin cushion measures about 3in. by 3in. by 1½in. (7.5cm by 7.5cm by 3.8cm). It is made by attaching a small piece of needlepoint onto the top of a padded linen cushion.

### Materials

You will need a piece of single canvas measuring at least 6in. (15cm) square; six different coloured skeins of embroidery silk; some linen material; a plastic bag; and some fine sawdust.

### Making the pin cushion

Mark out the design of the needlepoint on the canvas, leaving an unworked area on each side for the hems. Work over the canvas in graduated upright Gobelin stitches according to the chart given below, making certain that your embroidery yarns completely cover the canvas threads. Fill a small plastic bag with fine sawdust and pack it in tightly until it measures about 3in. (7.5cm) square. Secure the opening of the bag with some adhesive tape. Cut out two pieces of linen, one about 4in. (10cm) square and one about 13in. by 2½in. (33cm by 6.3cm). Turn in the hems and tack the strip of material around the sides of the square to form a three-dimensional "box" shape. Machine stitch over the tacking stitches and then unpick them. Turn the "box" right side out and place the bag of sawdust inside. Cut out another piece of linen about 4in. (10cm) square and place it on top of the bag of sawdust. Turn in the edges and sew it into position. You should now have a firmly padded cushion. Finally, slip stitch the needlepoint down onto the top, stretching it into shape as you go.

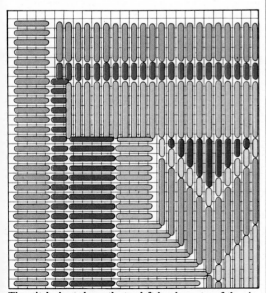

**The stitch chart shows the top left-hand quarter of the pin cushion; the rest of the design is a mirror-image repeat**

## Picture of cow

The finished picture measures about 6¼in. by 4¼in. (15.5cm by 10.5cm). It is worked on single canvas with 18 holes per in. (2.5cm) in stranded cottons. The stitches are shown right.

### Key to stitch chart

1 Tent stitch
2 Gobelin stitch
3 Diagonal stitch
4 Diagonal Gobelin filling stitch
5 Gobelin filling stitch
6 Graduated encroaching Gobelin stitch
7 French knots

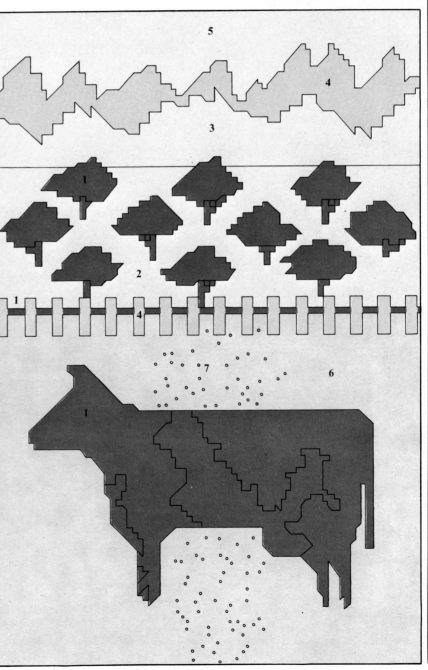

# Needlepoint belt

This decorative needlepoint belt is worked in graduated upright Gobelin stitches which follow a simple repeated chevron pattern (see page 350).

### Materials

You will need a strip of single-mesh canvas 40in. by 4in. (101.5cm by 10cm). It should be of fine gauge – about 24 threads per in. (48 per 5cm). You will also need a piece of suitably coloured linen backing and a piece of iron-on fabric, both the same size as the canvas. The needlepoint is worked in six different colours and you will need 26yds (24m) of stranded cotton for each colour. Finish off the belt with a flat rectangular buckle.

### Working the needlepoint stitches

Mark out the dimensions of the belt on the canvas – the length will vary according to your needs but the width should be 1½in. (3.8cm). Begin at the buckle end of the belt and follow the repeated pattern as indicated in the chart below. It is a good idea to use six blunt-ended tapestry needles, each threaded with one of the different colours. When finished, the belt must be blocked into shape (see blocking and setting, page 356).

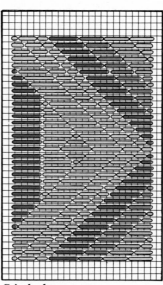

**Stitch chart**
*This basic pattern is repeated along the length of the belt.*

## Backing the belt

Before it can be worn, the finished belt must be lined with iron-on fabric and then backed with linen. This will make it stronger and help to protect it against wear and tear.

### How to back the belt

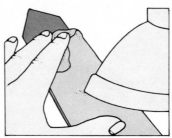

**1** *Lay the belt face down on a flat surface and press the iron-on fabric onto the back of the needlepoint. This will help to strengthen the work and guarantee that it stays flat.*

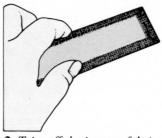

**2** *Trim off the iron-on fabric, cutting it as close to the stitching as possible. Now trim off the unworked canvas all the way around the edges of the belt to within about ¼in. (6mm) of the stitching. Fold back turnings and glue down.*

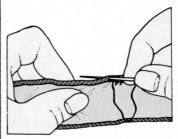

**3** *Cut out a piece of linen backing exactly ¼in. (6mm) larger all around than the belt. Turn in the hem and slip stitch the backing onto the back of the belt as shown.*

## Attaching the buckle

It is essential to choose a flat rectangular-shaped buckle which has a central bar the same width as the belt. The buckle is covered with needlepoint and attached with fabric.

### How to attach the buckle

**1** *Lay the buckle on a small piece of canvas and trace around the outline. Work over the shape of the buckle with needlepoint stitches in a colour and pattern to match the belt.*

**2** *When finished, cut around the shape leaving about ¼in. (6mm) extra around each edge. Using some strong glue, attach the needlepoint to the buckle. Turn the unworked edges to the back and stick them down firmly.*

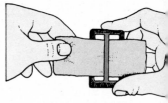

**3** *Attach the covered buckle to the belt by looping a piece of the backing fabric around its central bar, turning in the hems, stitching up the sides and sewing onto back of belt.*

# Needlepoint purse

This small quilted evening purse is made from a simple pattern and is decorated by attaching a rectangle of needlepoint onto the front flap. The checquered needlepoint design given here is worked in graduated upright Gobelin stitches (see page 350).

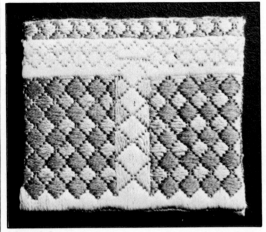

### Materials

For the needlepoint, you will need a piece of single-mesh canvas, 24 threads per in. (48 per 5cm), measuring about 6in. by 5¾in. (15cm by14·5cm) and five skeins of different coloured stranded cotton. For the purse, you will need a strip of satin fabric measuring 4¼in. by 14¼in. (10.6cm by 36.2cm) and cotton wadding measuring 5½in. by 3¼in. (14cm by 8.1cm).

## Working the needlepoint stitches

Mark out the shape of the needlepoint on the canvas, leaving an unworked edge on each side. The front of the purse should measure 3¼in. by 2¾in. (8.1cm by 7cm). Work the needlepoint stitches according to the chart below. As with the belt, and indeed with all needlepoint projects of this kind, use a separate needle for each colour so that you do not have to keep rethreading yarns. If, when you have completed the work, you find that it has become badly distorted, block and set it into shape (see page 356). Finally, trim the unworked edges of canvas to about ½in. (1.3cm) on each side.

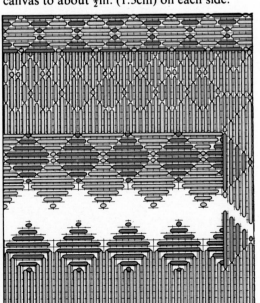

**Stitch chart**.
The chart shows how the stitches are worked on the left-hand half of the purse. The right-hand side is a mirror image. For the colours, see the illustration on page 350.

The purse itself is best made in a satin-like fabric. It can be padded and quilted using some cotton wadding. The rectangle of needlepoint forms the flap and is attached last.

### How to make the purse

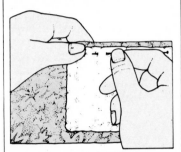

**1** *Take your strip of satin fabric and the piece of cotton wadding. Pin the cotton wadding to the wrong side of the fabric at one end as shown. This will form the padding for the finished purse.*

**2** *To obtain the quilted effect, mark diagonal quilting lines with chalk on the right side of the fabric above the section to which the cotton wadding is pinned. Using a fine, sharp needle, stitch along the chalk lines with either running or back stitch.*

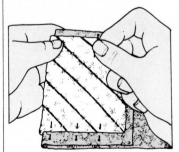

**3** *Fold right sides of the quilted section together so that there is exactly half of the cotton wadding showing on both sides. Pin in place.*

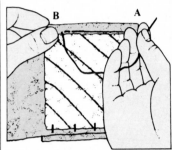

**4** *Leaving ½in. (1.3cm) seam allowance, stitch from the fold (A) along one edge of the cotton wadding to within ½in. (1.3cm) of the end of the fabric (B). Repeat for the other side, then trim off the seam allowance to ¼in. (6mm). Measure 2½in. (6.5cm) in from the seam line (B). Mark it as a fold line (C).*

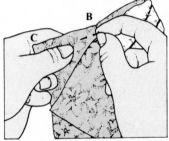

**5** *Double the fabric back on itself, right sides together, along the fold line (C). Leaving a seam allowance of ⅝in. (1.5cm), pin and then stitch along both sides from B to C. Trim the seam allowance to ¼in. (6mm).*

**6** *Turn the purse right side out and fit the lining inside. Attach the needlepoint to the final rectangle of fabric by turning in the canvas hems and the fabric hems and slip stitching the two together along the sides. Finish off with a popper.*

# Blocking

*Blocking* is the term given to smoothing the finished needlepoint or stretching it into shape. It is essential to take care over this since the final look of the work will depend on it being the correct shape and having an even finish. If a cardboard template is cut out using the original pattern or design, then the shape of the work can be checked against the template as it is stretched. Needlepoint is blocked face downwards unless it has been worked in looped stitches, in which case it is blocked face upwards to prevent the stitches from being squashed.

If the blocking is done correctly the needlepoint should not need ironing. However, should it be necessary, use a cool iron pressed lightly on to the work and lifted up and down, not rubbed across the surface, to ensure that the stitches are not flattened during the process.

### Preparing the work

The first thing to do is to make sure that there are no stitches missing from the finished needlepoint. This is done by holding the work up to the light. If daylight shows through, there is a missing stitch and it should be inserted at this stage. If the needlepoint has become dirty while being worked, it should be cleaned now before it is blocked. Detailed instructions for cleaning needlepoint are given on page 361.

### How to block

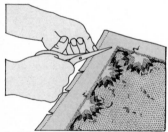

**1** *Place the needlepoint face downwards on a soft board which has been covered with polythene. If the canvas edge has a selvedge, cut a few nicks in it so it will stretch evenly.*

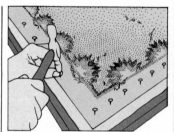

**3** *Ease work into the correct shape and insert more tacks lightly at 1in. (2.5cm) intervals around the edges, working from the centres towards the corners on all sides.*

**2** *Hammer a single tack lightly into the board at the top in the centre of the unworked area of canvas. Stretch the work gently, ensure that all the canvas threads are at right angles to each other, and tack at the centre bottom. Place 2 more tacks at the centre of the other 2 sides so that the needlepoint is firmly stretched.*

**4** *Work slowly and thoroughly, either measuring the needlepoint or checking its shape with the template, and adjusting the position of the tacks where necessary. Sponge lightly with cold water over areas which need a lot of stretching. When the work is finally in the correct shape, hammer in the tacks slightly more securely.*

# Setting

Once the needlepoint has been stretched into its correct shape, it must be set while still nailed down. In most cases, this can be done using water alone. However, if the piece is very badly distorted, it may have to be treated with a solution of starch.

### Setting with water

Sponge the back of work lightly with cold water. Simply leave it to dry at room temperature and out of direct sunlight. The drying process can take up to a week and it is important not to remove the work from the board until it is bone dry or you may find that it will become distorted again.

### Setting with starch

Make up a mild solution of starch. Sponge the solution lightly on to the back of the work and leave it to dry as above.

# Joining

If you have worked your needlepoint in several sections, block each piece separately before joining them together. A crewel needle and button thread are suitable for joining most pieces of needlepoint, but for heavy work it is better to use carpet thread. Pieces of work can be joined either on the straight or on the diagonal: the first method is the easier to work, but the second, if done well, is the more effective for joining the corners of additional needlepoint borders.

### How to join on the straight

**1** *Fold back the unworked area of canvas on the edge of one piece of needlepoint. Lay it face upwards on top of the unworked area of the other piece, matching up the pattern and placing it as near as possible to the needlepoint stitches. Pin together and then tack in position. Remove the pins.*

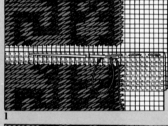

**2** *Slip stitch along the join, making sure that a stitch is made into each mesh of the canvas. Pull tight without puckering the canvas. Remove the tacking stitches.*

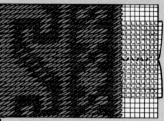

**3** *Work over the seam and any part of the canvas which may show. Use matching needlepoint stitches in the correct pattern and colour sequence and hold the folds of unworked canvas away from the back of the work so as not to stitch through a double thickness.*

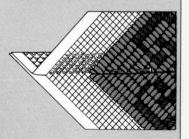

### How to join on the diagonal

*Lay the pieces on a flat surface, with the unworked canvas folded back, so that the diagonal edges meet to form a mitred corner. Join in the same way as above, taking great care to work into each mesh and to match up the pattern exactly.*

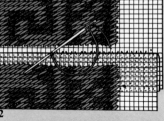

# *Mounting*

There are three ways of mounting a piece of needlepoint: on a stretcher; on a piece of hardboard covered with fabric; or directly on to hardboard.

Do not mount on to cardboard, since it contains acid which may damage the work and it retains moisture which could cause the work to rot. If you are going on to set the work in an overlapping frame once it has been mounted, make sure that the mount is slightly larger than the finished needlepoint otherwise some of the stitches will be obscured by the frame.

**Stretcher mount**
The illustration shows a needlepoint picture mounted on a square wooden stretcher. It is seen from the back.

## Mounting on a stretcher

This is by far the quickest and the easiest method of mounting a piece of finished needlepoint, although it is not the best method for permanent mounting. Since both sides of the work will remain exposed to the air, it will not be damp- or dust-proof; there is a possibility that the wooden stretcher may warp; and the tacks might rust and spoil the needlepoint by discolouring it.

### How to mount on a stretcher

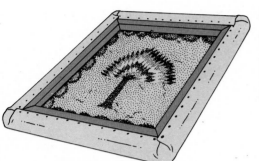

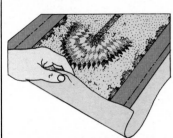

*1 Lay the needlepoint face downwards and place the wooden stretcher in position on top. Fold the unworked areas to the back of the stretcher.*

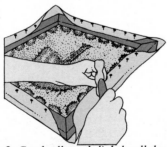

*3 Gradually tack lightly all the way around the sides, from the centres to the corners, checking as you go that the needlepoint is evenly stretched.*

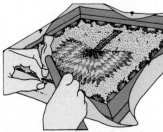

*2 Insert a tack lightly in the middle of each side, making sure that the canvas threads are at right angles to each other.*

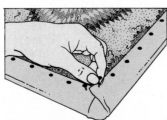

*4 Mitre the corners on to the stretcher with a triangular fold. When in position, hammer the tacks down firmly.*

## Mounting on hardboard

There are two methods of mounting needlepoint on to hardboard: it can either be stitched on to fabric which has first been secured to a board; or it can be stretched over uncovered hardboard and laced at the back. The first method takes longer but is particularly good for mounting fine work and small, shaped pieces. In both cases, use a piece of hardboard the same size as the needlepoint or, if you are going on to set it in an overlapping frame afterwards, a piece slightly larger than the design.

### How to mount on covered hardboard

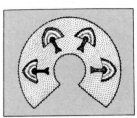

*1 Cut out a piece of fine linen or any fine natural-fibre fabric 3in. (7.5cm) larger all around than the hardboard. Stretch it tightly over the hardboard and secure it at the back with tape or glue. Place it under weights for 24 hours to ensure that the surface is smooth.*

*2 Place the work face upwards on to the covered surface, stretch it evenly and, when it is in the correct shape, pin it down. Then stitch it on to the fabric with a sewing needle or a curved needle and a strong but fine thread, using an overcasting or herringbone stitch.*

### How to mount directly on to hardboard

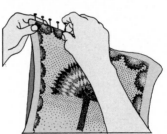

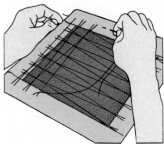

*1 Lay the work face upwards over the hardboard. Fold back 2 unworked sides of canvas and pin in the correct position on the edges of the hardboard.*

*3 Remove the pins, knot the thread at the starting point and tighten the lacing as shown so that the needlepoint is firmly stretched.*

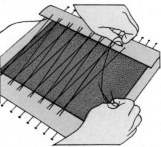

*2 Starting at the top left, sew the 2 sides together with long interlacing stitches. Pull the thread through from the starting point as you go.*

*4 Fold the unworked top and bottom edges of canvas to the back, turning the corners over in a simple square, and lace them together in the same way.*

# Framing

# Lining

Once you have mounted your work, framing it will not only display it at its best but will also protect it from dirt and from damage. Either make your own frame or buy one ready-made.

If you are going to cover the needlepoint with glass, it is important that the glass does not touch the work. If it does the stitches will become flattened. To avoid this, narrow strips of wood, mitred at the edges, are placed in each corner of the frame between the glass and the needlepoint. The strips can either be cut very small so that they do not show when the frame is finished, or they can be left partly exposed and then decorated by either painting or gilding them.

All needlepoint tapestry hangings must be lined before they are hung to give them extra strength and support. The linings must be made in a lighter fabric than the needlepoint or they will hang heavily and distort the work. Use a silk or fine cotton lining for needlepoint worked in silk thread, and brown holland for wool and cotton work. Before you attach a lining, wash the fabric at least once to prevent it shrinking later.

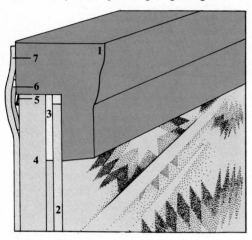

**Section through needlepoint mounted in an overlapping frame**

1 Wooden frame
2 Glass
3 Small strip of wood
4 Needlepoint mounted over a stretcher
5 Panel pin
6 Adhesive tape
7 Brown paper

***How to line a needlepoint tapestry hanging***

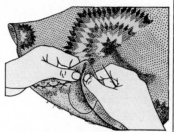 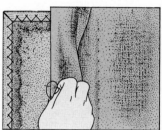

**1** *Turn the unworked areas of canvas to the back and stitch down with herringbone stitch, mitering the corners as shown.*

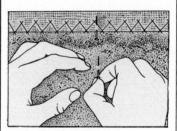

**2** *Lay the clean needlepoint face down on a flat surface. Mark the middle of the work by inserting a line of pins from top to bottom.*

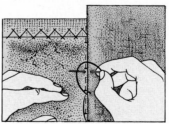

**3** *Cut out a piece of fabric for the lining, somewhat larger than the needlepoint tapestry. Lay it over the work so that the edges overlap. Fold the lining back on itself to the right along the vertical line of pins. Stitch the lining to the needlepoint along this line, starting 4in. (10cm) from the bottom and working up almost to the top. Use a sewing needle and button thread and work in locking stitch. Remove the pins.*

***How to frame the work with an overlapping frame***

 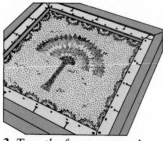

**1** *If necessary, set the small strips of wood in position in each corner of the frame. Then drop the mounted work face downwards into the frame so that the strips separate the needlepoint from the glass.*

**3** *Turn the frame over and check that the needlepoint is in the correct position. When it is, insert a few more pins at regular intervals around the sides to hold the work in place.*

**2** *Secure the work in place by nailing a panel pin or fine nail into the centre of each side of the frame.*

**4** *Seal the edges with adhesive tape to prevent dust from getting in. Then finish off by sticking a sheet of brown paper over the back of the frame.*

**4** *Spread the lining over the needlepoint. Then fold it back on itself to the right again, this time along a line several inches to the left of the row you have just stitched. Sew along the new fold as before so that the lining is slack enough not to pull or drag the tapestry.*

**5** *Continue folding and stitching to the edge of the needlepoint. Then go back and repeat the process on the right-hand side of the centre. When complete, work across in similarly spaced horizontal rows of stitches.*

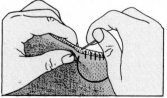

**6** *Turn in the sides and the top of the lining and slip stitch them to the canvas. Allow the lining to settle for a couple of days, adjust it if it is distorting the needlepoint anywhere, and then turn up the hem and slip stitch it into place.*

# Hanging needlepoint tapestries

When the tapestry has been lined it is ready to be hung. Do not hang in direct sunlight as this will cause the colours to fade. There are several different methods of hanging tapestries.

## Wooden strip and Velcro attachment

This method is particularly good for tapestries designed to cover a complete wall space. *Velcro* is a soft, pliable fabric with a hairy, hooked surface much like that of a burr or teasel.

### How to hang with the wooden strip and Velcro attachment

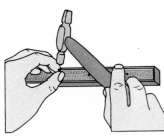

**1** *Cut out a wooden strip to the same width as the needlepoint tapestry. Secure a strip of Velcro to one side of the wood by nailing it on with upholstery tacks.*

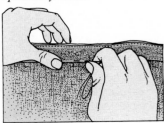

**2** *Sew a second strip of Velcro along the top edge of the lining. Stitch along both edges of the strip as shown.*

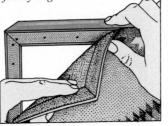

**3** *Screw the wood to the wall, and attach the tapestry to it by pressing the 2 strips of Velcro firmly together.*

**4** *If the tapestry is large and heavy make a wooden frame and screw it to the wall. Then attach Velcro to all 4 sides of tapestry and frame so that the weight is distributed evenly.*

## Curtain ring attachment

This method is very easy to do and simply involves the needlepoint tapestry being hung by curtain rings from a row of hooks screwed into the wall.

### How to hang with the curtain ring attachment

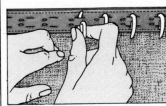

**1** *Either stitch curtain hooks at regular intervals along the top edge of the lining, or sew on a strip of standard heading tape and then slip the curtain hooks through it as shown.*

**2** *Screw hooks into the wall at the same intervals, after first drilling holes and inserting rawlplugs if necessary. Hang the tapestry by suspending the curtain hooks from them.*

## Sleeve attachment

This method involves hanging the tapestry from a rod slipped through a sleeve at the back of the lining. It is sometimes easier to machine stitch the sleeve on to the lining before the lining is sewn on to the tapestry; this will also give it extra strength. If the tapestry needs to be weighted further, then either place another rod in a sleeve at the bottom or attach some curtain weights at regular intervals.

### How to hang with the sleeve attachment

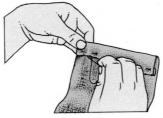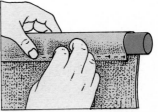

**1** *Use a rod about 4in. (10cm) longer than the width of the tapestry and a piece of the lining fabric or some webbing for the sleeve. Cut out a strip of fabric slightly longer than the width of the tapestry, and turn in each end and hem.*

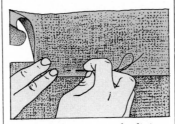

**2** *Stitch the strip to the lining about ¼in. (6mm) from the top edge of the tapestry.*

**3** *Place the rod in position, fold the strip over it and pin it along the bottom to form the sleeve. Remove the rod and stitch along the line of pins.*

**4** *Place the rod in the sleeve and suspend the tapestry from the wall either by ropes securely knotted to the ends of the rod or by chains fixed to hooks at either end.*

## Tabbed sleeve attachment

In this method, small pieces of material are sewn to the lining to make a tabbed sleeve. Because the tabs will show, they must be worked in a harmonizing fabric.

### How to hang with the tabbed sleeve attachment

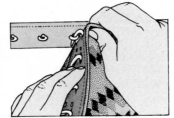

**1** *Cut out small pieces of fabric, gauging their length to the circumference of the rod. Fold them over and stitch to the top edge of the lining, overlapping the ends as shown.*

**2** *When you have sewn several of these tabs to the lining at regular intervals, insert the rod and hang the needlepoint in the same way as above.*

## Mitering corners

# Assembling and finishing

When the unworked sides of canvas are folded over and stitched to the back of the needlepoint, the corners will be neater if they are mitered. There are two alternative methods of doing this.

### How to make a triangular mitre

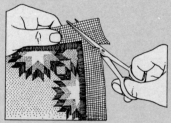

**1** *Trim off any selvedge. Cut a triangle off each corner to within about ¼in. (6mm) of the worked area.*

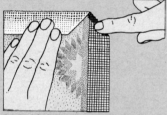

**2** *Fold the sides to the back of the work and stitch them down with herringbone stitch.*

### How to make a square mitre

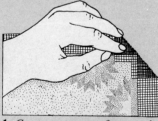

**1** *Cut out a square from each corner to within about ¼in. (6mm) of the worked area. Make triangular folds as shown.*

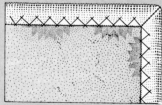

**2** *Fold the sides to the back and stitch them down as above.*

### Chairs

The simplest kind of chair to cover is the type with a drop-in seat pad. The needlepoint should be worked to the specific template for the chair and blocked before it is attached to the seat.

It is much more difficult to make a cover for dining chairs with stand-out seats or for armchairs. In both these cases, it is advisable to have your template designed by an upholsterer and then, when you have finished the needlepoint, to have him cover the chair.

### How to cover a drop-in seat

**1** *Remove the seat pad from the chair, and lay the needlepoint over it in position.*

**2** *Turn the pad over and nail the work to the frame, starting with 1 tack in the centre of each side. Make sure that the work is stretched evenly and is positioned correctly, then nail all the way around. If necessary, make a small cut at the corners with a very sharp knife to reduce any bulkiness.*

**3** *Finally, nail on a piece of suitable backing material, such as black calico, to the underside of the seat pad.*

### Clothes and accessories

Items such as clothes, bags and spectacle cases are usually made up from more than one piece of needlepoint. Each piece must be blocked and set separately before it is joined to the others. Pieces of lining fabric cut out using templates of the original design are joined together as well. The lining and needlepoint are laid right sides together, pinned and back stitched along the outside edges, leaving a space along one side. The turnings are trimmed to about ½in. (1.3cm), the work is turned right side out, and the final space is slip stitched together.

### Carpets and rugs

If the needlepoint tapestry is going to be made into a carpet or rug, it must first be blocked and set in the usual way and then finished and lined as follows before it can be used.

### How to finish and line carpets and rugs

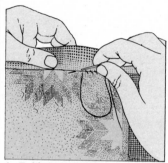

**1** *Fold the unworked canvas on each edge of the tapestry to the back of the work. Either slip stitch the edges down or secure them by facing them with 4 strips of webbing, 1 for each side of the work, using a sewing needle and strong carpet thread.*

**2** *Cut out a piece of thin carpet felt the same size as the work. Pin it in position to the back of the tapestry, making sure that it is straight, and slip stitch it into place all the way around the edge.*

**3** *Turn the tapestry face upwards again, and finish off by working matching needlepoint stitches along the edges to cover any exposed canvas threads.*

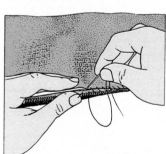

**4** *Finally, cut out a piece of hessian which is 2in. (5cm) larger all around than the carpet or rug. Spread out the needlepoint with the felt lining face upwards and make certain that it is straight and even. Turn in the extra 2in. (5cm) of the hessian and slip stitch it on to the back of the work.*

# Storing and cleaning

### Storing
Needlepoint is best stored away from the light. If the work cannot be laid flat, it should be rolled up. In the case of both lined and unlined pieces, this is done by rolling the work face outwards around a polythene-covered cylinder of newspapers, paper or cardboard. If this is done carefully it will guarantee that the surface of the stitching is kept smooth. Wrap in acid-free tissue paper or clean muslin.

### Cleaning
Routine cleaning of hangings, carpets and rugs can be done with a vacuum cleaner, although if the tapestry is old and fragile a nylon filament can be placed over the needlepoint. This process should remove the loose dust and dirt. However, if the needlepoint is so dirty that it needs to be washed, bear the following things in mind: first, if the work is very old, valuable and fragile, do not attempt to wash it yourself; second, if you do decide to wash it yourself, always check that the colours are fast by dabbing a small piece of dampened cotton wool onto the stitches at the back or the edge of the needlepoint; and third, it is always a good idea to make a cardboard template of the tapestry with which you can check the shape after washing.

*How to wash needlepoint tapestries*

**1** *Pour some softened warm water into a flat-bottomed bath, sink or dish which is large enough for the needlepoint to lie completely flat. Add a mild, soap-based washing agent and mix it up so that it forms suds. Do not use detergents of any kind.*

**2** *Lower the needlepoint face downwards into the water and allow it to become thoroughly saturated. Press a sponge gently up and down the back of the work, without rubbing or squeezing, and change the water if it becomes dirty.*

**3** *Let the dirty water drain away and rinse the work thoroughly in softened warm water. Repeat the process until there are no more soap suds. Finally, give the work one last rinse in distilled water or in water that has been boiled and then allowed to cool.*

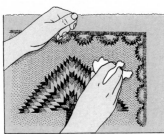

**4** *Drain away the last of the water, carefully remove the needlepoint and then lay it face upwards on a flat surface. Blot away the excess moisture with a small, clean piece of sponge and then block the work into shape using the template as a guide. Allow the needlepoint tapestry to dry thoroughly.*

# Repairing

If the needlepoint stitches have become frayed or have worn away, and the canvas threads are still in good condition, then unpick the damaged stitches and work new ones in their place. It is important to match carefully the type, the thickness and the colour of the threads.

If the needlepoint tapestry is only slightly damaged, it can probably be repaired by replacing any broken canvas threads and then covering over with matching needlepoint stitches. The method for doing this is outlined below. Larger holes can be repaired in the same way, although it is advisable to mount the damaged tapestry on a frame and support it beneath with a fabric such as linen scrim. You will find that repairing needlepoint mounted on a frame is not only easier but that, if the tension has been set correctly, it also retains its shape and should not require re-blocking when finished.

If the hole is too big to be replaced by darned threads, then it can be repaired by stitching a patch onto the back of the work, using exactly the same gauge canvas as the original and matching up the canvas threads in each direction. It is a method to avoid if possible, however, since the outline of the patch, where the two thicknesses of canvas overlap, will create a ridge in the surface of the needlepoint.

*How to replace broken canvas threads*

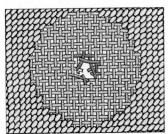

**1** *Carefully clear away about ½in. (1.3cm) all around the broken threads. Always cut away stitches from the back.*

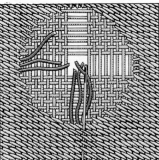

**2** *Push the ends of the broken canvas threads through to the back. Secure these ends by folding them back on themselves and weaving them into the backs of the remaining stitches as shown. This is best done by inserting a needle into the stitches first and then threading the loose ends through when it is in place.*

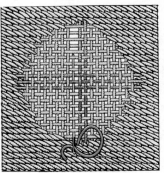

**3** *Thread the needle with either fine crochet cotton, some thin macramé string or a canvas thread unravelled from the unworked mesh at the edges of the work. Knot one end and insert the needle through the surface of the work about 3in. (7.5cm) below the broken area. Take it up to the hole and darn in the new threads so that they replace the missing ones exactly.*

**4** *Work matching needlepoint stitches over the repaired area. Cut away the knot from the surface of the work.*

# 6
# PATCHWORK

*including Quilting and Appliqué*

# History of patchwork

Patchwork, appliqué and quilting are all closely allied forms of needlework, and are often used together. They are probably amongst the oldest forms of stitching and were originally invented out of necessity rather than for adornment purposes. It was not till later on that they were extended for decorative uses. All started in ancient times: how long ago it is hard to determine, for although samples of each have been found, such as the patchworked and appliquéd funeral tent made for the Egyptian Queen Isi-em-Kebs in the late ninth century BC; an appliquéd felt saddle cover found in southern Siberia from the fifth or fourth century BC; and a Scytho-Siberian quilted carpet from the first century BC (the borders of which are decorated with appliquéd symbolic forms filled with quilted line designs worked in back stitch), the sophistication of these works hints at an earlier birth.

### Origins
Patchwork is made from fragments of fabric pieced together to make a whole. It was originally invented as a means either of making something serviceable out of scraps of scarce and precious fabric or of making an extended fabric by joining several lengths of narrow hand-woven widths together. Instances of this early patchwork can be seen on the sails of the Nile boats depicted on the wall paintings at Thebes.

Appliqué, which is made by stitching patches of fabric onto an existing ground fabric, was invented in order to make worn or holed fabrics good by covering them with patches. It later became more decorative when the patches were cut into shapes and their edges covered with couching. Appliqué, like patchwork, appears to have been used on the sails of the ancient Egyptian Nile boats, possibly as a form of identification, or as a mark of ownership. Later still, other forms of appliqué were made, such as inlay and reverse, and these were used only to make decorative designs and pictures.

Quilting, which was originally worked by stitching two layers of fabric together with a soft wadding in between, was introduced as the most practical way of obtaining warmth. Later, different and purely decorative forms of quilting were invented in which only two layers of fabric with no soft filling in between were stitched together with the stitching forming decorative patterns and giving a bubbled effect to the surface of the fabrics.

### Early development
All three crafts were developed and used for hundreds of years in North Africa, Turkestan, Persia, Syria, India and China but it was not until the eleventh century that they were developed for decorative purposes in Europe. Patchwork and appliqué came back from Palestine with the returning Crusaders who had been dazzled by the brightly patched and figured banners and the richly felt-appliquéd tents of the defeated Saracens. Both crafts were taken up and used in Europe from then onwards for all types of flags, banners, wall hangings, tablecloths, bed furnishings and church vestments. From then onwards to the present day appliqué has been considered the best technique for putting across visual ideas in needlework.

Practical forms of quilting had been used in Europe from a far earlier date. The Romans used it to make cushions, mattresses and primitive bedcoverings. It was also used as a protective covering by soldiers though the date of its protective use is hard to determine. But certainly Crusaders had come across it on a quilted shirts worn by the Saracens. From the eleventh century onwards quilted coats were worn by soldiers, and were used right up to the nineteenth century when they were worn by the early American soldiers in their battles with the Indians and were still considered sufficient protection against the arrows.

A decorative form of quilting was developed in Italy in the thirteenth century. This was known as *padded quilting* or *trapunto quilting* and, although the technique had long been used in Persia, India and Turkestan, it was given prominence by the fine designs worked on it in Italy. This form of quilting is made with only two layers of fabric stitched together and the design outlined in running stitches. Areas of the design are emphasized by stuffing them from the back to raise them. An early and perfect example of this type of work is the Sicilian quilt which shows episodes from the early life of Tristram. Trapunto quilting was also taken up and used in England for white bedcoverings, known as *counterpanes*, a derivation of quilt point or counter point. Yet another type of purely decorative quilting also came into prominence at this time. This was known as *cord quilting* or *Italian quilting* and though it too had long been used in Syria and Persia, where it was often worked on fine white linen with the design outlined in yellow stitching and the cording pattern made with different-coloured cords, it became fashionable and was worked into intricate designs by both the Portuguese and the Italians. Cord quilting is worked with only two layers of fabric and the design is stitched in channel lines which are later piped with cotton cords to raise them.

### Fifteenth and sixteenth centuries
In the fifteenth and sixteenth centuries appliqué was greatly used for all types of household furnishings, being a quick and easy way to achieve an effective and colourful embroidery. It was often used on velvet grounds with rich satin or gold leather patches cut into shapes and often couched with gold cords. Coats of arms, emblems, lettering, birds, animals and flowers were stitched onto the design with the designs becoming more and more complex by adding combinations of quilting and embroidery techniques to them. Chintz motifs, too, were cut out and applied with buttonhole stitches and this style became known as *broderie Perse*. Patchwork techniques also were used in an extremely sophisticated form at this time in India with the famous Kashmir shawls being woven into separate shapes and then sewn together like a jigsaw puzzle. So complicated were these patched shawls that it took six men three years to complete one and it is no wonder that when they were exported to England they sold at £700 each, which in those days was an enormous sum.

### Seventeenth century to present day
In the seventeenth century quilting was taken up and used on clothes of all types: suits, doublets, breeches and later petticoats. This popularity for quilted fashion continued to the eighteenth century when it gradually declined though quilted petticoats were still seen in country communities right up to the nineteenth century. On bedspreads, quilting was greatly used both on plain cream silk and in conjunction with embroidery. Its popularity continued until the middle of the eighteenth century when the textile industry developed new woven and printed fabric techniques. The novelty of these new fabrics became the fashion and patches and scraps of them were taken and pieced or applied together to make coverlets and wall hangings to echo the design of the brightly printed fabrics. This had the effect of overshadowing the much more delicate patterning of the quilting stitches. By the nineteenth century these too fell out of favour in Europe with the introduction of machine-made blankets. From then up to recent times there has been little interest in patchwork, quilting and appliqué in Europe though there was a brief burst of enthusiasm for a combination of patchwork and quilting in the middle of the nineteenth century. This type of work was known as *gathered patchwork* and was made of two layers of patches

stitched together, stuffed and then quilted. When a number of these stuffed and quilted patches had been made they were stitched together to make bedcovers.

However, quilting, patchwork and appliqué continued elsewhere and reached its height in quite another part of the world between 1775 and 1885. The techniques for all three had been taken to America by the early Dutch and English settlers and there they flourished into the most famous of all American Folk Art. It is easy to understand why this should have happened: times were extremely hard for the early pioneers, supplies were limited and these homely crafts thrived out of sheer necessity and also as a means of entertainment with social gatherings being arranged around quilting parties. These patched, appliquéd and quilted masterpieces were worked at first without designs, with the minimum of fancy fabrics and more often than not in the wilds of unexplored territory, an arrow's flight away from the native Indians. Later, different types of patchwork and appliquéd designs were developed and given such names as *barn raising,* *star of Bethlehem,* *rose of Sharon,* *log cabin* and many more besides. They were made for many different types of occasions and included wedding quilts for the bridal chamber, friendship quilts given as souvenirs with each block designed and signed by a different person and freedom quilts which were presented to young men at their coming of age.

By the twentieth century the hardships of the past were over: supplies were readily available, machines were capable of making blankets and eiderdowns and the need to create something beautiful out of very little or to make something warm and protective from the materials at hand no longer had any urgency. Indeed, all types of handwork were laid aside in favour of the new machine-made goods. This state of affairs continued right up to the middle of this century when a need to create something of one's own was once more felt. This, coupled with the fact that the mass-produced goods lacked originality, resulted in a resurgence of interest in many of the old crafts. Today, quilting, appliqué and patchwork are once more in demand and the following pages deal with all aspects of these three simple crafts which were born through need and developed over the years into some of the most beautiful examples of needlework, often without the sophisticated aids of patterns.

**Nineteenth-century appliqué quilt**
This quilt is worked in three colours of cotton in the prairie rose design.

**Late nineteenth-century patchwork**
This printed cotton patchwork is worked in the Star of Bethlehem pattern.

**Early nineteenth-century patchwork**
This English patchwork quilt is mainly worked in triangles and hexagons, with bird motifs.

**Early eighteenth-century English cover, worked in cord-quilted linen**

# Introduction to patchwork

Patchwork is made by joining many small patches of fabric together to make a complete mosaic pattern. The accuracy of joining, the choice of fabrics and the placing of the patches together are the three contributing factors which will make the finished work a thing of beauty. If these three factors are ignored then the result may well be an undistinguished mélange of scraps. All the patches should be accurately cut and folded so that they form clean, well-defined shapes which will fit together accurately to create the geometric patterns. The colour juxtapositions can either be contrasting or subtly shaded. It is more usual to use contrasts of dark and pale, alternating so that each patch is clearly defined. However, many pale patches can be assembled in blocks or medallions and then surrounded by a dark ground of patches or strips. Alternatively dark blocks can be assembled together against light ground patches. Equally, pale patches can be grouped together and gradually more intense colours can be added, row after row or circle after circle, to create sunblasts of colour. In the old days the patches were cut from the carefully collected pieces in the scrap bag which consisted of pieces left over from dressmaking or salvaged from clothes long worn out. Today, few people keep a scrap bag so it is more usual to make a patchwork from bought fabrics, which means that the exact colour scheme of a patchwork can be thought out and the fabrics bought in the colours to fit the scheme. Prints, too, need careful selection: small prints are ideal as they are proportionately right for the size of the patches, whereas large ones will overflow the patches and become meaningless.

## Fabrics

Any fabrics can be pieced together as long as they can be cut and sewn into but the ideal choices are those which are washable and finely woven so they give crisp fold lines, such as cottons – particularly fine cotton shirtings and prints which are washable and come in a vast number of different colours and prints. Fine linens, fine wools, silks and velvets are also good for patchworks but silks need a little more care in working as they are apt to be marked by pins and tacking threads: to avoid this the tacking should be done through the backing paper alone and not through the silk. Leather, too, is ideal for patchwork as it does not fray and therefore can be worked unfolded. Generally, patchworks should be made up in similar types of fabric so as to avoid washing difficulties later. It is also essential to make sure that all the pieces used are colour-fast: a test can easily be done before working by washing a scrap of fabric in warm water and leaving it to soak; if the colour comes off do not use it. The fabrics should all be of the same weight so that they will lie smoothly when joined. If this is not observed, and a mixture of heavy and lightweight fabrics are used together, the lighter ones will "bubble up", giving the patchwork an uneven surface. Similarly, fabrics of the same strength should be used together, otherwise the stronger ones will pull the weaker ones out of shape. However, if it is absolutely necessary to use different fabrics together these faults can be remedied by backing the weaker or lighter fabrics with a balancing fabric so that they are brought up to the same weight or strength as the others. Finally, if widely differing fabrics are used in the same piece they should all have the same washability or else be worked into a piece which will not need to be washed frequently but can be cleaned instead.

# Types of fabric

A selection of fabrics suitable for patchwork is illustrated below. This includes cottons, linens and silks. The fabrics best avoided, especially by the beginner, are: synthetics (which, due to their crease-resistant quality, will not fold); loose-woven fabrics, such as coarse linens, canvas and hessians which fray too easily; and stretch fabrics, such as jersey, which will not hold the shape of the geometric patches.

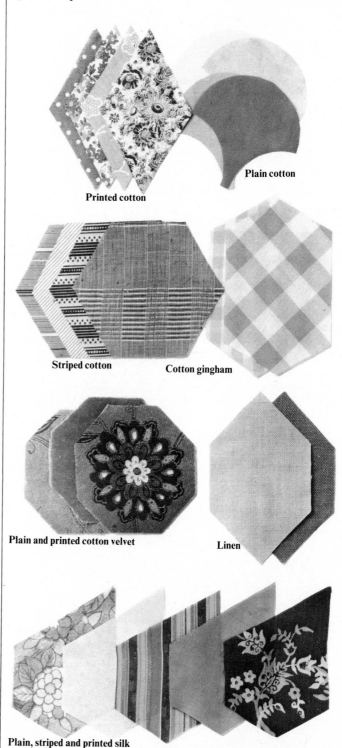

**Printed cotton**

**Plain cotton**

**Striped cotton**

**Cotton gingham**

**Plain and printed cotton velvet**

**Linen**

**Plain, striped and printed silk**

# *Templates*

Templates are the pattern shapes used to cut out the fabric and paper patches. They can either be made at home or bought at most needlework departments. The bought templates, made of plastic or metal, are usually sold in sets comprising a paper and a fabric template. Window templates are also available, which can be used for both, or simply to line up the print. Templates can also be found in sets of complementary shapes. A selection of generally available templates is shown below. (For making your own templates, see page 372.

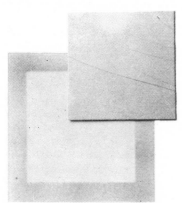

**Set of square templates for fabric and paper patches**

**Set of diamond templates for fabric and paper patches**

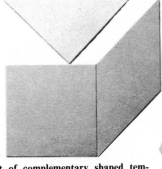

**Set of complementary shaped templates for paper patches**

**Set of hexagon templates for fabric and paper patches**

**Hexagon window template for both fabric and paper patches**

**Set of triangle templates for fabric and paper patches**

# *Implements*

When making patchwork it is important to use the correct type of paper for backing the fabric patches to ensure that these are given a smooth even surface and crisp fold lines. Although any stiff paper can be used, brown wrapping paper or paper from old letters and envelopes is ideal. (Thin card may even be used when working with heavy fabrics.) Other implements required are: adhesive tape, two pairs of sharp scissors (one for cutting fabric and the other for cutting paper – an artist's scalpel may be used instead of the latter), pins, fine needles and thread, a pencil and templates (see right).

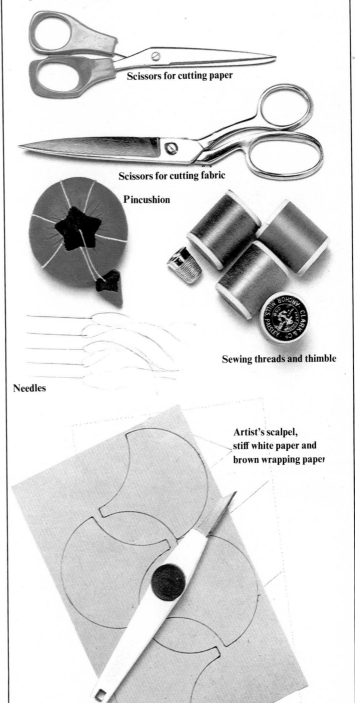

**Scissors for cutting paper**

**Scissors for cutting fabric**

**Pincushion**

**Sewing threads and thimble**

**Needles**

**Artist's scalpel, stiff white paper and brown wrapping paper**

# Templates

These are the pattern shapes which are used to cut both the fabric patches and the paper backings, and can either be made (see page 376) or bought. In the old days, before machine-made templates were readily available, all templates were made at home and cut from cardboard, hardboard, tin, zinc, pewter, copper, brass and even silver. The original patchworks, of course, did not require any templates at all, as these were made from random cut shapes which were stitched together in random formation rather like crazy paving stones – hence the name "crazy patchwork".

Later, people realized that it was easier to sew straight lines together, so squares and rectangles were used. These were cut from home-made templates which in turn had been cut from handy straight-edged articles, such as books (the family Bible being especially popular for the purpose). The resulting squares and rectangles were then halved and quartered, according to the size of the patches required. Later, even more shapes were introduced – such as triangles, diamonds, hexagons and octagons – all of which were developed from the original squares or rectangles. Finally, the circle was introduced, with templates for this being cut from such homely objects as wine glasses and egg cups. The shapes resulting from the circle template were the scallop, fan and shell (the hexagon and octagon can also be cut from the circle, see pages 380-381). Nowadays, machine-made templates can be bought in many different sizes and shapes (see opposite page). They are usually made of lightweight plastic or metal (which is much better than card as it will not lose its shape so easily when it is traced around repeatedly). Bought templates come in three forms: paper, fabric and window, of which there are two types. All are described below.

### Template for paper backing

This is the exact size of the finished patch, and identical sized paper pieces are cut from it, which are used for backing the patches of fabric. It can also be used for cutting out fabric patches by placing it on top of the fabric and cutting each patch individually, leaving ¼in. (6 mm) extra all around it to allow for the turned-in edges. The pieces of backing paper can also be used as templates themselves (see right).

### Template for fabric patches

This is made ¼in. (6 mm) bigger than the finished patch and is used to cut the fabric only. It is by far the most accurate way of cutting the patches to the correct size.

### Window template

There are two types of window template. One is an empty frame – the outer edge of which is the size of the unfolded fabric patch and the inner edge the size of the folded fabric or the paper backing. This type of window template can be used to cut the fabric by cutting around the outside edge, and the paper by drawing around the inner edge and then cutting. It is also used to frame up printed fabric so that the print on the patch will fall in the desired position. The second type of window template is made of clear plastic with a frosted frame. It is the same size as the unfolded fabric on the outside, and the see-through centre within the frame is the exact size of the folded patch. This type of window template is used for cutting the fabric and framing up the print within the clear area. When using this type you will also need to use the smaller paper template.

# Cutting paper and fabric patches

Although it is not absolutely necessary to use paper backings for the fabric patches it is far better to do so as the paper helps to retain the shape and firmness of the fabric patches and makes the joining together far easier. The paper backings are removed when the patchwork is completed (see pages 372-373).

### How to cut paper backing

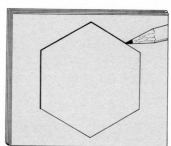

**1** *Fold a piece of paper so that several layers can be cut to shape at the same time, then place the template on the paper and draw around the edges with a pencil as close to the template as possible.*

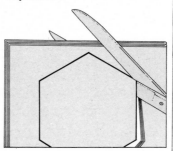

**2** *Cut through the layers of paper with either an artist's scalpel or scissors, making accurate and identical shapes, with the paper beneath.*

### How to cut printed fabric patches

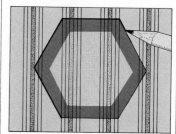

**1** *Place the various pieces of fabric on a flat surface. Then place the window template on top of the fabric and frame the print correctly, making sure that the grain of the fabric always runs in the same direction for each patch. Then pencil around template edges.*

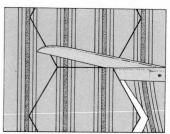

**2** *Cut along marked lines and when finished collect the various colour, print, shape and size groups together.*

## Paper patch templates

If a window or fabric template is not being used, then the paper patches themselves can be used as templates. This is done by placing a cut paper patch on top of the fabric and pinning it down, then cutting the fabric underneath ¼in. (6 mm) larger all around. Make sure that the grain of the fabric runs in the same direction for all the patches. This method is only recommended when using plain fabrics and simple-shaped patchworks.

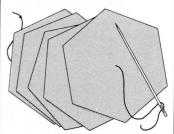

**3** *String the groups together by threading through the patches with a needle and knotted thread. This will make for easy selection when making up.*

### Working with plain fabrics

These are cut with the fabric template in the same way as described above, and do not need framing.

# Backing the patches

After the paper and fabric patches have been cut, the paper backing is then attached to the fabric patches.

### How to attach

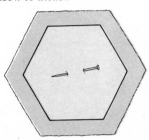

**1** *Lay fabric patches right side down on a flat surface and pin a paper patch to the centre of each, so that the edges of both patches lie parallel.*

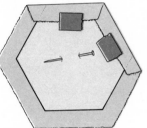

**2** *Fold the edges over one at a time and secure with a small piece of adhesive tape.*

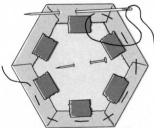

**3** *Then tack around the edges and remove adhesive tape.*

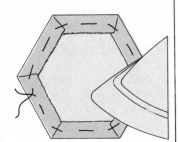

**4** *Press the folds into position with an iron in order to make clean lines. This will greatly help when stitching.*

# Special edge finishes

When attaching the paper backing to the fabric special care will be needed for folding the edges of specific shapes. For example, when working with triangles and diamonds the points must be sharply formed, and circles and curved shapes will need to be tacked around the edges before they are pinned down to the paper in order to make them fit smoothly.

### How to work with diamonds and triangles

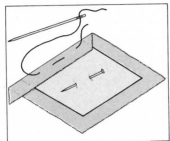

**1** *Pin the paper backing in position and fold and tack first side of diamond (or triangle).*

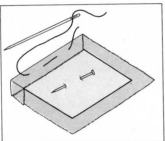

**2** *Then, before folding 2nd side, fold point of first side down on top of 2nd side.*

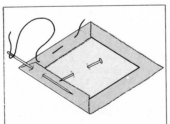

**3** *Fold and tack down 2nd side.*

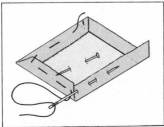

**4** *Fold back 3rd side, repeating the procedure for the point as in Step 2. Then tack down the final side of the patch.*

### How to work with circles and curved shapes

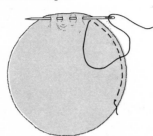

**1** *Work around the circular fabric patch with running stitches placed ⅛in. (3 mm) in from the edge and leave the thread hanging.*

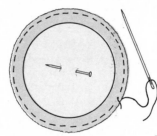

**2** *Pin paper patch to centre of fabric patch.*

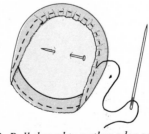

**3** *Pull thread to gather edge so that it folds neatly over the paper patch.*

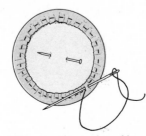

**4** *When circle is gathered knot thread and cut it off.*

# Template shapes

The patches used in patchwork can be made in a vast range of shapes. Below is a selection of template shapes most commonly used. See pages 384-391 for the different patterns which can be achieved.

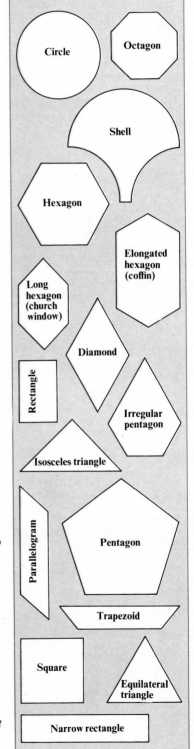

Circle

Octagon

Shell

Hexagon

Elongated hexagon (coffin)

Long hexagon (church window)

Diamond

Rectangle

Irregular pentagon

Isosceles triangle

Parallelogram

Pentagon

Trapezoid

Square

Equilateral triangle

Narrow rectangle

# Traditional patchworks

A careful study of old patchworks is extremely rewarding both as a guide to the placing of the patches and colours, and as a reference to textiles of the past. Indeed one of the ways of dating patchworks is from the textile scraps they contain. When the patchworks were used for quilted bed covers, the quilting stitches were either worked across the surface, ignoring the patched design, or made inside the patches. Sometimes, on plain fabric patchworks, very decorative quilting designs are worked inside the patches and along the borders.

Eighteenth-century English embroidered patchwork of brocades and velvets

Eighteenth-century shell patchwork made in printed fabrics from many parts of the world

Early nineteenth-century four-poster bed cover in East India company cottons

**Nineteenth-century American crazy patchwork**
*Worked in silks with embroidery motifs and edges. The border echoes colour of main design.*

**Mid-nineteenth century English military patchwork quilt**
*Military patchworks were made from scraps of uniforms and were often worked by soldiers.*

**Nineteenth-century American Amish quilted patchwork cover**
*This simple two-colour strip patchwork is quilted with circle and leaf patterns.*

**Nineteenth-century Indian army quilt worked in dyed wool serge**

**Nineteenth-century English quilt worked in printed cottons**

371

# Making templates

Templates, the shapes used to cut out the fabric and paper patches, can either be bought or made. Home-made templates have the advantage that they can be cut to the correct size and shape for any proposed patchwork. They can be made from cardboard, perspex, zinc, aluminium or harder metals such as tin, brass or copper. Cardboard, zinc and aluminium shapes can be cut with strong scissors. Perspex, however, needs a fine hacksaw while tin, brass and copper require metal shears. Home-made templates must be measured accurately and cut precisely so that the edges are straight and the angles correctly formed. If templates are badly cut the resulting patches will not fit together properly and will form an uneven surface.

### Cutting the template shapes

The template shape is first drawn on paper and cut out. The paper pattern is then stuck down to the material being used to make the template, and is carefully cut around. Any of the shapes shown on this and the following three pages can be used and cut in this way.

## Implements

When making templates you will need very sharp pencils, graph paper, a cutting board, and cutting implements as described above. Below are shown the implements needed for making accurate geometric shapes.

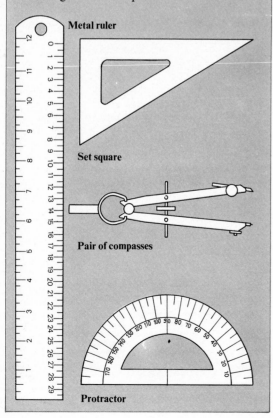

**Metal ruler**

**Set square**

**Pair of compasses**

**Protractor**

# Basic geometric shapes

It is useful to study the shape of geometric templates and their origins, for these all stem from either the square or the circle. An understanding of how these many shapes are related is a great help when planning an original patchwork. Squares, rectangles, triangles and diamond patterns can all be made from the basic square. The following templates have been cut from the same sized original square so that they can be used and fitted together.

### Squares

When making squares, use graph paper to mark out the sides. When this has been done the square can then be divided up in different ways to make smaller squares.

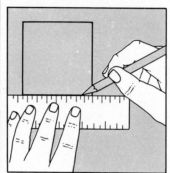

**The basic square**
Count the same number of graph squares on all 4 sides, mark the points and draw connecting lines.

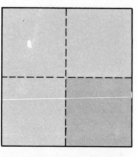

**Four squares**
Divide the square into quarters by drawing a vertical and a horizontal line from the middle of the existing lines.

**Sixteen squares**
Divide the square into quarters and then divide the quarters into quarters.

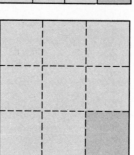

**Nine squares**
Divide the basic square into ninths by drawing 2 horizontal and 2 vertical lines from side to side.

# Rectangles

Rectangles can be made by dividing the basic square with horizontal or vertical lines. Smaller rectangles can be made from the basic rectangle shape, and strips in turn made from these. The latter are particularly useful in log cabin designs (see pages 394–395).

### How to make rectangles

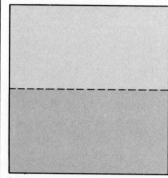

*Take the basic square and divide it in half from the middle of one side to the middle of the other side.*

### How to make small rectangles

*Divide the rectangle in half lengthwise as shown.*

### How to make strips

*Divide the smaller rectangle in half lengthwise.*

# Right-angled triangles

Right-angled triangles can be made by dividing the basic square with a diagonal line. Smaller right-angled triangles are made by halving these.

### How to make 2 right-angled triangles

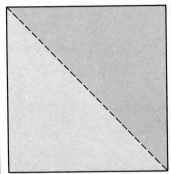

*Divide the basic square in half by drawing one diagonal line from corner to corner.*

### How to make 4 right-angled triangles

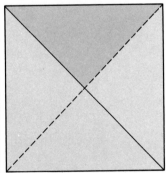

*Divide the basic square into quarters by drawing 2 diagonal lines from corner to corner.*

### How to make 8 right-angled triangles

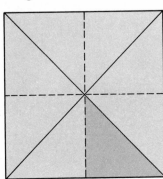

*Divide the basic square in eights with 2 diagonal lines and 1 horizontal and 1 vertical line.*

# Diamonds and triangles

Diamonds (rhomboids) are made from rectangles by drawing diagonal lines from the middle of the sides to the middle of the adjacent sides of the rectangle. Triangles are then automatically formed in the corners of the rectangle. The diamond itself can be divided in half to form either two isosceles or two obtuse-angled triangles. The rectangle and the diamond can be further divided to give several different shaped triangles.

### How to make a diamond and 4 right-angled triangles

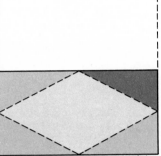

*First make a rectangle which is a half of a square. Then find the centre of all 4 sides of the rectangle and mark these points. Draw diagonals from one point to the next to make the diamond. This also forms the triangles around the perimeter of the diamond.*

### How to make 2 isosceles triangles

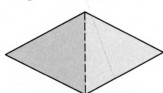

*Divide the diamond in half with a vertical line.*

### How to make 2 obtuse-angled triangles

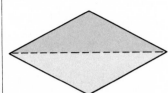

*Make a diamond as described above, and then divide it in half with a horizontal line.*

### How to make 4 right-angled and 2 obtuse-angled triangles

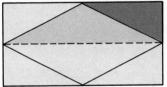

*Make a diamond in a rectangle and then divide it in half with a horizontal line.*

### How to make 8 isosceles and 8 right-angled triangles

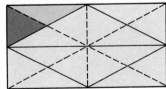

*Continue from the diagram above and make 1 vertical and 2 diagonal lines.*

## Making trapezoids

Trapezoids are formed around a small central square.

### How to make trapezoids
*Mark the basic square in quarters around the side lines. Then draw 2 diagonals from corner to corner. Next mark a square one quarter the size of the original lining it up with the quarter marks and diagonals.*

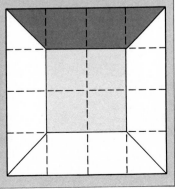

# Parallelograms

Parallelograms can be made from rectangles by drawing parallel diagonals at either end.

### How to make parallelograms

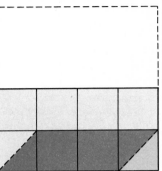

*Make a rectangle from the basic square and divide it in half lengthwise. Then mark it into 8 equal squares and draw diagonals across both of the end squares.*

### How to make wedges from parallelograms

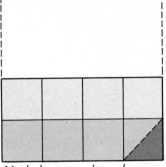

*Mark the rectangle as above and then draw one diagonal across the square at one end.*

### Parallelograms from 2 squares

Parallelograms can also be formed from two squares.

### How to make the parallelograms

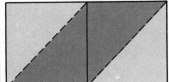

*Mark out two squares side by side and divide them both in half with diagonal lines.*

373

# Log cabin patchworks

When making log cabin designs it is important to make a really sharp difference in tone between the three design elements in each block with the light and dark sides being clearly defined both against each other and the neutral central square (see page 394 for log cabin instructions).

### American Mennonite design

In this design the strips on the dark sides are all kept to the same intensity of tone but the light sides use many different shades and tones of colours. The triangle border pattern uses colours from all three design elements.

**Chart of centre of design, right**

### American pineapple design

The final circuit of each block in the pineapple design shown on the right is finished at the corners with pink triangles so that when the blocks are joined together the triangles form squares. Small prints are effectively used with the same print being worked for a complete circuit to form an additional pattern within the patchwork.

**Single block of patchwork design, right**

American Mennonite log cabin patchwork, 1880

American mid-nineteenth century pineapple patchwork; dark areas are worked with different colours while light areas rely on prints to change the strips

# Decorative borders

The following borders can be used either to edge a plain solid fabric or as a contrast to a completed patchwork. They each form continuous patterns so therefore require a special treatment when the corners are reached. Suggested ways of filling the corners are given below but any block design can be used (see pages 384-391).

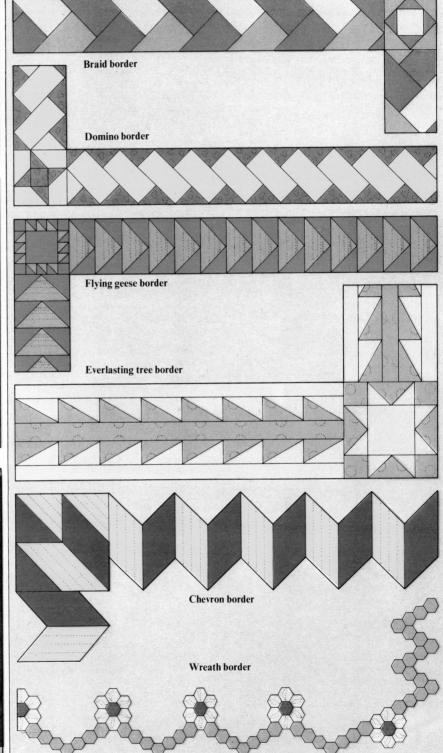

**Braid border**

**Domino border**

**Flying geese border**

**Everlasting tree border**

**Chevron border**

**Wreath border**

**Diagonal log cabin**

**Diagonal log cabin with subtly blended light tones**

**Light and dark squares alternate with light and dark triangles**

# Circles

## Making template shapes based on the circle

The circle is used for circular templates and also for making polygons such as hexagons, pentagons and octagons. In pure patchwork, circular or curved templates are rarely used (with the exception of shells) as the curved outlines are difficult to piece together. However, curved shapes are often used for applying to square patches which are then pieced together.

## Making a circle

Perfect circles are best made with a pair of compasses. Make sure that the paper is held securely and that the pencil end is sharp.

## How to make circles

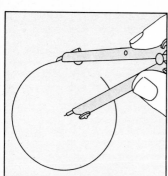

*Place the tip of the pair of compasses on the paper and describe an arc so that the pencil end marks out a full circle.*

## How to make shells

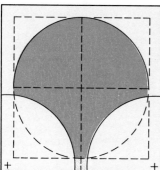

*Draw a circle on graph paper and then draw 2 small arcs below and to either side of it so that they cut into the large circle at the same positions on each side to form the shell.*

# Polygons

These are made by marking the circumference of the circle at equal distances and then drawing connecting lines from point to point. The number of intervals will be determined by the number of sides of the particular polygon. For example, six are needed to make the hexagon. In order to find the length of these intervals the full 360° of the circle is divided by the number of sides of the polygon and the result of this is then halved. The angle from this division is marked in a line from the base of the circle to the circumference and this line gives the measurement for the intervals.

## How to prepare the circle when making polygons

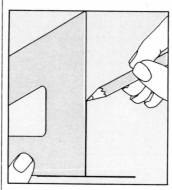

*1 Draw a horizontal line to act as the base line and then, using a set square, erect a perpendicular from it.*

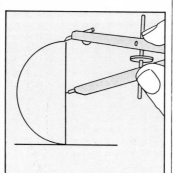

*2 Divide the required width of the shape being made in half in order to calculate the radius of the circle. Then draw a circle using the perpendicular to site the centre of the circle and the horizontal to base it on.*

# Hexagons

To measure the intervals for the six-sided hexagon the 360° of the circle is divided by six. The resulting 60° is then halved, to give an angle of 30°.

## How to mark the intervals

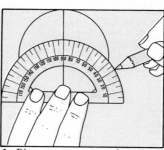

*1 Place protractor on base line with 90° line on perpendicular and mark 30° point.*

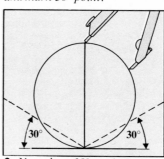

*2 Next draw 30° angle from base of perpendicular to 30° point. With a pair of compasses measure distance between base of perpendicular and point where 30° line intersects circumference. This distance gives the measurement for the intervals. Then, keeping pair of compasses fixed, mark next interval by placing tip on first intersection and marking next with pencil end. Continue in this way until six intervals have been marked.*

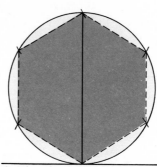

*3 Then draw six connecting lines from point to point to make hexagon.*

# Pentagons

To measure the intervals for the pentagon the 360° circle is divided by five and the resulting 72° is then halved, to give an angle of 36°.

## How to make the pentagon

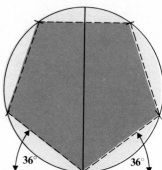

*Place protractor on base line with 90° line on perpendicular and mark 36° point. Next draw the 36° angle from the base line in the same way as for hexagons. Then mark the five intervals using the pair of compasses. Finally draw the five straight connecting lines from point to point to complete the pentagon.*

## Making octagons

To measure the intervals for the octagon the 360° circle is divided by eight and the resulting 45° is then halved, to give an angle of $22\frac{1}{2}°$.

## How to make the octagon

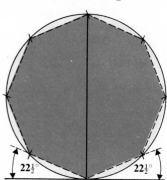

*Draw the $22\frac{1}{2}°$ angle from the base line in the same way as for hexagons. Then mark the eight intervals using the pair of compasses. Finally draw the eight straight connecting lines from point to point to complete the octagon.*

# Shapes from polygons

## Circular shapes

### Making shapes from hexagons

Polygons can be broken down into sections to form other geometric shapes.

#### How to make trapezoids

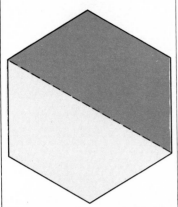

Divide the hexagon in half with one diagonal line.

#### How to make diamonds and equilateral triangles

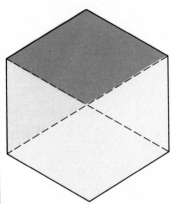

Draw two diagonal lines across the hexagon in each direction.

#### How to make diamonds

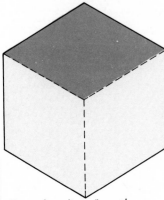

Draw three lines from the centre to alternate angles.

### Making stars from polygons

Polygons can be made into stars by dividing them first into triangles and then doubling the triangles to make diamonds.

#### How to make a six-pointed star from a hexagon

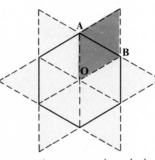

Draw a hexagon and mark the centre 0 and two adjacent angles A and B. Then draw lines 0A and 0B. The measurement of these lines will give the measurement for the other two sides of the diamond. Fix a pair of compasses to this measurement and using A as the centre draw an arc. Then using B as the centre draw a second arc intersecting the first. Draw lines from A and B to the point of intersection. This makes a diamond shape. Six diamonds pieced together in a circle form the stars.

#### How to make an eight-pointed star from an octagon

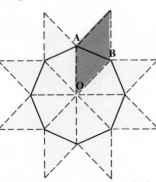

Draw an octagon and mark the centre 0 and two adjacent angles A and B. Draw in lines 0A and 0B. Draw arcs from A and B as above. Then draw lines from A and B to the point of intersection. Eight diamonds pieced together form the star.

As curved outlines are difficult to piece together for a whole patchwork, they are often made in such a way that they can be applied to square patches. These square patches are then sewn together to form the pattern. Simple arcs which form quarter circles are the basis of these circular shapes. But they can be divided and extended to form hearts, flowers and fans.

#### How to make small arcs

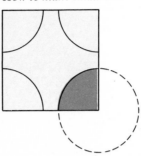

Make a square. Then, using the corner of the square for the centre, mark an arc.

#### How to make large arcs

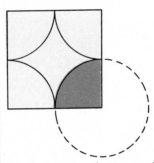

Mark the arc so that it exactly reaches the centre of the sides of the square.

#### How to make heart shapes

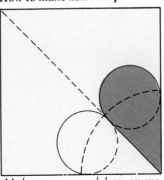

Make a square and draw an arc in the corner. Draw a diagonal line across it. Next, using the circumference of the arc to site the centres, draw two small circles carefully so that the circumference of each touches both the sides of the square and the diagonal line.

#### How to make flower shapes

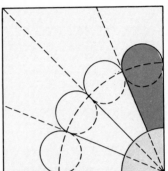

Draw a square and then in the corner of it draw a small arc. Draw a larger arc outside it. Then divide the small arc in half with a diagonal line. Draw one further diagonal on either side of this to divide the halves into quarters. Finally, using the larger arc to centre the circles, draw four small circles between the diagonal lines so that they touch. When four of these shapes are made and joined a flower shape is formed.

#### How to make a fan shape

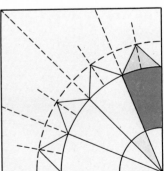

Draw a square and then draw an arc in the corner of it. Draw two larger arcs one outside the other. Next, draw a diagonal line across the square and follow this with two further diagonals to divide the square into four sections. Finally, divide the two arcs in each of these sections in half and draw diagonals to these points to form triangles.

# *Amish quilts*

Amish patchwork quilts are some of the most beautiful examples of the combined techniques of patchwork and quilting ever to be created. They are made by the Amish people, a religious community descended from the Swiss reformists. who came to America in the eighteenth century and settled principally in Ohio, Pennsylvania and Lousiana. They live their lives within a strict religious code, considering any form of adornment or decoration unnecessary and preferring plain and simple living. Their beliefs are reflected in their clothing which is made of plain but brightly coloured linens and cottons. It is from plain materials such as these that their patchworks are assembled into the masterpieces shown here. The quilting designs are worked with the same brilliance so that each pattern tells its own story and is defined on the plain ground.

**Sunshine and shadow, Pennsylvania, early twentieth century**

**Crazy patchwork, Lancaster County, Pennsylvania 1920**

**Star within a star, Iowa, 1935**

**Log cabin, Lancaster County, Pennsylvania, early twentieth century**

# Planning patchwork designs

When making an original patchwork it is best to plan it out on graph paper first. Cut the paper to the proposed measurement and then mark in the design with coloured pencils or inks. When buying the fabric for a patchwork the quantity required can be roughly estimated for this depends on the number, size and colouring of the patches. However, as a rough guide, take the measurements of the design as though it were going to be made in one piece and then add an extra yard for seams. The total is then divided proportionally according to the colours being used. On the following pages many different patterns are shown together with their templates.

## *The principles of patchwork design*

The colour, tone, print, texture and shape of the patches make the patchwork patterns, but simple patchworks can be made in two colours, cut into strips and joined together. More complicated patchworks can be composed of many colours and several different shapes and sizes of patches. The patchworks illustrated, left, give combinations of shapes, colours and textures without the use of prints.

**Barn raising variations**
This intricate looking pattern is simply formed with light and dark squares and right-angled triangles.

**Dutch tile pattern**
The pattern, left, is composed of octagons, squares and trapezoids in four tones.

**Crazy stars, Indiana, 1929**
*The above patchwork is made from diamond and square templates with some diamond patches pieced together in stripes. The border is quilted in shells, the ground in lozenges.*

**Barn raising**
*Barn raising designs were named after the community event of building a neighbour's barn.*

# *Joining the fabric patches*

When all the fabric patches have been prepared they are then joined together with small, evenly spaced overcasting stitches, securing the thread at the beginning and end with a back stitch. A fine needle and thread should be used to make the stitches as invisible as possible. The joining can be done in three ways: in rows, sections – or *blocks* as they are known – (see below) or in one continuous piece (see pages 382–383). The method used will depend on the type of patchwork made (specific instructions for more complex patterns are given on pages 392–395), and may vary slightly according to the shapes being joined (see right).

## *Joining in rows*

This is the best method to use for all-over patterns such as line and diagonal designs. It is worked by placing two patches face to face and oversewing neatly and closely along one edge, catching the fold of the fabric on each patch. Try to avoid sewing the paper patches underneath as it will then be easier to remove the paper when the joining has been completed. It also means that the paper patches can be used again for other patchworks. When the required number of rows has been made, join these together in the same way, placing first and second rows face to face and oversewing all the side edges together. Continue until the patchwork is complete.

## *Joining in blocks*

Blocks are made by joining a collection of patches together to form individual design units. The finished blocks are then joined together. Joining in blocks is the best method to use for medallion and section designs. Block joining is also easier if the work is to be carried around as the small blocks are easy to pick up and work from any point.

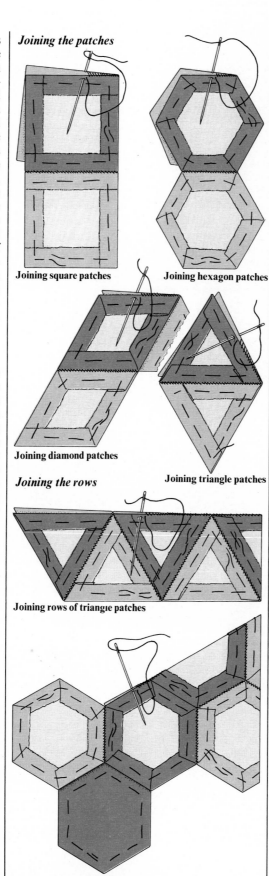

*Joining the patches*

Joining square patches

Joining hexagon patches

Joining diamond patches

*Joining the rows*

Joining triangle patches

Joining rows of triangle patches

Joining rows of hexagon patches

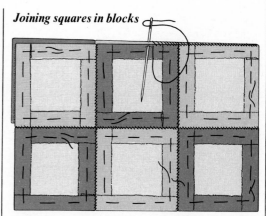

*Joining squares in blocks*

*Nine-square patch blocks are joined in three rows of three squares. Completed blocks are then joined together.*

*Joining hexagons in blocks*

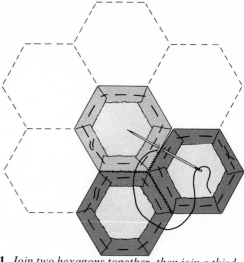

**1** *Join two hexagons together, then join a third hexagon to the sides of the first two.*

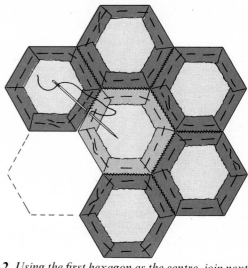

**2** *Using the first hexagon as the centre, join next four hexagons together in same way.*

# Machine joining

Although small patches need to be joined by hand, larger patches with sides over 1½in. (3.8cm) long can easily be joined by machine. This is especially true of large squares and rectangles which may not require a paper backing but can be machine stitched directly together, side seam to side seam, row by row, in the usual way.

### How to join squares and rectangles

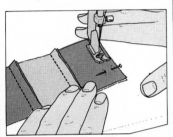

*1  Start by pinning the patches together and joining them in rows (as shown).*

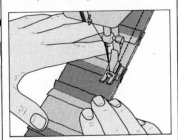

*2  When the rows are complete open up the seams and iron them flat. Then machine stitch the rows together.*

### How to join other shapes

*When the patches have been backed with paper and tacked in the usual way place them edge to edge right side up and machine stitch over them, using the swing needle attachment on your machine.*

# Finishing

When all the patches have been joined the patchwork must then be finished off and lined (see right). The finishing off process is carried out by pressing the whole patchwork into shape on a padded surface. If the patchwork has been worked in blocks, however, it may often be helpful to treat each section or block in this way before the final joining, to prevent the work from becoming too distorted.

### How to work

*1  Place the patchwork right side down on a padded surface. Stretch it out and pin it at the centre of each side and then at the corners. Then continue to pin along the sides until it is the required shape.*

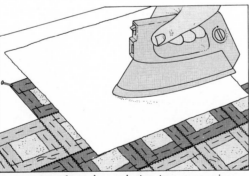

*2  Iron it under a damp cloth using a warm iron and leave it until it is dry.*

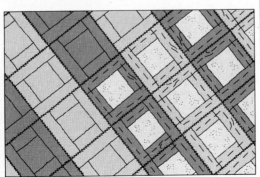

*3  Then remove the pins and the tacking thread. Take out the paper patches. If these have not been damaged they can be used again on other patchworks.*

# Lining

When the patchwork is finished it needs to be lined to both strengthen and neaten it. Lining alone is only suitable for small patchworks: larger items, such as bedcoverings, should be tied or quilted (see pages 396–405 for quilting) to keep the patchwork shape stabilized and to add warmth. The lining fabric must be appropriate to the materials which make up the patchwork and be firm enough to hold the top securely but not so heavy that it will pull away.

### How to work

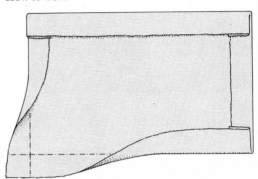

*1  Cut the lining fabric to the size of the patchwork, allowing an extra ½in. (1.3cm) seam allowance all round. Then lay it right side down on a flat surface. Fold in the seam allowance and press flat.*

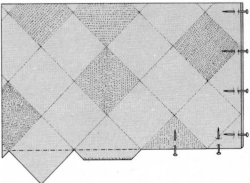

*2  Place the patchwork on top of the lining right side up so that the wrong side of it and the lining are together. Fold in edges of patchwork and press flat.*

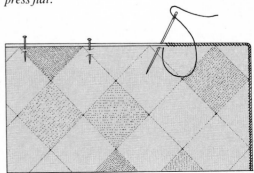

*3  Tack the two together. Then slip stitch the lining and patchwork together along all seams.*

# Joining from the centre outwards

Patchworks worked in this way can be designed on graph paper first so that the colouring will fall in the correct positions with the centre usually being the focal point.

**How to work**

**1** *Make a star or medallion using either hexagons, triangles or diamond patches and contrasting the colours as desired.*

**2** *Increase outwards, completing one circuit before starting on the next. Sunbursts are made using six- or eight-pointed stars at the centre of the design.*

**3** *Continue until the patchwork is required size. It can be left as a hexagon by placing diamond shapes sideways or cutting them in half.*

**Detail of tumbling blocks patchwork**

# Patterns in the round

**Hexagonal patchwork**
The hexagon shape can be made into a square by filling in the corners in pattern sequence. Note the way the colours are worked and the way the prints are placed to form rosettes and garlands.

**Late eighteenth-century English tumbling blocks patchwork in silks**
*The tumbling blocks are made with light, dark and neutral shades and the colour sequence is changed to make dark steps for the hexagon outline, light steps for the section divisions and light stars in each of the sections.*

## Colours, tones, textures and prints in patchwork

It is important to make a clear definition between each patch so that the pattern is effective. This definition is done by a change of colour, tone, texture or print. Patchworks can be made in tones of one colour throughout with the definition being made by a change of texture or print. Colours can be graded from patch to patch to give shaded effects. A series of coloured patches can be used in a contrast background to give silhouette shapes.

Printed fabrics can be cut so that the print makes a design: for example, they can be cut with the print in a central position to make a rosette with a single patch. Or diamonds or triangles can be cut so that the main part of the print falls at the angles of the patches so that, when joined together, these printed angles will form patterns on their own. Stripes can be used either to make patterns by positioning them together in different ways or by using broad to narrow stripes for optical effects. Prints, too, can be used to give a sense of distance by using tiny ones at the inside and gradually increasing the size until the biggest ones border the design.

Wedding quilt, English, 1870. The quilting is worked in lines and hearts .

Stars and check pattern, Welsh, 1890. The quilting is worked over the entire surface using matching threads for each patch.

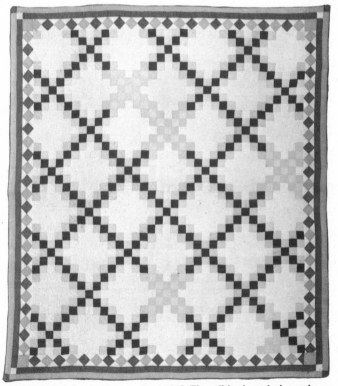

Double Irish chain pattern, American, 1865. The quilting is worked over the surface with white areas stitched in feather rosettes

383

*Squares*

Hit and miss

Checkerboard

Going down stairs

Strip pattern

Castellated pattern

Diagonal checkerboard

Framed squares

Irish chain

Double Irish chain

Diamonds

Burgoyne surrounded

Stairs

Mosaic

Variated mosaic

Circle mosaic

Undulating mosaic

Greek cross

Variation of Greek cross

*Rectangles*

Checks

Brick wall

Zigzag bricks

Turned rectangles

*Rectangles and squares*

Up and down

Roman squares

Flying squares

Domino

Children's delight

Patience corner

Puss in the corner

**Right-angled triangles**

Shark's teeth

Windmill

Pueblo triangles

Flying geese

River

Broken dishes

Dutchman's puzzle

Cotton reel

Windblown

Birds in air

Flock

Dutch windmill

High noon

Railroad crossing

Hourglass

**Equilateral triangles**

Triangles in rows

Triangles in diamond formation

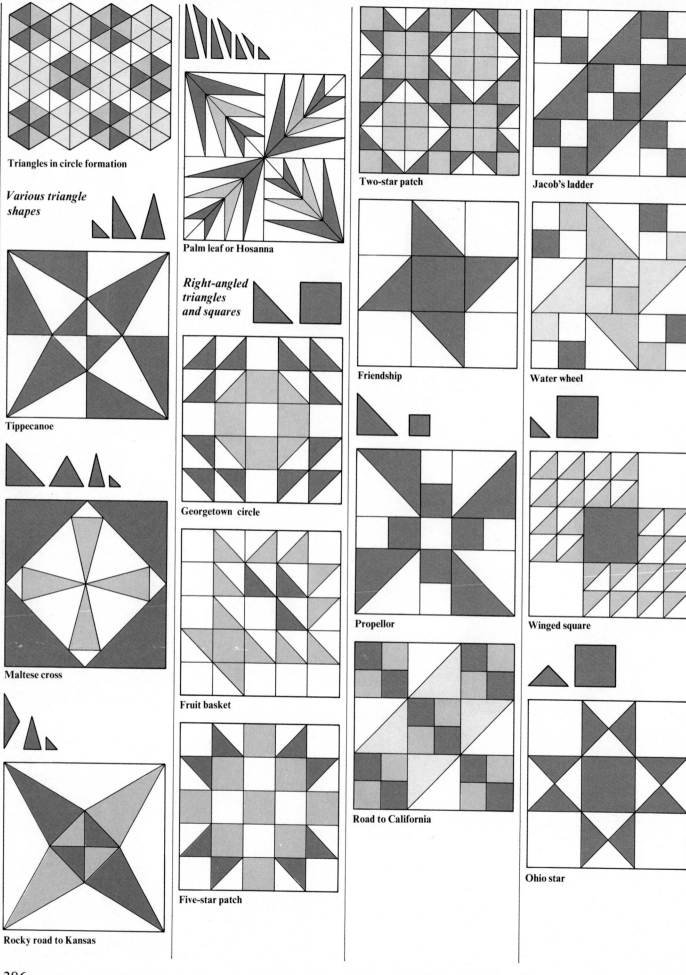

Triangles in circle formation

*Various triangle shapes*

Tippecanoe

Maltese cross

Rocky road to Kansas

Palm leaf or Hosanna

*Right-angled triangles and squares*

Georgetown circle

Fruit basket

Five-star patch

Two-star patch

Friendship

Propellor

Road to California

Jacob's ladder

Water wheel

Winged square

Ohio star

Variable star

Paving pattern

Window pane

Milky way

Prairie Queen

Double sawtooth

Blocks and stars

Paving stones

Paved block

Crows' cross

Eight-pointed star

Kansas trouble

Hovering hawks

Crosses and losses

Georgetown star

Northumberland star

Star block

Shark's tooth square

Rising star

*Triangles and rectangles*

Greek cross block

Red cross

Double T

Eight hands round

*Other triangle shapes and squares*

Flying Dutchman

Goose in the pond

Handy Andy

Lemoyne star

Tall pine tree

Sherman's march

Boxed square

54–40 or fight

*Triangles, rectangles and squares*

Weather vane

Rolling stone

Cross and crown

Grandmother's choice

Domino squares

**Diamonds**

Sunburst

Diamond star

Toy blocks

Star and blocks

**Diamonds, triangles and squares**

Eastern star

Storm at sea

**Parallelograms, squares and triangles**

Boxes

Clover

Pieced star

Spinning star

Road to Oklahoma

Columns

Ribbons

**Trapezoids, squares and triangles**

Susannah

389

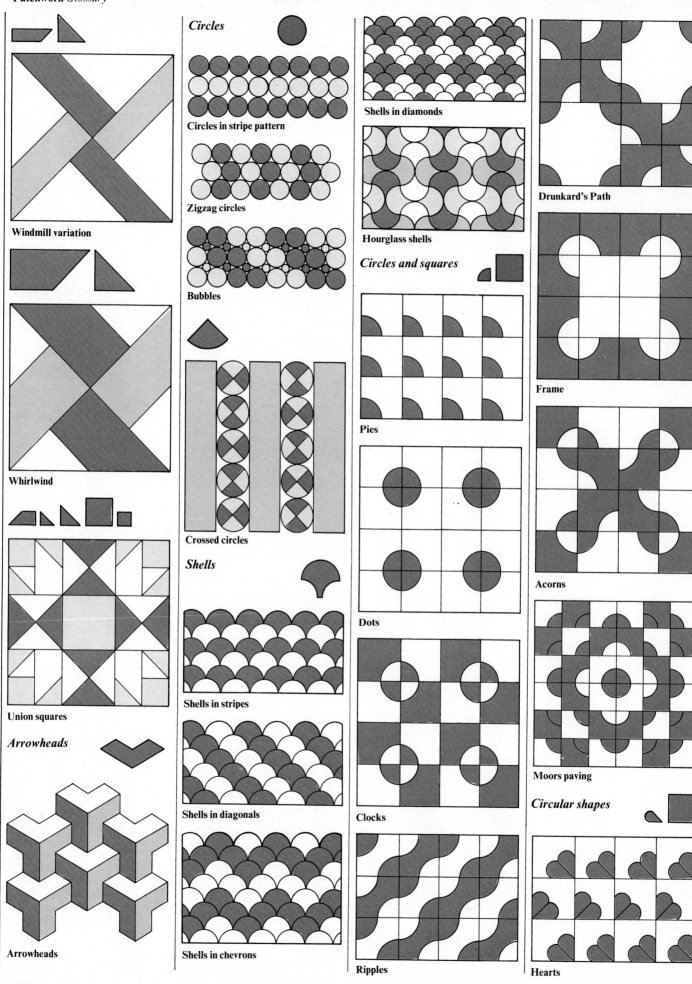

Windmill variation

Whirlwind

Union squares

*Arrowheads*

Arrowheads

*Circles*

Circles in stripe pattern

Zigzag circles

Bubbles

Crossed circles

*Shells*

Shells in stripes

Shells in diagonals

Shells in chevrons

Shells in diamonds

Hourglass shells

*Circles and squares*

Pies

Dots

Clocks

Ripples

Drunkard's Path

Frame

Acorns

Moors paving

*Circular shapes*

Hearts

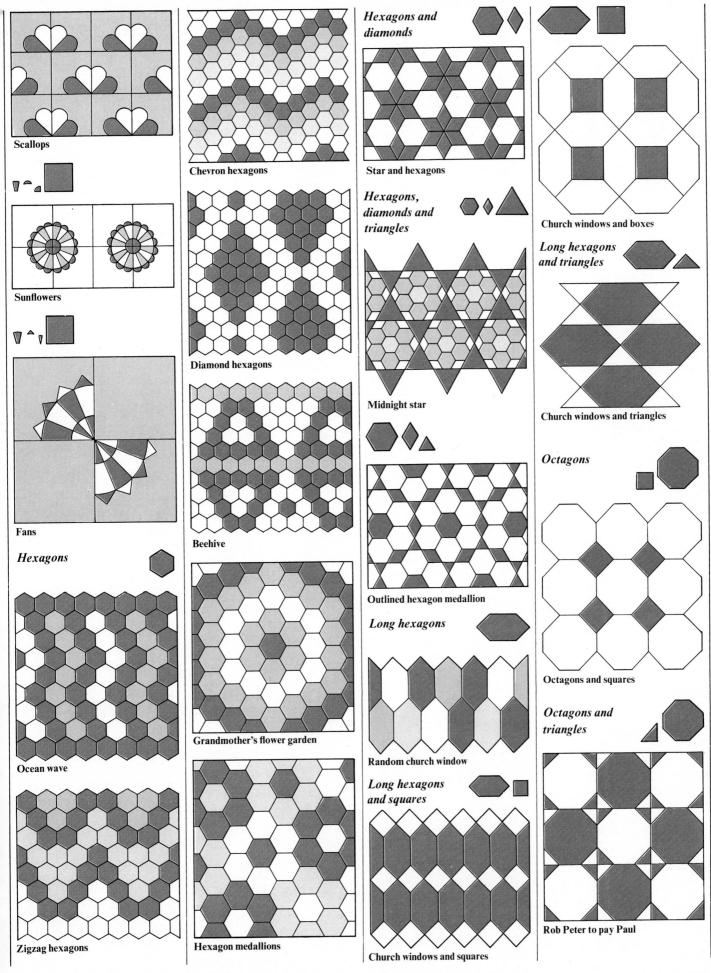

Scallops

Sunflowers

Fans

*Hexagons*

Ocean wave

Zigzag hexagons

Chevron hexagons

Diamond hexagons

Beehive

Grandmother's flower garden

Hexagon medallions

*Hexagons and diamonds*

Star and hexagons

*Hexagons, diamonds and triangles*

Midnight star

Outlined hexagon medallion

*Long hexagons*

Random church window

*Long hexagons and squares*

Church windows and squares

Church windows and boxes

*Long hexagons and triangles*

Church windows and triangles

*Octagons*

Octagons and squares

*Octagons and triangles*

Rob Peter to pay Paul

391

# Border patterns

Patchworks can be finished off quite simply with bound edges in the same way as quilts (see page 401). Bias bound edges are best used when only a narrow border is required or when the edge of the patchwork is curved or scalloped. Plain straight borders are attached in the same way and can be used when nothing more elaborate is required. These are made by cutting straight strips of fabric to the desired lengths and then attaching the first two strips to opposite sides of the patchwork. The second two are then attached to the remaining sides so that they cover the ends of the first two and are finished off by turning in the exposed edges at each end and securing these with a few slip stitches. More decorative borders can be made by working a contrasting patchwork pattern to the depth of the required border and then securing this with running stitches and placing the border face to face with the main patchwork. The simple patchwork borders shown below are all formed in block units so that when a corner is reached one block can be used to fill it. Alternatively a plain or patterned square can be used instead at each corner (see page 375 for further border patterns).

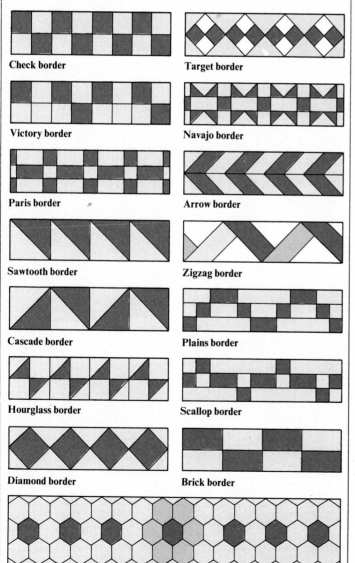

Check border

Target border

Victory border

Navajo border

Paris border

Arrow border

Sawtooth border

Zigzag border

Cascade border

Plains border

Hourglass border

Scallop border

Diamond border

Brick border

Rosette border

# Popular patchwork designs

Yo yo, cathedral window, crazy, shell and log cabin patchworks are all pieced together in different ways from standard patchwork and therefore each needs to be dealt with separately. Yo yo patchwork is made entirely for its decorative merit as it forms an open, lacy pattern and cannot be quilted to make a warm covering. Crazy, shell, log cabin and cathedral window patchworks are joined together so that the patches overlap and consequently they fall between the categories of patchwork and appliqué work.

### Yo yo patchwork
Yo yo patchwork is sometimes known as *openwork patchwork* because of the holes left between the patches when it is worked without a backing fabric. Yo yo patchwork is made by using a circular template of 3in. (7.5cm) to 6 in. (15cm) in diameter to cut the patches. These should first be cut out and arranged in colour groups. After all the patches have been gathered into shape, as described below, they can then be joined together and left. Alternatively they can be stitched down to a backing fabric which will both strengthen the work and fill in the holes.

***How to make yo yo patchwork***
**1** *Turn the fabric in ¼in. (6mm) and work evenly-spaced running stitches ⅛in. (3mm) from edge using a strong thread firmly secured at one end. Hold the patch right side down and begin the sewing with a couple of back stitches. Work running stitch around the edge.*

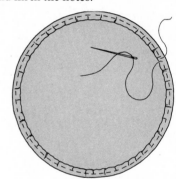

**2** *Then gather the edges up by gently but firmly pulling the thread. Continue pulling until the edges are in the centre and form a bathcap shape. Then secure the gathering thread with a couple of back stitches. Finally, arrange the gathers so that they are all straight and equally distributed around the circle.*

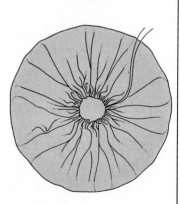

**3** *Flatten the patch by ironing it under a damp cloth with a warm iron making sure that the folded edge makes a well-formed circle. Gather all the patches in the same way and then arrange them in the patchwork pattern, side by side. Join with a few overcast stitches. If the patchwork is not to be lacy secure it to a suitable backing by stitching around the edges of the patches.*

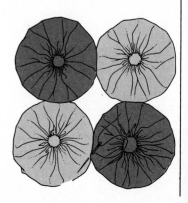

# Cathedral window patchwork

# Crazy patchwork

Cathedral window patchwork makes a quilted surface and is worked by folding squares of plain cotton or linen as frames over smaller squares of printed or contrasting coloured fabric. This produces a patchwork of rows of framed diamonds.

### How to make the patches

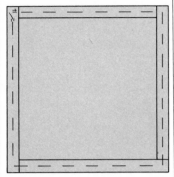

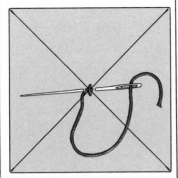

**1** *Cut squares of plain cotton and turn in ¼in. (6mm) all around and hem. Do not cut the squares too small as they will be folded down twice. For instance, if you start out with a patch 6¼in. (15.9cm) square, it will make a finished square which measures 3in. (7.9cm).*

**4** *Stitch corners to centre. Make the required number of squares and stitch together in rows. Then join rows together.*

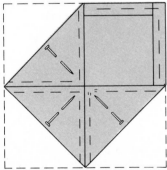

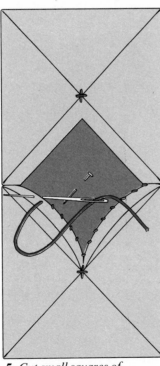

**2** *Then fold all 4 corners to the middle. Press the folds so that they lie flat and either pin or stitch down the corners to the centre of the patch.*

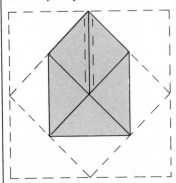

**3** *Fold all 4 of the corners of this square to the centre again and press the folds.*

**5** *Cut small squares of contrasting fabric on straight grain. They should be ¼in. (6mm) smaller than the diamond formed by the folds of the adjacent squares. Pin each on top of the seam of 2 folded squares. Fold edges of the squares over diamond patch. Hemstitch along the edge through all the layers of fabric. Then turn in and hem half-squares at the edges.*

Crazy patchwork is the original patchwork and was used as an economy measure either to patch up old bed quilts or to make something useful by salvaging fragments from worn-out clothes. It is assembled in jigsaw fashion from random-sized scraps of fabric which are joined together so that the edges overlap. These scraps are arranged and sewn onto a foundation of coarse cotton or cretonne. The edges of the individual patches can either be folded under or left raw and covered with embroidery stitches. The patchwork can be assembled in one piece or in individual blocks which are subsequently joined together. If individual blocks are made they can be worked in different shades so that the arrangement of the light and dark blocks forms a pattern (see page 371 for an example of crazy patchwork).

### Assembling the patches

When assembling the patches to cover the foundation fabric it is best to start at a corner. Place a right-angled patch on the corner of the foundation fabric. Then gradually build up the design placing the patches one after the other to overlap the edges of the previous patches, keeping the straight sides to the edges of the design. The design can be worked portion by portion, pinning and tacking one area before moving on to the next. Alternatively the patches can be arranged in position before any pinning or tacking begins. Use one of the methods below for finishing the edges of the patches.

### How to work with folded edges

*When all the pieces are in position tack them together, folding in the exposed raw edges with the needle while tacking. When tacking is completed hemstitch as invisibly as possible around all the overlapping edges. Stitch through the patches and the foundation fabric to secure them in place.*

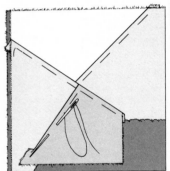

### How to work with raw edges

**1** *Pin and tack the patches in position as above but do not fold under the exposed raw edges. Stitch the patches together through the backing fabric using small even running stitches. These running stitches will make the patches more secure.*

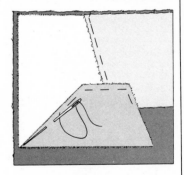

**2** *After all the patches have been tacked into position conceal the raw edges by working embroidery stitches over them. A variety of stitches would be suitable, including herringbone stitch (shown right), feather, or zigzag feather. The seams can also be concealed and decorated by couching a cord over them.*

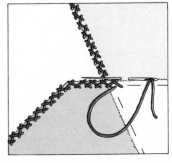

# Shell pattern patchwork

In shell pattern patchwork the stemmed shell shape forms the template but when the shell patterns are assembled the stem is concealed. There are two different ways of making the patches: with a fabric lining or with a paper backing. Fabric-lined patches are the most satisfactory as the lining helps to retain the shape of the patches during the joining process. The fabric patches should be cut in the usual way making sure that the grain of the fabric runs straight and parallel to the stem. Use the paper template to cut either paper patches or bonded fabric linings.

### Making fabric-lined patches

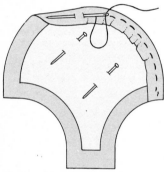

*Pin a fabric lining to the back of each patch. Fold over the curved edge and tack in place through hem and lining only.*

### Making paper-backed patches

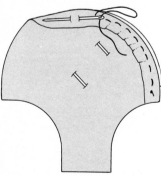

*Pin the paper patch to the front of the fabric patch. Fold the edge to the back using the paper patch to indicate the fold line. Tack around curved edge but not through the paper and then remove the paper.*

### Joining shell patches

The joining of shell patchwork requires accuracy so that the finished patchwork will be perfectly flat and even. Before the joining is begun the colour sequence which creates the pattern should be planned. Several patterns for shell patchwork are given on page 390 in the patchwork pattern glossary. The standard shell patterns are joined in rows as shown below but a variation of joining is given on page 390.

### How to join shell patches

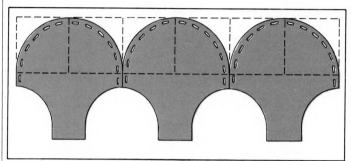

**1** *Place a row of prepared patches of the required length right side up on a cork board and pin them into position so that they are in a straight line with their sides touching.*

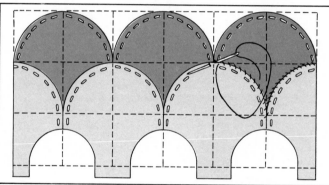

**2** *Then place the second row so that it overlaps the first, covering the stems. Pin it to the first row and then tack into position. Remove the pins and stitch neatly around the curves of the second row of shells, catching the fabric of the first row with each stitch. Continue in this way for the next and subsequent rows until the patchwork is the required length. Use half patches where necessary at the edges of the patchwork.*

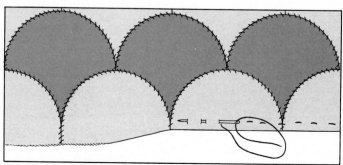

**3** *When the final row has been attached cut the stems off it. Fold the edges back and secure with small hem stitches. If paper backings were used remove all tacking stitches.*

## Log cabin patchwork

Log cabin patchworks were invented entirely for decorative reasons as they use a great deal of fabric and are very often worked in silks and velvets or with ribbons. They should be dry cleaned rather than washed as the strips are formed in folds and may lose their sharpness during washing. Log cabin patchworks are worked in square blocks composed half of light and half of dark strips stitched and folded around a small central square. The central square, which is the focal point of the block, should be in a colour contrasting with the light and the dark strips.

### Preparing the strips

The central square and strips are sewn one by one onto a foundation fabric. The strips are all cut to the same width but their length increases with each circuit. Their width should be twice the width of that shown on the template (see next page) plus ¼in. (6 mm) for overlapping with the next circuit. It is easiest to cut long strips to this width first, and then cut these into the correct lengths as the stitching progresses. The strips are stitched on in circuits in the order shown below.

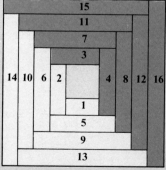

**Standard log cabin block**

### Joining the finished blocks

When the correct number of blocks have been made they are stitched together first in rows and then the rows are joined. The blocks are joined by placing them face to face and working running stitches.

# Log cabin blocks

Before the blocks are begun a template is drawn as a guide to the width and length of the circuits. Then a foundation square is cut and the strips are applied to it.

### How to make the template

Cut a square template from card or stiff paper to the size of the finished block plus $\frac{1}{2}$in. (1.3cm) seam allowance all around. Draw a small central square and then measure and draw radiating squares from this, making sure that they are the same distance apart. Use this template to position and cut the strips.

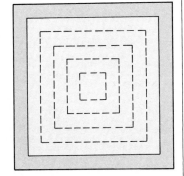

### How to apply the strips

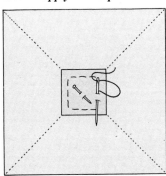

**1** Using the template cut a square of the foundation fabric. Draw 2 diagonal lines to help to position the corners of the strips. Next cut the small central square with $\frac{1}{4}$in. (6 mm) seam allowance. Pin this right side up to the centre of the large square and secure with even running stitches.

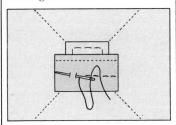

**2** Using the template as a guide cut the first circuit of dark and light strips allowing an extra $\frac{1}{4}$in (6 mm) at each end so that the next circuit will overlap it. Then place the first strip face down over the central square and secure with running stitches allowing a seam allowance the same width as finished strip.

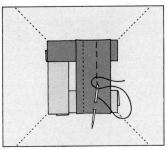

**3** Fold back the first strip and secure the second light strip in the same way.

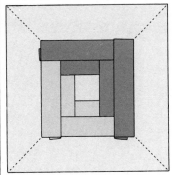

**4** Secure and fold the 2 dark strips in the same way.

**5** Secure the next and subsequent circuits in the same way but place the stitch line so that it overlaps the previous circuit by $\frac{1}{4}$in. (6 mm).

# Log cabin patterns

The positioning of the dark and light halves of the block in rows forms variations of the log cabin pattern.

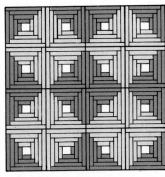

**Dark and light squares**

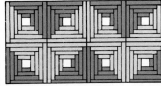

**Zigzags**

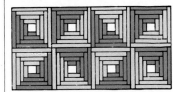

**Windmills**

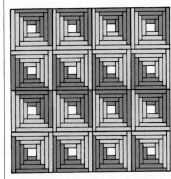

**Diamonds**

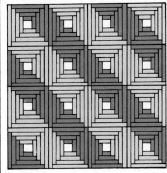

**Diagonals**

# Alternative blocks

### Courthouse steps

This pattern is made in the same way as the standard log cabin blocks except that the strips are attached in the order shown below. An optical variation of this pattern can be made by using four slightly different tones of one colour.

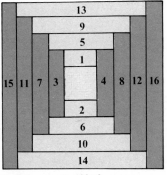

**Courthourse steps block**

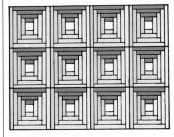

**Optical pattern**

### Radiating pineapple patterns

Strips can also be worked around a central square to radiate outwards both with straight and diagonal sides. These are made in the same way as the standard log cabin blocks except that at the end of each circuit four strips are placed diagonally at each corner.

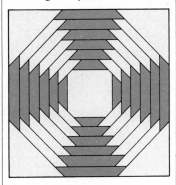

**Pineapple block**

# *Introduction to quilting*

The word "quilting" comes from the Latin *culcita* meaning a cushion or stuffed mattress. There are two distinctly different types of quilting. In one form, two layers of fabric are separated by a layer of wadding, and all three layers are stitched together. This type of quilting, known as *wadded* quilting, is sometimes called *English* quilting and is the earliest type. It was originated for the practical purpose of providing warmth or protection. The stitching patterns were handed down from generation to generation and the quilting was used largely for bedcovers and clothing, usually worked on white linen.

In the other form of quilting only two layers of fabric are used and it is purely decorative. The patterns are often pictorial. When the pattern consists of two narrow lines of stitching, a cord is inserted into the channels to raise the pattern on the surface. This type is known as *cord* or *Italian* quilting. In the other variation of this form, the design is stitched in outline through both layers and then raised by inserting a padding from the back of the work. This type is known as *padded* or *trapunto* quilting. Cord and trapunto quilting were also traditionally worked on white linen and, as in wadded quilting, the patterns were handed down through the centuries.

**Cord**
This form of raised quilting consists of two fabric layers threaded with cord.

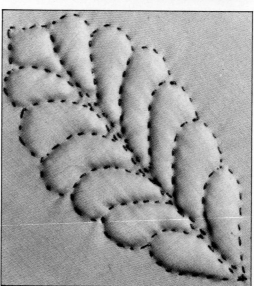

**Trapunto**
In this form of quilting the design is outlined with stitching and then stuffed with a soft padding.

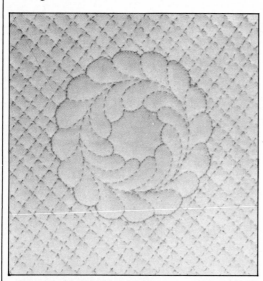

**Plain wadded**
This simply worked form of quilting consists of two fabric layers with a middle layer of padding.

**Patchworked wadded**
This form of quilting consists of two fabric layers and a padding-the top layer (and in this case the backing) of which is patchworked.

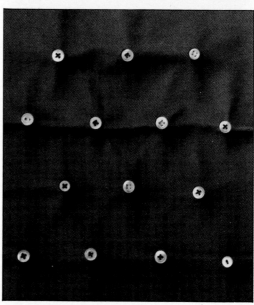

**Tied and buttoned**
In these forms of quilting the fabric layers are secured with buttons, bows or knots.

# Materials and implements

For quilting, a top or *ground* layer of fabric will be needed, with a backing or lining fabric of a suitable weight for the top fabric. Wadding will also be needed as an interlining or stuffing.

### Top and backing fabrics

The fabric chosen should be smooth, soft and closely woven and can be plain, printed, patchworked or embroidered. Try to avoid heavy or stiff fabrics or ones with a slippery surface because it is difficult to work quilting stitches through them. The most suitable fabrics are cotton, poplin, linen, dull satin and crêpe de chine. Printed designs lend themselves to quilting because they can be stitched directly around the existing designs. All fabrics should ideally be washable and also colourfast. If the fabric is not pre-shrunk it should be washed before starting to avoid distortion of the finished item.

### Interlinings

Cotton and synthetic paddings are the most commonly used forms of interlining for wadded quilting as they are cheap and easy to quilt with. One layer is usually sufficient, but up to three layers of padding can be used if necessary (more than this will make stitching too difficult).

Old blankets make very good interlinings but badly worn ones should be avoided as the uneven surface will result in an equally uneven surface to the quilting. One or more blankets can be used in layers, depending on how thick the quilted item is to be. Lightweight woollen lining is particularly useful for light quilts and clothing.

Cotton wool can also be used for padding quilted items and this is sold by the sheet. It is the best padding to use for trapunto work which has to be stuffed with a soft material. In wadded quilting, bear in mind that if it is used on large unstitched areas it is prone to shifting, and therefore matting, after a couple of washes. This is avoided in trapunto work because it is well stuffed.

For cord quilting, firm cotton cord gives the best results on linen and cotton (candlewick or upholstery cord can also be used). Specific quilting cord can be bought and, like other varieties, can be bought in varying thicknesses.

## Implements

The implements used for quilting are basically the same as for general sewing. Where they do differ is in their suitability for the fabric and the technique used.

### Needles and pins

The needles chosen, whether long or short, will depend on the thickness of the wadding and on the weight and type of fabric. Sharps are of medium length and can be used on most fabric weights. Betweens are smaller and are able to take fine stitches. Crewels are of medium length with a large eye. You will also need dressmaker's steel pins.

### Thread

A strong thread must be used for quilting stitches. A no. 40 sewing cotton is suitable for all cottons, linens and wool fabrics but silk thread should be used on silks.

## Additional equipment

For marking up designs a compass, ruler, set square, pencil or tailor's chalk may be needed. It is advisable to use a thimble to protect the finger pushing the needle through the fabric layers and to use a pincushion to keep the pins together and rust-free. Fabric tape will also be needed when mounting the quilting on the frame to secure it to the stretchers.

# Quilting frames

Frames are designed to hold single pieces or layers of fabric securely in place. Because they are held by the frame they are evenly stretched and kept under a consistent tension. This means that when they are removed from the frame the stitches appear in deeper relief. Hand stitched quilts and other large items are best worked on a frame otherwise it is too difficult to maintain the tension required to produce the stitches and prevent the fabric from slipping or puckering.

The use of a frame also ensures that the quilter's two hands are free to guide and make the stitches in the correct way. Small pieces of quilting can be worked on straight-sided or round embroidery frames. These are more convenient than the larger quilting frames because they can be carried around with the work mounted and ready for stitching.

### The quilting frame

The quilting frame consists of two long and two short pieces of wood which are slotted together to make a rectangular frame. The long pieces, known as *runners,* are slotted at either end and are set along the horizontal length of the frame. It is considered preferable to have the runners set so that they can take the complete length of the item being quilted to avoid any ridges or pulling of the fabric. If the fabric being quilted is too long for this then it will have to be set into the frame widthways. Webbing is nailed to the side of each runner and the backing of the quilted fabric is attached to it with overstitching.

The short pieces of wood, or *stretchers,* fit vertically into slots at the ends of the runners. They are drilled with holes into which wooden or metal pegs are placed to hold the rectangular frame at the required width.

The frame is then supported, either on the backs of two straight-backed chairs or with a trestle at each end. It is important that they are of a convenient height and that the frame is placed in a good light for the quilter.

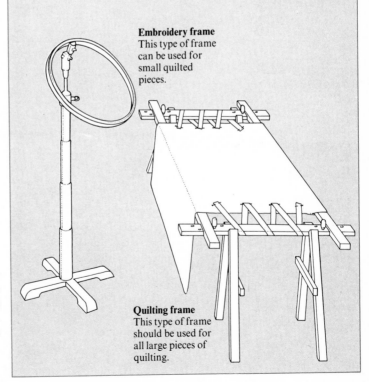

**Embroidery frame**
This type of frame can be used for small quilted pieces.

**Quilting frame**
This type of frame should be used for all large pieces of quilting.

# Quilting designs

# Making a paper pattern

Quilting was originally used for the purely practical purpose of joining three layers of fabric. The stitching then followed lozenge, diamond and square patterns without any regard to making it decorative. Circular patterns were later introduced giving a slightly more elaborate surface to the quilting. Finally, motifs were developed to act as focal points against the linear or circular background patterns.

### *Linear or circular patterns for grounds*

These can be worked uniformly over the quilt or in double lines to emphasize the pattern in certain places. A variety of different patterns can be used on the same design but these need to be carefully planned so that they work well together (see examples of these grounds below).

**Geometric ground patterns**

### *Template motifs*

Motifs can be made in many different shapes such as leaves, feathers, hearts and shells, but intricate shapes should be avoided as these will not come up well in the quilting. The templates can be used for both single motifs and for repeated border designs and several different sizes of template may be required to fill the quilted item correctly.

The template motifs can be filled with stitching to produce vein and feather effects. When filling the motif in this way the stitching should follow the longest possible design line. For example, when stitching in veins on a scallop design the stitching should work around the scallop and then down the vein lines. In this way no small lines are left to be filled in later.

### *Combining grounds with template shapes*

There should always be a clear contrast between the template shapes, which are the focal points, and the background patterning. This can best be achieved by using curved motifs against linear pattern backgrounds and vice versa. A central motif can be emphasized by either increasing or decreasing the background patterning around the centre.

The balance of design is as important as the contrast between the motif and the background. The overall design should be balanced so that the focal point is clearly defined and the surrounds well proportioned. When working flat designs for bed and cushion covers the centre should be the focal point, the ground patterning subdued and the borders pronounced. Smaller motifs can be placed at each corner to complement the central one. When working quilted curtains it is the border patterning which should be emphasized and this principle also applies to quilting clothes. For example, on a skirt the main design should be on the hemline or the skirt will appear top heavy. On jackets, waistcoats and shirts ground patterns can be used with special motifs worked on the pockets, and border patterns used for the edgings.

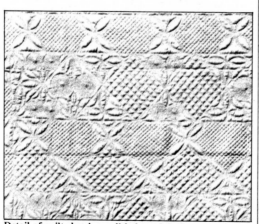

**Detail of quilt with central motif on linear ground**

**Detail of quilt showing well balanced design**

The design lines for wadded quilting are always marked on the top fabric. It is advisable, especially when learning to quilt, to work out the design on paper and then transfer it to the top fabric before it is mounted on the frame. The design can be drawn as you work but both skill and experience are needed for this to be successful.

### *Marking the design on paper*

First calculate the measurements of the finished quilted item and then mark them out onto a piece of paper the same size as the proposed design. Mark the centre point and the depth of the borders. Finally, draw two diagonal lines from the centre to the four corners. This will help you to plan any repeats in the design.

Calculate the size of template needed for the shaped motifs and the width of the filling patterns for the background stitching. Circular shapes can be drawn with a wine glass, cup, saucer or compasses. Straight lines should be drawn with a ruler. It is essential that these lines are accurately placed and equally spaced overall. When the motif is reached the line is stopped and then continued on the other side.

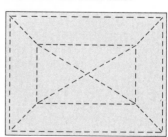

**Marking paper for design**

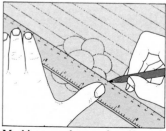

**Marking around a curved motif**

# Marking designs

The design can be marked with a needle, tailor's chalk or dressmaker's carbon.

### Using a needle

First lay the top fabric on a flat surface over a thick layer of padding, such as a blanket. The pattern is then marked with a needle using a template or ruler as a guide. The needle should be held nearly flat against the fabric and pushed down hard to make the creases as it moves around the template or ruler. Any mistakes can be removed by dampening and then pressing the crease with a cloth.

**Marking with a needle**

### Using tailor's chalk

The top fabric should be placed on a smooth, flat surface with no padding underneath. The template or ruler is drawn along gently.

### Using dressmaker's carbon

Lay top fabric on smooth, flat surface and place paper, carbon face down, on it. Use a pencil or tracing wheel to mark out the design.

### Marking in details

When the outlines of the templates have been marked the details can be filled in.

**Filling in motif details**

# Templates for designs

The simple outline shapes can be added to and filled in different ways to create different effects. The shapes illustrated below show how to build them up into richer designs by filling and adding to the original outlines and also how to use them for repeating border patterns.

### Motifs

These motifs can be worked large or small, as focal points or as corner motifs within borders.

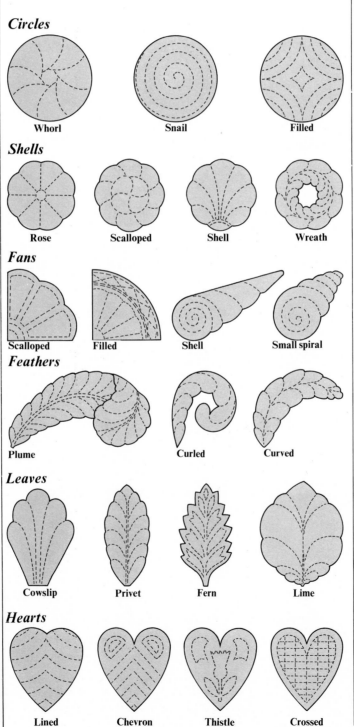

#### Circles
Whorl        Snail        Filled

#### Shells
Rose        Scalloped        Shell        Wreath

#### Fans
Scalloped        Filled        Shell        Small spiral

#### Feathers
Plume        Curled        Curved

#### Leaves
Cowslip        Privet        Fern        Lime

#### Hearts
Lined        Chevron        Thistle        Crossed

# Borders

These borders can be worked in a continuous line around the design or used with motifs at the corners.

### Scalloped borders

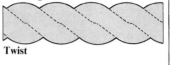

**Twist**

**Lined**

**Feather**

**Diamond chain**

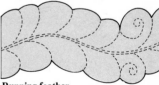

**Plaited chain**

### Undulating borders

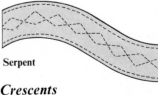

**Running feather**

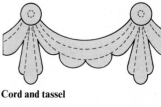

**Serpent**

### Crescents

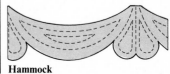

**Cord and tassel**

**Hammock**

399

# Quilting on a frame

The fabric to be quilted can either be mounted on a frame or stitched without any support. Generally, the larger the work the more advisable it is to mount it on a frame. This also enables more than one person to work at a time.

## Using a quilting frame

The fabric should be mounted carefully with each layer laid smooth and straight before the next one is placed on top. They must be mounted slackly or the stiches will not sink deeply into the fabric and the full quilted effect will be lost. Always cut the top and bottom layers with a 2in. (5cm) seam allowance and cut the padding to the size of the finished item.

### How to mount the fabric on the frame

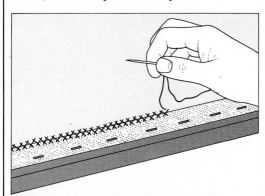

**1** *Herringbone stitch the side edges of the backing to the webbing on the runners. Roll one side around its runner until a convenient depth for working has been reached. This is usually about 18in. (46cm) although no more than 6in. (15cm) can be comfortably worked at a time. Slot stretchers onto the runners and peg the holes to secure the frame in position.*

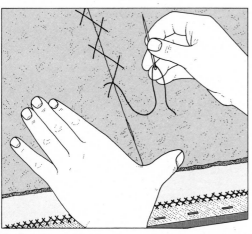

**2** *Cut the padding to the required size. Lay it down so that it lines up with the backing on the runner nearest to you and then smooth out any wrinkles. Tack any lengths together where necessary. When using loose wool make sure that the staples lie in the same direction.*

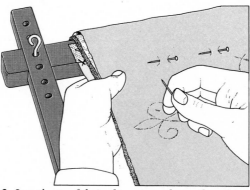

**3** *Lay the top fabric, face upwards, on the other 2 layers and allow the end to hang free on the far side. Tack through all 3 layers of fabric along the runner nearest to you. Smooth the cover and padding flat and then pin the 3 layers along the far runner. Be careful not to pull quilting too tight.*

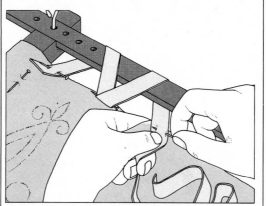

**4** *Tie the end of the fabric tape around the stretcher. Loop it over the top and pin through all 3 layers at the edge of the fabric. Take the tape back and over the stretcher. Continue to pin in this way at 3in. (7.5cm) intervals. Fasten other side in the same way.*

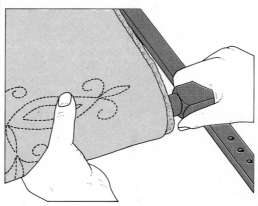

**5** *As each area of stitching is finished the pins and tape are removed and the backing on the far runner is unrolled. The work is then rolled around the runner nearest to you and the padding and top layers rearranged and smoothed out. The tape and pins are then put into position again. Follow this procedure until the quilting is finished.*

# Quilting without a frame

Simple quilting designs can be worked on a machine or held in the hand but great care will have to be taken in their preparation. This is necessary to ensure that the tension is consistent and that the fabric layers lie together smoothly. The top and backing fabrics are always cut with a 2in. (5cm) seam allowance but the padding is cut to the size of the finished quilt.

### How to prepare fabric

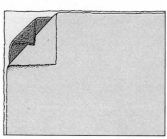

**1** *Place the backing wrong side up on a flat surface. Smooth it out and lay the padding on top. Smooth again, then place top fabric, right side up, on the other 2 layers.*

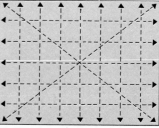

**2** *Work tacking stitches horizontally and vertically over the surface, starting at the centre and working outwards in each direction. Finish by working 2 diagonal lines from corner to corner. While tacking, constantly smooth the fabric to prevent creasing.*

### Starting to stitch

Do not tie a knot but insert the needle, piercing only the top fabric and work it through the padding for a short distance. Bring it out again at the starting point of the design line. Make a back stitch through the thread to anchor it firmly.

# Hand stitching

All intricate quilting designs need to be hand stitched: running and back stitch are most commonly used (see page 409). If the quilting is to be reversible then running stitches must be used. The stitches should be equal in length to the spaces left between them. They need not be small but they must be regular. Back stitch should only be used if the quilting is not reversible.

## Positioning the hands

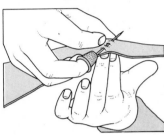

The position of the hands when quilting on a frame is important because they are not only used to work the stitching but also to press down on the layers to produce the correct quilted tension.

## Working the stitches

The needle should be inserted as upright as possible from the front of the work. Hold one hand below the frame and, as each stitch is made, feel where the needle is going to come through. Push it back up vertically through all the layers. Press down with the thumb of the other hand, just ahead of where the needle will emerge. Make several stitches before pulling the thread through.

To keep an even tension several needles can be kept in the work and used until the thread is finished. Finish with a couple of back stitches.

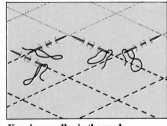

**Keeping needles in the work**

# Machine stitching

Machine quilting is quicker to do but is only suitable for simple designs. The same fabrics as those for hand quilting are used, but the padding must not be too thick or the fabrics will not be held securely by the presser foot.

It is essential when machine stitching to tack the fabric layers together thoroughly (see far left). Always use a suitable thread for the top fabric – for example, use silk thread on silk and synthetic thread on synthetic fabric. Select a medium stitch tension when using a normal machine foot and always stitch alternate quilting lines in opposite directions to prevent any wrinkling.

## Machine wadded quilting

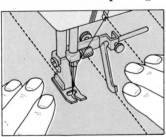

If using a normal machine foot, loosen the tension sufficiently to allow the quilting to move easily under the presser foot. Alternately, use a quilting foot. This has a special width guide for stitching so that the fabric does not have to be marked in advance.

## Machining raised quilting

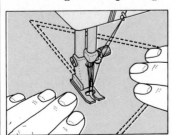

As only two fabrics are used in raised quilting, a normal machine foot can be used. Prepare the fabric (see far left) and select the correct thread for your fabric. A twin needle can be used to stitch the channel lines for cord quilting.

# Finishing off

Quilted fabrics can be finished in several ways. The edges can be turned under and stitched, piping cord can be inserted, or tape attached to the edges. Frame-worked fabrics are removed from the frame before finishing off the edges.

## How to finish the edges

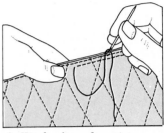 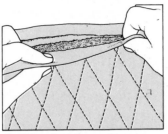

**1** *Trim the edges to ½in. (1.3cm) and fold the top fabric over the padding. Fold the bottom layer under the padding so that it will align neatly with the folded edge of the top fabric.*

**2** *Work a line of running stitches as near the edge as possible. Make a second line ⅛in. (3mm) further in from the first to secure the two edges. Continue in this way.*

## Piped edging

This gives a neat, firm edge to the quilting and there are two methods of working it. Always take care when stitching around corners that the quilting material does not pucker.

### How to insert piping cord between the edges

*Cover the length of piping cord with bias-cut fabric. Then turn under the edges and insert covered cord. Tack into place and then work 2 rows of running stitch along the edge to secure the piping.*

### How to attach piping to the backing

*Cover a length of piping cord with bias-cut fabric. Stitch covered cord to the folded edge of the backing fabric with running stitch. Fold back the edge of the top fabric and slip stitch to the base of the piping.*

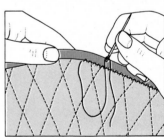

## Bound edging

Use tape or ribbon in contrasting colours to the main fabric to produce a decorative effect to the edges of the quilting.

### How to work

*With raw edges facing, place the tape wrong side uppermost along the top of the quilt edge. Work running stitches as near the edge as possible. Fold the tape over to the back of the quilt and slip stitch into position.*

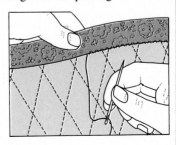

# Quilting

In wadded quilting two fabric layers enclose one of wadding, and all three are then stitched together with either running, back or machine stitch. The stitching is not only functional but also provides a textured pattern.

Detail of patchworked bedcover showing corner with fan motif bordered with semi-circular patterns

Tunic with wadded yoke worked in a simple geometric design

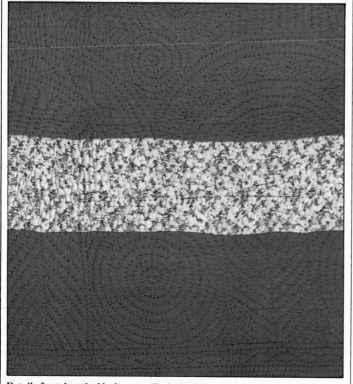

Detail of patchworked bedcover quilted with linear and curved patterns

Contemporary satin waistcoat worked with both back and machine stitch. The border is based on a wine glass pattern.

## Modern quilting designs

The traditional method of quilting can also be used in more adventurous ways. The top fabric can be dyed or tinted (using air-brush or normal dying techniques) and then stitched in the usual way. By doing this the quilting takes shape not only through the stitching but also through the patterning of the stitches.

**Air-brushed and machine stitched satin wall hanging**

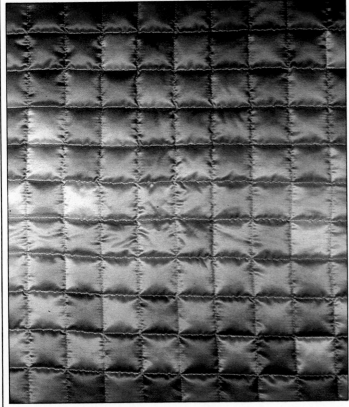

**Machine-quilted bed cover, imitating patchwork**

## Design motifs

Interesting designs can be produced by arranging individual motifs into composite shapes such as fans, clusters, stars, or flowers. These can be used as borders or central motifs, but care should be taken to ensure that the overall design is well-balanced. Mark out the design using one of the methods described on page 399 and then stitch.

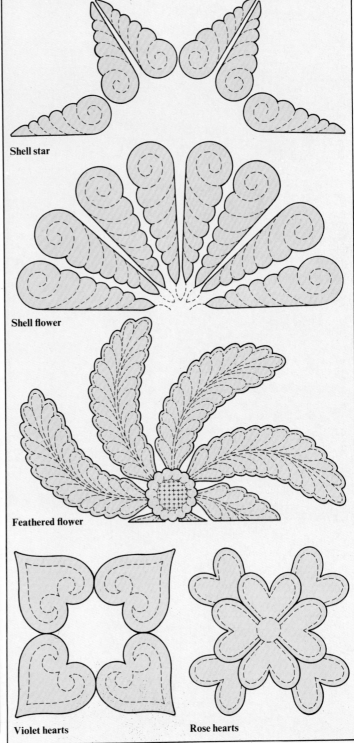

**Shell star**

**Shell flower**

**Feathered flower**

**Violet hearts**          **Rose hearts**

403

# Raised quilting

A purely decorative form of quilting can be worked in which only the design is padded. Two layers of fabric are used and the design stitched through both layers. For narrow, channel-like designs, a cord is threaded through the channel to raise it from the surface and this is known as *cord* or *Italian quilting*. If larger areas are to be raised a softer padding is usually used and inserted through the back of the work between the layers, and this is known as *stuffed* or *trapunto quilting*.

Some of the earliest examples of raised quilting show pictorial scenes and lettering worked in a raised design. Other motifs are very similar to those used in traditional wadded quilting. Cord and trapunto quilting were often used for decorating clothing. They were nearly always worked on plain white linen. Both these types of quilting need to be lined after the quilting has been completed if the back is going to show.

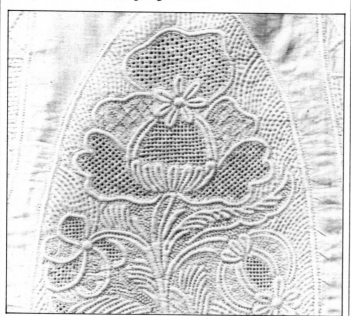

**Detail of eighteenth century cap showing cord quilting**

**Detail of late fourteenth century linen coverlet showing trapunto quilting**

# Cord quilting

The top fabric for a cord quilted design should be fine and closely woven so that the cord is sharply raised from the fabric to give a clear definition to the pattern. The backing fabric should be a fine loosely woven one such as linen scrim. The channels through which the cord is threaded are usually hand stitched using running stitch, but if the design is fairly simple it could be machine stitched. The cord used to stuff the design should be firm and strong - a piping cord is ideal. The channels through which it is threaded should be the same width as the cord itself to give a firmly raised effect. You will need a blunt-ended needle with a large eye for threading the cord.

### How to work cord quilting

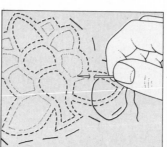

**1** Mark the design in double lines on the backing fabric, either free hand or tracing with dressmaker's carbon paper.

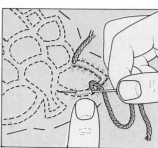

**3** Thread the cord onto a needle and insert through back of the work between the 2 lines of stitching and the layers of fabric, pulling it gently along the channels.

**2** Tack the 2 layers of fabric together, wrong sides facing. Mount onto a frame and stitch along the double outlines. When stitching is complete either loosen the frame or remove the fabric from it.

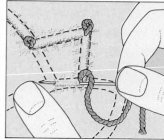

**4** If a sharp curve is reached, bring the needle through the back of the work, loop the cord a little at the angle and reinsert to continue piping. In this way the fabric will not pull or pucker. Stitch a lining to the backing fabric if necessary.

# Shadow quilting

A shadow effect in cord quilting can be achieved by using fine almost transparent white fabric on the top layer and a coloured piping cord or a tightly twisted wool. Work in the same way as for cord quilting. The result will be a softly coloured, raised design. Contrast channel stitching can be used for further effect.

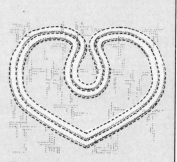

**Shadow quilting**

# Trapunto quilting

# Tied and buttoned quilting

This padded or stuffed form of raised quilting can be used on its own or in conjunction with the cord and wadded quilting to achieve special effects. The fabrics used are the same as those used for cord quilting. A crochet hook and a blunt-ended needle will be needed to insert the stuffing, which is generally a soft cotton wool, into the back of the work.

Tied quilting is another method of securing wadded quilting and is made by knotting the three layers together at intervals. It is serviceable rather than decorative and is quicker to work than stitched quilting. It can be made more decorative by using tightly knotted bows in different colours or by using buttons instead of knots.

### Making tied and buttoned quilting

The pattern is marked on the top fabric first and then all the layers are tacked firmly together (see page 400).

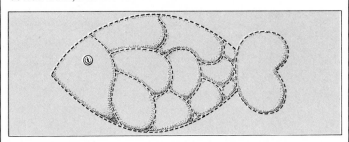

**Trapunto quilting**

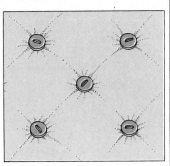

**Tied quilting**

**Buttoned quilting**

### How to work trapunto quilting

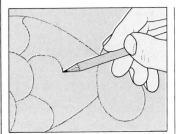

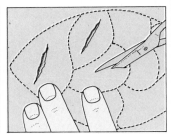

**1** Mark the design onto the front of the backing fabric, either drawing freehand or by tracing it with dressmaker's carbon.

**4** Slit the fabric at the back of the work where necessary, or if scrim is used, pull the threads apart with a crochet hook.

### How to work tied quilting

### How to work with buttoning

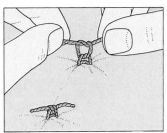

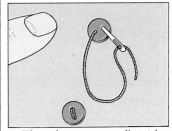

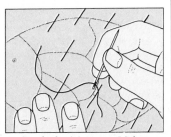

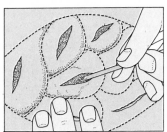

**2** Tack the 2 layers of fabric together, wrong sides facing, and mount onto a frame (see page 400 for instructions).

**5** Insert the padding with a crochet hook or a blunt needle taking care to position it evenly and not to overstuff the design.

**1** Thread the needle with the desired thread or threads. Make one stitch through all the layers, leaving a long loose end. Then make a back stitch and bring the needle out on the same side of the fabric.

**1** Thread a strong needle with buttontwist. Position one button on the top layer of fabric and secure it. Then place a second button immediately beneath it on the backing.

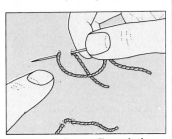

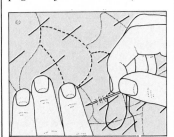

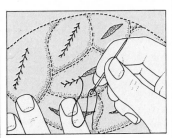

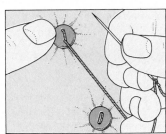

**3** Stitch along design outlines with small, even running stitches, working from the centre outwards·

**6** Slip stitch over the slits to close them. Stitch a lining to the backing fabric if it is necessary.

**2** Tie the ends together using a reef knot. Cut the threads to the desired length. If you do not want the ends to show thread them back between the layers. Alternatively, tie the ends together in tight bows for a more decorative effect.

**2** Stitch firmly through both buttons and all layers of the fabric, pulling the buttons down to make wells on both sides. Finish by passing the end of the thread between the layers of the quilted fabric. By using different coloured buttons arranged in pattern formation, a variety of designs can be made with this technique.

405

# American appliquéd quilts

This style of appliqué quilt, developed by North American women in the eighteenth and nineteenth centuries, is unique in the imaginative way that fabric scraps were assembled to produce simple and bold designs. The fabrics most commonly used, whether plain or patterned, were cotton, cambric and finely woven linen. These were cut to shape and then either stitched directly onto the main ground or onto individual blocks which were then pieced together.

Pennsylvania Dutch appliquéd quilt worked in plain and patterned fabric, central basket design, with flower motifs at corners, c. 1920

Nineteenth-century American appliqué quilt worked to commemorate William H. Harrisons' presidential campaign

# Modern appliqué

Any fabric which does not fray easily can be used for appliqué, with the motifs being either hand or machine stitched to the ground fabric. Surface appliqué can be worked in layers for special effects. it can also be raised by inserting a padding of cotton wool between the motif and the ground.

Simple felt appliqué picture depicting birds and flowers in a style similar to that used on traditional painted cabinets

Contemporary felt appliqué in traditional Swiss design secured with back stitch

Felt appliqué, making use of repeating curved motifs, in which the felt has been applied in layers and certain areas have been padded

Detail of cover imitating American quilt with appliquéd felt motifs applied with backstitch on a felt ground

Detail of panelled quilt with clouds and birds in flight.

Layered felt appliqué with both padding and embroidered details for flower stems and centres and for animal features

Padded appliqué border used to echo the design within

Hand stitched contemporary Norwegian design worked in toning shades of silk brocades used to catch the light.

Landscape in silks and brocades worked by the same artist as the above. Tiny appliqué dots are used on the print in the background

# Surface appliqué

This is the most popular and well known form of appliqué and is worked by applying cut out fabric shapes *(motifs)* to the surface of the ground fabric to produce an overall design or border pattern. This form of appliqué was frequently used for making bedcovers in the United States. Other forms of surface appliqué include embroidered appliqué, where the motif is entirely embroidered and then applied to the ground fabric; needlepoint appliqué, where the motif is worked in needlepoint stitches on tapestry canvas and then applied to the ground fabric and pattern cut appliqué, where the applied fabric is cut into a pattern and then attached to the ground fabric.

Before attaching appliqué motifs the edges should be secured to prevent fraying, either by folding the edges or by pasting a backing onto them. It is essential to make sure that the shapes are secured firmly to the ground fabric and that they are stitched to form well defined outlines. Surface appliqué should always be worked on a frame to provide sufficient tension.

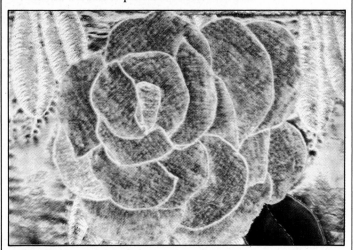

Appliquéd flower motif secured with satin stitch

## Fabrics for appliqué

Practically any fabric can be used for appliqué as long as it can be stitched but fabrics which fray easily should be avoided as they are difficult to work. The designs can be built up in tones of one colour, multicolours, or stripes, using contrasting or identical fabrics. The fabrics that can be used for appliqué include: gauze, organza, muslin, lawn, net, crêpe de chine, linen, cotton, georgette, satin, wool, velvet, corduroy, felt, leather, suede and plastic coated fabrics, such as vinyl.

### How to prepare the ground fabric

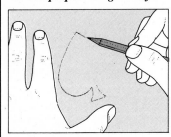 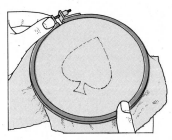

**1** *Mark the design on the ground fabric freehand or with dressmaker's carbon paper (see page 399).*

**2** *Loosely stretch the ground fabric on a frame, using an embroidery hoop or a rectangular frame.*

# Preparing the fabric

The fabric being applied has to be prepared to prevent the raw edges from fraying. This can be done either by pasting on a backing before cutting or by turning under the raw edges. When pasting, use a light paste to hold the fabric in place. Paste holland or lightweight canvas on wools and velvets; muslin on silks, cottons and linens and tissue on organzas. Turn under the edges of fine or lightweight fabrics.

### How to apply paste

**1** *Brush enough paste onto the backing to cover it evenly without penetrating the other side.*

**2** *As soon as the paste has been spread onto the backing place the appliqué fabric on top and smooth over gently, stroking the surface to remove air bubbles.*

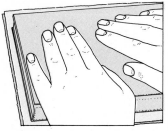

**3** *Press pasted fabrics under a board or heavy object. Leave until dry.*

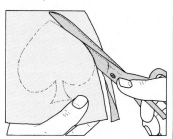

**4** *When the pasted fabrics are dry mark out the motifs and cut along the outlines.*

### How to turn under edges

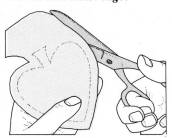

**1** *Mark the design onto the appliqué fabric. Then cut ⅟₄in. (6mm) out from the outlines to allow for turning under edges.*

**2** *Using sharp scissors take small snips around the edge of the curved outline to enable them to fold under easily.*

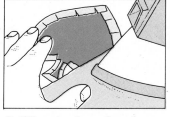

**3** *When the shapes have been cut fold the raw edges to the back and iron over them using a damp cloth.*

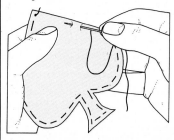

**4** *Then tack around the edges to complete the motifs which can then be applied.*

# Applying the motifs

# Stitching the motifs

The prepared motifs can either be pasted or tacked into position on the ground fabric. Motifs on heavily textured ground fabrics such as velvet, corduroy and brocade should be tacked into position.

Once the motifs have been secured on the ground fabric they can be stitched into place. Running stitch, back stitch, overcast stitch or chain stitch are the most commonly used. First sew any motifs which are to lie under parts of others (such as leaves under flower petals) using a thread which matches the fabric. Use bias strips for stems and connecting lines because they curve easily and lie flat on the ground fabric without puckering.

Felt, leather and bonded plastics need no preparation as they do not fray. They are the easiest fabrics to use when starting to appliqué and are therefore ideal for children to use when they begin.

## Pasting into position

The ground fabric should be laid on a flat surface and not placed in a frame if the motifs are to be secured by pasting.

### How to paste into position

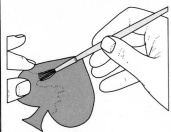

**1** *Apply a light paste to the back of the motifs using a small brush.*

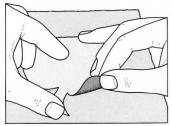

**2** *Place them into position on the ground fabric. Keep them in place with evenly distributed weights and leave to dry.*

## Tacking into position

When tacking motifs into position the ground fabric should be framed so the surface can be pinned without puckering.

### How to tack into position

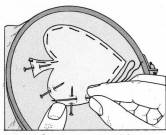

*Pin each piece into position on framed fabric and tack down.*

## Running stitch

This stitch is useful for securing fabric quickly or for marking outlines. On thick or quilted fabrics the stitches will have to be made individually.

### How to work

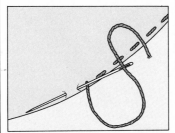

*Insert the needle from the back of the work. Take several small stitches onto the point of the needle before drawing the thread through the fabric.*

## Chain stitch

This stitch is more decorative but is equally suitable for securing. It is particularly good for curved and spiral shapes.

### How to work

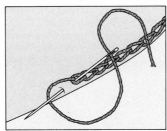

*Insert the needle from the back of the work. Make a small stitch forwards. Bring needle out and loop working thread, holding it in place. Pull the needle through, forming one chain. Insert the needle into the same hole from which it emerged. Bring it out a stitch length further on, over the thread as before and pull the needle through.*

## Overcast stitch

This method of stitching gives an almost invisible stitch on the turned under edges It can also be used on raw edges which fray easily.

### How to work

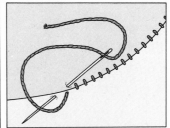

*Use the same colour thread as the appliqué fabric. Secure the thread under the appliqué motif. Pass the needle through the back of the fabric and into the appliqué motif, making diagonal stitches. Keep the stitches small and do not pull them too tight.*

## Back stitch

This is good for both turned under edges and raw edges which do not fray. It can also be used to emphasise the outlines of the motif.

### How to work

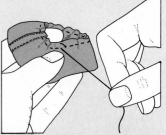

*Make a small stitch from left to right. Then make a double length stitch forwards on the wrong side of the work so that the needle emerges a stitch length in front of the first.*

### Applying the motifs

The shapes are cut out and placed into position on the marked ground fabric. They are then tacked into place. Beginners will find it easiest to use running stitch to secure them. Back, overcast, buttonhole or satin stitch can also be used. The motif can be decorated before it has been applied (see page 412).

### Relief appliqué

When working with fabrics which do not need any preparation, relief effects can be achieved by gathering areas of the appliqué motifs before stitching them to the ground. Rosettes of fabric, for example, can be made in this way by first cutting and joining a strip of fabric.

#### How to make relief rosettes

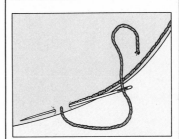

**1** *Cut out a strip and join into a circle. Work running stitches along one of the edges. Pull together firmly and then knot.*

**2** *Place rosette on the ground fabric and secure gathered edge with overcast stitching.*

# Plain fabrics for appliqué

The choice of fabrics plays as important a role as the cut shapes in appliqué. On this page all the contemporary designs shown use plain fabrics and the designs are emphasized with the clever choice of graded and contrasting colours. Texture too plays an important part and can be used to imitate or bring out a particular aspect of the appliquéd picture. For example, transparent fabrics can be used on the top of part of a design to give a glazed effect, pile fabrics for grasses, and moss and water silks for water.

**Pansy cushion**
The cusion, left, is worked in two colours of grey, with the outlines machined in white cotton and silver lurex.

The details of the animals and architecture are worked in embroidery, the bears in pile fabrics

Machine stitched appliqué with fabric and embroidered lettering. Note the use of gauze for the windscreen.

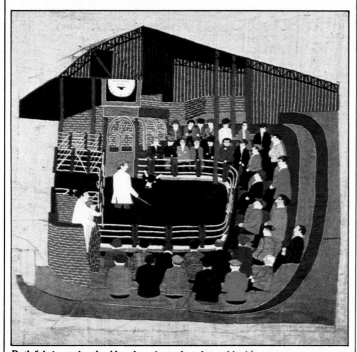

Both fabrics and embroidery have been cleverly used in this contemporary applique of a cattle sale

The graphic effect of the racing car design is emphasized by the plain background

# *Printed fabrics for appliqué*

Printed fabrics can be used to give a patterned effect within the appliqué motif, or individual motifs can be cut from it and applied to the ground fabric. Embroidery stitches can be used to fill in features or produce textured details. The examples below show how, in one cushion, textured, patterned fabric has been used to realistic effect in the bark of the tree and in the other, how the bird and tree have been cut directly from patterned fabric. Because they are surrounded with textured stitches they have been thrown into relief and made even more three-dimensional.

**The cushion design is enhanced by the unusual use of checked fabric for the trees and a realistic fabric for the bark**

**A small check design is used for the dress, a woven leaf pattern for the trees and a printed motif for the bird. The design, as a whole, seems to float on the velvet, which is stitched with French knots.**

**Flower vase hanging**
*Air-brush is used to bring out the design, which is further emphasized with quilting. The flowers on the vase are finished with embroidery.*

**Appliqué waistcoat**
*Plain and patterned fabrics, together with embroidery techniques, are used in clever juxtaposition on this design. Note the small print around the neckline and the use of braid for the button loops.*

411

# Decorative surface appliqué

Embroidered and needlepoint tapestry motifs and pattern cut fabric can all be used for surface appliqué. Embroidered and needlepoint motifs give the ground a textured look while pattern cut fabric gives it a lace-like appearance.

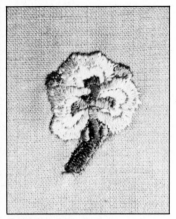

**Embroidered motif**

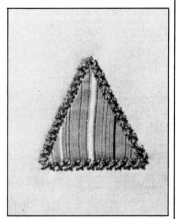

**Motif with herringbone stitch**

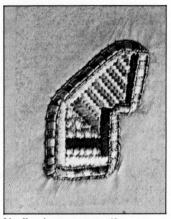

**Needlepoint tapestry motif**

**Motif with graded satin stitch**

## Embroidered motifs

Motifs of leaves, flowers, trees, figures and animals can be embroidered, cut to shape and then applied to the ground fabric. This type of appliqué was a very popular way of decorating bedhangings and curtains in the seventeenth and eighteenth century. Felt was also widely used: it was lightly embroidered, cut to shape and then arranged on the surface fabric.

### How to work

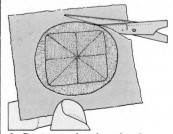

**1** *Design and embroider the motif onto a suitable fabric and then carefully cut around it using sharp scissors.*

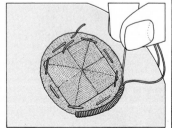

**2** *Pin and tack into position on the framed ground fabric and oversew the edges to secure them into place.*

# Needlepoint motifs

Needlepoint motifs, embroidered in silks or wools on fine gauge canvas, are particularly effective when applied to plain ground fabrics such as velvets, brocades and heavy silks. It is an excellent quick way of achieving the overall look of needlepoint without having to cover the background fabric.

### How to work

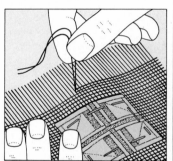

**1** *Work the needlepoint motif, on canvas and then pin and tack it into position on the framed ground fabric. Unravel the canvas threads around the edges of it.*

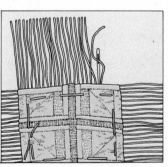

**2** *Using a large-eyed needle, take the canvas threads of the motif through to the back of the ground fabric.*

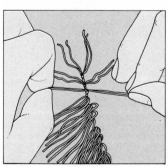

**3** *Knot the threads together in pairs, pulling them tight enough to secure them but not so tight as to pucker the ground fabric.*

# Pattern-cut appliqué

This type of work is often seen in Indian appliqué and it consists of a brightly coloured background fabric, which can be patchworked, covered with a plain fabric. The appliqué fabric is usually a white cotton and is folded and cut into holes in a pattern formation. The design is normally worked out first on paper and then transferred to the fabric.

### How to work

**1** *Take a piece of fabric exactly the same size as the coloured background fabric and fold in four.*

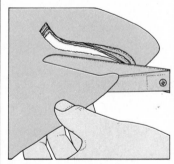

**2** *Snip out pieces at the appropriate points to achieve the chosen design.*

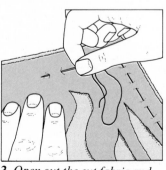

**3** *Open out the cut fabric and then pin it into position on the ground fabric. Tack, and then stitch around the holes using one of the methods described on the right.*

# Decorating the motif edges

After the motifs have been sewn down they can either be left plain or they can be worked over with embroidery stitches or couching to cover or decorate the edges.

## Embroidered edges

A large number of embroidery stitches can be used for edging motifs, the principal ones of which are shown below.

### Buttonhole stitch

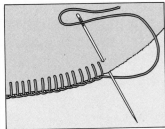

Bring needle through to surface at ·raw edge of motif. Insert through edge of motif and ground fabric and draw it through at raw edge with thread under needle. Continue in this way around the edge.

### Herringbone stitch

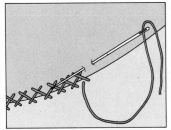

Bring needle through to surface on inner edge of motif then make a back stitch down to right over the raw edge and into the ground fabric. Next make a back stitch up to the right through the motif and ground fabric.

### Graded satin stitch

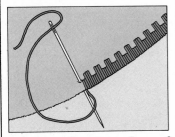

Bring needle to surface of motif and then work graded straight stitches over raw edge in pattern formation.

### Padded satin stitch

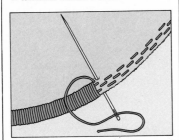

First work 3 or more lines of running stitches along the edge of the motif through both layers of fabric. These stitches act as a padding. Then cover them with closely worked satin stitches around the motif.

### Coral stitch

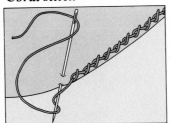

Bring needle to surface through the motif and make a small stitch downwards through both layers of fabric with thread over the needle. Bring the needle out with thread twisted as shown.

### Feather stitch

Bring needle out at arrow and insert at A. Hold thread down to left and bring needle out at B over thread. Next insert needle at C, hold thread down and bring needle out at D over thread. Continue in this way.

# Couched edges

Couching is an embroidery technique where cords, ribbons or threads are laid on the surface fabric and secured firmly and at regular intervals with visible or invisible couching stitches. It is a particularly effective way of decorating the edges of appliquéd motifs and can be worked in a variety of ways to provide different effects. For example it can be used to apparently diminish the motif by using the same colour threads as the ground fabric, or it can appear to enlarge it by using threads the same colour as the motif itself. The shape of the motif can also be emphasized by working the couching in a colour to contrast with both the motif and the ground. A more subtle effect can be achieved with a double line of couching – the inner line to match the motif and the outer to match the ground fabric.

In couching, the laid thread is loosely guided with the left hand while the right hand makes small overcast stitches with the couching thread. When using cords for couching the cord is opened a little at each stitch to allow the needle to slip through easily. Cords, ribbons and threads should always be laid directly over the raw edge to conceal it.

## How to work

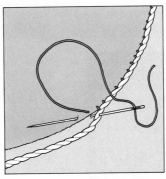

*Bring both the laid cord and the couching thread to the surface. Then secure the laid threads at regular intervals with couching stitches. Finish by taking threads to the back of the work and securing.*

# Openwork edges

Geometric designs on fine fabrics, such as organza, can be given open, lacy outlines by working around the edges using one of the following methods. Use a thick needle and a strong, fine thread.

### How to work chained border stitch

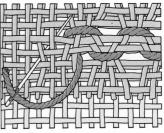

**1** *Work small horizontal stitches through the motif and ground fabrics, inserting the needle into the left side of the previous stitch and then pulling it tight to make the holes.*

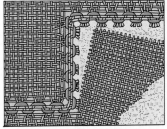

**2** *When stitching is complete trim the edge close to the motif.*

### How to work three-sided stitch

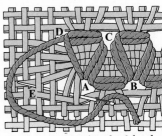

*Emerge at A and make 2 back stitches between A and B. Then make 2 back stitches between A and C, then between C and D and finally between D and A. When complete move onto E, ready to make 2 more back stitches between E and A. Continue in this way. When stitching is complete trim the edge close to the motif.*

# Reverse appliqué

Reverse appliqué in the San Blas islands resembles their traditional body painting designs. The examples on this page range from simple two layer, to more complicated multi-layered designs. Embroidery stitches are often used to finish off features in the designs. When working on reverse appliqué make sure that the outlines are simple and pronounced and that the fabrics do not fray easily. Quick and effective results in reverse appliqué can be achieved by using multi-coloured backing fabric. When the design is cut through the top layer different colours will show in different areas.

The rabbits are worked from red to green, black to yellow and the bird and cat are applied on top in two reverse layers. Teeth, eyes and squares are of surface appliqué

This design is worked on a printed background. In certain areas further layers of reverse appliqué have been worked

**San Blas Molas**
The simple two-layered Mola (above) uses pink as the top and blue for the backing. The multi-layered Mola (left) also makes use of surface appliqué.

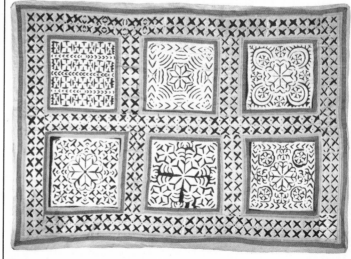

Indian canopy, worked in pattern cut appliqué. The design is cut on the top layer before it is applied.

# *Palestinian appliqué*

In Palestinian work of the type shown below, different forms of appliqué have been used together with embroidery stitches to give really rich effects. The base fabric of the dress is black with wide vertical stripes of purple, edged in yellow pin stripes. Surface appliqué in yellow, rust and green fabrics has been used on the bodice and panels and the hemline has been worked in pattern cut appliqué. Satin stitch has been used for the dot designs and triangular patterns have been edged with herringbone stitch.

**Traditional Palestinian dress, with corded neckline finished with tassels of silk and coloured beads**

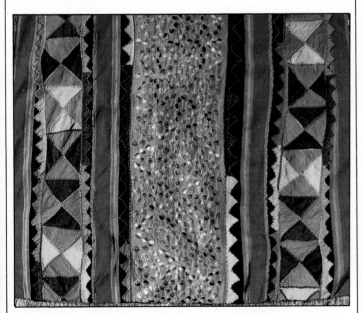

**Detail of bodice showing satin stitched dot design and triangles of surface appliqué set between purple stripes**

# *Stumpwork*

Stumpwork is a style of applied embroidery which was developed to give raised or relief effects. It began in the sixteenth century and was principally used to make pictures, frames and box covers. The early designs are unique; scale and proportion was disregarded but realism was pursued by working the focal points in relief.

## *Working stumpwork*

The design is first marked on the satin ground fabric and the relief motifs are then marked out on strong linen and worked separately. The linen is stretched on an embroidery frame and the motifs padded with wool, felt or string and secured with cross threads. They are then covered with needlepoint lace stitches or alternatively with fabric which has been cut to the motif shape and then embroidered. The completed motifs are then hem stitched to the ground fabric. Embroidery-covered wooden moulds can also be used for heads, hands and fruits and wiring can be used to produce free-standing parts of the design such as skirts or drapery. These are worked separately, stiffened around the edges with wire and then stitched into place.

**Late seventeenth-century English stumpwork panel** This example shows how hair or vegetation can be worked in relief stitches such as French or bullion knots. Seed pearls can be used for jewellery and pieces of tin for reflecting surfaces.

# Reverse appliqué

In reverse appliqué several layers are tacked together and the top fabric cut in patterns through different numbers of layers to reveal the fabrics below. This form of appliqué is seen in the designs of the Cuna Indians of the San Blas islands.

In a variation of this type of appliqué, known as patched reverse appliqué, different coloured patches are first applied to the backing fabric. The ground fabric is then tacked on top and cut in random patterns to allow the coloured patches to show through. The cut edges are turned under and slip stitched.

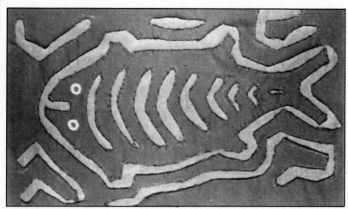

**Reverse appliqué worked in two colours**

## Fabrics
The best fabric to use in reverse appliqué is lightweight cotton. Because of the intricate cutting, fabrics which fray should be avoided. Very heavy fabrics should also be avoided because these will be too bulky when cut and turned under. Three to five layers of fabric can be used in this method of appliqué - the bottom layer acts as a lining and is never cut.

## How to work

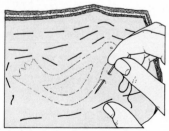

**1** *Mark the design on the top fabric. Lay the layers of fabric on top of each other, in the order in which they appear in the finished design and tack.*

**3** *Clip around edges. Turn under and stitch to the layer below using small stitches. Always complete stitching before starting another layer.*

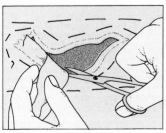

**2** *Cut through the top layer within the outlines using sharp scissors to make clean shapes.*

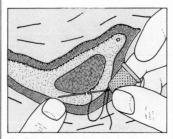

**4** *Continue to cut and stitch to a lower layer, thus building up the finished design.*

# Shadow appliqué

Shadow appliqué is made by joining two layers of transparent fabric with coloured motifs in between the two. The best fabrics to use are muslin, organdie or very light cotton.

**Reverse appliqué motif worked in two colours**

## How to work

**1** *Attach the coloured motifs to the base fabric with tacking. Then tack the ground and base fabric together.*

**2** *Outline the motifs in either buttonhole or graded satin stitch, using a contrasting thread to the ground or motif.*

**3** *When the motifs have been outlined fold the edges of the 2 main fabrics to the inside and hemstitch around all sides to join them. Remove tacking.*

# Insertion appliqué

This form of appliqué is used for borders and for inserting into curtains, bedspreads, table linen and lingerie. It is used on fine fabrics and should be worked on a frame.

### How to work solid motif on net ground

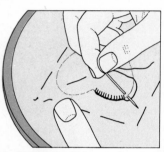

**1** *Mark the design on the ground fabric and then tack this on top of the net. Stitch over the outlines through both layers, using buttonhole stitch.*

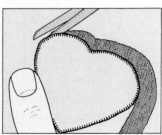

**2** *When complete, remove the tacking threads and cut away the surplus material outside the motif close to the design lines using blunt ended scissors.*

### How to work net motif on a solid ground

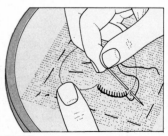

*Mark the design on the ground fabric and then tack the net on top of it. Stitch over the outlines through both layers of fabric using buttonhole stitch and then remove tacking threads. Using blunt ended scissors, cut away the ground from inside the motif and excess net around it.*

# Lace appliqué

In this type of appliqué a net or lace motif is applied to the surface of the ground fabric and outlined with stitches to secure it. The ground fabric is then cut away from beneath it.

### How to work lace insertion

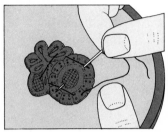

**1** *Firmly stretch the ground fabric onto a frame and then pin and tack the lace motif on top.*

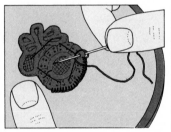

**2** *Work around the edges of the motif with buttonhole or satin stitch to cover the edges.*

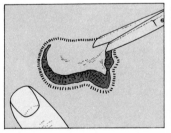

**3** *When the motif is completely outlined remove the fabric from the frame and cut away the ground fabric from beneath, using blunt ended scissors.*

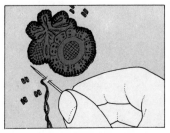

**4** *The edges can be further decorated with small dots or sprays of satin stitches.*

# Solid fabric insertion

This type of appliqué is particularly effective if two different types of fabric such as velvet and satin are used in the same colour.

### How to work

**1** *Mark the design onto both the ground and the chosen appliqué fabric. Tack the appliqué fabric face up on the ground fabric which should also be face up.*

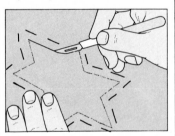

**2** *Cut through both layers with a sharp blade.*

**3** *Mount a supporting fabric on the frame and tack the ground fabric onto it. Drop motifs into the holes in ground fabric.*

**4** *Secure them with horizontal tacking stitches. Remove from frame and embroider edges.*

# Counterchange appliqué

This is a more elaborate form of solid fabric insertion but it is worked using the same basic principles. In counterchange the patterns are so designed that the motif is the exact counterpart of the ground. The idea is to produce two items with solid fabric insertions - the ground fabric of one being used as the motif of the other and vice versa. The effect can be produced either by using different colours or fabrics. The two pieces are joined and the seam covered with couching or embroidery.

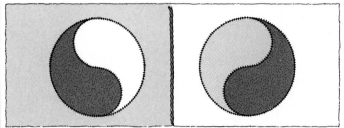

**Felt motifs worked in counterchange appliqué**

### How to work

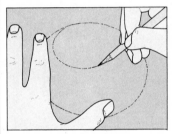

**1** *Take a piece of each different fabric and paste a backing onto them to prevent fraying (see page 408). Tack together and draw on design.*

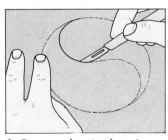

**2** *Pin onto drawing board, or flat cutting surface. Cut through both layers of fabric.*

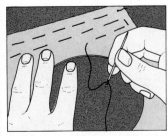

**3** *Mount a supporting fabric onto the frame and tack one of the ground fabrics on top of it.*

**4** *Drop the contrasting patch into the hole and secure it with horizontal tacking stitches.*

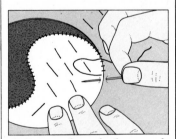

**5** *Remove from the frame and oversew the edges of the patch and ground fabric.*

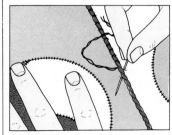

**6** *Join finished pieces and cover seam with couching or embroidery stitches (see page 413).*

417

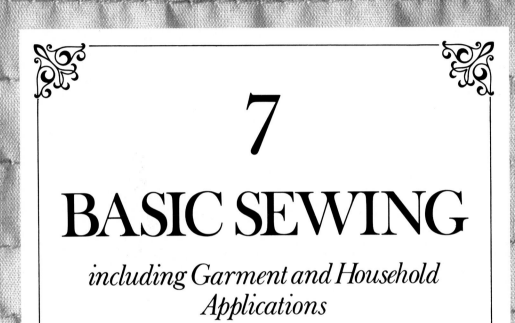

# 7

# BASIC SEWING

*including Garment and Household
Applications*

# *Introduction to basic sewing techniques*

Most people want to sew in order to make clothes or household items for themselves and their families. If you have never sewn before, begin by acquiring the basic skills and practising on simple projects. As a beginner it is best to choose a simple item with one major pattern piece. Any item which needs elaborate fitting and several pattern pieces is not suitable.

Whether you are making a simple or a complicated item you should always work methodically. Assemble your materials and basic implements on a cleared working surface. When using a bought pattern follow the advice on the envelope for suitable fabrics. These should be easy to handle, i.e. light- to medium-weight, non-slippery fabrics.

## *Basic sewing*

In the first part of this sewing section the basic principles of garment construction are given. These include advice on how to measure yourself in preparation to pattern buying; fabrics to buy; laying out your pattern; cutting and marking, and machining techniques. You are also shown how to make a simple toile to fit your figure. This can then be adapted to fit a variety of garments. In the second part you will find guides to constructing items from simple sheets to curtains and fitted bedspreads.

## *Implements*

There are certain essential implements for measuring, marking and cutting and these are illustrated on the right. A tape measure, preferably marked on both sides, is essential for taking body measurements. Buy a flexible tape with metal ends. A metre stick, of metal or wood, is useful for taking straight measurements or marking hems. If you buy a wooden one make sure that it is smooth or your fabric may be damaged.

### *Cutting equipment*

Good quality cutting implements are necessary to avoid damaging your fabric. They should be maintained by regular oiling and sharpening. Dressmaker's shears, with a bent handle, are best for cutting out patterns. The angled handles allow you to cut but still leave the fabric flat. Buy the 7in. to 8in. size (18cm to 20.5cm). Pinking shears are necessary for finishing raw edges on fabrics liable to fray. Do not use them to cut out patterns. The most common size is 7¼in. (19.5cm). Sewing scissors, 5in. to 6in. (14cm to 15cm) long, are useful for more delicate cutting and trimming. Embroidery scissors should be kept for needlework and buttonhole cutting and clipping.

### *Marking equipment*

The most common method of marking your fabric is with carbon and a tracing wheel. The wheel can be serrated or smooth-edged. The serrated wheel is the most commonly used but a smooth-edged wheel should be used on very delicate fabrics. Tailor's chalk, which comes in a variety of colours, is ideal for fitting but can also be used for construction marks.

### *Time-saving aids*

There is also a range of implements which, although not essential, make useful time-saving aids. A skirt marker, for example, allows you to mark a hem without any help; chalk is "puffed" onto your garment at a predetermined height; a hem gauge is handy for marking straight or curved hems, or changing pattern lengths. Electric scissors make quick work of cutting: they can be used on both heavy and light fabrics. A pin cushion, which can be combined with a sharpening bag, keeps needles and pins in an accessible, dry place. A needle threader eases the process of threading both hand and machine needles.

## *Measuring, marking and cutting implements*

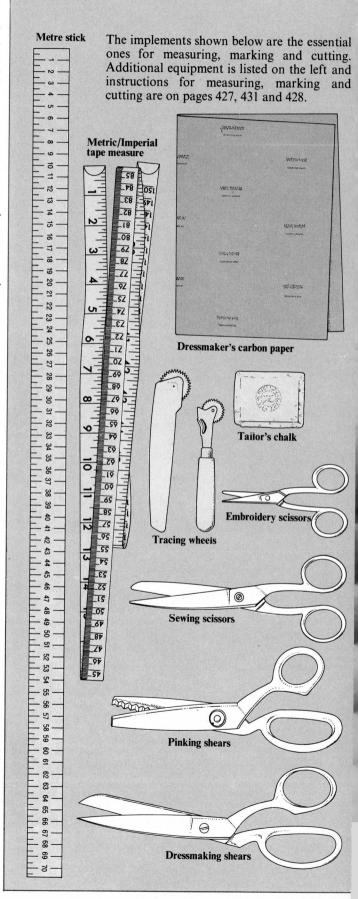

**Metre stick**

**Metric/Imperial tape measure**

The implements shown below are the essential ones for measuring, marking and cutting. Additional equipment is listed on the left and instructions for measuring, marking and cutting are on pages 427, 431 and 428.

**Dressmaker's carbon paper**

**Tailor's chalk**

**Tracing wheels**

**Embroidery scissors**

**Sewing scissors**

**Pinking shears**

**Dressmaking shears**

# Stitching implements

The most important implements you will need for hand sewing are needles and threads. The criteria which will affect your choice of these are given in the table below: for example, the type of fabric being sewn and the fabric weight and texture. Implements such as unpickers or thimbles, while not essential, are aids to easier and speedier sewing.

### Needles
Needle design varies according to purpose. Sharps, of medium length, can be used on most fabric weights. Betweens are smaller, allowing them to take fine stitches. Use long milliner's needles for tacking.

**Sharp**

**Between**

**Milliner**

### Pins
It is best to buy dressmaker's rustless, brass or stainless steel silk pins. Lengths vary from 1½in. (3.2cm) pins (used for heavy fabrics) to 1in. (2.5cm) extra fine pins suitable for delicate fabrics. Keep rust-free.

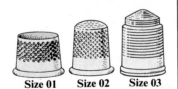

**1in. fine pin**

**Dressmaker's pin**

**Glass-headed pin**

### Unpicker
An unpicker has a sharp, curved head and is used to unpick seams. Insert the head into the seam to be undone, slitting threads as you do so.

**Unpicker**

### Thimbles
Thimbles fit on the middle finger of the hand which holds the needle. They enable you to push the needle through the fabric painlessly.

**Size 01**   **Size 02**   **Size 03**

### Threads
Select your thread according to fabric weight, colour and purpose (see chart). For example, do not use a fine silk thread on a heavy canvas because the threads will break too easily. Thread should be the same colour or a darker shade than your fabric.

| Thread type | When to use. |
| --- | --- |
| Tacking cotton | The loose twist allows easy breaking and is ideal for tacking. |
| General purpose cotton Size 50 | Machine and hand sewing on cottons, rayons, linens. When mercerized, it is smooth and silky. |
| General purpose silk Fine (size A) | Strong but flexible, used for silk or wool. It is fine enough to leave no holes or impressions after pressing. |
| General purpose nylon Fine (size A) | Use on light- to medium-weight synthetics (especially nylon knits). |
| General purpose polyester Size 50 | Suitable for most fabrics, especially woven synthetics, knits or stretch fabrics. |
| General purpose cotton-wrapped polyester Size 40 | Use on heavy vinyl or upholstery fabrics. |

# Pressing equipment

Pressing is an essential part of sewing. Every seam should be pressed as soon as it has been sewn, to give a clear, crisp line to the seam. Your pressing equipment should always be set up, ready for this purpose.

Below we show the implements which will help you to press your garments successfully. Your *iron* should be capable of both dry and steam ironing. It should have a wide range of temperatures, so that you can select the correct one for your fabric type. A spray attachment is useful for dry ironing. The *ironing board* should be adjustable to different heights and of a sturdy make. A padded cover is advisable and should be kept wrinkle-free to avoid pressing creases into your garment. *Pressing cloths* are most important. Use cheesecloth for lightweight fabrics and cotton or linen for heavier fabrics. When pressing curved areas use a *tailor's ham*. This is a firmly packed cushion with rounded ends. It represents the body's curves and fits into garment darts, princess seams or sleeves. A *sleeve board* provides two ironing surfaces. It is designed for pressing slim areas which cannot fit over the top of your ironing board, so that it is possible to press a single layer of fabric at a time, avoiding creases.

### Basic pressing equipment

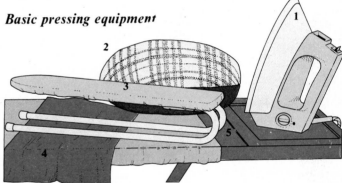

1 Steam iron   2 Tailor's ham   3 Sleeve board   4 Pressing cloth
5 Ironing board

### Optional aids
Other aids exist which are useful but not essential. A *pressing mitt* and a *seam roll* are similar in function and composition to the tailor's ham. The mitt can be slipped over your hand or on the tip of the sleeve board. Use on areas which your pressing ham cannot reach, or for sleeve caps. The seam roll is a firmly packed cylindrical cushion. Its main use is for pressing seams in narrow areas, like trousers or sleeves. As it is roll shaped only the seams get pressed, not the surrounding fabric. A *pressing pad* consists of a number of layers of soft fabric stitched together. Use for pressing monogrammed or sequinned fabric to prevent flattening. A *tailor's board* is made of wood, moulded into curves and straight lines. You can therefore press both curves and straight lines because of this. A *point presser* is also made of wood. Its upper surface has a pointed tip which can be used on corners, points and straight seams. Its lower surface can be used like a *dressmaker's clapper*. This is a solid block of wood, used most frequently in tailoring to produce creases in heavy fabric. The garment edge is first steamed and then pounded with the clapper. For pressing piled fabrics, use a *needleboard*. This is a flat surface covered with steel wires which will prevent the fabric from matting as it is pressed.

# Introduction to machine sewing

A number of different types of sewing machine are available, from the simplest hand-operated models to the latest electric ones which have a number of sophisticated attachments. Recent models fall into two categories: straight stitch or swing needle machines.

Straight stitch machines sew in a straight line, forwards or backwards. Stitch length can be adjusted. They are suitable for all basic home dressmaking, attaching shirring and elastic, some types of edge finishing and straight stitch embroidery.

Swing needle machines have a stitch width regulator which means that the needle can swing from side to side in a variety of widths. The machine can therefore produce both straight stitches and stitches like two-step, zigzag, overcasting, simple embroidery and buttonholes. Some swing needle machines are even more advanced and can produce three-step zigzag stitches, suitable for stretch material, and a wider range of decorative stitches (see special stitches page 424).

Choose a machine depending on the type of sewing you do and on whether you want to progress from simple sewing to more complicated tailored and embroidered garments. The principle of operation is the same for all types of machines. An instruction book is always included with the machine which will tell you exactly how it works, and how to look after it.

## Arranging seating and lighting

### Correct posture
Sitting correctly at your machine helps you to work comfortably and well. Position your chair so that you are sitting directly in front of the needle. Lean forward slightly towards your machine instead of sitting back in your chair. Your feet should be flat on the floor. If the machine has a foot control, operate it with one foot placed slightly forward. You can use whichever foot feels most comfortable. If the machine has a knee control place your left foot forward and press your right knee against the control.

**The correct position**

### Lighting your work
It is important to work in a well lit, shadow-free area, both for ease of sewing and to prevent eye strain. Try to place your machine in natural light. Even if your machine is near a window, additional lighting may be necessary to prevent shadows. An adjustable lamp will provide the best light and can be moved according to conditions. Most machines have a built in light to shine directly on the work.

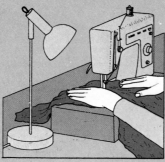
**Lighting your work**

# How the machine works

## Basic working parts of the machine

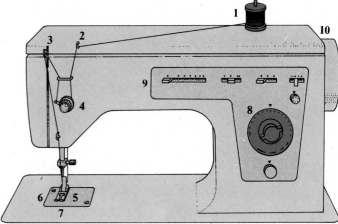

| | | |
|---|---|---|
| 1 **Spool pin** | 5 **Presser foot** | 9 **Stitch width** |
| 2 **Thread guide** | 6 **Feed** | **regulator** |
| 3 **Take-up lever** | 7 **Bobbin case** | 10 **Handwheel** |
| 4 **Tension disc** | 8 **Stitch length** | |
| **and regulator** | **regulator** | |

### Threading the machine
A sewing machine combines two separate threads to make stitches. The top reel of thread is fed through the fabric by a needle and looped with the bobbin thread to form a stitch. The fabric is guided through the machine by hand, and is held firm by a presser foot.

### Winding the bobbin
The bobbin on the machine will always need to be wound, but the position of the bobbin winder can vary. Some models wind the bobbin in the bobbin case, some on the machine top or side. Make sure it is evenly wound and not too full or the thread will break.

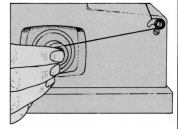
**Winding the bobbin**

### Threading the needle
To thread the needle, first raise it to expose the eye. Make sure the thread guide is at its highest position so the needle will not unthread as soon as you start machining. Follow the threading instructions for your machine. Thread direction varies according to the machine.

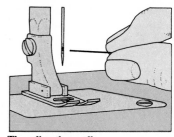
**Threading the needle**

### Drawing up the bobbin thread
With the thread in your left hand, turn the handwheel until the needle enters the bobbin case and returns to its highest position. As the needle rises it will pull up a loop of bobbin thread. Pull the loop to bring up the bobbin thread.

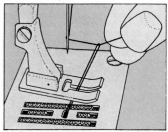
**Drawing up the bobbin thread**

# Tension

Most machines have tension controls for the needle and bobbin threads. A perfectly formed stitch can only be produced if the two tensions balance and the threads are drawn into the fabric to the same degree. A seam stitched with a balanced tension is twice as strong as one stitched with unbalanced tension.

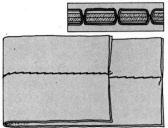
**Correct tension**

### Correct tension
When the pressure is correct on both threads the link formed with each stitch is centred between the fabric layers. Equal amounts of top and bottom thread should have been used to produce the stitches, and there should be no puckering of the fabric.

### Top thread too tight
Look at the position of the stitch links. With too much tension these will be nearer the top fabric. Excessive top tension results in too little thread for the stitch causing the fabric to pucker and the stitches to break easily. To correct, turn tension dial to lower number.

**Too much tension**

### Top thread too loose
When the stitch links appear near the bottom layer of fabric the top thread tension is too loose. Too little tension results in too much thread, producing a floppy and imprecise seam. The fabric may also pucker. To correct this, turn the tension dial to a higher number.

**Too little tension**

## Adjusting the tension
Adjust your tension as little as possible. There are two controls, one for top tension and one for bottom. Normally you will only need to use the top tension device alone.

### Top tension

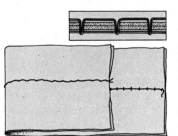

The top tension control is usually found on or close to the tension discs. Adjust the top tension to control the pull on the thread as it passes through the machine. With the machine threaded and the presser foot down, turn the tension dial as required.

### Bottom tension

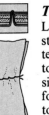

It is rarely necessary to alter the bottom tension, as adjustments to the top tension are normally sufficient. A screw on the side of the bobbin case controls tension. To increase tension, turn the screw clockwise. To decrease tension turn the screw anti-clockwise.

# Pressure and feed

Pressure and feed interact to produce even stitching. The presser foot exerts downward pressure on the fabric, so that the layers move through evenly. The feed plate exerts an upward force to move the fabric under the presser foot.

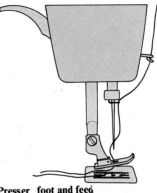
**Presser foot and feed**

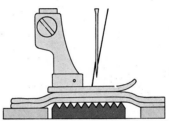
**Interaction of feed and presser foot**

### Presser foot and feed
As the needle enters the fabric so the feed is lowered, leaving the presser foot anchoring the fabric. As the needle comes up and out of the fabric the feed moves forward. This motion continues as the needle pulls the stitch up with it. As the stitch is being formed in the fabric the feed moves up to help the presser foot secure the fabric and then advances it one stitch length. The presser foot is adjusted by the pressure regulator while the feed is controlled by the stitch length regulator.

Regulate pressure according to fabric. A heavy fabric requires more pressure; a light fabric little pressure. Always test pressure and feed before starting to sew.

### Correct pressure
Pressure should be heavy enough to prevent slipping or "side creeping" but also light enough to move the fabric without marking it. Under the correct pressure, the fabric layers feed through the machine evenly and easily. The stitches are of an even length and tension and the fabric shows no sign of damage.

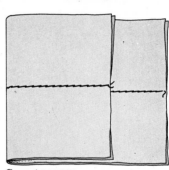
**Correct pressure**

### Too much pressure
With too much pressure the top fabric may slip while the bottom puckers up. The stitches may appear uneven in length and tension, or the fabric itself may be pinched up. Correct by dialling pressure regulator to a lower number.

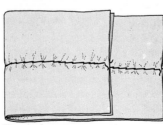
**Too much pressure**

### Too little pressure
Too little pressure causes irregular feeding. Stitches may be of uneven length and tension and in some cases the fabric may be caught and pulled into the bobbin area. Rectify by dialling pressure regulator to a higher number.

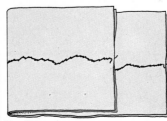
**Too little pressure**

# Machine stitching

### Types of stitches

A well-maintained machine will produce perfect stitches providing you use the right needle and thread for the fabric, with the correct tension.

The basic machine stitch is a running stitch. Use a short stitch length for sewing seams on lightweight fabrics; regular stitch length for general household sewing, and long stitch length for tacking, easing and gathering. Adjust length by moving the stitch length regulator higher or lower.

### Special stitches

Most machines are capable of special stitches. Zigzag and multistitch, in which both length and width can vary, are used for edging, mending, attaching elastic and fagotting. Overcasting stitch is used to produce neat durable seams on bulky fabrics and those which fray. Satin stitch, available on almost all modern machines, is used for buttonholing or edging.

### Learning to stitch

If you have never used a machine before, practise on a piece of paper, with the machine unthreaded. Always start to sew slowly, learning to control starting and stopping. Your speed will increase with practice.

### Starting to stitch

Raise the take-up lever to its highest position, pull the bobbin and top threads underneath and behind the presser foot. Then put the fabric underneath with the bulk of the fabric to the left and the seam edge to the right. Put the needle into the fabric where you want to begin. Lower the presser foot and start to sew.

### Finishing off

When you come to the end of your stitching line take the needle to its highest position and raise the presser foot. Withdraw your work by pulling it back and away from the needle. Leaving a short length, cut the two threads. Pull the needle thread through to the underside and then fasten the threads securely. Trim ends.

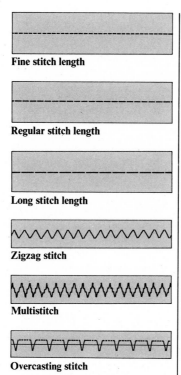
Fine stitch length

Regular stitch length

Long stitch length

Zigzag stitch

Multistitch

Overcasting stitch

Satin stitch

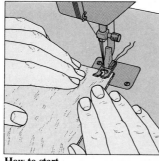
**How to start**

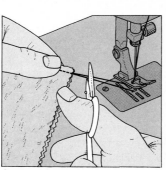
**Cutting the threads**

### Guiding the fabric

It is important to feed the fabric through the machine as evenly as possible. Gently put your left hand on the fabric (as shown in "starting to stitch"). Take care not to lean your left hand too heavily on the fabric as this will lead to uneven feeding and strain. Place your right hand 1½in. (4 cm) in front and to the right of the needle. As you depress the speed control, guide the fabric through with your fingers. Do not watch the needle, but concentrate on one point, such as the presser foot. Use the presser foot as a guide for straight stitching by maintaining an equal distance between it and the raw edge of the fabric seam allowance on your garment.

### Stitching corners

To stitch corners you will need to "pivot" the fabric. Stitch up to turning point, leaving the needle in the work. Raise the needle until it is about to leave the fabric. Raise the presser foot and pivot the fabric on the needle. Then lower the presser foot and continue. Reinforce at the corners by shortening the stitch length just before and after the point of the corner on your garment.

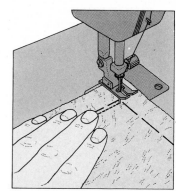
**Pivoting the fabric**

### Stitching on a curve

Stitching on a curved line can be done in one movement but if you need to adjust the angle of the fabric make sure the needle is in the fabric when you stop. Raise the presser foot and turn the fabric gently on the needle. Lower the presser foot and continue to sew until more adjustment is needed. Stitch slowly and smoothly, so as to avoid puckering the fabric as you sew.

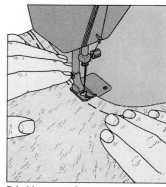
**Stitching around a curve**

## Top stitching your garment

Top stitching is used for decorative as well as functional purposes. Make all alterations to your garment before you top stitch it. Before starting to stitch, tack close to the proposed sewing line. Follow this line carefully. Use thicker or contrasting thread and the longer stitch setting when using as decoration. When using as a strengthener, set for the regular stitch length and sew through the seam allowances. Fasten threads on wrong side after pulling them through.

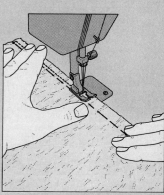
*Stitch close to tacking, using thicker or contrasting thread.*

# Selecting needles and thread | Machine attachments

## Choosing machine needles

The size and type of point are the determining factors in needle choice. Sizes range from 9 to 18 (the lower the number the finer the needle). To prevent damage to lightweight fabric use a fine needle. A heavier fabric will require a thicker needle to prevent needle deflection or breakage. The type of point is very important. A sharp-point needle is most commonly used and is recommended for all types of woven fabric. A ball-point needle has a rounded tip and is used when sewing knitwear because the point slides between the yarns instead of piercing them. A wedge-point needle is designed specifically for leathers and vinyls to minimize the risk of fabric splitting.

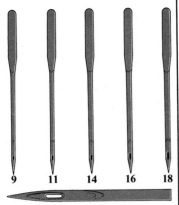

**9  11  14  16  18**

A sharp-point needle is recommended for woven fabrics

A ball-point needle should be used for knitted fabrics

A wedge-point needle is needed for leathers and vinyls

## Selecting threads

Choose thread according to the type of fabric being used. Use synthetic threads with man-made fibres and mercerized cotton or silk thread with cotton or linen. Woollen fabrics should be sewn with silk or synthetic threads as they are capable of stretching with the fabric. Choose thread which is one shade darker than your fabric because thread appears lighter when worked on a garment.

On all types of thread the higher the number on the label, the finer the thread. When stitched, the thread should be well set into the fabric to give a firm long-lasting seam. If the thread is too heavy for the fabric it will remain on the surface and wear out quickly, reducing the durability of your garment.

### Needle and thread selection chart

| Fabric | Thread | Needle | Stitches per in. (2.5cm) |
|---|---|---|---|
| **Lightweight** Chiffon, organza, fine lace, lawn, voile | Silk, size A, nylon, size A, mercerized cotton, extra fine (any fibre), size 60–100 | 9 or 11 | 10–15 |
| **Medium weight** Velvet, gingham, crepe, corduroy, stretch terry brocade, linen, some denims | Polyester, cotton-wrapped polyester, mercerized cotton, size 50–60 | 11 or 14 | 10–12 |
| **Heavy** Wide rib corduroy terry cloth | Polyester, cotton-wrapped polyester, heavy duty (any fibre), size 30–40 | 16 or 18 | 8–12 |
| **Very heavy** Canvas, upholstery fabric | Polyester, cotton-wrapped polyester, heavy duty (any fibre), size 20 | 16 or 18 | 8–12 |

Attachments greatly increase the versatility and efficiency of the machine. They are not strictly necessary, but they can save time and trouble. In addition to the ones described below, there is a wide variety of other attachments, such as a gathering foot, overedge foot, pin tuck foot, and cording foot. They are all variations on the presser foot. If the needle hole on the presser foot is small and round it is for straight stitching. If it is wide both straight and zigzag stitching can be made. Be sure to adjust stitch length and tension according to the attachment.

### Zip foot

A zip foot attachment can be used to sew any seam where there is a bulk of fabric on one side. There are two kinds of zip foot attachment: one with an adjustable foot, the other with a non-adjustable foot. The adjustable zip foot has indentations on either side. This enables you to sew to the left or right of the zip. To sew to the left of the zip, first raise the needle. Loosen the screw on the horizontal bar and position the needle above the right notch of the foot. Reverse the process for right-hand sewing.

**Zip foot**

### Buttonhole foot

Buttonhole attachments are used for making buttonholes or binding raw edges. These attachments are complicated to use on straight stitch machines. In such cases it is advisable to hand sew the buttonholes. On a swing needle machine the buttonhole attachment produces a simple buttonhole stitch by swinging the needle from side to side. Insert the attachment by removing the presser foot and putting the buttonhole attachment in its place. Consult your machine handbook for variations.

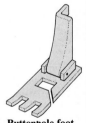

**Buttonhole foot**

### Overlock foot

An overlock foot is useful for producing a durable finish on seams which fray easily or are bulky. It is only suitable for use on a swing needle machine and is most effective when the fabric is positioned under the presser foot so that the stitches form slightly over the fabric edge. A metal bar holds the edge in place to make sure that the stitches are set correctly. Test that you have the correct positioning and stitch width before you start to sew. Insert the foot as instructed by your machine guide.

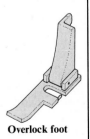

**Overlock foot**

### Embroidery foot

An embroidery thread foot is suitable for shirring fabric (shirring instructions are on page 444). Its design allows the elastic thread to pass easily under the presser foot. On swing needle machines the elastic is couched onto the fabric. The thread is fed through the presser foot hole and pulled gently. The more it is pulled the more the fabric gathers. On a straight stitch machine the elastic is wound around the bobbin. Insert the foot as instructed by your machine guide.

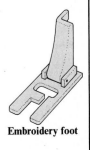

**Embroidery foot**

# Taking your measurements

### Taking measurements

Personal measurements must be taken before you buy or alter your pattern. Ask a friend to measure you, as this is easier and more accurate. If you are measuring for a dress, skirt or trousers wear your regular underwear. Take the vertical measurements first, then the horizontal ones. Keep the tape parallel to the ground and pull it taut. Write down your measurements and keep them for future reference.

### Bodice

Measure your waist, then from neck to waist and from the centre of your shoulder, over the bust point to the waistline. From the centre of the shoulder measure to the point of the bust. Measure from the neckline to the top of the sleeve and from the back shoulder to the waist. Measure your bust around the fullest part with the tape slightly higher at the back. Take the back measurement, halfway between the top of the armhole and underarm, with the arm slightly raised.

### Skirt

Take the waist measurement as for the bodice. Then the centre front waist to the hem, depending on the length desired. Also the centre back waist to the hem and side waist to hem. Take your hip measurement around the fullest part, approximately 9in. (23cm) below the waist. Take the yoke measurement from approximately 3in. (7.5cm) below the waistline.

### Sleeve

Measure from your shoulder to the wrist, with your arm bent to waist height. With the arm still bent measure shoulder to elbow and elbow to wrist. With the arm straightened, take your inside arm length from under the armhole to the wrist. Your upper arm measurement should be taken around the widest part of the arm. Measure around the elbow with the arm bent to waist height. Lastly, take your wrist measurement.

### Bodice and skirt measurement

1 **Point of bust** (shoulder to bust curve)

2 **Chest front** (armhole to armhole)

3 **Bust** (all around body)

4 **Neck to waist** (front)

5 **Waist** (front)

6 **Waist to hem** (front)

7 **Side waist to hem**

8 **Shoulder to waist** (front)

9 **Skirt yoke** (front)

10 **Hip** (front)

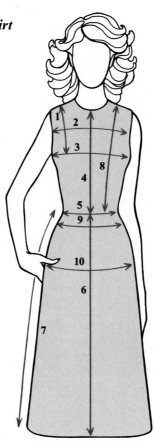

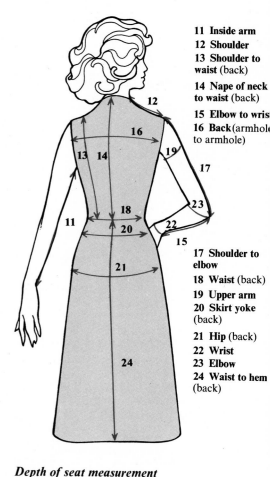

11 **Inside arm**

12 **Shoulder**

13 **Shoulder to waist** (back)

14 **Nape of neck to waist** (back)

15 **Elbow to wrist**

16 **Back** (armhole to armhole)

17 **Shoulder to elbow**

18 **Waist** (back)

19 **Upper arm**

20 **Skirt yoke** (back)

21 **Hip** (back)

22 **Wrist**

23 **Elbow**

24 **Waist to hem** (back)

### Inner and outer leg measurements

*Take waist and hip measurements (see left). Measure your inside leg from the inside top of the leg to the required height from the floor. Take your outside leg from the side waistline to the required height from the floor.*

1 **Waist**

2 **Hip**

3 **Inside leg**

4 **Outside leg**

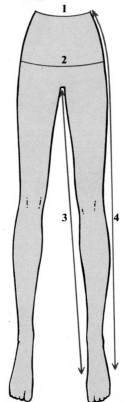

### Depth of seat measurement

*Sit on a chair with your back straight and measure from the side of your waist to the chair. Add $\frac{5}{8}$in. (1.5cm) for ease but for a full figure you will need to add more.*

1 **Waist**

2 **Depth of crotch**

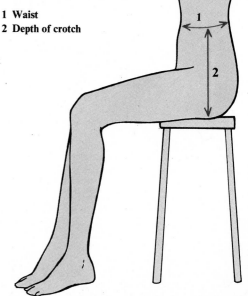

# Body measurement charts

### Men's

Men's pattern sizes are designed for men of average build and height about 5ft 10in. (1.78m), without shoes.

| Size | 34 cm | in | 36 cm | in | 38 cm | in | 40 cm | in | 42 cm | in | 44 cm | in |
|---|---|---|---|---|---|---|---|---|---|---|---|---|
| Chest | 87 | 34 | 92 | 36 | 97 | 38 | 102 | 40 | 107 | 42 | 112 | 44 |
| Waist | 71 | 28 | 76 | 30 | 81 | 32 | 87 | 34 | 92 | 36 | 99 | 39 |
| Hip (seat) | 89 | 35 | 94 | 37 | 99 | 39 | 104 | 41 | 109 | 43 | 114 | 45 |
| Neck band | 33.5 | 14 | 37 | 14½ | 38 | 15 | 39.5 | 15½ | 40.5 | 16 | 42 | 16½ |
| Shirt sleeve | 81 | 32 | 81 | 32 | 84 | 33 | 84 | 33 | 87 | 34 | 87 | 34 |

### Misses'

To suit heights 5ft 5in. to 5ft 6in. (1.65m to 1.68m). Designed for a well proportioned figure.

| Size | 6 cm | in | 8 cm | in | 10 cm | in | 12 cm | in | 14 cm | in | 16 cm | in |
|---|---|---|---|---|---|---|---|---|---|---|---|---|
| Bust | 78 | 30½ | 80 | 31½ | 83 | 32½ | 87 | 34 | 92 | 36 | 97 | 38 |
| Waist | 58 | 23 | 61 | 24 | 64 | 25 | 67 | 26½ | 71 | 28 | 76 | 30 |
| Hip | 83 | 32½ | 85 | 33½ | 88 | 34½ | 92 | 36 | 97 | 38 | 102 | 40 |
| Back waist length | 39.5 | 15½ | 40 | 15¾ | 40.5 | 16 | 41.5 | 16¼ | 42 | 16½ | 42.5 | 16¾ |

### Women's

To suit heights 5ft 5in. (1.65m to 1.68m) as in the misses' range but for a larger, more developed figure.

| Size | 38 cm | in | 40 cm | in | 42 cm | in | 44 cm | in | 46 cm | in | 48 cm | in |
|---|---|---|---|---|---|---|---|---|---|---|---|---|
| Bust | 107 | 42 | 112 | 44 | 117 | 46 | 122 | 48 | 127 | 50 | 132 | 52 |
| Waist | 89 | 35 | 94 | 37 | 99 | 39 | 105 | 41½ | 112 | 44 | 118 | 46½ |
| Hip | 112 | 44 | 117 | 46 | 122 | 48 | 127 | 50 | 132 | 52 | 137 | 54 |
| Back waist length | 44 | 17¼ | 44 | 17⅜ | 44.5 | 17½ | 45 | 17⅝ | 45 | 17¾ | 45.5 | 17⅞ |

### Junior petite

For an adolescent figure of 5ft (1.52m) with a small, highly-placed bust and short back length.

| Size | 3jp cm | in | 5jp cm | in | 7jp cm | in | 9jp cm | in | 11jp cm | in | 13jp cm | in |
|---|---|---|---|---|---|---|---|---|---|---|---|---|
| Bust | 78 | 30½ | 79 | 31 | 81 | 32 | 84 | 33 | 87 | 34 | 89 | 35 |
| Waist | 57 | 22½ | 58 | 23 | 61 | 24 | 64 | 25 | 66 | 26 | 69 | 27 |
| Hip | 80 | 31½ | 81 | 32 | 84 | 33 | 87 | 34 | 89 | 35 | 92 | 36 |
| Back waist length | 35.5 | 14 | 36 | 14¼ | 37 | 14½ | 37.5 | 14¾ | 38 | 15 | 39 | 15¼ |

### Half size

To suit heights 5ft 2in. to 5ft 5in. (1.57m to 1.60m) with a developed figure. Waist and hips are larger in proportion to the bust size in these patterns.

| Size | 10½ cm | in | 12½ cm | in | 14½ cm | in | 16½ cm | in | 18½ cm | in | 20½ cm | in |
|---|---|---|---|---|---|---|---|---|---|---|---|---|
| Bust | 84 | 33 | 89 | 35 | 94 | 37 | 99 | 39 | 104 | 41 | 109 | 43 |
| Waist | 69 | 27 | 74 | 29 | 79 | 31 | 84 | 33 | 89 | 35 | 96 | 37½ |
| Hip | 89 | 35 | 94 | 37 | 99 | 39 | 104 | 41 | 109 | 43 | 116 | 45½ |
| Back waist length | 38 | 15 | 39 | 15¼ | 39.5 | 15½ | 40 | 15¾ | 40.5 | 15⅞ | 40.5 | 16 |

# Understanding your pattern envelope

### Pattern size guidelines

Generally speaking you should take the same size in a pattern as in ready-to-wear. However, you must check your measurements with those on the back of the pattern envelope. Pattern size is based on bust measurement (i.e. a 34in. bust takes a size 12). If your basic measurements do not conform exactly to the pattern for jackets, dresses and coats buy the pattern size nearest to your bust measurement. It is easier to alter the waist and hips than the shoulders. It is important that the pattern fits well on the shoulders and around the armholes. Skirts, shorts and trousers are bought according to hip measurement. If your bust is larger in proportion to your other measurements than the pattern size specifies, and if the difference between your chest and bust is 4in. (10cm) buy a smaller pattern and increase bust allowance.

### Reading your pattern envelope information

Most important is the *yardage column*. Circle your size on the top row. Choose the garment view and width from the left column. Run your eye right, until you get to the column under your size. This number is the amount of fabric you will need to buy. There is also a *back view* to see fitting details; a *pattern piece* diagram and made-up measurements. Also check *suggested fabrics* to use for the design and *notions*.

**Misses' fashion basic dress with two necklines**

The dress has back zipper, set-in sleeves and optional front waistline darts. View 1 has lowered round neckline, patch pockets and short sleeves with turn back cuffs. View 2 has high round neckline and long sleeves.

**9 pieces given**

Extra fabric is needed to match plaids, stripes and one-way designs. Use nap fabric requirements and nap layouts for one-way design fabrics.
Not suitable for obvious diagonal fabrics.

| STANDARD BODY MEASUREMENTS | | | | |
|---|---|---|---|---|
| | Bust | 80(31½) | 83(32½) | 87(34) | 92(36) |
| | Waist | 61(24) | 64(25) | 67(26½) | 71(28) |
| | Hip–23cm(9") below waist | 85(33½) | 88(34½) | 92(36) | 97(38) |
| | Back–neck to waist | 40(15¾) | 40.5(16) | 41.5(16¼) | 42(16½) |

| Fabric required | Sizes | 8 | 10 | 12 | 14 |
|---|---|---|---|---|---|
| **View 1 Dress** | | | | | |
| 90cm(35"36") without nap | | 2.90(3⅛) | 2.90(3⅛) | 2.90(3⅛) | 2.90(3⅛) |
| 115cm(44"45") without nap | | 1.80(2) | 1.90(2) | 2.40(2⅝) | 2.40(2⅝) |
| 140cm(54") without nap | | 1.60(1¾) | 1.60(1¾) | 1.60(1¾) | 1.70(1⅞) |
| **View 2 Dress** | | | | | |
| 90cm(35"36") with or without nap | | 3.00(3¼) | 3.00(3¼) | 3.10(3⅜) | 3.10(3⅜) |
| 115cm(44"45") with nap | | 2.50(2¾) | 2.60(2⅞) | 2.70(3) | 2.80(3⅛) |
| 115cm(44"45") without nap | | 2.00(2¼) | 2.10(2⅜) | 2.60(2⅞) | 2.60(2⅞) |
| 150cm(58"60") without nap | | 1.70(1⅞) | 1.70(1⅞) | 1.70(1⅞) | 1.70(1⅞) |

**View 1 or 2 interfacing** – 0.20m(¼yd) of 64cm(25"), 82cm(32"), 90cm(35"36") woven or non-woven, fusible or non-fusible.

| Garment measurements | | | | |
|---|---|---|---|---|
| Finished back length of dress | 103(40½) | 104(41) | 106(41½) | 107(42) |
| Width of lower edge of dress | 120(47) | 122(48) | 126(49½) | 131(51½) |

**Sewing notions** – Thread, 55cm(22") zipper or invisible zipper, seam binding.
**Suggested fabrics** – Linen, silk linen, shantung, crepe, jersey, sateen, muslin.

# Types of fabric

The basic components of textile fabrics are fibres. These may be natural (wool, linen, cotton, silk) or synthetic (acrylic, polyester, acetate). All the natural fibres (with the exception of silk) are short and are called *staples*. The long continuous strands of silk and man-made fibres are called *filaments*. These staple and filament lengths are then twisted into yarns. The appearance and durability of the yarn is affected by the degree of twist. Gently twisted yarns are suitable for napped fabrics which are soft and rather weak. Tightly twisted yarns are used for smooth fabrics such as gaberdine. In general, the tighter the twist, the smoother and stronger the yarn.

### The different methods of construction

Fabric is formed using one of a variety of techniques. Weaving, knitting, felting and netting are the four basic ways of constructing fabric from which all other types are formed.

**Woven fabric**

#### Weaving

This is the most common method of forming fabric, whereby two sets of yarn are worked at right angles to each other. Warp yarns are stretched lengthwise on the loom and are raised and lowered by movable frames (harnesses). This allows weft yarns to be inserted crosswise by shuttles. All woven fabric has a selvedge.

#### Knitting

This method uses machines to produce a fabric of interlocking loops. Weft and warp knitting are the two basic techniques. Weft fabric is constructed with one continuous yarn forming loops crosswise. Stretch is greater across the fabric than down it. Although comfortable to wear, this fabric is prone to running and sagging. Warp knit fabric is made by forming loops lengthwise. Each yarn is controlled by its own needle. It follows a zigzag course, interlocking each loop with its neighbour down the length of the fabric. This produces durable, run-proof fabric.

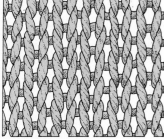

**Knitted fabric**

#### Felting

In this method moisture, heat and pressure are applied to short fibres to produce a matted layer. Felts do not fray, but they do tend to tear when they are damp.

**Felted fabric**

#### Netting

Here the yarns are held together by knots wherever they intersect. It can be as heavy as fishnet or as light as lace, depending on the fibre used.

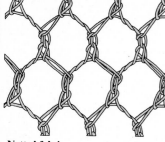

**Netted fabric**

# Choosing fabric

If you are using a bought pattern the pattern envelope usually contains a chart giving details of the amount of fabric you will need to buy. Advice on which type of fabric to buy is sometimes included. If so, follow it. Choose good quality fabric. Make sure that the weave is firm and that the threads do not shift when they are stretched. The weave should be even, so check it against the light for any unusually thin or thick areas, or holes. The dye should be even and look fresh. The fabric should be as crease resistant as possible. Take a corner of the fabric and crush it in your hand. The wrinkles should fall out. If they do not, any garment using such fabric will display the same amount of "wrinkle". Buy only the amount specified on the pattern envelope. If you are designing your own garment see page 430 for advice.

### Hints for beginners

Beginners should make garments using light- to medium-weight, non-slip fabrics such as cottons, brushed rayon, Viyella, polyester, light wool. These are the easiest to handle. Avoid very lightweight fabrics such as chiffon or georgette and heavyweight, loosely woven fabrics such as tweeds. Also avoid textured fabrics. Do not use heavily patterned fabric or fabric with a napped surface (where the pile runs in one direction only).

### Checking for suitability

Check the fabric's suitability for the pattern: i.e. if the pattern is gathered or pleated ensure that the fabric will adapt to the design. If in doubt ask the sales assistant for advice.

Check the fabric's suitability for you by draping the fabric near your face to see if the colour suits you. Boldly patterned fabric and very strongly coloured fabrics can be difficult to wear successfully. For example, a large person should avoid bold prints or horizontal bands as these are visually fattening. Take the bolt of cloth to the nearest long mirror and let the fabric fall against you in the same direction as the pattern to have an idea of the total look of the fabric.

| Simple garments and suitable materials for beginners | | |
|---|---|---|
| **Garments** | **Material** | **Linings** |
| **Dresses and skirts** | | |
| Pleated | Lightweight, firm woven without print | Lining helps give a light, soft fabric more body |
| Seamed | Lightweight, firm woven without print, or knitted | Lining can be a simple A shape |
| Plain | Lightweight or firm woven in any pattern, or knitted | |
| Gathered | Lightweight or soft fabric, any pattern or knitted | |
| **Capes and simple jackets** | Medium weight only. Firm woven best. Use strong zips | Usually lined in an appropriate fabric |
| **Nightclothes** | Lightweight, firm woven, knitted or synthetic | Unlined |
| **Tops and shirts** | | |
| Loose fitting | Lightweight, firm, soft or knitted | |
| Fitted | Large patterned fabric unsuitable. Firm woven or knitted best | |
| **Trousers** | Medium weight. Knits unsuitable. Strong zips needed for openings | Unlined |

# Special finishes

Fabric can be treated in a number of ways to adapt it for different purposes. These finishes vary enormously and will affect the way the fabric is cared for. The most common finishes are:

**Pre-shrunk** The fabric is shrunk beforehand and will not shrink more than one or two per cent.

**Flame resistant** The fabric is treated so that it will not burn once the source of the fire has been removed.

**Bonded** A rubberized backing is added to give it extra body.

**Waterproofed** A special finish makes sure that the fabric repels water.

**Laminated** A plastic coating on the fabric surface makes it water resistant.

**Crease resistant** A special finish helps to make the fabric crush-proof.

**Wash and wear** The fabric can be washed and worn without being ironed.

**Colourfast** This fabric will not fade with use if washed to instructions.

## Attention to fabric before (nd during sewing

All fabrics can shrink so they should be laundered according to instruction before sewing. Some fabrics, because of their construction, impose the following special sewing and cutting requirements.

**Synthetics** fray easily and should be cut with sharp scissors to prevent threads being caught and pulled. When sewing, a synthetic thread and a fine needle should always be used, and extra fabric left for turnings. It is also important to loosen the machine tension in order to avoid puckering. Any trimmings should also be synthetic fabric.

**Cotton** can shrink slightly so it should be washed according to instruction before sewing.

**Linen** is liable to fray so adequate turnings should be allowed and the fabric edges finished as appropriate.

# General care of fabric

To make sure that fabric lasts as long as possible, always launder it carefully, following any instructions. When you buy fabric check the bolt of cloth for washing instructions (whether it should be hand or machine washed or dry cleaned). Washing machine instructions appear as a numerical code corresponding to those displayed on the back of washing powder packets. These state which programme on the machine to use for a specific fabric (see right). If ever in doubt, either dry clean or test wash a small sample. Measure the length and breadth of the sample first and then check it after washing. If there is any discrepancy, dry clean.

## Cotton
Hand wash in hot water. Squeeze gently. Hang dry on a rust proof hanger. Pre-shrunk linen can be hand washed and dried like cotton. If not pre-shrunk, it must be dry cleaned.

## Wool
If hand washable, use a mild soap and luke-warm water. Soak for a few minutes and squeeze gently. Rinse thoroughly and then roll up in a towel to remove excess moisture. Always dry wool on a flat surface otherwise it may stretch and pull out of shape. Always check that dry cleaning is not advised.

## Synthetics
These will have to be treated according to their composition. Many synthetic fabrics these days are composed of several different fibres or a mixture of natural and synthetic fibres. Generally speaking synthetics can be divided into two main categories; those with a nylon or polyester base and those with a rayon base. Polyester and nylon can be washed in warm water, rinsed and dried on a metal hanger. Treat hand washable rayon gently. Wash with mild soap and lukewarm water if the instructions do not suggest dry cleaning.

## International codes
These symbols have been devised to give standardized washing information. We list specific washing and drying symbols above right. Below we show the basic symbols for washing, bleaching, ironing and dry cleaning. A cross through the symbol means "do not use", e.g. a crossed triangle means "do not bleach".

### The four main symbols

This symbol represents the washing process and all instructions relating to it.

The triangle represents chlorine bleaching and all instructions relating to it.

The iron is the symbol for ironing and all instructions relating to it.

The circle represents dry cleaning and all instructions relating to it.

## Laundering guide
The symbols for washing instructions, below, are international. They are reproduced on washing powder packets and give a reliable laundering guide.

White cotton and linen articles without special finishes.

Cotton, linen or viscose articles. No special finishes; colours fast at 60°C.

White nylon; white polyester and cotton mixtures.

Coloured nylon; cotton and viscose mixtures with special finishes; polyester/cotton mixtures.

Cotton, linen or viscose articles where colours are fast at 40°C, but not at 60°C.

Acrylic; acetate and triacetate, including mixtures with wool.

Wool; wool mixtures with cotton or viscose; silk.

Silk and printed acetate fabrics with colours not fast at 40°C.

Cotton articles with special finishes. Can be boiled but require drip drying.

Articles which must not be machine washed.

Do not wash.

## Pressing instructions
It is important to press your garment at each stage of its construction. Linen and cotton require a very hot iron, synthetic fabrics need little heat. Velvet and pile fabrics should be steamed to avoid flattening the pile. When pressing, put the iron on the fabric in the direction of the fabric grain. Lift and replace further up the garment. Use a pressing cloth on fabrics other than linen and cotton (a dry cloth with a steam iron and a moistened cloth with a dry iron). To avoid shine press the wrong side of the garment. Take care when ironing over bulky areas like pockets and zips. Do not press over pins. If you have one, use a pressing ham for curved areas.

### Pressing symbols

 Cotton, linen, viscose

 Synthetics.

 Polyester, mixtures, wool.

 Do not iron.

## Preparing the fabric

In any piece of fabric you buy the warp and weft threads (lengthwise and crosswise) should lie at right angles to each other. If they do not, the fabric is off-grain which means that it will then not hang properly when cut unless the fabric is pulled straight. Check before buying that there is no obvious distortion; for example, that the pattern has not been printed on off-grain fabric. Some fabrics with special finishes cannot be corrected because the yarns are locked.

To check the grain you must start with two weft threads. First find the straight crosswise grain by snipping through the selvedge with scissors and then grasp one thread running across the weave. Pull it gently allowing the fabric to gather on the thread. Cut carefully along this pulled thread as far as you can follow it. Repeat the cutting and pulling until you reach the other selvedge.

To straighten the grain, fold the fabric in half lengthwise. Pin the crosswise edges and the selvedges. Wrinkles will form. Dampen the lower layer of the fabric and using a steam iron, press along the lengthwise grain. If still off-grain, press the crosswise grain. Do not press the centre fold.

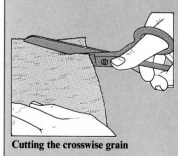

**Cutting the crosswise grain**

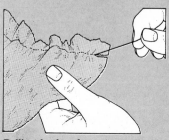

**Pulling the thread**

# Laying out the pattern pieces

If you are working from a bought pattern, your envelope will state how much fabric you need to buy, according to your size, the fabric width and whether it is napped or not. If you are working to your own design you can gauge this for yourself by pinning your pattern pieces to a sheet to see how much fabric you will have to buy. Having obtained the fabric, assemble all the equipment you will need for cutting and prepare a clear surface. Smooth out your pattern pieces, if necessary, with a warm, dry iron. Make any pattern alterations now (see pages 436–437).

If you are using a bought pattern, a guide will be included on how to lay out the fabric and deal with different fabric widths. These layouts differ for fabrics with or without nap.

It is important to keep the vertical line of the pattern pieces along the lengthwise grain of the fabric, unless the pattern suggests otherwise. Parts of the garment to be shaped without seams and darts are usually cut on the bias because of the added elasticity of the fabric. Any patterns cut on the bias take more fabric than those cut on a straight grain.

Prepare the fabric as shown left. Following your pattern instructions, lay out the pattern pieces across the width of your fabric ensuring that the pieces which need to lie on a fold do so. Leave enough space for turnings and pattern pieces like facings, which have to be used twice. Check that you have all the pattern pieces before you start work.

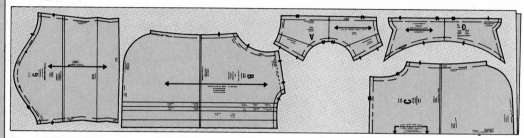

**Pattern laid on a fold on narrow fabric**

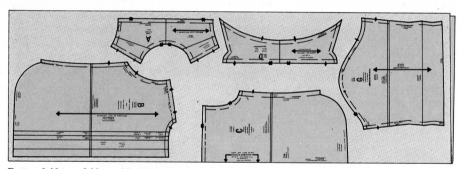

**Pattern laid on a fold on wide fabric**

### Construction marks

Every bought pattern has construction marks and it is essential to follow them. Some construction marks show you where to alter the pattern while others show you which pattern pieces should be matched and where.

**The cutting line** This is a continuous line on the outer edge of the pattern.

**The stitch line** This is a broken line about ⅝in. (1.5cm) from the cutting line, and marks the stitching line.

**The alteration line** This indicates where the pattern should be shortened or lengthened. It is symbolized by a double line.

**The fold line** This is represented by a line with arrows at right angles at either end, pointing to the pattern edge. It is always placed on a fold of material so that a double piece of fabric is produced when cut.

**The grain line** This appears as a line with arrows at either end. It always runs parallel to the

selvedge, following the true grain of the fabric.

**Easing line** This appears as a row of short broken lines with an arrow and a dot at each end.

**Gathering line** Two rows of short broken lines with arrows at each end. Dots mark the gathering points.

Other symbols, apart from the linear ones, are as follows.

**Balance marks** These are generally represented by notches, either single or double. Use these to match one piece of fabric to another. Dots of various sizes, squares and triangles also represent balance marks.

**Darts** These are represented by broken lines meeting at a point.

**Zip position** This is noted by a line of small triangles, showing the exact position of the zip.

**Buttonholes** The position and size of buttonholes is represented by a circle or dot with a horizontal line.

# Cutting the fabric

## Pinning

Having laid out your pieces correctly, pin them securely to the fabric. Place the pins, using as few as possible, diagonally well within the seam lines. This prevents puckering and avoids uneven cutting.

## Cutting

Before you begin, look at the cutting checklist. Always cut on a flat surface with sharp scissors. Open the blades wide and cut right to their points. Follow the seam allowance line, securing the fabric with one hand as you cut: Cut all the main pattern pieces first. Make sure that all necessary marks are transferred before unpinning, as shown right.

### Cutting checklist

**1** Do you have all the pattern pieces for the design? **2** Are the pattern pieces straight on the grain of the fabric? Make sure there are no flaws or creases in the fabric. **3** If the fabric has a nap, are the pattern pieces lying in one direction only? **4** If the fabric is printed, are the pattern pieces arranged so that the fabric design matches when joined together? **5** If the pattern is to be used double, is it lying with the appropriate pattern edge on the fabric fold? **6** Is the fabric folded with the right sides together unless otherwise instructed? **7** Is the fabric lying on an even surface?

## Laying out problem fabrics

Some fabrics, because of design or construction, require more careful laying out. These fabrics include those with a pile, patterns running in one direction, and checks and stripes. Consideration should also be taken when buying such fabrics. Like plain fabrics they should be pre-shrunk and their print and plaid should follow the true grain. Do not buy the fabric if it is printed off grain. Generally speaking, beginners should avoid such fabrics where possible because of the accuracy required in laying them out.

## Laying out napped fabrics or one-way designs

If you use a napped fabric like velvet, the pile must run the same way on each piece of the garment. Therefore the pattern pieces must be laid out so that they all follow the same direction. The pattern will take more fabric than one without nap because you cannot lay pattern pieces top to toe. You can test for nap by smoothing the fabric with your hand. If in doubt, ask the sales assistant. One-way designs are similarly laid out.

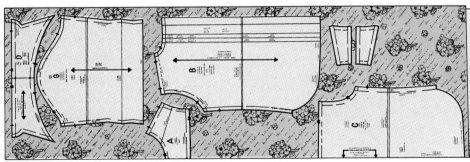

**Pattern laid out on a one-way design fabric**

## Laying out fabric with checks and stripes

Checks and stripes must match exactly at the side seams, centre seams or openings, waistlines, armholes and sleeves. The pattern pieces will need careful positioning to make sure that they match. The key to this is the notches. Shift pattern pieces so they align on the same check or stripe. It is sensible to choose patterns without too many seams for this reason. Be careful to match the checks and stripes at the line where the seam is stitched, rather than on the edge of the seam allowance. Most important, make any alterations to the pattern before laying out as this affects the way the design joins and therefore the match of the fabric.

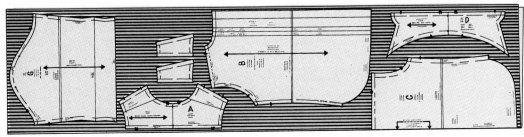

**Pattern laid out on striped fabric**

## Marking the fabric

Once you have cut out the pattern pieces, leave them pinned to your fabric so that you can transfer any marks. There are several ways of marking fabric. You can use tailor's tacks (see page 443), carbon paper or long tacking threads.

### Using a tracing wheel

You will need dressmaker's carbon paper and a tracing wheel. Put the carbon paper, coloured side down, on the wrong side of the fabric. With the pattern on top of the carbon paper, trace along the markings using a ruler as a guide. It is helpful to mark the ends of the darts, points of slashes and other small symbols with horizontal bars. To mark two layers at once use two pieces of carbon paper. Fold the fabric, right sides facing. Put the first piece of paper, coloured side down, between the top layer of fabric and the pattern piece. Place the other, coloured side up, under the bottom layer of fabric. Trace the markings as before.

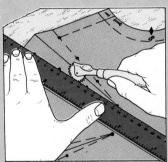

**Marking the fabric**
*Transfer marks with short firm strokes using a ruler as an accurate guide.*

### Thread tracing

A useful method for transferring marks onto the right side of the garment is thread tracing. It is used for pocket markings, centre front openings and button placements. Once the wrong side of the fabric has been marked and the pattern removed, tack over the lines with a contrasting thread. Remove when finished.

# Designing your own clothes from a toile

Most people use bought patterns to make garments. All bought patterns are in fact designed from a fabric replica of the body shaped to fit it. This replica, known as a *toile*, is taken apart and pressed, and the shapes and markings transferred to paper, making a basic paper pattern (see page 435). Toile is the name given to the prototype for a design; the *basic toile* is a basis from which other patterns can be developed.

It is not particularly difficult to make your own toile and therefore design some of your own clothes. Beginners, especially, would benefit greatly from making their own toile as it is a very useful exercise in learning how fabrics are moulded to the body, and in understanding how bought patterns are designed and constructed. However, although trousers can also be made from a basic toile, they are not very easy to cut. Beginners would be better off buying a trouser pattern and altering it if necessary.

## Making the toile

The fabric for making a toile will depend on the garment it is intended for. A soft but firm calico is normally used for a basic toile from which other patterns can be made. Muslin, heavy mull or even old sheets can also be used. Allow enough fabric for twice your own dress length and add 1ft (30.5cm) extra.

You can make a toile by shaping the fabric in sections on a stand which has been adjusted to your measurements. Alternatively, you can shape the fabric against your own figure in the same way, with the help of a friend. The steps given on the right indicate the stages of making a toile. Although it is not complicated, it does require patience to adjust so that it fits perfectly.

In order to mould the fabric to your body shape, you will have to work the fabric into small folds at tension points. You must do this without stretching the fabric. The folds are worked into neat points known as *darts*. On the basic toile these are known as *master darts* and show how much the fabric needs to be eased. The instructions given on the right indicate where they normally appear, but in fact they could be moved about to suit the particular design required.

Always remember to leave enough fabric for seam allowances, hems and turnings. Each piece of the toile pattern covers only half the area required, so remember that two pieces must be cut or the pattern must be placed on a fold line.

An important point to remember is to always keep the straight grain along the vertical line: use the selvedge or pull a thread to make sure of this (see page 430).

## Adapting the toile pattern

Any garment can be made by altering and adapting the toile pattern. You can either work from the basic toile pattern or make a new toile. If you just want to make simple pattern alterations, for example, a new toile will not be necessary; but if you want to try out something more adventurous, then it is worth making a new toile to see how the design hangs on you. If this is the case you should use an appropriate fabric, corresponding as closely as possible to the final garment fabric, e.g. soft muslin for a softly draped dress, or heavy calico for a coat or jacket.

## Working from an existing garment

You can also make a pattern from an existing garment by unpicking it and transferring the pattern pieces to paper in the same way, remembering to mark in the darts and leaving adequate seam allowances.

# The bodice back

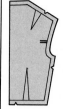

## Making the bodice back

The first step is to take your centre back measurement from the nape of the neck to the waist. Add 5in. (12.5cm). Then take a quarter of your bust measurement and add 2in. (5cm). Cut a rectangle of calico to these measurements with the lengthwise grain of the fabric down the centre back line.

### How to make the bodice back

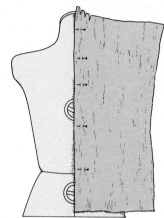

**1** *Pin the rectangle of fabric onto the back of the stand so that it lies with the top 1in. (2.5cm) above the neckline and with one long edge on the centre back as shown. Clip the excess fabric around the neck.*

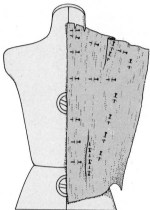

**3** *Smooth the fabric across the back of the stand and pin the fabric down the side seam to the waist. Pin any surplus fabric at the waist into a dart halfway between the centre back and the side seam. This dart should be 4in. to 6in. (10cm to 15cm) long. Work any surplus at armhole into shoulder dart.*

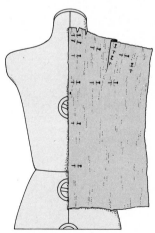

**2** *Check that the crosswise grain of the fabric is straight across the shoulder blade and pin it into place. Pin the fabric to the neckline and the outside point of the shoulder. Smooth the fabric to the centre of the shoulder line and pin any excess into a dart about 3in. (7.5cm) long. This should be halfway across shoulder line, at right angles to it.*

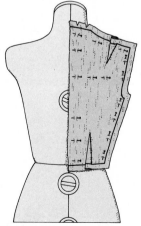

**4** *Draw a line along the outside edges and down each side of the pinned darts. Drop armhole line straight from the shoulder to halfway down the armhole and curve it to about 1in. (2.5cm) below the armhole line on the stand. Trim leaving ¾in. (2cm) all around for seam allowance.*

# *The bodice front*

***Making the bodice front***
You must take your neckline to waist measurement and add 7in. (17.5cm), and then take your bust measurement, divide it by 4 and add 4in. (10cm). Cut fabric to these measurements, as for bodice back.

***How to make the bodice front***

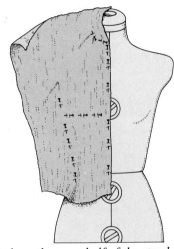

*1 Work on the same half of the stand as you did for the bodice back. Place the rectangle of fabric onto the front of the stand so that it lies with the top 5in. (12.5cm) of fabric above the neckline. Pin it down the centre front line and at the neckline. Clip the excess fabric around the neckline. With the crosswise grain straight over the bust, pin the fabric straight across the bust and from underarm point to waistline.*

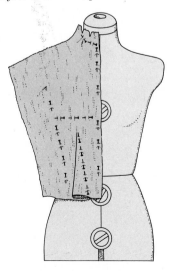

*2 Work the excess fabric between the centre front and the side seam into a dart at the waist, halfway between the centre and the side. For a good fit it should end 1in. to 1½in. (2.5cm to 4cm) below the bust point.*

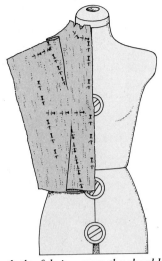

*3 Smooth the fabric across the shoulder, over the armhole, to the shoulder point. Work the excess fabric at the shoulder into a dart at the centre of the shoulder, to match the dart at the bodice back. The dart on the bodice front should end about ¾in. to 1in. (2cm to 2.5cm) above the bust point to obtain a good fit on the bust.*

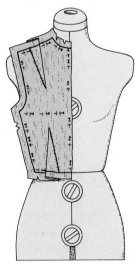

*4 Mark the seams and darts with a ballpoint pen. Then draw in the armhole, working gently into the hollow and curving the line to match that of the back armhole at the side seam. Trim off the excess fabric all round to ¾in. (2cm), and cut corresponding notches – single and double – in both back and front bodices at the shoulder and side seams. Clip the excess fabric around the armhole so that it lies flat against the stand.*

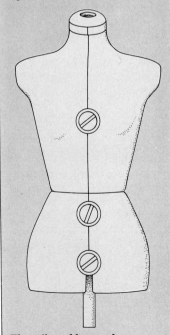

# The skirt toile

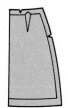

### Making the skirt back and front

To make the skirt back and front of the toile you must take your waist to hem measurement and add 4in. (10cm). Then take half your hip measurement, and cut a rectangle of calico to these measurements, so that the lengthwise grain of the fabric runs down the length of the rectangle. The difference in making the skirt back and front is in the darts.

### Making the skirt back

Place the rectangle with the long edge down the centre back line of the stand, so that it lies with the top 2in. (5cm) above the waistline at the side. Pin down the centre back. Smooth the fabric across the hipline with the sideways grain dropping slightly towards the side seam and pin into position. Smooth the fabric across the hip towards the waist and side seam and pin down the side seam to the hip line. Fold the excess fabric at the waist into a dart about 3in. (7.5cm) long. It should be halfway between the centre back and the side seam and should correspond to the dart in the bodice back. Pin the dart into position. Fold back any excess fabric at the side against the skirt, so that the side seam hangs vertically. With a ball-point pen mark the waistline dart. Trim excess fabric.

### Making the skirt front

Fold the excess fabric at the waist into a dart about 3in. (7.5cm) long, two thirds to three quarters of the way towards the side seam, and sloping towards it slightly. Pin into position. Fold back the excess fabric at the side as for the skirt back. Pin the side seams of the skirt together, then trim. Level the hem all around (this will produce a slight flare). Mark waistline dart, side seams and hem. Cut corresponding notches in the bodice and skirt at the waistline and in side seams.

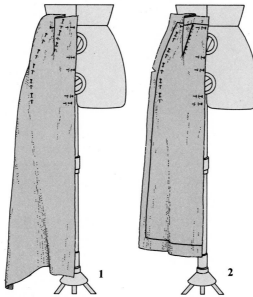

*A dart at the waistline of the skirt back shapes it into the curve of the back. The slight flare is achieved by folding the surplus at the side against the skirt (Fig. 1) and drawing the seam line from the point where the hemline is level. Trim surplus fabric (Fig. 2).*

*Smooth surplus fabric at the waistline into a dart which slopes slightly towards the side seam (Fig. 1). Draw the side seam as for the back, using the seam line on the back as a guide. Then trim surplus fabric (Fig. 2).*

# The sleeve toile

A sleeve toile is usually made by drafting a basic flat pattern to your own measurements (see page 426). This is then transferred to calico and fitted onto a stand or onto oneself with someone else's help.

### Marking out the basic measurements

Cut a rectangle of paper about 4in. (10cm) longer than the outside arm measurement and 4in. (10cm) wider than the upper arm measurement. Fold the paper in half lengthwise. Draw a horizontal line across the paper, 2in. (5cm) from one end and then mark it "wrist line". From the wrist line measure up half the underarm length, add 1in. (2.5cm) and square a line across. Mark this "elbow line". Again from the wrist line, measure up the underarm length, square a line across and mark it "underarm line". Finally, measure up the outside arm length from the wrist line, square a line across, and mark it "crown line".

On the elbow line, measuring across from the fold line, mark half the bent elbow measurement. On the underarm line, measuring across from the fold, mark half the upper arm measurement plus 1in. (2.5cm). Join the marks with a ruler. Extend the line to the wrist and crown lines to form the seam line. Cut down this seam line.

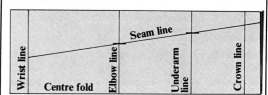

**The basic sleeve measurements marked on a folded piece of paper**

### Shaping the back armhole

Fold a line across the paper, halfway between the crown and underarm lines. Fold the seam line to meet the centre fold. From the intersection of these two folds mark B, $\frac{1}{2}$in. (1.3cm) towards the crown line. On the underarm line make a mark A, 1in. (2.5cm) in from the seam line. On the crown line mark C, $\frac{1}{4}$in. (6mm) from the centre fold line. Lightly connect these marks with straight lines. Halfway between B to C, mark $\frac{3}{8}$in. (1cm) above. Then draw a curved line to give the armhole shape.

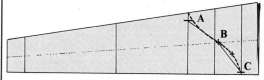

**Marking the folded piece of paper to produce the curved crown shape**

# Shaping and fitting the sleeve toile

## Transferring the toile to paper

### Shaping the front armhole

To make the front armhole, open out the paper and extend the lines across the paper. Measure off points corresponding to A, B and C of the back armhole and call them D, E and F. Halfway along and above D to E make a mark $\frac{3}{4}$in. (2cm) out. Halfway along and below E to F mark $\frac{1}{2}$in. (1.3cm). Connect marks with a curved line.

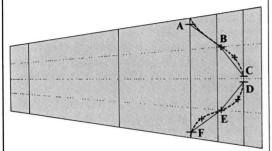

**Marking the folded piece of paper to produce the front armhole**

### Cutting out the toile

Cut out the sleeve shape and pin it to a suitably sized piece of calico. Draw around the sleeve shape. This is your seam line. Use tailor's tacks to notch points B and E on the sleeve toile and the centrefold line on the crown. Cut out the calico, leaving a seam allowance of $\frac{3}{4}$in. (2cm) all around.

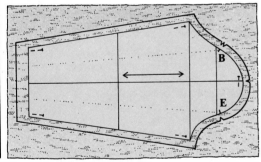

**The paper pattern pinned to calico**

## Points to remember

If the crown rolls too much, drop the armhole on the bodice a little. If the crown is too tight, raise the armhole on the bodice. If the sleeve swings backwards or forwards, reset considering only the grain line. Adjust the bodice seam line to match the underarm seam line. When all the faults are corrected, notch the crown and bodice in three places to give your balance marks. A single notch should be made on the top and front of the sleeve and corresponding points on the bodice. Make a double notch on the back crown and bodice.

### How to fit the sleeve

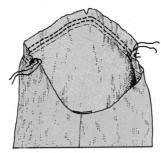

**1** *Tack the underarm seam, making sure that the front armhole will match the bodice front with the sleeve turned the right way out. Just outside the seam line on the crown, run a double row of gathering stitches between the tailor's tacks. With both ends secured draw up slightly from centre.*

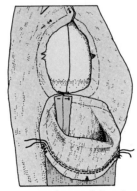

**2** *With the front of the sleeve to the bodice front, pin at the underarm point, matching the seams on the sleeve and bodice. From the underarm point, pin the front of armhole to the bodice until halfway up the armhole, making sure that the crosswise grain matches on both sleeve and bodice. Repeat with the back of armhole.*

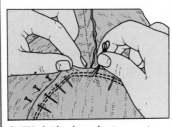

**3** *With the lengthwise grain hanging vertically, pin the crown into place, drawing up the gathering threads if necessary so that the sleeve is smooth across the crown.*

When you are sure that the main pattern pieces of the toile fit properly, you will have to transfer them onto paper. It is advisable to use strong brown paper as this will last longer; you will need a tracing wheel.

Check that you have marked all the seams and darts and cut all the corresponding notches, then unpin all the calico pieces and press them well. Pin each flat pattern piece of the toile onto the paper. With a tracing wheel, trace over the ballpoint marks of the darts and seam lines. Cut around each pattern piece, leaving the $\frac{3}{4}$in. (2cm) seam allowance. Unpin the calico and pencil in the tracing wheel marks on the paper.

Some of the toile pieces will be half patterns, while others will be cut twice, such as sleeves. Mark the paper patterns with "cut two" where necessary. Others may need to be cut along the centre fold, so mark that on the pattern pieces if necessary. Draw in the grain line, and identify each piece. Check that you have transferred all the dart marks and notches.

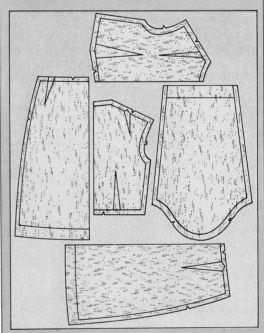

**Transferring your pattern pieces to strong brown paper**

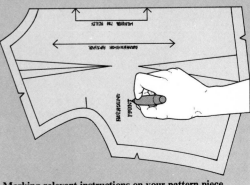

**Marking relevant instructions on your pattern piece.**

435

# Bodice front alterations

'Bought patterns rarely need much alteration on the bodice front because they are usually bought by the bust size measurement. If your bust size does change, you may need to alter your toile or pattern to increase the width and length for a full bust, or reduce the width for a smaller bust.

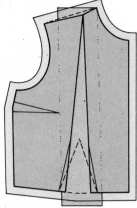
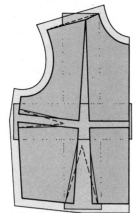

### How to increase width
Measure total front bodice alteration required. Add half to both bodice pieces. Draw a straight line through the centre of the waist dart to the shoulder seam. Cut along this line to within ⅛in. (3mm) of the pattern edge. Place tissue paper underneath and spread the 2 pattern pieces apart to the desired width. Redraw your dart.

### How to increase length
Draw a straight line across the bodice front, through the centre of the bust dart. Cut along this line. Place tissue paper underneath and spread the 2 pattern pieces apart to desired length. Pin tissue in place. Trim surplus and redraw the dart.

### How to reduce bodice width

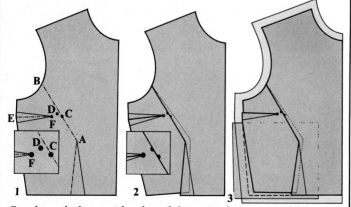

Cut through the outside edge of the waist dart to A and through to the point marked B on the armhole seam. Cut through the bust dart from E to F (Fig. 1). Measure half the total front reduction from the point marked C to the point marked D. Overlap the pattern pieces to D and secure. Overlap the bust dart so that the alteration is evened out (Fig. 2) between 2 darts. Secure overlaps and redraw original waistline (Fig. 3).

# Bodice back alterations

The bodice back may need to be altered for a number of reasons. The pattern will need to be made wider for a broad back or made longer for a rounded back. For a narrow back, the pattern width will need to be reduced. If you have a sway back or a very straight back the length may need to be reduced.

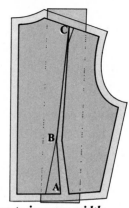
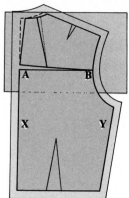

### How to increase width
Draw a straight line from B to the centre shoulder C. Then cut along the edge of the dart (from A to B) to the shoulder, ⅛in. (3mm) from point C. Place tissue paper underneath and spread pattern pieces apart to the desired width (half the total required). Pin tissue in place. Trim surplus then redraw the waistline and the dart.

### How to increase length
To add extra ease for rounded shoulders draw a straight line across the back (from A to B). Cut along this line. Mark and cut a line from halfway across the neckline almost to the first cut. With tissue in place, spread pattern to required amount. Redraw the centre back, keeping the line straight. To add length between armhole and waist, cut pattern from X to Y and spread apart. Trim and redraw as necessary.

### How to decrease back width

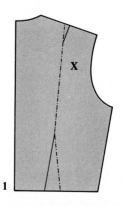
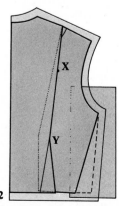

Draw a straight line from the outside edge of the waist dart to the centre of the shoulder (Fig. 1) and cut almost to top of line. Measure half the total amount of reduction from this line and mark X. Overlap the waist dart as far as the mark (X to Y) (Fig. 2) and pin into place. Redraw the waistline to the original measurement (Fig. 2, inset), but do not alter waist dart.

# Skirt alterations

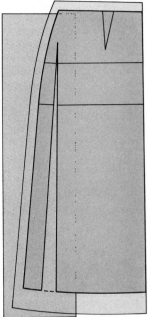

Skirt patterns often have to be altered to increase or reduce fullness at the hipline. Minor adjustments can be made by simply altering waist darts and side seams. When altering the skirt measurements at the waistline, all darts should be increased or reduced by the same amount. Adjust skirt length at hemline.

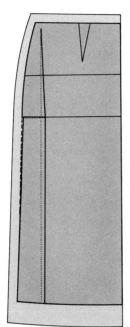

**How to increase width**
Both front and back skirt must be altered. Draw a straight line close to the side seam, extending from the bottom of the hem to the waistline. Cut along the line and place tissue paper underneath. Spread the pattern pieces apart by a quarter of total increase needed, and pin the tissue in place carefully. Trim off surplus and draw in extra width at the hem to retain the original skirt shape.

**How to reduce width**
Again, the alteration must be made to both front and back. Draw a straight line close to the side seam, extending from the bottom of the hem to the waistline. Cut along this line. Overlap the pieces at the hipline by a quarter of the total reduction needed, and pin in place. If a small bulge appears in the paper pattern at hip level, slash horizontally at the hip and overlap the pieces so that the pattern lies flat.

## Points to remember

1 *Always work with uncreased pattern pieces. Press them if necessary to smooth out the folds.*
2 *Remember that on some patterns, the reduction or increase will only be quarter or half of the total amount needed, depending on the position of the alteration and whether the pattern is cut out single or double.*
3 *Remember to transfer all marks onto the new pattern.*

# Sleeve and trouser alterations

Widen a sleeve by slashing lengthwise and inserting a piece of tissue; narrow the sleeve by slashing lengthwise and overlapping the pattern. The sleeve crown is then redrawn and the armhole on the bodice adjusted accordingly. Adjust the sleeve length in the same way.

### How to increase the upper arm width
*Draw a line from the centre of the wrist to the centre of the crown, and cut along this line. Place tissue underneath. Spread the pattern pieces apart to the required amount at the upper arm, tapering to a point at the wrist. Pin the tissue in place and trim off the excess. Straighten the shoulder line very slightly at the armhole edge.*

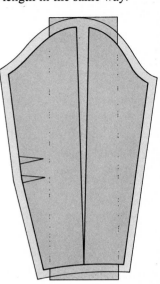

### Trouser alterations
Adjust trouser length as for a bodice, by either overlapping the pattern pieces to shorten them or spreading them apart to lengthen them. You may need to enlarge the seat of the trousers. In this case you must measure the crotch depth (see page 426) to gauge adjustment needed.

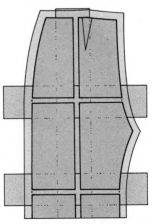

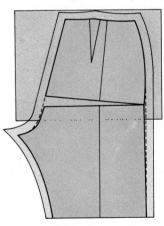

**How to increase width and length**
*Cut from the waistline to bottom of trouser leg. Place tissue underneath and spread pattern pieces. To increase length, slash horizontally at the desired point. Insert tissue, pin and redraw.*

**How to enlarge the seat of the trousers**
*Draw a straight line from the centre back across to side seam. Cut almost to end of line. Place tissue underneath, spread pattern pieces at the centre back. Pin, redraw centre back seam.*

# Hand sewing

### The first steps

Almost everything you sew needs some hand stitching, so you must be able to handle a needle and thread competently. The stitch tension should always be even, and the work finished off securely. Unless directed otherwise you should work from right to left, using an appropriate needle and thread. Start by inserting the needle into the wrong side of the fabric.

**1**

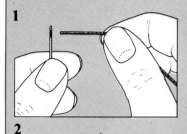

### How to thread a needle

**1** *With sharp scissors cut a length of thread about 24in. (60cm) long. With the needle in your left hand and the thread in your right hand, pass the thread through the eye of the needle.*

**2**

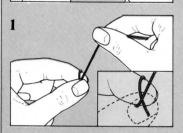

**2** *Transfer the needle from your left hand to your right hand. Then draw the thread through the eye of the needle and pull it halfway down the remaining supply of thread.*

**1**

### How to tie a knot

**1** *Hold the end of the thread between the thumb and forefinger of your left hand. With your right hand, bring the thread over and around the tip of the left forefinger, crossing the threads.*

**2**

**2** *With the long end of thread held taut in your right hand, roll the thread around the loop by pushing the thumb of your left hand up towards the tip of your left forefinger.*

**3**

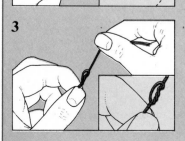

**3** *Slip the loop off your left forefinger, still holding the thread taut in your right hand. Pinch the loop with the thumb and forefinger of the left hand and pull the knot tight.*

### How to use a thimble

*Thimbles are graded in size from 0 to 6 and are usually made in plastic or metal.*
  *The thimble should be worn on the second finger of your sewing hand. Use to help the needle through the fabric.*

# Hand stitches

### Uneven tacking stitch

Uneven tacking stitch is used to mark or to hold fabrics together, only where there is no strain on the stitches. Use light-coloured or tacking thread for this.

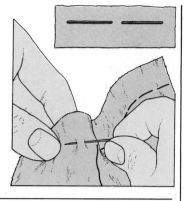

#### How to work the stitch

*Make a long stitch, about ½in. (1·3cm) on one side of the fabric and then a short stitch ¼in. (6mm) on the other side.*

### Tacking stitch

Tacking is used to hold fabric together temporarily, but more securely than uneven tacking. Use light-coloured or tacking thread for this.

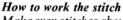

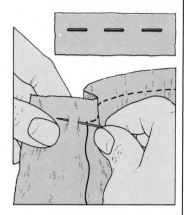

#### How to work the stitch

*Make even stitches about ¼in. to ⅜in. (6mm to 10mm) long. When easing one layer of fabric to another, hold the layer to be eased on top and gather this top layer of fabric gently as you stitch.*

### Running stitch

Running stitch is mainly used for gathering or shirring fabric. When used for both gathering and shirring make sure that enough thread is left to make an unbroken line of stitches.

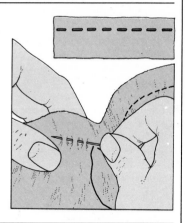

#### How to work the stitch

*Take several very small stitches onto the point of the needle before drawing the thread through the fabric.*

### Back stitch

Back stitch is useful for making strong seams and for finishing off a line of stitching.
  The stitches on the front of the work are small and appear continuous.

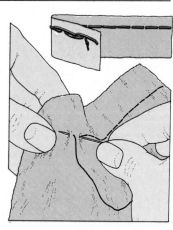

#### How to work the stitch

*Make a small stitch back from left to right. Then make a double length stitch forwards on the wrong side of the work so the needle emerges a stitch's length in front of the first one.*

## Half back stitch

Half back stitch is similar to back stitch but with a longer stitch at the back.

### How to work the stitch

*Make a small stitch back from left to right and then make a stitch forwards, two and a half times as long, on the wrong side of the work. Make another small stitch from left to right on the right side.*

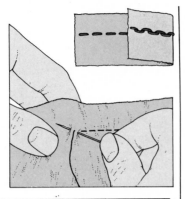

## Oversewing

Oversewing is used to finish seam edges on fabrics which fray easily.

### How to work the stitch

*Hold the fabric with the edge to be worked away from you. Insert the needle $\frac{1}{8}$in. to $\frac{1}{4}$in. (3mm to 6mm) from the edge and bring the thread over the edge of the fabric. Make the next stitch $\frac{1}{4}$in. (6mm) further on.*

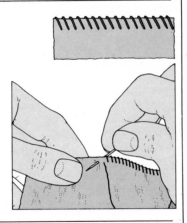

## Buttonhold stitch

Buttonhole stitch is worked with the needle pointing towards you, and the fabric edge away from you.

### How to work the stitch

*Insert the needle into the right side of the edge of the buttonhole. Bring it out $\frac{1}{8}$in. (3mm) below. Loop the thread hanging from the eye of the needle from right to left under the point of the needle and draw the needle upwards to knot the thread at the buttonhole edge.*

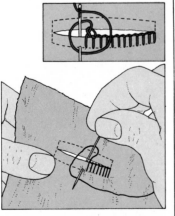

## Hem stitch

Hem stitch is used for hems on medium-weight or light-weight fabrics. The stitch size will depend on the fabric. The thread should not be pulled taut or the fabric will pucker.

### How to work the stitch

*With the work held as shown, pick up a thread of the single fabric on the needle point and then catch a thread of the fold on the point of the needle before pulling through.*

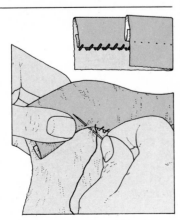

## Blind hemming stitch

Blind hemming is worked on the inside fold of the hem so that the stitches are almost invisible. The thread should not be pulled taut.

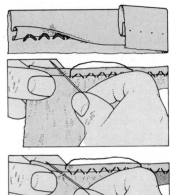

### How to work the stitch

*Holding the work with the fold of the hem towards you as shown, take a very small stitch inside the hem fold edge, picking up a thread of the single fabric on the point of the needle before taking another stitch on the inside hem fold of the garment.*

## Slip stitch

Slip stitch is used for flat hemming with a turned-in edge on light-weight to medium-weight fabrics. The thread should not be pulled taut, and the stitches should be worked about $\frac{1}{4}$in. (6mm) apart.

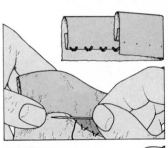

### How to work the stitch

*Pick up 1 or 2 threads of the single fabric and then slide the needle through the hem fold for about $\frac{1}{4}$in. (6mm). Draw the thread through.*

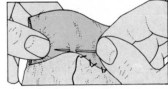

## Herringbone stitch

Herringbone is used for securing hems on heavy fabrics which do not fray easily and on stretch fabrics. It is worked from left to right.

### How to work the stitch

*Insert the needle through the inside of the hem turning, then right and down to make a small stitch in the single fabric. Move the needle diagonally up and right and take a small stitch from right to left in the hem fold, but not through it.*

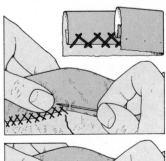

## Finishing off

To finish off any line of stitching, make two small back stitches (see instructions for back stitch) pulled tight.

## Left-handed instructions

If you are left handed hold the work in your right hand and work the needle and thread with your left hand. You should therefore work from left to right, reversing the instructions for right-handed workers.

# Seams

## General rules for making seams

A seam is made when you join two or more pieces of fabric together with a line of stitching. Seams are normally machine stitched, but you can handstitch a seam using back stitch (page 438).

Always make sure that the needle and thread used are appropriate for the fabric weight and texture (see page 425). Because the seams of a garment must withstand wear and tear, the beginning and end of the line of stitching should be secured with a few back stitches. Enough fabric should always be left between the line of stitching and the fabric edge to prevent fraying.

There are several different types of seams and the type of fabric and garment should determine the one you choose. A flat seam can be used on most garments and the seam edges should always be finished as appropriate for the fabric type.

Although a flat seam is always made with the right sides of the fabric facing, some other seams will need to be started with the wrong sides of the fabric facing. Follow the instructions carefully.

## Flat seam

A flat seam is the basic seam, joining the edges of two pieces of fabric. It is used on normal weight fabrics where there is no special strain on the seam. In most cases, plain straight stitch is used to stitch the seam

### How to make the seam

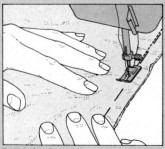

**1** *With the right sides of the fabric facing, pin the fabric together at both ends of the seam line and at intervals along the seam line, leaving an allowance of $\frac{3}{4}$in. (2cm).*

**3** *After removing the tacking stitches finish the seam edge by pinking it or as necessary for the fabric.*

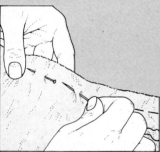

**2** *Tack close to the seam line and remove the pins. Then stitch along the seam line, back stitching a couple of stitches at each end to secure.*

**4** *Press the seam as stitched and then press it open as shown, using a pressing cloth between the iron and the fabric.*

# Types of seams

## French seam

This is a narrow seam used on fine fabrics or those which fray.

A French seam is generally used for fine fabrics or for those which fray easily. It is a seam within a seam and when finished should be about $\frac{1}{4}$in. (6mm) or less in width.

### How to make the seam

**1** *Place the wrong sides of the fabric together. Pin and tack in position close to the seam line. Stitch $\frac{1}{4}$in. (6mm) to the right of the seam line to the end of the seam. Press as stitched. Then trim the seam allowance to $\frac{1}{8}$in. (3mm).*

**2** *Press the seam open. Then turn the right sides of the fabric together. Fold on the stitch line and press. Tack in position.*

**3** *Stitch along the seam line and press as stitched.*

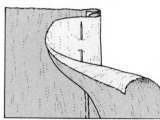

**1** Trimmed seam allowance.

**2** Fabric pinned in place.

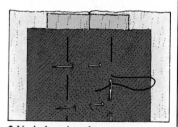

**3** Finished French seam.

## Channel seam

This is a decorative seam, designed to reveal a strip of fabric through the seam fold.

A channel seam is a decorative seam. It has a strip of fabric behind it which is visible through the seam fold, and can be made of contrasting fabric if desired.

### How to make the seam

**1** *With the right sides of the fabric together, pin and tack along the seam line. Press the seam open and cut an underlay of the same or contrasting fabric 1in. (2.5cm) wider than the two seam edges.*

**2** *With the wrong side of the work facing you, centre the right side of the underlay on the seam and pin in position. Tack and then stitch an equal distance each side from the seam depression.*

**3** *Remove the tacking and press as stitched.*

**1** Fabric tacked together.

**2** Underlay pinned to seam.

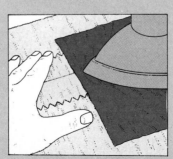

**3** Completed seam.

## Run and fell seam

This is a heavy duty seam, providing a neat finish for either side of the fabric.

A run and fell seam is a very strong neat seam which withstands heavy wear and frequent washing. You can choose which side of the seam you use on the right side of the fabric.

### How to make the seam

**1** *With the wrong sides of the fabric together, pin and tack along the seam line. Stitch along the seam line and press the seam open. Then press both seam edges over to one side. Trim the under seam allowance to half its width.*
**2** *Turn the upper seam allowance edge evenly over the trimmed edge and pin into place.*
**3** *Top stitch along the turned over edge, removing the pins, and press as stitched.*

1 Trimmed under seam.

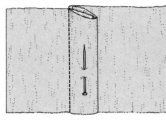

2 Upper seam pinned in place.

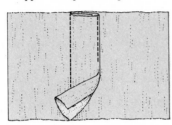

3 Top stitching.

## Tucked seam

This is a decorative seam. All edges should be finished before sewing.

A tucked seam is generally used as a design feature on a garment. If a tucked seam is used on fabric which frays easily, the seam edges should be finished by oversewing.

### How to make the seam

**1** *With the right side of the fabric facing you, turn under the seam allowance on one piece of fabric, and pin into place.*
**2** *Place the folded edge of the seam line on the right side of the second piece of fabric, keeping the raw edges together. Tack and stitch the desired width from the folded edge.*
**3** *Remove tacking threads and trim off the seam edge on the underneath of the seam. Press as stitched.*

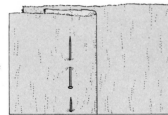

1 Pinned seam allowance.

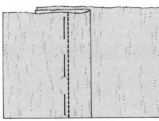

2 Seam tacked in position.

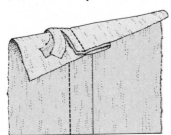

3 Trimmed seam edge.

## Mantua maker's seam

A mantua maker's seam is used to attach a frill to a straight piece of fabric.

### How to make the seam

**1** *With the right sides of the fabric together, tack along the seam line and stitch. Trim the frill seam allowance to $\frac{1}{4}$in. (6mm).*
**2** *Double fold the other seam allowance over the raw edge down to the seam line. Stitch close as possible to the seam line. Remove tacking, press the seam upwards away from the frill.*

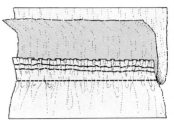

1 Stitched seam.

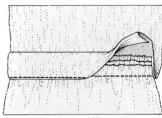

2 Seam folded double.

## Lapped seam

A lapped seam is used for joining sections of interfacing to avoid bulk.

### How to make the seam

*Lap one edge of the fabric over the other with the seam lines directly over each other. Tack and then stitch along the seam line with a wide zigzag stitch or a straight stitch. Trim the seam edges.*

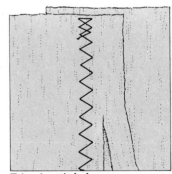

**Trimming stitched seam**

## Double stitch seam

A double stitched seam is used for sheer fabrics.

### How to make the seam

*With the right sides of the fabric together, tack and stitch along the seam line and press as stitched. Make a second line of stitching in the seam allowance $\frac{1}{4}$in. (6mm) from the first line, using a fine multistitch zigzag or straight stitch. Trim as shown.*

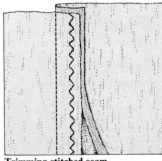

**Trimming stitched seam**

## Lingerie seam

A lingerie seam is used for making very fine seams.

### How to make the seam

*With the right sides of the fabric facing, pin, tack and then stitch along the seam line. Press as stitched. Pink the seam edges and press both seam allowances to one side. Stitch seam edge on right side with a fine zigzag.*

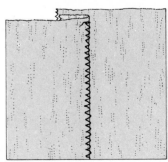

**Zigzagged seam edge**

441

# Special seams and seam finishes

Special types of seam have to be used on occasion. Their use depends on their position in the garment, on the fabric type, or on the amount of strain that will be put on them. Finish straight seams after pressing them open, but finish curved and corner seams beforehand. Seam finishes are designed to neaten seam edges and to prevent fraying.

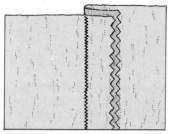

**Stretch fabric seam**

### Stretch fabric seam

Stretch fabric should be sewn with a stitch which allows the fabric to "give". A zigzag stitch is usual but you can use a special stretch stitch setting. Stitch as for a flat seam. If using a straight stitch, stretch the fabric as it passes under the needle to prevent puckering.

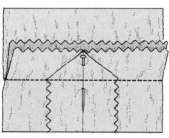

**Crossed seam**

### Crossed seam

Finish the seams before sewing them together. To ensure that the crossed seams align, insert the point of a fine pin into the stitching line at the crossing point before stitching. After stitching the seams, trim the allowances diagonally to reduce any bulk.

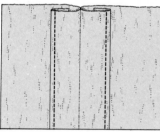

**Edge-stitched seam**

### Edge-stitched seam

This is a neat finish for light- to medium-weight, non-bulky fabrics. Fold under the edge of the seam allowance by $\frac{1}{8}$in. (3mm) and press into position. Working on the right side, stitch close to the edge of the turning. Press the finished seam so that it lies flat.

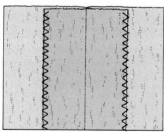

**Zigzag-edged seam**

### Zigzag-edged seam

This is a useful and quick method for finishing fabrics which fray. Set the machine to an appropriate stitch length and place the edge of the seam allowance, right side up, so that the needle sews once into the fabric and once outside it. Press the seam flat.

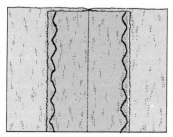

**Multistitch zigzag seam**

### Multistitch zigzag seam

Multistitch zigzag stretches, so this is an ideal finish for seams on jersey, double knit and other stretch fabrics. Place the edge to be neatened, right side up, under the machine and multistitch close to, but not over the edge. Press the finished seam so that it lies flat.

# Curved and corner seams

Curved pieces of fabric can be stitched together using a flat seam. However, special attention has to be paid to easing the curved pieces of fabric together as they are being sewn (see page 424 for machining instructions).

### *Stitching on a curve*

**Curved bust seam**

#### *How to make a curved seam*

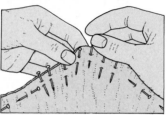

**1** Place fabric pieces together, right sides facing, and pin along seam line, easing fabric along the inside curve. Stitch along the seam line using a shorter stitch length than normal for your fabric.

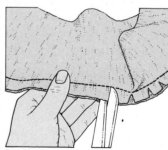

**2** Clip the seam allowance on the outside curve and notch the seam allowance on the inside curve so that it lies flat.

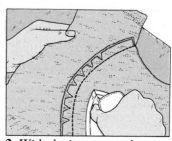

**3** With the iron correctly set, press seam flat to one side and then press it open.

### *Stitching corners*

**Corner armhole seam**

#### *How to make a corner seam*

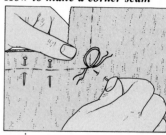

**1** Mark the corner points of your fabric pieces. With right sides facing, pin the corner point and one seam in place.

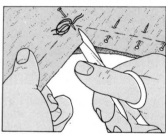

**2** Clip the top piece of fabric to the corner point. Stitch right to this point.

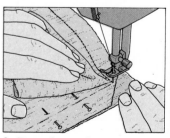

**3** Pivot the work. Pull the top layer of fabric around to align with the lower layer. Pin it into place and stitch to the end of the seam. Remove the marking thread and pins and press flat into place. Finish seams in the appropriate way.

# Shaping garments

**Gathering**

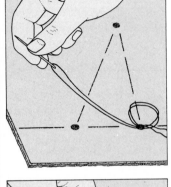

**Shirring**

**Pleats**

**Released tucks**

**Darts**

Fabric can be shaped in a number of different ways. It can be *gathered* or *shirred* by stitching and drawing up the fabric, or it can be folded into *pleats*, the width of which can vary from fine ones, known as *pin tucks*, to wide ones, known as *box pleats*. You can also cut and seam the fabric to shape it and control any extra fullness by making small, pointed folds of fabric which are known as *darts*.

### Types of fabric
The type of shaping will determine the design of the garment, and the type of fabric you use. Soft fabrics lend themselves to draped designs, so that gathers and unpressed pleats are particularly suitable. Crisper fabrics can be shaped with pressed pleats, by seams and darts. Very bulky fabrics will have to be shaped by cutting, seaming and darting. Patterned fabrics are not really suitable for elaborate seaming or pleating.

### Choosing designs
Apart from the considerations of the fabric, your own personal preference and your figure type will determine your choice. It is worth remembering that full garments can make people look shorter and wider, and narrow, fitted garments generally make people look taller and slimmer.

### Order of work
The instructions on page 466 will show you at which point in making up a garment the fabric should be shaped. However, it is worth remembering that all the relevant seams should be sewn, finished and pressed before the fabric is pleated or gathered.

### Estimating fabric
Pleats, tucks and gathering will require extra fabric – three times the width of each finished pleat or tuck and about half as much fabric again for gathering. If you are making your own design, you will have to estimate the amount of fabric yourself using this method for your calculations.

# Tailor's tacks

Tailor's tacks are used to mark double layers of fabric, especially where the areas have to be folded and stitched, such as in pleats, darts and tucks. They are also used to mark delicate fabrics which may be damaged by other methods. The pattern must always remain pinned to the fabric until all the marks have been transferred from it.

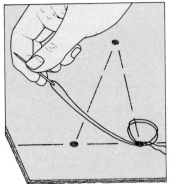

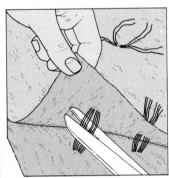

### How to make tailor's tacks
*1 With the sharp end of the needle, slit the pattern across the symbol to be marked. With a length of doubled, unknotted thread make a small stitch through the pattern and both layers of the fabric, leaving a 1in. (2.5cm) end. Make another stitch at the same point and leave a 2in. to 3in. (5cm to 7.5cm) loop and a 1in. (2.5cm) end.*

*2 When all the symbols have been marked in this way, lift the pattern off the fabric, taking care not to pull out the thread markings. Separate the layers of fabric to the limits of the thread and cut the loop joining the 2 pieces of fabric together. The threads left in the fabric will mark the appropriate joining points on your garment pieces.*

### Marking a fold line
Simplified tailor's tacks are used to mark a line of pleats. With a long piece of thread, make a small stitch on the pattern line through the fabric and pattern. Pull the needle and thread through, leaving a 1in. (2.5cm) thread end. Take similar stitches down the pleat lines, leaving the thread slack in between. Cut the thread at the centre points between the stitch and lift the pattern, taking care not to pull out markings.

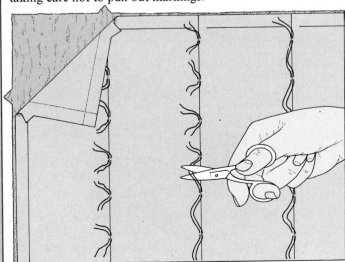

**Cutting the threads between the stitches before lifting the pattern**

## Dart finishes

Although there is usually no special finish to a dart before it is pressed, there are a few exceptions: for example to deep darts, used on heavy fabrics and contour and curved darts, used on light to medium weight fabrics.

### Deep dart

A dart which is made with a deep fold should be slashed through the fold to within ½in. (1.3cm) from the point and pressed open. If the fabric frays, overcast the edges.

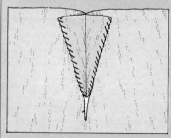

**A deep dart with overcast edges**

### Contour darts

Contour darts are pointed at each end. They should be clipped through almost to the stitching line at the widest point. A second line of stitching can be made at the curve as reinforcement.

**A contour dart clipped at centre**

### Curved dart

A curved dart should be trimmed to ⅝in. (1.5cm) from the point, and clipped at the curve. Reinforce the curve with a second line of stitching.

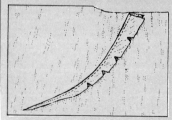

**A curved dart, notched on curved side**

## Darts

Darts are used to provide fullness at the bust, hip, shoulder and elbow. They can be curved or straight, single or double pointed but they must finish just short of the curve. Their width, length, shape and position will depend on the design and on the fit of the garment, and they may need to be altered. If so, then any corresponding darts should be re-aligned to match.

Unless used as a decorative feature, darts are made on the wrong side of the garment. They should taper to a fine point. Slashed darts should be pressed flat. Other darts should be pressed as stitched, over an ironing ham if necessary. Before making the dart, check that the fit of the garment is accurate. Make any alterations to the dart positions that are necessary. The darts should be finished as appropriate for the fabric (left).

### How to make a dart

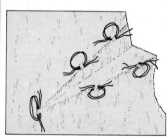

**1** Mark the dart with tailor's tacks or with a tracing wheel. Fold the dart carefully so that the markings match.

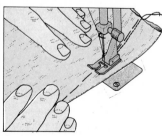

**2** Pin the dart and tack in position, starting at the seam edge and tapering the dart to a fine point. Remove any markings. Machine stitch starting at the seam edge, reinforcing at the point for a couple of stitches.

## Gathering and shirring

Gathering and shirring are both formed by drawing up the fabric on a row of stitches. Shirring gathers up the fabric on several rows of stitches and is used as a decorative feature.

### Gathering fabric

Gathering can be done by hand using a running stitch or on a machine with the longest stitch length. If you are hand stitching, make sure you take enough thread to complete a line.

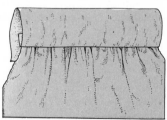

**Gathered fabric**

### How to gather fabric

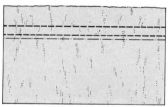

**1** Stitch just outside the seam line and make another row of stitches very close to the first row.

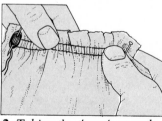

**2** Taking the threads at each end of the rows of stitching, draw up the threads to the required width. Fasten threads by winding around a pin.

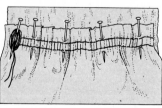

**3** Pin the gathered fabric to the ungathered fabric, with right sides together. Stitch on the seam line, with gathered fabric uppermost.

### Shirring fabric

To shir fabric, first follow the instructions for gathering (left), making two rows of stitching within the seam allowance.

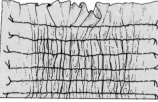

**Shirred fabric**

### How to shir fabric

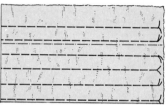

**1** Make 3 more rows of stitching, taking care to ensure the stitches are neat and even.

**2** Draw the shirred threads up to the desired width. Fold back the fabric edge and machine to secure shirring.

### Shirring with elastic thread

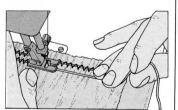

Shirring can be done with special elastic thread. This can either be threaded into the bobbin or, with a swing needle machine, it can be couched onto the fabric and oversewn with a zigzag stitch.

# *Knife, box and inverted pleats*

Pleats are folds in the fabric and are used to control fullness. They can be made in three ways: as *knife pleats* which have folds turning in one direction; as *box pleats* which have two folds of equal width turning away from each other; and as *inverted pleats* which are made in exactly the same way as box pleats but on the other side of the fabric. It is essential to mark the pleats accurately and evenly, to tack the pleats in position and to press them correctly.

## *Making knife pleats*

Knife pleats start across the back of a garment from left to right, becoming right to left facing across the front. Usually the last pleat covers any opening in the garment.

### *How to make the pleat*
**1** *Mark the pleat on the right side with simplified tailor's tacks, using a different coloured thread for fold and pleat edge lines.*

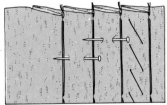

**2** *With the right side uppermost, fold pleats. Pin in position at right angles to the pleat. Secure the pleats with a diagonal stitch.*

## *Making box pleats*

Box pleats turn away from each other on the right side of the fabric and the underfold meets in the centre on the wrong side. They are most often used singly, as on the centre back of a shirt.

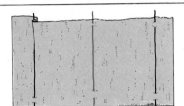

### *How to make the pleat*
**1** *Working on the right side of the fabric, make simplified tailor's tacks down the fold lines and pleat edge lines using different coloured threads on each of them.*

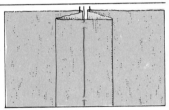

**2** *With the right side uppermost, fold the pleats to the marked lines, as shown, and pin at right angles to the pleats. Baste with diagonal stitching.*

## *Making inverted pleats*

Inverted pleats are made in exactly the same way as box pleats, except that the inverted pleat is on the right side of the fabric, and the box pleat on the wrong side.

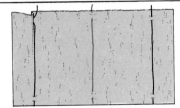

### *How to make the pleat*
**1** *Mark the pleats as for box pleats, on the right side of the fabric, and bring both pleats towards each other to the centre line.*

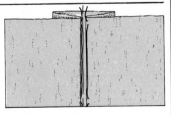

**2** *Work on the right side and fold the pleats as shown pinning at right angles to fold line. Secure the pleats as for box pleats.*

## *Stitching pleats*

All pleats can be pressed or unpressed, edges stitched all down to the hem, or partly edge stitched. If the pleat is to be pressed or stitched to the hem then the hem must be finished first. After the pleats have been tacked in position, stitch close to the edge of each pleat. Pressed pleats should be done with a pressing cloth to prevent fabric damage.

### *Edge stitched pleats*
*Edge stitch $\frac{1}{8}$in. (3mm) from the fold of the pleat and finish at appropriate point. Pull threads through to wrong side and tie.*

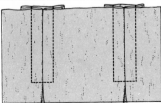

### *Box edged pleats*
*Mark the line for top stitching, and stitch carefully pivoting at the corners. Pull threads through to wrong side and tie.*

## *Tucks*

**Tucks can be used as a decorative finish or to control fullness.**

Tucks are a narrower version of knife pleats. The finest tucks are known as *pin tucks*. They can be made either horizontally or vertically on a garment, as a decorative feature on bodices, sleeves and yokes, for example. The tucks can be stitched all the way down to the hem or seam line or released at a certain point to give fullness, for example on a smock. The threads should be pulled to the wrong side and tied.

### *How to make tucks*

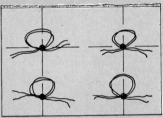

**1** *Mark the line for the fold of the tuck and the line to which it should be brought with rows of simplified tailor's tacks, in the same way as for knife pleats. Use different coloured threads for the 2 different lines.*

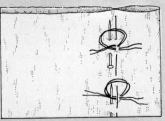

**2** *Fold the tucks and match the markings, keeping the tuck edges even. Pin and tack into position. Stitch down the tuck edge and reinforce with backstitching at either end. Remove the tacking threads.*

# Necklines and facings

## *Types of neckline*

Necklines, whatever their shape, will need to be finished, either by adding a collar (see page 448) or by applying a matching piece of fabric, known as a facing. The type of finish chosen will depend on the fabric and design of the garment. It can either be added to the neckline separately or cut as a piece with the garment.

Before any work is begun on the neckline, the bodice darts and shoulder seams should be stitched and finished. If the neckline has a zip fastener, it should be inserted before the neckline is finished.

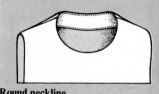

**Round neckline**

**Square neckline**

**V neckline**

**Slashed neckline**

**Rouleau bound neckline**

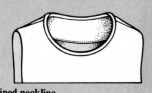

**Piped neckline**

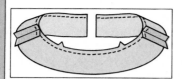

Most necklines will need a facing to finish them. Usually the facing is cut from a piece of the garment fabric to match the exact shape of the neckline. A second layer of fabric, known as an interfacing, can be applied to give the neckline edge a crisp finish (see page 464 for details).

## *How to face a round neckline*

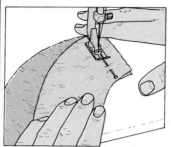

**1** *Join the facing at the shoulder seams and finish the seam edges. Press the seams open. Finish the edge of the facing by pinking the edge, and then turn it under by ¼in. (6mm) and edge stitch it.*

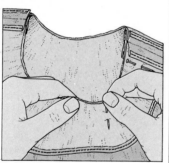

**2** *Pin the facing to the garment, right sides together, matching notches and shoulder seams. Stitch with short stitches around the neckline.*

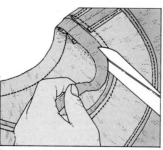

**3** *Trim the facing seam allowance to ⅛in. (3mm) and the garment neckline allowance to ¼in. (6mm). Clip into the seam allowance at regular intervals. Trim corners where the seams cross. Press.*

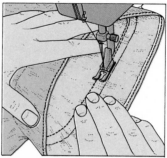

**4** *Pull the facing outside the neckline. On the right side of the facing stitch around the neckline, through the facing and the seam allowances, as close to the seam line as possible and press.*

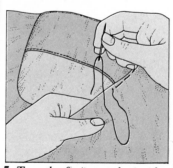

**5** *Turn the facing to the inside, rolling it under gently so that the seam line lies just to the inside of the neckline. Tack in position and press. Remove the tacking threads.*

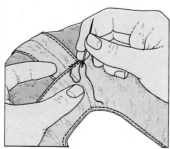

**6** *Catch the facing to the garment at the shoulder line seam with a few small slip stitches. Finish off after the zip has been inserted (see page 461).*

## *Facing a square neckline*

Follow the instructions for attaching a round facing. When stitching around the neckline, pivot the fabric on the needle at the corners and clip into the corners to within ⅛in. (3mm) of the seam line.

## *Facing a V neckline*

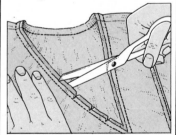

Follow the instructions for attaching a round facing, pivoting the fabric on the needle at the point of the V. Clip into the V as above.

## *Finishing off*

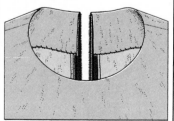

If a zip fastener is to be inserted into the opening, attach it before finishing off the facing (see page 461 for instructions). Then turn the ends of the facing seam allowance to the inside and catch it down to the zip with a few slip stitches.

# Extended facing

An extended facing can be cut out in one piece with the garment and folded to the inside. It is most often used on bodice fronts, for example on a slashed opening. Stitch and finish the shoulder seams of your garment as appropriate. Use tailor's tacks to mark the point of the front opening on the garment and the facing.

*How to make*

**1** *Fold the facing onto the neckline, right sides together, taking care to match seams and tailor's tacks. Tack and stitch. Reinforce for ½in. (1.3cm) on either side of the point with short stitches close to the first row of stitches.*

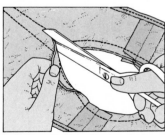

**2** *Using sharp scissors slash the opening to within ⅛in. (3mm) of the point. Trim the seam allowance.*

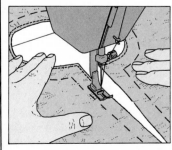

**3** *Turn the facing to the inside of your garment and finish off as for a round neckline facing, shown on the left.*

# Rouleau neckline

To make a rouleau bound neckline, a strip of bias cut fabric is applied to the neckline. It is normally cut four times wider than its finished visible width and 1½in. (4cm) longer than the neckline.

*How to make*

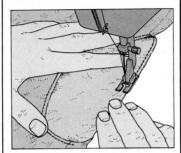

**1** *Cut away the neckline seam allowance and then stitch ⅜in. (5mm) from the edge to prevent stretching.*

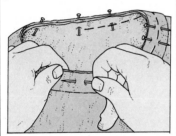

**2** *Fold the strip along the centre, wrong sides together and finger press lightly. Pin the two raw edges of the strip to the right side of the garment. Stretch bias on inside curve. If the neckline has no opening, join the bias ends at the shoulder seams and tack the strip to the neckline.*

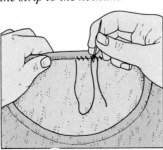

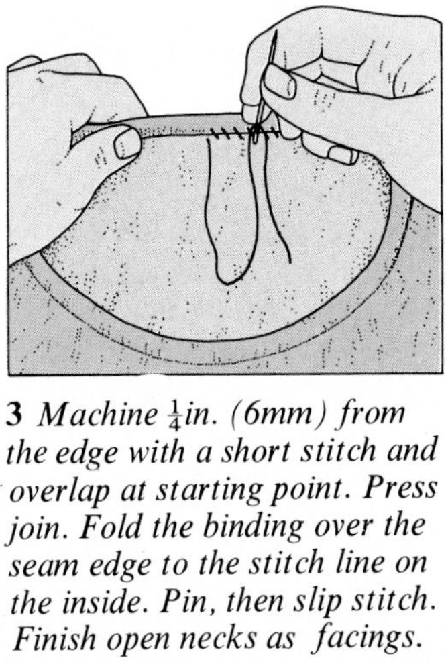

**3** *Machine ¼in. (6mm) from the edge with a short stitch and overlap at starting point. Press join. Fold the binding over the seam edge to the stitch line on the inside. Pin, then slip stitch. Finish open necks as facings.*

# Piped neckline

Piping can be added as a finish to a neckline which has a facing. The garment and the facing are prepared as usual by first stitching the shoulder seams of both the facing and the garment. If the neckline has an opening, finish the piped neckline by following the instructions for finishing a facing. To encase the piping cord in a bias cover see page 485. Make sure that the bias cover is 1½in. (4cm) longer than the neckline.

*How to make*

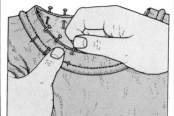

**1** *Make the piping (see page 485). Pin bias covered cord to the right side of the neckline, keeping the stitching line of the piping and neck seam line together. Ease the seam allowance of the cording so that it lies flat on the neckline.*

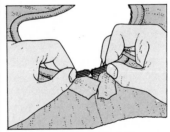

**2** *Pull the piping cord ⅝in. (1.5cm) out from the bias cover at either end and cut it so that the cord inside is exactly the length of the neckline (this prevents excess bulk at the seam). Curve the two ends of the bias slightly towards the seam line.*

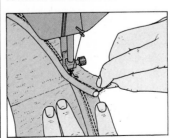

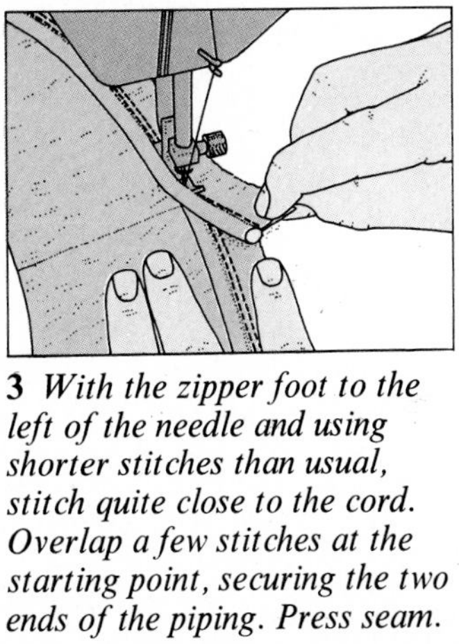

**3** *With the zipper foot to the left of the needle and using shorter stitches than usual, stitch quite close to the cord. Overlap a few stitches at the starting point, securing the two ends of the piping. Press seam.*

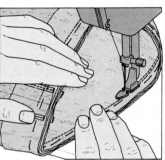

**4** *With right sides together pin and tack the facing to the neckline, matching the shoulder seams and centre lines. With the first row of stitching uppermost so that it can be used as a guide, stitch between the cord and the previous row of stitching.*

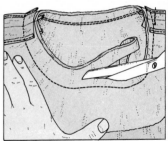

**5** *Trim the corded seam allowance to ⅛in. (3mm) and the garment and facing seam allowances to ¼in. (6mm). Clip into the inside curve and trim off the corners at the shoulder seams.*

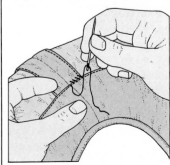

**6** *Press and turn the facing to the underside. Press again and finish off as for facings.*

## Types of collar

A collar is a decorative finish to a neckline on a garment. Styles of collar vary a great deal, but if only the outside edge of the collar is different, the method of application at the neckline will be the same. The construction of the two-piece (Peter Pan) collar, the roll collar, the stand collar and the shirt collar with a stand are shown on these two pages along with the methods for attaching the most commonly used collars. Cutting instructions appear on page 475.

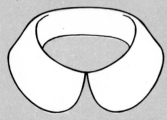

**Two-piece collar – Peter Pan style**

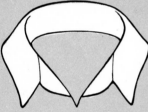

**Two-piece collar – Shirt style**

**Roll collar**

**Stand collar**

**Shirt collar with a stand**

## Constructing collars

The collar must fit perfectly, so the neckline of the garment and the neck-edge of the collar must match exactly. All matching notches should align and they should be clearly marked. Collar seam allowances are trimmed to the minimum to prevent bulk, and curves are clipped almost to the stitching line.

### Making a two-piece collar

A two-piece collar consists of an upper and under collar and an interfacing which exactly matches the collar shape.

### How to make the collar

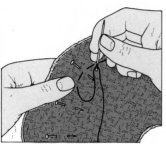

**1** *Pin and tack the interfacing to the wrong side of the upper collar. If you are using an iron-on interfacing, press it on the wrong side of the upper collar using a warm iron.*

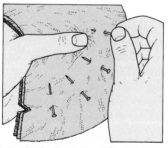

**2** *With the right sides facing, pin and tack the interfaced upper collar to the under collar around the outside edge only, leaving the neckline edge open.*

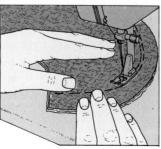

**3** *Stitch along the outside edge seam line, using a shorter stitch on any curved part of the collar to strengthen it (see page 424 for stitching on a curve).*

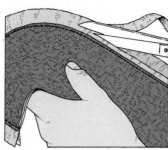

**4** *Trim the interfacing close to the stitching line. Then trim the seam allowance on the under collar to ⅛in. (3mm) and on the upper collar to ¼in. (6mm). Clip the curved part of the collar through the seam allowance almost to the stitching line.*

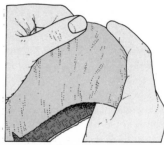

**5** *Press the collar, paying attention to the seam edges and turn it to the right side. Work the seam edges between the fingers and ease the seam line slightly to the underside. Tack close to the collar edge to hold it in place and press.*

**6** *On a pointed collar, first strengthen the corners with one or two shorter stitches across the corner. Then trim the seam allowances across at the point. Gently push the points out with tip of scissors.*

## Roll collar

A roll collar is made from one piece of fabric cut on the bias and folded in half before stitching. It is then worn folded in half again to give a softly finished neckline. A roll collar does not need an interfacing and can be attached with or without a facing.

### How to make the collar

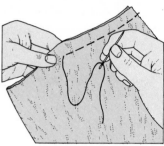

**1** *Fold the collar in half with the right sides together. Match the notches at the neckline edge and tack the 2 ends.*

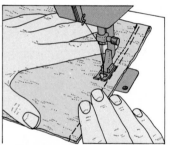

**2** *Stitch the ends together, leaving the neckline edge open.*

**3** *Trim the seam allowance of the inner collar to ⅛in. (3mm) and the outer collar seam allowance to ¼in. (6mm) and then cut across the seam allowances at the corners. Turn the collar through to the right side taking care to push the corners out well. Press stitched seams but not the fold of the collar, to retain the softly rolled finish.*

# Stand collar

This is a close-fitting collar which stands up stiffly against the neck. It is cut on the bias in two pieces with an opening at the front or the back. The interfacing should be pinned to the wrong side of the outer collar or an iron-on interfacing used. With right sides facing, the outer collar should be pinned and tacked to the inner collar. Stitch along the seam-line. Leave neck edge open.

*How to make the collar*

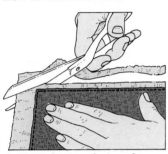

**1** *Trim the interfacing close to the stitching line. Trim the collar to ¼in. (6mm) on the seam edges. Trim the seam across and close to the stitching line at corners.*

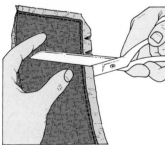

**2** *Clip into the curved edge almost to the stitching line.*

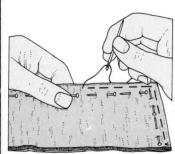

**3** *Turn the collar through to right side. Roll the seam slightly to the inside and pin and tack in position, then press. Remove tacking and press; attach to garment.*

# Shirt collar with stand

A shirt collar with a stand is a narrow version of the shirt collar, given height by being mounted on a narrow stand collar. Make the shirt collar, and prepare the stand by interfacing the wrong side of outer collar in the usual way.

*How to make the collar*

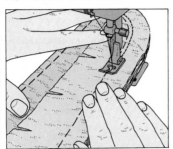

**1** *Insert the made up collar between the 2 pieces of the prepared stand, right sides facing, matching the markings. Pin and tack through all the thickness. Stitch along the seam line.*

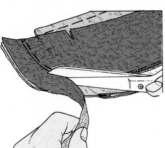

**2** *Trim all the interfacings and the seam allowances, and grade them. Then clip into the seam allowance to ease the seam and press.*

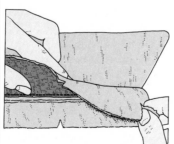

**3** *Turn the stand through to the right side and press in position. Make sure that the seam line rolls slightly to the inside of the stand ends. Attach to the garment using the first method on the right.*

# Attaching collars

### Attaching a collar without a facing

This is used to attach a collar to a garment without a neck facing. If the garment has an opening, the relevant seam should be finished before the collar is attached.

*How to attach the collar*

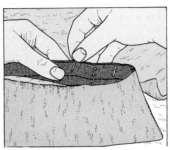

**1** *Place under collar on garment neckline, right sides and raw edges together. Make sure all the marks match. Pin the under collar only onto the garment.*

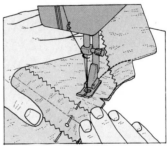

**2** *Stitch, then trim the seams to ¼in. (6mm) and press. Fold the collar up to a stand position. Press the seam again to tuck allowance into collar.*

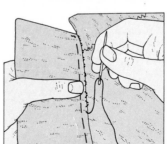

**3** *Turn under the seam allowance on the top collar. Pin and tack into place making sure the top collar has enough ease to roll over the under collar when it is turned down. Slip stitch and press along original stitching line.*

### Attaching a collar with a facing

If there are two collar pieces the neckline is usually faced. Prepare as for a self-neatening collar. Lay the facing over the outer collar with right sides together, matching any balance marks and fitting lines.

*How to attach the collar*

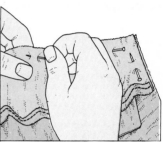

**1** *Pin into place and tack through all the thicknesses of fabric. Then stitch along the neckline in one continuous line, backstitching at the beginning and ends of seam.*

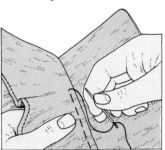

**2** *Trim turnings to ¼in. (6mm) then trim the corners and clip into the curve of the neckline, almost to the stitching line. Fold the facing to the inside of the garment and ease out the corners. Bring the stitched line onto the fold and press. Tack facing.*

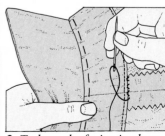

**3** *To keep the facing in place, slip stitch it to the seam allowances of the shoulder seams on the garment.*

## Types of sleeve

There are several different styles of sleeve but they have all evolved from the same three basic sleeve shapes.

The most common type of sleeve is the set-in one, where the sleeve is inserted into the armhole. The raglan sleeve is joined to the bodice by a seam running from the underarm to the neckline and the kimono sleeve is cut in one piece with the bodice.

**Faced armhole**

**Kimono sleeve**

**Set-in sleeve**

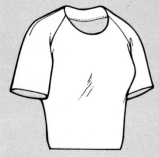

**Raglan sleeve**

# Attaching sleeve facings

The armhole of a sleeveless garment will need to be finished with a piece of the same fabric, cut to match the armhole shape. This is known as a *facing*, and it is stitched to the armhole edge and then turned inside the garment so that the join forms the finished edge of the armhole (see page 472 for cutting instructions).

### Applying a facing

Before applying the facing, join the shoulder and side seams of the bodice. Then join the shoulder and underarm seams of the facing. Finish all the seam edges and press the seams open.

Turning the garment to the right side, pin the facing to the armhole, right sides together, matching any notches and the seams. Tack in position and check the fit at this stage (see page 467 for fitting instructions).

*How to apply a facing*

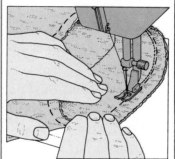

**1** *Stitch around the armhole and overlap a few stitches at the starting point. Press.*

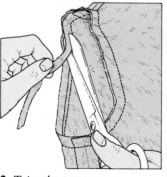

**2** *Trim the facing seam allowance to $\frac{1}{8}$ in. (3mm) and the garment seam allowance to $\frac{1}{4}$in. (6mm).*

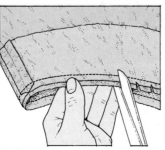

**3** *Slash the seam allowance on the inside curve and cut off corners where seams cross.*

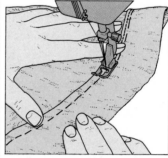

**4** *Pulling the facing outside the garment, understitch on the right side close to the seam line, through both layers of seam allowance. Press.*

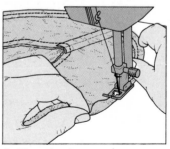

**5** *Turn the facing edge under along the outer edge and neaten it by edge stitching.*

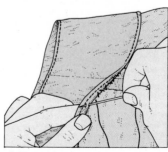

**6** *Turn the facing back into the armhole and press it in position. Using a blind hemming stitch, catch the facing to the shoulder and underarm seams.*

# Kimono sleeve

Kimono sleeves are usually cut in one piece with the body of the garment but they can be cut with a seam at the shoulder. If so, it is easier to stitch the underarm seam first.

*How to make a kimono sleeve*

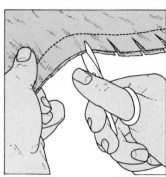

**1** *With the right sides of the garment facing, stitch the side and underarm seams together in one continuous line, shortening the stitch on the curve. Clip into the seam allowance at intervals and finish the seams; press open.*

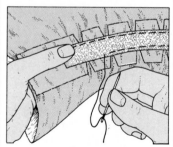

**2** *On the wrong side of the garment, tack a 6in. (15cm) piece of straight seam binding over the opened seam at the underarm curve.*

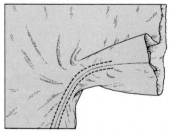

**3** *On the right side of the garment, stitch along the length of the binding on each side of the seam line, $\frac{1}{8}$in. (3mm) away from it. Pull the ends of the threads through to the wrong side and fasten.*

# Set-in sleeve

The set-in sleeve is cut separately from the garment and inserted into the armhole. The width and length of the sleeve can vary, but the principle of application remains the same. Any shaping must be done before the sleeve is inserted. If the sleeve has a squared armhole, follow the cornering instructions on page 424. Make sure the sleeve fits properly before stitching.

*How to make a set-in sleeve*

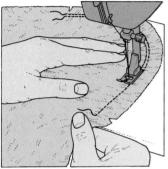

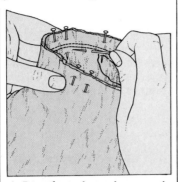

**1** *On the wrong side of the sleeve make 1 or 2 rows of gathering stitches within the seam allowance between the notches on the crown of the sleeve. Turning the sleeve to the right side, slip it into the armhole, right sides facing.*

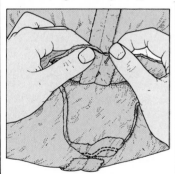

**2** *Working from the inside of the sleeve, pin at the underarm and shoulder seam points and at the notches.*

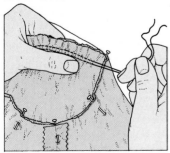

**3** *Gather up the fullness in the sleeve evenly towards the shoulder line, on both sides of the shoulder seam, until it fits exactly into the armhole.*

**4** *Distribute the gathers evenly and pin across the seam line at close intervals and tack the sleeve in position. Fasten the gathering threads.*

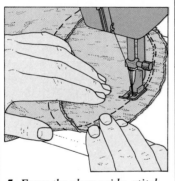

**5** *From the sleeve side, stitch along the seam line starting at the underarm seam and overlapping a few stitches at the end. Remove the gathering threads from the sleeve.*

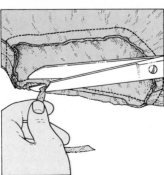

**6** *Trim and grade the seam allowances and cut off the corners where the seams cross at the shoulder and underarm points. Neaten the seam edges and press them flat.*

# Raglan sleeve

The raglan sleeve is cut separately from the body of the garment and is attached to the bodice at the back and front with a seam running from the neckline to the underarm sleeve. If the seam line is curved, follow the instructions for curved seams on page 424. The principle of application remains the same.

*How to make a raglan sleeve*

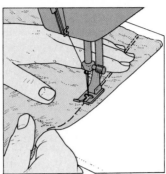

**1** *If the sleeve is cut in one piece, pin, tack and stitch the dart at the shoulder. If the sleeve is cut in 2 pieces, stitch the shoulder seam and finish it, pressing it open.*

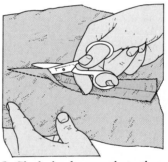

**2** *Slash the dart nearly to the point and press it open, finishing the edges as appropriate. Then stitch the underarm seams of the sleeve and bodice and neaten the seam edges. Press seams open.*

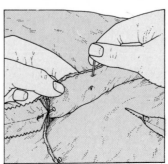

**3** *Turn the sleeve to the right side and pin to the bodice along the seam line with the right sides facing, matching notches and underarm seams.*

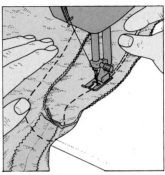

**4** *Tack and then stitch in one continuous line from one neck edge to the other. Remove the tacking threads.*

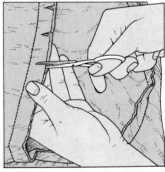

**5** *Slash the seam allowance at intervals on the inside curve and notch it on the outside curve, so that the seam lies flat when open. Cut off the corners where the seams cross at the underarm and neaten the seam edges as appropriate.*

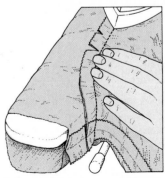

**6** *Press the seams open from the neckline to the armhole curve. Then turn the allowance towards the sleeve and press seam allowances to one side around the curve.*

## Types of cuff

Sleeves must be neatened to finish them. This can be done with either a simple hemmed finish or with a cuff, the design of which can vary considerably. The most common sleeve finishes are shown below (see page 458 for fastenings).

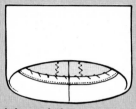

**Basic hemmed edge**

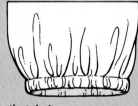

**Elasticated edge**

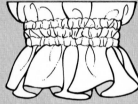

**Shirred cuff**

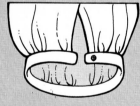

**Rouleau strip cuff**

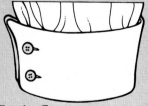

**French cuff**

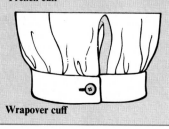

**Wrapover cuff**

## Sleeve finishes

The simplest method of finishing a sleeve is with a hemmed edge. This basic method of hemming can be adapted to produce several decorative finishes, such as the elasticated and the shirred sleeve edge.

### Making a hemmed edge

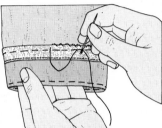

This is the simplest way of finishing a sleeve. Fold the hem evenly to the inside, tack and press. Attach seam binding to the raw edge of the hem. Join the ends of the binding together by folding one end under $\frac{1}{4}$in. (6mm) and overlapping it by $\frac{1}{2}$in. (1.2cm) at the sleeve seam. Press and pin the raw edge of the binding to the sleeve and slip stitch into place. Remove tackings. Press.

### Elasticating the edge

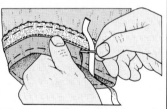

You can make a wide sleeve fit at the wrist by threading elastic through the hem to produce a tightly fitting cuff (see page 456 for threading instructions).

### Shirring the edge

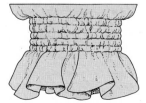

This is a variation on the elasticated cuff. It looks prettier and is more suitable on fine fabrics (see page 444 for shirring instructions).

## Sleeve openings

Long sleeves finished with a cuff need a slashed side opening to allow the hand to pass through easily. This opening must always be made and finished before the cuff is attached, either with a facing or a rouleau strip.

### How to make a facing strip

**1** Cut a strip of fabric as long as the opening, plus $1\frac{1}{4}$in. (3cm), and $2\frac{1}{2}$in. (6.3cm) wide. Edge stitch on 3 sides. With the centre of the strip over the slash line, tack to sleeve with right sides facing.

**2** Start stitching at the bottom of the sleeve. Keeping $\frac{1}{4}$in. (6mm) out from the tacking row, stitch along the V of the slash line. Take care not to pull or stretch the fabric as you stitch around the top curve of the facing strip.

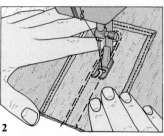

**3** Cut down the line of tacking to the point of stitching. Roll the facing to the wrong side of the sleeve, tack and then press into position. Slip stitch the facing to the sleeve but do not remove the tacking until the cuff has been attached.

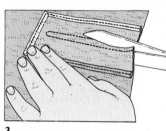

### How to make a rouleau strip

**1** Slash the opening to within $\frac{1}{4}$in. (6mm) of its top. Cut a strip of fabric on the true bias, twice as long as the opening plus $\frac{3}{4}$in. (2cm) and $1\frac{1}{4}$in. (3.2cm) wide. With right sides facing, place edge of the strip on left edge of opening.

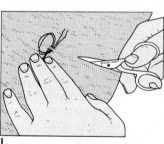

**2** Stitch $\frac{1}{4}$in. (6mm) from the raw edge. Curve the bias at the top of the opening to stitch around the point. Stitch to the end. Reinforce point of opening with a row of short stitches.

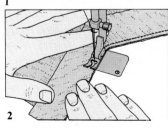

**3** Fold the strip in half, then over the raw edge of the opening to the wrong side of the sleeve. Pin and slip stitch to the row of machine stitching. Trim the ends to the edge of the sleeve. Fold rouleau strip to inside of sleeve on front edge only. Press.

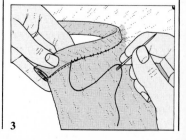

# Making cuffs

### Wrapover cuff

This cuff is often used on blouses and shirts. It is cut from a straight piece of fabric, and wraps over at the opening to be fastened with buttons or cuff links. Instructions for buttonholes are on page 459.

### *How to make a wrapover cuff*

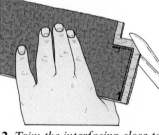

**1** *Tack the interfacing to the wrong side of the cuff. Fold the cuffs in half lengthwise, right sides facing. Tack the ends and stitch. On one end, stitch to mark for wrapover. Backstitch ½in. (1cm).*

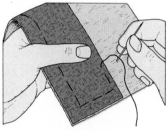

**2** *Trim the interfacing close to the stitching. Trim the seam allowance on the inner cuff to ⅛in. (3mm) and on the outer cuff to ¼in. (6mm). Cut diagonally across the corners, close to the stitching.*

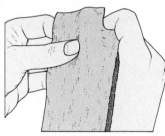

**3** *Press the seams, then turn the cuff to the right side. Pull the corners out to square them. Cut into the seam allowance at the wrapover mark, almost to the stitching. This will ease the stitching of cuff to sleeve. Press seams again.*

### French cuff

This is made from two pieces of fabric cut to twice the finished width. It folds back on itself to form a double cuff. It has four buttonholes for cuff links or button links.

### *How to make a French cuff*

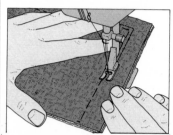

**1** *Tack the interfacing to the wrong side of the upper cuff. With right sides facing and notches matching, pin the outer to the inner cuff. Tack, then stitch around 3 sides, leaving open the edge to be stitched to the sleeve. Take one stitch across the corners and backstitch seam ends. Remove tacking; press.*

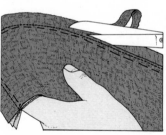

**2** *Trim the interfacing close to stitching. Trim the inner cuff seam edge to ⅛in. (3mm) and the outer cuff seam edge to ¼in. (6mm). Cut diagonally across the corners.*

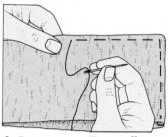

**3** *Press seams. Turn cuff through to the right side. Pull out the corners to square them. Roll the seam between thumb and forefinger, easing inner cuff. Tack and press.*

# Attaching cuffs

Before attaching a cuff to the sleeve, the sleeve seams must be stitched and the length of the sleeve checked. As the sleeve will be fuller than the cuff the fabric is usually gathered up to fit its width. Tucks and pleats can be used.

### *How to attach a basic cuff*

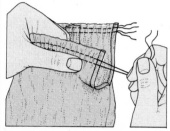

**1** *With the sleeve turned right side out, run a row of gathering stitches along the seam line at the bottom of the sleeve. Sew a second row ¼in. (6mm) nearer the raw edge. Draw up the gathering threads until sleeve edge fits the cuff.*

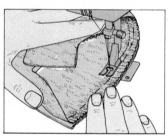

**2** *With right sides facing, pin the interfaced half of the cuff to the sleeve. Match the notches and adjust the gathers evenly. If the opening has a rouleau strip, keep the under edge flat and turn the front edge to the sleeve inside. Tack and stitch the cuff to the sleeve from the sleeve side. Trim seam allowance.*

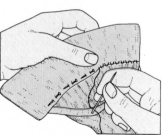

**3** *Press the seam. Turn the cuff up and press the seam edges towards the cuff. Working from the wrong side, fold the edge of the cuff under and slip stitch to the row of machine stitching.*

### *Attaching a rouleau cuff*

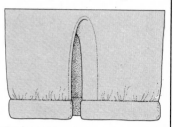

**Rouleau strip edge**

As an alternative to a cuff, you can bind the gathered edge of a sleeve with a rouleau strip. Make this in the same way as a rouleau strip for a neckline (see page 458 for instructions).

The sleeve may or may not have an opening, but if it has the rouleau strip is usually fastened with a press stud. It can also be fastened with loops and buttons. Align a row of buttons on the underside flap of your cuff opening. Sew loops in corresponding positions on the upper flap (see page 459 for instructions).

### *Attaching a wrapover cuff without an opening*

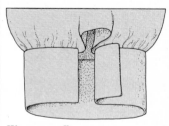

**Wrapover cuff**

It is also possible to attach a plain wrapover cuff to a sleeve which does not have an opening. In this case, the lower edge of the sleeve must be neatly hemmed before it is gathered. The cuff is gathered in the usual way, but the gathered sleeve is left slightly wider than the cuff. This leaves enough room for the hand to pass through when the cuff is fastened, while maintaining a secure finish.

## Types of pocket

Pockets should be large enough for the hand to fit into comfortably and they should always be firmly attached to the garment. They can also be decorative and often add a finishing touch to the garment. There are two basic ways of making pockets: either they can be made up first and then stitched onto the outside of the garment or they can be made as a part of the garment seam and concealed within it.

**Patch pocket**

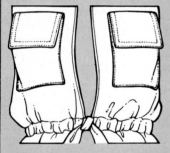

**Patch pocket with flap**

**Seamed pocket**

**Gathered pocket**

## Patch pocket

A patch pocket is made from one piece of fabric folded in two and stitched onto the garment. It can have square or rounded edges at the base.

*How to make the pocket*

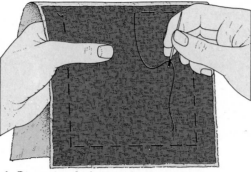

**1** *Pin and tack the interfacing to the wrong side of the outer pocket. Fold the pocket over so the right sides are together and pin into place. Stitch the pocket, leaving an opening for turning it right side out in the centre of the bottom edge. Backstitch ends of stitching.*

**2** *Trim the interfacing close to the stitching line and trim and grade the pocket seam allowances. Wedge-trim the corners or, if the corners are rounded, notch into the seam allowance at the curve. Pull the pocket through the opening, turning right side out and press. Slip stitch the hem of the opening.*

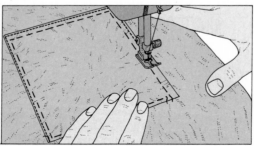

**3** *Pin and tack the pocket onto the garment. Start to stitch ⅜in. (1cm) from the top right hand corner and backstitch just into garment fabric to reinforce. Stitch close to pocket edge on 3 sides, finishing securely.*

## Patch pocket with flap

This is a variation of the patch pocket in which the pocket and the flap are constructed of double fabric and attached separately.

*How to make the flap*

**1** *Pin and tack the interfacing to the outer half of the flap on the wrong side and trim off the interfacing seam allowance. Fold the right sides together and pin. Stitch down the 2 sides on seam line and trim seam allowance as for the rest of the pocket.*

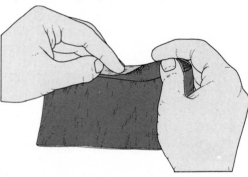

**2** *Remove the tacking and turn the flap through to right side and press. Turn the raw edges in by ¼in. (6mm) and press. Apply any decorative finish such as top stitching at this stage of making up.*

**3** *Place the flap in position on right side of the garment with the open edge just above the pocket top. Stitch along the seam line backstitching at the ends, then slip stitch the turned in edge to the garment. Fold the flap over the pocket and press.*

# Pocket in a seam

A concealed pocket is constructed from two pieces of fabric and is made in one with the garment. It is usually made of the garment fabric.

*How to make the pocket in a seam*

**1** *Place one piece of the pocket onto the garment between the points marking the pocket position. Pin and tack into place. Stitch ½in. (1cm) from the edge between the marks. Press then fold the pocket piece outside the seam line and press again. Repeat the process with the other pocket half.*

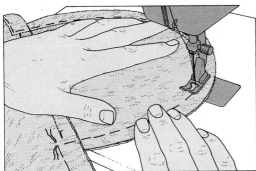

**2** *With right sides together, and markings matched, pin and tack along the seam line. Stitch on garment seam line to first mark, then stitch around the pocket to second mark. Pivot fabric on needle and stitch to end of seam. Press. Pink seams to prevent fraying.*

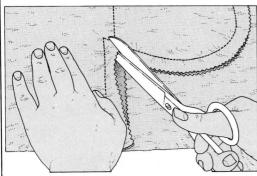

**3** *Turn the pocket towards the front of the garment and clip into the angle of the seam allowance of the back of the garment and the pocket. Press the seams open.*

# Gathered pocket

This is another way of adapting the patch pocket. It is a decorative pocket, made of a single layer of fabric stitched onto the garment and held by a fabric band or ribbon.

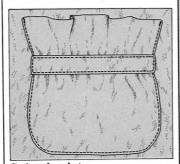

**Gathered pocket**

*How to make the gathered pocket*

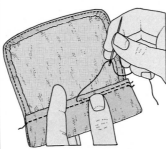

**1** *Finish all raw edges by turning under ¼in. (6mm), and run one row of gathering stitches just outside the seam line of the curved edge of the pocket. Fold over 2in. (5cm) at the top of the pocket for the frill and tack into place. Run 2 rows of gathering stitches through both layers of fabric at the bottom edge of the frill and draw up to the required width.*

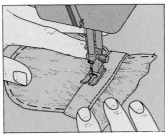

**2** *Tighten the gathering thread slightly on the curve. Turn in ½in. (1.3cm) seam allowance around the pocket. Tack and press. Stitch fabric band or ribbon over gathering for frill. Attach as for a patch pocket.*

# Decorative finishes

Simple designs can be made more interesting with decorative finishes of different kinds.

**Motif embroidery**
Whether hand- or machine-stitched, embroidery should be worked before the garment is made up.

**Ribbon**
Ribbon provides texture and colour on a garment. It can be applied by hand or machine.

**Rouleau strip with bias strip of different colour**
This is attached as for a rouleau strip neckline (see page 447).

**Contrasting fabrics**
These can be attached separately to the garment as an extended facing or as a turn back cuff.

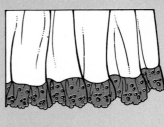

**Broderie anglaise**
Apply to any hem or band of fabric by hand or by machine.

**Lace trimmings**
These are made in a variety of widths, designs and weights. Apply to any hem or fabric band.

## Types of waist finishes

The simplest finish for skirts and trousers is a waistband. This must fit snugly and be firm enough to ensure that the garment hangs well from it. It can either be a plain, stiffened strip or it can be threaded with elastic. It is always attached after the garment is finished but before the hem is levelled. Waistbands can be decorative, depending on how they are sewn on the garment. Belts also provide a decorative and functional finish.

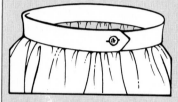

**Stiffened waistband**

**Elasticated waistband**

**Stiffened belt**

**Tie belt**

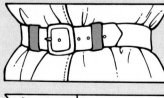

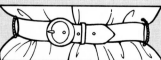

**Fabric and thread carriers**

## Stiffened waistband

A plain waistband must be strengthened with interfacing or other stiffening to maintain its shape and resist strain. Match all the corresponding notches and trim seams.

*How to make the waistband*

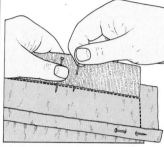

**1** Lay the waistband onto the skirt waist with right sides facing. Match the notches at the centre front, back and side seams. Pin and tack into place, then stitch. Pin the stiffening to the waistband as shown, with the edge on the line of stitching. Tack, then stitch close to edge from other side.

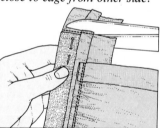

**2** Trim skirt seam close to the stitching. Trim waistband allowance $\frac{1}{8}$ in. (3mm) wider. Fold waistband against stiffening. Press the seams and the band away from the skirt. Fold band back on itself, against stiffening. Stitch each end of the band then trim the ends.

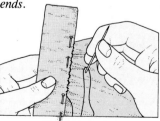

**3** Turn waistband to the right side. Trim seam allowance from the inside edge and turn it under. Pin into place on top of the row of stitching. Slip stitch the edge.

## Elasticated waistband

An elasticated waistband is simple to make and is particularly useful for children's clothes, gathered skirts and jersey fabrics where it provides a flexible and comfortable finish.

*How to make the waistband*

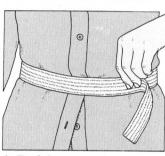

**1** Find the correct length of elastic by tying it around your waist so that it fits comfortably. Add 1in. (2.5cm). The casing should be twice the width of the elastic plus $\frac{1}{8}$in. (3mm) and twice the length, with sufficient fabric for turnings.

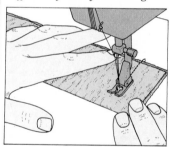

**2** Stitch the ends of the waistband together and press the seams open. With right sides facing, pin and tack it to the waistline and stitch. Press. Trim the skirt seam to $\frac{1}{8}$in. (3mm) and the waistband seam to $\frac{1}{4}$in. (6mm).

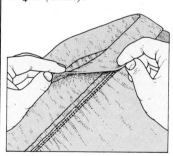

**3** Fold the waistband down. Turn under seam allowance to the line of stitching and pin in place. Slip stitch, leaving a gap at the joining seam through which the elastic will be threaded using a safety pin or bodkin.

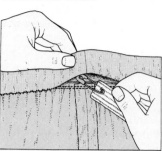

**4** Attach a safety pin or bodkin to the elastic to guide it through the casing. Secure the free end of the elastic to the casing with a pin to prevent the end of the elastic being drawn through by mistake. Then push the pin or bodkin through the gap in the stitching on the waistband.

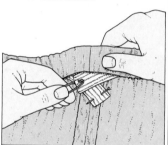

**5** Hold the front of the safety pin or bodkin firmly between the 2 layers of casing fabric. Gather the casing up onto the elastic. Continue until all the elastic has been threaded through the waistband casing and the 2 ends overlap.

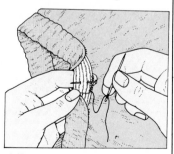

**6** Unpin the ends of the elastic and overlap them by 1in. (2.5 cm) and pin. Either oversew the edges very firmly or make two or three rows of zigzag stitches. Pull the casing back over the elastic and slip stitch neatly into place.

# Belts

Belts are traditionally used to hold loose garments in place, but they are also worn as a finishing touch to a tailored garment. There are two basic types: the simple tie belt and the stiffened belt, which is laced or fastened with a buckle. A tie belt is ideal for a full garment where it gathers the waistline gently into loose folds.

### Tie belt

This belt should be cut on the bias. It is made longer than the waist measurement so that the ends can be tied. The width of the belt can be altered to suit the style of the garment and personal preference. The ends can be finished with fringes or tassels or any other decoration.

Cut the fabric to twice the width of the finished belt, plus the seam allowances.

#### How to make the belt

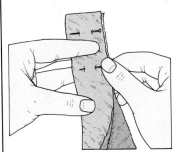

**1** *Fold the fabric in half lengthwise, with right sides facing. Pin and tack ¼in. (6 mm) from the raw edge, leaving one end open. Take care not to stretch the fabric. Stitch along the length of the belt and across one of the ends.*

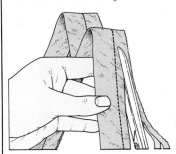

**2** *Trim the excess seam allowance and cut the corners diagonally. Turn the belt through to the right side. Turn under the raw edges at the open end and slip stitch into place. Press the finished belt.*

### Stiffened belt

There are many variations of the stiffened belt. It can be straight or curved and cut to a variety of widths. The instructions given are for a straight belt with a buckle.

#### How to make the belt

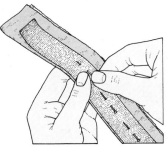

**1** *Fold the fabric in half lengthwise, right sides facing. Press the fabric lightly. Lay the stiffening, which is shaped at one end, with the edge along the folded edge and pin in place. Using the stiffening as a template, stitch around it. Start at the shaped end and work towards the buckle. Do not stitch the stiffening. Trim fabric to ⅛in. (3mm) and cut corners diagonally. Unpin stiffening and turn through to right side.*

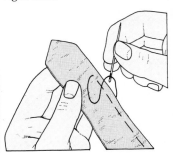

**2** *Insert stiffening, making sure the seam runs along its edge. Turn under and slip stitch the opening. Press. Tack and stitch close to the edge on the long sides and the shaped end. Attach buckle to other end (see method on the right).*

## Buckles, thread loop carriers and fabric carriers

Belts have to be held in position on the garment. Unless they are tie belts they are usually buckled and held in place on the garment by fabric or thread carriers. The carriers should be placed at the side seams and at the centre back on trousers and can be sewn before or after the garment is finished. To position the carriers fasten the belt and mark its width with pins.

### Fitting a buckle

Mark the centre front position on both ends of the belt. Trim the straight-edged end to measure 2in. (5cm) from the centre front line. Overstitch the ends.

**Overstitching the eyelet**

**Pushing prong into the belt end**

#### How to add the buckle

**1** *Pierce a hole, or eyelet, for the buckle on the centre front line of the straight end of the belt using a sharply pointed instrument. Buttonhole stitch around the eyelet (see page 439 for stitch instructions).*

**2** *Insert the buckle prong into this. Fold the flap down and secure. On the shaped end of the belt make another eyelet on the centre front mark. Punch one or two others to either side. Finish eyelets as before.*

### Thread carriers

These carriers are less noticeable than fabric ones and are only attached to the side seams. Do not use on trousers or on garments where they would be under any strain.

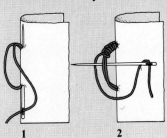

1       2

#### How to make the carrier

*Select button thread to match your garment. Anchor a double loop of thread across the waistline seam (Fig. 1). Reinforce the loop with blanket stitch (Fig. 2). These carriers can also be made using a machined chainstitch.*

### Fabric carriers

A fabric carrier provides a stronger loop for your belt and should be used if the belt is under any strain. Attach carrier by turning ends under ¼in. (6mm) and stitching in position.

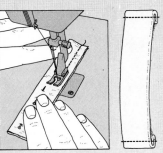

**Stitching the belt carrier**

#### How to make the carrier

*Cut a matching strip of fabric 1¼in. (3cm) wide and the depth of the belt plus 1½in. (4cm). Fold the strip lengthwise, pin and stitch ¼in. (6mm) from the raw edge. Trim seam allowance and turn to right side and press.*

*Fasten carrier to garment as described above.*

457

# Types of fastening

All garments will need openings at various points so that they can be put on and taken off easily. The openings can be fastened in a variety of ways – which type of fastening you choose will depend on the position of the fastening, the amount of strain put on it and whether the fastening is to form a decorative feature on the garment.

For long openings, zip fasteners are probably best because they open and close quickly and can take a lot of strain. Instructions for inserting them are on pages 460 and 461. Velcro – a burr-like fabric which sticks to itself – can always be used as a quick fastening device. It comes in tape form and can be stitched down on either side of the opening or overlap. Press stud tape is attached to the garment in the same way but forms a slightly firmer fastening than Velcro. It is ideal for fastening duvets and baby's sleeping suits.

For smaller openings, buttons, hooks and eyes or press studs can be used. They come in a wide variety of materials, colours, shapes and sizes.

One of the most important points to remember with all types of fastening is to make sure that the two sides of the opening match perfectly, and the two parts of the fastening meet without any puckering, pulling or gaping of the fabric. Most fastenings will have to take a certain amount of strain and the opening will often need to be faced and interfaced to provide a firm base for the fastener (see page 464 for instructions).

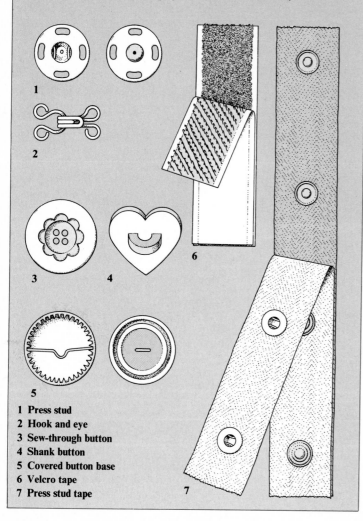

1 Press stud
2 Hook and eye
3 Sew-through button
4 Shank button
5 Covered button base
6 Velcro tape
7 Press stud tape

# Hooks and eyes

These are useful for extra fastenings, for example on waistbands and at necklines. The hook should be sewn first, and the position of the eye ascertained before it is sewn on.

### *How to sew on hooks and eyes*

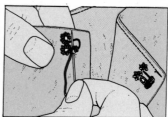

*Position the hook on the underside of the overlap ⅛in. (3mm) from the edge. Buttonhole stitch both holes on the hook and overcast the neck of the hook to keep it flat. Then position the eye on the other side of the opening and stitch in place.*

### *Press studs*

It is best to use these where there is not much strain at the opening. The ball of the stud is usually on the right side of the underlap and the socket on the wrong side of the overlap.

### *How to sew on press studs*

**1** *Mark the position for the stud taking care to match the lap of the opening. Make at least 4 stitches into each hole.*

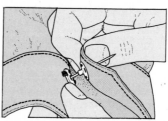

**2** *To sew on the socket, align the 2 parts of the press studs by putting the needle through the centres of both studs. Then stitch as in step 1.*

# Rouleau loops

Rouleau button loops can be made singly or in a row. They will need to be made along the faced edge of the garment. Once the loops have been made they have to be positioned on the garment and then stitched between the garment and the facing. The instructions for cutting the rouleau strips, which are always cut on the bias, are on page 472. Measure the diameter of the button and make a rouleau strip long enough both to take the button and to fasten to the garment.

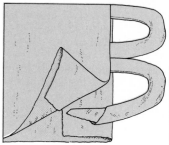

**Rouleau button loops**

### *How to attach rouleau loops*

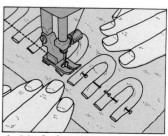

**1** *Mark the position for the loops on the fitting line on the right side of the garment. Pin them into position and machine into place with a row of stitching within the seam allowance.*

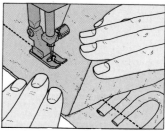

**2** *With the right sides of the garment facing stitch along the seam line. Fold the facing back, exposing the loops, and press the facing into position. Slip stitch into place.*

# Buttonholes

Buttonholes can either be hand-stitched (see page 439 for buttonhole instructions) or machine-stitched using a buttonhole attachment. Always make a test buttonhole first to check that it will fit the button. The size of the buttonhole will depend on the size and shape of the button.

## Making the buttonhole

The position and size of each buttonhole should be marked on the overlap with tacking thread. Two vertical lines of tacking threads are used to mark the ends of the buttonholes and a horizontal tacking line to mark the centre of each buttonhole where an opening will be slashed.

### How to make the buttonhole

1 *Mark one end of the buttonhole with vertical tacking. Mark centre with a horizontal line of stitches.*
2 *Using a short stitch sew $\frac{1}{8}$ in. (3mm) along each side of this horizontal line and across the other end of the buttonhole.*
3 *Slash carefully between the stitching with small sharp scissors. Overcast the raw edges using a matching thread to your garment fabric. Work from right to left on the lower edge of the slash. Insert the needle into the slash and bring it out at the line of tacking stitches below. Loop the thread around the needle point from left to right. Pull the needle away from you through the fabric, so that a knot forms exactly on the slash edge.*
4 *Stitch along the length of the slash using this technique. Make the stitches very close together to form a strong, secure edge. When you get to the corner, fan the stitches out. Make a bar of satin stitches at the other end of the buttonhole to reinforce it.*

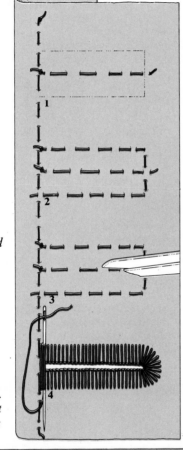

## Machine worked buttonholes

Machine worked buttonholes are slashed *after* the buttonhole is stitched.

### How to make the buttonhole

*Mark the buttonhole or buttonholes in the same way as for a handstitched buttonhole. Then, using the buttonhole attachment on the machine, work around the buttonhole position and slash carefully through the centre.*

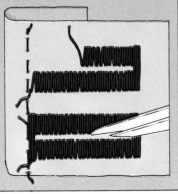

# Buttons

Buttons should be selected carefully to make sure that they suit both the weight and colour of the fabric. They should be sewn on securely using a strong, matching thread, leaving enough "give" in the thread to allow the buttonhole to close under the button without puckering the fabric. Make sure that the fabric to which the button is fastened has been suitably reinforced to prevent it tearing or pulling under strain (see page 464 for interfacing instructions).

## Positioning buttons

It is extremely important to position the buttons correctly after the buttonholes have been worked. Pin the opening overlaps together, then pin through the outer edge of each buttonhole to mark the correct position for each button.

## Sewing on buttons

Buttons are sewn on according to their construction. Some buttons are made with two or four holes, while other buttons have a metal shank underneath. If the buttons have padded fabric underneath they are treated as shank buttons.

### How to sew on sew-through buttons

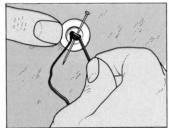

*Knot the thread and make a small stitch underneath the button to hide the knot. Then stitch in and out of the holes over a pin, leaving the thread fairly loose under the button. Wind the thread securely around the under threads and fasten off.*

### How to sew on shank buttons

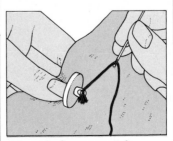

*Place the button at right angles to the fabric and then stitch through the loop of the shank and the garment several times before fastening off on the wrong side of the garment.*

## Making covered buttons

Covered buttons can make a decorative finish to a garment and are often fastened with matching rouleau loops. The buttons, which come in two parts and are made of metal, are sewn on as for shank buttons (see left).

### How to make the buttons

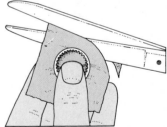

1 *Cut a circle of fabric half as large again as the button and place it over the top half of the button.*

2 *Fold the surplus fabric under the button and clip the bottom half to the top half, securing the fabric.*

## *Types of zip*

# *Zip fastenings*

### *Types of zip*

A standard zip is the type most commonly used on skirts, dresses and trousers. It can either be lapped or centred. The invisible zip is sometimes used on tailored skirts and dresses, where a standard zip opening might spoil the line of the garment. Open-ended zips are used, for example, on anoraks and sleeping bags because they unfasten to completely separate the zip.

The zips shown below are:
**1** Standard zip, centred. **2** Standard zip, lapped. **3** Invisible zip. **4** Open-ended zip.

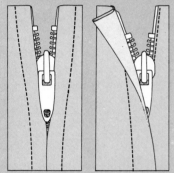

**1 Centred zip**      **2 Lapped zip**

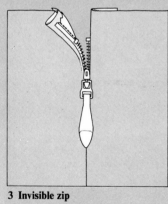

**3 Invisible zip**

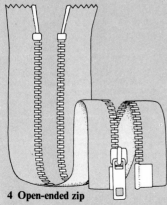

**4 Open-ended zip**

Zips are made in different weights for use on different types of garments and fabrics (see chart below). The heavier zips are naturally the strongest. They can have either metal or nylon teeth and the zip tape can be of cotton, nylon or a cotton/polyester mixture. Zips with synthetic tape should be used on synthetic fabric and those with metal teeth should be used on garments which will receive the heaviest wear.

Always insert your zip into flat, pressed seams. The zip length should be matched to the length of the opening and the opening should be large enough to allow easy access. Make sure that the hang of the garment is perfect before inserting the zip. Check that the seam allowance is $\frac{5}{8}$in. to $\frac{3}{4}$in. (15mm to 20mm). Tack each side of the zip opening and then press the seam before putting in the zip.

### Insertion tips

There are certain points which should be considered when inserting zips. Follow these tips and your garment will look more professional.

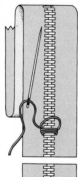

**1** Finish off all seams before inserting the zip.
**2** Pre-shrink the zip if the garment is washable. This will prevent puckering.
**3** Always try to pin from the bottom of the zip upwards.
**4** Use a zip foot when you are machine stitching. This will allow you to stitch on each side of the zip in one continuous movement.
**5** Shorten long zips at the bottom, by overstitching coils 1in. (2.5cm) below the desired new length. Cut off the excess.

**Shortening zip at the bottom**

### *Zip chart*

| Style | Weight | Length |
|---|---|---|
| Neckline | Very light to medium | 6″–9″ (15cm–23cm) |
| Skirt | Very light to medium | 4″–6″ (10cm–15cm) |
| Dress | Very light to medium | 12″–14″ (30.5cm–35.5cm) |
| Trousers | Medium to heavy | 9″–11″ (23cm–28cm) |
| Jeans | Heavy | 6″ (15cm) |

### *Centred zip*

This standard zip is placed in the seam with an equal width of seam allowance on each side. It is the easiest method of inserting zips and can be used on centre and back seams.

### *Inserting the zip*

Prepare and stitch the seam, leaving an opening for the zip the length of the zip teeth (Fig. 1). Press the seam allowance open so that the fold line forms the fitting line for the zip. Neaten the edges of the seam allowances using the appropriate method. Pin and tack along the fold lines (Fig. 2). Mark the end of the opening with a pin. Pin the zip into position with the teeth centred over the seam. The pins should be at right angles to the zip, alternating in direction (Fig. 3). Tack $\frac{1}{4}$in. (6mm) from zip teeth then remove pins. Stitch close to the tacking on the right side using the zip foot. Start at the top, stitch down the length of one side, pivot the fabric to turn and stitch across the bottom and then stitch up the other side (Fig. 4). Remove the tacking and press. Neaten the tape ends using the method appropriate for your garment and the zip type.

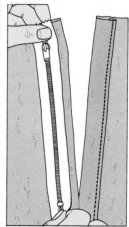
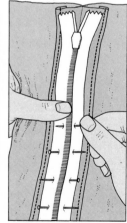

**1 Aligning the zip**      **3 Pinning the zip**

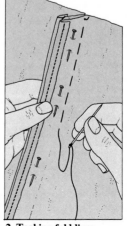
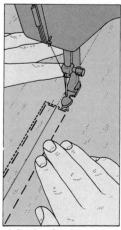

**2 Tacking fold lines**      **4 Sewing the zip**

## Lapped zip

This zip lies behind a flap formed by the seam allowance on one side. It is suitable for use on side and centre seams.

### Inserting the zip

Stitch seam up to the opening for the zip. This should be the same length as the teeth of the zip. Press the stitched seam allowance open as well as the overlapping section of the opening so that the fitting line lies on the fold (Fig. 1). From the right side of the garment place the zip under the seam opening (Fig. 2). Pin and tack the unpressed edge close to the teeth of the zip (Fig. 3). Lap the opposite seam allowance over the zip teeth, making sure that they are completely covered. Tack and stitch (Fig. 4).

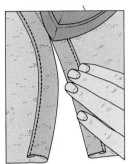

**1 Pressing opening**

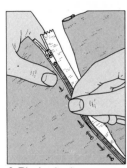

**3 Pinning in zip**

**2 Positioning zip**

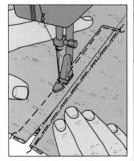

**4 Sewing lapped zip**

## Open-ended zip

This zip is best inserted before the garment has been hemmed. Usually centred, the teeth can be semi-concealed in the usual way, or exposed for a decorative finish.

### Inserting the zip

Align the lower end of the zip so that it tucks into the hem.

Tack the zip in place and turn the tape ends over at the top. Fold the facing and hem down over the tapes. Slip stitch into place, making sure that they do not interfere with the action of the zip.

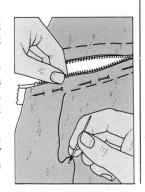

## Invisible zip

This zip provides an invisible fastening. All that shows from the right side of the garment is a plain seam and a pull tab, but no stitching. This is because the zip tapes are only stitched to the seam allowance of the open seam using a special zip foot attachment (the zip foot must be the one recommended for the brand of the zip that you buy). The zip is stitched in place before the remainder of the seam has been sewn.

### Inserting the zip

Press the zip tapes so that the coil stands away from the tapes. They will then feed through the zip foot smoothly (Fig. 1). Finish the seam edges where appropriate. Open the zip and place it face down on the right side of the garment. Place the coils on the proposed seam line with the tape in the seam allowance. Fit the groove on the right side of the foot over the coil. Stitch as far as the tab, keeping as close to the coil as possible (Fig. 2). Close the zip to position the coil on the other side and pin. Open the zip and stitch as on the other side, but with the left-hand groove over the coil (Fig. 3). To stitch the rest of the seam, first close the zip. Pin and tack the seam. Lower the needle into the end of zip stitching (Fig. 4). Stitch seam to the lower end, having made sure that it is connected to the stitching of the zip above it. Finish off the seam in the appropriate way for the fabric (see page 442).

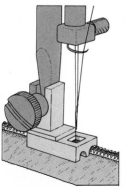

**1 Zip foot**

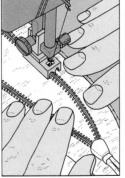

**3 Sewing right side**

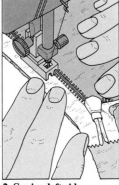

**2 Sewing left side**

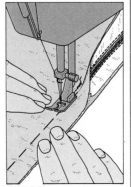

**4 Finishing seam**

## Neatening tape ends

Whether the zip is centred, lapped or open-ended, the ends have to be finished off neatly on the garment.

### Neatening standard zips

On trousers and skirts which are being fitted with standard zips, you must always insert the zip before the waistband is attached. This applies to both centred and lapped zips. The tape ends are enclosed between the waistband and the garment once the waistband has been attached.

On a neckline zip, whether it has been lapped or centred, the zip is inserted after the neckline has been faced. The zip fits between the facing and the garment and is slip stitched into place.

### Neatening open-ended zips

Open-ended zips are placed between the upper and lower hems of a garment. These are then slip stitched into place. Care should be taken to ensure that the facing and hems do not interfere with the action of the zip. It is best not to stitch any hem or facing in place on the garment beforehand.

### Neatening invisible tapes

Because of the method of insertion the tape ends are stitched along with the seam allowances.

Stitch the left tape to the left-hand seam allowance, close to the edge. Reposition the zip foot over the right zip tape and stitch in place. If the garment is to be faced the zip should be stitched into position first. After stitching the facing to the garment the raw edges of the facing should be folded against the zipper tapes and then slip stitched to them.

# Hems

The hem is the last step in garment making and is usually hand-stitched. To achieve a perfectly smooth hem use the right stitch for your fabric, never tighten the thread or the fabric will pucker, and always match seam and centre lines after turning up the hem. Stitches should never show on the right side (instructions for hand stitches are on pages 438–439).

### Preparing the hem for marking

Before marking the hem, make sure that the garment fits perfectly and hangs correctly. Any adjustment to the rest of the garment will affect the fall of the hem and therefore the look of the entire garment. If cut on the bias, hang the garment overnight before marking the skirt length. If the lining is attached to the skirt the two hems should be marked separately.

### Marking the hemline

As with other fitting stages, wear the underclothes and the shoes that you plan to wear with the garment. Similarly, any belt or sash should be worn as well. It is best to find someone to mark the hem for you. Use a chalk marker or a metre stick, measuring an even distance from the floor. The marker should move around the wearer to avoid any change in the hang of the skirt caused by movement. For full length skirts stand on a stool.

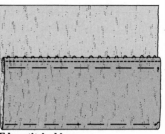

**Marking the hem with chalk**

### Turning the hem

Fold the hem on the chalk line and pin at right angles to the folded edge. Your skirt hem must be even all around so pin again until the hem measures the same distance from the ground all around. When you are sure the hem is level tack ¼in. (6mm) from the folded edge. Press to sharpen the creases, sliding the iron along the crosswise grain. Cut away surplus fabric and trim seam in hem fold to half its width.

The allowance left for a hem depends on its position on the garment and the type of fabric. Skirt hems and heavy fabrics will need deeper hems because the extra weight helps allow them to hang properly. Sleeves and fine fabrics only need narrow hems to secure them. Always sew the hem using the appropriate stitch, and make sure that only a thread of the garment fabric is taken onto the needle each time you take a stitch.

**Pinned and tacked hem**

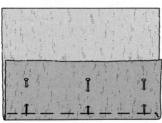

**Cutting away surplus fabric**

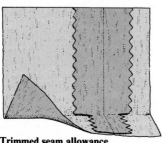

**Trimmed seam allowance**

# Hem finishes

A neat, level hem is essential for a professional finish to the garment. Having taken trouble to ensure the correct fit and hang of your garment you must choose the most appropriate method for finishing the hem. The actual shape of the skirt – whether it is gored, flared, circular or straight – as well as the type and weight of the fabric will help determine which method to use. It is best to finish off hems by hand if an invisible finish on the right side of the garment is required.

### Edge stitched hem

This is suitable for garments which are frequently laundered and for linings.

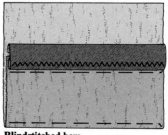

**Edge stitched hem**

#### Finishing the hem

Fold raw edge of the hem under ¼in. (6mm). Stitch near the edge of the fold and press. Pin the hem edge in place, matching seam and centre lines, then tack. Finish with slip stitch. Remove tacking and press the hem.

### Blindstitched hem

This is suitable for children's clothes and curtains. The stitching is inconspicuous on both sides of the garment.

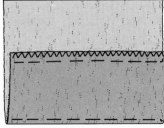

**Blindstitched hem**

#### Finishing the hem

The hem may be bound with straight or bias binding. Sew this ¼in. (6mm) from the raw edge of the hem using narrow zigzag stitch, then press. Tack the hem in place and then stitch using blind hemming stitch (see page 439). Press the finished hem.

### Herringbone hem

This is suitable for loosely woven fabrics. The raw edge should either be pinked or bias bound before it is stitched.

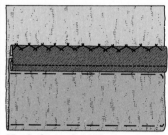

**Herringbone stitched hem**

#### Finishing the hem

Neaten the raw edge in the most suitable way for the fabric and tack into place. Stitch hem using herringbone stitch (see page 439), working from left to right. Press the finished hem.

### Zigzag hem

This is suitable for double knit fabrics because it prevents fraying and the stitch has as much "give" as the fabric.

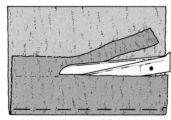

**Zigzag stitched hem**

#### Finishing the hem

Neaten the raw edge with multistitch or plain zigzag stitch. Press, then trim close to the stitching. Pin and tack the raw edge to the skirt, matching seam and centre lines. Finish with blind hemming stitch (page 439). Press the finished hem.

## *Flared and gored skirts*

The following method is suitable if the skirt is slightly flared or gored. The fullness of the hem is controlled by gathering the hem slightly.

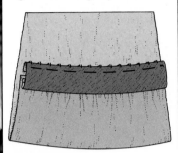

**Slightly flared hem**

### *Finishing the hem*

Run gathering stitches ¼in. (6mm) from the raw edge. Pin the hem to the skirt, matching centre and seam lines. Draw the gathering thread up slightly to ease the fullness and fit the skirt shape. Do not draw the hem in too much or the shape will be lost. Place the hem over a pressing mitt and shrink out fullness with a steam iron. Place bias binding over the gathering. Pin and tack the hem to the skirt. Press, shrinking the bias binding to the curve. Finish with blind hemming stitch (see page 439). Press the hem.

## *Circular hem*

For a smooth finish this hem should be made narrow. If the hem is left deep, there will be too much bulk for the hem to lie flat.

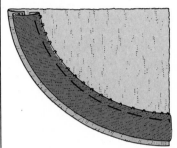

**Circular hem**

### *Finishing the hem*

After marking the hemline, trim away excess fabric to leave a turning of ½in. (1.3cm). Pin and stitch the bias binding, ¼in. (6mm) from the raw edge. Take care not to stretch the bias binding as you stitch. Press. Fold the fabric on the marked line. Pin and tack close to the fold, then press. Tack the raw edge to the skirt, close to the edge of the binding. Finish with blind hemming stitch or slip stitch (page 439). Remove tackings and press the length of the hem.

## *Machine stitched hem*

Machine-stitched hems are useful because they can be sewn quickly and they provide a strong finish. Care must be taken when machining the hem to ensure that the stitching is straight. This is important because the stitching will be visible on the right side. This hem is suitable for lingerie and frills. Trim the hem allowance to ¼in. (6mm). Double-fold the edge to ⅛in. (3mm) for about 2in. (5cm) and then press. Using the hemming foot on the machine, stitch through the creased fold for several stitches to secure the beginning of the hem.

### *Finishing the hem*

Take the thread ends in your left hand and guide the pressed edge under the hemming foot, thus forming a roll of fabric. Firm, crisp fabrics "roll" better with the foot raised; soft fabrics with the foot down. If fabric is cut on the bias stitch raw edge first.

**Machine-stitched hem**

## *Finishing corners*

It is worth taking trouble, when turning hem corners, to ensure there is no excess bulk and that you have sharp, square corners. They can be mitred or faced.

### *Mitred corner*

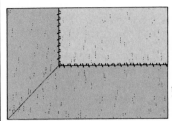

**Hem with a mitred corner**

### *How to make the corner*

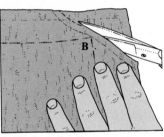

**1** *Turn under the raw edges and then turn the hem in the usual way. Press, then open out the fabric. At corner point of hem fold (B) draw a diagonal line across. Cut off corner fabric ¼in. (6mm) outside this line.*

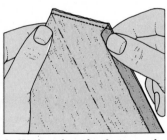

**2** *With right sides facing and raw edges turned under, fold across corner and stitch diagonal line. Turn corner through and finish off the hem.*

### *Faced corner*

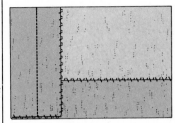

**Hem with a facing**

### *How to make the corner*

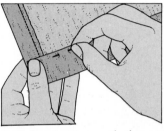

**1** *Before turning up the hem, fold the raw edge of the facing under ¾in. (2cm) then stitch. Pin and stitch the hem into place at the required depth.*

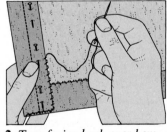

**2** *Turn facing back over hem to required width and slip stitch into place by first stitching along the bottom of the facing to secure it to the hem, and then stitching up the side of the facing.*

## *Pressing hems*

Hems should be steam pressed from the folded edge to the cut edge to shrink out any fullness at the cut edge and avoid wrinkles (see page 429 for pressing instructions). Press the hem when it has been tacked in place, and press again after stitching to remove thread marks.

**Pressing from folded to cut edge**

# Interfacing

An interfacing is an extra piece of fabric placed between the garment fabric and the facing. It reinforces and adds body and crispness to any faced part of the garment, preserving the shape and giving a sharper finish to the garment.

If you are using a bought pattern, it will include instructions for using an interfacing. When working from your own pattern, you should consider using interfacing whenever a faced edge needs extra strength, for example on collars, cuffs, buttonbands and lapels.

The type of interfacing you use will depend on the fabric and the type of garment. It should never be heavier than the garment fabric. Interfacings come in a variety of weights and degrees of firmness and can be either woven or non-woven. As well as the standard interfacing fabric you can buy an iron-on interfacing which can be applied by pressing it onto the fabric using a warm iron; the heat bonds the two layers together.

Where interfacings need to be seamed, a lapped seam should be used (see page 442) and then trimmed to a minimum at the seam allowances to avoid any unnecessary bulk.

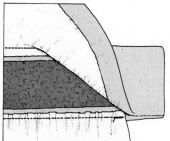

**Waistband reinforced and strengthened with interfacing**

**Trimming the pocket interfacing to reduce bulk**

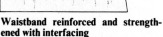

### Interfacing chart

| Fabric | Colour | Purpose | Points to note |
|---|---|---|---|
| Unbleached calico | Natural | Jackets, coats, loose weaves. Adds body without stiffness | Washable, dry cleanable. Shrink before applying |
| Batiste | White | Thin dresses and blouses | Washable. Shrink before applying |
| Medium stiff canvas | Beige | Lapels, fronts of heavyweight coats and jackets | Washable. Shrink before applying |
| Lawn | White or coloured | Cotton and washable dresses and blouses | Dry cleanable |
| Iron-on | White | Stiffening details in small areas: collars, cuffs, pocket flaps. Not for pure silks | Washable, dry cleanable |
| Vilene | White | Sheer cottons, light silks, drip-dry fabrics | Washable, dry cleanable |

# Lining

A lining neatens the inside of a garment by covering the seam edges. It also helps to prolong the life of a garment because it prevents the fabric from pulling out of shape. Lining is therefore particularly important when making garments from knitted or stretch fabrics, and on garments, or parts of garments, which will have a lot of hard wear.

Most outer garments, such as coats and jackets, need a lining both to hide the seam edges and to make sure that the fabrics of the inner and outer garments do not rub together.

The lining can either be made up with the garment and stitched to it as part of the construction process or the garment can be made up first and the lining attached to it separately. The best finish is obtained by facing the garment edges and attaching the lining to these. However, if you want to attach the lining directly to an edge (thus forming a facing), that edge must be left unfinished.

Lining fabrics should ideally be slippery and pliable. The most commonly used fabrics are imitation silks such as man-made crepe and taffeta. The lining's suitability regarding the weight and laundering needs should be considered.

### Making up the lining

Cut the lining pattern pieces from the garment pattern but omit the parts which do not require lining such as collars, cuffs and facings. Pleated or gathered garments will not require pleated or gathered linings, but the lining should be full enough to allow room for movement. Remember to transfer any markings onto the lining fabric and incorporate any alterations made.

### Finishing a lining hem

On skirts and dresses the lining will need to be hemmed separately from the garment. Before the lining is hemmed, the garment hem should be finished in the appropriate way. The hem linings on jackets and some coats are not hemmed separately. They are slip stitched to the finished hem of the outside fabric (see right).

### How to hem the lining

**1** *Turn the garment inside out and fold the excess lining fabric back at the hem, so that the hem of the lining is 1in. (2.5cm) from the hemline of the garment. Trim away surplus fabric.*

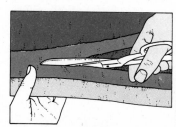

**2** *Pin the hem of the lining into position, easing any surplus fabric at the raw edge. Tack it into position taking care not to stitch through to the fabric of the garment. Then machine stitch around the hem to secure it.*

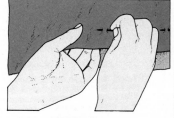

**3** *If you want to secure the lining hem to the garment at the side seams make several long stitches and reinforce these by working over them with blanket stitch.*

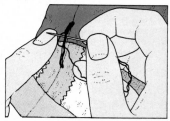

# Lining a garment

The lining should be made exactly the same size as the garment, minus the details such as pleats or gathers, and should fit without pulling or straining.

### Making up a lining

Make up the bodice and skirt of the lining separately but do not stitch the hems. Press all the seams open and the darts in the opposite direction to those on the outer garment. Turn it inside out and place on a stand if you have one.

### Attaching the bodice lining

Put the prepared bodice lining onto the garment with wrong sides facing. Pin into place (Fig. 1), matching the shoulder, side, centre and back seams, and all dart and style lines. Tack the lining to the seam allowance of the garment at the waistline and the armholes. Cut back the lining at the neckline so that it only overlaps the edge of the neck facing by ¾in. (2cm). Fold the neck edge of the lining to the inside and tack it to the neck facing (Fig. 2). Follow the same procedure at the armholes. If the garment has sleeves do not turn under the raw edges at the armholes.

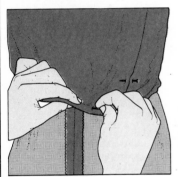

**1** *Pinning the bodice onto the garment, wrong sides facing.*

**2** *Tacking the lining at the neckline to the neck facing.*

### Attaching the skirt lining and zip

Place the skirt lining onto the skirt of the garment just above the stitching line at the waistline. Leave 1½in. (4cm) at either side of the zip fastener for the seam turning. Fold the bodice lining over the skirt lining at the waist seam line. Pin and then slip stitch into place (Fig. 1). If you are lining a skirt only, stitch the lining to the skirt at the waist before attaching the waistband. Fold back the seam allowance at either side of the zip fastener (Fig. 2) then hem stitch to the zip tapes. Press and remove all tacking stitches. Trim off any excess fabric and then finish hem lining as shown on the left.

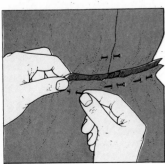

**1** *Pinning the skirt lining to the waist of the garment.*

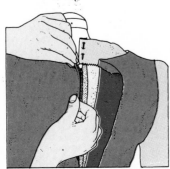

**2** *Turning under the seam allowance before securing zip.*

# Attaching a sleeve lining

The sleeve lining is attached after the main body of the garment has been lined. On some garments a sleeve lining will not be necessary even although the rest of the garment has to be lined. For short sleeves, the lining and outer garment may be stitched together to form the finished lower edge but on long sleeves the lining is attached to the facing at the wrist.

### Making a lining for a short sleeve

Make up the sleeve lining in the same way as the garment sleeve. Leave the edges unfinished. Turn the garment to the right side and place the lining over the garment sleeve. Make certain that you are matching the correct sleeve lining to the correct sleeve. With right sides facing stitch around sleeve hem edge.
Press; pull lining to the inside of the sleeve. Roll the sleeve hemline slightly to the inside, then tack into position and press. Turn inside out and then pin and tack the lining to the sleeve crown, starting at the underarm (Fig.1). Match all balance marks and ease excess fabric evenly then slip stitch (Fig. 2).

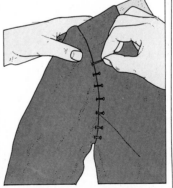

**1** *Pinning the crown of the sleeve lining to the bodice.*

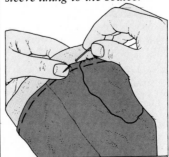

**2** *Pinning the bottom of the sleeve lining so that the cuff overlaps the bottom of the facing's raw edge.*

### Making a lining for a long sleeve

Make up the lining as for the garment sleeve. With the garment inside out pull the lining over the sleeve so that the wrong sides are facing. Make sure that you are matching the correct sleeve lining to the correct sleeve. Attach the lining at the armhole and crown as for the short sleeve lining. Pin a small pleat around the sleeve below the elbow (Fig. 1). Pin under the cuff edge of the lining so that it overlaps the raw edge of the facing by ½in. (1.3cm) (Fig. 2). Slip stitch in place then unpin the pleat and allow the fabric to fall free. Turn the sleeve and garment right side out.

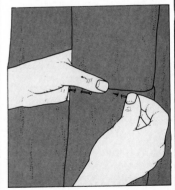

**1** *Pinning a pleat around the sleeve, just below the elbow, before securing the cuff.*

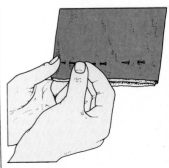

**2** *Slip stitching the lining to the facing at the wrist.*

# Making up four different garments

Making up any garment is a simple and straightforward process if properly organized. Think of the garment as a collection of units – the main pattern pieces such as the bodice and skirt and the smaller units such as facings, pockets, collars, cuffs and sleeves. Each of them should be made up first, and then attached to the other to form the completed garment. This method eliminates a great deal of wasted time and unnecessary handling.

There are a few simple rules which you should get into the habit of following because they will increase your efficiency and the professional look of your garment.

Always tack the garment together by hand and make any fitting alterations before machine stitching. Transfer alterations to a paper pattern immediately. Test the thread and stitch tension on a spare piece of fabric before you begin to stitch the garment.

Neaten all the seams as you stitch them and press each stage of the garment as it is completed. For example, press shoulder darts before you stitch shoulder seams.

## Blouse with button front and yoke

The back and front bodices are made up separately. They are joined and the sleeves inserted.

**Yoked blouse with button front**

### Making the garment
1 Gather the back bodice.
2 Attach the back bodice to the yoke piece.
3 Gather the front bodice pieces along the yoke.
4 Attach the front bodice pieces to the yoke pieces.
5 Neaten seam edges on yoke and bodice.
6 Prepare the facings for the button and buttonhole band.
7 Attach the facings.
8 Stitch the shoulder seams.
9 Neaten shoulder seams.
10 Make the collar and attach.
11 Make the sleeves.
12 Neaten seam edges.
13 Make up the cuffs.
14 Attach cuffs to sleeves.
15 Set in the sleeves.
16 Make any pockets.
17 Attach the pockets.
18 Finish the hem.
19 Make the buttonholes and sew on the buttons.

## Skirt with zip, waistband and concealed pockets

Simple skirts are made by stitching the side seams, attaching the waistband and inserting the zip. For a skirt with concealed pockets the skirt front and back are made up separately before being joined at the side seams.

**Skirt with zip, waistband and concealed pockets**

### Making the garment
1 Make the skirt front, including the front pocket pieces.
2 Make the back skirt, stitching only as far as the zip opening on the appropriate seam.
3 Attach the back pocket pieces to the garment.
4 Join the side seams, stitching around the pocket pieces to join them.
5 Make up the waistband.
6 Insert the zip.
7 Attach the waistband and complete it with a fastening.
8 Level the hem and stitch it.

## Trousers with a zip

The two legs are made up separately and the centre seam stitched later. This allows you to adjust the crotch seam.

**Trousers with zip opening**

### Making the garment
1 Stitch the darts in the front and back legs.
2 Join the fronts to the backs at the inner leg edges and side seams.
3 Make the pockets, if any.
4 Attach the pockets.
5 Stitch the centre seam in one continuous movement, allowing for the zip opening at the front. Attach the zip.
6 Make the waistband.
7 Attach the waistband and complete with a fastening.
8 Turn up the hems on each leg and stitch.

## Dress with centre back zip

The bodice and skirt are made up separately and then attached.

**Dress with centre back zip**

### Making the garment
1 Make darts in front bodice.
2 Make darts in back bodice.
3 Join and neaten the shoulder seams.
4 Make the collar.
5 Prepare the facing.
6 Attach the facing and collar.
7 Stitch the side seams.
8 Make the cuffs, with buttonholes if necessary.
9 Make the sleeves and neaten the seams.
10 Attach the cuffs to the sleeves.
11 Set in the sleeves.
12 Make the front skirt.
13 Make the pockets, if any.
14 Attach the pockets to the front skirt.
15 Stitch together the side seams of the skirt.
16 Attach the skirt to the bodice of the garment.
17 Stitch the centre back seam as far as the zip opening.
18 Insert the zip.
19 Make the belt.
20 Make the belt carriers if necessary.
21 Attach the belt carriers.
22 Level and stitch the hem.

466

# Fitting garments

One of the advantages of making your own garments is that they can be made to fit your figure exactly. To achieve this, first make sure that you take accurate body measurements. Secondly, check and adjust all pattern pieces before cutting. Finally, fit the tacked garment before sewing. This fitting should be made on your body not on a stand, so you will need the help of a friend to ensure an accurate fitting.

## Fitting adjustments

Fitting adjustments need to be made throughout the making up process, as soon as the main darts and seams have been tacked. Other seams and openings can be held together by pins. In theory, adjustments made to one side of the body should be matched exactly on the other. Most people, however, are not exactly symmetrical and adjustments may need to be made on one side only to achieve an even hang.

## The first fitting

When all the details have been checked and the garment has been tacked, you are ready for a proper fitting. Wear the underwear and shoes that you intend to wear with the garment. Try on the garment right side out, pin up the openings and put on a belt if there is to be one. If any adjustments have to be made, remove the tacking stitches and pin the corrections.

## Checking for comfort

The garment should feel comfortable when you sit, move, stretch, raise an arm or bend a knee. Try on a jacket over a blouse or skirt and a coat over a dress to ensure a proper fit. For a well-fitted look there should be a reasonable amount of ease at the bust; the waistline should fit snugly but without strain and the fabric should lie smoothly between waist and hip. If there is excess fabric at the back you may need to take in the side seam or raise the back at the waist. Any unsightly bulges or wrinkles should be removed by adjusting the appropriate dart or seam.

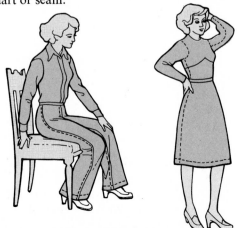

**Testing for comfort by sitting and stretching**

## Checking the grain lines

The centre back and front grain lines, which should have been marked with a line of tacking, should be straight and perpendicular to the floor (except for bias cut garments). The cross grain at the bust and hip lines should be parallel to the floor. The lengthwise sleeve grain should be vertical from the shoulder point to the elbow and the cross grain above the elbow should be parallel to the floor.

## Checking the stitching lines

By paying attention to the way you stitch seams and fitting lines together, you will produce a more professional looking garment.

**Shoulder seam**
The shoulder seam should be exactly on top of the shoulder and should not slope to front or back.

**Waistline**
This seam should be in the correct position naturally, although it may need to be raised or lowered according to the draping qualities of the fabric.

**Darts**
Bust darts should point to the fullest part of the bust. Sleeve darts should point to the elbow.

**Side seams**
Side seams should run in a straight, vertical line, at right angles to the floor (this also applies to back and front seams).

## Incorporating adjustments

Before you take off the garment, mark the new seam lines with chalk. Pin the seams again and tack them. Try on the garment again to check the new alterations. Stitch when you are satisfied with the fit.

## Adjusting the neckline fitting

The neckline must fit well if the garment is to look professional. Bear in mind that it will be ¾in. (2cm) wider all around when stitched because of the seam allowance.

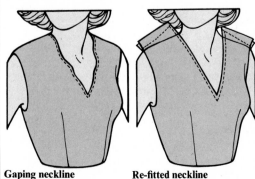

**Gaping neckline**     **Re-fitted neckline**
A gaping neckline can be adjusted by taking in the shoulder seams, making tucks around the neckline or taking it in at the centre back.

Minor alterations may have to be made to your garment after the first fitting but before final stitching takes place.

### Skirt back too tight

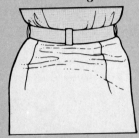

If the skirt is tight at hip level, wrinkles will appear below the waist. Release the centre back darts and then restitch them by curving them inwards to follow your own shape more accurately. The darts may also need shortening.

### Armholes too low

Any correction should be made at the crown of the armhole. Remove tacking stitches and re-position the armhole with the seam exactly on the shoulder top. Do not adjust the sleeve seam allowance.

### Badly positioned bust dart

The point of the bust dart should be at the fullest part of the bust. If the dart point is too high re-pin from the point, keeping the widest part of the dart in its original position.

## Cutting patterns

Cutting your own patterns can be one of the most satisfying parts of home sewing, because it gives you the opportunity to design your own clothes. The following pages provide a guide to simple pattern cutting, both from basic shapes such as circles and squares and from the basic toile (or *block*). This is shown on pages 432–435.

1 Circular poncho
2 Circular skirt
3 Square poncho
4 Loose fitting cape
5 Square-cut kimono

As you become more experienced you can adapt the basic block in any way you want by seaming, darting, gathering, pleating and tucking at different points, and by altering sleeve styles or the shape of the neckline.

The sewing instructions have all been given in the preceding pages. Make sure you follow the instructions on page 430 for cutting, marking and laying out your patterns.

Of the five patterns illustrated on this page, three are made from a basic square or circle and two are a simple adaptation of the basic block.

# Circular patterns

A circle provides a simple and quick shape for cutting out garments such as a skirt, a poncho or a cape. These can either be fully circular or semi-circular.

### Measuring out a circle
You will always need a square of paper at least 10in. to 20in. (25cm to 50cm) longer than the length of any garment you are making to allow for the opening. To make the circle, pin one end of the tape measure to the lower left hand corner of the paper. Then with the stretched tape measure and pencil in the same hand, mark off the length of the chosen garment down one side of the paper. Holding the tape stretched, draw a quarter circle.

To make a semi-circular pattern, place the quarter circle you have drawn on two layers of fabric, and to make a full circle, place the quarter circle on four layers of fabric.

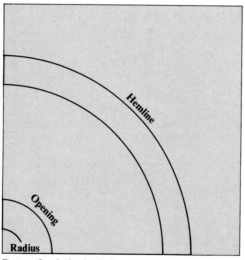

**Pattern for the basic circle**

### The opening
Any circular pattern you will make will need an opening – for a neckline on a poncho or a waistline on a circular skirt. To calculate the measurement of the opening you must first work out its radius. For a circular garment divide the desired size of opening by a quarter and that measurement by two thirds. For a semi-circular garment divide the opening by half and then by two thirds (see examples below). Measure out opening using the radius to draw a quarter circle as shown above.

*Radius for a circular garment*
Opening = 26in. (65cm); $\frac{1}{4}$ of 26in. (65cm) = 6in. (16.25cm); $\frac{2}{3}$ of 6in. (16.25cm) = 4in. (10.72 cm) radius

*Radius for a semi-circular garment*
Opening = 26in. (65cm); $\frac{1}{2}$ of 26in. (65cm) = 13in. (32.5cm); $\frac{2}{3}$ of 13in. (32.5cm) = $8\frac{2}{3}$in. (21.4cm) radius

### A circular poncho
This circular poncho has an opening in the centre for the head. The neckline can be slashed after the poncho has been cut.

### Cutting the poncho
Calculate the radius of your opening then draw in your neckline. Measure down from it to the desired length, allowing for turnings at the neckline and hem. Draw the quarter circle (see left) to give the poncho shape. Cut pattern by placing on four layers of fabric with folds as marked on the pattern.

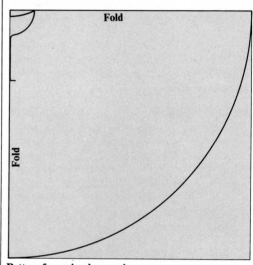

**Pattern for a circular poncho**

### Circular skirt
A circular skirt is another simple garment to make. It is made from a full circle with a waist opening, usually fastened with a zip.

### Cutting the skirt
Work out the radius of your waist measurement and then draw the opening required in the left-hand corner of the square paper pattern, which should be 10in. (25cm) longer than the length of the skirt. Draw a quarter circle the length of the garment plus a seam allowance. Lay the pattern on four layers of fabric with folds as shown on poncho pattern above. Make any necessary notches for matching side seams, and cut a waistband as shown on page 473.

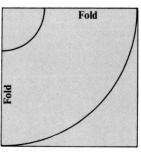

**Pattern for a circular skirt**

# Square patterns

### Loose-fitting cape

This cape is an extension of the flat collar and is cut using two pieces of your basic bodice block. It can be finished with a collar or faced.

### Cutting the cape

Place your bodice back pattern with the centre back along the edge of the paper. Pin into place. Mark in the "centre back fold". Place the shoulder of the front bodice pattern against the shoulder of the back bodice. Pin into place. Draw around both blocks and mark in the shoulder line. Extend this to form a construction line. The distance between the centre front and the edge of the paper gives you allowance for facings and overlaps. For an even hang all around measure and mark the length down the centre back from the neckline. Measure the remaining length from the cape hem to the back waistline. Apply this measurement to the centre front from the waist upwards. At the side seam you must allow for the angle of the shoulder or the cape will be too short at the sides. Measure the length along the side seam line from the neck point and add another 2in. to 2½in. (5cm to 6.5cm). Draw an evenly curved line to join these points and cut out pattern.

This simple shape is easy to cut and can be used to make ponchos, skirts and kimonos.

### Cutting a square pattern

Measure off the length of the garment from one corner, A, along the two edges of the paper. Remember to allow for neckline and hem turnings. Draw a line joining these two points, forming a triangle. This gives half of the square. To cut a full square, fold the fabric twice. Place the triangle on the fabric with the point A on the corner point of the folds.

### A square poncho

This shaped poncho is based on a square pattern. The neckline can either be round with a small slash for ease or it can be slit. The instructions given below are for a round neckline.

### Cutting the poncho

Decide on the length of the poncho and make up a square pattern, allowing for turnings. Draw the neckline in the same way as you would for a waistline (see far left). Cut out the neckline. The slash required for ease can be cut later.

### Square-cut kimono

This loose-fitting tunic is cut from the front skirt and bodice blocks only and can be cut to any fullness. The sleeves are cut as one with the bodice with a gusset inserted for ease.

### Cutting the kimono

Place the front skirt and bodice blocks on a sheet of paper, aligning the centre lines and abutting the waistlines. Trace around them and then draw a horizontal line at right angles to the centre front line through the neck point at the shoulder to the required sleeve length. Drop the armhole at least 1in. (2.5cm) and draw a line parallel to the shoulder line for the underarm seam. Draw a vertical line to produce sleeve hem. Measure the width of the bodice from the centre front line. It should be at least 1in. (2.5cm) wider than the bodice block, but if the hip is wider make it at least 1in. (2.5cm) more than the skirt block. Draw a vertical line at this width from the underarm seam to the hem of the tunic. Square a line across the bottom of the tunic. Draw in the shape of the neckline, making it large enough for your head to pass through with ease. For the back neck, trace the neckline shape from the back bodice by placing it neck point to neck point with the front bodice. Add ¾in. (2cm) seam allowance at the underarm and side seams, and 1in. (2.5cm) at the hem and sleeve ends. If the tunic is to be faced, add ¾in. (2cm) seam allowance at the neckline. If it is to be bound by a rouleau strip no allowance need be added. Mark in the straight grain parallel to the centre front line and cut out the pattern.

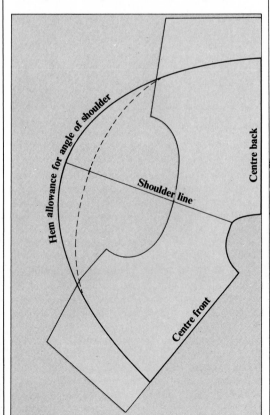

**Pattern for a loose-fitting cape**

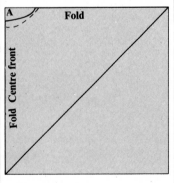

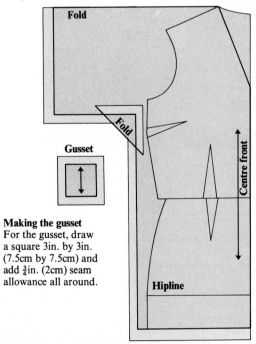

**Making the gusset**
For the gusset, draw a square 3in. by 3in. (7.5cm by 7.5cm) and add ¾in. (2cm) seam allowance all around.

**Pattern for a square-cut kimono**

# Patterns for shaped and gathered sleeves

You can easily design a wide range of sleeve styles by adapting your basic sleeve and bodice blocks. By cutting and spreading the sleeve block at the top or bottom you can add fullness to the crown or wrist and by extending the side seams of the bodice block you can produce kimono or batwing sleeves. Before you start to alter your sleeve you should bear in mind the style of the garment and the type of fabric being used. For example, a bishop sleeve would not be appropriate on a close-fitting dress, because of its fullness, but would suit a loosely draped garment made in a soft fabric.

Before starting to experiment with designs, transfer the block to another piece of paper so that the original block is left intact. Always remember to transfer any balance and cutting marks onto a duplicate block which you will use to try out your new ideas. As soon as you have decided on your new sleeve pattern trace it onto another clean sheet of paper. Store the basic sleeve block. The new sleeve style will be clean and ready to use.

### Puffed sleeve

This short sleeve is made by adding extra fullness at both the crown and lower edge of the sleeve. It should be finished with a bias strip or a straight, narrow band.

### Cutting the sleeve

Trace the sleeve block and cut it to the required length. Fold it into quarters lengthwise, then open it out and cut it along the fold lines. On another sheet of paper draw a vertical line a little longer than the sleeve. At right angles to it, draw a line to the same depth as, but longer than, the underarm line. Spread the pattern pieces across the underarm line with 2in. (5cm) between each piece. Pin into place. Measure 1½in. to 2¾in. (4cm to 7cm) from the shoulder point of the crown, depending on how high you want it to be. Draw a curve from this point, joining the outer sections of the pattern. Mark 2in. (5cm) below the centre of the lower edge of the sleeve. Draw a curved line to meet the side seam then draw in the straight grain. Add ¾in. (2cm) all around for the seam allowances. Transfer markings and cut out the new sleeve pattern.

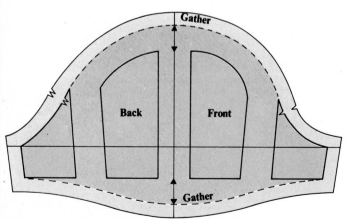

**Basic block cut and spread for a puffed sleeve pattern**

### Bishop sleeve with a plain head

This sleeve has a smooth crown and a full wrist. The cuff can be gathered or elasticated and the amount of fullness can be varied according to taste and fabric weight.

### Cutting the sleeve

Cut out a straight sleeve block with the underarm seams parallel from the underarm to the wrist. Fold the sleeve into quarters lengthwise and open out the pattern. Cut along the fold lines and place these pieces onto a longer sheet of paper, spreading them apart at their lower edges. As a rule, make the gap 1in. (2.5cm) at the front and centre slashes and 2in. (5cm) on the back line. Pin the pattern into place. Extend the underarm seam by 1in. (2.5cm) and the length of the three-quarter back line by 2in. (5cm). Draw a curved line along the lower edge and mark the opening 3in. (7.5cm) long. Add ¾in. (2cm) for the seam allowances all around. Mark the straight grain, shoulder point, balance marks and notches.

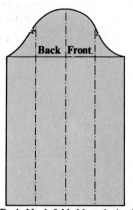
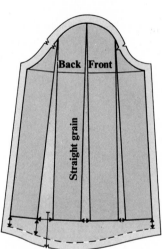

**Basic block folded lengthwise (above) and cut and spread to produce a bishop sleeve with a plain head (right)**

### Bishop sleeve with gathered head

Based on the plain bishop sleeve, this has additional fullness at the sleeve head which needs to be gathered so that the sleeve fits into the garment armhole.

### Cutting the sleeve

Make up the pattern as for the Bishop sleeve, but open up each section at the head by ½in. (1.3cm). Make a mark 2in. (5cm) above the shoulder point. Draw a curved line down from this point, as shown, to join the outer sections of the pattern then add ¾in. (2cm) turning all around for the seam allowances. Mark in the straight grain, shoulder point, balance marks and notches. Cut out the new pattern.

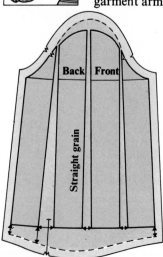

**Gathered head pattern**

# *Patterns for loose sleeves*

### *Cape sleeve*

This sleeve can be cut to any length. The extra fullness at the lower edge is not gathered up but left to hang freely. The lower edge is hemmed using the appropriate stitch.

#### *Cutting the sleeve*

Cut out a straight sleeve block to the length that you require. Fold the sheet into quarters lengthwise and then open it out and cut along the fold lines. Place the pattern onto another sheet of paper, spreading the pieces out evenly to give the required width at the lower edge. Keep the pieces together at the sleeve crown. Redraw the sleeve crown, curving the line across the indentations where the slashed pieces of the pattern meet. Add ¾in. (2cm) for the seam allowances at the crown and side seams. Add ⅜in. (1cm) to the lower edge for the rolled hem. Mark in the straight grain, shoulder point, balance marks and notches. Cut out the new pattern.

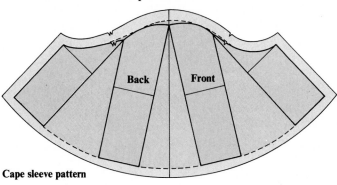

**Cape sleeve pattern**

### *Poncho sleeve*

Like the kimono sleeve, the poncho sleeve is formed by extending the bodice from the shoulder and waist. It can be finished with a hem or a facing.

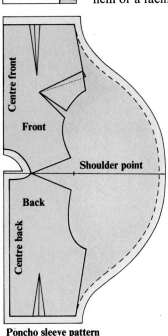

**Poncho sleeve pattern**

#### *Cutting the sleeve*

Lay the bodice pieces onto another sheet of paper so that the neck points meet. Pin into place. Draw a straight line at right angles to the centre back at the point where the neck edges meet. Extend this line to the required length, remembering to allow for the shoulder length. Draw a curved line, making it pass through the line denoting sleeve length. This will join the waistlines of both the bodices as shown on the left. Add ¾in. (2cm) all around for seam allowances. Mark in the straight grain line down the centre back line. Transfer balance marks and notches for matching and cut out·new sleeve pattern.

### *Kimono sleeve*

This loose-fitting sleeve is cut in one piece with the bodice by continuing the shoulder and underarm seams to the wrist. This produces a slightly shaped bodice with large, loose sleeves.

#### *Cutting the sleeve*

Place the back bodice block onto a larger sheet of paper. Pin it into place and extend the shoulder line to the full length of the sleeve. Mark the shoulder point C and the wrist point A. Mark in point B 1½in. (4cm) from, and at right angles to, A. Join point B to point C. Drop a line 4in. (10.2cm) from B, at right angles to BC. Mark the end of this line D. Measure down 1½in. (4cm) from the underarm point and mark this point G. Join D to G and then draw a curve between the bodice and the sleeve. Measure 8¾in. (21.5cm) from B along the line BC. Draw a line at right angles to BC so that it meets the line DG. This is the three-quarters sleeve line. Construct the bodice and the sleeve front in the same way. Drop the bust dart to just below the original one but keep the same bust point. Mark the grain line on the centre front and centre back bodice. Transfer all markings such as balance marks and notches and then cut out the new pattern.

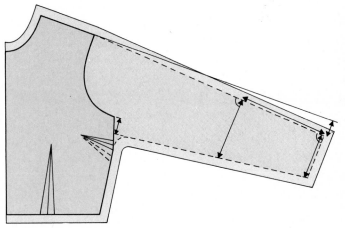

**Back kimono sleeve pattern**

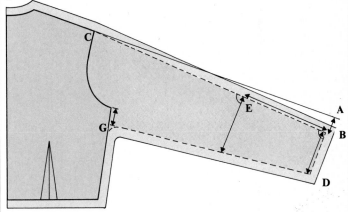

**Front kimono sleeve pattern**

# Bias strips

Bias strips are used for binding raw edges. If the binding is cut on true bias (see below) it will fold over smoothly without twisting or pulling. See below for instructions on making up bias strips.

### How to find the true bias

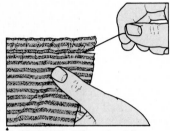

**1** *Make sure that the fabric edges are straight. Use the selvedge for one of your edges. Make sure that the other end is straight by pulling one of the cross threads (see page 430 for instructions).*

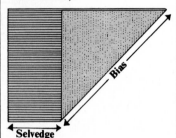

**2** *Lay the fabric out flat and fold it over with the straight end on the selvedge. Pin at right angles to the edge. The diagonal fold is the true bias. Rule off the width of your bias strips parallel to the bias.*

### How to cut and join the bias strips

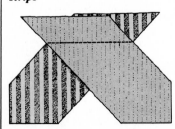

*Cut your bias strips to four times the final width (usually 1in. to 1¼in. (2.5cm to 3cm). Pin the lengthwise ends, with right sides facing, matching pattern if necessary. Stitch ¼in. (6mm) from the edge.*

# Facings

For a smooth, plain finish at necklines and armholes the edges should be neatened and strengthened with a facing. The facing should be made from the garment fabric and cut to exactly the same shape and size as the opening. Because of this, make sure of the fit of your garment before cutting the facing. If you have made any alterations to the pattern, matching facing may need to be cut.

On necklines, the facing will require an interfacing to add body. Cut to the exact shape of the facing, it is placed between the facing and the garment. The kind of interfacing used depends on the type and weight of the fabric as well as the style of the garment (see page 464). Iron-on interfacings can be bought and are pressed onto the fabric.

### Neckline facing

The facing can be made of two or three pieces, depending on whether or not there is a centre opening.

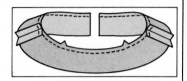

### How to cut the facing

**1** *Lay the bodice front on a piece of paper and pin into place. Trace around the shape of the neckline and include a seam allowance. Draw in the seam lines at the shoulder and centre front lines using dressmaker's carbon. Transfer balance marks.*

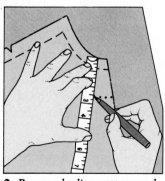

**2** *Remove bodice pattern and mark points around neck, 2½in. (6.5cm) from the traced line. This line will mark the depth of your neckline facing.*

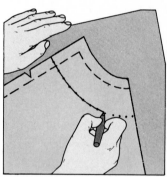

**3** *Join these points and mark in grain line at centre front.*

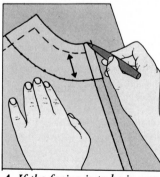

**4** *If the facing is to be in one piece, mark "fold" at the centre front. If you want a centre front opening add a seam allowance at the centre front and write "cut 2". Make the facing for the back neckline in the same way.*

### Armhole facing

Use this facing to finish the armhole on sleeveless garments. Like the neckline facing it should be cut with care so that it matches the opening exactly, thus preventing any puckering or pulling. Armhole facings are made in two pieces.

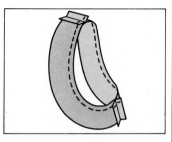

### Cutting the armhole facing

Place the bodice front onto a sheet of paper and pin into place. Trace around the shape of the armhole, including the seam allowances and side seams. Transfer any balance marks and mark in the position of the seam lines. Remove the bodice pattern and then mark points all around, 2½in. (6.5cm) from the traced armhole line. Join up these marks and draw in the seam lines at the shoulder and side seams. Draw in the grain line parallel to the centre front of the bodice block. Make facing for the back armhole in the same way as for the front.

### How to trace the armhole facing

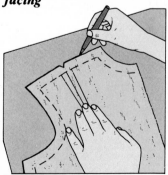

*Using a pen or chalk, trace around your bodice front pattern. Transfer any balance marks with dressmaker's carbon paper (see page 431 for instructions).*

# Waistbands

## Straight waistband with petersham

This waistband is cut from a simple rectangle on either the lengthwise or crosswise grain and is then stiffened with petersham. It can be made to any depth but this should be decided before you buy the stiffening.

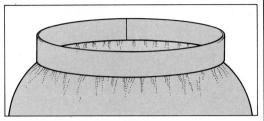

**Straight waistband with petersham**

## Cutting the waistband

On a sheet of paper draw out a rectangle the length of the waist measurement plus 1in. (2.5cm) for the underlap. Make it twice the depth of the stiffening and add ¾in. (2cm) for turnings all around. Mark in the straight grain along the length of the band and then mark in the centre front, centre back and side seams.

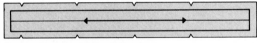

**Pattern for a straight waistband**

## Shaped waistband

The upper edge of this waistband is rounded at the centre front to accentuate the waist. It is cut on the straight grain but is made of two pieces, and stiffened with interfacing.

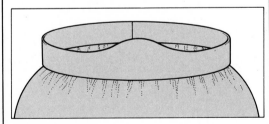

**Shaped waistband**

## Cutting the waistband

On a sheet of paper draw a rectangle the length of the waist measurement. Make it as wide as the deepest part of the belt. Shape one of the long edges into the curve desired and add 1in. (2.5cm) to one side of the centre back opening to allow for an underlap. Add ¾in. (2cm) for the seam allowance all around. Mark in the grain line along the length of the band, and the centre front and side seams. Write "cut 2" on the pattern.

**Pattern for a shaped waistband**

# Belts

## Stiffened belt

This is a standard belt, fastened with a buckle. It is cut on the straight grain to the depth required and stiffened or interfaced.

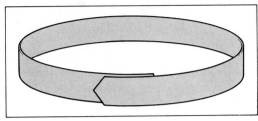

**Stiffened belt**

## Cutting the belt

On a sheet of paper draw a rectangle the length of the waist measurement plus 5in. (12.5cm). Make it twice the width required and add ¾in. (2cm) turnings all around. Shape one end into a point or curve for the belt end. Mark in the straight grain along the length of the belt. The interfacing should be cut to the same length as the belt, but to only half the width.

## Narrow tie belt

This can be as long or as wide as you want but it must be cut on the bias. This will allow the belt to curve around the waist without any pulling or puckering.

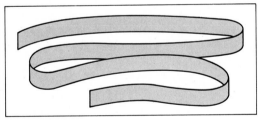

**Narrow tie belt**

## Cutting the belt

Fold the fabric to obtain the true bias (see instructions on the opposite page). Cut out bias strips which are twice the width of your belt plus 1½in. (4cm) for seam allowances (this provides an allowance of ¾in. (2cm) for each edge of the belt). The belt should be long enough to go around your waist and tie easily. Allow for ¾in. (2cm) seam allowance at the belt ends. To obtain the correct length for the belt it may be necessary to join a number of bias strips.

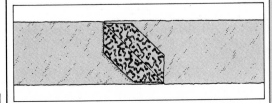

**Joining the bias strips to obtain the correct length for the tie belt**

The seam allowance on a pattern is usually ¾in. (2cm) and it is usually sufficient to neaten any raw edges. However, wherever the seam curves or where you need to eliminate any bulk, the resulting seam allowance must be trimmed to leave a neat, flat seam.

## Notching

If the seam allowance is on the inside of a curve, notch into it at regular intervals, almost to the stitching. This prevents puckering because it allows the fabric to overlap on the curve.

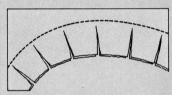

**Notched seam**

## Clipping

A seam allowance on the outer edge of a curve should be clipped to ease the fabric. It should be clipped at frequent intervals, as close to the stitching as possible.

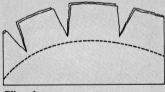

**Clipped seam**

## Grading

Grading is used on seam allowances to eliminate bulk where you have several fabric thicknesses, such as on collars and cuffs. Trim interfacing as close to the stitching as possible. Trim the under layer to within ⅛in. (3mm) of the stitching and the outer layer to within ¼in. (6mm).

**Graded seam**

# Cutting pockets

## Patch pocket

**Patch pocket without flap**    **Patch pocket with a flap**

The patch pocket should always be large enough for a hand to fit into easily. It can be cut either on the straight grain or on the bias. Extra care should be taken when using checked or patterned fabrics to make sure that they match the rest of the garment. When the pockets are being used in pairs you should also make sure that they match each other. Patch pockets can be interfaced or they can be left unlined.

### Cutting the pocket

Draw a rectangle the width of the pocket and twice the depth, plus a $\frac{3}{4}$in. (2cm) turning all around. For a rounded pocket, curve the corners at one end of the rectangle. The interfacing should be cut to the same width and the same depth as the finished pocket, with a $\frac{3}{4}$in. (2cm) turning all around.

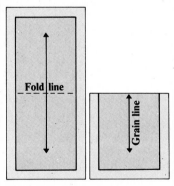

**Patch pocket and interfacing**

### Cutting the flap

Draw a rectangle the width of the pocket and twice the depth of the flap required, plus $\frac{3}{4}$in. (2cm) seam allowance all around. If rounded edges are made on the flap it must be cut in two pieces because you will not be able to fold it over. Cut the interfacing the same width and depth as the finished flap. Add a $\frac{3}{4}$in. (2cm) seam allowance all around.

## Pocket in a seam

This pocket is concealed by being stitched into the seam.

### Cutting the pocket

Draw a rectangle 6in. by 8in. (15cm by 20cm) and add $\frac{3}{4}$in. (2cm) seam allowance all around. Shape the pocket as shown and write "cut 2" on the pattern piece.

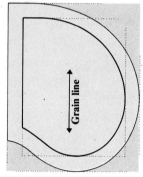

**Pocket in a seam pattern**

## Child's gathered pocket

This is a gathered version of the patch pocket. It can be held in place with a contrasting binding or with a strip of the same fabric, cut to fit.

### Cutting the pocket

Draw a $5\frac{1}{2}$in. (14cm) square and add $\frac{3}{8}$in. (1cm) seam allowance all around. Round off at one end as shown. Make the fold line for the turning 1in. (2.5cm) from the straight end and the gathering line 1in. (2.5cm) below this.

**Child's gathered pocket pattern**

# Cutting cuffs

## Wrapover cuff

This is a plain band cut on the straight grain with ends which overlap and is usually fastened with buttons. The cuff is made of one piece cut to twice the depth of the finished cuff and it should be interfaced.

### Cutting the cuff

Draw a rectangle the length of the wrist measurement plus $1\frac{1}{4}$in. (3.3cm) and twice the depth required. Add $\frac{3}{4}$in. (2cm) seam allowance all around. Draw in the straight grain down the depth of the cuff and the fold line at the centre along the length. Write "cut 2" and cut a double notch to match sleeve opening. Mark in buttonhole position. Cut interfacing to the same length and half the depth of the cuff.

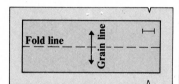

**Pattern for a wrapover cuff**

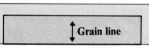

**Pattern for the interfacing**

## French cuff

Cut to twice the finished width, this cuff folds back on itself to form a double cuff. The ends do not overlap, but are fastened with links or buttons. Each cuff is made of two fabric pieces and an interfacing. Make four buttonholes.

### Cutting the cuff

Draw a rectangle twice the depth of the finished cuff, and the length of your wrist measurement plus $1\frac{1}{2}$in. (4cm). Add $\frac{3}{4}$in. (2cm) seam allowance all around. Draw in the "straight grain" down the depth of the cuff and the "fold line" at the centre along its length. Write "cut 4" and cut notches to match the sleeve opening. Mark in buttonhole positions. You will only need to cut two pieces of interfacing for this cuff.

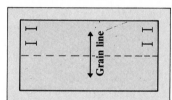

**Pattern for a French cuff**

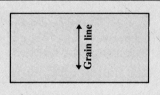

**Pattern for the interfacing**

## Rouleau strip cuff

A full sleeve can be finished with a simple rouleau strip edge which can be fastened with either a hook and eye, a button, a press stud or a rouleau loop.

### Cutting a rouleau strip

Take the wrist measurement and add 2in. (5cm) to allow for ease and a seam allowance plus enough length for a tie or button fastening. Take the finished width measurement required and multiply by 4 for a single thickness (instructions on page 472).

# *Cutting collars*

## *Stand collar*

This is one of the most basic types of collar to make. It will need an interfacing to give it a crisp finish. It can be cut with only one opening or with two.

### *Cutting the collar*

Cut a rectangle of paper half the length of the neckline and 1¾in. (4.5cm) deep, marking the shoulder seam, centre front and centre back. The centre front should be on the straight grain. Then from the front neckline mark points 1¼in. (4.5cm) and ¾in. (2cm) on the neck edge and slash the depth of the collar (Fig. 1). Overlap the slashes at upper edge by ¼in. (6mm). Draw round collar and mark shoulder point (Fig. 2). Draw ¾in. (2cm) seam allowance all round and if it is to have two openings mark as in Fig. 3. If the collar only has one opening, the centre back should be marked as in Fig. 4.

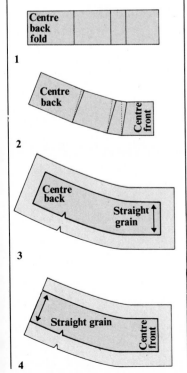

## *Shirt collar with a stand*

This consists of a basic collar and a separate stand and is used mostly on shirts. Both stand and collar pieces should be interfaced.

### *Cutting the collar*

Draw a rectangle to the length of half the neck measurement and 3in. (7.5cm) wide. Mark one end "centre back" and extend the other, the "centre front", by ¾in. (2cm). Measure the neck edge of the back bodice to the shoulder point and mark the position of the shoulder point on the collar pattern. Then draw a parallel line ¾in. (2cm) up from one long edge (this will be the neck edge) as far as the centre front line. Extend this line in a curve to the front of the extension (Fig. 1). Curve the neckline to the shoulder point ¾in. (2cm) above collar stand. This will be the collar. Trace two pieces of pattern separately, marking in the centre front. Also mark in the "straight grain" and "fold" at the centre back. Put notches at the shoulder point. Add ¾in. (2cm) seam allowance all around except at the centre back.

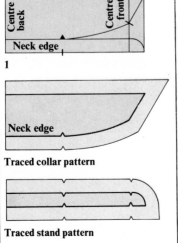

**Traced collar pattern**

**Traced stand pattern**

## *Peter Pan collar*

This is a simple collar which lies flat on the shoulder. It is made of two pieces of fabric which are interfaced. The pattern can be modified so that the collar stands up slightly.

### *Cutting the collar*

Lay the front and back bodices flat on a sheet of paper, abutting the shoulder seams. Draw around the neckline shape (Fig. 1). Remove the bodice pieces and draw in the desired collar shape. Add ¾in. (2cm) seam allowances all around. Mark the centre back with "straight grain" and "fold". Write "cut 2". Put notches halfway along the back neckline and the shoulder point on both collar and bodice patterns.

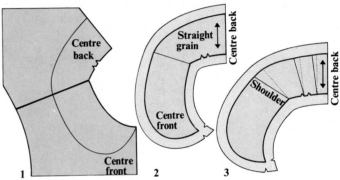

## *Peter Pan collar with slight stand*

If you want the collar to stand up slightly, shorten the outer edge. To do this, overlap the collar patterns marginally at the shoulder seam, keeping the neck points together (Fig. 2). The more the patterns overlap the shorter the outside edge will become and the higher the collar will stand. For a high stand, slash from the outer edge to the back neckline in two places and overlap the required amount on the outer edge only, keeping the same neck measurement (Fig. 3). Write "cut 2" on each pattern piece.

## *Roll collar*

This collar stands up against the neck and doubles back on itself. It is cut on the true bias and made from one piece of fabric. It needs no interfacing because it must roll softly.

### *Cutting the collar*

Draw a rectangle the length of the neckline with a width which is twice the sum of the stand and fall of the collar. Add ¾in. (2cm) turnings all around for the seam allowance. Mark in the "straight grain" on the true cross of the collar and "centre front" at the centre of the length. Make notches at the shoulder points.

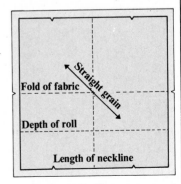

**Pattern for a roll collar**

# Patterns for simple garments

The possibilities for pattern alteration and cutting are endless once you have made your basic block. Some skill is required, so it is advisable for beginners to start with designs which need the minimum of modification. On these pages we give instructions for a simple flared skirt, a panelled skirt, a square-cut tunic and a princess line dress. These garments illustrate the construction of flared, loosely draped and fitted garments. The dresses can be further varied with the addition of collar,

sleeves and cuffs or by altering the necklines. Bear in mind the overall look of the garment before you change details like sleeves or collars.

When cutting patterns, remember to trace the basic block, minus seam allowances, onto a separate sheet of paper before cutting the pattern up. This keeps your basic block intact. Always make sure that you add hem and seam allowances where necessary, mark in the straight grain and transfer any other information needed for matching and shaping.

The pattern for this tunic is cut from the front blocks only.

### Cutting the tunic

Place the front bodice and skirt blocks on a sheet of paper, aligning the centre lines and abutting the waistlines. Trace around them. Draw a horizontal line at right angles to the centre front, through the neck point on the shoulder. Continue the line until the shoulder width has been reached. From here, drop a vertical line the length of the tunic. Square off a line across the bottom. Measure down from the shoulder line at the centre front and back to the depth of the neckline and mark "slash". Add 1in. (2.5cm) seam allowance at the side seam and hem. Mark in "gather", "fold" and depth of armhole. Cut out the new pattern.

### Flared skirt

It is a simple task to add fullness to the basic skirt block. It should only be slightly flared so that the sides do not fold back and spoil the line.

### Cutting the skirt

Fold the skirt block in half lengthwise and then slash down this line. Place the centre back piece on a sheet of paper and pin it into place. Without increasing the waist measurement, spread the outer pattern piece at the hemline by a quarter of the extra width needed. Trace around the pattern and add ¾in. (2cm) for a seam allowance at the side seam and waistline, and add 2in. (5cm) to the hem. If you are going to have a centre back opening, add ¾in. (2cm) to the centre back for the seam allowance. Transfer all notches and darts and then cut out the new pattern.

### Flared panelled skirt

This skirt is cut using a simple rectangle. It can be made up so that either the seams or the panels are at the centre front, back or sides.

### Cutting the skirt

Cut out a rectangle as wide as a quarter of your waist measurement and as long as your skirt length. Draw in the hip line. Fold it lengthwise into three equal parts and then cut along the fold lines. On a separate sheet of paper draw a straight line longer than the skirt length. This will be the straight grain line. Divide the centre piece into two equal parts with a pencil line down the centre. Place the pattern piece with the pencil line on the straight grain line and pin into place. Place the two outer pieces of the pattern on either side of the centre pattern. Without altering the waist measurement spread the lower edges equally until the hipline measures at least one quarter of your hip measurement plus ½in. (1.3cm). Pin into place. Draw around the pattern, curving the hemline slightly. Add ¾in. (2cm) for a seam allowance at the side seams and waistline, and add 1in. to 2in. (2.5cm to 5cm) at the hemline.

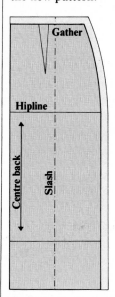

The basic skirt block should be folded (left) and then cut and spread for the flared skirt pattern (right).

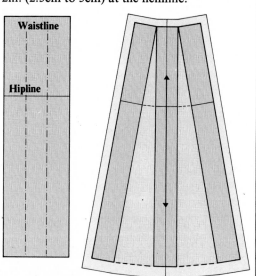

Pattern for the panelled flared skirt showing how it is folded (left) and then cut and spread (right)

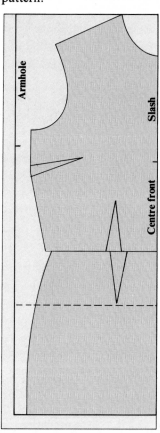

Pattern for the square-cut tunic

# Princess line dress

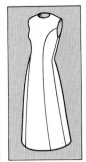

Using the basic bodice and skirt blocks, you can design this princess line dress. The fit of the body and flare of the skirt can be modified to suit your own personal taste.

### Cutting the dress
Place the skirt and bodice pieces on a sheet of paper, with the centre lines aligned and the seam lines abutting. The pattern pieces will overlap slightly at the side seam. Draw in the princess seam line from the armhole to the waist dart (pass very close to bust dart on front).

### Shaping the waist
To shape the waist, draw a vertical line from the top of the waist dart on the bodice to the hemline (AB). At the waistline, mark half the width of the dart on either side of this line (C and D). With a coloured pencil join the mark closest to the centre line (the inner mark) to the top of the dart. The more you take in, the closer the garment will fit.

### Marking the hemline
At the hemline, mark points at either side of the vertical line according to how much flare you want. Using the same coloured pencil, continue the line from the waist to the outer mark at the hemline. Taking a second colour, join the top of the bodice dart to the outer mark at the waistline, and continue it down to the inner mark at the hemline. Flare the hemline at the side seams by the same amount as the front panels, taking the flare from the hipline. Make a continuous line between the bodice and the skirt at the side seams (Fig. 1).

### Making the front bodice
On the front bodice, draw a line through the centre of the bust dart to the bust point and slash. Cut down the seam line from the armhole to the bust point and then close the bust dart (Fig. 2). This will open a new dart at the seam line. Pin it into position. Mark in straight grain on each panel, parallel to the centre line.

### Finishing the new pattern
Trace around each panel (Fig. 3) and add ¾in. (2cm) seam allowance to all vertical seams, except the centre front which will be placed on the fold. Add ¾in. (2cm) seam allowance at the shoulder seam, neckline and armhole and add 1in. to 2in. (2.5cm to 5cm) at the hemline. Draw in notches at bust (Fig. 4), waist, and hip levels. Cut out the new pattern. If the dress is to remain collarless and sleeveless, cut facings to fit them exactly (see page 472). Otherwise cut patterns for details such as collars, cuffs, sleeves, necklines and pockets as shown on pages 468–477.

# Godet

This flared piece of fabric can be fitted into a seam or simple slit cut in a skirt as a decorative finish, or to ease a tight skirt. Made from part of a circle, its width is determined by personal taste.

### Cutting the godet
Measure the slit and draw a straight line of this length onto a piece of paper. Using this same measurement, draw an arc on either side of the line. On the arc line, mark out half the width of the godet on either side of the vertical line. Join each of these points to the top of the godet, then cut out the new pattern.

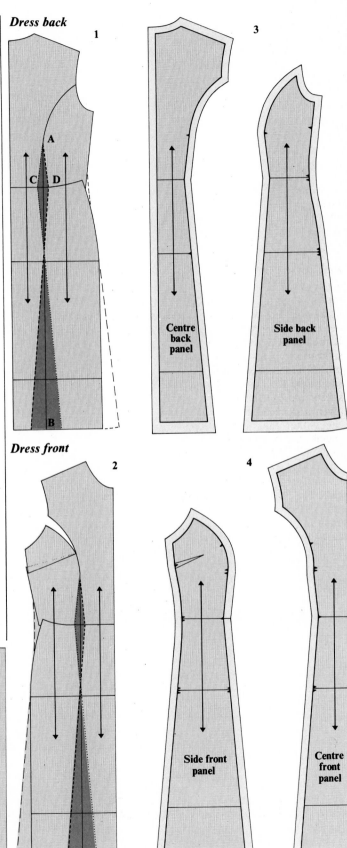

**Dress back**

1

3

Centre back panel

Side back panel

**Dress front**

2

4

Side front panel

Centre front panel

# Introduction to household sewing

There is a wide range of household items that are not difficult to sew. It is more economical to make rather than buy many articles, such as curtains, tablecloths, bedspreads, sheets, pillowcases and cushions and if you sew your own you have a wider choice of fabric.

The basic techniques for household sewing are the same as for dressmaking, so the introductory pages of the dressmaking section will provide the necessary information.

### Equipment

While the equipment is the same as for dressmaking, certain extra items will be needed, such as bias binding, wooden rings, braid and so on, where these are specified in the instructions.

### Fabrics

The type of fabric you use is extremely important in household sewing. Because most of the items will receive a lot of hard wear you will need to make sure that the fabric is suitable. It must also launder easily, so your first consideration when buying fabric for household use should be its practicability – the second should be the design. If required, tablecloths, sheets and pillowcases, for example, could be given a decorative finish (see far right) but check that the finish is appropriate for the article you are making: for example, do not put fine lace onto a heavily used item.

### Fabric requirement

For most household items the measurements are vital, so check these carefully before cutting out the fabric. Because these items are often large, you will frequently need to seam the fabric in order to achieve the desired width. If the pattern has a large print you will have to allow extra fabric for matching each new length of fabric. For example, if the fabric has a pattern which repeats itself at 10in. (25.5cm) intervals, allow for an extra 10in. (25.5cm) on each new length of fabric.

### Lining

Adding a lining will greatly increase the life of any item and this is particularly true for curtains. The lining protects the curtain fabric from the light and gives a neat finish to the inside. Always make sure when you buy lining fabric that it is suitable for the main fabric (see page 464) and that you buy enough.

### Sewing

The most important point to remember when sewing household items is to make sure that the seams are strong enough. Be sure to finish them off securely, backstitching to strengthen when necessary and finishing any raw edges which might otherwise fray.

# Round tablecloths

Round tablecloths can be cut to any size. Although it is best if the cloth can be cut from a single width of fabric, it may be necessary to join fabric (see opposite page). The cloth can just overlap the table or it can reach to the floor if a more formal effect is desired or the table base is to be concealed.

### Estimating the fabric requirement

The amount of fabric needed will depend on the depth of overhang from the table perimeter. A dining table usually requires an overhang of at least 9in. to 12in. (23cm to 31cm). To calculate the fabric requirement, measure the diameter of the table and add twice the overhang measurement plus twice the allowance for a hem – generally about 1in. (2.5cm). If the fabric needs to be joined in order to reach the required size follow the instructions given on the opposite page.

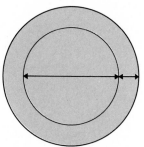

**Measuring a round tablecloth**

### Making the cloth

If your fabric is wide enough to cut the cloth in one piece, start by folding it into four. Draw a quarter circle directly onto the fabric with dressmaker's chalk (see page 468 for instructions). Cut out the cloth. Turn under the raw edge and then the hem allowance (the amount depends on the method of hemming). Pin, tack and stitch using the appropriate method for the fabric. Press the cloth and attach any decorative border if desired.

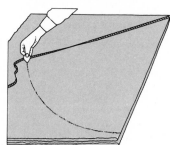

**Drawing a quarter circle**

### Hemming round tablecloths

Round tablecloths can be hemmed in the normal way by turning under the fabric or they can be secured with bias binding. If you are hemming the cloth directly, only leave ½in. (1.3cm) for the hem. If it is wider, the hem will be too bulky. Fold under ¼in. (6mm) and then another ¼in. (6mm); pin and then press into position before stitching close to the edge.

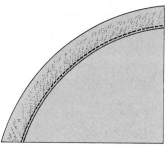

**Hem stitched without binding**

### Bias binding hem

Only ¼in. (6mm) should be left for this hem. Turn under ¼in. (6mm) and press. Open one side of the bias; fold under one of the ends by ⅜in. (1cm) and press. Refold the tape as it was originally and abut the edge to the fold line of the hem, on the right side. Stitch close to the edge of the tape. When you reach the starting point, fold the end of the tape under as before and overlap it slightly with the other tape end. Then turn the tape to the wrong side of the fabric, enclosing the raw edge of the hem. Pin the one edge of the bias tape to the fabric. Tack and then press lightly. Either machine or slip stitch into place.

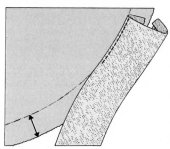

**Attaching the binding**

# Positioning fabric

If your fabric is not wide enough to cut the cloth in one piece you will have to join the fabric by seaming it. The seam joining the lengths of fabric should never be in the centre of the table. If a join is necessary one length of fabric should be cut in half lengthwise and each half of it attached to either side of the central panel. Depending on the size of the cloth and width of the fabric this may mean that some fabric will be wasted. If the fabric is patterned you should allow for one whole repeat of the pattern for matching.

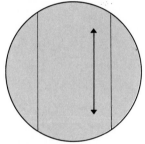

**Joining fabric pieces**

### Matching and joining widths of fabric

Place the two additional pieces on either side of the central panel, selvedge to selvedge. Make sure that the fabric runs the same way on all panels and that the pattern matches. Pin and tack the seams, then stitch and press them. Cut the fabric into a square to the dimensions of the cloth. Fold the square in four and follow the instructions for cutting round tablecloths (see left).

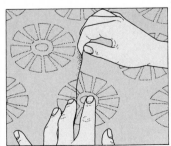

**Pattern matching**
*Turn under edge to match fabric pattern. Mark seam line. Unfold and join as instructed above.*

# Straight-sided tablecloths

Whether cut as squares or rectangles, these are the most common and useful types of tablecloth. They can be made in a variety of fabrics, cut to different lengths, and can be decorated by shaping or attaching one of the finishes on the right to their borders.

### Estimating the fabric requirement

For a square cloth measure the width and add twice the overhang plus 1in. (2.5cm) for the seam allowances. For a rectangular cloth, measure both the length and width of the table. Add twice the overhang allowance plus 1in. (2.5cm). Some fabrics such as heavy linen or those which fray easily need deeper hems. In such cases add twice hem depth.

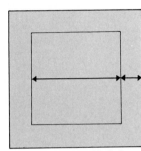

**Measuring a square tablecloth**

### Making the cloth

Cut out the cloth and turn under the raw edges and the hem allowance. If the corners are to be mitred follow the instructions below. Otherwise pin and tack the hem, then stitch it as appropriate. Press the cloth and attach any decorative finish before giving it a final pressing.

## Mitred corners

A cloth with a deep hem looks better if the corners are mitred. Turn raw edges under by ½in. (1.3cm) and press. Turn under your hem allowance and press. Open out the cloth, but leave the raw edges turned under. Fold back the corner of the fabric along the diagonal ABC, through the corner point. Open out again (Fig. 1). With the raw edges still turned under, cut off the corner ¼in. (6mm) outside the diagonal fold (Fig. 2). Fold fabric with right sides facing, so that points A and C meet and point B is on the fold line. Stitch along this line. Turn the fabric through to the right side and ease out the corner point with a needle. When all the corners have been mitred, stitch the hem in position (Fig. 3).

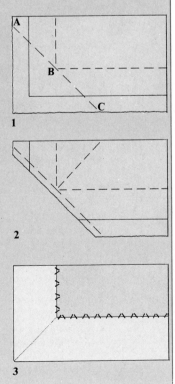

# Decorative additions

There are a variety of ways of finishing your tablecloth. It can be bordered with a fringe, tassels, braid, lace or a scalloped edge. Alternatively, it could be embroidered.

**Embroidered edge**

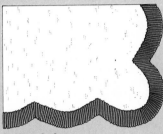

**Scalloped edge**

**Lace edge**

**Braid edge**

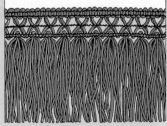

**Tasselled edge**

# Plain sheets

Plain rectangular sheets can be made in a variety of fabrics. The measurements will depend on the size of the bed.

### Estimating the fabric

It is usually best to buy sheeting fabric because it is made in suitable widths for different bed sizes – for example, single, double and king-size beds. The sheets must always be at least 28in. (71cm) wider than the mattress and 33in. (84cm) longer than it to ensure an adequate tuck-in. Add 4¾in. (12cm) to the length to allow for a hem of 2⅜in. (6cm) at either end.

### Making the sheet

Check that the fabric grain is straight (see page 430), then cut the fabric to the correct measurements with the fabric selvedge on the long side. Turn the raw edges under to the wrong side, at each end. Make the first fold ⅜in. (1cm) wide and then fold under again by a further 2⅝in. (6cm). Pin and tack into position. Stitch using straight or zigzag stitch (see page 424 for sewing instructions).

### Sheet size chart

The minimum sizes of sheets, duvets and pillowcases are listed below. The sizing for the sheets is based on the mattress thickness.

**Small single**

| | | in | cm |
|---|---|---|---|
| Sheet size | | 70 × 100 | 175 × 250 |
| Fitted sheet | | According to mattress size | |
| Pillowcase | | Standard sizes | |
| Duvet | | 53 × 75 | 135 × 190 |
| Mattress | | 3ft × 6ft 3in. | |
| | | 90cm × 190cm | |

**Standard single**

| | | in | cm |
|---|---|---|---|
| Sheet size | | 80 × 117 | 203 × 295 |
| Fitted Sheet | | According to mattress size | |
| Pillowcase | | Standard sizes | |
| Duvet | | 57 × 80 | 144 × 203 |
| Mattress | | 3ft 3in. × 6ft 6in. | |
| | | 100cm × 200cm | |

**Standard double**

| | | in | cm |
|---|---|---|---|
| Sheet size | | 108 × 117 | 270 × 295 |
| Fitted Sheet | | According to mattress size | |
| Pillowcase | | Standard sizes | |
| Duvet | | 78 × 80 | 198 × 203 |
| Mattress | | 5ft × 6ft 6in. | |
| | | 150cm × 200cm | |

**King size**

| | | in | cm |
|---|---|---|---|
| Sheet size | | 117 × 126 | 295 × 315 |
| Fitted sheet | | According to mattress size | |
| Pillowcase | | Standard sizes | |
| Duvet | | 90 × 80 | 230 × 203 |
| Mattress | | 6ft × 6ft 6in. | |
| | | 180cm × 200cm | |

# Fitted sheets

Fitted sheets are used only for the bottom sheet and are designed to fit the mattress exactly. This type of sheet is labour saving when used in conjunction with a duvet and is particularly useful for children's beds.

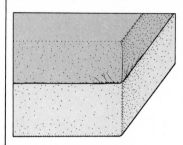

The fitted sheet is made to fit the mattress exactly by elasticating the corners. It gives a neat, smooth finish to the bottom sheet.

### Estimating the fabric

The length of sheeting required can be calculated by measuring the length and width of the bed and adding twice the depth of the mattress plus 7in. (18cm), for the tuck-in, to each measurement. Add 1in. (2.5cm) for hem.

### How to make the sheet

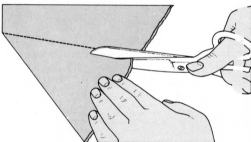

**1** *With the right sides facing, fold each corner across diagonally as shown, and mark a point 4½in. (11.5cm) from the corner point at one edge. Then stitch across the corner at right angles to this point. Trim the seam to within ¼in. (6mm) of the stitching line and finish the raw edges by oversewing. Repeat the same process at each corner. Fold over the raw edges by ¼in. (6mm) then ¾in. (2cm) all around, and then hem around the sheet leaving a small gap 10in. (25cm) from each corner.*

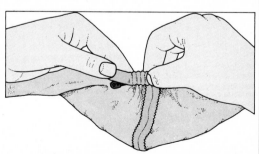

**2** *Cut elastic into four 10in. (25cm) strips and insert one end of each piece into each corner (see page 456 for threading instructions). Then draw the elastic along the hem edge, gathering up the corner as you do so. Fasten securely.*

Plain linen can be made more decorative by adding a special finish. For example, a simple decorative edge could be made by using special stitches on the machine to finish the hems. Alternatively, fabric borders can be stitched to the hem edge or motifs embroidered onto the linen.

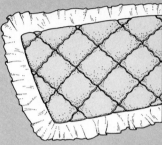

**Quilting**

**Coloured border**

**Hand embroidery**

**Machine embroidery**

# Pillowcases

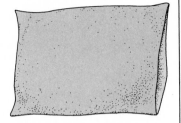

Pillowcases can be made from sheeting fabric. They look very effective when made in a contrasting fabric to the bottom sheet or in a matching fabric to the top sheet and duvet cover. Decorative finishes can be added (see left).

## Estimating the fabric

The finished pillowcase should be the same length and width as the pillow. The length of the fabric for the pillow should therefore measure twice the length of your pillow plus an allowance of 6¾in. (17cm) for a flap which holds the pillow in position. Add 2⅜in. (6cm) for the hem at the other end. The width should be the same as that of the pillow plus a 1in. (2.5cm) allowance for the seams.

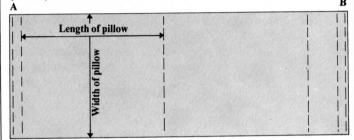

**Measuring the pillowcase**

## How to make the case

**1** *On the wrong side of the fabric turn under one of the short raw edges by ⅜in. (1cm) and press. Turn under a further 2in. (5cm), pin and stitch into position. Turn the other short edge under with a double hem of ⅜in. (1cm) and stitch. Turn the fabric to the right side.*

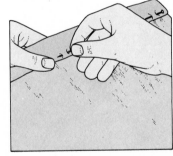

**2** *Fold edge A towards edge B to the desired length of the pillow. Fold B over A so that a flap is formed. Press into position. Pin along each of the longest edges and then stitch from the bottom of the pillow, over the flap to the top. Finish seams as appropriate (see page 440).*

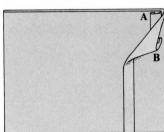

**3** *Turn the flap to the right side and push out the corners firmly with your finger as you do so. Then turn the whole case right side out and push out the other corners with scissors. Hand embroidered motifs can be stitched onto the pillow at this stage in making up.*

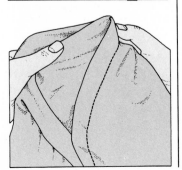

# Duvet covers

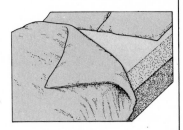

If you are using a duvet, it will need a cover. The fabric can be plain or patterned but it must always be washable, lightweight and hardwearing. The duvet cover is easy to make and can be closed with a tape or zip fastener.

## Estimating the fabric

Measure your duvet and add 1in. (2.5cm) to this measurement for the seam allowances. Sheeting fabric is usually the best buy because it is made in suitable sizes (see chart).

**Folding the duvet cover**

## Making the cover

Using fabric of the appropriate width, cut the duvet to the correct measurements. With right sides facing, pin all around the case, leaving an opening large enough to insert the duvet at one end, usually about 36in. (91.5cm). Stitch all around, backstitching when you get to the opening, and clip across the corner seam allowances. Finish the seams by pinking or zigzag stitching the edges.

## Closing the duvet

The duvet can be closed, either with a suitable length of hardwearing zip (see page 460 for instructions on inserting zips), or with Velcro or popper tape. Press the seam allowances flat and position one of the tapes on the underside of the seam opening. Pin and tack, then stitch it neatly top and bottom (Fig. 1). Align the other tape on the other side of the seam opening and stitch on, as before (Fig. 2).

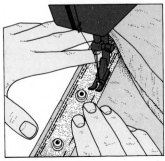 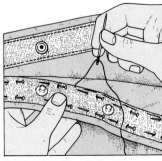

**1 Stitching popper tape**     **2 Stitching aligned edge**

481

## Types of bedspread

There are three basic types of bedspreads: *throwover, flounced* and *boxed*. The first is simply a flat piece of fabric which is draped over the bed. The other two have fitted sides which can be flounced or pleated at the corners.

They all consist of a full fabric width at the centre, to which side panels will often need to be attached; if so, the seams should be at an equal distance from the centre. Although any type of fabric can be used, firm fabric is more suitable because it gives a crisper finish; also, it does not need lining.

When calculating fabric requirements for any of these bedspreads you should always make up the bed fully (with pillows if the spread is to cover them) before measuring the bed's length, width and depth.

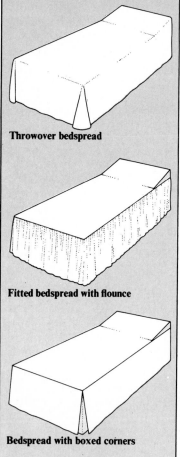

**Throwover bedspread**

**Fitted bedspread with flounce**

**Bedspread with boxed corners**

## Throwover bedspread

This simple bedspread is unfitted, but large enough to cover the bed and reach the floor. It can be neatened by giving it rounded corners.

### Calculating the fabric requirements

To calculate the correct fabric requirement you must first measure the bed. The width measurement is taken from the floor on one side, up across the bed and down to the floor on the other side. The length is measured from the bedhead, over the pillows, and to the floor at the foot of the bed. You should allow an extra 12in. (31cm) on the length if the spread is to be tucked under the pillows. You should also make an allowance for matching the pattern if a patterned fabric is used.

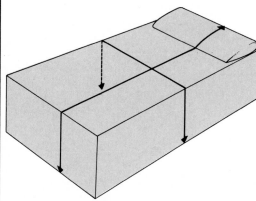

### Making the bedspread

Join the fabric as described on page 479. Hem the two long edges first by turning the raw edges under ⅟4in. (6mm) and pressing. Turn under again to make a ¾in. (2cm) hem. Pin, tack and stitch close to the turning, then press. Repeat the hemming on the two short sides, checking that the corners are square. Remove tacking and press again.

### Making rounded corners

After joining the pieces of fabric, place the spread on the bed and pin a curved line at the two corners at the foot of the bed. Remove the bedspread and neaten the curve using a round object. Hem as above, easing the rounded edges.

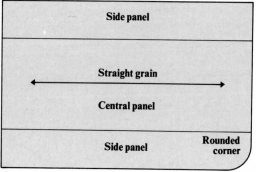

| Side panel | |
|---|---|
| Straight grain | |
| Central panel | |
| Side panel | Rounded corner |

## Fitted bedspread with flounce

A neater and more formal look can be achieved by making a fitted bedspread. The top central panel is exactly the same size as the top of the bed and a strip of fabric hangs from the edges to cover the sides. This can be gathered all round making a flounce, to which a gusset will have to be attached in order to accommodate the pillows.

### Calculating the fabric requirement

Measure the length and width of the top of the bed, adding 4in. (10cm) to the length for an overlap at the head of the bed, plus ¾in. (2cm) seam allowance all around. For the depth of the flounce, measure from the edge of the bed to the floor and add 2¾in. (7cm) for the hem and seam allowances. The length of the flounce before gathering will be one and a half to two times the measurement around three sides of the central panel – the two long edges and one short edge – plus ¾in. (2cm) for each joining seam and ¾in. (2cm) for the two sides of the bed. You will have to allow some extra fabric for the gusset (see below for fabric requirements and cutting instructions).

### Gussets

A gusset is an extra piece of fabric inserted at either side of the bed, which permits the central panel to accommodate the pillows and still enables the frill to hang parallel to the floor. There are two types: triangular and curved, although we shall concentrate mainly on the triangular gusset. The diagram below shows an example of each, together with the central panel of fabric. By matching the letters you can judge where to attach the gusset to the central panel.

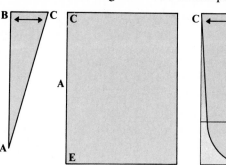

### Making the triangular gusset

This is particularly useful on wide single and double beds, where the pillows lie inside the edges of the bed. Draw a line on the paper pattern 16in. (40.6cm) long. Mark one end A and the other end B. From B and at right angles to AB draw a line 4½in. (10.8cm) long and mark the end of it C. Join A to C and mark the grain line parallel to BC (see above). Add ¾in. (2cm) turnings to all sides.

## Making the bedspread

In order to make the bedspread, the panels of fabric must first be joined together, and the gusset attached to them. The flounce is then made, and joined to the panel and the gusset.

### Joining the panels

Join the fabric in the usual way (see page 479). Fold this central panel in half lengthways and round off the two bottom corners slightly so that the flounce will gather and hang smoothly (see opposite page for rounding corners).

### Joining triangular gusset to the central panel

Pin and tack edge AB to central panel (see diagram on opposite page) 4in. (10cm) from head end of panel. The seam allowance beyond B is then left free for hemming. Stitch and press.

### Making the flounce

Using French seams (see page 440), join the pieces needed to make up the length of the flounce. Gather the top edge of the flounce, using two rows of gathering stitches just within the seam allowance, starting and finishing 1¼in. (3.2cm) from the raw edges at either end. (This allows for a ¾in. (2cm) turning allowance and the ½in. (1.3cm) finished hem width at the head end of the central panel.)

### How to join the flounce to the panel and triangular gusset

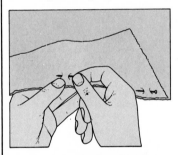

**1** *Adjust gathers evenly, then pin and tack the flounce to the central panel and pillow gusset, right sides facing. With the gusset uppermost, stitch the seam as far as point A (keeping the seam allowances out of the way) and backstitch. Repeat with second gusset.*

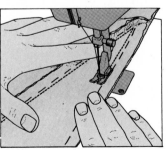

**2** *Restart stitching at A, continuing to end of flounce. Press turnings of gusset and flounce seam. Machine flounce and gusset turnings together, ⅜in. (1cm) outside stitching line, up to the raw edge of gusset turning beyond A.*

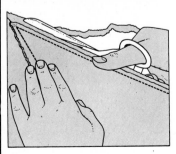

**3** *Trim away surplus to ⅛in. (3mm) outside stitching, and zigzag or overcast raw edges. Then make hems along sides of flounce and gusset, plus raw edge at head end of central panel and flounce. Neaten all flounces and central panel seams in the same way.*

# Fitted bedspread with boxed corners

### Fitted bedspread with boxed corners

This is a very neat bedspread, with a gusset for the pillows and box pleats at the corners.

### Calculating the fabric requirements

When making this type of bedspread, the fabric requirements should be calculated in the same way as for the fitted bedspread with a flounce for both the top of the spread and the triangular gusset. When the perimeter of the central panel has been measured, 16in. (40.5cm) should be added to this for each corner, making a total of 64in. (162.5cm).

### Making the bedspread

After making up the central panel in the usual way, the side strip with boxed corners is then made and attached to it.

### Making the boxed corners

Starting at central point C, mark B and D 8in. (20.5cm) away at each side, so that BD is 16in. (40.5cm) long. With right sides facing, fold B and D to meet at C. Pin along the folds and tack down through all three layers to hold them in place.

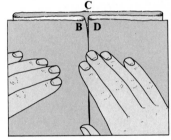

**Folding B and D to meet at C**

### How to join boxed corners to central panel

**1** *Tack boxed corner onto short side of central panel, matching C to corner point of panel, leaving ½in. (1.3cm) seam allowance. Stitch up to C, leaving ½in. (1.3cm) seam allowance.*

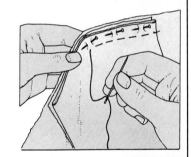

**2** *Pivot the work and turn the boxed corner so that it aligns with the long side of the central panel and stitch (see necklines, page 442, for technique).*

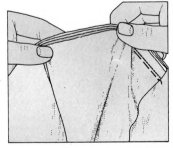

**3** *Snip the boxed corner to the edge of the stitching, and continue stitching to complete the second side of the spread. Attach the other corners in the same way. Finally, press and neaten all hems and press the pleats flat.*

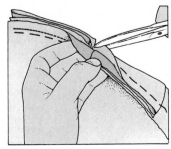

# Cushions

There are three main types of cushions: *scatter, boxed* and *bolster* cushions. Scatter cushions tend to be small, whereas boxed and bolster cushions are usually firm and large.

### Scatter cushions

These are usually used to brighten up a colour scheme and to provide more padding on chairs and sofas. They are usually soft and pliable, but they can be made larger and firmer to act as seating units in their own right.

### Boxed cushions

Boxed cushions are generally used on stools or window seats, or on hard chairs to make a seating unit with a firm base. They are usually firm and generally have a piped border for decoration, and to give a crisper edge to the cushion.

### Bolster cushions

Bolster cushions can be either used for decoration, like scatter cushions, in which case they are soft and fairly pliable, or to provide the back or arms to a sofa or day bed. They can be either tubular or shaped.

### The fabric

Almost any type of fabric can be used for making cushions, but if the cushions are to form part of a seating unit, they should obviously be covered in hardwearing material. The inner stuffing for the cushion will usually have its own cover, so that the outer cushion cover can be removed and laundered. The choice of stuffing depends on the type of cushion (for details, see page 487). Scatter cushions used for decoration can be made in quite delicate or lightweight fabric. They can be made plain or embroidered. If the latter, the embroidery should always be worked before the cover is made up, so first ascertain the amount of fabric required, and position the embroidery accordingly. If you are intending to pipe the edge of the cushion you will find it helpful to use a zip foot attachment on the machine when applying the piping (see far right).

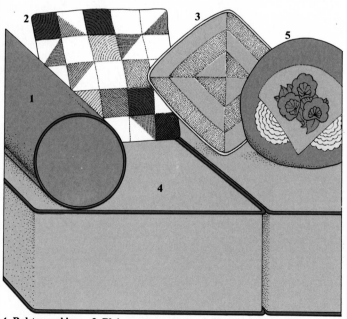

1 **Bolster cushion**   2 **Plain scatter cushion**   3 **Piped scatter cushion**
4 **Boxed cushion**   5 **Embroidered scatter cushion**

# Scatter cushions

Scatter cushions can be made to any size or shape you want. Generally, square or round cushions are the most popular but you can make rectangles or semi-circles or any other shape, as required.

### Estimating fabric for a square cushion

For a square cushion enough fabric for an inner and an outer cover will be needed. For a firm cushion, the inner cover should measure the same as the cushion pad, but for a softer cushion make the inner cover $\frac{1}{2}$in. (1.3cm) bigger all around. Cut the fabric accordingly, leaving a $\frac{1}{2}$in. (1.3cm) seam allowance all around.

### Estimating fabric for a round cushion

You will need enough fabric to cover the diameter of the circle plus $\frac{1}{2}$in. (1.3cm) for seam allowances. You must also allow for an extra seam allowance if you intend to use a zip for fastening the cover.

### Making a square inner cover

Cut two rectangles of fabric to the appropriate size and, with the right sides facing, pin and tack around, leaving $\frac{1}{2}$in. (1.3cm) seam allowances and a 4in. to 6in. (10cm to 15cm) opening on one side. Stitch, reinforcing corners. Turn right side out. Stuff filling into the cover and slip stitch the opening securely.

### Making a round inner cover

Cut the two circles and, with right sides facing, pin and tack as for a square cushion. Then stitch around the cushion, leaving a small opening. Make a second row of stitching inside the first and clip all round the cushion. Turn to right side and stuff filling into the cover. Then slip stitch the opening securely.

### Making outer covers

The outer cover for the square cushion is made in the same way as the inner cover. For the round cushion you should cut one full circle and two semi-circles to the required measurements, with extra seam allowances to allow for a central zip fastener (see below). You can finish the opening by using any of the methods shown below.

### Fastening the cover with Velcro

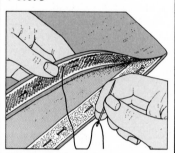

Tack and stitch a piece of Velcro tape to same measurement of the cushion opening onto the seam allowance.

### Fastening a round cover with a zip

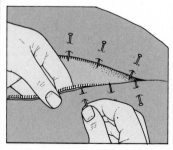

When making a circular cushion cover it will be easier to insert the zip across the underside of the cushion, for which you will need an extra seam. Attach zip onto seam allowances in usual way, then sew the two sides of the cushion together.

# *Piping scatter cushions*

Piped cushions can be made by stitching piping around the edges (see below for piping technique). Pipe the cushion before it is made up and then make up (see far left) and close by attaching with hooks and eyes or by using a zip.

## *Making the piping*

Piping is made up of a cord cased in a bias strip of fabric (see page 472). Several bias cut strips of fabric are joined together until there is enough fabric to cover the length of cord. Piping cord is usually made of twisted white cotton and comes in various diameters – from very fine for dressmaking to ⅜in. (10mm) for soft furnishings.

### *Estimating the fabric*

One yard (90cm) of 48in. (120cm) wide fabric will supply about 28yds (25.20m) of bias strip 1½in. (3.8cm) wide. The strips will have to be joined to make the casing, so you must take the seam allowances into account.

### *How to make the piping*

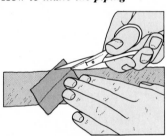

**1** *Sew pieces of bias strip together, clip the angle of the corners and trim as shown.*

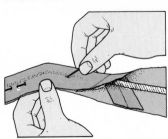

**2** *Place cord on wrong side of strip and fold strip in half over cord. Pin and stitch as close to cord as possible.*

## *Estimating the fabric for piped cushions*

To make the outer cover for a piped cushion you will need, for an 18in. (45cm) square cushion, 22in. (55cm) of 48in. (120cm) wide fabric (this allows for 2 extra strips of fabric 3in. (7.5cm) wide, for the straps); 2¼yards (2.10m) of number 2 piping cord; press studs, hooks and eyes or a 17in. (42.5cm) zip fastener. Extra allowance must be left for patterned fabrics.

## *Making outer covers for piped cushions*

The piping is made and attached to the edges of the cushions, and straps are then made and attached for the hooks and eyes.

### *How to attach the piping*

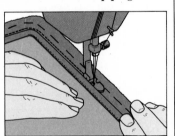

**1** *Trim the corners of both squares of the cover and make the piping (see left).*
*Starting at the middle of the side which will eventually be left open, pin, tack and stitch the piping around the edge of the case top on the right side, with raw edges facing.*

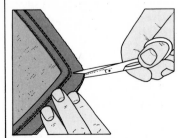

**2** *Clip edges of piping at corners to ease around curve.*

## *Using straps*

If the cushion is fastened with hooks and eyes, straps will be needed for a neater finish. These are made from two extra strips of fabric 3in. (7.5cm) wide. Trim these so that they are 2in. (5cm) shorter than the width of the case, and neaten all edges.

### *How to attach straps to piped cushion*

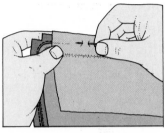

**1** *With right sides facing, pin, tack and stitch one strap directly to the case top on top of the stitching, holding the piping. Fold the strap over the raw edge to the wrong side of the fabric and turn in ½in. (1.3cm) of the raw edge of the strap. Hand stitch to seam line. Sew the other strap to the underside of case in same way.*

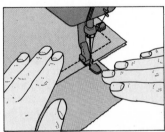

**2** *With right sides facing, pin both pieces of case together. Stitch on seam line around three sides and for 1½in. (3.8cm) at both ends of the fourth side.*
*Backstitch to secure straps and then stitch ½in. (1.3cm) in from the edge of the straps. Sew on the press studs or hooks and eyes, and then turn the cushion right side out.*

## *Using a zip fastener*

If using a zip you will not need the straps. Cut the fabric, make the piping and attach it to the case top as described left. Then make up cover around three sides before attaching zip to cover as described below, using the zip foot attachment on your sewing machine. Make sure that the corners are aligned before you begin stitching the zip.

### *How to attach the zip*

**1** *Pin, tack and stitch zip to opening, right sides facing. Stitch from one end of the teeth to the other but leave tape ends unstitched. Keep the stitching as close to the piping as possible. Open the zip and attach other side of the zip to underside of cushion in the same way.*

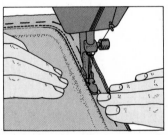

**2** *With right sides facing, tack and stitch top and underside together, at either end of the zip opening.*

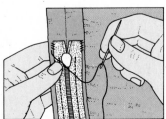

**3** *Neaten the raw edges and hand sew the zip tape ends to the seam allowance. Press on wrong side, then turn cover through to right side.*

# Boxed cushions

Boxed cushions can be round, rectangular or square. They usually have an inner and outer cover, the method of construction is the same for both covers.

**Piped boxed cover**

### The inner cover

Use a lightweight fabric for the inner cover. The amount needed is calculated in the same way as for the outer cover, except that no allowance need be made for extras such as piping or zips. The inner cover is stitched up on three sides and then filled.

### Estimating the fabric needed for both covers

Measure the top of the cushion pad and add ¾in. (2cm) for turnings all around. You will need two pieces of this size, cut on the straight grain. Take the depth of the pad and add 1in. (2.5cm) seam allowance. This will give you the depth of your boxing strips. The length of each piece of boxing strip should be 1½in. (3.8cm) longer than each side of the pad. You will need four of these boxing strips for the cover.

If the cover is to be piped allow extra for the casing (see page 485 for instructions). Measure the perimeter of the pad and add 4 in. (10cm) seam allowances. Cut two lengths of piping to this measurement for the pad top and bottom.

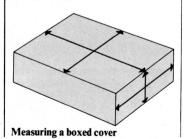

**Measuring a boxed cover**

## Permanent boxed cover with piping

Cut the fabric on the straight grain for the top and bottom pieces and the four side strips. Cut and make up piping on the bias (see page 485). Use bought foam shapes.

### How to make the piped cover

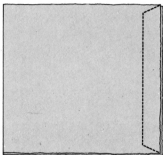

**1** Join the side strips by stitching their shortest sides together. Taper the seams into the corners of the strips as you stitch them together.

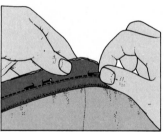

**2** Make up the piping casing on the bias of the fabric (see page 485). Then, with raw edges facing, place the casing on the right side of the side strip. Pin, tack and stitch the piping around each of the long edges ½in. (1.3cm) from the edge.

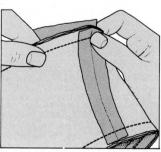

**3** With right sides facing, place the piped side strip so that the seams joining the individual strips are positioned at each corner of the cushion top.

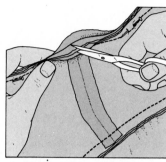

**4** Pin the fabric into place, clipping the piping casing at the corners to ease the piping around where necessary. The tapered seams on the side sections will allow sufficient ease without clipping.

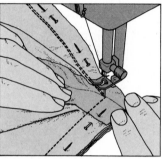

**5** Stitch the side section and top cover together, pivoting the fabric at the corners to get a neat squared seam (see page 424 for instructions). Neaten the raw edges in the appropriate way for the fabric.

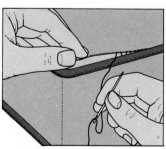

**6** Attach the bottom cover to the side sections as above, but leave a wide enough opening in one side to insert the pad. Neaten the seams as appropriate and press. Turn the cover inside out, insert the padding and then slip stitch the cover to the piping of the side strip to close opening.

## Removable cover with zip

Gauge the amount of fabric by measuring the cushion as for a permanent cover, but allow for a fifth strip which will be used for inserting the zip.

### How to make the cover

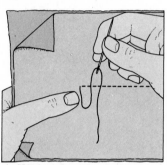

**1** With right sides facing, stitch two of the side strips down the centre of their length, using running stitch (see page 438).

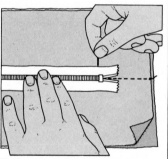

**2** Position the zip on the line of stitching, equidistant from each end. Then mark off the exact length of the zip teeth. Stitch to each of the marked points, backstitching to strengthen opening.

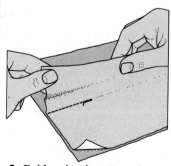

**3** Fold each side strip so that its wrong sides are facing. Insert the zip (see page 460) and remove running stitches. Make up the cover as described left.

# Bolster cushions

A bolster is a tubular cushion which normally has flat ends. These can be piped like boxed cushions. They are usually used as back supports on sofas and divan beds.

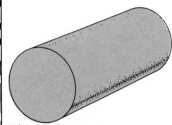

**Unpiped bolster cover**

*How to cut the cover*

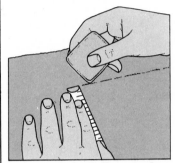

*1 Use tailor's chalk to mark a rectangle with one side 1in. (2.5cm) longer than the length of the bolster and the other 1¼in. (3.2cm) longer than the circumference of the bolster, to allow for the seams.*

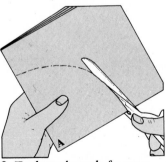

*2 To draw the ends for your bolster you will need a circular pattern. Take a square of paper and fold it in 4. From the corner, A, measure the radius of the ends and draw a quarter circle (see page 468). Cut out pattern and draw two circles.*

## Making the bolster covers

One of the simplest ways to make the pad is to stuff an inner cover very firmly with foam chips. You could also buy a thin sheet of foam to make your own bolster shape by cutting a rectangle and two circles and gluing them before stuffing with foam.

The inner and outer covers should be cut and made up in the same way. If the outer cover is to be removable, an extra rectangle of fabric the length of the opening and 3in. (7.5cm) wide should be cut. This provides the strap for your fastening.

*How to make the cover*

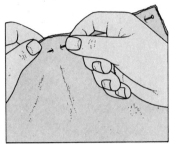

*1 Cut out the fabric for the bolster. With right sides facing, pin and stitch the longest sides of the rectangle together, ¼in. (6mm) from the raw edge.*

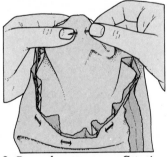

*2 Press the seam open. Starting at this central seam and with right sides facing, pin one of the circles to one end of the tube. Put a second pin directly opposite the first one and gradually work around the circle pinning evenly ½in. (1.3cm) from the raw edge. Clip into the fabric if necessary to ease it onto the round section. Tack and then stitch. Remove tacking then turn cover inside out. Insert the tube of foam or kapok into the hole at the top and ease the fabric down over it until it is firmly encased in the cylinder fabric.*

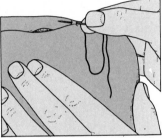

*3 Place the second circle, right side out, onto the open end of the tube. Turn under the raw edges, pin and slip stitch.*

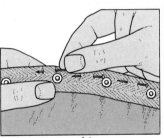

*4 For a removable cover, attach a strap along the side seam before it is stitched up (see page 485). Position the tape so that a wide enough gap is left to insert the bolster, with equal spaces left at each end. Pin then stitch the stud side of the tape to the right side of the strap. Attach socket side of the tape to the opposite edge.*

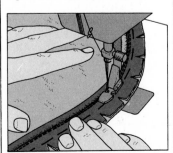

*5 If you want to add piping to the ends of the bolster, it should be stitched before you join the tubing to the circles (see piping boxed cushions).*

## Cushion fillings

The type of cushion filling you choose depends mainly on how firm you want the cushion to be and how much you can afford to spend on it.

### Feathers
Types of soft fillings include feathers (goose, duck or chicken) which are cheaper than down and can be bought as ready-made cushions. (They can also be bought by the pound from poultry farmers.) An 18in. (45cm) cushion needs 2lbs (1kilo) of feathers.

**Feathers**

### Kapok
Kapok and terylene fibre are cheap alternatives to feathers. Kapok, which is vegetable fibre, tends to become matted after a time. It is also not hand-washable. Terylene is a light filling which is washable and is also non-allergenic. 1lb (453g) will be sufficient for an 18in. to 20in. (45cm to 50cm) cushion.

**Kapok**

### Latex and foam
For firm cushions latex and foam foundations can be bought in a variety of shapes and sizes. This is very useful as one has the ready-made cushion shape which only needs covering.

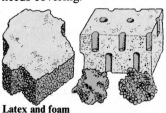

**Latex and foam**

## *Types of curtain*

Curtains can be of several different lengths usually sill length, apron length (hanging just below the sill) or floor length. Alternatively, the curtains can hang from a point halfway up the window. These are known as café curtains (see page 492). The choice of fabric, type of heading and length of curtains depends on the shape of the window and fabric washability and durability.

**Sill length curtains**

**Apron length curtains**

**Floor length curtains**

# *Measuring windows*

### *Measuring for curtains*

First decide on the length that the curtains are to be. This should be measured from the curtain track, preferably using a steel tape or long rule because these do not bend. Sill length curtains on inset windows should hang about 1in. (2.5cm) above the sill. Apron length curtains should hang 4in. to 9in. (10cm to 22.5cm) below the sill. Floor length curtains should clear the floor by 1in. (2.5cm). For the width, measure the full length of the curtain track.

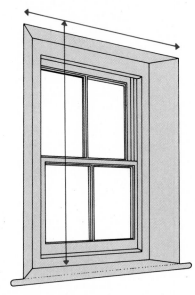

**Measuring for sill length curtains**

### *Calculating the fabric requirement*

Base the calculations for the width of your curtains on that of the curtain track. The type of heading being used and the weight of fabric will also affect how wide the fabric is to be. This is because of the amount of gathering necessary. Thin fabrics need to be two to three times the width of the track to look nicely full. Heavier fabrics on the other hand only need to be one and a half, to two times the width of the track. Allow another 2in. (5cm) for each side hem and 6in. (15cm) for curtain overlaps.

If the window is to have two curtains, divide the width of your curtain track by two to calculate the finished width of each curtain; if there are to be three curtains, divide it by three and so on. As most furnishing fabric is 48in. (120cm) wide, you will probably have to stitch together two or more fabric widths to produce the required measurement (see page 479 for instructions). Extra allowance must also be made for matching patterns. A simple guide is to allow one repeat pattern for each width of fabric. If two fabric widths are used for each of your two curtains, then four extra pattern repeats should be allowed for.

### *Measuring for blinds*

The same principles of measurement, namely length and width, apply to the measurement of blinds. Decide whether you want the blind to hang inside or outside the window recess and then measure accordingly. In both cases the brackets should be in position before you start your calculations and they should allow the roller to carry sufficient fabric as well as overlapping each side of the window by 1in. (2.5cm).

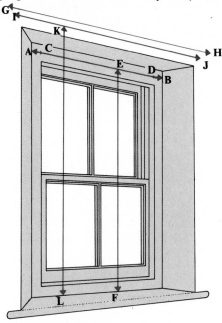

**Measuring window for roller blinds**

### *Measuring an inside recess*

The roller for your blind should extend from A to B, including the metal caps and pins. The fabric on the roller should extend from C to D, so that the total window area is covered. Add 2in. (5cm) for the side hem allowance. Measure the length of the blind from E to F, to the sill. Add 7in. (18cm) for attaching the fabric to the roller and making a pocket for the lath (a strip of wood inserted into the hem of the blind to provide weight).

### *Measuring an outside recess*

The roller and pins of the blind should extend from G to H, overlapping each side of the recess by at least 6in. (15cm). The total width of the fabric on the blind should be from I to J. Add 2in. (5cm) for the side hem allowance. Measure the length of the blind from K to L. It should overlap the recess by at least 2in. (5cm) and 7in. (18cm) should be added for attaching the fabric and making a pocket for the lath at the hem.

# Curtains

Making your own curtains is both economical and practical. Even simple curtains can be made to look very professional.

## Fabric

Whatever fabric you choose for your curtains, whether it is a heavy velvet or a thin cotton print, there are certain points to bear in mind before buying. Take into consideration how much and what type of wear they are liable to get: for example, it is sensible if you plan curtains for the kitchen to buy easily washable fabric as opposed to one which has to be dry cleaned. If the curtains are going to be exposed to strong sunlight, it is advisable to line them to help prevent the fabric from fading or rotting. Decide on the type of heading that the curtains will have before you buy the fabric because the type of heading will affect how much fabric you buy (the type and amount of pleating involved dictates the amount of fabric required).

## Curtain tracks

The curtain track is the rail which supports the curtains. It can be made of metal or plastic and comes in a variety of lengths. The tracks hold a series of runners to which the curtain is attached by hooks, suspended from a length of tape stitched to the head of the curtain. It is best to use metal tracks for heavy curtains and plastic tracks where a pliable rail is needed, for example fitting around a tight bay window.

Curtains can also be hung from decorative poles or rods. They can either be made of brass or wood. The curtains are hung from the poles by means of rings which are stitched to the curtains and threaded onto the pole. It is also quite common for net or lightweight curtains to be threaded directly onto spring tension rods which are then latched onto hooks either side of the window recess.

## Heading tapes

These tapes not only attach the curtain to the track by means of hooks, but also shape the top of the curtain. They consist of a length of tape, threaded top and bottom with cord. The tape is attached to the curtain and then gathered up, producing the pleats and also the pockets for the curtain hooks. The standard tape is available in a variety of widths and colours and can be used on all weights of curtain fabric. There is a special lightweight standard tape for use on nets and sheer fabrics. Pencil-pleat tape, which draws the fabric up into tightly rolled pleats, can be used on both lightweight and normal curtain fabric. It is unsuitable for use on heavy fabrics because of the tightness of the pleats. Use the thin, lightweight tape on nets and sheer fabrics and the stiffened tape on normal fabrics. Fanned pinch pleat tape comes in two depths – 1½in. (3.8cm) and 3½in. (9cm). It is attached, like the other tapes, along the top of the curtain. The cords are then drawn up, producing groups of pleats.

## Pelmets and valances

The curtain track, although usually hidden by the pleated heading of the curtain, can be covered by a *pelmet* or a *valance*. A pelmet is a wooden box which, when attached to the wall, surrounds and covers the track and top of the curtains. It can be covered with the same fabric as the curtains or left plain. A valance serves the same purpose as a pelmet, but is made of fabric. It can either be attached to the wall on a valance board or hung from a rod.

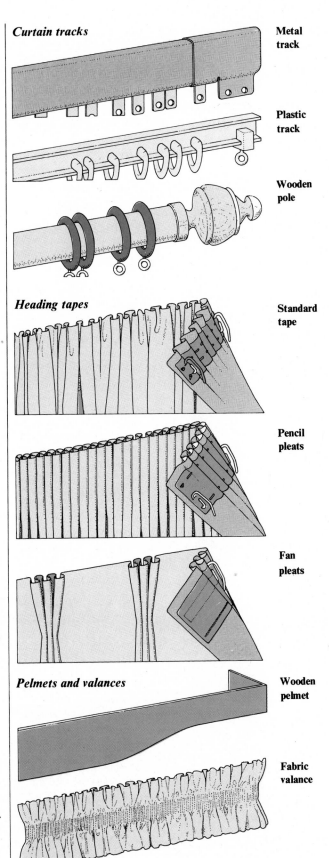

**Curtain tracks**

Metal track

Plastic track

Wooden pole

**Heading tapes**

Standard tape

Pencil pleats

Fan pleats

**Pelmets and valances**

Wooden pelmet

Fabric valance

# Unlined curtains

Curtains can be lined or unlined, depending on their purpose. Unlined curtains made in sheer fabric are particularly suitable for rooms where much light is needed, but lined curtains last longer, protect the curtain fabric and provide extra warmth.

## Making the curtains

Having measured the window and calculated the amount of fabric required (see page 489), the fabric can be cut into the appropriate lengths. Check to make sure that the fabric is pre-shrunk and that the cross grain is straight (see page 430). Then, on a smooth flat surface such as the floor, spread out and cut the fabric, bearing in mind the fabric repeats required for pattern matching (see page 479).

## Joining the fabric lengths

Position the lengths as required. Make sure that any part-widths of fabric are on the outside edge of the curtain. Then use a plain flat seam to join the selvedges or a run and fell seam for raw edges (see page 441).

If an invisible finish is required and you are using a run and fell seam, slip stitch the second line of stitching into place.

**Aligning part-widths of fabric**

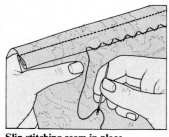

**Slip stitching seam in place**

## Curtain headings

The curtains can be attached with heading tape and hooks to a curtain track, or they can be attached to a rod with rings (see page 489). They can even be slotted directly onto a wire which is run through the hem pocket at the top of the curtain (see page 489). This last method is only suitable for lightweight curtains.

### Attaching standard tape

There are several types of heading tape but the method of attaching the tape is basically the same. The tape has two or three rows of gathering thread and slots into which the hooks will be inserted once the tape is attached.

### How to attach the tape

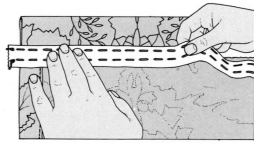

**1** *Cut the tape to the width of the curtain, leaving an allowance of 1in. (2.5cm) at either end as a turn-in. Knot one end of the tape securely but leave the other end free. Turn the top edge of the curtain under by 2in. (5cm) and tack into place. Position the tape on the curtain about 1in. to 1½in. (2.5cm to 3.8cm) below the heading of the curtain. Turn under each end of the tape and pin into position so that the knot at one end is enclosed and the cords at the other are free.*

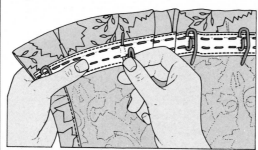

**2** *Pin and tack the tape on either side of the cords and at each end. Machine into place, working both rows of stitches in the same direction to prevent any drag on the fabric. Draw up the free ends of the cord until the curtain measures the right width and secure. Distribute the gathers evenly and fasten the surplus cord with a few stitches or a cord tidy. Insert curtain hooks at each end and then at equally spaced intervals, approximately 3in. (7.5cm) apart, along the tape.*

## How to hem the curtains

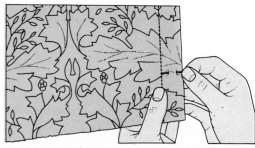

**1** *Hang the curtains up for a couple of days before turning up the bottom hem as some fabrics stretch when hung. Mark the required length on each side of the curtain and then unhook the curtains and mark the rest of the hem with pins or a line of tacking.*

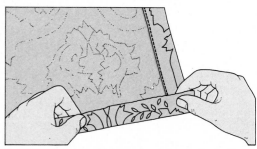

**2** *Turn the raw edges to the wrong side of the fabric by half the final depth. Press and then turn under the same amount again to make a double hem. Mitre the edges and insert weights into the corners, if necessary (mitering reduces bulk and weights improve hang). Pin, tack and then slip stitch into place. Machine stitch if an invisible finish is not required.*

## Making a double side seam

To prevent the edges of the curtains from pulling out of shape, a double hem should be made on the side seams.

### How to make the side seams

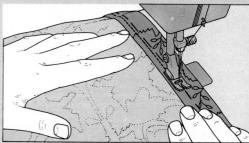

*Turn the fabric to the wrong side by 1in. (2.5cm) and press in place. Turn it under again by 1in. (2.5cm) and press and pin into place. Tack and then machine stitch, or stitch by hand if an invisible finish is needed.*

# Lined curtains

## Making up the curtains and the lining

Measure, cut out and join the fabric as for unlined curtains. Make the lining up in the same way but use only plain flat seams to join the fabric lengths. Make the side hems on the curtains as for the unlined ones, using loose cross stitch and ending 8in. (20cm) above the bottom edge of the curtain. This allows for the mitering of the hem later on.

### How to attach the lining

**1** *With wrong sides facing, place the lining on top of the curtain. Spread pieces out flat. Pin the two together down the centre line then turn back one half of the lining.*

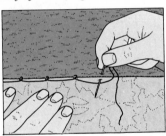

**2** *Lock stitch the lining to the curtain, starting 9in. (22.5cm) from the lower edge, working from left to right. Pick up one or two threads of the curtain and the lining with the needle, draw the thread around it and pull the needle through. Leave the thread fairly slack. Make stitches 2in. to 3in. (5cm to 7.5cm) apart. Repeat at wide intervals.*

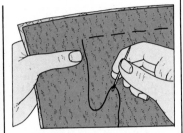

**3** *Tack the raw edge of the curtain and lining across the top of the curtain to within 3in. (7.5cm) of outer edges.*

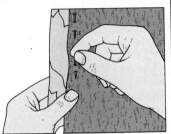

**4** *Trim away the lining at the sides so that it is ¼in. (6mm) short of the curtain edge. Turn the sides of the lining under ½in. (1.3cm). Pin and tack to the curtain so that there is a ¾in. (1.8cm) edge of curtain fabric. Slip stitch to within 8in. (20.5cm) of the bottom. Treat the curtain and lining as one and attach the heading tape.*

## Hemming the curtains

Hang the curtains for a few days before stitching the bottom hems. Mark off required length at outer edges. Take down curtains and mark rest of hem with pins or uneven tacking. Turn back half the depth of the bottom hem, press and mitre (see right). Fold the fabric along the hemline again. Pin, tack and slip stitch into place. Remove tacking and press. Turn up the lining to the back of the fabric – the hem fold should clear the bottom of the curtain by 1in. (2.5cm) – then finish the hem as for an unlined curtain. Slip stitch the lining to the curtain at the sides and for ½in. (1.3cm) where it covers bottom hem.

# Curtain headings

## Deep tape

Deep tape provides a stiffened stand up heading. When the curtains are drawn the curtain track is completely hidden.

### Making deep tape

Turn the top edge of the curtain to the wrong side by ½in. (1.3cm) and tack into place. Prepare and attach the tape in the same way as for the standard tape (see left) but align the tape so that it is level with curtain top.

### Detachable lining tape

This is an alternative finish for lined curtains in which the tape is stitched to the lining and then hooked to the curtains so that the lining can be easily removed and washed.

### How to attach the tape

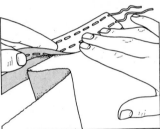

**1** *Pull the gathering cords free of the tape by 1½in. (3.8cm) at one end and knot firmly. Trim the cord to the desired width then fold under the knotted edge and machine the fold to secure it. With the right side of the lining towards you and the corded side uppermost, slip lining between tape sides.*

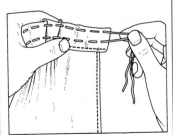

**2** *Leave 1in. (2.5cm) of the cord overlapping at the knotted end. Pin and tack along the bottom edge of the tape. Fold any excess tape to back of lining. Stitch, gather and finish as for standard tape.*

# Mitering a double folded hem

It will be necessary to mitre the corners of double folded hems, especially when the fabric is heavy.

### How to work

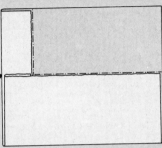

**1** *Hem the side of the curtains in the usual way but leave about 8in. (20.5cm) unhemmed at the bottom. Turn under the raw edge of this part of the curtain by 1in. (2.5cm). Turn up the bottom hem by half the final depth.*

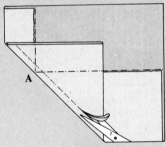

**2** *Fold in the corner to the wrong side of the curtain so that a diagonal line cuts through point A. Press so that a crease is formed. Cut along this crease line.*

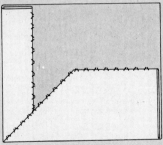

**3** *Fold the side hem to the wrong side by a further 1in. (2.5cm) and stitch in place. Fold up the bottom hem by its full depth and stitch in the appropriate way for the fabric. Slip stitch the mitred corner and hem together.*

## Types of café curtain

Café curtains can be made from lightweight fabric and fixed in position, or from heavier fabric and drawn if required. The curtains can be fixed partway down the window or even in two tiers. The curtain rod can slide into the plain or scalloped heading or can be attached to it with rings.

**Café curtains with plain heading**

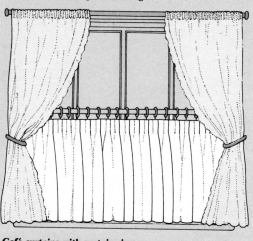

**Café curtains with curtain rings**

**Café curtains with straps**

## Plain heading

### Calculating fabric requirement

Fix the curtain rod in position and measure the width between the two fixing points. If you want the fabric to fall in loose folds, the total width of the curtains should be twice this measurement. Do not forget to allow enough fabric for matching patterns, as well as for seam allowances and possible shrinkage (see instructions on page 488).

### Making a plain heading

Wash and iron the fabric if it is not pre-shrunk. Join any widths of fabric at the selvedges using a plain seam. If any raw edges of the fabric are being joined use a run and fell seam (see page 441). Make the side seams as for unlined curtains with a 1in. (2.5cm) double hem. Turn down the raw edge at the top of the curtain, fold over the allowance required for inserting the rod, and pin and machine stitch the rod pocket in place. Insert the rod into the pocket and arrange the gathers evenly along the top. Leave the curtains to hang for a day or so before making up the hem as for unlined curtains (see instructions on page 490).

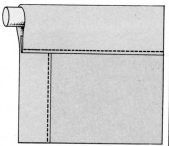

**Pocket for the curtain rod stitched into position to form a plain heading**

### Attaching the curtain with rings

If the curtains are to be fixed to the rod with rings, these should be sewn onto the wrong side of the heading at close intervals using strong button thread, as shown left.

## Scalloped heading

### Calculating fabric requirement

To make a scalloped heading on a café curtain you will first have to calculate the amount of fabric required. Fix the rod in position and measure the width between its two fixing points. The width of your curtain should be one and a half times this width plus 4in. (10cm) for turnings. If there are to be two curtains add an extra 4in. (10cm) to the width. For the length measure from the rod to the sill and add the depth of the scallops (see below). If you are hanging the curtain from rings you will need to add a further 2in. (5cm) for turnings. If you are hanging it from the straps alone, add the circumference of the rod plus 1in. (2.5cm) for ease. Add 4in. (10cm) for the hem on sill length curtains.

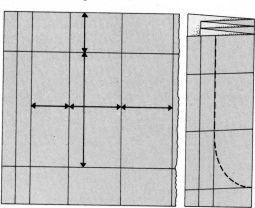

**Pattern for scalloped curtain**

### Making the pattern

Decide on the depth and width of your scallop – usually about 4in. (10cm) wide and half as deep. Divide the finished width of your curtain by the scallop and strap. This should leave enough for an extra strap at one end. The curtains must start and finish with a strap so reduce the width of scallops if necessary.

Take a strip of paper the width of the curtain minus turnings and 6in. (15cm) deeper than twice the depth of the scallops. Draw a line parallel to the top edge and 2in. (5cm) down from it. Measure off the depth of the scallop below this line and draw another parallel line. From the left, measure off half the width of the strap and draw a vertical line. Draw in another vertical line half a strap's width from this. From the second line, measure half the scallop width and draw a vertical line. Add half of strap to half of scallop and draw this in from the third line. Use this measurement to mark off the rest of the paper. At the end you will have the width of a strap; halve and draw a vertical line. Fold the paper on the third line from the left and then on every line so that you will be left with half a strap width at each end. With the paper still folded, draw a line for the scallop shape. Cut through all folds.

## Making a scalloped heading

Cut the fabric to the required measurements and join additional lengths where necessary. Make the side seams with a double 1in. (2.5cm) hem and press (see page 490). At the top of the curtain turn down the amount allowed for the scallop to the right side and press lightly. In effect this will be the facing in the shape of the scallops. If the fabric is flimsy attach a piece of iron-on interfacing the width of the curtain and slightly deeper than the scallops. Iron it on so that the edge is level with the folded edge of the curtain.

### How to make heading

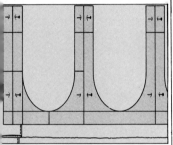

**1** *Unfold your pattern and pin it to the folded over edge of the curtain, aligning the top edge of the straps to the fold of the material.*

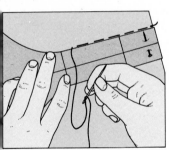

**2** *Using small stitches, tack around the edge of the pattern through both thicknesses of fabric. Take care as you tack around the curves.*

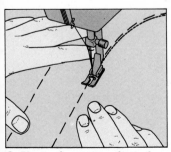

**3** *Unpin the pattern from the fabric, leaving the pattern marked out by tacking stitches. Machine alongside this tacking line, again taking care as you stitch around the curves. Do not stitch across top of straps.*

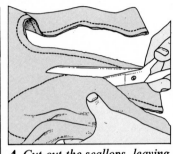

**4** *Cut out the scallops, leaving a ¼in. (6mm) seam allowance. If necessary notch the seam allowance around the curve and at the top corners (see page 473). Press the scalloped edge.*

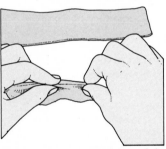

**5** *Turn the scalloped top of the curtain through to the right side and make sure that the corners are pushed out square. Roll the facing slightly towards the wrong side of the curtain and press into place.*

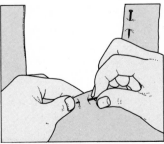

**6** *Pin and tack ¼in. (6mm) in from the edge of the scallops, then press the curtain heading. Turn under the raw edge of the facing by ½in. (1.3cm) to the wrong side. Pin and tack, and then slip stitch.*

# Roller blinds

These give a very neat, plain finish to a window. Blind fittings can be bought in kit form with fixing instructions included. The blinds can be hung inside or outside the window recess. If the blind is to hang inside the recess, make sure that it will not catch on any window fittings.

## Choosing the fabric

Closely woven fabrics such as canvas or heavy linen are the most suitable because they roll up easily on the blind. If you want to use sheer fabrics so that you get the maximum of light, you will have to stiffen the fabric. For bathrooms and kitchens, laminated fabric is ideal because it is waterproof and therefore easily cleaned.

## Measuring your blinds

Decide whether you want your blind to hang inside or outside the window recess. If it hangs inside the recess it looks neater, but you must always be sure that the blind will not catch on any window fittings (see page 488).

### How to make the roller blind

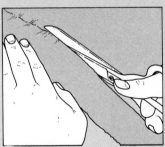

**1** *If the fabric is to hang vertically it is essential to square the fabric off with the selvedge (see page 472). Press out all creases.*

**2** *Press and hem the top of the blind by ½in. (1.3cm). The final width of the blind is the space between the end pins. Hem the blind at either side accordingly. Stitch both in place and stiffen the fabric if required. Measure for lath, allowing room for both lath and turning under raw edges.*

**3** *At the bottom of the blind, turn under the raw edges and then make a pocket to hold the lath. Machine the longest edge and slip stitch one side end.*

**4** *Cut the lath ½in. (1.3cm) shorter than the width of the blind and then insert it into the lath pocket. Slip stitch up pocket side. Thread and knot the cord through the pull-tab and screw onto the back of the blind. Align the top of the blind with the markings on the roller. Glue and tack to the roller. Wind up the fabric and place the roller on its bracket.*

# Darning and patching

Holes and tears can be mended either by darning or by patching. The method you choose will depend on the size of the tear, its position on the garment and on the type of fabric. Generally, if the tear is neat and unfrayed it can be darned but if it is large and rather ragged it should be patched. Bear in mind the amount of strain the mended tear will be under. For example, if the tear is next to an armhole, centre seam or other stress point it should be patched.

### Darning tears

If there is just a small tear in the fabric, the torn sides can be darned together. Do not attempt to use this method on fabrics which fray.

#### How to darn a tear

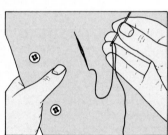

**1** *Use a very fine, sharp needle and matching thread for your fabric (for a good match, pull out a thread from a seam allowance). Keep the length of thread short and do not knot it. Pass the needle from the wrong side of the garment to the right side at the beginning of the tear, leaving ¼in. (6mm) of the thread underneath.*

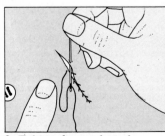

**2** *Taking diagonal stitches, pick up the threads, first to the right and then to the left until the whole tear has been joined. Fasten off on the wrong side of the garment.*

## Patching

Patches are generally used wherever a strong, durable repair is required. They should also be used on fabrics which fray, or where the hole is too large to be darned. Patches can also form a decorative finish to the garment instead of just being functional. Pieces of appliqué can be stitched over the hole once its raw edges have been turned under and neatened. If you do not want to use sew-on patches, iron-on patches are also available. These are pressed into position with a warm iron so the heat bonds the patch to the garment. Although they are quick and easy to apply to flat surfaces of a garment some areas will be inaccessible.

#### How to make a sew-on patch

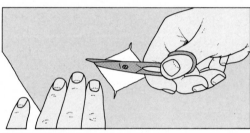

**1** *Trim the hole or tear into a neat square or rectangle. Clip into each of the corners by about ¼in. (6mm). Cut out a patch, at least 2in. (5cm) wider all around than the square. If possible, cut the patch from part of the same garment (such as the hem or facing).*

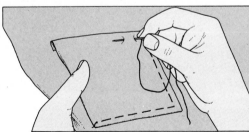

**2** *Turn under the raw edges of the patch. From the wrong side of the garment, with the wrong side of the patch uppermost, tack the patch over the hole.*

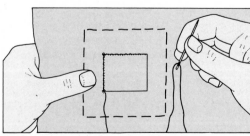

**3** *Turn the garment to the right side. Turn under the edges of the hole and slip stitch them neatly to the patch. Oversew the corners to reinforce them. The patch can also be top stitched from the right side.*

## Turning collars and cuffs

Very often the collar or cuffs of a shirt show signs of wear before the rest of the garment. Rather than discard the whole garment, you can turn the collar or the cuffs and lengthen the life of the article provided the underside of the collar or cuff is of the same fabric and without any special stitched features. The method is the same for both collar and cuffs except that when turning the collar, the marks should be made on the collar and neckband and the threads joining the two should be cut.

#### How to turn the cuff

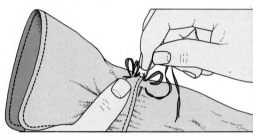

**1** *Fold the cuff in half and mark the centre line with tailor's tacks of contrasting thread. The mark must show on both sides of the cuff. Make a similar mark on the centre of the sleeve for the alignment of the turned cuff.*

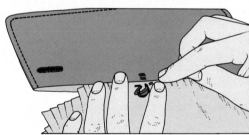

**2** *Using sharp pointed scissors or an unpicker, carefully cut the threads joining the cuff to the sleeve. Take out all the cut threads from the cuff. Reverse the cuff then replace it on the sleeve, matching markings.*

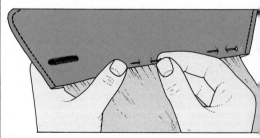

**3** *Pin the cuff into place. Then tack through all layers of fabric. Machine along the original line of stitching to complete the turned cuff.*

# Stain removal

It is always best to treat stains as soon as they occur because they are much more difficult to remove once dry. Any non-greasy stains should be sponged off with cool water, taking care not to rub in the stain any more. Washable fabrics should be soaked in cool water, then rinsed frequently. Non-washable fabrics should just be sponged gently. Greasy marks should be sprinkled with talcum powder and then treated with a dry cleaning agent such as carbon tetrachloride. Marks made by fruit or wine (unless they are on carpets or furniture) should be sprinkled with salt to prevent them spreading and then washed, where possible, in biological washing powder. Treat carpet or furniture stains with either carpet cleaner or borax solution. Stains made by unknown substances should be cleaned professionally.

### Blood
Rinse in cold water until the stain is partly removed, then wash in warm soapy water in the usual way. If badly stained rinse in cold, salted water and then wash in the usual way. If the stain is on heavy material make a thick paste of starch and warm water and apply this to it. Leave it to dry and then very gently shake the mixture off. Repeat this process several times if necessary.

### Candle wax
Harden the wax with an ice cube and scrape off excess. Place fabric between two sheets of blotting paper, then press with a warm iron, moving the blotting paper as it absorbs the wax. For coloured candle wax, remove the colouring with a sponge dipped in alcohol after the wax has been removed.

### Chewing gum
Soften the gum with carbon tetrachloride or methylated spirits and then pick it off the garment.

### Chocolate and cocoa
Cover the stain with borax and wash in cold water. For delicate fabrics sponge with warm water, taking care to rinse the sponge between each application. Use glycerine or bleach on stubborn stains.

### Coffee and tea
Treat the stain immediately with a borax or peroxide solution. Dried-in stains should be treated with glycerine to loosen them. Coffee and tea stains on wool or silk should be dealt with as for chocolate.

### Deodorant
Use a vinegar solution, or methylated spirits on stubborn stains.

### Egg
Wherever possible, use a biological washing powder. Otherwise use warm water for egg whites and detergent lather for yolks. Use a grease solvent on stubborn stains.

### Fruit and wine
Cover the stain with table salt and rub over it with a piece of damp soap. Leave for a few hours and then rinse. For silk and wool cover the stain with borax and wash in warm water. For white cotton and linen apply lemon to the stain and pour hot water onto it.

### Glue
Soak washables in very hot water with a little detergent until the glue dissolves. Sponge severe stains with vinegar.

### Grease
Remove as much as possible with an absorbent then use carbon tetrachloride. Use eucalyptus oil on black oil and tar. On dried-in stains apply a paste of talcum powder and carbon tetrachloride. Brush off when dry.

### Indelible pen
Soak stains for three to five minutes in alcohol, then wash in warm soapy water.

### Ink
Rinse and wash washable fabrics as soon as possible. Use methylated spirits for ballpoint or felt tip pens.

### Lipstick
Use vaseline, eucalyptus oil or glycerine on the mark and then wash, if possible, with warm soapy water. Sponge with carbon tetrachloride when dry.

### Mildew
Fresh stains can be easily removed by washing in warm, soapy water. Mildew on white is best removed with lemon juice and then dried in the sun.

### Milk
Rinse washables in cool water, then biological washing powder. Use borax on dried-in stains and a grease solvent on non-washables.

### Perspiration
Use a biological washing powder, borax or a vinegar solution on the stain.

### Rust
For rust stains on white spread the stained area over a bowl of steaming water and squeeze lemon juice on it. Leave for a few minutes, then rinse in hot water. Repeat several times if necessary. Alternatively you can moisten stain with salt and lemon juice, adding more lemon juice as it dries. Wash in warm soapy water.

### Scorch marks
Wash as quickly as possible in warm soapy water or moisten with a mixture of salt and fresh lemon juice applied to the stain. For wool wet the stain, apply powdered chalk and then dry in the sun. For white flannel rub fresh lemon juice and pulp into the scorch mark at once, then dry in the sun.

### Shoe polish
Use a grease solvent and then methylated spirits to remove any remaining colour.

### Vomit
For washables, use a biological powder. Use salt solution on non-washables and a grease solvent on any remaining stain on the fabric.

### Water marks
Sponge the entire surface evenly, moistening fabric but not soaking it, then press. For silk, satin and velvet shake the fabric over steam. Cover the spout with a cloth. Keep water boiling until the fabric is thoroughly steamed.

Whichever stain remover you use always work from the wrong side of the fabric (this is not always possible, for example on carpets. Never saturate the carpet with solvent because the carpet backing must never get wet). To avoid leaving a ring, apply the solvent in a circle around the stain and work towards the centre. Always test chemicals first on a hidden part of the fabric and rinse it thoroughly. Many solvents are both poisonous and inflammable so keep them out of the reach of children.

### Absorbents
Talcum powder, French chalk.

### Acetone
This should never be used on acetate, triacetate or viscose rayon. Amyl acetate can be used on these fabrics instead. Test before use.

### Borax
Make a solution of one dessert spoon of borax to $\frac{1}{2}$ pint ($\frac{1}{4}$ litre) of warm water. Soak stain if possible, otherwise sponge. For large stains, rub borax on dampened stain and leave for half an hour, then rinse carefully.

### Detergents
These can either contain soap, or be soapless. When dealing with non-washable fabrics only the lather of the soap detergent should be used. Heavy-duty detergents contain a mild bleach which can be used on some stains. Enzyme detergents soak out protein stains such as blood and egg.

### Dry cleaner
These are grease solvents sold under varying brand names. Apply to dry surfaces.

### Eucalyptus oil
Used neat for tar and oil stains.

### Methylated spirits
Test before use. Use undiluted.

### Peroxide
Use on whites, one part to four parts water.

### Vinegar
Use one part to four parts water. Counteracts discolouration of the fabric.

# KNITTING INDEX

Numbers in *italic* indicate text
and illustrations

# CROCHET INDEX

# KNOTTED AND WOVENWORK INDEX

# EMBROIDERY INDEX

# NEEDLEPOINT INDEX

# PATCHWORK INDEX

# BASIC SEWING INDEX

# ACKNOWLEDGMENTS

In the making of this book I have been supported, aided and sometimes carried by the technical knowledge and friendship of Sally Harding who is responsible for many of the needlework samples. I also relied on the work of Lesley Walker for the sewing material and Ena Richards and Brenda Sparkes for knotting and weaving.

I have also had generous contributions of materials from Millwards, C. & J. Coats, and DMC whose yarn, threads and needles were used on many of the working samples. Artists such as Kaffe Fassett, Lillian Delevoryas, Jonathan Langley, Jon Sandsmark and many others have lent their work for photography and these pieces are mentioned in the picture credits.

I would also like to thank the editors, art editors and designers who put the book together so skilfully. Without their intelligence, dedication and inventiveness, this gigantic task would never have been accomplished.

Finally, I would also like to thank the team of illustrators who have so carefully studied the stitches and meticulously drawn each and every one in the style and technical perfection of draughtsmen from the finest periods of historical art.

**Judy Brittain**


Dorling Kindersley Limited would like to thank the following:

**Overall technical consultant**
Sally Harding

**Section advisors:** Lesley Walker *(Sewing)*; Ena Richards *(Knotted and Woven Work)*; Brenda Sparkes *(Knitting and Weaving)*; Janet Haigh *(Needlepoint and Rugmaking)*; Penny Baker *(Machine Knitting)*; Diana Thornton *(Needlepoint)*; Jean Litchfield *(Knitting and Crochet)*; Lesley Prescott *(Knitting)*.

**Contributors and suppliers**
Byzantium, Margaret Stuart, J. & P. Coats, Millwards, Scottish Merchant, Kaffe Fassett *(Knitting)*; Lady Mary Strachey, Browns, DMC *(Crochet)*; The Rope Shop, Joan Buckle, Mollie Geller, Lucinda Stevens, Olga Catterson *(Knotted and Wovenwork)*; Jonathan Langley, Belinda Montagu, Geraldine Gillett *(Embroidery)*; Lillian Delevoryas, Kaffe Fassett, DMC *(Needlepoint)*; Strawberry Fayre, Paul Taylor, Rachel Smith, Belinda Montagu, Lucy Goffin, Geraldine Gillett *(Patchwork, Appliqué and Quilting)*; Mary-Lynn Stadler-Forbes *(Sewing)*. Special thanks to Moira MacNeill, Sue Joiner and Barbara Dawson for advice and help, and to DMC.

**Project designers and makers**
*Knitting:* Sally Harding, Mary Tebbs, Brenda Sparkes, Lesley Prescott.
*Crochet:* Cecilia Lundstrom, Mary Tebbs, Sally Harding, Jean Lichfield, Christalla Sariyannis.
*Knotted and Wovenwork:* I. Konior, Pamela Smith, Joan Buckle, Stephanie Todd, Olga Catterson, Janet Haigh, Brenda Sparkes.
*Embroidery:* Sally Harding, Christalla Sariyannis, Jane Iles, Geraldine Gillett, Barbara Dawson, Jonathan Langley, Belinda Montagu.
*Needlepoint:* Janet Haigh, Mary Pick, Diana Thornton, Jane Iles, Gisela Banbury, Rachel Smith.
*Patchwork:* Rachel Smith, Geraldine Gillett.
*Sewing:* Lesley Walker.

**Typesetting**
Typesetting Services Ltd.
C. E. Dawkins Ltd.
Whitecross Graphics

**Reproduction**
F. E. Burman Limited.

**Illustrators and studio services**
Lindsay Blow
Michael Craig
Shirley Curzon
Eugene Fleury
Gilchrist Studios
Tony Graham
Sally Launder
Richard Lewis
Coral Mula
Negs
Ann Savage

**Photography**
Elly Beintema
John Cousins
Peter Mackertitch

**Picture credits**
All original photography was done by John Cousins except the knitting chapter which was photographed by Peter Mackertitch who also took the following photographs: pages 130 (TR), 135 (TR), 143 (TL), 147 (TR), 155, 161.

In the list below, the name of the worker is italicized and the name of the photographer or picture source, if different from above, is in roman. Abbreviations are as follows: T: top; B: bottom; R: right; L: left; C: centre.

1. Victoria and Albert Museum 2. Angelo Hornak 6. *Lillian Delevoryas* (TL); *Joen Zinni Lask* [21 Antiques (C)] 3. Victoria and Albert Museum (T) Museum of London (C) Victoria and Albert Museum (B) 62. *Kaffe Fassett* (TR) 63. *Sally Harding* (CR) 67. *Sally Harding* 70. *Sally Harding* 71. *Sally Harding* 75. *Brenda Sparkes* 78. *Brenda Sparkes* (R) 79. *Brenda Sparkes* 97. J. & P. Coats (BR) 100. *Brenda Sparkes* 101. *Brenda Sparkes* 110. Victoria and Albert Museum (CB) 111. *Birgitta Bjerke* 135. *Sally Harding/Christalla Sariyanniis* 139. DMC 143. *Mollie Geller* (R) 146. DMC (TL); Browns (BR) 147. *Lady Mary Strachey* (TL) 150. DMC (BL) 151. *Mrs. M. Tebbs* (R) 155. *Cecilia Lundstrom* 161. *Sally Harding* 173. *Pam Smith* 174. Victoria and Albert Museum (L) 183. *Pam Smith* 184. *Stephanie Todd* 185. *Stephanie Todd* 190. The Rope Shop 198. *M. Konior* (L) 204. *Pam Smith* (L) 205. *Diana Thornton* 207. Picturepoint 208. *Janet Haigh* 209. *Janet Haigh* 210. *Janet Haigh* 211. *Janet Haigh* 212. *Janet Haigh* 225. *Brenda Sparkes* 229. Michael Holford (T); Patcham Park (C), Victoria and Albert Museum 230. Cooper Bridgeman Library (BL); Angelo Hornak (TR); Victoria and Albert Museum (BR) 231. C. M. Dixon (TL); Angelo Hornak (BL, TR, C, CB); Ianthe Ruthven (BR) 238. *Sally Harding* (T); *Sally Harding* (C); Ianthe Ruthven (B) 239. *Jonathan Langley* (T); I. Ruthven (C); Victoria and Albert Museum (R) 240. Victoria and Albert Museum 241. Victoria and Albert Museum 242. Victoria and Albert Museum (C & R) 245. Victoria and Albert Museum 246. Victoria and Albert Museum 251. Victoria and Albert Museum (C) 254. Victoria and Albert (BR) 258. *Sally Harding* (TL, BC); *Jane Iles* (TC) 259. *Sally Harding* 260. Werner Forman 262. Picturepoint (BL); Angelo Hornak (TL); Michael Holford (R) 263. Cooper Bridgeman (TL); Michael Holford (BL); Ianthe Ruthven (BR) 265. Werner Forman Archive 266. Alan Hutchinson Library (TC); Angelo Hornak (BC); Ianthe Ruthven (TR); Michael Holford (BR) 272. Victoria and Albert Museum (BL) 274. *Geraldine Gillett* 286. Victoria and Albert Museum; Elly Beintema 290. Werner Forman Archive (BL); *Sally Harding* (TR); Ianthe Ruthven (BR) 291. *Jonathan Langley* 294. Mallett & Son (TR); Ianthe Ruthven (CR); Angelo Hornak (BR) 295. Michael Holford (TL); Ianthe Ruthven (BL); *Sally Harding* (R) 296. Alan Hutchinson 297. Ianthe Ruthven 298. Ianthe Ruthven (TL); Victoria and Albert Museum (BL) 308. Parham Park Collection 309. Cooper Bridgeman Library 310. Victoria and Albert Museum (T); Metropolitan Museum of Art (gift of Mrs. J. Insley Blair 1930) 315. *Mary Pick* (TL); *Diana Thornton* (TR & B) 318. *Diana Thornton* 319. *Janet Haigh* 329. DMC 331. Angelo Hornak (Victoria and Albert Museum) 338–9. *Gisela Banbury* 342. *Lillian Delevoryas* (T); *Janet Haigh* 343. *Lillian Delevoryas* 344. *Janet Haigh* 346. *Janet Haigh* 347. *Janet Haigh* (TL); *Lillian Delevoryas* (TR); *Lillian Delevoryas* (BL); *Janet Haigh* (BR) 348. *Lillian Delevoryas* 350. *Diana Thornton;* DMC (R); 365. Victoria and Albert Museum 370. Victoria and Albert Museum (TR) 371. Cooper Bridgeman Library (TL); Angelo Hornak (BR) 402. *Paul Taylor and Ron Simpson* (TL) (BL); *Lucy Goffin* (TR); *Geraldine Gillett* (BR) 403. *Diana Harrison* 404. Victoria and Albert Museum 406. *Paul Taylor and Ron Simpson* (TL); Cooper Bridgeman (TR); *Linda Brill* 407. *Linda Brill* (LT, CB); *Jon Sandsmark* 410. *Glenys de Sida* (L); *Patrick and Debbie Buchan* (R) 411. *Lillian Delevoryas; Lucy Goffin* (R) 414. Ianthe Ruthven (TL, TR, CR); Freda Craft Stores (BL, BR) 415. Angelo Hornak (TL, BL); Victoria and Albert Museum.